THEORETICAL ASTRONOMY

RELATING TO THE

MOTIONS OF THE HEAVENLY BODIES

REVOLVING AROUND THE SUN IN ACCORDANCE WITH THE LAW OF UNIVERSAL GRAVITATION

EMBRACING

A SYSTEMATIC DERIVATION OF THE FORMULÆ FOR THE CALCULATION OF THE GEOCENTRIC AND HELIOCENTRIC PLACES, FOR THE DETERMINATION OF THE ORBITS OF PLANETS AND COMETS, FOR THE CORRECTION OF APPROXIMATE ELEMENTS, AND FOR THE COMPUTATION OF SPECIAL PERTURBATIONS; TOGETHER WITH THE THEORY OF THE COMBINATION OF OBSERVATIONS AND THE METHOD OF LEAST SQUARES.

With Numerical Examples and Auxiliary Tables

BY

JAMES C. WATSON

DIRECTOR OF THE OBSERVATORY AT ANN ARBOR, AND PROFESSOR OF ASTRONOMY IN THE UNIVERSITY OF MICHIGAN.

PHILADELPHIA

J. B. LIPPINCOTT & CO.

LONDON: TRUBNER & CO.

1868

PREFACE.

THE discovery of the great law of nature, the law of gravitation, by NEWTON, prepared the way for the brilliant achievements which have distinguished the history of astronomical science. A first essential, however, to the solution of those recondite problems which were to exhibit the effect of the mutual attraction of the bodies of our system, was the development of the infinitesimal calculus; and the labors of those who devoted themselves to pure analysis have contributed a most important part in the attainment of the high degree of perfection which characterizes the results of astronomical investigations. Of the earlier efforts to develop the great results following from the law of gravitation, those of EULER stand pre-eminent, and the memoirs which he published have, in reality, furnished the germ of all subsequent investigations in celestial mechanics. In this connection also the names of BERNOUILLI, CLAIRAUT, and D'ALEMBERT deserve the most honorable mention as having contributed also, in a high degree, to give direction to the investigations which were to unfold so many mysteries of nature. By means of the researches thus inaugurated, the great problems of mechanics were successfully solved, many beautiful theorems relating to the planetary motions demonstrated, and many useful formulæ developed.

It is true, however, that in the early stage of the science methods were developed which have since been found to be impracticable, even if not erroneous; still, enough was effected to direct attention in the proper channel, and to prepare the way for the more complete labors of LAGRANGE and LAPLACE. The genius and the analytical skill of these extraordinary men gave to the progress of Theoretical Astronomy the most rapid strides; and the intricate investigations which they successfully performed, served constantly to educe new discoveries, so that of all the problems relating to the mutual attraction of the several planets but little more remained to be accomplished by their successors than to develop and simplify the methods which they made known, and to introduce such modifications as should be indicated by experience or rendered possible by the latest discoveries in the domain of pure analysis.

The problem of determining the elements of the orbit of a comet moving in a parabola, by means of observed places, which had been considered by NEWTON, EULER, BOSCOVICH, LAMBERT, and others, received from LAGRANGE and LAPLACE the most careful consideration in the light of all that had been previously done. The solution given by the former is analytically complete, but far from being practically complete; that given by the latter is especially simple and practical so far as regards the labor of computation; but the results obtained by it are so affected by the unavoidable errors of observation as to be often little more than rude approximations. The method which was found to answer best in actual practice, was that proposed by OLBERS in his work entitled *Leichteste und bequemste Methode die Bahn eines Cometen zu berechnen*, in which, by making use of a beautiful theorem of parabolic motion demonstrated by EULER and also by LAMBERT, and by adopting a method of trial and error in the numerical solution of certain equations, he was enabled to effect a solution which could be performed with remarkable ease. The accuracy of the results obtained by OLBERS's method, and the facility of its application, directed the attention of LEGENDRE, IVORY, GAUSS, and ENCKE to this subject, and by them the method was extended and generalized, and rendered applicable in the exceptional cases in which the other methods failed.

It should be observed, however, that the knowledge of one element, the eccentricity, greatly facilitated the solution; and, although elliptic elements had been computed for some of the comets, the first hypothesis was that of parabolic motion, so that the subsequent process required simply the determination of the corrections to be applied to these elements in order to satisfy the observations. The more difficult problem of determining all the elements of planetary motion directly from three observed places, remained unsolved until the discovery of *Ceres* by PIAZZI in 1801, by which the attention of GAUSS was directed to this subject, the result of which was the subsequent publication of his *Theoria Motus Corporum Cœlestium*, a most able work, in which he gave to the world, in a finished form, the results of many years of attention to the subject of which it treats. His method for determining all the elements directly from given observed places, as given in the *Theoria Motus*, and as subsequently given in a revised form by ENCKE, leaves scarcely any thing to be desired on this topic. In the same work he gave the first explanation of the method of least squares, a method which has been of inestimable service in investigations depending on observed data.

The discovery of the minor planets directed attention also to the methods of determining their perturbations, since those applied in the case of the major planets were found to be inapplicable. For a long time astronomers were content simply to compute the special perturbations of these bodies from epoch to epoch, and it was not until the commencement of the brilliant researches by HANSEN that serious hopes were entertained of being able to compute successfully the general perturbations of these bodies. By devising an entirely new mode of considering the perturbations, namely, by determining what may be called the perturbations of the time, and thus passing from the undisturbed place to the disturbed place, and by other ingenious analytical and mechanical devices, he succeeded in effecting a solution of this most difficult problem, and his latest works contain all the formulæ which are required for the cases actually occurring. The refined and difficult analysis and the laborious calculations involved were such that, even after HANSEN's methods were made known, astronomers still adhered to the method of special perturbations by the variation of constants as developed by LAGRANGE.

The discovery of *Astræa* by HENCKE was speedily followed by the discovery of other planets, and fortunately indeed it so happened that the subject of special perturbations was to receive a new improvement. The discovery by BOND and ENCKE of a method by which we determine at once the variations of the rectangular co-ordinates of the disturbed body by integrating the fundamental equations of motion by means of mechanical quadrature, directed the attention of HANSEN to this phase of the problem, and soon after he gave formulæ for the determination of the perturbations of the latitude, the mean anomaly, and the logarithm of the radius-vector, which are exceedingly convenient in the process of integration, and which have been found to give the most satisfactory results. The formulæ for the perturbations of the latitude, true longitude, and radius-vector, to be integrated in the same manner, were afterwards given by BRÜNNOW.

Having thus stated briefly a few historical facts relating to the problems of theoretical astronomy, I proceed to a statement of the object of this work. The discovery of so many planets and comets has furnished a wide field for exercise in the calculations relating to their motions, and it has occurred to me that a work which should contain a development of all the formulæ required in determining the orbits of the heavenly bodies directly from given observed places, and in correcting these orbits by means of more extended discussions of series of observations, including also the determination of the perturbations, together with a complete collection of auxiliary tables, and also such practical directions as might guide the inexperienced computer, might add very materially to the progress of the science by attracting the attention of a greater number of competent computers. Having carefully read the works of the great masters, my plan was to prepare a complete work on this subject, commencing with the fundamental principles of dynamics, and systematically treating, from one point of view, all the problems presented. The scope and the arrangement of the work will be best understood after an examination of its contents; and let it suffice to add that I have endeavored to keep constantly in view the wants of the computer, providing for the exceptional cases as they occur, and giving all the formulæ which appeared to me to be best adapted to the problems under consideration. I have not thought it worth while to trace out the geometrical signification of many of the auxiliary quantities introduced. Those who are curious in such matters may readily derive many beautiful theorems from a consideration of the relations of some of these auxiliaries. For convenience, the formulæ are numbered consecutively through each chapter, and the references to those of a preceding chapter are defined by adding a subscript figure denoting the number of the chapter.

Besides having read the works of those who have given special attention to these problems, I have consulted the *Astronomische Nachrichten*, the *Astronomical Journal*, and other astronomical periodicals, in which is to be found much valuable information resulting from the experience of those who have been or are now actively engaged in astronomical pursuits. I must also express my obligations to the publishers,

Messrs. J. B. LIPPINCOTT & Co., for the generous interest which they have manifested in the publication of the work, and also to Dr. B. A. GOULD, of Cambridge, Mass., and to Dr. OPPOLZER, of Vienna, for valuable suggestions.

For the determination of the time from the perihelion and of the true anomaly in very eccentric orbits I have given the method proposed by BESSEL in the *Monatliche Correspondenz*, vol. xii.,—the tables for which were subsequently given by BRÜNNOW in his *Astronomical Notices*,—and also the method proposed by GAUSS, but in a more convenient form. For obvious reasons, I have given the solution for the special case of parabolic motion before completing the solution of the general problem of finding all of the elements of the orbit by means of three observed places. The differential formulæ and the other formulæ for correcting approximate elements are given in a form convenient for application, and the formulæ for finding the chord or the time of describing the subtended arc of the orbit, in the case of very eccentric orbits, will be found very convenient in practice.

I have given a pretty full development of the application of the theory of probabilities to the combination of observations, endeavoring to direct the attention of the reader, as far as possible, to the sources of error to be apprehended and to the most advantageous method of treating the problem so as to eliminate the effects of these errors. For the rejection of doubtful observations, according to theoretical considerations, I have given the simple formula, suggested by CHAUVENET, which follows directly from the fundamental equations for the probability of errors, and which will answer for the purposes here required as well as the more complete criterion proposed by PEIRCE. In the chapter devoted to the theory of special perturbations I have taken particular pains to develop the whole subject in a complete and practical form, keeping constantly in view the requirements for accurate and convenient numerical application. The time is adopted as the independent variable in the determination of the perturbations of the elements directly, since experience has established the convenience of this form; and should it be desired to change the independent variable and to use the differential coefficients with respect to the eccentric anomaly, the equations between this function and the mean motion will enable us to effect readily the required transformation.

The numerical examples involve data derived from actual observations, and care has been taken to make them complete in every respect, so as to serve as a guide to the efforts of those not familiar with these calculations; and when different fundamental planes are spoken of, it is presumed that the reader is familiar with the elements of spherical astronomy, so that it is unnecessary to state, in all cases, whether the centre of the sphere is taken at the centre of the earth, or at any other point in space.

The preparation of the Tables has cost me a great amount of labor, logarithms of ten decimals being employed in order to be sure of the last decimal given. Several of those in previous use have been recomputed and extended, and others here given for the first time have been prepared with special care. The adopted value of the constant of the solar attraction is that given by GAUSS, which, as will appear, is not accurately in accordance with the adoption of the mean distance of the earth from the sun as the unit of space; but until the absolute value of the earth's mean motion is known, it is best, for the sake of uniformity and accuracy, to retain GAUSS's constant.

The preparation of this work has been effected amid many interruptions, and with other labors constantly pressing me, by which the progress of its publication has been somewhat delayed, even since the stereotyping was commenced, so that in some cases I have been anticipated in the publication of formulæ which would have here appeared for the first time. I have, however, endeavored to perform conscientiously the self-imposed task, seeking always to secure a logical sequence in the development of the formulæ, to preserve uniformity and elegance in the notation, and to elucidate the successive steps in the analysis, so that the work may be read by those who, possessing a respectable mathematical education, desire to be informed of the means by which astronomers are enabled to arrive at so many grand results connected with the motions of the heavenly bodies, and by which the grandeur and sublimity of creation are unveiled. The labor of the preparation of the work will have been fully repaid if it shall be the means of directing a more general attention to the study of the wonderful mechanism of the heavens, the contemplation of which must ever serve to impress upon the mind the reality of the perfection of the OMNIPOTENT, the LIVING GOD!

OBSERVATORY, ANN ARBOR, June, 1867.

CONTENTS.

THEORETICAL ASTRONOMY.

CHAPTER I.

INVESTIGATION OF THE FUNDAMENTAL EQUATIONS OF MOTION, AND OF THE FORMULÆ FOR DETERMINING, FROM KNOWN ELEMENTS, THE HELIOCENTRIC AND GEOCENTRIC PLACES OF A HEAVENLY BODY, ADAPTED TO NUMERICAL COMPUTATION FOR CASES OF ANY ECCENTRICITY WHATEVER.

CHAPTER II.

INVESTIGATION OF THE DIFFERENTIAL FORMULÆ WHICH EXPRESS THE RELATION BETWEEN THE GEOCENTRIC OR HELIOCENTRIC PLACES OF A HEAVENLY BODY AND THE VARIATIONS OF THE ELEMENTS OF ITS ORBIT.

CHAPTER III.

INVESTIGATION OF FORMULÆ FOR COMPUTING THE ORBIT OF A COMET MOVING IN A PARABOLA, AND FOR CORRECTING APPROXIMATE ELEMENTS BY THE VARIATION OF THE GEOCENTRIC DISTANCE.

CHAPTER IV.

DETERMINATION, FROM THREE COMPLETE OBSERVATIONS, OF THE ELEMENTS OF THE ORBIT OF A HEAVENLY BODY, INCLUDING THE ECCENTRICITY OR FORM OF THE CONIC SECTION.

CHAPTER V.

DETERMINATION OF THE ORBIT OF A HEAVENLY BODY FROM FOUR OBSERVATIONS, OF WHICH THE SECOND AND THIRD MUST BE COMPLETE.

CHAPTER VI.

INVESTIGATION OF VARIOUS FORMULÆ FOR THE CORRECTION OF THE APPROXIMATE ELEMENTS OF THE ORBIT OF A HEAVENLY BODY.

CHAPTER VII.

METHOD OF LEAST SQUARES, THEORY OF THE COMBINATION OF OBSERVATIONS, AND DETERMINATION OF THE MOST PROBABLE SYSTEM OF ELEMENTS FROM A SERIES OF OBSERVATIONS.

CHAPTER VIII.

INVESTIGATION OF VARIOUS FORMULÆ FOR THE DETERMINATION OF THE SPECIAL PERTURBATIONS OF A HEAVENLY BODY.

TABLES.

THEORETICAL ASTRONOMY.

CHAPTER I.

INVESTIGATION OF THE FUNDAMENTAL EQUATIONS OF MOTION, AND OF THE FORMULÆ FOR DETERMINING, FROM KNOWN ELEMENTS, THE HELIOCENTRIC AND GEOCENTRIC PLACES OF A HEAVENLY BODY, ADAPTED TO NUMERICAL COMPUTATION FOR CASES OF ANY ECCENTRICITY WHATEVER.

1. THE study of the motions of the heavenly bodies does not require that we should know the ultimate limit of divisibility of the matter of which they are composed,—whether it may be subdivided indefinitely, or whether the limit is an indivisible, impenetrable atom. Nor are we concerned with the relations which exist between the separate atoms or molecules, except so far as they form, in the aggregate, a definite body whose relation to other bodies of the system it is required to investigate. On the contrary, in considering the operation of the laws in obedience to which matter is aggregated into single bodies and systems of bodies, it is sufficient to conceive simply of its divisibility to a limit which may be regarded as infinitesimal compared with the finite volume of the body, and to regard the magnitude of the element of matter thus arrived at as a mathematical point.

An element of matter, or a material body, cannot give itself motion; neither can it alter, in any manner whatever, any motion which may have been communicated to it. This tendency of matter to resist all changes of its existing state of rest or motion is known as *inertia*, and is the fundamental law of the motion of bodies. Experience invariably confirms it as a law of nature; the continuance of motion as resistances are removed, as well as the sensibly unchanged motion of the heavenly bodies during many centuries, affording the most convincing proof of its universality. Whenever, therefore, a material point experiences any change of its state as respects rest or motion, the cause must be attributed to the operation of something external to the element itself, and which we designate by the word *force*. The nature of forces is generally unknown, and we estimate them by the effects which they produce. They are thus rendered comparable with some unit, and may be expressed by abstract numbers.

2. If a material point, free to move, receives an impulse by virtue of the action of any force, or if, at any instant, the force by which motion is communicated shall cease to act, the subsequent motion of the point, according to the law of inertia, must be rectilinear and *uniform*, equal spaces being described in equal times. Thus, if s, v, and t represent, respectively, the *space*, the *velocity*, and the *time*, the measure of v being the space described in a unit of time, we shall have, in this case,

$$s = vt.$$

It is evident, however, that the space described in a unit of time will vary with the intensity of the force to which the motion is due, and, the nature of the force being unknown, we must necessarily compare the velocities communicated to the point by different forces, in order to arrive at the relation of their effects. We are thus led to regard the force as proportional to the velocity; and this also has received the most indubitable proof as being a law of nature. Hence, the principles of the composition and resolution of forces may be applied also to the composition and resolution of velocities.

If the force acts incessantly, the velocity will be accelerated, and the force which produces this motion is called an *accelerating* force. In regard to the mode of operation of the force, however, we may consider it as acting absolutely without cessation, or we may regard it as acting instantaneously at successive infinitesimal intervals represented by dt, and hence the motion as uniform during each of these intervals. The latter supposition is that which is best adapted to the requirements of the infinitesimal calculus; and, according to the fundamental principles of this calculus, the finite result will be the same as in the case of a force whose action is absolutely incessant. Therefore, if we represent the element of space by ds, and the element of time by dt, the instantaneous velocity will be

$$v = \frac{ds}{dt},$$

which will vary from one instant to another.

3. Since the force is proportional to the velocity, its measure at any instant will be determined by the corresponding velocity. If the accelerating force is constant, the motion will be uniformly accelerated; and if we designate the *acceleration* due to the force by f, the unit of f being the velocity generated in a unit of time, we shall have

$$v = ft.$$

If, however, the force be variable, we shall have, at any instant, the relation

$$f = \frac{dv}{dt},$$

the force being regarded as constant in its action during the element of time dt. The instantaneous value of v gives, by differentiation,

$$\frac{dv}{dt} = \frac{d^2s}{dt^2},$$

and hence we derive

$$f = \frac{d^2s}{dt^2}; \qquad (1)$$

so that, in varied motion, the acceleration due to the force is measured by the second differential of the space divided by the square of the element of time.

4. By the *mass* of the body we mean its absolute quantity of matter. The *density* is the mass of a unit of volume, and hence the entire mass is equal to the volume multiplied by the density. If it is required to compare the forces which act upon different bodies, it is evident that the masses must be considered. If equal masses receive impulses by the action of instantaneous forces, the forces acting on each will be to each other as the velocities imparted; and if we consider as the unit of force that which gives to a unit of mass the unit of velocity, we have for the measure of a force F, denoting the mass by M,

$$F = Mv.$$

This is called the *quantity of motion* of the body, and expresses its capacity to overcome inertia. By virtue of the inert state of matter, there can be no action of a force without an equal and contrary reaction; for, if the body to which the force is applied is fixed, the equilibrium between the resistance and the force necessarily implies the development of an equal and contrary force; and, if the body be free to move, in the change of state, its inertia will oppose equal and contrary resistance. Hence, as a necessary consequence of inertia, it follows that action and reaction are simultaneous, equal, and contrary.

If the body is acted upon by a force such that the motion is varied, the accelerating force upon each element of its mass is represented by $\frac{dv}{dt}$, and the entire *motive force* F is expressed by

$$F = M\frac{dv}{dt},$$

M being the sum of all the elements, or the mass of the body. Since

$$v = \frac{ds}{dt},$$

this gives

$$F = M\frac{d^2s}{dt^2},$$

which is the expression for the intensity of the motive force, or of the force of inertia developed. For the unit of mass, the measure of the force is

$$\frac{d^2s}{dt^2};$$

and this, therefore, expresses that part of the intensity of the motive force which is impressed upon the unit of mass, and is what is usually called the *accelerating force.*

5. The force in obedience to which the heavenly bodies perform their journey through space, is known as the *attraction of gravitation;* and the law of the operation of this force, in itself simple and unique, has been confirmed and generalized by the accumulated researches of modern science. Not only do we find that it controls the motions of the bodies of our own solar system, but that the revolutions of binary systems of stars in the remotest regions of space proclaim the universality of its operation. It unfailingly explains all the phenomena observed, and, outstripping observation, it has furnished the means of predicting many phenomena subsequently observed. The law of this force is that *every particle of matter is attracted by every other particle by a force which varies directly as the mass and inversely as the square of the distance of the attracting particle.*

This reciprocal action is instantaneous, and is not modified, in any degree, by the interposition of other particles or bodies of matter. It is also absolutely independent of the nature of the molecules themselves, and of their aggregation.

If we consider two bodies the masses of which are m and m', and whose magnitudes are so small, relatively to their mutual distance ρ, that we may regard them as material points, according to the law of gravitation, the action of m on each molecule or unit of m' will be $\frac{m}{\rho^2}$, and the total force on m' will be

$$m'\frac{m}{\rho^2}.$$

The action of m' on each molecule of m will be expressed by $\frac{m'}{\rho^2}$, and its total action by

$$m\,\frac{m'}{\rho^2}.$$

The absolute or moving force with which the masses m and m' tend toward each other is, therefore, the same on each body, which result is a necessary consequence of the equality of action and reaction. The velocities, however, with which these bodies would approach each other must be different, the velocity of the smaller mass exceeding that of the greater, and in the ratio of the masses moved. The expression for the velocity of m', which would be generated in a unit of time if the force remained constant, is obtained by dividing the absolute force exerted by m by the mass moved, which gives

$$\frac{m}{\rho^2},$$

and this is, therefore, the measure of the acceleration due to the action of m at the distance ρ. For the acceleration due to the action of m' we derive, in a similar manner,

$$\frac{m'}{\rho^2}.$$

6. Observation shows that the heavenly bodies are nearly spherical in form, and we shall therefore, preparatory to finding the equations which express the relative motions of the bodies of the system, determine the attraction of a spherical mass of uniform density, or varying from the centre to the surface according to any law, for a point exterior to it.

If we suppose a straight line to be drawn through the centre of the sphere and the point attracted, the total action of the sphere on the point will be a force acting along this line, since the mass of the sphere is symmetrical with respect to it. Let dm denote an element of the mass of the sphere, and ρ its distance from the point attracted; then will

$$\frac{dm}{\rho^2}$$

express the action of this element on the point attracted. If we suppose the density of the sphere to be constant, and equal to unity, the element dm becomes an element of volume, and will be expressed by

$$dm = dx\,dy\,dz;$$

x, y, and z being the co-ordinates of the element referred to a system of rectangular co-ordinates. If we take the origin of co-ordinates at the centre of the sphere, and introduce polar co-ordinates, so that

$$x = r\cos\varphi\cos\theta,$$
$$y = r\cos\varphi\sin\theta,$$
$$z = r\sin\varphi,$$

the expression for dm becomes

$$dm = r^2\cos\varphi\,dr\,d\varphi\,d\theta;$$

and its action on the point attracted is

$$df = \frac{r^2\cos\varphi\,dr\,d\varphi\,d\theta}{\rho^2}.$$

If we suppose the axis of z to be directed to the point attracted, the co-ordinates of this point will be

$$x' = 0, \qquad y' = 0, \qquad z' = a,$$

a being the distance of the point from the centre of the sphere, and, since

$$\rho^2 = (x - x')^2 + (y - y')^2 + (z - z')^2,$$

we shall have

$$\rho^2 = a^2 - 2ar\sin\varphi + r^2.$$

The component of the force df in the direction of the line a, joining the point attracted and the centre of the sphere, is

$$df\cos\gamma,$$

where γ is the angle at the point attracted between the element dm and the centre of the sphere. It is evident that the sum of all the components which act in the direction of the line a will express the total action of the sphere, since the sum of those which act perpendicular to this line, taken so as to include the entire mass of the sphere, is zero.

But we have

$$a = z + \rho \cos \gamma,$$

and hence

$$\cos \gamma = \frac{a - r \sin \varphi}{\rho}.$$

The differentiation of the expression for ρ^2, with respect to a, gives

$$\frac{d\rho}{da} = \frac{a - r \sin \varphi}{\rho} = \cos \gamma.$$

Therefore, if we denote the attraction of the sphere by A, we shall have, by means of the values of df and $\cos \gamma$,

$$dA = \frac{r^2 \cos \varphi \, dr \, d\varphi \, d\theta}{\rho^2} \cdot \frac{d\rho}{da},$$

or

$$dA = - r^2 \cos \varphi \, dr \, d\varphi \, d\theta \frac{d\frac{1}{\rho}}{da}.$$

The polar co-ordinates r, φ, and θ are independent of a, and hence

$$dA = - \frac{d\frac{r^2 \cos \phi \, dr \, d\phi \, d\theta}{\rho}}{da}.$$

Let us now put

$$dV = \frac{r^2 \cos \varphi \, dr \, d\varphi \, d\theta}{\rho}, \tag{2}$$

and we shall have

$$A = - \frac{dV}{da}.$$

Consequently, to find the total action of the sphere on the given point, we have only to find V by means of equation (2), the limits of the integration being taken so as to include the entire mass of the sphere, and then find its differential coefficient with respect to a.

If we integrate equation (2) first with reference to θ, for which ρ is constant, between the limits $\theta = 0$ and $\theta = 2\pi$, we get

$$V = 2\pi \iint \frac{r^2 \cos \varphi \, dr \, d\varphi}{\rho}.$$

This must be integrated between the limits $\varphi = + \frac{1}{2}\pi$ and $\varphi = - \frac{1}{2}\pi$;

but since ρ is a function of φ, if we differentiate the expression for ρ^2 with respect to φ, we have

$$r \cos \varphi \, d\varphi = -\frac{\rho}{a} \, d\rho,$$

and hence

$$V = -\frac{2\pi}{a} \iint r \, dr \, d\rho.$$

Corresponding to the limits of φ we have $\rho = a - r$, and $\rho = a + r$; and taking the integral with respect to ρ between these limits, we obtain

$$V = -\frac{4\pi}{a} \int r^2 \, dr.$$

Integrating, finally, between the limits $r = 0$ and $r = r_{,}$, we get

$$V = -\tfrac{4}{3} \frac{\pi r_{,}^3}{a},$$

$r_{,}$ being the radius of the sphere, and, if we denote its entire mass by m, this becomes

$$V = -\frac{m}{a}.$$

Therefore,

$$A = -\frac{dV}{da} = \frac{m}{a^2},$$

from which it appears that the action of a homogeneous spherical mass on a point exterior to it, is the same as if the entire mass were concentrated at its centre. If, in the integration with respect to r, we take the limits r' and r'', we obtain

$$A = \tfrac{4}{3} \frac{\pi \left(r''^3 - r'^3\right)}{a^2},$$

and, denoting by m_0 the mass of a spherical shell whose radii are r'' and r', this becomes

$$A = \frac{m_0}{a^2}.$$

Consequently, the attraction of a homogeneous spherical shell on a point exterior to it, is the same as if the entire mass were concentrated at its centre.

The supposition that the point attracted is situated within a spherical shell of uniform density, does not change the form of the general equation; but, in the integration with reference to ρ, the limits will be $\rho = r + a$, and $\rho = r - a$, which give

$$V = -4\pi \int r\, dr;$$

and this being independent of a, we have

$$A = -\frac{dV}{da} = 0.$$

Whence it follows that a point placed in the interior of a spherical shell is equally attracted in all directions, and that, if not subject to the action of any extraneous force, it will be in equilibrium in every position.

7. Whatever may be the law of the change of the density of the heavenly bodies from the surface to the centre, we may regard them as composed of homogeneous, concentric layers, the density varying only from one layer to another, and the number of the layers may be indefinite. The action of each of these will be the same as if its mass were united at the centre of the shell; and hence the total action of the body will be the same as if the entire mass were concentrated at its centre of gravity. The planets are indeed not exactly spheres, but oblate spheroids differing but little from spheres; and the error of the assumption of an exact spherical form, so far as relates to their action upon each other, is extremely small, and is in fact compensated by the magnitude of their distances from each other; for, whatever may be the form of the body, if its dimensions are small in comparison with its distance from the body which it attracts, it is evident that its action will be sensibly the same as if its entire mass were concentrated at its centre of gravity. If we suppose a system of bodies to be composed of spherical masses, each unattended with any satellite, and if we suppose that the dimensions of the bodies are small in comparison with their mutual distances, the formation of the equations for the motion of the bodies of the system will be reduced to the consideration of the motions of simple points endowed with forces of attraction corresponding to the respective masses. Our solar system is, in reality, a compound system, the several systems of primary and satellites corresponding nearly to the case supposed; and, before proceeding with the formation of the equations which are applicable to the general case, we will consider, at first, those for a simple system of bodies, considered as points and subject to their mutual actions and the action of the forces which correspond to the

actual velocities of the different parts of the system for any instant. It is evident that we cannot consider the motion of any single body as free, and subject only to the action of the primitive impulsion which it has received and the accelerating forces which act upon it; but, on the contrary, the motion of each body will depend on the force which acts upon it directly, and also on the reaction due to the other bodies of the system. The consideration, however, of the variations of the motion of the several bodies of the system is reduced to the simple case of equilibrium by means of the general principle that, if we assign to the different bodies of the system motions which are modified by their mutual action, we may regard these motions as composed of those which the bodies actually have and of other motions which are destroyed, and which must therefore necessarily be such that, if they alone existed, the system would be in equilibrium. We are thus enabled to form at once the equations for the motion of a system of bodies. Let m, m', m'', &c. be the masses of the several bodies of the system, and x, y, z, x', y', z', &c. their co-ordinates referred to any system of rectangular axes. Further, let the components of the total force acting upon a unit of the mass of m, or of the accelerating force, resolved in directions parallel to the co-ordinate axes, be denoted by X, Y, and Z, respectively, then will

$$mX, \qquad mY, \qquad mZ,$$

be the forces which act upon the body in the same directions. The velocities of the body m at any instant, in directions parallel to the co-ordinate axes, will be

$$\frac{dx}{dt}, \qquad \frac{dy}{dt}, \qquad \frac{dz}{dt};$$

and the corresponding forces are

$$m\frac{dx}{dt}, \qquad m\frac{dy}{dt}, \qquad m\frac{dz}{dt}.$$

By virtue of the action of the accelerating force, these forces for the next instant become

$$m\frac{dx}{dt} + mXdt, \qquad m\frac{dy}{dt} + mYdt, \qquad m\frac{dz}{dt} + mZdt,$$

which may be written respectively:

$$m\frac{dx}{dt}+md\frac{dx}{dt}-md\frac{dx}{dt}+mXdt,$$
$$m\frac{dy}{dt}+md\frac{dy}{dt}-md\frac{dy}{dt}+mYdt,$$
$$m\frac{dz}{dt}+md\frac{dz}{dt}-md\frac{dz}{dt}+mZdt.$$

The actual velocities for this instant are

$$\frac{dx}{dt}+d\frac{dx}{dt},\qquad \frac{dy}{dt}+d\frac{dy}{dt},\qquad \frac{dz}{dt}+d\frac{dz}{dt};$$

and the corresponding forces are

$$m\frac{dx}{dt}+md\frac{dx}{dt},\qquad m\frac{dy}{dt}+md\frac{dy}{dt},\qquad m\frac{dz}{dt}+md\frac{dz}{dt}.$$

Comparing these with the preceding expressions for the forces, it appears that the forces which are destroyed, in directions parallel to the co-ordinate axes, are

$$\begin{aligned}&-md\frac{dx}{dt}+mXdt,\\ &-md\frac{dy}{dt}+mYdt,\\ &-md\frac{dz}{dt}+mZdt.\end{aligned}\tag{3}$$

In the same manner we find for the forces which will be destroyed in the case of the body m':

$$-m'd\frac{dx'}{dt}+m'X'dt,$$
$$-m'd\frac{dy'}{dt}+m'Y'dt,$$
$$-m'd\frac{dz'}{dt}+m'Z'dt;$$

and similarly for the other bodies of the system. According to the general principle above enunciated, the system under the action of these forces alone, will be in equilibrium. The conditions of equilibrium for a system of points of invariable but arbitrary form, and subject to the action of forces directed in any manner whatever, are

$$\Sigma X_{,}=0,\qquad \Sigma Y_{,}=0,\qquad \Sigma Z_{,}=0,$$
$$\Sigma(Y_{,}x-X_{,}y)=0,\qquad \Sigma(X_{,}z-Z_{,}x)=0,\qquad \Sigma(Z_{,}y-Y_{,}z)=0;$$

in which $X_{,}$, $Y_{,}$, $Z_{,}$, denote the components, resolved parallel to the co-ordinate axes, of the forces acting on any point, and x, y, z, the co-ordinates of the point. These equations are equally applicable to the case of the equilibrium at any instant of a system of variable form; and substituting in them the expressions (3) for the forces destroyed in the case of a system of bodies, we shall have

$$\begin{aligned}
&\Sigma m\frac{d^2x}{dt^2} - \Sigma mX = 0,\\
&\Sigma m\frac{d^2y}{dt^2} - \Sigma mY = 0,\\
&\Sigma m\frac{d^2z}{dt^2} - \Sigma mZ = 0,\\
&\Sigma m\left(x\frac{d^2y}{dt^2} - y\frac{d^2x}{dt^2}\right) - \Sigma m\,(Yx - Xy) = 0,\\
&\Sigma m\left(z\frac{d^2x}{dt^2} - x\frac{d^2z}{dt^2}\right) - \Sigma m\,(Xz - Zx) = 0,\\
&\Sigma m\left(y\frac{d^2z}{dt^2} - z\frac{d^2y}{dt^2}\right) - \Sigma m\,(Zy - Yz) = 0;
\end{aligned} \qquad (4)$$

which are the general equations for the motions of a system of bodies.

8. Let $x_{\prime}$, $y_{\prime}$, $z_{\prime}$, be the co-ordinates of the centre of gravity of the system, and, by differentiation of the equations for the co-ordinates of the centre of gravity, which are

$$x_{\prime} = \frac{\Sigma mx}{\Sigma m}, \qquad y_{\prime} = \frac{\Sigma my}{\Sigma m}, \qquad z_{\prime} = \frac{\Sigma mz}{\Sigma m},$$

we get

$$\frac{d^2x_{\prime}}{dt^2} = \frac{\Sigma m\frac{d^2x}{dt^2}}{\Sigma m}, \qquad \frac{d^2y_{\prime}}{dt^2} = \frac{\Sigma m\frac{d^2y}{dt^2}}{\Sigma m}, \qquad \frac{d^2z_{\prime}}{dt^2} = \frac{\Sigma m\frac{d^2z}{dt^2}}{\Sigma m}.$$

Introducing these values into the first three of equations (4), they become

$$\frac{d^2x_{\prime}}{dt^2} = \frac{\Sigma mX}{\Sigma m}; \qquad \frac{d^2y_{\prime}}{dt^2} = \frac{\Sigma mY}{\Sigma m}, \qquad \frac{d^2z_{\prime}}{dt^2} = \frac{\Sigma mZ}{\Sigma m}; \qquad (5)$$

from which it appears that the centre of gravity of the system moves in space as if the masses of the different bodies of which it is composed, were united in that point, and the forces directly applied to it.

If we suppose that the only accelerating forces which act on the bodies of the system, are those which result from their mutual action, we have the obvious relation:

$$mX = -m'X', \qquad mY = -m'Y', \qquad mZ = -m'Z',$$

and similarly for any two bodies; and, consequently,

$$\Sigma mX = 0, \qquad \Sigma mY = 0, \qquad \Sigma mZ = 0;$$

so that equations (5) become

$$\frac{d^2x_{,}}{dt^2} = 0, \qquad \frac{d^2y_{,}}{dt^2} = 0, \qquad \frac{d^2z_{,}}{dt^2} = 0.$$

Integrating these once, and denoting the constants of integration by c, c', c'', we find, by combining the results,

$$\frac{dx_{,}^2 + dy_{,}^2 + dz_{,}^2}{dt^2} = v^2 = c^2 + c'^2 + c''^2;$$

and hence the absolute motion of the centre of gravity of the system, when subject only to the mutual action of the bodies which compose it, must be uniform and rectilinear. Whatever, therefore, may be the relative motions of the different bodies of the system, the motion of its centre of gravity is not thereby affected.

9. Let us now consider the last three of equations (4), and suppose the system to be submitted only to the mutual action of the bodies which compose it, and to a force directed toward the origin of co-ordinates. The action of m' on m, according to the law of gravitation, is expressed by $\frac{m'}{\rho^2}$, in which ρ denotes the distance of m from m'. To resolve this force in directions parallel to the three rectangular axes, we must multiply it by the cosine of the angle which the line joining the two bodies makes with the co-ordinate axes respectively, which gives

$$X = \frac{m'(x' - x)}{\rho^3}, \qquad Y = \frac{m'(y' - y)}{\rho^3}, \qquad Z = \frac{m'(z' - z)}{\rho^3}.$$

Further, for the components of the accelerating force of m on m', we have

$$X' = \frac{m(x - x')}{\rho^3}, \qquad Y' = \frac{m(y - y')}{\rho^3}, \qquad Z' = \frac{m(z - z')}{\rho^3}.$$

Hence we derive

$$m(Yx - Xy) + m'(Y'x' - X'y') = 0,$$

and generally

$$\Sigma m(Yx - Xy) = 0. \tag{6}$$

In a similar manner, we find

$$\begin{aligned}\Sigma m\,(Xz - Zx) &= 0,\\ \Sigma m\,(Zy - Yz) &= 0.\end{aligned}\tag{7}$$

These relations will not be altered if, in addition to their reciprocal action, the bodies of the system are acted upon by forces directed to the origin of co-ordinates. Thus, in the case of a force acting upon m, and directed to the origin of co-ordinates, we have, for its action alone,

$$Yx = Xy, \qquad Xz = Zx, \qquad Zy = Yz,$$

and similarly for the other bodies. Hence these forces disappear from the equations, and, therefore, when the several bodies of the system are subject only to their reciprocal action and to forces directed to the origin of co-ordinates, the last three of equations (4) become

$$\begin{aligned}\Sigma m\left(x\frac{d^2y}{dt^2} - y\frac{d^2x}{dt^2}\right) &= 0,\\ \Sigma m\left(z\frac{d^2x}{dt^2} - x\frac{d^2z}{dt^2}\right) &= 0,\\ \Sigma m\left(y\frac{d^2z}{dt^2} - z\frac{d^2y}{dt^2}\right) &= 0,\end{aligned}$$

the integration of which gives

$$\begin{aligned}\Sigma m\,(xdy - ydx) &= cdt,\\ \Sigma m\,(zdx - xdz) &= c'dt,\\ \Sigma m\,(ydz - zdy) &= c''dt,\end{aligned}\tag{8}$$

c, c', and c'' being the constants of integration. Now, $xdy - ydx$ is double the area described about the origin of co-ordinates by the projection of the radius-vector, or line joining m with the origin of co-ordinates, on the plane of xy during the element of time dt; and, further, $zdx - xdz$ and $ydz - zdy$ are respectively double the areas described, during the same time, by the projection of the radius-vector on the planes of xz and yz. The constant c, therefore, expresses the sum of the products formed by multiplying the *areal velocity* of each body, in the direction of the co-ordinate plane xy, by its mass; and c', c'', express the same sum with reference to the co-ordinate planes xz and yz respectively. Hence the sum of the areal velocities of the several bodies of the system about the origin of co-ordinates, each multiplied by the corresponding mass, is constant; and the sum of the areas traced, each multiplied by the corresponding mass, is proportional to the time. If the only forces which operate, are those resulting from the mutual action of the bodies which compose the system, this result is correct whatever may be the point in space taken as the origin of co-ordinates.

The areas described by the projection of the radius-vector of each body on the co-ordinate planes, are the projections, on these planes, of the areas actually described in space. We may, therefore, conceive of a resultant, or principal plane of projection, such that the sum of the areas traced by the projection of each radius-vector on this plane, when projected on the three co-ordinate planes, each being multiplied by the corresponding mass, will be respectively equal to the first members of the equations (8). Let α, β, and γ be the angles which this principal plane makes with the co-ordinate planes xy, xz, and yz, respectively; and let S denote the sum of the areas traced on this plane, in a unit of time, by the projection of the radius-vector of each of the bodies of the system, each area being multiplied by the corresponding mass. The sum S will be found to be a maximum, and its projections on the co-ordinate planes, corresponding to the element of time dt, are

$$S \cos \alpha \, dt, \qquad S \cos \beta \, dt, \qquad S \cos \gamma \, dt.$$

Therefore, by means of equations (8), we have

$$c = S \cos \alpha, \qquad c' = S \cos \beta, \qquad c'' = S \cos \gamma,$$

and, since $\cos^2 \alpha + \cos^2 \beta + \cos^2 \gamma = 1$,

$$S^2 = c^2 + c'^2 + c''^2.$$

Hence we derive

$$\cos \alpha = \frac{c}{\sqrt{c^2 + c'^2 + c''^2}}, \qquad \cos \beta = \frac{c'}{\sqrt{c^2 + c'^2 + c''^2}},$$

$$\cos \gamma = \frac{c''}{\sqrt{c^2 + c'^2 + c''^2}}.$$

These angles, being therefore constant and independent of the time, show that this principal plane of projection remains constantly parallel to itself during the motion of the system in space, whatever may be the relative positions of the several bodies; and for this reason it is called the *invariable plane* of the system. Its position with reference to any known plane is easily determined when the velocities, in directions parallel to the co-ordinate axes, and the masses and co-ordinates of the several bodies of the system, are known. The values of c, c', c'' are given by equations (8), and hence the values of α, β, and γ, which determine the position of the invariable plane.

Since the positions of the co-ordinate planes are arbitrary, we may suppose that of xy to coincide with the invariable plane, which gives $\cos\beta = 0$ and $\cos\gamma = 0$, and, therefore, $c' = 0$ and $c'' = 0$. Further, since the positions of the axes of x and y in this plane are arbitrary, it follows that for every plane perpendicular to the invariable plane, the sum of the areas traced by the projections of the radii-vectores of the several bodies of the system, each multiplied by the corresponding mass, is zero. It may also be observed that the value of S is constant whatever may be the position of the co-ordinate planes, and that its value is necessarily greater than that of either of the quantities in the second member of the equatity:

$$S^2 = c^2 + c'^2 + c''^2,$$

except when two of them are each equal to zero. It is, therefore, a maximum, and the invariable plane is also the plane of maximum areas.

10. If we suppose the origin of co-ordinates itself to move with uniform and rectilinear motion in space, the relations expressed by equations (8) will remain unchanged. Thus, let $x_{,}$, $y_{,}$, $z_{,}$ be the co-ordinates of the movable origin of co-ordinates, referred to a fixed point in space taken as the origin; and let x_0, y_0, z_0, x_0', y_0', z_0', &c. be the co-ordinates of the several bodies referred to the movable origin. Then, since the co-ordinate planes in one system remain always parallel to those of the other system of co-ordinates, we shall have

$$x = x_{,} + x_0, \qquad y = y_{,} + y_0, \qquad z = z_{,} + z_0,$$

and similarly for the other bodies of the system. Introducing these values of x, y, and z into the first three of equations (4), they become

$$\Sigma m\left(\frac{d^2x_{,}}{dt^2} + \frac{d^2x_0}{dt^2}\right) - \Sigma mX = 0,$$
$$\Sigma m\left(\frac{d^2y_{,}}{dt^2} + \frac{d^2y_0}{dt^2}\right) - \Sigma mY = 0,$$
$$\Sigma m\left(\frac{d^2z_{,}}{dt^2} + \frac{d^2z_0}{dt^2}\right) - \Sigma mZ = 0.$$

The condition of uniform rectilinear motion of the movable origin gives

$$\frac{d^2x_{,}}{dt^2} = 0, \qquad \frac{d^2y_{,}}{dt^2} = 0, \qquad \frac{d^2z_{,}}{dt^2} = 0,$$

and the preceding equations become

$$\Sigma m \frac{d^2x_0}{dt^2} - \Sigma mX = 0,$$
$$\Sigma m \frac{d^2y_0}{dt^2} - \Sigma mY = 0, \qquad (9)$$
$$\Sigma m \frac{d^2z_0}{dt^2} - \Sigma mZ = 0.$$

Substituting the same values in the last three of equations (4), observing that the co-ordinates $x_{,}$, $y_{,}$, $z_{,}$ are the same for all the bodies of the system, and reducing the resulting equations by means of equations (9), we get

$$\Sigma m\left(x_0 \frac{d^2y_0}{dt^2} - y_0 \frac{d^2x_0}{dt^2}\right) - \Sigma m\,(Yx_0 - Xy_0) = 0,$$
$$\Sigma m\left(z_0 \frac{d^2x_0}{dt^2} - x_0 \frac{d^2z_0}{dt^2}\right) - \Sigma m\,(Xz_0 - Zx_0) = 0, \qquad (10)$$
$$\Sigma m\left(y_0 \frac{d^2z_0}{dt^2} - z_0 \frac{d^2y_0}{dt^2}\right) - \Sigma m\,(Zy_0 - Yz_0) = 0.$$

Hence it appears that the form of the equations for the motion of the system of bodies, remains unchanged when we suppose the origin of co-ordinates to move in space with a uniform and rectilinear motion.

11. The equations already derived for the motions of a system of bodies, considered as reduced to material points, enable us to form at once those for the motion of a solid body. The mutual distances of the parts of the system are, in this case, invariable, and the masses of the several bodies become the elements of the mass of the solid body. If we denote an element of the mass by dm, the equations (5) for the motion of the centre of gravity of the body become

$$m\frac{d^2x_{,}}{dt^2} = \int Xdm, \qquad m\frac{d^2y_{,}}{dt^2} = \int Ydm, \qquad m\frac{d^2z_{,}}{dt^2} = \int Zdm, \qquad (11)$$

the summation, or integration with reference to dm, being taken so as to include the entire mass of the body, from which it appears that the centre of gravity of the body moves in space as if the entire mass were concentrated in that point, and the forces applied to it directly.

If we take the origin of co-ordinates at the centre of gravity of the body, and suppose it to have a rectilinear, uniform motion in space, and denote the co-ordinates of the element dm, in reference to this origin, by x_0, y_0, z_0, we have, by means of the equations (10),

$$\int\left(x_0\frac{d^2y_0}{dt^2}-y_0\frac{d^2x_0}{dt^2}\right)dm-\int(Yx_0-Xy_0)\,dm=0,$$
$$\int\left(z_0\frac{d^2x_0}{dt^2}-x_0\frac{d^2z_0}{dt^2}\right)dm-\int(Xz_0-Zx_0)\,dm=0, \qquad (12)$$
$$\int\left(y_0\frac{d^2z_0}{dt^2}-z_0\frac{d^2y_0}{dt^2}\right)dm-\int(Zy_0-Yz_0)\,dm=0,$$

the integration with respect to dm being taken so as to include the entire mass of the body. These equations, therefore, determine the motion of rotation of the body around its centre of gravity regarded as fixed, or as having a uniform rectilinear motion in space. Equations (11) determine the position of the centre of gravity for any instant, and hence for the successive instants at intervals equal to dt; and we may consider the motion of the body during the element of time dt as rectilinear and uniform, whatever may be the form of its trajectory. Hence, equations (11) and (12) completely determine the position of the body in space,—the former relating to the motion of translation of the centre of gravity, and the latter to the motion of rotation about this point. It follows, therefore, that for any forces which act upon a body we can always decompose the actual motion into those of the translation of the centre of gravity in space, and of the motion of rotation around this point; and these two motions may be considered independently of each other, the motion of the centre of gravity being independent of the form and position of the body about this point.

If the only forces which act upon the body are the reciprocal action of the elements of its mass and forces directed to the origin of coordinates, the second terms of equations (12) become each equal to zero, and the results indicated by equations (8) apply in this case also. The parts of the system being invariably connected, the plane of maximum areas, or *invariable plane*, is evidently that which is perpendicular to the axis of rotation passing through the centre of gravity, and therefore, in the motion of translation of the centre of gravity in space, the axis of rotation remains constantly parallel to itself. Any extraneous force which tends to disturb this relation will necessarily develop a contrary reaction, and hence a rotating body resists any change of its plane of rotation not parallel to itself. We may observe, also, that on account of the invariability of the mutual distances of the elements of the mass, according to equations (8), the motion of rotation must be uniform.

12. We shall now consider the action of a system of bodies on a

distant mass, which we will denote by M. Let $x_0, y_0, z_0, x_0', y_0', z_0'$, &c. be the co-ordinates of the several bodies of the system referred to its centre of gravity as the origin of co-ordinates; $x_,, y_,$, and $z_,$ the co-ordinates of the centre of gravity of the system referred to the centre of gravity of the body M. The co-ordinates of the body m, of the system, referred to this origin, will therefore be

$$x = x_, + x_0, \qquad y = y_, + y_0, \qquad z = z_, + z_0,$$

and similarly for the other bodies of the system. If we denote by r the distance of the centre of gravity of m from that of M, the accelerating force of the former on an element of mass at the centre of gravity of the latter, resolved parallel to the axis of x, will be

$$\frac{mx}{r^3},$$

and, therefore, that of the entire system on the element of M, resolved in the same direction, will be

$$\Sigma\frac{mx}{r^3}.$$

We have also

$$r^2 = (x_, + x_0)^2 + (y_, + y_0)^2 + (z_, + z_0)^2,$$

and, if we denote by $r_,$ the distance of the centre of gravity of the system from M,

$$r_,^2 = x_,^2 + y_,^2 + z_,^2.$$

Therefore

$$\frac{x}{r^3} = (x_, + x_0)\left(r_,^2 + 2\left(x_,x_0 + y_,y_0 + z_,z_0\right) + r_0^2\right)^{-\frac{3}{2}}.$$

We shall now suppose the mutual distances of the bodies of the system to be so small in comparison with the distance $r_,$ of its centre of gravity from that of M, that terms of the order r_0^2 may be neglected; a condition which is actually satisfied in the case of the secondary systems belonging to the solar system. Hence, developing the second factor of the second member of the last equation, and neglecting terms of the order r_0^2, we shall have

$$\frac{x}{r^3} = \frac{x_,}{r_,^3} + \frac{x_0}{r_,^3} - \frac{3x_,(x_,x_0 + y_,y_0 + z_,z_0)}{r_,^5},$$

and

$$\Sigma\frac{mx}{r^3} = x_,\frac{\Sigma m}{r_,^3} + \frac{\Sigma mx_0}{r_,^3} - \frac{3x_,}{r_,^5}\left(x_,\Sigma mx_0 + y_,\Sigma my_0 + z_,\Sigma mz_0\right).$$

But, since x_0, y_0, z_0, are the co-ordinates in reference to the centre of gravity of the system as origin, we have

$$\Sigma m x_0 = 0, \qquad \Sigma m y_0 = 0, \qquad \Sigma m z_0 = 0,$$

and the preceding equation reduces to

$$\Sigma \frac{mx}{r^3} = x_{,} \frac{\Sigma m}{r_{,}^{\,3}}.$$

In a similar manner, we find

$$\Sigma \frac{my}{r^3} = y_{,} \frac{\Sigma m}{r_{,}^{\,3}}, \qquad \Sigma \frac{mz}{r^3} = z_{,} \frac{\Sigma m}{r_{,}^{\,3}}.$$

The second members of these equations are the expressions for the total accelerating force due to the action of the bodies of the system on M, resolved parallel to the co-ordinate axes respectively, when we consider the several masses to be collected at the centre of gravity of the system. Hence we conclude that when an element of mass is attracted by a system of bodies so remote from it that terms of the order of the squares of the co-ordinates of the several bodies, referred to the centre of gravity of the system as the origin of co-ordinates, may be neglected in comparison with the distance of the system from the point attracted, the action of the system will be the same as if the masses were all united at its centre of gravity.

If we suppose the masses m, m', m'', &c. to be the elements of the mass of a single body, the form of the equations remains unchanged; and hence it follows that the mass M is acted upon by another mass, or by a system of bodies, as if the entire mass of the body, or of the system, were collected at its centre of gravity. It is evident, also, that reciprocally in the case of two systems of bodies, in which the mutual distances of the bodies are small in comparison with the distance between the centres of gravity of the two systems, their mutual action is the same as if all the several masses in each system were collected at the common centre of gravity of that system; and the two centres of gravity will move as if the masses were thus united.

13. The results already obtained are sufficient to enable us to form the equations for the motions of the several bodies which compose the solar system. If these bodies were exact spheres, which could be considered as composed of homogeneous concentric spherical shells, the density varying only from one layer to another, the action of

each on an element of the mass of another would be the same as if the entire mass of the attracting body were concentrated at its centre of gravity. The slight deviation from this law, arising from the ellipsoidal form of the heavenly bodies, is compensated by the magnitude of their mutual distances; and, besides, these mutual distances are so great that the action of the attracting body on the entire mass of the body attracted, is the same as if the latter were concentrated at its centre of gravity. Hence the consideration of the reciprocal action of the single bodies of the system, is reduced to that of material points corresponding to their respective centres of gravity, the masses of which, however, are equivalent to those of the corresponding bodies. The mutual distances of the bodies composing the secondary systems of planets attended with satellites are so small, in comparison with the distances of the different systems from each other and from the other planets, that they act upon these, and are reciprocally acted upon, in nearly the same manner as if the masses of the secondary systems were united at their common centres of gravity, respectively. The motion of the centre of gravity of a system consisting of a planet and its satellites is not affected by the reciprocal action of the bodies of that system, and hence it may be considered independently of this action. The difference of the action of the other planets on a planet and its satellites will simply produce inequalities in the relative motions of the latter bodies as determined by their mutual action alone, and will not affect the motion of their common centre of gravity. Hence, in the formation of the equations for the motion of translation of the centres of gravity of the several planets or secondary systems which compose the solar system, we have simply to consider them as points endowed with attractive forces corresponding to the several single or aggregated masses. The investigation of the motion of the satellites of each of the planets thus attended, forms a problem entirely distinct from that of the motion of the common centre of gravity of such a system. The consideration of the motion of rotation of the several bodies of the solar system about their respective centres of gravity, is also independent of the motion of translation. If the resultant of all the forces which act upon a planet passed through the centre of gravity, the motion of rotation would be undisturbed; and, since this resultant in all cases very nearly satisfies this condition, the disturbance of the motion of rotation is very slight. The inequalities thus produced in the motion of rotation are, in fact, sensible, and capable of being indicated by observation, only in the case of the earth and moon. It has, indeed, been rigidly demonstrated that the axis of rotation of the earth relative to the body itself is fixed, so that the poles of rotation and the terrestrial equator preserve constantly the same position in reference to the surface; and that also the velocity of rotation is constant. This assures us of the permanency of geographical positions, and, in connection with the fact that the change of the length of the mean solar day arising from the variation of the obliquity of the ecliptic and in the length of the tropical year, due to the action of the sun, moon, and planets upon the earth, is absolutely insensible, —amounting to only a small fraction of a second in a million of years,—assures us also of the permanence of the interval which we adopt as the unit of time in astronomical investigations.

14. Placed, as we are, on one of the bodies of the system, it is only possible to deduce from observation the relative motions of the different heavenly bodies. These relative motions in the case of the comets and primary planets are referred to the centre of the sun, since the centre of gravity of this body is near the centre of gravity of the system, and its preponderant mass facilitates the integration of the equations thus obtained. In the case, however, of the secondary systems, the motions of the satellites are considered in reference to the centre of gravity of their primaries. We shall, therefore, form the equations for the motion of the planets relative to the centre of gravity of the sun; for which it becomes necessary to consider more particularly the relation between the heterogeneous quantities, space, time, and mass, which are involved in them. Each denomination, being divided by the unit of its kind, is expressed by an abstract number; and hence it offers no difficulty by its presence in an equation. For the unit of space we may arbitrarily take the mean distance of the earth from the sun, and the mean solar day may be taken as the unit of time. But, in order that when the space is expressed by 1, and the time by 1, the force or velocity may also be expressed by 1, if the unit of space is first adopted, the relation of the time and the mass—which determines the measure of the force—will be such that the units of both cannot be arbitrarily chosen. Thus, if we denote by f the acceleration due to the action of the mass m on a material point at the distance a, and by f' the acceleration corresponding to another mass m' acting at the same distance, we have the relation

$$\frac{f}{f'}=\frac{m}{m'};$$

and hence, since the acceleration is proportional to the mass, it may be taken as the measure of the latter. But we have, for the measure of f,

$$f = \frac{d^2s}{dt^2}.$$

Integrating this, regarding f as constant, and the point to move from a state of rest, we get

$$s = \tfrac{1}{2}ft^2. \tag{13}$$

The acceleration in the case of a variable force is, at any instant, measured by the velocity which the force acting at that instant would generate, if supposed to remain constant in its action, during a unit of time. The last equation gives, when $t = 1$,

$$f = 2s;$$

and hence the acceleration is also measured by double the space which would be described by a material point, from a state of rest, during a unit of time, the force being supposed constant in its action during this time. In each case the duration of the unit of time is involved in the measure of the acceleration, and hence in that of the mass on which the acceleration depends; and the unit of mass, or of the force, will depend on the duration which is chosen for the unit of time. In general, therefore, we regard as the unit of mass that which, acting constantly at a distance equal to unity on a material point free to move, will give to this point, in a unit of time, a velocity which, if the force ceased to act, would cause it to describe the unit of distance in the unit of time.

Let the unit of time be a mean solar day; k^2 the acceleration due to the force exerted by the mass of the sun at the unit of distance; and f the acceleration corresponding to the distance r; then will

$$f = \frac{k^2}{r^2},$$

and k^2 becomes the measure of the mass of the sun. The unit of mass is, therefore, equal to the mass of the sun taken as many times as k^2 is contained in unity. Hence, when we take the mean solar day as the unit of time, the mass of the sun is measured by k^2; by which we are to understand that if the sun acted during a mean solar day, on a material point free to move, at a distance constantly equal to the mean distance of the earth from the sun, it would, at the end of that time, have communicated to the point a velocity which, if the force did not thereafter act, would cause it to describe, in a unit of time, the space expressed by k^2.

The acceleration due to the action of the sun at the unit of distance is designated by k^2, since the square root of this quantity appears frequently in the formulæ which will be derived.

If we take arbitrarily the mass of the sun as the unit of mass, the unit of time must be determined. Let t denote the number of mean solar days which must be taken for the unit of time when the unit of mass is the mass of the sun. The space which the force due to this mass, acting constantly on a material point at a distance equal to the mean distance of the earth from the sun, would cause the point to describe in the time t, is, according to equation (13),

$$s = \tfrac{1}{2}k^2t^2.$$

But, since t expresses the number of mean solar days in the unit of time, the measure of the acceleration corresponding to this unit is $2s$, and this being the unit of force, we have

$$k^2t^2 = 1;$$

and hence

$$t = \frac{1}{k}.$$

Therefore, if the mass of the sun is regarded as the unit of mass, the number of mean solar days in the unit of time will be equal to unity divided by the square root of the acceleration due to the force exerted by this mass at the unit of distance. The numerical value of k will be subsequently found to be 0.0172021, which gives 58.13244 mean solar days for the unit of time, when the mass of the sun is taken as the unit of mass.

15. Let x, y, z be the co-ordinates of a heavenly body referred to the centre of gravity of the sun as the origin of co-ordinates; r its *radius-vector*, or distance from this origin; and let m denote the quotient obtained by dividing its mass by that of the sun; then, taking the mean solar day as the unit of time, the mass of the sun is expressed by k^2, and that of the planet or comet by mk^2. For a second body let the co-ordinates be x', y', z'; the distance from the sun, r'; and the mass, $m'k^2$; and similarly for the other bodies of the system. Let the co-ordinates of the centre of gravity of the sun referred to any fixed point in space be ξ, η, ζ, the co-ordinate planes being parallel to those of x, y, and z, respectively; then will the

acceleration due to the action of m on the sun be expressed by $\frac{mk^2}{r^2}$, and the three components of this force in directions parallel to the co-ordinate axes, respectively, will be

$$mk^2\frac{x}{r^3}, \qquad mk^2\frac{y}{r^3}, \qquad mk^2\frac{z}{r^3}.$$

The action of m' on the sun will be expressed by

$$m'k^2\frac{x'}{r'^3}, \qquad m'k^2\frac{y'}{r'^3}, \qquad m'k^2\frac{z'}{r'^3},$$

and hence the acceleration due to the combined and simultaneous action of the several bodies of the system on the sun, resolved parallel to the co-ordinate axes, will be

$$k^2\Sigma\frac{mx}{r^3}, \qquad k^2\Sigma\frac{my}{r^3}, \qquad k^2\Sigma\frac{mz}{r^3}.$$

The motion of the centre of gravity of the sun, relative to the fixed origin, will, therefore, be determined by the equations

$$\frac{d^2\xi}{dt^2} = k^2\Sigma\frac{mx}{r^3}, \qquad \frac{d^2\eta}{dt^2} = k^2\Sigma\frac{my}{r^3}, \qquad \frac{d^2\zeta}{dt^2} = k^2\Sigma\frac{mz}{r^3}. \quad (14)$$

Let ρ denote the distance of m from m'; ρ' its distance from m'', adding an accent for each successive body considered; then will the action of the bodies m', m'', &c. on m be

$$k^2\Sigma\frac{m'}{\rho^2},$$

of which the three components parallel to the co-ordinate axes, respectively, are

$$k^2\Sigma m'\frac{x'-x}{\rho^3}, \qquad k^2\Sigma m'\frac{y'-y}{\rho^3}, \qquad k^2\Sigma m'\frac{z'-z}{\rho^3}.$$

The action of the sun on m, resolved in the same manner, is expressed by

$$-\frac{k^2x}{r^3}, \qquad -\frac{k^2y}{r^3}, \qquad -\frac{k^2z}{r^3},$$

which are negative, since the force tends to diminish the co-ordinates x, y, and z. The three components of the total action of the other bodies of the system on m are, therefore,

$$-\frac{k^2x}{r^3}+k^2\Sigma\frac{m'(x'-x)}{\rho^3},$$
$$-\frac{k^2y}{r^3}+k^2\Sigma\frac{m'(y'-y)}{\rho^3},$$
$$-\frac{k^2z}{r^3}+k^2\Sigma\frac{m'(z'-z)}{\rho^3};$$

and, since the co-ordinates of m referred to the fixed origin are

$$\xi+x, \qquad \eta+y, \qquad \zeta+z,$$

the equations which determine the absolute motion are

$$\begin{aligned}
\frac{d^2\xi}{dt^2}+\frac{d^2x}{dt^2}+\frac{k^2x}{r^3}&=k^2\Sigma\frac{m'(x'-x)}{\rho^3},\\
\frac{d^2\eta}{dt^2}+\frac{d^2y}{dt^2}+\frac{k^2y}{r^3}&=k^2\Sigma\frac{m'(y'-y)}{\rho^3},\\
\frac{d^2\zeta}{dt^2}+\frac{d^2z}{dt^2}+\frac{k^2z}{r^3}&=k^2\Sigma\frac{m'(z'-z)}{\rho^3},
\end{aligned} \tag{15}$$

the symbol of summation in the second members relating simply to the masses and co-ordinates of the several bodies which act on m, exclusive of the sun. Substituting for $\frac{d^2\xi}{dt^2}$, $\frac{d^2\eta}{dt^2}$, and $\frac{d^2\zeta}{dt^2}$ their values given by equations (14), we get

$$\begin{aligned}
\frac{d^2x}{dt^2}+k^2(1+m)\frac{x}{r^3}&=k^2\Sigma m'\left(\frac{x'-x}{\rho^3}-\frac{x'}{r'^3}\right),\\
\frac{d^2y}{dt^2}+k^2(1+m)\frac{y}{r^3}&=k^2\Sigma m'\left(\frac{y'-y}{\rho^3}-\frac{y'}{r'^3}\right),\\
\frac{d^2z}{dt^2}+k^2(1+m)\frac{z}{r^3}&=k^2\Sigma m'\left(\frac{z'-z}{\rho^3}-\frac{z'}{r'^3}\right).
\end{aligned} \tag{16}$$

Since x, y, z are the co-ordinates of m relative to the centre of gravity of the sun, these equations determine the motion of m relative to that point. The second members may be put in another form, which greatly facilitates the solution of some of the problems relating to the motion of m. Thus, let us put

$$\Omega=\frac{m'}{1+m}\left(\frac{1}{\rho}-\frac{xx'+yy'+zz'}{r'^3}\right)+\frac{m''}{1+m}\left(\frac{1}{\rho'}-\frac{xx''+yy''+zz''}{r''^3}\right)+\ldots\text{\&c.}, \tag{17}$$

and we shall have for the partial differential coefficient of this with respect to x,

$$\left(\frac{d\Omega}{dx}\right)=\frac{m'}{1+m}\left(-\frac{1}{\rho^2}\cdot\frac{d\rho}{dx}-\frac{x'}{r'^3}\right)+\frac{m''}{1+m}\left(-\frac{1}{\rho'^2}\frac{d\rho'}{dx}-\frac{x''}{r''^3}\right)+\ldots\text{\&c.}$$

But, since

$$\rho^2 = (x' - x)^2 + (y' - y)^2 + (z' - z)^2,$$
$$\rho'^2 = (x'' - x)^2 + (y'' - y)^2 + (z'' - z)^2,$$

we have

$$\frac{d\rho}{dx} = -\frac{x' - x}{\rho}, \qquad \frac{d\rho'}{dx} = -\frac{x'' - x}{\rho'},$$

and hence we derive

$$\left(\frac{d\Omega}{dx}\right) = \frac{m'}{1+m}\left(\frac{x' - x}{\rho^3} - \frac{x'}{r'^3}\right) + \frac{m''}{1+m}\left(\frac{x'' - x}{\rho'^3} - \frac{x''}{r''^3}\right) + \ldots \&c.$$

or

$$(1 + m)\left(\frac{d\Omega}{dx}\right) = \Sigma m'\left(\frac{x' - x}{\rho^3} - \frac{x'}{r'^3}\right).$$

We find, also, in the same manner, for the partial differential coefficients with respect to y and z,

$$(1 + m)\left(\frac{d\Omega}{dy}\right) = \Sigma m'\left(\frac{y' - y}{\rho^3} - \frac{y'}{r'^3}\right),$$
$$(1 + m)\left(\frac{d\Omega}{dz}\right) = \Sigma m'\left(\frac{z' - z}{\rho^3} - \frac{z'}{r'^3}\right).$$

The equations (16), therefore, become

$$\begin{aligned} \frac{d^2x}{dt^2} + k^2(1 + m)\frac{x}{r^3} &= k^2(1 + m)\left(\frac{d\Omega}{dx}\right), \\ \frac{d^2y}{dt^2} + k^2(1 + m)\frac{y}{r^3} &= k^2(1 + m)\left(\frac{d\Omega}{dy}\right), \\ \frac{d^2z}{dt^2} + k^2(1 + m)\frac{z}{r^3} &= k^2(1 + m)\left(\frac{d\Omega}{dz}\right). \end{aligned} \tag{18}$$

It will be observed that the second members of equations (16) express the difference between the action of the bodies m', m'', &c. on m and on the sun, resolved parallel to the co-ordinate axes respectively. The mutual distances of the planets are such that these quantities are generally very small, and we may, therefore, in a first approximation to the motion of m relative to the sun, neglect the second members of these equations; and the integrals which may then be derived, express what is called the *undisturbed* motion of m. By means of the results thus obtained for the several bodies successively, the approximate values of the second members of equations (16) may be found, and hence a still closer approximation to the actual motion of m. The force whose components are expressed by the second members of these equations is called the *disturbing force;*

and, using the second form of the equations, the function Ω, which determines these components, is called the *perturbing function.* The complete solution of the problem is facilitated by an artifice of the infinitesimal calculus, known as the variation of parameters, or of constants, according to which the complete integrals of equations (16) are of the same form as those obtained by putting the second members equal to zero, the arbitrary constants, however, of the latter integration being regarded as variables. These constants of integration are the *elements* which determine the motion of m relative to the sun, and when the disturbing force is neglected the elements are pure constants. The variations of these, or of the co-ordinates, arising from the action of the disturbing force are, in almost all cases, very small, and are called the *perturbations.* The problem which first presents itself is, therefore, the determination of all the circumstances of the undisturbed motion of the heavenly bodies, after which the action of the disturbing forces may be considered.

It may be further remarked that, in the formation of the preceding equations, we have supposed the different bodies to be free to move, and, therefore, subject only to their mutual action. There are, indeed, facts derived from the study of the motion of the comets which seem to indicate that there exists in space a *resisting medium* which opposes the free motion of all the bodies of the system. If such a medium actually exists, its effect is very small, so that it can be sensible only in the case of rare and attenuated bodies like the comets, since the accumulated observations of the different planets do not exhibit any effect of such resistance. But, if we assume its existence, it is evidently necessary only to add to the second members of equations (16) a force which shall represent the effect of this resistance,—which, therefore, becomes a part of the disturbing force,—and the motion of m will be completely determined.

16. When we consider the undisturbed motion of a planet or comet relative to the sun, or simply the motion of the body relative to the sun as subject only to the reciprocal action of the two bodies, the equations (16) become

$$\begin{aligned}\frac{d^2x}{dt^2}+k^2(1+m)\frac{x}{r^3}&=0,\\ \frac{d^2y}{dt^2}+k^2(1+m)\frac{y}{r^3}&=0,\\ \frac{d^2z}{dt^2}+k^2(1+m)\frac{z}{r^3}&=0.\end{aligned}\tag{19}$$

The equations for the undisturbed motion of a satellite relative to its primary are of the same form, the value of k^2, however, being in this case the acceleration due to the force exerted by the mass of the primary at the unit of distance, and m the ratio of the mass of the satellite to that of the primary.

The integrals of these equations introduce six arbitrary constants of integration, which, when known, will completely determine the undisturbed motion of m relative to the sun.

If we multiply the first of these equations by y, and the second by x, and subtract the last product from the first, we shall find, by integrating the result,

$$\frac{xdy - ydx}{dt} = c,$$

c being an arbitrary constant.

In a similar manner, we obtain

$$\frac{xdz - zdx}{dt} = c', \qquad \frac{ydz - zdy}{dt} = c''.$$

If we multiply these three equations respectively by z, $-y$, and x, and add the products, we obtain

$$cz - c'y + c''x = 0.$$

This, being the equation of a plane passing through the origin of co-ordinates, shows that the path of the body relative to the sun is a plane curve, and that *the plane of the orbit passes through the centre of the sun.*

Again, if we multiply the first of equations (19) by $2dx$, the second by $2dy$, and the third by $2dz$, take the sum and integrate, we shall find

$$\frac{dx^2 + dy^2 + dz^2}{dt^2} + 2k^2(1 + m)\int\frac{xdx + ydy + zdz}{r^3} = 0.$$

But, since $r^2 = x^2 + y^2 + z^2$, we shall have, by differentiation,

$$rdr = xdx + ydy + zdz.$$

Therefore, introducing this value into the preceding equation, we obtain

$$\frac{dx^2 + dy^2 + dz^2}{dt^2} - \frac{2k^2(1 + m)}{r} + h = 0, \qquad (20)$$

h being an arbitrary constant.

If we add together the squares of the expressions for c, c', and c'', and put $c^2 + c'^2 + c''^2 = 4f^2$, we shall have

$$\frac{(x^2+y^2+z^2)(dx^2+dy^2+dz^2)}{dt^2} - \frac{(xdx+ydy+zdz)^2}{dt^2} = 4f^2;$$

or

$$r^2\frac{dx^2+dy^2+dz^2}{dt^2} - \frac{r^2dr^2}{dt^2} = 4f^2. \qquad (21)$$

If we represent by dv the infinitely small angle contained between two consecutive radii-vectores r and $r + dr$, since $dx^2 + dy^2 + dz^2$ is the square of the element of path described by the body, we shall have

$$dx^2 + dy^2 + dz^2 = dr^2 + r^2dv^2.$$

Substituting this value in the preceding equation, it becomes

$$r^2dv = 2fdt. \qquad (22)$$

The quantity r^2dv is double the area included by the element of path described in the element of time dt, and by the radii-vectores r and $r + dr$; and f, therefore, represents the *areal velocity*, which, being a constant, shows that the *radius-vector of a planet or comet describes equal areas in equal intervals of time.*

From the equations (20) and (21) we find, by elimination,

$$dt = \frac{rdr}{\sqrt{2rk^2(1+m) - hr^2 - 4f^2}}. \qquad (23)$$

Substituting this value of dt in equation (22), we get

$$dv = \frac{2fdr}{r\sqrt{2rk^2(1+m) - hr^2 - 4f^2}}, \qquad (24)$$

which gives, in order to find the maximum and minimum values of r,

$$\frac{dr}{dv} = \frac{r\sqrt{2rk^2(1+m) - hr^2 - 4f^2}}{2f} = 0,$$

or

$$2rk^2(1+m) - hr^2 - 4f^2 = 0.$$

Therefore

$$\frac{k^2(1+m)}{h} + \sqrt{-\frac{4f^2}{h} + \frac{k^4(1+m)^2}{h^2}},$$

and

$$\frac{k^2(1+m)}{h} - \sqrt{-\frac{4f^2}{h} + \frac{k^4(1+m)^2}{h^2}},$$

are, respectively, the maximum and minimum values of r. The points of the orbit, or trajectory of the body relative to the sun, corresponding to these values of r, are called the *apsides;* the former, the *aphelion,* and the latter, the *perihelion.* If we represent these values, respectively, by $a(1+e)$ and $a(1-e)$, we shall have

$$h = \frac{k^2(1+m)}{a}; \qquad 4f^2 = ak^2(1+m)(1-e^2) = k^2p(1+m),$$

in which $p = a(1-e^2)$. Introducing these values into the equation (24), it becomes

$$dv = \frac{\sqrt{p}\,dr}{r\sqrt{2r - \frac{1}{a}r^2 - p}} = -\frac{\frac{p}{e}\,d\frac{1}{r}}{\sqrt{1-\left(\frac{p}{e}\cdot\frac{1}{r}-\frac{1}{e}\right)^2}},$$

the integral of which gives

$$v = \omega + \cos^{-1}\frac{1}{e}\left(\frac{p}{r}-1\right),$$

ω being an arbitrary constant. Therefore we shall have

$$\frac{1}{e}\left(\frac{p}{r}-1\right) = \cos(v-\omega),$$

from which we derive

$$r = \frac{p}{1+e\cos(v-\omega)},$$

which is the polar equation of a conic section, the pole being at the focus, p being the semi-parameter, e the eccentricity, and $v-\omega$ the angle at the focus between the radius-vector and a fixed line, in the plane of the orbit, making the angle ω with the semi-transverse axis a.

If the angle $v-\omega$ is counted from the perihelion, we have $\omega = 0$, and

$$r = \frac{p}{1+e\cos v}. \tag{25}$$

The angle v is called the *true anomaly.*

Hence we conclude that *the orbit of a heavenly body revolving around the sun is a conic section with the sun in one of the foci.* Observation shows that the planets revolve around the sun in ellipses, usually of small eccentricity, while the comets revolve either in ellipses of great eccentricity, in parabolas, or in hyperbolas, a circumstance which, as we shall have occasion to notice hereafter, greatly lessens the amount of labor in many computations respecting their motion.

Introducing into equation (23) the values of h and $4f^2$ already found, we obtain

$$dt = \frac{\sqrt{a}}{k\sqrt{1+m}} \cdot \frac{rdr}{\sqrt{a^2e^2 - (a-r)^2}},$$

which may be written

$$dt = -\frac{a^{\frac{3}{2}}}{k\sqrt{1+m}} \cdot \frac{\left(1 - \frac{a-r}{a}\right) d\left(\frac{a-r}{ae}\right)}{\sqrt{1 - \left(\frac{a-r}{ae}\right)^2}},$$

or

$$dt = \frac{a^{\frac{3}{2}}}{k\sqrt{1+m}} \left(\frac{-d\left(\frac{a-r}{ae}\right)}{\sqrt{1-\left(\frac{a-r}{ae}\right)^2}} + e\,\frac{\frac{a-r}{ae}\,d\left(\frac{a-r}{ae}\right)}{\sqrt{1-\left(\frac{a-r}{ae}\right)^2}} \right),$$

the integration of which gives

$$t = \frac{a^{\frac{3}{2}}}{k\sqrt{1+m}} \left(\cos^{-1}\left(\frac{a-r}{ae}\right) - e\sqrt{1-\left(\frac{a-r}{ae}\right)^2} \right) + C. \qquad (26)$$

In the perihelion, $r = a(1-e)$, and the integral reduces to $t' = C$; therefore, if we denote the time from the perihelion by t_0, we shall have

$$t_0 = \frac{a^{\frac{3}{2}}}{k\sqrt{1+m}} \left(\cos^{-1}\left(\frac{a-r}{ae}\right) - e\sqrt{1-\left(\frac{a-r}{ae}\right)^2} \right). \qquad (27)$$

In the aphelion, $r = a(1+e)$; and therefore we shall have, for the time in which the body passes from the perihelion to the aphelion, $t_0 = \frac{1}{2}\tau$, or

$$\tfrac{1}{2}\tau = \frac{a^{\frac{3}{2}}}{k\sqrt{1+m}}\pi,$$

τ being the periodic time, or time of one revolution of the planet around the sun, a the semi-transverse axis of the orbit, or *mean distance* from the sun, and π the semi-circumference of a circle whose radius is unity. Therefore we shall have

$$\tau^2 = 4\pi^2 \frac{a^3}{k^2(1+m)}. \qquad (28)$$

For a second planet, we shall have

$$\tau'^2 = 4\pi^2 \frac{a'^3}{k^2(1+m')};$$

and, consequently, between the mean distances and periodic times of any two planets, we have the relation

$$\frac{(1+m)\tau^2}{(1+m')\tau'^2} = \frac{a^3}{a'^3}. \tag{29}$$

If the masses of the two planets m and m' are very nearly the same, we may take $1+m = 1+m'$; and hence, in this case, it follows that *the squares of the periodic times are to each other as the cubes of the mean distances from the sun.* The same result may be stated in another form, which is sometimes more convenient. Thus, since πab is the area of the ellipse, a and b representing the semi-axes, we shall have

$$\frac{\pi ab}{\tau} = f = \text{areal velocity};$$

and, since $b^2 = a^2(1-e^2)$, we have

$$f = \frac{\pi a^{\frac{3}{2}} a^{\frac{1}{2}} (1-e^2)^{\frac{1}{2}}}{\tau} = \frac{\pi a^{\frac{3}{2}} \sqrt{p}}{\tau},$$

which becomes, by substituting the value of τ already found,

$$f = \tfrac{1}{2} k \sqrt{p(1+m)}. \tag{30}$$

In like manner, for a second planet, we have

$$f' = \tfrac{1}{2} k \sqrt{p'(1+m')};$$

and, if the masses are such that we may take $1+m$ sensibly equal to $1+m'$, it follows that, in this case, *the areas described in equal times, in different orbits, are proportional to the square roots of their parameters.*

17. We shall now consider the signification of some of the constants of integration already introduced. Let i denote the inclination of the orbit of m to the plane of xy, which is thus taken as the plane of reference, and let Ω be the angle formed by the axis of x and the line of intersection of the plane of the orbit with the plane of xy; then will the angles i and Ω determine the position of the plane of

the orbit in space. The constants c, c', and c'', involved in the equation

$$cz - c'y + c''x = 0,$$

are, respectively, double the projections, on the co-ordinate planes, xy, xz, and yz, of the areal velocity f; and hence we shall have

$$c = 2f \cos i.$$

The projection of $2f$ on a plane passing through the intersection of the plane of the orbit with the plane of xy, and perpendicular to the latter, is

$$2f \sin i;$$

and the projection of this on the plane of xz, to which it is inclined at an angle equal to Ω, gives

$$c' = 2f \sin i \cos \Omega.$$

Its projection on the plane of yz gives

$$c'' = 2f \sin i \sin \Omega.$$

Hence we derive

$$z \cos i - y \sin i \cos \Omega + x \sin i \sin \Omega = 0, \tag{31}$$

which is the equation of the plane of the orbit; and, by means of the value of f in terms of p, and the values of c, c', c'', we derive, also,

$$\begin{aligned} x\frac{dy}{dt} - y\frac{dx}{dt} &= k\sqrt{p\,(1+m)} \cos i, \\ x\frac{dz}{dt} - z\frac{dx}{dt} &= k\sqrt{p\,(1+m)} \cos \Omega \sin i, \\ y\frac{dz}{dt} - z\frac{dy}{dt} &= k\sqrt{p\,(1+m)} \sin \Omega \sin i. \end{aligned} \tag{32}$$

These equations will enable us to determine Ω, i, and p, when, for any instant, the mass and co-ordinates of m, and the components of its velocity, in directions parallel to the co-ordinate axes, are known. The constants a and e are involved in the value of p, and hence four constants, or *elements*, are introduced into these equations, two of which, a and e, relate to the form of the orbit, and two, Ω and i, to the position of its plane in space. If we measure the angle $v - \omega$ from the point in which the orbit intersects the plane of xy, the constant ω will determine the position of the orbit in its own plane. Finally, the constant of integration C, in equation (26), is the time of passage through the perihelion; and this determines the position of the body in its orbit. When these six constants are known, the undisturbed orbit of the body is completely determined.

Let V denote the velocity of the body in its orbit; then will equation (20) become

$$V^2 = k^2 (1 + m) \left(\frac{2}{r} - \frac{1}{a} \right).$$

At the perihelion, r is a minimum, and hence, according to this equation, the corresponding value of V is a maximum. At the aphelion, V is a minimum.

In the parabola, $a = \infty$, and hence

$$V = k \sqrt{1 + m} \sqrt{\frac{2}{r}},$$

which will determine the velocity at any instant, when r is known. It will be observed that the velocity, corresponding to the same value of r, in an elliptic orbit is less than in a parabolic orbit, and that, since a is negative in the hyperbola, the velocity in a hyperbolic orbit is still greater than in the case of the parabola. Further, since the velocity is thus found to be independent of the eccentricity, the direction of the motion has no influence on the species of conic section described.

If the position of a heavenly body at any instant, and the direction and magnitude of its velocity, are given, the relations already derived will enable us to determine the six constant elements of its orbit. But since we cannot know in advance the magnitude and direction of the primitive impulse communicated to the body, it is only by the aid of observation that these elements can be derived; and therefore, before considering the formulæ necessary to determine unknown elements by means of observed positions, we will investigate those which are necessary for the determination of the heliocentric and geocentric places of the body, assuming the elements to be known. The results thus obtained will facilitate the solution of the problem of finding the unknown elements from the data furnished by observation.

18. To determine the value of k, which is a constant for the solar system, we have, from equation (28),

$$k = \frac{2\pi}{\tau} \cdot \frac{a^{\frac{3}{2}}}{\sqrt{1 + m}}.$$

In the case of the earth, $a=1$, and therefore

$$k=\frac{2\pi}{\tau\sqrt{1+m}}.$$

In reducing this formula to numbers we should properly use, for τ, the absolute length of the sidereal year, which is invariable. The effect of the action of the other bodies of the system on the earth is to produce a very small secular change in its mean longitude corresponding to any fixed date taken as the epoch of the elements; and a correction corresponding to this secular variation should be applied to the value of τ derived from observation. The effect of this correction is to slightly increase the observed value of τ; but to determine it with precision requires an exact knowledge of the masses of all the bodies of the system, and a complete theory of their relative motions,—a problem which is yet incompletely solved. Astronomical usage has, therefore, sanctioned the employment of the value of k found by means of the length of the sidereal year derived directly from observation. This is virtually adopting as the unit of space a distance which is very little less than the absolute, invariable mean distance of the earth from the sun; but, since this unit may be arbitrarily chosen, the accuracy of the results is not thereby affected.

The value of τ from which the adopted value of k has been computed, is 365.2563835 mean solar days; and the value of the combined mass of the earth and moon is

$$m=\frac{1}{354710}.$$

Hence we have $\log\tau=2.5625978148$; $\log\sqrt{1+m}=0.0000006122$; $\log 2\pi=0.7981798684$; and, consequently,

$$\log k=8.2355814414.$$

If we multiply this value of k by 206264.81, the number of seconds of arc corresponding to the radius of a circle, we shall obtain its value expressed in seconds of arc in a circle whose radius is unity, or on the orbit of the earth supposed to be circular. The value of k in seconds is, therefore,

$$\log k=3.5500065746.$$

The quantity $\frac{2\pi}{\tau}$ expresses the mean angular motion of a planet in a mean solar day, and is usually designated by μ. We shall, therefore, have

$$\mu = \frac{k\sqrt{1+m}}{a^{\frac{3}{2}}}, \tag{33}$$

for the expression for the *mean daily motion* of a planet.

Since, in the case of the earth, $\sqrt{1+m}$ differs very little from 1, it will be observed that k very nearly expresses the mean angular motion of the earth in a mean solar day.

In the case of a small planet or of a comet, the mass m is so small that it may, without sensible error, be neglected; and then we shall have

$$\mu = \frac{k}{a^{\frac{3}{2}}}. \tag{34}$$

For the old planets whose masses are considerable, the rigorous expression (33) must be used.

19. Let us now resume the polar equation of the ellipse, the pole being at the focus, which is

$$r = \frac{a(1-e^2)}{1 + e\cos v}.$$

If we represent by φ the angle included between the conjugate axis and a line drawn from the extremity of this axis to the focus, we shall have

$$\sin\varphi = e;$$

and, since $a(1-e^2)$ is half the parameter of the transverse axis, which we have designated by p, we have

$$r = \frac{p}{1 + \sin\varphi\cos v}.$$

The angle φ is called the *angle of eccentricity*.

Again, since $p = a(1-e^2) = a\cos^2\varphi$, we have

$$r = \frac{a\cos^2\varphi}{1 + \sin\varphi\cos v} \tag{35}$$

It is evident, from this equation, that the maximum value of r in an elliptic orbit corresponds to $v = 180°$, and that the minimum value of r corresponds to $v = 0$. It therefore increases from the perihelion to the aphelion, and then decreases as the planet approaches the perihelion.

In the case of the parabola, $\varphi = 90°$, and $\sin\varphi = e = 1$; consequently,

$$r = \frac{p}{1 + \cos v}.$$

But, since $1 + \cos v = 2\cos^2\frac{1}{2}v$, if we put $q = \frac{1}{2}p$, we shall have

$$r = \frac{q}{\cos^2\frac{1}{2}v}, \tag{36}$$

in which q is the *perihelion distance*. In this case, therefore, when $v = \pm 180°$, r will be infinite, and the comet will never return, but course its way to other systems.

The angle φ cannot be applied to the case of the hyperbola, since in a hyperbolic orbit e is greater than 1; and, therefore, the eccentricity cannot be expressed by the sine of an arc. If, however, we designate by ψ the angle which the asymptote to the hyperbola makes with the transverse axis, we shall have

$$e\cos\psi = 1.$$

Introducing this value of e into the polar equation of the hyperbola, it becomes

$$r = \frac{p\cos\psi}{\cos v + \cos\psi}.$$

But, since $\cos v + \cos\psi = 2\cos\frac{1}{2}(v + \psi)\cos\frac{1}{2}(v - \psi)$, this gives

$$r = \frac{p\cos\psi}{2\cos\frac{1}{2}(v + \psi)\cos\frac{1}{2}(v - \psi)}. \tag{37}$$

It appears from this formula that r increases with v, and becomes infinite when $1 + e\cos v = 0$, or $\cos v = -\cos\psi$, in which case $v = 180° - \psi$: consequently, the maximum positive value of v is represented by $180° - \psi$, and the maximum negative value by $-(180° - \psi)$. Further, it is evident that the orbit will be that branch of the hyperbola which corresponds to the focus in which the sun is placed, since, under the operation of an attractive force, the path of the body must be concave toward the centre of attraction. A body subject to a force of repulsion of the same intensity, and varying according to the same law, would describe the other branch of the curve.

The problem of finding the position of a heavenly body as seen from any point of reference, consists of two parts: first, the determination of the place of the body in its orbit; and then, by means of this and of the elements which fix the position of the plane of the orbit, and that of the orbit in its own plane, the determination of the position in space.

In deriving the formulæ for finding the place of the body in its orbit, we will consider each species of conic section separately, commencing with the ellipse.

20. Since the value of $a - r$ can never exceed the limits $-ae$ and $+ae$, we may introduce an auxiliary angle such that we shall have

$$\frac{a-r}{ae} = \cos E.$$

This auxiliary angle E is called the *eccentric anomaly;* and its geometrical signification may be easily known from its relation to the true anomaly. Introducing this value of $\frac{a-r}{ae}$ into the equation (27) and writing $t - T$ in place of t_0, T being the *time of perihelion passage,* and t the time for which the place of the planet in its orbit is to be computed, we obtain

$$\frac{k\sqrt{1+m}}{a^{\frac{3}{2}}}(t-T) = E - e\sin E. \tag{38}$$

But $\frac{k\sqrt{1+m}}{a^{\frac{3}{2}}}$ = *mean daily motion* of the planet $= \mu$; therefore

$$\mu(t-T) = E - e\sin E.$$

The quantity $\mu(t-T)$ represents what would be the angular distance from the perihelion if the planet had moved uniformly in a circular orbit whose radius is a, its mean distance from the sun. It is called the *mean anomaly,* and is usually designated by M. We shall, therefore, have

$$M = \mu(t-T),$$
$$M = E - e\sin E. \tag{39}$$

When the planet or comet is in its perihelion, the true anomaly, mean anomaly, and eccentric anomaly are each equal to zero. All three of these increase from the perihelion to the aphelion, where they are each equal to 180°, and decrease from the aphelion to the perihelion, provided that they are considered negative. From the perihelion to the aphelion v is greater than E, and E is greater than M. The same relation holds true from the aphelion to the perihelion, if we regard, in this case, the values of v, E, and M as negative.

As soon as the auxiliary angle E is obtained by means of the mean motion and eccentricity, the values of r and v may be derived. For this purpose there are various formulæ which may be applied in practice, and which we will now develop.

The equation

$$\frac{a-r}{ae} = \cos E,$$

gives

$$r = a(1 - e\cos E). \tag{40}$$

This also gives

$$\frac{a-r}{e} - ae = a\cos E - ae,$$

or

$$\frac{p-r}{e} = a\cos E - ae,$$

which, by means of equation (25), reduces to

$$r\cos v = a\cos E - ae. \tag{41}$$

If we square both members of equations (40) and (41), and subtract the latter result from the former, we get

$$r^2\sin^2 v = a^2(1-e^2)\sin^2 E,$$

or

$$r\sin v = a\sqrt{1-e^2}\sin E = b\sin E. \tag{42}$$

By means of the equations (41) and (42) it may be easily shown that the auxiliary angle E, or eccentric anomaly, is the angle at the centre of the ellipse between the semi-transverse axis, and a line drawn from the centre to the point where the prolongation of the ordinate perpendicular to this axis, and drawn through the place of the body, meets the circumference of the circumscribed circle.

Equations (40) and (41) give

$$r(1 \mp \cos v) = a(1 \pm e)(1 \mp \cos E).$$

By using first the upper sign, and then the lower sign, we obtain, by reduction,

$$\begin{aligned} \sqrt{r}\sin\tfrac{1}{2}v &= \sqrt{a(1+e)}\sin\tfrac{1}{2}E, \\ \sqrt{r}\cos\tfrac{1}{2}v &= \sqrt{a(1-e)}\cos\tfrac{1}{2}E, \end{aligned} \tag{43}$$

which are convenient for the calculation of r and v, and especially so when several places are required. By division, these equations give

$$\tan\tfrac{1}{2}v = \sqrt{\frac{1+e}{1-e}}\tan\tfrac{1}{2}E. \tag{44}$$

Since $e = \sin\varphi$, we have

$$\frac{1-e}{1+e} = \frac{1-\sin\varphi}{1+\sin\varphi} = \tan^2(45^\circ - \tfrac{1}{2}\varphi).$$

Consequently,

$$\tan\tfrac{1}{2}E = \tan(45^\circ - \tfrac{1}{2}\varphi)\tan\tfrac{1}{2}v. \tag{45}$$

Again,

$$\sqrt{1+e} = \sqrt{1+\sin\varphi} = \sqrt{1 + 2\sin\tfrac{1}{2}\varphi\cos\tfrac{1}{2}\varphi},$$

which may be written

$$\sqrt{1+e} = \sqrt{\sin^2\tfrac{1}{2}\varphi + \cos^2\tfrac{1}{2}\varphi + 2\sin\tfrac{1}{2}\varphi\cos\tfrac{1}{2}\varphi},$$

or

$$\sqrt{1+e} = \sin\tfrac{1}{2}\varphi + \cos\tfrac{1}{2}\varphi.$$

In a similar manner we find

$$\sqrt{1-e} = -\sin\tfrac{1}{2}\varphi + \cos\tfrac{1}{2}\varphi.$$

From these two equations we obtain

$$\begin{aligned} \sqrt{1+e} + \sqrt{1-e} &= 2\cos\tfrac{1}{2}\varphi, \\ \sqrt{1+e} - \sqrt{1-e} &= 2\sin\tfrac{1}{2}\varphi, \end{aligned} \tag{46}$$

which are convenient in many transformations of equations involving e or φ.

Equation (42) gives

$$\sin E = \frac{r\sin v}{b} = \frac{p\sin v}{b(1+e\cos v)};$$

but $p = a\cos^2\varphi$, and $b = a\cos\varphi$, hence

$$\sin E = \frac{r\sin v}{a\cos\varphi} = \frac{\cos\varphi\sin v}{1+e\cos v}. \tag{47}$$

Equation (41) gives

$$\cos E = \frac{r\cos v + ae}{a} = \frac{p\cos v}{a(1+e\cos v)} + e,$$

or

$$\cos E = \frac{p\cos v + ae + ae^2\cos v}{a(1+e\cos v)};$$

and, putting $a\cos^2\varphi$ instead of p, and $\sin\varphi$ for e, we get

$$\cos E = \frac{\cos v + e}{1+e\cos v}. \tag{48}$$

If we multiply the first of equations (43) by $\cos\tfrac{1}{2}E$, and the second by $\sin \frac{1}{2}E$, successively add and subtract the products, and reduce by means of the preceding equations, we obtain

$$\sin \tfrac{1}{2}(v+E) = \sqrt{\frac{a}{r}} \cos \tfrac{1}{2}\varphi \sin E,$$

$$\sin \tfrac{1}{2}(v-E) = \sqrt{\frac{a}{r}} \sin \tfrac{1}{2}\varphi \sin E. \tag{49}$$

The perihelion distance, in an elliptic orbit, is given by the equation

$$q = a(1-e).$$

21. The difference between the true and the mean anomaly, or $v - M$, is called the *equation of the centre*, and is positive from the perihelion to the aphelion, and negative from the aphelion to the perihelion. When the body is in either apsis, the equation of the centre will be equal to zero.

We have, from equation (39),

$$E = M + e \sin E.$$

Expanding this by Lagrange's theorem, we get

$$F(E) = F(M) + \sin M \frac{dF(M)}{dM} \cdot \frac{e}{1} + \frac{d}{dM}\left(\sin^2 M \frac{dF(M)}{dM}\right)\frac{e^2}{1 \cdot 2}$$
$$+ \frac{d^2}{dM^2}\left(\sin^3 M \frac{dF(M)}{dM}\right)\frac{e^3}{1 \cdot 2 \cdot 3} + \ldots \tag{50}$$

Let us now take, equation (40),

$$F(E) = (1 - e \cos E)^{-2} = \frac{a^2}{r^2},$$

and, consequently,

$$F(M) = (1 - e \cos M)^{-2}.$$

Therefore we shall have

$$\frac{a^2}{r^2} = (1 - e \cos M)^{-2} - 2e^2 \sin^2 M (1 - e \cos M)^{-3}$$
$$- e^3 \frac{d}{dM}\left(\sin^3 M (1 - e \cos M)^{-3}\right) - \ldots .$$

Expanding these terms, and performing the operations indicated, we get

$$\frac{a^2}{r^2} = 1 + 2e \cos M + \frac{e^2}{2}(6 \cos^2 M - 4 \sin^2 M)$$
$$+ \frac{e^3}{4}(16 \cos^3 M - 36 \sin^2 M \cos M) + \ldots,$$

which reduces to

$$\frac{a^2}{r^2}=1+2e\cos M+\frac{e^2}{2}(1+5\cos 2M)+\frac{e^3}{4}(13\cos 3M+3\cos M)+\ldots \quad (51)$$

Equation (22) gives

$$dv=\frac{2fdt}{r^2},$$

and, since $f=\frac{1}{2}k\sqrt{p(1+m)}$, we have

$$dv=\frac{k\sqrt{p(1+m)}}{r^2}\,dt, \quad (52)$$

or

$$dv=\frac{k\sqrt{1+m}}{a^{\frac{3}{2}}}\cdot\frac{a^2}{r^2}\sqrt{1-e^2}\,dt.$$

But $\frac{k\sqrt{1+m}}{a^{\frac{3}{2}}}=\mu$, and therefore

$$dv=\sqrt{1-e^2}\,\frac{a^2}{r^2}\,\mu dt=\sqrt{1-e^2}\,\frac{a^2}{r^2}\,dM.$$

By expanding the factor $\sqrt{1-e^2}$, we obtain

$$\sqrt{1-e^2}=1-\tfrac{1}{2}e^2-\tfrac{1}{8}e^4-\ldots,$$

and hence

$$dv=(1-\tfrac{1}{2}e^2-\ldots)\,\frac{a^2}{r^2}\,dM.$$

Substituting for $\frac{a^2}{r^2}$ its value from equation (51), and integrating, we get, since $v=0$ when $M=0$,

$$v-M=2e\sin M+\tfrac{5}{4}e^2\sin 2M+\frac{e^3}{12}(13\sin 3M-3\sin M)+\ldots \quad (53)$$

which is the expression for the *equation of the centre* to terms involving e^3. In the same manner, this series may be extended to higher powers of e.

When the eccentricity is very small, this series converges very rapidly; and the value of $v-M$ for any planet may be arranged in a table with the argument M.

For the purpose, however, of computing the places of a heavenly body from the elements of its orbit, it is preferable to solve the equations which give v and E directly; and when the eccentricity is very great, this mode is indispensable, since the series will not in that case be sufficiently convergent.

It will be observed that the formula which must be used in obtaining the eccentric anomaly from the mean anomaly is transcendental, and hence it can only be solved either by series or by trial. But fortunately, indeed, it so happens that the circumstances of the celestial motions render these approximations very rapid, the orbits being usually either nearly circular, or else very eccentric.

If, in equation (50), we put $F(E) = E$, and consequently $F(M) = M$, we shall have, performing the operations indicated and reducing,

$$E = M + e \sin M + \tfrac{1}{2}e^2 \sin 2M + \&c. \qquad (54)$$

Let us now denote the approximate value of E computed from this equation by E_0, then will

$$E_0 + \Delta E_0 = E,$$

in which ΔE_0 is the correction to be applied to the assumed value of E. Substituting this in equation (39), we get

$$M = E_0 + \Delta E_0 - e \sin E_0 - e \cos E_0 \Delta E_0;$$

and, denoting by M_0 the value of M corresponding to E_0, we shall also have

$$M_0 = E_0 - e \sin E_0.$$

Subtracting this equation from the preceding one, we obtain

$$\frac{M - M_0}{1 - e \cos E_0} = \Delta E_0.$$

It remains, therefore, only to add the value of ΔE_0 found from this formula to the first assumed value of E, or to E_0, and then, using this for a new value of E_0, to proceed in precisely the same manner for a second approximation, and so on, until the correct value of E is obtained. When the values of E for a succession of dates, at equal intervals, are to be computed, the assumed values of E_0 may be obtained so closely by interpolation that the first approximation, in the manner just explained, will give the correct value; and in nearly every case two or three approximations in this manner will suffice.

Having thus obtained the value of E corresponding to M for any instant of time, we may readily deduce from it, by the formulæ already investigated, the corresponding values of r and v.

In the case of an ellipse of very great eccentricity, corresponding to the orbits of many of the comets, the most convenient method of computing r and v, for any instant, is somewhat different. The manner of proceeding in the computation in such cases we shall consider hereafter; and we will now proceed to investigate the formulæ for determining r and v, when the orbit is a parabola, the formulæ for elliptic motion not being applicable, since, in the parabola, $a=\infty$, and $e=1$.

22. Observation shows that the masses of the comets are insensible in comparison with that of the sun; and, consequently, in this case, $m=0$ and equation (52), putting for p its value $2q$, becomes

$$k\sqrt{2q}\, dt = r^2 dv,$$

or

$$k\sqrt{2q}\, dt = \frac{2q^2}{\cos^4 \frac{1}{2}v} \tfrac{1}{2} dv,$$

which may be written

$$\frac{kdt}{\sqrt{2}\, q^{\frac{3}{2}}} = \tfrac{1}{2}(1+\tan^2 \tfrac{1}{2}v)\sec^2 \tfrac{1}{2}v dv = (1+\tan^2 \tfrac{1}{2}v)\, d\tan \tfrac{1}{2}v.$$

Integrating this expression between the limits T and t, we obtain

$$\frac{k(t-T)}{\sqrt{2}\, q^{\frac{3}{2}}} = \tan \tfrac{1}{2}v + \tfrac{1}{3}\tan^3 \tfrac{1}{2}v, \qquad (55)$$

which is the expression for the relation between the true anomaly and the time from the perihelion, in a parabolic orbit.

Let us now represent by τ_0 the time of describing the arc of a parabola corresponding to $v=90°$; then we shall have

$$\frac{k\tau_0}{\sqrt{2}\, q^{\frac{3}{2}}} = \frac{4}{3},$$

or

$$\frac{3k}{\sqrt{2}} = \frac{4\, q^{\frac{3}{2}}}{\tau_0}.$$

Now, $\frac{3k}{\sqrt{2}}$ is constant, and its logarithm is 8.5621876983; and if we take $q=1$, which is equivalent to supposing the comet to move in a parabola whose perihelion distance is equal to the semi-transverse axis of the earth's orbit, we find

$$\log \tau_0^{\text{days}} = 2.03987229, \text{ or } \tau_0 = 109.61558 \text{ days};$$

that is, a comet moving in a parabola whose perihelion distance is equal to the mean distance of the earth from the sun, requires 109.61558 days to describe an arc corresponding to $v = 90°$.

Equation (55) contains only such quantities as are comparable with each other, and by it $t - T$, the time from the perihelion, may be readily found when the remaining terms are known; but, in order to find v from this formula, it will be necessary to solve the equation of the third degree, $\tan \frac{1}{2}v$ being the unknown quantity. If we put $x = \tan \frac{1}{2}v$, this equation becomes

$$x^3 + 3x - a = 0,$$

in which a is the known quantity, and is negative before, and positive after, the perihelion passage. According to the general principle in the theory of equations that in every equation, whether complete or incomplete, the number of positive roots cannot exceed the number of variations of sign, and that the number of negative roots cannot exceed the number of variations of sign, when the signs of the terms containing the odd powers of the unknown quantity are changed, it follows that when a is positive, there is one positive root and no negative root. When a is negative, there is one negative root and no positive root; and hence we conclude that equation (55) can have but one real root.

We may dispense with the direct solution of this equation by forming a table of the values of v corresponding to those of $t - T$ in a parabola whose perihelion distance is equal to the mean distance of the earth from the sun. This table will give the time corresponding to the anomaly v in any parabola, whose perihelion distance is q, by multiplying by $q^{\frac{3}{2}}$, the time which corresponds to the same anomaly in the table. We shall have the anomaly v corresponding to the time $t - T$ by dividing $t - T$ by $q^{\frac{3}{2}}$, and seeking in the table the anomaly corresponding to the time resulting from this division.

A more convenient method, however, of finding the true anomaly from the time, and the reverse, is to use a table of the form generally known as Barker's Table. The following will explain its construction:—

Multiplying equation (55) by 75, we obtain

$$\frac{75k}{\sqrt{2}\,q^{\frac{3}{2}}}(t - T) = 75 \tan \tfrac{1}{2}v + 25 \tan^3 \tfrac{1}{2}v.$$

Let us now put

$$M = 75 \tan \tfrac{1}{2}v + 25 \tan^3 \tfrac{1}{2}v,$$

and $C_0 = \frac{75k}{\sqrt{2}}$, which is a constant quantity; then will

$$\frac{C_0}{q^{\frac{3}{2}}}(t-T) = M.$$

The value of C_0 is

$$\log C_0 = 9.9601277069.$$

Again, let us take

$$m = \frac{C_0}{q^{\frac{3}{2}}},$$

which is called the mean daily motion in the parabola; then will

$$M = m\,(t-T) = 75 \tan \tfrac{1}{2}v + 25 \tan^3 \tfrac{1}{2}v.$$

If we now compute the values of M corresponding to successive values of v from $v = 0°$ to $v = 180°$, and arrange them in a table with the argument v, we may derive at once, from this table, for the time $(t - T)$ either M when v is known, or v when $M = m\,(t - T)$ is known. It may also be observed that when $t - T$ is negative, the value of v is considered as being negative, and hence it is not necessary to pay any further attention to the algebraic sign of $t - T$ than to give the same sign to the value of v obtained from the table.

Table VI. gives the values of M for values of v from 0° to 180°, with differences for interpolation, the application of which will be easily understood.

23. When v approaches near to 180°, this table will be extremely inconvenient, since, in this case, the differences between the values of M for a difference of one minute in the value of v increase very rapidly; and it will be very troublesome to obtain the value of v from the table with the requisite degree of accuracy. To obviate the necessity of extending this table, we proceed in the following manner:—

* Equation (55) may be written

$$\frac{k\,(t-T)}{\sqrt{2}\,q^{\frac{3}{2}}} = \tfrac{1}{3} \tan^3 \tfrac{1}{2}v\,(1 + 3 \cot^2 \tfrac{1}{2}v);$$

and, multiplying and dividing the second member by $(1 + \cot^2 \tfrac{1}{2}v)^3$, we shall have

$$\frac{k\,(t-T)}{\sqrt{2}\,q^{\frac{3}{2}}} = \tfrac{1}{3} \tan^3 \tfrac{1}{2}v\,(1 + \cot^2 \tfrac{1}{2}v)^3 \,\frac{1 + 3 \cot^2 \tfrac{1}{2}v}{(1 + \cot^2 \tfrac{1}{2}v)^3}.$$

* This is Bessel's method, given in Astr. Nach. No. 520 together with the table which appears as Table VII in this volume.

But $1 + \cot^2 \frac{1}{2}v = \dfrac{2}{\sin v \tan \frac{1}{2}v}$ and consequently

$$\frac{k\,(t - T)}{\sqrt{2}\, q^{\frac{3}{2}}} = \frac{8}{3 \sin^3 v} \cdot \frac{1 + 3 \cot^2 \frac{1}{2}v}{(1 + \cot^2 \frac{1}{2}v)^3}.$$

Now, when v approaches near to $180°$, $\cot \frac{1}{2}v$ will be very small, and the second factor of the second member of this equation will nearly $= 1$. Let us therefore denote by w the value of v on the supposition that this factor is equal to unity, which will be strictly true when $v = 180°$, and we shall have, for the correct value of v, the following equation:

$$v = w + \Delta_0,$$

Δ_0 being a very small quantity. We shall therefore have

$$\frac{8}{\sin^3 w} = 3 \tan \tfrac{1}{2}(w + \Delta_0) + \tan^3 \tfrac{1}{2}(w + \Delta_0),$$

and, putting $\tan \frac{1}{2}w = \theta$, and $\tan \frac{1}{2}\Delta_0 = x$, we get, from this equation,

$$\frac{(1 + \theta^2)^3}{\theta^3} = 3\,\frac{\theta + x}{1 - \theta x} + \frac{(\theta + x)^3}{(1 - \theta x)^3}.$$

Multiplying this through by $\theta^3 (1 - \theta x)^3$, expanding and reducing, there results the following equation:

$$1 + 3\theta^2 = 3\theta\,(1 + 4\theta^2 + 2\theta^4 + \theta^6)\,x - 3\theta^2 (1 + 4\theta^2 + 2\theta^4 + \theta^6)\,x^2 + \theta^3 (2 + 6\theta^2 + 3\theta^4 + \theta^6)\,x^3.$$

Dividing through by the coefficient of x, we obtain

$$\frac{1 + 3\theta^2}{3\theta\,(1 + 4\theta^2 + 2\theta^4 + \theta^6)} = x - \theta x^2 + \frac{\theta^2 (2 + 6\theta^2 + 3\theta^4 + \theta^6)\,x^3}{3\,(1 + 4\theta^2 + 2\theta^4 + \theta^6)}.$$

Let us now put

$$\frac{1 + 3\theta^2}{3\theta\,(1 + 4\theta^2 + 2\theta^4 + \theta^6)} = y;$$

then, substituting this in the preceding equation, inverting the series and reducing, we obtain finally

$$x = y + \theta y^2 + \frac{\theta^2 (4 + 18\theta^2 + 9\theta^4 + 5\theta^6)}{3\,(1 + 4\theta^2 + 2\theta^4 + \theta^6)}\, y^3 + \&c.$$

But $\tan \frac{1}{2}\Delta_0 = x$, therefore

$$\Delta_0 = 2x - \tfrac{2}{3}x^3 + \ldots..$$

Substituting in this the value of x above found, and reducing, we obtain

$$\Delta_0 = 2y + 2\theta y^2 + \frac{-2 + 32\theta^4 + 16\theta^6 + 10\theta^8}{3(1 + 4\theta^2 + 2\theta^4 + \theta^6)} y^3 + \&c.$$

For all the cases in which this equation is to be applied, the third term of the second member will be insensible, and we shall have, to a sufficient degree of approximation,

$$\Delta_0 = 2y + 2\theta y^2.$$

Table VII. gives the values of Δ_0, expressed in seconds of arc, corresponding to consecutive values of w from $w = 155°$ to $w = 180°$. In the application of this table, we have only to compute the value of M precisely as for the case in which Table VI. is to be used, namely,

$$M = m(t - T);$$

then will w be given by the formula

$$\sin w = \sqrt[3]{\frac{200}{M}},$$

since we have already found

$$\frac{k(t-T)}{\sqrt{2}\, q^{\frac{3}{2}}} = \frac{8}{3\sin^3 w},$$

or

$$\sin w = \sqrt[3]{\frac{8q^{\frac{3}{2}}\sqrt{2}}{3(t-T)k}} = \sqrt[3]{\frac{200}{M}}.$$

Having computed the value of w from this equation, Table VII. will furnish the corresponding value of Δ_0; and then we shall have, for the correct value of the true anomaly,

$$v = w + \Delta_0,$$

which will be precisely the same as that obtained directly from Table VI., when the second and higher orders of differences are taken into account.

If v is given and the time $t - T$ is required, the table will give, by inspection, an approximate value of Δ_0, using v as argument, and then w is given by

$$w = v - \Delta_0.$$

The exact value of Δ_0 is then found from the table, and hence we derive that of w; and finally $t - T$ from

$$t - T = \frac{200}{C_0} \cdot \frac{q^{\frac{3}{2}}}{\sin^3 w}.$$

24. The problem of finding the time $t - T$ when the true anomaly is given, may also be solved conveniently, and especially so when v is small, by the following process:—

Equation (55) is easily transformed into

$$\frac{3k(t-T)}{\sqrt{2}\, q^{\frac{3}{2}}} = \frac{\sin \frac{1}{2}v}{\cos^3 \frac{1}{2}v} (3 - 2 \sin^2 \tfrac{1}{2}v),$$

from which we obtain, since $q = r \cos^2 \frac{1}{2}v$,

$$\frac{3k(t-T)}{2\, r^{\frac{3}{2}}} = 3\left(\frac{\sin \frac{1}{2}v}{\sqrt{2}}\right) - 4\left(\frac{\sin \frac{1}{2}v}{\sqrt{2}}\right)^3.$$

Let us now put

$$\sin x = \frac{\sin \frac{1}{2}v}{\sqrt{2}},$$

and we have

$$\frac{3k(t-T)}{2\, r^{\frac{3}{2}}} = 3 \sin x - 4 \sin^3 x = \sin 3x.$$

Consequently,

$$t - T = \frac{2}{3k} r^{\frac{3}{2}} \sin 3x,$$

which admits of an accurate and convenient numerical solution. To facilitate the calculation we put

$$N = \frac{\sin 3x}{\sin v},$$

the values of which may be tabulated with the argument v. When $v = 0$, we shall have $N = \frac{3}{4}\sqrt{2}$, and when $v = 90$, we have $N = 1$; from which it appears that the value of N changes slowly for values of v from 0° to 90°. But when $v = 180°$, we shall have $N = \infty$; and hence, when v exceeds 90°, it becomes necessary to introduce an auxiliary different from N. We shall, therefore, put in this case,

$$N' = N \sin v = \sin 3x;$$

from which it appears that $N'=1$ when $v=90°$, and that $N'=\frac{1}{2}\sqrt{2}$ when $v=180°$. Therefore we have, finally, when v is less than 90°,

$$t-T=\frac{2}{3k}Nr^{\frac{3}{2}}\sin v,$$

and, when v is greater than 90°,

$$t-T=\frac{2}{3k}N'r^{\frac{3}{2}},$$

in which $\log\frac{2}{3k}=1.5883272995$, from which $t-T$ is easily derived when v is known.

Table VIII. gives the values of N, with differences for interpolation, for values of v from $v=0°$ to $v=90°$, and the values of N' for those of v from $v=90°$ to $v=180°$.

25. We shall now consider the case of the hyperbola, which differs from the ellipse only that e is greater than 1; and, consequently, the formulæ for elliptic and hyperbolic motion will differ from each other only that certain quantities which are positive in the ellipse are negative or imaginary in the hyperbola. We may, however, introduce auxiliary quantities which will serve to preserve the analogy between the two, and yet to mark the necessary distinctions.

For this purpose, let us resume the equation

$$r=\frac{p\cos\psi}{2\cos\frac{1}{2}(v+\psi)\cos\frac{1}{2}(v-\psi)}.$$

When $v=0$, the factors $\cos\frac{1}{2}(v+\psi)$ and $\cos\frac{1}{2}(v-\psi)$ in the denominator will be equal; and since the limits of the values of v are $180°-\psi$ and $-(180°-\psi)$, it follows that the first factor will vanish for the maximum positive value of v, and that the second factor will vanish for the maximum negative value of v, and, therefore, that, in either case, $r=\infty$.

In the hyperbola, the semi-transverse axis is negative, and, consequently, we have, in this case,

$$p=a(e^2-1), \qquad \text{or } a=p\cot^2\psi.$$

We have, also, for the perihelion distance,

$$q=a(e-1).$$

Let us now put

$$\tan\tfrac{1}{2}F=\tan\tfrac{1}{2}v\sqrt{\frac{e-1}{e+1}}, \tag{56}$$

which is analogous to the formula for the eccentric anomaly E in an ellipse; and, since $e=\frac{1}{\cos\psi}$, we shall have

$$\frac{e-1}{e+1}=\frac{1-\cos\psi}{1+\cos\psi}=\tan^2\tfrac{1}{2}\psi,$$

and, consequently,

$$\tan\tfrac{1}{2}F=\tan\tfrac{1}{2}v\tan\tfrac{1}{2}\psi. \tag{57}$$

We shall now introduce an auxiliary quantity σ, such that

$$\sigma=\tan(45^\circ+\tfrac{1}{2}F)=\frac{1+\tan\frac{1}{2}F}{1-\tan\frac{1}{2}F},$$

whence we derive

$$\tan\tfrac{1}{2}F=\frac{\sigma-1}{\sigma+1}, \tag{58}$$

and also

$$\sigma=\frac{\cos\frac{1}{2}(v-\psi)}{\cos\frac{1}{2}(v+\psi)}. \tag{59}$$

This last equation shows that $\sigma=1$ when the comet is in its perihelion; $\sigma=\infty$ when $v=180^\circ-\psi$; and $\sigma=0$ when $v=-(180^\circ-\psi)$.

Since $\tan F=\frac{2\tan\frac{1}{2}F}{1-\tan^2\frac{1}{2}F}$, we shall have

$$\tan F=\frac{2\left(\frac{\sigma-1}{\sigma+1}\right)}{1-\left(\frac{\sigma-1}{\sigma+1}\right)^2}=\tfrac{1}{2}\left(\sigma-\frac{1}{\sigma}\right). \tag{60}$$

Squaring this equation, adding 1 to both members, and reducing we obtain

$$\frac{1}{\cos F}=\tfrac{1}{2}\left(\sigma+\frac{1}{\sigma}\right). \tag{61}$$

Replacing σ in this equation by its value from equation (59), we get

$$\frac{1}{\cos F}=\frac{\cos^2\frac{1}{2}(v+\psi)+\cos^2\frac{1}{2}(v-\psi)}{2\cos\frac{1}{2}(v+\psi)\cos\frac{1}{2}(v-\psi)},$$

or

$$\frac{1}{\cos F}=\frac{1+\cos v\cos\psi}{2\cos\frac{1}{2}(v+\psi)\cos\frac{1}{2}(v-\psi)}=\frac{(e+\cos v)\cos\psi}{2\cos\frac{1}{2}(v+\psi)\cos\frac{1}{2}(v-\psi)}$$

which reduces to

$$\frac{1}{\cos F}=\frac{r(e+\cos v)}{p}. \tag{62}$$

If we add ∓ 1 to both members of this equation, we shall have

$$\frac{1 \mp \cos F}{\cos F} = \frac{r(e \mp 1)(1 \mp \cos v)}{p}.$$

Taking first the upper sign, and then the lower sign, and reducing, we get

$$\sqrt{r} \sin \tfrac{1}{2}v = \frac{\sqrt{a(e+1)}}{\sqrt{\cos F}} \sin \tfrac{1}{2}F;$$

$$\sqrt{r} \cos \tfrac{1}{2}v = \frac{\sqrt{a(e-1)}}{\sqrt{\cos F}} \cos \tfrac{1}{2}F. \qquad (63)$$

These equations for finding r and v, it will be observed, are analogous to those previously investigated for an elliptic orbit. These equations give, by division,

$$\tan \tfrac{1}{2}v = \sqrt{\frac{e+1}{e-1}} \tan \tfrac{1}{2}F,$$

which is identical with the equation (56), and may be employed to verify the computation of r and v.

Multiplying the last of equations (63) by the first, putting for $e^2 - 1$ its value $\tan^2 \psi$, and reducing, we obtain

$$r \sin v = a \tan \psi \tan F = \tfrac{1}{2}a \tan \psi \left(\sigma - \frac{1}{\sigma} \right). \qquad (64)$$

Further, we have

$$r \cos v = \frac{p \cos v}{1 + e \cos v} = ae - \frac{ar(e + \cos v)}{p},$$

which, combined with equation (62), gives

$$r \cos v = a\left(e - \frac{1}{\cos F} \right) = \tfrac{1}{2}a\left(2e - \sigma - \frac{1}{\sigma} \right). \qquad (65)$$

If we square these values of $r \sin v$ and $r \cos v$, add the results together, reduce, and extract the square root, we find

$$r = a\left(\frac{e}{\cos F} - 1 \right) = \tfrac{1}{2}a\left(e\left(\sigma + \frac{1}{\sigma} \right) - 2 \right). \qquad (66)$$

We might also introduce the auxiliary quantity σ into the equations (63); but such a transformation is hardly necessary, and, if at all desirable, it can be easily effected by means of the formulæ which we have already derived.

26. Let us now resume the equation

$$\sigma = \frac{\cos \frac{1}{2}(v - \psi)}{\cos \frac{1}{2}(v + \psi)}.$$

Differentiating this, regarding ψ as constant, we have

$$d\sigma = \frac{\sin \psi}{2 \cos^2 \frac{1}{2}(v + \psi)} dv,$$

and, dividing this equation by the preceding one, we get

$$\frac{d\sigma}{\sigma} = \frac{\sin \psi}{2 \cos \frac{1}{2}(v + \psi) \cos \frac{1}{2}(v - \psi)} dv.$$

But

$$r = \frac{p \cos \psi}{2 \cos \frac{1}{2}(v + \psi) \cos \frac{1}{2}(v - \psi)},$$

consequently,

$$\frac{d\sigma}{\sigma} = \frac{r \tan \psi}{p} dv,$$

which gives

$$r^2 dv = \frac{pr}{\sigma \tan \psi} d\sigma.$$

Substituting this value of r^2dv in equation (22), and putting instead of $2f$ its value $k\sqrt{p}$, from equation (30), the mass being considered as insensible in comparison with that of the sun, we get

$$k\sqrt{p}\, dt = \frac{pr}{\sigma \tan \psi} d\sigma.$$

Then, substituting for r its value from equation (66), and for p its value $a \tan^2 \psi$, we have

$$k\sqrt{p}\, dt = a^2 \tan \psi \left(\tfrac{1}{2}e \left(1 + \frac{1}{\sigma^2}\right) - \frac{1}{\sigma} \right) d\sigma.$$

Integrating this between the limits T and t, we obtain

$$k\sqrt{p}\,(t - T) = a^2 \tan \psi \left(\tfrac{1}{2}e \left(\sigma - \frac{1}{\sigma}\right) - \log_e \sigma \right), \qquad (67)$$

in which $\log_e \sigma$ is the Naperian or hyperbolic logarithm of σ. Since $\sqrt{p} = \sqrt{a} \tan \psi$, if we put

$$\nu = \frac{k}{a^{\frac{3}{2}}},$$

in which ν is the mean daily motion; and if we also put

$$\nu(t-T)=N_0,$$

in which N_0 corresponds to the mean anomaly M in an ellipse, we shall have, from equation (67),

$$N_0=\tfrac{1}{2}e\left(\sigma-\frac{1}{\sigma}\right)-\log_e\sigma. \tag{68}$$

If we multiply both members of this equation by $\lambda=0.434294482$, the modulus of the common system of logarithms, and put

$$N=N_0\lambda=\frac{\lambda k}{a^{\frac{3}{2}}}(t-T),$$

we shall have

$$N=\tfrac{1}{2}e\lambda\left(\sigma-\frac{1}{\sigma}\right)-\log\sigma;$$

wherein $\log\lambda=9.6377843113$, and $\log\lambda k=7.8733657527$.

Let us now introduce F into this formula; and for this purpose we have

$$\tan F=\tfrac{1}{2}\left(\sigma-\frac{1}{\sigma}\right),$$

and also

$$\log\sigma=\log\tan\left(45^\circ+\tfrac{1}{2}F\right).$$

Therefore we obtain

$$N=e\lambda\tan F-\log\tan\left(45^\circ+\tfrac{1}{2}F\right). \tag{69}$$

This equation will give, directly, the time $t-T$ from the perihelion, when a, e, and F are known; but, since it is transcendental, in the solution of the inverse problem, that of finding the true anomaly and radius-vector from the time, the value of F can only be found by successive approximations.

If we differentiate the last equation, regarding N and F as variable, we get

$$dN=\frac{\lambda}{\cos^2F}(e-\cos F)\,dF.$$

Hence, if we denote an approximate value of F by $F_{,}$, and the corresponding value of N by $N_{,}$, the correction $\Delta F_{,}$ to the assumed value of F may be computed by the formula

$$\Delta F_{,}=\frac{(N-N_{,})\cos^2F_{,}}{\lambda(e-\cos F_{,})}.$$

This correction being applied to $F_{,}$, a nearer approximation to the true value of F will be obtained; and by repeating the operation there results a still closer approximation. This process may be continued until the exact value of F is found, and, when several successive places are required, the first assumed value may be estimated, in advance, so closely that a very few trials will suffice. In practice, however, cases will rarely occur in which this formula will be applied, since the probability of hyperbolic motion is small, and, whenever any positive indication of an eccentricity greater than 1 has been found to exist, it has only been after a very accurate series of observations has been introduced as the basis of the calculation. For a majority of the cases which do really occur, the most accurate and convenient method of finding r and v will be explained hereafter.

27. If we consider the equation

$$M = E - e \sin E,$$

we shall see that, when logarithms of six or seven decimals are used, the error which may exist in the determination of E when M and e are given, will increase as e increases, but in a much greater ratio; and, when the eccentricity becomes nearly equal to that of the parabola, the error may be very great. In the case of hyperbolic motion, also, the numerical solution of equation (69), when $e - 1$ is very small, and with the ordinary logarithmic tables, becomes very uncertain. This can only be remedied, when equations (39) and (69) are employed, by using more extended logarithmic tables; and when the orbit differs only in an extremely slight degree from a parabola, even with the most extended logarithmic tables which have been constructed, the error may be very large. For this reason we have recourse to other methods, which will give the required accuracy without introducing inconveniences which are proportionally great.

We shall, therefore, now proceed to develop the formulæ for finding the true anomaly in ellipses and hyperbolas which differ but little from the parabola, such that they will furnish the required accuracy, when the exact solution of equations (39) or (69) with the logarithmic tables in common use is impossible.

For this purpose, let us resume equation (22), which, by substituting for $2f$ its value $k\sqrt{p}$, the mass of the comet being neglected in comparison with that of the sun, becomes

$$k\sqrt{p}\, dt = r^2 dv,$$

or

$$k\sqrt{p}\,dt = p^2 \frac{dv}{(1 + e\cos v)^2}.$$

Let us now put $u = \tan\frac{1}{2}v$, and we shall have

$$\cos v = \frac{1 - u^2}{1 + u^2}\,;\ dv = \frac{2du}{1 + u^2}.$$

Substituting these values in the preceding equation, and putting $\frac{1-e}{1+e} = i$, we get

$$k\sqrt{p}\,dt = \frac{2p^2}{(1+e)^2}\,\frac{(1 + u^2)\,du}{(1 + iu^2)^2},$$

or, since $p = q\,(1 + e)$,

$$\frac{k\sqrt{1 + e}\,dt}{2q^{\frac{3}{2}}} = \frac{(1 + u^2)\,du}{(1 + iu^2)^2}.$$

Let us now develop the second member into a series. This may be written thus:

$$du\,(1 + u^2)\,(1 + iu^2)^{-2};$$

and developing the last factor into a series, we obtain

$$(1 + iu^2)^{-2} = 1 - 2iu^2 + 3i^2u^4 - 4i^3u^6 + \&c.$$

Consequently,

$$(1 + u^2)\,(1 + iu^2)^{-2} = 1 + u^2 - 2i\,(u^2 + u^4) + 3i^2\,(u^4 + u^6) \\ - 4i^3\,(u^6 + u^8) + \ldots.$$

Multiplying this equation through by du, and integrating between the limits T and t, the result is

$$\frac{k\,(t - T)\sqrt{1 + e}}{2q^{\frac{3}{2}}} = u + \tfrac{1}{3}u^3 - 2i\,(\tfrac{1}{3}u^3 + \tfrac{1}{5}u^5) + 3i^2\,(\tfrac{1}{5}u^5 + \tfrac{1}{7}u^7) \\ - 4i^3\,(\tfrac{1}{7}u^7 + \tfrac{1}{9}u^9) + \&c. \qquad (70)$$

In the case of the parabola, $e = 1$ and $i = 0$, and this equation becomes identical with (55).

Let us now put

$$\frac{k\,(t - T)\sqrt{1 + e}}{2q^{\frac{3}{2}}} = U + \tfrac{1}{3}U^3, \qquad (71)$$

and also

$$U = \tan \tfrac{1}{2} V;$$

then the angle V will not be the true anomaly in the parabola, but an angle derived from the solution of a cubic equation of the same form as that for finding the parabolic anomaly; and its value may be found by means of Table VI., if we use for M the value computed from

$$M = \frac{75k(t-T)}{\sqrt{2}\, q^{\frac{3}{2}}} \cdot \sqrt{\frac{1+e}{2}}.$$

Let U be expanded into a series of the form

$$U = u + \alpha i + \beta i^2 + \gamma i^3 + \ldots\ldots,$$

which is evidently admissible, α, β, γ, ... being functions of u and independent of i. It remains now to determine the values of the coefficients α, β, γ, &c., and, in doing so, it will only be necessary to consider terms of the third order, or those involving i^3, since, for nearly all of those cases in which the eccentricity is such that terms of the order i^4 will sensibly affect the result, the general formulæ already derived, with the ordinary means of solution, will give the required accuracy. We shall, therefore, have

$$U + \tfrac{1}{3}U^3 = u + \alpha i + \beta i^2 + \gamma i^3 + \tfrac{1}{3}(u + \alpha i + \beta i^2 + \gamma i^3)^3,$$

or, again neglecting terms of the order i^4,

$$U + \tfrac{1}{3}U^3 = u + \tfrac{1}{3}u^3 + i(1+u^2)\,\alpha + i^2(u\alpha^2 + (1+u^2)\,\beta)$$
$$+ i^3(\tfrac{1}{3}\alpha^3 + 2u\alpha\beta + (1+u^2)\,\gamma).$$

But we have already found, (70),

$$\frac{k(t-T)\sqrt{1+e}}{2q^{\frac{3}{2}}} = U + \tfrac{1}{3}U^3 = u + \tfrac{1}{3}u^3 - 2i(\tfrac{1}{3}u^3 + \tfrac{1}{5}u^5)$$
$$+ 3i^2(\tfrac{1}{5}u^5 + \tfrac{1}{7}u^7) - 4i^3(\tfrac{1}{7}u^7 + \tfrac{1}{9}u^9).$$

Since the first members of these equations are identical, it follows, by the principle of indeterminate coefficients, that the coefficients of the like powers of i are equal, and we shall, therefore, have

$$(1+u^2)\,\alpha = -2(\tfrac{1}{3}u^3 + \tfrac{1}{5}u^5),$$
$$u\alpha^2 + (1+u^2)\,\beta = +3(\tfrac{1}{5}u^5 + \tfrac{1}{7}u^7),$$
$$\tfrac{1}{3}\alpha^3 + 2u\alpha\beta + (1+u^2)\,\gamma = -4(\tfrac{1}{7}u^7 + \tfrac{1}{9}u^9).$$

From the first of these equations we find

$$\alpha = -\frac{2\left(\frac{1}{3}u^3 + \frac{1}{5}u^5\right)}{1 + u^2}.$$

The second equation gives

$$\beta = \frac{3\left(\frac{1}{5}u^5 + \frac{1}{7}u^7\right) - u\alpha^2}{1 + u^2},$$

or, substituting for α its value just found, and reducing,

$$\beta = \frac{3\left(\frac{1}{5}u^5 + \frac{373}{945}u^7 + \frac{97}{315}u^9 + \frac{47}{525}u^{11}\right)}{(1 + u^2)^3}.$$

We have also

$$\gamma = \frac{-4\left(\frac{1}{7}u^7 + \frac{1}{9}u^9\right) - \frac{1}{3}\alpha^3 - 2\alpha\beta u}{1 + u^2};$$

and hence, substituting the values of α and β already found, and reducing, we obtain finally

$$\gamma = \frac{-4\left(\frac{1}{7}u^7 + \frac{1298}{2835}u^9 + \frac{10174}{14175}u^{11} + \frac{196}{315}u^{13} + \frac{2213}{7875}u^{15} + \frac{82}{1575}u^{17}\right)}{(1 + u^2)^5}.$$

Again, we have

$$\tan^{-1} U = \tan^{-1}(u + \alpha i + \beta i^2 + \gamma i^3).$$

Developing this, and neglecting terms of the order i^4, we get

$$\tan^{-1} U = \tan^{-1} u + \frac{1}{1+u^2}(\alpha i + \beta i^2 + \gamma i^3) - \frac{u}{(1+u^2)^2}(\alpha^2 i^2 + 2\alpha\beta i^3) + \frac{u^2 - \frac{1}{3}}{(1+u^2)^3}\alpha^3 i^3.$$

Now, since $u = \tan\frac{1}{2}v$ and $U = \tan\frac{1}{2}V$, we shall have

$$V = v + \frac{2}{1+u^2}(\alpha i + \beta i^2 + \gamma i^3) - \frac{2u}{(1+u^2)^2}(\alpha^2 i^2 + 2\alpha\beta i^3) + \frac{2\left(u^2 - \frac{1}{3}\right)}{(1+u^2)^3}\alpha^3 i^3,$$

or

$$V = v + \frac{2\alpha}{1+u^2}i + \left(\frac{2\beta}{1+u^2} - \frac{2\alpha^2 u}{(1+u^2)^2}\right)i^2 + \left(\frac{2\gamma}{1+u^2} - \frac{4\alpha\beta u}{(1+u^2)^2} + \frac{2\left(u^2 - \frac{1}{3}\right)}{(1+u^2)^3}\alpha^3\right)i^3. \tag{72}$$

Substituting in this equation the values of α, β, and γ already found, and reducing, we obtain finally

$$V = v - \frac{\frac{4}{3}u^3 + \frac{4}{5}u^5}{(1+u^2)^2}i + \frac{\frac{6}{5}u^5 + \frac{466}{315}u^7 + \frac{82}{105}u^9 + \frac{38}{175}u^{11}}{(1+u^2)^4}i^2 - \frac{\frac{8}{7}u^7 + \frac{5288}{2835}u^9 + \frac{26384}{14175}u^{11} + \frac{464}{315}u^{13} + \frac{5128}{7875}u^{15} + \frac{904}{7875}u^{17}}{(1+u^2)^6}i^3. \tag{73}$$

This equation can be used whenever the true anomaly in the ellipse or hyperbola is given, and the time from the perihelion is to be determined. Having found the value of V, we enter Table VI. with the argument V and take out the corresponding value of M; and then we derive $t - T$ from

$$t - T = \frac{M q^{\frac{3}{2}}}{C_0} \sqrt{\frac{2}{1+e}},$$

in which $\log C_0 = 9.96012771$.

For the converse of this, in which the time from the perihelion is given and the true anomaly is required, it is necessary to express the difference $v - V$ in a series of ascending powers of i, in which the coefficients are functions of U. Let us, therefore, put

$$u = U + \alpha' i + \beta' i^2 + \gamma' i^3 + \&c.$$

Substituting this value of u in equation (70), and neglecting terms multiplied by i^4 and higher powers of i, we get

$$\begin{aligned}\frac{k(t-T)\sqrt{1+e}}{2q^{\frac{3}{2}}} = U + \tfrac{1}{3}U^3 &+ (\alpha'(1+U^2) - \tfrac{2}{3}U^3 - \tfrac{2}{5}U^5)\, i \\ &+ (\beta'(1+U^2) + U\alpha'^2 - 2U^2\alpha'(1+U^2) + \tfrac{3}{5}U^5 + \tfrac{3}{7}U^7)\, i^2 \\ &+ (\gamma'(1+U^2) + \tfrac{1}{3}\alpha'^3 + 2U\alpha'\beta' + 3U^4\alpha'(1+U^2) - 2\beta' U^2(1+U^2) \\ &\quad - 4U^3\alpha'^2 - 2U\alpha'^2 - \tfrac{4}{7}U^7 - \tfrac{4}{9}U^9)\, i^3.\end{aligned}$$

But, since the first member of this equation is equal to $U + \frac{1}{3}U^3$, we shall have, by the principle of indeterminate coefficients,

$$\begin{aligned}&\alpha'(1+U^2) - \tfrac{2}{3}U^3 - \tfrac{2}{5}U^5 = 0, \\ &\beta'(1+U^2) + U\alpha'^2 - 2U^2\alpha'(1+U^2) + \tfrac{3}{5}U^5 + \tfrac{3}{7}U^7 = 0, \\ &\gamma'(1+U^2) + \tfrac{1}{3}\alpha'^3 + 2U\alpha'\beta' + 3U^4\alpha'(1+U^2) - 2\beta' U^2(1+U^2) \\ &\qquad - 4U^3\alpha'^2 - 2U\alpha'^2 - \tfrac{4}{7}U^7 - \tfrac{4}{9}U^9 = 0.\end{aligned}$$

From these equations, we find

$$\alpha' = \frac{\frac{2}{3}U^3 + \frac{2}{5}U^5}{1+U^2},$$

$$\beta' = \frac{\frac{11}{15}U^5 + \frac{439}{315}U^7 + \frac{33}{35}U^9 + \frac{37}{175}U^{11}}{(1+U^2)^3},$$

$$\gamma' = \frac{\frac{292}{315}U^7 + \frac{7928}{2835}U^9 + \frac{10328}{2835}U^{11} + \frac{432}{175}U^{13} + \frac{6692}{7875}U^{15} + \frac{184}{1575}U^{17}}{(1+U^2)^5}.$$

If we interchange v and V in equation (72), it becomes, writing α', β', γ' for α, β, γ,

$$v = V + \frac{2\alpha'}{1+U^2}i + \left(\frac{2\beta'}{1+U^2} - \frac{2\alpha'^2 U}{(1+U^2)^2}\right)i^2$$
$$+ \left(\frac{2\gamma'}{1+U^2} - \frac{4\alpha'\beta' U}{(1+U^2)^2} + \frac{2(U^2-\frac{1}{3})}{(1+U^2)^3}\alpha'^3\right)i^3.$$

Substituting in this equation the above values of α', β', and γ', and reducing, we obtain, finally,

$$v = V + \frac{\frac{4}{3}U^3 + \frac{4}{5}U^5}{(1+U^2)^2}i + \frac{\frac{22}{15}U^5 + \frac{598}{315}U^7 + \frac{86}{105}U^9 + \frac{18}{175}U^{11}}{(1+U^2)^4}i^2$$
$$+ \frac{\frac{584}{315}U^7 + \frac{9752}{2835}U^9 + \frac{37328}{14175}U^{11} + \frac{1648}{1575}U^{13} + \frac{1768}{7875}U^{15} + \frac{184}{7875}U^{17}}{(1+U^2)^6}i^3, \quad (74)$$

by means of which v may be determined, the angle V being taken from Table VI., so as to correspond with the value of M derived from

$$M = (t-T)\frac{C_0}{q^{\frac{3}{2}}} \cdot \sqrt{\frac{1+e}{2}}.$$

Equations (73) and (74) are applicable, without any modification, to the case of a hyperbolic orbit which differs but little from the parabola. In this case, however, e is greater than unity, and, consequently, i is negative.

28. In order to render these formulæ convenient in practice, tables may be constructed in the following manner:—

Let $x = v$ or V, and $\tan\frac{1}{2}x = \theta$, and let us put

$$A = \frac{\frac{4}{3}\theta^3 + \frac{4}{5}\theta^5}{100(1+\theta^2)^2}s,$$
$$B = \frac{\frac{22}{15}\theta^5 + \frac{598}{315}\theta^7 + \frac{86}{105}\theta^9 + \frac{18}{175}\theta^{11}}{10000(1+\theta^2)^4}s,$$
$$B' = \frac{\frac{6}{5}\theta^5 + \frac{466}{315}\theta^7 + \frac{82}{105}\theta^9 + \frac{38}{175}\theta^{11}}{10000(1+\theta^2)^4}s,$$
$$C = \frac{\frac{584}{315}\theta^7 + \frac{9752}{2835}\theta^9 + \frac{37328}{14175}\theta^{11} + \frac{1648}{1575}\theta^{13} + \frac{1768}{7875}\theta^{15} + \frac{184}{7875}\theta^{17}}{1000000(1+\theta^2)^6}s,$$
$$C' = \frac{\frac{8}{7}\theta^7 + \frac{5288}{2835}\theta^9 + \frac{26384}{14175}\theta^{11} + \frac{464}{315}\theta^{13} + \frac{5128}{7875}\theta^{15} + \frac{904}{7875}\theta^{17}}{1000000(1+\theta^2)^6}s,$$

wherein s expresses the number of seconds corresponding to the length of arc equal to the radius of a circle, or $\log s = 5.31442513$. We shall, therefore, have:—

When $x = V$,

$$v = V + A(100i) + B(100i)^2 + C(100i)^3;$$

and, when $x = v$,

$$V = v - A(100i) + B'(100i)^2 - C'(100i)^3.$$

Table IX. gives the values of A, B, B', C, and C' for consecutive values of x from $x = 0°$ to $x = 149°$, with differences for interpolation.

When the value of v has been found, that of r may be derived from the formula

$$r = \frac{q(1+e)}{1 + e\cos v}.$$

Similar expressions arranged in reference to the ascending powers of $(1 - e)$ or of $\left(\left(\frac{2}{1+e}\right)^{\frac{1}{2}} - 1\right)$ may be derived, but they do not converge with sufficient rapidity; for, although $\left(\left(\frac{2}{1+e}\right)^{\frac{1}{2}} - 1\right)$ is less than i, yet the coefficients are, in each case, so much greater than those of the corresponding powers of i, that three terms will not afford the same degree of accuracy as the same number of terms in the expressions involving i.

29. Equations (73) and (74) will serve to determine v or $t - T$ in nearly all cases in which, with the ordinary logarithmic tables, the general methods fail. However, when the orbit differs considerably from a parabola, and when v is of considerable magnitude, the results obtained by means of these equations will not be sufficiently exact, and we must employ other methods of approximation in the case that the accurate numerical solution of the general formulæ is still impossible. It may be observed that when E or F exceeds 50° or 60°, the equations (39) and (69) will furnish accurate results, even when e differs but little from unity. Still, a case may occur in which the perihelion distance is very small and in which v may be very great before the disappearance of the comet, such that neither the general method, nor the special method already given, will enable us to determine v or $t - T$ with accuracy; and we shall, therefore, investigate another method, which will, in all cases, be sufficiently exact when the general formulæ are inapplicable directly. For this purpose, let us resume the equation

$$\frac{k(t-T)}{a^{\frac{3}{2}}} = E - e\sin E,$$

which, since $q = a(1 - e)$, may be written

$$\frac{k(t-T)\sqrt{1-e}}{q^{\frac{3}{2}}} = \frac{1}{10}(9E + \sin E) + \frac{1}{10}\cdot\frac{1+9e}{1-e}(E - \sin E).$$

If we put

$$A = 15\,\frac{E - \sin E}{9E + \sin E},$$

we shall have

$$\frac{k(t-T)\sqrt{1-e}}{2q^{\frac{3}{2}}}\cdot\frac{20\sqrt{A}}{9E + \sin E} = A^{\frac{1}{2}} + \frac{1}{3}\cdot\frac{1+9e}{5(1-e)}A^{\frac{3}{2}}.$$

Let us now put

$$B = \frac{9E + \sin E}{20\sqrt{A}},$$

and

$$\tan^2 \tfrac{1}{2}w = \frac{1+9e}{5(1-e)}A;$$

then we have

$$\frac{k(t-T)}{\sqrt{2}\,q^{\frac{3}{2}}}\cdot\frac{\sqrt{\frac{1}{10}(1+9e)}}{B} = \tan\tfrac{1}{2}w + \tfrac{1}{3}\tan^3\tfrac{1}{2}w. \tag{75}$$

When B is known, the value of w may, according to this equation, be derived directly from Table VI. with the argument

$$M = \frac{75k(t-T)}{\sqrt{2}\,q^{\frac{3}{2}}}\cdot\frac{\sqrt{\frac{1}{10}(1+9e)}}{B},$$

and then from w we may find the value of A. It remains, therefore, to find the value of B; and then that of v from the resulting value of A.

Now, we have

$$\sin E = \frac{2\tan\frac{1}{2}E}{1+\tan^2\frac{1}{2}E},$$

and if we put $\tan^2\frac{1}{2}E = \tau$, we get

$$\sin E = \frac{2\tau^{\frac{1}{2}}}{1+\tau} = 2\tau^{\frac{1}{2}}(1 - \tau + \tau^2 - \tau^3 + \&c.).$$

We have, also,

$$E = 2\tan^{-1}\tau^{\frac{1}{2}} = 2\tau^{\frac{1}{2}}(1 - \tfrac{1}{3}\tau + \tfrac{1}{5}\tau^2 - \tfrac{1}{7}\tau^3 + \&c.).$$

Therefore,

$$15(E - \sin E) = 2\tau^{\frac{1}{2}}(10\tau - \tfrac{60}{5}\tau^2 + \tfrac{90}{7}\tau^3 - \tfrac{120}{9}\tau^4 + \&c.),$$

and

$$9E + \sin E = 2\tau^{\frac{1}{2}}(10 - \tfrac{12}{3}\tau + \tfrac{14}{5}\tau^2 - \tfrac{16}{7}\tau^3 + \tfrac{18}{9}\tau^4 - \&c.).$$

Hence, by division,

$$15\frac{E - \sin E}{9E + \sin E} = A = \tau - \tfrac{4}{5}\tau^2 + \tfrac{24}{35}\tau^3 - \tfrac{1592}{2625}\tau^4 + \tfrac{78856}{144375}\tau^5 - \tfrac{10899688}{21896875}\tau^6 + \&c.;$$

and, inverting this series, we get

$$\frac{A}{\tau} = 1 - \tfrac{4}{5}A + \tfrac{8}{175}A^2 + \tfrac{8}{525}A^3 + \tfrac{1896}{336875}A^4 + \tfrac{28744}{13138125}A^5 + \&c.,$$

which converges rapidly, and from which the value of $\frac{A}{\tau}$ may be found.

Let us now put

$$\frac{A}{\tau} = \frac{1}{C^2},$$

then the values of C may be tabulated with the argument A; and, besides, it is evident that as long as A is small C^2 will not differ much from $1 + \frac{4}{5}A$.

Next, to find B, we have

$$A^{\frac{1}{2}} = \tau^{\frac{1}{2}}(1 - \tfrac{2}{5}\tau + \tfrac{46}{175}\tau^2 - \tfrac{104}{525}\tau^3 + \tfrac{161002}{1010625}\tau^4 - \&c.),$$

and hence

$$\frac{\frac{1}{20}(9E + \sin E)}{\sqrt{A}} = B = 1 + \tfrac{3}{175}\tau^2 - \tfrac{62}{2625}\tau^3 + \tfrac{9007}{336875}\tau^4 - \&c.;$$

from which we easily find

$$B = 1 + \tfrac{3}{175}A^2 + \tfrac{2}{525}A^3 + \tfrac{471}{336875}A^4 + \&c.$$

If we compare equations (44) and (56), we get

$$\tan\tfrac{1}{2}E = \sqrt{-1}\,\tan\tfrac{1}{2}F.$$

Hence, in the case of a hyperbolic orbit, if we put $\tan^2\frac{1}{2}F = \tau'$, we must write $-\tau'$ in place of τ in the formulæ already derived; and, from the series which gives A in terms of τ, it appears that A is in this case negative. Therefore, if we distinguish the equations for hyperbolic motion from those for elliptic motion by writing A', B', and C' in place of A, B, and C, respectively, we shall have

$$\frac{1}{C'^2} = \frac{A'}{\tau'} = 1 + \tfrac{4}{5}A' + \tfrac{8}{175}A'^2 - \tfrac{8}{525}A'^3 + \tfrac{1896}{336875}A'^4 - \tfrac{28744}{13138125}A'^5 + \&c.,$$

$$B' = 1 + \tfrac{3}{175}A'^2 - \tfrac{2}{525}A'^3 + \tfrac{471}{336875}A'^4 - \&c.$$

Table X. contains the values of $\log B$ and $\log C$ for the ellipse and the hyperbola, with the argument A, from $A = 0$ to $A = 0.3$. For every case in which A exceeds 0.3, the general formulæ (39) and (69) may be conveniently applied, as already stated.

The equation

$$\tan \tfrac{1}{2}v = \sqrt{\frac{1+e}{1-e}} \tan \tfrac{1}{2}E$$

gives

$$\tan^2 \tfrac{1}{2}v = \frac{1+e}{1-e} A C^2,$$

or, substituting the value of A in terms of w,

$$\tan \tfrac{1}{2}v = C \tan \tfrac{1}{2}w \sqrt{\frac{5(1+e)}{1+9e}}. \tag{76}$$

The last of equations (43) gives

$$r \cos^2 \tfrac{1}{2}v = q \cos^2 \tfrac{1}{2}E = \frac{q}{1 + \tan^2 \tfrac{1}{2}E}.$$

Hence we derive

$$r = \frac{q}{(1 + A C^2) \cos^2 \tfrac{1}{2}v}. \tag{77}$$

The equation for v in a hyperbolic orbit is of precisely the same form as (76), the accents being omitted, and the value of A being computed from

$$A = \frac{5(e-1)}{1+9e} \tan^2 \tfrac{1}{2}w. \tag{78}$$

For the radius-vector in a hyperbolic orbit, we find, by means of the last of equations (63),

$$r = \frac{q}{(1 - A C^2) \cos^2 \tfrac{1}{2}v}. \tag{79}$$

When $t - T$ is given and r and v are required, we first assume $B = 1$, and enter Table VI. with the argument

$$M = \frac{C_0 (t-T)}{q^{\frac{3}{2}}} \cdot \frac{\sqrt{\tfrac{1}{10}(1+9e)}}{B},$$

in which $\log C_0 = 9.96012771$, and take out the corresponding value of w. Then we derive A from the equation

$$A = \frac{5(1-e)}{1+9e} \tan^2 \tfrac{1}{2}w,$$

in the case of the ellipse, and from (78) in the case of a hyperbolic orbit. With the resulting value of A, we find from Table X. the corresponding value of $\log B$, and then, using this in the expression for M, we repeat the operation. The second result for A will not require any further correction, since the error of the first assumption of $B = 1$ is very small; and, with this as argument, we derive the value of $\log C$ from the table, and then v and r by means of the equations (76) and (77) or (79).

When the true anomaly is given, and the time $t - T$ is required, we first compute τ from

$$\tau = \frac{1-e}{1+e} \tan^2 \tfrac{1}{2}v,$$

in the case of the ellipse, or from

$$\tau = \frac{e-1}{e+1} \tan^2 \tfrac{1}{2}v,$$

in the case of the hyperbola. Then, with the value of τ as argument, we enter the second part of Table X. and take out an approximate value of A, and, with this as argument, we find $\log B$ and $\log C$. The equation

$$A = \frac{\tau}{C^2}$$

will show whether the approximate value of A used in finding $\log C$ is sufficiently exact, and, hence, whether the latter requires any correction. Next, to find w, we have

$$\tan \tfrac{1}{2}w = \frac{\tan \frac{1}{2}v}{C} \cdot \sqrt{\frac{1+9e}{5(1+e)}};$$

and, with w as argument, we derive M from Table VI. Finally, we have

$$t - T = \frac{MBq^{\frac{3}{2}}}{C_0 \sqrt{\frac{1}{10}(1+9e)}}, \tag{80}$$

by means of which the time from the perihelion may be accurately determined.

30. We have thus far treated of the motion of the heavenly bodies, relative to the sun, without considering the positions of their orbits in space; and the elements which we have employed are the eccentricity and semi-transverse axis of the orbit, and the mean anomaly at a given epoch, or, what is equivalent, the time of passing the perihelion. These are the elements which determine the position of the body in its orbit at any given time. It remains now to fix its position in space in reference to some other point in space from which we conceive it to be seen. To accomplish this, the position of its orbit in reference to a known plane must be given; and the elements which determine this position are the longitude of the perihelion, the longitude of the ascending node, and the inclination of the plane of the orbit to the known plane, for which the plane of the ecliptic is usually taken. These three elements will enable us to determine the co-ordinates of the body in space, when its position in its orbit has been found by means of the formulæ already investigated.

The *longitude of the ascending node,* or longitude of the point through which the body passes from the south to the north side of the ecliptic, which we will denote by ☊, is the angular distance of this point from the vernal equinox. The line of intersection of the plane of the orbit with the fundamental plane is called the *line of nodes.*

The angle which the plane of the orbit makes with the plane of the ecliptic, which we will denote by i, is called the *inclination* of the orbit. It will readily be seen that, if we suppose the plane of the orbit to revolve about the line of nodes, when the angle i exceeds 180°, ☊ will no longer be the longitude of the ascending node, but will become the longitude of the descending node, or of the point through which the planet passes from the north to the south side of the ecliptic, which is denoted by ☋, and which is measured, as in the case of ☊, from the vernal equinox.

It will easily be understood that, when seen from the sun, so long as the inclination of the orbit is less than 90°, the motion of the body will be in the same direction as that of the earth, and it is then said to be *direct.* When the inclination is 90°, the motion will be at right angles to that of the earth; and when i exceeds 90°, the motion in longitude will be in a direction opposite to that of the earth, and it is then called *retrograde.* It is customary, therefore, to extend the inclination of the orbit only to 90°, and if this angle exceeds a right angle, to regard its supplement as the inclination of the orbit, noting simply the distinction that the motion is *retrograde.*

The *longitude of the perihelion*, which is denoted by π, fixes the position of the orbit in its own plane, and is, in the case of direct motion, the sum of the longitude of the ascending node and the angular distance, measured in the direction of the motion, of the perihelion from this node. It is, therefore, the angular distance of the perihelion from a point in the orbit whose angular distance back from the ascending node is equal to the longitude of this node; or it may be measured on the ecliptic from the vernal equinox to the ascending node, then on the plane of the orbit from the node to the place of the perihelion.

In the case of retrograde motion, the longitudes of the successive points in the orbit, in the direction of the motion, decrease, and the point in the orbit from which these longitudes in the orbit are measured is taken at an angular distance from the ascending node equal to the longitude of that node, but taken, from the node, in the same direction as the motion. Hence, in this case, the longitude of the perihelion is equal to the longitude of the ascending node diminished by the angular distance of the perihelion from this node.

It may, perhaps, seem desirable that the distinctions, *direct* and *retrograde* motion, should be abandoned, and that the inclination of the orbit should be measured from 0° to 180°, since in this case one set of formulæ would be sufficient, while in the common form two sets are in part required. However, the custom of astronomers seems to have sanctioned these distinctions, and they may be perpetuated or not, as may seem advantageous.

Further, we may remark that in the case of direct motion the sum of the true anomaly and longitude of the perihelion is called the *true longitude in the orbit;* and that the sum of the mean anomaly and longitude of the perihelion is called the *mean longitude*, an expression which can occur only in the case of elliptic orbits.

In the case of retrograde motion the longitude in the orbit is equal to the longitude of the perihelion minus the true anomaly.

31. We will now proceed to derive the formulæ for determining the co-ordinates of a heavenly body in space, when its position in its orbit is known.

For the co-ordinates of the position of the body at the time t, we have

$$x = r \cos v,$$
$$y = r \sin v,$$

the line of apsides being taken as the axis of x, and the origin being taken at the centre of the sun.

If we take the line of nodes as the axis of x, we shall have

$$x = r\cos(v + \omega),$$
$$y = r\sin(v + \omega),$$

ω being the arc of the orbit intercepted between the place of the perihelion and of the node, or the angular distance of the perihelion from the node.

Now, we have $\omega = \pi - \Omega$ in the case of direct motion, and $\omega = \Omega - \pi$ in the case of retrograde motion; and hence the last equations become

$$x = r\cos(v \pm \pi \mp \Omega)$$
$$y = r\sin(v \pm \pi \mp \Omega)$$

the upper and lower signs being taken, respectively, according as the motion is direct or retrograde. The arc $v \pm \pi \mp \Omega = u$ is called the *argument of the latitude.*

Let us now refer the position of the body to three co-ordinate planes, the origin being at the centre of the sun, the ecliptic being taken as the plane of xy, and the axis of x, in the line of nodes. Then we shall have

$$x' = r\cos u,$$
$$y' = \pm r\sin u\cos i,$$
$$z' = r\sin u\sin i.$$

If we denote the heliocentric latitude and longitude of the body, at the time t, by b and l, respectively, we shall have

$$x' = r\cos b\cos(l - \Omega),$$
$$y' = r\cos b\sin(l - \Omega),$$
$$z' = r\sin b,$$

and, consequently,

$$\cos u = \cos b\cos(l - \Omega),$$
$$\pm\sin u\cos i = \cos b\sin(l - \Omega), \qquad (81)$$
$$\sin u\sin i = \sin b.$$

From these we derive

$$\tan(l - \Omega) = \pm\tan u\cos i,$$
$$\tan b = \pm\tan i\sin(l - \Omega), \qquad (82)$$

which serve to determine l and b, when Ω, u, and i are given. Since

$\cos b$ is always positive, it follows that $l - \Omega$ and u must lie in the same quadrant when i is less than $90°$; but if i is greater than $90°$, or the motion is retrograde, $l - \Omega$ and $360° - u$ will belong to the same quadrant. Hence the ambiguity which the determination of $l - \Omega$ by means of its tangent involves, is wholly avoided.

If we use the distinction of retrograde motion, and consider i always less than $90°$, $l - \Omega$ and $-u$ will lie in the same quadrant.

32. By multiplying the first of the equations (81) by $\sin u$, and the second by $\cos u$, and combining the results, considering only the upper sign, we derive

$$\cos b \sin(u - l + \Omega) = 2 \sin u \cos u \sin^2 \tfrac{1}{2}i,$$

or

$$\cos b \sin(u - l + \Omega) = \sin 2u \sin^2 \tfrac{1}{2}i.$$

In a similar manner, we find

$$\cos b \cos(u - l + \Omega) = \cos^2 u + \sin^2 u \cos i,$$

which may be written

$$\cos b \cos(u - l + \Omega) = \tfrac{1}{2}(1 + \cos 2u) + \tfrac{1}{2}(1 - \cos 2u) \cos i,$$

or

$$\cos b \cos(u - l + \Omega) = \tfrac{1}{2}(1 + \cos i) + \tfrac{1}{2}(1 - \cos i) \cos 2u;$$

and hence

$$\cos b \cos(u - l + \Omega) = \cos^2 \tfrac{1}{2}i + \sin^2 \tfrac{1}{2}i \cos 2u.$$

If we divide this equation by the value of $\cos b \sin(u - l + \Omega)$ already found, we shall have

$$\tan(u - l + \Omega) = \frac{\tan^2 \frac{1}{2}i \sin 2u}{1 + \tan^2 \frac{1}{2}i \cos 2u}. \qquad (83)$$

The angle $u - l + \Omega$ is called the *reduction to the ecliptic;* and the expression for it may be arranged in a series which converges rapidly when i is small, as in the case of the planets. In order to effect this development, let us first take the equation

$$\tan y = \frac{n \sin x}{1 + n \cos x}.$$

Differentiating this, regarding y and n as variables, and reducing, we find

$$\frac{dy}{dn} = \frac{\sin x}{1 + 2n \cos x + n^2},$$

which gives, by division, or by the method of indeterminate coefficients,

$$\frac{dy}{dn} = \sin x - n \sin 2x + n^2 \sin 3x - n^3 \sin 4x + \&c.$$

Integrating this expression, we get, since $y = 0$ when $x = 0$,

$$y = n \sin x - \tfrac{1}{2} n^2 \sin 2x + \tfrac{1}{3} n^3 \sin 3x - \tfrac{1}{4} n^4 \sin 4x + \ldots, \qquad (84)$$

which is the general form of the development of the above expression for $\tan y$. The assumed expression for $\tan y$ corresponds exactly with the formula for the reduction to the ecliptic by making $n = \tan^2 \frac{1}{2} i$ and $x = 2u$; and hence we obtain

$$u - l + \Omega = \tan^2 \tfrac{1}{2} i \sin 2u - \tfrac{1}{2} \tan^4 \tfrac{1}{2} i \sin 4u + \tfrac{1}{3} \tan^6 \tfrac{1}{2} i \sin 6u$$
$$- \tfrac{1}{4} \tan^8 \tfrac{1}{2} i \sin 8u + \tfrac{1}{5} \tan^{10} \tfrac{1}{2} i \sin 10u - \&c. \qquad (85)$$

When the value of i does not exceed 10° or 12°, the first two terms of this development will be sufficient. To express $u - l + \Omega$ in seconds of arc, the value derived from the second member of this equation must be multiplied by 206264.81, the number of seconds corresponding to the radius of a circle.

If we denote by R_e the reduction to the ecliptic, we shall have

$$l = u + \Omega - R_e = v + \pi - R_e.$$

But we have $v = M +$ the equation of the centre; hence

$$l = M + \pi + \text{equation of the centre} - \text{reduction to the ecliptic},$$

and, putting $L = M + \pi =$ mean longitude, we get

$$l = L + \text{equation of centre} - \text{reduction to ecliptic}. \qquad (86)$$

In the tables of the motion of the planets, the equation of the centre (53) is given in a table with M as the argument; and the reduction to the ecliptic is given in a table in which i and u are the arguments.

33. In determining the place of a heavenly body directly from the elements of its orbit, there will be no necessity for computing the reduction to the ecliptic, since the heliocentric longitude and latitude may be readily found by the formulæ (82). When the heliocentric place has been found, we can easily deduce the corresponding geocentric place.

Let x, y, z be the rectangular co-ordinates of the planet or comet referred to the centre of the sun, the plane of xy being in the ecliptic, the positive axis of x being directed to the vernal equinox, and the positive axis of z to the north pole of the ecliptic. Then we shall have

$$x = r\cos b\cos l,$$
$$y = r\cos b\sin l,$$
$$z = r\sin b.$$

Again, let X, Y, Z be the co-ordinates of the centre of the sun referred to the centre of the earth, the plane of XY being in the ecliptic, and the axis of X being directed to the vernal equinox; and let $\odot$ denote the geocentric longitude of the sun, R its distance from the earth, and Σ its latitude. Then we shall have

$$X = R\cos\Sigma\cos\odot,$$
$$Y = R\cos\Sigma\sin\odot,$$
$$Z = R\sin\Sigma.$$

Let x', y', z' be the co-ordinates of the body referred to the centre of the earth; and let λ and β denote, respectively, the geocentric longitude and latitude, and Δ, the distance of the planet or comet from the earth. Then we obtain

$$\begin{aligned} x' &= \Delta\cos\beta\cos\lambda, \\ y' &= \Delta\cos\beta\sin\lambda, \\ z' &= \Delta\sin\beta. \end{aligned} \qquad (87)$$

But, evidently, we also have

$$x' = x + X, \qquad y' = y + Y, \qquad z' = z + Z,$$

and, consequently,

$$\begin{aligned} \Delta\cos\beta\cos\lambda &= r\cos b\cos l + R\cos\Sigma\cos\odot, \\ \Delta\cos\beta\sin\lambda &= r\cos b\sin l + R\cos\Sigma\sin\odot, \\ \Delta\sin\beta &= r\sin b \qquad\quad + R\sin\Sigma. \end{aligned} \qquad (88)$$

If we multiply the first of these equations by $\cos\odot$, and the second by $\sin\odot$, and add the products; then multiply the first by $\sin\odot$, and the second by $\cos\odot$, and subtract the first product from the second, we get

$$\begin{aligned} \Delta\cos\beta\cos(\lambda - \odot) &= r\cos b\cos(l - \odot) + R\cos\Sigma, \\ \Delta\cos\beta\sin(\lambda - \odot) &= r\cos b\sin(l - \odot), \\ \Delta\sin\beta &= r\sin b + R\sin\Sigma. \end{aligned} \qquad (89)$$

It will be observed that this transformation is equivalent to the supposition that the axis of x, in each of the co-ordinate systems, is directed to a point whose longitude is $\odot$, or that the system has been revolved about the axis of z to a new position for which the axis of abscissas makes the angle $\odot$ with that of the primitive system. We may, therefore, in general, in order to effect such a transformation in systems of equations thus derived, simply diminish the longitudes by the given angle.

The equations (89) will determine λ, β, and Δ when r, b, and l have been derived from the elements of the orbit, the quantities R, $\odot$, and Σ being furnished by the solar tables; or, when Δ, β, and λ are given, these equations determine l, b, and r. The latitude Σ of the sun never exceeds $\pm\, 0''.9$, and, therefore, it may in most cases be neglected, so that $\cos\Sigma = 1$ and $\sin\Sigma = 0$, and the last equations become

$$\begin{aligned} \Delta \cos\beta \cos(\lambda - \odot) &= r \cos b \cos(l - \odot) + R, \\ \Delta \cos\beta \sin(\lambda - \odot) &= r \cos b \sin(l - \odot), \\ \Delta \sin\beta &= r \sin b. \end{aligned} \tag{90}$$

If we suppose the axis of x to be directed to a point whose longitude is Ω, or to the ascending node of the planet or comet, the equations (88) become

$$\begin{aligned} \Delta \cos\beta \cos(\lambda - \Omega) &= r \cos u + R \cos\Sigma \cos(\odot - \Omega), \\ \Delta \cos\beta \sin(\lambda - \Omega) &= \pm\, r \sin u \cos i + R \cos\Sigma \sin(\odot - \Omega), \\ \Delta \sin\beta &= r \sin u \sin i + R \sin\Sigma, \end{aligned} \tag{91}$$

by means of which β and λ may be found directly from Ω, i, r, and u.

If it be required to determine the geocentric right ascension and declination, denoted respectively by α and δ, we may convert the values of β and λ into those of α and δ. To effect this transformation, denoting by ε the obliquity of the ecliptic, we have

$$\begin{aligned} \cos\delta \cos\alpha &= \cos\beta \cos\lambda, \\ \cos\delta \sin\alpha &= \cos\beta \sin\lambda \cos\varepsilon - \sin\beta \sin\varepsilon, \\ \sin\delta &= \cos\beta \sin\lambda \sin\varepsilon + \sin\beta \cos\varepsilon. \end{aligned}$$

Let us now take

$$\begin{aligned} n \sin N &= \sin\beta, \\ n \cos N &= \cos\beta \sin\lambda, \end{aligned}$$

and we shall have

$$\begin{aligned} \cos\delta \cos\alpha &= \cos\beta \cos\lambda, \\ \cos\delta \sin\alpha &= n \cos(N + \varepsilon), \\ \sin\delta &= n \sin(N + \varepsilon). \end{aligned}$$

Therefore, we obtain

$$\tan N = \frac{\tan\beta}{\sin\lambda}, \qquad \tan\alpha = \frac{\cos(N+\varepsilon)}{\cos N}\tan\lambda, \qquad (92)$$
$$\tan\delta = \tan(N+\varepsilon)\sin\alpha.$$

We also have

$$\frac{\cos(N+\varepsilon)}{\cos N} = \frac{\cos\delta\sin\alpha}{\cos\beta\sin\lambda},$$

which will serve to check the calculation of α and δ. Since $\cos\delta$ and $\cos\beta$ are always positive, $\cos\alpha$ and $\cos\lambda$ must have the same sign, and thus the quadrant in which α is to be taken, is determined.

For the solution of the inverse problem, in which α and δ are given and the values of λ and β are required, it is only necessary to interchange, in these equations, α and λ, δ and β, and to write $-\varepsilon$ in place of ε.

34. Instead of pursuing the tedious process, when several places are required, of computing first the heliocentric place, then the geocentric place referred to the ecliptic, and, finally, the geocentric right ascension and declination, we may derive formulæ which, when certain constant auxiliaries have once been computed, enable us to derive the geocentric place directly, referred either to the ecliptic or to the equator.

We will first consider the case in which the ecliptic is taken as the fundamental plane. Let us, therefore, resume the equations

$$\begin{aligned} x' &= r\cos u, \\ y' &= \pm r\sin u\cos i, \\ z' &= r\sin u\sin i, \end{aligned}$$

in which the axis of x is supposed to be directed to the ascending node of the orbit of the body. If we now pass to a new system x, y, z,—the origin and the axis of z remaining the same,—in which the axis of x is directed to the vernal equinox, we shall move it back, in a negative direction, equal to the angle Ω, and, consequently,

$$\begin{aligned} x &= x'\cos\Omega - y'\sin\Omega, \\ y &= x'\sin\Omega + y'\cos\Omega, \\ z &= z'. \end{aligned}$$

Therefore, we obtain

$$\begin{aligned} x &= r(\cos u\cos\Omega \mp \sin u\cos i\sin\Omega), \\ y &= r(\pm\sin u\cos i\cos\Omega + \cos u\sin\Omega), \qquad (93) \\ z &= r\sin u\sin i, \end{aligned}$$

which are the expressions for the heliocentric co-ordinates of a planet or comet referred to the ecliptic, the positive axis of x being directed to the vernal equinox. The upper sign is to be used when the motion is direct, and the lower sign when it is retrograde.

Let us now put

$$\begin{aligned} \cos \Omega &= \sin a \sin A, \\ \mp \cos i \sin \Omega &= \sin a \cos A, \\ \sin \Omega &= \sin b \sin B, \\ \pm \cos i \cos \Omega &= \sin b \cos B, \end{aligned} \tag{94}$$

in which $\sin a$ and $\sin b$ are positive, and the expressions for the co-ordinates become

$$\begin{aligned} x &= r \sin a \sin (A + u), \\ y &= r \sin b \sin (B + u), \\ z &= r \sin i \sin u. \end{aligned} \tag{95}$$

The auxiliary quantities a, b, A, and B, it will be observed, are functions of Ω and i, and, in computing an ephemeris, are constant so long as these elements are regarded as constant. They are called the *constants for the ecliptic.*

To determine them, we have, from equations (94),

$$\cot A = \mp \tan \Omega \cos i, \qquad \cot B = \pm \cot \Omega \cos i,$$

$$\sin a = \frac{\cos \Omega}{\sin A}, \qquad \sin b = \frac{\sin \Omega}{\sin B};$$

the upper sign being used when the motion is direct, and the lower sign when it is retrograde.

The auxiliaries $\sin a$ and $\sin b$ are always positive, and, therefore, $\sin A$ and $\cos \Omega$, $\sin B$ and $\sin \Omega$, respectively, must have the same signs. The quadrants in which A and B are situated, are thus determined.

From the equations (94) we easily find

$$\begin{aligned} \cos a &= \sin i \sin \Omega, \\ \cos b &= - \sin i \cos \Omega. \end{aligned} \tag{96}$$

If we add to the heliocentric co-ordinates of the body the co-ordinates of the sun referred to the earth, for which the equations have already been given, we shall have

$$\begin{aligned} x + X &= \Delta \cos \beta \cos \lambda, \\ y + Y &= \Delta \cos \beta \sin \lambda, \\ z + Z &= \Delta \sin \beta, \end{aligned} \tag{97}$$

which suffice to determine λ, β, and Δ. The values of α and δ may be derived from these by means of the equations (92).

35. We shall now derive the formulæ for determining α and δ directly. For this purpose, let x, y, z be the heliocentric co-ordinates of the body referred to the equator, the positive axis of x being directed to the vernal equinox. To pass from the system of co-ordinates referred to the ecliptic to those referred to the equator as the fundamental plane, we must revolve the system negatively around the axis of x, so that the axes of z and y in the new system make the angle ε with those of the primitive system, ε being the obliquity of the ecliptic. In this case, we have

$$\begin{aligned} x'' &= x, \\ y'' &= y \cos\varepsilon - z \sin\varepsilon, \\ z'' &= y \sin\varepsilon + z \cos\varepsilon. \end{aligned}$$

Substituting for x, y, and z their values from equations (93), and omitting the accents, we get

$$\begin{aligned} x &= r \cos u \cos \Omega \mp r \sin u \cos i \sin \Omega, \\ y &= r \cos u \sin \Omega \cos\varepsilon + r \sin u\,(\pm \cos i \cos \Omega \cos\varepsilon - \sin i \sin\varepsilon), \\ z &= r \cos u \sin \Omega \sin\varepsilon + r \sin u\,(\pm \cos i \cos \Omega \sin\varepsilon + \sin i \cos\varepsilon). \end{aligned} \tag{98}$$

These are the expressions for the heliocentric co-ordinates of the planet or comet referred to the equator. To reduce them to a convenient form for numerical calculation, let us put

$$\begin{aligned} \cos \Omega &= \sin a \sin A, \\ \mp \cos i \sin \Omega &= \sin a \cos A, \\ \sin \Omega \cos\varepsilon &= \sin b \sin B, \\ \pm \cos i \cos \Omega \cos\varepsilon - \sin i \sin\varepsilon &= \sin b \cos B, \\ \sin \Omega \sin\varepsilon &= \sin c \sin C, \\ \pm \cos i \cos \Omega \sin\varepsilon + \sin i \cos\varepsilon &= \sin c \cos C; \end{aligned} \tag{99}$$

and the expressions for the co-ordinates reduce to

$$\begin{aligned} x &= r \sin a \sin (A + u), \\ y &= r \sin b \sin (B + u), \\ z &= r \sin c \sin (C + u). \end{aligned} \tag{100}$$

The auxiliary quantities, a, b, c, A, B, and C, are constant so long as Ω and i remain unchanged, and are called *constants for the equator.*

It will be observed that the equations involving a and A, regarding the motion as direct, correspond to the relations between the parts of a quadrantal triangle of which the sides are i and a, the angle included between these sides being that which we designate by A, and the angle opposite the side a being $90° - \Omega$. In the case of b and B, the relations are those of the parts of a spherical triangle of which the sides are b, i, and $90° + \varepsilon$, B being the angle included by i and b, and $180° - \Omega$ the angle opposite the side b. Further, in the case of c and C, the relations are those of the parts of a spherical triangle of which the sides are c, i, and ε, the angle C being that included by the sides i and c, and $180° - \Omega$ that included by the sides i and ε. We have, therefore, the following additional equations:

$$\begin{aligned} \cos a &= \sin i \sin \Omega, \\ \cos b &= -\cos \Omega \sin i \cos \varepsilon - \cos i \sin \varepsilon, \\ \cos c &= -\cos \Omega \sin i \sin \varepsilon + \cos i \cos \varepsilon. \end{aligned} \tag{101}$$

In the case of retrograde motion, we must substitute in these $180° - i$ in place of i.

The geometrical signification of the auxiliary constants for the equator is thus made apparent. The angles a, b, and c are those which a line drawn from the origin of co-ordinates perpendicular to the plane of the orbit on the north side, makes with the positive co-ordinate axes, respectively; and A, B, and C are the angles which the three planes, passing through this line and the co-ordinate axes, make with a plane passing through this line and perpendicular to the line of nodes.

In order to facilitate the computation of the constants for the equator, let us introduce another auxiliary quantity E_0, such that

$$\begin{aligned} \sin i &= e_0 \sin E_0, \\ \pm \cos i \cos \Omega &= e_0 \cos E_0, \end{aligned}$$

e_0 being always positive. We shall, therefore, have

$$\tan E_0 = \pm \frac{\tan i}{\cos \Omega}.$$

Since both e_0 and $\sin i$ are positive, the angle E_0 cannot exceed 180°; and the algebraic sign of $\tan E_0$ will show whether this angle is to be taken in the first or second quadrant.

The first two of equations (99) give

$$\cot A = \mp \tan \Omega \cos i;$$

and the first gives

$$\sin a = \frac{\cos \Omega}{\sin A}.$$

From the fourth of equations (99), introducing e_0 and E_0, we get

$$\sin b \cos B = e_0 \cos E_0 \cos \varepsilon - e_0 \sin E_0 \sin \varepsilon = e_0 \cos (E_0 + \varepsilon).$$

But

$$\sin b \sin B = \sin \Omega \cos \varepsilon;$$

therefore

$$\cot B = \frac{e_0}{\sin \Omega} \cdot \frac{\cos (E_0 + \varepsilon)}{\cos \varepsilon} = \pm \frac{\cos i}{\tan \Omega \cos E_0} \cdot \frac{\cos (E_0 + \varepsilon)}{\cos \varepsilon}.$$

We have, also,

$$\sin b = \frac{\sin \Omega \cos \varepsilon}{\sin B}.$$

In a similar manner, we find

$$\cot C = \pm \frac{\cos i}{\tan \Omega \cos E_0} \cdot \frac{\sin (E_0 + \varepsilon)}{\sin \varepsilon},$$

and

$$\sin c = \frac{\sin \Omega \sin \varepsilon}{\sin C}.$$

The auxiliaries $\sin a$, $\sin b$, and $\sin c$ are always positive, and, therefore, $\sin A$ and $\cos \Omega$, $\sin B$ and $\sin \Omega$, and also $\sin C$ and $\sin \Omega$, must have the same signs, which will determine the quadrant in which each of the angles A, B, and C is situated.

If we multiply the last of equations (99) by the third, and the fifth of these equations by the fourth, and subtract the first product from the last, we get, by reduction,

$$\sin b \sin c \sin (C - B) = - \sin i \sin \Omega.$$

But

$$\sin a \cos A = \mp \cos i \sin \Omega;$$

and hence we derive

$$\frac{\sin b \sin c \sin (C - B)}{\sin a \cos A} = \pm \tan i,$$

which serves to check the accuracy of the numerical computation of the constants, since the value of $\tan i$ obtained from this formula must agree exactly with that used in the calculation of the values of these constants.

If we put $A' = A \pm \pi \mp \Omega$, $B' = B \pm \pi \mp \Omega$, and $C' = C \pm \pi \mp \Omega$, the upper or lower sign being used according as the motion is direct or retrograde, we shall have

$$x = r \sin a \sin (A' + v),$$
$$y = r \sin b \sin (B' + v), \qquad (102)$$
$$z = r \sin c \sin (C' + v),$$

a transformation which is perhaps unnecessary, but which is convenient when a series of places is to be computed.

It will be observed that the formulæ for computing the constants a, b, c, A, B, and C, in the case of direct motion, are converted into those for the case in which the distinction of retrograde motion is adopted, by simply using $180° - i$ instead of i.

36. When the heliocentric co-ordinates of the body have been found, referred to the equator as the fundamental plane, if we add to these the geocentric co-ordinates of the sun referred to the same fundamental plane, the sum will be the geocentric co-ordinates of the body referred also to the equator.

For the co-ordinates of the sun referred to the centre of the earth, we have, neglecting the latitude of the sun,

$$X = R \cos \odot,$$
$$Y = R \sin \odot \cos \varepsilon,$$
$$Z = R \sin \odot \sin \varepsilon = Y \tan \varepsilon,$$

in which R represents the radius-vector of the earth, $\odot$ the sun's longitude, and ε the obliquity of the ecliptic.

We shall, therefore, have

$$x + X = \Delta \cos \delta \cos \alpha,$$
$$y + Y = \Delta \cos \delta \sin \alpha, \qquad (103)$$
$$z + Z = \Delta \sin \delta,$$

which suffice to determine α, δ, and Δ.

If we have regard to the latitude of the sun in computing its geocentric co-ordinates, the formulæ will evidently become

$$X = R \cos \odot \cos \Sigma,$$
$$Y = R \sin \odot \cos \Sigma \cos \varepsilon - R \sin \Sigma \sin \varepsilon, \qquad (104)$$
$$Z = R \sin \odot \cos \Sigma \sin \varepsilon + R \sin \Sigma \cos \varepsilon,$$

in which, since Σ can never exceed $\pm 0''.9$, $\cos \Sigma$ is very nearly equal to 1, and $\sin \Sigma = \Sigma$.

The longitudes and latitudes of the sun may be derived from a solar ephemeris, or from the solar tables. The principal astronomical ephemerides, such as the *Berliner Astronomisches Jahrbuch*, the *Nautical Almanac*, and the *American Ephemeris and Nautical Al-*

manac, contain, for each year for which they are published, the equatorial co-ordinates of the sun, referred both to the mean equinox and equator of the beginning of the year, and to the apparent equinox of the date, taking into account the latitude of the sun.

37. In the case of an elliptic orbit, we may determine the co-ordinates directly from the eccentric anomaly in the following manner:—

The equations (102) give, accenting the letters a, b, and c,

$$\begin{aligned} x &= r\cos v\sin a'\sin A' + r\sin v\sin a'\cos A', \\ y &= r\cos v\sin b'\sin B' + r\sin v\sin b'\cos B', \\ z &= r\cos v\sin c'\sin C' + r\sin v\sin c'\cos C'. \end{aligned}$$

Now, since $r\cos v = a\cos E - ae$, and $r\sin v = a\cos\varphi\sin E$, we shall have

$$\begin{aligned} x &= a\sin a'\sin A'\cos E - ae\sin a'\sin A' + a\cos\varphi\sin a'\cos A'\sin E, \\ y &= a\sin b'\sin B'\cos E - ae\sin b'\sin B' + a\cos\varphi\sin b'\cos B'\sin E, \\ z &= a\sin c'\sin C'\cos E - ae\sin c'\sin C' + a\cos\varphi\sin c'\cos C'\sin E. \end{aligned}$$

Let us now put

$$\begin{aligned} a\cos\varphi\sin a'\cos A' &= \lambda_x\cos L_x, \\ a\sin a'\sin A' &= \lambda_x\sin L_x, \\ -ae\sin a'\sin A' &= -e\lambda_x\sin L_x = \nu_x; \\ a\cos\varphi\sin b'\cos B' &= \lambda_y\cos L_y, \\ a\sin b'\sin B' &= \lambda_y\sin L_y, \\ -ae\sin b'\sin B' &= -e\lambda_y\sin L_y = \nu_y; \\ a\cos\varphi\sin c'\cos C' &= \lambda_z\cos L_z, \\ a\sin c'\sin C' &= \lambda_z\sin L_z, \\ -ae\sin c'\sin C' &= -e\lambda_z\sin L_z = \nu_z; \end{aligned}$$

in which $\sin a'$, $\sin b'$, and $\sin c'$ have the same values as in equations (102), the accents being added simply to mark the necessary distinction in the notation employed in these formulæ. We shall, therefore, have

$$\begin{aligned} x &= \lambda_x\sin(L_x + E) + \nu_x, \\ y &= \lambda_y\sin(L_y + E) + \nu_y, \\ z &= \lambda_z\sin(L_z + E) + \nu_z. \end{aligned} \qquad (105)$$

By means of these formulæ, the co-ordinates are found directly from the eccentric anomaly, when the constants λ_x, λ_y, λ_z, L_x, L_y, L_z, ν_x, ν_y, and ν_z, have been computed from those already found, or from a, b, c, A, B, and C. This method is very convenient when a great number of geocentric places are to be computed; but, when only a few places are required, the additional labor of computing so many auxiliary quantities will not be compensated by the facility afforded in the numerical calculation, when these constants have been determined. Further, when the ephemeris is intended for the comparison of a series of observations in order to determine the corrections to be applied to the elements by means of the differential formulæ which we shall investigate in the following chapter, it will always be advisable to compute the co-ordinates by means of the radius-vector and true anomaly, since both of these quantities will be required in finding the differential coefficients.

38. In the case of a hyperbolic orbit, the co-ordinates may be computed directly from F, since we have

$$r\cos v = a(e - \sec F),$$
$$r\sin v = a\tan\psi\tan F;$$

and, consequently,

$$x = ae\sin a'\sin A' - a\sec F\sin a'\sin A' + a\tan\psi\tan F\sin a'\cos A',$$
$$y = ae\sin b'\sin B' - a\sec F\sin b'\sin B' + a\tan\psi\tan F\sin b'\cos B',$$
$$z = ae\sin c'\sin C' - a\sec F\sin c'\sin C' + a\tan\psi\tan F\sin c'\cos C'.$$

Let us now put

$$ae\sin a'\sin A' = \lambda_x,$$
$$-a\sin a'\sin A' = \mu_x,$$
$$a\tan\psi\sin a'\cos A' = \nu_x;$$
$$ae\sin b'\sin B' = \lambda_y,$$
$$-a\sin b'\sin B' = \mu_y,$$
$$a\tan\psi\sin b'\cos B' = \nu_y;$$
$$ae\sin c'\sin C' = \lambda_z,$$
$$-a\sin c'\sin C' = \mu_z,$$
$$a\tan\psi\sin c'\cos C' = \nu_z.$$

Then we shall have

$$x = \lambda_x + \mu_x\sec F + \nu_x\tan F,$$
$$y = \lambda_y + \mu_y\sec F + \nu_y\tan F, \qquad (106)$$
$$z = \lambda_z + \mu_z\sec F + \nu_z\tan F.$$

In a similar manner we may derive expressions for the co-ordinates, in the case of a hyperbolic orbit, when the auxiliary quantity σ is used instead of F.

39. If we denote by π', ☊$'$, and i' the elements which determine the position of the orbit in space when referred to the equator as the

fundamental plane, and by ω_0 the angular distance between the ascending node of the orbit on the ecliptic and its ascending node on the equator, being measured positively from the equator in the direction of the motion, we shall have

$$\pi' = \pi - \Omega + \Omega' + \omega_0.$$

To find Ω' and i', we have, from the spherical triangle formed by the intersection of the planes of the orbit, ecliptic, and equator with the celestial vault,

$$\begin{aligned}\cos i' &= \cos i \cos \varepsilon - \sin i \sin \varepsilon \cos \Omega, \\ \sin i' \sin \Omega' &= \sin i \sin \Omega, \\ \sin i' \cos \Omega' &= \cos i \sin \varepsilon + \sin i \cos \varepsilon \cos \Omega.\end{aligned}$$

Let us now put

$$\begin{aligned}n \sin N &= \cos i; \\ n \cos N &= \sin i \cos \Omega,\end{aligned}$$

and these equations reduce to

$$\begin{aligned}\cos i' &= n \sin (N - \varepsilon), \\ \sin i' \sin \Omega' &= \sin i \sin \Omega, \\ \sin i' \cos \Omega' &= n \cos (N - \varepsilon);\end{aligned}$$

from which we find

$$\tan N = \frac{\cot i}{\cos \Omega}, \qquad \tan \Omega' = \frac{\cos N}{\cos (N - \varepsilon)} \tan \Omega,$$
$$\cot i' = \tan (N - \varepsilon) \cos \Omega'. \qquad (107)$$

Since $\sin i$ is always positive, $\cos N$ and $\cos \Omega$ must have the same signs. To prove the numerical calculation, we have

$$\frac{\sin i \cos \Omega}{\sin i' \cos \Omega'} = \frac{\cos N}{\cos (N - \varepsilon)},$$

the value of the second member of which must agree with that used in computing Ω'.

In order to find ω_0, we have, from the same triangle,

$$\begin{aligned}\sin \omega_0 \sin i' &= \sin \Omega \sin \varepsilon, \\ \cos \omega_0 \sin i' &= \cos \varepsilon \sin i + \sin \varepsilon \cos i \cos \Omega.\end{aligned}$$

Let us now take

$$\begin{aligned}m \sin M &= \cos \varepsilon, \\ m \cos M &= \sin \varepsilon \cos \Omega;\end{aligned}$$

and we obtain

$$\cot M = \tan \varepsilon \cos \Omega,$$
$$\tan \omega_0 = \frac{\cos M}{\cos (M - i)} \tan \Omega, \tag{108}$$

and, also, to check the calculation,

$$\frac{\sin \varepsilon \cos \Omega}{\sin i' \cos \omega_0} = \frac{\cos M}{\cos (M - i)}.$$

If we apply Gauss's analogies to the same spherical triangle, we get

$$\begin{aligned} \cos \tfrac{1}{2}i' \sin \tfrac{1}{2}(\Omega' + \omega_0) &= \sin \tfrac{1}{2}\Omega \cos \tfrac{1}{2}(i - \varepsilon), \\ \cos \tfrac{1}{2}i' \cos \tfrac{1}{2}(\Omega' + \omega_0) &= \cos \tfrac{1}{2}\Omega \cos \tfrac{1}{2}(i + \varepsilon), \\ \sin \tfrac{1}{2}i' \sin \tfrac{1}{2}(\Omega' - \omega_0) &= \sin \tfrac{1}{2}\Omega \sin \tfrac{1}{2}(i - \varepsilon), \\ \sin \tfrac{1}{2}i' \cos \tfrac{1}{2}(\Omega' - \omega_0) &= \cos \tfrac{1}{2}\Omega \sin \tfrac{1}{2}(i + \varepsilon). \end{aligned} \tag{109}$$

The quadrant in which $\frac{1}{2}(\Omega' + \omega_0)$ or $\frac{1}{2}(\Omega' - \omega_0)$ is situated, must be so taken that $\sin \frac{1}{2}i'$ and $\cos \frac{1}{2}i'$ shall be positive; and the agreement of the values of the latter two quantities, computed by means of the value of $\frac{1}{2}i'$ derived from $\tan \frac{1}{2}i'$, will serve to check the accuracy of the numerical calculation.

For the case in which the motion is regarded as retrograde, we must use $180^\circ - i$ instead of i in these equations, and we have, also,

$$\pi' = \pi - \Omega + \Omega' - \omega_0.$$

We may thus find the elements π', Ω', and i', in reference to the equator, from the elements referred to the ecliptic; and using the elements so found instead of π, Ω, and i, and using also the places of the sun referred to the equator, we may derive the heliocentric and geocentric places with respect to the equator by means of the formulæ already given for the ecliptic as the fundamental plane.

If the position of the orbit with respect to the equator is given, and its position in reference to the ecliptic is required, it is only necessary to interchange Ω and Ω', as well as i and $180^\circ - i'$, ε remaining unchanged, in these equations. These formulæ may also be used to determine the position of the orbit in reference to any plane in space; but the longitude Ω must then be measured from the place of the descending node of this plane on the ecliptic. The value of Ω, therefore, which must be used in the solution of the equations is, in this case, equal to the longitude of the ascending node of the orbit on the ecliptic diminished by the longitude of the descending node of the new plane of reference on the ecliptic. The quantities Ω', i', and ω_0 will have the same signification in reference to this plane that they have in reference to the equator, with this distinction, however, that ☊′ is measured from the descending node of this new plane of reference on the ecliptic; and ε will in this case denote the inclination of the ecliptic to this plane.

40. We have now derived all the formulæ which can be required in the case of undisturbed motion, for the computation of the heliocentric or geocentric place of a heavenly body, referred either to the ecliptic or equator, or to any other known plane, when the elements of its orbit are known; and the formulæ which have been derived are applicable to every variety of conic section, thus including all possible forms of undisturbed orbits consistent with the law of universal gravitation. The circle is an ellipse of which the eccentricity is zero, and, consequently, $M = v = u$, and $r = a$, for every point of the orbit. There is no instance of a circular orbit yet known; but in the case of the discovery of the asteroid planets between Mars and Jupiter it is sometimes thought advisable, in order to facilitate the identification of comparison stars for a few days succeeding the discovery, to compute circular elements, and from these an ephemeris.

The elements which determine the form of the orbit remain constant so long as the system of elements is regarded as unchanged; but those which determine the position of the orbit in space, π, ☊, and i, vary from one epoch to another on account of the change of the relative position of the planes to which they are referred. Thus the inclination of the orbit will vary slowly, on account of the change of the position of the ecliptic in space, arising from the perturbations of the earth by the other planets; while the longitude of the perihelion and the longitude of the ascending node will vary, both on account of this change of the position of the plane of the ecliptic, and also on account of precession and nutation. If π, ☊, and i are referred to the true equinox and ecliptic of any date, the resulting heliocentric places will be referred to the same equinox and ecliptic; and, further, in the computation of the geocentric places, the longitudes of the sun must be referred to the same equinox, so that the resulting geocentric longitudes or right ascensions will also be referred to that equinox. It will appear, therefore, that, on account of these changes in the values of π, ☊, and i, the auxiliaries $\sin a$, $\sin b$, $\sin c$, A, B, and C, introduced into the formulæ for the coordinates, will not be constants in the computation of the places for a series of dates, unless the elements are referred constantly, in the calculation, to a fixed equinox and ecliptic. It is customary, therefore, to reduce the elements to the ecliptic and mean equinox of the beginning of the year for which the ephemeris is required, and then to compute the places of the planet or comet referred to this equinox, using, in the case of the right ascension and declination, the mean obliquity of the ecliptic for the date of the fixed equinox adopted, in the computation of the auxiliary constants and of the co-ordinates of the sun. The places thus found may be reduced to the true equinox of the date by the well-known formulæ for precession and nutation. Thus, for the reduction of the right ascension and declination from the mean equinox and equator of the beginning of the year to the apparent or true equinox and equator of any date, usually the date to which the co-ordinates of the body belong, we have

$$\begin{aligned} \Delta\alpha &= f + g\sin(G+\alpha)\tan\delta, \\ \Delta\delta &= g\cos(G+\alpha), \end{aligned} \qquad (110)$$

for which the quantities f, g, and G are derived from the data given either in the solar and lunar tables, or in astronomical ephemerides, such as have already been mentioned.

The problem of reducing the elements from the ecliptic of one date t to that of another date t' may be solved by means of equations (109), making, however, the necessary distinction in regard to the point from which Ω and Ω' are measured. Let θ denote the longitude of the descending node of the ecliptic of t' on that of t, and let η denote the angle which the planes of the two ecliptics make with each other, then, in the equations (109), instead of Ω we must write $\Omega - \theta$, and, in order that Ω' shall be measured from the vernal equinox, we must also write $\Omega' - \theta$ in place of Ω'. Finally, we must write η instead of ε, and $\Delta\omega$ for ω_0, which is the variation in the value of ω in the interval $t' - t$ on account of the change of the position of the ecliptic; then the equations become

$$\begin{aligned} \cos\tfrac{1}{2}i'\sin\tfrac{1}{2}(\Omega' - \theta + \Delta\omega) &= \sin\tfrac{1}{2}(\Omega - \theta)\cos\tfrac{1}{2}(i - \eta), \\ \cos\tfrac{1}{2}i'\cos\tfrac{1}{2}(\Omega' - \theta + \Delta\omega) &= \cos\tfrac{1}{2}(\Omega - \theta)\cos\tfrac{1}{2}(i + \eta), \\ \sin\tfrac{1}{2}i'\sin\tfrac{1}{2}(\Omega' - \theta - \Delta\omega) &= \sin\tfrac{1}{2}(\Omega - \theta)\sin\tfrac{1}{2}(i - \eta), \\ \sin\tfrac{1}{2}i'\cos\tfrac{1}{2}(\Omega' - \theta - \Delta\omega) &= \cos\tfrac{1}{2}(\Omega - \theta)\sin\tfrac{1}{2}(i + \eta). \end{aligned} \qquad (111)$$

These equations enable us to determine accurately the values of Ω', i', and $\Delta\omega$, which give the position of the orbit in reference to the ecliptic corresponding to the time t', when θ and η are known. The longitudes, however, will still be referred to the same mean equinox as before, which we suppose to be that of t; and, in order to refer them to the mean equinox of the epoch t', the amount of the precession in longitude during the interval $t'-t$ must also be applied.

If the changes in the values of the elements are not of considerable magnitude, it will be unnecessary to apply these rigorous formulæ, and we may derive others sufficiently exact, and much more convenient in application. Thus, from the spherical triangle formed by the intersection of the plane of the orbit and of the planes of the two ecliptics with the celestial vault, we get

$$\sin\eta\cos(\Omega-\theta)=-\cos i'\sin i+\sin i'\cos i\cos\Delta\omega,$$

from which we easily derive

$$\sin(i'-i)=\sin\eta\cos(\Omega-\theta)+2\sin i'\cos i\sin^2\tfrac{1}{2}\Delta\omega. \qquad (112)$$

We have, further,

$$\sin\Delta\omega\sin i'=\sin\eta\sin(\Omega-\theta),$$

or

$$\sin\Delta\omega=\sin\eta\,\frac{\sin(\Omega-\theta)}{\sin i'}. \qquad (113)$$

We have, also, from the same triangle,

$$\sin\Delta\omega\cos i'=-\cos(\Omega-\theta)\sin(\Omega'-\theta)$$
$$+\sin(\Omega-\theta)\cos(\Omega'-\theta)\cos\eta,$$

which gives

$$\sin(\Omega'-\Omega)=-\sin\Delta\omega\cos i'-2\sin(\Omega-\theta)\cos(\Omega'-\theta)\sin^2\tfrac{1}{2}\eta,$$

or

$$\sin(\Omega'-\Omega)=-\sin\eta\sin(\Omega-\theta)\cot i'$$
$$-2\sin(\Omega-\theta)\cos(\Omega'-\theta)\sin^2\tfrac{1}{2}\eta. \qquad (114)$$

Finally, we have

$$\pi'-\pi=\Omega'-\Omega+\Delta\omega.$$

Since η is very small, these equations give, if we apply also the precession in longitude so as to reduce the longitudes to the mean equinox of the date t',

$$\Delta\omega=\eta\,\frac{\sin(\Omega-\theta)}{\sin i'},$$

$$i'=i+\eta\cos(\Omega-\theta)+\tfrac{1}{4}\frac{\Delta\omega^2}{s}\sin 2i,$$

$$\Omega'=\Omega+(t'-t)\frac{dl}{dt}-\eta\sin(\Omega-\theta)\cot i'-\tfrac{1}{4}\frac{\eta^2}{s}\sin 2(\Omega-\theta), \qquad (115)$$

$$\pi'=\pi+(t'-t)\frac{dl}{dt}+\eta\sin(\Omega-\theta)\tan\tfrac{1}{2}i'-\tfrac{1}{4}\frac{\eta^2}{s}\sin 2(\Omega-\theta);$$

in which $\frac{dl}{dt}$ is the annual precession in longitude, and in which $s = 206264''.8$. In most cases, the last terms of the expressions for i', Ω', and π', being of the second order, may be neglected.

For the case in which the motion is regarded as retrograde, we must put $180° - i$ and $180° - i'$, instead of i and i', respectively, in the equations for $\Delta\omega$, i', and Ω'; and for π', in this case, we have

$$\pi' - \pi = \Omega' - \Omega - \Delta\omega,$$

which gives

$$\pi' = \pi + (t' - t)\frac{dl}{dt} - \eta \sin(\Omega - \theta)\tan\tfrac{1}{2}i' - \tfrac{1}{4}\frac{\eta^2}{s}\sin 2(\Omega - \theta).$$

If we adopt Bessel's determination of the luni-solar precession and of the variation of the mean obliquity of the ecliptic, we have, at the time $1750 + \tau$,

$$\frac{dl}{dt} = 50''.21129 + 0.''0002442966\tau,$$

$$\frac{d\eta}{dt} = 0''.48892 - 0.''000006143\tau,$$

and, consequently,

$$\eta = (0.''48892 - 0.''000006143\tau)\,(t' - t);$$

and in the computation of the values of these quantities we must put $\tau = \frac{1}{2}(t' + t) - 1750$, t and t' being expressed in years.

The longitude of the descending node of the ecliptic of the time t on the ecliptic of 1750.0 is also found to be

$$351°\ 36'\ 10'' - 5''.21\,(t - 1750),$$

which is measured from the mean equinox of the beginning of the year 1750.

The longitude of the descending node of the ecliptic of t' on that of t, measured from the same mean equinox, is equal to this value diminished by the angular distance between the descending node of the ecliptic of t on that of 1750 and the descending node of the ecliptic of t' on that of t, which distance is, neglecting terms of the second order,

$$5''.21\,(t' - 1750);$$

and the result is

$$351°\ 36'\ 10'' - 5''.21\,(t - 1750) - 5''.21\,(t' - 1750),$$

or

$$351°\ 36'\ 10'' - 10''.42\,(t - 1750) - 5''.21\,(t' - t).$$

To reduce this longitude to the mean equinox at the time t, we must add the general precession during the interval $t - 1750$, or

$$50''.21\,(t - 1750),$$

so that we have, finally,

$$\theta = 351^\circ\ 36'\ 10'' + 39''.79\,(t - 1750) - 5''.21\,(t' - t).$$

When the elements π, Ω, and i have been thus reduced from the ecliptic and mean equinox to which they are referred, to those of the date for which the heliocentric or geocentric place is required, they may be referred to the apparent equinox of the date by applying the nutation in longitude. Then, in the case of the determination of the right ascension and declination, using the apparent obliquity of the ecliptic in the computation of the co-ordinates, we directly obtain the place of the body referred to the apparent equinox. But, in computing a series of places, the changes which thus take place in the elements themselves from date to date induce corresponding changes in the auxiliary quantities a, b, c, A, B, and C, so that these are no longer to be considered as constants, but as continually changing their values by small differences. The differential formulæ for the computation of these changes, which are easily derived from the equations (99), will be given in the next chapter; but they are perhaps unnecessary, since it is generally most convenient, in the cases which occur, to compute the auxiliaries for the extreme dates for which the ephemeris is required, and to interpolate their values for intermediate dates.

It is advisable, however, to reduce the elements to the ecliptic and mean equinox of the beginning of the year for which the ephemeris is required, and using the mean obliquity of the ecliptic for that epoch, in the computation of the auxiliary constants for the equator, the resulting geocentric right ascensions and declinations will be referred to the same equinox, and they may then be reduced to the apparent equinox of the date by applying the corrections for precession and nutation.

The places which thus result are *free from parallax and aberration.* In comparing observations with an ephemeris, the correction for parallax is applied directly to the observed apparent places, since this correction varies for different places on the earth's surface. The correction for aberration may be applied in two different modes. We may subtract from the time of observation the time in which the light from the planet or comet reaches the earth, and the true place for this reduced time is identical with the apparent place for the time of observation; or, in case we know the daily or hourly motion of the body in right ascension and declination, we may compute the motion during the interval which is required for the light to pass from the body to the earth, which, being applied to the observed place, gives the true place for the time of observation.

We may also include the aberration directly in the ephemeris by using the time $t - 497^s.78\Delta$ in computing the geocentric places for the time t, or by subtracting from the place free from aberration, computed for the time t, the motion in α and δ during the interval $497^s.78\Delta$, in which expression Δ is the distance of the body from the earth, and 497.78 the number of seconds in which light traverses the mean distance of the earth from the sun.

It is customary, however, to compute the ephemeris free from aberration and to subtract the *time of aberration*, $497^s.78\Delta$, from the time of observation when comparing observations with an ephemeris, according to the first method above mentioned. The places of the sun used in computing its co-ordinates must also be free from aberration; and if the longitudes derived from the solar tables include aberration, the proper correction must be applied, in order to obtain the true longitude required.

41. EXAMPLES.—We will now collect together, in the proper order for numerical calculation, some of the principal formulæ which have been derived, and illustrate them by numerical examples, commencing with the case of an elliptic orbit. Let it be required to find the geocentric right ascension and declination of the planet *Eurynome* (79), for mean midnight at Washington, for the date 1865 February 24, the elements of the orbit being as follows:—

$$\begin{aligned}
\text{Epoch} &= 1864 \text{ Jan. } 1.0 \text{ Greenwich mean time.} \\
M &= 1^\circ\ 29'\ 40''.21 \\
\pi &= 44\ \ 20\ \ 33\ .09 \\
\Omega &= 206\ \ 42\ \ 40\ .13 \\
i &= 4\ \ 36\ \ 50\ .51
\end{aligned} \left.\begin{matrix} \\ \\ \\ \end{matrix}\right\} \text{Ecliptic and Mean Equinox, 1864.0.}$$

$$\begin{aligned}
\varphi &= 11\ \ 15\ \ 51\ .02 \\
\log a &= 0.3881319 \\
\log \mu &= 2.9678088 \\
\mu &= 928''.55745
\end{aligned}$$

When a series of places is to be computed, the first thing to be done is to compute the auxiliary constants used in the expressions for the co-ordinates, and although but a single place is required in the problem proposed, yet we will proceed in this manner, in order to exhibit the application of the formulæ. Since the elements π, Ω, and i are referred to the ecliptic and mean equinox of 1864.0, we will first reduce them to the ecliptic and mean equinox of 1865.0. For this reduction we have $t = 1864.0$, and $t' = 1865.0$, which give

$$\frac{dl}{dt} = 50''.239, \qquad \theta = 352^\circ\ 51'\ 41'', \qquad \eta = 0''.4882.$$

Substituting these values in the equations (115), we obtain

$$i' - i = \Delta i = -\ 0''.40, \qquad \Delta\Omega = +\ 53''.61, \qquad \Delta\pi = +\ 50''.23;$$

and hence the elements which determine the position of the orbit in reference to the ecliptic of 1865.0 are

$$\pi = 44^\circ\ 21'\ 23''.32, \qquad \Omega = 206^\circ\ 43'\ 33''.74, \qquad i = 4^\circ\ 36'\ 50''.11.$$

For the same instant we derive, from the *American Ephemeris and Nautical Almanac,* the value of the mean obliquity of the ecliptic, which is

$$\varepsilon = 23^\circ\ 27'\ 24''.03.$$

The auxiliary constants for the equator are then found by means of the formulæ

$$\cot A = -\tan\Omega\cos i, \qquad \tan E_0 = \frac{\tan i}{\cos\Omega},$$

$$\cot B = \frac{\cos i}{\tan\Omega\cos E_0}\cdot\frac{\cos(E_0+\varepsilon)}{\cos\varepsilon},$$

$$\cot C = \frac{\cos i}{\tan\Omega\cos E_0}\cdot\frac{\sin(E_0+\varepsilon)}{\sin\varepsilon},$$

$$\sin a = \frac{\cos\Omega}{\sin A}, \qquad \sin b = \frac{\sin\Omega\cos\varepsilon}{\sin B}, \qquad \sin c = \frac{\sin\Omega\sin\varepsilon}{\sin C}.$$

The angle E_0 is always less than 180°, and the quadrant in which it is to be taken, is indicated directly by the algebraic sign of $\tan E_0$. The values of $\sin a$, $\sin b$, and $\sin c$ are always positive, and, therefore, the angles A, B, and C must be so taken, with respect to the quadrant in which each is situated, that $\sin A$ and $\cos\Omega$, $\sin B$ and $\sin\Omega$, and also $\sin C$ and $\sin\Omega$, shall have the same signs. From these we derive

$$\begin{aligned} A &= 296^\circ\ 39'\ \ 5''.07, & \log\sin a &= 9.9997156,\\ B &= 205\ \ 55\ \ 27\ .14, & \log\sin b &= 9.9748254,\\ C &= 212\ \ 32\ \ 17\ .74, & \log\sin c &= 9.5222192. \end{aligned}$$

Finally, the calculation of these constants is proved by means of the formula

$$\tan i = \frac{\sin b \sin c \sin (C - B)}{\sin a \cos A},$$

which gives $\log \tan i = 8.9068875$, agreeing with the value 8.9068876 derived directly from i.

Next, to find r and u. The date 1865 February 24.5 mean time at Washington reduced to the meridian of Greenwich by applying the difference of longitude, $5^h\ 8^m\ 11^s.2$, becomes 1865 February 24.714018 mean time at Greenwich. The interval, therefore, from the epoch for which the mean anomaly is given and the date for which the geocentric place is required, is 420.714018 days; and multiplying the mean daily motion, $928''.55745$, by this number, and adding the result to the given value of M, we get the mean anomaly for the required place, or

$$M = 1^\circ\ 29'\ 40''.21 + 108^\circ\ 30'\ 57''.14 = 110^\circ\ 0'\ 37''.35.$$

The eccentric anomaly E is then computed by means of the equation

$$M = E - e \sin E,$$

the value of e being expressed in seconds of arc. For *Eurynome* we have $\log \sin \varphi = \log e = 9.2907754$, and hence the value of e expressed in seconds is

$$\log e = 4.6052005.$$

By means of the equation (54) we derive an approximate value of E, namely,

$$E_0 = 119^\circ\ 49'\ 24'',$$

the value of e^2 expressed in seconds being $\log e^2 = 3.895976$; and with this we get

$$M_0 = E_0 - e \sin E_0 = 110^\circ\ 6'\ 50''.$$

Then we have

$$\Delta E_0 = \frac{M - M_0}{1 - e \cos E_0} = -\frac{372''.7}{1.097} = -339''.7,$$

which gives, for a second approximation to the value of E,

$$E_0 = 119^\circ\ 43'\ 44''.3.$$

This gives $M_0 = 110^\circ\ 0'\ 36''.98$, and hence

$$\Delta E_0 = +\frac{0''.37}{1.097} = +0''.34.$$

Therefore, we have, for a third approximation to the value of E,

$$E = 119^\circ\ 43'\ 44''.64,$$

which requires no further correction, since it satisfies the equation between M and E.

To find r and v, we have

$$\sqrt{r}\sin\tfrac{1}{2}v = \sqrt{a(1+e)}\sin\tfrac{1}{2}E,$$
$$\sqrt{r}\cos\tfrac{1}{2}v = \sqrt{a(1-e)}\cos\tfrac{1}{2}E.$$

The values of the first factors in the second members of these equations are: $\log\sqrt{a(1+e)} = 0.2328104$, and $\log\sqrt{a(1-e)} = 0.1468741$; and we obtain

$$v = 129^\circ\ 3'\ 50''.52, \qquad \log r = 0.4282854.$$

Since $\pi - \Omega = 197^\circ\ 37'\ 49''.58$, we have

$$u = v + \pi - \Omega = 326^\circ\ 41'\ 40''.10.$$

The heliocentric co-ordinates in reference to the equator as the fundamental plane are then derived from the equations

$$x = r\sin a\sin(A+u),$$
$$y = r\sin b\sin(B+u),$$
$$z = r\sin c\sin(C+u),$$

which give, for *Eurynome*,

$$x = -2.6611270, \qquad y = +0.3250277, \qquad z = +0.0119486.$$

The *American Nautical Almanac* gives, for the equatorial co-ordinates of the sun for 1865 February 24.5 mean time at Washington, referred to the mean equinox and equator of the beginning of the year,

$$X = +0.9094557, \qquad Y = -0.3599298, \qquad Z = -0.1561751.$$

Finally, the geocentric right ascension, declination, and distance are given by the equations

$$\tan\alpha = \frac{y+Y}{x+X}, \qquad \tan\delta = \frac{z+Z}{y+Y}\sin\alpha = \frac{z+Z}{x+X}\cos\alpha, \qquad \Delta = \frac{z+Z}{\sin\delta},$$

the first form of the equation for $\tan\delta$ being used when $\sin\alpha$ is greater than $\cos\alpha$.

The value of Δ must always be positive; and δ cannot exceed $\pm 90^\circ$, the minus sign indicating south declination. Thus, we obtain

$$\alpha = 181^\circ\ 8'\ 29''.29, \qquad \delta = -4^\circ\ 42'\ 21''.56, \qquad \log \varDelta = 0.2450054.$$

To reduce α and δ to the true equinox and equator of February 24.5, we have, from the *Nautical Almanac*,

$$f = +16''.80, \qquad \log g = 1.0168, \qquad G = 45^\circ\ 16';$$

and, substituting these values in equations (110), the result is

$$\Delta\alpha = +17''.42, \qquad \Delta\delta = -7''.17.$$

Hence the geocentric place, referred to the true equinox and equator of the date, is

$$\alpha = 181^\circ\ 8'\ 46''.71, \qquad \delta = -4^\circ\ 42'\ 28''.73, \qquad \log \varDelta = 0.2450054.$$

When only a single place is required, it is a little more expeditious to compute r from

$$r = a(1 - e \cos E),$$

and then $v - E$ from

$$\sin \tfrac{1}{2}(v - E) = \sqrt{\frac{a}{r}} \sin \tfrac{1}{2}\varphi \sin E.$$

Thus, in the case of the required place of *Eurynome*, we get

$$\log r = 0.4282852, \qquad v - E = 9^\circ\ 20'\ 5''.92,$$
$$v = 129^\circ\ 3'\ 50''.56,$$

agreeing with the values previously determined. The calculation may be proved by means of the formula

$$\sin \tfrac{1}{2}(v + E) = \sqrt{\frac{a}{r}} \cos \tfrac{1}{2}\varphi \sin E.$$

In the case of the values just found, we have

$$\tfrac{1}{2}(v + E) = 124^\circ\ 23'\ 47''.60, \qquad \log \sin \tfrac{1}{2}(v + E) = 9.9165316,$$

while the second member of this equation gives

$$\log \sin \tfrac{1}{2}(v + E) = 9.9165316.$$

In the calculation of a single place, it is also very little shorter to compute first the heliocentric longitude and latitude by means of the equations (82), then the geocentric latitude and longitude by means of (89) or (90), and finally convert these into right ascension and declination by means of (92). When a large number of places are to be computed, it is often advantageous to compute the heliocentric co-ordinates directly from the eccentric anomaly by means of the equations (105).

The calculation of the geocentric place in reference to the ecliptic is, in all respects, similar to that in which the equator is taken as the fundamental plane, and does not require any further illustration.

The determination of the geocentric or heliocentric place in the cases of parabolic and hyperbolic motion differs from the process indicated in the preceding example only in the calculation of r and v. To illustrate the case of parabolic motion, let $t - T = 75.364$ days; $\log q = 9.9650486$; and let it be required to find r and v.

First, we compute m from

$$m = \frac{C_0}{q^{\frac{3}{2}}},$$

in which $\log C_0 = 9.9601277$, and the result is

$$\log m = 0.0125548.$$

Then we find M from

$$M = m(t - T),$$

which gives

$$\log M = 1.8897187.$$

From this value of $\log M$ we derive, by means of Table VI.,

$$v = 79° \; 55' \; 57''.26.$$

Finally, r is found from

$$r = \frac{q}{\cos^2 \frac{1}{2}v},$$

which gives

$$\log r = 0.1961120.$$

For the case of hyperbolic motion, let there be given $t - T = 65.41236$ days; $\psi = 37° \; 35' \; 0''.0$, or $\log e = 0.1010188$; and $\log a = 0.6020600$, to find r and v. First, we compute N from

$$N = \frac{\lambda k}{a^{\frac{3}{2}}}(t - T),$$

in which $\log \lambda = 9.6377843$, and we obtain

$$\log N = 8.7859356; \qquad N = 0.06108514.$$

The value of F must now be found from the equation

$$N = e\lambda \tan F - \log \tan (45° + \tfrac{1}{2} F).$$

If we assume $F = 30°$, a more approximate value may be derived from

$$\tan F_{,} = \frac{N + \log \tan 60°}{e\lambda},$$

which gives $F_{,} = 28° \ 40' \ 23''$, and hence $N_{,} = 0.072678$. Then we compute the correction to be applied to this value of F, by means of the equation

$$\Delta F_{,} = \frac{(N - N_{,}) \cos^2 F_{,}}{\lambda (e - \cos F_{,})} s,$$

wherein $s = 206264''.8$; and the result is

$$\Delta F_{,} = 4.6097 \, (N - N_{,}) \, s = -3° \ 3' \ 43''.0.$$

Hence, for a second approximation to the value of F, we have

$$F_{,} = 25° \ 36' \ 40''.0.$$

The corresponding value of N is $N_{,} = 0.0617653$, and hence

$$\Delta F_{,} = 5.199 \, (N - N_{,}) \, s = -12' \ 9''.4.$$

The third approximation, therefore, gives $F_{,} = 25° \ 24' \ 30''.6$, and, repeating the operation, we get

$$F = 25° \ 24' \ 27''.74.$$

which requires no further correction.

To find r, we have

$$r = a \left(\frac{e}{\cos F} - 1 \right),$$

which gives

$$\log r = 0.2008544.$$

Then, v is derived from

$$\tan \tfrac{1}{2} v = \cot \tfrac{1}{2} \psi \ \tan \tfrac{1}{2} F,$$

and we find

$$v = 67° \ 3' \ 0''.0.$$

When several places are required, it is convenient to compute v and r by means of the equations

$$\sqrt{r} \sin \tfrac{1}{2} v = \frac{\sqrt{a(e + 1)}}{\sqrt{\cos F}} \sin \tfrac{1}{2} F,$$

$$\sqrt{r} \cos \tfrac{1}{2} v = \frac{\sqrt{a(e - 1)}}{\sqrt{\cos F}} \cos \tfrac{1}{2} F.$$

For the given values of a and e we have $\log \sqrt{a(e+1)} = 0.4782649$, $\log \sqrt{a(e-1)} = 0.0100829$, and hence we derive

$$v = 67^\circ\ 2'\ 59''.92, \qquad \log r = 0.2008545.$$

It remains yet to illustrate the calculation of v and r for elliptic and hyperbolic orbits in which the eccentricity differs but little from unity. First, in the case of elliptic motion, let $t - T = 68.25$ days; $e = 0.9675212$; and $\log q = 9.7668134$. We compute M from

$$M = (t - T)\frac{C_0}{q^{\frac{3}{2}}}\sqrt{\frac{1+e}{2}},$$

wherein $\log C_0 = 9.9601277$, which gives

$$\log M = 2.1404550.$$

With this as argument we get, from Table VI.,

$$V = 101^\circ\ 38'\ 3''.74,$$

and then with this value of V as argument we find, from Table IX.,

$$A = 1540''.08, \qquad B = 9''.506, \qquad C = 0''.062.$$

Then we have $\log i = \log \dfrac{1-e}{1+e} = 8.217680$, and from the equation

$$v = V + A(100i) + B(100i)^2 + C(100i)^3,$$

we get

$$v = V + 42'\ 22''.28 + 25''.90 + 0''.28 = 102^\circ\ 20'\ 52''.20.$$

The value of r is then found from

$$r = \frac{q(1+e)}{1 + e\cos v},$$

namely,

$$\log r = 0.1614051.$$

We may also determine r and v by means of Table X. Thus, we first compute M from

$$M = \frac{C_0(t-T)}{q^{\frac{3}{2}}} \cdot \frac{\sqrt{\frac{1}{10}(1+9e)}}{B}.$$

Assuming $B = 1$, we get $\log M = 2.13757$, and, entering Table VI. with this as argument, we find $w = 101^\circ\ 25'$. Then we compute A from

$$A = \frac{5(1-e)}{1+9e}\tan^2 \tfrac{1}{2}w,$$

which gives $A = 0.024985$. With this value of A as argument, we find, from Table X.,

$$\log B = 0.0000047.$$

The exact value of M is then found to be

$$\log M = 2.1375635,$$

which, by means of Table VI., gives

$$w = 101^\circ\ 24'\ 36''.26.$$

By means of this we derive

$$A = 0.02497944,$$

and hence, from Table X.,

$$\log C = 0.0043771.$$

Then we have

$$\tan \tfrac{1}{2}v = C \tan \tfrac{1}{2}w \sqrt{\frac{5(1+e)}{1+9e}},$$

which gives

$$v = 102^\circ\ 20'\ 52''.20,$$

agreeing exactly with the value already found. Finally, r is given by

$$r = \frac{q}{(1 + AC^2)\cos^2 \frac{1}{2}v},$$

from which we get

$$\log r = 0.1614052.$$

Before the time of perihelion passage, $t - T$ is negative; but the value of v is computed as if this were positive, and is then considered as negative.

In the case of hyperbolic motion, i is negative, and, with this distinction, the process when Table IX. is used is precisely the same as for elliptic motion; but when table X. is used, the value of A must be found from

$$A = \frac{5(e-1)}{(1+9e)} \tan^2 \tfrac{1}{2}w,$$

and that of r from

$$r = \frac{q}{(1 - AC^2)\cos^2 \frac{1}{2}v},$$

the values of $\log B$ and $\log C$ being taken from the columns of the table which belong to hyperbolic motion.

In the calculation of the position of a comet in space, if the motion is retrograde and the inclination is regarded as less than 90°, the distinctions indicated in the formulæ must be carefully noted.

42. When we have thus computed the places of a planet or comet for a series of dates equidistant, we may readily interpolate the places for intermediate dates by the usual formulæ for interpolation. The interval between the dates for which the direct computation is made should also be small enough to permit us to neglect the effect of the fourth differences in the process of interpolation. This, however, is not absolutely necessary, provided that a very extended series of places is to be computed, so that the higher orders of differences may be taken into account. To find a convenient formula for this interpolation, let us denote any date, or argument of the function, by $a + n\omega$, and the corresponding value of the co-ordinate, or of the function, for which the interpolation is to be made, by $f(a + n\omega)$. If we have computed the values of the function for the dates, or arguments, $a - \omega$, a, $a + \omega$, $a + 2\omega$, &c., we may assume that an expression for the function which exactly satisfies these values will also give the exact values corresponding to any intermediate value of the argument. If we regard n as variable, we may expand the function into the series

$$f(a + n\omega) = f(a) + An + Bn^2 + Cn^3 + \&c. \qquad (116)$$

and if we regard the fourth differences as vanishing, it is only necessary to consider terms involving n^3 in the determination of the unknown coefficients A, B, and C. If we put n successively equal to -1, 0, 1, and 2, and then take the successive differences of these values, we get

	I. Diff.	II. Diff.	III. Diff.
$f(a-\omega) = f(a) - A + B - C$			
	$A - B + C$		
$f(a) = f(a)$		$2B$	
	$A + B + C$		$6C$
$f(a+\omega) = f(a) + A + B + C$		$2B + 6C$	
	$A + 3B + 7C$		
$f(a+2\omega) = f(a) + 2A + 4B + 8C$			

If we symbolize, generally, the difference $f(a + n\omega) - f(a + (n-1)\omega)$ by $f'(a + (n - \frac{1}{2})\omega)$, the difference $f'(a + (n + \frac{1}{2})\omega) - f'(a + (n - \frac{1}{2})\omega)$ by $f''(a + n\omega)$, and similarly for the successive orders of differences, these may be arranged as follows:—

Argument.	Function.	I. Diff.	II. Diff.	III. Diff.
$a - \omega$	$f(a - \omega)$			
		$f'(a - \frac{1}{2}\omega)$		
a	$f(a)$		$f''(a)$	
		$f'(a + \frac{1}{2}\omega)$		$f'''(a + \frac{1}{2}\omega)$
$a + \omega$	$f(a + \omega)$		$f''(a + \omega)$	
		$f'(a + \frac{3}{2}\omega)$		
$a + 2\omega$	$f(a + 2\omega)$			

Comparing these expressions for the differences with the above, we get

$$C = \tfrac{1}{6} f'''(a + \tfrac{1}{2}\omega), \qquad B = \tfrac{1}{2} f''(a),$$
$$A = f'(a + \tfrac{1}{2}\omega) - \tfrac{1}{2} f''(a) - \tfrac{1}{6} f'''(a + \tfrac{1}{2}\omega),$$

which, from the manner in which the differences are formed, give

$$C = \tfrac{1}{6}(f''(a + \omega) - f''(a)), \qquad B = \tfrac{1}{2} f''(a),$$
$$A = f(a + \omega) - f(a) - \tfrac{1}{2} f''(a) - \tfrac{1}{6}(f''(a + \omega) - f''(a)).$$

To find the value of the function corresponding to the argument $a + \frac{1}{2}\omega$, we have $n = \frac{1}{2}$, and, from (116),

$$f(a + \tfrac{1}{2}\omega) = f(a) + \tfrac{1}{2}A + \tfrac{1}{4}B + \tfrac{1}{8}C.$$

Substituting in this the values of A, B, and C, last found, and reducing, we get

$$f(a + \tfrac{1}{2}\omega) = \tfrac{1}{2}(f(a + \omega) + f(a)) - \tfrac{1}{8}(\tfrac{1}{2}(f''(a + \omega) + f''(a))),$$

in which only fourth differences are neglected, and, since the place of the argument for $n = 0$ is arbitrary, we have, therefore, generally,

$$f(a + (n + \tfrac{1}{2})\omega) = \tfrac{1}{2}(f(a + (n + 1)\omega) + f(a + n\omega)) - \tfrac{1}{8}(\tfrac{1}{2}(f''(a + (n + 1)\omega) + f''(a + n\omega))). \qquad (117)$$

Hence, to interpolate the value of the function corresponding to a date midway between two dates, or values of the argument, for which the values are known, we take the arithmetical mean of these two known values, and from this we subtract one-eighth of the arithmetical mean of the second differences which are found on the same horizontal line as the two given values of the function.

By extending the analytical process here indicated so as to include the fourth and fifth differences, the additional term to be added to equation (117) is found to be

$$+ \tfrac{3}{128}(\tfrac{1}{2}(f^{\text{iv}}(a + (n + 1)\omega) + f^{\text{iv}}(a + n\omega))),$$

and the correction corresponding to this being applied, only sixth differences will be neglected.

It is customary in the case of the comets which do not move too rapidly, to adopt an interval of four days, and in the case of the asteroid planets, either four or eight days, between the dates for which the direct calculation is made. Then, by interpolating, in the case of an interval ω, equal to four days, for the intermediate dates, we obtain a series of places at intervals of two days; and, finally, interpolating for the dates intermediate to these, we derive the places at intervals of one day. When a series of places has been computed, the use of differences will serve as a check upon the accuracy of the calculation, and will serve to detect at once the place which is not correct, when any discrepancy is apparent. The greatest discordance will be shown in the differences on the same horizontal line as the erroneous value of the function; and the discordance will be greater and greater as we proceed successively to take higher orders of differences. In order to provide against the contingency of systematic error, duplicate calculation should be made of those quantities in which such an error is likely to occur.

The ephemerides of the planets, to be used for the comparison of observations, are usually computed for a period of a few weeks before and after the time of opposition to the sun; and the time of the opposition may be found in advance of the calculation of the entire ephemeris. Thus, we find first the date for which the mean longitude of the planet is equal to the longitude of the sun increased by 180°; then we compute the equation of the centre at this time by means of the equation (53), using, in most cases, only the first term of the development, or

$$v - M = 2e \sin M,$$

e being expressed in seconds. Next, regarding this value as constant, we find the date for which

$$L + \text{equation of the centre}$$

is equal to the longitude of the sun increased by 180°; and for this date, and also for another at an interval of a few days, we compute u, and hence the heliocentric longitudes by means of the equation

$$\tan(l - \Omega) = \tan u \cos i.$$

Let these longitudes be denoted by l and l', the times to which they correspond by t and t', and the longitudes of the sun for the same times by $\odot$ and $\odot'$; then for the time t_0, for which the heliocentric longitudes of the planet and the earth are the same, we have

$$t_0 = t + \frac{l - 180° - \odot}{(\odot' - \odot) - (l' - l)}(t' - t),$$

or (118)

$$t_0 = t' + \frac{l' - 180° - \odot'}{(\odot' - \odot) - (l' - l)}(t' - t),$$

the first of these equations being used when $l - 180° - \odot$ is less than $l' - 180° - \odot'$. If the time t_0 differs considerably from t or t', it may be necessary, in order to obtain an accurate result, to repeat the latter part of the calculation, using t_0 for t, and taking t' at a small interval from this, and so that the true time of opposition shall fall between t and t'. The longitudes of the planet and of the sun must be measured from the same equinox.

When the eccentricity is considerable, it will facilitate the calculation to use two terms of equation (53) in finding the equation of the centre, and, if e is expressed in seconds, this gives

$$v - M = 2e \sin M + \frac{5}{4} \cdot \frac{e^2}{s} \sin 2M,$$

s being the number of seconds corresponding to a length of arc equal to the radius, or 206264″.8; and the value of $v - M$ will then be expressed in seconds of arc. In all cases in which circular arcs are involved in an equation, great care must be taken, in the numerical application, in reference to the homogeneity of the different terms. If the arcs are expressed by an abstract number, or by the length of arc expressed in parts of the radius taken as the unit, to express them in seconds we must multiply by the number 206264.8; but if the arcs are expressed in seconds, each term of the equation must contain only one concrete factor, the other concrete factors, if there be any, being reduced to abstract numbers by dividing each by s the number of seconds in an arc equal to the radius.

43. It is unnecessary to illustrate further the numerical application of the various formulæ which have been derived, since by reference to the formulæ themselves the course of procedure is obvious. It may be remarked, however, that in many cases in which auxiliary angles have been introduced so as to render the equations convenient for logarithmic calculation, by the use of tables which determine the logarithms of the sum or difference of two numbers when the logarithms of these numbers are given, the calculation is abbreviated, and is often even more accurately performed than by the aid of the auxiliary angles.

The logarithm of the sum of two numbers may be found by means of the tables of common logarithms. Thus, we have

$$\log(a + b) = \log a\left(1 + \frac{b}{a}\right) = \log b\left(1 + \frac{a}{b}\right).$$

If we put

$$\log \tan x = \tfrac{1}{2}(\log b - \log a),$$

we shall have

$$\log(a+b) = \log a - 2\log\cos x,$$

or

$$\log(a+b) = \log b - 2\log\sin x.$$

The first form is used when $\cos x$ is greater than $\sin x$, and the second form when $\cos x$ is less than $\sin x$.

It should also be observed that in the solution of equations of the form of (89), after $\tan(\lambda - \odot)$—using the notation of this particular case—has been found by dividing the second equation by the first, the second members of these equations being divided by $\cos(\lambda - \odot)$ and $\sin(\lambda - \odot)$, respectively, give two values of $\varDelta\cos\beta$, which should agree within the limits of the unavoidable errors of the logarithmic tables; but, in order that the errors of these tables shall have the least influence, the value derived from the first equation is to be preferred when $\cos(\lambda - \odot)$ is greater than $\sin(\lambda - \odot)$, and that derived from the second equation when $\cos(\lambda - \odot)$ is less than $\sin(\lambda - \odot)$. The value of $\varDelta$, if the greatest accuracy possible is required, should be derived from $\varDelta\cos\beta$ when β is less than 45°, and from $\varDelta\sin\beta$ when β is greater than 45°.

In the application of numbers to equations (109), when the values of the second members have been computed, we first, by division, find $\tan\frac{1}{2}(\Omega' + \omega_0)$ and $\tan\frac{1}{2}(\Omega' - \omega_0)$; then, if $\sin\frac{1}{2}(\Omega' + \omega_0)$ is greater than $\cos\frac{1}{2}(\Omega' + \omega_0)$, we find $\cos\frac{1}{2}i'$ from the first equation; but if $\sin\frac{1}{2}(\Omega' + \omega_0)$ is less than $\cos\frac{1}{2}(\Omega' + \omega_0)$, we find $\cos\frac{1}{2}i'$ from the second equation. The same principle is applied in finding $\sin\frac{1}{2}i'$ by means of the third and fourth equations. Finally, from $\sin\frac{1}{2}i'$ and $\cos\frac{1}{2}i'$ we get $\tan\frac{1}{2}i'$, and hence i'. The check obtained by the agreement of the values of $\sin\frac{1}{2}i'$ and $\cos\frac{1}{2}i'$, with those computed from the value of i' derived from $\tan\frac{1}{2}i'$, does not absolutely prove the calculation. This proof, however, may be obtained by means of the equation

$$\sin i' \sin \Omega' = \sin i \sin \Omega,$$

or by

$$\sin i' \sin \omega_0 = \sin \varepsilon \sin \Omega.$$

In all cases, care should be taken in determining the quadrant in which the angles sought are situated, the criteria for which are fixed either by the nature of the problem directly, or by the relation of the algebraic signs of the trigonometrical functions involved.

CHAPTER II.

INVESTIGATION OF THE DIFFERENTIAL FORMULÆ WHICH EXPRESS THE RELATION BETWEEN THE GEOCENTRIC OR HELIOCENTRIC PLACES OF A HEAVENLY BODY AND THE VARIATION OF THE ELEMENTS OF ITS ORBIT.

44. In many calculations relating to the motion of a heavenly body, it becomes necessary to determine the variations which small increments applied to the values of the elements of its orbit will produce in its geocentric or heliocentric place. The form, however, in which the problem most frequently presents itself is that in which approximate elements are to be corrected by means of the differences between the places derived from computation and those derived from observation. In this case it is required to find the variations of the elements such that they will cause the differences between calculation and observation to vanish; and, since there are six elements, it follows that six separate equations, involving the variations of the elements as the unknown quantities, must be formed. Each longitude or right ascension, and each latitude or declination, derived from observation, will furnish one equation; and hence at least three complete observations will be required for the solution of the problem. When more than three observations are employed, and the number of equations exceeds the number of unknown quantities, the equations of condition which are obtained must be reduced to six final equations, from which, by elimination, the corrections to be applied to the elements may be determined.

If we suppose the corrections which must be applied to the elements, in order to satisfy the data furnished by observation, to be so small that their squares and higher powers may be neglected, the variations of those elements which involve angular measure being expressed in parts of the radius as unity, the relations sought may be determined by differentiating the various formulæ which determine the position of the body. Thus, if we represent by θ any co-ordinate of the place of the body computed from the assumed elements of the orbit, we shall have, in the case of an elliptic orbit,

$$\theta = f(\pi, \Omega, i, \varphi, M_0, \mu),$$

M_0 being the mean anomaly at the epoch T. Let θ' denote the value of this co-ordinate as derived directly or indirectly from observation; then, if we represent the variations of the elements by $\Delta\pi$, $\Delta\Omega$, Δi, &c., and if we suppose these variations to be so small that their squares and higher powers may be neglected, we shall have

$$\theta' - \theta = \Delta\theta = \frac{d\theta}{d\pi}\Delta\pi + \frac{d\theta}{d\Omega}\Delta\Omega + \frac{d\theta}{di}\Delta i + \frac{d\theta}{d\varphi}\Delta\varphi$$
$$+ \frac{d\theta}{dM_0}\Delta M_0 + \frac{d\theta}{d\mu}\Delta\mu. \qquad (1)$$

The differential coefficients $\frac{d\theta}{d\pi}$, $\frac{d\theta}{d\Omega}$, &c. must now be derived from the equations which determine the place of the body when the elements are known.

We shall first take the equator as the plane to which the positions of the body are referred, and find the differential coefficients of the geocentric right ascension and declination with respect to the elements of the orbit, these elements being referred to the ecliptic as the fundamental plane. Let x, y, z be the heliocentric co-ordinates of the body in reference to the equator, and we have

$$\theta = f(x, y, z),$$

or

$$d\theta = \frac{d\theta}{dx}dx + \frac{d\theta}{dy}dy + \frac{d\theta}{dz}dz.$$

Hence we obtain

$$\frac{d\theta}{d\pi} = \frac{d\theta}{dx}\cdot\frac{dx}{d\pi} + \frac{d\theta}{dy}\cdot\frac{dy}{d\pi} + \frac{d\theta}{dz}\cdot\frac{dz}{d\pi}; \qquad (2)$$

and similarly for the differential coefficients of θ with respect to the other elements. We must, therefore, find the partial differential coefficients of θ with respect to x, y, and z, and then the partial differential coefficients of these co-ordinates with respect to the elements. In the case of the right ascension we put $\theta = \alpha$, and in the case of the declination we put $\theta = \delta$.

45. If we differentiate the equations

$$x + X = \Delta \cos\delta \cos\alpha,$$
$$y + Y = \Delta \cos\delta \sin\alpha,$$
$$z + Z = \Delta \sin\delta,$$

regarding X, Y, and Z as constant, we find

$$dx = \cos\alpha\cos\delta\, d\Delta - \Delta\sin\alpha\cos\delta\, d\alpha - \Delta\cos\alpha\sin\delta\, d\delta,$$
$$dy = \sin\alpha\cos\delta\, d\Delta + \Delta\cos\alpha\cos\delta\, d\alpha - \Delta\sin\alpha\sin\delta\, d\delta,$$
$$dz = \sin\delta\, d\Delta + \Delta\cos\delta\, d\delta.$$

From these equations, by elimination, we obtain

$$\cos\delta\, d\alpha = -\frac{\sin\alpha}{\Delta}dx + \frac{\cos\alpha}{\Delta}dy, \qquad (3)$$
$$d\delta = -\frac{\cos\alpha\sin\delta}{\Delta}dx - \frac{\sin\alpha\sin\delta}{\Delta}dy + \frac{\cos\delta}{\Delta}dz.$$

Therefore, the partial differential coefficients of α and δ with respect to the heliocentric co-ordinates are

$$\begin{aligned} &\cos\delta\frac{d\alpha}{dx} = -\frac{\sin\alpha}{\Delta}, && \frac{d\delta}{dx} = -\frac{\cos\alpha\sin\delta}{\Delta}, \\ &\cos\delta\frac{d\alpha}{dy} = \frac{\cos\alpha}{\Delta}, && \frac{d\delta}{dy} = -\frac{\sin\alpha\sin\delta}{\Delta}, \\ &\cos\delta\frac{d\alpha}{dz} = 0, && \frac{d\delta}{dz} = \frac{\cos\delta}{\Delta}. \end{aligned} \qquad (4)$$

Next, to find the partial differential coefficients of the co-ordinates x, y, z, with respect to the elements, if we differentiate the equations $(100)_1$, observing that $\sin a$, $\sin b$, $\sin c$, A, B, C, are functions of Ω and i, we get

$$dx = \frac{x}{r}dr + x\cot(A+u)\,du + \frac{dx}{d\Omega}d\Omega + \frac{dx}{di}di,$$
$$dy = \frac{y}{r}dr + y\cot(B+u)\,du + \frac{dy}{d\Omega}d\Omega + \frac{dy}{di}di,$$
$$dz = \frac{z}{r}dr + z\cot(C+u)\,du + \frac{dz}{d\Omega}d\Omega + \frac{dz}{di}di.$$

To find the expressions for $\frac{dx}{d\Omega}$, $\frac{dx}{di}$, &c., we have the equations

$$x = r\cos u\cos\Omega - r\sin u\sin\Omega\cos i,$$
$$y = r\cos u\sin\Omega\cos\varepsilon + r\sin u\cos\Omega\cos i\cos\varepsilon - r\sin u\sin i\sin\varepsilon,$$
$$z = r\cos u\sin\Omega\sin\varepsilon + r\sin u\cos\Omega\cos i\sin\varepsilon + r\sin u\sin i\cos\varepsilon,$$

which give, by differentiation,

$$\frac{dx}{d\Omega} = -r\cos u\sin\Omega - r\sin u\cos\Omega\cos i,$$
$$\frac{dy}{d\Omega} = r\cos u\cos\Omega\cos\varepsilon - r\sin u\sin\Omega\cos i\cos\varepsilon,$$

$$\frac{dz}{d\Omega} = r \cos u \cos \Omega \sin \varepsilon - r \sin u \sin \Omega \cos i \sin \varepsilon,$$

$$\frac{dx}{di} = r \sin u \sin \Omega \sin i,$$

$$\frac{dy}{di} = - r \sin u \cos \Omega \sin i \cos \varepsilon - r \sin u \cos i \sin \varepsilon,$$

$$\frac{dz}{di} = - r \sin u \cos \Omega \sin i \sin \varepsilon + r \sin u \cos i \cos \varepsilon.$$

The first three of these equations immediately reduce to

$$\frac{dx}{d\Omega} = - y \cos \varepsilon - z \sin \varepsilon, \qquad \frac{dy}{d\Omega} = x \cos \varepsilon, \qquad \frac{dz}{d\Omega} = x \sin \varepsilon; \tag{5}$$

and since

$$\begin{aligned} \cos a &= \sin \Omega \sin i, \\ \cos b &= - \cos \Omega \sin i \cos \varepsilon - \cos i \sin \varepsilon, \\ \cos c &= - \cos \Omega \sin i \sin \varepsilon + \cos i \cos \varepsilon, \end{aligned}$$

we have, also,

$$\frac{dx}{di} = r \sin u \cos a, \qquad \frac{dy}{di} = r \sin u \cos b, \qquad \frac{dz}{di} = r \sin u \cos c.$$

Further, we have

$$du = dv + d\pi - d\Omega,$$

and hence, finally,

$$\begin{aligned} dx &= \frac{x}{r} dr + x \cot (A + u)\, dv + x \cot (A + u)\, d\pi \\ &\quad + (- x \cot (A + u) - y \cos \varepsilon - z \sin \varepsilon)\, d\Omega + r \sin u \cos a\, di, \\ dy &= \frac{y}{r} dr + y \cot (B + u)\, dv + y \cot (B + u)\, d\pi \\ &\quad + (- y \cot (B + u) + x \cos \varepsilon)\, d\Omega + r \sin u \cos b\, di, \\ dz &= \frac{z}{r} dr + z \cot (C + u)\, dv + z \cot (C + u)\, d\pi \\ &\quad + (- z \cot (C + u) + x \sin \varepsilon)\, d\Omega + r \sin u \cos c\, di. \end{aligned} \tag{6}$$

These equations give, for the partial differential coefficients of the heliocentric co-ordinates with respect to the elements,

$$\frac{dx}{d\pi} = \frac{dx}{dv} = x \cot (A + u), \qquad \frac{dy}{d\pi} = \frac{dy}{dv} = y \cot (B + u),$$

$$\frac{dz}{d\pi} = \frac{dz}{dv} = z \cot (C + u);$$

$$\frac{dx}{d\Omega} = -x\cot(A+u) - y\cos\varepsilon - z\sin\varepsilon, \qquad \frac{dy}{d\Omega} = -y\cot(B+u) + x\cos\varepsilon,$$

$$\frac{dz}{d\Omega} = -z\cot(C+u) + x\sin\varepsilon;$$

$$\frac{dx}{di} = r\sin u\cos a, \qquad \frac{dy}{di} = r\sin u\cos b, \qquad \frac{dz}{di} = r\sin u\cos c; \quad (7)$$

$$\frac{dx}{dr} = \frac{x}{r}, \qquad \frac{dy}{dr} = \frac{y}{r}, \qquad \frac{dz}{dr} = \frac{z}{r}.$$

When the direct inclination is greater than 90°, if we introduce the distinction of retrograde motion, we have

$$du = dv - d\pi + d\Omega,$$

and hence

$$\frac{dx}{d\pi} = -\frac{dx}{dv} = -x\cot(A+u), \qquad \frac{dy}{d\pi} = -\frac{dy}{dv} = -y\cot(B+u),$$

$$\frac{dz}{d\pi} = -\frac{dz}{dv} = -z\cot(C+u); \quad (8)$$

$$\frac{dx}{d\Omega} = \frac{dx}{dv} - y\cos\varepsilon - z\sin\varepsilon, \qquad \frac{dy}{d\Omega} = \frac{dy}{dv} + x\cos\varepsilon, \qquad \frac{dz}{d\Omega} = \frac{dz}{dv} + x\sin\varepsilon.$$

The expressions for $\frac{dx}{dr}$, $\frac{dy}{dr}$, and $\frac{dz}{dr}$ remain unchanged; and we have, also,

$$\frac{dx}{di} = -r\sin u\cos a, \quad \frac{dy}{di} = -r\sin u\cos b, \quad \frac{dz}{di} = -r\sin u\cos c. \quad (9)$$

It is advisable, in order to avoid the use of two sets of formulæ, in part, to regard the motion as direct and the inclination as susceptible of any value from 0° to 180°. If the elements which are given are for retrograde motion, we take the supplement of i instead of i; and if we designate the longitude of the perihelion, when the motion is considered as being retrograde, by (π), we shall have

$$\pi = 2\Omega - (\pi).$$

If we introduce, as one of the elements of the orbit, the distance of the perihelion from the ascending node, we have

$$du = dv + d\omega,$$

and, hence,

$$\frac{dx}{d\omega} = \frac{dx}{dv} = x\cot(A+u), \qquad \frac{dy}{d\omega} = \frac{dy}{dv} = y\cot(B+u),$$

$$\frac{dz}{d\omega} = \frac{dz}{dv} = z\cot(C+u). \quad (10)$$

The values of $\frac{dx}{d\Omega}$, $\frac{dy}{d\Omega}$, and $\frac{dz}{d\Omega}$ must, in this case, be found by means of the equations (5).

By means of these expressions for the differential coefficients of the co-ordinates x, y, z, with respect to the various elements, and those given by (4), we may derive the differential coefficients of the geocentric right ascension and declination with respect to the elements Ω, i, and π or ω, and also with respect to r and v, by writing successively α and δ in place of θ, and Ω, i, &c., in place of π in the equation (2). The quantities r and v, however, are functions of the remaining elements φ, M_0, and μ; and we have

$$dr = \frac{dr}{d\varphi} d\varphi + \frac{dr}{dM_0} dM_0 + \frac{dr}{d\mu} d\mu,$$

$$dv = \frac{dv}{d\varphi} d\varphi + \frac{dv}{dM_0} dM_0 + \frac{dv}{d\mu} d\mu.$$

Therefore, the partial differential coefficients of x, with respect to the elements φ, M_0, and μ, are

$$\begin{aligned} \frac{dx}{d\varphi} &= \frac{dx}{dr}\cdot\frac{dr}{d\varphi} + \frac{dx}{dv}\cdot\frac{dv}{d\varphi}, \\ \frac{dx}{dM_0} &= \frac{dx}{dr}\cdot\frac{dr}{dM_0} + \frac{dx}{dv}\cdot\frac{dv}{dM_0}, \\ \frac{dx}{d\mu} &= \frac{dx}{dr}\cdot\frac{dr}{d\mu} + \frac{dx}{dv}\cdot\frac{dv}{d\mu}. \end{aligned} \tag{11}$$

The expressions for the partial differential coefficients in the case of the co-ordinates y and z are of precisely the same form, and are obtained by writing, successively, y and z in place of x. The values of $\frac{dx}{dr}$, $\frac{dx}{dv}$, $\frac{dy}{dr}$, $\frac{dy}{dv}$, $\frac{dz}{dr}$, and $\frac{dz}{dv}$ are given by the equations (7), and when the expressions for $\frac{dr}{d\varphi}$, $\frac{dv}{d\varphi}$, $\frac{dr}{dM_0}$, $\frac{dv}{dM_0}$, $\frac{dr}{d\mu}$, and $\frac{dv}{d\mu}$ have been found, the partial differential coefficients of the heliocentric co-ordinates with respect to the elements φ, M_0, and μ will be completely determined, and hence, by means of (2), making the necessary changes, the differential coefficients of α and δ with respect to these elements.

46. If we differentiate the equation

$$M = E - e \sin E,$$

we shall have

$$dM = dE(1 - e\cos E) - \cos\varphi \sin E\, d\varphi.$$

But, since $1 - e\cos E = \frac{r}{a}$, and $\cos\varphi \sin E = \frac{r}{a}\sin v$, this reduces to

$$dM = \frac{r}{a}dE - \frac{r}{a}\sin v\, d\varphi,$$

or

$$dE = \frac{a}{r}dM + \sin v\, d\varphi.$$

If we take the logarithms of both members of the equation

$$\tan\tfrac{1}{2}v = \tan\tfrac{1}{2}E \tan(45° + \tfrac{1}{2}\varphi),$$

and differentiate, we find

$$\frac{dv}{2\sin\frac{1}{2}v\cos\frac{1}{2}v} = \frac{dE}{2\sin\frac{1}{2}E\cos\frac{1}{2}E} + \frac{d\varphi}{2\sin(45° + \frac{1}{2}\varphi)\cos(45° + \frac{1}{2}\varphi)},$$

which reduces to

$$dv = \frac{\sin v}{\sin E}dE + \frac{\sin v}{\cos\varphi}d\varphi.$$

Introducing into this equation the value of dE, already found, and replacing $\sin E$ by $\frac{r\sin v}{a\cos\varphi}$, we get

$$dv = \frac{a^2\cos\varphi}{r^2}dM + \frac{\sin v}{\cos\varphi}\left(\frac{a\cos^2\varphi}{r} + 1\right)d\varphi.$$

But since $a\cos^2\varphi = p$, and $\frac{p}{r} = 1 + \sin\varphi\cos v$, this becomes

$$dv = \frac{a^2\cos\varphi}{r^2}dM + \left(\frac{2}{\cos\varphi} + \tan\varphi\cos v\right)\sin v\, d\varphi. \qquad (12)$$

If we differentiate the equation

$$r = a(1 - e\cos E),$$

we shall have

$$dr = \frac{r}{a}da + ae\sin E\, dE - a\cos\varphi\cos E\, d\varphi;$$

and substituting for dE its value in terms of dM and $d\varphi$, the result is

$$dr = \frac{r}{a}da + a\tan\varphi\sin v\, dM + (ae\sin E\sin v - a\cos\varphi\cos E)\, d\varphi. \qquad (13)$$

Now, since $\sin E = \frac{\sin v \cos \varphi}{1 + e \cos v}$, and $\cos E = \frac{\cos v + e}{1 + e \cos v}$, we shall have

$$ae \sin E \sin v - a \cos \varphi \cos E = \frac{ae \cos \varphi \sin^2 v}{1 + e \cos v} - \frac{a \cos \varphi (\cos v + e)}{1 + e \cos v},$$

which reduces to

$$ae \sin E \sin v - a \cos \varphi \cos E = - a \cos \varphi \cos v$$

Hence, the expression for dr becomes

$$dr = \frac{r}{a} da + a \tan \varphi \sin v \, dM - a \cos \varphi \cos v \, d\varphi. \tag{14}$$

Further, we have

$$M = M_0 + \mu (t - T),$$

T being the epoch for which the mean anomaly is M_0, and

$$\mu = \frac{k \sqrt{1 + m}}{a^{\frac{3}{2}}}.$$

Differentiating these expressions, we get

$$dM = dM_0 + (t - T) \, d\mu,$$
$$\frac{da}{a} = - \tfrac{2}{3} \cdot \frac{d\mu}{\mu};$$

and substituting these values in the expressions for dr and dv, we have, finally,

$$dr = a \tan \varphi \sin v \, dM_0 + \left(a \tan \varphi \sin v \, (t - T) - \frac{2r}{3\mu} \right) d\mu$$
$$- a \cos \varphi \cos v \, d\varphi, \tag{15}$$
$$dv = \frac{a^2 \cos \varphi}{r^2} dM_0 + \frac{a^2 \cos \varphi}{r^2} (t - T) \, d\mu + \left(\frac{2}{\cos \varphi} + \tan \varphi \cos v \right) \sin v \, d\varphi.$$

From these equations for dr and dv we obtain the following values of the partial differential coefficients:—

$$\frac{dr}{d\varphi} = - a \cos \varphi \cos v, \qquad \frac{dv}{d\varphi} = \left(\frac{2}{\cos \varphi} + \tan \varphi \cos v \right) \sin v,$$
$$\frac{dr}{dM_0} = a \tan \varphi \sin v, \qquad \frac{dv}{dM_0} = \frac{a^2 \cos \varphi}{r^2}, \tag{16}$$
$$\frac{dr}{d\mu} = a \tan \varphi \sin v \, (t - T) - \frac{2r}{3\mu} 206264.8, \qquad \frac{dv}{d\mu} = \frac{a^2 \cos \varphi}{r^2} (t - T).$$

It will be observed that in the last term of the expression for $\frac{dr}{d\mu}$ we have supposed μ to be expressed in seconds of arc, and hence the factor 206264.8 is introduced in order to render the equation homogeneous.

47. The formulæ already derived are sufficient to find the variations of the right ascension and declination corresponding to the variations of the elements in the case of the elliptic orbit of a planet; but in the case of ellipses of great eccentricity, and also in the cases of parabolic and hyperbolic motion, these formulæ for the differential coefficients require some modification, which we now proceed to develop.

First, then, in the case of parabolic motion, $\sin\varphi = 1$, and instead of M_0 and μ we shall introduce the elements T and q, the differential coefficients relating to π, Ω, and i remaining unchanged from their form as already derived.

If we differentiate the equation

$$\frac{k(t-T)}{\sqrt{2}} = q^{\frac{3}{2}}(\tan\tfrac{1}{2}v + \tfrac{1}{3}\tan^3\tfrac{1}{2}v),$$

regarding T, q, and v as variable, we shall have

$$-\frac{kdT}{\sqrt{2}} = \tfrac{3}{2}\frac{k(t-T)}{q\sqrt{2}}dq + \tfrac{1}{2}q^{\frac{3}{2}}\sec^4\tfrac{1}{2}v,$$

or, since $r^2 = q^2\sec^4\frac{1}{2}v$,

$$-\frac{kdT}{\sqrt{2}} = \tfrac{3}{2}\frac{k(t-T)}{q\sqrt{2}}dq + \tfrac{1}{2}\frac{r^2}{q^{\frac{1}{2}}}dv.$$

Multiplying through by $\frac{2q^{\frac{1}{2}}}{r^2}$, and reducing, we get

$$dv = -\frac{k\sqrt{2q}}{r^2}dT - \frac{3k(t-T)}{r^2\sqrt{2q}}dq. \tag{17}$$

Instead of q, we may use $\log q$, and the equation will, therefore, become

$$dv = -\frac{k\sqrt{2q}}{r^2}dT - \frac{3k(t-T)\sqrt{2q}}{2r^2\lambda_0}d\log q, \tag{18}$$

in which λ_0 is the modulus of the system of logarithms.

If we take the logarithms of both members of the equation

$$r = \frac{q}{\cos^2 \frac{1}{2}v},$$

and differentiate, we find

$$dr = \frac{r}{q}\, dq + r \tan \tfrac{1}{2}v\, dv.$$

Introducing into this equation the value of dv from (17), we get

$$dr = r\left(\frac{1}{q} - \frac{3k(t-T)\tan \frac{1}{2}v}{r^2 \sqrt{2q}}\right) dq - \frac{k\sqrt{2q}\tan \frac{1}{2}v}{r}\, dT. \tag{19}$$

Now, since $\dfrac{k(t-T)}{\sqrt{2q}} = q(\tan \frac{1}{2}v + \frac{1}{3}\tan^3 \frac{1}{2}v)$, and $q = r\cos^2 \frac{1}{2}v$, we have

$$\frac{1}{q} - \frac{3k(t-T)\tan \frac{1}{2}v}{r^2\sqrt{2q}} = \frac{1}{r}(1 + \tan^2 \tfrac{1}{2}v - 3\sin^2 \tfrac{1}{2}v - \sin^2 \tfrac{1}{2}v \tan^2 \tfrac{1}{2}v)$$
$$= \frac{\cos v}{r}.$$

We also have

$$\frac{k\sqrt{2q}}{r}\tan \tfrac{1}{2}v = \frac{k\sqrt{2q}\cos^2 \frac{1}{2}v \tan \frac{1}{2}v}{q} = \frac{k \sin v}{\sqrt{2q}}.$$

Therefore, equation (19) reduces to

$$dr = \cos v\, dq - \frac{k\sin v}{\sqrt{2q}}\, dT. \tag{20}$$

If we introduce $d \log q$ instead of dq, this equation becomes

$$dr = \frac{q\cos v}{\lambda_0}\, d\log q - \frac{k \sin v}{\sqrt{2q}}\, dT. \tag{21}$$

From the equations (17), (18), (20), and (21), we derive

$$\begin{aligned}
\frac{dr}{dT} &= -\frac{k\sin v}{\sqrt{2q}}, & \frac{dv}{dT} &= -\frac{k\sqrt{2q}}{r^2}, \\
\frac{dr}{dq} &= \cos v, & \frac{dv}{dq} &= -\frac{3k(t-T)}{r^2\sqrt{2q}}, \\
\frac{dr}{d\log q} &= \frac{q\cos v}{\lambda_0}, & \frac{dv}{d\log q} &= -\frac{3k(t-T)\sqrt{2q}}{2\lambda_0 r^2};
\end{aligned} \tag{22}$$

and then we have, for the differential coefficients of x with respect to T and q or $\log q$,

$$\frac{dx}{dT}=\frac{dx}{dr}\cdot\frac{dr}{dT}+\frac{dx}{dv}\cdot\frac{dv}{dT},\qquad \frac{dx}{dq}=\frac{dx}{dr}\cdot\frac{dr}{dq}+\frac{dx}{dv}\cdot\frac{dv}{dq},$$

$$\frac{dx}{d\log q}=\frac{dx}{dr}\cdot\frac{dr}{d\log q}+\frac{dx}{dv}\cdot\frac{dv}{d\log q},$$

and similarly for the differential coefficients of y and z with respect to these elements. The expressions for the partial differential coefficients of x, y, and z, respectively, with respect to r and v are the same as already found in the case of elliptic motion. We shall thus obtain the equations which express the relation between the variations of the geocentric places of a comet and the variation of the parabolic elements of its orbit, and which may be employed either to correct the approximate elements by means of equations of condition furnished by comparison of the computed place with the observed place, or to determine the change in the geocentric right ascension and declination corresponding to given increments assigned to the elements.

48. We may also, in the case of an elliptic orbit, introduce T, q, and e instead of the elements φ, M_0, and μ. If we differentiate the expression

$$q=a(1-e),$$

we shall have

$$da=\frac{a}{q}\,dq+\frac{a^2}{q}\,de.$$

We have, also,

$$M=k\sqrt{1+m}\,a^{-\frac{3}{2}}(t-T),$$

in which T is the time of perihelion passage, and

$$dM=-k\sqrt{1+m}\,a^{-\frac{3}{2}}\,dT-\tfrac{3}{2}k\sqrt{1+m}\,a^{-\frac{5}{2}}(t-T)\,da.$$

Hence we derive

$$dM=-k\sqrt{1+m}\,a^{-\frac{3}{2}}\,dT-\tfrac{3}{2}\,\frac{k\sqrt{1+m}\,a^{-\frac{3}{2}}}{q}(t-T)\,dq$$
$$-\tfrac{3}{2}\,\frac{k\sqrt{1+m}\,a^{-\frac{1}{2}}}{q}(t-T)\,de.$$

Substituting this value of dM in equation (12), replacing $\sin\varphi$ by e, and reducing, we get

$$dv=-\frac{k\sqrt{p(1+m)}}{r^2}\,dT-\tfrac{3}{2}\,\frac{k\sqrt{p(1+m)}}{qr^2}(t-T)\,dq$$
$$-\left(p\,\frac{\frac{3}{2}k\sqrt{p(1+m)}}{qr^2}(t-T)-\left(\frac{p}{r}+1\right)\sin v\right)\frac{1}{1-e^2}\,de. \qquad (23)$$

In a similar manner, by substituting the values of da and dM in equation (14), and reducing, we find

$$dr = -\frac{k\sqrt{1+m}}{\sqrt{p}}\, e \sin v\, dT$$
$$+\left(\frac{r}{q} - \tfrac{3}{2}\frac{k\sqrt{1+m}\,(t-T)}{\sqrt{2}\,q^{\frac{3}{2}}}\sqrt{\frac{2}{1+e}}\, e\sin v\right) dq$$
$$+\left(p\left(\frac{r}{q} - \cos v\right) - \tfrac{3}{2}k\sqrt{p(1+m)}\,(t-T)\frac{e\sin v}{q}\right)\frac{1}{1-e^2}\, de. \quad (24)$$

These equations, (23) and (24), will furnish the expressions for the partial differential coefficients $\frac{dv}{dT}, \frac{dv}{dq}, \frac{dv}{de}, \frac{dr}{dT}, \frac{dr}{dq}$, and $\frac{dr}{de}$, which are required in finding the differential coefficients of the heliocentric co-ordinates with respect to the elements T, q, and e, these quantities being substituted for M_0, μ, and φ, respectively, in the equations (11).

49. When the orbit is a hyperbola, we introduce, in place of M_0, μ, and φ, the elements T, q, and ψ.

If we differentiate the equation

$$N_0 = e \tan F - \log_e \tan(45^\circ + \tfrac{1}{2}F),$$

we shall have

$$dN_0 = \left(\frac{e}{\cos F} - 1\right)\frac{dF}{\cos F} + \tan F\, de,$$

which is easily transformed into

$$dN_0 = \frac{r}{a}\cdot\frac{dF}{\cos F} + \tan F\frac{\tan\psi}{\cos\psi}\, d\psi,$$

or

$$\frac{dF}{\sin F} = \frac{a}{r\tan F}\, dN_0 - \frac{a}{r}\cdot\frac{\tan\psi}{\cos\psi}\, d\psi.$$

Let us now take the logarithms of both members of the equation

$$\tan\tfrac{1}{2}F = \tan\tfrac{1}{2}v\,\tan\tfrac{1}{2}\psi,$$

and differentiate, and we shall have

$$dv = \sin v\frac{dF}{\sin F} - \frac{\sin v}{\sin\psi}\, d\psi.$$

Introducing into this equation the value of $\frac{dF}{\sin F}$ already found, we get

$$dv = \frac{a\sin v}{r\tan F}\, dN_0 - \left(\frac{a\sin v}{r}\cdot\frac{\tan\psi}{\cos\psi} + \frac{\sin v}{\sin\psi}\right) d\psi.$$

But, since $r \sin v = a \tan \psi \tan F$, and $p = a \tan^2 \psi$, this reduces to

$$dv = \frac{a^{\frac{3}{2}}}{r^2} \sqrt{p}\, dN_0 - \left(\frac{p}{r} + 1 \right) \frac{\sin v}{\sin \psi} d\psi. \qquad (25)$$

If we differentiate the equation

$$r = a \left(\frac{e}{\cos F} - 1 \right),$$

we get

$$dr = \frac{r}{a} da + ae \tan^2 F \frac{dF}{\sin F} + \frac{a}{\cos F} \cdot \frac{\tan \psi}{\cos \psi} d\psi.$$

Substituting in this equation the value of $\frac{dF}{\sin F}$, we obtain

$$dr = \frac{r}{a} da + \frac{a^2 e \tan F}{r} dN_0 - \left(\frac{a^2 e \tan^2 F}{r} - \frac{a}{\cos F} \right) \frac{\tan \psi}{\cos \psi} d\psi,$$

which is easily reduced to

$$dr = \frac{r}{a} da + a \frac{\sin v}{\sin \psi} dN_0 + \frac{p}{r} \left(\frac{r}{\cos F} - \frac{ae}{\cos^2 F} + ae \right) \frac{d\psi}{\sin \psi}.$$

But, since

$$\frac{r}{\cos F} = \frac{ae}{\cos^2 F} - \frac{a}{\cos F},$$

this reduces to

$$dr = \frac{r}{a} da + \frac{a \sin v}{\sin \psi} dN_0 + \frac{pa}{r} \left(e - \frac{1}{\cos F} \right) \frac{d\psi}{\sin \psi},$$

or

$$dr = \frac{r}{a} da + a \frac{\sin v}{\sin \psi} dN_0 + p \frac{\cos v}{\sin \psi} d\psi. \qquad (26)$$

Now, since $q = a(e - 1)$, we have

$$dq = \frac{q}{a} da + \frac{a \tan \psi}{\cos \psi} d\psi,$$

or

$$da = \frac{a}{q} dq - \frac{a^{\frac{3}{2}} \sqrt{p}}{q \cos \psi} d\psi.$$

We have, also,

$$N_0 = ka^{-\frac{3}{2}} (t - T),$$

and hence

$$dN_0 = - ka^{-\frac{3}{2}} dT - \tfrac{3}{2} ka^{-\frac{5}{2}} (t - T)\, da.$$

By substituting the value of da, this becomes

$$dN_0 = - ka^{-\frac{3}{2}} dT - \frac{\frac{3}{2} ka^{-\frac{3}{2}} (t - T)}{q} dq + \frac{\frac{3}{2} k (t - T) \sqrt{p}}{aq \cos \psi} d\psi.$$

Substituting this value of dN_0 in equation (25), and reducing, we obtain

$$dv = -\frac{k\sqrt{p}}{r^2}\,dT - \frac{\frac{3}{2}k\sqrt{p}\,(t-T)}{qr^2}\,dq$$
$$+\left(\frac{\frac{3}{2}kp^{\frac{3}{2}}(t-T)}{qr^2} - \left(\frac{p}{r}+1\right)\sin v\right)\frac{d\psi}{\sin\psi}. \qquad (27)$$

In a similar manner, substituting in equation (26) the values of da and dN_0, and reducing, we get

$$dr = -\frac{k}{\sqrt{p}}\cdot\frac{\sin v}{\cos\psi}\,dT + \left(\frac{r}{q} - \frac{3}{2}\,\frac{k(t-T)}{\sqrt{2}\,q^{\frac{3}{2}}}\cdot\frac{\sin v}{\cos\frac{1}{2}\psi\,\sqrt{\cos\psi}}\right)dq$$
$$+\left(\frac{\frac{3}{2}k\sqrt{p}\,(t-T)}{q}\cdot\frac{\sin v}{\cos\psi} - \left(\frac{r}{q}-\cos v\right)p\right)\frac{d\psi}{\sin\psi}. \qquad (28)$$

The equations (27) and (28) will furnish the expressions for the partial differential coefficients of r and v with respect to the elements T, q, and ψ, required in forming the equations for $\cos\delta\,d\alpha$ and $d\delta$. It will be observed that these equations are analogous to the equations (23) and (24), and that by introducing the relation between e and ψ, and neglecting the mass, they become identical with them. We might, indeed, have derived the equations (27) and (28) directly from (23) and (24) by substituting for e its value in terms of ψ; but the differential formulæ which have resulted in deriving them directly from the equations for hyperbolic motion, will not be superfluous.

50. It is evident, from an inspection of the terms of equations (23), (24), (27), and (28) which contain de and $d\psi$, that when the value of e is very nearly equal to unity, the coefficients for these differentials become indeterminate. It becomes necessary, therefore, to develop the corresponding expressions for the case in which these equations are insufficient. For this purpose, let us resume the equation

$$\frac{k(t-T)\,(1+e)^{\frac{1}{2}}}{2q^{\frac{3}{2}}} = u + \tfrac{1}{3}u^3 - 2i\left(\tfrac{1}{3}u^3 + \tfrac{1}{5}u^5\right) + 3i^2\left(\tfrac{1}{5}u^5 + \tfrac{1}{7}u^7\right) - \&c.,$$

in which $u = \tan\frac{1}{2}v$, and $i = \dfrac{1-e}{1+e}$. Then, since

$$i = \tfrac{1}{2}(1-e) + \tfrac{1}{4}(1-e)^2 + \&c.,$$

$$\sqrt{\frac{2}{1+e}} = \sqrt{\frac{1}{1-\frac{1}{2}(1-e)}} = 1 + \tfrac{1}{4}(1-e) + \tfrac{3}{32}(1-e)^2 + \&c.,$$

we shall have

$$\frac{k(t-T)}{\sqrt{2}\,q^{\frac{3}{2}}} = u + \tfrac{1}{3}u^3 + (\tfrac{1}{4}u - \tfrac{1}{4}u^3 - \tfrac{1}{5}u^5)(1-e)$$
$$+ (\tfrac{3}{32}u - \tfrac{7}{32}u^3 + \tfrac{3}{28}u^7)(1-e)^2 + \&c. \qquad (29)$$

If it is required to find the expression for $\frac{dv}{de}$ in the case of the variation of the elements of parabolic motion, or when $1-e$ is very small, we may regard the coefficient of $1-e$ as constant, and neglect terms multiplied by the square and higher powers of $1-e$. By differentiating the equation (29) according to these conditions, and regarding u and e as variable, we get

$$0 = (1+u^2)\,du - (\tfrac{1}{4}u - \tfrac{1}{4}u^3 - \tfrac{1}{5}u^5)\,de;$$

and, since $du = \frac{1}{2}(1+u^2)\,dv$, this gives

$$\frac{dv}{de} = \frac{\tfrac{1}{2}u - \tfrac{1}{2}u^3 - \tfrac{2}{5}u^5}{(1+u^2)^2}. \qquad (30)$$

The values of the second member, corresponding to different values of v, may be tabulated with the argument v; but a table of this kind is by no means indispensable, since the expression for $\frac{dv}{de}$ may be changed to another form which furnishes a direct solution with the same facility. Thus, by division, we have

$$\frac{dv}{de} = -\tfrac{2}{5}u + \tfrac{9}{10}\,\frac{u + \tfrac{1}{3}u^3}{(1+u^2)^2},$$

and since, in the case of parabolic motion,

$$\frac{k(t-T)}{\sqrt{2}\,q^{\frac{3}{2}}} = u + \tfrac{1}{3}u^3, \qquad r^2 = q^2(1+u^2)^2,$$

this becomes

$$\frac{dv}{de} = \tfrac{9}{20}\,\frac{k(t-T)}{r^2}\sqrt{2q} - \tfrac{2}{5}\tan\tfrac{1}{2}v. \qquad (31)$$

If we differentiate the equation

$$r = \frac{q(1+e)}{1+e\cos v},$$

regarding r, v, and e as variables, we shall have

$$\frac{dr}{de} = \frac{2r^2\sin^2\tfrac{1}{2}v}{q(1+e)^2} + \frac{r^2 e\sin v}{q(1+e)}\cdot\frac{dv}{de}. \qquad (32)$$

In the case of parabolic motion, $e=1$, and this equation is easily transformed into

$$\frac{dr}{de}=\tfrac{1}{2}r\tan\tfrac{1}{2}v\left(\tan\tfrac{1}{2}v+2\frac{dv}{de}\right). \qquad (33)$$

Substituting for $\frac{dv}{de}$ its value from (31), and reducing, we get

$$\frac{dr}{de}=\tfrac{9}{20}\frac{k(t-T)}{\sqrt{2q}}\sin v+\tfrac{1}{10}r\tan^2\tfrac{1}{2}v. \qquad (34)$$

The equations (31) and (34) furnish the values of $\frac{dv}{de}$ and $\frac{dr}{de}$ to be used in forming the expressions for the variation of the place of the body when the parabolic eccentricity is changed to the value $1+de$. When the eccentricity to which the increment is assigned differs but little from unity, we may compute the value of $\frac{dv}{de}$ directly from equation (30). A still closer approximation would be obtained by using an additional term of (29) in finding the expression for $\frac{dv}{de}$; but a more convenient formula may be derived, of which the numerical application is facilitated by the use of Table IX. Thus, if we differentiate the equation

$$v=V+A\,(100i)+B\,(100i)^2+C(100i)^3,$$

regarding the coefficients A, B, and C as constant, and introducing the value of i in terms of e, we have

$$\frac{dv}{de}=\frac{dV}{de}-\frac{200A}{s(1+e)^2}-\frac{400B}{s(1+e)^2}(100i)-\frac{600C}{s(1+e)^2}(100i)^2,$$

in which $s=206264.8$, the values of A, B, and C, as derived from the table, being expressed in seconds. To find $\frac{dV}{de}$, we have

$$\frac{k(t-T)\sqrt{1+e}}{2q^{\frac{3}{2}}}=\tan\tfrac{1}{2}V+\tfrac{1}{3}\tan^3\tfrac{1}{2}V,$$

which gives, by differentiation,

$$\frac{k(t-T)}{2q^{\frac{3}{2}}}\cdot\frac{de}{\sqrt{1+e}}=\frac{dV}{\cos^4\frac{1}{2}V};$$

and if we introduce the expression for the value of M used as the argument in finding V by means of Table VI., the result is

$$\frac{dV}{de}=\frac{M\cos^4\frac{1}{2}V}{75(1+e)}.$$

Hence we have

$$\frac{dv}{de}=\frac{M\cos^4\frac{1}{2}V}{75(1+e)}-\frac{200A}{s(1+e)^2}-\frac{400B}{s(1+e)^2}(100i)-\frac{600C}{s(1+e)^2}(100i)^2, \quad (35)$$

by means of which the value of $\frac{dv}{de}$ is readily found.

When the eccentricity differs so much from that of the parabola that the terms of the last equation are not sufficiently convergent, the expression for $\frac{dv}{de}$, which will furnish the required accuracy, may be derived from the equations $(75)_1$ and $(76)_1$. If we differentiate the first of these equations with respect to e, since B may evidently be regarded as constant, we get

$$\frac{dw}{de}=\tfrac{9}{10}\frac{k(t-T)}{\sqrt{2}\,q^{\frac{3}{2}}}\cdot\frac{\cos^4\frac{1}{2}w}{B\sqrt{\frac{1}{10}(1+9e)}}. \quad (36)$$

If we take the logarithms of both members of equation $(76)_1$, and differentiate, we get

$$\frac{dv}{\sin v}=\frac{dC}{C}+\frac{dw}{\sin w}-\frac{4de}{(1+e)(1+9e)}. \quad (37)$$

To find the differential coefficient of C with respect to e, it will be sufficient to take

$$\frac{1}{C^2}=1-\tfrac{4}{5}A,$$

which gives

$$\frac{dC}{C}=\tfrac{2}{5}C^2\,dA.$$

The equation

$$A=\frac{5(1-e)}{(1+9e)}\tan^2\tfrac{1}{2}w$$

gives

$$dA=-\frac{50}{(1+9e)^2}\tan^2\tfrac{1}{2}w\,de+\frac{A\,dw}{\tan\frac{1}{2}w\cos^2\frac{1}{2}w};$$

and hence we obtain

$$\frac{dC}{C}=-\frac{20C^2}{(1+9e)^2}\tan^2\tfrac{1}{2}w\,de+\tfrac{4}{5}\frac{AC^2}{\sin w}\,dw.$$

Substituting this value in equation (37), we get

$$\frac{dv}{de}=-\frac{20C^2}{(1+9e)^2}\sin v\tan^2\tfrac{1}{2}w+\frac{C^2\sin v}{\sin w}\cdot\frac{dw}{de}-\frac{4\sin v}{(1+e)(1+9e)};$$

and substituting, finally, the value of $\frac{dw}{de}$, we obtain

$$\frac{dv}{de} = \tfrac{9}{20} \cdot \frac{k(t-T)}{\sqrt{2}\, q^{\frac{3}{2}}} \cdot \frac{C^2 \sin v}{B\sqrt{\tfrac{1}{10}(1+9e)}} \cdot \frac{\cos^2 \frac{1}{2}w}{\tan \frac{1}{2}w} - \frac{20\, C^2}{(1+9e)^2} \sin v \tan^2 \tfrac{1}{2}w$$
$$- \frac{4 \sin v}{(1+e)(1+9e)},$$

which, by means of $(76)_1$, reduces to

$$\frac{dv}{de} = \tfrac{9}{20} \cdot \frac{k(t-T)}{\sqrt{2}\, q^{\frac{3}{2}}} \cdot \frac{C^2 \sin v}{B\sqrt{\tfrac{1}{10}(1+9e)}} \cdot \frac{\cos^2 \frac{1}{2}w}{\tan \frac{1}{2}w} - \frac{8 \tan \frac{1}{2}v}{(1+e)(1+9e)}. \quad (38)$$

If we introduce the quantity M which is used as the argument in finding w by means of Table VI., this equation becomes

$$\frac{dv}{de} = \frac{9}{2(1+9e)} \cdot \frac{M \cos^2 \frac{1}{2}w}{75 \tan \frac{1}{2}w} C^2 \sin v - \frac{8 \tan \frac{1}{2}v}{(1+e)(1+9e)}. \quad (39)$$

This equation remains unchanged in the case of hyperbolic motion, the value of C being taken from the column of the table which corresponds to this case; and it will furnish the correct value of $\frac{dv}{de}$ in all cases in which the last term of equation (23) is not conveniently applicable. The value of $\frac{dr}{de}$ is then given by the equation (32).

When the eccentricity differs very little from unity, we may put $B = 1$, and

$$\tan \tfrac{1}{2}w = \tan \tfrac{1}{2}v \sqrt{\tfrac{1}{10}(1+9e)},$$
$$\cos^2 \tfrac{1}{2}w = C^2 \cos^2 \tfrac{1}{2}v.$$

Then we shall have

$$\frac{M \cos^2 \frac{1}{2}w}{75 \tan \frac{1}{2}w} C^2 \sin v = \frac{2k(t-T)}{\sqrt{2}\, q^{\frac{3}{2}}} \cos^4 \tfrac{1}{2}w.$$

The equation

$$\frac{q}{r} = (1 + AC^2) \cos^2 \tfrac{1}{2}v = (1 + \tfrac{1}{5}A) \cos^2 \tfrac{1}{2}w,$$

gives

$$\frac{q^2}{r^2} = (1 + \tfrac{2}{5}A) \cos^4 \tfrac{1}{2}w = C \cos^4 \tfrac{1}{2}w.$$

Hence we derive

$$\frac{M \cos^2 \frac{1}{2}w}{75 \tan \frac{1}{2}w} C^2 \sin v = \frac{k(t-T)\sqrt{p}}{r^2} \cdot \sqrt{\frac{2}{C^2(1+e)}}.$$

If we substitute this value in equation (39), and put $C^2(1+e)=2$, we get

$$\frac{dv}{de}=\frac{9}{2(1+9e)}\cdot\frac{k\sqrt{p}}{r^2}(t-T)-\frac{8\tan\frac{1}{2}v}{(1+e)(1+9e)}, \qquad (40)$$

and when $e=1$, this becomes identical with equation (31).

51. Examples.—We will now illustrate, by numerical examples, the formulæ for the calculation of the variations of the geocentric right ascension and declination arising from small increments assigned to the elements. Let it be required to find for the date 1865 February 24.5 mean time at Washington, the differential coefficients of the right ascension and declination of the planet *Eurynome* (79) with respect to the elements of its orbit, using the data and results given in Art. 41. Thus we have

$$\alpha=181^\circ\ 8'\ 29''.29, \quad \delta=-4^\circ\ 42'\ 21''.56, \quad \log\Delta=0.2450054,$$
$$\log r=0.428285, \quad v=129^\circ\ 3'\ 50''.5, \quad u=326^\circ\ 41'\ 40''.1,$$
$$A=296^\circ\ 39'\ 5''.0, \quad B=205^\circ\ 55'\ 27''.1, \quad C=212^\circ\ 32'\ 17''.7,$$
$$\log\sin a=9.999716, \quad \log\sin b=9.974825, \quad \log\sin c=9.522219,$$
$$\log x=0.425066_n, \quad \log y=9.511920, \quad \log z=8.077315,$$
$$\varepsilon=23^\circ\ 27'\ 24''.0, \quad t-T=420.714018.$$

First, by means of the equations (4), we compute the following values:—

$$\log\cos\delta\frac{d\alpha}{dx}=8.054308, \qquad \log\frac{d\delta}{dx}=8.668959_n,$$
$$\log\cos\delta\frac{d\alpha}{dy}=9.754919_n, \qquad \log\frac{d\delta}{dy}=6.968348_n,$$
$$\log\frac{d\delta}{dz}=9.753529.$$

Then we find the differential coefficients of the heliocentric co-ordinates, with respect to π, ☊, i, v, and r, from the formulæ (7), which give

$$\log\frac{dx}{d\pi}=\log\frac{dx}{dv}=9.491991_n, \qquad \log\frac{dy}{d\pi}=\log\frac{dy}{dv}=0.399496_n,$$
$$\log\frac{dz}{d\pi}=\log\frac{dz}{dv}=9.950466_n;$$

$$\log\frac{dx}{d☊}=7.876553, \quad \log\frac{dy}{d☊}=8.830941, \quad \log\frac{dz}{d☊}=9.222898_n,$$
$$\log\frac{dx}{di}=8.726364, \quad \log\frac{dy}{di}=9.687577, \quad \log\frac{dz}{di}=0.142443_n,$$
$$\log\frac{dx}{dr}=9.996780_n, \quad \log\frac{dy}{dr}=9.083635, \quad \log\frac{dz}{dr}=7.649030.$$

In computing the values of $\frac{dx}{di}$, $\frac{dy}{di}$, and $\frac{dz}{di}$, those of $\cos a$, $\cos b$, and $\cos c$ may generally be obtained with sufficient accuracy from $\sin a$, $\sin b$, and $\sin c$. Their algebraic signs, however, must be strictly attended to. The quantities $\sin a$, $\sin b$, and $\sin c$ are always positive; and the algebraic signs of $\cos a$, $\cos b$, and $\cos c$ are indicated at once by the equations $(101)_1$, from which, also, their numerical values may be derived. In the case of the example proposed, it will be observed that $\cos a$ and $\cos b$ are negative, and that $\cos c$ is positive.

To find the values of $\cos\delta\frac{d\alpha}{d\pi}$ and $\frac{d\delta}{d\pi}$, we have, according to equation (2),

$$\cos\delta\frac{d\alpha}{d\pi}=\cos\delta\frac{d\alpha}{dx}\cdot\frac{dx}{d\pi}+\cos\delta\frac{d\alpha}{dy}\cdot\frac{dy}{d\pi}, \qquad (41)$$

$$\frac{d\delta}{d\pi}=\frac{d\delta}{dx}\cdot\frac{dx}{d\pi}+\frac{d\delta}{dy}\cdot\frac{dy}{d\pi}+\frac{d\delta}{dz}\cdot\frac{dz}{d\pi},$$

which give

$$\cos\delta\frac{d\alpha}{d\pi}=\cos\delta\frac{d\alpha}{dv}=+1.42345, \qquad \frac{d\delta}{d\pi}=\frac{d\delta}{dv}=-0.48900.$$

In the case of ☊, i, and r, we write these quantities successively in place of π in the equations (41), and hence we derive

$$\cos\delta\frac{d\alpha}{d\Omega}=-0.03845, \qquad \frac{d\delta}{d\Omega}=-0.09533,$$

$$\cos\delta\frac{d\alpha}{di}=-0.27641, \qquad \frac{d\delta}{di}=-0.78993,$$

$$\cos\delta\frac{d\alpha}{dr}=-0.08020, \qquad \frac{d\delta}{dr}=+0.04873.$$

Next, from (16), we compute the following values:—

$$\log\frac{dr}{d\varphi}=0.179155, \qquad \log\frac{dr}{dM_0}=9.577453, \qquad \log\frac{dr}{d\mu}=2.376581_n,$$

$$\log\frac{dv}{d\varphi}=0.171999, \qquad \log\frac{dv}{dM_0}=9.911247, \qquad \log\frac{dv}{d\mu}=2.535234.$$

We may now find $\frac{dx}{d\varphi}$, $\frac{dx}{dM_0}$, &c. by means of the equations (11), and thence the values of $\cos\delta\frac{d\alpha}{d\varphi}$, $\frac{d\delta}{d\varphi}$, &c.; but it is most convenient to derive these values directly from $\cos\delta\frac{d\alpha}{dr}$, $\cos\delta\frac{d\alpha}{dv}$, $\frac{d\delta}{dr}$, and $\frac{d\delta}{dv}$, in connection with the numerical values last found, according to the equations which result from the analytical substitution of the expressions for $\frac{dx}{d\varphi}$, $\frac{dy}{d\varphi}$, $\frac{dz}{d\varphi}$, &c., in equation (2), writing successively φ, M_0, and μ in place of π. Thus, we have

$$\cos\delta\frac{d\alpha}{d\varphi}=\cos\delta\frac{d\alpha}{dr}\cdot\frac{dr}{d\varphi}+\cos\delta\frac{d\alpha}{dv}\cdot\frac{dv}{d\varphi},$$
$$\frac{d\delta}{d\varphi}=\frac{d\delta}{dr}\cdot\frac{dr}{d\varphi}+\frac{d\delta}{dv}\cdot\frac{dv}{d\varphi}, \qquad (42)$$

and similarly for M_0 and μ, which give

$$\cos\delta\frac{d\alpha}{d\varphi}=+1.99400, \qquad \frac{d\delta}{d\varphi}=-0.65307,$$
$$\cos\delta\frac{d\alpha}{dM_0}=+1.13004, \qquad \frac{d\delta}{dM_0}=-0.38023,$$
$$\cos\delta\frac{d\alpha}{d\mu}=+507.264, \qquad \frac{d\delta}{d\mu}=-179.315.$$

Therefore, according to (1), we shall have

$$\cos\delta\,\Delta\alpha=+1.42345\Delta\pi-0.03845\Delta\Omega-0.27641\Delta i+1.99400\Delta\varphi+1.13004\Delta M_0+507.264\Delta\mu,$$
$$\Delta\delta=-0.48900\Delta\pi-0.09533\Delta\Omega-0.78993\Delta i-0.65307\Delta\varphi-0.38023\Delta M_0-179.315\Delta\mu.$$

To prove the calculation of the coefficients in these equations, we assign to the elements the increments

$$\Delta M_0=+10'', \quad \Delta\pi=-20'', \quad \Delta\Omega=-10'', \quad \Delta i=+10'',$$
$$\Delta\varphi=+10'', \quad \Delta\mu=+0''.01,$$

so that they become

Epoch = 1864 Jan. 1.0 Greenwich mean time.

$$\begin{aligned}M_0 &= 1^\circ\ 29'\ 50''.21\\ \pi &= 44\ \ 20\ \ 13\ .09\\ \Omega &= 206\ \ 42\ \ 30\ .13\\ i &= 4\ \ 37\ \ 0\ .51\\ \varphi &= 11\ \ 16\ \ 1\ .02\\ \log a &= 0.3881288\\ \mu &= 928.56745\end{aligned}$$

(π, Ω, i: Mean Equinox 1864.0)

With these elements we compute the geocentric place for 1865 February 24.5 mean time at Washington; and the result is

$$\alpha=181^\circ\ 8'\ 34''.81, \qquad \delta=-4^\circ\ 42'\ 30''.58, \qquad \log\Delta=0.2450284,$$

which are referred to the mean equinox and equator of 1865.0. The difference between these values of α and δ and those already given, as derived from the unchanged elements, gives

$$\Delta\alpha = +5''.52, \qquad \cos\delta\,\Delta\alpha = +5''.50, \qquad \Delta\delta = -9''.02,$$

and the direct substitution of the assumed values of $\Delta\pi$, $\Delta\Omega$, Δi, &c. in the equations for $\cos\delta\,\Delta\alpha$ and $\Delta\delta$, gives

$$\cos\delta\,\Delta\alpha = +5''.46, \qquad \Delta\delta = -9''.29.$$

The agreement of these results is sufficiently close to show that the computation of the differential coefficients has been correctly performed, the difference being due chiefly to terms of the second order.

When the differential coefficients are required for several dates, if we compute their values for successive dates at equal intervals, the use of differences will serve to check the accuracy of the calculation; but, to provide against the possibility of a systematic error, it may be advisable to calculate at least one place directly from the changed elements. Throughout the calculation of the various differential coefficients, great care must be taken in regard to the algebraic signs involved in the successive numerical substitutions. In the example given, we have employed logarithms of six decimal places; but it would have been sufficient if logarithms of five decimals had been used; and such is generally the case.

It will be observed that the calculation of the coefficients of $\Delta\pi$, $\Delta\Omega$, and Δi is independent of the form of the orbit, depending simply on the position of the plane of the orbit and on the position of the orbit in this plane. Hence, in the case of parabolic and hyperbolic orbits, the only deviation from the process already illustrated is in the computation of the coefficients of the variations of the elements which determine the magnitude and form of the orbit and the position of the body in its orbit at a given epoch. In all cases, the values of $\cos\delta\frac{d\alpha}{dv}$, $\cos\delta\frac{d\alpha}{dr}$, $\frac{d\delta}{dv}$, and $\frac{d\delta}{dr}$ are determined as already exemplified. If we introduce the elements T, q, and e, we shall have

$$\cos\delta\frac{d\alpha}{dT} = \cos\delta\frac{d\alpha}{dr}\cdot\frac{dr}{dT} + \cos\delta\frac{d\alpha}{dv}\cdot\frac{dv}{dT},$$

$$\frac{d\delta}{dT} = \frac{d\delta}{dr}\cdot\frac{dr}{dT} + \frac{d\delta}{dv}\cdot\frac{dv}{dT}, \tag{43}$$

and similarly for the differential coefficients with respect to q and e.

The mode of calculating the values of $\frac{dr}{dT}, \frac{dv}{dT}, \frac{dr}{dq}, \frac{dv}{dq}, \frac{dr}{de}$, and $\frac{dv}{de}$ depends on the nature of the orbit.

In the case of passing from one system of parabolic elements to another system of parabolic elements, the coefficients of Δe vanish. To illustrate the calculation of $\frac{dr}{dT}, \frac{dv}{dT}$, &c. in the case of parabolic motion, let us resume the values $t - T = 75.364$ days, and $\log q = 9.9650486$, from which we have found

$$\log r = 0.1961120, \qquad v = 79^\circ\ 55'\ 57''.26.$$

Then, by means of the equations (22), we find

$$\log \frac{dr}{dT} = 8.095802_n, \qquad \log \frac{dr}{dq} = 9.242547,$$
$$\log \frac{dv}{dT} = 7.976397_n, \qquad \log \frac{dv}{dq} = 0.064602_n.$$

If, instead of dq, we introduce $d \log q$, we shall have

$$\log \frac{dr}{d \log q} = 9.569812, \qquad \log \frac{dv}{d \log q} = 0.391867_n.$$

From these, by means of (43), we obtain the differential coefficients of α and δ with respect to T and q or $\log q$. The same values are also used when the variation of the parabolic eccentricity is taken into account. But in this case we compute also $\frac{dv}{de}$ from equation (31) and $\frac{dr}{de}$ from (33) or (34), which give, for $v = 79^\circ\ 55'\ 57''.3$,

$$\log \frac{dv}{de} = 8.147367_n, \qquad \log \frac{dr}{de} = 9.726869.$$

In the case of very eccentric orbits, the values of $\frac{dr}{dT}, \frac{dv}{dT}$, &c. are found from

$$\frac{dv}{dT} = -\frac{k\sqrt{p}}{r^2}, \qquad \frac{dr}{dT} = -\frac{k}{\sqrt{p}} e \sin v, \tag{44}$$
$$\frac{dv}{dq} = -\tfrac{3}{2}\frac{k\sqrt{p}}{qr^2}(t-T), \qquad \frac{dr}{dq} = \frac{r}{q} - \tfrac{3}{2}\frac{k(t-T)}{q\sqrt{p}} e \sin v$$
$$\frac{dr}{dq} = \frac{r}{q} + \frac{r^2 e \sin v}{p} \cdot \frac{dv}{dq},$$

the mass being neglected.

To illustrate the application of these formulæ, let us resume the values, $t - T = 68.25$ days, $e = 0.9675212$, and $\log q = 9.7668134$, from which we have found (Art. 41)

$$v = 102^\circ\ 20'\ 52''.20, \qquad \log r = 0.1614052.$$

Hence we derive

$$\log p = 0.0607328,$$

and

$$\log \frac{dv}{dT} = 7.943137_n, \qquad \log \frac{dr}{dT} = 8.180711_n,$$

$$\log \frac{dv}{dq} = 0.186517_n, \qquad \log \frac{dr}{dq} = 0.186517_n.$$

If we wish to obtain the differential coefficients of v and r with respect to $\log q$ instead of q, we have

$$\frac{dv}{d \log q} = \frac{q}{\lambda_0} \cdot \frac{dv}{dq}, \qquad \frac{dr}{d \log q} = \frac{q}{\lambda_0} \cdot \frac{dr}{dq},$$

in which λ_0 is the modulus of the system of logarithms.

Then we compute the value of $\frac{dv}{de}$ by means of the equation (30). (35), (39), or (40). The correct value as derived from (39) is

$$\frac{dv}{de} = -0.24289.$$

The values derived from (35), omitting the last term, from (40) and from (30), are, respectively, -0.24440, -0.24291, and -0.23531. The close agreement of the value derived from (40) with the correct value is accidental, and arises from the particular value of v, which is here such as to make the assumptions, according to which equation (40) is derived from (39), almost exact.

Finally, the value of $\frac{dr}{de}$ may be found by means of (32), which gives

$$\frac{dr}{de} = +0.70855.$$

When, in addition to the differential coefficients which depend on the elements T, q, and e, those which depend on the position of the orbit in space have been found, the expressions for the variation of the geocentric right ascension and declination become

$$\cos\delta\,\Delta\alpha = \cos\delta\frac{d\alpha}{d\pi}\Delta\pi + \cos\delta\frac{d\alpha}{d\Omega}\Delta\Omega + \cos\delta\frac{d\alpha}{di}\Delta i + \cos\delta\frac{d\alpha}{dT}\Delta T$$
$$+ \cos\delta\frac{d\alpha}{dq}\Delta q + \cos\delta\frac{d\alpha}{de}\Delta e,$$
$$\Delta\delta = \frac{d\delta}{d\pi}\Delta\pi + \frac{d\delta}{d\Omega}\Delta\Omega + \frac{d\delta}{di}\Delta i + \frac{d\delta}{dT}\Delta T + \frac{d\delta}{dq}\Delta q + \frac{d\delta}{de}\Delta e.$$

If we introduce $\log q$ instead of q, the terms containing q become respectively $\cos\delta\frac{d\alpha}{d\log q}\Delta\log q$ and $\frac{d\delta}{d\log q}\Delta\log q$. It should be observed that if $\Delta\pi$, $\Delta\Omega$, and Δi are expressed in seconds, in order that these equations may be homogeneous, the terms containing ΔT, Δq, and Δe must be multiplied by 206264.8; but if $\Delta\pi$, $\Delta\Omega$, and Δi are expressed in parts of the radius as unity, the resulting values of $\cos\delta\,\Delta\alpha$ and $\Delta\delta$ must be multiplied by 206264.8 in order to express them in seconds of arc.

The most general application of the equations for $\cos\delta\,\Delta\alpha$ and $\Delta\delta$ in terms of the variations of the elements is for the cases in which the values of $\cos\delta\,\Delta\alpha$ and of $\Delta\delta$ are already known by comparison of the computed place of the body with the observed place, and in which it is required to find the values of $\Delta\pi$, $\Delta\Omega$, Δi, &c., which, being applied to the elements, will make the computed and the observed places agree. When the variations of all the elements of the orbit are taken into account, at least six equations thus derived are necessary, and, if more than six equations are employed, they must first be reduced to six final equations, from which, by elimination, the values of the unknown quantities $\Delta\pi$, $\Delta\Omega$, &c. may be found. In all such cases, the values of $\Delta\alpha$ and $\Delta\delta$, as derived from the comparison of the computed with the observed place, are expressed in seconds of arc; and if the elements involved are expressed in seconds of arc, the coefficients of the several terms of the equations must be abstract numbers. But if some of the elements are not expressed in seconds, as in the case of T, q, and e, the equations formed must be rendered homogeneous. For this purpose we multiply the coefficients of the variations of those elements which are not expressed in seconds of arc by 206264.8. Further, it is generally inconvenient to express the variations ΔT, Δq, and Δe in parts of the units of T, q, and e, respectively; and, to avoid this inconvenience, we may express these variations in terms of certain parts of the actual units. Thus, in the case of T, we may adopt as the unit of ΔT the nth part of a mean solar day, and the coefficients of the terms of the equations for $\cos\delta\,\Delta\alpha$ and $\Delta\delta$ which involve ΔT

must evidently be divided by n. In the same manner, it appears that if we adopt as the unit of Δq the unit of the mth decimal place of its value expressed in parts of the unit of q, we must divide its coefficient by 10^m, and similarly in the case of Δe, so that the equations become

$$\cos\delta\,\Delta\alpha = \cos\delta\frac{d\alpha}{d\pi}\Delta\pi + \cos\delta\frac{d\alpha}{d\Omega}\Delta\Omega + \cos\delta\frac{d\alpha}{di}\Delta i + \frac{s}{n}\cos\delta\frac{d\alpha}{dT}\Delta T$$
$$+ \frac{s}{10^m}\cos\delta\frac{d\alpha}{dq}\Delta q + \frac{s}{10^{m'}}\cos\delta\frac{d\alpha}{de}\Delta e, \quad (45)$$
$$\Delta\delta = \frac{d\delta}{d\pi}\Delta\pi + \frac{d\delta}{d\Omega}\Delta\Omega + \frac{d\delta}{di}\Delta i + \frac{s}{n}\cdot\frac{d\delta}{dT}\Delta T + \frac{s}{10^m}\frac{d\delta}{dq}\Delta q$$
$$+ \frac{s}{10^{m'}}\frac{d\delta}{de}\Delta e,$$

in which $s = 206264.8$. When $\log q$ is introduced in place of q, the coefficients of $\Delta\log q$ are multiplied by the same factor as in the case of Δq, the unit of $\Delta\log q$ being the unit of the mth decimal place of the logarithms. The equations are thus rendered homogeneous, and also convenient for the numerical solution in finding the values of the unknown quantities $\Delta\pi$, $\Delta\Omega$, Δi, ΔT, &c. When ΔT, Δq, and Δe have been found by means of the equations thus formed, the corrections to be applied to the corresponding elements are $\frac{\Delta T}{n}$, $\frac{\Delta q}{10^m}$, and $\frac{\Delta e}{10^{m'}}$. In the same manner, we may adopt as the unknown quantity, instead of the actual variation of any one of the elements of the orbit, n times that variation, in which case its coefficient in the equations must be divided by n.

The value of $\Delta\alpha$, derived by taking the difference between the computed and the observed place, is affected by the uncertainty necessarily incident to the determination of α by observation. The unavoidable error of observation being supposed the same in the case of α as in the case of δ, when expressed in parts of the same unit, it is evident that an error of a given magnitude will produce a greater apparent error in α than in δ, since in the case of α it is measured on a small circle, of which the radius is $\cos\delta$; and hence, in order that the difference between computation and observation in α and δ may have the same influence in the determination of the corrections to be applied to the elements, we introduce $\cos\delta\,\Delta\alpha$ instead of $\Delta\alpha$. The same principle is applied in the case of the longitude and of all corresponding spherical co-ordinates.

52. The formulæ already given will determine also the variations of the geocentric longitude and latitude corresponding to small increments assigned to the elements of the orbit of a heavenly body. In this case we put $\varepsilon = 0$, and compute the values of A, B, $\sin a$, and $\sin b$ by means of the equations $(94)_1$. We have also $C = 0$, $\sin c = \sin i$, and, in place of α and δ, respectively, we write λ and β. But when the elements are referred to the same fundamental plane as the geocentric places of the body, the formulæ which depend on the position of the plane of the orbit may be put in a form which is more convenient for numerical application.

If we differentiate the equations

$$\begin{aligned} x' &= r \cos u \cos \Omega - r \sin u \sin \Omega \cos i, \\ y' &= r \cos u \sin \Omega + r \sin u \cos \Omega \cos i, \\ z' &= r \sin u \sin i, \end{aligned}$$

we obtain

$$\begin{aligned} dx' &= \frac{x'}{r} dr - r(\sin u \cos \Omega + \cos u \sin \Omega \cos i)\, du \\ &\quad - r(\cos u \sin \Omega + \sin u \cos \Omega \cos i)\, d\Omega + r \sin u \sin \Omega \sin i\, di, \\ dy' &= \frac{y'}{r} dr - r(\sin u \sin \Omega - \cos u \cos \Omega \cos i)\, du \\ &\quad + r(\cos u \cos \Omega - \sin u \sin \Omega \cos i)\, d\Omega - r \sin u \cos \Omega \sin i\, di, \\ dz' &= \frac{z'}{r} dr + r \cos u \sin i\, du + r \sin u \cos i\, di, \end{aligned} \tag{46}$$

in which x', y', z' are the heliocentric co-ordinates of the body in reference to the ecliptic, the positive axis of x being directed to the vernal equinox. Let us now suppose the place of the body to be referred to a system of co-ordinates in which the ecliptic remains as the plane of xy, but in which the positive axis of x is directed to the point whose longitude is Ω; then we shall have

$$\begin{aligned} dx &= dx' \cos \Omega + dy' \sin \Omega, \\ dy &= - dx' \sin \Omega + dy' \cos \Omega, \\ dz &= dz', \end{aligned}$$

and the preceding equations give

$$\begin{aligned} dx &= \frac{x}{r} dr - r \sin u\, du - r \sin u \cos i\, d\Omega, \\ dy &= \frac{y}{r} dr + r \cos u \cos i\, du + r \cos u\, d\Omega - r \sin u \sin i\, di, \\ dz &= \frac{z}{r} dr + r \cos u \sin i\, du + r \sin u \cos i\, di. \end{aligned} \tag{47}$$

This transformation, it will be observed, is equivalent to diminishing the longitudes in the equations (46) by the angle ☊ through which the axis of x has been moved.

Let $X_{,}$, $Y_{,}$, $Z_{,}$ denote the heliocentric co-ordinates of the earth referred to the same system of co-ordinates, and we have

$$\begin{aligned} x + X_{,} &= \Delta \cos\beta \cos(\lambda - \Omega), \\ y + Y_{,} &= \Delta \cos\beta \sin(\lambda - \Omega), \\ z + Z_{,} &= \Delta \sin\beta, \end{aligned}$$

in which λ is the geocentric longitude and β the geocentric latitude. In differentiating these equations so as to find the relation between the variations of the heliocentric co-ordinates and the geocentric longitude and latitude, we must regard ☊ as constant, since it indicates here the position of the axis of x in reference to the vernal equinox, and this position is supposed to be fixed. Therefore, we shall have

$$\begin{aligned} dx &= \cos\beta\cos(\lambda-\Omega)\,d\Delta - \Delta\sin\beta\cos(\lambda-\Omega)\,d\beta - \Delta\cos\beta\sin(\lambda-\Omega)\,d\lambda, \\ dy &= \cos\beta\sin(\lambda-\Omega)\,d\Delta - \Delta\sin\beta\sin(\lambda-\Omega)\,d\beta + \Delta\cos\beta\cos(\lambda-\Omega)\,d\lambda, \\ dz &= \sin\beta\,d\Delta + \Delta\cos\beta\,d\beta, \end{aligned}$$

from which, by elimination, we find

$$\cos\beta\,d\lambda = -\frac{\sin(\lambda-\Omega)}{\Delta}dx + \frac{\cos(\lambda-\Omega)}{\Delta}dy,$$

$$d\beta = -\frac{\sin\beta\cos(\lambda-\Omega)}{\Delta}dx - \frac{\sin\beta\sin(\lambda-\Omega)}{\Delta}dy + \frac{\cos\beta}{\Delta}dz.$$

These equations give

$$\begin{aligned} \cos\beta\frac{d\lambda}{dx} &= -\frac{\sin(\lambda-\Omega)}{\Delta}, & \frac{d\beta}{dx} &= -\frac{\sin\beta\cos(\lambda-\Omega)}{\Delta}, \\ \cos\beta\frac{d\lambda}{dy} &= \frac{\cos(\lambda-\Omega)}{\Delta}, & \frac{d\beta}{dy} &= -\frac{\sin\beta\sin(\lambda-\Omega)}{\Delta}, \quad (48) \\ \cos\beta\frac{d\lambda}{dz} &= 0, & \frac{d\beta}{dz} &= \frac{\cos\beta}{\Delta}. \end{aligned}$$

If we introduce the distance ω between the ascending node and the place of the perihelion as one of the elements of the orbit, we have

$$du = dv + d\omega,$$

and the equations (47) give

$$\frac{dx}{dr} = \frac{x}{r} = \cos u, \qquad \frac{dy}{dr} = \frac{y}{r} = \sin u\cos i, \qquad \frac{dz}{dr} = \frac{z}{r} = \sin u \sin i;$$

$$\frac{dx}{dv} = \frac{dx}{d\omega} = -r\sin u, \quad \frac{dy}{dv} = \frac{dy}{d\omega} = r\cos u\cos i, \quad \frac{dz}{dv} = \frac{dz}{d\omega} = r\cos u\sin i,$$

$$\frac{dx}{d\Omega}=-r\sin u\cos i,\quad \frac{dy}{d\Omega}=r\cos u,\quad \frac{dz}{d\Omega}=0;\tag{49}$$
$$\frac{dx}{di}=0,\quad \frac{dy}{di}=-r\sin u\sin i,\quad \frac{dz}{di}=r\sin u\cos i.$$

If we introduce π, the longitude of the perihelion, we have

$$du=dv+d\pi-d\Omega,$$

and hence the expressions for the partial differential coefficients of the heliocentric co-ordinates with respect to π and Ω become

$$\frac{dx}{d\pi}=-r\sin u,\quad \frac{dy}{d\pi}=r\cos u\cos i,\quad \frac{dz}{d\pi}=r\cos u\sin i;$$
$$\frac{dx}{d\Omega}=2r\sin u\sin^2\tfrac{1}{2}i,\quad \frac{dy}{d\Omega}=2r\cos u\sin^2\tfrac{1}{2}i,\quad \frac{dz}{d\Omega}=-r\cos u\sin i.\tag{50}$$

When the direct inclination exceeds 90° and the motion is regarded as being retrograde, we find, by making the necessary distinctions in regard to the algebraic signs in the general equations,

$$\frac{dx}{di}=0,\quad \frac{dy}{di}=r\sin u\sin i,\quad \frac{dz}{di}=-r\sin u\cos i;\tag{51}$$

and the expressions for $\frac{dx}{dr}$, $\frac{dx}{dv}$, $\frac{dx}{d\Omega}$, $\frac{dy}{dr}$, &c. are derived directly from (49) by writing $180°-i$ in place of i. If we introduce the longitude of the perihelion, we have, in this case,

$$du=dv-d\pi+d\Omega,$$

and hence

$$\frac{dx}{d\pi}=r\sin u,\quad \frac{dy}{d\pi}=r\cos u\cos i,\quad \frac{dz}{d\pi}=-r\cos u\sin i;$$
$$\frac{dx}{d\Omega}=-2r\sin u\sin^2\tfrac{1}{2}i,\quad \frac{dy}{d\Omega}=2r\cos u\sin^2\tfrac{1}{2}i,\quad \frac{dz}{d\Omega}=r\cos u\sin i.\tag{52}$$

But, to prevent confusion and the necessity of using so many formulæ, it is best to regard i as admitting any value from 0° to 180°, and to transform the elements which are given with the distinction of retrograde motion into those of the general case by taking $180°-i$ instead of i, and $2\Omega-\pi$ instead of π, the other elements remaining the same in both cases.

53. The equations already derived enable us to form those for the differential coefficients of λ and β with respect to r, v, Ω, i, and ω or π, by writing successively λ and β in place of θ, and Ω, i, &c. in

place of π in equation (2). The expressions for the differential coefficients of r and v, with respect to the elements which determine the form of the orbit and the position of the body in its orbit, being independent of the position of the plane of the orbit, are the same as those already given; and hence, according to (42) and (43), we may derive the values of the partial differential coefficients of λ and β with respect to these elements. The numerical application, however, is facilitated by the introduction of certain auxiliary quantities. Thus, if we substitute the values given by (48) and (49) in the equations

$$\cos\beta\frac{d\lambda}{dv}=\cos\beta\frac{d\lambda}{dx}\cdot\frac{dx}{dv}+\cos\beta\frac{d\lambda}{dy}\cdot\frac{dy}{dv},$$
$$\frac{d\beta}{dv}=\frac{d\beta}{dx}\cdot\frac{dx}{dv}+\frac{d\beta}{dy}\cdot\frac{dy}{dv}+\frac{d\beta}{dz}\cdot\frac{dz}{dv},$$

and put

$$\begin{aligned}\cos i\cos(\lambda-\Omega)&=A_0\sin A,\\ \sin(\lambda-\Omega)&=A_0\cos A,\\ \sin i&=n\sin N,\\ -\sin(\lambda-\Omega)\cos i&=n\cos N,\end{aligned}\tag{53}$$

in which A_0 and n are always positive, they become

$$\cos\beta\frac{d\lambda}{dv}=\cos\beta\frac{d\lambda}{d\omega}=\frac{r}{\Delta}A_0\sin(A+u),$$
$$\frac{d\beta}{dv}=\frac{d\beta}{d\omega}=\frac{r}{\Delta}(\sin\beta\cos(\lambda-\Omega)\sin u+n\cos u\sin(N+\beta)).$$

Let us also put

$$\begin{aligned}n\sin(N+\beta)&=B_0\sin B,\\ \sin\beta\cos(\lambda-\Omega)&=B_0\cos B,\end{aligned}\tag{54}$$

and we have

$$\begin{aligned}\cos\beta\frac{d\lambda}{dv}&=\cos\beta\frac{d\lambda}{d\omega}=\frac{r}{\Delta}A_0\sin(A+u),\\ \frac{d\beta}{dv}&=\frac{d\beta}{d\omega}=\frac{r}{\Delta}B_0\sin(B+u).\end{aligned}\tag{55}$$

The expressions for $\cos\beta\frac{d\lambda}{dr}$ and $\frac{d\beta}{dr}$ give, by means of the same auxiliary quantities,

$$\begin{aligned}\cos\beta\frac{d\lambda}{dr}&=-\frac{A_0}{\Delta}\cos(A+u),\\ \frac{d\beta}{dr}&=-\frac{B_0}{\Delta}\cos(B+u).\end{aligned}\tag{56}$$

In the same manner, if we put

$$\left.\begin{aligned}\cos(\lambda - \Omega) &= C_0 \sin C,\\ \cos i \sin(\lambda - \Omega) &= C_0 \cos C;\\ \cos i &= D_0 \sin D,\\ \sin(\lambda - \Omega)\sin i &= D_0 \cos D;\end{aligned}\right\} \qquad (57)$$

we obtain

$$\left.\begin{aligned}\cos\beta \frac{d\lambda}{d\Omega} &= \frac{r}{\Delta} C_0 \sin(C + u),\\ \frac{d\beta}{d\Omega} &= -\frac{r}{\Delta} A_0 \sin\beta \cos(A + u);\\ \cos\beta \frac{d\lambda}{di} &= -\frac{r}{\Delta} \sin i \sin u \cos(\lambda - \Omega),\\ \frac{d\beta}{di} &= \frac{\Delta}{r} D_0 \sin u \sin(D + \beta).\end{aligned}\right\} \qquad (58)$$

If we substitute the expressions (55) and (56) in the equations

$$\begin{aligned}\cos\beta \frac{d\lambda}{d\varphi} &= \cos\beta \frac{d\lambda}{dr} \cdot \frac{dr}{d\varphi} + \cos\beta \frac{d\lambda}{dv} \cdot \frac{dv}{d\varphi},\\ \frac{d\beta}{d\varphi} &= \frac{d\beta}{dr} \cdot \frac{dr}{d\varphi} + \frac{d\beta}{dv} \cdot \frac{dv}{d\varphi},\end{aligned}$$

and put

$$\left.\begin{aligned}-\frac{dr}{d\varphi} &= f \sin F = a \cos\varphi \cos v,\\ r\frac{dv}{d\varphi} &= f \cos F = \left(\frac{2}{\cos\varphi} + \tan\varphi \cos v\right) r \sin v,\end{aligned}\right\} \qquad (59)$$

we get

$$\left.\begin{aligned}\cos\beta \frac{d\lambda}{d\varphi} &= \frac{f}{\Delta} A_0 \sin(A + F + u),\\ \frac{d\beta}{d\varphi} &= \frac{f}{\Delta} B_0 \sin(B + F + u).\end{aligned}\right\} \qquad (60)$$

In a similar manner, if we put

$$\left.\begin{aligned}-\frac{dr}{dM_0} &= g \sin G = -a \tan\varphi \sin v,\\ r\frac{dv}{dM_0} &= g \cos G = \frac{a^2 \cos\varphi}{r},\\ -\frac{dr}{d\mu} &= h \sin H = -\left(a \tan\varphi \sin v (t - T) - \frac{2r}{3\mu} 206264.8\right),\\ r\frac{dv}{d\mu} &= h \cos H = \frac{a^2 \cos\varphi}{r}(t - T),\end{aligned}\right\} \qquad (61)$$

we obtain

$$
\begin{aligned}
\cos\beta\frac{d\lambda}{dM_0} &= \frac{g}{\varDelta}A_0\sin(A+G+u), \\
\frac{d\beta}{dM_0} &= \frac{g}{\varDelta}B_0\sin(B+G+u); \\
\cos\beta\frac{d\lambda}{d\mu} &= \frac{h}{\varDelta}A_0\sin(A+H+u), \\
\frac{d\beta}{d\mu} &= \frac{h}{\varDelta}B_0\sin(B+H+u).
\end{aligned}
\qquad (62)
$$

The quadrants in which the auxiliary angles must be taken are determined by the condition that A_0, B_0, C_0, f, g, and h are always positive.

54. If the elements T, q, and e are introduced in place of M_0, μ, and φ, we must put

$$
\begin{aligned}
f\sin F &= -\frac{dr}{de}, & f\cos F &= r\frac{dv}{de}, \\
g\sin G &= -\frac{dr}{dT}, & g\cos G &= r\frac{dv}{dT}, \\
h\sin H &= -\frac{dr}{dq}, & h\cos H &= r\frac{dv}{dq},
\end{aligned}
\qquad (63)
$$

and the equations become

$$
\begin{aligned}
\cos\beta\frac{d\lambda}{de} &= \frac{f}{\varDelta}A_0\sin(A+F+u), \\
\frac{d\beta}{de} &= \frac{f}{\varDelta}B_0\sin(B+F+u); \\
\cos\beta\frac{d\lambda}{dT} &= \frac{g}{\varDelta}A_0\sin(A+G+u), \\
\frac{d\beta}{dT} &= \frac{g}{\varDelta}B_0\sin(B+G+u); \\
\cos\beta\frac{d\lambda}{dq} &= \frac{h}{\varDelta}A_0\sin(A+H+u), \\
\frac{d\beta}{dq} &= \frac{h}{\varDelta}B_0\sin(B+H+u).
\end{aligned}
\qquad (64)
$$

In the numerical application of these formulæ, the values of the second members of the equations (63) are found as already exemplified for the cases of parabolic orbits and of elliptic and hyperbolic orbits in which the eccentricity differs but little from unity. In the same manner, the differential coefficients of λ and β with respect to any other elements which determine the form of the orbit may be computed.

In the case of a parabolic orbit, if the parabolic eccentricity is supposed to be invariable, the terms involving e vanish. Further, in the case of parabolic elements, we have

$$g \sin G = -\frac{dr}{dT} = \frac{k \sin v}{\sqrt{2q}} = -r \tan \tfrac{1}{2}v \frac{dv}{dT},$$

$$g \cos G = r\frac{dv}{dT},$$

which give

$$\tan G = -\tan \tfrac{1}{2}v.$$

Hence there results $G = 180° - \frac{1}{2}v$, and $g = k\sqrt{\frac{2}{r}}$, which is the expression for the linear velocity of a comet moving in a parabola. Therefore,

$$\begin{aligned} \cos\beta \frac{d\lambda}{dT} &= -\frac{k\sqrt{2}}{\Delta\sqrt{r}} A_0 \sin(A + u - \tfrac{1}{2}v), \\ \frac{d\beta}{dT} &= -\frac{k\sqrt{2}}{\Delta\sqrt{r}} B_0 \sin(B + u - \tfrac{1}{2}v). \end{aligned} \tag{65}$$

For the case in which the motion is considered as being retrograde, $180° - i$ must be used instead of i in computing the values of A_0, A, n, N, C_0, and C, and the equations (55), (56), and the first two of (58), remain unchanged. But, for the differential coefficients with respect to i, the values of D_0 and D must be found from the last two of equations (57), using the given value of i directly; and then we shall have

$$\begin{aligned} \cos\beta \frac{d\lambda}{di} &= \frac{r}{\Delta} \sin i \sin u \cos(\lambda - \Omega), \\ \frac{d\beta}{di} &= -\frac{r}{\Delta} D_0 \sin u \sin(D + \beta). \end{aligned} \tag{66}$$

55. Examples.—The equations thus derived for the differential coefficients of λ and β with respect to the elements of the orbit, referred to the ecliptic as the fundamental plane, are applicable when any other plane is taken as the fundamental plane, if we consider λ and β as having the same signification in reference to the new plane that they have in reference to the ecliptic, the longitudes, however, being measured from the place of the descending node of this plane on the ecliptic. To illustrate their numerical application, let it be required to find the differential coefficients of the geocentric right ascension and declination of *Eurynome* (79) with respect to the elements of its orbit referred to the equator, for the date 1865 February 24.5 mean time at Washington, using the data given in Art. 41.

In the first place, the elements which are referred to the ecliptic must be referred to the equator as the fundamental plane; and, by means of the equations $(109)_1$, we obtain

$$\Omega' = 353^\circ\ 45'\ 35''.87, \qquad i' = 19^\circ\ 26'\ 25''.76, \qquad \omega_0 = 212^\circ\ 32'\ 17''.71,$$

and

$$\omega' = \omega + \omega_0 = 50^\circ\ 10'\ 7''.29,$$

which are the elements which determine the position of the orbit in space when the equator is taken as the fundamental plane. These elements are referred to the mean equinox and equator of 1865.0. Writing α and δ in place of λ and β, and Ω', i', ω' in place of Ω, i, and ω, respectively, we have

$$\begin{aligned} A_0 \sin A &= \cos(\alpha - \Omega')\cos i', & A_0 \cos A &= \sin(\alpha - \Omega'); \\ n\ \sin N &= \sin i', & n\ \cos N &= -\cos i' \sin(\alpha - \Omega'); \\ B_0 \sin B &= n \sin(N + \delta), & B_0 \cos B &= \sin\delta \cos(\alpha - \Omega'); \\ C_0 \sin C &= \cos(\alpha - \Omega'), & C_0 \cos C &= \sin(\alpha - \Omega')\cos i'; \\ D_0 \sin D &= \cos i', & D_0 \cos D &= \sin i' \sin(\alpha - \Omega'); \end{aligned}$$

$$\begin{aligned} f \sin F &= a \cos\varphi \cos v, \\ f \cos F &= \left(\frac{2}{\cos\varphi} + \tan\varphi \cos v\right) r \sin v; \\ g \sin G &= -a \tan\varphi \sin v, \\ g \cos G &= \frac{a^2 \cos\varphi}{r}; \\ h \sin H &= -\left(a \tan\varphi \sin v\,(t - T) - \frac{2r}{3\mu}\,206264.8\right), \\ h \cos H &= \frac{a^2 \cos\varphi}{r}(t - T). \end{aligned}$$

The values of A_0, n, B_0, C_0, D_0, f, g, and h must always be positive, thus determining the quadrants in which the angles A, B, &c. must be taken; and these equations give

$$\begin{aligned} \log A_0 &= 9.97497, & A &= 262^\circ\ 10'\ 40'', \\ \log B_0 &= 9.52100, & B &= 75\ \ 48\ \ 35\ , \\ \log C_0 &= 9.99961, & C &= 263\ \ \ 2\ \ \ 6\ , \\ \log D_0 &= 9.97497, & D &= 92\ \ 35\ \ 47\ , \\ \log f &= 0.62946, & F &= 339\ \ 14\ \ \ 0\ , \\ \log g &= 0.34593, & G &= 350\ \ 11\ \ 16\ , \\ \log h &= 2.97759, & H &= 14\ \ 30\ \ 48\ , \end{aligned}$$

$$u' = v + \omega' = 179^\circ\ 13'\ 58''.$$

Substituting these values in the equations (55), (58), (60), and (62), and writing α and δ instead of λ and β, and u' in place of u, we find

$$\cos\delta\frac{d\alpha}{d\omega'} = +\,1.4235, \qquad \frac{d\delta}{d\omega'} = -\,0.4890,$$
$$\cos\delta\frac{d\alpha}{d\Omega'} = +\,1.5098, \qquad \frac{d\delta}{d\Omega'} = +\,0.0176,$$
$$\cos\delta\frac{d\alpha}{di'} = +\,0.0067, \qquad \frac{d\delta}{di'} = +\,0.0193,$$
$$\cos\delta\frac{d\alpha}{d\varphi} = +\,1.9940, \qquad \frac{d\delta}{d\varphi} = -\,0.6530,$$
$$\cos\delta\frac{d\alpha}{dM_0} = +\,1.1300, \qquad \frac{d\delta}{dM_0} = -\,0.3802,$$
$$\cos\delta\frac{d\alpha}{d\mu} = +\,507.25, \qquad \frac{d\delta}{d\mu} = -\,179.34;$$

and hence

$$\cos\delta\,\Delta\alpha = +\,1.4235\,\Delta\omega' + 1.5098\,\Delta\Omega' + 0.0067\,\Delta i' + 1.9940\,\Delta\varphi + 1.1300\,\Delta M_0 + 507.25\,\Delta\mu,$$
$$\Delta\delta = -\,0.4890\,\Delta\omega' + 0.0176\,\Delta\Omega' + 0.0193\,\Delta i' - 0.6530\,\Delta\varphi - 0.3802\,\Delta M_0 - 179.34\,\Delta\mu.$$

If we put

$$\Delta\omega' = -\,6''.64, \qquad \Delta\Omega' = -\,14''.12, \qquad \Delta i' = -\,8''.86,$$
$$\Delta\varphi = +\,10'', \qquad \Delta M_0 = +\,10'', \qquad \Delta\mu = +\,0''.01,$$

we get

$$\cos\delta\,\Delta\alpha = +\,5''.47, \qquad \Delta\delta = -\,9''.29;$$

and the values calculated directly from the elements corresponding to the increments thus assigned, are

$$\cos\delta\,\Delta\alpha = +\,5''.50, \qquad \Delta\delta = -\,9''.02.$$

The agreement of these results is sufficiently close to prove the calculation of the coefficients in the equations for $\cos\delta\,\Delta\alpha$ and $\Delta\delta$.

When the values of $\Delta\omega'$, $\Delta\Omega'$, and $\Delta i'$ are small, the corresponding values of $\Delta\omega$, $\Delta\Omega$, and Δi may be determined by means of differential formulæ. From the spherical triangle formed by the intersection of the planes of the orbit, ecliptic, and equator with the celestial vault, we have

$$\begin{aligned}
\cos i &= \cos i'\cos\varepsilon + \sin i'\sin\varepsilon\cos\Omega', \\
\sin i\cos\Omega &= -\cos i'\sin\varepsilon + \sin i'\cos\varepsilon\cos\Omega', \\
\sin i\sin\Omega &= \sin i'\sin\Omega', \\
\sin i\sin\omega_0 &= \sin\Omega'\sin\varepsilon, \\
\sin i\cos\omega_0 &= \cos\varepsilon\sin i' - \sin\varepsilon\cos i'\cos\Omega',
\end{aligned} \qquad (67)$$

from which the values of Ω, i, and ω_0 may be found from those of Ω' and i'. If we differentiate the first of these equations, regarding ε as constant, and reduce by means of the other given relations, we get

$$di = \cos\omega_0 \, di' + \sin\omega_0 \sin i' \, d\Omega'. \tag{68}$$

Interchanging i and $180° - i'$, and also Ω and Ω', we obtain

$$di' = \cos\omega_0 \, di - \sin\omega_0 \sin i \, d\Omega.$$

Eliminating di from these equations, and introducing the value

$$\frac{\sin i'}{\sin i} = \frac{\sin\Omega}{\sin\Omega'},$$

the result is

$$d\Omega = \frac{\sin\Omega}{\sin\Omega'} \cos\omega_0 \, d\Omega' - \frac{\sin\omega_0}{\sin i} \, di'. \tag{69}$$

If we differentiate the expression for $\cos\omega_0$ derived from the same spherical triangle, and reduce, we find

$$d\omega_0 = \cos i \, d\Omega - \cos i' \, d\Omega'.$$

Substituting for $d\Omega$ its value given by the preceding equation, and reducing by means of

$$\sin\Omega' \cos i' = \sin\Omega \cos\omega_0 \cos i - \cos\Omega \sin\omega_0,$$

we get

$$d\omega_0 = \frac{\sin\omega_0}{\sin\Omega'} \cos\Omega \, d\Omega' - \frac{\sin\omega_0}{\sin i} \cos i \, di'. \tag{70}$$

The equations (68), (69), and (70) give the partial differential coefficients of Ω, i, and ω_0 with respect to Ω' and i', and if we suppose the variations of the elements, expressed in parts of the radius as unity, to be so small that their squares may be neglected, we shall have

$$\begin{aligned}
\Delta\omega_0 &= \frac{\sin\omega_0}{\sin\Omega'} \cos\Omega \, \Delta\Omega' - \frac{\sin\omega_0}{\sin i} \cos i \, \Delta i', \\
\Delta\Omega &= \frac{\sin\Omega}{\sin\Omega'} \cos\omega_0 \, \Delta\Omega' - \frac{\sin\omega_0}{\sin i} \Delta i', \\
\Delta i &= \sin\omega_0 \sin i' \, \Delta\Omega' + \cos\omega_0 \, \Delta i', \\
\Delta\omega &= \Delta\omega' - \Delta\omega_0.
\end{aligned} \tag{71}$$

If we apply these formulæ to the case of *Eurynome*, the result is

$$\begin{aligned}
\Delta\omega_0 &= -4.420\Delta\Omega' + 6.665\Delta i', \\
\Delta\Omega &= -3.488\Delta\Omega' + 6.686\Delta i', \\
\Delta i &= -0.179\Delta\Omega' - 0.843\Delta i';
\end{aligned}$$

and if we assign the values

$$\Delta \Omega' = -14''.12, \qquad \Delta i' = -8''.86, \qquad \Delta\omega' = -6''.64,$$

we get

$$\Delta\omega_0 = +3''.36, \quad \Delta\Omega = -10''.0, \quad \Delta i = +10''.0, \quad \Delta\omega = -10''.0,$$

and, hence, the elements which determine the position of the orbit in reference to the ecliptic.

The elements ω', Ω', and i' may also be changed into those for which the ecliptic is the fundamental plane, by means of equations which may be derived from $(109)_1$ by interchanging Ω and Ω' and $180° - i'$ and i.

56. If we refer the geocentric places of the body to a plane whose inclination to the plane of the ecliptic is i, and the longitude of whose ascending node on the ecliptic is Ω,—which is equivalent to taking the plane of the orbit corresponding to the unchanged elements as the fundamental plane,—the equations are still further simplified. Let x', y', z' be the heliocentric co-ordinates of the body referred to a system of co-ordinates for which the plane of the unchanged orbit is the plane of xy, the positive axis of x being directed to the ascending node of this plane on the ecliptic; and let x, y, z be the heliocentric co-ordinates referred to a system in which the plane of xy is the plane of the ecliptic, the positive axis of x being directed to the point whose longitude is Ω. Then we shall have

$$\begin{aligned} dx' &= dx, \\ dy' &= dy \cos i + dz \sin i, \\ dz' &= -dy \sin i + dz \cos i. \end{aligned}$$

Substituting for dx, dy, and dz their values given by the equations (47), we get

$$\begin{aligned} dx' &= \frac{x'}{r} dr - r \sin u \, du - r \sin u \cos i \, d\Omega, \\ dy' &= \frac{y'}{r} dr + r \cos u \, du + r \cos u \cos i \, d\Omega, \\ dz' &= \frac{z'}{r} dr - r \cos u \sin i \, d\Omega + r \sin u \, di. \end{aligned}$$

It will be observed that we have, so long as the elements remain unchanged,

$$x' = r \cos u, \qquad y' = r \sin u, \qquad z' = 0,$$

and hence, omitting the accents, so that x, y, z will refer to the plane of the unchanged orbit as the plane of xy, the preceding equations give

$$\begin{aligned} dx &= \cos u\, dr - r \sin u\, du - r \sin u \cos i\, d\Omega, \\ dy &= \sin u\, dr + r \cos u\, du + r \cos u \cos i\, d\Omega, \\ dz &= - r \cos u \sin i\, d\Omega + r \sin u\, di. \end{aligned}$$

The value of ω is subject to two distinct changes, the one arising from the variation of the position of the orbit in its own plane, and the other, from the variation of the position of the plane of the orbit. Let us take a fixed line in the plane of the orbit and directed from the centre of the sun to a point the angular distance of which, back from the place of the ascending node on the ecliptic, we shall designate by σ; and let the angle between this fixed line and the semi-transverse axis be designated by χ. Then we have

$$\chi = \omega + \sigma.$$

The fixed line thus taken is supposed to be so situated that, so long as the position of the plane of the orbit remains unchanged, we have

$$\sigma = \Omega, \qquad \chi = \pi.$$

But if the elements which fix the position of the plane of the orbit are supposed to vary, we have the relations

$$\begin{aligned} d\sigma &= \cos i\, d\Omega, \\ d\omega &= d\chi - \cos i\, d\Omega, \\ d\pi &= d\chi + (1 - \cos i)\, d\Omega = d\chi + 2 \sin^2 \tfrac{1}{2} i\, d\Omega. \end{aligned} \tag{72}$$

Now, since $u = v + \omega$, we have

$$u = v + \chi - \sigma,$$

and

$$du = dv + d\chi - d\sigma = dv + d\chi - \cos i\, d\Omega.$$

Substituting this value of du in the equations for dx, dy, dz, they reduce to

$$\begin{aligned} dx &= \cos u\, dr - r \sin u\, dv - r \sin u\, d\chi, \\ dy &= \sin u\, dr + r \cos u\, dv + r \cos u\, d\chi, \\ dz &= - r \cos u \sin i\, d\Omega + r \sin u\, di. \end{aligned} \tag{73}$$

The inclination is here supposed to be susceptible of any value from 0° to 180°, and if the elements are given with the distinction of retrograde motion we must use $180° - i$ instead of i.

Let us now denote by θ the geocentric longitude of the body measured in the plane of the unchanged orbit (which is here taken as the fundamental plane) from the ascending node of this plane on the ecliptic, and let the geocentric latitude in reference to the same plane be denoted by η. Then we shall have

$$\begin{aligned} x + X &= \varDelta \cos\eta \cos\theta, \\ y + Y &= \varDelta \cos\eta \sin\theta, \\ z + Z &= \varDelta \sin\eta, \end{aligned}$$

in which X, Y, Z are the geocentric co-ordinates of the sun referred to the same system of co-ordinates as x, y, and z. These equations give, by differentiation,

$$\begin{aligned} dx &= \cos\eta \cos\theta \, d\varDelta - \varDelta \sin\eta \cos\theta \, d\eta - \varDelta \cos\eta \sin\theta \, d\theta, \\ dy &= \cos\eta \sin\theta \, d\varDelta - \varDelta \sin\eta \sin\theta \, d\eta + \varDelta \cos\eta \cos\theta \, d\theta, \\ dz &= \sin\eta \, d\varDelta + \varDelta \cos\eta \, d\eta; \end{aligned}$$

and hence we obtain

$$\begin{aligned} \cos\eta \, d\theta &= -\frac{\sin\theta}{\varDelta} dx + \frac{\cos\theta}{\varDelta} dy, \\ d\eta &= -\frac{\sin\eta \cos\theta}{\varDelta} dx - \frac{\sin\eta \sin\theta}{\varDelta} dy + \frac{\cos\eta}{\varDelta} dz. \end{aligned}$$

These give

$$\begin{aligned} &\cos\eta \frac{d\theta}{dx} = -\frac{\sin\theta}{\varDelta}, \qquad \cos\eta \frac{d\theta}{dy} = \frac{\cos\theta}{\varDelta}, \qquad \cos\eta \frac{d\theta}{dz} = 0; \\ &\frac{d\eta}{dx} = -\frac{\sin\eta \cos\theta}{\varDelta}, \qquad \frac{d\eta}{dy} = -\frac{\sin\eta \sin\theta}{\varDelta}, \qquad \frac{d\eta}{dz} = \frac{\cos\eta}{\varDelta}; \end{aligned} \tag{74}$$

and from (73) we get

$$\begin{aligned} &\frac{dx}{dr} = \cos u, \qquad \frac{dy}{dr} = \sin u, \qquad \frac{dz}{dr} = 0; \\ &\frac{dx}{dv} = \frac{dx}{d\chi} = -r \sin u, \qquad \frac{dy}{dv} = \frac{dy}{d\chi} = r \cos u, \qquad \frac{dz}{dv} = \frac{dz}{d\chi} = 0; \\ &\frac{dx}{d\Omega} = 0, \qquad \frac{dy}{d\Omega} = 0, \qquad \frac{dz}{d\Omega} = -r \cos u \sin i; \\ &\frac{dx}{di} = 0, \qquad \frac{dy}{di} = 0, \qquad \frac{dz}{di} = r \sin u. \end{aligned} \tag{75}$$

Substituting the values thus found, in the equations

$$\begin{aligned} \cos\eta \frac{d\theta}{dv} &= \cos\eta \frac{d\theta}{dx} \cdot \frac{dx}{dv} + \cos\eta \frac{d\theta}{dy} \cdot \frac{dy}{dv}, \\ \frac{d\eta}{dv} &= \frac{d\eta}{dx} \cdot \frac{dx}{dv} + \frac{d\eta}{dy} \cdot \frac{dy}{dv} + \frac{d\eta}{dz} \cdot \frac{dz}{dv}, \end{aligned}$$

we get

$$\cos\eta\frac{d\theta}{dv}=\cos\eta\frac{d\theta}{d\chi}=\frac{r}{\varDelta}\cos(\theta-u),$$
$$\frac{d\eta}{dv}=\frac{d\eta}{d\chi}=-\frac{r}{\varDelta}\sin\eta\sin(\theta-u). \tag{76}$$

In a similar manner, we derive

$$\cos\eta\frac{d\theta}{dr}=-\frac{1}{\varDelta}\sin(\theta-u),\qquad \frac{d\eta}{dr}=-\frac{1}{\varDelta}\sin\eta\cos(\theta-u),$$
$$\cos\eta\frac{d\theta}{d\Omega}=0,\qquad \frac{d\eta}{d\Omega}=-\frac{r}{\varDelta}\cos\eta\sin i\cos u, \tag{77}$$
$$\cos\eta\frac{d\theta}{di}=0,\qquad \frac{d\eta}{di}=+\frac{r}{\varDelta}\cos\eta\sin u.$$

If we introduce the elements φ, M_0, and μ, which determine r and v, we have, from

$$\cos\eta\frac{d\theta}{d\varphi}=\cos\eta\frac{d\theta}{dr}\cdot\frac{dr}{d\varphi}+\cos\eta\frac{d\theta}{dv}\cdot\frac{dv}{d\varphi},$$
$$\frac{d\eta}{d\varphi}=\frac{d\eta}{dr}\cdot\frac{dr}{d\varphi}+\frac{d\eta}{dv}\cdot\frac{dv}{d\varphi},$$

if we introduce also the auxiliary quantities f and F, as determined by means of the equations (59),

$$\cos\eta\frac{d\theta}{d\varphi}=\frac{f}{\varDelta}\cos(\theta-u-F),\qquad \frac{d\eta}{d\varphi}=-\frac{f}{\varDelta}\sin\eta\sin(\theta-u-F). \tag{78}$$

Finally, using the auxiliaries g, h, G, and H, according to the equations (61), we get

$$\cos\eta\frac{d\theta}{dM_0}=\frac{g}{\varDelta}\cos(\theta-u-G),\qquad \frac{d\eta}{dM_0}=-\frac{g}{\varDelta}\sin\eta\sin(\theta-u-G),$$
$$\cos\eta\frac{d\theta}{d\mu}=\frac{h}{\varDelta}\cos(\theta-u-H),\qquad \frac{d\eta}{d\mu}=-\frac{h}{\varDelta}\sin\eta\sin(\theta-u-H). \tag{79}$$

If we express r and v in terms of the elements T, q, and e, the values of the auxiliaries f, g, h, F, &c. must be found by means of (64); and, in the same manner, any other elements which determine the form of the orbit and the position of the body in its orbit, may be introduced.

The partial differential coefficients with respect to the elements having been found, we have

$$\cos\eta\,\Delta\theta=\cos\eta\frac{d\theta}{d\chi}\Delta\chi+\cos\eta\frac{d\theta}{d\varphi}\Delta\varphi+\cos\eta\frac{d\theta}{dM_0}\Delta M_0+\cos\eta\frac{d\theta}{d\mu}\Delta\mu,$$
$$\Delta\eta=\frac{d\eta}{d\Omega}\Delta\Omega+\frac{d\eta}{di}\Delta i+\frac{d\eta}{d\chi}\Delta\chi+\frac{d\eta}{d\varphi}\Delta\varphi+\frac{d\eta}{dM_0}\Delta M_0+\frac{d\eta}{d\mu}\Delta\mu,$$

from which it appears that, by the introduction of χ as one of the elements of the orbit, when the geocentric places are referred directly to the plane of the unchanged orbit as the fundamental plane, the variation of the geocentric longitude in reference to this plane depends on only four elements.

57. It remains now to derive the formulæ for finding the values of η and θ from those of λ and β. Let x_0, y_0, z_0 be the geocentric co-ordinates of the body referred to a system in which the ecliptic is the plane of xy, the positive axis of x being directed to the point whose longitude is ☊; and let x_0', y_0', z_0' be the geocentric co-ordinates of the body referred to a system in which the axis of x remains the same, but in which the plane of the unchanged orbit is the plane of xy; then we shall have

$$\begin{aligned} x_0 &= \varDelta \cos\beta \cos(\lambda - ☊), & x_0' &= \varDelta \cos\eta \cos\theta, \\ y_0 &= \varDelta \cos\beta \sin(\lambda - ☊), & y_0' &= \varDelta \cos\eta \sin\theta, \\ z_0 &= \varDelta \sin\beta, & z_0' &= \varDelta \sin\eta, \end{aligned}$$

and also

$$\begin{aligned} x_0' &= x_0, \\ y_0' &= y_0 \cos i + z_0 \sin i, \\ z_0' &= -y_0 \sin i + z_0 \cos i. \end{aligned}$$

Hence we obtain

$$\begin{aligned} \cos\eta \cos\theta &= \cos\beta \cos(\lambda - ☊), \\ \cos\eta \sin\theta &= \cos\beta \sin(\lambda - ☊) \cos i + \sin\beta \sin i, \\ \sin\eta &= -\cos\beta \sin(\lambda - ☊) \sin i + \sin\beta \cos i. \end{aligned} \tag{80}$$

These equations correspond to the relations between the parts of a spherical triangle of which the sides are i, $90° - \eta$, and $90° - \beta$, the angles opposite to $90° - \eta$ and $90° - \beta$ being respectively $90° + (\lambda - ☊)$ and $90° - \theta$. Let the other angle of the triangle be denoted by γ, and we have

$$\begin{aligned} \cos\eta \sin\gamma &= \sin i \cos(\lambda - ☊), \\ \cos\eta \cos\gamma &= \sin i \sin(\lambda - ☊) \sin\beta + \cos i \cos\beta. \end{aligned} \tag{81}$$

The equations thus obtained enable us to determine η, θ, and γ from λ and β. Their numerical application is facilitated by the introduction of auxiliary angles. Thus, if we put

$$\begin{aligned} n \sin N &= \sin\beta, \\ n \cos N &= \cos\beta \sin(\lambda - ☊), \end{aligned} \tag{82}$$

in which n is always positive, we get

$$\begin{aligned}\cos\eta\cos\theta &= \cos\beta\cos(\lambda - \Omega),\\ \cos\eta\sin\theta &= n\cos(N - i),\\ \sin\eta &= n\sin(N - i),\end{aligned} \qquad (83)$$

from which η and θ may be readily found. If we also put

$$\begin{aligned}n'\sin N' &= \cos i,\\ n'\cos N' &= \sin i\sin(\lambda - \Omega),\end{aligned} \qquad (84)$$

we shall have

$$\begin{aligned}\cot N' &= \tan i\sin(\lambda - \Omega),\\ \tan\gamma &= \frac{\cos N'}{\cos(N' + \beta)}\cot(\lambda - \Omega).\end{aligned} \qquad (85)$$

If γ is small, it may be found from the equation

$$\sin\gamma = \frac{\sin i\cos(\lambda - \Omega)}{\cos\eta}. \qquad (86)$$

The quadrants in which the angles sought must be taken, are easily determined by the relations of the quantities involved ; and the accuracy of the numerical calculation may be checked as already illustrated for similar cases.

If we apply Gauss's analogies to the same spherical triangle, we get

$$\begin{aligned}&\sin(45° - \tfrac{1}{2}\eta)\sin(45° - \tfrac{1}{2}(\theta + \gamma)) =\\ &\qquad\cos(45° + \tfrac{1}{2}(\lambda - \Omega))\sin(45° - \tfrac{1}{2}(\beta + i)),\\ &\sin(45° - \tfrac{1}{2}\eta)\cos(45° - \tfrac{1}{2}(\theta + \gamma)) =\\ &\qquad\sin(45° + \tfrac{1}{2}(\lambda - \Omega))\sin(45° - \tfrac{1}{2}(\beta - i)),\\ &\cos(45° - \tfrac{1}{2}\eta)\sin(45° - \tfrac{1}{2}(\theta - \gamma)) = \qquad (87)\\ &\qquad\cos(45° + \tfrac{1}{2}(\lambda - \Omega))\cos(45° - \tfrac{1}{2}(\beta + i)),\\ &\cos(45° - \tfrac{1}{2}\eta)\cos(45° - \tfrac{1}{2}(\theta - \gamma)) =\\ &\qquad\sin(45° + \tfrac{1}{2}(\lambda - \Omega))\cos(45° - \tfrac{1}{2}(\beta - i)),\end{aligned}$$

from which we may derive η, θ, and γ.

When the problem is to determine the corrections to be applied to the elements of the orbit of a heavenly body, in order to satisfy given observed places, it is necessary to find the expressions for $\cos\eta\,\Delta\theta$ and $\Delta\eta$ in terms of $\cos\beta\,\Delta\lambda$ and $\Delta\beta$. If we differentiate the first and second of equations (80), regarding Ω and i (which here determine the position of the fundamental plane adopted) as constant, eliminate the terms containing $d\eta$ from the resulting equations, and reduce by means of the relations of the parts of the spherical triangle, we get

$$\cos\eta\, d\theta = \cos\gamma \cos\beta\, d\lambda + \sin\gamma\, d\beta.$$

Differentiating the last of equations (80), and reducing, we find

$$d\eta = -\sin\gamma \cos\beta\, d\lambda + \cos\gamma\, d\beta.$$

The equations thus derived give the values of the differential coefficients of θ and η with respect to λ and β; and if the differences $\Delta\lambda$ and $\Delta\beta$ are small, we shall have

$$\begin{aligned} \cos\eta\, \Delta\theta &= \cos\gamma \cos\beta\, \Delta\lambda + \sin\gamma\, \Delta\beta, \\ \Delta\eta &= -\sin\gamma \cos\beta\, \Delta\lambda + \cos\gamma\, \Delta\beta. \end{aligned} \tag{88}$$

The value of γ required in the application of numbers to these equations may generally be derived with sufficient accuracy from (86), the algebraic sign of $\cos\gamma$ being indicated by the second of equations (81); and the values of η and θ required in the calculation of the differential coefficients of these quantities with respect to the elements of the orbit, need not be determined with extreme accuracy.

58. Example.—Since the spherical co-ordinates which are furnished directly by observation are the right ascension and declination, the formulæ will be most frequently required in the form for finding η and θ from α and δ. For this purpose, it is only necessary to write α and δ in place of λ and β, respectively, and also Ω', i', ω', χ', and u' in place of Ω, i, ω, χ, and u, in the equations which have been derived for the determination of η and θ, and for the differential coefficients of these quantities with respect to the elements of the orbit.

To illustrate this clearly, let it be required to find the expressions for $\cos\eta\, \Delta\theta$ and $\Delta\eta$ in terms of the variations of the elements in the case of the example already given; for which we have

$$\omega' = 50°\ 10'\ 7''.29, \qquad \Omega' = 353°\ 45'\ 35''.87, \qquad i' = 19°\ 26'\ 25''.76.$$

These are the elements which determine the position of the orbit of *Eurynome* (79), referred to the mean equinox and equator of 1865.0. We have, further,

$$\begin{aligned} &\log f = 0.62946, &&\log g = 0.34593, &&\log h = 2.97759, \\ &F = 339°\ 14'\ 0'', &&G = 350°\ 11'\ 16'', &&H = 14°\ 30'\ 48'', \\ &&&u' = 179°\ 13'\ 58''. \end{aligned}$$

In the first place, we compute η, θ, and γ by means of the formulæ

(83) and (85), or by means of (87), writing α, δ, Ω', and i' instead of λ, β, Ω, and i, respectively. Hence we obtain

$$\theta = 188^\circ\, 31'\, 9'', \qquad \eta = -1^\circ\, 59'\, 28'', \qquad \gamma = -19^\circ\, 17'\, 7''.$$

Since the equator is here considered as the fundamental plane, the longitude θ is measured on the equator from the place of the ascending node of the orbit on this plane. The values of the differential coefficients are then found by means of the formulæ

$$\begin{aligned}
\cos\eta \frac{d\theta}{d\Omega'} &= 0, & \frac{d\eta}{d\Omega'} &= -\frac{r}{\Delta}\cos\eta\sin i'\cos u', \\
\cos\eta \frac{d\theta}{di'} &= 0, & \frac{d\eta}{di'} &= +\frac{r}{\Delta}\cos\eta\sin u', \\
\cos\eta \frac{d\theta}{d\chi'} &= \frac{r}{\Delta}\cos(\theta - u'), & \frac{d\eta}{d\chi'} &= -\frac{r}{\Delta}\sin\eta\sin(\theta - u'), \\
\cos\eta \frac{d\theta}{d\varphi} &= \frac{f}{\Delta}\cos(\theta - u' - F), & \frac{d\eta}{d\varphi} &= -\frac{f}{\Delta}\sin\eta\sin(\theta - u' - F), \\
\cos\eta \frac{d\theta}{dM_0} &= \frac{g}{\Delta}\cos(\theta - u' - G), & \frac{d\eta}{dM_0} &= -\frac{g}{\Delta}\sin\eta\sin(\theta - u' - G), \\
\cos\eta \frac{d\theta}{d\mu} &= \frac{h}{\Delta}\cos(\theta - u' - H), & \frac{d\eta}{d\mu} &= -\frac{h}{\Delta}\sin\eta\sin(\theta - u' - H),
\end{aligned}$$

which give

$$\begin{aligned}
\cos\eta \frac{d\theta}{d\Omega'} &= 0, & \frac{d\eta}{d\Omega'} &= +0.5072, \\
\cos\eta \frac{d\theta}{di'} &= 0, & \frac{d\eta}{di'} &= +0.0204, \\
\cos\eta \frac{d\theta}{d\chi'} &= +1.5051, & \frac{d\eta}{d\chi'} &= +0.0086, \\
\cos\eta \frac{d\theta}{d\varphi} &= +2.0978, & \frac{d\eta}{d\varphi} &= +0.0422, \\
\cos\eta \frac{d\theta}{dM_0} &= +1.1922, & \frac{d\eta}{dM_0} &= +0.0143, \\
\cos\eta \frac{d\theta}{d\mu} &= +538.00, & \frac{d\eta}{d\mu} &= -1.71.
\end{aligned}$$

Therefore, the equations for $\cos\eta\,\Delta\theta$ and $\Delta\eta$ become

$$\begin{aligned}
\cos\eta\,\Delta\theta &= +1.5051\,\Delta\chi' + 2.0978\,\Delta\varphi + 1.1922\,\Delta M_0 + 538.00\,\Delta\mu, \\
\Delta\eta &= +0.0086\,\Delta\chi' + 0.0422\,\Delta\varphi + 0.0143\,\Delta M_0 - 1.71\,\Delta\mu \\
&\quad + 0.5072\,\Delta\Omega' + 0.0204\,\Delta i'.
\end{aligned}$$

If we assign to the elements of the orbit the variations

$$\Delta\omega' = -6''.64, \qquad \Delta\Omega' = -14''.12, \qquad \Delta i' = -8''.86,$$
$$\Delta\varphi = +10'', \qquad \Delta M_0 = +10'', \qquad \Delta\mu = +0''.01,$$

we have

$$\Delta\chi' = \Delta\omega' + \cos i' \,\Delta\Omega' = -19''.96;$$

and the preceding equations give

$$\cos\eta \,\Delta\theta = +8''.24, \qquad \Delta\eta = -6''.96.$$

With the same values of $\Delta\omega'$, $\Delta\Omega'$, &c., we have already found

$$\cos\delta \,\Delta\alpha = +5''.47, \qquad \Delta\delta = -9''.29,$$

which, by means of the equations (88), writing α and δ in place of λ and β, give

$$\cos\eta \,\Delta\theta = +8''.23, \qquad \Delta\eta = -6''.96.$$

59. In special cases, in which the differences between the calculated and the observed values of two spherical co-ordinates are given, and the corrections to be applied to the assumed elements are sought, it may become necessary, on account of difficulties to be encountered in the solution of the equations of condition, to introduce other elements of the orbit of the body. The relation of the elements chosen to those commonly used will serve, without presenting any difficulty, for the transformation of the equations into a form adapted to the special case. Thus, in the case of the elements which determine the form of the orbit, we may use a or $\log a$ instead of μ, and the equation

$$\mu = \frac{k\sqrt{1+m}}{a^{\frac{3}{2}}}$$

gives

$$d\mu = -\tfrac{3}{2}\frac{\mu}{a}\,da = -\tfrac{3}{2}\frac{\mu}{\lambda_0}\,d\log a, \tag{89}$$

in which λ_0 is the modulus of the system of logarithms. Therefore, the coefficient of $\Delta\mu$ is transformed into that of $\Delta \log a$ by multiplying it by $-\tfrac{3}{2}\frac{\mu}{\lambda_0}$; and if the unit of the mth decimal place of the logarithms is taken as the unit of $\Delta \log a$, the coefficient must be also multiplied by 10^{-m}. The homogeneity of the equation is not disturbed, since μ is here supposed to be expressed in seconds.

If we introduce $\log p$ as one of the elements, from the equation

$$p = a\cos^2\varphi$$

we get

$$d \log p = -\tfrac{2}{3}\frac{\lambda_0}{\mu}\, d\mu - 2\lambda_0 \tan\varphi\, d\varphi,$$

or

$$d\mu = -\tfrac{3}{2}\frac{\mu}{\lambda_0}\, d\log p - 3\mu \tan\varphi\, d\varphi. \qquad (90)$$

Hence it appears that the coefficients of $\Delta \log p$ are the same as those of $\Delta \log a$, but since p is also a function of φ, the coefficients of $\Delta\varphi$ are changed; and if we denote by $\cos\delta\left(\frac{d\alpha}{d\varphi}\right)$ and $\left(\frac{d\delta}{d\varphi}\right)$ the values of the partial differential coefficients when the element μ is used in connection with φ, we shall have, for the case under consideration,

$$\cos\delta\frac{d\alpha}{d\varphi} = \cos\delta\left(\frac{d\alpha}{d\varphi}\right) - 3\frac{\mu}{s}\tan\varphi\cos\delta\frac{d\alpha}{d\mu},$$

$$\frac{d\delta}{d\varphi} = \left(\frac{d\delta}{d\varphi}\right) - 3\frac{\mu}{s}\tan\varphi\frac{d\delta}{d\mu},$$

in which $s = 206264''.8$. If the values of the differential coefficients with respect to μ and φ have not already been found, it will be advantageous to compute the values of $\frac{dr}{d\varphi}, \frac{dv}{d\varphi}, \frac{dr}{d\log p}$, and $\frac{dv}{d\log p}$ by means of the expressions which may be derived by substituting in the equations (15) the value of $d\mu$ given by (90), and then we may compute directly the values of $\cos\delta\frac{d\alpha}{d\varphi}$, $\cos\delta\frac{d\alpha}{d\log p}$, $\frac{d\delta}{d\varphi}$, and $\frac{d\delta}{d\log p}$.

In place of M_0, it is often convenient to introduce L_0, the mean longitude for the epoch; and since

$$L_0 = M_0 + \pi,$$

we have

$$dL_0 = dM_0 + d\pi = dM_0 + d\omega + d\Omega,$$

and, when χ is used,

$$dL_0 = dM_0 + d\chi + (1 - \cos i)\, d\Omega.$$

Instead of the elements Ω and i which indicate the position of the plane of the orbit, we may use

$$b = \sin i \sin\Omega, \qquad c = \sin i \cos\Omega,$$

and the expressions for the relations between the differentials of b and c and those of i and Ω are easily derived. The cosines of the angles which the line of apsides or any other line in the orbit makes with the three co-ordinate axes, may also be taken as elements of the orbit in the formation of the equations for the variation of the geocentric place.

60. The equations (48), by writing l and b in place of λ and β, respectively, will give the values of the differential coefficients of the heliocentric longitude and latitude with respect to x, y, and z. Combining these with the expressions for the differential coefficients of the heliocentric co-ordinates with respect to the elements of the orbit, we obtain the values of $\cos b\ \Delta l$ and Δb in terms of the variations of the elements.

The equations for dx, dy, and dz in terms of du, $d\Omega$, and di, may also be used to determine the corrections to be applied to the co-ordinates in order to reduce them from the ecliptic and mean equinox of one epoch to those of another, or to the apparent equinox of the date. In this case, we have

$$du = d\pi - d\Omega.$$

When the auxiliary constants A, B, a, b, &c. are introduced, to find the variations of these arising from the variations assigned to the elements, we have, from the equations $(99)_1$,

$$\begin{aligned}
\cot A &= -\tan\Omega\cos i,\\
\cot B &= \cot\Omega\cos i - \sin i\ \mathrm{cosec}\,\Omega\tan\varepsilon,\\
\cot C &= \cot\Omega\cos i + \sin i\ \mathrm{cosec}\,\Omega\cot\varepsilon,
\end{aligned}$$

in which i may have any value from 0° to 180°. If we differentiate these, regarding all the quantities involved as variable, and reduce by means of the values of $\sin a$, $\sin b$, and $\sin c$, we get

$$\begin{aligned}
dA &= \frac{\cos i}{\sin^2 a}\,d\Omega - \frac{\sin A}{\sin a}\sin\Omega\sin i\,di,\\
dB &= \frac{\cos\varepsilon}{\sin^2 b}(\cos i\cos\varepsilon - \sin i\sin\varepsilon\cos\Omega)\,d\Omega\\
&\quad + \frac{\sin B}{\sin b}(\cos\Omega\sin i\cos\varepsilon + \cos i\sin\varepsilon)\,di + \frac{\sin i\sin\Omega}{\sin^2 b}\,d\varepsilon,\\
dC &= \frac{\sin\varepsilon}{\sin^2 c}(\cos i\sin\varepsilon + \sin i\cos\varepsilon\cos\Omega)\,d\Omega\\
&\quad + \frac{\sin C}{\sin c}(\cos\Omega\sin i\sin\varepsilon - \cos i\cos\varepsilon)\,di + \frac{\sin i\sin\Omega}{\sin^2 c}\,d\varepsilon;
\end{aligned}$$

and these, by means of $(101)_1$, reduce to

$$dA = \frac{\cos i}{\sin^2 a} d\Omega - \sin A \cot a \, di,$$

$$dB = \frac{\cos \varepsilon \cos c}{\sin^2 b} d\Omega - \sin B \cot b \, di + \frac{\cos a}{\sin^2 b} d\varepsilon, \tag{91}$$

$$dC = -\frac{\sin \varepsilon \cos b}{\sin^2 c} d\Omega - \sin C \cot c \, di + \frac{\cos a}{\sin^2 c} d\varepsilon.$$

Let us now differentiate the equations $(101)_1$, using only the upper sign, and the result is

$$\begin{aligned} da &= -\sin i \sin A \, d\Omega + \cos A \, di, \\ db &= -\sin i \sin B \, d\Omega + \cos B \, di + \cos c \operatorname{cosec} b \, d\varepsilon, \\ dc &= -\sin i \sin C \, d\Omega + \cos C \, di - \cos b \operatorname{cosec} c \, d\varepsilon. \end{aligned}$$

If we multiply the first of these equations by $\cot a$, the second by $\cot b$, and the third by $\cot c$, and denote by λ_0 the modulus of the system of logarithms, we get

$$\begin{aligned} d \log \sin a &= -\lambda_0 \sin i \cot a \sin A \, d\Omega + \lambda_0 \cot a \cos A \, di, \\ d \log \sin b &= -\lambda_0 \sin i \cot b \sin B \, d\Omega + \lambda_0 \cot b \cos B \, di + \lambda_0 \frac{\cos b \cos c}{\sin^2 b} d\varepsilon, \\ d \log \sin c &= -\lambda_0 \sin i \cot c \sin C \, d\Omega + \lambda_0 \cot c \cos C \, di - \lambda_0 \frac{\cos b \cos c}{\sin^2 c} d\varepsilon. \end{aligned} \tag{92}$$

The equations (91) and (92) furnish the differential coefficients of A, B, C, $\log \sin a$, &c. with respect to Ω, i, and ε; and if the variations assigned to Ω, i, and ε are so small that their squares may be neglected, the same equations, writing ΔA, $\Delta \Omega$, Δi, &c. instead of the differentials, give the variations of the auxiliary constants. In the case of equations (92), if the variations of Ω, i, and ε are expressed in seconds, each term of the second member must be divided by 206264.8, and if the variations of $\log \sin a$, $\log \sin b$, and $\log \sin c$ are required in units of the mth decimal place of the logarithms, each term of the second member must also be divided by 10^m.

If we differentiate the equations $(81)_1$, and reduce by means of the same equations, we easily find

$$\begin{aligned} \cos b \, dl &= \cos i \sec b \, du + \cos b \, d\Omega - \sin b \cos(l - \Omega) \, di, \\ db &= \sin i \cos(l - \Omega) \, du + \sin(l - \Omega) \, di, \end{aligned} \tag{93}$$

which determine the relations between the variations of the elements of the orbit and those of the heliocentric longitude and latitude.

By differentiating the equations $(88)_1$, neglecting the latitude of the sun, and considering λ, β, Δ, and $\odot$ as variables, we derive, after reduction,

$$\begin{aligned} \cos\beta\, d\lambda &= \frac{R}{\Delta}\cos(\lambda - \odot)\, d\odot, \\ d\beta &= -\frac{R}{\Delta}\sin\beta \sin(\lambda - \odot)\, d\odot, \end{aligned} \tag{94}$$

which determine the variation of the geocentric latitude and longitude arising from an increment assigned to the longitude of the sun. It appears, therefore, that an error in the longitude of the sun will produce the greatest error in the computed geocentric longitude of a heavenly body when the body is in opposition.

CHAPTER III.

INVESTIGATION OF FORMULÆ FOR COMPUTING THE ORBIT OF A COMET MOVING IN A PARABOLA, AND FOR CORRECTING APPROXIMATE ELEMENTS BY THE VARIATION OF THE GEOCENTRIC DISTANCE.

61. THE observed spherical co-ordinates of the place of a heavenly body furnish each one equation of condition for the correction of the elements of its orbit approximately known, and similarly for the determination of the elements in the case of an orbit wholly unknown; and since there are six *elements*, neglecting the mass,—which must always be done in the first approximation, the perturbations not being considered,—three complete observations will furnish the six equations necessary for finding these unknown quantities. Hence, the data required for the determination of the orbit of a heavenly body are three complete observations, namely, three observed longitudes and the corresponding latitudes, or any other spherical co-ordinates which completely determine three places of the body as seen from the earth. Since these observations are given as made at some point or at different points on the earth's surface, it becomes necessary in the first place to apply the corrections for parallax. In the case of a body whose orbit is wholly unknown, it is impossible to apply the correction for parallax directly to the place of the body; but an equivalent correction may be applied to the places of the earth, according to the formulæ which will be given in the next chapter. However, in the first determination of approximate elements of the orbit of a comet, it will be sufficient to neglect entirely the correction for parallax. The uncertainty of the observed places of these bodies is so much greater than in the case of well-defined objects like the planets, and the intervals between the observations which will be generally employed in the first determination of the orbit will be so small, that an attempt to represent the observed places with extreme accuracy will be superfluous.

When approximate elements have been derived, we may find the distances of the comet from the earth corresponding to the three observed places, and hence determine the parallax in right ascension and in declination for each observation by means of the usual formulæ. Thus, we have

$$\Delta\alpha = -\frac{\pi\rho\cos\varphi'}{\varDelta} \cdot \frac{\sin(\alpha - \Theta)}{\cos\delta},$$

$$\tan\gamma = \frac{\tan\varphi'}{\cos(\alpha - \Theta)},$$

$$\Delta\delta = \frac{\pi\rho\sin\varphi'}{\varDelta} \cdot \frac{\sin(\gamma - \delta)}{\sin\gamma},$$

in which α is the right ascension, δ the declination, $\varDelta$ the distance of the comet from the earth, φ' the geocentric latitude of the place of observation, Θ the sidereal time corresponding to the time of observation, ρ the radius of the earth expressed in parts of the equatorial radius, and π the equatorial horizontal parallax of the sun.

In order to obtain the most accurate representation of the observed place by means of the elements computed, the correction for aberration must also be applied. When the distance $\varDelta$ is known, the time of observation may be corrected for the time of aberration; but if $\varDelta$ is not approximately known, this correction may be neglected in the first approximation.

The transformation of the observed right ascension and declination into latitude and longitude is effected by means of the equations which may be derived from $(92)_1$ by interchanging α and λ, δ and β, and writing $-\varepsilon$ instead of ε. Thus, we have

$$\begin{aligned} \tan N &= \frac{\tan\delta}{\sin\alpha}, \\ \tan\lambda &= \frac{\cos(N - \varepsilon)}{\cos N}\tan\alpha, \\ \tan\beta &= \tan(N - \varepsilon)\sin\lambda, \end{aligned} \qquad (1)$$

and also

$$\frac{\cos(N - \varepsilon)}{\cos N} = \frac{\cos\beta\sin\lambda}{\cos\delta\sin\alpha},$$

which will serve to check the numerical calculation of λ and β. Since $\cos\beta$ and $\cos\delta$ are always positive, $\cos\lambda$ and $\cos\alpha$ must have the same sign, thus determining the quadrant in which λ is to be taken.

62. As soon as these preliminary corrections and transformations have been effected, and the times of observation have been reduced to the same meridian, the longitudes having been reduced to the

same equinox, we are prepared to proceed with the determination of the elements of the orbit. For this purpose, let t, t', t'' be the times of observation, r, r', r'' the radii-vectores of the body, and u, u', u'' the corresponding arguments of the latitude, R, R', R'' the distances of the earth from the sun, and $\odot$, $\odot'$, $\odot''$ the longitudes of the sun corresponding to these times.

Let $[rr']$ denote double the area of the triangle formed between the radii-vectores r, r' and the chord of the orbit between the corresponding places of the body, and similarly for the other triangles thus formed. The angle at the sun in this triangle is the difference between the corresponding arguments of the latitude, and we shall have

$$\begin{aligned}[rr'] &= rr' \sin(u' - u), \\ [rr''] &= rr'' \sin(u'' - u), \\ [r'r''] &= r'r'' \sin(u'' - u'),\end{aligned} \tag{2}$$

If we designate by x, y, z, x', y', z', x'', y'', z'' the heliocentric coordinates of the body at the times t, t', and t'', we shall have

$$\begin{aligned}x &= r \sin a \sin(A + u), \\ x' &= r' \sin a \sin(A + u'), \\ x'' &= r'' \sin a \sin(A + u''),\end{aligned}$$

in which a and A are auxiliary constants which are functions of the elements Ω and i, and these elements may refer to any fundamental plane whatever. If we multiply the first of these equations by $\sin(u'' - u')$, the second by $-\sin(u'' - u)$, and the third by $\sin(u' - u)$, and add the products, we find, after reduction,

$$\frac{x}{r}\sin(u'' - u') - \frac{x'}{r'}\sin(u'' - u) + \frac{x''}{r''}\sin(u' - u) = 0,$$

which, by introducing the values of $[rr']$, $[rr'']$, and $[r'r'']$, becomes

$$[r'r'']\,x - [rr'']\,x' + [rr']\,x'' = 0.$$

If we put

$$n = \frac{[r'r'']}{[rr'']}, \qquad n'' = \frac{[rr']}{[rr'']}, \tag{3}$$

we get

$$nx - x' + n''x'' = 0. \tag{4}$$

In precisely the same manner, we find

$$\begin{aligned}ny - y' + n''y'' &= 0, \\ nz - z' + n''z'' &= 0.\end{aligned} \tag{5}$$

Since the coefficients in these equations are independent of the positions of the co-ordinate planes, except that the origin is at the centre of the sun, it is evident that the three equations are identical, and express simply the condition that the plane of the orbit passes through the centre of the sun; and the last two might have been derived from the first by writing successively y and z in place of x.

Let λ, λ', λ'' be the three observed longitudes, β, β', β'' the corresponding latitudes, and $\varDelta$, $\varDelta'$, $\varDelta''$ the distances of the body from the earth; and let

$$\varDelta \cos\beta = \rho, \qquad \varDelta' \cos\beta' = \rho', \qquad \varDelta'' \cos\beta'' = \rho'',$$

which are called *curtate* distances. Then we shall have

$$\begin{aligned} x &= \rho\cos\lambda - R\cos\odot, & x' &= \rho'\cos\lambda' - R'\cos\odot', \\ y &= \rho\sin\lambda - R\sin\odot, & y' &= \rho'\sin\lambda' - R'\sin\odot', \\ z &= \rho\tan\beta, & z' &= \rho'\tan\beta', \end{aligned}$$

$$\begin{aligned} x'' &= \rho''\cos\lambda'' - R''\cos\odot'', \\ y'' &= \rho''\sin\lambda'' - R''\sin\odot'', \\ z'' &= \rho''\tan\beta'', \end{aligned}$$

in which the latitude of the sun is neglected. The data may be so transformed that the latitude of the sun becomes 0, as will be explained in the next chapter; but in the computation of the orbit of a comet, in which this preliminary reduction has not been made, it will be unnecessary to consider this latitude which never exceeds 1″, while its introduction into the formulæ would unnecessarily complicate some of those which will be derived. If we substitute these values of x, x', &c. in the equations (4) and (5), they become

$$\begin{aligned} 0 &= n(\rho\cos\lambda - R\cos\odot) - (\rho'\cos\lambda' - R'\cos\odot') \\ &\qquad + n''(\rho''\cos\lambda'' - R''\cos\odot''), \\ 0 &= n(\rho\sin\lambda - R\sin\odot) - (\rho'\sin\lambda' - R'\sin\odot') \\ &\qquad + n''(\rho''\sin\lambda'' - R''\sin\odot''), \\ 0 &= n\rho\tan\beta - \rho'\tan\beta' + n''\rho''\tan\beta''. \end{aligned} \tag{6}$$

These equations simply satisfy the condition that the plane of the orbit passes through the centre of the sun, and they only become distinct or independent of each other when n and n'' are expressed in functions of the time, so as to satisfy the conditions of undisturbed motion in accordance with the law of gravitation. Further, they involve five unknown quantities in the case of an orbit wholly unknown, namely, n, n'', ρ, ρ', and ρ''; and if the values of n and n'' are first found, they will be sufficient to determine ρ, ρ', and ρ''.

The determination, however, of n and n'' to a sufficient degree of accuracy, by means of the intervals of time between the observations, requires that ρ' should be approximately known, and hence, in general, it will become necessary to derive first the values of n, n'', and ρ'; after which those of ρ and ρ'' may be found from equations (6) by elimination. But since the number of equations will then exceed the number of unknown quantities, we may combine them in such a manner as will diminish, in the greatest degree possible, the effect of the errors of the observations. In special cases in which the conditions of the problem are such that when the ratio of two curtate distances is known, the distances themselves may be determined, the elimination must be so performed as to give this ratio with the greatest accuracy practicable.

63. If, in the first and second of equations (6), we change the direction of the axis of x from the vernal equinox to the place of the sun at the time t', and again in the second, from the equinox to the second place of the body, we must diminish the longitudes in these equations by the angle through which the axis of x has been moved, and we shall have

$$\begin{aligned}
0 &= n(\rho\cos(\lambda-\odot')-R\cos(\odot'-\odot))-(\rho'\cos(\lambda'-\odot')-R') \\
&\quad +n''(\rho''\cos(\lambda''-\odot')-R''\cos(\odot''-\odot')), \\
0 &= n(\rho\sin(\lambda-\odot')+R\sin(\odot'-\odot))-\rho'\sin(\lambda'-\odot') \\
&\quad +n''(\rho''\sin(\lambda''-\odot')-R''\sin(\odot''-\odot')), \\
0 &= n(\rho\sin(\lambda'-\lambda)+R\sin(\odot-\lambda'))-R'\sin(\odot'-\lambda') \\
&\quad -n''(\rho''\sin(\lambda''-\lambda')-R''\sin(\odot''-\lambda')), \\
0 &= n\rho\tan\beta-\rho'\tan\beta'+n''\rho''\tan\beta''.
\end{aligned} \tag{7}$$

If we multiply the second of these equations by $\tan\beta'$, and the fourth by $-\sin(\lambda'-\odot')$, and add the products, we get

$$\begin{aligned}
0 &= n''\rho''(\tan\beta'\sin(\lambda''-\odot')-\tan\beta''\sin(\lambda'-\odot')) \\
&\quad -n''R''\sin(\odot''-\odot')\tan\beta'+n\rho(\tan\beta'\sin(\lambda-\odot')-\tan\beta\sin(\lambda'-\odot')) \\
&\quad +nR\sin(\odot'-\odot)\tan\beta'.
\end{aligned} \tag{8}$$

Let us now denote double the area of the triangle formed by the sun and two places of the earth corresponding to R and R' by $[RR']$, and we shall have

$$[RR'] = RR'\sin(\odot'-\odot),$$

and similarly

$$\begin{aligned}
[RR''] &= RR''\sin(\odot''-\odot), \\
[R'R''] &= R'R''\sin(\odot''-\odot').
\end{aligned}$$

Then, if we put

$$N = \frac{[R'R'']}{[RR'']}, \qquad N'' = \frac{[RR']}{[RR'']}, \tag{9}$$

we obtain

$$R'' \sin(\odot'' - \odot') = R \sin(\odot' - \odot)\,\frac{N}{N''}.$$

Substituting this in the equation (8), and dividing by the coefficient of ρ'', the result is

$$\rho'' = \rho\,\frac{n}{n''}\cdot\frac{\tan\beta' \sin(\lambda - \odot') - \tan\beta \sin(\lambda' - \odot')}{\tan\beta'' \sin(\lambda' - \odot') - \tan\beta' \sin(\lambda'' - \odot')}$$
$$+ \left(\frac{n}{n''} - \frac{N}{N''}\right)\frac{R \sin(\odot' - \odot)\tan\beta'}{\tan\beta'' \sin(\lambda' - \odot') - \tan\beta' \sin(\lambda'' - \odot')}.$$

Let us also put

$$M' = \frac{\tan\beta' \sin(\lambda - \odot') - \tan\beta \sin(\lambda' - \odot')}{\tan\beta'' \sin(\lambda' - \odot') - \tan\beta' \sin(\lambda'' - \odot')},$$
$$M'' = \frac{\sin(\odot' - \odot)\tan\beta'}{\tan\beta'' \sin(\lambda' - \odot') - \tan\beta' \sin(\lambda'' - \odot')}, \tag{10}$$

and the preceding equation reduces to

$$\rho'' = \frac{n}{n''}M'\rho + \left(\frac{n}{n''} - \frac{N}{N''}\right)M''R. \tag{11}$$

We may transform the values of M' and M'' so as to be better adapted to logarithmic calculation with the ordinary tables. Thus, if w' denotes the inclination to the ecliptic of a great circle passing through the second place of the comet and the second place of the sun, the longitude of its ascending node will be $\odot'$, and we shall have

$$\sin(\lambda' - \odot')\tan w' = \tan\beta'. \tag{12}$$

Let β_0, β_0'' be the latitudes of the points of this circle corresponding to the longitudes λ and λ'', and we have, also,

$$\tan\beta_0 = \sin(\lambda - \odot')\tan w',$$
$$\tan\beta_0'' = \sin(\lambda'' - \odot')\tan w'. \tag{13}$$

Substituting these values for $\tan\beta'$, $\sin(\lambda - \odot')$ and $\sin(\lambda'' - \odot')$ in the expressions for M' and M'', and reducing, they become

$$M' = \frac{\sin(\beta_0 - \beta)}{\sin(\beta'' - \beta_0'')}\cdot\frac{\cos\beta''\cos\beta_0''}{\cos\beta_0\cos\beta},$$
$$M'' = \tan w' \sin(\odot' - \odot)\,\frac{\cos\beta''\cos\beta_0''}{\sin(\beta'' - \beta_0'')}. \tag{14}$$

When the value of $\frac{n}{n''}$ has been found, equation (11) will give the relation between ρ and ρ'' in terms of known quantities. It is evident, however, from equations (14), that when the apparent path of the comet is in a plane passing through the second place of the sun, since, in this case, $\beta = \beta_0$ and $\beta'' = \beta_0''$, we shall have $M' = \frac{0}{0}$ and $M'' = \infty$. In this case, therefore, and also when $\beta_0 - \beta$ and $\beta'' - \beta_0''$ are very nearly 0, we must have recourse to some other equation which may be derived from the equations (7), and which does not involve this indetermination.

It will be observed, also, that if, at the time of the middle observation, the comet is in opposition or conjunction with the sun, the values of M' and M'' as given by equation (14) will be indeterminate in form, but that the original equations (10) will give the values of these quantities provided that the apparent path of the comet is not in a great circle passing through the second place of the sun. These values are

$$M' = -\frac{\sin(\lambda - \odot')}{\sin(\lambda'' - \odot')}, \qquad M'' = -\frac{\sin(\odot' - \odot)}{\sin(\lambda'' - \odot')}.$$

Hence it appears that whenever the apparent path of the body is nearly in a plane passing through the place of the sun at the time of the middle observation, the errors of observation will have great influence in vitiating the resulting values of M' and M''; and to obviate the difficulties thus encountered, we obtain from the third of equations (7) the following value of ρ'':—

$$\rho'' = \rho \frac{n}{n''} \cdot \frac{\sin(\lambda' - \lambda)}{\sin(\lambda'' - \lambda')}$$
$$+ \frac{\frac{n}{n''} R \sin(\odot - \lambda') - \frac{1}{n''} R' \sin(\odot' - \lambda') + R'' \sin(\odot'' - \lambda')}{\sin(\lambda'' - \lambda')}. \qquad (15)$$

We may also eliminate ρ between the first and fourth of equations (7). If we multiply the first by $\tan\beta'$, and the second by $-\cos(\lambda' - \odot')$, and add the products, we obtain

$$0 = n''\rho''(\tan\beta' \cos(\lambda'' - \odot') - \tan\beta'' \cos(\lambda' - \odot'))$$
$$- n''R'' \tan\beta' \cos(\odot'' - \odot') + n\rho(\tan\beta' \cos(\lambda - \odot') - \tan\beta \cos(\lambda' - \odot'))$$
$$- nR \tan\beta' \cos(\odot' - \odot) + R' \tan\beta',$$

from which we derive

$$\rho'' = \rho\frac{n}{n''}\cdot\frac{\tan\beta'\cos(\lambda - \odot') - \tan\beta\cos(\lambda' - \odot')}{\tan\beta''\cos(\lambda' - \odot') - \tan\beta'\cos(\lambda'' - \odot')}$$
$$- \frac{R''\tan\beta'\cos(\odot'' - \odot') + \frac{n}{n''}R\tan\beta'\cos(\odot' - \odot) - \frac{1}{n''}R'\tan\beta'}{\tan\beta''\cos(\lambda' - \odot') - \tan\beta'\cos(\lambda'' - \odot')}. \tag{16}$$

Let us now denote by I' the inclination to the ecliptic of a great circle passing through the second place of the comet and that point of the ecliptic whose longitude is $\odot' - 90°$, which will therefore be the longitude of its ascending node, and we shall have

$$\cos(\lambda' - \odot')\tan I' = \tan\beta'; \tag{17}$$

and, if we designate by $\beta_{\prime}$ and $\beta_{\prime\prime}$ the latitudes of the points of this circle corresponding to the longitudes λ and λ'', we shall also have

$$\begin{aligned}\tan\beta_{\prime} &= \cos(\lambda - \odot')\tan I',\\ \tan\beta_{\prime\prime} &= \cos(\lambda'' - \odot')\tan I'.\end{aligned} \tag{18}$$

Introducing these values into equation (16), it reduces to

$$\rho'' = \rho\frac{n}{n''}\cdot\frac{\sin(\beta_{\prime} - \beta)}{\sin(\beta'' - \beta_{\prime\prime})}\cdot\frac{\cos\beta''\cos\beta_{\prime\prime}}{\cos\beta\cos\beta_{\prime}}$$
$$- \frac{\tan I'\cos\beta''\cos\beta_{\prime\prime}}{\sin(\beta'' - \beta_{\prime\prime})}\left(R''\cos(\odot'' - \odot') + \frac{n}{n''}R\cos(\odot' - \odot) - \frac{R'}{n''}\right), \tag{19}$$

from which it appears that this equation becomes indeterminate when the apparent path of the body is in a plane passing through that point of the ecliptic whose longitude is equal to the longitude of the second place of the sun diminished by 90°. In this case we may use equation (11) provided that the path of the comet is not nearly in the ecliptic. When the comet, at the time of the second observation, is in quadrature with the sun, equation (19) becomes indeterminate in form, and we must have recourse to the original equation (16), which does not necessarily fail in this case.

When both equations (11) and (16) are simultaneously nearly indeterminate, so as to be greatly affected by errors of observation, the relation between ρ and ρ'' must be determined by means of equation (15), which fails only when the motion of the comet in longitude is very small. It will rarely happen that all three equations, (14), (15), and (16), are inapplicable, and when such a case does occur it will indicate that the data are not sufficient for the determination of the elements of the orbit. In general, equation (16) or (19) is to be used when the motion of the comet in latitude is considerable, and equation (15) when the motion in longitude is greater than in latitude.

64. The formulæ already derived are sufficient to determine the relation between ρ'' and ρ when the values of n and n'' are known, and it remains, therefore, to derive the expressions for these quantities.

If we put

$$\begin{aligned} k(t'-t) &= \tau'', \\ k(t''-t') &= \tau, \\ k(t''-t) &= \tau', \end{aligned} \tag{20}$$

and express the values of x, y, z, x'', y'', z'' in terms of x', y', z' by expansion into series, we have

$$\begin{aligned} x &= x' - \frac{dx'}{dt}\cdot\frac{\tau''}{k} + \frac{1}{1.2}\cdot\frac{d^2x'}{dt^2}\cdot\frac{\tau''^2}{k^2} - \frac{1}{1.2.3}\cdot\frac{d^3x'}{dt^3}\cdot\frac{\tau''^3}{k^3} + \&c., \\ x'' &= x' + \frac{dx'}{dt}\cdot\frac{\tau}{k} + \frac{1}{1.2}\cdot\frac{d^2x'}{dt^2}\cdot\frac{\tau^2}{k^2} + \frac{1}{1.2.3}\cdot\frac{d^3x'}{dt^3}\cdot\frac{\tau^3}{k^3} + \&c., \end{aligned} \tag{21}$$

and similar expressions for y, y'', z, and z''. We shall, however, take the plane of the orbit as the fundamental plane, in which case z, z', and z'' vanish.

The fundamental equations for the motion of a heavenly body relative to the sun are, if we neglect its mass in comparison with that of the sun,

$$\begin{aligned} \frac{d^2x'}{dt^2} + \frac{k^2x'}{r'^3} &= 0, \\ \frac{d^2y'}{dt^2} + \frac{k^2y'}{r'^3} &= 0. \end{aligned}$$

If we differentiate the first of these equations, we get

$$\frac{d^3x'}{dt^3} = \frac{3k^2x'}{r'^4}\cdot\frac{dr'}{dt} - \frac{k^2}{r'^3}\cdot\frac{dx'}{dt}.$$

Differentiating again, we find

$$\frac{d^4x'}{dt^4} = \left(\frac{k^4}{r'^6} - \frac{12k^2}{r'^5}\left(\frac{dr'}{dt}\right)^2 + \frac{3k^2}{r'^4}\cdot\frac{d^2r'}{dt^2}\right)x' + \frac{6k^2}{r'^4}\cdot\frac{dr'}{dt}\cdot\frac{dx'}{dt}.$$

Writing y instead of x, we shall have the expressions for $\frac{d^3y'}{dt^3}$ and $\frac{d^4y'}{dt^4}$. Substituting these values of the differential coefficients in equations (21), and the corresponding expressions for y and y'', and putting

$$
\begin{aligned}
a &= 1 - \tfrac{1}{2}\frac{\tau''^2}{r'^3} - \tfrac{1}{2}\frac{\tau''^3}{kr'^4}\cdot\frac{dr'}{dt} + \tfrac{1}{24}\left(\frac{1}{r'^6} - \frac{12}{k^2r'^5}\left(\frac{dr'}{dt}\right)^2 + \frac{3}{k^2r'^4}\cdot\frac{d^2r'}{dt^2}\right)\tau''^4 \ldots, \\
b &= \frac{\tau''}{k} - \tfrac{1}{6}\frac{\tau''^3}{kr'^3} - \tfrac{1}{4}\frac{\tau''^4}{k^2r'^4}\cdot\frac{dr'}{dt}\ldots, \qquad (22) \\
a'' &= 1 - \tfrac{1}{2}\frac{\tau^2}{r'^3} + \tfrac{1}{2}\frac{\tau^3}{kr'^4}\cdot\frac{dr'}{dt} + \tfrac{1}{24}\left(\frac{1}{r'^6} - \frac{12}{k^2r'^5}\left(\frac{dr'}{dt}\right)^2 + \frac{3}{k^2r'^4}\cdot\frac{d^2r'}{dt^2}\right)\tau^4 \ldots, \\
b'' &= \frac{\tau}{k} - \tfrac{1}{6}\frac{\tau^3}{kr'^3} + \tfrac{1}{4}\frac{\tau^4}{k^2r'^4}\cdot\frac{dr'}{dt}\ldots\ldots,
\end{aligned}
$$

we obtain

$$
x = ax' - b\frac{dx'}{dt}, \qquad x'' = a''x' + b''\frac{dx'}{dt},
$$

$$
y = ay' - b\frac{dy'}{dt}, \qquad y'' = a''y' + b''\frac{dy'}{dt}.
$$

From these equations we easily derive

$$
\begin{aligned}
y'x - x'y &= b\,\frac{x'dy' - y'dx'}{dt}, \\
y''x' - x'y' &= b''\,\frac{x'dy' - y'dx'}{dt}, \qquad (23) \\
y''x - x''y &= (ab'' + a''b)\,\frac{x'dy' - y'dx'}{dt}.
\end{aligned}
$$

The first members of these equations are double the areas of the triangles formed by the radii-vectores and the chords of the orbit between the places of the comet or planet. Thus,

$$
y'x - x'y = [rr'], \qquad y''x' - x''y' = [r'r''], \qquad y''x - x''y = [rr''], \qquad (24)
$$

and $x'dy' - y'dx'$ is double the area described by the radius-vector during the element of time dt, and, consequently, $\dfrac{x'dy' - y'dx'}{dt}$ is double the areal velocity. Therefore we shall have, neglecting the mass of the body,

$$
\frac{x'dy' - y'dx'}{dt} = 2f = k\sqrt{p},
$$

in which p is the semi-parameter of the orbit. The equations (23), therefore, become

$$
[rr'] = bk\sqrt{p}, \qquad [r'r''] = b''k\sqrt{p}, \qquad [rr''] = (ab'' + a''b)\,k\sqrt{p}.
$$

Substituting for a, b, a'', b'' their values from (22), we find, since $\tau' = \tau + \tau''$,

$$
\begin{aligned}
[rr'] &= \tau'' \sqrt{p}\left(1 - \tfrac{1}{6}\frac{\tau''^2}{r'^3} - \tfrac{1}{4}\frac{\tau''^3}{kr'^4}\cdot\frac{dr'}{dt}\ldots\ldots\right),\\
[r'r''] &= \tau\ \sqrt{p}\left(1 - \tfrac{1}{6}\frac{\tau^2}{r'^3} + \tfrac{1}{4}\frac{\tau^3}{kr'^4}\cdot\frac{dr'}{dt}\ldots\ldots\right),\\
[rr''] &= \tau'\ \sqrt{p}\left(1 - \tfrac{1}{6}\frac{\tau'^2}{r'^3} + \tfrac{1}{4}\frac{\tau'^2(\tau-\tau'')}{kr'^4}\cdot\frac{dr'}{dt}\ldots\right).
\end{aligned}
\tag{25}
$$

From these equations the values of $n = \dfrac{[r'r'']}{[rr'']}$ and $n'' = \dfrac{[rr']}{[rr'']}$ may be derived; and the results are

$$
\begin{aligned}
n &= \frac{\tau}{\tau'}\left(1 + \tfrac{1}{6}\frac{\tau''(\tau'+\tau)}{r'^3} + \tfrac{1}{4}\frac{\tau''(\tau''^2+\tau\tau''-\tau^2)}{kr'^4}\cdot\frac{dr'}{dt}\ldots\right),\\
n'' &= \frac{\tau''}{\tau'}\left(1 + \tfrac{1}{6}\frac{\tau(\tau'+\tau'')}{r'^3} - \tfrac{1}{4}\frac{\tau(\tau^2+\tau\tau''-\tau''^2)}{kr'^4}\cdot\frac{dr'}{dt}\ldots\right),
\end{aligned}
\tag{26}
$$

which values are exact to the third powers of the time, inclusive.

In the case of the orbit of the earth, the term of the third order, being multiplied by the very small quantity $\dfrac{dR'}{dt}$, is reduced to a superior order, and, therefore, it may be neglected, so that in this case we shall have, to the same degree of approximation as in (26),

$$
\begin{aligned}
N &= \frac{\tau}{\tau'}\left(1 + \tfrac{1}{6}\frac{\tau''(\tau'+\tau)}{R'^3}\ldots\right),\\
N'' &= \frac{\tau''}{\tau'}\left(1 + \tfrac{1}{6}\frac{\tau(\tau'+\tau'')}{R'^3}\ldots\right).
\end{aligned}
\tag{27}
$$

From the equations (26) or from (25), since $\dfrac{n}{n''} = \dfrac{[r'r'']}{[rr']}$, we find

$$
\frac{n}{n''} = \frac{\tau}{\tau''}\left(1 - \tfrac{1}{6}\frac{\tau^2-\tau''^2}{r'^3} + \tfrac{1}{4}\frac{\tau^3+\tau''^3}{kr'^4}\cdot\frac{dr'}{dt}\ldots\right). \tag{28}
$$

Since this equation involves r' and $\dfrac{dr'}{dt}$, it is evident that the value of $\dfrac{n}{n''}$, in the case of an orbit wholly unknown, can be determined only by successive approximations. In the first approximation to the elements of the orbit of a heavenly body, the intervals between the observations will usually be small, and the series of terms of (28) will converge rapidly, so that we may take

$$
\frac{n}{n''} = \frac{\tau}{\tau''},
$$

and similarly

$$\frac{N}{N''}=\frac{\tau}{\tau''}.$$

Hence the equation (11) reduces to

$$\rho''=\frac{\tau}{\tau''}M'\rho. \tag{29}$$

It will be observed, further, that if the intervals between the observations are equal, the term of the second order in equation (28) vanishes, and the supposition that $\frac{n}{n''}=\frac{\tau}{\tau''}$ is correct to terms of the third order. It will be advantageous, therefore, to select observations whose intervals approach nearest to equality. But if the observations available do not admit of the selection of those which give nearly equal intervals, and these intervals are necessarily very unequal, it will be more accurate to assume

$$\frac{n}{n''}=\frac{N}{N''},$$

and compute the values of N and N'' by means of equations (9), since, according to (27) and (28), if r' does not differ much from R', the error of this assumption will only involve terms of the third order, even when the values of τ and τ'' differ very much.

Whenever the values of ρ and ρ'' can be found when that of their ratio is given, we may at once derive the corresponding values of r and r'', as will be subsequently explained.

The values of r and r'' may also be expressed in terms of r' by means of series, and we have

$$r\;=r'-\frac{dr'}{dt}\cdot\frac{\tau''}{k}+\tfrac{1}{2}\frac{d^2r'}{dt^2}\cdot\frac{\tau''^2}{k^2}-\&c.,$$

$$r''=r'+\frac{dr'}{dt}\cdot\frac{\tau}{k}+\tfrac{1}{2}\frac{d^2r'}{dt^2}\cdot\frac{\tau^2}{k^2}+\&c.,$$

from which we derive

$$r''-r=\frac{\tau+\tau''}{k}\cdot\frac{dr'}{dt},$$

neglecting terms of the third order. Therefore

$$\frac{dr'}{dt}=\frac{k\,(r''-r)}{\tau'}; \tag{30}$$

and when the intervals are equal, this value is exact to terms of the fourth order. We have, also,

$$r + r'' = 2r' + \frac{\tau - \tau''}{k} \cdot \frac{dr'}{dt},$$

which gives

$$r' = \tfrac{1}{2}(r + r'') - \tfrac{1}{2}(r'' - r)\frac{\tau - \tau''}{\tau'}. \tag{31}$$

Therefore, when r and r'' have been determined by a first approximation, the approximate values of r' and $\frac{dr'}{dt}$ are obtained from these equations, by means of which the value of $\frac{n}{n''}$ may be recomputed from equation (28). We also compute

$$\frac{N}{N''} = \frac{R'R'' \sin(\odot'' - \odot')}{RR' \sin(\odot' - \odot)}, \tag{32}$$

and substitute in equation (11) the values of $\frac{n}{n''}$ and $\frac{N}{N''}$ thus found.

If we designate by M the ratio of the curtate distances ρ and ρ'', we have

$$M = \frac{\rho''}{\rho} = M'\frac{n}{n''} + M''\left(\frac{n}{n''} - \frac{N}{N''}\right)\frac{R}{\rho}. \tag{33}$$

In the numerical application of this, the approximate value of ρ will be used in computing the last term of the second member.

In the case of the determination of an orbit when the approximate elements are already known, the value of $\frac{n}{n''}$ may be computed from

$$\frac{n}{n''} = \frac{r'r'' \sin(v'' - v')}{rr' \sin(v' - v)}, \tag{34}$$

and that of $\frac{N}{N''}$ from (32); and the value of M derived by means of these from (33) will not require any further correction.

65. When the apparent path of the body is such that the value of M', as derived from the first of equations (10), is either indeterminate or greatly affected by errors of observation, the equations (15) and (16) must be employed. The last terms of these equations may be changed to a form which is more convenient in the approximations to the value of the ratio of ρ'' to ρ.

Let Y, Y', Y'' be the ordinates of the sun when the axis of abscissas is directed to that point in the ecliptic whose longitude is λ', and we have

$$Y = R \sin(\odot - \lambda'),$$
$$Y' = R' \sin(\odot' - \lambda'),$$
$$Y'' = R'' \sin(\odot'' - \lambda').$$

Now, in the last term of equation (15), it will be sufficient to put

$$\frac{n}{n''} = \frac{N}{N''},$$

and, introducing Y, Y', Y'', it becomes

$$\left(\frac{N}{N''} Y - \frac{1}{n''} Y' + Y''\right) \operatorname{cosec} (\lambda'' - \lambda'). \qquad (35)$$

It now remains to find the value of $\frac{1}{n''}$. From the second of equations (26) we find, to terms of the second order inclusive,

$$\frac{1}{n''} = \frac{\tau'}{\tau''}\left(1 - \tfrac{1}{6}\frac{\tau(\tau' + \tau'')}{r'^3}\right).$$

We have, also,

$$\frac{1}{N''} = \frac{\tau'}{\tau''}\left(1 - \tfrac{1}{6}\frac{\tau(\tau' + \tau'')}{R'^3}\right),$$

and hence

$$\frac{1}{n''} = \frac{1}{N''} - \tfrac{1}{6}\frac{\tau'}{\tau''}\tau(\tau' + \tau'')\left(\frac{1}{r'^3} - \frac{1}{R'^3}\right).$$

Therefore, the expression (35) becomes

$$\frac{1}{N'' \sin(\lambda'' - \lambda')}\left(NY - Y' + N''Y'' + \tfrac{1}{6}\frac{\tau'}{\tau''}\tau(\tau' + \tau'')\left(\frac{1}{r'^3} - \frac{1}{R'^3}\right)N''Y'\right).$$

But, according to equations (5),

$$NY - Y' + N''Y'' = 0,$$

and the foregoing expression reduces to

$$+\tfrac{1}{6}\frac{\tau\tau'}{\tau''}(\tau' + \tau'')\left(\frac{1}{r'^3} - \frac{1}{R'^3}\right)\frac{R' \sin(\odot' - \lambda')}{\sin(\lambda'' - \lambda')},$$

since $Y' = R' \sin(\odot' - \lambda')$. Hence the equation (15) becomes

$$\rho'' = \rho\frac{n}{n''} \cdot \frac{\sin(\lambda' - \lambda)}{\sin(\lambda'' - \lambda')} - \tfrac{1}{6}\frac{\tau\tau'}{\tau''}(\tau' + \tau'')\left(\frac{1}{r'^3} - \frac{1}{R'^3}\right)\frac{R' \sin(\lambda' - \odot')}{\sin(\lambda'' - \lambda')}. \qquad (36)$$

If we put

$$M_0 = \frac{n}{n''} \cdot \frac{\sin(\lambda' - \lambda)}{\sin(\lambda'' - \lambda')},$$

$$F = 1 - \tfrac{1}{6} \frac{n''}{n} \cdot \frac{\tau\tau'}{\tau''} (\tau' + \tau'') \frac{\sin(\lambda' - \odot')}{\sin(\lambda' - \lambda)} \cdot \frac{R'}{\rho} \left(\frac{1}{r'^3} - \frac{1}{R'^3} \right),$$

we have

$$\frac{\rho''}{\rho} = M = M_0 F. \tag{37}$$

Let us now consider the equation (16), and let us designate by X, X', X'' the abscissas of the earth, the axis of abscissas being directed to that point of the ecliptic for which the longitude is $\odot'$, then

$$\begin{aligned} X &= R \cos(\odot - \odot'), \\ X' &= R', \\ X'' &= R'' \cos(\odot'' - \odot'). \end{aligned}$$

It will be sufficient, in the last term of (16), to put

$$\frac{n}{n''} = \frac{N}{N''},$$

and for $\frac{1}{n''}$ its value in terms of N'' as already found. Then, since

$$NX - X' + N''X'' = 0,$$

this term reduces to

$$-\tfrac{1}{6} \frac{\tau\tau'}{\tau''} (\tau' + \tau'') \left(\frac{1}{r'^3} - \frac{1}{R'^3} \right) \frac{R' \tan\beta'}{\tan\beta'' \cos(\lambda' - \odot') - \tan\beta' \cos(\lambda'' - \odot')};$$

and if we put

$$\begin{aligned} M_0' &= \frac{n}{n''} \cdot \frac{\tan\beta' \cos(\lambda - \odot') - \tan\beta \cos(\lambda' - \odot')}{\tan\beta'' \cos(\lambda' - \odot') - \tan\beta' \cos(\lambda'' - \odot')}, \\ F' &= 1 - \tfrac{1}{6} \frac{n''}{n} \cdot \frac{\tau\tau'}{\tau''} (\tau + \tau'') \left(\frac{1}{r'^3} - \frac{1}{R'^3} \right) \frac{\tan\beta'}{\tan\beta' \cos(\lambda - \odot') - \tan\beta \cos(\lambda' - \odot')} \cdot \frac{R'}{\rho}, \end{aligned} \tag{38}$$

the equation (16) becomes

$$M = \frac{\rho''}{\rho} = M_0' F'. \tag{39}$$

In the numerical application of these formulæ, if the elements are not approximately known, we first assume

$$\frac{n}{n''} = \frac{\tau}{\tau''},$$

when the intervals are nearly equal, and

$$\frac{n}{n''} = \frac{N}{N''},$$

as given by (32), when the intervals are very unequal, and neglect the factors F and F'. The values of ρ and ρ'' which are thus obtained, enable us to find an approximate value of r', and with this a more exact value of $\frac{n}{n''}$ may be found, and also the value of F or F'.

Whenever equation (11) is not materially affected by errors of observation, it will furnish the value of M with more accuracy than the equations (37) and (39), since the neglected terms will not be so great as in the case of these equations. In general, therefore, it is to be preferred, and, in the case in which it fails, the very circumstance that the geocentric path of the body is nearly in a great circle, makes the values of F and F' differ but little from unity, since, in order that the apparent path of the body may be nearly in a great circle, r' must differ very little from R'.

66. When the value of M has been found, we may proceed to determine, by means of other relations between ρ and ρ'', the values of the quantities themselves.

The co-ordinates of the first place of the earth referred to the third, are

$$\begin{aligned} x_{,} &= R'' \cos \odot'' - R \cos \odot, \\ y_{,} &= R'' \sin \odot'' - R \sin \odot. \end{aligned} \tag{40}$$

If we represent by g the chord of the earth's orbit between the places corresponding to the first and third observations, and by G the longitude of the first place of the earth as seen from the third, we shall have

$$x_{,} = g \cos G, \qquad y_{,} = g \sin G,$$

and, consequently,

$$\begin{aligned} R'' \cos (\odot'' - \odot) - R &= g \cos (G - \odot), \\ R'' \sin (\odot'' - \odot) \qquad &= g \sin (G - \odot). \end{aligned} \tag{41}$$

If ψ represents the angle at the earth between the sun and comet at the first observation, and if we designate by w the inclination to the ecliptic of a plane passing through the places of the earth, sun, and comet or planet for the first observation, the longitude of the ascending node of this plane on the ecliptic will be $\odot$, and we shall have, in accordance with equations $(81)_1$,

$$\begin{aligned} \cos \psi &= \cos \beta \cos (\lambda - \odot), \\ \sin \psi \cos w &= \cos \beta \sin (\lambda - \odot), \\ \sin \psi \sin w &= \sin \beta, \end{aligned}$$

from which

$$\tan w = \frac{\tan \beta}{\sin(\lambda - \odot)},$$
$$\tan \psi = \frac{\tan(\lambda - \odot)}{\cos w}. \tag{42}$$

Since $\cos \beta$ is always positive, $\cos \psi$ and $\cos(\lambda - \odot)$ must have the same sign; and, further, ψ cannot exceed 180°.

In the same manner, if w'' and ψ'' represent analogous quantities for the time of the third observation, we obtain

$$\tan w'' = \frac{\tan \beta''}{\sin(\lambda'' - \odot'')},$$
$$\tan \psi'' = \frac{\tan(\lambda'' - \odot'')}{\cos w''}, \tag{43}$$
$$\cos \psi'' = \cos \beta'' \cos(\lambda'' - \odot'').$$

We also have

$$r^2 = \Delta^2 + R^2 - 2\Delta R \cos \psi,$$

which may be transformed into

$$r^2 = (\rho \sec \beta - R \cos \psi)^2 + R^2 \sin^2 \psi; \tag{44}$$

and in a similar manner we find

$$r''^2 = (\rho'' \sec \beta'' - R'' \cos \psi'')^2 + R''^2 \sin^2 \psi''. \tag{45}$$

Let $\varkappa$ designate the chord of the orbit of the body between the first and third places, and we have

$$\varkappa^2 = (x'' - x)^2 + (y'' - y)^2 + (z'' - z)^2.$$

But

$$x = \rho \cos \lambda - R \cos \odot,$$
$$y = \rho \sin \lambda - R \sin \odot,$$
$$z = \rho \tan \beta,$$

and, since $\rho'' = M\rho$,

$$x'' = M\rho \cos \lambda'' - R'' \cos \odot'',$$
$$y'' = M\rho \sin \lambda'' - R'' \sin \odot'',$$
$$z'' = M\rho \tan \beta''$$

from which we derive, introducing g and G,

$$x'' - x = M\rho \cos \lambda'' - \rho \cos \lambda - g \cos G,$$
$$y'' - y = M\rho \sin \lambda'' - \rho \sin \lambda - g \sin G,$$
$$z'' - z = M\rho \tan \beta'' - \rho \tan \beta.$$

Let us now put

$$\begin{aligned} M\rho\cos\lambda'' - \rho\cos\lambda &= \rho h\cos\zeta\cos H, \\ M\rho\sin\lambda'' - \rho\sin\lambda &= \rho h\cos\zeta\sin H, \\ M\rho\tan\beta'' - \rho\tan\beta &= \rho h\sin\zeta. \end{aligned} \tag{46}$$

Then we have

$$\begin{aligned} x'' - x &= \rho h\cos\zeta\cos H - g\cos G, \\ y'' - y &= \rho h\cos\zeta\sin H - g\sin G, \\ z'' - z &= \rho h\sin\zeta. \end{aligned}$$

Squaring these values, and adding, we get, by reduction,

$$\varkappa^2 = \rho^2h^2 - 2g\,\rho h\cos\zeta\cos(G - H) + g^2; \tag{47}$$

and if we put

$$\cos\zeta\cos(G - H) = \cos\varphi, \tag{48}$$

we have

$$\varkappa^2 = (\rho h - g\cos\varphi)^2 + g^2\sin^2\varphi. \tag{49}$$

If we multiply the first of equations (46) by $\cos\lambda''$, and the second by $\sin\lambda''$, and add the products; then multiply the first by $\sin\lambda''$, and the second by $\cos\lambda''$, and subtract, we obtain

$$\begin{aligned} h\cos\zeta\cos(H - \lambda'') &= M - \cos(\lambda'' - \lambda), \\ h\cos\zeta\sin(H - \lambda'') &= \sin(\lambda'' - \lambda), \\ h\sin\zeta \qquad\qquad &= M\tan\beta'' - \tan\beta, \end{aligned} \tag{50}$$

by means of which we may determine h, ζ, and H.

Let us now put

$$\begin{aligned} g\sin\varphi &= A, \\ R\sin\psi &= B, \qquad & h\cos\beta &= b, \\ R''\sin\psi'' &= B'', \qquad & \frac{h\cos\beta''}{M} &= b'', \\ g\cos\varphi - bR\cos\psi &= c, \qquad & g\cos\varphi - b''R''\cos\psi'' &= c'', \\ & \rho h - g\cos\varphi = d, \end{aligned} \tag{51}$$

and the equations (44), (45), and (49) become

$$\begin{aligned} \varkappa &= \sqrt{d^2 + A^2}, \\ r &= \sqrt{\left(\frac{d + c}{b}\right)^2 + B^2}, \\ r'' &= \sqrt{\left(\frac{d + c''}{b''}\right)^2 + B''^2}. \end{aligned} \tag{52}$$

The equations thus derived are independent of the form of the orbit, and are applicable to the case of any heavenly body revolving around the sun. They will serve to determine r and r'' in all cases in which the unknown quantity d can be determined. If ρ is known,

d becomes known directly; but in the case of an unknown orbit, these equations are applicable only when ρ or d may be determined directly or indirectly from the data furnished by observation.

67. Since the equations (52) involve two radii-vectores r and r'' and the chord $\varkappa$ joining their extremities, it is evident that an additional equation involving these and known quantities will enable us to derive d, if not directly, at least by successive approximations. There is, indeed, a remarkable relation existing between two radii-vectores, the chord joining their extremities, and the time of describing the part of the orbit included by these radii-vectores. In general, the equation which expresses this relation involves also the semi-transverse axis of the orbit; and hence, in the case of an unknown orbit, it will not be sufficient, in connection with the equations (52), for the determination of d, unless some assumption is made in regard to the value of the semi-transverse axis. For the special case of parabolic motion, the semi-transverse axis is infinite, and the resulting equation involves only the time, the two radii-vectores, and the chord of the part of the orbit included by these. It is, therefore, adapted to the determination of the elements when the orbit is supposed to be a parabola, and, though it is transcendental in form, it may be easily solved by trial. To determine this expression, let us resume the equations

$$\frac{k(t-T)}{\sqrt{2}\,q^{\frac{3}{2}}} = \tan \tfrac{1}{2}v + \tfrac{1}{3} \tan^3 \tfrac{1}{2}v$$

and, for the time t'',

$$\frac{k(t''-T)}{\sqrt{2}\,q^{\frac{3}{2}}} = \tan \tfrac{1}{2}v'' + \tfrac{1}{3} \tan^3 \tfrac{1}{2}v''.$$

Subtracting the former from the latter, and reducing, we obtain

$$\frac{3k(t''-t)}{\sqrt{2}\,q^{\frac{3}{2}}} = \frac{\sin \frac{1}{2}(v''-v)}{\cos \frac{1}{2}v'' \cos \frac{1}{2}v}\left(\frac{r''}{q} + \frac{\cos \frac{1}{2}(v''-v)}{\cos \frac{1}{2}v'' \cos \frac{1}{2}v} + \frac{r}{q}\right),$$

and, since $r = q \sec^2 \frac{1}{2}v$, this gives

$$\frac{3k(t''-t)}{\sqrt{2}} = \frac{\sin \frac{1}{2}(v''-v)\sqrt{rr''}}{\sqrt{q}}\left(r + r'' + \cos \tfrac{1}{2}(v''-v)\sqrt{rr''}\right). \quad (53)$$

But we have, also, from the triangle formed by the chord $\varkappa$ and the radii-vectores r and r'',

$$\begin{aligned}\varkappa^2 &= r^2 + r''^2 - 2rr'' \cos(v''-v) \\ &= (r+r'')^2 - 4rr'' \cos^2 \tfrac{1}{2}(v''-v).\end{aligned}$$

Therefore,

$$\cos \tfrac{1}{2}(v'' - v) = \pm \frac{\sqrt{(r + r'' + \varkappa)(r + r'' - \varkappa)}}{2\sqrt{rr''}}.$$

Let us now put

$$r + r'' + \varkappa = m^2, \qquad r + r'' - \varkappa = n^2,$$

m and n being positive quantities. Then we shall have

$$\begin{aligned} r + r'' &= \tfrac{1}{2}(m^2 + n^2), \\ 2 \cos \tfrac{1}{2}(v'' - v)\sqrt{rr''} &= \pm\, mn; \end{aligned} \qquad (54)$$

and, since m and n are always positive, it follows that the upper sign must be used when $v'' - v$ is less than 180°, and the lower sign when $v'' - v$ is greater than 180°. Combining the last equation with (53), the result is

$$3k(t'' - t) = \frac{\sin \frac{1}{2}(v'' - v)\sqrt{rr''}}{\sqrt{2q}}(m^2 + n^2 \pm mn). \qquad (55)$$

Now we have

$$\sin \tfrac{1}{2}(v'' - v) = \sin \tfrac{1}{2}v'' \cos \tfrac{1}{2}v - \cos \tfrac{1}{2}v'' \sin \tfrac{1}{2}v.$$

Squaring this, and reducing, we get

$$\sin^2 \tfrac{1}{2}(v'' - v) = \cos^2 \tfrac{1}{2}v + \cos^2 \tfrac{1}{2}v'' - 2 \cos \tfrac{1}{2}v'' \cos \tfrac{1}{2}v \cos \tfrac{1}{2}(v'' - v),$$

or, introducing r and q,

$$\sin^2 \tfrac{1}{2}(v'' - v) = \frac{q}{r} + \frac{q}{r''} \mp q\frac{mn}{rr''}.$$

Therefore,

$$\sin \tfrac{1}{2}(v'' - v) = \frac{\sqrt{2q}}{2\sqrt{rr''}}(m \mp n).$$

Introducing this value into equation (55), we find

$$6k(t'' - t) = m^3 \mp n^3.$$

Replacing m and n by their values expressed in terms of r, r'', and $\varkappa$, this becomes

$$6k(t'' - t) = (r + r'' + \varkappa)^{\frac{3}{2}} \mp (r + r'' - \varkappa)^{\frac{3}{2}}, \qquad (56)$$

the upper sign being used when $v'' - v$ is less than 180°. This equation expresses the relation between the time of describing any parabolic arc and the rectilinear distances of its extremities from each other and from the sun, and enables us at once, when three of these quantities are given, to find the fourth, independent of either the perihelion distance or the position of the perihelion with respect to the arc described.

68. The transcendental form of the equation (56) indicates that, when either of the quantities in the second member is to be found, it must be solved by successive trials; and, to facilitate these approximations, it may be transformed as follows:—

Since the chord $\varkappa$ can never exceed $r + r''$, we may put

$$\frac{\varkappa}{r + r''} = \sin\gamma', \tag{57}$$

and, since $\varkappa$, r, and r'' are positive, $\sin\gamma'$ must always be positive. The value of γ' must, therefore, be within the limits 0° and 180°. From the last equation we obtain

$$\cos^2\gamma' = \frac{(r + r'')^2 - \varkappa^2}{(r + r'')^2};$$

and substituting for $\varkappa^2$ its value given by

$$\varkappa^2 = (r + r'')^2 - 4rr''\cos^2\tfrac{1}{2}(v'' - v),$$

this becomes

$$\cos^2\gamma' = \frac{4rr''\cos^2\frac{1}{2}(v'' - v)}{(r + r'')^2}.$$

Therefore, we have

$$\cos\gamma' = \cos\tfrac{1}{2}(v'' - v)\,\frac{2\sqrt{rr''}}{r + r''}, \tag{58}$$

and also

$$\tan\gamma' = \frac{\varkappa}{2\sqrt{rr''}\cos\frac{1}{2}(v'' - v)}. \tag{59}$$

Hence it appears that when $v'' - v$ is less than 180°, γ' belongs to the first quadrant, and that when $v'' - v$ is greater than 180°, $\cos\gamma'$ is negative, and γ' belongs to the second quadrant.

If we introduce γ' into the expressions for m^2 and n^2, they become

$$m^2 = (r + r'')(1 + \sin\gamma'),$$
$$n^2 = (r + r'')(1 - \sin\gamma'),$$

which give

$$m^2 = (r + r'')(\cos\tfrac{1}{2}\gamma' + \sin\tfrac{1}{2}\gamma')^2,$$
$$n^2 = (r + r'')(\pm\cos\tfrac{1}{2}\gamma' \mp \sin\tfrac{1}{2}\gamma')^2;$$

and, since γ' is greater than 90° when $v'' - v$ exceeds 180°, the equation (56) becomes

$$\frac{6\tau'}{(r + r'')^{\frac{3}{2}}} = (\cos\tfrac{1}{2}\gamma' + \sin\tfrac{1}{2}\gamma')^3 - (\cos\tfrac{1}{2}\gamma' - \sin\tfrac{1}{2}\gamma')^3.$$

From this equation we get

$$\frac{6\tau'}{(r + r'')^{\frac{3}{2}}} = 6 \cos^2 \tfrac{1}{2}\gamma' \sin \tfrac{1}{2}\gamma' + 2 \sin^3 \tfrac{1}{2}\gamma',$$

or

$$\frac{6\tau'}{(r + r'')^{\frac{3}{2}}} = 6 \sin \tfrac{1}{2}\gamma' - 4 \sin^3 \tfrac{1}{2}\gamma';$$

and this, again, may be transformed into

$$\frac{6\tau'}{2^{\frac{3}{2}}(r + r'')^{\frac{3}{2}}} = 3\left(\frac{\sin \frac{1}{2}\gamma'}{\sqrt{2}}\right) - 4\left(\frac{\sin \frac{1}{2}\gamma'}{\sqrt{2}}\right)^3. \qquad (60)$$

Let us now put

$$\sin x = \frac{\sin \frac{1}{2}\gamma'}{\sqrt{2}}, \qquad (61)$$

or

$$\sin \tfrac{1}{2}\gamma' = \sqrt{2} \sin x,$$

and we have

$$\frac{3\tau'}{\sqrt{2}(r + r'')^{\frac{3}{2}}} = 3 \sin x - 4 \sin^3 x = \sin 3x. \qquad (62)$$

When $v'' - v$ is less than 180°, γ' must be less than 90°, and hence, in this case, $\sin x$ cannot exceed the value $\frac{1}{2}$, or x must be within the limits 0° and 30°. When $v'' - v$ is greater than 180°, the angle γ' is within the limits 90° and 180°, and corresponding to these limits, the values of $\sin x$ are, respectively, $\frac{1}{2}$ and $\frac{1}{2}\sqrt{2}$. Hence, in the case that $v'' - v$ exceeds 180°, it follows that x must be within the limits 30° and 45°.

The equation

$$\frac{3\tau'}{\sqrt{2}(r + r'')^{\frac{3}{2}}} = \sin 3x$$

is satisfied by the values $3x$ and $180° - 3x$; but when the first gives x less than 15°, there can be but one solution, the value $180° - 3x$ being in this case excluded by the condition that $3x$ cannot exceed 135°. When x is greater than 15°, the required condition will be satisfied by $3x$ or by $180° - 3x$, and there will be two solutions, corresponding respectively to the cases in which $v'' - v$ is less than 180°, and in which $v'' - v$ is greater than 180°. Consequently, when it is not known whether the heliocentric motion during the interval $t'' - t$ is greater or less than 180°, and we find $3x$ greater than 45°, the same data will be satisfied by these two different solutions. In practice, however, it is readily known which of the two solutions must be adopted, since, when the interval $t'' - t$ is not very large, the heliocentric motion cannot exceed 180°, unless the perihelion distance is very small; and the known circumstances will generally show whether such an assumption is admissible.

We shall now put

$$\eta = \frac{2\tau'}{(r + r'')^{\frac{3}{2}}}, \tag{63}$$

and we obtain

$$\sin 3x = \frac{3\eta}{\sqrt{8}}. \tag{64}$$

We have, also,

$$\sin \tfrac{1}{2}\gamma' = \sqrt{2} \sin x,$$

and hence

$$\cos \tfrac{1}{2}\gamma' = \sqrt{1 - 2\sin^2 x} = \sqrt{\cos 2x}.$$

Therefore

$$\sin \gamma' = 2^{\frac{3}{2}} \sin x \sqrt{\cos 2x},$$

and, since $\varkappa = (r + r'') \sin \gamma'$, we have

$$\varkappa = 2^{\frac{3}{2}} (r + r'') \sin x \sqrt{\cos 2x}.$$

If we put

$$\mu = \frac{3 \sin x}{\sin 3x} \sqrt{\cos 2x}, \tag{65}$$

the preceding equation reduces to

$$\varkappa = \frac{2\tau'}{\sqrt{(r + r'')}} \mu. \tag{66}$$

From equation (64) it appears that η must be within the limits 0 and $\frac{1}{3}\sqrt{8}$. We may, therefore, construct a table which, with η as the argument, will give the corresponding value of μ, since, with a given value of η, $3x$ may be derived from equation (64), and then the value of μ from (65). Table XI. gives the values of μ corresponding to values of η from 0.0 to 0.9.

69. In determining an orbit wholly unknown, it will be necessary to make some assumption in regard to the approximate distance of the comet from the sun. In this case the interval $t'' - t$ will generally be small, and, consequently, $\varkappa$ will be small compared with r and r''. As a first assumption we may take $r = 1$, or $r + r'' = 2$, and $\mu = 1$, and then find $\varkappa$ from the formula

$$\varkappa = \tau' \sqrt{2}.$$

With this value of $\varkappa$ we compute d, r, and r'' by means of the equations (52). Having thus found approximate values of r and r'', we compute η by means of (63), and with this value we enter Table XI. and take out the corresponding value of μ. A second value for $\varkappa$ is then found from (66), with which we recompute r and r'', and proceed as before, until the values of these quantities remain unchanged. The final values will exactly satisfy the equation (56), and will enable us to complete the determination of the orbit.

After three trials the value of $r + r''$ may be found very nearly correct from the numbers already derived. Thus, let y be the true value of $\log(r + r'')$, and let Δy be the difference between any assumed or approximate value of y and the true value, or

$$y_0 = y + \Delta y.$$

Then if we denote by y_0' the value which results by direct calculation from the assumed value y_0, we shall have

$$y_0' - y_0 = f(y_0) = f(y + \Delta y).$$

Expanding this function, we have

$$y_0' - y_0 = f(y) + A\,\Delta y + B\,\Delta y^2 + \&c.$$

But, since the equations (52) and (66) will be exactly satisfied when the true value of y is used, it follows that

$$f(y) = 0,$$

and hence, when Δy is very small, so that we may neglect terms of the second order, we shall have

$$y_0' - y_0 = A\,\Delta y = A\,(y_0 - y).$$

Let us now denote three successive approximate values of $\log(r + r'')$ by y_0, y_0', y_0'', and let

$$y_0' - y_0 = a, \qquad y_0'' - y_0' = a';$$

then we shall have

$$a = A\,(y_0 - y),$$
$$a' = A\,(y_0' - y).$$

Eliminating A from these equations, we get

$$y\,(a' - a) = a'y_0 - ay_0',$$

from which

$$y = y_0' - \frac{aa'}{a' - a} = y_0'' - \frac{a'^2}{a' - a}. \tag{67}$$

Unless the assumed values are considerably in error, the value of y or of $\log(r+r'')$ thus found will be sufficiently exact; but should it be still in error, we may, from the three values which approximate nearest to the truth, derive y with still greater accuracy. In the numerical application of this equation, a and a' may be expressed in units of the last decimal place of the logarithms employed.

The solution of equation (56), to find $t''-t$ when $\varkappa$ is known, is readily effected by means of Table VIII. Thus we have

$$\frac{3\tau'}{\sqrt{2}\,(r+r'')^{\frac{3}{2}}}=\sin 3x,$$

and, when γ' is less than 90°, if we put

$$N=\frac{\sin 3x}{\sin\gamma'},$$

we get

$$\tau'=\tfrac{1}{3}\sqrt{2}\,N\sin\gamma'\,(r+r'')^{\frac{3}{2}}, \tag{68}$$

or

$$\tau'=\tfrac{1}{3}\sqrt{2}\,N\varkappa\sqrt{r+r''}.$$

When γ' exceeds 90°, we put

$$N'=\sin 3x,$$

and we have

$$\tau'=\tfrac{1}{3}\sqrt{2}\,N'(r+r'')^{\frac{3}{2}}, \tag{69}$$

in which $\log\frac{1}{3}\sqrt{2}=9.6733937$. With the argument γ' we take from Table VIII. the corresponding value of N or N', and by means of these equations $\tau'=k\,(t''-t)$ is at once derived.

The inverse problem, in which τ' is known and $\varkappa$ is required, may also be solved by means of the same table. Thus, we may for a first approximation put

$$\varkappa=\tau'\sqrt{2},$$

and with this value of $\varkappa$ compute d, r, and r''. The value of γ' is then found from

$$\sin\gamma'=\frac{\varkappa}{r+r''},$$

and the table gives the corresponding value of N or N'. A second approximation to $\varkappa$ will be given by the equation

$$\varkappa=\frac{3}{\sqrt{2}}\cdot\frac{\tau'}{N\sqrt{r+r''}},$$

or by

$$\varkappa = \frac{3}{\sqrt{2}} \cdot \frac{\tau' \sin \gamma'}{N' \sqrt{r + r''}},$$

in which $\log \frac{3}{\sqrt{2}} = 0.3266063$. Then we recompute d, r, and r'', and proceed as before until $\varkappa$ remains unchanged. The approximations are facilitated by means of equation (67).

It will be observed that d is computed from

$$d = \pm \sqrt{\varkappa^2 - A^2},$$

and it should be known whether the positive or negative sign must be used. It is evident from the equation

$$d = \rho h - g \cos \varphi,$$

since ρ, h, and g are positive quantities, that so long as φ (which must be within the limits 0° and 180°) exceeds 90°, the value of d must be positive; and therefore φ must be less than 90°, and $g \cos \varphi$ greater than ρh, in order that d may be negative. The equation (47) shows that when $\varkappa$ is greater than g, we have

$$g \cos \varphi < \tfrac{1}{2} \rho h,$$

and hence d must in this case be positive. But when $\varkappa$ is less than g, either the positive or the negative value of d will answer to the given value of φ, and the sign to be adopted must be determined from the physical conditions of the problem.

If we suppose the chords g and $\varkappa$ to be proportional to the linear velocities of the earth and comet at the middle observation, we have, the eccentricity of the earth's orbit being neglected,

$$\varkappa = g \sqrt{\frac{2}{r'}},$$

which shows that $\varkappa$ is greater than g, and that d is positive, so long as r' is less than 2. The comets are rarely visible at a distance from the earth which much exceeds the distance of the earth from the sun, and a comet whose radius-vector is 2 must be nearly in opposition in order to satisfy this condition of visibility. Hence cases will rarely occur in which d can be negative, and for those which do occur it will generally be easy to determine which sign is to be used. However, if d is very small, it may be impossible to decide which of the two solutions is correct without comparing the resulting elements with other and more distant observations.

70. When the values of r and r'' have been finally determined, as just explained, the exact value of d may be computed, and then we have

$$\rho = \frac{d + g\cos\varphi}{h}, \qquad (70)$$
$$\rho'' = M\rho,$$

from which to find ρ and ρ''.

According to the equations $(90)_1$, we have

$$\begin{aligned} r\cos b\cos(l - \odot) &= \rho\cos(\lambda - \odot) - R, \\ r\cos b\sin(l - \odot) &= \rho\sin(\lambda - \odot), \\ r\sin b &= \rho\tan\beta, \end{aligned} \qquad (71)$$

and also

$$\begin{aligned} r''\cos b''\cos(l'' - \odot'') &= \rho''\cos(\lambda'' - \odot'') - R'', \\ r''\cos b''\sin(l'' - \odot'') &= \rho''\sin(\lambda'' - \odot''), \\ r''\sin b'' &= \rho''\tan\beta'', \end{aligned} \qquad (72)$$

in which l and l'' are the heliocentric longitudes and b, b'' the corresponding heliocentric latitudes of the comet. From these equations we find r, r'', l, l'', b, and b''; and the values of r and r'' thus found, should agree with the final values already obtained. When l'' is less than l, the motion of the comet is retrograde, or, rather, when the motion is such that the heliocentric longitude is diminishing instead of increasing.

From the equations $(82)_1$, we have

$$\begin{aligned} \pm\tan i\sin(l - \Omega) &= \tan b, \\ \pm\tan i\sin(l'' - \Omega) &= \tan b'', \end{aligned} \qquad (73)$$

which may be written

$$\pm\tan i\left(\sin(l - x)\cos(x - \Omega) + \sin(x - \Omega)\cos(l - x)\right) = \tan b,$$
$$\pm\tan i\left(\sin(l'' - x)\cos(x - \Omega) + \sin(x - \Omega)\cos(l'' - x)\right) = \tan b''.$$

Multiplying the first of these equations by $\sin(l'' - x)$, and the second by $-\sin(l - x)$, and adding the products, we get

$$\pm\tan i\sin(x - \Omega)\sin(l'' - l) = \tan b\sin(l'' - x) - \tan b''\sin(l - x);$$

and in a similar manner we find

$$\pm\tan i\cos(x - \Omega)\sin(l'' - l) = \tan b''\cos(l - x) - \tan b\cos(l'' - x).$$

Now, since x is entirely arbitrary, we may put it equal to l, and we have

$$\tan i \sin(l - \Omega) = \pm \tan b,$$
$$\tan i \cos(l - \Omega) = \pm \frac{\tan b'' - \tan b \cos(l'' - l)}{\sin(l'' - l)}, \tag{74}$$

the lower sign being used when it is desired to introduce the distinction of retrograde motion.

The formulæ will be better adapted to logarithmic calculation if we put $x = \frac{1}{2}(l'' + l)$, whence $l'' - x = \frac{1}{2}(l'' - l)$ and $l - x = \frac{1}{2}(l - l'')$; and we obtain

$$\begin{aligned}\tan i \sin\left(\tfrac{1}{2}(l'' + l) - \Omega\right) &= \pm \frac{\sin(b'' + b)}{2\cos b \cos b'' \cos\frac{1}{2}(l'' - l)},\\ \tan i \cos\left(\tfrac{1}{2}(l'' + l) - \Omega\right) &= \pm \frac{\sin(b'' - b)}{2\cos b \cos b'' \sin\frac{1}{2}(l'' - l)}.\end{aligned} \tag{75}$$

These equations may also be derived directly from (73) by addition and subtraction. Thus we have

$$\pm \tan i\left(\sin(l'' - \Omega) + \sin(l - \Omega)\right) = \tan b'' + \tan b,$$
$$\pm \tan i\left(\sin(l'' - \Omega) - \sin(l - \Omega)\right) = \tan b'' - \tan b;$$

and, since

$$\sin(l'' - \Omega) + \sin(l - \Omega) = 2\sin\tfrac{1}{2}(l'' + l - 2\Omega)\cos\tfrac{1}{2}(l'' - l),$$
$$\sin(l'' - \Omega) - \sin(l - \Omega) = 2\cos\tfrac{1}{2}(l'' + l - 2\Omega)\sin\tfrac{1}{2}(l'' - l),$$

these become

$$\begin{aligned}\tan i \sin\left(\tfrac{1}{2}(l'' + l) - \Omega\right) &= \pm \frac{\frac{1}{2}(\tan b'' + \tan b)}{\cos\frac{1}{2}(l'' - l)},\\ \tan i \cos\left(\tfrac{1}{2}(l'' + l) - \Omega\right) &= \pm \frac{\frac{1}{2}(\tan b'' - \tan b)}{\sin\frac{1}{2}(l'' - l)},\end{aligned} \tag{76}$$

which may be readily transformed into (75). However, since b and b'' will be found by means of their tangents in the numerical application of equations (71) and (72), if addition and subtraction logarithms are used, the equations last derived will be more convenient than in the form (75).

As soon as Ω and i have been computed from the preceding equations, we have, for the determination of the arguments of the latitude u and u'',

$$\tan u = \pm \frac{\tan(l - \Omega)}{\cos i}, \qquad \tan u'' = \pm \frac{\tan(l'' - \Omega)}{\cos i}. \tag{77}$$

Now we have

$$u = v + \omega,$$

in which $\omega = \pi - \Omega$ in the case of direct motion, and $\omega = \Omega - \pi$

when the distinction of retrograde motion is adopted; and we shall have

$$u'' - u = v'' - v,$$

and, consequently,

$$\varkappa^2 = r^2 + r''^2 - 2rr'' \cos(u'' - u), \tag{78}$$

or

$$\varkappa^2 = (r'' - r\cos(u'' - u))^2 + r^2 \sin^2(u'' - u). \tag{79}$$

The value of $\varkappa$ derived from this equation should agree with that already found from (66).

We have, further,

$$r = q \sec^2 \tfrac{1}{2}(u - \omega), \qquad r'' = q \sec^2 \tfrac{1}{2}(u'' - \omega),$$

or

$$\frac{1}{\sqrt{q}} \cos \tfrac{1}{2}(u - \omega) = \frac{1}{\sqrt{r}}, \qquad \frac{1}{\sqrt{q}} \cos \tfrac{1}{2}(u'' - \omega) = \frac{1}{\sqrt{r''}}.$$

By addition and subtraction, we get, from these equations,

$$\frac{1}{\sqrt{q}} \left(\cos \tfrac{1}{2}(u'' - \omega) + \cos \tfrac{1}{2}(u - \omega)\right) = \frac{1}{\sqrt{r''}} + \frac{1}{\sqrt{r}},$$
$$\frac{1}{\sqrt{q}} \left(\cos \tfrac{1}{2}(u'' - \omega) - \cos \tfrac{1}{2}(u - \omega)\right) = \frac{1}{\sqrt{r''}} - \frac{1}{\sqrt{r}},$$

from which we easily derive

$$\begin{aligned} \frac{2}{\sqrt{q}} \cos \tfrac{1}{2}\left(\tfrac{1}{2}(u'' + u) - \omega\right) \cos \tfrac{1}{4}(u'' - u) &= \frac{1}{\sqrt{r}} + \frac{1}{\sqrt{r''}}, \\ \frac{2}{\sqrt{q}} \sin \tfrac{1}{2}\left(\tfrac{1}{2}(u'' + u) - \omega\right) \sin \tfrac{1}{4}(u'' - u) &= \frac{1}{\sqrt{r}} - \frac{1}{\sqrt{r''}}. \end{aligned} \tag{80}$$

But

$$\frac{1}{\sqrt{r}} \mp \frac{1}{\sqrt{r''}} = \frac{1}{\sqrt[4]{rr''}} \left(\sqrt[4]{\frac{r''}{r}} \mp \sqrt[4]{\frac{r}{r''}}\right),$$

and if we put

$$\tan(45° + \theta') = \sqrt[4]{\frac{r''}{r}},$$

since $\sqrt[4]{\frac{r''}{r}}$ will not differ much from 1, θ' will be a small angle; and we shall have, since $\tan(45° + \theta') - \cot(45° + \theta') = 2 \tan 2\theta'$,

$$\sqrt[4]{\frac{r''}{r}} - \sqrt[4]{\frac{r}{r''}} = 2 \tan 2\theta',$$
$$\sqrt[4]{\frac{r''}{r}} + \sqrt[4]{\frac{r}{r''}} = 2 \sec 2\theta',$$

Therefore, the equations (80) become

$$\begin{aligned}\frac{1}{\sqrt{q}}\sin\tfrac{1}{2}\left(\tfrac{1}{2}(u''+u)-\omega\right)&=\frac{\tan 2\theta'}{\sin\frac{1}{4}(u''-u)\sqrt[4]{rr''}},\\ \frac{1}{\sqrt{q}}\cos\tfrac{1}{2}\left(\tfrac{1}{2}(u''+u)-\omega\right)&=\frac{\sec 2\theta'}{\cos\frac{1}{4}(u''-u)\sqrt[4]{rr''}},\end{aligned}\tag{81}$$

from which the values of q and ω may be found. Then we shall have, for the longitude of the perihelion

$$\pi=\omega+\Omega,$$

when the motion is direct, and

$$\pi=\Omega-\omega,$$

when i unrestricted exceeds 90° and the distinction of retrograde motion is adopted.

It remains now to find T, the time of perihelion passage. We have

$$v=u-\omega,\qquad v''=u''-\omega.$$

With the resulting values of v and v'' we may find, by means of Table VI., the corresponding values of M (which must be distinguished from the symbol M already used to denote the ratio of the curtate distances), and if these values are designated by M and M'', we shall have

$$t-T=\frac{M}{m},\qquad t''-T=\frac{M''}{m},$$

or

$$T=t-\frac{M}{m}=t''-\frac{M''}{m},$$

in which $m=\frac{C_0}{q^{\frac{3}{2}}}$, and $\log C_0=9.9601277$. When v is negative, the corresponding value of M is negative. The agreement between the two values of T will be a final proof of the accuracy of the numerical calculation.

The value of T when the true anomaly is small, is most readily and accurately found by means of Table VIII., from which we derive the two values of N and compute the corresponding values of T from the equation

$$T=t-\frac{2}{3k}Nr^{\frac{3}{2}}\sin v,$$

in which $\log\frac{2}{3k}=1.5883273$. When v is greater than 90°, we derive the values of N' from the table, and compute the corresponding values of T from

$$T = t - \frac{2}{3k} N' r^{\frac{3}{2}}.$$

71. The elements q and T may be derived directly from the values of r, r'', and $\varkappa$, as derived from the equations (52), without first finding the position of the plane of the orbit and the position of the orbit in its own plane. Thus, the equations (80), replacing u and u'' by their values $v + \omega$ and $v'' + \omega''$, become

$$\begin{aligned} \frac{2}{\sqrt{q}} \sin \tfrac{1}{4} (v'' + v) \sin \tfrac{1}{4} (v'' - v) &= \frac{1}{\sqrt{r}} - \frac{1}{\sqrt{r''}}, \\ \frac{2}{\sqrt{q}} \cos \tfrac{1}{4} (v'' + v) \cos \tfrac{1}{4} (v'' - v) &= \frac{1}{\sqrt{r}} + \frac{1}{\sqrt{r''}}. \end{aligned} \qquad (82)$$

Adding together the squares of these, and reducing, we get

$$\frac{1}{q} = \frac{\frac{1}{r} + \frac{1}{r''} - \frac{2}{\sqrt{rr''}} \cos \frac{1}{2} (v'' - v)}{\sin^2 \frac{1}{2} (v'' - v)},$$

or

$$q = \frac{rr'' \sin^2 \frac{1}{2} (v'' - v)}{r'' + r - 2\sqrt{rr''} \cos \frac{1}{2} (v'' - v)}.$$

Combining this equation with (59), the result is

$$q = \frac{rr'' \sin^2 \frac{1}{2} (v'' - v)}{r + r'' - \varkappa \cot \gamma'},$$

and hence, since $\varkappa = (r + r'') \sin \gamma'$,

$$q = \frac{rr''}{\varkappa} \sin^2 \tfrac{1}{2} (v'' - v) \cot \tfrac{1}{2} \gamma'. \qquad (83)$$

We have, further, from (78),

$$\varkappa^2 = (r'' - r)^2 + 4rr'' \sin^2 \tfrac{1}{2} (v'' - v),$$

from which, putting

$$\sin \nu = \frac{r'' - r}{\varkappa}, \qquad (84)$$

we derive

$$\cos \nu = \frac{2\sqrt{rr''}}{\varkappa} \sin \tfrac{1}{2} (v'' - v). \qquad (85)$$

Therefore, the equation (83) becomes

$$q = \tfrac{1}{2}(r + r'') \cos^2 \tfrac{1}{2}\gamma' \cos^2 \nu, \tag{86}$$

by means of which q is derived directly from r, r'', and $\varkappa$, the value of ν being found by means of the formula (84), so that $\cos \nu$ is positive.

When γ' cannot be found with sufficient accuracy from the equation

$$\sin \gamma' = \frac{\varkappa}{r + r''},$$

we may use another form. Thus, we have

$$1 + \sin \gamma' = \frac{r + r'' + \varkappa}{r + r''}, \qquad 1 - \sin \gamma' = \frac{r + r'' - \varkappa}{r + r''},$$

which give, by division,

$$\tan(45^\circ + \tfrac{1}{2}\gamma') = \sqrt{\frac{r + r'' + \varkappa}{r + r'' - \varkappa}}. \tag{87}$$

In a similar manner, we derive

$$\tan(45^\circ + \tfrac{1}{2}\nu) = \sqrt{\frac{\varkappa + (r'' - r)}{\varkappa - (r'' - r)}}. \tag{88}$$

In order to find the time of perihelion passage, it is necessary first to derive the values of v and v''. The equations (59) and (85) give, by multiplication,

$$\tan \tfrac{1}{2}(v'' - v) = \tan \gamma' \cos \nu, \tag{89}$$

from which $v'' - v$ may be computed. From (82) we get

$$\tan \tfrac{1}{4}(v'' + v) \tan \tfrac{1}{4}(v'' - v) = \frac{\sqrt{\frac{r''}{r}} - 1}{\sqrt{\frac{r''}{r}} + 1}.$$

If we put

$$\tan \chi' = \sqrt{\frac{r''}{r}}, \tag{90}$$

this equation reduces to

$$\tan \tfrac{1}{4}(v'' + v) = \tan(\chi' - 45^\circ) \cot \tfrac{1}{4}(v'' - v), \tag{91}$$

and the equations (81) give, also,

$$\tan \tfrac{1}{4}(v'' + v) = \cot \tfrac{1}{4}(v'' - v) \sin 2\theta',$$

either of which may be used to find $v'' + v$.

From the equations

$$\frac{\cos\frac{1}{2}v}{\sqrt{q}} = \frac{1}{\sqrt{r}}, \qquad \frac{\cos\frac{1}{2}v''}{\sqrt{q}} = \frac{1}{\sqrt{r''}},$$

by multiplying the first by $\sin\frac{1}{2}v''$ and the second by $-\sin\frac{1}{2}v$, adding the products and reducing, we easily find

$$\frac{\sin\frac{1}{2}(v''-v)\sin\frac{1}{2}v}{\sqrt{q}} = \frac{\cos\frac{1}{2}(v''-v)}{\sqrt{r}} - \frac{1}{\sqrt{r''}}.$$

Hence we have

$$\begin{aligned} \frac{1}{\sqrt{q}}\sin\tfrac{1}{2}v &= \frac{\cot\frac{1}{2}(v''-v)}{\sqrt{r}} - \frac{1}{\sqrt{r''}\sin\frac{1}{2}(v''-v)}, \\ \frac{1}{\sqrt{q}}\cos\tfrac{1}{2}v &= \frac{1}{\sqrt{r}}, \end{aligned} \tag{92}$$

which may be used to compute q, v, and v'' when $v''-v$ is known.

When $\frac{1}{2}(v''-v)$ and $\frac{1}{2}(v''+v)$, and hence v'' and v, have been determined, the time of perihelion passage must be found, as already explained, by means of Table VI. or Table VIII.

It is evident, therefore, that in the determination of an orbit, as soon as the numerical values of r, r'', and $\varkappa$ have been derived from the equations (52), instead of completing the calculation of the elements of the orbit, we may find q and T, and then, by means of these, the values of r' and v' may be computed directly. When this has been effected, the values of n and n'' may be found from (3), or that of $\frac{n}{n''}$ from (34). Then we compute ρ by means of the first of equations (70), and the corrected value of M from (33), or, in the special cases already examined, from the equations (37) and (39). In this way, by successive approximations, the determination of parabolic elements from given data may be carried to the limit of accuracy which is consistent with the assumption of parabolic motion. In the case, however, of the equations (37) and (39), the neglected terms may be of the second order, and, consequently, for the final results it will be necessary, in order to attain the greatest possible accuracy, to derive

$$M = \frac{\rho''}{\rho}$$

from (15) and (16). When the final value of M has been found, the determination of the elements is completed by means of the formulæ already given.

72. EXAMPLE.—To illustrate the application of the formulæ for the calculation of the parabolic elements of the orbit of a comet by a numerical example, let us take the following observations of the Fifth Comet of 1863, made at Ann Arbor:—

Ann Arbor M. T.	α	δ
1864 Jan. 10 $6^h\ 57^m\ 20^s.5$	$19^h\ 14^m\ 4^s.92$	$+34°\ 6'\ 27''.4$,
13 6 11 54 .7	19 25 2 .84	36 36 52 .8,
16 6 35 11 .6	19 41 4 .54	$+39$ 41 26 .9.

These places are referred to the apparent equinox of the date and are already corrected for parallax and aberration by means of approximate values of the geocentric distances of the comet. But if approximate values of these distances are not already known, the corrections for parallax and aberration may be neglected in the first determination of the approximate elements of the unknown orbit of a comet. If we convert the observed right ascensions and declinations into the corresponding longitudes and latitudes by means of equations (1), and reduce the times of observation to the meridian of Washington, we get

Washington M. T.	λ	β
1864 Jan. 10 $7^h\ 24^m\ 3^s$	$297°\ 53'\ 7''.6$	$+55°\ 46'\ 58''.4$,
13 6 38 37	302 57 51 .3	57 39 35 .9,
16 7 1 54	310 31 52 .3	$+59$ 38 18 .7.

Next, we reduce these places by applying the corrections for precession and nutation to the mean equinox of 1864.0, and reduce the times of observation to decimals of a day, and we have

$$t = 10.30837, \quad \lambda = 297°\ 52'\ 51''.1, \quad \beta = +55°\ 46'\ 58''.4,$$
$$t' = 13.27682, \quad \lambda' = 302\ \ 57\ \ 34\ .4, \quad \beta' = \ \ 57\ \ 39\ \ 35\ .9,$$
$$t'' = 16.29299, \quad \lambda'' = 310\ \ 31\ \ 35\ .0, \quad \beta'' = +59\ \ 38\ \ 18\ .7.$$

For the same times we find, from the *American Nautical Almanac*,

$$\odot = 290°\ 6'\ 27''.4, \qquad \log R = 9.992763,$$
$$\odot' = 293\ \ 7\ \ 57\ .1, \qquad \log R' = 9.992830,$$
$$\odot'' = 296\ \ 12\ \ 15\ .7, \qquad \log R'' = 9.992916,$$

which are referred to the mean equinox of 1864.0. It will generally be sufficient, in a first approximation, to use logarithms of five decimals; but, in order to exhibit the calculation in a more complete form, we shall retain six places of decimals.

Since the intervals are very nearly equal, we may assume

$$\frac{n}{n''} = \frac{\tau}{\tau''} = \frac{N}{N''}.$$

Then we have

$$M = \frac{t''-t'}{t'-t} \cdot \frac{\tan\beta' \sin(\lambda - \odot') - \tan\beta \sin(\lambda' - \odot')}{\tan\beta'' \sin(\lambda' - \odot') - \tan\beta' \sin(\lambda'' - \odot')},$$

and

$$\begin{aligned}
g \sin(G - \odot) &= R'' \sin(\odot'' - \odot), \\
g \cos(G - \odot) &= R'' \cos(\odot'' - \odot) - R; \\
h \cos\zeta \cos(H - \lambda'') &= M - \cos(\lambda'' - \lambda), \\
h \cos\zeta \sin(H - \lambda'') &= \sin(\lambda'' - \lambda), \\
h \sin\zeta \qquad\qquad &= M \tan\beta'' - \tan\beta;
\end{aligned}$$

from which to find M, G, g, H, ζ, and h. Thus we obtain

$$\begin{aligned}
\log M &= 9.829827, & H &= 94^\circ\ 24'\ \ 1''.8, \\
G &= 22^\circ\ 58'\ 1''.7, & \zeta &= -40\ \ 28\ \ 21\ .9, \\
\log g &= 9.019613, & \log h &= 9.688532.
\end{aligned}$$

Since $\frac{\Delta''}{\Delta} = M\frac{\cos\beta}{\cos\beta''} = 0.752$, it appears that the comet, at the time of these observations, was rapidly approaching the earth. The quadrants in which $G - \odot$ and $H - \lambda''$ must be taken, are determined by the condition that g and $h \cos\zeta$ must always be positive. The value of M should be checked by duplicate calculation, since an error in this will not be exhibited until the values of λ' and β' are computed from the resulting elements.

Next, from

$$\cos\psi = \cos\beta \cos(\lambda - \odot), \qquad \cos\psi'' = \cos\beta'' \cos(\lambda'' - \odot''),$$
$$\cos\varphi = \cos\zeta \cos(G - H),$$

we compute $\cos\psi$, $\cos\psi''$, and $\cos\varphi$; and then from

$$\begin{aligned}
g \sin\varphi &= A, & h \cos\beta &= b, \\
R \sin\psi &= B, & \frac{h\cos\beta''}{M} &= b'', \\
R'' \sin\psi'' &= B'', & & \\
g\cos\varphi - bR\cos\psi &= c, & g\cos\varphi - b''R''\cos\psi'' &= c'',
\end{aligned}$$

we obtain A, B, B'', &c. It will generally be sufficiently exact to find $\sin\psi$ and $\sin\psi''$ from $\cos\psi$ and $\cos\psi''$; but if more accurate values of ψ and ψ'' are required, they may be obtained by means of the equations (42) and (43). Thus we derive

$$\begin{aligned}
\log A &= 9.006485, & \log B &= 9.912052, & \log B'' &= 9.933366, \\
\log b &= 9.438524, & & & \log b'' &= [illegible].562387, \\
c &= -0.125067, & & & c'' &= [illegible]\ 0.150562.
\end{aligned}$$

Then we have

$$\tau' = k(t'' - t), \qquad \eta = \frac{2\tau'}{(r + r'')^{\frac{3}{2}}},$$

$$\varkappa = \frac{2\tau'}{\sqrt{r + r''}}\mu, \qquad d = \sqrt{\varkappa^2 - A^2},$$

$$r = \sqrt{\left(\frac{d + c}{b}\right)^2 + B^2}, \qquad r'' = \sqrt{\left(\frac{d + c''}{b''}\right)^2 + B''^2},$$

from which to find, by successive trials, the values of r, r'', and $\varkappa$, that of μ being found from Table XI. with the argument η. First, we assume

$$\log \varkappa = \log \tau' \sqrt{2} = 9.163132,$$

and with this we obtain

$$\log r = 9.913895, \qquad \log r'' = 9.938040, \qquad \log(r + r'') = 0.227165.$$

This value of $\log(r + r'')$ gives $\eta = 0.094$, and from Table XI. we find $\log \mu = 0.000160$. Hence we derive

$$\log \varkappa = 9.200220, \qquad \log r = 9.912097, \qquad \log r'' = 9.935187,$$
$$\log(r + r'') = 0.224825.$$

Repeating the operation, using the last value of $\log(r + r'')$, we get

$$\log \varkappa = 9.201396, \qquad \log r = 9.912083, \qquad \log r'' = 9.935117,$$
$$\log(r + r'') = 0.224783.$$

The correct value of $\log(r + r'')$ may now be found by means of the equation (67). Thus, we have, in units of the sixth decimal place of the logarithms,

$$a = 224825 - 227165 = -2340, \qquad a' = 224783 - 224825 = -42,$$

and the correction to the last value of $\log(r + r'')$ becomes

$$-\frac{a'^2}{a' - a} = -0.8.$$

Therefore,

$$\log(r + r'') = 0.224782,$$

and, recomputing η, μ, $\varkappa$, r, and r'', we get, finally,

$$\log \varkappa = 9.201419, \qquad \log r = 9.912083, \qquad \log r'' = 9.935116,$$
$$\log(r + r'') = 0.224782.$$

The agreement of the last value of $\log(r + r'')$ with the preceding one shows that the results are correct. Further, it appears from the values of r and r'' that the comet had passed its perihelion and was receding from the sun.

By means of the values of r and r'' we might compute approximate values of r' and $\frac{dr'}{dt}$ from the equations (30) and (31), and then a more approximate value of $\frac{n}{n''}$ from (28), that of $\frac{N}{N''}$ being found from (32). But, since r' differs but little from R', the difference between $\frac{n}{n''}$ and $\frac{N}{N''}$ is very small, so that it is not necessary to consider the second term of the second member of the equation (33); and, since the intervals are very nearly equal, the error of the assumption

$$\frac{n}{n''} = \frac{\tau}{\tau''}$$

is of the third order. It should be observed, however, that an error in the value of M affects H, ζ, h, and hence also A, b, b'', c, and c'', and the resulting value of ρ may be affected by an error which considerably exceeds that of M. It is advantageous, therefore, to select observations which furnish intervals as nearly equal as possible in order that the error of M may be small, otherwise it may become necessary to correct M and to repeat the calculation of r, r'', and $\varkappa$. We may also compute the perihelion distance and the time of perihelion passage from r, r'', and $\varkappa$ by means of the equations (86), (89), and (91) in connection with Tables VI. and VIII. Then r' and v' may be computed directly, and the complete expression for M may be employed.

In the first determination of the elements, and especially when the corrections for parallax and aberration have been neglected, it is unnecessary to attempt to arrive at the limit of accuracy attainable, since, when approximate elements have been found, the observations may be more conveniently reduced, and those which include a longer interval may be used in a more complete calculation. Hence, as soon as r, r'', and $\varkappa$ have been found, the curtate distances are next determined, and then the elements of the orbit. To find ρ and ρ'', we have

$$d = +\,0.122395,$$

the positive sign being used since $\varkappa$ is greater than g, and the formulæ

$$\rho = \frac{d + g\cos\varphi}{h}, \qquad \rho'' = M\rho,$$

give

$$\log\rho = 9.480952, \qquad \log\rho'' = 9.310779.$$

From these values of ρ and ρ'', it appears that the comet was very near the earth at the time of the observations.

The heliocentric places are then found by means of the equations (71) and (72). Thus we obtain

$$l = 106^\circ\ 40'\ 50''.5, \qquad b = +33^\circ\ 1'\ 10''.6, \qquad \log r = 9.912082,$$
$$l'' = 112\ \ 31\ \ 9\ .9, \qquad b'' = +23\ \ 55\ \ 5\ .8, \qquad \log r'' = 9.935116.$$

The agreement of these values of r and r'' with those previously found, checks the accuracy of the calculation. Further, since the heliocentric longitudes are increasing, the motion is *direct*.

The longitude of the ascending node and the inclination of the orbit may now be found by means of the equations (74), (75), or (76); and we get

$$\Omega = 304^\circ\ 43'\ 11''.5, \qquad i = 64^\circ\ 31'\ 21''.7.$$

The values of u and u'' are given by the formulæ

$$\tan u = \frac{\tan (l - \Omega)}{\cos i}, \qquad \tan u'' = \frac{\tan (l'' - \Omega)}{\cos i},$$

u and $l - \Omega$ being in the same quadrant in the case of direct motion. Thus we obtain

$$u = 142^\circ\ 52'\ 12''.4, \qquad u'' = 153^\circ\ 18'\ 49''.4.$$

Then the equation

$$\varkappa^2 = (r'' - r\cos (u'' - u))^2 + r^2 \sin^2 (u'' - u)$$

gives

$$\log \varkappa = 9.201423,$$

and the agreement of this value of $\varkappa$ with that previously found, proves the calculation of Ω, i, u, and u''.

From the equations

$$\tan (45^\circ + \theta') = \sqrt[4]{\frac{r''}{r}},$$

$$\frac{1}{\sqrt{q}} \sin \tfrac{1}{2} \left(\tfrac{1}{2} (u'' + u) - \omega\right) = \frac{\tan 2\theta'}{\sin \frac{1}{4} (u'' - u) \sqrt[4]{rr''}},$$

$$\frac{1}{\sqrt{q}} \cos \tfrac{1}{2} \left(\tfrac{1}{2} (u'' + u) - \omega\right) = \frac{\sec 2\theta'}{\cos \frac{1}{4} (u'' - u) \sqrt[4]{rr''}},$$

we get

$$\theta' = 0^\circ\ 22'\ 47''.4, \qquad \omega = 115^\circ\ 40'\ 6''.3, \qquad \log q = 9.887378.$$

Hence we have

$$\pi = \omega + \Omega = 60^\circ\ 23'\ 17''.8,$$

and

$$v = u - \omega = 27^\circ\ 12'\ 6''.1, \qquad v'' = u'' - \omega = 37^\circ\ 38'\ 43''.1.$$

Then we obtain

$$\log m = 9.9601277 - \tfrac{3}{2}\log q = 0.129061,$$

and, corresponding to the values of v and v'', Table VI. gives

$$\log M = 1.267163, \qquad \log M'' = 1.424152.$$

Therefore, for the time of perihelion passage, we have

$$T = t - \frac{M}{m} = t - 13.74364,$$

and

$$T = t'' - \frac{M''}{m} = t'' - 19.72836.$$

The first value gives $T = 1863$ Dec. 27.56473, and the second gives $T =$ Dec. 27.56463. The agreement between these results is the final proof of the calculation of the elements from the adopted value of $M = \frac{\rho''}{\rho}$.

If we find T by means of Table VIII., we have

$$\log N = 0.021616, \qquad \log N'' = 0.018210,$$

and the equation

$$T = t - \frac{2}{3k} N r^{\frac{3}{2}} \sin v = t'' - \frac{2}{3k} N'' r''^{\frac{3}{2}} \sin v'',$$

in which $\log \frac{2}{3k} = 1.5883273$, gives for T the values Dec. 27.56473 and Dec. 27.56469.

Collecting together the several results obtained, we have the following elements:

$$\begin{aligned} T &= 1863 \text{ Dec. } 27.56471 \text{ Washington mean time.} \\ \pi &= \left.\begin{aligned} &60^\circ\ 23'\ 17''.8 \\ &304\ \ 43\ \ 11\ .5 \\ &64\ \ 31\ \ 21\ .7 \end{aligned}\right\} \text{Ecliptic and Mean Equinox 1864.0,} \\ \log q &= 9.887378. \end{aligned}$$

(the three lines of the brace being π, ☊, i)

Motion Direct.

73. The elements thus derived will, in all cases, exactly represent the extreme places of the comet, since these only have been used in finding the elements after ρ and ρ'' have been found. If, by means

of these elements, we compute n and n'', and correct the value of M, the elements which will then be obtained will approximate nearer the true values; and each successive correction will furnish more accurate results. When the adopted value of M is exact, the resulting elements must by calculation reproduce this value, and since the computed values of λ, λ'', β, and β'' will be the same as the observed values, the computed values of λ' and β' must be such that when substituted in the equation for M, the same result will be obtained as when the observed values of λ' and β' are used. But, according to the equations (13) and (14), the value of M depends only on the inclination to the ecliptic of a great circle passing through the places of the sun and comet for the time t', and is independent of the angle at the earth between the sun and comet. Hence, the spherical coordinates of any point of the great circle joining these places of the sun and comet will, in connection with those of the extreme places, give the same value of M, and when the exact value of M has been used in deriving the elements, the computed values of λ' and β' must give the same value for w' as that which is obtained from observation. But if we represent by ψ' the angle at the earth between the sun and comet at the time t', the values of ψ' derived by observation and by computation from the elements will differ, unless the middle place is exactly represented. In general, this difference will be small, and since w' is constant, the equations

$$\begin{aligned} \cos\psi' &= \cos\beta' \cos(\lambda' - \odot'), \\ \sin\psi' \cos w' &= \cos\beta' \sin(\lambda' - \odot'), \\ \sin\psi' \sin w' &= \sin\beta', \end{aligned} \tag{93}$$

give, by differentiation,

$$\begin{aligned} \cos\beta'\, d\lambda' &= \cos w' \sec\beta'\, d\psi', \\ d\beta' &= \sin w' \cos(\lambda' - \odot')\, d\psi'. \end{aligned} \tag{94}$$

From these we get

$$\frac{\cos\beta'\, d\lambda'}{d\beta'} = \frac{\tan(\lambda' - \odot')}{\sin\beta'},$$

which expresses the ratio of the residual errors in longitude and latitude, for the middle place, when the correct value of M has been used.

Whenever these conditions are satisfied, the elements will be correct on the hypothesis of parabolic motion, and the magnitude of the final residuals in the middle place will depend on the deviation of the actual orbit of the comet from the parabolic form. Further, when elements have been derived from a value of M which has not been finally corrected, if we compute λ' and β' by means of these elements, and then

$$\tan w' = \frac{\tan \beta'}{\sin(\lambda' - \odot')}, \tag{95}$$

the comparison of this value of $\tan w'$ with that given by observation will show whether any further correction of M is necessary, and if the difference is not greater than what may be due to unavoidable errors of calculation, we may regard M as exact.

To compare the elements obtained in the case of the example given with the middle place, we find

$$v' = 32^\circ\ 31'\ 13''.5, \qquad u' = 148^\circ\ 11'\ 19''.8, \qquad \log r' = 9.922836.$$

Then from the equations

$$\tan(l' - \Omega) = \cos i \tan u',$$
$$\tan b' = \tan i \sin(l' - \Omega),$$

we derive

$$l' = 109^\circ\ 46'\ 48''.3, \qquad b' = 28^\circ\ 24'\ 56''.0.$$

By means of these and the values of $\odot'$ and R', we obtain

$$\lambda' = 302^\circ\ 57'\ 41''.1, \qquad \beta' = 57^\circ\ 39'\ 37''.0;$$

and, comparing these results with the observed values of λ' and β', the residuals for the middle place are found to be

Comp. — Obs.

$$\cos \beta' \Delta\lambda' = +3''.6, \qquad \Delta\beta = +1''.1.$$

The ratio of these remaining errors, after making due allowance for unavoidable errors of calculation, shows that the adopted value of M is not exact, since the error of the longitude should be less than that of the latitude.

The value of w' given by observation is

$$\log \tan w' = 0.966314,$$

and that given by the computed values of λ' and β' is

$$\log \tan w' = 0.966247.$$

The difference being greater than what can be attributed to errors of calculation, it appears that the value of M requires further correction. Since the difference is small, we may derive the correct value of M by using the same assumed value of $\frac{n}{n''}$, and, instead of the value of $\tan w'$ derived from observation, a value differing as much from this in a contrary direction as the computed value differs. Thus, in the present example, the computed value of $\log \tan w'$ is 0.000067 less than the observed value, and, in finding the new value of M, we must use

$$\log \tan w' = 0.966381$$

in computing β_0 and β_0'' involved in the first of equations (14). If the first of equations (10) is employed, we must use, instead of $\tan \beta'$ as derived from observation,

$$\tan \beta' = \tan w' \sin (\lambda' - \odot'),$$

or

$$\log \tan \beta' = 0.966381 + \log \sin (\lambda' - \odot') = 0.198559,$$

the observed value of λ' being retained. Thus we derive

$$\log M = 9.829586,$$

and if the elements of the orbit are computed by means of this value, they will represent the middle place in accordance with the condition that the difference between the computed and the observed value of $\tan w'$ shall be zero.

A system of elements computed with the same data from $\log M = 9.822906$ gives for the error of the middle place,

C. — O.

$$\cos \beta' \Delta \lambda' = -1' \, 26''.2, \qquad \Delta \beta' = -40''.1.$$

If we interpolate by means of the residuals thus found for two values of M, it appears that a system of elements computed from

$$\log M = 9.829586$$

will almost exactly represent the middle place, so that the data are completely satisfied by the hypothesis of parabolic motion.

The equations (34) and (32) give

$$\log \frac{n}{n''} = 0.006955, \qquad \log \frac{N}{N''} = 0.006831,$$

and from (10) we get

$$\log M' = 9.822906, \qquad \log M'' = 9.663729_n.$$

Then by means of the equation (33) we derive, for the corrected value of M,

$$\log M = 9.829582,$$

which differs only in the sixth decimal place from the result obtained by varying $\tan w'$ and retaining the approximate values $\frac{n}{n''} = \frac{\tau}{\tau''} = \frac{N}{N''}$.

74. When the approximate elements of the orbit of a comet are known, they may be corrected by using observations which include a longer interval of time. The most convenient method of effecting this correction is by the variation of the geocentric distance for the time of one of the extreme observations, and the formulæ which may be derived for this purpose are applicable, without modification, to any case in which it is possible to determine the elements of the orbit of a comet on the supposition of motion in a parabola. Since there are only five elements to be determined in the case of parabolic motion, if the distance of the comet from the earth corresponding to the time of one complete observation is known, one additional complete observation will enable us to find the elements of the orbit. Therefore, if the elements are computed which result from two or more assumed values of Δ differing but little from the correct value, by comparison of intermediate observations with these different systems of elements, we may derive that value of the geocentric distance of the comet for which the resulting elements will best represent the observations.

In order that the formulæ may be applicable to the case of any fundamental plane, let us consider the equator as this plane, and, supposing the data to be three complete observations, let A, A', A'' be the right ascensions, and D, D', D'' the declinations of the sun for the times t, t', t''. The co-ordinates of the first place of the earth referred to the third are

$$\begin{aligned} x &= R'' \cos D'' \cos A'' - R \cos D \cos A, \\ y &= R'' \cos D'' \sin A'' - R \cos D \sin A, \\ z &= R'' \sin D'' \qquad\qquad\quad - R \sin D. \end{aligned}$$

If we represent by g the chord of the earth's orbit between the places for the first and third observations, and by G and K, respectively, the right ascension and declination of the first place of the earth as seen from the third, we shall have

$$\begin{aligned} x &= g \cos K \cos G, \\ y &= g \cos K \sin G, \\ z &= g \sin K, \end{aligned}$$

and, consequently,

$$\begin{aligned} g\cos K\cos(G-A) &= R''\cos D''\cos(A''-A)-R\cos D,\\ g\cos K\sin(G-A) &= R''\cos D''\sin(A''-A),\\ g\sin K &= R''\sin D''-R\sin D,\end{aligned} \tag{96}$$

from which g, K, and G may be found.

If we designate by $x_{,}$, $y_{,}$, $z_{,}$ the co-ordinates of the first place of the comet referred to the third place of the earth, we shall have

$$\begin{aligned} x_{,} &= \Delta\cos\delta\cos\alpha+g\cos K\cos G,\\ y_{,} &= \Delta\cos\delta\sin\alpha+g\cos K\sin G,\\ z_{,} &= \Delta\sin\delta\qquad\quad +g\sin K.\end{aligned}$$

Let us now put

$$\begin{aligned} x_{,} &= h'\cos\zeta'\cos H',\\ y_{,} &= h'\cos\zeta'\sin H',\\ z_{,} &= h'\sin\zeta',\end{aligned}$$

and we get

$$\begin{aligned} h'\cos\zeta'\cos(H'-G) &= \Delta\cos\delta\cos(\alpha-G)+g\cos K,\\ h'\cos\zeta'\sin(H'-G) &= \Delta\cos\delta\sin(\alpha-G),\\ h'\sin\zeta' &= \Delta\sin\delta+g\sin K,\end{aligned} \tag{97}$$

from which to determine H', ζ', and h'.

If we represent by φ' the angle at the third place of the earth between the actual first and third places of the comet in space, we obtain

$$\cos\varphi'=\cos\zeta'\cos H'\cos\delta''\cos\alpha''+\cos\zeta'\sin H'\cos\delta''\sin\alpha''+\sin\zeta'\sin\delta'',$$

or

$$\cos\varphi'=\cos\zeta'\cos\delta''\cos(\alpha''-H')+\sin\zeta'\sin\delta''; \tag{98}$$

and if we put

$$\begin{aligned} e\sin f &= \sin\delta'',\\ e\cos f &= \cos\delta''\cos(\alpha''-H')\end{aligned}$$

this becomes

$$\cos\varphi'=e\cos(\zeta'-f). \tag{99}$$

Then we shall have

$$\varkappa^2=h'^2+\Delta''^2-2h'\Delta''\cos\varphi'$$

or

$$\varkappa^2=(\Delta''-h'\cos\varphi')^2+h'^2\sin^2\varphi', \tag{100}$$

in which Δ'' is the distance of the comet from the earth corresponding to the last observation. We have, also, from equations (44) and (45),

$$\begin{aligned} r^2 &= (\Delta-R\cos\psi)^2+R^2\sin^2\psi,\\ r''^2 &= (\Delta''-R''\cos\psi'')^2+R''^2\sin^2\psi'',\end{aligned} \tag{101}$$

in which ψ is the angle at the earth between the sun and comet at the time t, and ψ'' the same angle at the time t''. To find their values, we have

$$\begin{aligned}\cos\psi &= \cos D\cos\delta\cos(\alpha - A) + \sin D\sin\delta,\\ \cos\psi'' &= \cos D''\cos\delta''\cos(\alpha'' - A'') + \sin D''\sin\delta'',\end{aligned} \tag{102}$$

which may be still further reduced by the introduction of auxiliary angles as in the case of equation (98).

Let us now put

$$\begin{aligned} h'\sin\varphi' &= C, & h'\cos\varphi' &= c,\\ R\sin\psi &= B, & R\cos\psi &= b,\\ R''\sin\psi'' &= B'', & R''\cos\psi'' &= b'', \end{aligned} \tag{103}$$

and we shall have

$$\begin{aligned} \varkappa &= \sqrt{(\varDelta'' - c)^2 + C^2},\\ r &= \sqrt{(\varDelta - b)^2 + B^2},\\ r'' &= \sqrt{(\varDelta'' - b'')^2 + B''^2}. \end{aligned} \tag{104}$$

These equations, together with (56), will enable us to determine $\varDelta''$ by successive trials when $\varDelta$ is given.

We may, therefore, assume an approximate value of $\varDelta''$ by means of the approximate elements known, and find r'' from the last of these equations, the value of r having been already found from the assumed value of $\varDelta$. Then $\varkappa$ is obtained from the equation

$$\varkappa = \frac{2\tau'}{\sqrt{r + r''}}\mu,$$

μ being found by means of Table XI., and a second approximation to the value of $\varDelta''$ from

$$\varDelta'' = c \pm \sqrt{\varkappa^2 - C^2}. \tag{105}$$

The approximate elements will give $\varDelta''$ near enough to show whether the upper or lower sign must be used. With the value of $\varDelta''$ thus found we recompute r'' and $\varkappa$ as before, and in a similar manner find a still closer approximation to the correct value of $\varDelta''$. A few trials will generally give the correct result.

When $\varDelta''$ has thus been determined, the heliocentric places are found by means of the formulæ

$$\begin{aligned} r\cos b\cos(l - A) &= \varDelta\cos\delta\cos(\alpha - A) - R\cos D,\\ r\cos b\sin(l - A) &= \varDelta\cos\delta\sin(\alpha - A),\\ r\sin b &= \varDelta\sin\delta - R\sin D; \end{aligned} \tag{106}$$

$$\begin{aligned} r'' \cos b'' \cos(l'' - A'') &= \Delta'' \cos \delta'' \cos(\alpha'' - A'') - R'' \cos D'', \\ r'' \cos b'' \sin(l'' - A'') &= \Delta'' \cos \delta'' \sin(\alpha'' - A''), \\ r'' \sin b'' &= \Delta'' \sin \delta'' - R'' \sin D'', \end{aligned} \tag{107}$$

in which b, b'', l, l'' are the heliocentric spherical co-ordinates referred to the equator as the fundamental plane. The values of r and r'' found from these equations must agree with those obtained from (104).

The elements of the orbit may now be determined by means of the equations (75), (77), and (81), in connection with Tables VI. and VIII., as already explained. The elements thus derived will be referred to the equator, or to a plane passing through the centre of the sun and parallel to the earth's equator, and they may be transformed into those for the ecliptic as the fundamental plane by means of the equations $(109)_1$.

75. With the resulting elements we compute the place of the comet for the time t' and compare it with the corresponding observed place, and if we denote the computed right ascension and declination by α_0' and δ_0', respectively, we shall have

$$\alpha' + a' = \alpha_0', \qquad \delta' + d' = \delta_0',$$

in which a' and d' denote the differences between computation and observation. Next we assume a second value of Δ, which we represent by $\Delta + \delta\Delta$, and compute the corresponding system of elements. Then we have

$$\alpha' + a'' = \alpha_0', \qquad \delta' + d'' = \delta_0',$$

a'' and d'' denoting the differences between computation and observation for the second system of elements. We also compute a third system of elements with the distance $\Delta - \delta\Delta$, and denote the differences between computation and observation by a and d; then we shall have

$$a = f(\Delta - \delta\Delta), \qquad a' = f(\Delta), \qquad a'' = f(\Delta + \delta\Delta),$$

and similarly for d, d', and d''. If these three numbers are exactly represented by the expression

$$m + n\frac{x}{\delta\Delta} + o\left(\frac{x}{\delta\Delta}\right)^2,$$

in which $\Delta + x$ is the general value of the argument, since the values of a, a', and a'' will be such that the third differences may be neglected, this formula may be assumed to express exactly any value of the function corresponding to a value of the argument not differing much from Δ, or within the limits $x = -\delta\Delta$ and $x = +\delta\Delta$, the assumed values $\Delta - \delta\Delta$, Δ, and $\Delta + \delta\Delta$ being so taken that the correct value of Δ shall be either within these limits or very nearly so.

To find the coefficients m, n, and o, we have

$$m - n + o = a, \qquad m = a', \qquad m + n + o = a'',$$

whence

$$m = a', \qquad n = \tfrac{1}{2}(a'' - a), \qquad o = \tfrac{1}{2}(a'' + a) - a'.$$

Now, in order that the middle place may be exactly represented in right ascension, we must have

$$o\left(\frac{x}{\delta\Delta}\right)^2 + n\left(\frac{x}{\delta\Delta}\right) + m = 0,$$

from which we find

$$\frac{x}{\delta\Delta} = -\frac{1}{2o}\left(n - \sqrt{n^2 - 4mo}\right) = p,$$

or

$$x - p\delta\Delta = 0.$$

In the same manner, the condition that the middle place shall be exactly represented in declination, gives

$$x - p'\delta\Delta = 0.$$

In order that the orbit shall exactly represent the middle place, both conditions must be satisfied simultaneously; but it will rarely happen that this can be effected, and the correct value of x must be found from those obtained by the separate conditions. The arithmetical mean of the two values of x will not make the sum of the squares of the residuals a minimum, and, therefore, give the most probable value, unless the variation of $\cos\delta'\,\Delta\alpha'$, for a given increment assigned to Δ, is the same as that of $\Delta\delta'$. But if we denote the value of x for which the error in α' is reduced to zero by x', and that for which $\Delta\delta' = 0$, by x'', the most probable value of x will be

$$x = \frac{n^2 x' + n'^2 x''}{n^2 + n'^2}, \tag{108}$$

in which $n = \frac{1}{2}(a'' - a)$ and $n' = \frac{1}{2}(d'' - d)$. It should be observed that, in order that the differences in right ascension and declination shall have equal influence in determining the value of x, the values of a, a', and a'' must be multiplied by $\cos\delta'$. The value of $\delta\Delta$ is most conveniently expressed in units of the last decimal place of the logarithms employed.

If the elements are already known so approximately that the first assumed value of $\varDelta$ differs so little from the true value that the second differences of the residuals may be neglected, two assumptions in regard to the value of $\varDelta$ will suffice. Then we shall have $o = 0$, and hence

$$m = a', \qquad n = a'' - a'.$$

The condition that the middle place shall be exactly represented, gives the two equations

$$\begin{aligned} (a'' - a')\,x + a'\delta\varDelta &= 0, \\ (d'' - d')\,x + d'\delta\varDelta &= 0. \end{aligned} \tag{109}$$

The combination of these equations according to the method of least squares will give the most probable value of x, namely, that for which the sum of the squares of the residuals will be a minimum.

Having thus determined the most probable value of x, a final system of elements computed with the geocentric distance $\varDelta + x$, corresponding to the time t, will represent the extreme places exactly, and will give the least residuals in the middle place consistent with the supposition of parabolic motion. It is further evident that we may use any number of intermediate places to correct the assumed value of $\varDelta$, each of which will furnish two equations of condition for the determination of x, and thus the elements may be found which will represent a series of observations.

76. Example.—The formulæ thus derived for the correction of approximate parabolic elements by varying the geocentric distance, are applicable to the case of any fundamental plane, provided that α, δ, A, D, &c. have the same signification with respect to this plane that they have in reference to the equator. To illustrate their numerical application, let us take the following normal places of the Great Comet of 1858, which were derived by comparing an ephemeris with several observations made during a few days before and after the date of each normal, and finding the mean difference between computation and observation:

Washington M. T.	α	δ
1858 June 11.0	141° 18′ 30″.9	+ 24° 46′ 25″.4,
July 13.0	144 32 49 .7	27 48 0 .8,
Aug. 14.0	152 14 12 .0	+ 31 21 47 .9,

which are referred to the apparent equinox of the date. These places are free from aberration.

We shall take the ecliptic for the fundamental plane, and converting these right ascensions and declinations into longitudes and latitudes, and reducing to the ecliptic and mean equinox of 1858.0, the times of observation being expressed in days from the beginning of the year, we get

$$t = 162.0, \qquad \lambda = 135^\circ\ 51'\ 44''.2, \qquad \beta = +\ 9^\circ\ 6'\ 57''.8,$$
$$t' = 194.0, \qquad \lambda' = 137\ \ 39\ \ 41\ .2, \qquad \beta' = \ \ 12\ \ 55\ \ 9\ .0,$$
$$t'' = 226.0, \qquad \lambda'' = 142\ \ 51\ \ 31\ .8, \qquad \beta'' = +\ 18\ \ 36\ \ 28\ .7.$$

From the *American Nautical Almanac* we obtain, for the true places of the sun,

$$\odot = 80^\circ\ 24'\ 32''.4, \qquad \log R = 0.006774,$$
$$\odot' = 110\ \ 55\ \ 51\ .2, \qquad \log R' = 0.007101,$$
$$\odot'' = 141\ \ 33\ \ 2\ .0, \qquad \log R'' = 0.005405,$$

the longitudes being referred to the mean equinox 1858.0.

When the ecliptic is the fundamental plane, we have, neglecting the sun's latitude, $D = 0$, and we must write λ and β in place of α and δ, and $\odot$ in place of A, in the equations which have been derived for the equator as the fundamental plane. Therefore, we have

$$g \cos(G - \odot) = R'' \cos(\odot'' - \odot) - R,$$
$$g \sin(G - \odot) = R'' \sin(\odot'' - \odot);$$

$$\cos\psi = \cos\beta \cos(\lambda - \odot), \qquad \cos\psi'' = \cos\beta'' \cos(\lambda'' - \odot'')$$
$$R \cos\psi = b, \qquad R'' \cos\psi'' = b'',$$
$$R \sin\psi = B, \qquad R'' \sin\psi'' = B'',$$

from which to find G, g, b, B, b'', and B'', all of which remain unchanged in the successive trials with assumed values of $\varDelta$. Thus we obtain

$$G = 201^\circ\ 7'\ 57''.4, \qquad \log B = 9.925092, \qquad b = +\ 0.568719,$$
$$\log g = 0.013500, \qquad \log B'' = 9.510309, \qquad b'' = +\ 0.959342.$$

Then we assume, by means of approximate elements already known,

$$\log \varDelta = 0.397800,$$

and from

$$h' \cos\zeta' \cos(H' - G) = \varDelta \cos\beta \cos(\lambda - G) + g,$$
$$h' \cos\zeta' \sin(H' - G) = \varDelta \cos\beta \sin(\lambda - G),$$
$$h' \sin\zeta' = \varDelta \sin\beta,$$

we find H', ζ', and h'. These give

$$H' = 153^\circ\ 46'\ 20''.5, \qquad \zeta' = +\ 7^\circ\ 24'\ 16''.4, \qquad \log h' = 0.487484.$$

Next, from

$$\cos\varphi' = \cos\zeta' \cos\beta'' \cos(\lambda'' - H') + \sin\zeta' \sin\beta'',$$

$$h' \cos\varphi' = c, \qquad h' \sin\varphi' = C,$$

we get

$$\log C = 9.912519, \qquad c = +\,2.961673;$$

and from

$$r = \sqrt{(\varDelta - b)^2 + B^2},$$

we find

$$\log r = 0.323446.$$

Then we have

$$\varDelta'' = c \pm \sqrt{\varkappa^2 - C^2}, \qquad r'' = \sqrt{(\varDelta'' - b'')^2 + B''^2},$$

$$\tau' = k(t'' - t), \qquad \eta = \frac{2\tau'}{(r + r'')^{\frac{3}{2}}}, \qquad \varkappa = \frac{2\tau'}{\sqrt{r + r''}}\mu,$$

from which to find $\varDelta''$, r'', and $\varkappa$. First, by means of the approximate elements, we assume

$$\log \varDelta'' = 0.310000,$$

which gives $\log r'' = 0.053000$, and hence we have

$$\eta = 0.3783, \qquad \log\mu = 0.002706, \qquad \log\varkappa = 0.090511.$$

With this value of $\varkappa$ we obtain from the expression for $\varDelta''$, the lower sign being used, since $\varDelta''$ is less than c,

$$\log \varDelta'' = 0.309717.$$

Repeating the calculation of r'', μ, and $\varkappa$, and then finding $\varDelta''$ again, the result is

$$\log \varDelta'' = 0.309647.$$

Then, by means of the formula (67), we may find the correct value. Thus we have, in units of the sixth decimal place,

$$a = 309717 - 310000 = -\,283, \qquad a' = 309647 - 309717 = -\,70,$$

and for the correction to the last result for $\log \varDelta''$ we have

$$-\frac{a'^2}{a' - a} = -\,23.$$

Therefore,

$$\log \varDelta'' = 0.309624.$$

By means of this value we get

$$\log r'' = 0.052350, \qquad \log\varkappa = 0.090628,$$

and this value of $\varkappa$ gives, finally,

$$\log \varDelta'' = 0.309623, \qquad \log r'' = 0.052348.$$

The heliocentric places of the comet are now found from the equations (71) and (72), writing $\varDelta \cos\beta$ and $\varDelta'' \cos\beta''$ for ρ and ρ'', respectively. Thus we obtain

$$\begin{array}{lll} l\ = 159^\circ\ 43'\ 14''.2, & b\ = +\ 10^\circ\ 50'\ 14''.0, & \log r\ = 0.323447, \\ l'' = 144\ \ 17\ \ 47\ .8, & b'' = +\ 35\ \ 14\ \ 28\ .7, & \log r'' = 0.052347. \end{array}$$

The agreement of these results for r and r'' with those already obtained, proves the accuracy of the calculation. Since the heliocentric longitudes are diminishing, the motion is *retrograde.*

Then from (74) we get

$$\Omega = 165^\circ\ 17'\ 30''.3, \qquad i = 63^\circ\ 6'\ 32''.5;$$

and from

$$\tan u = -\frac{\tan(l - \Omega)}{\cos i}, \qquad \tan u'' = -\frac{\tan(l'' - \Omega)}{\cos i},$$

we obtain

$$u = 12^\circ\ 10'\ 12''.6, \qquad u'' = 40^\circ\ 18'\ 51''.2,$$

the values of $-u$ and $l - \Omega$ being in the same quadrant when the motion is retrograde. The equation (79) gives $\log \varkappa = 0.090630$, which agrees with the value already found.

The formulæ (81) give

$$\omega = 129^\circ\ 6'\ 46''.3, \qquad \log q = 9.760326,$$

and hence we have

$$v = u - \omega = -\ 116^\circ\ 56'\ 33''.7, \qquad v'' = u'' - \omega = -\ 88^\circ\ 47'\ 55''.1,$$

from which we get

$$T = 1858 \text{ Sept. } 29.4274.$$

From these elements we find

$$\log r' = 0.212844, \qquad v' = -\ 107^\circ\ 7'\ 34''.0, \qquad u' = 21^\circ\ 59'\ 12''.3,$$

and from

$$\tan(l' - \Omega) = -\cos i \tan u',$$
$$\tan b' = -\tan i \sin(l' - \Omega),$$

we get

$$l' = 154^\circ\ 56'\ 33''.4, \qquad b' = +\ 19^\circ\ 30'\ 22''.1.$$

By means of these and the values of $\odot'$ and R', we obtain

$$\lambda' = 137° \, 39' \, 13''.3, \qquad \beta' = +12° \, 54' \, 45''.3,$$

and comparing these results with observation, we have, for the error of the middle place,

$$\text{C.} - \text{O.}$$
$$\cos\beta' \, \Delta\lambda' = -27''.2, \qquad \Delta\beta' = -23''.7.$$

From the relative positions of the sun, earth, and comet at the time t'' it is easily seen that, in order to diminish these residuals, the geocentric distance must be increased, and therefore we assume, for a second value of Δ,

$$\log \Delta = 0.398500,$$

from which we derive

$$H' = 153° \, 44' \, 57''.6, \qquad \zeta' = +7° \, 24' \, 26''.1, \qquad \log h' = 0.488026,$$
$$\log C = 9.912587, \qquad \log c = 0.472115, \qquad \log r = 0.324207,$$
$$\log \Delta'' = 0.311054, \qquad \log r'' = 0.054824, \qquad \log \varkappa = 0.089922.$$

Then we find the heliocentric places

$$l = 159° \, 40' \, 33''.8, \qquad b = +10° \, 50' \, 8''.6, \qquad \log r = 0.324207,$$
$$l'' = 144 \;\; 17 \;\; 12 .1, \qquad b'' = +35 \;\; 8 \;\; 37 .8, \qquad \log r'' = 0.054825,$$

and from these,

$$\Omega = 165° \, 15' \, 41''.1, \qquad i = 63° \, 2' \, 49''.2,$$
$$u = 12 \;\; 10 \;\; 30 .8, \qquad u'' = 40 \;\; 13 \;\; 26 .0,$$
$$\omega = 128 \;\; 54 \;\; 44 .4, \qquad \log q = 9.763620,$$
$$T = 1858 \text{ Sept. } 29.8245, \qquad \log r' = 0.214116,$$
$$v' = -106° \, 55' \, 43''.8, \qquad u' = 21° \, 59' \, 0''.6,$$
$$l' = 154 \;\; 53 \;\; 32 .3, \qquad b' = +19 \;\; 29 \;\; 31 .9,$$
$$\lambda' = 137 \;\; 39 \;\; 39 .7, \qquad \beta' = +12 \;\; 55 \;\; 2 .9.$$

Therefore, for the second assumed value of Δ, we have

$$\text{C.} - \text{O.}$$
$$\cos\beta' \, \Delta\lambda' = -1''.5, \qquad \Delta\beta' = -6''.1.$$

Since these residuals are very small, it will not be necessary to make a third assumption in regard to Δ, but we may at once derive the correction to be applied to the last assumed value by means of the equations (109). Thus we have

$$a' = -1.5, \qquad a'' = -27.2, \qquad d' = -6.1, \qquad d'' = -23.7,$$
$$\delta \log \Delta = -0.000700,$$

and, expressing $\delta \log \varDelta$ in units of the sixth decimal place, these equations give

$$25.7x - 1050 = 0.$$
$$17.6x - 4270 = 0.$$

Combining these according to the method of least squares, we get

$$x = \frac{105 \times 2.57 + 427 \times 1.76}{(2.57)^2 + (1.76)^2} = +106.$$

Hence the corrected value of $\log \varDelta$ is

$$\log \varDelta = 0.398500 + 0.000106 = 0.398606.$$

With this value of $\log \varDelta$ the final elements are computed as already illustrated, and the following system is obtained:—

$$\begin{aligned} T &= 1858 \text{ Sept. } 29.88617 \text{ Washington mean time.} \\ \pi &= 36^\circ\ 22'\ 36''.9 \\ \Omega &= 165\ \ 15\ \ 24\ .8 \\ i &= 63\ \ \ 2\ \ 14\ .2 \\ \log q &= 9.764142 \end{aligned} \quad \left.\begin{matrix} \\ \pi \\ \Omega \end{matrix}\right\} \text{Mean Equinox 1858.0.}$$

Motion Retrograde.

If the distinction of retrograde motion is not adopted, and we regard i as susceptible of any value from 0° to 180°, we shall have

$$\pi = 294^\circ\ \ 8'\ 12''.7,$$
$$i = 116\ \ 57\ \ 45\ .8,$$

the other elements remaining the same.

The comparison of the middle place with these final elements gives the following residuals:—

C. — O.

$$\cos\beta\,\Delta\lambda = +0''.2, \qquad \Delta\beta = -4''.3.$$

These errors are so small that the orbit indicated by the observed places on which the elements are based differs very little from a parabola.

When, instead of a single place, a series of intermediate places is employed to correct the assumed value of $\varDelta$, it is best to adopt the equator as the fundamental plane, since an error in α or δ will affect both λ and β; and, besides, incomplete observations may also be used when the fundamental plane is that to which the observations are directly referred. Further, the entire group of equations of condition for the determination of x, according to the formulæ (109), must be combined by multiplying each equation by the coefficient of x in that equation and taking the sum of all the equations thus formed as the final equation from which to find x, the observations being supposed equally good.

CHAPTER IV.

DETERMINATION, FROM THREE COMPLETE OBSERVATIONS, OF THE ELEMENTS OF THE ORBIT OF A HEAVENLY BODY, INCLUDING THE ECCENTRICITY OR FORM OF THE CONIC SECTION.

77. THE formulæ which have thus far been derived for the determination of the elements of the orbit of a heavenly body by means of observed places, do not suffice, in the form in which they have been given, to determine an orbit entirely unknown, except in the particular case of parabolic motion, for which one of the elements becomes known. In the general case, it is necessary to derive at least one of the curtate distances without making any assumption as to the form of the orbit, after which the others may be found. But, preliminary to a complete investigation of the elements of an unknown orbit by means of three complete observations of the body, it is necessary to provide for the corrections due to parallax and aberration, so that they may be applied in as advantageous a manner as possible.

When the elements are entirely unknown, we cannot correct the observed places directly for parallax and aberration, since both of these corrections require a knowledge of the distance of the body from the earth. But in the case of the aberration we may either correct the time of observation for the time in which the light from the body reaches the earth, or we may consider the observed place corrected for the actual aberration due to the combined motion of the earth and of light as the true place at the instant when the light left the planet or comet, but as seen from the place which the earth occupies at the time of the observation. When the distance is unknown, the latter method must evidently be adopted, according to which we apply to the observed apparent longitude and latitude the actual aberration of the fixed stars, and regard this place as corresponding to the time of observation corrected for the time of aberration, to be effected when the distances shall have been found, but using for the place of the earth that corresponding to the time of observation. It will appear, therefore, that only that part of the calculation of the elements which involves the times of observation will have to be repeated after the corresponding distances of the body from the earth have been found. First, then, by means of the apparent obliquity of the ecliptic, the observed apparent right ascension and declination must be converted into apparent longitude and latitude. Let λ_0 and β_0, respectively, denote the observed apparent longitude and latitude; and let $\odot_0$ be the true longitude of the sun, Σ_0 its latitude, and R_0 its distance from the earth, corresponding to the time of observation. Then, if λ and β denote the longitude and latitude of the planet or comet corrected for the actual aberration of the fixed stars, we shall have

$$\begin{aligned} \lambda - \lambda_0 &= +\, 20''.445 \cos(\lambda - \odot_0) \sec\beta + 0''.343 \cos(\lambda - 281^\circ) \sec\beta, \\ \beta - \beta_0 &= -\, 20''.445 \sin(\lambda - \odot_0) \sin\beta - 0''.343 \sin(\lambda - 281^\circ) \sin\beta. \end{aligned} \quad (1)$$

In computing the numerical values of these corrections, it will be sufficiently accurate to use λ_0 and β_0 instead of λ and β in the second members of these equations, and the last terms may, in most cases, be neglected. The values of λ and β thus derived give the true place of the body at the time $t - 497^s.78\varDelta$, but as seen from the place of the earth at the time t.

When the distance of the planet or comet is unknown, it is impossible to reduce the observed place to the centre of the earth; but if we conceive a line to be drawn from the body through the true place of observation, it is evident that were an observer at the point of intersection of this line with the plane of the ecliptic, or at any point in the line, the body would be seen in the same direction as from the actual place of observation. Hence, instead of applying any correction for parallax directly to the observed apparent place, we may conceive the place of the observer to be changed from the actual place to this point of intersection with the ecliptic, and, therefore, it becomes necessary to determine the position of this point by means of the data furnished by observation.

Let θ_0 be the sidereal time corresponding to the time t_0 of observation, φ' the geocentric latitude of the place of observation, and ρ_0 the radius of the earth at the place of observation, expressed in parts of the equatorial radius as unity. Then θ_0 is the right ascension and φ' the declination of the zenith at the time t_0. Let l_0 and b_0 denote these quantities converted into longitude and latitude, or the longitude and latitude of the geocentric zenith at the time t_0. The rectangular co-ordinates of the place of observation referred to the centre of the earth and expressed in parts of the mean distance of the earth from the sun as the unit, will be

$$x_0 = \rho_0 \sin \pi_0 \cos b_0 \cos l_0,$$
$$y_0 = \rho_0 \sin \pi_0 \cos b_0 \sin l_0,$$
$$z_0 = \rho_0 \sin \pi_0 \sin b_0,$$

in which $\pi_0 = 8''.57116$.

Let Δ_0 be the distance of the planet or comet from the true place of the observer, and $\Delta_{,}$ its distance from the point in the ecliptic to which the observation is to be reduced. Then will the co-ordinates of the place of observation, referred to this point in the ecliptic, be

$$x_{,} = (\Delta_{,} - \Delta_0) \cos \beta \cos \lambda,$$
$$y_{,} = (\Delta_{,} - \Delta_0) \cos \beta \sin \lambda,$$
$$z_{,} = (\Delta_{,} - \Delta_0) \sin \beta,$$

the axis of x being directed to the vernal equinox. Let us now designate by $\odot$ the longitude of the sun as seen from the point of reference in the ecliptic, and by R its distance from this point. Then will the heliocentric co-ordinates of this point be

$$X = -R \cos \odot,$$
$$Y = -R \sin \odot,$$
$$Z = 0.$$

The heliocentric co-ordinates of the centre of the earth are

$$X_0 = -R_0 \cos \Sigma_0 \cos \odot_0,$$
$$Y_0 = -R_0 \cos \Sigma_0 \sin \odot_0,$$
$$Z_0 = -R_0 \sin \Sigma_0.$$

But the heliocentric co-ordinates of the true place of observation will be

$$X + x_{,}, \qquad Y + y_{,}, \qquad Z + z_{,},$$

or

$$X_0 + x_0, \qquad Y_0 + y_0, \qquad Z_0 + z_0,$$

and, consequently, we shall have

$$R \cos \odot - (\Delta_{,} - \Delta_0) \cos \beta \cos \lambda = R_0 \cos \Sigma_0 \cos \odot_0 - \rho_0 \sin \pi_0 \cos b_0 \cos l_0,$$
$$R \sin \odot - (\Delta_{,} - \Delta_0) \cos \beta \sin \lambda = R_0 \cos \Sigma_0 \sin \odot_0 - \rho_0 \sin \pi_0 \cos b_0 \sin l_0,$$
$$-(\Delta_{,} - \Delta_0) \sin \beta = R_0 \sin \Sigma_0 - \rho_0 \sin \pi_0 \sin b_0.$$

If we suppose the axis of x to be directed to the point whose longitude is $\odot_0$, these become

$$\begin{aligned}
R\cos(\odot-\odot_0)-(\varDelta_\prime-\varDelta_0)\cos\beta\cos(\lambda-\odot_0)&=\\
&R_0\cos\Sigma_0-\rho_0\sin\pi_0\cos b_0\cos(l_0-\odot_0),\\
R\sin(\odot-\odot_0)-(\varDelta_\prime-\varDelta_0)\cos\beta\sin(\lambda-\odot_0)&=\\
&-\rho_0\sin\pi_0\cos b_0\sin(l_0-\odot_0),\\
-(\varDelta_\prime-\varDelta_0)\sin\beta&=R_0\sin\Sigma_0-\rho_0\sin\pi_0\sin b_0,
\end{aligned}\tag{2}$$

from which R and $\odot$ may be determined. Let us now put

$$(\varDelta_\prime-\varDelta_0)\cos\beta=D;\tag{3}$$

then, since π_0, Σ_0, and $\odot-\odot_0$ are small, these equations may be reduced to

$$\begin{aligned}
R&=D\cos(\lambda-\odot_0)-\pi_0\rho_0\cos b_0\cos(l_0-\odot_0)+R_0,\\
R(\odot-\odot_0)&=D\sin(\lambda-\odot_0)-\pi_0\rho_0\cos b_0\sin(l_0-\odot_0),\\
0&=D\tan\beta\qquad\qquad-\pi_0\rho_0\sin b_0+R_0\Sigma_0.
\end{aligned}$$

Hence we shall have, if π_0 and Σ_0 are expressed in seconds of arc,

$$\begin{aligned}
D&=\frac{\pi_0\rho_0\sin b_0-R_0\Sigma_0}{206264.8}\cot\beta,\\
R&=R_0+D\cos(\lambda-\odot_0)-\frac{\pi_0\rho_0\cos b_0\cos(l_0-\odot_0)}{206264.8},\\
\odot&=\odot_0+\frac{206264.8\,D\sin(\lambda-\odot_0)-\pi_0\rho_0\cos b_0\sin(l_0-\odot_0)}{R},
\end{aligned}\tag{4}$$

from which we may derive the values of $\odot$ and R which are to be used throughout the calculation of the elements as the longitude and distance of the sun, instead of the corresponding places referred to the centre of the earth. The point of reference being in the plane of the ecliptic, the latitude of the sun as seen from this point is zero, which simplifies some of the equations of the problem, since, if the observations had been reduced to the centre of the earth, the sun's latitude would be retained.

We may remark that the body would not be seen, at the instant of observation, from the point of reference in the direction actually observed, but at a time different from t_0, to be determined by the interval which is required for the light to pass over the distance $\varDelta_\prime-\varDelta_0$. Consequently we ought to add to the time of observation the quantity

$$(\varDelta_\prime-\varDelta_0)\,497^s.78=497^s.78\,D\sec\beta,\tag{5}$$

which is called the *reduction of the time;* but unless the latitude of the body should be very small, this correction will be insensible.

The value of λ derived from equations (1) and the longitude $\odot$

derived from (4) should be reduced by applying the correction for nutation to the mean equinox of the date, and then both these and the latitude β should be reduced by applying the correction for precession to the ecliptic and mean equinox of a fixed epoch, for which the beginning of the year is usually chosen.

In this way each observed apparent longitude and latitude is to be corrected for the aberration of the fixed stars, and the corresponding places of the sun, referred to the point in which the line drawn from the body through the place of observation on the earth's surface intersects the plane of the ecliptic, are derived from the equations (4). Then the places of the sun and of the planet or comet are reduced to the ecliptic and mean equinox of a fixed date, and the results thus obtained, together with the times of observation, furnish the data for the determination of the elements of the orbit.

When the distance of the body corresponding to each of the observations shall have been determined, the times of observation may be corrected for the time of aberration. This correction is necessary, since the adopted places of the body are the true places for the instant when the light was emitted, corresponding respectively to the times of observation diminished by the time of aberration, but as seen from the places of the earth at the actual times of observation, respectively.

When $\beta = 0$, the equations (4) cannot be applied, and when the latitude is so small that the reduction of the time and the correction to be applied to the place of the sun are of considerable magnitude, it will be advisable, if more suitable observations are not available, to neglect the correction for parallax and derive the elements, using the uncorrected places. The distances of the body from the earth which may then be derived, will enable us to apply the correction for parallax directly to the observed places of the body.

When the approximate distances of the body from the earth are already known, and it is required to derive new elements of the orbit from given observed places or from normal places derived from many observations, the observations may be corrected directly for parallax, and the times corrected for the time of aberration. We shall then have the true places of the body as seen from the centre of the earth, and if these places are adopted, it will be necessary, for the most accurate solution possible, to retain the latitude of the sun in the formulæ which may be required. But since some of these formulæ acquire greater simplicity when the sun's latitude is not introduced, if, in this case, we reduce the geocentric places to the point in which a perpendicular let fall from the centre of the earth to the plane of the ecliptic cuts that plane, the longitude of the sun will remain unchanged, the latitude will be zero, and the distance R will also be unchanged, since the greatest geocentric latitude of the sun does not exceed 1″. Then the longitude of the planet or comet as seen from this point in the ecliptic will be the same as seen from the centre of the earth, and if $\varDelta_{,}$ is the distance of the body from this point of reference, and $\beta_{,}$ its latitude as seen from this point, we shall have

$$\varDelta_{,} \cos\beta_{,} = \varDelta \cos\beta,$$
$$\varDelta_{,} \sin\beta_{,} = \varDelta \sin\beta - R_0 \sin\Sigma_0,$$

from which we easily derive the correction $\beta_{,} - \beta$, or $\Delta\beta$, to be applied to the geocentric latitude. Thus, we find

$$\Delta\beta = -\frac{R_0\,\Sigma_0}{\varDelta_{,}}\cos\beta, \tag{6}$$

Σ_0 being expressed in seconds. This correction having been applied to the geocentric latitude, the latitude of the sun becomes

$$\Sigma = 0.$$

The correction to be applied to the time of observation (already diminished by the time of aberration) due to the distance $\varDelta_{,} - \varDelta_0$ will be absolutely insensible, its maximum value not exceeding $0^s.002$. It should be remarked also that before applying the equation (6), the latitude Σ_0 should be reduced to the fixed ecliptic which it is desired to adopt for the definition of the elements which determine the position of the plane of the orbit.

78. When these preliminary corrections have been applied to the data, we are prepared to proceed with the calculation of the elements of the orbit, the necessary formulæ for which we shall now investigate. For this purpose, let us resume the equations $(6)_3$; and, if we multiply the first of these equations by $\tan\beta\sin\lambda'' - \tan\beta''\sin\lambda$, the second by $\tan\beta''\cos\lambda - \tan\beta\cos\lambda''$, and the third by $\sin(\lambda - \lambda'')$, and add the products, we shall have

$$\begin{aligned} 0 = nR\,&(\tan\beta''\sin(\lambda - \odot) - \tan\beta\sin(\lambda'' - \odot)) \\ &- \rho'\,(\tan\beta\sin(\lambda'' - \lambda') - \tan\beta'\sin(\lambda'' - \lambda) + \tan\beta''\sin(\lambda' - \lambda)) \\ &- R'\,(\tan\beta''\sin(\lambda - \odot') - \tan\beta\sin(\lambda'' - \odot')) \\ &+ n''R''\,(\tan\beta''\sin(\lambda - \odot'') - \tan\beta\sin(\lambda'' - \odot'')). \end{aligned} \tag{7}$$

It should be observed that when the correction for parallax is applied to the place of the sun, ρ' is the projection, on the plane of the ecliptic, of the distance of the body from the point of reference to which the observation has been reduced.

Let us now designate by K the longitude of the ascending node, and by I the inclination to the ecliptic, of a great circle passing through the first and third observed places of the body, and we have

$$\begin{aligned} \tan\beta\ &= \sin(\lambda - K)\tan I, \\ \tan\beta'' &= \sin(\lambda'' - K)\tan I. \end{aligned} \tag{8}$$

Introducing these values of $\tan\beta$ and $\tan\beta''$ into the equation (7), since

$$\begin{aligned} &\sin(\lambda - \odot)\sin(\lambda'' - K) - \sin(\lambda'' - \odot)\sin(\lambda - K) = \\ &\qquad\qquad - \sin(\lambda'' - \lambda)\sin(\odot - K), \\ &\sin(\lambda' - \lambda)\sin(\lambda'' - K) + \sin(\lambda'' - \lambda')\sin(\lambda - K) = \\ &\qquad\qquad + \sin(\lambda'' - \lambda)\sin(\lambda' - K), \\ &\sin(\lambda - \odot')\sin(\lambda'' - K) - \sin(\lambda'' - \odot')\sin(\lambda - K) = \\ &\qquad\qquad - \sin(\lambda'' - \lambda)\sin(\odot' - K), \\ &\sin(\lambda - \odot'')\sin(\lambda'' - K) - \sin(\lambda'' - \odot'')\sin(\lambda - K) = \\ &\qquad\qquad - \sin(\lambda'' - \lambda)\sin(\odot'' - K), \end{aligned}$$

we obtain, by dividing through by $\sin(\lambda'' - \lambda)\tan I$,

$$\begin{aligned} 0 = nR\sin(\odot - K) &+ \rho'\left(\sin(\lambda' - K) - \tan\beta'\cot I\right) \\ &- R'\sin(\odot' - K) + n''R''\sin(\odot'' - K). \end{aligned} \tag{9}$$

Let β_0 denote the latitude of that point of the great circle passing through the first and third places which corresponds to the longitude λ', then

$$\tan\beta_0 = \sin(\lambda' - K)\tan I,$$

and the coefficient of ρ' in equation (9) becomes

$$\frac{\sin(\beta_0 - \beta')}{\cos\beta_0\cos\beta'\tan I}.$$

Therefore, if we put

$$a_0 = \frac{\sin(\beta' - \beta_0)}{\cos\beta_0\tan I}, \tag{10}$$

we shall have

$$\begin{aligned} \rho'\sec\beta' = -\frac{R'\sin(\odot' - K)}{a_0} &+ n\frac{R\sin(\odot - K)}{a_0} \\ &+ n''\frac{R''\sin(\odot'' - K)}{a_0}. \end{aligned} \tag{11}$$

This formula will give the value of ρ', or of Δ', when the values of n and n'' have been determined, since a_0 and K are derived from the data furnished by observation.

To find K and I, we obtain from equations (8) by a transformation precisely similar to that by which the equations $(75)_3$ were derived,

$$\begin{aligned}\tan I \sin\left(\tfrac{1}{2}(\lambda''+\lambda)-K\right)&=\frac{\sin(\beta''+\beta)}{2\cos\beta\cos\beta''}\sec\tfrac{1}{2}(\lambda''-\lambda),\\ \tan I\cos\left(\tfrac{1}{2}(\lambda''+\lambda)-K\right)&=\frac{\sin(\beta''-\beta)}{2\cos\beta\cos\beta''}\operatorname{cosec}\tfrac{1}{2}(\lambda''-\lambda).\end{aligned}\qquad(12)$$

We may also compute K and I from the equations which may be derived from $(74)_3$ and $(76)_3$ by making the necessary changes in the notation, and using only the upper sign, since I is to be taken always less than 90°.

Before proceeding further with the discussion of equation (11), let us derive expressions for ρ and ρ'' in terms of ρ', the signification of ρ and ρ'', when the corrections for parallax are applied to the places of the sun, being as already noticed in the case of ρ'.

79. If we multiply the first of equations $(6)_3$ by $\sin\odot''\tan\beta''$, the second by $-\cos\odot''\tan\beta''$, and the third by $\sin(\lambda''-\odot'')$, and add the products, we get

$$\begin{aligned}0=n\rho\left(\tan\beta''\sin(\odot''-\lambda)-\tan\beta\sin(\odot''-\lambda'')\right)-nR\tan\beta''\sin(\odot''-\odot)\\ -\rho'\left(\tan\beta''\sin(\odot''-\lambda')-\tan\beta'\sin(\odot''-\lambda'')\right)+R'\tan\beta''\sin(\odot''-\odot'),\end{aligned}\qquad(13)$$

which may be written

$$\begin{aligned}0=n\rho\left(\tan\beta\sin(\lambda''-\odot'')-\tan\beta''\sin(\lambda-\odot'')\right)-nR\tan\beta''\sin(\odot''-\odot)\\ +\rho'\left(\tan\beta''\sin(\lambda'-\odot'')-\tan\beta_0\sin(\lambda''-\odot'')\right)\\ -\rho'(\tan\beta'-\tan\beta_0)\sin(\lambda''-\odot'')+R'\tan\beta''\sin(\odot''-\odot').\end{aligned}$$

Introducing into this the values of $\tan\beta$, $\tan\beta''$, and $\tan\beta_0$ in terms of I and K, and reducing, the result is

$$\begin{aligned}0=n\rho\sin(\lambda''-\lambda)\sin(\odot''-K)-nR\sin(\odot''-\odot)\sin(\lambda''-K)\\ -\rho'\sin(\lambda''-\lambda')\sin(\odot''-K)-\rho'a_0\sec\beta'\sin(\lambda''-\odot'')\\ +R'\sin(\odot''-\odot')\sin(\lambda''-K).\end{aligned}$$

Therefore we obtain

$$\begin{aligned}\rho=\frac{\rho'}{n}\left(\frac{\sin(\lambda''-\lambda')}{\sin(\lambda''-\lambda)}+\frac{a_0\sec\beta'}{\sin(\lambda''-\lambda)}\cdot\frac{\sin(\lambda''-\odot'')}{\sin(\odot''-K)}\right)\\ -\frac{\sin(\lambda''-K)}{n}\cdot\frac{R'\sin(\odot''-\odot')-nR\sin(\odot''-\odot)}{\sin(\lambda''-\lambda)\sin(\odot''-K)}.\end{aligned}$$

But, by means of the equations $(9)_3$, we derive

$$R'\sin(\odot''-\odot')-nR\sin(\odot''-\odot)=(N-n)R\sin(\odot''-\odot),$$

and the preceding equation reduces to

$$\rho=\frac{\rho'}{n}\left(\frac{\sin(\lambda''-\lambda')}{\sin(\lambda''-\lambda)}+\frac{a_0\sec\beta'}{\sin(\lambda''-\lambda)}\cdot\frac{\sin(\lambda''-\odot'')}{\sin(\odot''-K)}\right)$$
$$+\left(1-\frac{N}{n}\right)\frac{R\sin(\odot''-\odot)\sin(\lambda''-K)}{\sin(\lambda''-\lambda)\sin(\odot''-K)}. \qquad (14)$$

To obtain an expression for ρ'' in terms of ρ', if we multiply the first of equations $(6)_3$ by $\sin\odot\tan\beta$, the second by $-\cos\odot\tan\beta$, and the third by $\sin(\lambda-\odot)$, and add the products, we shall have

$$0=n''\rho''(\tan\beta\sin(\lambda''-\odot)-\tan\beta''\sin(\lambda-\odot))-n''R''\tan\beta\sin(\odot''-\odot)$$
$$-\rho'(\tan\beta\sin(\lambda'-\odot)-\tan\beta'\sin(\lambda-\odot))+R'\tan\beta\sin(\odot'-\odot). \qquad (15)$$

Introducing the values of $\tan\beta$, $\tan\beta'$, and $\tan\beta''$ in terms of K and I, and reducing precisely as in the case of the formula already found for ρ, we obtain

$$\rho''=\frac{\rho'}{n''}\left(\frac{\sin(\lambda'-\lambda)}{\sin(\lambda''-\lambda)}-\frac{a_0\sec\beta'}{\sin(\lambda''-\lambda)}\cdot\frac{\sin(\lambda-\odot)}{\sin(\odot-K)}\right)$$
$$+\left(1-\frac{N''}{n''}\right)\frac{R''\sin(\odot''-\odot)\sin(\lambda-K)}{\sin(\lambda''-\lambda)\sin(\odot-K)}. \qquad (16)$$

Let us now put, for brevity,

$$b=\frac{R\sin(\odot-K)}{a_0},\qquad c=\frac{R'\sin(\odot'-K)}{a_0},$$
$$d=\frac{R''\sin(\odot''-K)}{a_0},\qquad f=\frac{\sec\beta'}{\sin(\lambda''-\lambda)},\qquad h=\frac{RR''\sin(\odot''-\odot)}{a_0\sin(\lambda''-\lambda)},$$
$$M_1=\frac{\sin(\lambda''-\lambda')}{\sin(\lambda''-\lambda)}+f\frac{R''\sin(\lambda''-\odot'')}{d}, \qquad (17)$$
$$M_1''=\frac{\sin(\lambda'-\lambda)}{\sin(\lambda''-\lambda)}-f\frac{R\sin(\lambda-\odot)}{b},$$
$$M_2=\frac{h\sin(\lambda''-K)}{d},\qquad M_2''=\frac{h\sin(\lambda-K)}{b},$$

and the equations (11), (14), and (16) become

$$\rho'\sec\beta'=-c+nb+n''d,$$
$$\rho=M_1\,\frac{\rho'}{n}+M_2\left(1-\frac{N}{n}\right), \qquad (18)$$
$$\rho''=M_1''\frac{\rho'}{n''}+M_2''\left(1-\frac{N''}{n''}\right).$$

If n and n'' are known, these equations will, in most cases, be sufficient to determine ρ, ρ', and ρ''.

80. It will be apparent, from a consideration of the equations which have been derived for ρ, ρ', and ρ'', that under certain circumstances they are inapplicable in the form in which they have been given, and that in some cases they become indeterminate. When the great circle passing through the first and third observed places of the body passes also through the second place, we have $a_0 = 0$, and equation (11) reduces to

$$n''R''\sin(\odot'' - K) + nR\sin(\odot - K) = R'\sin(\odot' - K).$$

If the ratio of n'' to n is known, this equation will determine the quantities themselves, and from these the radius-vector r' for the middle place may be found. But if the great circle which thus passes through the three observed places passes also through the second place of the sun, we shall have $K = \odot'$, or $K = 180° + \odot'$, and hence

$$n''R''\sin(\odot'' - \odot') - nR\sin(\odot' - \odot) = 0,$$

or

$$\frac{n''}{n} = \frac{R\sin(\odot' - \odot)}{R''\sin(\odot'' - \odot')},$$

from which it appears that the solution of the problem is in this case impossible.

If the first and third observed places coincide, we have $\lambda = \lambda''$ and $\beta = \beta''$, and each term of equation (7) reduces to zero, so that the problem becomes absolutely indeterminate. Consequently, if the data are nearly such as to render the solution impossible, according to the conditions of these two cases of indetermination, the elements which may be derived will be greatly affected by errors of observation. If, however, λ is equal to λ'' and β'' differs from β, it will be possible to derive ρ', and hence ρ and ρ''; but the formulæ which have been given require some modification in this particular case. Thus, when $\lambda = \lambda''$, we have $K = \lambda'' = \lambda$, $I = 90°$, and $\beta_0 = 90°$, and hence a_0, as determined by equation (10), becomes $\frac{0}{0}$. Still, in this case it is not indeterminate, since, by recurring to the original equation (9), the coefficient of ρ', which is $-a_0 \sec\beta'$, gives

$$a_0 = \sin\beta' \cot I - \cos\beta' \sin(\lambda' - K), \tag{19}$$

and when $\lambda = \lambda''$, it becomes simply

$$a_0 = -\cos\beta' \sin(\lambda' - K).$$

Whenever, therefore, the difference $\lambda''-\lambda$ is very small compared with the motion in latitude, a_0 should be computed by means of the equation (19) or by means of the expression which is obtained directly from the coefficient of ρ' in equation (7).

When $\lambda=\lambda''=K$, the values of M_1, M_1'', M_2, and M_2'' cannot be found by means of the equations (17); but if we use the original form of the expressions for ρ and ρ'' in terms of ρ', as given by equations (13) and (15), without introducing the auxiliary angles, we shall have

$$\rho=\frac{\rho'}{n}\cdot\frac{\tan\beta'\sin(\lambda''-\odot'')-\tan\beta''\sin(\lambda'-\odot'')}{\tan\beta\sin(\lambda''-\odot'')-\tan\beta''\sin(\lambda-\odot'')} \\ +\left(1-\frac{N}{n}\right)\frac{R\tan\beta''\sin(\odot''-\odot)}{\tan\beta\sin(\lambda''-\odot'')-\tan\beta''\sin(\lambda-\odot'')},$$

$$\rho''=\frac{\rho'}{n''}\cdot\frac{\tan\beta\sin(\lambda'-\odot)-\tan\beta'\sin(\lambda-\odot)}{\tan\beta\sin(\lambda''-\odot)-\tan\beta''\sin(\lambda-\odot)} \\ +\left(1-\frac{N''}{n''}\right)\frac{R''\tan\beta\sin(\odot''-\odot)}{\tan\beta\sin(\lambda''-\odot)-\tan\beta''\sin(\lambda-\odot)}.$$

Hence

$$\begin{aligned} M_1&=\frac{\tan\beta'\sin(\lambda''-\odot'')-\tan\beta''\sin(\lambda'-\odot'')}{\tan\beta\sin(\lambda''-\odot'')-\tan\beta''\sin(\lambda-\odot'')}, \\ M_1''&=\frac{\tan\beta\sin(\lambda'-\odot)-\tan\beta'\sin(\lambda-\odot)}{\tan\beta\sin(\lambda''-\odot)-\tan\beta''\sin(\lambda-\odot)}, \\ M_2&=\frac{R\tan\beta''\sin(\odot''-\odot)}{\tan\beta\sin(\lambda''-\odot'')-\tan\beta''\sin(\lambda-\odot'')}, \\ M_2''&=\frac{R''\tan\beta\sin(\odot''-\odot)}{\tan\beta\sin(\lambda''-\odot)-\tan\beta''\sin(\lambda-\odot)}, \end{aligned} \qquad (20)$$

are the expressions for M_1, M_1'', M_2, and M_2'' which must be used when $\lambda=\lambda''$ or when λ is very nearly equal to λ''; and then ρ and ρ'' will be obtained from equations (18). These expressions will also be used when $\lambda''-\lambda=180°$, this being an analogous case.

When the great circle passing through the first and third observed places of the body also passes through the first or the third place of the sun, the last two of the equations (18) become indeterminate, and other formulæ must be derived. If we multiply the second of equations $(7)_3$ by $\tan\beta''$ and the fourth by $-\sin(\lambda''-\odot')$, and add the products, then multiply the second of these equations by $\tan\beta$ and the fourth by $-\sin(\lambda-\odot')$, and add, and finally reduce by means of the relation

$$NR\sin(\odot'-\odot)=N''R''\sin(\odot''-\odot'),$$

we get

$$\rho = \frac{\rho'}{n} \cdot \frac{\tan\beta'' \sin(\lambda' - \odot') - \tan\beta' \sin(\lambda'' - \odot')}{\tan\beta'' \sin(\lambda - \odot') - \tan\beta \sin(\lambda'' - \odot')}$$
$$+ \left(\frac{n''}{n} - \frac{N''}{N}\right) \frac{R'' \tan\beta'' \sin(\odot'' - \odot')}{\tan\beta'' \sin(\lambda - \odot') - \tan\beta \sin(\lambda'' - \odot')},$$
$$\rho'' = \frac{\rho'}{n''} \cdot \frac{\tan\beta' \sin(\lambda - \odot') - \tan\beta \sin(\lambda' - \odot')}{\tan\beta'' \sin(\lambda - \odot') - \tan\beta \sin(\lambda'' - \odot')} \tag{21}$$
$$+ \left(\frac{n}{n''} - \frac{N}{N''}\right) \frac{R \tan\beta \sin(\odot' - \odot)}{\tan\beta'' \sin(\lambda - \odot') - \tan\beta \sin(\lambda'' - \odot')}.$$

These equations are convenient for determining ρ and ρ'' from ρ'; but they become indeterminate when the great circle passing through the extreme places of the body also passes through the second place of the sun. Therefore they will generally be inapplicable for the cases in which the equations (18) fail.

If we eliminate ρ'' from the first and second of the equations $(6)_3$ we get

$$0 = n\rho \sin(\lambda'' - \lambda) - nR \sin(\lambda'' - \odot) - \rho' \sin(\lambda'' - \lambda')$$
$$+ R' \sin(\lambda'' - \odot') - n''R'' \sin(\lambda'' - \odot''),$$

from which we derive

$$\rho = \frac{\rho'}{n} \cdot \frac{\sin(\lambda'' - \lambda')}{\sin(\lambda'' - \lambda)} \tag{22}$$
$$+ \frac{nR \sin(\lambda'' - \odot) - R' \sin(\lambda'' - \odot') + n''R'' \sin(\lambda'' - \odot'')}{n \sin(\lambda'' - \lambda)}.$$

Eliminating ρ between the same equations, the result is

$$\rho'' = \frac{\rho'}{n''} \cdot \frac{\sin(\lambda' - \lambda)}{\sin(\lambda'' - \lambda)} \tag{23}$$
$$- \frac{nR \sin(\lambda - \odot) - R' \sin(\lambda - \odot') + n''R'' \sin(\lambda - \odot'')}{n'' \sin(\lambda'' - \lambda)}.$$

These formulæ will enable us to determine ρ and ρ'' from ρ' in the special cases in which the equations (18) and (21) are inapplicable; but, since they do not involve the third of equations $(6)_3$, they are not so well adapted to a complete solution of the problem as the formulæ previously given whenever these may be applied.

If we eliminate successively ρ'' and ρ between the first and fourth of the equations $(7)_3$, we get

$$\rho = \frac{\rho'}{n} \cdot \frac{\tan\beta'' \cos(\lambda' - \odot') - \tan\beta' \cos(\lambda'' - \odot')}{\tan\beta'' \cos(\lambda - \odot') - \tan\beta \cos(\lambda'' - \odot')}$$
$$+ \frac{\tan\beta''}{n} \cdot \frac{nR \cos(\odot' - \odot) - R' + n''R'' \cos(\odot'' - \odot')}{\tan\beta'' \cos(\lambda - \odot') - \tan\beta \cos(\lambda'' - \odot')},$$
$$\rho'' = \frac{\rho'}{n''} \cdot \frac{\tan\beta' \cos(\lambda - \odot') - \tan\beta \cos(\lambda' - \odot')}{\tan\beta'' \cos(\lambda - \odot') - \tan\beta \cos(\lambda'' - \odot')} \tag{24}$$
$$- \frac{\tan\beta}{n''} \cdot \frac{nR \cos(\odot' - \odot) - R' + n''R'' \cos(\odot'' - \odot')}{\tan\beta'' \cos(\lambda - \odot') - \tan\beta \cos(\lambda'' - \odot')},$$

which may also be used to determine ρ and ρ'' when the equations (18) and (21) cannot be applied. When the motion in latitude is greater than in longitude, these equations are to be preferred instead of (22) and (23.)

81. It would appear at first, without examining the quantities involved in the formula for ρ', that the equations $(26)_3$ will enable us to find n and n'' by successive approximations, assuming first that

$$n = \frac{\tau}{\tau'}, \qquad n'' = \frac{\tau''}{\tau'},$$

and from the resulting value of ρ' determining r', and then carrying the approximation to the values of n and n'' one step farther, so as to include terms of the second order with reference to the intervals of time between the observations. But if we consider the equation (10), we observe that a_0 is a very small quantity depending on the difference $\beta' - \beta_0$, and therefore on the deviation of the observed path of the body from the arc of a great circle, and, as this appears in the denominator of terms containing n and n'' in the equation (11), it becomes necessary to determine to what degree of approximation these quantities must be known in order that the resulting value of ρ' may not be greatly in error.

To determine the relation of a_0 to the intervals of time between the observations, we have, from the coefficient of ρ' in equation (7),

$$a_0 \sec \beta' = \tan \beta \sin (\lambda'' - \lambda') - \tan \beta' \sin (\lambda'' - \lambda) + \tan \beta'' \sin (\lambda' - \lambda).$$

We may put

$$\begin{aligned} \tan \beta \ &= \tan \beta' - A\tau'' + B\tau''^2 - \ldots., \\ \tan \beta'' &= \tan \beta' + A\tau + B\tau^2 + \ldots., \end{aligned}$$

and hence we have

$$\begin{aligned} a_0 \sec \beta' = &\left(\sin (\lambda'' - \lambda') - \sin (\lambda'' - \lambda) + \sin (\lambda' - \lambda)\right) \tan \beta' \\ &+ \left(\tau \sin (\lambda' - \lambda) - \tau'' \sin (\lambda'' - \lambda')\right) A + \left(\tau^2 \sin (\lambda' - \lambda) + \tau''^2 \sin (\lambda'' - \lambda')\right) B + \ldots, \end{aligned}$$

which is easily transformed into

$$\begin{aligned} a_0 \sec \beta' = &\ 4 \sin \tfrac{1}{2} (\lambda' - \lambda) \sin \tfrac{1}{2} (\lambda'' - \lambda') \sin \tfrac{1}{2} (\lambda'' - \lambda) \tan \beta' \qquad (25) \\ &+ \left(\tau \sin (\lambda' - \lambda) - \tau'' \sin (\lambda'' - \lambda')\right) A + \left(\tau^2 \sin (\lambda' - \lambda) + \tau''^2 \sin (\lambda'' - \lambda')\right) B + \ldots. \end{aligned}$$

If we suppose the intervals to be small, we may also put

$$\sin \tfrac{1}{2} (\lambda'' - \lambda) = \tfrac{1}{2} (\lambda'' - \lambda),$$

and

$$\sin (\lambda'' - \lambda) = \lambda'' - \lambda, \qquad \sin (\lambda' - \lambda) = \lambda' - \lambda.$$

Further, we may put

$$\lambda = \lambda' - A'\tau'' + B'\tau''^2 - \ldots.,$$
$$\lambda'' = \lambda' + A'\tau + B'\tau^2 + \ldots..$$

Substituting these values in the equation (25), neglecting terms of the fourth order with respect to τ, and reducing, we get

$$a_0 = \tau\tau'\tau'' \left(\tfrac{1}{2}A'^3 \tan\beta' + A'B - AB'\right) \cos\beta'.$$

It appears, therefore, that a_0 is at least of the third order with reference to the intervals of time between the observations, and that an error of the second order in the assumed values of n and n'' may produce an error of the order zero in the value of ρ' as derived from equation (11) even under the most favorable circumstances. Hence, in general, we cannot adopt the values

$$n = \frac{\tau}{\tau'}, \qquad n'' = \frac{\tau''}{\tau'},$$

omitting terms of the second order, without affecting the resulting value of ρ' to such an extent that it cannot be regarded even as an approximation to the true value; and terms of at least the second order must be included in the first assumed values of n and n''.

The equation $(28)_3$ gives

$$\frac{n''}{n} = \frac{\tau''}{\tau}\left(1 + \tfrac{1}{6}\frac{\tau^2 - \tau''^2}{r'^3}\right), \tag{26}$$

omitting the term multiplied by $\frac{dr'}{dt}$, which term is of the third order with respect to the times; and hence in this value of $\frac{n}{n''}$ only terms of at least the fourth order are neglected. Again, from the equations $(26)_3$ we derive, since $\tau' = \tau + \tau''$,

$$n + n'' = 1 + \frac{\tau\tau''}{2r'^3}, \tag{27}$$

in which only terms of the fourth order have been neglected. Now the first of equations (18) may be written:

$$\rho' \sec\beta' = (n + n'')\frac{b + \dfrac{n''}{n}d}{1 + \dfrac{n''}{n}} - c, \tag{28}$$

in which, if we introduce the values of $\frac{n''}{n}$ and $n + n''$ as given by (26) and (27), only terms of the fourth order with respect to the times will be neglected, and consequently the resulting value of ρ' will be affected with only an error of the second order when a_0 is of the third order. Further, if the intervals between the observations are not very unequal, $\tau^2 - \tau''^2$ will be a quantity of an order superior to τ^2, and when these intervals are equal, we have, to terms of the fourth order,

$$\frac{n''}{n} = \frac{\tau''}{\tau}.$$

The equation (27) gives

$$2r'^3(n + n'' - 1) = \tau\tau''.$$

Hence, if we put

$$P = \frac{n''}{n}, \qquad Q = 2r'^3(n + n'' - 1), \tag{29}$$

we may adopt, for a first approximation to the value of ρ',

$$P = \frac{\tau''}{\tau}, \qquad Q = \tau\tau'', \tag{30}$$

and ρ' will be affected with an error of the first order when the intervals are unequal; but of the second order only when the intervals are equal. It is evident, therefore, that, in the selection of the observations for the determination of an unknown orbit, the intervals should be as nearly equal as possible, since the nearer they approach to equality the nearer the truth will be the first assumed values of P and Q, thus facilitating the successive approximations; and when a_0 is a very small quantity, the equality of the intervals is of the greatest importance.

From the equations (29) we get

$$n = \frac{1}{1+P}\left(1 + \frac{Q}{2r'^3}\right), \qquad n'' = nP; \tag{31}$$

and introducing P and Q in (28), there results

$$\rho' \sec\beta' = \left(1 + \frac{Q}{2r'^3}\right)\frac{b + Pd}{1 + P} - c. \tag{32}$$

This equation involves both ρ' and r' as unknown quantities, but by means of another equation between these quantities ρ' may be eliminated, thus giving a single equation from which r' may be found, after which ρ' may also be determined.

82. Let ψ' represent the angle at the earth between the sun and planet or comet at the second observation, and we shall have, from the equations $(93)_3$,

$$\tan w' = \frac{\tan \beta'}{\sin (\lambda' - \odot')},$$
$$\tan \psi' = \frac{\tan (\lambda' - \odot')}{\cos w'}, \tag{33}$$
$$\cos \psi' = \cos \beta' \cos (\lambda' - \odot'),$$

by means of which we may determine ψ', which cannot exceed 180°. Since $\cos \beta'$ is always positive, $\cos \psi'$ and $\cos (\lambda' - \odot')$ must have the same sign.

We also have

$$r'^2 = \Delta'^2 + R'^2 - 2\Delta' R' \cos \psi',$$

which may be put in the form

$$r'^2 = (\rho' \sec \beta' - R' \cos \psi')^2 + R'^2 \sin^2 \psi',$$

from which we get

$$\rho' \sec \beta' = R' \cos \psi' \pm \sqrt{r'^2 - R'^2 \sin^2 \psi'}. \tag{34}$$

Substituting for $\rho' \sec \beta'$ its value given by equation (32), we have

$$\left(1 + \frac{Q}{2r'^3}\right) \frac{b + Pd}{1 + P} - c = R' \cos \psi' \pm \sqrt{r'^2 - R'^2 \sin^2 \psi'}.$$

For brevity, let us put

$$c_0 = \frac{b + Pd}{1 + P},$$
$$c_0 - c = k_0, \tag{35}$$
$$-\tfrac{1}{2} c_0 Q = l_0,$$

and we shall have

$$k_0 - \frac{l_0}{r'^3} = R' \cos \psi' \pm \sqrt{r'^2 - R'^2 \sin^2 \psi'}. \tag{36}$$

When the values of P and Q have been found, this equation will give the value of r' in terms of quantities derived directly from the data furnished by observation. We shall now represent by z' the angle at the planet between the sun and earth at the time of the second observation, and we shall have

$$r' = \frac{R' \sin \psi'}{\sin z'}. \tag{37}$$

Substituting this value of r', in the preceding equation, there results

$$(k_0 - R'\cos\psi')\sin z' \mp R'\sin\psi'\cos z' = \frac{l_0\sin^4 z'}{R'^3\sin^3\psi'}, \tag{38}$$

and if we put

$$\begin{aligned} \eta_0 \sin\zeta &= R'\sin\psi', \\ \eta_0\cos\zeta &= k_0 - R'\cos\psi', \\ m_0 &= \frac{l_0}{\eta_0 R'^3\sin^3\psi'}, \end{aligned} \tag{39}$$

the condition being imposed that m_0 shall always be positive, we have, finally,

$$\sin(z' \mp \zeta) = m_0 \sin^4 z'. \tag{40}$$

In order that m_0 may be positive, the quadrant in which ζ is taken must be such that η_0 shall have the same sign as l_0, since $\sin\psi'$ is always positive.

From equation (37) it appears that $\sin z'$ must always be positive, or $z' < 180°$; and further, in the plane triangle formed by joining the actual places of the earth, sun, and planet or comet corresponding to the middle observation, we have

$$\varDelta' = \frac{r'\sin(z'+\psi')}{\sin\psi'} = \frac{R'\sin(z'+\psi')}{\sin z'}.$$

Therefore,

$$\rho' = \frac{R'\sin(z'+\psi')}{\sin z'}\cos\beta', \tag{41}$$

and, since ρ' is always positive, it follows that $\sin(z'+\psi')$ must be positive, or that z' cannot exceed $180° - \psi'$.

When the planet or comet at the time of the middle observation is both in the node and in opposition or conjunction with the sun, we shall have $\beta' = 0$, $\psi' = 180°$ when the body is in opposition, and $\psi' = 0°$ when it is in conjunction. Consequently, it becomes impossible to determine r' by means of the angle z'; but in this case the equation (36) gives

$$k_0 - \frac{l_0}{r'^3} = -R' + r',$$

when the body is in opposition, the lower sign being excluded by the condition that the value of the first member of the equation must be positive, and for $\psi' = 0$,

$$k_0 - \frac{l_0}{r'^3} = R' \pm r',$$

the upper sign being used when the sun is between the earth and the planet, and the lower sign when the planet is between the earth and the sun. It is hardly necessary to remark that the case of an observation at the superior conjunction when $\beta' = 0$, is physically impossible. The value of r' may be found from these equations by trial; and then we shall have

$$\rho' = r' - R'$$

when the body is in opposition, and

$$\rho' = R' - r'$$

when it is in inferior conjunction with the sun.

For the case in which the great circle passing through the extreme observed places of the body passes also through the middle place, which gives $a_0 = 0$, let us divide equation (32) through by c, and we have

$$\left(1 + \frac{Q}{2r'^3}\right)\frac{\frac{b}{c} + P\frac{d}{c}}{1 + P} - 1 = \frac{\rho' \sec \beta'}{c},$$

The equations (17) give

$$\frac{b}{c} = \frac{R \sin(\odot - K)}{R' \sin(\odot' - K)}, \qquad \frac{d}{c} = \frac{R'' \sin(\odot'' - K)}{R' \sin(\odot' - K)},$$

and if we put

$$\frac{\frac{b}{c} + P\frac{d}{c}}{1 + P} = C_0,$$

we shall have

$$\left(1 + \frac{Q}{2r'^3}\right) C_0 - 1 = 0,$$

since $c = \infty$ when $a_0 = 0$. Hence we derive

$$r' = \sqrt[3]{\frac{\frac{1}{2} C_0 Q}{1 - C_0}}. \qquad (42)$$

But when the great circle passing through the three observed places passes also through the second place of the sun, both c and C_0 become indeterminate, and thus the solution of the problem, with the given data, becomes impossible.

83. The equation (40) must give four roots corresponding to each sign, respectively; but it may be shown that of these eight roots at least four will, in every case, be imaginary. Thus, the equation may be written

$$m_0 \sin^4 z' - \sin z' \cos \zeta = \mp \cos z' \sin \zeta,$$

and, by squaring and reducing, this becomes

$$m_0^2 \sin^8 z' - 2m_0 \cos \zeta \sin^5 z' + \sin^2 z' - \sin^2 \zeta = 0.$$

When ζ is within the limits $-90°$ and $+90°$, $\cos \zeta$ will be positive, and, m_0 being always positive, it appears from the algebraic signs of the terms of the equation, according to the theory of equations, that in this case there cannot be more than four real roots, of which three will be positive and one negative. When ζ exceeds the limits $-90°$ and $+90°$, $\cos \zeta$ will be negative, and hence, in this case also, there cannot be more than four real roots, of which one will be positive and three negative. Further, since $\sin^2 \zeta$ is real and positive, there must be at least two real roots—one positive and the other negative—whether $\cos \zeta$ be negative or positive.

We may also remark that, in finding the roots of the equation (40), it will only be necessary to solve the equation

$$\sin (z' - \zeta) = m_0 \sin^4 z', \tag{43}$$

since the lower sign in (40) follows directly from this by substituting $180° - z'$ in place of z'; and hence the roots derived from this will comprise all the real roots belonging to the general form of the equation.

The observed places of the heavenly body only give the direction in space of right lines passing through the places of the earth and the corresponding places of the body, and any three points, one in each of these lines, which are situated in a plane passing through the centre of the sun, and which are at such distances as to fulfil the condition that the areal velocity shall be constant, according to the relation expressed by the equation $(30)_{\text{II}}$, must satisfy the analytical conditions of the problem. It is evident that the three places of the earth may satisfy these conditions; and hence there may be one root of equation (43) which will correspond to the orbit of the earth, or give

$$\rho' = 0.$$

Further, it follows from the equation (37) that this root must be

$$z' = 180° - \psi';$$

and such would be strictly the case if, instead of the assumed values of P and Q, their exact values for the orbit of the earth were adopted, and if the observations were referred directly to the centre of the earth, in the correction for parallax, neglecting also the perturbations in the motion of the earth.

In the case of the earth,

$$n'' = N'' = \frac{RR' \sin(\odot' - \odot)}{RR'' \sin(\odot'' - \odot)},$$

$$n = N \ = \frac{R'R'' \sin(\odot'' - \odot')}{RR'' \sin(\odot'' - \odot)},$$

and the complete values of P and Q become

$$P = \frac{RR' \sin(\odot' - \odot)}{R'R'' (\sin(\odot'' - \odot')},$$

$$Q = 2R'^3 \left(\frac{RR' \sin(\odot' - \odot) + R'R'' \sin(\odot'' - \odot')}{RR'' \sin(\odot'' - \odot)} - 1 \right);$$

and since the approximate values

$$P = \frac{\tau''}{\tau}, \qquad Q = \tau\tau''$$

differ but little from these, as will appear from the equations $(27)_3$, there will be one root of equation (43) which gives z' nearly equal to $180° - \psi'$. This root, however, cannot satisfy the physical conditions of the problem, which will require that the rays of light in coming from the planet or comet to the earth shall proceed from points which are at a considerable distance from the eye of the observer. Further, the negative values of $\sin z'$ are excluded by the nature of the problem, since r' must be positive, or $z' < 180°$; and of the three positive roots which may result from equation (43), that being excluded which gives z' very nearly equal to $180° - \psi'$, there will remain two, of which one will be excluded if it gives z' greater than $180° - \psi'$, and the remaining one will be that which belongs to the orbit of the planet or comet. It may happen, however, that neither of these two roots is greater than $180° - \psi'$, in which case both will satisfy the physical conditions of the problem, and hence the observations will be satisfied by two wholly different systems of elements. It will then be necessary to compare the elements computed from each of the two values of z' with other observations in order to decide which actually belongs to the body observed.

In the other case, in which $\cos \zeta$ is negative, the negative roots being excluded by the condition that r' is positive, the positive root must in most cases belong to the orbit of the earth, and the three observations do not then belong to the same body. However, in the case of the orbit of a comet, when the eccentricity is large, and the intervals between the observations are of considerable magnitude, if the approximate values of P and Q are computed directly, by means of approximate elements already known, from the equations

$$P = \frac{rr' \sin(u' - u)}{r'r'' \sin(u'' - u')},$$
$$Q = 2r'^3 \left(\frac{rr' \sin(u' - u) + r'r'' \sin(u'' - u')}{rr'' \sin(u'' - u)} - 1 \right), \qquad (44)$$

it may occur that $\cos\zeta$ is negative, and the positive root will actually belong to the orbit of the comet. The condition that one value of z' shall be very nearly equal to $180° - \psi'$, requires that the adopted values of P and Q shall differ but little from those derived directly from the places of the earth; and in the case of orbits of small eccentricity this condition will always be fulfilled, unless the intervals between the observations and the distance of the planet from the sun are both very great. But if the eccentricity is large, the difference may be such that no root will correspond to the orbit of the earth.

84. We may find an expression for the limiting values of m_0 and ζ, within which equation (43) has four real roots, and beyond which there are only two, one positive and one negative. This change in the number of real roots will take place when there are two equal roots, and, consequently, if we proceed under the supposition that equation (43) has two equal roots, and find the values of m_0 and ζ which will accord with this supposition, we may determine the limits required.

Differentiating equation (43) with respect to z', we get

$$\cos(z' - \zeta) = 4m_0 \sin^3 z' \cos z';$$

and, in the case of equal roots, the value of z' as derived from this must also satisfy the original equation

$$\sin(z' - \zeta) = m_0 \sin^4 z'.$$

To find the values of m_0 and ζ which will fulfil this condition, if we eliminate m_0 between these equations, we have

$$\sin z' \cos(z' - \zeta) = 4 \cos z' \sin(z' - \zeta),$$

from which we easily find

$$\sin(2z' - \zeta) = \tfrac{5}{3} \sin\zeta. \qquad (45)$$

This gives the value of ζ in terms of z' for which equation (43) has equal roots, and at which it ceases to have four real roots. To find the corresponding expression for m_0, we have

$$m_0 = \frac{\sin(z' - \zeta)}{\sin^4 z'} = \frac{\cos(z' - \zeta)}{4\sin^3 z' \cos z'},$$

in which we must use the value of ζ given by the preceding equation. Now, since $\sin(2z' - \zeta)$ must be within the limits -1 and $+1$, the limiting values of $\sin\zeta$ will be $+\frac{3}{5}$ and $-\frac{3}{5}$, or ζ must be within the limits $+36°\ 52'.2$ and $-36°\ 52'.2$, or $143°\ 7'.8$ and $216°\ 52'.2$. If ζ is not contained within these limits, the equation cannot have equal roots, whatever may be the value of m_0, and hence there can only be two real roots, of which one will be positive and one negative. If for a given value of ζ we compute z' from equation (45), and call this z_0', or

$$\sin(2z_0' - \zeta) = \tfrac{5}{3}\sin\zeta,$$

we may find the limits of the values of m_0, within which equation (43) has four real roots. The equation for z_0' will be satisfied by the values

$$2z_0' - \zeta, \qquad 180° - (2z_0' - \zeta);$$

and hence there will be two values of m_0, which we will denote by m_1 and m_2, for which, with a given value of ζ, equation (43) will have equal roots. Thus we shall have

$$m_1 = \frac{\sin(z_0' - \zeta)}{\sin^4 z_0'},$$

and, putting in this equation $180° - (2z_0' - \zeta)$ instead of $2z_0' - \zeta$, or $90° - (z_0' - \zeta)$ in place of z_0',

$$m_2 = \frac{\cos z_0'}{\cos^4(z_0' - \zeta)}.$$

It follows, therefore, that for any given value of ζ, if m_0 is not within the limits assigned by the values of m_1 and m_2, equation (43) will only have two real roots, one positive and one negative, of which the latter is excluded by the nature of the problem, and the former may belong to the orbit of the earth. But if P and Q differ so much from their values in the case of the orbit of the earth that z' is not very nearly equal to $180° - \psi'$, the positive root, when ζ exceeds the limits $+36°\ 52'.2$ and $-36°\ 52'.2$, may actually satisfy the conditions of the problem, and belong to the orbit of the body observed.

When ζ is within the limits 143° 7′.8 and 216° 52′.2, there will be four real roots, one positive and three negative, if m_0 is within the limits m_1 and m_2; but, if m_0 surpasses these limits, there will be only two real roots.

Table XII. contains for values of ζ from $-36°$ 52′.2 to $+36°$ 52′.2 the values of m_1 and m_2, and also the values of the four real roots corresponding respectively to m_1 and m_2.

In every case in which equation (43) has three positive roots and one negative root, the value of m_0 must be within the limits indicated by m_1 and m_2, and the values of z' will be within the limits indicated by the quantities corresponding to m_1 and m_2 for each root, which we designate respectively by z_1', z_2', z_3', and z_4'. The table will show, from the given values of m_0 and $180° - \psi'$, whether the problem admits of two distinct solutions, since, excluding the value of z', which is nearly equal to $180° - \psi'$, and corresponds to the orbit of the earth, and also that which exceeds 180°, it will appear at once whether one or both of the remaining two values of z' will satisfy the condition that z' shall be less than $180° - \psi'$. The table will also indicate an approximate value of z', by means of which the equation (43) may be solved by a few trials.

For the root of the equation (43) which corresponds to the orbit of the earth, we have $\rho' = 0$, and hence from (36) we derive

$$k_0 = \frac{l_0}{R'^3}.$$

Substituting this value for k_0 in the general equation (32), we have

$$\rho' \sec\beta' = l_0\left(\frac{1}{R'^3} - \frac{1}{r'^3}\right);$$

and, since ρ' must be positive, the algebraic sign of the numerical value of l_0 will indicate whether r' is greater or less than R'. It is easily seen, from the formulæ for l_0, b, d, &c., that in the actual application of these formulæ, the intervals between the observations not being very large, l_0 will be positive when $\beta' - \beta_0$ and $\sin(\odot' - K)$ have contrary signs, and negative when $\beta' - \beta_0$ has the same sign as $\sin(\odot' - K)$. Hence, when $\odot' - K$ is less than 180°, r' must be less than R' if $\beta' - \beta_0$ is positive, but greater than R' if $\beta' - \beta_0$ is negative. When $\odot' - K$ exceeds 180°, r' will be greater than R' if $\beta' - \beta_0$ is positive, and less than R' if $\beta' - \beta_0$ is negative. We may, therefore, by means of a celestial globe, determine by inspection whether the distance of a comet from the sun is greater or less than that of the earth from the sun. Thus, if we pass a great circle through the two extreme observed places of the comet, r' must be greater than R' when the place of the comet for the middle observation is on the same side of this great circle as the point of the ecliptic which corresponds to the place of the sun. But when the middle place and the point of the ecliptic corresponding to the place of the sun are on opposite sides of the great circle passing through the first and third places of the comet, r' must be less than R'.

85. From the values of ρ' and r' derived from the assumed values $P = \frac{\tau''}{\tau}$ and $Q = \tau\tau''$, we may evidently derive more approximate values of these quantities, and thus, by a repetition of the calculation, make a still closer approximation to the true value of ρ'. To derive other expressions for P and Q which are exact, provided that r' and ρ' are accurately known, let us denote by s'' the ratio of the sector of the orbit included by r and r' to the triangle included by the same radii-vectores and the chord joining the first and second places; by s' the same ratio with respect to r and r'', and by s this ratio with respect to r' and r''. These ratios s, s', s'' must necessarily be greater than 1, since every part of the orbit is concave toward the sun. According to the equation $(30)_1$, we have for the areas of the sectors, neglecting the mass of the body,

$$\tfrac{1}{2}\tau''\sqrt{p}, \qquad \tfrac{1}{2}\tau'\sqrt{p}, \qquad \tfrac{1}{2}\tau\sqrt{p},$$

and therefore we obtain

$$s''[rr'] = \tau''\sqrt{p}, \qquad s'[rr''] = \tau'\sqrt{p}, \qquad s[r'r''] = \tau\sqrt{p}. \tag{46}$$

Then, since

$$n = \frac{[r'r'']}{[rr'']}, \qquad n'' = \frac{[rr']}{[rr'']},$$

we shall have

$$n = \frac{\tau}{\tau'}\cdot\frac{s'}{s}, \qquad n'' = \frac{\tau''}{\tau'}\cdot\frac{s'}{s''}, \tag{47}$$

and, consequently,

$$\begin{aligned} P &= \frac{\tau''}{\tau}\cdot\frac{s}{s''}, \\ Q &= \frac{\tau\tau''}{ss''}\left(\frac{s's''}{\tau'\tau''} + \frac{ss'}{\tau\tau'} - \frac{ss''}{\tau\tau''}\right)2r'^3. \end{aligned} \tag{48}$$

Substituting for s, s', and s'' their values from (46), we have

$$Q = 2pr'^3\,\frac{[r'r''] + [rr'] - [rr'']}{[rr']\,.\,[rr'']\,.\,[r'r'']}\cdot\frac{\tau\tau''}{ss''}. \tag{49}$$

The angular distance between the perihelion and node being denoted by ω, the polar equation of the conic section gives

$$\frac{p}{r} = 1 + e\cos(u - \omega),$$
$$\frac{p}{r'} = 1 + e\cos(u' - \omega), \qquad (50)$$
$$\frac{p}{r''} = 1 + e\cos(u'' - \omega).$$

If we multiply the first of these equations by $\sin(u'' - u')$, the second by $-\sin(u'' - u)$, and the third by $\sin(u' - u)$, add the products and reduce, we get

$$\frac{p}{r}\sin(u'' - u') - \frac{p}{r'}\sin(u'' - u) + \frac{p}{r''}\sin(u' - u) = \sin(u'' - u') - \sin(u'' - u) + \sin(u' - u);$$

and, since

$$\sin(u'' - u') = 2\sin\tfrac{1}{2}(u'' - u')\cos\tfrac{1}{2}(u'' - u'),$$
$$\sin(u'' - u) - \sin(u' - u) = 2\sin\tfrac{1}{2}(u'' - u')\cos\tfrac{1}{2}(u'' + u' - 2u),$$

the second member reduces to

$$4\sin\tfrac{1}{2}(u'' - u')\sin\tfrac{1}{2}(u'' - u)\sin\tfrac{1}{2}(u' - u).$$

Therefore, we shall have

$$p = \frac{4rr'r''\sin\frac{1}{2}(u'' - u')\sin\frac{1}{2}(u'' - u)\sin\frac{1}{2}(u' - u)}{r'r''\sin(u'' - u') - rr''\sin(u'' - u) + rr'\sin(u' - u)}.$$

If we multiply both numerator and denominator of this expression by

$$2rr'r''\cos\tfrac{1}{2}(u'' - u')\cos\tfrac{1}{2}(u'' - u)\cos\tfrac{1}{2}(u' - u),$$

it becomes, introducing $[rr']$, $[rr'']$, and $[r'r'']$,

$$p = \frac{[r'r''] \, . \, [rr''] \, . \, [rr']}{[r'r''] + [rr'] - [rr'']} \cdot \frac{1}{2rr'r''\cos\frac{1}{2}(u'' - u')\cos\frac{1}{2}(u'' - u)\cos\frac{1}{2}(u' - u)}.$$

Substituting this value of p in equation (49), it reduces to

$$Q = \frac{\tau\tau''}{ss''} \cdot \frac{r'^2}{rr''\cos\frac{1}{2}(u'' - u')\cos\frac{1}{2}(u'' - u)\cos\frac{1}{2}(u' - u)}. \qquad (51)$$

86. If we compare the equations (47) with the formula $(28)_3$, we derive

$$\frac{s''}{s} = 1 - \tfrac{1}{6}\frac{\tau^2 - \tau''^2}{r'^3} + \tfrac{1}{4}\frac{(\tau^3 + \tau''^3)}{kr'^4} \cdot \frac{dr'}{dt} \ldots . \qquad (52)$$

Consequently, in the first approximation, we may take

$$\frac{s''}{s} = 1.$$

If the intervals of the times are not very unequal, this assumption will differ from the truth only in terms of the third order with respect to the time, and in terms of the fourth order if the intervals are equal, as has already been shown. Hence, we adopt for the first approximation,

$$P = \frac{\tau''}{\tau}, \qquad Q = \tau\tau'',$$

the values of τ and τ'' being computed from the uncorrected times of observation, which may be denoted by t_0, t_0', and t_0''. With the values of P and Q thus found, we compute r', and from this ρ', ρ, and ρ'', by means of the formulæ already derived.

The heliocentric places for the first and third observations may now be found from the formulæ $(71)_3$ and $(72)_3$, and then the angle $u'' - u$ between the radii-vectores r and r'' may be obtained in various ways, precisely as the distance between two points on the celestial sphere is obtained from the spherical co-ordinates of these points. When $u'' - u$ has been found, we have

$$\begin{aligned} \sin(u'' - u') &= \frac{nr}{r'} \sin(u'' - u), \\ \sin(u' - u) &= \frac{n''r''}{r'} \sin(u'' - u), \end{aligned} \qquad (53)$$

from which $u'' - u'$ and $u' - u$ may be computed. From these results the ratios s and s'' may be computed, and then new and more approximate values of P and Q. The value of $u'' - u$, found by taking the sum of $u'' - u'$ and $u' - u$ as derived from (53), should agree with that used in the second members of these equations, within the limits of the errors which may be attributed to the logarithmic tables.

The most advantageous method of obtaining the angles between the radii-vectores is to find the position of the plane of the orbit directly from l, l'', b, and b'', and then compute u, u', and u'' directly from Ω and i, according to the first of equations $(82)_1$. It will be expedient also to compute r', l' and b' from ρ', λ', and β', and the agreement of the value of r', thus found, with that already obtained from equation (37), will check the accuracy of part of the numerical calculation. Further, since the three places of the body must be in a plane passing through the centre of the sun, whether P and Q are exact or only approximate, we must also have

$$\tan b' = \tan i \sin (l' - \Omega),$$

and the value of b' derived from this equation must agree with that computed directly from ρ', or at least the difference should not exceed what may be due to the unavoidable errors of logarithmic calculation.

We may now compute n and n'' directly from the equations

$$n = \frac{r'r'' \sin (u'' - u')}{rr'' \sin (u'' - u)}, \qquad n'' = \frac{rr' \sin (u' - u)}{rr'' \sin (u'' - u)}; \qquad (54)$$

but when the values of u, u', and u'' are those which result from the assumed values of P and Q, the resulting values of n and n'' will only satisfy the condition that the plane of the orbit passes through the centre of the sun. If substituted in the equations (29), they will only reproduce the assumed values of P and Q, from which they have been derived, and hence they cannot be used to correct them. If, therefore, the numerical calculation be correct, the values of n and n'' obtained from (54) must agree with those derived from equations (31), within the limits of accuracy admitted by the logarithmic tables.

The differences $u'' - u'$ and $u' - u$ will usually be small, and hence a small error in either of these quantities may considerably affect the resulting values of n and n''. In order to determine whether the error of calculation is within the limits to be expected from the logarithmic tables used, if we take the logarithms of both members of the equations (54) and differentiate, supposing only n, n'', and u' to vary, we get

$$d \log_e n = - \cot (u'' - u')\, du',$$
$$d \log_e n'' = + \cot (u' - u)\, du'.$$

Multiplying these by 0.434294, the modulus of the common system of logarithms, and expressing du' in seconds of arc, we find, in units of the seventh decimal place of common logarithms,

$$d \log n = - 21.055 \cot (u'' - u')\, du',$$
$$d \log n'' = + 21.055 \cot (u' - u)\, du'.$$

If we substitute in these the differences between $\log n$ and $\log n''$ as found from the equations (54), and the values already obtained by means of (31), the two resulting values of du' should agree, and the magnitude of du' itself will show whether the error of calculation exceeds the unavoidable errors due to the limited extent of the logarithmic tables. When the agreement of the two results for n and n'' is in accordance with these conditions, and no error has been made in computing n and n'' from P and Q by means of the equations (31), the accuracy of the entire calculation, both of the quantities which depend on the assumed values of P and Q, and of those which are obtained independently from the data furnished by observation, is completely proved.

87. Since the values of n and n'' derived from equations (54) cannot be used to correct the assumed values of P and Q, from which r, r', u, u', &c. have been computed, it is evidently necessary to compute the values for a second approximation by means of the series given by the equations $(26)_3$, or by means of the ratios s and s''. The expressions for n and n'' arranged in a series with respect to the time involve the differential coefficients of r' with respect to t, and, since these are necessarily unknown, and cannot be conveniently determined, it is plain that if the ratios s and s'' can be readily found from r, r', r'', u, u', u'', and τ, τ', τ'', so as to involve the relation between the times of observation and the places in the orbit, they may be used to obtain new values of P and Q by means of equations (48) and (51), to be used in a second approximation.

Let us now resume the equation

$$M = E - e \sin E,$$

or

$$\frac{k(t-T)}{a^{\frac{3}{2}}} = E - e \sin E,$$

and also for the third place

$$\frac{k(t''-T)}{a^{\frac{3}{2}}} = E'' - e \sin E''.$$

Subtracting, we get

$$\frac{\tau'}{a^{\frac{3}{2}}} = E'' - E - 2e \sin \tfrac{1}{2}(E''-E) \cos \tfrac{1}{2}(E''+E). \tag{55}$$

This equation contains three unknown quantities, a, e, and the difference $E''-E$. We can, however, by means of expressions involving r, r'', u, and u'', eliminate a and e. Thus, since $p = a(1-e^2)$, we have

$$\tau'\sqrt{p} = a^2\sqrt{1-e^2}\,(E''-E-2e \sin \tfrac{1}{2}(E''-E) \cos \tfrac{1}{2}(E''+E)). \tag{56}$$

From the equations

$$\sqrt{r}\sin\tfrac{1}{2}v=\sqrt{a(1+e)}\sin\tfrac{1}{2}E,\qquad \sqrt{r''}\sin\tfrac{1}{2}v''=\sqrt{a(1+e)}\sin\tfrac{1}{2}E'',$$
$$\sqrt{r}\cos\tfrac{1}{2}v=\sqrt{a(1-e)}\cos\tfrac{1}{2}E,\qquad \sqrt{r''}\cos\tfrac{1}{2}v''=\sqrt{a(1-e)}\cos\tfrac{1}{2}E'',$$

since $v''-v=u''-u$, we easily derive

$$\sqrt{rr''}\sin\tfrac{1}{2}(u''-u)=a\sqrt{1-e^2}\sin\tfrac{1}{2}(E''-E), \tag{57}$$

and also

$$a\cos\tfrac{1}{2}(E''-E)-ae\cos\tfrac{1}{2}(E''+E)=\sqrt{rr''}\cos\tfrac{1}{2}(u''-u),$$

or

$$e\cos\tfrac{1}{2}(E''+E)=\cos\tfrac{1}{2}(E''-E)-\frac{\sqrt{rr''}\cos\tfrac{1}{2}(u''-u)}{a}. \tag{58}$$

Substituting this value of $e\cos\tfrac{1}{2}(E''+E)$ in equation (56), we get

$$\begin{aligned}\tau'\sqrt{p}&=a^2\sqrt{1-e^2}\,(E''-E-\sin(E''-E))\\&\quad+2a\sqrt{1-e^2}\sin\tfrac{1}{2}(E''-E)\cos\tfrac{1}{2}(u''-u)\sqrt{rr''},\end{aligned}$$

and substituting, in the last term of this, for $a\sqrt{1-e^2}$, its value from (57), the result is

$$\tau'\sqrt{p}=a^2\sqrt{1-e^2}\,(E''-E-\sin(E''-E))+rr''\sin(u''-u). \tag{59}$$

From (57) we obtain

$$a^2\sqrt{1-e^2}=\frac{1}{p}\cdot\frac{(\sqrt{rr''}\sin\tfrac{1}{2}(u''-u))^3}{\sin^3\tfrac{1}{2}(E''-E)},$$

or

$$a^2\sqrt{1-e^2}=\left(\frac{rr''\sin(u''-u)}{2\sqrt{rr''}\cos\tfrac{1}{2}(u''-u)}\right)^3\frac{1}{p\sin^3\tfrac{1}{2}(E''-E)}.$$

Therefore, the equation (59) becomes

$$\tau'\sqrt{p}=\frac{1}{p}\cdot\frac{E''-E-\sin(E''-E)}{\sin^3\tfrac{1}{2}(E''-E)}\left(\frac{[rr'']}{2\sqrt{rr''}\cos\tfrac{1}{2}(u''-u)}\right)^3+[rr'']. \tag{60}$$

Let $\varkappa'$ be the chord of the orbit between the first and third places, and we shall have

$$\varkappa'^2=(r+r'')^2-4rr''\cos^2\tfrac{1}{2}(u''-u).$$

Now, since the chord $\varkappa'$ can never exceed $r+r''$, we may put

$$\varkappa'=(r+r'')\sin\gamma', \tag{61}$$

and from this, in combination with the preceding equation, we derive

$$2\sqrt{rr''}\cos\tfrac{1}{2}(u''-u)=(r+r'')\cos\gamma'. \tag{62}$$

Substituting this value, and $[rr''] = \frac{\tau'}{s'}\sqrt{p}$, in equation (60), it reduces to

$$\frac{E''-E-\sin(E''-E)}{\sin^3\frac{1}{2}(E''-E)}\cdot\frac{\tau'^2}{(r+r'')^3\cos^3\gamma'}\cdot\frac{1}{s'^3}+\frac{1}{s'}=1. \tag{63}$$

The elements a and e are thus eliminated, but the resulting equation involves still the unknown quantities $E''-E$ and s'. It is necessary, therefore, to derive an additional equation involving the same unknown quantities in order that $E''-E$ may be eliminated, and that thus the ratio s', which is the quantity sought, may be found.

From the equations

$$r = a - ae\cos E, \qquad r'' = a - ae\cos E'',$$

we get

$$r''+r = 2a - 2ae\cos\tfrac{1}{2}(E''+E)\cos\tfrac{1}{2}(E''-E).$$

Substituting in this the value of $e\cos\frac{1}{2}(E''+E)$ from (58), we have

$$r''+r = 2a\sin^2\tfrac{1}{2}(E''-E) + 2\sqrt{rr''}\cos\tfrac{1}{2}(u''-u)\cos\tfrac{1}{2}(E''-E),$$

and substituting for $\sin\frac{1}{2}(E''-E)$ its value from (57), there results

$$r''+r = \frac{2rr''\sin^2\frac{1}{2}(u''-u)}{p} + 2\sqrt{rr''}\cos\tfrac{1}{2}(u''-u)\left(1-2\sin^2\tfrac{1}{4}(E''-E)\right).$$

But, since

$$\frac{2rr''\sin^2\frac{1}{2}(u''-u)}{p} = \frac{([rr''])^2}{2prr''\cos^2\frac{1}{2}(u''-u)} = \frac{2\tau'^2}{s'^2}\left(\frac{1}{2\sqrt{rr''}\cos\frac{1}{2}(u''-u)}\right)^2,$$

we have

$$r+r'' = \frac{2\tau'^2}{s'^2}\cdot\frac{1}{(r+r'')^2\cos^2\gamma'} + (r+r'')\cos\gamma'\left(1-2\sin^2\tfrac{1}{4}(E''-E)\right),$$

from which we derive

$$\sin^2\tfrac{1}{4}(E''-E) = \frac{1}{s'^2}\cdot\frac{\tau'^2}{(r+r'')^3\cos^3\gamma'} - \frac{\sin^2\frac{1}{2}\gamma'}{\cos\gamma'}, \tag{64}$$

which is the additional equation required, involving $E''-E$ and s' as unknown quantities.

Let us now put

$$\begin{aligned} y' &= \frac{\sin^3\frac{1}{2}(E''-E)}{E''-E-\sin(E''-E)}, \\ m' &= \frac{\tau'^2}{(r+r'')^3\cos^3\gamma'}, \\ l' &= \frac{\sin^2\frac{1}{2}\gamma'}{\cos\gamma'}, \\ x' &= \sin^2\tfrac{1}{4}(E''-E), \end{aligned} \tag{65}$$

and the equations (63) and (64) become

$$\frac{m'}{y'}\cdot\frac{1}{s'^3}+\frac{1}{s'}=1,$$
$$x'=\frac{m'}{s'^2}-y'. \qquad (66)$$

When the value of y' is known, the first of these equations will enable us to determine s', and hence the value of x', or $\sin^2\frac{1}{4}(E''-E)$, from the last equation.

The calculation of γ' may be facilitated by the introduction of an additional auxiliary quantity. Thus, let

$$\tan\chi'=\sqrt{\frac{r''}{r}}, \qquad (67)$$

and from (62) we find

$$\cos\gamma'=\cos\tfrac{1}{2}(u''-u)\,\frac{2\sqrt{rr''}}{r+r''}=2\cos\tfrac{1}{2}(u''-u)\cos^2\chi'\tan\chi',$$

or

$$\cos\gamma'=\sin 2\chi'\cos\tfrac{1}{2}(u''-u). \qquad (68)$$

We have, also,

$$\varkappa'^2=(r+r'')^2-4rr''\cos^2\tfrac{1}{2}(u''-u),$$

which gives

$$\varkappa'^2=(r-r'')^2+4rr''\sin^2\tfrac{1}{2}(u''-u).$$

Multiplying this equation by $\cos^2\frac{1}{2}(u''-u)$ and the preceding one by $\sin^2\frac{1}{2}(u''-u)$, and adding, we get

$$\varkappa'^2=(r+r'')^2\sin^2\tfrac{1}{2}(u''-u)+(r-r'')^2\cos^2\tfrac{1}{2}(u''-u). \qquad (69)$$

From (67) we get

$$\cos^2\chi'=\frac{r}{r+r''}, \qquad \sin^2\chi'=\frac{r''}{r+r''},$$

and, therefore,

$$\cos 2\chi'=\frac{r-r''}{r+r''},$$

so that equation (69) may be written

$$\frac{\varkappa'^2}{(r+r'')^2}=\sin^2\gamma'=\sin^2\tfrac{1}{2}(u''-u)+\cos^2 2\chi'\cos^2\tfrac{1}{2}(u''-u).$$

We may, therefore, put

$$\begin{aligned}\sin\gamma'\cos G'&=\sin\tfrac{1}{2}(u''-u),\\ \sin\gamma'\sin G'&=\cos\tfrac{1}{2}(u''-u)\cos 2\chi',\\ \cos\gamma'&=\cos\tfrac{1}{2}(u''-u)\sin 2\chi',\end{aligned} \qquad (70)$$

from which γ' may be derived by means of its tangent, so that $\sin\gamma'$ shall be positive. The auxiliary angle G' will be of subsequent use in determining the elements of the orbit from the final hypothesis for P and Q.

88. We shall now consider the auxiliary quantity y' introduced into the first of equations (66). For brevity, let us put

$$g = \tfrac{1}{2}(E'' - E),$$

and we shall have

$$y' = \frac{\sin^3 g}{2g - \sin 2g}.$$

This gives, by differentiation,

$$\frac{dy'}{y'} = 3 \cot g \, dg - \frac{4 \sin^2 g \, dg}{2g - \sin 2g},$$

or

$$\frac{dy'}{dg} = 3y' \cot g - 4y'^2 \operatorname{cosec} g.$$

The last of equations (65) gives $x' = \sin^2 \tfrac{1}{2}g$, and hence

$$\frac{dg}{dx'} = 2 \operatorname{cosec} g.$$

Therefore we have

$$\frac{dy'}{dx'} = \frac{6y' \cos g - 8y'^2}{\sin^2 g} = \frac{3(1 - 2x')\,y' - 4y'^2}{2x'(1 - x')}.$$

It is evident that we may expand y' into a series arranged in reference to the ascending powers of x', so that we shall have

$$y' = \alpha + \beta x' + \gamma x'^2 + \delta x'^3 + \varepsilon x'^4 + \zeta x'^5 + \&c.$$

Differentiating, we get

$$\frac{dy'}{dx'} = \beta + 2\gamma x' + 3\delta x'^2 + 4\varepsilon x'^3 + 5\zeta x'^4 + \&c.,$$

and substituting for $\frac{dy'}{dx'}$ the value already obtained, there results

$$\begin{aligned} 2\beta x' + (4\gamma - 2\beta)\,x'^2 + (6\delta - 4\gamma)\,x'^3 + (8\varepsilon - 6\delta)\,x'^4 + (10\zeta - 8\varepsilon)\,x'^5 + \&c. \\ = (3\alpha - 4\alpha^2) + (3\beta - 6\alpha - 8\alpha\beta)\,x' + (3\gamma - 6\beta - 4\beta^2 - 8\alpha\gamma)\,x'^2 \\ + (3\delta - 6\gamma - 8\beta\gamma - 8\alpha\delta)\,x'^3 + (3\varepsilon - 6\delta - 4\gamma^2 - 8\beta\delta - 8\alpha\varepsilon)\,x'^4 \\ + (3\zeta - 6\varepsilon - 8\gamma\delta - 8\beta\varepsilon - 8\alpha\zeta)\,x'^5 + \&c. \end{aligned}$$

Since the coefficients of like powers of x' must be equal, we have

$$3\alpha - 4\alpha^2 = 0, \qquad 3\beta - 6\alpha - 8\alpha\beta = 2\beta,$$
$$3\gamma - 6\beta - 4\beta^2 - 8\alpha\gamma = 2(2\gamma - \beta), \ \&c.;$$

and hence we derive

$$\alpha = \tfrac{3}{4}, \qquad \beta = -\tfrac{9}{10}, \qquad \gamma = \tfrac{9}{175}, \qquad \delta = \tfrac{26}{875},$$
$$\varepsilon = \tfrac{6228}{336875}, \qquad \zeta = \tfrac{265896}{21896875}, \qquad \eta = \tfrac{191139024}{22991171875}.$$

Therefore we have

$$y' = \tfrac{3}{4} - \tfrac{9}{10}x' + \tfrac{9}{175}x'^2 + \tfrac{26}{875}x'^3 + \tfrac{6228}{336875}x'^4 + \tfrac{265896}{21896875}x'^5 + \tfrac{191139024}{22991171875}x'^6 + \&c. \tag{71}$$

If we multiply through by $\tfrac{10}{9}$, and put

$$\xi' = \tfrac{2}{35}x'^2 + \tfrac{52}{1575}x'^3 + \tfrac{1384}{67375}x'^4 + \tfrac{59088}{4379375}x'^5 + \tfrac{38278048}{4138509375}x'^6 + \&c., \tag{72}$$

we obtain

$$\tfrac{10}{9}y' - \tfrac{5}{6} + x' = \xi'. \tag{73}$$

Combining this with the second of equations (66), the result is

$$\tfrac{10}{9}y' + \frac{m'}{s'^2} = \tfrac{5}{6} + j' + \xi'.$$

If we put

$$\eta' = \frac{m'}{\tfrac{5}{6} + j' + \xi'}, \tag{74}$$

we shall have

$$\tfrac{9}{10}\,\frac{m'}{y'} = \frac{\eta' s'^2}{s'^2 - \eta'}.$$

But from the first of equations (66) we get

$$\frac{m'}{y'} = s'^2(s' - 1);$$

and therefore we have

$$\eta' = \frac{s'^2(s'-1)}{s' + \tfrac{1}{9}}. \tag{75}$$

As soon as η' is known, this equation will give the corresponding value of s'.

Since ξ' is a quantity of the fourth order in reference to the difference $\tfrac{1}{2}(E'' - E)$, we may evidently, for a first approximation to the value of η', take

$$\eta' = \frac{m'}{\tfrac{5}{6} + j'},$$

and with this find s' from (75), and the corresponding value of x' from the last of equations (66). With this value of x' we find the corresponding value of ξ', and recompute η', s', and x'; and, if the value of ξ' derived from the last value of x' differs from that already used, the operation must be repeated.

It will be observed that the series (72) for ξ' converges with great rapidity, and that for $E''-E=94°$ the term containing x'^6 amounts to only one unit of the seventh decimal place in the value of ξ'. Table XIV. gives the values of ξ' corresponding to values of x' from 0.0 to 0.3, or from $E''-E=0$ to $E''-E=132°\ 50'.6$. Should a case occur in which $E''-E$ exceeds this limit, the expression

$$y'=\frac{\sin^3\frac{1}{2}(E''-E)}{E''-E-\sin(E''-E)}$$

may then be computed accurately by means of the logarithmic tables ordinarily in use. An approximate value of x' may be easily found with which y' may be computed from this equation, and then ξ' from (73). With the value of ξ' thus found, η' may be computed from (74), and thus a more approximate value of x' is immediately obtained.

The equation (75) is of the third degree, and has, therefore, three roots. Since s' is always positive, and cannot be less than 1, it follows from this equation that η' is always a positive quantity. The equation may be written thus:

$$s'^3-s'^2-\eta's'-\tfrac{1}{9}\eta'=0,$$

and there being only one variation of sign, there can be only one positive root, which is the one to be adopted, the negative roots being excluded by the nature of the problem. Table XIII. gives the values of $\log s'^2$ corresponding to values of η' from $\eta'=0$ to $\eta'=0.6$. When η' exceeds the value 0.6, the value of s' must be found directly from the equation (75).

89. We are now enabled to determine whether the orbit is an ellipse, parabola, or hyperbola. In the ellipse $x=\sin^2\frac{1}{4}(E''-E)$ is positive. In the parabola the eccentric anomaly is zero, and hence $x=0$. In the hyperbola the angle which we call the eccentric anomaly, in the case of elliptic motion, becomes imaginary, and hence, since $\sin\frac{1}{4}(E''-E)$ will be imaginary, x' must be negative. It follows, therefore, that if the value of x' derived from the equation

$$x'=\frac{m'}{s'^2}-l'$$

is positive, the orbit is an ellipse; if equal to zero, the orbit is a parabola; and if negative, it is a hyperbola.

For the case of parabolic motion we have $x' = 0$, and the second of equations (66) gives

$$s'^2 = \frac{m'}{j'}. \tag{76}$$

If we eliminate s' by means of both equations, since, in this case, $y' = \frac{3}{4}$, we get

$$m'^{\frac{1}{2}} = j'^{\frac{1}{2}} + \tfrac{4}{3} j'^{\frac{3}{2}}.$$

Substituting in this the values of m and j given by (65), we obtain

$$\frac{3\tau'}{(r + r'')^{\frac{3}{2}}} = 3 \sin \tfrac{1}{2}\gamma' \cos \gamma' + 4 \sin^3 \tfrac{1}{2}\gamma',$$

which gives

$$\frac{6\tau'}{(r + r'')^{\frac{3}{2}}} = 6 \sin \tfrac{1}{2}\gamma' \cos^2 \tfrac{1}{2}\gamma' + 2 \sin^3 \tfrac{1}{2}\gamma',$$

or

$$\frac{6\tau'}{(r + r'')^{\frac{3}{2}}} = (\sin \tfrac{1}{2}\gamma' + \cos \tfrac{1}{2}\gamma')^3 + (\sin \tfrac{1}{2}\gamma' - \cos \tfrac{1}{2}\gamma')^3.$$

This may evidently be written

$$\frac{6\tau'}{(r + r'')^{\frac{3}{2}}} = (1 + \sin \gamma')^{\frac{3}{2}} \mp (1 - \sin \gamma')^{\frac{3}{2}},$$

the upper sign being used when γ' is less than 90°, and the lower sign when it exceeds 90°. Multiplying through by $(r + r'')^{\frac{3}{2}}$, and replacing $(r + r'') \sin \gamma$ by $\varkappa$, we obtain

$$6\tau' = (r + r'' + \varkappa)^{\frac{3}{2}} \mp (r + r'' - \varkappa)^{\frac{3}{2}},$$

which is identical with the equation $(56)_3$ for the special case of parabolic motion.

Since x' is negative in the case of hyperbolic motion, the value of ξ' determined by the series (72) will be different from that in the case of elliptic motion. Table XIV. gives the value of ξ' corresponding to both forms; but when x' exceeds the limits of this table, it will be necessary, in the case of the hyperbola also, to compute the value of ξ' directly, using additional terms of the series, or we may modify the expression for y' in terms of E'' and E so as to be applicable.

If we compare equations $(44)_1$ and $(56)_1$, we get

$$\tan \tfrac{1}{2}E = \sqrt{-1} \tan \tfrac{1}{2}F;$$

and hence, from $(58)_1$,

$$\tan \tfrac{1}{2}E = \frac{\sigma - 1}{\sigma + 1} \sqrt{-1}.$$

We have, also, by comparing $(65)_1$ with $(41)_1$, since a is negative in the hyperbola,

$$\cos E = \frac{\sigma^2 + 1}{2\sigma},$$

which gives

$$\sin E = \frac{\sigma^2 - 1}{2\sigma} \sqrt{-1}.$$

Now, since

$$\cos E + \sqrt{-1} \sin E = e^{E\sqrt{-1}},$$

in which e is the base of Naperian logarithms, we have

$$E\sqrt{-1} = \log_e (\cos E + \sqrt{-1} \sin E),$$

which reduces to

$$E\sqrt{-1} = \log_e \frac{1}{\sigma},$$

or

$$E = \sqrt{-1} \log_e \sigma.$$

By means of these relations between E and σ, the expression for y' may be transformed so as not to involve imaginary quantities. Thus we have

$$E'' - E = (\log_e \sigma'' - \log_e \sigma) \sqrt{-1} = \sqrt{-1} \log_e \frac{\sigma''}{\sigma},$$

$$\sin (E'' - E) = \sin E'' \cos E - \cos E'' \sin E = \frac{\sigma''^2 - \sigma^2}{2\sigma\sigma''} \sqrt{-1}.$$

From the value of $\cos E$ we easily derive

$$\sin \tfrac{1}{2}E = \frac{\sigma - 1}{2\sqrt{\sigma}} \sqrt{-1}, \qquad \cos \tfrac{1}{2}E = \frac{\sigma + 1}{2\sqrt{\sigma}},$$

and hence

$$\sin \tfrac{1}{2}(E'' - E) = \frac{\sigma'' - \sigma}{2\sqrt{\sigma\sigma''}} \sqrt{-1}.$$

Therefore the expression for y' becomes

$$y' = -\frac{(\sigma'' - \sigma)^3}{(\sqrt{\sigma\sigma''})^3 \log_e \frac{\sigma''}{\sigma} - 4\sqrt{\sigma\sigma''}\,(\sigma''^2 - \sigma^2)}.$$

Since the auxiliary quantity σ in the hyperbola is always positive, let us now put

$$\frac{\sigma''}{\sigma}=A^2,$$

and we have

$$y'=\frac{\frac{1}{4}(A-\frac{1}{A})^3}{A^2-\frac{1}{A^2}-4\log_e A}, \tag{77}$$

from which y' may be derived when A is known.

We have, further,

$$\sin^2\tfrac{1}{4}(E''-E)=\tfrac{1}{2}(1-\cos\tfrac{1}{2}(E''-E))=\tfrac{1}{2}\left(1-\frac{\sigma''+\sigma}{2\sqrt{\sigma\sigma''}}\right);$$

and therefore

$$x'=-\frac{(\sqrt{\sigma''}-\sqrt{\sigma})^2}{4\sqrt{\sigma\sigma''}}, \tag{78}$$

or

$$x'=-\tfrac{1}{4}\left(\sqrt{A}-\frac{1}{\sqrt{A}}\right)^2. \tag{79}$$

These expressions for y' and x' enable us to find ξ' when x' exceeds the limits of the table. Thus, we obtain an approximate value of x' by putting

$$\eta'=\frac{m'}{\frac{5}{6}+j''}$$

from which we first find s' and then x' from the second of equations (66). Then we compute A from the formula (79), which gives

$$A=1-2x'+2\sqrt{x'^2-x'}, \tag{80}$$

y' from (77), and ξ' from (73). A repetition of the calculation, using the value of ξ' thus found, will give a still closer approximation to the correct values of x' and s'; and this process should be continued until ξ' remains unchanged.

90. The formulæ for the calculation of s' will evidently give the value of s if we use τ, r', r'', u', and u'', the necessary changes in the notation being indicated at once; and in the same manner using τ'', r, r', u, and u', we obtain s''. From the values of s and s'' thus found, more accurate values of P and Q may be computed by means of the equations (48) and (51). We may remark, however, that if the times of the observations have not been already corrected for the

time of aberration, as in the case of the determination of an unknown orbit, this correction may now be applied as determined by means of the values of ρ, ρ', and ρ'' already obtained. Thus, if t_0, t_0', and t_0'' are the uncorrected times of observation, the corrected values will be

$$\begin{aligned} t &= t_0 - C\rho \sec\beta, \\ t' &= t_0' - C\rho' \sec\beta', \\ t'' &= t_0'' - C\rho'' \sec\beta'', \end{aligned} \tag{81}$$

in which $\log C = 7.760523$, expressed in parts of a day; and from these values of t, t', t'' we recompute τ, τ', and τ'', which values will require no further correction, since ρ, ρ', and ρ'', derived from the first approximation, are sufficient for this purpose. With the new values of P and Q we recompute r, r', r'', and u, u', u'' as before, and thence again P and Q, and if the last values differ from the preceding, we proceed in the same manner to a third approximation, which will usually be sufficient unless the interval of time between the extreme observations is considerable. If it be found necessary to proceed further with the approximations to P and Q after the calculation of these quantities in the third approximation has been effected, instead of employing these directly for the next trial, we may derive more accurate values from those already obtained. Thus, let x and y be the true values of P and Q respectively, with which, if the calculation be repeated, we should derive the same values again. Let Δx and Δy be the differences between any assumed values of x and y and the true values, or

$$x_0 = x + \Delta x, \qquad y_0 = y + \Delta y.$$

Then, if we denote by x_0', y_0' the values which result by direct calculation from the assumed values x_0 and y_0, we shall have

$$x_0' - x_0 = f(x_0, y_0) = f(x + \Delta x, y + \Delta y).$$

Expanding this function, we get

$$x_0' - x_0 = f(x, y) + A\Delta x + B\Delta y + C\Delta x^2 + D\Delta x\,\Delta y + E\Delta y^2 + \ldots,$$

and if Δx and Δy are very small, we may neglect terms of the second order. Further, since the employment of x and y will reproduce the same values, we have

$$f(x, y) = 0,$$

and hence, since $\Delta x = x_0 - x$ and $\Delta y = y_0 - y$,

$$x_0' - x_0 = A(x_0 - x) + B(y_0 - y).$$

In a similar manner, we obtain

$$y_0' - y_0 = A'(x_0 - x) + B'(y_0 - y).$$

Let us now denote the values resulting from the first assumption for P and Q by P_1 and Q_1, those resulting from P_1, Q_1 by P_2, Q_2, and from P_2, Q_2 by P_3, Q_3; and, further, let

$$\begin{array}{lll} P_1 - P = a, & P_2 - P_1 = a', & P_3 - P_2 = a'', \\ Q_1 - Q = b, & Q_2 - Q_1 = b', & Q_3 - Q_2 = b''. \end{array}$$

Then, by means of the equations for $x_0' - x_0$ and $y_0' - y_0$, we shall have

$$\begin{array}{ll} a = A(P - x) + B(Q - y), & b = A'(P - x) + B'(Q - y), \\ a' = A(P_1 - x) + B(Q_1 - y), & b' = A'(P_1 - x) + B'(Q_1 - y), \\ a'' = A(P_2 - x) + B(Q_2 - y), & b'' = A'(P_2 - x) + B'(Q_2 - y). \end{array}$$

If we eliminate A, B, A', and B' from these equations, the results are

$$x = \frac{P(a'b'' - a''b') + P_1(a''b - ab'') + P_2(ab' - a'b)}{(a'b'' - a''b') + (a''b - ab'') + (ab' - a'b)},$$

$$y = \frac{Q(a'b'' - a''b') + Q_1(a''b - ab'') + Q_2(ab' - a'b)}{(a'b'' - a''b') + (a''b - ab'') + (ab' - a'b)},$$

from which we get

$$\begin{aligned} x &= P_3 - \frac{(a'' + a')(a'b'' - a''b') + a''(a''b - ab'')}{(a'b'' - a''b') + (a''b - ab'') + (ab' - a'b)}, \\ y &= Q_3 - \frac{(b'' + b')(a'b'' - a''b') + b''(a''b - ab'')}{(a'b'' - a''b') + (a''b - ab'') + (ab' - a'b)}. \end{aligned} \qquad (82)$$

In the numerical application of these formulæ it will be more convenient to use, instead of the numbers P, P_1, P_2, Q, Q_1, &c., the logarithms of these quantities, so that $a = \log P_1 - \log P$, $b = \log Q_1 - \log Q$, and similarly for a', b', a'', b'',—which may also be expressed in units of the last decimal place of the logarithms employed,—and we shall thus obtain the values of $\log x$ and $\log y$. With these values of $\log x$ and $\log y$ for $\log P$ and $\log Q$ respectively, we proceed with the final calculation of r, r', r'', and u, u', u''.

When the eccentricity is small and the intervals of time between the observations are not very great, it will not be necessary to employ the equations (82); but if the eccentricity is considerable, and if, in addition to this, the intervals are large, they will be required. It may also occur that the values of P and Q derived from the last hypothesis as corrected by means of these formulæ, will differ so much from the values found for x and y, on account of the neglected terms of the second order, that it will be necessary to recompute these quantities, using these last values of P and Q in connection with the three preceding ones in the numerical solution of the equations (82).

91. It remains now to complete the determination of the elements of the orbit from these final values of P and Q. As soon as Ω, i, and u, u', u'' have been found, the remaining elements may be derived by means of r, r', and $u'-u$, and also from r', r'', and $u''-u'$; or, which is better, we will obtain them from the extreme places, and, if the approximation to P and Q is complete, the results thus found will agree with those resulting from the combination of the middle place with either extreme.

We must, therefore, determine s' and x' from r, r'', and $u''-u$, by means of the formulæ already derived, and then, from the second of equations (46), we have

$$p=\left(\frac{s'rr''\sin(u''-u)}{\tau'}\right)^2, \tag{83}$$

from which to obtain p. If we compute s and s'' also, we shall have

$$p=\left(\frac{sr'r''\sin(u''-u')}{\tau}\right)^2=\left(\frac{s''rr'\sin(u'-u)}{\tau''}\right)^2,$$

and the mean of the two values of p obtained from this expression should agree with that found from (83), thus checking the calculation and showing the degree of accuracy to which the approximation to P and Q has been carried.

The last of equations (65) gives

$$\sin\tfrac{1}{4}(E''-E)=\sqrt{x'}, \tag{84}$$

from which $E''-E$ may be computed. Then, from equation (57), since $e=\sin\varphi$, we have

$$a\cos\varphi=\frac{\sin\frac{1}{2}(u''-u)}{\sin\frac{1}{2}(E''-E)}\sqrt{rr''} \tag{85}$$

for the calculation of $a\cos\varphi$. But $p=a(1-e^2)=a\cos^2\varphi$, whence

$$\cos\varphi=\frac{p}{a\cos\varphi}, \tag{86}$$

which may be used to determine φ when e is very nearly equal to unity; and then e may be found from

$$e=1-2\sin^2(45^\circ-\tfrac{1}{2}\varphi).$$

The equations (50) give

$$e\cos(u-\omega)=\frac{p}{r}-1,$$

$$e\cos(u''-\omega)=\frac{p}{r''}-1,$$

and from these, by addition and subtraction, we derive

$$\begin{aligned}2e\cos\tfrac{1}{2}(u''-u)\cos\left(\tfrac{1}{2}(u''+u)-\omega\right)&=\frac{p}{r}+\frac{p}{r''}-2,\\2e\sin\tfrac{1}{2}(u''-u)\sin\left(\tfrac{1}{2}(u''+u)-\omega\right)&=\frac{p}{r}-\frac{p}{r''},\end{aligned}\qquad(87)$$

by means of which e and ω may be found.

Since

$$\cos 2\chi'=\frac{r-r''}{r+r''},\qquad\qquad \sin 2\chi'=\frac{2\sqrt{rr''}}{r+r''},$$

we have

$$\begin{aligned}\frac{p}{r}+\frac{p}{r''}-2&=\frac{2p}{\sqrt{rr''}\sin 2\chi'}-2,\\\frac{p}{r}-\frac{p}{r''}&=-\frac{2p\cot 2\chi'}{\sqrt{rr''}},\end{aligned}$$

and from equations (70),

$$\cot 2\chi'=\frac{\sin\frac{1}{2}(u''-u)\tan G'}{\cos\gamma'},\qquad\qquad \sin 2\chi'=\frac{\cos\gamma'}{\cos\frac{1}{2}(u''-u)}.$$

Therefore the formulæ (87) reduce to

$$\begin{aligned}e\sin\left(\omega-\tfrac{1}{2}(u''+u)\right)&=\frac{p}{\cos\gamma'\sqrt{rr''}}\tan G',\\e\cos\left(\omega-\tfrac{1}{2}(u''+u)\right)&=\frac{p}{\cos\gamma'\sqrt{rr''}}-\sec\tfrac{1}{2}(u''-u),\end{aligned}\qquad(88)$$

from which also e and ω may be derived. Then

$$\sin\varphi=e,$$

and the agreement of $\cos\varphi$ as derived from this value of φ with that given by (86) will serve as a further proof of the calculation. The longitude of the perihelion will be given by

$$\pi=\omega+\Omega,$$

or, when i exceeds 90°, and the distinction of retrograde motion is adopted, by $\pi=\Omega-\omega$.

To find a, we have

$$a = \frac{p}{\cos^2 \varphi} = \frac{(a \cos \varphi)^2}{p},$$

or it may be computed directly from the equation

$$a = \frac{\tau'^2}{4s'^2 rr'' \cos^2 \frac{1}{2}(u'' - u) \sin^2 \frac{1}{2}(E'' - E)}, \tag{89}$$

which results from the substitution, in the last term of the preceding equation, of the expressions for $a \cos \varphi$ and p given by (83) and (85). Then for the mean daily motion we have

$$\mu = \frac{k}{a^{\frac{3}{2}}}.$$

We have now only to find the mean anomaly corresponding to any epoch, and the elements are completely determined. For the true anomalies we have

$$v = u - \omega, \qquad v' = u' - \omega, \qquad v'' = u'' - \omega;$$

and if we compute r, r', r'' from these by means of the polar equation of the conic section, the results should agree with the values of the same quantities previously obtained. According to the equation $(45)_1$, we have

$$\begin{aligned} \tan \tfrac{1}{2}E &= \tan (45° - \tfrac{1}{2}\varphi) \tan \tfrac{1}{2}v, \\ \tan \tfrac{1}{2}E' &= \tan (45° - \tfrac{1}{2}\varphi) \tan \tfrac{1}{2}v', \\ \tan \tfrac{1}{2}E'' &= \tan (45° - \tfrac{1}{2}\varphi) \tan \tfrac{1}{2}v'', \end{aligned} \tag{90}$$

from which to find E, E', and E''. The difference $E'' - E$ should agree with that derived from equation (84) within the limits of accuracy afforded by the logarithmic tables. Then, to find the mean anomalies, we have

$$\begin{aligned} M &= E - e \sin E, \\ M' &= E' - e \sin E', \\ M'' &= E'' - e \sin E''; \end{aligned} \tag{91}$$

and, if M_0 denotes the mean anomaly corresponding to any epoch T, we have, also,

$$\begin{aligned} M_0 &= M - \mu (t - T) \\ &= M' - \mu (t' - T) \\ &= M'' - \mu (t'' - T), \end{aligned}$$

in the application of which the values of t, t', and t'' must be those which have been corrected for the time of aberration. The agreement of the three values of M_0 will be a final test of the accuracy of the entire calculation. If the final values of P and Q are exact, this proof will be complete within the limits of accuracy admitted by the logarithmic tables.

When the eccentricity is such that the equations (91) cannot be solved with the requisite degree of accuracy, we must proceed according to the methods already given for finding the time from the perihelion in the case of orbits differing but little from the parabola. For this purpose, Tables IX. and X. will be employed. As soon as v, v', and v'' have been determined, we may find the auxiliary angle V for each observation by means of Table IX.; and, with V as the argument, the quantities M, M', M'' (which are not the mean anomalies) must be obtained from Table VI. Then, the perihelion distance having been computed from

$$q = \frac{p}{1+e},$$

we shall have

$$T = t - \frac{Mq^{\frac{3}{2}}}{C_0}\sqrt{\frac{2}{1+e}} = t' - \frac{M'q^{\frac{3}{2}}}{C_0}\sqrt{\frac{2}{1+e}} = t'' - \frac{M''q^{\frac{3}{2}}}{C_0}\sqrt{\frac{2}{1+e}}; \quad (92)$$

in which $\log C_0 = 9.96012771$ for the determination of the time of perihelion passage. The times t, t', t'' must be those which have been corrected for the time of aberration, and the agreement of the three values of T is a final proof of the numerical calculation.

If Table X. is used, as soon as the true anomalies have been found, the corresponding values of $\log B$ and $\log C$ must be derived from the table. Then w is computed from

$$\tan \tfrac{1}{2}w = \frac{\tan \frac{1}{2}v}{C}\sqrt{\frac{1+9e}{5(1+e)}},$$

and similarly for w' and w''; and, with these as arguments, we derive M, M', M'' from Table VI. Finally, we have

$$T = t - \frac{MBq^{\frac{3}{2}}}{C_0\sqrt{\frac{1}{10}(1+9e)}} = t' - \frac{M'B'q^{\frac{3}{2}}}{C_0\sqrt{\frac{1}{10}(1+9e)}} = t'' - \frac{M''B''q^{\frac{3}{2}}}{C_0\sqrt{\frac{1}{10}(1+9e)}}, \quad (93)$$

for the time of perihelion passage, the value of C_0 being the same as in (92).

When the orbit is a parabola, $e = 1$ and $p = 2q$, and the elements q and ω can be derived from r, r'', u, and u'' by means of the equations (76), (83), and (88), or by means of the formulæ already given for the special case of parabolic motion.

92. Since certain quantities which are real in the ellipse and parabola become imaginary in the case of the hyperbola, the formulæ already given for determining the elements from r, r'', u, and u'' require some modification when applied to a hyperbolic orbit.

When s' and x' have been found, p, e, and ω may be derived from equations (83) and (87) or (88) precisely as in the case of an elliptic orbit. Since $x' = \sin^2 \frac{1}{4}(E'' - E)$, we easily find

$$\sin \tfrac{1}{2}(E'' - E) = 2\sqrt{x' - x'^2},$$

and equation (85) becomes

$$a \cos \varphi = \frac{\sin \frac{1}{2}(u'' - u)\sqrt{rr''}}{2\sqrt{x' - x'^2}}. \tag{94}$$

But in the hyperbola x' is negative, and hence $\sqrt{x' - x'^2}$ will be imaginary; and, further, comparing the values of p in the ellipse and hyperbola, we have $\cos^2\varphi = -\tan^2\psi$, or

$$\cos \varphi = \sqrt{-1} \tan \psi.$$

Therefore the equation for $a \cos \varphi$ becomes

$$a \tan \psi = \frac{\sin \frac{1}{2}(u'' - u)\sqrt{rr''}}{2\sqrt{x'^2 - x'}}, \tag{95}$$

if a is considered as being positive, from which $a \tan \psi$ may be obtained. Then, since $p = a \tan^2 \psi$, we have

$$\tan \psi = \frac{p}{a \tan \psi}, \tag{96}$$

for the determination of ψ, and the value of e computed from

$$e = \sec \psi = \sqrt{1 + \tan^2 \psi}$$

should agree with that derived from equation (88). When e differs but little from unity, it is conveniently and accurately computed from

$$e = 1 + 2 \sin^2 \tfrac{1}{2}\psi \sec \psi.$$

The value of a may be found from

$$a = p \cot^2 \psi = \frac{(a \tan \psi)^2}{p}, \tag{97}$$

or from

$$a = \frac{\tau'^2}{16 s'^2 r r'' \cos^2 \frac{1}{2}(u'' - u)(x'^2 - x')},$$

which is derived directly from (89), observing that the elliptic semi-transverse axis becomes negative in the case of the hyperbola.

As soon as ω has been found, we derive from u, u', and u'' the corresponding values of v, v', and v'', and then compute the values of F, F', and F'' by means of the formula $(57)_1$; after which, by means of the equation $(69)_1$, the corresponding values of N, N', and N'' will be obtained. Finally, the time of perihelion passage will be given by

$$T = t - \frac{a^{\frac{3}{2}}}{\lambda_0 k} N = t' - \frac{a^{\frac{3}{2}}}{\lambda_0 k} N' = t'' - \frac{a^{\frac{3}{2}}}{\lambda_0 k} N''$$

wherein $\log \lambda_0 k = 7.87336575$.

The cases of hyperbolic orbits are rare, and in most of those which do occur the eccentricity will not differ much from that of the parabola, so that the most accurate determination of T will be effected by means of Tables IX. and X. as already illustrated.

93. Example.—To illustrate the application of the principal formulæ which have been derived in this chapter, let us take the following observations of *Eurynome* (79):

Ann Arbor M. T.	(79) α	(79) δ
1863 Sept. 14 $15^h\ 53^m\ 37^s.2$	$1^h\ 0^m\ 44^s.91$	$+9°\ 53'\ 30''.8$,
21 9 46 18 .0	0 57 3 .57	9 13 5 .5,
28 8 49 29 .2	0 52 18 .90	+8 22 8 .7.

The apparent obliquity of the ecliptic for these dates was, respectively, 23° 27′ 20″.75, 23° 27′ 20″.71, and 23° 27′ 20″.65; and, by means of these, converting the observed right ascensions and declinations into apparent longitudes and latitudes, we get—

Ann Arbor M. T.	Longitude.	Latitude.
1863 Sept. 14 $15^h\ 53^m\ 37^s.2$	17° 47′ 37″.60	+3° 8′ 43″.19,
21 9 46 18 .0	16 41 36 .20	2 52 27 .46,
28 8 49 29 .2	15 16 56 .35	+2 32 42 .98.

For the same dates we obtain from the *American Nautical Almanac* the following places of the sun:

True Longitude.	Latitude.	$\log R_0$.
172° 1′ 42″.1	— 0.07	0.0022140,
178 37 17 .2	+ 0.77	0.0013857,
185 26 54 .8	+ 0.67	0.0005174.

Since the elements are supposed to be wholly unknown, the places of the planet must be corrected for the aberration of the fixed stars as given by equations (1). Thus we find for the corrections to be applied to the longitudes, respectively,

$$-18''.48, \qquad -19''.49, \qquad -20''.8,$$

and for the latitudes,

$$+0''.47, \qquad +0''.30, \qquad +0''.14.$$

When these corrections are applied, we obtain the true places of the planet for the instants when the light was emitted, but as seen from the places of the earth at the instants of observation.

Next, each place of the sun must be reduced from the centre of the earth to the point in which a line drawn from the planet through the place of the observer cuts the plane of the ecliptic. For this purpose we have, for Ann Arbor,

$$\varphi' = 42^\circ\ 5'.4, \qquad \log \rho_0 = 9.99935;$$

and the mean time of observation being converted into sidereal time gives, for the three observations,

$$\theta_0 = 3^h\ 29^m\ 1^s, \qquad \theta_0' = 21^h\ 48^m\ 17^s, \qquad \theta_0'' = 21^h\ 18^m\ 55^s,$$

which are the right ascensions of the geocentric zenith, of which φ' is in each case the declination. From these we derive the longitude and latitude of the zenith for each observation, namely,

$$l_0 = 60^\circ\ 33'.9, \qquad l_0' = 347^\circ\ 0'.4, \qquad l_0'' = 342^\circ\ 59'.2,$$
$$b_0 = +22\ \ 25\ .0, \qquad b_0' = +50\ \ 15\ .8, \qquad b_0'' = +53\ \ 41\ .6.$$

Then, by means of equations (4), we obtain

$$\Delta\odot_0 = -18''.92, \qquad \Delta\odot' = -36''.94, \qquad \Delta\odot'' = -25''.76,$$
$$\Delta \log R_0 = -0.0001084, \qquad \Delta \log R_0' = -0.0002201,$$
$$\Delta \log R_0'' = -0.0002796.$$

For the reduction of time, we have the values $+0^s.15$, $+0^s.28$, and $+0^s.34$, which are so small that they may be neglected.

Finally, the longitudes of both the sun and planet are reduced to the mean equinox of 1863.0 by applying the corrections

$$-50''.95, \qquad -51''.52, \qquad -52''.14;$$

and the latitudes of the planet are reduced to the ecliptic of the same date by applying the corrections $-0''.15$, $-0''.14$, and $-0''.14$, respectively.

Collecting together and applying the several corrections thus obtained for the places of the sun and of the planet, reducing the uncorrected times of observation to the meridian of Washington, and expressing them in days from the beginning of the year, we have the following data:—

$$\begin{array}{lll} t_0 = 257.68079, & \lambda = 17^\circ\ 46'\ 28''.17, & \beta = +3^\circ\ \ 8'\ 43''.51, \\ t_0' = 264.42570, & \lambda' = 16\ \ 40\ \ 25\ .19, & \beta' = \quad 2\ \ 52\ \ 27\ .62, \\ t_0'' = 271.38625, & \lambda'' = 15\ \ 15\ \ 44\ .03, & \beta'' = +2\ \ 32\ \ 42\ .98, \end{array}$$

$$\begin{array}{ll} \odot = 172^\circ\ \ 0'\ 32''.23, & \log R = 0.0021056, \\ \odot' = 178\ \ 35\ \ 48\ .74, & \log R' = 0.0011656, \\ \odot'' = 185\ \ 25\ \ 36\ .90, & \log R'' = 0.0002378. \end{array}$$

The numerical values of the several corrections to be applied to the data furnished by observation and by the solar tables should be checked by duplicate calculation, since an error in any of these reductions will not be indicated until after the entire calculation of the elements has been effected.

By means of the equations

$$N = \frac{R'R'' \sin(\odot'' - \odot')}{RR'' \sin(\odot'' - \odot)}, \qquad N'' = \frac{RR' \sin(\odot' - \odot)}{RR'' \sin(\odot'' - \odot)},$$

$$\tan w' = \frac{\tan \beta'}{\sin(\lambda' - \odot')}, \qquad \tan \psi' = \frac{\tan(\lambda' - \odot')}{\cos w'},$$

we obtain

$$\log N = 9.7087449, \qquad \log N'' = 9.6950091,$$
$$\psi' = 161^\circ\ 42'\ 13''.16,$$
$$\log(R' \sin \psi') = 9.4980010, \qquad \log(R' \cos \psi') = 9.9786355_n.$$

The quadrant in which ψ' must be taken is determined by the conditions that ψ' must be less than 180°, and that $\cos\psi'$ and $\cos(\lambda' - \odot')$ must have the same sign. Then from

$$\tan I \sin\left(\tfrac{1}{2}(\lambda'' + \lambda) - K\right) = \frac{\sin(\beta'' + \beta)}{2\cos\beta\cos\beta''} \sec\tfrac{1}{2}(\lambda'' - \lambda),$$

$$\tan I \cos\left(\tfrac{1}{2}(\lambda'' + \lambda) - K\right) = \frac{\sin(\beta'' - \beta)}{2\cos\beta\cos\beta''} \operatorname{cosec}\tfrac{1}{2}(\lambda'' - \lambda);$$

$$\tan\beta_0 = \sin(\lambda' - K)\tan I, \qquad a_0 = \frac{\sin(\beta' - \beta_0)}{\cos\beta_0 \tan I},$$

$$b = \frac{R\sin(\odot - K)}{a_0}, \qquad c = \frac{R'\sin(\odot' - K)}{a_0},$$

$$d = \frac{R''\sin(\odot'' - K)}{a_0}, \qquad f = \frac{\sec\beta'}{\sin(\lambda'' - \lambda)}, \qquad h = \frac{RR''\sin(\odot'' - \odot)}{a_0\sin(\lambda'' - \lambda)},$$

we compute K, I, β_0, a_0, b, c, d, f, and h. The angle I must be less than 90°, and the value of β_0 must be determined with the greatest possible accuracy, since on this the accuracy of the resulting elements principally depends. Thus we obtain

$$K = 4°\ 47'\ 29''.48, \qquad \log\tan I = 9.3884640,$$
$$\beta_0 = 2°\ 52'\ 59''\tfrac{215}{419}, \qquad \log a_0 = 6.8013583_n,$$
$$\log b = 2.5456342_n, \qquad \log c = 2.2328550_n,$$
$$\log d = 1.2437914, \qquad \log f = 1.3587437_n, \qquad \log h = 3.9247691.$$

The formulæ

$$M_1 = \frac{\sin(\lambda'' - \lambda')}{\sin(\lambda'' - \lambda)} + f\frac{R''\sin(\lambda'' - \odot'')}{d},$$

$$M_1'' = \frac{\sin(\lambda' - \lambda)}{\sin(\lambda'' - \lambda)} - f\frac{R\sin(\lambda - \odot)}{b},$$

$$M_2 = \frac{h\sin(\lambda'' - K)}{d}, \qquad M_2'' = \frac{h\sin(\lambda - K)}{b},$$

give

$$\log M_1 = 9.8946712, \qquad \log M_1'' = 9.6690383,$$
$$\log M_2 = 1.9404111, \qquad \log M_2'' = 0.7306625_n.$$

The quantities thus far obtained remain unchanged in the successive approximations to the values of P and Q.

For the first hypothesis, from

$$\tau = k(t_0'' - t_0'), \qquad \tau'' = k(t_0' - t_0),$$

$$P = \frac{\tau''}{\tau}, \qquad Q = \tau\tau'',$$

$$c_0 = \frac{b + Pd}{1 + P}, \qquad k_0 = c_0 - c, \qquad l_0 = -\tfrac{1}{2}c_0 Q,$$

$$\eta_0 \sin\zeta = R'\sin\psi',$$
$$\eta_0 \cos\zeta = k_0 - R'\cos\psi',$$

$$m_0 = \frac{l_0}{\eta_0 R'^3 \sin^3\psi'},$$

we obtain

$$\log \tau = 9.0782249, \qquad \log \tau'' = 9.0645575,$$
$$\log P = 9.9863326, \qquad \log Q = 8.1427824,$$
$$\log c_0 = 2.2298567_n, \qquad \log k_0 = 0.0704470,$$
$$\log l_0 = 0.0716091, \qquad \log \eta_0 = 0.3326925,$$
$$\zeta = 8^\circ\ 24'\ 49''.74, \qquad \log m_0 = 1.2449136.$$

The quadrant in which ζ must be situated is determined by the condition that η_0 shall have the same sign as l_0.

The value of z' must now be found by trial from the equation

$$\sin(z' - \zeta) = m_0 \sin^4 z'.$$

Table XII. shows that of the four roots of this equation one exceeds 180°, and is therefore excluded by the condition that $\sin z'$ must be positive, and that two of these roots give z' greater than $180^\circ - \psi'$, and are excluded by the condition that z' must be less than $180^\circ - \psi'$. The remaining root is that which belongs to the orbit of the planet, and it is shown to be approximately 10° 40′; but the correct value is found from the last equation by a few trials to be

$$z' = 9^\circ\ 1'\ 22''.96.$$

The root which corresponds to the orbit of the earth is 18° 20′ 41″, and differs very little from $180^\circ - \psi'$.

Next, from

$$r' = \frac{R' \sin \psi'}{\sin z'}, \qquad \rho' = \frac{R' \sin(z' + \psi')}{\sin z'} \cos \beta',$$
$$n = \frac{1}{1+P}\left(1 + \frac{Q}{2r'^3}\right), \qquad n'' = nP,$$
$$\rho = M_1 \frac{\rho'}{n} + M_2\left(1 - \frac{N}{n}\right),$$
$$\rho'' = M_1'' \frac{\rho'}{n''} + M_2''\left(1 - \frac{N''}{n''}\right),$$

we derive

$$\log r' = 0.3025672, \qquad \log \rho' = 0.0123991,$$
$$\log n = 9.7061229, \qquad \log n'' = 9.6924555,$$
$$\log \rho = 0.0254823, \qquad \log \rho'' = 0.0028859.$$

The values of the curtate distances having thus been found, the heliocentric places for the three observations are now computed from

$$
\begin{aligned}
r \cos b \cos (l - \odot) &= \rho \cos (\lambda - \odot) - R, \\
r \cos b \sin (l - \odot) &= \rho \sin (\lambda - \odot), \\
r \sin b &= \rho \tan \beta; \\
r' \cos b' \cos (l' - \odot') &= \rho' \cos (\lambda' - \odot') - R', \\
r' \cos b' \sin (l' - \odot') &= \rho' \sin (\lambda' - \odot'), \\
r' \sin b' &= \rho' \tan \beta'; \\
r'' \cos b'' \cos (l'' - \odot'') &= \rho'' \cos (\lambda'' - \odot'') - R'', \\
r'' \cos b'' \sin (l'' - \odot'') &= \rho'' \sin (\lambda'' - \odot''), \\
r'' \sin b'' &= \rho'' \tan \beta'',
\end{aligned}
$$

which give

$l = 5^\circ\ 14'\ 39''.53,$	$\log \tan b = 8.4615572,$	$\log r = 0.3040994,$
$l' = 7\ \ 45\ \ 11\ .28,$	$\log \tan b' = 8.4107555,$	$\log r' = 0.3025673,$
$l'' = 10\ \ 21\ \ 34\ .57,$	$\log \tan b'' = 8.3497911,$	$\log r'' = 0.3011010.$

The agreement of the value of $\log r'$ thus obtained with that already found, is a proof of part of the calculation. Then, from

$$\tan i \sin \left(\tfrac{1}{2}(l'' + l) - \Omega\right) = \frac{\tan b'' + \tan b}{2 \cos \frac{1}{2}(l'' - l)},$$

$$\tan i \cos \left(\tfrac{1}{2}(l'' + l) - \Omega\right) = \frac{\tan b'' - \tan b}{2 \sin \frac{1}{2}(l'' - l)},$$

$$\tan u = \frac{\tan (l - \Omega)}{\cos i}, \quad \tan u' = \frac{\tan (l' - \Omega)}{\cos i}, \quad \tan u'' = \frac{\tan (l'' - \Omega)}{\cos i},$$

we get

$$\Omega = 207^\circ\ 2'\ 38''.16, \qquad i = 4^\circ\ 27'\ 23''.84,$$

$$u = 158^\circ\ 8'\ 25''.78, \qquad u' = 160^\circ\ 39'\ 18''.13, \qquad u'' = 163^\circ\ 16'\ 4''.42.$$

The equation

$$\tan b' = \tan i \sin (l' - \Omega)$$

gives $\log \tan b' = 8.4107514$, which differs 0.0000041 from the value already found directly from ρ'. This difference, however, amounts to only $0''.05$ in the value of the heliocentric latitude, and is due to errors of calculation. If we compute n and n'' from the equations

$$n = \frac{r'r'' \sin (u'' - u')}{rr'' \sin (u'' - u)}, \qquad n'' = \frac{rr' \sin (u' - u)}{rr'' \sin (u'' - u)},$$

the results should agree with the values of these quantities previously computed directly from P and Q. Using the values of u, u', and u'' just found, we obtain

$$\log n = 9.7061158, \qquad \log n'' = 9.6924683,$$

which differ in the last decimal places from the values used in finding ρ and ρ''. According to the equations

$$d \log n = -21.055 \cot(u''-u')\, du',$$
$$d \log n'' = +21.055 \cot(u'-u)\, du',$$

the differences of $\log n$ and $\log n''$ being expressed in units of the seventh decimal place, the correction to u' necessary to make the two values of $\log n$ agree is $-0''.15$; but for the agreement of the two values of $\log n''$, u' must be diminished by $0''.26$, so that it appears that this proof is not complete, although near enough for the first approximation. It should be observed, however, that a great circle passing through the extreme observed places of the planet passes very nearly through the third place of the sun, and hence the values of ρ and ρ'' as determined by means of the last two of equations (18) are somewhat uncertain. In this case it would be advisable to compute ρ and ρ'', as soon as ρ' has been found, by means of the equations (22) and (23). Thus, from these equations we obtain

$$\log \rho = 0.0254918, \qquad \log \rho'' = 0.0028874,$$

and hence

$$l = 5^\circ\ 14'\ 40''.05, \qquad \log \tan b = 8.4615619, \qquad \log r = 0.3041042,$$
$$l'' = 10\ \ 21\ \ 34\ .19, \qquad \log \tan b'' = 8.3497919, \qquad \log r'' = 0.3011017,$$
$$\Omega = 207^\circ\ 2'\ 32''.97, \qquad i = 4^\circ\ 27'\ 25''.13,$$
$$u = 158^\circ\ 8'\ 31''.47, \qquad u' = 160^\circ\ 39'\ 23''.31, \qquad u'' = 163^\circ\ 16'\ 9''.22.$$

The value of $\log \tan b'$ derived from λ' and these values of Ω and i, is 8.4107555, agreeing exactly with that derived from ρ' directly. The values of n and n'' given by these last results for u, u' and u'', are

$$\log n = 9.7061144, \qquad \log n'' = 9.6924640;$$

and this proof will be complete if we apply the correction $du' = -0''.18$ to the value of u', so that we have

$$u'' - u' = 2^\circ\ 36'\ 46''.09, \qquad u' - u = 2^\circ\ 30'\ 51''.66.$$

The results which have thus been obtained enable us to proceed to a second approximation to the correct values of P and Q, and we may also correct the times of observation for the time of aberration by means of the formulæ

$$t = t_0 - C\rho \sec \beta, \qquad t' = t_0' - C\rho' \sec \beta', \qquad t'' = t_0'' - C\rho'' \sec \beta'',$$

wherein $\log C = 7.760523$, expressed in parts of a day. Thus we get

$$t = 257.67467, \qquad t' = 264.41976, \qquad t'' = 271.38044,$$

and hence

$\log \tau = 9.0782331, \qquad \log \tau' = 9.3724848, \qquad \log \tau'' = 9.0645692.$

Then, to find the ratios denoted by s and s'', we have

$$\tan \chi = \sqrt{\frac{r''}{r'}},$$

$$\begin{aligned} \sin \gamma \cos G &= \sin \tfrac{1}{2}(u'' - u'), \\ \sin \gamma \sin G &= \cos \tfrac{1}{2}(u'' - u') \cos 2\chi, \\ \cos \gamma &= \cos \tfrac{1}{2}(u'' - u') \sin 2\chi; \end{aligned}$$

$$\tan \chi'' = \sqrt{\frac{r'}{r}},$$

$$\begin{aligned} \sin \gamma'' \cos G'' &= \sin \tfrac{1}{2}(u' - u), \\ \sin \gamma'' \sin G'' &= \cos \tfrac{1}{2}(u' - u) \cos 2\chi'', \\ \cos \gamma'' &= \cos \tfrac{1}{2}(u' - u) \sin 2\chi''; \end{aligned}$$

$$m = \frac{\tau^2}{(r' + r'')^3 \cos^3 \gamma}, \qquad j = \frac{\sin^2 \frac{1}{2}\gamma}{\cos \gamma},$$

$$m'' = \frac{\tau''^2}{(r + r')^3 \cos^3 \gamma''}, \qquad j'' = \frac{\sin^2 \frac{1}{2}\gamma''}{\cos \gamma''},$$

from which we obtain

$$\begin{aligned} \chi &= 44^\circ\ 57'\ 6''.00, & \chi'' &= 44^\circ\ 56'\ 57''.50, \\ \gamma &= 1\ \ 18\ \ 35\ .90, & \gamma'' &= 1\ \ 15\ \ 40\ .69, \\ \log m &= 6.3482114, & \log m'' &= 6.3163548, \\ \log j &= 6.1163135, & \log j'' &= 6.0834230. \end{aligned}$$

From these, by means of the equations

$$\eta = \frac{m}{\frac{5}{6} + j + \xi}, \qquad x = \frac{m}{s^2} - j,$$

$$\eta'' = \frac{m''}{\frac{5}{6} + j'' + \xi''}, \qquad x'' = \frac{m''}{s''^2} - j'',$$

using Tables XIII. and XIV., we compute s and s''. First, in the case of s, we assume

$$\eta = \frac{m}{\frac{5}{6} + j} = 0.0002675,$$

and, with this as the argument, Table XIII. gives $\log s^2 = 0.0002581$. Hence we obtain $x' = 0.000092$, and, with this as the argument, Table XIV. gives $\xi = 0.00000001$; and, therefore, it appears that a repetition of the calculation is unnecessary. Thus we obtain

$$\log s = 0.0001290, \qquad \log s'' = 0.0001200.$$

When the intervals are small, it is not necessary to use the formulæ in the complete form here given, since these ratios may then be found by a simpler process, as will appear in the sequel. Then, from

$$P = \frac{\tau''}{\tau} \cdot \frac{s}{s''},$$

$$Q = \frac{\tau\tau''}{ss''} \cdot \frac{r'^2}{rr'' \cos\frac{1}{2}(u''-u') \cos\frac{1}{2}(u''-u) \cos\frac{1}{2}(u'-u)},$$

we find

$$\log P = 9.9863451, \qquad \log Q = 8.1431341,$$

with which the second approximation may be completed. We now compute c_0, k_0, l_0, z', &c. precisely as in the first approximation; but we shall prefer, for the reason already stated, the values of ρ and ρ'' computed by means of the equations (22) and (23) instead of those obtained from the last two of the formulæ (18). The results thus derived are as follows:—

$$\log c_0 = 2.2298499_n, \qquad \log k_0 = 0.0714280,$$
$$\log l_0 = 0.0719540, \qquad \log \eta_0 = 0.3332233,$$
$$\zeta = 8^\circ\ 24'\ 12''.48, \qquad \log m_0 = 1.2447277,$$
$$z' = 9^\circ\ 0'\ 30''.84,$$
$$\log r' = 0.3032587, \qquad \log \rho' = 0.0137621,$$
$$\log n = 9.7061153, \qquad \log n'' = 9.6924604,$$
$$\log \rho = 0.0269143, \qquad \log \rho'' = 0.0041748,$$
$$l = 5^\circ\ 15'\ 57''.26, \qquad \log\tan b = 8.4622524, \qquad \log r = 0.3048368,$$
$$l' = 7\ \ 46\ \ 2\ .76, \qquad \log\tan b' = 8.4114276, \qquad \log r' = 0.3032587,$$
$$l'' = 10\ \ 22\ \ 0\ .91, \qquad \log\tan b'' = 8.3504332, \qquad \log r'' = 0.3017481,$$
$$\Omega = 207^\circ\ 0'\ 0''.72, \qquad i = 4^\circ\ 28'\ 35''.20,$$
$$u = 158^\circ\ 12'\ 19''.54, \qquad u' = 160^\circ\ 42'\ 45''.82, \qquad u'' = 163^\circ\ 19'\ 7''.14.$$

The agreement of the two values of $\log r'$ is complete, and the value of $\log\tan b'$ computed from

$$\tan b' = \tan i \sin(l' - \Omega),$$

is $\log\tan b' = 8.4114279$, agreeing with the result derived directly from ρ'. The values of n and n'' obtained from the equations (54) are

$$\log n = 9.7061156, \qquad \log n'' = 9.6924603,$$

which agree with the values already used in computing ρ and ρ'', and the proof of the calculation is complete. We have, therefore,

$$u'' - u' = 2^\circ\ 36'\ 21''.32, \quad u' - u = 2^\circ\ 30'\ 26''.28, \quad u'' - u = 5^\circ\ 6'\ 47''.60.$$

From these values of $u'' - u'$ and $u' - u$, we obtain

$$\log s = 0.0001284, \qquad \log s'' = 0.0001193,$$

and, recomputing P and Q, we get

$$\log P = 9.9863452, \qquad \log Q = 8.1431359,$$

which differ so little from the preceding values of these quantities that another approximation is unnecessary. We may, therefore, from the results already derived, complete the determination of the elements of the orbit.

The equations

$$\tan \chi' = \sqrt{\frac{r''}{r}},$$

$$\sin \gamma' \cos G' = \sin \tfrac{1}{2}(u'' - u),$$

$$\sin \gamma' \sin G' = \cos \tfrac{1}{2}(u'' - u) \cos 2\chi',$$

$$\cos \gamma' = \cos \tfrac{1}{2}(u'' - u) \sin 2\chi',$$

$$m' = \frac{\tau'^2}{(r + r'')^3 \cos^3 \gamma'}, \qquad j' = \frac{\sin^2 \frac{1}{2}\gamma'}{\cos \gamma'},$$

give

$$\chi' = 44^\circ\ 53'\ 53''.25, \qquad \gamma' = 2^\circ\ 33'\ 52''.97, \qquad \log \tan G' = 8.9011435,$$

$$\log m' = 6.9332999, \qquad \log j' = 6.7001345.$$

From these, by means of the formulæ

$$\eta' = \frac{m'}{\frac{5}{6} + j' + \xi'}, \qquad x' = \frac{m'}{s'^2} - j',$$

and Tables XIII. and XIV., we obtain

$$\log s'^2 = 0.0009908, \qquad \log x' = 6.5494116.$$

Then from

$$p = \left(\frac{s' r r'' \sin(u'' - u)}{\tau'}\right)^2,$$

we get

$$\log p = 0.3691818.$$

The values of $\log p$ given by

$$p = \left(\frac{s r' r'' \sin(u'' - u')}{\tau}\right)^2 = \left(\frac{s'' r r' \sin(u' - u)}{\tau''}\right)^2$$

are 0.3691824 and 0.3691814, the mean of which agrees with the result obtained from $u'' - u$, and the differences between the separate results are so small that the approximation to P and Q is sufficient.

The equations

$$\sin \tfrac{1}{4}(E'' - E) = \sqrt{x'},$$

$$a \cos \varphi = \frac{\sin \frac{1}{2}(u'' - u)}{\sin \frac{1}{2}(E'' - E)} \sqrt{r r''},$$

$$\cos \varphi = \frac{p}{a \cos \varphi},$$

give

$$\tfrac{1}{4}(E''-E)=1^\circ\ 4'\ 42''.903, \qquad \log(a\cos\varphi)=0.3770315,$$
$$\log\cos\varphi=9.9921503.$$

Next, from

$$e\sin\big(\omega-\tfrac{1}{2}(u''+u)\big)=\frac{p}{\cos\gamma'\sqrt{rr''}}\tan G',$$

$$e\cos\big(\omega-\tfrac{1}{2}(u''+u)\big)=\frac{p}{\cos\gamma'\sqrt{rr''}}-\sec\tfrac{1}{2}(u''-u),$$

we obtain

$$\omega=190^\circ\ 15'\ 39''.57, \qquad \log e=\log\sin\varphi=9.2751434,$$
$$\varphi=\ 10\ \ 51\ \ 39\ .62, \qquad \pi=\omega+\Omega=37^\circ\ 15'\ 40''.29.$$

This value of φ gives $\log\cos\varphi=9.9921501$, agreeing with the result already found.

To find a and μ, we have

$$a=\frac{p}{\cos^2\varphi}, \qquad \mu=\frac{k}{a^{\frac{3}{2}}},$$

the value of k expressed in seconds of arc being $\log k=3.5500066$, from which the results are

$$\log a=0.3848816, \qquad \log\mu=2.9726842.$$

The true anomalies are given by

$$v=u-\omega, \qquad v'=u'-\omega, \qquad v''=u''-\omega,$$

according to which we have

$$v=327^\circ\ 56'\ 39''.97, \qquad v'=330^\circ\ 27'\ 6''.25, \qquad v''=333^\circ\ 3'\ 27''.57.$$

If we compute r, r', and r'' from these values by means of the polar equation of the ellipse, we get

$$\log r=0.3048367, \qquad \log r'=0.3032586, \qquad \log r''=0.3017481,$$

and the agreement of these results with those derived directly from ρ, ρ', and ρ'' is a further proof of the calculation.

The equations

$$\tan\tfrac{1}{2}E\ =\tan(45^\circ-\tfrac{1}{2}\varphi)\tan\tfrac{1}{2}v,$$
$$\tan\tfrac{1}{2}E'\ =\tan(45^\circ-\tfrac{1}{2}\varphi)\tan\tfrac{1}{2}v',$$
$$\tan\tfrac{1}{2}E''=\tan(45^\circ-\tfrac{1}{2}\varphi)\tan\tfrac{1}{2}v''$$

give

$$E=333^\circ\ 17'\ 28''.18, \qquad E'=335^\circ\ 24'\ 38''.00, \qquad E''=337^\circ\ 36'\ 19''.78.$$

The value of $\frac{1}{4}(E'' - E)$ thus obtained differs only $0''.003$ from that computed directly from x'.

Finally, for the mean anomalies we have

$$M = E - e \sin E, \qquad M' = E' - e \sin E', \qquad M'' = E'' - e \sin E'',$$

from which we get

$$M = 338^\circ\ 8'\ 36''.71, \qquad M' = 339^\circ\ 54'\ 10''.61, \qquad M'' = 341^\circ\ 43'\ 6''.97;$$

and if M_0 denotes the mean anomaly for the date $T = 1863$ Sept. 21.5 Washington mean time, from the formulæ

$$\begin{aligned} M_0 &= M \;\;\; - \mu(t - T) \\ &= M' \;\; - \mu(t' - T) \\ &= M'' - \mu(t'' - T), \end{aligned}$$

we obtain the three values $339^\circ\ 55'\ 25''.97$, $339^\circ\ 55'\ 25''.96$, and $339^\circ\ 55'\ 25''.96$, the mean of which gives

$$M_0 = 339^\circ\ 55'\ 25''.96.$$

The agreement of the three results for M_0 is a final proof of the accuracy of the entire calculation of the elements.

Collecting together the separate results obtained, we have the following elements:

$$\begin{aligned} \text{Epoch} &= 1863 \text{ Sept. } 21.5 \text{ Washington mean time.} \\ M &= 339^\circ\ 55'\ 25''.96 \\ \pi &= \;\;37\ \ 15\ \ 40\ .29 \\ \Omega &= 207\ \ \ 0\ \ \ 0\ .72 \\ i &= \;\;\;4\ \ 28\ \ 35\ .20 \\ \varphi &= \;\;10\ \ 51\ \ 39\ .62 \\ \log a &= 0.3848816 \\ \log \mu &= 2.9726842 \\ \mu &= 939''.04022. \end{aligned}$$

(π, Ω, i:) Ecliptic and Mean Equinox 1863.0.

If we compute the geocentric right ascension and declination of the planet directly from these elements for the dates of the observations, as corrected for the time of aberration, and then reduce the observations to the centre of the earth by applying the corrections for parallax, the comparison of the results thus obtained will show how closely the elements represent the places on which they are based. Thus, we compute first the auxiliary constants for the equator, using the mean obliquity of the ecliptic,

$$\varepsilon = 23^\circ\ 27'\ 24''.96,$$

and the following expressions for the heliocentric co-ordinates of the planet are obtained:

$$x = r\,[9.9997272] \sin(296° \; 55' \; 46''.05 + u),$$
$$y = r\,[9.9744699] \sin(206 \;\; 12 \;\; 42\;.79 + u),$$
$$z = r\,[9.5249539] \sin(212 \;\; 39 \;\; 14\;.62 + u).$$

The numbers enclosed in the brackets are the logarithms of $\sin a$, $\sin b$, and $\sin c$, respectively; and these equations give the co-ordinates referred to the mean equinox and equator of 1863.0.

The places of the sun for the corrected times of observation, and referred to the mean equinox of 1863.0, are

True Longitude.	Latitude.	Log R.
172° 0′ 29″.5	— 0″.07	0.0022146,
178 36 4 .5	+ 0 .77	0.0013864,
185 25 42 .0	+ 0 .67	0.0005182.

If we compute from these values, by means of the equations $(104)_1$, the co-ordinates of the sun, and combine them with the corresponding heliocentric co-ordinates of the planet, we obtain the following geocentric places of the planet:

$$\alpha = 15° \; 10' \; 29''.06, \qquad \delta = +9° \; 53' \; 16''.72, \qquad \log \Delta = 0.02726,$$
$$\alpha' = 14 \;\; 15 \;\; 0\;.22, \qquad \delta' = \;\; 9 \;\; 12 \;\; 51\;.29, \qquad \log \Delta' = 0.01410,$$
$$\alpha'' = 13 \;\; 3 \;\; 49\;.47, \qquad \delta'' = +8 \;\; 21 \;\; 54\;.46, \qquad \log \Delta'' = 0.00433.$$

To reduce these places to the apparent equinox of the date of observation, the corrections

$$+48''.14, \qquad +48''.54, \qquad +48''.91,$$

must be applied to the right ascensions, respectively, and

$$+18''.55, \qquad +18''.92, \qquad +19''.31,$$

to the declinations. Thus we obtain:

Washington M. T.	Comp. α.	Comp. δ.
1863 Sept. 14.67467	$1^h \; 0^m \; 45^s.15$	+ 9° 53′ 35″.3,
21.41976	0 57 3 .25	9 13 10 .2,
28.38044	0 52 18. 56	+ 8 22 13 .8.

The corrections to be applied to the respective observations, in order to reduce them to the centre of the earth, are $+0^s.24$, $-0^s.31$, $-0^s.34$ in right ascension, and $+4''.5$, $+4''.8$, $+5''.1$ in declination, so that we have, for the same dates,

Observed α.	Observed δ.
$1^h\ 0^m\ 45^s.15$	$+9^\circ\ 53'\ 35''.3$,
0 57 3 .26	9 13 10 .3,
0 52 18 .56	+8 22 13 .8.

The comparison of these with the computed values shows that the extreme places are exactly represented, while the difference in the middle place amounts to only $0^s.01$ in right ascension, and to $0''.1$ in declination. It appears, therefore, that the observations are completely satisfied by the elements obtained, and that the preliminary corrections for aberration and parallax, as determined by the equations (1) and (4), have been correctly computed.

It cannot be expected that a system of elements derived from observations including an interval of only fourteen days, will be so exact as the results which are obtained from a series of observations or from those including a much longer interval of time; and although the elements which have been derived completely represent the data, yet, on account of the smallness of $\beta' - \beta_0$, this difference being only $31''.893$, the slight errors of observation have considerable influence in the final results.

When approximate elements are already known, so that the correction for parallax may be applied directly to the observations, in order to take into account the latitude of the sun, the observed places of the body must be reduced, by means of equation (6), to the point in which a perpendicular let fall from the centre of the earth to the plane of the ecliptic cuts that plane. The times of observation must also be corrected for the time of aberration, and the corresponding places of both the planet and the sun must be reduced to the ecliptic and mean equinox of a fixed epoch; and further, the reduction to the fixed ecliptic should precede the application of equation (6).

If the intervals between the times of observation are considerable, it may become necessary to make three or more approximations to the values of P and Q, and in this case the equations (82) may be applied. But when approximate elements are already known, it will be advantageous to compute the first assumed values of P and Q directly from these elements by means of the equations (44) or by means of (48) and (51); and the ratios s and s'' may be found directly from the equations (46). In the case of very eccentric orbits this is indispensable, if it be desired to avoid prolixity in the numerical calculation, since otherwise the successive approximations to P and Q will slowly approach the limits required.

The various modifications of the formulæ for certain special cases, as well as the formulæ which must be used in the case of parabolic and hyperbolic orbits, and of those differing but little from the parabola, have been given in a form such that they require no further illustration.

94. In the determination of an unknown orbit, if the intervals are considerably unequal, it will be advantageous to correct the first assumed value of P before completing the first approximation in the manner already illustrated. The assumption of

$$Q = \tau\tau''$$

is correct to terms of the fourth order with respect to the time, and for the same degree of approximation to P we must, according to equation $(28)_3$, use the expression

$$P = \frac{\tau''}{\tau}\left(1 + \tfrac{1}{6}\,\frac{\tau^2 - \tau''^2}{r'^3}\right),$$

which becomes equal to $\dfrac{\tau''}{\tau}$ only when the intervals are equal. The first assumed values

$$P = \frac{\tau''}{\tau}, \qquad Q = \tau\tau'',$$

furnish, with very little labor, an approximate value of r'; and then, with the values of P and Q, derived from

$$P = \frac{\tau''}{\tau}\left(1 + \tfrac{1}{6}\,\frac{\tau^2 - \tau''^2}{r'^3}\right), \qquad Q = \tau\tau'', \tag{98}$$

the entire calculation should be completed precisely as in the example given. Thus, in this example, the first assumed values give

$$\log r' = 0.30257,$$

and, recomputing P by means of the first of these equations, we get

$$\log P = 9.9863404, \qquad \log Q = 8.1427822,$$

with which, if the first approximation to the elements be completed, the results will differ but little from those obtained, without this correction, from the second hypothesis. If the times had been already corrected for the time of aberration, the agreement would be still closer.

The comparison of equations (46) with $(25)_3$ gives, to terms of the fourth order,

$$s = 1 + \tfrac{1}{6}\frac{\tau^2}{r'^3}, \qquad s' = 1 + \tfrac{1}{6}\frac{\tau'^2}{r'^3}, \qquad s'' = 1 + \tfrac{1}{6}\frac{\tau''^2}{r'^3},$$

and, if the intervals are equal, this value of s' is correct to terms of the fifth order. Since

$$\log_e s = \log_e (1 + (s-1)) = s - 1 - \tfrac{1}{2}(s-1)^2 + \&c.,$$

we have, neglecting terms of the fourth order,

$$\log s = \frac{\lambda_0}{6} \cdot \frac{\tau^2}{r'^3}, \tag{99}$$

in which $\log \tfrac{1}{6}\lambda_0 = 8.8596330$. We have, also, to the same degree of approximation,

$$\log s' = \frac{\lambda_0}{6} \cdot \frac{\tau'^2}{r'^3}, \qquad \log s'' = \frac{\lambda_0}{6} \cdot \frac{\tau''^2}{r'^3}. \tag{100}$$

For the values

$\log \tau = 9.0782331,$ $\log \tau' = 9.3724848,$ $\log \tau'' = 9.0645692,$
$\log r' = 0.3032587,$

these formulæ give

$\log s = 0.0001277,$ $\log s' = 0.0004953,$ $\log s'' = 0.0001199,$

which differ but little from the correct values 0.0001284, 0.0004954, and 0.0001193 previously obtained.

Since

$$\sec^3 \gamma' = 1 + 6 \sin^2 \tfrac{1}{2}\gamma' + \&c.,$$

the second of equations (65) gives

$$m' = \frac{\tau'^2}{(r + r'')^3} + \frac{6\tau'^2}{(r + r'')^3} \sin^2 \tfrac{1}{2}\gamma' + \&c.$$

Substituting this value in the first of equations (66), we get

$$s'^2 (s' - 1) = \frac{\tau'^2}{y'(r + r'')^3} + \frac{6\tau'^2}{y'(r + r'')^3} \sin^2 \tfrac{1}{2}\gamma' + \&c.$$

If we neglect terms of the fourth order with respect to the time, it will be sufficient in this equation to put $y' = \tfrac{3}{4}$, according to (71), and hence we have

$$s'^2 (s' - 1) = \tfrac{4}{3} \frac{\tau'^2}{(r + r'')^3};$$

and, since $s' - 1$ is of the second order with respect to τ', we have, to terms of the fourth order,

$$s'^2 (s' - 1) = \log_e s'.$$

Therefore,

$$\log s' = \tfrac{4}{3}\lambda_0 \frac{\tau'^2}{(r+r'')^3}, \tag{101}$$

which, when the intervals are small, may be used to find s' from r and r''. In the same manner, we obtain

$$\log s = \tfrac{4}{3}\lambda_0 \frac{\tau^2}{(r'+r'')^3}, \qquad \log s'' = \tfrac{4}{3}\lambda_0 \frac{\tau''^2}{(r+r')^3}. \tag{102}$$

For logarithmic calculation, when addition and subtraction logarithms are not used, it is more convenient to introduce the auxiliary angles χ, χ', and χ'', by means of which these formulæ become

$$\log s = \tfrac{4}{3}\lambda_0 \frac{\tau^2 \cos^6\chi}{r'^3}, \quad \log s' = \tfrac{4}{3}\lambda_0 \frac{\tau'^2 \cos^6\chi'}{r^3}, \quad \log s'' = \tfrac{4}{3}\lambda_0 \frac{\tau''^2 \cos^6\chi''}{r^3}, \tag{103}$$

in which $\log \tfrac{4}{3}\lambda_0 = 9.7627230$. For the first approximation these equations will be sufficient, even when the intervals are considerable, to determine the values of s and s'' required in correcting P and Q.

The values of τ, τ', τ'', and r' above given, in connection with

$$\log r = 0.3048368, \qquad \log r'' = 0.3017481,$$

give

$$\log s = 0.0001284, \qquad \log s' = 0.0004951, \qquad \log s'' = 0.0001193.$$

These results for $\log s$ and $\log s''$ are correct, and that for $\log s'$ differs only 3 in the seventh decimal place from the correct value.

CHAPTER V.

DETERMINATION OF THE ORBIT OF A HEAVENLY BODY FROM FOUR OBSERVATIONS, OF WHICH THE SECOND AND THIRD MUST BE COMPLETE.

95. THE formulæ given in the preceding chapter are not sufficient to determine the elements of the orbit of a heavenly body when its apparent path is in the plane of the ecliptic. In this case, however, the position of the plane of the orbit being known, only four elements remain to be determined, and four observed longitudes will furnish the necessary equations. There is no instance of an orbit whose inclination is zero; but, although no such case may occur, it may happen that the inclination is very small, and that the elements derived from three observations will on this account be uncertain, and especially so, if the observations are not very exact. The difficulty thus encountered may be remedied by using for the data in the determination of the elements one or more additional observations, and neglecting those latitudes which are regarded as most uncertain. The formulæ, however, are most convenient, and lead most expeditiously to a knowledge of the elements of an orbit wholly unknown, when they are made to depend on four observations, the second and third of which must be complete; but of the extreme observations only the longitudes are absolutely required.

The preliminary reductions to be applied to the data are derived precisely as explained in the preceding chapter, preparatory to a determination of the elements of the orbit from three observations.

Let t, t', t'', t''' be the times of observation, r, r', r'', r''' the radii-vectores of the body, u, u', u'', u''' the corresponding arguments of the latitude, R, R', R'', R''' the distances of the earth from the sun, and $\odot$, $\odot'$, $\odot''$, $\odot'''$ the longitudes of the sun corresponding to these times. Let us also put

$$[r'r'''] = r'r''' \sin(u''' - u'),$$
$$[r''r'''] = r''r''' \sin(u''' - u''),$$

and

$$n' = \frac{[r''r''']}{[r'r''']} \qquad n''' = \frac{[r'r'']}{[r'r''']}. \tag{1}$$

Then, according to the equations $(5)_3$, we shall have

$$\begin{aligned} nx \;-x' + n''x'' &= 0, \\ ny \;-y' + n''y'' &= 0, \\ n'x' - x'' + n'''x''' &= 0, \\ n'y' - y'' + n'''y''' &= 0. \end{aligned} \tag{2}$$

Let λ, λ', λ'', λ''' be the observed longitudes, β, β', β'', β''' the observed latitudes corresponding to the times t, t', t'', t''', respectively, and Δ, Δ', Δ'', Δ''' the distances of the body from the earth. Further, let

$$\Delta''' \cos\beta''' = \rho''',$$

and for the last place we have

$$\begin{aligned} x''' &= \rho''' \cos\lambda''' - R''' \cos\odot''', \\ y''' &= \rho''' \sin\lambda''' - R''' \sin\odot'''. \end{aligned}$$

Introducing these values of x''' and y''', and the corresponding values of x, x', x'', y, y', y'' into the equations (2), they become

$$\begin{aligned} 0 &= n(\rho\cos\lambda - R\cos\odot) - (\rho'\cos\lambda' - R'\cos\odot') \\ &\qquad\qquad + n''(\rho''\cos\lambda'' - R''\cos\odot''), \\ 0 &= n(\rho\sin\lambda - R\sin\odot) - (\rho'\sin\lambda' - R'\sin\odot') \\ &\qquad\qquad + n''(\rho''\sin\lambda'' - R''\sin\odot''), \\ 0 &= n'(\rho'\cos\lambda' - R'\cos\odot') - (\rho''\cos\lambda'' - R''\cos\odot'') \\ &\qquad\qquad + n'''(\rho'''\cos\lambda''' - R'''\cos\odot'''), \\ 0 &= n'(\rho'\sin\lambda' - R'\sin\odot') - (\rho''\sin\lambda'' - R''\sin\odot'') \\ &\qquad\qquad + n'''(\rho'''\sin\lambda''' - R'''\sin\odot'''). \end{aligned} \tag{3}$$

If we multiply the first of these equations by $\sin\lambda$, and the second by $-\cos\lambda$, and add the products, we get

$$\begin{aligned} 0 = nR\sin(\lambda - \odot) &- (\rho'\sin(\lambda' - \lambda) + R'\sin(\lambda - \odot')) \\ &+ n''(\rho''\sin(\lambda'' - \lambda) + R''\sin(\lambda - \odot'')); \end{aligned} \tag{4}$$

and in a similar manner, from the third and fourth equations, we find

$$\begin{aligned} 0 = n'(\rho'\sin(\lambda''' - \lambda') &- R'\sin(\lambda''' - \odot')) \\ - (\rho''\sin(\lambda''' - \lambda'') &- R''\sin(\lambda''' - \odot'')) - n'''R'''\sin(\lambda''' - \odot'''). \end{aligned} \tag{5}$$

Whenever the values of n, n', n'', and n''' are known, or may be determined in functions of the time so as to satisfy the conditions of motion in a conic section, these equations become distinct or independent of each other; and, since only two unknown quantities ρ'

and ρ'' are involved in them, they will enable us to determine these curtate distances.

Let us now put

$$\begin{array}{ll} \cos\beta' \sin(\lambda'-\lambda) = A, & \cos\beta'' \sin(\lambda''-\lambda) = B, \\ \cos\beta'' \sin(\lambda'''-\lambda'') = C, & \cos\beta' \sin(\lambda'''-\lambda') = D, \end{array} \tag{6}$$

and the preceding equations give

$$\begin{aligned} A\rho' \sec\beta' - Bn''\rho'' \sec\beta'' &= nR\sin(\lambda-\odot) - R'\sin(\lambda-\odot') \\ &\qquad + n''R''\sin(\lambda-\odot''), \\ Dn'\rho' \sec\beta' - C\rho'' \sec\beta'' &= n'R'\sin(\lambda'''-\odot') - R''\sin(\lambda'''-\odot'') \\ &\qquad + n'''R'''\sin(\lambda'''-\odot'''). \end{aligned} \tag{7}$$

If we assume for n and n'' their values in the case of the orbit of the earth, which is equivalent to neglecting terms of the second order in the equations $(26)_3$, the second member of the first of these equations reduces rigorously to zero; and in the same manner it can be shown that when similar terms of the second order in the corresponding expressions for n' and n'' are neglected, the second member of the last equation reduces to zero. Hence the second member of each of these equations will generally differ from zero by a quantity which is of at least the second order with respect to the intervals of time between the observations. The coefficients of ρ' and ρ'' are of the first order, and it is easily seen that if we eliminate ρ'' from these equations, the resulting equation for ρ' is such that an error of the second order in the values of n and n'' may produce an error of the order zero in the result for ρ', so that it will not be even an approximation to the correct value; and the same is true in the case of ρ''. It is necessary, therefore, to retain terms of the second order in the first assumed values for n, n', n'', and n'''; and, since the terms of the second order involve r' and r'', we thus introduce two additional unknown quantities. Hence two additional equations involving r', r'', ρ', ρ'' and quantities derived from observation, must be obtained, so that by elimination the values of the quantities sought may be found.

From equation $(34)_4$ we have

$$\rho' \sec\beta' = R'\cos\psi' \pm \sqrt{r'^2 - R'^2\sin^2\psi'}, \tag{8}$$

which is one of the equations required; and similarly we find, for the other equation,

$$\rho'' \sec\beta'' = R''\cos\psi'' \pm \sqrt{r''^2 - R''^2\sin^2\psi''}. \tag{9}$$

Introducing these values into the equations (7), and putting

$$\begin{aligned} x' &= \pm \sqrt{r'^2 - R'^2 \sin^2 \psi'}, \\ x'' &= \pm \sqrt{r''^2 - R''^2 \sin^2 \psi''}, \end{aligned} \qquad (10)$$

we get

$$\begin{aligned} Ax' - Bn''x'' = nR \sin(\lambda - \odot) - R' \sin(\lambda - \odot') \\ + n''R'' \sin(\lambda - \odot'') - AR' \cos \psi' + n''BR'' \cos \psi'', \\ Dn'x' - Cx'' = n'R' \sin(\lambda''' - \odot') - R'' \sin(\lambda''' - \odot'') \\ + n'''R''' \sin(\lambda''' - \odot''') - n'DR' \cos \psi' + CR'' \cos \psi''. \end{aligned}$$

Let us now put

$$\frac{B}{A} = h', \qquad \frac{D}{C} = h'',$$

or

$$h' = \frac{\cos \beta'' \sin(\lambda'' - \lambda)}{\cos \beta' \sin(\lambda' - \lambda)}, \qquad h'' = \frac{\cos \beta' \sin(\lambda''' - \lambda')}{\cos \beta'' \sin(\lambda''' - \lambda'')},$$

$$\begin{aligned} R' \cos \psi' + \frac{R' \sin(\lambda - \odot')}{A} &= a', \\ R'' \cos \psi'' - \frac{R'' \sin(\lambda''' - \odot'')}{C} &= a'', \\ h'R'' \cos \psi'' + \frac{R'' \sin(\lambda - \odot'')}{A} &= c', \\ h''R' \cos \psi' - \frac{R' \sin(\lambda''' - \odot')}{C} &= c'', \end{aligned} \qquad (11)$$

$$\frac{R \sin(\lambda - \odot)}{A} = d', \qquad \frac{R''' \sin(\lambda''' - \odot''')}{C} = -d'',$$

and we have

$$\begin{aligned} x' &= h'n''x'' + nd' - a' + n''c', \\ x'' &= h''n'x' + n'''d'' - a'' + n'c''. \end{aligned} \qquad (12)$$

These equations will serve to determine x' and x'', and hence r' and r'', as soon as the values of n, n', n'', and n''' are known.

96. In order to include terms of the second order in the values of n and n'', we have, from the equations $(26)_3$,

$$n = \frac{\tau}{\tau'}\left(1 + \tfrac{1}{6}\frac{\tau''(\tau' + \tau)}{r'^3}\right), \qquad n'' = \frac{\tau''}{\tau'}\left(1 + \tfrac{1}{6}\frac{\tau(\tau' + \tau'')}{r'^3}\right),$$

and, putting

$$P' = \frac{n}{n''}, \qquad Q' = (n + n'' - 1) r'^3, \qquad (13)$$

these give

$$P' = \frac{\tau}{\tau''}\left(1 - \tfrac{1}{6}\frac{\tau^2 - \tau''^2}{r'^3}\right),$$
$$Q' = \tfrac{1}{2}\tau\tau''. \tag{14}$$

Let us now put

$$\tau''' = k(t''' - t''), \qquad \tau_0' = k(t''' - t'), \tag{15}$$

and, making the necessary changes in the notation in equations $(26)_3$, we obtain

$$n''' = \frac{\tau}{\tau_0'}\left(1 + \tfrac{1}{6}\frac{\tau'''(\tau_0' + \tau)}{r''^3} - \tfrac{1}{4}\frac{\tau'''(\tau'''^2 + \tau'''\tau - \tau^2)}{kr''^4}\cdot\frac{dr''}{dt}\cdots\right),$$
$$n' = \frac{\tau'''}{\tau_0'}\left(1 + \tfrac{1}{6}\frac{\tau(\tau_0' + \tau''')}{r''^3} + \tfrac{1}{4}\frac{\tau(\tau^2 + \tau\tau''' - \tau'''^2)}{kr''^4}\cdot\frac{dr''}{dt}\cdots\right). \tag{16}$$

From these we get, including terms of the second order,

$$n''' = \frac{\tau}{\tau_0'}\left(1 + \tfrac{1}{6}\frac{\tau'''(\tau_0' + \tau)}{r''^3}\right), \qquad n' = \frac{\tau'''}{\tau_0'}\left(1 + \tfrac{1}{6}\frac{\tau(\tau_0' + \tau''')}{r''^3}\right),$$

and hence, if we put

$$P'' = \frac{n'''}{n'}, \qquad Q'' = (n' + n''' - 1)\, r''^3, \tag{17}$$

we shall have, since $\tau_0' = \tau + \tau'''$,

$$P'' = \frac{\tau}{\tau'''}\left(1 - \tfrac{1}{6}\frac{\tau^2 - \tau'''^2}{r''^3}\right),$$
$$Q'' = \tfrac{1}{2}\tau\tau'''. \tag{18}$$

When the intervals are equal, we have

$$P' = \frac{\tau}{\tau''}, \qquad P'' = \frac{\tau}{\tau'''},$$

and these expressions may be used, in the case of an unknown orbit, for the first approximation to the values of these quantities.

The equations (13) and (17) give

$$n'' = \frac{1}{1 + P'}\left(1 + \frac{Q'}{r'^3}\right),$$
$$n = n''P';$$
$$n' = \frac{1}{1 + P''}\left(1 + \frac{Q''}{r''^3}\right),$$
$$n''' = n'P''; \tag{19}$$

and, introducing these values, the equations (12) become

$$x = \frac{1}{1+P'}\left(1+\frac{Q'}{r'^3}\right)(h'x''+P'd'+c') - a',$$
$$x'' = \frac{1}{1+P''}\left(1+\frac{Q''}{r''^3}\right)(h''x'+P''d''+c'') - a''. \qquad (20)$$

Let us now put

$$\frac{P'd'+c'}{1+P'} = c_0', \qquad \frac{h'}{1+P'} = f',$$
$$\frac{P''d''+c''}{1+P''} = c_0'', \qquad \frac{h''}{1+P''} = f'', \qquad (21)$$

and we shall have

$$x' = \left(1+\frac{Q'}{r'^3}\right)(f'x''+c_0') - a',$$
$$x'' = \left(1+\frac{Q''}{r''^3}\right)(f''x'+c_0'') - a''. \qquad (22)$$

We have, further, from equations (10),

$$r'^3 = (x'^2 + R'^2 \sin^2\psi')^{\frac{3}{2}},$$
$$r''^3 = (x''^2 + R''^2 \sin^2\psi'')^{\frac{3}{2}}, \qquad (23)$$

If we substitute these values of r'^3 and r''^3 in equations (22), the two resulting equations will contain only two unknown quantities x' and x'', when P', P'', Q', and Q'' are known, and hence they will be sufficient to solve the problem. But if we effect the elimination of either of the unknown quantities directly, the resulting equation becomes of a high order. It is necessary, therefore, in the numerical application, to solve the equations (22) by successive trials, which may be readily effected.

If z' represents the angle at the planet between the sun and the earth at the time of the second observation, and z'' the same angle at the time of the third observation, we shall have

$$r' = \frac{R'\sin\psi'}{\sin z'},$$
$$r'' = \frac{R''\sin\psi''}{\sin z''}. \qquad (24)$$

Substituting these values of r' and r'' in equations (10), we get

$$x' = r'\cos z',$$
$$x'' = r''\cos z'', \qquad (25)$$

and hence

$$\tan z' = \frac{R' \sin \psi'}{x'},$$
$$\tan z'' = \frac{R'' \sin \psi''}{x''} \tag{26}$$

by means of which we may find z' and z'' as soon as x' and x'' shall have been determined; and then r' and r'' are obtained from (24) or (25). The last equations show that when x' is negative, z' must be greater than 90°, and hence that in this case r' is less than R'.

In the numerical application of equations (22), for a first approximation to the values of x' and x'', since Q' and Q'' are quantities of the second order with respect to τ or τ''', we may generally put

$$Q' = 0, \qquad Q'' = 0;$$

and we have

$$x' = f'x'' + c_0' - a',$$
$$x'' = f''x' + c_0'' - a'',$$

or, by elimination,

$$x' = \frac{c_0' + f'c_0'' - f'a'' - a'}{1 - f'f''},$$
$$x'' = \frac{c_0'' + f''c_0' - f''a' - a''}{1 - f'f''}.$$

With the approximate values of x' and x'' derived from these equations, we compute first r' and r'' from the equations (26) and (24), and then new values of x' and x'' from (22), the operation being repeated until the true values are obtained. To facilitate these approximations, the equations (22) give

$$x'' = \frac{x' + a'}{f'\left(1 + \frac{Q'}{r'^3}\right)} - \frac{c_0'}{f'},$$
$$x' = \frac{x'' + a''}{f''\left(1 + \frac{Q''}{r''^3}\right)} - \frac{c_0''}{f''}. \tag{27}$$

Let an approximate value of x' be designated by x_0', and let the value of x'' derived from this by means of the first of equations (27) be designated by x_0''. With the value of x_0'' for x'' we derive a new value of x' from the second of these equations, which we denote by x_1'. Then, recomputing x'' and x', we obtain a third approximate value of the latter quantity, which may be designated by x_2'; and, if we put

$$x_1' - x_0' = a_0, \qquad x_2' - x_1' = a_0',$$

we shall have, according to the equation $(67)_3$, the necessary changes being made in the notation,

$$x' = x_1' - \frac{a_0 a_0'}{a_0' - a_0} = x_2' - \frac{a_0'^2}{a_0' - a_0}. \tag{28}$$

The value of x' thus obtained will give, by means of the first of equations (27), a new value of x'', and the substitution of this in the last of these equations will show whether the correct result has been found. If a repetition of the calculation be found necessary, the three values of x' which approximate nearest to the true value will, by means of (28), give the correct result. In the same manner, if we assume for x'' the value derived by putting $Q' = 0$ and $Q'' = 0$, and compute x', three successive approximate results for x'' will enable us to interpolate the correct value.

When the elements of the orbit are already approximately known, the first assumed value of x' should be derived from

$$x' = \sqrt{r'^2 - R'^2 \sin^2 \psi'}$$

instead of by putting Q' and Q'' equal to zero.

97. It should be observed that when $\lambda' = \lambda$ or $\lambda''' = \lambda''$, the equations (22) are inapplicable, but that the original equations (7) give, in this case, either ρ'' or ρ' directly in terms of n and n'' or of n' and n''' and the data furnished by observation. If we divide the first of equations (22) by h', we have

$$\frac{x'}{h'} = \left(1 + \frac{Q'}{r'^3}\right)\left(\frac{f'}{h'} x'' + \frac{c_0'}{h'}\right) - \frac{a'}{h'}.$$

The equations (21) give

$$\frac{f'}{h'} = \frac{1}{1 + P'}, \qquad \frac{c_0'}{h'} = \frac{P' \dfrac{d'}{h'} + \dfrac{c'}{h'}}{1 + P'},$$

and from (11) we get

$$\begin{aligned} \frac{a'}{h'} &= \frac{R' \cos \psi'}{h'} + \frac{R' \sin (\lambda - \odot')}{B}, \\ \frac{c'}{h'} &= R'' \cos \psi'' + \frac{R'' \sin (\lambda - \odot'')}{B}, \\ \frac{d'}{h'} &= \frac{R \sin (\lambda - \odot)}{B}. \end{aligned} \tag{29}$$

Then, if we put

$$C_0' = P' \frac{d'}{h'} + \frac{c'}{h'},$$

its value may be found from the results for $\frac{c'}{h'}$ and $\frac{d'}{h'}$ derived by means of these equations, and we shall have

$$\frac{x'}{h'} = \frac{1}{1+P'}\left(1 + \frac{Q'}{r'^3}\right)(x'' + C_0') - \frac{a'}{h'}. \tag{30}$$

When $\lambda' = \lambda$, we have $h' = \infty$, and this formula becomes

$$0 = \left(1 + \frac{Q'}{r'^3}\right)(x'' + C_0') - \frac{a'}{h'}(1 + P'),$$

the value of $\frac{a'}{h'}$ being given by the first of equations (29) This equation and the second of equations (22) are sufficient to determine x' and x'' in the special case under consideration.

The second of equations (22) may be treated in precisely the same manner, so that when $\lambda''' = \lambda''$, it becomes

$$0 = \left(1 + \frac{Q''}{r''^3}\right)(x' + C_0'') - \frac{a''}{h''}(1 + P''),$$

and this must be solved in connection with the first of these equations in order to find x' and x''.

98. As soon as the numerical values of x' and x'' have been derived, those of r' and r'' may be found by means of the equations (26) and (24). Then, according to $(41)_4$, we have

$$\begin{aligned} \rho' &= \frac{R' \sin(z' + \psi')}{\sin z'} \cos\beta', \\ \rho'' &= \frac{R'' \sin(z'' + \psi'')}{\sin z''} \cos\beta''. \end{aligned} \tag{31}$$

The heliocentric places are then found from ρ' and ρ'' by means of the equations $(71)_3$, and the values of r' and r'' thus obtained should agree with those already derived. From these places we compute the position of the plane of the orbit, and thence the arguments of the latitude for the times t' and t''.

The values of r', r'', u', u'', n, n'', n', and n''' enable us to determine r, r''', u, and u'''. Thus, we have

$$[r'r''] = r'r'' \sin(u'' - u'),$$

and, from the equations (1) and $(3)_3$,

$$[rr'] \;\;\;= \frac{n''}{n}[r'r''],$$

$$[rr''] \;\;= \frac{1}{n}[r'r''],$$

$$[r''r'''] = \frac{n'}{n'''}[r'r''],$$

$$[r'r'''] = \frac{1}{n'''}[r'r''].$$

Therefore,

$$\begin{aligned} r\sin(u'-u) &= \frac{n''}{n}r''\sin(u''-u'),\\ r\sin(u''-u) &= \frac{1}{n}r'\sin(u''-u'),\\ r'''\sin(u'''-u'') &= \frac{n'}{n'''}r'\sin(u''-u'),\\ r'''\sin(u'''-u') &= \frac{1}{n'''}r''\sin(u''-u'). \end{aligned} \tag{32}$$

From the first and second of these equations, by addition and subtraction, we get

$$\begin{aligned} r\sin\big((u'-u)+\tfrac{1}{2}(u''-u')\big) &= \frac{r'+n''r''}{n}\sin\tfrac{1}{2}(u''-u'),\\ r\cos\big((u'-u)+\tfrac{1}{2}(u''-u')\big) &= \frac{r'-n''r''}{n}\cos\tfrac{1}{2}(u''-u'), \end{aligned} \tag{33}$$

from which we may find r, $u'-u$, and $u = u'-(u'-u)$.

In a similar manner, from the third and fourth of equations (32), we obtain

$$\begin{aligned} r'''\sin\big((u'''-u'')+\tfrac{1}{2}(u''-u')\big) &= \frac{r''+n'r'}{n'''}\sin\tfrac{1}{2}(u''-u'),\\ r'''\cos\big((u'''-u'')+\tfrac{1}{2}(u''-u')\big) &= \frac{r''-n'r'}{n'''}\cos\tfrac{1}{2}(u''-u'), \end{aligned} \tag{34}$$

from which to find r''' and u'''.

When the approximate values of r, r', r'', r''', and u, u', u'', u''' have been found, by means of the preceding equations, from the assumed values of P', P'', Q', and Q'', the second approximation to the elements may be commenced. But, in the case of an unknown orbit, it will be expedient to derive, first, approximate values of r' and r'', using

$$P' = \frac{\tau}{\tau''}, \qquad\qquad P'' = \frac{\tau}{\tau'''},$$

and then recompute P' and P'' by means of the equations (14) and

(18), before finding u' and u''. The terms of the second order will thus be completely taken into account in the first approximation.

99. If the times of observation have not been corrected for the time of aberration, as in the case of an orbit wholly unknown, this correction may be applied before the second approximation to the elements is effected, or at least before the final approximation is commenced. For this purpose, the distances of the body from the earth for the four observations must be determined; and, since the curtate distances ρ' and ρ'' are already given, there remain only ρ and ρ''' to be found. If we eliminate ρ' from the first two of equations (3), the result is

$$\rho = \rho'' \frac{n'' \sin(\lambda'' - \lambda')}{n \sin(\lambda' - \lambda)} + \frac{nR \sin(\lambda' - \odot) - R' \sin(\lambda' - \odot') + n''R'' \sin(\lambda' - \odot'')}{n \sin(\lambda' - \lambda)}; \tag{35}$$

and, by eliminating ρ'' from the last two of these equations, we also obtain

$$\rho''' = \rho' \frac{n' \sin(\lambda'' - \lambda')}{n''' \sin(\lambda''' - \lambda'')} - \frac{n'R' \sin(\lambda'' - \odot') - R'' \sin(\lambda'' - \odot'') + n'''R''' \sin(\lambda'' - \odot''')}{n''' \sin(\lambda''' - \lambda'')}, \tag{36}$$

by means of which ρ and ρ''' may be found. The combination of the first and second of equations (3) gives

$$\rho = \frac{\rho'}{n} \cos(\lambda' - \lambda) - \frac{n''\rho''}{n} \cos(\lambda'' - \lambda) + \frac{nR \cos(\lambda - \odot) - R' \cos(\lambda - \odot') + n''R'' \cos(\lambda - \odot'')}{n}. \tag{37}$$

and from the third and fourth we get

$$\rho''' = \frac{\rho''}{n'''} \cos(\lambda''' - \lambda'') - \frac{n'\rho'}{n'''} \cos(\lambda''' - \lambda') + \frac{n'R' \cos(\lambda''' - \odot') - R'' \cos(\lambda''' - \odot'') + n'''R''' \cos(\lambda''' - \odot''')}{n'''}. \tag{38}$$

Further, instead of these, any of the various formulæ which have been given for finding the ratio of two curtate distances, may be employed; but, if the latitudes β, β', &c. are very small, the values of ρ and ρ''' which depend on the differences of the observed longitudes of the body must be preferred.

The values of ρ and ρ''' may also be derived by computing the heliocentric places of the body for the times t and t''' by means of the equations $(82)_1$, and then finding the geocentric places, or those which belong to the points to which the observations have been reduced, by means of $(90)_1$, writing ρ in place of $\varDelta \cos \beta$. This process affords a verification of the numerical calculation, namely, the values of λ and λ''' thus found should agree with those furnished by observation, and the agreement of the computed latitudes β and β''' with those observed, in case the latter are given, will show how nearly the position of the plane of the orbit as derived from the second and third observations represents the extreme latitudes. If it were not desirable to compute λ and λ''' in order to check the calculation, even when β and β''' are given by observation, we might derive ρ and ρ''' from the equations

$$\begin{aligned} \rho &= r \sin u \sin i \cot \beta, \\ \rho''' &= r''' \sin u''' \sin i \cot \beta''', \end{aligned} \tag{39}$$

when the latitudes are not very small.

In the final approximation to the elements, and especially when the position of the plane of the orbit cannot be obtained with the required precision from the second and third observations, it will be advantageous, provided that the data furnish the extreme latitudes β and β''', to compute ρ and ρ''' as soon as ρ' and ρ'' have been found, and then find l, l''', b, and b''' directly from these by means of the formulæ $(71)_3$. The values of Ω and i may thus be obtained from the extreme places, or, the heliocentric places for the times t' and t'' being also computed directly from ρ' and ρ'', from those which are best suited to this purpose. But, since the data will be more than sufficient for the solution of the problem, when the extreme latitudes are used, if we compute the heliocentric latitudes b' and b'' from the equations

$$\begin{aligned} \tan b' &= \tan i \sin (l' - \Omega), \\ \tan b'' &= \tan i \sin (l'' - \Omega), \end{aligned}$$

they will not agree exactly with the results obtained directly from ρ' and ρ'', unless the four observations are completely satisfied by the elements obtained. The values of r' and r'', however, computed directly from ρ' and ρ'' by means of $(71)_3$, must agree with those derived from x' and x''.

The corrections to be applied to the times of observation on account of aberration may now be found. Thus, if t_0, t_0', t_0'', and t_0''' are the uncorrected times of observation, the corrected values will be

$$\begin{aligned} t &= t_0 - C\rho \sec\beta, \\ t' &= t_0' - C\rho' \sec\beta', \\ t'' &= t_0'' - C\rho'' \sec\beta'', \\ t''' &= t_0''' - C\rho''' \sec\beta''', \end{aligned} \tag{40}$$

wherein $\log C = 7.760523$, and from these we derive the corrected values of τ, τ', τ'', τ''', and τ_0'.

100. To find the values of P', P'', Q', and Q'', which will be exact when r, r', r'', r''', and u, u', u'', u''' are accurately known, we have, according to the equations $(47)_4$ and $(51)_4$, since $Q' = \frac{1}{2}Q$,

$$\begin{aligned} P' &= \frac{\tau}{\tau''} \cdot \frac{s''}{s}, \\ Q' &= \tfrac{1}{2}\frac{\tau\tau''}{ss''} \cdot \frac{r'^2}{rr'' \cos\frac{1}{2}(u''-u') \cos\frac{1}{2}(u''-u) \cos\frac{1}{2}(u'-u)}. \end{aligned} \tag{41}$$

In a similar manner, if we designate by s''' the ratio of the sector formed by the radii-vectores r'' and r''' to the triangle formed by the same radii-vectores and the chord joining their extremities, we find

$$\begin{aligned} P'' &= \frac{\tau}{\tau'''} \cdot \frac{s'''}{s}, \\ Q'' &= \tfrac{1}{2}\frac{\tau\tau'''}{ss'''} \cdot \frac{r''^2}{r'r''' \cos\frac{1}{2}(u'''-u'') \cos\frac{1}{2}(u'''-u') \cos\frac{1}{2}(u''-u')}. \end{aligned} \tag{42}$$

The formulæ for finding the value of s''' are obtained from those for s by writing χ''', γ''', G''', &c. in place of χ, γ, G, &c., and using r'', r''', $u'''-u''$ instead of r', r'', and $u''-u'$, respectively.

By means of the results obtained from the first approximation to the values of P', P'', Q', and Q'', we may, from equations (41) and (42), derive new and more nearly accurate values of these quantities, and, by repeating the calculation, the approximations to the exact values may be carried to any extent which may be desirable. When three approximate values of P' and Q', and of P'' and Q'', have been derived, the next approximation will be facilitated by the use of the formulæ $(82)_4$, as already explained.

When the values of P', P'', Q', and Q'' have been derived with sufficient accuracy, we proceed from these to find the elements of the orbit. After ☊, i, r, r', r'', r''', u, u', u'', and u''' have been found, the remaining elements may be derived from any two radii-vectores and the corresponding arguments of the latitude. It will be most accurate, however, to derive the elements from r, r''', u, and u'''. If the values of P', P'', Q', and Q'' have been obtained with great accuracy, the results derived from any two places will agree with those obtained from the extreme places.

In the first place, from

$$\tan\chi_0 = \sqrt{\frac{r'''}{r}},$$

$$\begin{aligned} \sin\gamma_0\cos G_0 &= \sin\tfrac{1}{2}(u'''-u), \\ \sin\gamma_0\sin G_0 &= \cos\tfrac{1}{2}(u'''-u)\cos 2\chi_0, \\ \cos\gamma_0 &= \cos\tfrac{1}{2}(u'''-u)\sin 2\chi_0, \end{aligned} \qquad (43)$$

we find γ_0 and G_0. Then we have

$$\tau_0 = k(t'''-t),$$

$$m_0 = \frac{\tau_0^2}{(r+r''')^3\cos^3\gamma_0}, \qquad j_0 = \frac{\sin^2\frac{1}{2}\gamma_0}{\cos\gamma_0}, \qquad (44)$$

$$\eta_0 = \frac{m_0}{\frac{5}{6}+j_0+\xi_0}, \qquad x_0 = \frac{m_0}{s_0^2} - j_0,$$

from which, by means of Tables XIII. and XIV., to find s_0 and x_0.

We have, further,

$$p = \left(\frac{s_0\, rr'''\sin(u'''-u)}{\tau_0}\right)^2,$$

and the agreement of the value of p thus found with the separate results for the same quantity obtained from the combination of any two of the four places, will show the extent to which the approximation to P', P'', Q', and Q'' has been carried. The elements are now to be computed from the extreme places precisely as explained in the preceding chapter, using r''' in the place of r'' in the formulæ there given and introducing the necessary modifications in the notation, which have been already suggested and which will be indicated at once.

101. Example.—For the purpose of illustrating the application of the formulæ for the calculation of an orbit from four observations, let us take the following normal places of *Eurynome* (79) derived by comparing a series of observations with an ephemeris computed from approximate elements.

Greenwich M. T.	α	δ
1863 Sept. 20.0	14° 30′ 35″.6	+ 9° 23′ 49″.7,
Dec. 9.0	9 54 17 .0	2 53 41 .8,
1864 Feb. 2.0	28 41 34 .1	9 6 2 .8,
April 30.0	74 29 58 .9	+ 19 35 41 .5.

These normals give the geocentric places of the planet referred to the mean equinox and equator of 1864.0, and free from aberration. For the mean obliquity of the ecliptic of 1864.0, the *American Nautical Almanac* gives

$$\varepsilon = 23^\circ\ 27'\ 24''.49,$$

and, by means of this, converting the observed right ascensions and declinations, as given by the normal places, into longitudes and latitudes, we get

Greenwich M. T.	λ	β
1863 Sept. 20.0	16° 59′ 9″.42	+ 2° 56′ 44″.58,
Dec. 9.0	10 14 17 .57	— 1 15 48 .82,
1864 Feb. 2.0	29 53 21 .99	2 29 57 .38,
April 30.0	75 23 46 .90	— 3 4 44 .49.

These places are referred to the ecliptic and mean equinox of 1864.0, and, for the same dates, the geocentric latitudes of the sun referred also to the ecliptic of 1864.0 are

$$+0''.60, \qquad +0''.53, \qquad +0''.36, \qquad +0''.19.$$

For the reduction of the geocentric latitudes of the planet to the point in which a perpendicular let fall from the centre of the earth to the plane of the ecliptic cuts that plane, the equation $(6)_4$ gives the corrections $-0''.57$, $-0''.38$, $-0''.18$, and $-0''.07$ to be applied to these latitudes respectively, the logarithms of the approximate distances of the planet from the earth being

$$0.02618, \qquad 0.13355, \qquad 0.29033, \qquad 0.44990.$$

Thus we obtain

$$\begin{array}{lll}
t = 0.0, & \lambda = 16^\circ\ 59'\ 9''.42, & \beta = +2^\circ\ 56'\ 44''.01, \\
t' = 80.0, & \lambda' = 10\ \ 14\ \ 17\ .57, & \beta' = -1\ \ 15\ \ 49\ .20, \\
t'' = 135.0, & \lambda'' = 29\ \ 53\ \ 21\ .99, & \beta'' = -2\ \ 29\ \ 57\ .56, \\
t''' = 223.0, & \lambda''' = 75\ \ 23\ \ 46\ .90, & \beta''' = -3\ \ \ 4\ \ 44\ .56;
\end{array}$$

and, for the same times, the true places of the sun referred to the mean equinox of 1864.0 are

$$\begin{array}{ll}
\odot = 177^\circ\ \ 0'\ 58''.6, & \log R = 0.0015899. \\
\odot' = 256\ \ 58\ \ 35\ .9, & \log R' = 9.9932638, \\
\odot'' = 312\ \ 57\ \ 49\ .8, & \log R'' = 9.9937748, \\
\odot''' = 40\ \ 21\ \ 26\ .8, & \log R''' = 0.0035149,
\end{array}$$

From the equations

$$\tan w' = \frac{\tan\beta'}{\sin(\lambda' - \odot')}, \qquad \tan\psi' = \frac{\tan(\lambda' - \odot')}{\cos w'},$$

$$\tan w'' = \frac{\tan\beta''}{\sin(\lambda'' - \odot'')}, \qquad \tan\psi'' = \frac{\tan(\lambda'' - \odot'')}{\cos w''},$$

we obtain

$$\psi' = 113^\circ\ 15'\ 20''.10, \qquad \log(R'\cos\psi') = 9.5896777_n,$$
$$\log(R'\sin\psi') = 9.9564624,$$
$$\psi'' = 76\ \ 56\ \ 17\ .75, \qquad \log(R''\cos\psi'') = 9.3478848,$$
$$\log(R''\sin\psi'') = 9.9823904.$$

The quadrant in which ψ' must be taken, is indicated by the condition that $\cos\psi'$ and $\cos(\lambda' - \odot')$ must have the same sign. The same condition exists in the case of ψ''. Then, the formulæ

$$A = \cos\beta'\sin(\lambda' - \lambda), \qquad B = \cos\beta''\sin(\lambda'' - \lambda),$$
$$C = \cos\beta''\sin(\lambda''' - \lambda''), \qquad D = \cos\beta'\sin(\lambda''' - \lambda'),$$
$$\frac{B}{A} = h', \qquad \frac{D}{C} = h'',$$
$$a' = R'\cos\psi' + \frac{R'\sin(\lambda - \odot')}{A},$$
$$a'' = R''\cos\psi'' - \frac{R''\sin(\lambda''' - \odot'')}{C},$$
$$c' = h'R''\cos\psi'' + \frac{R''\sin(\lambda - \odot'')}{A},$$
$$c'' = h''R'\cos\psi' - \frac{R'\sin(\lambda''' - \odot')}{C},$$
$$d' = \frac{R\sin(\lambda - \odot)}{A}, \qquad d'' = -\frac{R'''\sin(\lambda''' - \odot''')}{C},$$

give the following results:—

$$\log A = 9.0699254_n, \qquad \log C = 9.8528803,$$
$$\log B = 9.3484939, \qquad \log D = 9.9577271,$$
$$\log h' = 0.2785685_n, \qquad \log h'' = 0.1048468,$$
$$\log a' = 0.8834880_n, \qquad \log a'' = 9.9752915_n,$$
$$\log c' = 0.9012910_n, \qquad \log c'' = 9.7267348_n,$$
$$\log d' = 0.4650841, \qquad \log d'' = 9.9096469_n.$$

We are now prepared to make the first hypothesis in regard to the values of P', Q', P'', and Q''. If the elements were entirely unknown, it would be necessary, in the first instance, to assume for these quantities the values given by the expressions

$$P' = \frac{\tau}{\tau''}, \qquad Q' = \tfrac{1}{2}\tau\tau'',$$

$$P'' = \frac{\tau}{\tau'''}, \qquad Q'' = \tfrac{1}{2}\tau\tau''';$$

then approximate values of r' and r'' are readily obtained by means of the equations (27), (26), and (24) or (25). The first assumed value of x' to be used in the second member of the first of equations (27), is obtained from the expression which results from (22) by putting $Q' = 0$ and $Q'' = 0$, namely,

$$x' = \frac{c_0' + f'c_0'' - f'a'' - a'}{1 - f'f''};$$

after which the values of x' and x'' will be obtained by trial from (27). It should be remarked, further, that in the first determination of an orbit entirely unknown, the intervals of time between the observations will generally be small, and hence the value of x' derived from the assumption of $Q' = 0$ and $Q'' = 0$ will be sufficiently approximate to facilitate the solution of equations (27).

As soon as the approximate values of r' and r'' have thus been found, those of P' and P'' must be recomputed from the expressions

$$P' = \frac{\tau}{\tau''}\left(1 - \tfrac{1}{6}\,\frac{\tau^2 - \tau''^2}{r'^3}\right), \qquad P'' = \frac{\tau}{\tau'''}\left(1 - \tfrac{1}{6}\,\frac{\tau^2 - \tau'''^2}{r''^3}\right).$$

With the results thus derived for P' and P'', and with the values of Q' and Q'' already obtained, the first approximation to the elements must be completed.

When the elements are already approximately known, the first assumed values of P', P'', Q', and Q'' should be computed by means of these elements. Thus, from

$$n = \frac{r'r'' \sin(v'' - v')}{rr'' \sin(v'' - v)}, \qquad n'' = \frac{rr' \sin(v' - v)}{rr'' \sin(v'' - v)},$$

$$n' = \frac{r''r''' \sin(v''' - v'')}{r'r''' \sin(v''' - v')}, \qquad n''' = \frac{r'r'' \sin(v'' - v')}{r'r''' \sin(v''' - v')},$$

we find n, n', n'', and n'''. The approximate elements of *Eurynome* give

$$\begin{aligned} v &= 322^\circ\ 55'\ 9''.3, & \log r &= 0.308327, \\ v' &= 353\ \ 19\ \ 26\ .3, & \log r' &= 0.294225, \\ v'' &= 14\ \ 45\ \ 8\ .5, & \log r'' &= 0.296088, \\ v''' &= 47\ \ 23\ \ 32\ .8, & \log r''' &= 0.317278, \end{aligned}$$

and hence we obtain

$$\log n = 9.653052, \qquad \log n'' = 9.806836,$$
$$\log n' = 9.825408, \qquad \log n''' = 9.633171.$$

Then, from

$$P' = \frac{n}{n''}, \qquad Q' = (n + n'' - 1)\, r'^3,$$
$$P'' = \frac{n'''}{n'}, \qquad Q'' = (n' + n''' - 1)\, r''^3,$$

we get

$$\log P' = 9.846216, \qquad \log Q' = 9.840771,$$
$$\log P'' = 9.807763, \qquad \log Q'' = 9.882480.$$

The values of these quantities may also be computed by means of the equations (41) and (42).

Next, from

$$c_0' = \frac{P'd' + c'}{1 + P'}, \qquad f' = \frac{h'}{1 + P'},$$
$$c_0'' = \frac{P''d'' + c''}{1 + P''}, \qquad f'' = \frac{h''}{1 + P''},$$

we find

$$\log c_0' = 0.541344_n, \qquad \log f' = 0.047658_n,$$
$$\log c_0'' = 9.807665_n, \qquad \log f'' = 9.889385.$$

Then we have

$$x'' = \frac{x' + a'}{f'\left(1 + \frac{Q'}{r'^3}\right)} - \frac{c_0'}{f'},$$
$$x' = \frac{x'' + a''}{f''\left(1 + \frac{Q''}{r''^3}\right)} - \frac{c_0''}{f''},$$

$$\tan z' = \frac{R' \sin \psi'}{x'}, \qquad \tan z'' = \frac{R'' \sin \psi''}{x''},$$
$$r' = \frac{R' \sin \psi'}{\sin z'} = \frac{x'}{\cos z'}, \qquad r'' = \frac{R'' \sin \psi''}{\sin z''} = \frac{x''}{\cos z''},$$

from which to find r' and r''. In the first place, from

$$x' = \sqrt{r'^2 - R'^2 \sin^2 \psi'},$$

we obtain the approximate value

$$\log x' = 0.242737.$$

Then the first of the preceding equations gives

$$\log x'' = 0.237687.$$

From this we get

$$z'' = 29^\circ\ 3'\ 11''.7, \qquad \log r'' = 0.296092;$$

and then the equation for x' gives

$$\log x' = 0.242768.$$

Hence we have

$$z' = 27^\circ\ 20'\ 59''.6, \qquad \log r' = 0.294249;$$

and, repeating the operation, using these results for x' and r', we get

$$\log x'' = 0.237678, \qquad \log x' = 0.242757.$$

The correct value of $\log x'$ may now be found by means of equation (28). Thus, in units of the sixth decimal place, we have

$$a_0 = 242768 - 242737 = +31, \qquad a_0' = 242757 - 242768 = -11,$$

and for the correction to be applied to the last value of $\log x'$, in units of the sixth decimal place,

$$\Delta \log x' = -\frac{a_0'^2}{a_0' - a_0} = +3.$$

Therefore, the corrected value is

$$\log x' = 0.242760,$$

and from this we derive

$$\log x'' = 0.237681.$$

These results satisfy the equations for x' and x'', and give

$$z' = 27^\circ\ 21'\ 1''.2, \qquad \log r' = 0.294242,$$
$$z'' = 29\ \ 3\ \ 12\ .9, \qquad \log r'' = 0.296087.$$

To find the curtate distances for the first and second observations, the formulæ are

$$\rho' = \frac{R' \sin(z' + \psi')}{\sin z'} \cos\beta', \qquad \rho'' = \frac{R'' \sin(z'' + \psi'')}{\sin z''} \cos\beta'',$$

which give

$$\log \rho' = 0.133474, \qquad \log \rho'' = 0.289918.$$

Then, by means of the equations

$$\begin{aligned}
r' \cos b' \cos (l' - \odot') &= \rho' \cos (\lambda' - \odot') - R', \\
r' \cos b' \sin (l' - \odot') &= \rho' \sin (\lambda' - \odot'), \\
r' \sin b' &= \rho' \tan \beta',
\end{aligned}$$

$$\begin{aligned}
r'' \cos b'' \cos (l'' - \odot'') &= \rho'' \cos (\lambda'' - \odot'') - R'', \\
r'' \cos b'' \sin (l'' - \odot'') &= \rho'' \sin (\lambda'' - \odot''), \\
r'' \sin b'' &= \rho'' \tan \beta'',
\end{aligned}$$

we find the following heliocentric places:

$$\begin{aligned}
l' &= 37^\circ\ 35'\ 26''.4, & \log \tan b' &= 8.182861_n, & \log r' &= 0.294243, \\
l'' &= 58\ \ 58\ \ 15\ .3, & \log \tan b'' &= 8.634209_n, & \log r'' &= 0.296087.
\end{aligned}$$

The agreement of these values of $\log r'$ and $\log r''$ with those obtained directly from x' and x'' is a partial proof of the numerical calculation.

From the equations

$$\begin{aligned}
\tan i \sin \left(\tfrac{1}{2}(l'' + l') - \Omega\right) &= \tfrac{1}{2}(\tan b'' + \tan b') \sec \tfrac{1}{2}(l'' - l'), \\
\tan i \cos \left(\tfrac{1}{2}(l'' + l') - \Omega\right) &= \tfrac{1}{2}(\tan b'' - \tan b') \operatorname{cosec} \tfrac{1}{2}(l'' - l'),
\end{aligned}$$

$$\tan u' = \frac{\tan (l' - \Omega')}{\cos i}, \qquad \tan u'' = \frac{\tan (l'' - \Omega)}{\cos i},$$

we obtain

$$\begin{aligned}
\Omega &= 206^\circ\ 42'\ 24''.0, & i &= 4^\circ\ 36'\ 47''.2, \\
u' &= 190\ \ 55\ \ 6\ .6 & u'' &= 212\ \ 20\ \ 53\ .5.
\end{aligned}$$

Then, from

$$\begin{aligned}
n'' &= \frac{1}{1 + P'}\left(1 + \frac{Q'}{r'^3}\right), & n &= n''P', \\
n' &= \frac{1}{1 + P''}\left(1 + \frac{Q''}{r''^3}\right), & n''' &= n'P'',
\end{aligned}$$

we get

$$\begin{aligned}
\log n'' &= 9.806832, & \log n &= 9.653048, \\
\log n' &= 9.825408, & \log n''' &= 9.633171,
\end{aligned}$$

and the equations

$$\begin{aligned}
r \sin \left((u' - u) + \tfrac{1}{2}(u'' - u')\right) &= \frac{r' + n''r''}{n} \sin \tfrac{1}{2}(u'' - u'), \\
r \cos \left((u' - u) + \tfrac{1}{2}(u'' - u')\right) &= \frac{r' - n''r''}{n} \cos \tfrac{1}{2}(u'' - u'), \\
r''' \sin \left((u''' - u'') + \tfrac{1}{2}(u'' - u')\right) &= \frac{r'' + n'r'}{n'''} \sin \tfrac{1}{2}(u'' - u'), \\
r''' \cos \left((u''' - u'') + \tfrac{1}{2}(u'' - u')\right) &= \frac{r'' - n'r'}{n'''} \cos \tfrac{1}{2}(u'' - u'),
\end{aligned}$$

give

$$\log r = 0.308379, \qquad u = 160^\circ\ 30'\ 57''.6,$$
$$\log r''' = 0.317273, \qquad u''' = 244\ \ 59\ \ 32\ .5.$$

Next, by means of the formulæ

$$\tan(l - \Omega) = \cos i \tan u, \qquad \tan b = \tan i \sin(l - \Omega),$$
$$\tan(l''' - \Omega) = \cos i \tan u''', \qquad \tan b''' = \tan i \sin(l''' - \Omega),$$
$$\rho \cos(\lambda - \odot) = r \cos b \cos(l - \odot) + R,$$
$$\rho \sin(\lambda - \odot) = r \cos b \sin(l - \odot),$$
$$\rho \tan \beta = r \sin b;$$

$$\rho''' \cos(\lambda''' - \odot''') = r''' \cos b''' \cos(l''' - \odot''') + R''',$$
$$\rho''' \sin(\lambda''' - \odot''') = r''' \cos b''' \sin(l''' - \odot'''),$$
$$\rho''' \tan \beta''' = r''' \sin b''',$$

we obtain

$$l = 7^\circ\ 16'\ 51''.8, \qquad l''' = 91^\circ\ 37'\ 40''.0,$$
$$b = +\ 1\ \ 32\ \ 14\ .4, \qquad b''' = -\ 4\ \ 10\ \ 47\ .4,$$
$$\lambda = 16\ \ 59\ \ 9\ .0, \qquad \lambda''' = 75\ \ 23\ \ 46\ .9,$$
$$\beta = +\ 2\ \ 56\ \ 40\ .1, \qquad \beta''' = -\ 3\ \ 4\ \ 43\ .4,$$
$$\log \rho = 0.025707, \qquad \log \rho''' = 0.449258.$$

The value of λ''' thus obtained agrees exactly with that given by observation, but λ differs $0''.4$ from the observed value. This difference does not exceed what may be attributed to the unavoidable errors of calculation with logarithms of six decimal places. The differences between the computed and the observed values of β and β''' show that the position of the plane of the orbit, as determined by means of the second and third places, will not completely satisfy the extreme places.

The four curtate distances which are thus obtained enable us, in the case of an orbit entirely unknown, to complete the correction for aberration according to the equations (40).

The calculation of the quantities which are independent of P', P'', Q', and Q'', and which are therefore the same in the successive hypotheses, should be performed as accurately as possible. The value of $\frac{c_0'}{f'}$, required in finding x'' from x', may be computed directly from

$$\frac{c_0'}{f'} = P' \frac{d'}{h'} + \frac{c'}{h'},$$

the values of $\frac{d'}{h'}$ and $\frac{c'}{h'}$ being found by means of the equations (29);

and a similar method may be adopted in the case of $\frac{c_0''}{f''}$. Further, in the computation of x' and x'', it may in some cases be advisable to employ one or both of the equations (22) for the final trial. Thus, in the present case, x'' is found from the first of equations (27) by means of the difference of two larger numbers, and an error in the last decimal place of the logarithm of either of these numbers affects in a greater degree the result obtained. But as soon as r'' is known so nearly that the logarithm of the factor $1+\frac{Q''}{r''^3}$ remains unchanged, the second of equations (22) gives the value of x'' by means of the sum of two smaller numbers. In general, when two or more formulæ for finding the same quantity are given, of those which are otherwise equally accurate and convenient for logarithmic calculation, that in which the number sought is obtained from the sum of smaller numbers should be preferred instead of that in which it is obtained by taking the difference of larger numbers.

The values of r, r', r'', r''', and u, u', u'', u''', which result from the first hypothesis, suffice to correct the assumed values of P', P'', Q', and Q''. Thus, from

$$\tau = k(t''-t'), \qquad \tau'' = k(t'-t), \qquad \tau''' = k(t'''-t''),$$

$$\tan\chi = \sqrt{\frac{r''}{r'}}, \qquad \tan\chi'' = \sqrt{\frac{r'}{r}}, \qquad \tan\chi''' = \sqrt{\frac{r'''}{r''}},$$

$$\begin{aligned}
\sin\gamma\cos G &= \sin\tfrac{1}{2}(u''-u'), & \sin\gamma''\cos G'' &= \sin\tfrac{1}{2}(u'-u),\\
\sin\gamma\sin G &= \cos\tfrac{1}{2}(u''-u')\cos 2\chi, & \sin\gamma''\sin G'' &= \cos\tfrac{1}{2}(u'-u)\cos 2\chi'',\\
\cos\gamma &= \cos\tfrac{1}{2}(u''-u')\sin 2\chi, & \cos\gamma'' &= \cos\tfrac{1}{2}(u'-u)\sin 2\chi'',
\end{aligned}$$

$$\begin{aligned}
\sin\gamma'''\cos G''' &= \sin\tfrac{1}{2}(u'''-u''),\\
\sin\gamma'''\sin G''' &= \cos\tfrac{1}{2}(u'''-u'')\cos 2\chi'''\\
\cos\gamma''' &= \cos\tfrac{1}{2}(u'''-u'')\sin 2\chi''';
\end{aligned}$$

$$m = \frac{\tau^2\cos^6\chi}{r'^3\cos^3\gamma}, \qquad m'' = \frac{\tau''^2\cos^6\chi''}{r^3\cos^3\gamma''}, \qquad m''' = \frac{\tau'''^2\cos^6\chi'''}{r''^3\cos^3\gamma'''},$$

$$j = \frac{\sin^2\frac{1}{2}\gamma}{\cos\gamma}, \qquad j'' = \frac{\sin^2\frac{1}{2}\gamma''}{\cos\gamma''}, \qquad j''' = \frac{\sin^2\frac{1}{2}\gamma'''}{\cos\gamma'''},$$

$$\eta = \frac{m}{\frac{5}{6}+j+\xi}, \qquad \eta'' = \frac{m''}{\frac{5}{6}+j''+\xi''}, \qquad \eta''' = \frac{m'''}{\frac{5}{6}+j'''+\xi'''},$$

$$x = \frac{m}{s^2}-j, \qquad x'' = \frac{m''}{s''^2}-j'', \qquad x''' = \frac{m'''}{s'''^2}-j''',$$

in connection with Tables XIII. and XIV. we find s, s'', and s'''. The results are

$\log\tau = 9.9759441,$ $\quad \log\tau'' = 0.1386714,$ $\quad \log\tau''' = 0.1800641,$

$\chi = 45^\circ\ 3'\ 39''.1,$ $\quad \chi'' = 44^\circ\ 32'\ 1''.4,$ $\quad \chi''' = 45^\circ\ 41'\ 55''.2,$

$\gamma = 10\ \ 42\ \ 55\ .9,$ $\quad \gamma'' = 15\ \ 13\ \ 45\ .0,$ $\quad \gamma''' = 16\ \ 22\ \ 48\ .5,$

$\log m = 8.186217,$ $\quad \log m'' = 8.516727,$ $\quad \log m''' = 8.590596,$

$\log j = 7.948097,$ $\quad \log j'' = 8.260013,$ $\quad \log j''' = 8.325365,$

$\log s = 0.0085248,$ $\quad \log s'' = 0.0174621,$ $\quad \log s''' = 0.0204063.$

Then, by means of the formulæ

$$P' = \frac{\tau}{\tau''}\cdot\frac{s''}{s},$$

$$Q' = \tfrac{1}{2}\,\frac{\tau\tau''}{ss''}\cdot\frac{r'^2}{rr''\cos\frac{1}{2}(u''-u')\cos\frac{1}{2}(u''-u)\cos\frac{1}{2}(u'-u)},$$

$$P'' = \frac{\tau}{\tau'''}\cdot\frac{s'''}{s},$$

$$Q'' = \tfrac{1}{2}\,\frac{\tau\tau'''}{ss'''}\cdot\frac{r''^2}{r'r'''\cos\frac{1}{2}(u'''-u'')\cos\frac{1}{2}(u'''-u')\cos\frac{1}{2}(u''-u')},$$

we obtain

$\log P' = 9.8462100,$ $\quad \log Q' = 9.8407536,$

$\log P'' = 9.8077615,$ $\quad \log Q'' = 9.8824728,$

with which the next approximation may be completed.

We now recompute c_0', c_0'', f', f'', x', x'', &c. precisely as already illustrated; and the results are

$\log c_0' = 0.5413485_n,$ $\quad \log c_0'' = 9.8076649_n,$

$\log f' = 0.0476614_n,$ $\quad \log f'' = 9.8893851,$

$\log x' = 0.2427528,$ $\quad \log x'' = 0.2376752,$

$z' = 27^\circ\ 21'\ 2''.71,$ $\quad z'' = 29^\circ\ 3'\ 14''.09,$

$\log r' = 0.2942369,$ $\quad \log r'' = 0.2960826,$

$\log \rho' = 0.1334635,$ $\quad \log \rho'' = 0.2899124,$

$\log n = 9.6530445,$ $\quad \log n'' = 9.8068345,$

$\log n' = 9.8254092,$ $\quad \log n''' = 9.6331707.$

Then we obtain

$l' = 37^\circ\ 35'\ 27''.88,$ $\quad \log\tan b' = 8.1828572_n,$ $\quad \log r' = 0.2942369,$

$l'' = 58\ \ 58\ \ 16\ .48,$ $\quad \log\tan b'' = 8.6342073_n,$ $\quad \log r'' = 0.2960827.$

These results for $\log r'$ and $\log r''$ agree with those obtained directly from z' and z'', thus checking the calculation of ψ' and ψ'' and of the heliocentric places.

Next, we derive

$\Omega = 206^\circ\ 42'\ 25''.89,$ $\quad i = 4^\circ\ 36'\ 47''.20,$

$u' = 190\ \ 55\ \ 6\ .27,$ $\quad u'' = 212\ \ 20\ \ 52\ .96,$

and from $u''-u'$, r', r'', n, n'', n', and n''', we obtain

$$\log r = 0.3083734, \qquad u = 160^\circ\ 30'\ 55''.45,$$
$$\log r''' = 0.3172674, \qquad u''' = 244\ \ 59\ \ 31\ .98.$$

For the purpose of proving the accuracy of the numerical results, we compute also, as in the first approximation,

$$l = 7^\circ\ 16'\ 51''.54, \qquad l''' = 91^\circ\ 37'\ 41''.20,$$
$$b = +\ 1\ \ 32\ \ 14\ .07, \qquad b''' = -\ 4\ \ 10\ \ 47\ .36,$$
$$\lambda = 16\ \ 59\ \ 9\ .38, \qquad \lambda''' = 75\ \ 23\ \ 46\ .99,$$
$$\beta = +\ 2\ \ 56\ \ 39\ .54, \qquad \beta''' = -\ 3\ \ 4\ \ 43\ .33,$$
$$\log \rho = 0.0256960, \qquad \log \rho''' = 0.4492539.$$

The values of λ and λ''' thus found differ, respectively, only $0''.04$ and $0''.09$ from those given by the normal places, and hence the accuracy of the entire calculation, both of the quantities which are independent of P', P'', Q', and Q'', and of those which depend on the successive hypotheses, is completely proved. This condition, however, must always be satisfied whatever may be the assumed values of P', P'', Q', and Q''.

From r, r', u, u', &c., we derive

$$\log s = 0.0085254, \qquad \log s'' = 0.0174637, \qquad \log s''' = 0.0204076,$$

and hence the corrected values of P', P'', Q', and Q'' become

$$\log P' = 9.8462110, \qquad \log Q' = 9.8407524,$$
$$\log P'' = 9.8077622, \qquad \log Q'' = 9.8824726.$$

These values differ so little from those for the second approximation, the intervals of time between the observations being very large, that a further repetition of the calculation is unnecessary, since the results which would thus be obtained can differ but slightly from those which have been derived. We shall, therefore, complete the determination of the elements of the orbit, using the extreme places. Thus, from

$$\tau_0 = k(t''' - t), \qquad \tan\chi_0 = \sqrt{\frac{r'''}{r}},$$

$$\sin\gamma_0 \cos G_0 = \sin\tfrac{1}{2}(u''' - u),$$
$$\sin\gamma_0 \sin G_0 = \cos\tfrac{1}{2}(u''' - u)\cos 2\chi_0,$$
$$\cos\gamma_0 = \cos\tfrac{1}{2}(u''' - u)\sin 2\chi_0,$$

$$m_0 = \frac{\tau_0^{\,2}}{(r + r''')^3 \cos^3\gamma_0}, \qquad j_0 = \frac{\sin^2\frac{1}{2}\gamma_0}{\cos\gamma_0},$$

$$\eta_0 = \frac{m_0}{\frac{5}{6} + j_0 + \xi_0}, \qquad x_0 = \frac{m_0}{s_0^{\,2}} - j_0,$$

we get

$$\log \tau_0 = 0.5838863, \qquad \log \tan G_0 = 8.0521953_n,$$
$$\gamma_0 = 42^\circ\ 14'\ 30''.17, \qquad \log m_0 = 9.7179026,$$
$$\log s_0^{\,2} = 0.2917731, \qquad \log x_0 = 8.9608397.$$

The formula

$$p = \left(\frac{s_0 r r''' \sin (u''' - u)}{\tau_0} \right)^2$$

gives

$$\log p = 0.3712401;$$

and if we compute the same quantity by means of

$$p = \left(\frac{s r' r'' \sin (u'' - u')}{\tau} \right)^2 = \left(\frac{s'' r r' \sin (u' - u)}{\tau''} \right)^2 = \left(\frac{s''' r'' r''' \sin (u''' - u'')}{\tau'''} \right)^2,$$

the separate results are, respectively, 0.3712397, 0.3712418, and 0.3712414. The differences between these results are very small, and arise both from the unavoidable errors of calculation and from the deviation of the adopted values of P', P'', Q', and Q'' from the limit of accuracy attainable with logarithms of seven decimal places. A variation of only $0''.2$ in the values of $u' - u$ and $u''' - u''$ will produce an entire accordance of the particular results.

From the equations

$$\sin \tfrac{1}{4} (E''' - E) = \sqrt{x_0},$$
$$a \cos \varphi = \frac{\sin \frac{1}{2} (u''' - u)}{\sin \frac{1}{2} (E''' - E)} \sqrt{r r'''},$$
$$\cos \varphi = \frac{p}{a \cos \varphi},$$

we obtain

$$\tfrac{1}{4} (E''' - E) = 17^\circ\ 35'\ 42''.12, \qquad \log (a \cos \varphi) = 0.3796883,$$
$$\log \cos \varphi = 9.9915518.$$

The formulæ

$$e \sin \left(\omega - \tfrac{1}{2} (u''' + u)\right) = \frac{p}{\cos \gamma_0 \sqrt{r r'''}} \tan G_0,$$
$$e \cos \left(\omega - \tfrac{1}{2} (u''' + u)\right) = \frac{p}{\cos \gamma_0 \sqrt{r r'''}} - \sec \tfrac{1}{2} (u''' - u),$$

give

$$\omega = 197^\circ\ 38'\ 8''.48, \qquad \log e = \log \sin \varphi = 9.2907881,$$
$$\varphi = 11^\circ\ 15'\ 52''.22, \qquad \pi = \omega + \Omega = 44^\circ\ 20'\ 34''.37.$$

This result for φ gives $\log \cos \varphi = 9.9915521$, which differs only 3 in the last decimal place from the value found from p and $a \cos \varphi$. Then, from

20

$$a = \frac{p}{\cos^2 \varphi}, \qquad \mu = \frac{k}{a^{\frac{3}{2}}},$$

the value of k being expressed in seconds of arc, or $\log k = 3.5500066$, we get

$$\log a = 0.3881359, \qquad \log \mu = 2.9678027.$$

For the eccentric anomalies we have

$$\begin{aligned} \tan \tfrac{1}{2} E &= \tan \tfrac{1}{2}(u - \omega) \tan (45^\circ - \tfrac{1}{2}\varphi), \\ \tan \tfrac{1}{2} E' &= \tan \tfrac{1}{2}(u' - \omega) \tan (45^\circ - \tfrac{1}{2}\varphi), \\ \tan \tfrac{1}{2} E'' &= \tan \tfrac{1}{2}(u'' - \omega) \tan (45^\circ - \tfrac{1}{2}\varphi), \\ \tan \tfrac{1}{2} E''' &= \tan \tfrac{1}{2}(u''' - \omega) \tan (45^\circ - \tfrac{1}{2}\varphi), \end{aligned}$$

from which the results are

$$\begin{aligned} E &= 329^\circ\ 11'\ 46''.01, \qquad & E'' &= 12^\circ\ \ 5'\ 33''.63, \\ E' &= 354\ \ 29\ \ 11\ .84, & E''' &= 39\ \ 34\ \ 34\ .65. \end{aligned}$$

The value of $\frac{1}{4}(E''' - E)$ thus derived differs only $0''.03$ from that obtained directly from x_0.

For the mean anomalies, we have

$$\begin{aligned} M &= E - e \sin E, \qquad & M'' &= E'' - e \sin E'', \\ M' &= E' - e \sin E', & M''' &= E''' - e \sin E''', \end{aligned}$$

which give

$$\begin{aligned} M &= 334^\circ\ 55'\ 39''.32, \qquad & M'' &= \ \ 9^\circ\ 44'\ 52''.82, \\ M' &= 355\ \ 33\ \ 42\ .97, & M''' &= 32\ \ 26\ \ 44\ .74. \end{aligned}$$

Finally, if M_0 denotes the mean anomaly for the epoch $T = 1864$ Jan. 1.0 mean time at Greenwich, from

$$\begin{aligned} M_0 &= M - \mu(t - T) = M' - \mu(t' - T) \\ &= M'' - \mu(t'' - T) = M''' - \mu(t''' - T), \end{aligned}$$

we obtain the four values

$$\begin{aligned} M_0 = 1^\circ\ 29'\ 39''&.40 \\ 39\ &.49 \\ 39\ &.40 \\ 39\ &.40, \end{aligned}$$

the agreement of which completely proves the entire calculation of the elements from the data. Collecting together the several results, we have the following elements:

$$\begin{aligned} \text{Epoch} &= 1864 \text{ Jan. } 1.0 \text{ Greenwich mean time.} \\ M &= \quad 1^\circ\ 29'\ 39''.42 \\ \pi &= \quad 44\ \ 20\ \ 34\ .37 \\ \Omega &= 206\ \ 42\ \ 25\ .89 \\ i &= \quad 4\ \ 36\ \ 47\ .20 \\ \varphi &= \quad 11\ \ 15\ \ 52\ .22 \\ \log a &= 0.3881359 \\ \log \mu &= 2.9678027 \\ \mu &= 928''.54447. \end{aligned} \quad \left.\begin{matrix} \\ \\ \end{matrix}\right\} \text{Ecliptic and Mean Equinox 1864.0.}$$

102. The elements thus derived completely represent the four observed longitudes and the latitudes for the second and third places, which are the actual data of the problem; but for the extreme latitudes the residuals are, computation minus observation,

$$\Delta\beta = -4''.47, \qquad \Delta\beta''' = +1''.23.$$

These remaining errors arise chiefly from the circumstance that the position of the plane of the orbit cannot be determined from the second and third places with the same degree of precision as from the extreme places. It would be advisable, therefore, in the final approximation, as soon as ρ', ρ'', n, n'', n', and n''' are obtained, to compute from these and the data furnished directly by observation the curtate distances for the extreme places. The corresponding heliocentric places may then be found, and hence the position of the plane of the orbit as determined by the first and fourth observations. Thus, by means of the equations (37) and (38), we obtain

$$\log \rho = 0.0256953, \qquad \log \rho''' = 0.4492542.$$

With these values of ρ and ρ''', the following heliocentric places are obtained:

$$\begin{aligned} l &= 7^\circ\ 16'\ 51''.54, & \log \tan b &= 8.4289064, & \log r &= 0.3083732, \\ l''' &= 91\ \ 37\ \ 40\ .96, & \log \tan b''' &= 8.8638549_n, & \log r''' &= 0.3172678. \end{aligned}$$

Then from

$$\begin{aligned} \tan i \sin\left(\tfrac{1}{2}(l''' + l) - \Omega\right) &= \tfrac{1}{2}(\tan b''' + \tan b) \sec \tfrac{1}{2}(l''' - l), \\ \tan i \cos\left(\tfrac{1}{2}(l''' + l) - \Omega\right) &= \tfrac{1}{2}(\tan b''' - \tan b) \operatorname{cosec} \tfrac{1}{2}(l''' - l), \end{aligned}$$

we get

$$\Omega = 206^\circ\ 42'\ 45''.23, \qquad i = 4^\circ\ 36'\ 49''.76.$$

For the arguments of the latitude the results are

$$u = 160^\circ\ 30'\ 35''.99, \qquad u''' = 244^\circ\ 59'\ 12''.53.$$

The equations

$$\tan b' = \tan i \sin (l' - \Omega),$$
$$\tan b'' = \tan i \sin (l'' - \Omega),$$

give

$$\log \tan b' = 8.1827129_n, \qquad \log \tan b'' = 8.6342104_n,$$

and the comparison of these results with those derived directly from ρ' and ρ'' exhibits a difference of $+1''.04$ in b', and of $-0''.06$ in b''. Hence, the position of the plane of the orbit as determined from the extreme places very nearly satisfies the intermediate latitudes.

If we compute the remaining elements by means of these values of r, r''', and u, u''', the separate results are:

$$\begin{aligned} \log \tan G_0 &= 8.0522282_n, & \log m_0 &= 9.7179026, \\ \log s_0^2 &= 0.2917731, & \log x_0 &= 8.9608397, \\ \log p &= 0.3712405, & \tfrac{1}{4}(E'' - E) &= 17^\circ\ 35'\ 42''.12, \\ \log (a \cos \varphi) &= 0.3796884, & \log \cos \varphi &= 9.9915521, \\ \omega &= 197^\circ\ 37'\ 47''.72, & \log e &= 9.2907906, \\ \varphi &= 11\ \ 15\ \ 52\ .46, & \log \cos \varphi &= 9.9915520, \\ \log a &= 0.3881365, & \log \mu &= 2.9678019, \\ E &= 329^\circ\ 11'\ 47''.24, & E''' &= 39^\circ\ 34'\ 35''.70, \\ M &= 334\ \ 55\ \ 40\ .46, & M''' &= 32\ \ 26\ \ 45\ .49, \\ M_0 &= 1\ \ 29\ \ 40\ .36, & M_0 &= 1\ \ 29\ \ 40\ .37. \end{aligned}$$

Hence, the elements are as follows:

$$\begin{aligned} \text{Epoch} &= 1864 \text{ Jan. } 1.0 \text{ Greenwich mean time.} \\ M &= 1^\circ\ 29'\ 40''.36 \\ \pi &= 44\ \ 20\ \ 32\ .95 \\ \Omega &= 206\ \ 42\ \ 45\ .23 \\ i &= 4\ \ 36\ \ 49\ .76 \\ \varphi &= 11\ \ 15\ \ 52\ .46 \\ \log a &= 0.3881365 \\ \mu &= 928''.5427. \end{aligned}$$

(π, Ω, i:) Ecliptic and Mean Equinox 1864.0.

It appears, therefore, that the principal effect of neglecting the extreme latitudes in the determination of an orbit from four observations is on the inclination of the orbit and on the longitude of the ascending node, the other elements being very slightly changed. The elements thus derived represent the extreme places exactly, and if we compute the second and third places directly from these elements, we obtain

$$\begin{aligned} M' &= 355^\circ\ 33'\ 43''.88, & M'' &= 9^\circ\ 44'\ 53''.73, \\ E' &= 354\ \ 29\ \ 12\ .93, & E'' &= 12\ \ 5\ \ 34\ .81, \\ v' &= 353\ \ 16\ \ 59\ .07, & v'' &= 14\ \ 42\ \ 45\ .96, \end{aligned}$$

$\log r' = 0.2942366,$ $\qquad$ $\log r'' = 0.2960826,$

$u' = 190° \; 54' \; 46''.79,$ $\qquad$ $u'' = 212° \; 20' \; 33''.68,$

$l' = 37 \; 35 \; 27 \; .75,$ $\qquad$ $l'' = 58 \; 58 \; 16 \; .50,$

$b' = -\; 0 \; 52 \; 21 \; .25,$ $\qquad$ $b'' = -\; 2 \; 27 \; 59 \; .06,$

$\lambda' = 10 \; 14 \; 17 \; .35,$ $\qquad$ $\lambda'' = 29 \; 53 \; 21 \; .99,$

$\beta' = -\; 1 \; 15 \; 47 \; .67,$ $\qquad$ $\beta'' = -\; 2 \; 29 \; 57 \; .62,$

$\log \rho' = 0.1334634,$ $\qquad$ $\log \rho'' = 0.2899122.$

Hence, the residuals for the second and third places of the planet are—

Comp. — Obs.

$\Delta\lambda' = -\,0''.22, \qquad \Delta\beta' = +\,1''.53,$

$\Delta\lambda'' = \;\; 0\;.00, \qquad \Delta\beta'' = -\,0\;.06;$

and the elements very nearly represent the four normal places. Since the interval between the extreme places is 223 days, these elements must represent, within the limits of the errors of observation, the entire series of observations on which the normals are based. It may be observed, also, that the successive approximations, in the case of intervals which are very large, do not converge with the same degree of rapidity as when the intervals are small, and that in such cases the numerical calculation is very much abbreviated by the determination, in the first instance, of the assumed values of P', P'', Q', and Q'' by means of approximate elements already known. For the first determination of an unknown orbit, the intervals will generally be so small that the first assumed values of these quantities, as determined by the equations

$$P' = \frac{\tau}{\tau''}\left(1 - \tfrac{1}{6}\frac{\tau^2 - \tau''^2}{r'^3}\right), \qquad Q' = \tfrac{1}{2}\tau\tau'',$$

$$P'' = \frac{\tau}{\tau'''}\left(1 - \tfrac{1}{6}\frac{\tau^2 - \tau'''^2}{r''^3}\right), \qquad Q'' = \tfrac{1}{2}\tau\tau''',$$

will not differ much from the correct values, and two or three hypotheses, or even less, will be sufficient. But when the intervals are large, and especially if the eccentricity is also considerable, several hypotheses may be required, the last of which will be facilitated by using the equations $(82)_4$.

The application of the formulæ for the determination of an orbit from four observations, is not confined to orbits whose inclination to the ecliptic is very small, corresponding to the cases in which the method of finding the elements by means of three observations fails, or at least becomes very uncertain. On the contrary, these formulæ apply equally well in the case of orbits of any inclination whatever, and since the labor of computing an orbit from four observations does not much exceed that required when only three observed places are used, while the results must evidently be more approximate, it will be expedient, in very many cases, to use the formulæ given in this chapter both for the first approximation to an unknown orbit and for the subsequent determination from more complete data.

CHAPTER VI.

INVESTIGATION OF VARIOUS FORMULÆ FOR THE CORRECTION OF THE APPROXIMATE ELEMENTS OF THE ORBIT OF A HEAVENLY BODY.

103. In the case of the discovery of a planet, it is often convenient, before sufficient data have been obtained for the determination of elliptic elements, to compute a system of circular elements, an ephemeris computed from these being sufficient to follow the planet for a brief period, and to identify the comparison stars used in differential observations. For this purpose, only two observed places are required, there being but four elements to be determined, namely, ☊, i, a, and, for any instant, the longitude in the orbit. As soon as a has been found, the geocentric distances of the planet for the instants of observation may be obtained by means of the formulæ

$$\begin{aligned} \Delta &= R\cos\psi + \sqrt{a^2 - R^2\sin^2\psi}, \\ \Delta'' &= R''\cos\psi'' + \sqrt{a^2 - R''^2\sin^2\psi''}, \end{aligned} \qquad (1)$$

the values of ψ and ψ'' being computed from the equations $(42)_3$ and $(43)_3$. For convenient logarithmic calculation, we may first find z and z'' from

$$\sin z = \frac{R\sin\psi}{a}, \qquad \sin z'' = \frac{R''\sin\psi''}{a}, \qquad (2)$$

since the formulæ will generally be required for cases such that these angles may be obtained with sufficient accuracy by means of their sines. Then we have

$$\rho = \frac{R\sin(z+\psi)}{\sin z}\cos\beta, \qquad \rho'' = \frac{R''\sin(z''+\psi'')}{\sin z''}\cos\beta'', \qquad (3)$$

from which to find ρ and ρ''. These having been found, we have

$$\begin{aligned} \tan(l - \odot) &= \frac{\rho\sin(\lambda - \odot)}{\rho\cos(\lambda - \odot) - R}, \\ \sin b &= \frac{\rho\tan\beta}{a}, \end{aligned} \qquad (4)$$

for the determination of l and b, and similarly for l'' and b''. The inclination of the orbit and the longitude of the ascending node are then found by means of the formulæ $(75)_3$, and the arguments of the latitude by means of $(77)_3$. Since $u''-u$ is the distance on the celestial sphere between two points of which the heliocentric spherical co-ordinates are l, b, and l'', b'', we have, also, the equations

$$\begin{aligned}
\sin(u''-u)\sin B &= \cos b''\sin(l''-l),\\
\sin(u''-u)\cos B &= \cos b\sin b''-\sin b\cos b''\cos(l''-l),\\
\cos(u''-u) &= \sin b\sin b''+\cos b\cos b''\cos(l''-l),
\end{aligned}$$

for the determination of $u''-u$, the angle opposite the side $90°-b''$ of the spherical triangle being denoted by B. The solution of these equations is facilitated by the introduction of auxiliary angles, as already illustrated for similar cases.

In a circular orbit, the eccentricity being equal to zero, $u''-u$ expresses the mean motion of the planet during the interval $t''-t$, and we must also have

$$t''-t=\frac{a^{\frac{3}{2}}}{k}(u''-u), \tag{5}$$

the value of k being expressed in seconds of arc, or $\log k=3.5500066$.

These formulæ will be applied only when the interval $t''-t$ is small, and for the case of the asteroid planets we may first assume

$$a=2.7,$$

which is about the average mean distance of the group. With this we compute ρ and ρ'' by means of the equations (2) and (3), and the corresponding heliocentric places by means of (4). If the inclination is small, $u''-u$ will differ very little from $l''-l$. Therefore, in the first approximation, when the heliocentric longitudes have been found, the corresponding value of $t''-t$ may be obtained from equation (5), writing $l''-l$ in place of $u''-u$. If this comes out less than the actual interval between the times of observation, we infer that the assumed value of a is too small; but if it comes out greater, the assumed value of a is too large. The value to be used in a repetition of the calculation may be computed from the expression

$$\log a=\tfrac{2}{3}\left(\log(t''-t)+\log k-\log(u''-u)\right),$$

the difference $u''-u$ being expressed in seconds of arc. With this we recompute ρ, ρ'', l, and l'', and find also b, b'', Ω, i, u, and u''. Then, if the value of a computed from the last result for $u''-u$ differs from the last assumed value, a further repetition of the calculation becomes necessary. But when three successive approximate values of a have been found, the correct value may be readily interpolated according to the process already illustrated for similar cases.

As soon as the value of a has been obtained which completely satisfies equation (5), this result and the corresponding values of Ω, i, and the argument of the latitude for a fixed epoch, complete the system of circular elements which will exactly satisfy the two observed places. If we denote by u_0 the argument of the latitude for the epoch T, we shall have, for any instant t,

$$u = u_0 + \mu (t - T),$$

μ being the mean or actual daily motion computed from

$$\mu = \frac{k}{a^{\frac{3}{2}}}.$$

The value of u thus found, and $r = a$, substituted in the formulæ for computing the places of a heavenly body, will furnish the approximate ephemeris required.

The corrections for parallax and aberration are neglected in the first determination of circular elements; but as soon as these approximate elements have been derived, the geocentric distances may be computed to a degree of accuracy sufficient for applying these corrections directly to the observed places, preparatory to the determination of elliptic elements. The assumption of $r' = a$ will also be sufficient to take into account the term of the second order in the first assumed value of P, according to the first of equations $(98)_4$.

104. When approximate elements of the orbit of a heavenly body have been determined, and it is desired to correct them so as to satisfy as nearly as possible a series of observations including a much longer interval of time than in the case of the observations used in finding these approximate elements, a variety of methods may be applied. For a very long series of observations, the approximate elements being such that the squares of the corrections which must be applied to them may be neglected, the most complete method is to form the equations for the variations of any two spherical co-ordinates which fix the place of the body in terms of the variations of the six elements of the orbit; and the differences between the computed places for different dates and the corresponding observed places thus furnish equations of condition, the solution of which gives the corrections to be applied to the elements. But when the observations do not in-

clude a very long interval of time, instead of forming the equations for the variations of the geocentric places in terms of the variations of the elements of the orbit, it will be more convenient to form the equations for these variations in terms of quantities, less in number, from which the elements themselves are readily obtained. If no assumption is made in regard to the form of the orbit, the quantities which present the least difficulties in the numerical calculation are the geocentric distances of the body for the dates of the extreme observations, or at least for the dates of those which are best adapted to the determination of the elements. As soon as these distances are accurately known, the two corresponding complete observations are sufficient to determine all the elements of the orbit.

The approximate elements enable us to assume, for the dates t and t'', the values of Δ and Δ''; and the elements computed from these by means of the data furnished by observation, will exactly represent the two observed places employed. Further, the elements may be supposed to be already known to such a degree of approximation that the squares and products of the corrections to be applied to the assumed values of Δ and Δ'' may be neglected, so that we shall have, for any date,

$$\begin{aligned} \cos\delta\,\Delta\alpha &= \cos\delta\frac{d\alpha}{d\Delta}\,\Delta\Delta + \cos\delta\frac{d\alpha}{d\Delta''}\,\Delta\Delta'', \\ \Delta\delta &= \frac{d\delta}{d\Delta}\,\Delta\Delta + \frac{d\delta}{d\Delta''}\,\Delta\Delta''. \end{aligned} \tag{6}$$

If, therefore, we compare the elements computed from Δ and Δ'' with any number of additional or intermediate observed places, each observed spherical co-ordinate will furnish an equation of condition for the correction of the assumed distances. But in order that the equations (6) may be applied, the numerical values of the partial differential coefficients of α and δ with respect to Δ and Δ'' must be found. Ordinarily, the best method of effecting the determination of these is to compute three systems of elements, the first from Δ and Δ'', the second from $\Delta + D$ and Δ'', and the third from Δ and $\Delta'' + D''$, D and D'' being small increments assigned to Δ and Δ'' respectively. If now, for any date t', we compute α' and δ' from each system of elements thus obtained, we may find the values of the differential coefficients sought. Thus, let the spherical co-ordinates for the time t' computed from the first system be denoted by α' and δ'; those computed from the second system of elements, by $\alpha' + a\sec\delta'$ and $\delta' + d$; and those from the third system, by $\alpha' + a''\sec\delta'$ and $\delta' + d''$. Then we shall have

$$\cos\delta'\frac{d\alpha'}{d\Delta}=\frac{a}{D},\qquad \frac{d\delta'}{d\Delta}=\frac{d}{D},$$
$$\cos\delta'\frac{d\alpha'}{d\Delta''}=\frac{a''}{D''},\qquad \frac{d\delta'}{d\Delta''}=\frac{d''}{D''};\tag{7}$$

and the equations (6) give

$$\cos\delta'\,\Delta\alpha'=\frac{a}{D}\Delta\Delta+\frac{a''}{D''}\Delta\Delta'',$$
$$\Delta\delta'=\frac{d}{D}\Delta\Delta+\frac{d''}{D''}\Delta\Delta''.\tag{8}$$

In the same manner, computing the places for various dates, for which observed places are given, by means of each of the three systems of elements, the equations for the correction of Δ and Δ'', as determined by each of the additional observations employed, may be formed.

105. For the purpose of illustrating the application of this method, let us suppose that three observed places are given, referred to the ecliptic as the fundamental plane, and that the corrections for parallax, aberration, precession, and nutation have all been duly applied. By means of the approximate elements already known, we compute the values of Δ and Δ'' for the extreme places, and from these the heliocentric places are obtained by means of the equations $(71)_3$ and $(72)_3$, writing $\Delta\cos\beta$ and $\Delta''\cos\beta''$ in place of ρ and ρ''. The values of ☊, i, u, and u'' will be obtained by means of the formulæ $(76)_3$ and $(77)_3$; and from r, r'' and $u''-u$ the remaining elements of the orbit are determined as already illustrated. The first system of elements is thus obtained. Then we assign an increment to Δ, which we denote by D, and with the geocentric distances $\Delta+D$ and Δ'' we compute in precisely the same manner a second system of elements. Next, we assign to Δ'' an increment D'', and from Δ and $\Delta''+D''$ a third system of elements is derived. Let the geocentric longitude and latitude for the date of the middle observation computed from the first system of elements be designated, respectively, by λ_1' and β_1'; from the second system of elements, by λ_2' and β_2'; and from the third system, by λ_3' and β_3'. Then from

$$a\;=(\lambda_2'-\lambda_1')\cos\beta_1',\qquad d\;=\beta_2'-\beta_1',$$
$$a''=(\lambda_3'-\lambda_1')\cos\beta_1',\qquad d''=\beta_3'-\beta_1',\tag{9}$$

we compute a, a'', d, and d'', and by means of these and the values of D and D'' we form the equations

$$\frac{a}{D}\Delta\varDelta + \frac{a''}{D''}\Delta\varDelta'' = \cos\beta'\,\Delta\lambda',$$
$$\frac{d}{D}\Delta\varDelta + \frac{d''}{D''}\Delta\varDelta'' = \Delta\beta', \qquad (10)$$

for the determination of the corrections to be applied to the first assumed values of $\varDelta$ and $\varDelta''$, by means of the differences between observation and computation. The observed longitude and latitude being denoted by λ' and β', respectively, we shall have

$$\cos\beta'\,\Delta\lambda' = (\lambda' - \lambda_1')\cos\beta',$$
$$\Delta\beta' = \beta' - \beta_1', \qquad (11)$$

for finding the values of the second members of the equations (10), and then by elimination we obtain the values of the corrections $\Delta\varDelta$ and $\Delta\varDelta''$ to be applied to the assumed values of the distances. Finally, we compute a fourth system of elements corresponding to the geocentric distances $\varDelta + \Delta\varDelta$ and $\varDelta'' + \Delta\varDelta''$ either directly from these values, or by interpolation from the three systems of elements already obtained; and, if the first assumption is not considerably in error, these elements will exactly represent the middle place. It should be observed, however, that if the second system of elements represents the middle place better than the first system, λ_2' and β_2' should be used instead of λ_1' and β_1' in the equations (11), and, in this case, the final system of elements must be computed with the distances $\varDelta + D + \Delta\varDelta$ and $\varDelta'' + \Delta\varDelta''$. Similarly, if the middle place is best represented by the third system of elements, the corrections will be obtained for the distances used in the third hypothesis.

If the computation of the middle place by means of the final elements still exhibits residuals, on account of the neglected terms of the second order, a repetition of the calculation of the corrections $\Delta\varDelta$ and $\Delta\varDelta''$, using these residuals for the values of the second members of the equations (10), will furnish the values of the distances for the extreme places with all the precision desired. The increments D and D'' to be assigned successively to the first assumed values of $\varDelta$ and $\varDelta''$ may, without difficulty, be so taken that the true elements shall differ but little from one of the three systems computed; and in all the formulæ it will be convenient to use, instead of the geocentric distances themselves, the logarithms of these distances, and to express the variations of these quantities in units of the last decimal place of the logarithms.

These formulæ will generally be applied for the correction of approximate elements by means of several observed places, which may be either single observations or normal places, each derived from several observations, and the two places selected for the computation of the elements from $\varDelta$ and $\varDelta''$ should not only be the most accurate possible, but they should also be such that the resulting elements are not too much affected by small errors in these geocentric places. They should moreover be as distant from each other as possible, the other considerations not being overlooked. When the three systems of elements have been computed, each of the remaining observed places will furnish two equations of condition, according to equations (10), for the determination of the corrections to be applied to the assumed values of the geocentric distances; and, since the number of equations will thus exceed the number of unknown quantities, the entire group must be combined according to the method of least squares. Thus, we multiply each equation by the coefficient of $\Delta\varDelta$ in that equation, taken with its proper algebraic sign, and the sum of all the equations thus formed gives one of the final equations required. Then we multiply each equation by the coefficient of $\Delta\varDelta''$ in that equation, taken also with its proper algebraic sign, and the sum of all these gives the second equation required. From these two final equations, by elimination, the most probable values of $\Delta\varDelta$ and $\Delta\varDelta''$ will be obtained; and a system of elements computed with the distances thus corrected will exactly represent the two fundamental places selected, while the sum of the squares of the residuals for the other places will be a minimum. The observations are thus supposed to be equally good; but if certain observed places are entitled to greater influence than the others, the relative precision of these places must be taken into account in the combination of the equations of condition, the process for which will be fully explained in the next chapter.

When a number of observed places are to be used for the correction of the approximate elements of the orbit of a planet or comet, it will be most convenient to adopt the equator as the fundamental plane. In this case the heliocentric places will be computed from the assumed values of $\varDelta$ and $\varDelta''$, and the corresponding geocentric right ascensions and declinations by means of the formulæ $(106)_3$ and $(107)_3$; and the position of the plane of the orbit as determined from these by means of the equations $(76)_3$ will be referred to the equator as the fundamental plane. The formation of the equations of condition for the corrections $\Delta\varDelta$ and $\Delta\varDelta''$ to be applied to the assumed values of the distances will then be effected precisely as in the case of λ and β, the necessary changes being made in the notation. In a similar manner, the calculation may be effected for any other fundamental plane which may be adopted.

It should be observed, further, that when the ecliptic is taken as the fundamental plane, the geocentric latitudes should be corrected by means of the equation $(6)_4$, in order that the latitudes of the sun shall vanish, otherwise, for strict accuracy, the heliocentric places must be determined from Δ and Δ'' in accordance with the equations $(89)_1$.

106. The partial differential coefficients of the two spherical coordinates with respect to Δ and Δ'' may be computed directly by means of differential formulæ; but, except for special cases, the numerical calculation is less expeditious than in the case of the indirect method, while the liability of error is much greater. If we adopt the plane of the orbit as determined by the approximate values of Δ and Δ'' as the fundamental plane, and introduce χ as one of the elements of the orbit, as in the equations $(72)_2$, the variation of the geocentric longitude θ measured in this plane, neglecting terms of the second order, depends on only four elements; and in this case the differential formulæ may be applied with facility. Thus, if we express r and v in terms of the elements φ, M_0, and μ, we shall have

$$\frac{dr}{d\Delta}=\frac{dr}{d\varphi}\cdot\frac{d\varphi}{d\Delta}+\frac{dr}{dM_0}\cdot\frac{dM_0}{d\Delta}+\frac{dr}{d\mu}\cdot\frac{d\mu}{d\Delta},$$

and

$$\frac{dv}{d\Delta}=\frac{dv}{d\varphi}\cdot\frac{d\varphi}{d\Delta}+\frac{dv}{dM_0}\cdot\frac{dM_0}{d\Delta}+\frac{dv}{d\mu}\cdot\frac{d\mu}{d\Delta},$$

or

$$\frac{d(v+\chi)}{d\Delta}=\frac{d\chi}{d\Delta}+\frac{dv}{d\varphi}\cdot\frac{d\varphi}{d\Delta}+\frac{dv}{dM_0}\cdot\frac{dM_0}{d\Delta}+\frac{dv}{d\mu}\cdot\frac{d\mu}{d\Delta},$$

In like manner, we have

$$\frac{dr''}{d\Delta}=\frac{dr''}{d\varphi}\cdot\frac{d\varphi}{d\Delta}+\frac{dr''}{dM_0}\cdot\frac{dM_0}{d\Delta}+\frac{dr''}{d\mu}\cdot\frac{d\mu}{d\Delta},$$

$$\frac{d(v''+\chi)}{d\Delta}=\frac{dv''}{d\varphi}\cdot\frac{d\varphi}{d\Delta}+\frac{dv''}{dM_0}\cdot\frac{dM_0}{d\Delta}+\frac{dv''}{d\mu}\cdot\frac{d\mu}{d\Delta}+\frac{d\chi}{d\Delta}.$$

As soon as the values of $\frac{dr}{d\Delta}$, $\frac{d(v+\chi)}{d\Delta}$, $\frac{dr''}{d\Delta}$, and $\frac{d(v''+\chi)}{d\Delta}$ are known, the equations necessary for finding the differential coefficients of the elements χ, φ, M_0, and μ with respect to Δ are thus provided. In the case under consideration, when an increment is assigned to Δ, the value of Δ'' remaining unchanged, r'' and $v''+\chi$ are not changed, and hence

$$\frac{dr''}{d\Delta}=0, \qquad \frac{d\,(v''+\chi)}{d\Delta}=0.$$

To find $\frac{dr}{d\Delta}$ and $\frac{d\,(v+\chi)}{d\Delta}$, from the equations

$$\Delta \cos\eta \cos\theta = x + X,$$
$$\Delta \cos\eta \sin\theta = y + Y,$$

in which η is the geocentric latitude in reference to the plane of the orbit computed from Δ and Δ'' as the fundamental plane, and X, Y the geocentric co-ordinates of the sun referred to the same plane, we get

$$dx = \cos\eta \cos\theta\, d\Delta,$$
$$dy = \cos\eta \sin\theta\, d\Delta,$$

or, substituting for dx and dy their values given by $(73)_2$,

$$\cos\eta\cos\theta\, d\Delta = \cos u\, dr - r\sin u\, d\,(v+\chi),$$
$$\cos\eta\sin\theta\, d\Delta = \sin u\, dr + r\cos u\, d\,(v+\chi).$$

Eliminating, successively, $d\,(v+\chi)$ and dr, we get

$$\begin{aligned}\frac{dr}{d\Delta} &= \cos\eta\cos(\theta-u),\\ \frac{d\,(v+\chi)}{d\Delta} &= \frac{1}{r}\cos\eta\sin(\theta-u).\end{aligned} \tag{12}$$

Therefore, we shall have

$$\begin{aligned}\frac{d\chi}{d\Delta}+\frac{dv}{d\varphi}\cdot\frac{d\varphi}{d\Delta}+\frac{dv}{dM_0}\cdot\frac{dM_0}{d\Delta}+\frac{dv}{d\mu}\cdot\frac{d\mu}{d\Delta} &= \frac{1}{r}\cos\eta\sin(\theta-u),\\ \frac{dr}{d\varphi}\cdot\frac{d\varphi}{d\Delta}+\frac{dr}{dM_0}\cdot\frac{dM_0}{d\Delta}+\frac{dr}{d\mu}\cdot\frac{d\mu}{d\Delta} &= \cos\eta\cos(\theta-u),\\ \frac{d\chi}{d\Delta}+\frac{dv''}{d\varphi}\cdot\frac{d\varphi}{d\Delta}+\frac{dv''}{dM_0}\cdot\frac{dM_0}{d\Delta}+\frac{dv''}{d\mu}\cdot\frac{d\mu}{d\Delta} &= 0,\\ \frac{dr''}{d\varphi}\cdot\frac{d\varphi}{d\Delta}+\frac{dr''}{dM_0}\cdot\frac{dM_0}{d\Delta}+\frac{dr''}{d\mu}\cdot\frac{d\mu}{d\Delta} &= 0;\end{aligned} \tag{13}$$

and if we compute the numerical values of the differential coefficients of r, r'', v, and v'' with respect to the elements φ, M_0, and μ, these equations will furnish, by elimination, the values of the four unknown quantities $\frac{d\chi}{d\Delta}$, $\frac{d\varphi}{d\Delta}$, $\frac{dM_0}{d\Delta}$, and $\frac{d\mu}{d\Delta}$.

In precisely the same manner we derive the following equations for the determination of the partial differential coefficients of these elements with respect to Δ'':—

$$\begin{aligned}
\frac{d\chi}{d\Delta''} + \frac{dv}{d\varphi}\cdot\frac{d\varphi}{d\Delta''} + \frac{dv}{dM_0}\cdot\frac{dM_0}{d\Delta''} + \frac{dv}{d\mu}\cdot\frac{d\mu}{d\Delta''} &= 0, \\
\frac{dr}{d\varphi}\cdot\frac{d\varphi}{d\Delta''} + \frac{dr}{dM_0}\cdot\frac{dM_0}{d\Delta''} + \frac{dr}{d\mu}\cdot\frac{d\mu}{d\Delta''} &= 0, \\
\frac{d\chi}{d\Delta''} + \frac{dv''}{d\varphi}\cdot\frac{d\varphi}{d\Delta''} + \frac{dv''}{dM_0}\cdot\frac{dM_0}{d\Delta''} + \frac{dv''}{d\mu}\cdot\frac{d\mu}{d\Delta''} &= \frac{1}{r''}\cos\eta''\sin(\theta''-u''). \\
\frac{dr''}{d\varphi}\cdot\frac{d\varphi}{d\Delta''} + \frac{dr''}{dM_0}\cdot\frac{dM_0}{d\Delta''} + \frac{dr''}{d\mu}\cdot\frac{d\mu}{d\Delta''} &= \cos\eta''\cos(\theta''-u'').
\end{aligned} \tag{14}$$

Since the geocentric latitude η is affected chiefly by a change of the position of the plane of the orbit, while the variation of the longitude θ is independent of ☊ and i when the squares and products of the variations of the elements are neglected, if we determine the elements which exactly represent the places to which Δ and Δ'' belong, as well as the longitudes for two additional places, or, if we determine those which satisfy the two fundamental places and the longitudes for any number of additional observed places, so that the sum of the squares of their residuals shall be a minimum, the results thus obtained will very nearly satisfy the several latitudes.

Let θ' denote the geocentric longitude of the body, referred to the plane of the orbit computed from Δ and Δ'' as the fundamental plane, for the date t' of any one of the observed places to be used for correcting these assumed distances. Then, to find the partial differential coefficients of θ' with respect to Δ and Δ'', we have

$$\begin{aligned}
\cos\eta'\frac{d\theta'}{d\Delta} &= \cos\eta'\frac{d\theta'}{d\chi}\cdot\frac{d\chi}{d\Delta} + \cos\eta'\frac{d\theta'}{d\varphi}\cdot\frac{d\varphi}{d\Delta} + \cos\eta'\frac{d\theta'}{dM_0}\cdot\frac{dM_0}{d\Delta} \\
&\quad + \cos\eta'\frac{d\theta'}{d\mu}\cdot\frac{d\mu}{d\Delta}, \\
\cos\eta'\frac{d\theta'}{d\Delta''} &= \cos\eta'\frac{d\theta'}{d\chi}\cdot\frac{d\chi}{d\Delta''} + \cos\eta'\frac{d\theta'}{d\varphi}\cdot\frac{d\varphi}{d\Delta''} + \cos\eta'\frac{d\theta'}{dM_0}\cdot\frac{dM_0}{d\Delta''} \\
&\quad + \cos\eta'\frac{d\theta'}{d\mu}\cdot\frac{d\mu}{d\Delta''},
\end{aligned} \tag{15}$$

and by means of the results thus derived, we form the equation

$$\cos\eta'\,\Delta\theta' = \cos\eta'\frac{d\theta'}{d\Delta}\Delta\Delta + \cos\eta'\frac{d\theta'}{d\Delta''}\Delta\Delta''. \tag{16}$$

A fourth observed place will furnish, in the same manner, the additional equation required for finding $\Delta\Delta$ and $\Delta\Delta''$. If more than two observations are used in addition to the fundamental places on which the assumed elements as derived from $\varDelta$ and $\varDelta''$ are based, the several longitudes will furnish each an equation of condition, and the most probable values of $\Delta\varDelta$ and $\Delta\varDelta''$ will be obtained by combining the entire group of equations of condition according to the method of least squares.

107. In the actual application of these formulæ to the correction of the approximate elements, after all the preliminary corrections have been applied to the data, we select the proper observed places for determining the elements from the corresponding assumed distances $\varDelta$ and $\varDelta''$, according to the conditions which have already been stated, and from these we derive the six elements of the orbit. Since the data furnished directly by observation are the right ascensions and the declinations of the body, the elements will be derived in reference to the equator as the plane to which the inclination and the longitude of the ascending node belong. These elements will exactly represent the two fundamental places, and, if the assumed distances $\varDelta$ and $\varDelta''$ are not much in error, they will also very nearly satisfy the remaining places.

We now adopt as the fundamental plane the plane of the approximate orbit thus determined, and by means of the equations $(83)_2$ and $(85)_2$, or by means of $(87)_2$, writing α, δ, Ω', and i' in place of λ, β, Ω, and i, respectively, we compute the values of θ, η, and γ for the dates of the several places to be employed. Then the residuals for each of the observed places are found from the formulæ

$$\begin{aligned}\cos\eta\,\Delta\theta &= \sin\gamma\,\Delta\delta + \cos\gamma\cos\delta\,\Delta\alpha,\\ \Delta\eta &= \cos\gamma\,\Delta\delta - \sin\gamma\cos\delta\,\Delta\alpha,\end{aligned}\tag{17}$$

the values of $\Delta\alpha$ and $\Delta\delta$ for each place being found by subtracting from the observed right ascension and declination, respectively, the right ascension and declination computed by means of the elements derived from $\varDelta$ and $\varDelta''$. The values of θ, η, and γ being required only for finding $\cos\eta\,\Delta\theta$, $\Delta\eta$, and the differential coefficients of θ and η, with respect to the elements of the orbit, need not be determined with great accuracy.

Next, we compute $\dfrac{dr}{d\varDelta}$ and $\dfrac{d(v+\chi')}{d\varDelta}$ from equations (12), and from $(16)_2$ the values of $\dfrac{dr}{d\varphi}$, $\dfrac{dr''}{d\varphi}$, $\dfrac{dv}{d\varphi}$, $\dfrac{dv''}{d\varphi}$, $\dfrac{dr}{dM_0}$, &c., by means of which, using the value of u in reference to the equator, we form the equations (13). The accent is added to χ to indicate that it refers to the equator as the plane for defining the elements. Thus we obtain four equations, from which, by elimination, the values of the differential coefficients of χ', φ, M_0, and μ with respect to $\varDelta$ may be obtained. In the numerical solution, by subtracting the third equation from the first, the unknown quantity $\frac{d\chi'}{d\varDelta}$ is immediately eliminated, so that we have three equations to find the three unknown quantities $\frac{d\varphi}{d\varDelta}$, $\frac{dM_0}{d\varDelta}$, and $\frac{d\mu}{d\varDelta}$. These having been found, $\frac{d\chi'}{d\varDelta}$ may be obtained from the first or from the third equation.

In the same manner we form the equations (14), and thence derive the values of $\frac{d\chi'}{d\varDelta''}$, $\frac{d\varphi}{d\varDelta''}$, $\frac{dM_0}{d\varDelta''}$, and $\frac{d\mu}{d\varDelta''}$. Then, by means of the formulæ $(76)_2$, $(78)_2$, and $(79)_2$, we compute for the date of each place to be employed in correcting the assumed distances the values of $\cos\eta'\frac{d\theta'}{d\chi'}$, $\cos\eta'\frac{d\theta'}{d\varphi'}$, &c., and hence from (15) the values of $\cos\eta'\frac{d\theta'}{d\varDelta}$ and $\cos\eta'\frac{d\theta'}{d\varDelta''}$. The results thus obtained, together with the residuals computed by means of the equations (17), enable us to form, according to (16), the equations of condition for finding the values of the corrections $\Delta\varDelta$ and $\Delta\varDelta''$. The solution of all the equations thus formed, according to the method of least squares, will give the most probable values of these quantities, and the system of elements which corresponds to the distances thus corrected will very nearly satisfy the entire series of observations. Since the values of $\cos\eta'\,\Delta\theta'$ are expressed in seconds of arc, the resulting values of $\Delta\varDelta$ and $\Delta\varDelta''$ will also be expressed in seconds of arc in a circle whose radius is equal to the mean distance of the earth from the sun. To express them in parts of the unit of space, we must divide their values in seconds of arc by 206264.8.

The corrections to be applied to the elements computed from $\varDelta$ and $\varDelta''$, in order to satisfy the corrected values $\varDelta+\Delta\varDelta$ and $\varDelta''+\Delta\varDelta''$, may be computed by means of the partial differential coefficients already derived. Thus, in the case of χ', we have

$$\Delta\chi' = \frac{d\chi'}{d\varDelta}\Delta\varDelta + \frac{d\chi'}{d\varDelta''}\Delta\varDelta'',$$

from which to find $\Delta\chi'$; and in a similar manner $\Delta\varphi$, ΔM_0, and $\Delta\mu$ may be obtained. If, from the values of $\frac{d\,(v+\chi')}{d\varDelta}$ and $\frac{d\,(v''+\chi')}{d\varDelta''}$, we compute

$$\Delta v = \frac{d(v+\chi')}{d\varDelta}\Delta\varDelta - \Delta\chi',$$
$$\Delta v'' = \frac{d(v''+\chi')}{d\varDelta''}\Delta\varDelta'' - \Delta\chi',$$

and apply these corrections to the values of v and v'' found from $\varDelta$ and $\varDelta''$, we obtain the true anomalies corresponding to the distances $\varDelta + \Delta\varDelta$ and $\varDelta'' + \Delta\varDelta''$. The corrections to be applied to the values of r and r'' derived from $\varDelta$ and $\varDelta''$ are given by

$$\Delta r = \frac{dr}{d\varDelta}\Delta\varDelta, \qquad \Delta r'' = \frac{dr''}{d\varDelta''}\Delta\varDelta''.$$

If $\Delta\varDelta$ and $\Delta\varDelta''$ are expressed in seconds of arc, the corresponding values of Δr and $\Delta r''$ must be divided by 206264.8. The corrected results thus obtained should agree with the values of r and r'' computed directly from the corrected values of v, v'', p, and e by means of the polar equation of the conic section. Finally, we have

$$dz = \sin\eta\, d\varDelta,$$

and similarly for dz''; and the last of equations $(73)_2$ gives

$$\begin{aligned} r\sin u\,\Delta i' - r\cos u\sin i'\,\Delta\Omega' &= \sin\eta\,\Delta\varDelta, \\ r''\sin u''\,\Delta i' - r''\cos u''\sin i'\,\Delta\Omega' &= \sin\eta''\,\Delta\varDelta'', \end{aligned} \tag{18}$$

from which to find $\Delta i'$ and $\Delta\Omega'$, u and u'' being the arguments of the latitude in reference to the equator. We have also, according to $(72)_2$,

$$\Delta\omega' = \Delta\chi' - \cos i'\,\Delta\Omega',$$
$$\Delta\pi' = \Delta\chi' + 2\sin^2\tfrac{1}{2}i'\,\Delta\Omega',$$

from which to find the corrections to be applied to ω' and π'. The elements which refer to the equator may then be converted into those for the ecliptic by means of the formulæ which may be derived from $(109)_1$ by interchanging Ω and Ω' and $180° - i'$ and i.

The final residuals of the longitudes may be obtained by substituting the adopted values of $\Delta\varDelta$ and $\Delta\varDelta''$ in the several equations of condition, or, which affords a complete proof of the accuracy of the entire calculation, by direct calculation from the corrected elements; and the determination of the remaining errors in the values of η will show how nearly the position of the plane of the orbit corresponding to the corrected distances satisfies the intermediate latitudes.

Instead of φ, M_0, and μ, we may introduce any other elements which determine the form and magnitude of the orbit, the necessary changes being made in the formulæ. Thus, if we use the elements T, q, and e, these must be written in place of M_0, μ, and φ, respectively, in the equations (13), (14), and (15), and the partial differential coefficients of r, r'', v, and v'' with respect to these elements must be computed by means of the various differential formulæ which have already been investigated. Further, in all these cases, the homogeneity of the formulæ must be carefully attended to.

108. The approximate elements of the orbit of a heavenly body may also be corrected by varying the elements which fix the position of the plane of the orbit. Thus, if the observed longitude and latitude and the values of ☊ and i are given, the three equations $(91)_1$ will contain only three unknown quantities, namely, Δ, r, and u, and the values of these may be found by elimination. When the observed latitude β is corrected by means of the formula $(6)_4$, the latitudes of the sun disappear from these equations, and if we multiply the first by $\sin(\odot - ☊)\sin\beta$, the second (using only the upper sign) by $-\cos(\odot - ☊)\sin\beta$, and the third by $-\sin(\lambda - \odot)\cos\beta$, and add the products, we get

$$\tan u = \frac{\sin\beta\sin(\odot - ☊)}{\cos i\sin\beta\cos(\odot - ☊) - \sin i\cos\beta\sin(\lambda - \odot)}, \tag{19}$$

from which u may be found. If we multiply the second of these equations by $\sin\beta$, and the third by $-\cos\beta\sin(\lambda - ☊)$, and add the products, we find

$$r = \frac{R\sin(\odot - ☊)}{\sin u\,(\sin i\cot\beta\sin(\lambda - ☊) - \cos i)}. \tag{20}$$

The expression for r in terms of the known quantities may also be found by combining the first and second, or by combining the first and third, of equations $(91)_1$. If we put

$$n\cos N = \sin\beta\cos(\odot - ☊),$$
$$n\sin N = \cos\beta\sin(\lambda - \odot),$$

the formula for u becomes

$$\tan u = \frac{\cos N}{\cos(N+i)}\tan(\odot - ☊). \tag{21}$$

The last of equations $(91)_1$ shows that $\sin u$ and $\sin\beta$ must have the same sign, and thus the quadrant in which u must be taken is determined. Putting, also,

$$m\cos M = \sin u,$$
$$m\sin M = \sin u\cot\beta\sin(\lambda - ☊),$$

we have

$$r = -\frac{\cos M}{\cos(M+i)} \cdot \frac{R \sin(\odot - \Omega)}{\sin u}. \tag{22}$$

When any other plane is taken as the fundamental plane, the latitude of the sun (which will then refer to this plane) will be retained in the equations $(91)_1$ and in the resulting expressions for u and r.

The value of u may also be obtained by first computing w and ψ by means of the equations $(42)_3$, and then, if z denotes the angle at the planet or comet between the earth and sun, the values of u and z, as may be readily seen, will be determined by means of the relations of the parts of a spherical triangle of which the sides are $180° - (z + \psi)$, $180° + \odot - \Omega$, and u, the angle opposite to the side u being that which we designate by w, and the side $180° + \odot - \Omega$ being included by this and the inclination i. Let $S = 180° - (z + \psi)$, and, according to Napier's analogies, this spherical triangle gives

$$\begin{aligned} \tan \tfrac{1}{2}(S + u) &= \frac{\cos \frac{1}{2}(i - w)}{\cos \frac{1}{2}(i + w)} \cot \tfrac{1}{2}(\Omega - \odot), \\ \tan \tfrac{1}{2}(S - u) &= \frac{\sin \frac{1}{2}(i - w)}{\sin \frac{1}{2}(i + w)} \cot \tfrac{1}{2}(\Omega - \odot), \end{aligned} \tag{23}$$

from which S and u are readily found. Then we have

$$\begin{aligned} z &= 180° - \psi - S, \\ r &= \frac{R \sin \psi}{\sin z}, \end{aligned} \tag{24}$$

to find r.

If we assume approximate values of Ω and i, as given by a system of elements already known, the equations here given enable us to find r, u, r'', and u'' from λ, β and λ'', β'', corresponding to the dates t and t'' of the fundamental places selected, and from these results for two radii-vectores and arguments of the latitude, the remaining elements may be derived. From these the geocentric place of the body may be found for the date t' of any intermediate or additional observed place, and the difference between the computed and the observed place will indicate the degree of precision of the assumed values of Ω and i. Then we assign to Ω the increment $\delta\Omega$, i remaining unchanged, and compute a second system of elements, and from these the geocentric place for the time t'. We also compute a third system from Ω and $i + \delta i$, and by a process entirely analogous to that already indicated in the case of the variation of two geocentric distances, we obtain the numerical values of the differential coefficients of λ' and β' with respect to ☊ and i. Thus the equations

$$\cos\beta'\,\Delta\lambda' = \cos\beta'\frac{d\lambda'}{d☊}\Delta☊ + \cos\beta'\frac{d\lambda'}{di}\Delta i,$$
$$\Delta\beta' = \frac{d\beta'}{d☊}\Delta☊ + \frac{d\beta'}{di}\Delta i, \qquad (25)$$

for finding the corrections Δ☊ and Δi to be applied to the assumed values of these elements, will be formed; and each additional observation or normal place will furnish two equations of condition for the determination of these corrections.

If the observed right ascensions and declinations are used directly instead of the longitudes and latitudes, the elements ☊ and i must be referred to the equator as the fundamental plane, and the declinations of the sun will appear in the formulæ for u and r obtained from the equations $(91)_1$, thus rendering them more complex. Their derivation offers no difficulty, being similar in all respects to that of the equations (19) and (20), and since they will be rarely, if ever, required, it is not necessary to give the process here in detail. In general, the equations (23) and (24) will be most convenient for finding r and u from the geocentric spherical co-ordinates and the elements ☊ and i, since w, ψ, w'', and ψ'' remain unchanged for the three hypotheses.

When the equator is taken as the fundamental plane, ψ is the distance between two points on the celestial sphere for which the geocentric spherical co-ordinates are A, D and α, δ, those of the sun being denoted by A and D. Hence we shall have

$$\sin\psi\sin B = \cos\delta\sin(\alpha - A),$$
$$\sin\psi\cos B = \cos D\sin\delta - \sin D\cos\delta\cos(\alpha - A), \qquad (26)$$
$$\cos\psi = \sin D\sin\delta + \cos D\cos\delta\cos(\alpha - A),$$

from which to find ψ and B, the angle opposite to the side $90° - \delta$ of the spherical triangle being denoted by B. Let K denote the right ascension of the ascending node on the equator of a great circle passing through the places of the sun and comet or planet for the time t, and let w_0 denote its inclination to the equator; then we shall have

$$\sin w_0\cos(A - K) = \cos B,$$
$$\sin w_0\sin(A - K) = \sin B\sin D, \qquad (27)$$
$$\cos w_0 = \sin B\cos D,$$

from which to find w_0 and K. In a similar manner, we may compute the values of $u''-u$, Ω, and i from the heliocentric spherical co-ordinates l, b and l'', b''.

From the equations

$$\begin{aligned}\tan\tfrac{1}{2}(S_0+u) &= \frac{\cos\frac{1}{2}(i'-w_0)}{\cos\frac{1}{2}(i'+w_0)}\cot\tfrac{1}{2}(\Omega'-K),\\ \tan\tfrac{1}{2}(S_0-u) &= \frac{\sin\frac{1}{2}(i'-w_0)}{\sin\frac{1}{2}(i'+w_0)}\cot\tfrac{1}{2}(\Omega'-K),\end{aligned} \tag{28}$$

the accents being added to distinguish the elements in reference to the equator from those with respect to the ecliptic, the values of S_0 and u (in reference to the equator) may be found. Let s_0 denote the angular distance between the place of the sun and that point of the equator for which the right ascension is K, and the equation

$$\cot s_0 = \cos w_0 \cot(K-A) \tag{29}$$

gives the value of s_0, the quadrant in which it is situated being determined by the condition that $\cos s_0$ and $\cos(K-A)$ shall have the same sign. Then we have $S=S_0-s_0$, and

$$\begin{aligned} z &= 180^\circ - \psi - S_0 + s_0,\\ r &= \frac{R\sin\psi}{\sin z},\end{aligned} \tag{30}$$

from which to find r.

109. In both the method of the variation of two geocentric distances and that of the variation of Ω and i, instead of using the geocentric spherical co-ordinates given by an intermediate observation, in forming the equations for the corrections to be applied to the assumed quantities, we may use any other two quantities which may be readily found from the data furnished by observation. Thus, if we compute r' and u' for the date of a third observation directly from each of the three systems of elements, the differences between the successive results will furnish the numerical values of the partial differential coefficients of r' and u' with respect to $\varDelta$ and $\varDelta''$, or with respect to Ω and i, as the case may be. Then, computing the values of r' and u' from the observed geocentric spherical co-ordinates by means of the values of Ω and i for the system of elements to be corrected, the differences between the results thus derived and those obtained directly from the elements enable us to form the equations

$$\begin{aligned}\frac{du'}{d\varDelta}\Delta\varDelta + \frac{du'}{d\varDelta''}\Delta\varDelta'' &= \Delta u',\\ \frac{dr'}{d\varDelta}\Delta\varDelta + \frac{dr'}{d\varDelta''}\Delta\varDelta'' &= \Delta r',\end{aligned} \tag{31}$$

or the corresponding expressions in the case of the variation of ☊ and i, by means of which the corrections to be applied to the assumed values will be determined. In the numerical application of these equations, $\Delta u'$ being expressed in seconds of arc, $\Delta r'$ should also be expressed in seconds, and the resulting values of $\Delta \varDelta$ and $\Delta \varDelta''$ will be converted into those expressed in parts of the unit of space by dividing them by 206264.8.

When only three observed places are to be used for correcting an approximate orbit, from the values of r, r', r'' and u, u', u'' obtained by means of the formulæ which have been given, we may find p and a or $\frac{1}{a}$—the latter in the case of very eccentric orbits—from the first and second places, and also from the first and third places. If these results agree, the elements do not require any correction; but if a difference is found to exist, by computing the differences, in the case of each of these two elements, for three hypotheses in regard to $\varDelta$ and $\varDelta''$ or in regard to ☊ and i, the equations may be formed by means of which the corrections to be applied to the assumed values of the two geocentric distances, or to those of ☊ and i, will be obtained.

110. The formulæ which have thus far been given for the correction of an approximate orbit by varying the geocentric distances, depend on two of these distances when no assumption is made in regard to the form of the orbit, and these formulæ apply with equal facility whether three or more than three observed places are used. But when a series of places can be made available, the problem may be successfully treated in a manner such that it will only be necessary to vary one geocentric distance. Thus, let x, y, z be the rectangular heliocentric co-ordinates, and r the radius-vector of the body at the time t, and let X, Y, Z be the geocentric co-ordinates of the sun at the same instant. Let the geocentric co-ordinates of the body be designated by x_0, y_0, z_0, and let the plane of the equator be taken as the fundamental plane, the positive axis of x being directed to the vernal equinox. Further, let ρ denote the projection of the radius-vector of the body on the plane of the equator, or the curtate distance with respect to the equator; then we shall have

$$x_0 = \rho \cos \alpha, \qquad y_0 = \rho \sin \alpha, \qquad z_0 = \rho \tan \delta. \tag{32}$$

If we represent the right ascension of the sun by A, and its declination by D, we also have

$$X = R\cos D\cos A, \qquad Y = R\cos D\sin A, \qquad Z = R\sin D. \quad (33)$$

The fundamental equations for the undisturbed motion of the planet or comet, neglecting its mass in comparison with that of the sun, are

$$\frac{d^2x}{dt^2} + \frac{k^2x}{r^3} = 0, \qquad \frac{d^2y}{dt^2} + \frac{k^2y}{r^3} = 0, \qquad \frac{d^2z}{dt^2} + \frac{k^2z}{r^3} = 0;$$

but since

$$x = x_0 - X, \qquad y = y_0 - Y, \qquad z = z_0 - Z,$$

and, neglecting also the mass of the earth,

$$\frac{d^2X}{dt^2} + \frac{k^2X}{R^3} = 0, \qquad \frac{d^2Y}{dt^2} + \frac{k^2Y}{R^3} = 0, \qquad \frac{d^2Z}{dt^2} + \frac{k^2Z}{R^3} = 0,$$

these become

$$\begin{aligned} \frac{d^2x_0}{dt^2} + \frac{k^2x_0}{r^3} + k^2X\left(\frac{1}{R^3} - \frac{1}{r^3}\right) &= 0, \\ \frac{d^2y_0}{dt^2} + \frac{k^2y_0}{r^3} + k^2Y\left(\frac{1}{R^3} - \frac{1}{r^3}\right) &= 0, \\ \frac{d^2z_0}{dt^2} + \frac{k^2z_0}{r^3} + k^2Z\left(\frac{1}{R^3} - \frac{1}{r^3}\right) &= 0. \end{aligned} \quad (34)$$

Substituting for x_0, y_0, and z_0 their values in terms of α and δ, and putting

$$k^2X\left(\frac{1}{R^3} - \frac{1}{r^3}\right) = \xi, \qquad k^2Y\left(\frac{1}{R^3} - \frac{1}{r^3}\right) = \eta, \qquad k^2Z\left(\frac{1}{R^3} - \frac{1}{r^3}\right) = \zeta, \quad (35)$$

we get

$$\begin{aligned} \frac{d^2x_0}{dt^2} + \frac{k^2\rho}{r^3}\cos\alpha + \xi &= 0, \\ \frac{d^2y_0}{dt^2} + \frac{k^2\rho}{r^3}\sin\alpha + \eta &= 0, \\ \frac{d^2z_0}{dt^2} + \frac{k^2\rho}{r^3}\tan\delta + \zeta &= 0. \end{aligned} \quad (36)$$

Differentiating the equations (32) with respect to t, we find

$$\begin{aligned} \frac{dx_0}{dt} &= \cos\alpha\frac{d\rho}{dt} - \rho\sin\alpha\frac{d\alpha}{dt}, \\ \frac{dy_0}{dt} &= \sin\alpha\frac{d\rho}{dt} + \rho\cos\alpha\frac{d\alpha}{dt}, \\ \frac{dz_0}{dt} &= \tan\delta\frac{d\rho}{dt} + \rho\sec^2\delta\frac{d\delta}{dt}. \end{aligned} \quad (37)$$

Differentiating again with respect to t, and substituting in the equations (36) the values thus found, the results are

$$\begin{aligned}
&\left(\frac{k^2\rho}{r^3}+\frac{d^2\rho}{dt^2}-\rho\frac{d\alpha^2}{dt^2}\right)\cos\alpha-\left(\rho\frac{d^2\alpha}{dt^2}+2\frac{d\rho}{dt}\cdot\frac{d\alpha}{dt}\right)\sin\alpha+\xi=0,\\
&\left(\frac{k^2\rho}{r^3}+\frac{d^2\rho}{dt^2}-\rho\frac{d\alpha^2}{dt^2}\right)\sin\alpha+\left(\rho\frac{d^2\alpha}{dt^2}+2\frac{d\rho}{dt}\cdot\frac{d\alpha}{dt}\right)\cos\alpha+\eta=0, \qquad (38)\\
&\left(\frac{k^2\rho}{r^3}+\frac{d^2\rho}{dt^2}\right)\tan\delta+2\sec^2\delta\frac{d\delta}{dt}\cdot\frac{d\rho}{dt}+2\rho\sec^2\delta\tan\delta\frac{d\delta^2}{dt^2}+\rho\sec^2\delta\frac{d^2\delta}{dt^2}+\zeta=0.
\end{aligned}$$

If we multiply the first of these equations by $\sin\alpha$, and the second by $-\cos\alpha$, and add the products, we obtain

$$\frac{d\rho}{dt}=\tfrac{1}{2}\frac{\xi\sin\alpha-\eta\cos\alpha-\rho\dfrac{d^2\alpha}{dt^2}}{\dfrac{d\alpha}{dt}}.$$

Now, from (35) we get

$$\xi\sin\alpha-\eta\cos\alpha=k^2\left(\frac{1}{R^3}-\frac{1}{r^3}\right)R\cos D\sin(\alpha-A),$$

and the preceding equation becomes

$$\frac{d\rho}{dt}=\tfrac{1}{2}\frac{k^2\left(\dfrac{1}{R^3}-\dfrac{1}{r^3}\right)R\cos D\cos(\alpha-A)-\rho\dfrac{d^2\alpha}{dt^2}}{\dfrac{d\alpha}{dt}}. \qquad (39)$$

The value of $\frac{d\rho}{dt}$ thus found is independent of the differential coefficients of δ with respect to t. To find another value of $\frac{d\rho}{dt}$, using all three of equations (38), we multiply the first of these equations by $\sin A\tan\delta$, the second by $-\cos A\tan\delta$, and the third by $-\sin(\alpha-A)$. Then, adding the products, since $\xi\sin A=\eta\cos A$, the result is

$$\begin{aligned}
&2\frac{d\rho}{dt}\left(\cot(\alpha-A)\frac{d\alpha}{dt}-\cot\delta\sec^2\delta\frac{d\delta}{dt}\right)=\\
&\qquad\rho\left(\frac{d\alpha^2}{dt^2}-\cot(\alpha-A)\frac{d^2\alpha}{dt^2}+\sec^2\delta\left(2\frac{d\delta^2}{dt^2}+\cot\delta\frac{d^2\delta}{dt^2}\right)\right)+\zeta\cot\delta,
\end{aligned}$$

from which we get

$$\frac{d\rho}{dt}=\tfrac{1}{2}\rho\frac{\dfrac{d\alpha^2}{dt^2}-\cot(\alpha-A)\dfrac{d^2\alpha}{dt^2}+\sec^2\delta\left(2\dfrac{d\delta^2}{dt^2}+\cot\delta\dfrac{d^2\delta}{dt^2}\right)+\dfrac{\zeta}{\rho}\cot\delta}{\cot(\alpha-A)\dfrac{d\alpha}{dt}-\cot\delta\sec^2\delta\dfrac{d\delta}{dt}}. \qquad (40)$$

When the ecliptic is taken as the fundamental plane, the last term of the numerator of the second member of this equation vanishes, and the epuation may be written

$$\frac{d\rho}{dt} = C\rho, \tag{41}$$

the coefficient C being independent of ρ.

111. When the value of ρ is given, that of $\frac{d\rho}{dt}$ will be determined in terms of the data furnished directly by observation and of the differential coefficients of α and δ with respect to t from equation (39), or from (40), the latter being preferred when the motion of the body in right ascension is very slow. The value of $\frac{d\rho}{dt}$ having been found, we may compute the velocities of the body in directions parallel to the co-ordinate axes. Thus, since

$$x_0 = x + X, \qquad y_0 = y + Y, \qquad z_0 = z + Z,$$

the equations (37) give

$$\begin{aligned}
\frac{dx}{dt} &= \cos\alpha\frac{d\rho}{dt} - \rho\sin\alpha\frac{d\alpha}{dt} - \frac{dX}{dt},\\
\frac{dy}{dt} &= \sin\alpha\frac{d\rho}{dt} + \rho\cos\alpha\frac{d\alpha}{dt} - \frac{dY}{dt},\\
\frac{dz}{dt} &= \tan\delta\frac{d\rho}{dt} + \rho\sec^2\delta\frac{d\delta}{dt} - \frac{dZ}{dt},
\end{aligned} \tag{42}$$

by means of which $\frac{dx}{dt}$, $\frac{dy}{dt}$, and $\frac{dz}{dt}$ may be determined.

To find the values of $\frac{dX}{dt}$, $\frac{dY}{dt}$, and $\frac{dZ}{dt}$, the equations

$$\begin{aligned}
X &= R\cos\odot,\\
Y &= R\sin\odot\cos\varepsilon,\\
Z &= R\sin\odot\sin\varepsilon,
\end{aligned}$$

give, by differentiation,

$$\begin{aligned}
\frac{dX}{dt} &= \cos\odot\frac{dR}{dt} - R\sin\odot\frac{d\odot}{dt},\\
\frac{dY}{dt} &= \sin\odot\cos\varepsilon\frac{dR}{dt} + R\cos\odot\cos\varepsilon\frac{d\odot}{dt},\\
\frac{dZ}{dt} &= \sin\odot\sin\varepsilon\frac{dR}{dt} + R\cos\odot\sin\varepsilon\frac{d\odot}{dt}.
\end{aligned} \tag{43}$$

Now, according to equation $(52)_1$, we have

$$\frac{d\odot}{dt} = \frac{k\sqrt{(1-e_0^2)(1+m_0)}}{R^2}, \tag{44}$$

m_0 denoting the mass of the earth, and e_0 the eccentricity of its orbit. The polar equation of the conic section gives

$$\frac{dr}{dt} = \frac{r^2 e \sin v}{p} \cdot \frac{dv}{dt}.$$

Let Γ denote the longitude of the sun's perigee, and this equation gives

$$\frac{dR}{dt} = \frac{R^2 e_0 \sin(\odot - \Gamma)}{1-e_0^2} \cdot \frac{d\odot}{dt} = \frac{k\sqrt{1+m_0}}{\sqrt{1-e_0^2}} e_0 \sin(\odot - \Gamma). \tag{45}$$

If we neglect the square of the eccentricity of the earth's orbit, we have simply

$$\frac{d\odot}{dt} = \frac{k\sqrt{1+m_0}}{R^2}, \quad \frac{dR}{dt} = k\sqrt{1+m_0}\, e_0 \sin(\odot - \Gamma). \tag{46}$$

The values of $\frac{a\odot}{dt}$ and $\frac{dR}{dt}$ having been found by means of these formulæ, the equations (43) give the required results for $\frac{dX}{dt}$, $\frac{dY}{dt}$, and $\frac{dZ}{dt}$, and hence, by means of (42), we obtain the velocities of the comet or planet in directions parallel to the co-ordinate axes.

112. The values of x, y, and z may be derived by means of the equations

$$x = \Delta \cos\delta \cos\alpha - X,$$
$$y = \Delta \cos\delta \sin\alpha - Y,$$
$$z = \Delta \sin\delta - Z,$$

and from these, in connection with the corresponding velocities, the elements of the orbit may be found. The equations $(32)_1$ give immediately the values of the inclination, the semi-parameter, and the right ascension of the ascending node on the equator. Then, the position of the plane of the orbit being known, we may compute r and u directly from the geocentric right ascension and declination by means of the equations (28) and (30). But if we use the values of the heliocentric co-ordinates directly, multiplying the first of equations $(93)_1$ by $\cos \Omega$, and the second by $\sin \Omega$, and adding the products, we have

$$r \sin u = z \operatorname{cosec} i,$$
$$r \cos u = x \cos \Omega + y \sin \Omega, \qquad (47)$$

from which r and u may be found, the argument of the latitude u being referred to the plane of xy as the fundamental plane. The equation

$$r^2 = x^2 + y^2 + z^2$$

gives

$$\frac{dr}{dt} = \frac{x}{r} \cdot \frac{dx}{dt} + \frac{y}{r} \cdot \frac{dy}{dt} + \frac{z}{r} \cdot \frac{dz}{dt}, \qquad (48)$$

and, since

$$\frac{dr}{dt} = \frac{r^2 e \sin v}{p} \cdot \frac{dv}{dt}, \qquad \frac{dv}{dt} = \frac{k\sqrt{p}}{r^2},$$

we shall have

$$e \sin v = \frac{\sqrt{p}}{k} \cdot \frac{dr}{dt},$$
$$e \cos v = \frac{p}{r} - 1, \qquad (49)$$

from which to find e and v. Then the distance between the perihelion and the ascending node is given by

$$\omega = u - v.$$

The semi-transverse axis is obtained from p and e by means of the relation

$$a = \frac{p}{1 - e^2}.$$

Finally, from the value of v the eccentric anomaly and thence the mean anomaly may be found, and the latter may then be referred to any epoch by means of the mean motion determined from a.

In the case of very eccentric orbits, the perihelion distance will be given by

$$q = \frac{p}{1 + e};$$

and the time of perihelion passage may be found from v and e by means of Table IX. or Table X., as already illustrated.

The equation $(21)_1$ gives, if we substitute for f its value in terms of p, denote by V the linear velocity of the planet or comet, and neglect the mass,

$$V^2 r^2 - r^2 \frac{dr^2}{dt^2} = k^2 p.$$

Let ψ_0 denote the angle which the tangent to the orbit at the extremity of the radius-vector makes with the prolongation of this radius-vector, and we shall have

$$rV\cos\psi_0 = r\frac{dr}{dt} = x\frac{dx}{dt} + y\frac{dy}{dt} + z\frac{dz}{dt},$$

so that the preceding equation gives

$$k^2p = V^2r^2\sin^2\psi_0.$$

Hence we derive the equations

$$\begin{aligned} Vr\sin\psi_0 &= k\sqrt{p}, \\ Vr\cos\psi_0 &= x\frac{dx}{dt} + y\frac{dy}{dt} + z\frac{dz}{dt}, \end{aligned} \tag{50}$$

from which Vr and ψ_0 may be found. Then, since

$$V^2 = k^2\left(\frac{2}{r} - \frac{1}{a}\right),$$

we shall have

$$\frac{k^2}{a} = \frac{2k^2}{r} - V^2, \tag{51}$$

by means of which a may be determined, and then e may be found by means of this and the value of p.

The equations (49) and (50) give

$$\begin{aligned} e\sin(u-\omega) &= \frac{V^2}{k^2}r\sin\psi_0\cos\psi_0, \\ e\cos(u-\omega) &= \frac{V^2}{k^2}r\sin^2\psi_0 - 1, \end{aligned}$$

and, since

$$\frac{V^2}{k^2} = \frac{2}{r} - \frac{1}{a},$$

these are easily transformed into

$$\begin{aligned} 2ae\sin(u-\omega) &= (2a-r)\sin 2\psi_0, \\ 2ae\cos(u-\omega) &= -(2a-r)\cos 2\psi_0 - r. \end{aligned}$$

If we multiply the first of these equations by $-\cos u$ and the second by $\sin u$, and add the products; then multiply the first by $\sin u$ and the second by $\cos u$, and add, we obtain

$$\begin{aligned} 2ae\sin\omega &= -(2a-r)\sin(2\psi_0 + u) - r\sin u, \\ 2ae\cos\omega &= -(2a-r)\cos(2\psi_0 + u) - r\cos u, \end{aligned} \tag{52}$$

These equations give the values of ω and e.

113. We have thus derived all the formulæ necessary for finding the elements of the orbit of a heavenly body from one geocentric distance, provided that the first and second differential coefficients of α and δ with respect to the time are accurately known. It remains,

therefore, to devise the means by which these differential coefficients may be determined with accuracy from the data furnished by observation. The approximate elements derived from three or from a small number of observations will enable us to correct the entire series of observations for parallax and aberration, and to form the normal places which shall represent the series of observed places. We may now assume that the deviation of the spherical co-ordinates computed by means of the approximate elements from those which would be obtained if the true elements were used, may be exactly represented by the formula

$$\Delta\theta = A + Bh + Ch^2, \qquad (53)$$

h denoting the interval between the time at which the deviation is expressed by A and the time for which this difference is $\Delta\theta$. The differences between the normal places and those computed with the approximate elements to be corrected, will then suffice to form equations of condition by means of which the values of the coefficients A, B, and C may be determined. The epoch for which $h = 0$ may be chosen arbitrarily, but it will generally be advantageous to fix it at or near the date of the middle observed place. If three observed places are given, the difference between the observed and the computed value of each right ascension will give an equation of condition, according to (53), and the three equations thus formed will furnish the numerical values of A, B, and C. These having been determined, the equation (53) will give the correction to be applied to the computed right ascension for any date within the limits of the extreme observations of the series. When more than three normal places are determined, the resulting equations of condition may be reduced by the method of least squares to three final equations, from which, by elimination, the most probable values of A, B, and C will be derived. In like manner, the corrections to be applied to the computed latitudes may be determined. These corrections being applied, the ephemeris thus obtained may be assumed to represent the apparent path of the body with great precision, and may be employed as an auxiliary in determining the values of the differential coefficients of α and δ with respect to t.

Let $f(a)$ denote the right ascension of the body at the middle epoch or that for which $h = 0$, and let $f(a \pm n\omega)$ denote the value of α for any other date separated by the interval $n\omega$, in which ω is the interval between the successive dates of the ephemeris. Then, if we put n successively equal to 1, 2, 3, &c., we shall have

Function.	I. Diff.	II. Diff.	III. Diff.	IV. Diff.	V. Diff.
$f(a-3\omega)$					
	$f'(a-\frac{5}{2}\omega)$				
$f(a-2\omega)$		$f''(a-2\omega)$			
	$f'(a-\frac{3}{2}\omega)$		$f'''(a-\frac{3}{2}\omega)$		
$f(a-\omega)$		$f''(a-\omega)$		$f^{\text{iv}}(a-\omega)$	
	$f'(a-\frac{1}{2}\omega)$		$f'''(a-\frac{1}{2}\omega)$		$f^{\text{v}}(a-\frac{1}{2}\omega)$
$f(a)$		$f''(a)$		$f^{\text{iv}}(a)$	
	$f'(a+\frac{1}{2}\omega)$		$f'''(a+\frac{1}{2}\omega)$		$f^{\text{v}}(a+\frac{1}{2}\omega)$.
$f(a+\omega)$		$f''(a+\omega)$		$f^{\text{iv}}(a+\omega)$	
	$f'(a+\frac{3}{2}\omega)$		$f'''(a+\frac{3}{2}\omega)$		
$f(a+2\omega)$		$f''(a+2\omega)$			
	$f'(a+\frac{5}{2}\omega)$				
$f(a+3\omega)$					

The series of functions and differences may be extended in the same manner in either direction. If we expand $f(a+n\omega)$ into a series, the result is

$$f(a+n\omega)=\alpha+\frac{d\alpha}{dt}n\omega+\tfrac{1}{2}\frac{d^2\alpha}{dt^2}n^2\omega^2+\tfrac{1}{6}\frac{d^3\alpha}{dt^3}n^3\omega^3+\tfrac{1}{24}\frac{d^4\alpha}{dt^4}n^4\omega^4+\&\text{c.},$$

or, putting for brevity $A=\frac{d\alpha}{dt}\omega$, $B=\frac{1}{2}\frac{d^2\alpha}{dt^2}\omega^2$, &c.,

$$f(\alpha+n\omega)=\alpha+An+Bn^2+Cn^3+Dn^4+\&\text{c.}$$

If we now put n successively equal to $-4, -3, -2, -1, -0, +1$, &c., we obtain the values of $f(a-4\omega), f(a-3\omega), \ldots\ldots f(a+4\omega)$ in terms of A, B, C, &c. Then, taking the successive orders of differences and symbolizing them as indicated above, we obtain a series of equations by means of which A, B, C, &c. will be determined in terms of the successive orders of differences. Finally, replacing A, B, C, &c. by the quantities which they represent, and putting

$$\tfrac{1}{2}f'(a-\tfrac{1}{2}\omega)+\tfrac{1}{2}f'(a+\tfrac{1}{2}\omega)\ \ =f'(a),$$
$$\tfrac{1}{2}f'''(a-\tfrac{1}{2}\omega)+\tfrac{1}{2}f'''(a+\tfrac{1}{2}\omega)=f'''(a),\ \&\text{c.},$$

we obtain

$$\begin{aligned}
\frac{d\alpha}{dt}&=\frac{1}{\omega}\left(f'(a)-\tfrac{1}{6}f'''(a)+\tfrac{1}{30}f^{\text{v}}(a)-\tfrac{1}{140}f^{\text{vii}}(a)+\&\text{c.}\right),\\
\frac{d^2\alpha}{dt^2}&=\frac{1}{\omega^2}\left(f''(a)-\tfrac{1}{12}f^{\text{iv}}(a)+\tfrac{1}{90}f^{\text{vi}}(a)-\tfrac{1}{560}f^{\text{viii}}(a)+\&\text{c.}\right),\\
\frac{d^3\alpha}{dt^3}&=\frac{1}{\omega^3}\left(f'''(a)-\tfrac{1}{4}f^{\text{v}}(a)+\tfrac{7}{120}f^{\text{vii}}(a)-\&\text{c.}\right),\\
\frac{d^4\alpha}{dt^4}&=\frac{1}{\omega^4}\left(f^{\text{iv}}(a)-\tfrac{1}{6}f^{\text{vi}}(a)+\tfrac{7}{240}f^{\text{viii}}(a)-\&\text{c.}\right),\qquad(54)\\
\frac{d^5\alpha}{dt^5}&=\frac{1}{\omega^5}\left(f^{\text{v}}(a)-\tfrac{1}{3}f^{\text{vii}}(a)+\&\text{c.}\right),\\
\frac{d^6\alpha}{dt^6}&=\frac{1}{\omega^6}\left(f^{\text{vi}}(a)-\tfrac{1}{4}f^{\text{viii}}(a)+\&\text{c.}\right),\\
\frac{d^7\alpha}{dt^7}&=\frac{1}{\omega^7}\left(f^{\text{vii}}(a)-\&\text{c.}\right),\qquad \frac{d^8\alpha}{dt^8}=\frac{1}{\omega^8}\left(f^{\text{viii}}(a)-\&\text{c.}\right),
\end{aligned}$$

by means of which the successive differential coefficients of α with respect to t may be determined. The derivation of these coefficients in the case of δ is entirely analogous to the process here indicated for α. Since the successive differences will be expressed in seconds of arc, the resulting values of the differential coefficients of α and δ with respect to t will also be expressed in seconds, and must be divided by 206264.8 in order to express them abstractly.

We may adopt directly the values of $\frac{d\alpha}{dt}, \frac{d^2\alpha}{dt^2}, \frac{d\delta}{dt}$, and $\frac{d^2\delta}{dt^2}$ determined by means of the corrected ephemeris, or, if the observed places do not include a very long interval, we may determine only the values of $\frac{d^3\alpha}{dt^3}, \frac{d^4\alpha}{dt^4}$, &c. by means of the ephemeris, and then find $\frac{d\alpha}{dt}$ and $\frac{d^2\alpha}{dt^2}$ directly from the normal places or observations. Thus, let $\alpha, \alpha', \alpha''$ be three observed right ascensions corresponding to the times t, t', t'', and we shall have

$$\alpha = \alpha' - \frac{d\alpha'}{dt}(t'-t) + \tfrac{1}{2}\frac{d^2\alpha'}{dt^2}(t'-t)^2 - \tfrac{1}{6}\frac{d^3\alpha'}{dt^3}(t'-t)^3 + \tfrac{1}{24}\frac{d^4\alpha'}{dt^4}(t'-t)^4 - \&c.,$$

$$\alpha'' = \alpha' + \frac{d\alpha'}{dt}(t''-t') + \tfrac{1}{2}\frac{d^2\alpha'}{dt^2}(t''-t')^2 + \tfrac{1}{6}\frac{d^3\alpha'}{dt^3}(t''-t')^3 + \tfrac{1}{24}\frac{d^4\alpha'}{dt^4}(t''-t')^4 + \&c.,$$

which give

$$\begin{aligned} \frac{d\alpha'}{dt} - \tfrac{1}{2}(t'-t)\frac{d^2\alpha'}{dt^2} &= \frac{\alpha'-\alpha}{t'-t} - \tfrac{1}{6}(t'-t)^2\frac{d^3\alpha'}{dt^3} + \tfrac{1}{24}(t'-t)^3\frac{d^4\alpha'}{dt^4} - \&c., \\ \frac{d\alpha'}{dt} + \tfrac{1}{2}(t''-t')\frac{d^2\alpha'}{dt^2} &= \frac{\alpha''-\alpha'}{t''-t'} - \tfrac{1}{6}(t''-t')^2\frac{d^3\alpha'}{dt^3} - \tfrac{1}{24}(t''-t')^3\frac{d^4\alpha'}{dt^4} - \&c. \end{aligned} \tag{55}$$

These equations, being solved numerically, will give the values of $\frac{d\alpha'}{dt}$ and $\frac{d^2\alpha'}{dt^2}$, and we may thus by triple combinations of the observed places, using always the same middle place, form equations of condition for the determination of the most probable values of these differential coefficients by the solution of the equations according to the method of least squares.

In a similar manner the values of $\frac{d\delta}{dt}$ and $\frac{d^2\delta}{dt}$ may be derived.

114. In applying these formulæ to the calculation of an orbit, after the normal places have been derived, an ephemeris should be computed at intervals of four or eight days, arranging it so that one of the dates shall correspond to that of the middle observation or normal place. This ephemeris should be computed with the utmost

care, since it is to be employed as an auxiliary in determining quantities on which depends the accuracy of the final results. The comparison of the ephemeris with the observed places will furnish, by means of equations of the form

$$A + Bh + Ch^2 = \Delta\alpha',$$
$$A' + B'h + C'h^2 = \Delta\delta',$$

h being the interval between the middle date t' and that of the place used, the values of A, B, C, A', &c.; and the corrections to be applied to the ephemeris will be determined by

$$A + Bn\omega + Cn^2\omega^2 = \Delta\alpha,$$
$$A' + B'n\omega + C'n^2\omega^2 = \Delta\delta.$$

The unit of h may be ten days, or any other convenient interval, observing, however, that $n\omega$ in the last equations must be expressed in parts of the same unit. With the ephemeris thus corrected, we compute the values of $\frac{d\alpha}{dt}$, $\frac{d^2\alpha}{dt^2}$, $\frac{d\delta}{dt}$, and $\frac{d^2\delta}{dt^2}$ as already explained. These differential coefficients should be determined with great care, since it is on their accuracy that the subsequent calculation principally depends. We compute, also, the velocities $\frac{dX}{dt}$, $\frac{dY}{dt}$, and $\frac{dZ}{dt}$ by means of the formulæ (43), $\frac{d\odot}{dt}$ and $\frac{dR}{dt}$ being computed from (46). The quantities thus far derived remain unchanged in the two hypotheses with regard to $\varDelta$.

Then we assume an approximate value of $\varDelta$, and compute

$$\rho = \varDelta \cos\delta;$$

and by means of the equation (40) or (39) we compute the value of $\frac{d\rho}{dt}$. It will be observed that if we put the equation (40) in the form

$$\frac{d\rho}{dt} = \frac{P}{Q}\rho + \frac{\zeta}{Q}\cot\delta,$$

the coefficient $\frac{P}{Q}$ remains the same in the two hypotheses. The three equations (38) may be so combined that the resulting value of $\frac{d\rho}{dt}$ will not contain $\frac{d^2\alpha}{dt^2}$. This transformation is easily effected, and may be advantageous in special cases for which the value of $\frac{d^2\alpha}{dt^2}$ is very uncertain.

The heliocentric spherical co-ordinates will be obtained from the assumed value of $\varDelta$ by means of the equations $(106)_3$, and the rectangular co-ordinates from

$$x = r\cos b\cos l,$$
$$y = r\cos b\sin l,$$
$$z = r\sin b.$$

The velocities $\frac{dx}{dt}$, $\frac{dy}{dt}$, and $\frac{dz}{dt}$ will be given by (42), and from these and the co-ordinates x, y, z the elements of the orbit will be computed by means of the equations $(32)_1$, (47), (49), &c. With the elements thus derived we compute the geocentric places for the dates of the normals, and find the differences between computation and observation. Then a second system of elements is computed from $\varDelta + \delta\varDelta$, and compared with the observed places. Let the difference between computation and observation for either of the two spherical co-ordinates be denoted by n for the first system of elements, and by n' for the second system. The final correction to be applied to $\varDelta$, in order that the observed place may be exactly represented, will be determined by

$$\frac{\Delta\varDelta}{\delta\varDelta}(n' - n) + n = 0. \tag{56}$$

Each observed right ascension and each observed declination will thus furnish an equation of condition for the determination of $\Delta\varDelta$, observing that the residuals in right ascension should in each case be multiplied by $\cos\delta$. Finally, the elements which correspond to the geocentric distance $\varDelta + \Delta\varDelta$ will be determined either directly or by interpolation, and these must represent the entire series of observed places.

115. The equations $(52)_3$ enable us to find two radii-vectores when the ratio of the corresponding curtate distances is known, provided that an additional equation involving r, r'', $\varkappa$, and known quantities is given. For the special case of parabolic motion, this additional equation involves only the interval of time, the two radii-vectores, and the chord joining their extremities. The corresponding equation for the general conic section involves also the semi-transverse axis of the orbit, and hence, if the ratio M of the curtate distances is known, this equation will, in connection with the equations $(52)_3$, enable us to find the values of r and r'' corresponding to a given value of a. To derive this expression, let us resume the equations

$$\frac{\tau'}{a^{\frac{3}{2}}} = E'' - E - 2e \sin \tfrac{1}{2}(E'' - E) \cos \tfrac{1}{2}(E'' + E),$$
$$r + r'' = 2a - 2ae \cos \tfrac{1}{2}(E'' - E) \cos \tfrac{1}{2}(E'' + E). \qquad (57)$$

For the chord $\varkappa$ we have

$$\varkappa^2 = (r + r'')^2 - 4rr'' \cos^2 \tfrac{1}{2}(u'' - u),$$

which, by means of $(58)_4$, gives

$$\kappa^2 = (r + r'')^2 - 4a^2 \left(\cos^2 \tfrac{1}{2}(E'' - E) - 2e \cos \tfrac{1}{2}(E'' - E) \cos \tfrac{1}{2}(E'' + E) + e^2 \cos^2 \tfrac{1}{2}(E'' + E)\right);$$

and, substituting for $r + r''$ its value given by the last of equations (57), we get

$$\varkappa^2 = 4a^2 \sin^2 \tfrac{1}{2}(E'' - E) \left(1 - e^2 \cos^2 \tfrac{1}{2}(E'' + E)\right). \qquad (58)$$

Let us now introduce an auxiliary angle h, such that

$$\cos h = e \cos \tfrac{1}{2}(E'' + E),$$

the condition being imposed that h shall be less than 180°, and put

$$g = \tfrac{1}{2}(E'' - E);$$

then the equations (57) and (58) become

$$\frac{\tau'}{a^{\frac{3}{2}}} = 2g - 2 \sin g \cos h,$$
$$r + r'' = 2a(1 - \cos g \cos h), \qquad (59)$$
$$\varkappa = 2a \sin g \sin h.$$

Further, let us put

$$h - g = \delta, \qquad h + g = \varepsilon,$$

and the last two of equations (59) give

$$r + r'' + \varkappa = 4a \sin^2 \tfrac{1}{2}\varepsilon,$$
$$r + r'' - \varkappa = 4a \sin^2 \tfrac{1}{2}\delta. \qquad (60)$$

Introducing δ and ε into the first of equations (59), it becomes

$$\frac{\tau'}{a^{\frac{3}{2}}} = (\varepsilon - \sin \varepsilon) - (\delta - \sin \delta). \qquad (61)$$

The formulæ (60) enable us to determine ε and δ from $r + r''$, $\varkappa$, and a, and then the time $\tau' = k(t'' - t)$ may be determined from (61). Since, according to $(58)_4$,

$$\sqrt{rr''} \cos \tfrac{1}{2}(u'' - u) = a(\cos g - \cos h) = 2_a \sin \tfrac{1}{2}\varepsilon \sin \tfrac{1}{2}\delta,$$

and since $\sin \frac{1}{2}\varepsilon$ is necessarily positive, it appears that when $u'' - u$ exceeds $180°$, the value of $\sin \frac{1}{2}\delta$ must be negative, and when $u'' - u = 180°$, we have $\delta = 0$; and thus the quadrant in which δ must be taken is determined. It will be observed that the value of $\frac{1}{2}\varepsilon$, as given by the first of equations (60), may be either in the first or the second quadrant; but, in the actual application of the formulæ, the ambiguity is easily removed by means of the known circumstances in regard to the motion of the body during the interval $t'' - t$.

In the application of the equations $(52)_3$, by means of an approximate value of $\varkappa$ we compute d, and thence r and r''. Then we compute ε and δ corresponding to the given value of a, and from (61) we derive the value of

$$t'' - t = \frac{\tau'}{k}.$$

If this agrees with the observed interval $t'' - t$, the assumed value of $\varkappa$ is correct; but if a difference exists, by varying $\varkappa$ we may readily find, by a few trials, the value which will exactly satisfy the equations. The formulæ $(70)_3$ will then enable us to determine the curtate distances ρ and ρ'', and from these and the observed spherical co-ordinates the elements of the orbit may be found.

As soon as the values of u and u'' have been computed, since $\varepsilon - \delta = E'' - E$, we have, according to equation $(85)_4$,

$$\cos \varphi = \frac{\sin \frac{1}{2}(u'' - u)}{a \sin \frac{1}{2}(\varepsilon - \delta)} \sqrt{rr''},$$

which may be used to determine φ when the orbit is very eccentric. To find p and q, we have

$$p = a \cos^2 \varphi, \qquad q = 2a \sin^2 (45° - \tfrac{1}{2}\varphi);$$

and the value of ω may be found by means of the equations $(87)_4$ or $(88)_4$.

116. The process here indicated will be applied chiefly in the determination of the orbits of comets, and generally for cases in which a is large. In such cases the angles ε and δ will be small, so that the slightest errors will have considerable influence in vitiating the value of $t'' - t$ as determined by equation (61); but if we transform this equation so as to eliminate the divisor $a^{\frac{3}{2}}$ in the first member, the uncertainty of the solution may be overcome. The difference $\varepsilon - \sin \varepsilon$

may be expressed by a series which converges rapidly when ε is small. Thus, let us put

$$\varepsilon - \sin\varepsilon = y\sin^3\tfrac{1}{2}\varepsilon, \qquad x = \sin^2\tfrac{1}{4}\varepsilon,$$

and we have

$$\frac{dy}{d\varepsilon} = 2\operatorname{cosec}\tfrac{1}{2}\varepsilon - \tfrac{3}{2}y\cot\tfrac{1}{2}\varepsilon,$$

$$\frac{d\varepsilon}{dx} = 4\operatorname{cosec}\tfrac{1}{2}\varepsilon.$$

Therefore

$$\frac{dy}{dx} = \frac{8 - 6y\cos\frac{1}{2}\varepsilon}{\sin^2\frac{1}{2}\varepsilon} = \frac{4 - 3y(1-2x)}{2x(1-x)}.$$

If we suppose y to be expanded into a series of the form

$$y = \alpha + \beta x + \gamma x^2 + \delta x^3 + \text{\&c.},$$

we get, by differentiation,

$$\frac{dy}{dx} = \beta + 2\gamma x + 3\delta x^2 + \text{\&c.},$$

and substituting for $\frac{dy}{dx}$ the value already obtained, the result is

$$\begin{aligned} 2\beta x + (4\gamma - 2\beta)x^2 + (6\delta - 4\gamma)x^3 + \text{\&c.} = 4 - 3\alpha &+ (6\alpha - 3\beta)x \\ &+ (6\beta - 3\gamma)x^2 + (6\gamma - 3\delta)x^3 + \text{\&c.} \end{aligned}$$

Therefore we have

$$4 - 3\alpha = 0, \qquad 6\alpha - 3\beta = 2\beta,$$
$$6\beta - 3\gamma = 4\gamma - 2\beta, \qquad 6\gamma - 3\delta = 6\delta - 4\gamma,$$

from which we get

$$\alpha = \tfrac{4}{3}, \qquad \beta = \frac{4\,.\,6}{3\,.\,5}, \qquad \gamma = \frac{4\,.\,6\,.\,8}{3\,.\,5\,.\,7}, \qquad \delta = \frac{4\,.\,6\,.\,8\,.\,10}{3\,.\,5\,.\,7\,.\,9}, \text{ \&c.}$$

Hence we obtain

$$\varepsilon - \sin\varepsilon = \tfrac{4}{3}\sin^3\tfrac{1}{2}\varepsilon\left(1 + \tfrac{6}{5}\sin^2\tfrac{1}{4}\varepsilon + \frac{6\,.\,8}{5\,.\,7}\sin^4\tfrac{1}{4}\varepsilon + \frac{6\,.\,8\,.\,10}{5\,.\,7\,.\,9}\sin^6\tfrac{1}{4}\varepsilon + \text{\&c.}\right), \quad (62)$$

and, in like manner,

$$\delta - \sin\delta = \tfrac{4}{3}\sin^3\tfrac{1}{2}\delta\left(1 + \tfrac{6}{5}\sin^2\tfrac{1}{4}\delta + \frac{6\,.\,8}{5\,.\,7}\sin^4\tfrac{1}{4}\delta + \frac{6\,.\,8\,.\,10}{5\,.\,7\,.\,9}\sin^6\tfrac{1}{4}\delta + \text{\&c.}\right), \quad (63)$$

which, for brevity, may be written

$$\begin{aligned} \varepsilon - \sin\varepsilon &= \tfrac{4}{3}Q\sin^3\tfrac{1}{2}\varepsilon, \\ \delta - \sin\delta &= \tfrac{4}{3}Q'\sin^3\tfrac{1}{2}\delta, \end{aligned} \quad (64)$$

Combining these expressions with (61), and substituting for $\sin \frac{1}{2}\varepsilon$ and $\sin \frac{1}{2}\delta$ their values given by the equations (60), there results

$$6\tau' = Q(r + r'' + \varkappa)^{\frac{3}{2}} \mp Q'(r + r'' - \varkappa)^{\frac{3}{2}}, \tag{65}$$

the upper sign being used when the heliocentric motion of the body is less than 180°, and the lower sign when it is greater than 180°. The coefficients Q and Q' represent, respectively, the series of terms enclosed in the parentheses in the second members of the equations (62) and (63), and it is evident that their values may be tabulated with the argument ε or δ, as the case may be. It will be observed, however, that the first two terms of the value of Q are identical with the first two terms of the expansion of $(\cos \frac{1}{4}\varepsilon)^{-\frac{12}{5}}$ into a series of ascending powers of $\sin \frac{1}{4}\varepsilon$, while the difference is very small between the coefficients of the third terms. Thus, we have

$$(\cos \tfrac{1}{4}\varepsilon)^{-\frac{12}{5}} = (1 - \sin^2 \tfrac{1}{4}\varepsilon)^{-\frac{6}{5}} = 1 + \tfrac{6}{5}\sin^2 \tfrac{1}{4}\varepsilon + \frac{6\,.\,11}{5\,.\,10}\sin^4 \tfrac{1}{4}\varepsilon + \frac{6\,.\,11\,.\,16}{5\,.\,10\,.\,15}\sin^6 \tfrac{1}{4}\varepsilon + \&c.,$$

and if we put

$$Q = \frac{B_0}{(\cos \frac{1}{4}\varepsilon)^{\frac{12}{5}}}, \tag{66}$$

we shall have

$$B_0 = 1 + \tfrac{9}{175}\sin^4 \tfrac{1}{4}\varepsilon + \tfrac{142}{2625}\sin^6 \tfrac{1}{4}\varepsilon + \&c. \tag{67}$$

In a similar manner, if we put

$$Q' = \frac{B_0'}{(\cos \frac{1}{4}\delta)^{\frac{12}{5}}}, \tag{68}$$

we find

$$B_0' = 1 + \tfrac{9}{175}\sin^4 \tfrac{1}{4}\delta + \tfrac{142}{2625}\sin^6 \tfrac{1}{4}\delta + \&c. \tag{69}$$

Table XV. gives the values of B_0 or B_0' corresponding to ε or δ from 0° to 60°.

For the case of parabolic motion we have

$$Q = 1, \qquad Q' = 1,$$

and the equation (65) becomes identical with $(56)_3$.

In the application of these formulæ, we first compute ε and δ by means of the equations (60), and then, having found B_0 and B_0' by means of Table XV., we compute the values of Q and Q' from (66) and (68). Finally, the time $\tau' = k(t'' - t)$ will be obtained from (65), and the difference between this result and the observed interval will indicate whether the assumed value of $\varkappa$ must be increased or diminished. A few trials will give the correct result.

117. Since the interval of time $t''-t$ cannot be determined with sufficient accuracy from (65) when the chord $\varkappa$ is very small, it becomes necessary to effect a further transformation of this equation. Thus, let us put

$$Q-Q'=6P, \qquad x=\sin^2\tfrac{1}{4}\varepsilon, \qquad x'=\sin^2\tfrac{1}{4}\delta,$$

and we shall have

$$P=\tfrac{1}{5}(x-x')\left(1+\tfrac{8}{7}(x+x')+\frac{8\,.\,10}{7\,.\,9}(x^2+xx'+x'^2)+\&c.\right).$$

Now, when $\varkappa$ is very small, we may put

$$\cos\tfrac{1}{4}\varepsilon=\cos\tfrac{1}{4}\delta,$$

and hence

$$x-x'=\sin^2\tfrac{1}{4}\varepsilon-\sin^2\tfrac{1}{4}\delta=\frac{\sin^2\frac{1}{2}\varepsilon-\sin^2\frac{1}{2}\delta}{4\cos^2\frac{1}{4}\varepsilon},$$

which, by means of equations (60), becomes

$$x-x'=\frac{\varkappa}{8a\cos^2\frac{1}{4}\varepsilon}.$$

Therefore we have, when $\varkappa$ is very small,

$$P=\frac{\varkappa}{40a\cos^2\frac{1}{4}\varepsilon}\left(1+\tfrac{16}{7}\sin^2\tfrac{1}{4}\varepsilon+\tfrac{80}{21}\sin^4\tfrac{1}{4}\varepsilon+\&c.\right) \tag{70}$$

If we put

$$\tau_0'=\frac{\tau'-P(r+r''-\varkappa)^{\frac{3}{2}}}{Q}, \tag{71}$$

the equation (65) becomes, using only the upper sign,

$$(r+r''+\varkappa)^{\frac{3}{2}}-(r+r''-\varkappa)^{\frac{3}{2}}=6\tau_0', \tag{72}$$

which is of the same form as $(56)_3$. Hence, according to the equations $(63)_3$ and $(66)_3$, we shall have

$$\varkappa=\frac{2\tau_0'}{\sqrt{r+r''}}\,\mu, \tag{73}$$

the value of μ being found from Table XI. with the argument

$$\eta=\frac{2\tau_0'}{(r+r'')^{\frac{3}{2}}}. \tag{74}$$

It remains, therefore, simply to find a convenient expression for τ_0', and the determination of $\varkappa$ is effected by a process precisely the same as in the special case of parabolic motion.

Let us now put

$$\frac{P}{Q}=\frac{\varkappa}{40a}\cdot\frac{N}{\cos^4\frac{1}{4}\varepsilon},$$

and we shall have

$$N=\frac{\cos^2\frac{1}{4}\varepsilon}{Q}\left(1+\frac{2\,.\,8}{7}\sin^2\tfrac{1}{4}\varepsilon+\frac{3\,.\,8\,.\,10}{7\,.\,9}\sin^4\tfrac{1}{4}\varepsilon+\frac{4\,.\,8\,.\,10\,.\,12}{7\,.\,9\,.\,11}\sin^6\tfrac{1}{4}\varepsilon+\&c.\right),$$

or, substituting for Q its value in terms of $\sin\frac{1}{4}\varepsilon$,

$$N=1+\tfrac{3}{35}\sin^2\tfrac{1}{4}\varepsilon+\tfrac{26}{525}\sin^4\tfrac{1}{4}\varepsilon+\tfrac{2076}{67375}\sin^6\tfrac{1}{4}\varepsilon+\&c. \qquad (75)$$

Therefore, if we put

$$\Delta\tau_0'=\frac{\varkappa}{40a}\cdot\frac{N}{\cos^4\frac{1}{4}\varepsilon}(r+r''-\varkappa)^{\frac{3}{2}}, \qquad (76)$$

the expression for τ_0' becomes

$$\tau_0'=\frac{\tau'}{Q}-\Delta\tau_0'. \qquad (77)$$

Table XV. gives the value of $\log N$ corresponding to values of ε from $\varepsilon=0$ to $\varepsilon=60^\circ$.

If the chord $\varkappa$ is given, and the interval of time $t''-t$ is required, we compute $\Delta\tau_0'$ by means of (76), and, having found τ_0' from

$$\tau_0'=\frac{\varkappa\sqrt{r+r''}}{2\mu},$$

as in the case of parabolic motion, we have

$$t''-t=\frac{Q\,(\tau_0'+\Delta\tau_0')}{k}.$$

It should be observed that although equation (76) is derived for the case of a small value of $\varkappa$, yet it is applicable whenever the difference $\varepsilon-\delta$ is very small, whatever may be the value of $\varkappa$. For orbits which differ but little from the parabolic form, it will in all cases be sufficient to use this expression for $\Delta\tau_0'$; and for cases in which the difference between ε and δ is such that the assumption of $\cos\frac{1}{4}\varepsilon=\cos\frac{1}{4}\delta$, $x+x'=2x$, &c., made in deriving equation (70), does not afford the required accuracy, we may compute both Q and Q' directly, and then we have

$$\Delta\tau_0' = \tfrac{1}{6}\left(1 - \frac{Q'}{Q}\right)(r + r'' - \varkappa)^{\frac{3}{2}}. \tag{78}$$

The values of the factor $\frac{1}{6}\left(1 - \frac{Q'}{Q}\right)$ may be tabulated directly with $\frac{r+r''}{4a}$ as the vertical argument and $\frac{\varkappa}{4a}$ as the horizontal argument; but for the few cases in which the value of N given by the equation (75) is not sufficiently accurate, it will be easy to compute Q and Q' by means of the formulæ (66) and (68), and then find $\Delta\tau_0'$ from (78). Further, when there is any doubt as to the accuracy of the result given by (76), for the final trial in finding $\varkappa$ from $r + r''$ and τ_0 by means of the equations (73) and (74), it will be advisable to compute $\Delta\tau_0'$ from (78).

It appears, therefore, that for nearly all the cases which actually occur the determination of the value of $\varkappa$, corresponding to given values of a and $M = \frac{\rho''}{\rho}$, is reduced by means of the equation (72) to the method which is adopted in the case of parabolic orbits.

The calculation of the numerical values of $r + r'' + \varkappa$ and $r + r'' - \varkappa$ will be most conveniently effected by the aid of addition and subtraction logarithms. If the tables of common logarithms are used, we may first compute

$$\sin\gamma' = \frac{\varkappa}{r + r''},$$

and then we have

$$r + r'' + \varkappa = 2(r + r'')\sin^2(45° + \tfrac{1}{2}\gamma'),$$
$$r + r'' - \varkappa = 2(r + r'')\cos^2(45° + \tfrac{1}{2}\gamma').$$

118. In the case of hyperbolic motion, the semi-transverse axis is negative, and the values of $\sin\frac{1}{2}\varepsilon$ and $\sin\frac{1}{2}\delta$ given by the equations (60) become imaginary, so that it is no longer possible to compute the interval of time from $r + r''$ and $\varkappa$ by means of the auxiliary angles ε and δ. Let us, therefore, put

$$\sin^2\tfrac{1}{2}\varepsilon = -m^2, \qquad \sin^2\tfrac{1}{2}\delta = -n^2;$$

then, when a is negative, m and n will be real. Now we have

$$\tfrac{1}{2}\varepsilon = \sin^{-1}\sqrt{-m^2}, \qquad \tfrac{1}{2}\delta = \sin^{-1}\sqrt{-n^2},$$

and

$$\tfrac{1}{2}\varepsilon\sqrt{-1} = \log_e(\cos\tfrac{1}{2}\varepsilon + \sqrt{-1}\sin\tfrac{1}{2}\varepsilon).$$

Hence we derive

$$\varepsilon = 2 \sin^{-1} \sqrt{-m^2} = \frac{2}{\sqrt{-1}} \log_e (\sqrt{1 + m^2} + m),$$

$$\delta = 2 \sin^{-1} \sqrt{-n^2} = \frac{2}{\sqrt{-1}} \log_e (\sqrt{1 + n^2} + n).$$

Substituting these values in the equation (61), and writing $-a$ instead of a, since

$$\sin \varepsilon = 2m \sqrt{-1} \cdot \sqrt{1 + m^2},$$

we shall have

$$\begin{aligned} \frac{\tau'}{a^{\frac{3}{2}}} = 2m \sqrt{1 + m^2} - 2 \log_e (\sqrt{1 + m^2} + m) \\ \mp (2n \sqrt{1 + n^2} - 2 \log_e (\sqrt{1 + n^2} + n)), \end{aligned} \tag{79}$$

the upper sign being used when the heliocentric motion is less than 180°, and the lower sign when it is greater than 180°. Therefore, if we compute m and n from

$$m = \sqrt{\frac{r + r'' + \varkappa}{4a}}, \qquad n = \sqrt{\frac{r + r'' - \varkappa}{4a}}, \tag{80}$$

regarding the hyperbolic semi-transverse axis a as positive, the formula (79) will determine the interval of time $\tau' = k(t'' - t)$.

The first two terms of the second member of equation (79) may be expressed in a series of ascending powers of m, and the last two terms in a series of ascending powers of n. Thus, if we put

$$\log_e (\sqrt{1 + m^2} + m) = \alpha m + \beta m^2 + \gamma m^3 + \delta m^4 + \&c.,$$

we get, by differentiation,

$$\frac{1}{\sqrt{1 + m^2}} = \alpha + 2\beta m + 3\gamma m^2 + 4\delta m^3 + 5\varepsilon m^4 + \&c.;$$

and since

$$\frac{1}{\sqrt{1 + m^2}} = 1 - \tfrac{1}{2} m^2 + \frac{1 \cdot 3}{2 \cdot 4} m^4 - \frac{1 \cdot 3 \cdot 5}{2 \cdot 4 \cdot 6} m^6 + \&c.,$$

we have

$$\alpha = 1, \qquad \beta = 0, \qquad \gamma = -\tfrac{1}{3} \cdot \tfrac{1}{2}, \qquad \delta = 0, \qquad \varepsilon = \tfrac{1}{5} \frac{1 \cdot 3}{2 \cdot 4}, \ \&$$

Hence we obtain

$$2 \log_e (\sqrt{1 + m^2} + m) = 2m - \tfrac{1}{3} m^3 + \tfrac{1}{5} \cdot \tfrac{3}{4} m^5 - \tfrac{1}{7} \frac{3 \cdot 5}{4 \cdot 6} m^7 + \&c.$$

We have, also,

$$2m\sqrt{1+m^2} = 2m + m^3 - \tfrac{1}{4}m^5 + \frac{1\cdot 3}{4\cdot 6}m^7 - \&c.$$

Therefore,

$$2m\sqrt{1+m^2} - 2\log_e(\sqrt{1+m^2}+m) = \tfrac{4}{3}m^3\left(1 - \tfrac{3}{5}\cdot\tfrac{1}{2}m^2 + \tfrac{3}{7}\frac{1\cdot 3}{2\cdot 4}m^4 - \&c.\right), \tag{81}$$

and similarly

$$2n\sqrt{1+n^2} - 2\log_e(\sqrt{1+n^2}+n) = \tfrac{4}{3}n^3\left(1 - \tfrac{3}{5}\cdot\tfrac{1}{2}n^2 + \tfrac{3}{7}\frac{1\cdot 3}{2\cdot 4}n^4 - \&c.\right). \tag{82}$$

Substituting these values in the equation (79), and denoting the series of terms enclosed in the parentheses by Q and Q', respectively, we get

$$6\tau' = Q(r + r'' + \varkappa)^{\frac{3}{2}} \mp Q'(r + r'' - \varkappa)^{\frac{3}{2}} \tag{83}$$

which is identical with equation (65). If we replace m^2 by $-\sin^2\tfrac{1}{2}\varepsilon$ and n^2 by $-\sin^2\tfrac{1}{2}\delta$ in the expressions for Q and Q', as given by (81) and (82), we shall have the expressions for these quantities in terms of $\sin\tfrac{1}{2}\varepsilon$ and $\sin\tfrac{1}{2}\delta$, respectively, instead of $\sin\tfrac{1}{4}\varepsilon$ and $\sin\tfrac{1}{4}\delta$ as given by the equations (62) and (63), namely,

$$\begin{aligned} Q &= 1 + \tfrac{3}{5}\cdot\tfrac{1}{2}\sin^2\tfrac{1}{2}\varepsilon + \tfrac{3}{7}\frac{1\cdot 3}{2\cdot 4}\sin^4\tfrac{1}{2}\varepsilon + \tfrac{3}{9}\frac{1\cdot 3\cdot 5}{2\cdot 4\cdot 6}\sin^6\tfrac{1}{2}\varepsilon + \&c., \\ Q' &= 1 + \tfrac{3}{5}\cdot\tfrac{1}{2}\sin^2\tfrac{1}{2}\delta + \tfrac{3}{7}\frac{1\cdot 3}{2\cdot 4}\sin^4\tfrac{1}{2}\delta + \tfrac{3}{9}\frac{1\cdot 3\cdot 5}{2\cdot 4\cdot 6}\sin^6\tfrac{1}{2}\delta + \&c. \end{aligned} \tag{84}$$

For the case of an elliptic orbit it is most convenient to use the equations (66) and (68) in finding Q and Q'; but, since the cases of hyperbolic motion are rare, while for those which do occur the eccentricity is very little greater than that of the parabola, it will be sufficient to tabulate Q directly with the argument m. The same table, using n as the argument, will give the value of Q'. Table XVI. gives the values of Q corresponding to values of m from $m = 0$ to $m = 0.2$.

When the values of $r + r''$, τ', and a are given, and the chord $\varkappa$ is required, we may compute $\Delta\tau_0'$ from (78), τ_0' from (77), and finally $\varkappa$ from (73).

It may be remarked, also, that the formulæ for the relation between τ', $r + r''$, $\varkappa$, and a suffice to find by trial the value of a when $r + r''$ and $\varkappa$ are given. Hence, in the computation of an orbit from assumed values of $\varDelta$ and $\varDelta''$, the value of $\varkappa$ may be computed from r, r'', and $u''-u$, and then a may be found in the manner here indicated.

If we substitute in the equations (84) the values of $\sin\frac{1}{2}\varepsilon$ and $\sin\frac{1}{2}\delta$ in terms of $r+r''$, $\varkappa$, and a, and then substitute the resulting values of Q and Q' in the equation (65), we obtain

$$6k(t''-t) = (r+r''+\varkappa)^{\frac{3}{2}} \mp (r+r''-\varkappa)^{\frac{3}{2}} + \tfrac{3}{40}\frac{1}{a}\left((r+r''+\varkappa)^{\frac{5}{2}} \mp (r+r''-\varkappa)^{\frac{5}{2}}\right)$$
$$+ \tfrac{9}{896}\frac{1}{a^2}\left((r+r''+\varkappa)^{\frac{7}{2}} \mp (r+r''-\varkappa)^{\frac{7}{2}}\right) + \&c., \qquad (85)$$

the lower sign being used when $u''-u$ exceeds 180°. When the eccentricity is very nearly equal to unity, this series converges with great rapidity. In the case of hyperbolic motion, the sign of a must be changed.

119. The formulæ thus derived for the determination of the chord $\varkappa$ for the cases of elliptic and hyperbolic orbits, enable us to correct an approximate orbit by varying the semi-transverse axis a and the ratio M of two curtate distances. But since the formulæ will generally be applied for the correction of approximate parabolic elements, or those which are nearly parabolic, it will be expedient to use $\frac{1}{a}$ and M as the quantities to be determined.

In the first place, we compute a system of elements from M and $f=\frac{1}{a}$; and, for the determination of the auxiliary quantities preliminary to the calculation of the values of r, r'', and $\varkappa$, the equations $(41)_3$, $(50)_3$, and $(51)_3$ will be employed when the ecliptic is the fundamental plane. But when the equator is taken as the fundamental plane, we must first compute g, K, and G by means of the equations $(96)_3$. Then, by a process entirely analogous to that by which the equations $(47)_3$ and $(50)_3$ were derived, we obtain

$$\begin{aligned} h\cos\zeta\cos(H-\alpha'') &= M-\cos(\alpha''-\alpha), \\ h\cos\zeta\sin(H-\alpha'') &= \sin(\alpha''-\alpha), \\ h\sin\zeta &= M\tan\delta''-\tan\delta, \end{aligned} \qquad (86)$$

from which to find H, ζ, and h; and also

$$\cos\varphi = \cos\zeta\cos K\cos(G-H)+\sin\zeta\sin K, \qquad (87)$$

from which to find φ. In this case, ζ and H will be referred to the equator as the fundamental plane. The angles ψ and ψ'' will be obtained from the equations $(102)_3$, or from equations of the form of (26), and finally the auxiliary quantities A, B, B'', &c. will be obtained from $(51)_3$, writing δ and δ'' in place of β and β'', respectively.

As soon as these auxiliary quantities have been determined, by means of $(52)_3$ the value of $\varkappa$ must be found which will exactly satisfy equation (65). To effect this, we first compute ε from

$$\sin \tfrac{1}{2}\varepsilon = \sqrt{\tfrac{1}{4}f(r + r'' + \varkappa)},$$

and, if it be required, we also find δ from

$$\sin \tfrac{1}{2}\delta = \sqrt{\tfrac{1}{4}f(r + r'' - \varkappa)},$$

using approximate values of $r + r''$ and $\varkappa$. Then we find Q from (66), and $\Delta\tau_0'$ from (76) or from (78), the logarithms of the auxiliary quantities B_0 and N being found by means of Table XV. with the argument ε. The value of τ_0' having been found from (77), the equations (73) and (74), in connection with Table XI., enable us to obtain a closer approximation to the correct value of $\varkappa$. With this we compute new values of r and r'', and repeat the determination of $\varkappa$. A few trials will generally give the correct result, and these trials may be facilitated by the use of the formula $(67)_3$. It will be observed, also, that Q and $\Delta\tau_0'$ are very slightly changed by a small change in the values of $r + r''$ and $\varkappa$, so that a repetition of the calculation of these quantities only becomes necessary for the final trial in finding the value of $\varkappa$ which completely satisfies the equations $(52)_3$ and (65). When the value of a is such that the values of Q and N exceed the limits of Table XV., the equation (61) may be employed, and, in the case of hyperbolic motion, when Q and Q' exceed the limits of Table XVI., we may employ the complete expression for the time τ' in terms of m and n as given by (79).

The values of r, r'', and $\varkappa$ having thus been found, the equations

$$d = \sqrt{\varkappa^2 - A^2}, \qquad \rho = \frac{d + g\cos\varphi}{h}, \qquad \rho'' = M\rho,$$

will determine the curtate distances ρ and ρ''. When the equator is the fundamental plane, we have

$$\rho = \Delta\cos\delta, \qquad \rho'' = \Delta''\cos\delta''.$$

From ρ, ρ'', and the corresponding geocentric spherical co-ordinates, the radii-vectores and the heliocentric spherical co-ordinates l, l'', b, and b'' will be obtained, and thence Ω, i, u, u'', and the remaining elements of the orbit, as already illustrated. In the case of elliptic motion, if we compute the auxiliary quantities ε and δ by means of the equations (60), we shall have

$$e \sin \tfrac{1}{2}(E'' + E) = \frac{r'' - r}{2a \sin \frac{1}{2}(\varepsilon - \delta)},$$
$$e \cos \tfrac{1}{2}(E'' + E) = \cos \tfrac{1}{2}(\varepsilon + \delta),$$

from which e and $\frac{1}{2}(E'' + E)$ may be found, and hence, since $\frac{1}{2}(E'' - E) = \frac{1}{2}(\varepsilon - \delta)$, we derive E and E''. The values of q and v may then be found directly from these and quantities already obtained. Thus, the last of equations $(43)_1$ gives

$$\frac{\cos \frac{1}{2}v}{\sqrt{q}} = \frac{\cos \frac{1}{2}E}{\sqrt{r}}, \qquad \frac{\cos \frac{1}{2}v''}{\sqrt{q}} = \frac{\cos \frac{1}{2}E''}{\sqrt{r''}}.$$

Multiplying the first of these expressions by $\sin \frac{1}{2}v''$, and the second by $-\sin \frac{1}{2}v$, adding the products, and reducing, we obtain

$$\frac{\sin \frac{1}{2}(v'' - v) \sin \frac{1}{2}v}{\sqrt{q}} = \frac{\cos \frac{1}{2}(v'' - v) \cos \frac{1}{2}E}{\sqrt{r}} - \frac{\cos \frac{1}{2}E''}{\sqrt{r''}}.$$

Therefore, we shall have

$$\begin{aligned} \frac{1}{\sqrt{q}} \sin \tfrac{1}{2}v &= \frac{\cos \frac{1}{2}E}{\sqrt{r} \tan \frac{1}{2}(u'' - u)} - \frac{\cos \frac{1}{2}E''}{\sqrt{r''} \sin \frac{1}{2}(u'' - u)}, \\ \frac{1}{\sqrt{q}} \cos \tfrac{1}{2}v &= \frac{\cos \frac{1}{2}E}{\sqrt{r}}, \end{aligned} \tag{88}$$

from which q and v may be found as soon as $\cos \frac{1}{2}E$ and $\cos \frac{1}{2}E''$ are known. In the case of parabolic motion the eccentric anomaly is equal to zero, and these equations become identical with $(92)_3$. The angular distance of the perihelion from the ascending node will be obtained from

$$\omega = u - v.$$

Since $r = a - ae \cos E$, and $q = a(1 - e)$, we have

$$\cos E = \frac{1 - \frac{r}{a}}{1 - \frac{q}{a}} = 1 - \frac{\frac{r}{q} - 1}{\frac{a}{q} - 1},$$

and hence

$$\begin{aligned} \cos^2 \tfrac{1}{2}E &= 1 - \tfrac{1}{2} \frac{\frac{r}{q} - 1}{\frac{a}{q} - 1}, \\ \cos^2 \tfrac{1}{2}E'' &= 1 - \tfrac{1}{2} \frac{\frac{r''}{q} - 1}{\frac{a}{q} - 1}. \end{aligned} \tag{89}$$

When the eccentricity is nearly equal to unity, the value of q given by approximate elements will be sufficient to compute $\cos\frac{1}{2}E$ and $\cos\frac{1}{2}E''$ by means of these equations, and the results thus derived will be substituted in the equations (88), from which a new value of q results. If this should differ considerably from that used in computing $\cos\frac{1}{2}E$ and $\cos\frac{1}{2}E''$, a repetition of the calculation will give the correct result.

In the case of hyperbolic motion, although E and E'' are imaginary, we may compute the numerical values of $\cos\frac{1}{2}E$ and $\cos\frac{1}{2}E''$ from the equations (89), regarding a as negative, and the results will be used for the corresponding quantities in (88) in the computation of q and v for the hyperbolic orbit.

Next, we compute a second system of elements from M and $f+\delta f$, and a third system from $M+\delta M$ and f, δf and δM denoting the arbitrary increments assigned to f and M respectively. The comparison of these three systems of elements with additional observed places of the comet, will enable us to form the equations of condition for the determination of the most probable values of the corrections ΔM and Δf to be applied to M and f respectively. The formation of these equations is effected in precisely the same manner as in the case of the variation of the geocentric distances or of Ω and i, and it does not require any further illustration. The final elements will be obtained from $M+\Delta M$, and $f+\Delta f$, either directly or by interpolation. We may remark, further, that it will be convenient to use $\log M$ as the quantity to be corrected, and to express the variations of $\log M$ in units of the last decimal place of the logarithms.

When the orbit differs very little from the parabolic form, it will be most expeditious to make two hypotheses in regard to M, putting in each case $\frac{1}{a}=0$, and only compute elliptic or hyperbolic elements in the third hypothesis, for which we use M and $f=\delta f$. The first and second systems of elements will thus be parabolic.

120. Instead of M and $\frac{1}{a}$ we may use Δ and $\frac{1}{a}$ as the quantities to be corrected. In this case we assume an approximate value of Δ by means of elements already known, and by means of $(96)_3$, $(98)_3$, $(102)_3$, and $(103)_3$, we compute the auxiliary quantities C, B, B'', &c., required in the solution of the equations $(104)_3$. We assume, also, an approximate value of Δ'' and compute the corresponding value of r'', the value of r having been already found from the assumed value of Δ. Then, by trial, we find the value of $\varkappa$ which, in connection with

the assumed value of $\frac{1}{a}$, will satisfy the equations $(104)_3$ and (65) or (61). The corresponding value of Δ'' is given by

$$\Delta'' = c \pm \sqrt{\varkappa^2 - C^2}.$$

When Δ'' has thus been determined, the heliocentric places will be obtained by means of the equations $(106)_3$ and $(107)_3$, and, finally, the corresponding elements of the orbit will be computed. If the ecliptic is taken as the fundamental plane, we put $D = 0$, $A = \odot$, and write λ and β in place of α and δ respectively.

If we now compute a second system of elements from $\Delta + \delta\Delta$ and $f = \frac{1}{a}$, and a third system from Δ and $f + \delta f$, the comparison of the three systems of elements with additional observed places will furnish the equations of condition for the determination of the corrections $\Delta\Delta$ and Δf to be applied to Δ and $\frac{1}{a}$ respectively.

When the eccentricity is very nearly equal to unity, we may assume $f = 0$ for the first and second hypotheses, and only compute elliptic or hyperbolic elements for the third hypothesis.

121. The comparison of the several observed places of a heavenly body with one of the three systems of elements obtained by varying the two quantities selected for correction, or, when the required differential coefficients are known, with any other system of elements such that the squares and products of the corrections may be neglected, gives a series of equations of the form

$$mx + ny = p,$$
$$m'x + n'y = p', \text{ \&c.},$$

in which x and y denote the final corrections to be applied to the two assumed quantities respectively. The combination of these equations which gives the most probable values of the unknown quantities, is effected according to the method of least squares. Thus, we multiply each equation by the coefficient of x in that equation, and the sum of all the equations thus formed gives the first normal equation. Then we multiply each equation of condition by the coefficient of y in that equation, and the sum of all the products gives the second normal equation. Let these equations be expressed thus:—

$$[mm]\, x + [mn]\, y = [mp],$$
$$[mn]\, x + [nn]\, y = [np],$$

in which $[mm] = m^2 + m'^2 + m''^2 + \&c.$, $[mn] = mn + m'n' + m''n'' + \&c.$, and similarly for the other terms. These two final equations give, by elimination, the most probable values of x and y, namely, those for which the sum of the squares of the residuals will be a minimum. It is, however, often convenient to determine x in terms of y, or y in terms of x, so that we may find the influence of a variation of one of the unknown quantities on the differences between computation and observation when the most probable value of the other unknown quantity is used. Thus, if it be desired to find x in terms of y, the most probable value of x will be

$$x = \frac{[mp]}{[mm]} - \frac{[mn]}{[mm]} y.$$

If we substitute this value of x in the original equations of condition, the remaining differences between computation and observation will be expressed in terms of the unknown quantity y, or in the form

$$\Delta\theta = m_0 + n_0 y. \tag{90}$$

Then, by assigning different values to y, we may find the corresponding residuals, and thus determine to what extent the correction y may be varied without causing these residuals to surpass the limits of the probable errors of observation.

In the determination of the orbit of a comet there must be more or less uncertainty in the value of a, and if y denotes the correction to be applied to the assumed value of $\frac{1}{a}$, we may thus determine the probable limits within which the true value of the periodic time must be found. In the case of a comet which is identified, by the similarity of elements, with one which has previously appeared, if we compute the system of elements which will best satisfy the series of observations, the supposition being made that the comet has performed but one revolution around the sun during the intervening interval, it will be easy to determine whether the observations are better satisfied by assuming that two or more revolutions have been completed during this interval. Thus, let T denote the periodic time assumed, and the relation between T and a is expressed by

$$T = \frac{2\pi a^{\frac{3}{2}}}{k},$$

in which π denotes the semi-circumference of a circle whose radius is unity. Let the periodic time corresponding to $\frac{1}{a}+y$ be denoted by $\frac{T}{z}$: then we shall have

$$y=\frac{1}{a}z^{\frac{2}{3}}-\frac{1}{a},$$

and the equations for the residuals are transformed into the form

$$\Delta\theta=(m_0-n_0f)+n_0fz^{\frac{2}{3}}. \tag{91}$$

If we now assign to z, successively, the values 1, 2, 3, &c., the residuals thus obtained will indicate the value of z which best satisfies the series of observations, and hence how many revolutions of the comet have taken place during the interval denoted by T.

122. In the determination of the orbit of a comet from three observed places, a hypothesis in regard to the semi-transverse axis may with facility be introduced simultaneously with the computation of the parabolic elements. The numerical calculation as far as the formation of the equations $(52)_3$ will be precisely the same for both the parabolic and the elliptic or hyperbolic elements. Then in the one case we find the values of r, r'', and $\varkappa$ which will satisfy equation $(56)_3$, and in the other case we find those which will satisfy the equation (65), as already explained. From the results thus obtained, the two systems of elements will be computed. Let $f=\frac{1}{a}$, then in the case of the system of parabolic elements we have $f=0$, and the comparison of the middle place with these and also with the elliptic or hyperbolic elements will give the value of

$$\frac{d\theta}{df}=\frac{\theta_2-\theta_1}{f},$$

in which θ_1 denotes the geocentric spherical co-ordinate computed from the parabolic elements, and θ_2 that computed from the other system of elements. Further, let $\Delta\theta$ denote the difference between computation and observation for the middle place, and the correction to be applied to f, in order that the computed and the observed values of θ may agree, will be given by

$$\frac{d\theta}{df}\Delta f+\Delta\theta=0.$$

Hence, the two observed spherical co-ordinates for the middle place will give two equations of condition from which Δf may be found, and the corresponding elements will be those which best represent the observations, assuming the adopted value of M to be correct.

123. The first determination of the approximate elements of the orbit of a comet is most readily effected by adopting the ecliptic as the fundamental plane. In the subsequent correction of these elements, by varying $\frac{1}{a}$ and M or Δ, it will often be convenient to use the equator as the fundamental plane, and the first assumption in regard to M will be made by means of the values of the distances given by the approximate elements already known. But if it be desired to compute M directly from three observed places in reference to the equator, without converting the right ascensions and declinations into longitudes and latitudes, the requisite formulæ may be derived by a process entirely analogous to that employed when the curtate distances refer to the ecliptic. The case may occur in which only the right ascension for the middle place is given, so that the corresponding longitude cannot be found. It will then be necessary to adopt the equator as the fundamental plane in determining a system of parabolic elements by means of two complete observations and this incomplete middle place. If we substitute the expressions for the heliocentric co-ordinates in reference to the equator in the equations $(4)_3$ and $(5)_3$, we shall have

$$\begin{aligned} 0 &= n(\rho\cos\alpha - R\cos D\cos A) - (\rho'\cos\alpha' - R'\cos D'\cos A') \\ &\qquad + n''(\rho''\cos\alpha'' - R''\cos D''\cos A''), \\ 0 &= n(\rho\sin\alpha - R\cos D\sin A) - (\rho'\sin\alpha' - R'\cos D'\sin A') \qquad (92) \\ &\qquad + n''(\rho''\sin\alpha'' - R''\cos D''\sin A''), \\ 0 &= n(\rho\tan\delta - R\sin D) - (\rho'\tan\delta' - R'\sin D') \\ &\qquad + n''(\rho''\tan\delta'' - R''\sin D''), \end{aligned}$$

in which ρ, ρ', ρ'' denote the curtate distances with respect to the equator, A, A', A'' the right ascensions of the sun, and D, D', D'' its declinations. These equations correspond to $(6)_3$, and may be treated in a similar manner.

From the first and second of equations (92) we get

$$\begin{aligned} 0 = n\,(\rho\sin(\alpha'-\alpha) - R\cos D\sin(\alpha'-A)) + R'\cos D'\sin(\alpha'-A') \\ - n''\,(\rho''\sin(\alpha''-\alpha') + R''\cos D''\sin(\alpha'-A'')), \end{aligned}$$

and hence

$$M = \frac{\rho''}{\rho} = \frac{n}{n''}\cdot\frac{\sin(\alpha'-\alpha)}{\sin(\alpha''-\alpha')} \qquad (93)$$
$$-\frac{nR\cos D\sin(\alpha'-A) - R'\cos D'\sin(\alpha'-A') + n''R''\cos D''\sin(\alpha'-A'')}{\rho n''\sin(\alpha''-\alpha')}.$$

This formula, being independent of the declination δ', may be used to compute M when only the right ascension for the middle place is given. For the first assumption in the case of an unknown orbit, we take

$$M = \frac{t''-t'}{t'-t} \cdot \frac{\sin(\alpha'-\alpha)}{\sin(\alpha''-\alpha')},$$

and, by means of the results obtained from this hypothesis, the complete expression (93) may be computed. By a process identical with that employed in deriving the equation $(36)_3$, we derive, from (93), the expression

$$\rho'' = \rho \frac{n}{n''} \cdot \frac{\sin(\alpha'-\alpha)}{\sin(\alpha''-\alpha')} \qquad (94)$$

$$- \tfrac{1}{6} \frac{\tau\tau'}{\tau''} (\tau' + \tau'') \left(\frac{1}{r'^3} - \frac{1}{R'^3} \right) \frac{R' \cos D' \sin(\alpha' - A')}{\sin(\alpha''-\alpha')};$$

and, putting

$$M_0 = \frac{n}{n''} \cdot \frac{\sin(\alpha'-\alpha)}{\sin(\alpha''-\alpha')},$$

$$F = 1 - \tfrac{1}{6} \frac{n''}{n} \cdot \frac{\tau\tau'}{\tau''} (\tau' + \tau'') \frac{\cos D' \sin(\alpha' - A')}{\sin(\alpha'-\alpha)} \cdot \frac{R'}{\rho} \left(\frac{1}{r'^3} - \frac{1}{R'^3} \right),$$

we have

$$M = \frac{\rho''}{\rho} = M_0 F. \qquad (95)$$

The calculation of the auxiliary quantities in the equations $(52)_3$ will be effected by means of the formulæ $(96)_3$, (86), (87), $(102)_3$, and $(51)_3$. The heliocentric places for the times t and t'' will be given by $(106)_3$ and $(107)_3$, and from these the elements of the orbit will be found according to the process already illustrated.

124. The methods already given for the correction of the approximate elements of the orbit of a heavenly body by means of additional observations or normal places, are those which will generally be applied. There are, however, modifications of these which may be advantageous in rare and special cases, and which will readily suggest themselves. Thus, if it be desired to correct approximate elements by varying two radii-vectores r and r'', we may assume an approximate value of each of these, and the three equations $(88)_1$ will contain only the three unknown quantities Δ, b, and l. By elimination, these unknown quantities may be found, and in like manner the

values of Δ'', b'', and l''. It will be most convenient to compute the angles ψ and ψ'', and then find z and z'' from

$$\sin z = \frac{R \sin \psi}{r}, \qquad \sin z'' = \frac{R'' \sin \psi''}{r''},$$

or, putting $x^2 = r^2 - R^2 \sin^2 \psi$, and $x''^2 = r''^2 - R''^2 \sin^2 \psi''$, from

$$\tan z = \frac{R \sin \psi}{x}, \qquad \tan z'' = \frac{R'' \sin \psi''}{x''}.$$

The curtate distances will be given by the equations (3), and the heliocentric spherical co-ordinates by means of (4), writing r in place of a. From these $u'' - u$ may be found, and by means of the values of r, r'', and $u'' - u$ the determination of the elements of the orbit may be completed. Then, assigning to r an increment δr, we compute a second system of elements, and from r and $r'' + \delta r''$ a third system. The comparison of these three systems of elements with an additional or intermediate observed place will furnish the equations for the determination of the corrections Δr and $\Delta r''$ to be applied to r and r'', respectively. The comparison of the middle place may be made with the observed geocentric spherical co-ordinates directly, or with the radius-vector and argument of the latitude computed directly from the observed co-ordinates; and in the same manner any number of additional observed places may be employed in forming the equations of condition for the determination of Δr and $\Delta r''$.

Instead of r and r'', we may take the projections of these radii-vectores on the plane of the ecliptic as the quantities to be corrected. Let these projected distances of the body from the sun be denoted by r_0 and r_0'', respectively; then, by means of the equations $(88)_1$, we obtain

$$\sin (l - \lambda) = \frac{R \sin (\lambda - \odot)}{r_0}, \tag{96}$$

from which l may be found; and in a similar manner we may find l''. If we put

$$x_0^2 = r_0^2 - R^2 \sin^2 (\lambda - \odot),$$

we have

$$\tan (l - \lambda) = \frac{R \sin (\lambda - \odot)}{x_0}. \tag{97}$$

Let S denote the angle at the sun between the earth and the place of the planet or comet projected on the plane of the ecliptic; then we shall have

$$S = 180^\circ + \odot - l,$$
$$\rho = \frac{R \sin(l - \odot)}{\sin(l - \lambda)}, \qquad (98)$$

and

$$\tan b = \frac{\rho \tan \beta}{r_0}, \qquad (99)$$

by means of which the heliocentric latitudes b and b'' may be found. The calculation of the elements and the correction of r_0 and r_0'' are then effected as in the case of the variation of r and r''.

In the case of parabolic motion, the eccentricity being known, we may take q and T as the quantities to be corrected. If we assume approximate values of these elements, r, r', r'', and v, v', v'' will be given immediately. Then from r, r', r'' and the observed spherical co-ordinates of the body we may compute the values of $u'' - u'$ and $u' - u$. In the same manner, by means of the observed places, we compute the angles $u''-u'$ and $u'-u$ corresponding to $q + \delta q$ and T, and to q and $T + \delta T$, δq and δT denoting the arbitrary increments assigned to q and T, respectively. The comparison of the heliocentric motion, during the intervals $t'' - t'$ and $t' - t$, thus obtained, in the case of each of the three systems of elements, from the observed geocentric places with the corresponding results given by

$$u'' - u' = v'' - v', \qquad u' - u = v' - v,$$

enables us to form the equations by which we may find the corrections Δq and ΔT to be applied to the assumed values of q and T, respectively, in order that the values of $u'' - u'$ and $u' - u$ computed by means of the observed places shall agree with those given by the true anomalies computed directly from q and T.

CHAPTER VII.

METHOD OF LEAST SQUARES, THEORY OF THE COMBINATION OF OBSERVATIONS, AND DETERMINATION OF THE MOST PROBABLE SYSTEM OF ELEMENTS FROM A SERIES OF OBSERVATIONS.

125. WHEN the elements of the orbit of a heavenly body are known to such a degree of approximation that the squares and products of the corrections which should be applied to them may be neglected, by computing the partial differential coefficients of these elements with respect to each of the observed spherical co-ordinates, we may form, by means of the differences between computation and observation, the equations for the determination of these corrections. Three complete observations will furnish the six equations required for the determination of the corrections to be applied to the six elements of the orbit; but, if more than three complete places are given, the number of equations will exceed the number of unknown quantities, and the problem will be more than determinate. If the observed places were absolutely exact, the combination of the equations of condition in any manner whatever would furnish the values of these corrections, such that each of these equations would be completely satisfied. The conditions, however, which present themselves in the actual correction of the elements of the orbit of a heavenly body by means of given observed places, are entirely different. When the observations have been corrected for all known instrumental errors, and when all other known corrections have been duly applied, there still remain those accidental errors which arise from various causes, such as the abnormal condition of the atmosphere, the imperfections of vision, and the imperfections in the performance of the instrument employed. These accidental and irregular errors of observation cannot be eliminated from the observed data, and the equations of condition for the determination of the corrections to be applied to the elements of an approximate orbit cannot be completely satisfied by any system of values assigned to the unknown quantities unless the number of equations is the same as the number of these unknown quantities. It becomes an important problem, therefore, to determine the particular combination of these equations of condition, by means of which

the resulting values of the unknown quantities will be those which, while they do not completely satisfy the several equations, will afford the highest degree of probability in favor of their accuracy. It will be of interest also to determine, as far as it may be possible, the degree of accuracy which may be attributed to the separate results. But, in order to simplify the more general problem, in which the quantities sought are determined indirectly by observation, it will be expedient to consider first the simpler case, in which a single quantity is obtained directly by observation.

126. If the accidental errors of observation could be obviated, the different determinations of a magnitude directly by observation would be identical; but since this is impossible when an extreme limit of precision is sought, we adopt a *mean* or average value to be derived from the separate results obtained. The adopted value may or may not agree with any individual result, since it is only necessary that the residuals obtained by comparing the adopted value with the observed values shall be such as to make this adopted value the *most probable* value. It is evident, from the very nature of the case, that we approach here the confines of the unknown, and, before we proceed further, something additional must be assumed.

However irregular and uncertain the law of the accidental errors of observation may be, we may at least assume that small errors are more probable than large errors, and that errors surpassing a certain limit will not occur. We may also assume that in the case of a large number of observations, errors in excess will occur as frequently as errors in defect, so that, in general, positive and negative residuals of equal absolute value are equally probable. It appears, therefore, that the relative frequency of the occurrence of an accidental error $\varDelta$ in the observed value will depend on the magnitude of this error, and may be expressed by $\varphi(\varDelta)$. This function will also express the probability of an error $\varDelta$ in an observed value. At the limit beyond which an error of the magnitude $\varDelta$ can never occur, we must have $\varphi(\varDelta)=0$: when $\varDelta=0$, the value of $\varphi(\varDelta)$ must be a maximum, and for equal positive and negative values of $\varDelta$ the values of $\varphi(\varDelta)$ must be the same. Hence, in a given series of observations, the number m of observations being supposed to be large, the number of times in which the error $\varDelta$ occurs will be expressed by $m\varphi(\varDelta)$, and the number of times in which the error $\varDelta'$ occurs will be expressed by $m\varphi(\varDelta')$, so that we shall have

$$m=m\varphi(\varDelta)+m\varphi(\varDelta')+m\varphi(\varDelta'')+\&c.,$$

or

$$\Sigma\varphi(\Delta) = 1.$$

The sum Σ must be taken between the limits for which the accidental errors of observation are considered possible; but since the assignment of these limits is, in a certain sense, arbitrary, we must evidently have

$$\sum_{\Delta=-\infty}^{\Delta=+\infty}\varphi(\Delta) = 1, \tag{1}$$

the value of $\varphi(\Delta)$ being absolutely zero for the limits $+\infty$ and $-\infty$.

Within any given limits there are an infinite number of values, any one of which may possibly be the true value of Δ, and hence the number of the functions expressed by $\varphi(\Delta)$ must be infinite. The probability of an error Δ is expressed by $\varphi(\Delta)$, and will be the same as the probability that the error is contained within the limits Δ and $\Delta + d\Delta$. The latter is expressed by the sum of all the functions $\varphi(\Delta)$ between the limits Δ and $\Delta + d\Delta$, or by

$$\varphi(\Delta)\, d\Delta.$$

We conclude, therefore, that the probability that an error falls between the limits a and b is expressed by the integral

$$\int_a^b \varphi(\Delta)\, d\Delta,$$

and this integral, taken so as to include all possible accidental errors of observation, is, according to equation (1),

$$\int_{-\infty}^{+\infty}\varphi(\Delta)\, d\Delta = 1. \tag{2}$$

According to the theory of probabilities, the probability that the errors Δ, Δ', &c. occur simultaneously is equal to the continued product of the probabilities of the occurrence of these errors separately. Let P denote the probability that these errors occur at the same time in the given series of observed values, and we have

$$P = \varphi(\Delta) \,.\, \varphi(\Delta') \,.\, \varphi(\Delta'') \,.....\tag{3}$$

The most probable value of the quantity sought, which we will denote by x, must evidently be that which makes P a maximum. If we take the logarithms of both members of equation (3), and differentiate, the condition of a maximum gives

$$0 = \frac{d \log \varphi(\Delta)}{d\Delta} \cdot \frac{d\Delta}{dx} + \frac{d \log \varphi(\Delta')}{d\Delta'} \cdot \frac{d\Delta'}{dx} + \&c. \tag{4}$$

Let n, n', n'', &c. be the observed values of x, and m the number of observations; then we have

$$\Delta = n - x, \qquad \Delta' = n' - x, \qquad \Delta'' = n'' - x, \ \&c.,$$

and hence

$$\frac{d\Delta}{dx} = \frac{d\Delta'}{dx} = \frac{d\Delta''}{dx} \ldots\ldots = -1.$$

Therefore the equation (4) becomes

$$0 = \frac{d \log \varphi(n - x)}{d(n - x)} + \frac{d \log \varphi(n' - x)}{d(n' - x)} + \&c. \tag{5}$$

This equation will serve to determine the value of x as soon as the form of the function symbolized by φ is known. It becomes necessary, therefore, to make some further assumption in regard to the errors Δ, Δ', Δ'', &c., in order that the form of this function may be determined; and, although the hypothesis which presents itself gives directly the most probable value of x, since the function $\varphi(\Delta)$ is supposed to be general, we may thus, by the special case, determine the form of this function; and the result will be applicable when, instead of the value of a single quantity, it is required to find the most probable values of several unknown quantities determined indirectly by observation.

127. The principle may be received as an axiom, that when a series of observed values of a quantity is given, if the circumstances under which the separate observations were made are similar, so that there is no reason for preferring one result to another, the most probable value of the quantity sought is the *arithmetical mean* of the several results. Hence we have

$$x = \frac{n + n' + n'' + \ldots.}{m},$$

m being the number of observed values. This expression gives

$$0 = (n - x) + (n' - x) + (n'' - x) + \&c., \tag{6}$$

from which it appears that the algebraic sum of the residuals is equal to zero. The equation (5) may be written

$$0 = (n-x)\frac{d\log\varphi(n-x)}{(n-x)\,d(n-x)} + (n'-x)\frac{d\log\varphi(n'-x)}{(n'-x)\,d(n'-x)} + \&c.,$$

and the comparison of this with (6) shows that

$$\frac{d\log\varphi(n-x)}{(n-x)\,d(n-x)} = \frac{d\log\varphi(n'-x)}{(n'-x)\,d(n'-x)}\ldots. = k, \qquad (7)$$

k being a constant quantity. Hence we derive

$$d\log_e\varphi(\varDelta) = k\varDelta\, d\varDelta,$$

the integration of which gives

$$\log_e\varphi(\varDelta) = \tfrac{1}{2}k\varDelta^2 + \log_e c,$$

$\log_e c$ being the constant of integration. From this equation there results

$$\varphi(\varDelta) = ce^{\frac{1}{2}k\Delta^2}, \qquad (8)$$

in which e is the base of Naperian logarithms. Since $\varphi(\varDelta)$ diminishes as $\varDelta$ increases, the quantity k must be essentially negative, and if we put $\frac{1}{2}k = -h^2$, we shall have

$$\varphi(\varDelta) = ce^{-h^2\Delta^2}. \qquad (9)$$

If we substitute this value of $\varphi(\varDelta)$ in the equation (2), we have

$$c\int_{-\infty}^{+\infty} e^{-h^2\Delta^2}\, d\varDelta = 1,$$

or, putting also $t = h\varDelta$,

$$\frac{c}{h}\int_{-\infty}^{+\infty} e^{-t^2}\, dt = 1. \qquad (10)$$

This equation will give the value of the constant c, provided that the value of the integral

$$\int_0^\infty e^{-t^2}\, dt$$

is known. Since the definite integral is independent of the variable, let us multiply it by a similar one, in which y is the variable; so that we have

$$\left(\int_0^\infty e^{-t^2}\, dt\right)^2 = \int_0^\infty e^{-t^2}\, dt\int_0^\infty e^{-y^2}\, dy = \int_0^\infty\int_0^\infty e^{-(t^2+y^2)}\, dt\, dy,$$

in which the order of integration is indifferent. If we put $y = tz$, we have, since t is regarded as constant in the integration with respect to y,

$$dy = tdz;$$

and hence

$$\left(\int_0^\infty e^{-t^2}\,dt\right)^2 = \int_0^\infty dz \int_0^\infty e^{-(1+z^2)t^2}\,tdt.$$

Then, since we have, in general,

$$\int_0^\infty e^{-ax^2}\,xdx = \frac{1}{2a},$$

the preceding equation gives

$$\left(\int_0^\infty e^{-t^2}\,dt\right)^2 = \int_0^\infty \frac{dz}{2(1+z^2)} = \tfrac{1}{2}\left[\tan^{-1} z\right]_{z=0}^{z=\infty} = \tfrac{1}{4}\pi,$$

in which π denotes the semi-circumference of a circle whose radius is unity. Therefore we have

$$\int_0^\infty e^{-t^2}\,dt = \tfrac{1}{2}\sqrt{\pi}, \tag{11}$$

and the equation (10) gives

$$c = \frac{h}{\sqrt{\pi}}. \tag{12}$$

Hence, the expression for $\varphi(\Delta)$ becomes

$$\varphi(\Delta) = \frac{h}{\sqrt{\pi}}\,e^{-h^2\Delta^2}. \tag{13}$$

The constant h, according to the relation $h^2 = -\frac{1}{2}k$, must depend on the nature of the observations, and will be the same in the case of systems of observations in which the probability of an error Δ is the same. Since $h^2\Delta^2$ must necessarily be an abstract number, Δ and $\frac{1}{h}$ must be homogeneous.

128. In a given series of observations, the probability that for any observation the error will be within the limits $-\delta$ and $+\delta$ will be expressed by

$$\frac{h}{\sqrt{\pi}}\int_{-\delta}^{+\delta} e^{-h^2\Delta^2}\,d\Delta; \tag{14}$$

and in another series of observations, more or less precise, the probability that the error of an observation is within the limits $-\delta'$ and $+\delta'$ will be

$$\frac{h'}{\sqrt{\pi}}\int_{-\delta'}^{+\delta'} e^{-h'^2\Delta^2}\,d\Delta. \tag{15}$$

Since

$$\frac{h}{\sqrt{\pi}}\int_{-\delta}^{+\delta} e^{-h^2\Delta^2}\,d\Delta = \frac{1}{\sqrt{\pi}}\int_{-h\delta}^{+h\delta} e^{-h^2\Delta^2}\,d\,(h\Delta),$$

it appears that the integrals (14) and (15) are equal when $h\delta = h'\delta'$. Hence, if we put $h' = 2h$, these integrals will be equal when $\delta = 2\delta'$, and an error of a given magnitude in the first series will have the same probability as an error of half that magnitude in the second series. The second series of observations will therefore be twice as accurate as the first series, and the constant h may be called the *measure of precision* of the observations. The greater the degree of precision of the observations, the greater will be the value of h.

The relative accuracy of two series of observations may also be determined by a comparison of the errors which are committed with equal facility in each series. If we arrange the errors of the several observations in each series in the order of their absolute magnitude without reference to the algebraic sign, the errors which occupy the same position in reference to the extremes in each case will serve to determine the relation sought. We select that, however, which occupies the middle place in the series of errors thus arranged, and since the number of errors which exceed this is the same as the number of errors less than this, if we designate the error which occupies the middle place by r, the probability that an error is within the limits $-r$ and $+r$ will be equal to $\frac{1}{2}$. The probability of an error greater than r being the same as the probability of an error less than r, the error r is called the *probable error*.

The relation between r and h is easily determined. Thus, we have

$$\frac{h}{\sqrt{\pi}}\int_{-r}^{+r} e^{-h^2\Delta^2}\,d\Delta = \tfrac{1}{2},$$

or, putting $h\Delta = t$,

$$\int_0^{hr} e^{-t^2}\,dt = \frac{\sqrt{\pi}}{4} = 0.44311. \tag{16}$$

If we expand e^{-t^2} into a series of ascending powers of t, multiply by dt, and integrate between the limits 0 and T, we get

$$\int_0^T e^{-t^2}\,dt = T - \tfrac{1}{3}T^3 + \tfrac{1}{5}\frac{T^5}{1\,.\,2} - \tfrac{1}{7}\frac{T^7}{1\,.\,2\,.\,3} + \tfrac{1}{9}\frac{T^9}{1\,.\,2\,.\,3\,.\,4} - \&c., \quad (17)$$

which converges rapidly when T is small. To find the value of T which corresponds to the value 0.44311 assigned to the integral, we compute the value of the series (17) for the values 0.45, 0.47, and 0.49 assigned to T, successively, and from the results thus obtained it is easily seen that when the sum of the terms of the series is 0.44311, we have

$$T = hr = 0.47694,$$

or

$$r = \frac{0.47694}{h}, \quad (18)$$

which determines the relation between the probable error and the measure of precision.

The probability that the error of an observation, without regard to sign, does not exceed nr, is expressed by

$$\frac{2}{\sqrt{\pi}}\int_0^{nhr} e^{-t^2}\,dt, \quad (19)$$

and this integral, therefore, indicates the ratio of the number of observations affected with an error which does not exceed nr to the whole number of observations. Hence, if we assign different values to n, the integral (19) computed for the several assumed values of

$$nhr = 0.47694n$$

will give the relative number of errors of a given magnitude. Thus, if we put $n = \frac{1}{2}$, we obtain

$$\frac{2}{\sqrt{\pi}}\int_0^{0.2385} e^{-t^2}\,dt = 0.264.$$

from which it appears that in a series of 1000 observations there ought to be 264 observations in which the error does not exceed $\frac{1}{2}r$. It has been found, in this manner, that in the case of an extended series of observations the number of errors of a given magnitude assigned by theory agrees very closely with that actually given by the series of observations; and hence we conclude that the error committed in extending the limits of the summation in the expression (1) to $-\infty$ and $+\infty$, instead of the finite limits which it is presumed that the actual errors cannot exceed, is very slight, so that the form of the function $\varphi(\Delta)$ which has been derived may be regarded as that which best satisfies all the conditions of the problem.

129. The relative accuracy of different series of observations may also be indicated by means of what are called the *mean error* and the *mean of the errors* for each series, the former being the error whose square is equal to the mean of the squares of all the errors of the series, and the latter the mean of these errors without reference to their algebraic sign.

Let ε denote the mean error; then, since the number of observations having the error Δ is $m\varphi(\Delta)$, we shall have, according to the definition,

$$\varepsilon^2 = \frac{\Delta^2 m\varphi(\Delta) + \Delta'^2 m\varphi(\Delta') + \&c.}{m} = \Sigma\, \Delta^2\varphi(\Delta).$$

But the number of possible errors being infinite, the probability of an error Δ is expressed by $\varphi(\Delta)\, d\Delta$, and we have

$$\varepsilon^2 = \int_{-\infty}^{+\infty} \Delta^2\varphi(\Delta)\, d\Delta = \frac{h}{\sqrt{\pi}} \int_{-\infty}^{+\infty} e^{-h^2\Delta^2}\, \Delta^2 d\Delta,$$

which gives

$$\varepsilon^2 = \frac{1}{2h^2}. \tag{20}$$

Hence, by means of (18), we have

$$\begin{aligned} \varepsilon &= \frac{1}{h\sqrt{2}} = 1.4826r, \\ r &= 0.67449\varepsilon, \end{aligned} \tag{21}$$

which determine the relation between ε and r.

Let η denote the mean of the errors, and we shall have

$$\eta = \int_0^{\infty} 2\Delta\,\varphi(\Delta)\, d\Delta = \frac{2h}{\sqrt{\pi}} \int_0^{\infty} e^{-h^2\Delta^2}\, \Delta d\Delta,$$

which gives

$$\eta = \frac{1}{h\sqrt{\pi}}. \tag{22}$$

Therefore, we have

$$\begin{aligned} \eta &= 1.1829r, \\ r &= 0.8453\eta, \end{aligned} \tag{23}$$

for the relation between r and η.

130. Let us denote by v, v', v'', &c. the differences between any assumed value of x and the observed values for a given series of observations, the number of observations being denoted by m; then, if we put

$$[vv] = v^2 + v'^2 + v''^2 + \&c., \tag{24}$$

and similarly in the case of the sum of any other series of similar terms, we shall have for the probability of the value $x_{,}$,

$$P = \frac{h^m}{\sqrt{\pi^m}} e^{-h^2 [vv]}, \tag{25}$$

and this probability will be a maximum when $[vv]$ is a minimum. Now we have

$$v = n - x_{,}, \qquad v' = n' - x_{,}, \qquad v'' = n'' - x_{,}, \ \&c.,$$

n, n', n'', &c. being the observed values of x, and hence

$$\begin{aligned} [vv] &= [nn] - 2[n]\, x_{,} + m x_{,}^2 \\ &= [nn] - \frac{[n]^2}{m} + m\left(x_{,} - \frac{[n]}{m}\right)^2. \end{aligned}$$

It appears, therefore, that $[vv]$ will be a minimum when

$$x_{,} = \frac{[n]}{m}, \tag{26}$$

and this is a necessary consequence of the assumption that the arithmetical mean of the observations gives the most probable value of x, according to which the form of the function $\varphi(\Delta)$ was derived. But although the arithmetical mean is the most probable value, yet we cannot affirm that this is the exact value, so long as the number of observations is finite. It becomes important, therefore, to determine the degree of precision of the arithmetical mean.

Let x_0 denote the most probable value of x, for which the residuals are v, v', v'', &c., and let $x_0 + \delta$ be any other value of x. Then, since we may put

$$[v] = v + v' + v'' + \ldots. = 0,$$

and

$$[vv] = m\varepsilon^2,$$

the probability of the value $x_0 + \delta$ will be

$$P' = \frac{h^m}{\sqrt{\pi^m}} e^{-mh^2(\varepsilon^2 + \delta^2)}.$$

The probability that the error of the arithmetical mean is zero is indicated by

$$P = \frac{h^m}{\sqrt{\pi^m}} e^{-mh^2\varepsilon^2},$$

and we have

$$P' = Pe^{-mh^2\delta^2}.$$

In the case of a single observation, if P denotes the probability of the error zero, and P' the probability of the error δ, we have

$$P' = Pe^{-h^2\delta^2}.$$

Hence it appears that if h_0 denotes the measure of precision of the arithmetical mean of m observations, the relation between h_0 and h, the measure of precision of an observation, is given by

$$h_0^2 = mh^2; \qquad (27)$$

and if r_0 is the probable error of the arithmetical mean, and ε_0 its mean error, we have, according to the equations (18) and (20),

$$r_0 = \frac{r}{\sqrt{m}}, \qquad \varepsilon_0 = \frac{\varepsilon}{\sqrt{m}}. \qquad (28)$$

These expressions determine the probable and the mean error of the arithmetical mean of a number of observations when these errors in the case of a single observation are known.

131. The expressions for the relation between the mean and probable errors have been derived for the case of a very large number of observations, a number so great that the error of the arithmetical mean becomes equal to zero. In the case of a limited number of observed values of x, the residuals given by comparing the arithmetical mean with the several observations will not, in general, give the true errors of the observations; but the greater the number of observations, the nearer will these residuals approach the absolute errors. If Δ, Δ', Δ'', &c. are the actual errors of the observations, and v, v', v'', &c. those which result from the most probable value of x, we shall have, denoting the arithmetical mean by x_0, and the true value by $x_0 + \delta$,

$$\Delta = v - \delta, \qquad \Delta' = v' - \delta, \qquad \Delta'' = v'' - \delta, \text{ \&c.};$$

and hence

$$m\varepsilon^2 = [\Delta\Delta] = [vv] + m\delta^2. \tag{29}$$

This equation will enable us to determine the mean error of an observation when δ is given; but, since this is necessarily unknown, some assumption in regard to its value must be made. If we assume it to be equal to the mean error of the arithmetical mean, the remaining error will be wholly insensible, and hence the equation (29) becomes

$$m\varepsilon^2 = [vv] + m\varepsilon_0^2 = [vv] + \varepsilon^2.$$

Therefore, we shall have

$$\varepsilon = \sqrt{\frac{[vv]}{m-1}}, \tag{30}$$

and, according to (21),

$$r = 0.6745\sqrt{\frac{[vv]}{m-1}}. \tag{31}$$

These equations give the values of the mean and probable errors of a single observation in terms of the actual residuals found by comparing the arithmetical mean with the several observed values.

The probable and the mean error of the arithmetical mean will be given by

$$\left.\begin{aligned} \varepsilon_0 &= \sqrt{\frac{[vv]}{m(m-1)}}, \\ r_0 &= 0.6745\sqrt{\frac{[vv]}{m(m-1)}}. \end{aligned}\right\} \tag{32}$$

When the number of observations is very large, the probable error of an observation and also that of the arithmetical mean may be determined by means of the mean of the errors. If we suppose the number of positive errors to be the same as the number of negative errors, the mean of the errors without reference to the algebraic sign gives

$$\eta = \frac{[v]}{m},$$

and hence we have, according to (23),

$$r = 0.8453\,\frac{[v]}{m}. \tag{33}$$

For the mean error of an observation we have

$$\varepsilon = \eta\sqrt{\tfrac{1}{2}\pi} = 1.2533\,\frac{[v]}{m}. \tag{34}$$

If the number of observations is very great, the results given by these equations will agree with those given by (30) and (31); but for any limited series of observed values, the results obtained by means of the mean error will afford the greatest accuracy.

132. The relative accuracy of two or more observed values of a quantity may be expressed by means of what are called their *weights.* If the observations are made under precisely similar circumstances, so that there is no reason for preferring one to the other, they are said to have the same weight. The weight must therefore depend on the measure of precision of the observations, and hence on their probable errors. The unit of the weight is entirely arbitrary, since only the relative weights are required, and if we denote the weight by p, the value of p indicates the number of observations of equal accuracy which must be combined in order that their arithmetical mean may have the same degree of precision as the observation whose weight is p. Hence, if the weight of a single observation is 1, the arithmetical mean of m such observations will have the weight m. Let the probable error of an observation of the weight unity be denoted by r, and the probable error of that whose weight is p' by r'; then, according to the first of equations (28), we shall have

$$r' = \frac{r}{\sqrt{p'}},$$

or

$$r^2 = p'r'^2.$$

For the case of an observation whose weight is p'' and whose probable error is r'', we have

$$r^2 = p''r''^2 = p'r'^2,$$

from which it appears that *the weights of two observations are to each other inversely as the squares of their probable or mean errors, and, according to* (18), *directly as the squares of their measures of precision.*

Let us now consider two values of x, which may be designated by x' and x'', the mean errors of these values being, respectively, ε' and ε''; then, if we put

$$X = x' \pm x''$$

and suppose that both x' and x'' have been derived from a large number m of observations (and the same number in each case), so that the residuals $v_{,,}$ $v_{,}'$, v''', &c. in the case of x' and the residuals $v_{,}$, $v_{,}'$, $v_{,}''$, &c. in the case of x'' may be regarded as the actual errors of observation, the errors of the value of X, as determined from the several observations, will be

$$v \pm v_{,}, \qquad v' \pm v_{,}', \qquad v'' \pm v_{,}'', \text{ \&c.}$$

Let the mean error of X be denoted by E; then we have

$$mE^2 = \Sigma(v \pm v_{,})^2 = [vv] \pm 2[vv_{,}] + [v_{,}v_{,}];$$

and since the number of observed values is supposed to be so great that the frequency of negative products $vv_{,}$ is the same as that of the similar positive products, so that $[vv_{,}] = 0$, this equation gives

$$mE^2 = m\varepsilon'^2 + m\varepsilon''^2,$$

or

$$E^2 = \varepsilon'^2 + \varepsilon''^2.$$

Combining X with a third value x''' whose mean error is ε''', the mean error of $x' \pm x'' \pm x'''$ will be found in the same manner to be equal to $\varepsilon'^2 + \varepsilon''^2 + \varepsilon'''^2$; and hence we have, for the algebraic sum of any number of separate values,

$$E = \sqrt{\varepsilon^2 + \varepsilon'^2 + \varepsilon''^2 + \text{\&c.}}, \tag{35}$$

and, according to the last of equations (21),

$$R = \sqrt{r^2 + r'^2 + r''^2 + \text{\&c.}}, \tag{36}$$

R being the probable error of the algebraic sum. If the probable errors of the several values are the same, we have

$$r = r' = r'' = \text{\&c.}$$

and the probable error of the sum of m values will be given by

$$R = r\sqrt{m}.$$

Hence the probable error of the arithmetical mean of m observed values will be

$$r_0 = \frac{R}{m} = \frac{r}{\sqrt{m}},$$

which agrees with the first of equations (28).

Let P denote the weight of the sum X, p' the weight of x', and p'' that of x''; then we shall have

$$\frac{p'}{P} = \frac{r'^2 + r''^2}{r'^2}, \qquad \frac{p''}{P} = \frac{r'^2 + r''^2}{r''^2},$$

from which we get

$$P = \frac{p'p''}{p' + p''}. \tag{37}$$

Since the unit of weight is arbitrary, we may take

$$p' = \frac{1}{r'^2}, \qquad p'' = \frac{1}{r''^2}, \text{ \&c.};$$

and hence we have, for the weight of the algebraic sum of any number of values,

$$P = \frac{1}{R^2} = \frac{1}{r'^2 + r''^2 + r'''^2 + \text{\&c.}}, \tag{38}$$

or, whatever may be the unit of weight adopted,

$$P = \frac{1}{\frac{1}{p'} + \frac{1}{p''} + \frac{1}{p'''} + \ldots}. \tag{39}$$

In the case of a series of observed values of a quantity, if we designate by r' the probable error of a residual found by comparing the arithmetical mean with an observed value, by r the probable error of the observation, by x_0 the arithmetical mean, and by n any observed value, the probable error of

$$n = x_0 + v,$$

according to (36), will be

$$r^2 = r_0^2 + r'^2 = \frac{r^2}{m} + r'^2,$$

r_0 being the probable error of the arithmetical mean. Hence we derive

$$r = r'\sqrt{\frac{m}{m-1}};$$

and if we adopt the value

$$r' = 0.8453\,\frac{[v]}{m},$$

the expression for the probable error of an observation becomes

$$r = 0.8453\,\frac{[v]}{\sqrt{m(m-1)}}, \tag{40}$$

in which $[v]$ denotes the sum of the residuals regarded as positive, and m the number of observations.

133. Let n, n', n'', &c. denote the observed values of x, and let p, p', p'', &c. be their respective weights; then, according to the defi-

nition of the weight, the value n may be regarded as the arithmetical mean of p observations whose weight is unity, and the same is true in the case of n', n'', &c. We thus resolve the given values into $p+p'+p''+\ldots.$ observations of the weight unity, and the arithmetical mean of all these gives, for the most probable value of x,

$$x_0 = \frac{pn+p'n'+p''n''+\text{\&c.}}{p+p'+p''+\text{\&c.}} = \frac{[pn]}{[p]}. \tag{41}$$

The unit of weight being entirely arbitrary, it is evident that the relation given by this equation is correct as well when the quantities p, p', p'', &c. are fractional as when they are whole numbers. The weight of x_0 as determined by (41) is expressed by the sum

$$p+p'+p''+p'''+\text{\&c.},$$

and the probable error of x_0 is given by

$$r_0 = \frac{r_{,}}{\sqrt{p+p'+p''+\ldots}} = \frac{r_{,}}{\sqrt{[p]}}, \tag{42}$$

when $r_{,}$ denotes the probable error of an observation whose weight is unity. The value of $r_{,}$ must be found by means of the observations themselves. Thus, there will be p residuals expressed by $n-x_0$, p' residuals expressed by $n'-x_0$, and similarly in the case of n'', n''', &c. Hence, according to equation (31), we shall have

$$r_{,} = 0.6745\sqrt{\frac{[pvv]}{m-1}}, \tag{43}$$

in which m denotes the number of values to be combined, or the number of quantities n, n', n'', &c. For the mean error of x_0, we have the equations

$$\begin{aligned} \varepsilon_{,} &= \sqrt{\frac{[pvv]}{m-1}}, \\ \varepsilon_0 &= \frac{\varepsilon_{,}}{\sqrt{[p]}} = \sqrt{\frac{[pvv]}{(m-1)[p]}}. \end{aligned} \tag{44}$$

If different determinations of the quantity x are given, for which the probable errors are r, r', r'', &c., the reciprocals of the squares of these probable errors may be taken as the weights of the respective values n, n', n'', &c., and we shall have

$$x_0 = \frac{\frac{n}{r^2}+\frac{n'}{r'^2}+\frac{n''}{r''^2}+\ldots.}{\frac{1}{r^2}+\frac{1}{r'^2}+\frac{1}{r''^2}+\ldots.}, \tag{45}$$

with the probable error

$$r_0 = \frac{1}{\sqrt{\frac{1}{r^2} + \frac{1}{r'^2} + \frac{1}{r''^2} + \ldots}}. \qquad (46)$$

The mean errors may be used in these equations instead of the probable errors.

134. The results thus obtained for the case of the direct observation of the quantity sought, are applicable to the determination of the conditions for finding the most probable values of several unknown quantities when only a certain function of these quantities is directly observed. In the actual application of the formulæ it will always be possible to reduce the problem to the case in which the quantity observed is a linear function of the quantities sought. Thus, let V be the quantity observed, and ξ, η, ζ, &c. the unknown quantities to be determined, so that we have

$$V = f(\xi, \eta, \zeta, \ldots).$$

Let ξ_0, η_0, ζ_0, &c. be approximate values of these quantities supposed to be already known by means of previous calculation, and let x, y, z, &c. denote, respectively, the corrections which must be applied to these approximate values in order to obtain their true values. Then, if we suppose that the previous approximation is so close that the squares and products of the several corrections may be neglected, we have

$$V - V_0 = \frac{dV}{d\xi}x + \frac{dV}{d\eta}y + \frac{dV}{d\zeta}z + \ldots,$$

and thus the equation is reduced to a linear form. Hence, in general, if we denote by n the difference between the computed and the observed value of the function, and similarly in the case of each observation employed, the equations to be solved are of the following form:—

$$\begin{aligned} ax + by + cz + du + ew + ft + n &= 0, \\ a'x + b'y + c'z + d'u + e'w + f't + n' &= 0, \\ a''x + b''y + c''z + d''u + e''w + f''t + n'' &= 0, \\ \&c. \qquad\qquad \&c. & \end{aligned} \qquad (47)$$

which may be extended so as to include any number of unknown quantities. If the number of equations is the same as the number of unknown quantities, the resulting values of these will exactly satisfy the several equations; but if the number of equations exceeds the number of unknown quantities, there will not be any system of values for these which will reduce the second members absolutely to zero, and we can only determine the values for which the errors for the several equations, which may be denoted by v, v', v'', &c., will be those which we may regard as belonging to the most probable values of the unknown quantities.

Let Δ, Δ', Δ'', &c. be the actual errors of the observed quantities; then the probability that these occur in the case of the observations used in forming the equations of condition, will be expressed by

$$P = \varphi(\Delta) \, . \, \varphi(\Delta') \, . \, \varphi(\Delta'') \ldots ,$$

and the most probable values of the unknown quantities will be those which make P a maximum. The form of the function $\varphi(\Delta)$ has been already found to be

$$\varphi(\Delta) = \frac{h}{\sqrt{\pi}} e^{-h^2\Delta^2},$$

and hence we shall have

$$P = \frac{hh'h'' \ldots}{\sqrt{\pi^m}} e^{-(h^2\Delta^2 + h'^2\Delta'^2 + h''^2\Delta''^2 + \&c.)},$$

m being the number of observations or equations of condition. In order that P may be a maximum, the value of

$$h^2\Delta^2 + h'^2\Delta'^2 + h''^2\Delta''^2 + \&c.$$

must be a minimum. If the observations are equally good, the expression for P becomes

$$P = \frac{h^m}{\sqrt{\pi^m}} e^{-h^2(\Delta^2 + \Delta'^2 + \Delta''^2 + \&c.)},$$

and the condition of a maximum probability requires that

$$\Delta^2 + \Delta'^2 + \Delta''^2 + \&c.$$

shall be a minimum. Hence it appears that when the observations are equally precise, the most probable values of the unknown quantities are those which render the sum of the squares of the residuals a minimum, and that, in general, if each error is multiplied by its measure of precision, the sum of the squares of the products thus formed must be a minimum.

If we denote the actual residuals by v, v', v'', &c., and regard the observations as having the same measure of precision, the condition that the sum of their squares shall be a minimum gives

$$\frac{d[vv]}{dx} = 0, \qquad \frac{d[vv]}{dy} = 0, \qquad \frac{d[vv]}{dz} = 0, \text{ \&c.},$$

or

$$
\begin{aligned}
v\frac{dv}{dx}+v'\frac{dv'}{dx}+v''\frac{dv''}{dx}+\ldots\ldots&=0,\\
v\frac{dv}{dy}+v'\frac{dv'}{dy}+v''\frac{dv''}{dy}+\ldots\ldots&=0,\\
v\frac{dv}{dz}+v'\frac{dv'}{dz}+v''\frac{dv''}{dz}+\ldots\ldots&=0,\\
\&c. \qquad\qquad \&c.
\end{aligned}
\tag{48}
$$

If we differentiate the equations

$$
\begin{aligned}
ax+by+cz+du+ew+ft+n&=v,\\
a'x+b'y+c'z+d'u+e'w+f't+n'&=v',\\
a''x+b''y+c''z+d''u+e''w+f''t+n''&=v'',\\
\&c. \qquad\qquad \&c.
\end{aligned}
\tag{49}
$$

with respect to x, y, z, &c., successively, we obtain

$$
\begin{aligned}
&\frac{dv}{dx}=a, &&\frac{dv'}{dx}=a', &&\frac{dv''}{dx}=a'',\ \&c.\\
&\frac{dv}{dy}=b, &&\frac{dv'}{dy}=b', &&\frac{dv''}{dy}=b'',\ \&c.\\
&\&c. &&\&c. &&\&c.
\end{aligned}
\tag{50}
$$

Introducing these values into the equations (48), and substituting for v, v', v'', &c. their values given by (49), we get

$$
\begin{aligned}
[aa]x+[ab]y+[ac]z+[ad]u+[ae]w+[af]t+[an]&=0,\\
[ab]x+[bb]y+[bc]z+[bd]u+[be]w+[bf]t+[bn]&=0,\\
[ac]x+[bc]y+[cc]z+[cd]u+[ce]w+[cf]t+[cn]&=0,\\
[ad]x+[bd]y+[cd]z+[dd]u+[de]w+[df]t+[dn]&=0,\\
[ae]x+[be]y+[ce]z+[de]u+[ee]w+[ef]t+[en]&=0,\\
[af]x+[bf]y+[cf]z+[df]u+[ef]w+[ff]t+[fn]&=0,
\end{aligned}
\tag{51}
$$

in which

$$
\begin{aligned}
[aa]&=aa+a'a'+a''a''+\ldots\ldots\\
[ab]&=ab+a'b'+a''b''+\ldots\ldots\\
[ac]&=ac+a'c'+a''c''+\ldots\ldots\\
[bb]&=bb+b'b'+b''b''+\ldots\ldots\\
\&c.& \qquad\qquad \&c.
\end{aligned}
\tag{52}
$$

The equations of condition are thus reduced to the same number as the number of the unknown quantities, and the solution of these will give the values for which the sum of the squares of the residuals will be a minimum. These final equations are called *normal equations.*

When the observations are not equally precise, in accordance with the condition that $h^2v^2+h'^2v'^2+h''^2v''^2+$ &c. shall be a minimum, each equation of condition must be multiplied by the measure of precision of the observation; or, since the weight is proportional to the square of the measure of precision, each equation of condition must be multiplied by the square root of the weight of the observation, and the several equations of condition, being thus reduced to the same unit of weight, must be combined as indicated by the equations (51).

135. It will be observed that the formation of the first normal equation is effected by multiplying each equation of condition by the coefficient of x in that equation and then taking the sum of all the equations thus formed. The second normal equation is obtained in the same manner by multiplying by the coefficient of y; and thus by multiplying by the coefficient of each of the unknown quantities the several normal equations are formed. These equations will generally give, by elimination, a system of determinate values of the unknown quantities x, y, z, &c. But if one of the normal equations may be derived from one of the others by multiplying it by a constant, or if one of the equations may be derived by a combination of two or more of the remaining equations, the number of distinct relations will be less than the number of unknown quantities, and the problem will thus become indeterminate. In this case an unknown quantity may be expressed in the form of a linear function of one or more of the other unknown quantities. Thus, if the number of independent equations is one less than the number of unknown quantities, the final expressions for all of these quantities except one, will be of the form

$$x = \alpha + \beta t, \qquad y = \alpha' + \beta' t, \qquad z = \alpha'' + \beta'' t, \text{ \&c.} \qquad (53)$$

The coefficients α, β, α', β', &c. depend on the known terms and coefficients in the normal equations, and if by any means t can be determined independently, the values of x, y, z, &c. become determinate. It is evident, further, that when two of the normal equations may be rendered nearly identical by the introduction of a constant factor, the problem becomes so nearly indeterminate that in the numerical application the resulting values of the unknown quantities will be very uncertain, so that it will be necessary to express them as in the equations (53).

The indetermination in the case of the normal equations results necessarily from a similarity in the original equations of condition, and when the problem becomes nearly indeterminate, the identity of the equations will be closer in the normal equations than in the equations of condition from which they are derived. It should be observed, also, that when we express x, y, z, &c. in terms of t, as in (53), the normal equation in t, which is the one formed by multiplying by the coefficient of t in each of the equations of condition, is not required.

136. The elimination in the solution of the equations (51) is most conveniently effected by the method of substitution. Thus, the first of these equations gives

$$x = -\frac{[ab]}{[aa]}y - \frac{[ac]}{[aa]}z - \frac{[ad]}{[aa]}u - \frac{[ae]}{[aa]}w - \frac{[af]}{[aa]}t - \frac{[an]}{[aa]};$$

and if we substitute this for x in each of the remaining normal equations, and put

$$\begin{aligned} &[bb] - \frac{[ab]}{[aa]}[ab] = [bb.1], \qquad [bc] - \frac{[ab]}{[aa]}[ac] = [bc.1], \\ &[bd] - \frac{[ab]}{[aa]}[ad] = [bd.1], \qquad [be] - \frac{[ab]}{[aa]}[ae] = [be.1], \\ &[bf] - \frac{[ab]}{[aa]}[af] = [bf.1]; \end{aligned} \tag{54}$$

$$\begin{aligned} &[cc] - \frac{[ac]}{[aa]}[ac] = [cc.1], \qquad [cd] - \frac{[ac]}{[aa]}[ad] = [cd.1], \\ &[ce] - \frac{[ac]}{[aa]}[ae] = [ce.1], \qquad [cf] - \frac{[ac]}{[aa]}[af] = [cf.1]; \end{aligned} \tag{55}$$

$$\begin{aligned} &[dd] - \frac{[ad]}{[aa]}[ad] = [dd.1], \qquad [de] - \frac{[ad]}{[aa]}[ae] = [de.1], \\ &[df] - \frac{[ad]}{[aa]}[af] = [df.1]; \end{aligned} \tag{56}$$

$$\begin{aligned} &[ee] - \frac{[ae]}{[aa]}[ae] = [ee.1], \qquad [ef] - \frac{[ae]}{[aa]}[af] = [ef.1], \\ &[ff] - \frac{[af]}{[aa]}[af] = [ff.1]; \end{aligned} \tag{57}$$

$$\begin{aligned} &[bn] - \frac{[ab]}{[aa]}[an] = [bn.1], \qquad [cn] - \frac{[ac]}{[aa]}[an] = [cn.1], \\ &[dn] - \frac{[ad]}{[aa]}[an] = [dn.1], \qquad [en] - \frac{[ae]}{[aa]}[an] = [en.1], \\ &[fn] - \frac{[af]}{[aa]}[an] = [fn.1], \end{aligned} \tag{58}$$

we obtain

$$\begin{aligned}
&[bb.1]\,y + [bc.1]\,z + [bd.1]\,u + [be.1]\,w + [bf.1]\,t + [bn.1] = 0,\\
&[bc.1]\,y + [cc.1]\,z + [cd.1]\,u + [ce.1]\,w + [cf.1]\,t + [cn.1] = 0,\\
&[bd.1]\,y + [cd.1]\,z + [dd.1]\,u + [de.1]\,w + [df.1]\,t + [dn.1] = 0,\\
&[be.1]\,y + [ce.1]\,z + [de.1]\,u + [ee.1]\,w + [ef.1]\,t + [en.1] = 0,\\
&[bf.1]\,y + [cf.1]\,z + [df.1]\,u + [ef.1]\,w + [ff.1]\,t + [fn.1] = 0.
\end{aligned} \tag{59}$$

These equations are symmetrical, and of the same form as the normal equations, the coefficients being distinguished by writing the numeral 1 within the brackets.

The unknown quantity x is thus eliminated, and by a similar process y may be eliminated from the equations (59), the resulting equations being rendered symmetrical in form by the introduction of the numeral 2 within the brackets. Thus, we put

$$\begin{aligned}
&[cc.1] - \frac{[bc.1]}{[bb.1]}[bc.1] = [cc.2], \qquad [cd.1] - \frac{[bc.1]}{[bb.1]}[bd.1] = [cd.2],\\
&[ce.1] - \frac{[bc.1]}{[bb.1]}[be.1] = [ce.2], \qquad [cf.1] - \frac{[bc.1]}{[bb.1]}[bf.1] = [cf.2];
\end{aligned} \tag{60}$$

$$\begin{aligned}
&[dd.1] - \frac{[bd.1]}{[bb.1]}[bd.1] = [dd.2], \qquad [de.1] - \frac{[bd.1]}{[bb.1]}[be.1] = [de.2],\\
&[df.1] - \frac{[bd.1]}{[bb.1]}[bf\,1] = [df.2];
\end{aligned} \tag{61}$$

$$\begin{aligned}
&[ee.1] - \frac{[be.1]}{[bb.1]}[be.1] = [ee.2], \qquad [ef.1] - \frac{[be.1]}{[bb.1]}[bf.1] = [ef.2]\\
&[ff.1] - \frac{[bf.1]}{[bb.1]}[bf.1] = [ff.2];
\end{aligned} \tag{62}$$

$$\begin{aligned}
&[cn.1] - \frac{[bc.1]}{[bb.1]}[bn.1] = [cn.2], \qquad [dn.1] - \frac{[bd.1]}{[bb.1]}[bn.1] = [dn.2],\\
&[en.1] - \frac{[be.1]}{[bb.1]}[bn.1] = [en.2], \qquad [fn.1] - \frac{[bf.1]}{[bb.1]}[bn.1] = [fn.2],
\end{aligned} \tag{63}$$

and the equations become

$$\begin{aligned}
&[cc.2]\,z + [cd.2]\,u + [ce.2]\,w + [cf.2]\,t + [cn.2] = 0,\\
&[cd.2]\,z + [dd.2]\,u + [de.2]\,w + [df.2]\,t + [dn.2] = 0,\\
&[ce.2]\,z + [de.2]\,u + [ee.2]\,w + [ef.2]\,t + [en.2] = 0,\\
&[cf.2]\,z + [df.2]\,u + [ef.2]\,w + [ff.2]\,t + [fn.2] = 0.
\end{aligned} \tag{64}$$

To eliminate z from these equations, we put

$$\begin{aligned}
&[dd.2] - \frac{[cd.2]}{[cc.2]}[cd.2] = [dd.3], \qquad [de.2] - \frac{[cd.2]}{[cc.2]}[ce.2] = [de.3],\\
&[df.2] - \frac{[cd.2]}{[cc.2]}[cf.2] = [df.3];
\end{aligned} \tag{65}$$

$$[ee.2] - \frac{[ce.2]}{[cc.2]}[ce.2] = [ee.3], \qquad [ef.2] - \frac{[ce.2]}{[cc.2]}[cf.2] = [ef.3],$$
$$[ff.2] - \frac{[cf.2]}{[cc.2]}[cf.2] = [ff.3]; \qquad (66)$$

$$[dn.2] - \frac{[cd.2]}{[cc.2]}[cn.2] = [dn.3], \qquad [en.2] - \frac{[ce.2]}{[cc.2]}[cn.2] = [en.3],$$
$$[fn.2] - \frac{[cf.2]}{[cc.2]}[cn.2] = [fn.3], \qquad (67)$$

and we have

$$\begin{aligned}
[dd.3]\,u + [de.3]\,w + [df.3]\,t + [dn.3] &= 0,\\
[de.3]\,u + [ee.3]\,w + [ef.3]\,t + [en.3] &= 0,\\
[df.3]\,u + [ef.3]\,w + [ff.3]\,t + [fn.3] &= 0,
\end{aligned} \qquad (68)$$

Again we put, in a similar manner,

$$[ee.3] - \frac{[de.3]}{[dd.3]}[de.3] = [ee.4], \qquad [ef.3] - \frac{[de.3]}{[dd.3]}[df.3] = [ef.4],$$
$$[ff.3] - \frac{[df.3]}{[dd.3]}[df.3] = [ff.4], \qquad [en.3] - \frac{[de.3]}{[dd.3]}[dn.3] = [en.4], \qquad (69)$$
$$[fn.3] - \frac{[df.3]}{[dd.3]}[dn.3] = [fn.4];$$

and the equations are

$$\begin{aligned}
[ee.4]\,w + [ef.4]\,t + [en.4] &= 0,\\
[ef.4]\,w + [ff.4]\,t + [fn.4] &= 0.
\end{aligned} \qquad (70)$$

Finally, to eliminate w, we put

$$[ff.4] - \frac{[ef.4]}{[ee.4]}[ef.4] = [ff.5], \qquad [fn.4] - \frac{[ef.4]}{[ee.4]}[en.4] = [fn.5], \qquad (71)$$

and the resulting equation is

$$[ff.5]\,t + [fn.5] = 0, \qquad (72)$$

which gives

$$t = -\frac{[fn.5]}{[ff.5]}. \qquad (73)$$

The value of t thus found enables us to derive that of w by means of the first of equations (70). The value of w being found, that of u will be obtained from the first of equations (68). In like manner, the remaining unknown quantities will be determined by means of the equations (64), (59), and (51). The determination of the unknown quantities is thus reduced to the solution of the following system of equations:

$$\begin{aligned}
x+\frac{[ab]}{[aa]}y+\frac{[ac]}{[aa]}z+\frac{[ad]}{[aa]}u+\frac{[ae]}{[aa]}w+\frac{[af]}{[aa]}t+\frac{[an]}{[aa]}&=0,\\
y+\frac{[bc.1]}{[bb.1]}z+\frac{[bd.1]}{[bb.1]}u+\frac{[be.1]}{[bb.1]}w+\frac{[bf.1]}{[bb.1]}t+\frac{[bn.1]}{[bb.1]}&=0,\\
z+\frac{[cd.2]}{[cc.2]}u+\frac{[ce.2]}{[cc.2]}w+\frac{[cf.2]}{[cc.2]}t+\frac{[cn.2]}{[cc.2]}&=0,\\
u+\frac{[de.3]}{[dd.3]}w+\frac{[df.3]}{[dd.3]}t+\frac{[dn.3]}{[dd.3]}&=0,\\
w+\frac{[ef.4]}{[ee.4]}t+\frac{[en.4]}{[ee.4]}&=0,\\
t+\frac{[fn.5]}{[ff.5]}&=0,
\end{aligned} \tag{74}$$

the coefficients of which will have been found in the process of determining the several auxiliary quantities. It will be observed, further, that both in the normal equations and in those which result after each successive elimination, the coefficients which appear in a horizontal line, with the exception of the coefficient involving the absolute terms of the equations of condition, are found also in the corresponding vertical line. The form of the notation $[bb.1]$, $[bc.1]$, &c. may be symbolized thus:

$$[\beta\gamma.\mu]-\frac{[\alpha\beta.\mu]}{[\alpha\alpha.\mu]}[\alpha\gamma.\mu]=[\beta\gamma.(\mu+1)], \tag{75}$$

in which α, β, γ, denote any three letters, and μ any numeral.

The equations (74) are derived for the case of six unknown quantities, which is the number usually to be determined in the correction of the elements of the orbit of a heavenly body; but there will be no difficulty in extending the process indicated to the case of a greater number of unknown quantities, except that the number of auxiliaries symbolized generally by (75) increases very rapidly when the number of unknown quantities is increased.

137. In the numerical application of the formulæ, when so many quantities are to be computed, it becomes important to be able to check the accuracy of the calculation in its successive stages. First, then, to prove the calculation of the coefficients in the normal equations, we put

$$\begin{aligned}
a+b+c+d+e+f&=s,\\
a'+b'+c'+d'+e'+f'&=s', \text{ \&c.}
\end{aligned}$$

If we multiply each of the sums thus formed by the corresponding absolute term n, and take the sum of all the products, we have

$$[an] + [bn] + [cn] + [dn] + [en] + [fn] = [sn]. \qquad (76)$$

In a similar manner, multiplying by each of the coefficients in the original equations of condition, we find

$$\begin{aligned} [aa] + [ab] + [ac] + [ad] + [ae] + [af] &= [as], \\ [ab] + [bb] + [bc] + [bd] + [be] + [bf] &= [bs], \\ [ac] + [bc] + [cc] + [cd] + [ce] + [cf] &= [cs], \\ [ad] + [bd] + [cd] + [dd] + [de] + [df] &= [ds], \\ [ae] + [be] + [ce] + [de] + [ee] + [ef] &= [es], \\ [af] + [bf] + [cf] + [df] + [ef] + [ff] &= [fs]. \end{aligned} \qquad (77)$$

Hence it appears that if we compute the sums s, s', s'', s''', &c., and form $[as]$, $[bs]$, $[cs]$, &c. simultaneously with the calculation of the coefficients in the normal equations, the equation (76) must be satisfied when the absolute terms of the normal equations are correct; and the equations (77) must be satisfied when the coefficients of the unknown quantities in the normal equations are correct.

The accuracy of the calculation of the auxiliary quantities symbolized by the equation (75) may be proved in a similar manner. Thus, we have

$$[bs.1] = [bs] - \frac{[ab]}{[aa]}[as],$$

which, by means of the first and second of equations (77), becomes

$$[bs.1] = [bb] - \frac{[ab]}{[aa]}[ab] + [bc] - \frac{[ab]}{[aa]}[ac] + [bd] - \frac{[ab]}{[aa]}[ad] + [be] - \frac{[ab]}{[aa]}[ae] + [bf] - \frac{[ab]}{[aa]}[af],$$

or

$$[bs.1] = [bb.1] + [bc.1] + [bd.1] + [be.1] + [bf.1]; \qquad (78)$$

and similarly we derive the expressions for $[cs.1]$, $[ds.1]$, &c. It is obvious, therefore, that the calculation of the coefficients in the equations (59), (64), (68), and (70) will be checked as in the case of the coefficients in the normal equations, the auxiliaries depending on s being determined as if s, s', s'', &c. were the coefficients of an additional unknown quantity in the several equations of condition. Hence we must have, finally,

$$[fs.5] = [ff.5], \qquad [sn.5] = [fn.5]. \qquad (79)$$

If we multiply each of the equations (49) by its v, and take the sum of the several products, we get

$$[av]\,x + [bv]\,y + [cv]\,z + [dv]\,u + [ev]\,w + [fv]\,t + [vn] = [vv].$$

But, according to the equations (48) and (50), we have, for the most probable values of the unknown quantities,

$$[av] = 0, \qquad [bv] = 0, \qquad [cv] = 0, \text{ \&c.};$$

and hence

$$[vn] = [vv]. \tag{80}$$

If we multiply each of the equations (49) by its n, and take the sum of all the products thus formed, substituting $[vv]$ for $[vn]$, there results

$$[an]\,x + [bn]\,y + [cn]\,z + [dn]\,u + [en]\,w + [fn]\,t + [nn] = [vv].$$

Substituting in this the value of x given by the first normal equation, it becomes

$$[bn.1]\,y + [cn.1]\,z + [dn.1]\,u + [en.1]\,w + [fn.1]\,t + [nn.1] = [vv],$$

in which

$$[nn.1] = [nn] - \frac{[an]}{[aa]}\,[an]. \tag{81}$$

Substituting, further, for y its value given by the first of equations (59), and continuing the process as in the elimination of the unknown quantities by successive substitution, we obtain the following equations:

$$\begin{aligned} [cn.2]\,z + [dn.2]\,u + [en.2]\,w + [fn.2]\,t + [nn.2] &= [vv], \\ [dn.3]\,u + [en.3]\,w + [fn.3]\,t + [nn.3] &= [vv], \\ [en.4]\,w + [fn.4]\,t + [nn.4] &= [vv], \\ [fn.5]\,t + [nn.5] &= [vv], \\ [nn.6] &= [vv]. \end{aligned} \tag{82}$$

The expressions for the auxiliaries $[nn.2]$, $[nn.3]$, &c. are

$$[nn.2] = [nn.1] - \frac{[bn.1]}{[bb.1]}\,[bn.1], \qquad [nn.3] = [nn.2] - \frac{[cn.2]}{[cc.2]}\,[cn.2],$$

$$[nn.4] = [nn.3] - \frac{[dn.3]}{[dd.3]}\,[dn.3], \qquad [nn.5] = [nn.4] - \frac{[en.4]}{[ee.4]}\,[en.4],$$

$$[nn.6] = [nn.5] - \frac{[fn.5]}{[ff.5]}\,[fn.5]. \tag{83}$$

The process here indicated may be readily extended to the case of a greater number of unknown quantities, and we have, in general, when μ denotes the number of unknown quantities,

$$[vv] = [nn.\mu]. \tag{84}$$

This equation affords a complete verification of the entire numerical calculation involved in the determination of the unknown quantities from the original equations of condition. Thus, after the elimination has been completed, we substitute the resulting values of x, y, z, &c. in the equations of condition, and derive the corresponding values of the residuals v, v', v'', &c. Then, taking the sum of the squares of these, the equation (84) must be satisfied within the limits of the unavoidable errors of calculation with the logarithmic tables employed. If this condition is satisfied, it may be inferred that the entire calculation of the values of the unknown quantities from the given equations of condition is correct.

138. If the values of x, y, z, &c. thus found were the absolutely exact values, the residuals v, v', v'', &c. would be the actual errors of observation. But since the results obtained only furnish the most probable values of the unknown quantities, the final residuals may differ slightly from the accidental errors of observation. Further, it is evident that the degree of precision with which the several unknown quantities may be determined by means of the data of the problem may be very different, so that it is desirable to be able to determine the relative weights of the different results.

It will be observed that the expressions for either of the unknown quantities resulting from the elimination of the others is a linear function of n, n', n'', &c., so that we have

$$x + \alpha n + \alpha' n' + \alpha'' n'' + \alpha''' n''' + \ldots = 0, \tag{85}$$

in which the coefficients α, α', α'', &c. are functions of the several coefficients of the unknown quantities in the equations of condition. If we now suppose the equations of condition to be reduced to the same unit of weight, the mean error of the several absolute terms of the equations will be the same, and will be the mean error of an observation whose weight is unity. Thus, if ε denotes the mean error of an observation of the weight unity, the mean error of αn will be $\alpha\varepsilon$, that of $\alpha' n'$ will be $\alpha'\varepsilon'$, and similarly for the other terms of (85); and, according to the equation (35), the mean error of x will be

$$\varepsilon_x = \varepsilon \sqrt{\alpha^2 + \alpha'^2 + \alpha''^2 + \&c.} = \varepsilon \sqrt{[\alpha\alpha]}. \tag{86}$$

Hence the weight of x will be expressed by

$$p_x = \frac{1}{[\alpha\alpha]}. \tag{87}$$

Let $x_{,}$ denote the true value of x, namely, that which would be obtained if the true values of v, v', v'', &c. were retained in the second members of the equations of condition instead of putting them equal to zero; then it is evident that the expression for $x_{,}$ must be that which would result by substituting $n - v$ in place of n in the formulæ for the most probable value as determined from the actual data. Hence we have

$$x_{,} + \alpha(n - v) + \alpha'(n' - v') + \ldots. = 0,$$

and comparing this with the expression (85), we obtain

$$x_{,} = x + [\alpha v].$$

Substituting in this the values of v, v', v'', &c. given by the equations (49), there results

$$x_{,} = x + [\alpha a]\, x_{,} + [\alpha b]\, y_{,} + [\alpha c]\, z_{,} + [\alpha d]\, u_{,} + [\alpha e]\, w_{,} + [\alpha f]\, t_{,} + [\alpha n],$$

and since, according to (85), $x + [\alpha n] = 0$, in order to satisfy this expression for $x_{,}$, we must evidently have

$$[\alpha a] = 1, \quad [\alpha b] = 0, \quad [\alpha c] = 0, \quad [\alpha d] = 0, \quad [\alpha e] = 0, \quad [\alpha f] = 0. \quad (88)$$

Since the values of the unknown quantities as determined by the normal equations must be the same by whatever mode the elimination may have been performed, let us suppose the method of indeterminate multipliers to be applied for the determination of x, and let these multipliers be designated by q, q', q'', &c.; then, the values of these factors are determined by the condition that the coefficient of x in the final equation shall be unity, and that the coefficients of the other unknown quantities shall be zero. Hence we shall have

$$\begin{aligned}
&[aa]\, q + [ab]\, q' + [ac]\, q'' + [ad]\, q''' + \ldots. = 1,\\
&[ab]\, q + [bb]\, q' + [bc]\, q'' + [bd]\, q''' + \ldots. = 0,\\
&[ac]\, q + [bc]\, q' + [cc]\, q'' + [cd]\, q''' + \ldots. = 0,\\
&\qquad\quad \&c. \qquad\qquad\quad \&c.
\end{aligned} \quad (89)$$

and also, retaining the residuals v, v', v'', &c. in the formation of the normal equations,

$$x_{,} + [an]\, q + [bn]\, q' + [cn]\, q'' + \ldots = [av]\, q + [bv]\, q' + [cv]\, q'' + \ldots \quad (90)$$

Therefore, since

$$x_{,} + [\alpha n] = [\alpha v],$$

and since the first member of this equation must be identical with the first member of (90), we have

$$[av]\, q + [bv]\, q' + [cv]\, q'' + \ldots = \alpha v + \alpha' v' + \alpha'' v'' + \ldots,$$

which gives, by expanding the several sums,

$$\begin{aligned} aq &+ bq' + cq'' + dq''' + \ldots = \alpha, \\ a'q &+ b'q' + c'q'' + d'q''' + \ldots = \alpha', \\ a''q &+ b''q' + c''q'' + d''q''' + \ldots = \alpha'', \\ &\text{\&c.} \qquad\qquad \text{\&c.} \end{aligned} \tag{91}$$

Multiplying each of these equations by its α, and adding the products, the result is

$$[\alpha a]\,q + [\alpha b]\,q' + [\alpha c]\,q'' + [\alpha d]\,q''' + \ldots = [\alpha\alpha],$$

which, by means of the equations (88), reduces to

$$q = \frac{1}{p_x}. \tag{92}$$

Hence it appears that the eliminating factor q is the reciprocal of the weight of x, and, since the coefficients of q, q', q'', &c. in the equations (89) are the same as those of x, y, z, &c. in the normal equations, that if we put $[an] = -1$, $[bn] = 0$, $[cn] = 0$, &c., in the normal equations, the resulting value of x will be the reciprocal of the weight of the most probable of this quantity.

The equation (90) shows that if, in the general elimination, by whatever method it may have been effected, we write $[av]$, $[bv]$, &c. instead of zero in the second members of the normal equations respectively, the coefficient of $[av]$ is the reciprocal of the weight of x. It is obvious that it will not be necessary to know the numerical values of $[av]$, $[bv]$, &c., since only the coefficient q is required. The most probable value of x is found from (90) by the condition of a minimum of the squares of the residuals, namely, that

$$[av] = 0, \qquad [bv] = 0, \qquad [cv] = 0, \qquad \text{\&c.}$$

The process here indicated for the determination of the weight of the final value of x is general, and applies to the case of any other unknown quantity provided that the necessary changes are made in the notation. Thus, the reciprocal of the weight of y is determined by writing, in the normal equations, -1 in place of $[bn]$, and putting $[an]$, $[cn]$, &c. equal to zero, and completing the elimination. It is also the coefficient of $[bv]$ in the value of y when the elimination is effected with the symbols $[av]$, $[bv]$, &c. retained in the second members of the normal equations.

139. It may be easily shown that when the elimination is effected by the method of successive substitution, as already explained, the

coefficient of the unknown quantity which is made the last in the elimination, in the final equation for its determination, is equal to the weight of the resulting value of that quantity. Thus, in the case of the equations for six unknown quantities, since the reciprocal of the weight of the most probable value of t is the value of t obtained from the normal equations by putting $[fn] = -1$, and $[an]$, $[bn]$, $[cn]$, &c. equal to zero, the equations (63), (67), (69), and (71) show that we have

$$[fn] = [fn.1] = [fn.2] = [fn.3] = [fn.4] = [fn.5] = -1,$$

and hence, according to (72), for the reciprocal of the weight of t,

$$[ff.5]\frac{1}{p_t} - 1 = 0,$$

which gives

$$p_t = [ff.5]. \tag{93}$$

The weight of t is therefore equal to its coefficient in the final equation which results from the elimination of the other unknown quantities by successive substitution. Hence, by repeating the elimination, successively changing the order of the quantities, so that each of the unknown quantities may have the last place, the weights will be determined independently, and the agreement of the several sets of values for the unknown quantities will be a proof of the accuracy of the calculation. It is not necessary, however, to make so many repetitions of the elimination, since, in each case, the weights of two of the unknown quantities will be given by means of the auxiliaries used in the elimination. Thus, the reciprocal of the weight of w is obtained by putting $[en] = -1$, and the other absolute terms of the normal equations equal to zero, and finding the corresponding value of w. This operation gives

$$[en.4] = -1, \qquad [fn.4] = 0, \qquad [fn.5] = \frac{[ef.4]}{[ee.4]}.$$

Hence the equation (73) becomes

$$t = -\frac{[ef.4]}{[ee.4]\,[ff.5]};$$

and substituting this value of t in the last of equations (70), we get

$$[ef.4]\frac{1}{p_w} - \frac{[ff.4]\,[ef.4]}{[ff.5]\,[ee.4]} = 0,$$

or

$$p_w = \frac{[ff.5]}{[ff.4]}[ee.4], \tag{94}$$

which gives the weight of w in terms of the auxiliary quantities required in the determination of its most probable value.

If the order of elimination is now completely reversed, so that x is made the last in the elimination, the weights of x and y will be determined by the equations

$$p_x = [aa.5], \qquad p_y = \frac{[aa.5]}{[aa.4]}[bb.4]. \tag{95}$$

A third elimination, in which z and u are the unknown quantities first determined, will give the weights of these determinations. It appears, therefore, that when only four unknown quantities are to be found, a single repetition of the elimination, the order of the quantities being completely reversed, will furnish at once the weights of the several results, and check the accuracy of the calculation. When there are only two unknown quantities, the elimination gives directly the values of these quantities and also of their weights.

140. In the case of three or more unknown quantities, the weights of all the results may be determined without repeating the elimination when certain additional auxiliary quantities have been found. The weights of the two which are first determined are given in terms of the auxiliaries required in the elimination, that of the quantity which is next found will require the value of an additional auxiliary quantity, the succeeding one will require two additional auxiliaries, and so on. The equations (74) show that when the substitution is effected analytically the final value of x will have the denominator

$$D = [aa]\,[bb.1]\,[cc.2]\,[dd.3]\,[ee.4]\,[ff.5],$$

and this denominator, being the determinant formed from all the coefficients in the normal equations, must evidently have the same value whatever may be the order in which the unknown quantities are eliminated. Let us now suppose that each of the unknown quantities is, in succession, made the last in the elimination, and let the auxiliaries in each elimination be distinguished from those when t is last eliminated by annexing the letter which is the coefficient of the quantity first determined; then we shall have

$$\begin{aligned} D &= [aa]\,[bb.1]\,[cc.2]\,[dd.3]\,[ee.4]\,[ff.5] \\ &= [aa]_e\,[bb.1]_e\,[cc.2]_e\,[dd.3]_e\,[ff.4]_e\,[ee.5] \\ &= [aa]_d\,[bb.1]_d\,[cc.2]_d\,[ee.3]_d\,[ff.4]_d\,[dd.5] \\ &= [aa]_c\,[bb.1]_c\,[dd.2]_c\,[ee.3]_c\,[ff.4]_c\,[cc.5] \\ &= [aa]_b\,[cc.1]_b\,[dd.2]_b\,[ee.3]_b\,[ff.4]_b\,[bb.5] \\ &= [bb]_a\,[cc.1]_a\,[dd.2]_a\,[ee.3]_a\,[ff.4]_a\,[aa.5]. \end{aligned}$$

It will be observed, however, that when the order of elimination is changed, only those auxiliaries which involve the coefficient of the quantity which is made the last in the changed order will be changed. Hence, if we add the distinguishing letter only to those auxiliaries which have a different value in the new order, we have

$$\begin{aligned} D &= [aa]\,[bb.1]\,[cc.2]\,[dd.3]\,[ee.4]\,[ff.5] \\ &= [aa]\,[bb.1]\,[cc.2]\,[dd.3]\,[ff.4]\,[ee.5] \\ &= [aa]\,[bb.1]\,[cc.2]\,[ee.3]\,[ff.4]_d\,[dd.5] \\ &= [aa]\,[bb.1]\,[dd.2]\,[ee.3]_c\,[ff.4]_c\,[cc.5] \\ &= [aa]\,[cc.1]\,[dd.2]_b\,[ee.3]_b\,[ff.4]_b\,[bb.5] \\ &= [bb]\,[cc.1]_a\,[dd.2]_a\,[ee.3]_a\,[ff.4]_a\,[aa.5], \end{aligned}$$

and from these equations we obtain

$$\begin{aligned} p_t &= [ff.5], \\ p_w &= [ee.5] = \frac{[ff.5]}{[ff.4]}\,[ee.4], \\ p_u &= [dd.5] = \frac{[ff.5]}{[ff.4]_d}\cdot\frac{[ee.4]}{[ee.3]}\,[dd.3], \\ p_z &= [cc.5] = \frac{[ff.5]}{[ff.4]_c}\cdot\frac{[ee.4]}{[ee.3]_c}\cdot\frac{[dd.3]}{[dd.2]}\,[cc.2], \\ p_y &= [bb.5] = \frac{[ff.5]}{[ff.4]_b}\cdot\frac{[ee.4]}{[ee.3]_b}\cdot\frac{[dd.3]}{[dd.2]_b}\cdot\frac{[cc.2]}{[cc.1]}\,[bb.1], \\ p_x &= [aa.5] = \frac{[ff.5]}{[ff.4]_a}\cdot\frac{[ee.4]}{[ee.3]_a}\cdot\frac{[dd.3]}{[dd.2]_a}\cdot\frac{[cc.2]}{[cc.1]_a}\cdot\frac{[bb.1]}{[bb]}\,[aa], \end{aligned} \tag{96}$$

by means of which the weights of the six unknown quantities may be determined. The process here indicated may be readily extended to the case of a greater number of unknown quantities. The equation for p_w is identical with (94), the expression for p_u introduces the new auxiliary quantity $[ff.4]_d$, and that for p_z introduces two new auxiliaries.

The expressions for the new auxiliaries $[ff.4]_d$, $[ff.4]_c$, $[ee.3]_c$, &c. are easily formed by observing that all the auxiliaries as far as those which are designated by the numeral 4 are not affected by putting e or f last, that, as far as those which contain the numeral 3, it makes no difference whether d, e, or f is placed last, that those distinguished by the numerals 1 and 2 are not affected by making c, d, e, or f the last, and that those designated by the numeral 1 are unchanged unless a is made the last. Thus, we obtain

$$[ff.4]_d = [ff.3] - \frac{[ef.3]}{[ee.3]}\,[ef.3], \tag{97}$$

and, also,

$$
\begin{aligned}
[ef.3]_c &= [ef.2] - \frac{[de.2]}{[dd.2]}[df.2], &\qquad [ff.3]_c &= [ff.2] - \frac{[df.2]}{[dd.2]}[ef.2], \\
[ee.3]_c &= [ee.2] - \frac{[de.2]}{[dd.2]}[de.2], &\qquad [ff.4]_c &= [ff.3]_c - \frac{[ef.3]_c}{[ee.3]_c}[ef.3]_c.
\end{aligned}
\tag{98}
$$

In like manner we may derive the expressions for the new auxiliaries introduced into the equations for p_y and p_x. It will be expedient, however, in the actual application of the formulæ, to eliminate first in the order x, y, z, u, w, t, and the weights of the results for u, w, and t will be obtained by means of the first three of equations (96), the single additional auxiliary required being found by means of (97). Then the elimination should be performed in the order t, w, u, z, y, x, and we shall have

$$
\begin{aligned}
p_x &= [aa.5], &\qquad p_z &= \frac{[aa.5]}{[aa.4]_c}\cdot\frac{[bb.4]}{[bb.3]}[cc.3], \\
p_y &= \frac{[aa.5]}{[aa.4]}[bb.4], &\qquad [aa.4]_c &= [aa.3] - \frac{[ab.3]}{[bb.3]}[ab.3],
\end{aligned}
\tag{99}
$$

by means of which the weights of x, y, and z will be determined. The agreement of the two sets of values of the unknown quantities will prove the accuracy of the numerical calculation in the process of elimination.

141. The weights of the most probable values of the unknown quantities may also be computed separately when certain auxiliary factors have been found, and these factors are those which are introduced when the equations (74) are solved by the method of indeterminate multipliers instead of by successive substitution. Thus, in order to find x, let the first of these equations be multiplied by 1, the second by A', the third by A'', the fourth by A''', and so on, and let the sum of all these products be taken; then the equations of condition for the determination of the several eliminating factors will be

$$
\begin{aligned}
0 &= \frac{[ab]}{[aa]} + A', \\
0 &= \frac{[ac]}{[aa]} + \frac{[bc.1]}{[bb.1]}A' + A'', \\
0 &= \frac{[ad]}{[aa]} + \frac{[bd.1]}{[bb.1]}A' + \frac{[cd.2]}{[cc.2]}A'' + A''', \\
0 &= \frac{[ae]}{[aa]} + \frac{[be.1]}{[bb.1]}A' + \frac{[ce.2]}{[cc.2]}A'' + \frac{[de.3]}{[dd.3]}A''' + A^{\text{iv}}, \\
0 &= \frac{[af]}{[aa]} + \frac{[bf.1]}{[bb.1]}A' + \frac{[cf.2]}{[cc.2]}A'' + \frac{[df.3]}{[dd.3]}A''' + \frac{[ef.4]}{[ee.4]}A^{\text{iv}} + A^{\text{v}}.
\end{aligned}
\tag{100}
$$

To determine y from the last five of equations (74), let the eliminating factors be denoted by B'', B''', B^{iv}, and B^{v}, and we shall have

$$\begin{aligned}
0 &= \frac{[bc.1]}{[bb.1]} + B'', \\
0 &= \frac{[bd.1]}{[bb.1]} + \frac{[cd.2]}{[cc.2]} B'' + B''', \\
0 &= \frac{[be.1]}{[bb.1]} + \frac{[ce.2]}{[cc.2]} B'' + \frac{[de.3]}{[dd.3]} B''' + B^{iv}, \\
0 &= \frac{[bf.1]}{[bb.1]} + \frac{[cf.2]}{[cc.2]} B'' + \frac{[df.3]}{[dd.3]} B''' + \frac{[ef.4]}{[ee.4]} B^{iv} + B^{v}.
\end{aligned} \tag{101}$$

In a similar manner, we obtain the following equations for the determination of the eliminating factors necessary for finding the values of the remaining unknown quantities:

$$\begin{aligned}
0 &= \frac{[cd.2]}{[cc.2]} + C''', \\
0 &= \frac{[ce.2]}{[cc.2]} + \frac{[de.3]}{[dd.3]} C''' + C^{iv}, \\
0 &= \frac{[cf.2]}{[cc.2]} + \frac{[df.3]}{[dd.3]} C''' + \frac{[ef.4]}{[ee.4]} C^{iv} + C^{v}; \\
0 &= \frac{[de.3]}{[dd.3]} + D^{iv}, \\
0 &= \frac{[df.3]}{[dd.3]} + \frac{[ef.4]}{[ee.4]} D^{iv} + D^{v}, \\
0 &= \frac{[ef.4]}{[ee.4]} + E^{v}.
\end{aligned} \tag{102}$$

The expressions for the values of the unknown quantities will therefore become

$$\begin{aligned}
-x &= \frac{[an]}{[aa]} + \frac{[bn.1]}{[bb.1]} A' + \frac{[cn.2]}{[cc.2]} A'' + \frac{[dn.3]}{[dd.3]} A''' + \frac{[en.4]}{[ee.4]} A^{iv} + \frac{[fn.5]}{[ff.5]} A^{v}, \\
-y &= \frac{[bn.1]}{[bb.1]} + \frac{[cn.2]}{[cc.2]} B'' + \frac{[dn.3]}{[dd.3]} B''' + \frac{[en.4]}{[ee.4]} B^{iv} + \frac{[fn.5]}{[ff.5]} B^{v}, \\
-z &= \frac{[cn.2]}{[cc.2]} + \frac{[dn.3]}{[dd.3]} C''' + \frac{[en.4]}{[ee.4]} C^{iv} + \frac{[fn.5]}{[ff.5]} C^{v}, \\
-u &= \frac{[dn.3]}{[dd.3]} + \frac{[en.4]}{[ee.4]} D^{iv} + \frac{[fn.5]}{[ff.5]} D^{v}, \\
-w &= \frac{[en.4]}{[ee.4]} + \frac{[fn.5]}{[ff.5]} E^{v}, \\
-t &= \frac{[fn.5]}{[ff.5]}.
\end{aligned} \tag{103}$$

The first of these equations will give the reciprocal of the weight of x, when we put $[an] = -1$, and the other absolute terms of the normal equations equal to zero; the second will give the reciprocal of the weight of y by putting $[bn] = -1$, and the other absolute terms of the normal equations equal to zero; and, continuing the process, finally the last equation will give the reciprocal of the weight of t when we put $[fn] = -1$, and $[an]$, $[bn]$, $[cn]$, &c. equal to zero. It remains, therefore, to determine the particular values of $[bn.1]$, $[cn.2]$, &c., and the expressions for the weights will be complete.

If we multiply the first of equations (100) by $[an]$, it becomes

$$[bn.1] = [an]\,A' + [bn]. \tag{104}$$

Multiplying the second of equations (100) by $[an]$, and the first of (101) by $[bn]$, adding the products, and introducing the value of $[bn.1]$ just found, we get

$$[cn] - [cn.1] + \frac{[bc.1]}{[bb.1]}\,[bn.1] + [an]\,A'' + [bn]\,B'' = 0,$$

which reduces to

$$[an]\,A'' + [bn]\,B'' + [cn] = [cn.2]. \tag{105}$$

Multiplying the third of equations (100) by $[an]$, the second of (101) by $[bn]$, and the first of (102) by $[cn]$, adding the products, and reducing by means of (104) and (105), we obtain

$$\begin{aligned} 0 = [dn] - [dn.1] &+ \frac{[bd.1]}{[bb.1]}\,[bn.1] \\ &+ \frac{[cd.2]}{[cc.2]}\,[cn.2] + [an]\,A''' + [bn]\,B''' + [cn]\,C''', \end{aligned}$$

which, by means of the expressions for the auxiliaries, is further reduced to

$$[an]\,A''' + [bn]\,B''' + [cn]\,C''' + [dn] = [dn.3]. \tag{106}$$

In a similar manner we find, from the remaining equations of (100), (101), and (102), the following expressions:

$$\begin{aligned} &[an]\,A^{\text{iv}} + [bn]\,B^{\text{iv}} + [cn]\,C^{\text{iv}} + [dn]\,D^{\text{iv}} + [en] = [en.4], \\ &[an]\,A^{\text{v}} + [bn]\,B^{\text{v}} + [cn]\,C^{\text{v}} + [dn]\,D^{\text{v}} + [en]\,E^{\text{v}} + [fn] = [fn.5]. \end{aligned} \tag{107}$$

The equations (104), (105), (106), and (107), enable us to find the particular values of $[bn.1]$, $[cn.2]$, &c. required in the expressions for the reciprocals of the weights. Thus, for the weight of x, we have

$$[an] = -1, \qquad [bn] = [cn] = [dn] = [en] = [fn] = 0;$$

and these equations give

$$[bn.1] = -A', \qquad [cn.2] = -A'', \qquad [dn.3] = -A''',$$
$$[en.4] = -A^{\text{iv}}, \qquad [fn.5] = -A^{\text{v}}.$$

For the case of the weight of y, we have

$$[bn] = -1, \qquad [an] = [cn] = [dn] = [en] = [fn] = 0,$$

and the same equations give

$$[bn.1] = -1, \qquad [cn.2] = -B'', \qquad [dn.3] = -B''',$$
$$[en.4] = -B^{\text{iv}}, \qquad [fn.5] = -B^{\text{v}}.$$

We have, also, for the weight of z,

$$[cn.2] = -1, \qquad [dn.3] = -C''', \qquad [en.4] = -C^{\text{iv}}, \qquad [fn.5] = -C^{\text{v}};$$

for the weight of u,

$$[dn.3] = -1, \qquad [en.4] = -D^{\text{iv}}, \qquad [fn.5] = -D^{\text{v}};$$

for the weight of w,

$$[en.4] = -1, \qquad [fn.5] = -E^{\text{v}};$$

and finally, for the weight of t,

$$[fn.5] = -1.$$

Introducing these particular values into the equations (103), the corresponding values of the unknown quantities are the reciprocals of the weights of their most probable values, respectively; and hence we derive

$$\left.\begin{aligned}
\frac{1}{p_x} &= \frac{1}{[aa]} + \frac{A'A'}{[bb.1]} + \frac{A''A''}{[cc.2]} + \frac{A'''A'''}{[dd.3]} + \frac{A^{\text{iv}}A^{\text{iv}}}{[ee.4]} + \frac{A^{\text{v}}A^{\text{v}}}{[ff.5]}, \\
\frac{1}{p_y} &= \frac{1}{[bb.1]} + \frac{B''B''}{[cc.2]} + \frac{B'''B'''}{[dd.3]} + \frac{B^{\text{iv}}B^{\text{iv}}}{[ee.4]} + \frac{B^{\text{v}}B^{\text{v}}}{[ff.5]}, \\
\frac{1}{p_z} &= \frac{1}{[cc.2]} + \frac{C'''C'''}{[dd.3]} + \frac{C^{\text{iv}}C^{\text{iv}}}{[ee.4]} + \frac{C^{\text{v}}C^{\text{v}}}{[ff.5]}, \\
\frac{1}{p_u} &= \frac{1}{[dd.3]} + \frac{D^{\text{iv}}D^{\text{iv}}}{[ee.4]} + \frac{D^{\text{v}}D^{\text{v}}}{[ff.5]}, \\
\frac{1}{p_w} &= \frac{1}{[ee.4]} + \frac{E^{\text{v}}E^{\text{v}}}{[ff.5]}, \\
\frac{1}{p_t} &= \frac{1}{[ff.5]}.
\end{aligned}\right\} \quad (108)$$

The equations (103) and (108) will serve to determine separately the value of each unknown quantity and also that of its weight, the auxiliary factors A', A'', B'', &c. having been found from the equations (100), (101), and (102). If we reverse the operation and recompose the equations (74) by means of the expressions for the unknown quantities given by (103), the conditions which immediately follow furnish another series of equations for the determination of the auxiliary factors. The equations thus derived will give first the values of A', B'', C''', D^{iv}, and E^{v}; then, those of A'', B''', C^{iv}, D^{v}; and so on. They are equally as convenient as those already given, provided that the values of all the unknown quantities are required as well as their respective weights.

142. The formulæ already given for the relations between the data of the problem and the weights of the most probable values of the unknown quantities, are those which are of the greatest practical value. It will be apparent from what has been derived that there must be a variety of methods which may be applied, but that all of these methods involve essentially the same numerical operations. The peculiar symmetry of the normal equations affords also a variety of expressions applicable to the different phases under which the problem presents itself.

According to the general theory of elimination, the expression for any unknown quantity, as determined from the normal equations, may be put in the form

$$x = -\frac{A}{D}[an] - \frac{A'}{D}[bn] - \frac{A''}{D}[cn] - \&c., \tag{109}$$

in which D is the determinant formed from all the coefficients of the unknown quantities in the normal equations, and in which A, A', A'', &c. are the partial determinants required in the elimination. Thus, A is the determinant formed from the coefficients of all the unknown quantities except x, in all the equations except the first; A' is the determinant formed from the coefficients of y, z, &c. in all the equations except the second; and the values of A'', A''', &c. are formed in a similar manner. Now, since the value of x which results when we put $[an] = -1$, and the other absolute terms of the normal equations equal to zero, is the reciprocal of the weight of the most probable value of this unknown quantity as given by (109), we have

$$p_x = \frac{D}{A}. \tag{110}$$

In like manner, the expression for the most probable value of y will be

$$y = -\frac{B}{D}[an] - \frac{B'}{D}[bn] - \frac{B''}{D}[cn] - \&c., \tag{111}$$

B, B', B'', &c. being the partial determinants formed when the coefficients of y are omitted; and for its weight we have

$$p_y = \frac{D}{B'}. \tag{112}$$

The formulæ for the most probable value of z and for its weight are entirely analogous to those for x and y, so that the process here indicated may be extended to the case of any number of unknown quantities. It appears, therefore, that the weight of the most probable value of any unknown quantity is found by dividing the complete determinant of all the coefficients by the partial determinant formed when we omit the normal equation corresponding particularly to this unknown quantity, and when we omit also the coefficients of this quantity in the remaining normal equations.

The peculiar arrangement of the coefficients in the normal equations abbreviates somewhat the expressions for the several determinants. Thus, in the case of three unknown quantities, we have

$$A = [bb][cc] - [bc]^2, \quad B' = [aa][cc] - [ac]^2, \quad C'' = [aa][bb] - [ab]^2,$$
$$D = [aa][bb][cc] + 2[ab][bc][ac] - [aa][bc]^2 - [bb][ac]^2 - [cc][ab]^2,$$

which are all the quantities required for finding simply the weights of the most probable values of x, y, and z. The expression for the weight of z is

$$p_z = \frac{D}{C''}.$$

When there are but two unknown quantities, we have

$$A = [bb], \qquad B' = [aa], \qquad D = [aa][bb] - [ab]^2,$$

and hence

$$p_x = \frac{[aa][bb] - [ab]^2}{[bb]}, \qquad p_y = \frac{[aa][bb] - [ab]^2}{[aa]}.$$

When the number of unknown quantities is increased, the expressions for the determinants necessarily become much more complicated, and hence the convenience of other auxiliary quantities is manifest.

143. The case has been already alluded to in which the determination of the values of the unknown quantities is rendered uncertain by the similarity of the signs and coefficients in the normal equations,

and in which the problem becomes nearly indeterminate. Sometimes it will be possible to overcome the difficulty thus encountered by a suitable change of the elements to be determined; but, generally, for a complete and satisfactory solution, additional data will be required. It often happens, however, that several of the unknown quantities may be accurately determined from the given equations when the values of the others are known, but that the certainty of the determination of the same quantities is very greatly impaired when all the unknown quantities are derived simultaneously from the same equations. Let us suppose that one of the unknown quantities is, from the very nature of the problem, not susceptible of an accurate determination from the data employed. The equations will then present themselves in a form approaching that in which the number of independent relations is one less than the number of unknown quantities, so that it will be necessary to determine the other unknown quantities in terms of that whose value is necessarily uncertain. In this case the elimination should be so arranged that the quantity which is regarded as uncertain is that whose value would be first determined. Then, if its coefficient in the final equation, corresponding to (72), is very small, a circumstance which indicates at once the existence of the uncertainty when it is not otherwise suspected, the process of elimination should not be completed, and the auxiliary quantities should be determined only as far as those required in the formation of the equation which corresponds to the first of (70). Thus, let t be the uncertain quantity, and we have

$$w = -\frac{[ef.4]}{[ee.4]}t - \frac{[en.4]}{[ee.4]},$$

which must be substituted for w in the first of equations (68). We thus obtain w, u, z, y, and x as functions of t. If the solution is effected by means of the equations (103), let x_0, y_0, z_0, &c. denote the values of these unknown quantities when we put $t=0$; and then we shall have

$$\begin{aligned} x_0 &= -\frac{[an]}{[aa]} - \frac{[bn.1]}{[bb.1]}A' - \frac{[cn.2]}{[cc.2]}A'' - \frac{[dn.3]}{[dd.3]}A''' - \frac{[en.4]}{[ee.4]}A^{\text{iv}}, \\ y_0 &= -\frac{[bn.1]}{[bb.1]} - \frac{[cn.2]}{[cc.2]}B'' - \frac{[dn.3]}{[dd.3]}B''' - \frac{[en.4]}{[ee.4]}B^{\text{iv}}, \qquad (113) \\ z_0 &= -\frac{[cn.2]}{[cc.2]} - \frac{[dn.3]}{[dd.3]}C''' - \frac{[en.4]}{[ee.5]}C^{\text{iv}}, \end{aligned}$$

$$u_0 = -\frac{[dn.3]}{[dd.3]} - \frac{[en.4]}{[ee.4]} D^{\text{iv}},$$
$$w_0 = -\frac{[en.4]}{[ee.4]}. \tag{113}$$

and hence

$$x = x_0 + A^{\text{v}}t, \qquad y = y_0 + B^{\text{v}}t, \qquad z = z_0 + C^{\text{v}}t,$$
$$u = u_0 + D^{\text{v}}t, \qquad w = w_0 + E^{\text{v}}t. \tag{114}$$

As soon as t is determined by some independent condition or relation, these equations will give the corresponding values of x, y, z, &c. The mean errors of x_0, y_0, z_0, &c. having been determined by neglecting t entirely, if we denote the mean error of the final adopted value of t by ε_t, the mean errors of the corresponding values of the other variables will be given by

$$\varepsilon_x^2 = (\varepsilon_x)^2 + A^{\text{v}}A^{\text{v}}\varepsilon_t^2, \quad \varepsilon_y^2 = (\varepsilon_y)^2 + B^{\text{v}}B^{\text{v}}\varepsilon_t^2, \quad \varepsilon_z^2 = (\varepsilon_z)^2 + C^{\text{v}}C^{\text{v}}\varepsilon_t^2,$$
$$\varepsilon_u^2 = (\varepsilon_u)^2 + D^{\text{v}}D^{\text{v}}\varepsilon_t^2, \qquad \varepsilon_w^2 = (\varepsilon_w)^2 + E^{\text{v}}E^{\text{v}}\varepsilon_t^2, \tag{115}$$

in which (ε_x), (ε_y), &c. denote the mean errors of x_0, y_0, &c. These formulæ show, also, that when one of the variables is neglected, the equations assign too great a degree of precision to the results thus obtained.

When there are two or more unknown quantities which cannot be determined from the data with sufficient certainty, the problem must be treated in a manner entirely analogous to that here indicated; but, since cases of this kind will rarely, if ever, occur, it is not necessary to pursue the subject further.

144. The weights which are obtained for the most probable values of the unknown quantities enable us to find the mean and probable errors of these values. Let ε denote the mean error of an observation whose weight is unity; then the mean error of x will be

$$\varepsilon_x = \frac{\varepsilon}{\sqrt{p_x}}, \tag{116}$$

and, in like manner, the expressions for the mean errors of y, z, u, &c. will be

$$\varepsilon_y = \frac{\varepsilon}{\sqrt{p_y}}, \qquad \varepsilon_z = \frac{\varepsilon}{\sqrt{p_z}}, \qquad \varepsilon_u = \frac{\varepsilon}{\sqrt{p_u}}, \text{ \&c.} \tag{117}$$

It remains, therefore, to determine the value of ε by means of the final residuals obtained by comparing the observed values of the function with those given by the most probable values of the variables. If these residuals were the actual fortuitous errors of observation, the mean error of an observation would be

$$\varepsilon = \sqrt{\frac{[vv]}{m}},$$

m being the number of equations of condition. This value is evidently an approximation to the correct result; but since by supposing the residuals v, v', v'', &c. to be the actual errors of the several observed values of the function, we assign too high a degree of precision to the several results, the true value of ε must necessarily be greater than that given by this equation. Let the true values of the unknown quantities be $x + \Delta x$, $y + \Delta y$, $z + \Delta z$, &c., the substitution of which in the several equations of condition would give the residuals $\varDelta$, $\varDelta'$, $\varDelta''$, &c.; then we shall have

$$\begin{aligned} a\Delta x + b\Delta y + c\Delta z + d\Delta u \ldots . + v &= \varDelta, \\ a'\Delta x + b'\Delta y + c'\Delta z + d'\Delta u \ldots . + v' &= \varDelta', \\ \&c. \qquad\qquad &\&c. \end{aligned} \tag{118}$$

If we multiply each of these equations by its $\varDelta$, and take the sum of all the products, we get

$$[a\varDelta]\Delta x + [b\varDelta]\Delta y + [c\varDelta]\Delta z + [d\varDelta]\Delta u + \ldots . + [v\varDelta] = [\varDelta\varDelta].$$

But if we multiply each of the same equations by its v, take the sum of the products, and reduce by means of (48) and (50), we obtain

$$[vv] = [v\varDelta];$$

and hence we derive

$$[\varDelta\varDelta] = [vv] + [a\varDelta]\Delta x + [b\varDelta]\Delta y + [c\varDelta]\Delta z + [d\varDelta]\Delta u + \ldots . \tag{119}$$

If we form the normal equations from (118), it will be observed that they are of the same form as the normal equations formed from the original equations of condition, provided that we write $-\varDelta$ in place of n; and hence, according to (85), we have

$$\Delta x = \alpha\varDelta + \alpha'\varDelta' + \alpha''\varDelta'' + \ldots . .$$

We have, also,

$$[a\varDelta] = a\varDelta + a'\varDelta' + a''\varDelta'' + \ldots . .,$$

and the product of these equations gives

$$\begin{aligned} [a\varDelta]\Delta x = a\alpha\varDelta^2 + a'\alpha'\varDelta'^2 + a''\alpha''\varDelta''^2 + \ldots . \\ + a\alpha'\varDelta\varDelta' + a\alpha''\varDelta\varDelta'' + \ldots . \end{aligned}$$

The mean value of the terms containing $\varDelta\varDelta'$, $\varDelta\varDelta''$, &c. is zero, and for the mean values of Δ^2, Δ'^2, Δ''^2, &c. we must, in each case, write ε^2. Hence the mean value of the product $[a\Delta]\,\Delta x$ will be

$$[aa]\,\varepsilon^2,$$

and this, by means of the first of equations (88), is further reduced to

$$[a\Delta]\,\Delta x = \varepsilon^2.$$

In a similar manner, we obtain the value ε^2 for the mean value of each of the products $[b\Delta]\,\Delta y$, $[c\Delta]\,\Delta z$, &c. Now, the terms added to $[vv]$ in the second member of the equation (119) are necessarily very small, and, although their exact value cannot be determined, we may without sensible error adopt the mean values of the several terms as here determined, so that the equation becomes

$$[\Delta\Delta] = [vv] + \mu\varepsilon^2, \tag{120}$$

μ being the number of unknown quantities. Therefore, since $[\Delta\Delta] = m\varepsilon^2$, we shall have

$$\varepsilon = \sqrt{\frac{[vv]}{m-\mu}} = \sqrt{\frac{[nn.\mu]}{m-\mu}}, \tag{121}$$

by means of which the mean error of an observation whose weight is unity may be determined. When $\mu = 1$, this equation becomes identical with (30).

For the determination of the probable errors of the final values of the unknown quantities, if r denotes the probable error of an observation of the weight unity, we have the following equations:—

$$r = 0.67449\sqrt{\frac{[vv]}{m-\mu}},$$
$$r_x = \frac{r}{\sqrt{p_x}}, \qquad r_y = \frac{r}{\sqrt{p_y}}, \ \text{\&c.} \tag{122}$$

145. The formulæ which result from the theory of errors according to which the method of least squares is derived, enable us to combine the data furnished by observation so as to overcome, in the greatest degree possible, the effect of those accidental errors which no refinement of theory can successfully eliminate. The problem of the correction of the approximate elements of the orbit of a heavenly body by means of a series of observed places, requires the application of nearly all the distinct results which have been derived. The first approximate elements of the orbit of the body will be determined from three or four observed places according to the methods which

have been already explained. In the case of a planet, if the inclination is not very small, the method of three geocentric places may be employed, but it will, in general, afford greater accuracy and require but little additional labor to base the first determination on four observed places, according to the process already illustrated. In the case of a comet, the first assumption made is that the orbit is a parabola, and the elements derived in accordance with this hypothesis may be successively corrected, until it is apparent whether it is necessary to make any further assumption in regard to the value of the eccentricity. In all cases, the approximate elements derived from a few places should be further corrected by means of more extended data before any attempt is made to obtain a more complete determination of the elements. The various methods by which this preliminary correction may be effected have been already sufficiently developed.

The fundamental places adopted as the basis of the correction may be single observed places separated by considerable intervals of time; but it will be preferable to use places which may be regarded as the average of a number of observations made on the same day or during a few days before and after the date of the average or *normal* place. The ephemeris computed from the approximate elements known may be assumed to represent the actual path so closely that, for an interval of a few days, the difference between computation and observation may be regarded as being constant, or at least as varying proportionally to the time. Let n, n', n'', &c. be the differences between computation and observation, in the case of either spherical co-ordinate, for the dates t, t', t'', &c., respectively; then, if the interval between the extreme observations to be combined in the formation of the normal place is not too great, and if we regard the observations as equally precise, the normal difference n_0 between computation and observation will be found by taking the arithmetical mean of the several values of n, and this being applied with the proper sign to the computed spherical co-ordinate for the date t_0, which is the mean of t, t', t'', &c., will give the corresponding normal place. But when different weights p, p', p'', &c. are assigned to the observations, the value of n_0 must be found from

$$n_0 = \frac{np + n'p' + n''p'' + \ldots}{p + p' + p'' + \ldots}, \tag{123}$$

and the weight of this value will be equal to the sum

$$p + p' + p'' + \ldots.$$

The date of the normal place will be determined by

$$t_0 = \frac{pt + p't' + p''t'' + \dots}{p + p' + p'' + \dots}. \tag{124}$$

If the error of the ephemeris can be considered as nearly constant, it is not necessary to determine t_0 with great precision, since any date not differing much from the average of all may be adopted with sufficient accuracy. It should be observed further that, in order to obtain the greatest accuracy practicable, the spherical co-ordinates of the body for the date t_0 should be computed directly from the elements, so that the resulting normal place may be as free as possible from the effect of neglected differences in the interpolation of the ephemeris.

When the differences between the computed and the observed places to be combined for the formation of a normal place cannot be considered as varying proportionally to the time, we may derive the error of the ephemeris from an equation of the form of $(53)_6$, namely,

$$\Delta\theta = A + B\tau + C\tau^2,$$

the coefficients A, B, and C being found from equations of condition formed by means of the several known values of $\Delta\theta$ in the case of each of the spherical co-ordinates.

146. In this way we obtain normal places at convenient intervals throughout the entire period during which the body was observed. From three or more of these normal places, a new system of elements should be computed by means of some one of the methods which have already been given; and these fundamental places being judiciously selected, the resulting elements will furnish a pretty close approximation to the truth, so that the residuals which are found by comparing them with all the directly observed places may be regarded as indicating very nearly the actual errors of those places. We may then proceed to investigate the character of the observations more fully. But since the observations will have been made at many different places, by different observers, with instruments of different sizes, and under a variety of dissimilar attendant circumstances, it may be easily understood that the investigation will involve much that is vague and uncertain. In the theory of errors which has been developed in this chapter, it has been assumed that all constant errors have been duly eliminated, and that the only errors which remain are those accidental errors which must ever continue in a greater or less degree undetermined. The greater the number and

perfection of the observations employed, the more nearly will these errors be determined, and the more nearly will the law of their distribution conform to that which has been assumed as the basis of the method of least squares.

When all known errors have been eliminated, there may yet remain constant errors, and also other errors whose law of distribution is peculiar, such as may arise from the idiosyncrasies of the different observers, from the systematic errors of the adopted star-places in the case of differential observations, and from a variety of other sources; and since the observations themselves furnish the only means of arriving at a knowledge of these errors, it becomes important to discuss them in such a manner that all errors which may be regarded, in a sense more or less extended, as *regular* may be eliminated. When this has been accomplished, the residuals which still remain will enable us to form an estimate of the degree of accuracy which may be attributed to the different series of observations, in order that they may not only be combined in the most advantageous manner, but that also no refinements of calculation may be introduced which are not warranted by the quality of the material to be employed.

The necessity of a preliminary calculation in which a high degree of accuracy is already obtained, is indicated by the fact that, however conscientious the observer may be, his judgment is unconsciously warped by an inherent desire to produce results harmonizing well among themselves, so that a limited series of places may agree to such an extent that the probable error of an observation as derived from the relative discordances would assign a weight vastly in excess of its true value. The combination, however, of a large number of independent data, by exhibiting at least an approximation to the absolute errors of the observations, will indicate nearly what the measure of precision should be. As soon, therefore, as provisional elements which nearly represent the entire series of observations have been found, an attempt should be made to eliminate all errors which may be accurately or approximately determined. The places of the comparison-stars used in the observations should be determined with care from the data available, and should be reduced, by means of the proper systematic corrections, to some standard system. The reduction of the mean places of the stars to apparent places should also be made by means of uniform constants of reduction. The observations will thus be uniformly reduced. Then the perturbations arising from the action of the planets should be computed by means of formulæ which will be investigated in the next chapter, and the observed places should be freed from these perturbations so as to give the places for a system of osculating elements for a given date.

147. The next step in the process will be to compare the provisional elements with the entire series of observed places thus corrected; and in the calculation of the ephemeris it will be advantageous to correct the places of the sun given by the tables whenever observations are available for that purpose. Then, selecting one or more epochs as the origin, if we compute the coefficients A, B, C in the equation

$$\Delta\theta = A + B\tau + C\tau^2, \tag{125}$$

in the case of each of the spherical co-ordinates, by means of equations of condition formed from all the observations, the standard ephemeris may be corrected so that it may be regarded as representing the actual path of the body during the period included by the observations. When the number of observations is considerable, it will be more convenient to divide the observations into groups, and use the differences between computation and observation for provisional normal places in the formation of the equations of condition for the determination of A, B, and C. It thus appears that the corrected ephemeris which is so essential to a determination of the constant errors peculiar to each series of observations, is obtained without first having determined the most probable system of elements. The corrections computed by means of the equation (125) being applied to the several residuals of each series, we obtain what may be regarded as the actual errors of these observations. The arithmetical or probable mean of the corrected residuals for the series of observations made by each observer may be regarded as the average error of observation for that series. The mean of the average errors of the several series may be regarded as the actual constant error pertaining to all the observations, and the comparison of this final mean with the means found for the different series, respectively, furnishes the probable value of the constant errors due to the peculiarities of the observers; and the constant correction thus found for each observer should be applied to the corresponding residuals already obtained.

In this investigation, if the number of comparisons or the number of wires taken is known, relative weights proportional to the number of comparisons may be adopted for the combination of the residuals for each series. In this manner, observations which, on account of the peculiarities of the observers, are in a certain sense heterogeneous, may be rendered homogeneous, being reduced to a standard which approaches the absolute in proportion as the number and perfection of the distinct series combined are increased. Whatever constant error remains will be very small, and, besides, will affect all places alike.

The residuals which now remain must be regarded as consisting of the actual errors of observation and of the error of the adopted place of the comparison-star. Hence they will not give the probable error of observation, and will not serve directly for assigning the measures of precision of the series of observations by each observer. Let us, therefore, denote by ε_s the mean error of the place of the comparison-star, by $\varepsilon_{,}$ the mean error of a single comparison; then will $\frac{\varepsilon_{,}}{\sqrt{m}}$ be the mean error of m comparisons, and the mean error of the resulting place of the body will, according to equation (35), be given by

$$\varepsilon_0^2 = \frac{\varepsilon_{,}^2}{m} + \varepsilon_s^2. \tag{126}$$

The value of ε_0, in the case of each series, will be found by means of the residuals finally corrected for the constant errors, and the value of ε_s is supposed to be determined in the formation of the catalogue of star-places adopted. Hence the actual mean error of an observation consisting of a single comparison will be

$$\varepsilon_{,} = \sqrt{m(\varepsilon_0^2 - \varepsilon_s^2)}. \tag{127}$$

The value of $\varepsilon_{,}$ for each observer having been found in accordance with this equation, the mean error of an observation consisting of m comparisons will be

$$\frac{\varepsilon_{,}}{\sqrt{m}}.$$

The mean error of an observation whose weight is unity being denoted by ε, the weight of an observation based on m comparisons will be

$$p = \frac{m\varepsilon^2}{\varepsilon_{,}^2}. \tag{128}$$

The value of ε may be arbitrarily assigned, and we may adopt for it $\pm 10''$ or any other number of seconds for which the resulting values of p will be convenient numbers.

When all the observations are differential observations, and the stars of comparison are included in the fundamental list, if we do not take into account the number of comparisons on which each observed place depends, it will not be necessary to consider ε_s, and we may then derive ε, directly from the residuals corrected for constant errors. Further, in the case of meridian observations, the error which corresponds to ε_s will be extremely small, and hence it is only when these are combined with equatorial observations, or when equatorial observations based on different numbers of comparisons are combined, that the separation of the errors into the two component parts becomes necessary for a proper determination of the relative weights.

According to the complete method here indicated, after having eliminated as far as possible all constant errors, including the corrections assigned by equation (125) to be applied to the provisional ephemeris, we find the value of ε, given by the equation

$$n\varepsilon_{,}^2 = [mvv] - [m]\,\varepsilon_s^2, \qquad (129)$$

in which n denotes the number of observations; m, m', m'', &c. the number of comparisons for the respective observations; and v, v', v'', &c. the corresponding residuals. Then, by means of equation (128), assuming a convenient number for ε, we compute the weight of each observation. Thus, for example, let the residuals and corresponding values of m be as follows:—

$\Delta\theta$	m	$\Delta\theta$	m
$+2''.0$	5,	$-1''.0$	7,
$-1\;.8$	5,	$+1\;.5$	5,
$-0\;.4$	10,	$+4\;.1$	8,
$-5\;.5$	5,	$0\;.0$	5.

Let the mean error of the place of a comparison-star be

$$\varepsilon_s = \pm 2''.0;$$

then we have $n = 8$, and, according to (129),

$$8\varepsilon_{,}^2 = 341.78 - 200.0,$$

which gives

$$\varepsilon_{,} = \pm 4''.2.$$

Let us now adopt as the unit of weight that for which the mean error is

$$\varepsilon = \pm 3''.0;$$

then we obtain by means of equation (128), for the weights of the observations,

2.5, 2.5, 5.1, 2.5, 3.6, 2.5, 4.1, 2.5,

respectively.

In this manner the weights of the observations in the series made by each observer must be determined, using throughout the same value of ε. Then the differences between the places computed from the provisional elements to be corrected and the observed places corrected for the constant error of the observer, must be combined according to the equations (123) and (125), the adopted values of p, p', p'', &c. being those found from (128). Thus will be obtained the final residuals for the formation of the equations of condition from which to derive the most probable value of the corrections to be applied to the elements. The relative weights of these normals will be indicated by the sums formed by adding together the weights of the observations combined in the formation of each normal, and the unit of weight will depend on the adopted value of ε. If it be desired to adopt a different unit of weight in the case of the solution of the equations of condition, such, for example, that the weight of an equation of average precision shall be unity, we may simply divide the weights of the normals by any number p_0 which will satisfy the condition imposed. The mean error of an observation whose weight is unity will then be given by

$$\frac{\varepsilon}{\sqrt{p_0}},$$

the value of ε being that used in the determination of the weights p, p', &c.

148. The observations of comets are liable to be affected by other errors in addition to those which are common to these and to planetary observations. Different observers will fix upon different points as the proper point to be observed, and all of these may differ from the actual position of the centre of gravity of the comet; and further, on account of changes in the physical appearance of the comet, the same observer may on different nights select different points. These circumstances concur to vitiate the normal places, inasmuch as the resulting errors, although in a certain sense fortuitous, are yet such that the law of their distribution is evidently different from that which is adopted as the basis of the method of least squares. The impossibility of assigning the actual limits and the law of distribution of many errors of this class, renders it necessary to adopt empirical methods, the success of which will depend on the discrimination of the computer.

If ε_0 denotes the mean error of an observation based on m comparisons, and ε_c the mean error to be feared on account of the peculiarities of the physical appearance of the comet,

$$\varepsilon_0^2 + \varepsilon_c^2.$$

will express the mean error of the residuals; and if n of these residuals are combined in the formation of a normal place, the mean error of the normal will be given by

$$\varepsilon_n^2 = \frac{[\varepsilon_0^2]}{n} + \varepsilon_c^2. \tag{130}$$

The value of ε_c^2 may be determined approximately from the data furnished by the observations. Thus, if the mean error of a single comparison, for the different observers, has been determined by means of the differences between single comparisons and the arithmetical mean of a considerable number of comparisons, and if the mean error of the place of a comparison-star has also been determined, the equation (126) will give the corresponding value of ε_0^2; then the actual differences between computation and observation obtained by eliminating the error of the ephemeris and such constant errors as may be determined, will furnish an approximate value of ε_c by means of the formula

$$\varepsilon_c^2 = \frac{[vv]}{n} - \varepsilon_0^2,$$

in which n denotes the number of observations combined.

Sometimes, also, in the case of comets, in order to detect the operation of any abnormal force or circumstance producing different effects in different parts of the orbit, it may be expedient to divide the observations into two distinct groups, the first including the observations made before the time of perihelion passage, and the other including those subsequent to that epoch.

149. The circumstances of the problem will often suggest appropriate modifications of the complete process of determining the relative weights of the observations to be combined, or indeed a relaxation from the requirements of the more rigorous method. Thus, if on account of the number or quality of the data it is not considered necessary to compute the relative weights with the greatest precision attainable, it will suffice, when the discussion of the observations has been carried to an extent sufficient to make an approximate estimate of the relative weights, to assume, without considering the number of comparisons, a weight 1 for the observations at one observatory, a

weight $\frac{3}{4}$ for another class of observations, $\frac{1}{2}$ for a third class, and so on. It should be observed, also, that when there are but few observations to be combined, the application of the formulæ for the mean or probable errors may be in a degree fallacious, the resulting values of these errors being little more than rude approximations; still the mean or probable errors as thus determined furnish the most reliable means of estimating the relative weights of the observations made by different observers, since otherwise the scale of weights would depend on the arbitrary discretion of the computer. Further, in a complete investigation, even when the very greatest care has been taken in the theoretical discussion, on account of independent known circumstances connected with some particular observation, it may be expedient to change arbitrarily the weight assigned by theory to certain of the normal places. It may also be advisable to reject entirely those observations whose weight is less than a certain limit which may be regarded as the standard of excellence below which the observations should be rejected; and it will be proper to reject observations which do not afford the data requisite for a homogeneous combination with the others according to the principles already explained. But in all cases the rejection of apparently doubtful observations should not be carried to any considerable extent unless a very large number of good observations are available. The mere apparent discrepancy between any residual and the others of a series, is not in itself sufficient to warrant its rejection unless facts are known which would independently assign to it a low degree of precision.

A doubtful observation will have the greatest influence in vitiating the resulting normal place when but a small number of observed places are combined; and hence, since we cannot assume that the law of the distribution of errors, according to which the method of least squares is derived, will be complied with in the case of only a few observations, it will not in general be safe to reject an observation provided that it surpasses a limit which is fixed by the adopted theory of errors. If the number of observations is so large that the distribution of the errors may be assumed to conform to the theory adopted, it will be possible to assign a limit such that a residual which surpasses it may be rejected. Thus, in a series of m observations, according to the expression (19), the number of errors greater than nr will be

$$m\left(1-\frac{2}{\sqrt{\pi}}\int_0^{nhr} e^{-t^2}\,dt\right);$$

and when n has a value such that the value of this expression is less than 0.5, the error nr will have a greater probability against it than for it, and hence it may be rejected. The expression for finding the limiting value of n therefore becomes

$$\frac{2}{\sqrt{\pi}}\int_0^{nhr} e^{-t^2}\,dt = 1 - \frac{1}{2m}. \tag{131}$$

By means of this equation we derive for given values of m the corresponding values of $nhr = 0.47694n$, and hence the values of n. For convenient application, it will be preferable to use ε instead of r, and if we put $n' = 0.67449n$, the limiting error will be $n'\varepsilon$, and the values of n' corresponding to given values of m will be as exhibited in the following table.

TABLE.

m	n'	m	n'	m	n'	m	n'
6	1.732	20	2.241	55	2.608	90	2.773
8	1.863	25	2.326	60	2.638	95	2.791
10	1.960	30	2.394	65	2.665	100	2.807
12	2.037	35	2.450	70	2.690	200	3.020
14	2.100	40	2.498	75	2.713	300	3.143
16	2.154	45	2.539	80	2.734	400	3.224
18	2.200	50	2.576	85	2.754	500	3.289

According to this method, we first find the mean error of an observation by means of all the residuals. Then, with the value of m as the argument, we take from the table the corresponding value of n', and if one of the residuals exceeds the value $n'\varepsilon$ it must be rejected. Again, finding a new value of ε from the remaining $m - 1$ residuals, and repeating the operation, it will be seen whether another observation should be rejected; and the process may be continued until a limit is reached which does not require the further rejection of observations. Thus, for example, in the case of 50 observations in which the residuals $-11''.5$ and $+7''.8$ occur, let the sum of the squares of the residuals be

$$[vv] = 320.4.$$

Then, according to equation (30), we shall have

$$\varepsilon = \pm 2''.56.$$

Corresponding to the value $m = 50$, the table gives $n' = 2.576$, and the limiting value of the error becomes

$$n'\varepsilon = 6''.6\,;$$

and hence the residuals $-11''.5$ and $+7''.8$ are rejected. Recomputing the mean error of an observation, we have

$$\varepsilon = \sqrt{\frac{320.4 - 193.09}{47}} = \pm\, 1''.65.$$

In the formation of a normal place, when the mean error of an observation has been inferred from only a small number of observations, according to what has been stated, it will not be safe to rely upon the equation (131) for the necessity of the rejection of a doubtful observation. But if any abnormal influence is suspected, or if any antecedent discussion of observations by the same observer, made under similar circumstances, seems to indicate that an error of a given magnitude is highly improbable, the application of this formula will serve to confirm or remove the doubt already created. Much will therefore depend on the discrimination of the computer, and on his knowledge of the various sources of error which may conspire continuously or discontinuously in the production of large apparent errors. It is the business of the observer to indicate the circumstances peculiar to the phenomenon observed, the instruments employed, and the methods of observation; and the discussion of the data thus furnished by different observers, as far as possible in accordance with the strict requirements of the adopted theory of errors, will furnish results which must be regarded as the best which can be derived from the evidence contributed by all the observations.

150. When the final normal places have been derived, the differences between these and the corresponding places computed from the provisional elements to be corrected, taken in the sense computation minus observation, give the values of n, n', n'', &c. which are the absolute terms of the equations of condition. By means of these elements we compute also the values of the differential coefficients of each of the spherical co-ordinates with respect to each of the elements to be corrected. These differential coefficients give the values of the coefficients a, b, c, a', b', &c. in the equations of condition. The mode of calculating these coefficients, for different systems of co-ordinates, and the mode of forming the equations of condition, have been fully developed in the second chapter. It is of great import-

ance that the numerical values of these coefficients should be carefully checked by direct calculation, assigning variations to the elements, or by means of differences when this test can be successfully applied. In assigning increments to the elements in order to check the formation of the equations, they should not be so large that the neglected terms of the second order become sensible, nor so small that they do not afford the required certainty by means of the agreement of the corresponding variations of the spherical co-ordinates as obtained by substitution and by direct calculation.

As soon as the equations of condition have been thus formed, we multiply each of them by the square root of its weight as given by the adopted relative weights of the normal places; and these equations will thus be reduced to the same weight. In general, the numerical values of the coefficients will be such that it will be convenient, although not essential, to adopt as the unit of weight that which is the average of the weights of the normals, so that the numbers by which most of the equations will be multiplied will not differ much from unity. The reduction of the equations to a uniform measure of precision having been effected, it remains to combine them according to the method of least squares in order to derive the most probable values of the unknown quantities, together with the relative weights of these values. It should be observed, however, that the numerical calculation in the combination and solution of these equations, and especially the required agreement of some of the checks of the calculation, will be facilitated by having the numerical values of the several coefficients not very unequal. If, therefore, the coefficient a of any unknown quantity x is in each of the equations numerically much greater or much less than in the case of the other unknown quantities, we may adopt as the corresponding unknown quantity to be determined, not x but νx, ν being any entire or fractional number such that the new coefficients $\frac{a}{\nu}$, $\frac{a'}{\nu}$, &c. shall be made to agree in magnitude with the other coefficients. The unknown quantity whose value will then be derived by the solution of the equations will be νx, and the corresponding weight will be that of νx. To find the weight of x from that of νx, we have the equation

$$p_x = \nu^2 p_{\nu x}. \tag{132}$$

In the same manner, the coefficient of any other unknown quantity may be changed, and the coefficients of all the unknown quantities may thus be made to agree in magnitude within moderate limits, the advantage of which, in the numerical solution of the equations, will be apparent by a consideration of the mode of proving the calculation of the coefficients in the normal equations. It will be expedient, also, to take for ν some integral power of 10, or, when a fractional value is required, the corresponding decimal. It may be remarked, further, that the introduction of ν is generally required only when the coefficient of one of the unknown quantities is very large, as frequently happens in the case of the variation of the mean daily motion μ.

When the coefficients of some of the unknown quantities are extremely small in all the equations of condition to be combined, an approximate solution, and often one which is sufficiently accurate for the purposes required, may be obtained by first neglecting these quantities entirely, and afterwards determining them separately. In general, however, this can only be done when it is certainly known that the influence of the neglected terms is not of sensible magnitude, or when at least approximate values of these terms are already given. When we adopt the approximate plane of the orbit as the fundamental plane, the equations for the longitude involve only four elements, and the coefficients of the variations of these elements in the equations for the latitudes are always very small. Hence, for an approximate solution, we may first solve the equations involving four unknown quantities as furnished by the longitudes, and then, substituting the resulting values in the equations for the latitudes, they will contain but two unknown quantities, namely, those which give the corrections to be applied to Ω and i.

151. When the number of equations of condition is large, the computation of the numerical values of the coefficients in the normal equations will entail considerable labor; and hence it is desirable to arrange the calculation in a convenient form, applying also the checks which have been indicated. The most convenient arrangement will be to write the logarithms of the absolute terms n, n', n'', &c. in a horizontal line, directly under these the logarithms of the coefficients a, a', a'', &c., then the logarithms of b, b', b'', &c., and so on. Then writing, in a corresponding form, the values of $\log n$, $\log n'$, &c. on a slip of paper, by bringing this successively over each line, the sums $[nn]$, $[an]$, $[bn]$, &c. will be readily formed. Again, writing on another slip of paper the logarithms of a, a', a'', &c., and placing this slip successively over the lines containing the coefficients, we derive the values $[aa]$, $[ab]$, $[ac]$, &c. The multiplication by b, c, d,

&c. successively is effected in a similar manner; and thus will be derived $[bb]$, $[bc]$, $[bd]$, &c., and finally $[ff]$ in the case of six unknown quantities. In forming these sums, in the cases of sums of positive and negative quantities, it is convenient as well as conducive to accuracy to write the positive values in one vertical column and the negative values in a separate column, and take the difference of the sums of the numbers in the respective columns. The proof of the calculation of the coefficients of the normal equations is effected by introducing s, s', s'', &c., the algebraic sums of all the coefficients in the respective equations of condition, and treating these as the coefficients of an additional unknown quantity, thus forming directly the sums $[sn]$, $[as]$, $[bs]$, $[cs]$, &c. Then, according to the equations (76) and (77), the values thus found should agree with those obtained by taking the corresponding sums of the coefficients in the normal equations.

The normal equations being thus derived, the next step in the process is the determination of the values of the auxiliary quantities necessary for the formation of the equations (74). An examination of the equations (54), (55), &c., by means of which these auxiliaries are determined, will indicate at once a convenient and systematic arrangement of the numerical calculation. Thus, we first write in a horizontal line the values of $[aa]$, $[ab]$, $[ac]$, ... $[as]$, $[an]$, and directly under them the corresponding logarithms. Next, we write under these, commencing with $[ab]$, the values of $[bb]$, $[bc]$, $[bd]$, .. $[bs]$, $[bn]$; then, adding the logarithm of the factor $\frac{[ab]}{[aa]}$ to the logarithms of $[ab]$, $[ac]$, &c. successively, we write the value of $\frac{[ab]}{[aa]}[ab]$ under $[bb]$, that of $\frac{[ab]}{[aa]}[ac]$ under $[bc]$, and so on. Subtracting the numbers in this line from those in the line above, the differences give the values of $[bb.1]$, $[bc.1]$, ... $[bs.1]$, $[bn.1]$, to be written in the next line, and the logarithms of these we write directly under them. Then we write in a horizontal line the values of $[cc]$, $[cd]$, .. $[cs]$, $[cn]$, placing $[cc]$ under $[bc.1]$, and, having added the logarithm of $\frac{[ac]}{[aa]}$ to the logarithms of $[ac]$, $[ad]$, &c. in succession, we derive, according to the equations (55) and (58), the values of $[cc.1]$, $[cd.1]$, .. $[cs.1]$, $[cn.1]$, which are to be placed under the corresponding quantities $[cc]$, $[cd]$, &c. Next, we subtract from these, respectively, the products

$$\frac{[bc.1]}{[bb.1]}[bc.1], \qquad \frac{[bc.1]}{[bb.1]}[bd.1], \ldots \frac{[bc.1]}{[bb.1]}[bs.1], \qquad \frac{[bc.1]}{[bb.1]}[bn.1],$$

and thus derive the values of $[cc.2]$, $[cd.2]$, .. $[cs.2]$, $[cn.2]$, which are to be written in the next horizontal line and under them their logarithms. Then we introduce, in a similar manner, the coefficients $[dd]$, $[de]$, .. $[dn]$, writing $[dd]$ under $[cd.2]$; and from each of these in succession we subtract the products

$$\frac{[ad]}{[aa]}[ad], \ldots \frac{[ad]}{[aa]}[as], \qquad \frac{[ad]}{[aa]}[an],$$

thus finding the values of $[dd.1]$, $[de.1]$, .. $[dn.1]$. From these we subtract the products

$$\frac{[bd.1]}{[bb.1]}[bd.1], \qquad \frac{[bd.1]}{[bb.1]}[be.1], \ldots \frac{[bd.1]}{[bb.1]}[bn.1],$$

respectively, which operation gives the values of $[dd.2]$, $[de.2]$, ... $[dn.2]$. From these results we subtract the products

$$\frac{[cd.2]}{[cc.2]}[cd.2], \qquad \frac{[cd.2]}{[cc.2]}[ce.2], \ldots \frac{[cd.2]}{[cc.2]}[cn.2],$$

and derive $[dd.3]$, $[de.3]$, .. $[dn.3]$ under which we write the corresponding logarithms. Then we introduce $[ee]$, $[ef]$, $[es]$, and $[en]$, writing $[ee]$ under $[de.3]$. First, subtracting $\frac{[ae]}{[aa]}[ae]$, $\frac{[ae]}{[aa]}[af]$, .. $\frac{[ae]}{[aa]}[an]$, we get $[ee.1]$, $[ef.1]$, $[es.1]$, and $[en.1]$; then subtracting from these the products

$$\frac{[be.1]}{[bb.1]}[be.1], \qquad \frac{[be.1]}{[bb.1]}[bf.1], \ldots \frac{[be.1]}{[bb.1]}[bn.1],$$

we obtain the values of $[ee.2]$, $[ef.2]$, $[es.2]$, and $[en.2]$. Again, subtracting

$$\frac{[ce.2]}{[cc.2]}[ce.2], \qquad \frac{[ce.2]}{[cc.2]}[cf.2], \ldots \frac{[ce.2]}{[cc.2]}[cn.2],$$

we have the values of $[ee.3]$, $[ef.3]$, $[es.3]$, $[en.3]$; and finally, subtracting from these the products

$$\frac{[de.3]}{[dd.3]}[de.3], \qquad \frac{[de.3]}{[dd.3]}[df.3], \ldots \frac{[de.3]}{[dd.3]}[dn.3],$$

we derive the results for $[ee.4]$, $[ef.4]$, $[es.4]$, and $[en.4]$; under which the corresponding logarithms are to be written.

If there are six unknown quantities to be determined, we must further write in a horizontal line the values of $[ff]$, $[fs]$, and $[fn]$, placing $[ff]$ under $[ef.4]$, and by means of five successive subtractions entirely analogous to what precedes, and as indicated by the remaining equations for the auxiliaries, we obtain the values of $[ff.5]$, $[fs.5]$, and $[fn.5]$.

The values of $[bs.1]$, $[cs.1]$, $[cs.2]$, &c. serve to check the calculation of the successive auxiliary coefficients. Thus we must have

$$
\begin{aligned}
[bb.1] + [bc.1] + [bd.1] + [be.1] + [bf.1] &= [bs.1] \\
[bc.1] + [cc.1] + [cd.1] + [ce.1] + [cf.1] &= [cs.1], \text{ \&c.,} \\
[cc.2] + [cd.2] + [ce.2] + [cf.2] &= [cs.2], \\
[cd.2] + [dd.2] + [de.2] + [df.2] &= [ds.2], \text{ \&c.}
\end{aligned}
$$

Hence it appears that when the numerical calculation is arranged as above suggested, the auxiliary containing s must, in each line, be equal to the sum of all the terms to the left of it in the same line and of those terms containing the same distinguishing numeral found in a vertical column over the last quantity at the left of this line.

There will yet remain only the auxiliaries which are derived from $[sn]$ and $[nn]$ to be determined. These additional auxiliaries will be found by means of the formulæ

$$
\begin{aligned}
&[sn.1] = [sn] - \frac{[an]}{[aa]}[as], &\quad& [sn.2] = [sn.1] - \frac{[bn.1]}{[bb.1]}[bs.1], \\
&[sn.3] = [sn.2] - \frac{[cn.2]}{[cc.2]}[cs.2], && [sn.4] = [sn.3] - \frac{[dn.3]}{[dd.3]}[ds.3], \qquad (133) \\
&[sn.5] = [sn.4] - \frac{[en.4]}{[ee.4]}[es.4], && [sn.6] = [sn.5] - \frac{[fn.5]}{[ff.5]}[fs.5],
\end{aligned}
$$

and the equations (81) and (83). The arrangement of the numerical process should be similar to that already explained.

The values of $[sn.1]$, $[sn.2]$, &c. check the accuracy of the results for $[bn.1]$, $[cn.1]$, $[cn.2]$, $[dn.3]$, &c. by means of the equations

$$
\begin{aligned}
[bn.1] + [cn.1] + [dn.1] + [en.1] + [fn.1] &= [sn.1], \\
[cn.2] + [dn.2] + [en.2] + [fn.2] &= [sn.2], \\
[dn.3] + [en.3] + [fn.3] &= [sn.3], \qquad (134) \\
[en.4] + [fn.4] &= [sn.4], \\
[fn.5] &= [sn.5].
\end{aligned}
$$

It appears further, that, in the case of six unknown quantities, since $[fs.5] = [ff.5]$, we have $[sn.6] = 0$.

Having thus determined the numerical values of the auxiliaries required, we are prepared to form at once the equations (74), by means of which the values of the unknown quantities will be determined by successive substitution, first finding t from the last of these equations, then substituting this result in the equation next to the last and thus deriving the value of w, and so on until all the unknown quantities have been determined. It will be observed that the logarithms of the coefficients of the unknown quantities in these equations will have been already found in the computation of the auxiliaries.

If we add together the several equations of (74), first clearing them of fractions, we get

$$\begin{aligned} 0 = [aa]\,x &+ ([ab] + [bb.1])\,y + ([ac] + [bc.1] + [cc.2])\,z \\ &+ ([ad] + [bd.1] + [cd.2] + [dd.3])\,u \\ &+ ([ae] + [be.1] + [ce.2] + [de.3] + [ee.4])\,w \qquad (135) \\ &+ ([af] + [bf.1] + [cf.2] + [df.3] + [ef.4] + [ff.5])\,t \\ &+ [an] + [bn.1] + [cn.2] + [dn.3] + [en.4] + [fn.5]; \end{aligned}$$

and this equation must be satisfied by the values of x, y, z, &c. found from (74).

152. EXAMPLE.—The arrangement of the calculation in the case of any other number of unknown quantities is precisely similar; and to illustrate the entire process let us take the following equations, each of which is already multiplied by the square root of its weight:—

$$\begin{aligned} 0.707x + 2.052y - 2.372z - 0.221u + 6''.58 &= 0, \\ 0.471x + 1.347y - 1.715z - 0.085u + 1\,.63 &= 0, \\ 0.260x + 0.770y - 0.356z + 0.483u - 4\,.40 &= 0, \\ 0.092x + 0.343y + 0.235z + 0.469u - 10\,.21 &= 0, \\ 0.414x + 1.204y - 1.506z - 0.205u + 3\,.99 &= 0, \\ 0.040x + 0.150y + 0.104z + 0.206u - 4\,.34 &= 0. \end{aligned}$$

First, we derive

$$\begin{array}{lllll} & [nn] = 204.313, & & & \\ [an] = +\ 4.815, & [aa] = +0.971, & & & \\ [bn] = +12.961, & [ab] = +2.821, & [bb] = +8.208, & & \\ [cn] = -25.697, & [ac] = -3.175, & [bc] = -9.168, & [cc] = +11.028, & \\ [dn] = -10.218, & [ad] = -0.104, & [bd] = -0.251, & [cd] = +0.938, & [dd] = +0.594, \\ [sn] = -18.139, & [as] = +0.513, & [bs] = +1.610, & [cs] = -0.377, & [ds] = +1.177. \end{array}$$

The values of $[sn]$, $[as]$, $[bs]$, $[cs]$, and $[ds]$, found by taking the sums of the normal coefficients, agree exactly with the values computed directly, thus proving the calculation of these coefficients. The normal equations are, therefore,

$$\begin{aligned}
0.971x + 2.821y - 3.175z - 0.104u + 4.815 &= 0, \\
2.821x + 8.208y - 9.168z - 0.251u + 12.961 &= 0, \\
-3.175x - 9.168y + 11.028z + 0.938u - 25.697 &= 0, \\
-0.104x - 0.251y + 0.938z + 0.594u - 10.218 &= 0.
\end{aligned}$$

It will be observed that the coefficients in these equations are numerically greater than in the equations of condition; and this will generally be the case. Hence, if we use logarithms of five decimals in forming the normal equations, it will be expedient to use tables of six or seven decimals in the solution of these equations.

Arranging the process of elimination in the most convenient form, the successive results are as follows:—

$[bb.1] = +0.0123$,	$[bc.1] = +0.0562$,	$[bd.1] = +0.0511$,	$[bs.1] = +0.1196$,	$[bn.1] = -\ 1.0278$,
	$[cc.1] = +0.6463$,	$[cd.1] = +0.5979$,	$[cs.1] = +1.3004$,	$[cn.1] = -\ 9.9528$,
	$[cc.2] = +0.3895$,	$[cd.2] = +0.3644$,	$[cs.2] = +0.7539$,	$[cn.2] = -\ 5.2567$,
		$[dd.1] = +0.5829$,	$[ds.1] = +1.2319$,	$[dn.1] = -\ 9.7023$,
		$[dd.2] = +0.3706$,	$[ds.2] = +0.7350$,	$[dn.2] = -\ 5.4323$,
		$[dd.3] = +0.0297$,	$[ds.3] = +0.0297$	$[dn.3] = -\ 0.5143$,
			$[nn.1] = 180.436$,	$[sn.1] = -20.6828$,
			$[nn.2] = 94.552$,	$[sn.2] = -10.6889$,
			$[nn.3] = 23.608$,	$[sn.3] = -\ 0.5143$,
			$[nn.4] = 14.698$,	$[sn.4] = 0$.

The several checks agree completely, and only the value of $[nn.4]$ remains to be proved. The equations (74) therefore give

$$\begin{aligned}
x + 2.9052y - 3.2698z - 0.1071u + 4.9588 &= 0, \\
y + 4.5691z + 4.1545u - 83.5610 &= 0, \\
z + 0.9356u - 13.4960 &= 0, \\
u - 17.3165 &= 0,
\end{aligned}$$

and from these we get

$$u = +17''.316, \quad z = -2''.705, \quad y = +23''.977, \quad x = -81''.608.$$

Then the equation (135) becomes

$$0 = +0.9710x + 2.8333y - 2.7293z + 0.3412u - 1.9838,$$

which is satisfied by the preceding values of the unknown quantities.

If we substitute these values of x, y, z, and u in the equations of condition already reduced to the same weight by multiplication by the square roots of their weights, we obtain the residuals

$$+0''.67, \quad -1''.34, \quad +2''.17, \quad -2''.01, \quad -0''.40, \quad -0''.72,$$

The sum of the squares of these gives

$$[vv] = [nn.4] = 11.672,$$

and the difference between this result and the value 14.698 already found is due to the decimals neglected in the computation of the numerical values of the several auxiliaries. The sum of all the equations of condition gives generally

$$[a]x + [b]y + [c]z + [d]u + \ldots . + [n] = [v], \qquad (136)$$

which may be used to check the substitution of the numerical values in the determination of v, v', &c. Thus, we have, for the values here given,

$$1.984x + 5.866y - 5.610z + 0.647u - 6.75 = [v] = -1.''63.$$

It remains yet to determine the relative weights of the resulting values of the unknown quantities. For this purpose we may apply any of the various methods already given. The weights of u and z may be found directly from the auxiliaries whose values have been computed. Thus, we have

$$p_u = [dd.3] = 0.0297, \qquad p_z = \frac{[dd.3]}{[dd.2]}[cc.2] = 0.0312.$$

If we now completely reverse the order of elimination from the normal equations, and determine x first, we obtain the values

$$[bb.2] = +0.0425, \qquad [aa.2] = +0.0033,$$
$$[aa.3] = +0.00056, \qquad [nn.4] = 14.665,$$

and also

$$x = -82.''750, \quad y = +24.''365, \quad z = -2.''699, \quad u = +17.''272.$$

The small differences between these results and those obtained by the first elimination arise from the decimals neglected. This second elimination furnishes at once the weights of x and y, namely,

$$p_x = [aa.3] = 0.00056, \qquad p_y = \frac{[aa.3]}{[aa.2]}[bb.2] = 0.0072.$$

We may also compute the weights by means of the equations (96). Thus, to find the weight of y, we have

$$[dd.2]_b = [dd.1] - \frac{[cd.1]}{[cc.1]}[cd.1] = +0.02977,$$

and hence

$$p_y = \frac{[dd.3]}{[dd.2]_b} \cdot \frac{[cc.2]}{[cc.1]}[bb.1] = 0.0074.$$

The equations (103) and (108) are convenient for the determination of the values and weights of the unknown quantities separately.

Thus, by means of the values of the auxiliaries obtained in the first elimination, we find from the equations (100), (101), and (102),

$$A' = -2.9052, \qquad A'' = +16.5442, \qquad A''' = -3.3012,$$
$$B'' = -4.5691, \qquad B''' = +\ 0.1202, \qquad C''' = -0.9356,$$

and then the equations (103) and (108) give

$$x = -81''.609, \quad y = +23''.977, \quad z = -2''.705, \quad u = +17''.316,$$
$$p_x = 0.00057, \quad p_y = 0.0074, \quad p_z = 0.0312, \quad p_u = 0.0297,$$

agreeing with the results obtained by means of the other methods. The weights are so small that it may be inferred at once that the values of x, y, z, and u are very uncertain, although they are those which best satisfy the given equations. It will be observed that if we multiply the first normal equation by 2.9, the resulting equation will differ very little from the second normal equation, and hence we have nearly the case presented in which the number of independent relations is one less than the number of unknown quantities.

The uncertainty of the solution will be further indicated by determining the probable errors of the results, although on account of the small number of equations the probable or mean errors obtained may be little more than rude approximations. Thus, adopting the value of $[vv]$ obtained by direct substitution, we have

$$\varepsilon = \sqrt{\frac{[nn.4]}{m-\mu}} = \sqrt{\frac{11.672}{6-4}} = 2.416,$$

and hence

$$r = \pm 1''.629,$$

which is the probable error of the absolute term of an equation of condition whose weight is unity. Then the equations

$$r_x = \frac{r}{\sqrt{p_x}}, \qquad r_y = \frac{r}{\sqrt{p_y}}, \qquad r_z = \frac{r}{\sqrt{p_z}}, \ \&c.,$$

give

$$r_x = \pm 68''.25, \qquad r_y = \pm 18''.94, \qquad r_z = \pm 9''.22, \qquad r_u = \pm 9''.45.$$

It thus appears that the probable error of z exceeds the value obtained for the quantity itself, and that although the sum of the squares of the residuals is reduced from 204.31 to 11.67, the results are still quite uncertain.

153. The certainty of the solution will be greatest when the coefficients in the equations of condition and also in the normal equations

differ very considerably both in magnitude and in sign. In the correction of the elements of the orbit of a planet when the observations extend only over a short interval of time, the coefficients will generally change value so slowly that the equations for the direct determination of the corrections to be applied to the elements will not afford a satisfactory solution. In such cases it will be expedient to form the equations for the determination of a less number of quantities from which the corrected elements may be subsequently derived. Thus we may determine the corrections to be applied to two assumed geocentric distances or to any other quantities which afford the required convenience in the solution of the problem, various formulæ for which have been given in the preceding chapter. The quantities selected for correction should be known functions of the elements, and such that the equations to be solved, in order to combine all the observed places, shall not be subject to any uncertainty in the solution. But when the observations extend over a long period, the most complete determination of the corrections to be applied to the provisional elements will be obtained by forming the equations for these variations directly, and combining them as already explained. A complete proof of the accuracy of the entire calculation will be obtained by computing the normal places directly from the elements as finally corrected, and comparing the residuals thus derived with those given by the substitution of the adopted values of the unknown quantities in the original equations of condition.

If the elements to be corrected differ so much from the true values that the squares and products of the corrections are of sensible magnitude, so that the assumption of a linear form for the equations does not afford the required accuracy, it will be necessary to solve the equations first provisionally, and, having applied the resulting corrections to the elements, we compute the places of the body directly from the corrected elements, and the differences between these and the observed places furnish new values of n, n', n'', &c., to be used in a repetition of the solution. The corrections which result from the second solution will be small, and, being applied to the elements as corrected by the first solution, will furnish satisfactory results. In this new solution it will not in general be necessary to recompute the coefficients of the unknown quantities in the equations of condition, since the variations of the elements will not be large enough to affect sensibly the values of their differential coefficients with respect to the observed spherical co-ordinates. Cases may occur, however, in which it may become necessary to recompute the coefficients of one or more of the unknown quantities, but only when these coefficients are very considerably changed by a small variation in the adopted values of the elements employed in the calculation. In such cases the residuals obtained by substitution in the equations of condition will not agree with those obtained by direct calculation unless the corrections applied to the corresponding elements are very small. It may also be remarked that often, and especially in a repetition of the solution so as to include terms of the second order, it will be sufficiently accurate to relax a little the rigorous requirements of a complete solution, and use, instead of the actual coefficients, equivalent numbers which are more convenient in the numerical operations required. Although the greatest confidence should be placed in the accuracy of the results obtained as far as possible in strict accordance with the requirements of the theory, yet the uncertainty of the determination of the relative weights in the combination of a series of observations, as well as the effect of uneliminated constant errors, may at least warrant a little latitude in the numerical application, provided that the weights of the results are not thereby much affected. A constant error may in fact be regarded as an unknown quantity to be determined, and since the effect of the omission of one of the unknown quantities is to diminish the probable errors of the resulting values of the others, it is evident that, on account of the existence of constant errors not determined, the values of the variables obtained by the method of least squares from different corresponding series of observations may differ beyond the limits which the probable errors of the different determinations have assigned. Further, it should be observed that, on account of the unavoidable uncertainty in the estimation of the weights of the observations in the preliminary combination, the probable error of an observed place whose weight is unity as determined by the final residuals given by the equations of condition, may not agree exactly with that indicated by the prior discussion of the observations.

154. In the case of very eccentric orbits in which the corrections to be applied to certain elements are not indicated with certainty by the observations, it will often become necessary to make that whose weight is very small the last in the elimination, and determine the other corrections as functions of this one; and whenever the coefficients of two of the unknown quantities are nearly equal or have nearly the same ratio to each other in all the different equations of condition, this method is indispensable unless the difficulty is reme-

died by other means, such as the introduction of different elements or different combinations of the same elements. The equations (113) furnish the values of the unknown quantities when we neglect that which is to be determined independently; and then the equations (114) give the required expressions for the complete values of these quantities. Thus, when a comet has been observed only during a brief period, the ellipticity of the orbit, however, being plainly indicated by the observations, the determination of the correction to be applied to the mean daily motion as given by the provisional elements, in connection with the corrections of the other elements, will necessarily be quite uncertain, and this uncertainty may very greatly affect all the results. Hence the elimination will be so arranged that $\Delta\mu$ shall be the last, and the other corrections will be determined as functions of this quantity. The substitution of the results thus derived in the equations of condition will give for each residual an expression of the following form:—

$$\Delta\theta = v_0 + \gamma\Delta\mu.$$

Therefore we shall have

$$[vv] = [v_0 v_0] + 2\,[v_0\gamma]\,\Delta\mu + [\gamma\gamma]\,\Delta\mu^2, \tag{137}$$

which may be applied more conveniently in the equivalent form

$$[vv] = [v_0 v_0] - \frac{[v_0\gamma]}{[\gamma\gamma]}[v_0\gamma] + [\gamma\gamma]\left(\Delta\mu + \frac{[v_0\gamma]}{[\gamma\gamma]}\right)^2. \tag{138}$$

The most probable value of $\Delta\mu$ will be that which renders $[vv]$ a minimum, or

$$\Delta\mu = -\frac{[v_0\gamma]}{[\gamma\gamma]}, \tag{139}$$

and the corresponding value of the sum of the squares of the residuals is

$$[vv] = [v_0 v_0] - \frac{[v_0\gamma]}{[\gamma\gamma]}[v_0\gamma]. \tag{140}$$

The correction given by equation (139) having been applied to μ, the result may be regarded as the most probable value of that element, and the corresponding values of the corrections of the other elements as determined by the equations (114) having been also duly applied, we obtain the most probable system of elements. These, however, may still be expressed in the form

$$\Omega + A_0\Delta\mu, \qquad i + B_0\Delta\mu, \qquad \pi + C_0\Delta\mu, \text{ \&c.}$$

the coefficients A_0, B_0, C_0, &c. being those given by the equations (114), and thus the elements may be derived which correspond to any assumed value of μ differing from its most probable value. The unknown quantity $\Delta\mu$ will also be retained in the values of the residuals. Hence, if we assign small increments to μ, it may easily be seen how much this element may differ from its most probable value without giving results for the residuals which are incompatible with the evidence furnished by the observations.

If the dimensions of the orbit are expressed by means of the elements q and e, it may occur that the latter will not be determined with certainty by the observations, and hence it should be treated as suggested in the case of μ; and we proceed in a similar manner when the correction to be applied to a given value of the semi-transverse axis a is one of the unknown quantities to be determined.

CHAPTER VIII.

INVESTIGATION OF VARIOUS FORMULÆ FOR THE DETERMINATION OF THE SPECIAL PERTURBATIONS OF A HEAVENLY BODY.

155. WE have thus far considered the circumstances of the undisturbed motion of the heavenly bodies in their orbits; but a complete determination of the elements of the orbit of any body revolving around the sun, requires that we should determine the alterations in its motion due to the action of the other bodies of the system. For this purpose, we shall resume the general equations $(18)_1$, namely,

$$\begin{aligned}\frac{d^2x}{dt^2}+k^2(1+m)\frac{x}{r^3}&=k^2(1+m)\frac{d\Omega}{dx},\\ \frac{d^2y}{dt^2}+k^2(1+m)\frac{y}{r^3}&=k^2(1+m)\frac{d\Omega}{dy},\\ \frac{d^2z}{dt^2}+k^2(1+m)\frac{z}{r^3}&=k^2(1+m)\frac{d\Omega}{dz},\end{aligned}\qquad(1)$$

which determine the motion of a heavenly body relative to the sun when subject to the action of the other bodies of the system. We have, further,

$$\Omega=\frac{m'}{1+m}\left(\frac{1}{\rho}-\frac{xx'+yy'+zz'}{r'^3}\right)+\frac{m''}{1+m}\left(\frac{1}{\rho'}-\frac{xx''+yy''+zz''}{r''^3}\right)+\&c.,$$

which is called the *perturbing function*, of which the partial differential coefficients, with respect to the co-ordinates, are

$$\begin{aligned}\frac{d\Omega}{dx}&=\frac{m'}{1+m}\left(\frac{x'-x}{\rho^3}-\frac{x'}{r'^3}\right)+\frac{m''}{1+m}\left(\frac{x''-x}{\rho'^3}-\frac{x''}{r''^3}\right)+\&c.,\\ \frac{d\Omega}{dy}&=\frac{m'}{1+m}\left(\frac{y'-y}{\rho^3}-\frac{y'}{r'^3}\right)+\frac{m''}{1+m}\left(\frac{y''-y}{\rho'^3}-\frac{y''}{r''^3}\right)+\&c.,\\ \frac{d\Omega}{dz}&=\frac{m'}{1+m}\left(\frac{z'-z}{\rho^3}-\frac{z'}{r'^3}\right)+\frac{m''}{1+m}\left(\frac{z''-z}{\rho'^3}-\frac{z''}{r''^3}\right)+\&c.,\end{aligned}\qquad(2)$$

and in which m', m'', &c. denote the ratios of the masses of the several disturbing planets to the mass of the sun, and m the ratio of the mass of the disturbed planet to that of the sun. These partial differential coefficients, when multiplied by $k^2(1+m)$, express the sum of the components of the disturbing force resolved in directions parallel to the three rectangular axes respectively.

When we neglect the consideration of the perturbations, the general equations of motion become

$$\begin{aligned} \frac{d^2x_0}{dt^2} + k^2(1+m)\frac{x_0}{r_0^3} &= 0, \\ \frac{d^2y_0}{dt^2} + k^2(1+m)\frac{y_0}{r_0^3} &= 0, \\ \frac{d^2z_0}{dt^2} + k^2(1+m)\frac{z_0}{r_0^3} &= 0, \end{aligned} \qquad (3)$$

the complete integration of which furnishes as arbitrary constants of integration the six elements which determine the orbitual motion of a heavenly body. But if we regard these elements as representing the actual orbit of the body for a given instant of time t, and conceive of the effect of the disturbing forces due to the action of the other bodies of the system, it is evident that, on account of the change arising from the force thus introduced, the body at another instant different from the first will be moving in an orbit for which the elements are in some degree different from those which satisfy the original equations. Although the action of the disturbing force is continuous, we may yet regard the elements as unchanged during the element of time dt, and as varying only after each interval dt. Let us now designate by t_0 the epoch to which the elements of the orbit belong, and let these elements be designated by M_0, π_0, Ω_0, i_0, e_0, and a_0; then will the equations (3) be exactly satisfied by means of the expressions for the co-ordinates in terms of these rigorously-constant elements. These elements will express the motion of the body subject to the action of the disturbing forces only during the infinitesimal interval dt, and at the time $t_0 + dt$ it will commence to describe a new orbit of which the elements will differ from these constant elements by increments which are called the *perturbations*.

According to the principle of the variation of parameters, or of the constants of integration, the differential equations (1) will be satisfied by integrals of the same form as those obtained when the second members are put equal to zero, provided only that the arbitrary constants of the latter integration are no longer regarded as pure constants but as subject to variation. Consequently, if we denote the variable elements by M, π, Ω, i, e, and a, they will be connected with the constant elements, or those which determine the orbit at the instant t_0, by the equations

$$
\begin{aligned}
M &= M_0 + \int \frac{dM}{dt}\,dt, & \pi &= \pi_0 + \int \frac{d\pi}{dt}\,dt, & \Omega &= \Omega_0 + \int \frac{d\Omega}{dt}\,dt, \\
i &= i_0 + \int \frac{di}{dt}\,dt, & e &= e_0 + \int \frac{de}{dt}\,dt, & a &= a_0 + \int \frac{da}{dt}\,dt,
\end{aligned} \tag{4}
$$

in which $\frac{dM}{dt}, \frac{d\pi}{dt}$, &c. denote the differential coefficients of the elements depending on the disturbing forces. When these differential coefficients are known, we may determine, by simple quadrature, the perturbations δM, $\delta\pi$, &c. to be added to the constant elements in order to obtain those corresponding to any instant for which the place of the body is required. These differential coefficients, however, are functions of the partial differential coefficients of $\varOmega$ with respect to the elements, and before the integration can be performed it becomes necessary to find the expressions for these partial differential coefficients. For this purpose we expand the function $\varOmega$ into a converging series and then differentiate each term of this series relatively to the elements. This function is usually developed into a converging series arranged in reference to the ascending powers of the eccentricities and inclinations, and so as to include an indefinite number of revolutions; and the final integration will then give what are called the *absolute* or *general perturbations*. When the eccentricities and inclinations are very great, as in the case of the comets, this development and analytical integration, or quadrature, becomes no longer possible, and even when it is possible it may, on account of the magnitude of the eccentricity or inclination, become so difficult that we are obliged to determine, instead of the absolute perturbations, what are called the *special perturbations*, by methods of approximation known as *mechanical quadratures*, according to which we determine the variations of the elements from one epoch t_0 to another epoch t. This method is applicable to any case, and may be advantageously employed even when the determination of the absolute perturbations is possible, and especially when a series of observations extending through a period of many years is available and it is desired to determine, for any instant t_0, a system of elements, usually called *osculating elements*, on which the complete theory of the motion may be based.

Instead of computing the variations of the elements of the orbit directly, we may find the perturbations of any known functions of these elements; and the most direct and simple method is to determine the variations, due to the action of the disturbing forces, of any system of three co-ordinates by means of which the position of the body or the elements themselves may be found. We shall, therefore, derive various formulæ for this purpose before investigating the formulæ for the direct variation of the elements.

156. Let x_0, y_0, z_0 be the rectangular co-ordinates of the body at the time t computed by means of the osculating elements M_0, π_0, Ω_0, &c., corresponding to the epoch t_0. Let x, y, z be the actual co-ordinates of the disturbed body at the time t; and we shall have

$$x = x_0 + \delta x, \qquad y = y_0 + \delta y, \qquad z = z_0 + \delta z,$$

δx, δy, and δz being the perturbations of the rectangular co-ordinates from the epoch t_0 to the time t. If we substitute these values of x, y, and z in the equations (1), and then subtract from each the corresponding one of equations (3), we get

$$\begin{aligned}
\frac{d^2\delta x}{dt^2} + k^2(1+m)\left(\frac{x_0+\delta x}{r^3} - \frac{x_0}{r_0^{\,3}}\right) &= k^2(1+m)\frac{d\Omega}{dx},\\
\frac{d^2\delta y}{dt^2} + k^2(1+m)\left(\frac{y_0+\delta y}{r^3} - \frac{y_0}{r_0^{\,3}}\right) &= k^2(1+m)\frac{d\Omega}{dy},\\
\frac{d^2\delta z}{dt^2} + k^2(1+m)\left(\frac{z_0+\delta z}{r^3} - \frac{z_0}{r_0^{\,3}}\right) &= k^2(1+m)\frac{d\Omega}{dz}.
\end{aligned} \tag{5}$$

Let us now put $r = r_0 + \delta r$; then to terms of the order δr^2, which is equivalent to considering only the first power of the disturbing force, we have

$$\begin{aligned}
\frac{x_0+\delta x}{r^3} - \frac{x_0}{r_0^{\,3}} &= \frac{1}{r_0^{\,3}}\left(\delta x - 3\frac{x_0}{r_0}\delta r\right),\\
\frac{y_0+\delta y}{r^3} - \frac{y_0}{r_0^{\,3}} &= \frac{1}{r_0^{\,3}}\left(\delta y - 3\frac{y_0}{r_0}\delta r\right),\\
\frac{z_0+\delta z}{r^3} - \frac{z_0}{r_0^{\,3}} &= \frac{1}{r_0^{\,3}}\left(\delta z - 3\frac{z_0}{r_0}\delta r\right),
\end{aligned}$$

and hence

$$\begin{aligned}
\frac{d^2\delta x}{dt^2} &= k^2(1+m)\frac{d\Omega}{dx} + \frac{k^2(1+m)}{r_0^{\,3}}\left(3\frac{x_0}{r_0}\delta r - \delta x\right),\\
\frac{d^2\delta y}{dt^2} &= k^2(1+m)\frac{d\Omega}{dy} + \frac{k^2(1+m)}{r_0^{\,3}}\left(3\frac{y_0}{r_0}\delta r - \delta y\right),\\
\frac{d^2\delta z}{dt^2} &= k^2(1+m)\frac{d\Omega}{dz} + \frac{k^2(1+m)}{r_0^{\,3}}\left(3\frac{z_0}{r_0}\delta r - \delta z\right).
\end{aligned} \tag{6}$$

We have also from

$$r^2 = x^2 + y^2 + z^2,$$

neglecting terms of the second order,

$$\delta r = \frac{x_0}{r_0}\delta x + \frac{y_0}{r_0}\delta y + \frac{z_0}{r_0}\delta z. \tag{7}$$

The integration of the equations (6) will give the perturbations δx, δy, and δz to be applied to the rectangular co-ordinates x_0, y_0, z_0 computed by means of the osculating elements, in order to find the actual co-ordinates of the body for the date to which the integration belongs. But since the second members contain the quantities δx, δy, δz which are sought, the integration must be effected indirectly by successive approximations; and from the manner in which these are involved in the second members of the equations, it will appear that this integration is possible.

If we consider only a single disturbing planet, according to the equations (2), we shall have

$$
\begin{aligned}
k^2(1+m)\frac{d\Omega}{dx} &= m'k^2\left(\frac{x'-x}{\rho^3}-\frac{x'}{r'^3}\right),\\
k^2(1+m)\frac{d\Omega}{dy} &= m'k^2\left(\frac{y'-y}{\rho^3}-\frac{y'}{r'^3}\right),\\
k^2(1+m)\frac{d\Omega}{dz} &= m'k^2\left(\frac{z'-z}{\rho^3}-\frac{z'}{r'^3}\right),
\end{aligned} \tag{8}
$$

and these forces we will designate by X, Y, and Z respectively; then, if in these expressions we neglect the terms of the order of the square of the disturbing force, writing x_0, y_0, z_0 in place of x, y, z, the equations (6) become

$$
\begin{aligned}
\frac{d^2\delta x}{dt^2} &= X_0 + \frac{k^2(1+m)}{r_0^3}\left(3\frac{x_0}{r_0}\delta r - \delta x\right),\\
\frac{d^2\delta y}{dt^2} &= Y_0 + \frac{k^2(1+m)}{r_0^3}\left(3\frac{y_0}{r_0}\delta r - \delta y\right),\\
\frac{d^2\delta z}{dt^2} &= Z_0 + \frac{k^2(1+m)}{r_0^3}\left(3\frac{z_0}{r_0}\delta r - \delta z\right),
\end{aligned} \tag{9}
$$

which are the equations for computing the perturbations of the rectangular co-ordinates with reference only to the first power of the masses or disturbing forces. We have, further,

$$\rho^2 = (x'-x)^2 + (y'-y)^2 + (z'-z)^2, \tag{10}$$

in which, when terms of the second order are neglected, we use the values x_0, y_0, z_0 for x, y, and z respectively.

157. From the values of δx, δy, and δz computed with regard to the first power of the masses we may, by a repetition of part of the calculation, take into account the squares and products and even the higher powers of the disturbing forces. The equations (5) may be written thus:—

$$\frac{d^2\delta x}{dt^2} = X + \frac{k^2(1+m)}{r_0^3}\left(\left(1-\frac{r_0^3}{r^3}\right)x - \delta x\right),$$
$$\frac{d^2\delta y}{dt^2} = Y + \frac{k^2(1+m)}{r_0^3}\left(\left(1-\frac{r_0^3}{r^3}\right)y - \delta y\right), \qquad (11)$$
$$\frac{d^2\delta z}{dt^2} = Z + \frac{k^2(1+m)}{r_0^3}\left(\left(1-\frac{r_0^3}{r^3}\right)z - \delta z\right),$$

in which nothing is neglected. In the application of these formulæ, as soon as δx, δy, and δz have been found for a few successive intervals, we may readily derive approximate values of these quantities for the date next following, and with these find

$$x = x_0 + \delta x, \qquad y = y_0 + \delta y, \qquad z = z_0 + \delta z,$$

and hence the complete values of the forces X, Y, and Z, by means of the equations (8). To find an expression for the factor

$$1 - \frac{r_0^3}{r^3}$$

which will be convenient in the numerical calculation, we have

$$r^2 = (x_0 + \delta x)^2 + (y_0 + \delta y)^2 + (z_0 + \delta z)^2$$
$$= r_0^2 + 2x_0\delta x + 2y_0\delta y + 2z_0\delta z + \delta x^2 + \delta y^2 + \delta z^2,$$

and therefore

$$\frac{r^2}{r_0^2} = 1 + 2\frac{(x^0 + \frac{1}{2}\delta x)\,\delta x + (y_0 + \frac{1}{2}\delta y)\,\delta y + (z_0 + \frac{1}{2}\delta z)\,\delta z}{r_0^2}.$$

Let us now put

$$q = \frac{x_0 + \frac{1}{2}\delta x}{r_0^2}\,\delta x + \frac{y_0 + \frac{1}{2}\delta y}{r_0^2}\,\delta y + \frac{z_0 + \frac{1}{2}\delta z}{r_0^2}\,\delta z, \qquad (12)$$

and

$$fq = 1 - \frac{r_0^3}{r^3} = 1 - (1 + 2q)^{-\frac{3}{2}};$$

then we shall have

$$f = 3\left(1 - \frac{5}{2}q + \frac{5\,.\,7}{2\,.\,3}q^2 - \frac{5\,.\,7\,.\,9}{2\,.\,3\,.\,4}q^3 + \&c.\right), \qquad (13)$$

and the values of f may be tabulated with the argument q. The equations (11) therefore become

$$\frac{d^2\delta x}{dt^2} = X + \frac{k^2(1+m)}{r_0^3}(fqx - \delta x),$$
$$\frac{d^2\delta y}{dt^2} = Y + \frac{k^2(1+m)}{r_0^3}(fqy - \delta y), \qquad (14)$$
$$\frac{d^2\delta z}{dt^2} = Z + \frac{k^2(1+m)}{r_0^3}(fqz - \delta z).$$

The coefficients of δx, δy, and δz in equation (12) may be found at once, with sufficient accuracy, by means of the approximate values of these quantities; and having found the value of f corresponding to the resulting value of q, the numerical values of $\frac{d^2\delta x}{dt^2}$, $\frac{d^2\delta y}{dt^2}$, and $\frac{d^2\delta z}{dt^2}$, which include the squares and products of the masses, will be obtained. The integration of these will give more exact values of δx, δy, and δz, and then, recomputing q and the other quantities which require correction, a still closer approximation to the exact values of the perturbations will result.

Table XVII. gives the values of $\log f$ for positive or negative values of q at intervals of 0.0001 from $q = 0$ to $q = 0.03$. Unless the perturbations are very large, q will be found within the limits of this table; and in those cases in which it exceeds the limits of the table, the value of

$$fq = 1 - \frac{r_0^{\,3}}{r^3}$$

may be computed directly, using the value of r in terms of r_0 and δx, δy, δz.

In the application of the preceding formulæ, the positions of the disturbed and disturbing bodies may be referred to any system of rectangular co-ordinates. It will be advisable, however, to adopt either the plane of the equator or that of the ecliptic as the fundamental plane, the positive axis of x being directed to the vernal equinox. By choosing the plane of the elliptic orbit at the time t_0 as the plane of xy, the co-ordinate z will be of the order of the perturbations, and the calculation of this part of the action of the disturbing force will be very much abbreviated; but unless the inclination is very large there will be no actual advantage in this selection, since the computation of the values of the components of the disturbing forces will require more labor than when either the equator or the ecliptic is taken as the fundamental plane. The perturbations computed for one fundamental plane may be converted into those referred to another plane or to a different position of the axes in the same plane by means of the formulæ which give the transformation of the co-ordinates directly.

158. We shall now investigate the formulæ for the integration of the linear differential equations of the second order which express the variation of the co-ordinates, and generally the formulæ for finding the integrals of expressions of the form $\int f(x)\,dx$ and $\iint f(x)\,dx^2$

when the values of $f(x)$ are computed for successive values of x increasing in arithmetical progression. First, therefore, we shall find the integral of $f(x)\,dx$ within given limits.

Within the limits for which x is continuous, we have

$$f(x) = \alpha + \beta x + \gamma x^2 + \delta x^3 + \phi x^4 + \ldots; \qquad (15)$$

and if we consider only three terms of this series, the resulting equation

$$f(x) = \alpha + \beta x + \gamma x^2$$

is that of the common parabola of which the abscissa is x and the ordinate $f(x)$, and the integral of $f(x)\,dx$ is the area included by the abscissa, two ordinates, and the included arc of this curve. Generally, therefore, we may consider the more complete expression for $f(x)$ as the equation of a parabolic curve whose degree is one less than the number of terms taken. Hence, if we take n terms of the series as the value of $f(x)$, we shall derive the equation for a parabola whose degree is $n - 1$, and which has n points in common with the curve represented by the exact value of $f(x)$.

If we multiply equation (15) by dx and integrate between the limits 0 and x', we get

$$\int_0^{x'} f(x)\,dx = \alpha x' + \tfrac{1}{2}\beta x'^2 + \tfrac{1}{3}\gamma x'^3 + \tfrac{1}{4}\delta x'^4 + \ldots. \qquad (16)$$

If now the values of $f(x)$ for different values of x from 0 to x' are known, each of these, by means of equation (15), will furnish an equation for the determination of α, β, γ, &c.; and the number of terms which may be taken will be equal to the number of different known values of $f(x)$. As soon as α, β, γ, &c. have thus been found, the equation (16) will give the integral required.

If the values of $f(x)$ are computed for values of x at equal intervals and we integrate between the limits $x = 0$, and $x = n\Delta x$, Δx being the constant interval between the successive values of $f(x)$ and n the number of intervals from the beginning of the integration, we obtain

$$\int_0^{n\Delta x} f(x)\,dx = \alpha n\Delta x + \tfrac{1}{2}\beta n^2\Delta x^2 + \tfrac{1}{3}\gamma n^3\Delta x^3 + \&c.$$

Let us now suppose a quadratic parabola to pass through the points of the curve represented by $f(x)$, corresponding to $x = 0$, $x = \Delta x$, and $x = 2\Delta x$; then will the area included by the arc of this parabola, the extreme ordinates, and the axis of abscissas be

$$\int_0^{2\Delta x} f(x)\,dx = \Delta x\,(2\alpha + 2\beta\Delta x + \tfrac{8}{3}\gamma\Delta x^2).$$

The equation of the curve gives, if we designate the ordinates of the three successive points by y_0, y_1, and y_2,

$$\alpha = y_0, \qquad \beta = -\frac{1}{2\Delta x}(y_2 - y_1 + y_0), \qquad \gamma = \frac{1}{2\Delta x^2}(y_2 - 2y_1 + y_0),$$

and hence we derive

$$\int_0^{2\Delta x} f(x)\,dx = \tfrac{1}{3}\Delta x\,(y_0 + 4y_1 + y_2).$$

In a similar manner, the area included by the ordinates y_2 and y_4,—corresponding to $x = 2\Delta x$ and $x = 4\Delta x$,—the axis of abscissas, and the parabola passing through the three points corresponding to y_2, y_3, and y_4, is found to be

$$\int_{2\Delta x}^{4\Delta x} f(x)\,dx = \tfrac{1}{3}\Delta x\,(y_2 + 4y_3 + y_4);$$

and hence we have, finally,

$$\int_{(n-2)\Delta x}^{n\Delta x} f(x)\,dx = \tfrac{1}{3}\Delta x\,(y_{n-2} + 4y_{n-1} + y_n).$$

The sum of all these gives

$$\int_0^{n\Delta x} f(x)\,dx = \tfrac{1}{3}\Delta x\big((y_0 + y_n) + 4(y_1 + y_3 + y_5 + \ldots y_{n-1}) + 2(y_2 + y_4 + \ldots y_{n-2})\big), \qquad (17)$$

by means of which the approximate value of the integral within the given limits may be found.

If we consider the curve which passes through four points corresponding to y_0, y_1, y_2, and y_3, we have

$$y = f(x) = \alpha + \beta x + \gamma x^2 + \delta x^3$$

for the equation of the curve, and hence, giving to x the values 0, Δx, $2\Delta x$, and $3\Delta x$, successively, we easily find

$$\alpha = y_0,$$
$$\beta = \frac{1}{6\Delta x}(2y_3 - 9y_2 + 18y_1 - 11y_0),$$
$$\gamma = \frac{1}{2\Delta x^2}(-y_3 + 4y_2 - 5y_1 + 2y_0),$$
$$\delta = \frac{1}{6\Delta x^3}(y_3 - 3y_2 + 3y_1 - y_0).$$

Therefore we shall have

$$\int_0^{3\Delta x} f(x)\,dx = \tfrac{3}{8}\,\Delta x\,(y_0 + 3y_1 + 3y_2 + y_3). \tag{18}$$

In like manner, by taking successively an additional term of the series, we may derive

$$\begin{aligned} \int_0^{4\Delta x} f(x)\,dx &= \frac{2\Delta x}{45}(7y_0 + 32y_1 + 12y_2 + 32y_3 + 7y_4), \\ \int_0^{5\Delta x} f(x)\,dx &= \frac{5\Delta x}{288}(19y_0 + 75y_1 + 50y_2 + 50y_3 + 75y_4 + 19y_5). \end{aligned} \tag{19}$$

This process may be continued so as to include the extreme values of x for which $f(x)$ is known; but in the calculation of perturbations it will be more convenient to use the finite differences of the function instead of the function itself directly. We may remark, further, that the intervals of quadrature when the function itself is used, may be so determined that the degree of approximation will be much greater than when these intervals are uniform.

159. Let us put $\Delta x = \omega$, and let the value of x for which $n = 0$ be designated by a; then will the general value be

$$f(x) = f(a + n\omega),$$

ω being the constant interval at which the values of $f(x)$ are given. Hence we shall have

$$dx = \omega dn,$$
$$\int f(x)\,dx = \omega \int f(a + n\omega)\,dn.$$

If we expand the function $f(a + n\omega)$, we have

$$f(a+n\omega) = f(a) + n\omega\frac{df(a)}{da} + \frac{n^2\omega^2}{1\,.\,2}\cdot\frac{d^2f(a)}{da^2} + \frac{n^3\omega^3}{1.2.3}\cdot\frac{d^3f(a)}{da^3} + \&c., \tag{20}$$

and hence

$$\int f(a+n\omega)\,dn = C + nf(a) + \tfrac{1}{2}n^2\omega\frac{df(a)}{da} + \tfrac{1}{6}n^3\omega^2\frac{d^2f(a)}{da^2} + \tfrac{1}{24}n^4\omega^3\frac{d^3f(a)}{da^3} + \&c., \qquad (21)$$

C being the constant of integration. The equations $(54)_6$ give

$$\begin{aligned}
\omega\frac{df(a)}{da} &= f'(a) - \tfrac{1}{6}f'''(a) + \tfrac{1}{30}f^{\text{v}}(a) - \tfrac{1}{140}f^{\text{vii}}(a) + \ldots,\\
\omega^2\frac{d^2f(a)}{da^2} &= f''(a) - \tfrac{1}{12}f^{\text{iv}}(a) + \tfrac{1}{90}f^{\text{vi}}(a) - \tfrac{1}{560}f^{\text{viii}}(a) + \ldots,\\
\omega^3\frac{d^3f(a)}{da^3} &= f'''(a) - \tfrac{1}{4}f^{\text{v}}(a) + \tfrac{7}{120}f^{\text{vii}}(a) - \ldots,\\
\omega^4\frac{d^4f(a)}{da^4} &= f^{\text{iv}}(a) - \tfrac{1}{6}f^{\text{vi}}(a) + \tfrac{7}{240}f^{\text{viii}}(a) - \ldots,\\
\omega^5\frac{d^5f(a)}{da^5} &= f^{\text{v}}(a) - \tfrac{1}{3}f^{\text{vii}}(a) + \ldots,\\
\omega^6\frac{d^6f(a)}{da^6} &= f^{\text{vi}}(a) - \tfrac{1}{4}f^{\text{viii}}(a) + \ldots,
\end{aligned} \qquad (22)$$

in which the functional symbols in the second members denote the different orders of finite differences of the function. Hence we obtain

$$\begin{aligned}
\int f(a+n\omega)\,dn = C &+ nf(a)\\
&+ \tfrac{1}{2}n^2(f'(a) - \tfrac{1}{6}f'''(a) + \tfrac{1}{30}f^{\text{v}}(a) - \tfrac{1}{140}f^{\text{vii}}(a) + \ldots)\\
&+ \tfrac{1}{6}n^3(f''(a) - \tfrac{1}{12}f^{\text{iv}}(a) + \tfrac{1}{90}f^{\text{vi}}(a) - \tfrac{1}{560}f^{\text{viii}}(a) + \ldots)\\
&+ \tfrac{1}{24}n^4(f'''(a) - \tfrac{1}{4}f^{\text{v}}(a) + \tfrac{7}{120}f^{\text{vii}}(a) - \ldots)\\
&+ \tfrac{1}{120}n^5(f^{\text{iv}}(a) - \tfrac{1}{6}f^{\text{vi}}(a) + \tfrac{7}{240}f^{\text{viii}}(a) - \ldots)\\
&+ \tfrac{1}{720}n^6(f^{\text{v}}(a) - \tfrac{1}{3}f^{\text{vii}}(a) + \ldots)\\
&+ \tfrac{1}{5040}n^7(f^{\text{vi}}(a) - \tfrac{1}{4}f^{\text{viii}}(a) + \ldots)\\
&+ \tfrac{1}{40320}n^8f^{\text{vii}}(a) - \ldots + \tfrac{1}{362880}n^9f^{\text{viii}}(a) - \&c.
\end{aligned} \qquad (23)$$

If we take the integral between the limits $-n'$ and $+n'$, the terms containing the even powers of n disappear. Further, since the values of the function are supposed to be known for a series of values of n at intervals of a unit, it will evidently be convenient to determine the integral between the required limits by means of the sum of a series of integrals whose limits are successively increased by a unit, such that the difference between the superior and the inferior limit of each integral shall be a unit. Hence we take the first integral between the limits $-\frac{1}{2}$ and $+\frac{1}{2}$, and the equation (23) gives, after reduction,

$$\int_{-\frac{1}{2}}^{+\frac{1}{2}} f(a + n\omega)\, dn = f(a) + \tfrac{1}{24} f''(a) - \tfrac{17}{5760} f^{\text{iv}}(a) + \tfrac{367}{967680} f^{\text{vi}}(a) - \tfrac{27859}{464486400} f^{\text{viii}}(a) + \&c. \quad (24)$$

It is evident that by writing, in succession, $a + \omega$, $a + 2\omega$, ... $a + i\omega$ in place of a, we simply add 1 to each limit successively, so that we have

$$\int_{i-\frac{1}{2}}^{i+\frac{1}{2}} f(a + n\omega)\, dn = \int_{-\frac{1}{2}}^{+\frac{1}{2}} f\big((a + i\omega) + (n - i)\,\omega\big)\, d(n - i)$$
$$= f(a+i\omega) + \tfrac{1}{24} f''(a+i\omega) - \tfrac{17}{5760} f^{\text{iv}}(a+i\omega) + \tfrac{367}{967680} f^{\text{vi}}(a+i\omega) - \&c.$$

But since

$$\int_{-\frac{1}{2}}^{i+\frac{1}{2}} f(a+n\omega)\, dn = \int_{-\frac{1}{2}}^{\frac{1}{2}} f(a+n\omega)\, dn + \int_{\frac{1}{2}}^{\frac{3}{2}} f(a+n\omega)\, dn \ldots\ldots + \int_{i-\frac{1}{2}}^{i+\frac{1}{2}} f(a+n\omega)\, dn,$$

if we give to i successively the values 0, 1, 2, 3, &c. in the preceding equation, and add the results, we get

$$\int_{-\frac{1}{2}}^{i+\frac{1}{2}} f(a + n\omega)\, dn = \sum_{n=0}^{n=i} f(a + n\omega) + \tfrac{1}{24} \sum_{n=0}^{n=i} f''(a + n\omega) - \tfrac{17}{5760} \sum_{n=0}^{n=i} f^{\text{iv}}(a + n\omega) + \tfrac{367}{967680} \sum_{n=0}^{n=i} f^{\text{vi}}(a + n\omega) - \&c. \quad (25)$$

Let us now consider the functions $f(a), f(a + n\omega)$, &c. as being themselves the finite differences of other functions symbolized by $'f$, the first of which is entirely arbitrary, so that we may put, in accordance with the adopted notation,

$$f(a) = {}'f(a + \tfrac{1}{2}\omega) - {}'f(a - \tfrac{1}{2}\omega),$$
$$f(a + \omega) = {}'f(a + \tfrac{3}{2}\omega) - {}'f(a + \tfrac{1}{2}\omega),$$
$$\ldots \qquad \ldots \qquad \ldots$$
$$f(a + n\omega) = {}'f\big(a + (n + \tfrac{1}{2})\,\omega\big) - {}'f\big(a + (n - \tfrac{1}{2})\,\omega\big).$$

Therefore we shall have

$$\sum_{n=0}^{n=i} f(a + n\omega) = {}'f\big(a + (i + \tfrac{1}{2})\,\omega\big) - {}'f(a - \tfrac{1}{2}\omega),$$

and also

$$\sum_{n=0}^{n=i} f''(a + n\omega) = f'\big(a + (i + \tfrac{1}{2})\,\omega\big) - f'(a - \tfrac{1}{2}\omega),$$
$$\sum_{n=0}^{n=i} f^{\text{iv}}(a + n\omega) = f'''\big(a + (i + \tfrac{1}{2})\,\omega\big) - f'''(a - \tfrac{1}{2}\omega), \ \&c.$$

Further, since the quantity $'f(a-\frac{1}{2}\omega)$ is entirely arbitrary, we may assign to it a value such that the sum of all the terms of the equation which have the argument $a-\frac{1}{2}\omega$ shall be zero, namely,

$$'f(a-\tfrac{1}{2}\omega)=-\tfrac{1}{24}f'(a-\tfrac{1}{2}\omega)+\tfrac{17}{5760}f'''(a-\tfrac{1}{2}\omega)-\tfrac{367}{967680}f^{\text{v}}(a-\tfrac{1}{2}\omega)+\&\text{c.} \qquad (26)$$

Substituting these values in (25), it reduces to

$$\begin{aligned}\int_{a-\frac{1}{2}\omega}^{a+(i+\frac{1}{2})\omega} f(x)\,dx &= \omega\int_{-\frac{1}{2}}^{i+\frac{1}{2}} f(a+n\omega)\,dn \\ &= \omega\{'f(a+(i+\tfrac{1}{2})\omega)+\tfrac{1}{24}f'(a+(i+\tfrac{1}{2})\omega) \\ &\quad -\tfrac{17}{5760}f'''(a+(i+\tfrac{1}{2})\omega)+\tfrac{367}{967680}f^{\text{v}}(a+(i+\tfrac{1}{2})\omega)-\&\text{c.}\}\end{aligned} \qquad (27)$$

In the calculation of the perturbations of a heavenly body, the dates for which the values of the function are computed may be so arranged that for $n=-\frac{1}{2}$, corresponding to the inferior limit, the integral shall be equal to zero, the epoch of $f(a-\frac{1}{2}\omega)$ being that of the osculating elements. It will be observed that the equation (26) expresses this condition, the constant of integration being included in $'f(a-\frac{1}{2}\omega)$. If, instead of being equal to zero, the integral has a given value when $n=-\frac{1}{2}$, it is evidently only necessary to add this value to $'f(a-\frac{1}{2}\omega)$ as given by (26).

160. The interval ω and the arguments of the function may always be so taken that the equation (27) will furnish the required integral, either directly or by interpolation; but it will often be convenient to integrate for other limits directly, thus avoiding a subsequent interpolation. The derivation of the required formulæ of integration may be effected in a manner entirely analogous to that already indicated. Thus, let it be required to find the expression for the integral taken between the limits $-\frac{1}{2}$ and i.

The general formula (23) gives

$$\begin{aligned}\int_0^{\frac{1}{2}} f(a+n\omega)\,dn &= \tfrac{1}{2}f(a)+\tfrac{1}{8}f'(a)+\tfrac{1}{48}f''(a)-\tfrac{7}{384}f'''(a)-\tfrac{17}{11520}f^{\text{iv}}(a) \\ &\quad +\tfrac{163}{46080}f^{\text{v}}(a)+\tfrac{367}{1935360}f^{\text{vi}}(a)-\&\text{c.};\end{aligned}$$

and since, according to the notation adopted,

$$\begin{aligned} f'(a) &= \tfrac{1}{2}(f'(a-\tfrac{1}{2}\omega)+f'(a+\tfrac{1}{2}\omega)) \\ &= f'(a+\tfrac{1}{2}\omega) \quad -\tfrac{1}{2}f''(a), \\ f'''(a) &= f'''(a+\tfrac{1}{2}\omega) \quad -\tfrac{1}{2}f^{\text{iv}}(a), \\ f^{\text{v}}(a) &= f^{\text{v}}(a+\tfrac{1}{2}\omega) \quad -\tfrac{1}{2}f^{\text{vi}}(a),\ \&\text{c.},\end{aligned} \qquad (28)$$

this becomes

$$\int_0^{\frac{1}{2}} f(a+n\omega)\,dn = \tfrac{1}{2}f(a) + \tfrac{1}{8}f'(a+\tfrac{1}{2}\omega) - \tfrac{1}{24}f''(a) - \tfrac{7}{384}f'''(a+\tfrac{1}{2}\omega) \qquad (29)$$
$$+ \tfrac{11}{1440}f^{\text{iv}}(a) + \tfrac{163}{46080}f^{\text{v}}(a+\tfrac{1}{2}\omega) - \tfrac{191}{120960}f^{\text{vi}}(a) - \&c.$$

Therefore we obtain

$$\int_i^{i+\frac{1}{2}} f(a+n\omega)\,dn = \tfrac{1}{2}f(a+i\omega) + \tfrac{1}{8}f'\big(a+(i+\tfrac{1}{2})\,\omega\big) - \tfrac{1}{24}f''(a+i\omega)$$
$$- \tfrac{7}{384}f'''\big(a+(i+\tfrac{1}{2})\,\omega\big) + \tfrac{11}{1440}f^{\text{iv}}(a+i\omega) + \tfrac{163}{46080}f^{\text{v}}\big(a+(i+\tfrac{1}{2})\,\omega\big) \qquad (30)$$
$$- \tfrac{191}{120960}f^{\text{vi}}(a+i\omega) - \&c.$$

Now we have

$$\int_{-\frac{1}{2}}^{i} f(a+n\omega)\,dn = \int_{-\frac{1}{2}}^{i+\frac{1}{2}} f(a+n\omega)\,dn - \int_{i}^{i+\frac{1}{2}} f(a+n\omega)\,dn;$$

and if we substitute the values already found for the terms in the second member, and also

$$\begin{aligned} f(a+i\omega) &= {}'f\big(a+(i+\tfrac{1}{2})\,\omega\big) - {}'f\big(a+(i-\tfrac{1}{2})\,\omega\big), \\ f''(a+i\omega) &= f'\big(a+(i+\tfrac{1}{2})\,\omega\big) - f'\big(a+(i-\tfrac{1}{2})\,\omega\big), \\ f^{\text{iv}}(a+i\omega) &= f'''\big(a+(i+\tfrac{1}{2})\,\omega\big) - f'''\big(a+(i-\tfrac{1}{2})\,\omega\big), \\ f^{\text{vi}}(a+i\omega) &= f^{\text{v}}\big(a+(i+\tfrac{1}{2})\,\omega\big) - f^{\text{v}}\big(a+(i-\tfrac{1}{2})\,\omega\big), \&c. \end{aligned} \qquad (31)$$

we get

$$\int_{a-i\omega}^{a+i\omega} f(x)\,dx = \omega\int_{-\frac{1}{2}}^{i} f(a+n\omega)\,dn \qquad (32)$$
$$= \omega\,\big\{\tfrac{1}{2}{}'f\big(a+(i+\tfrac{1}{2})\,\omega\big) + \tfrac{1}{2}{}'f\big(a+(i-\tfrac{1}{2})\,\omega\big) - \tfrac{1}{24}f'\big(a+(i+\tfrac{1}{2})\,\omega\big)$$
$$- \tfrac{1}{24}f'\big(a+(i-\tfrac{1}{2})\,\omega\big) + \tfrac{11}{1440}f'''\big(a+(i+\tfrac{1}{2})\,\omega\big) + \tfrac{11}{1440}f'''\big(a+(i-\tfrac{1}{2})\,\omega\big)$$
$$- \tfrac{191}{120960}f^{\text{v}}\big(a+(i+\tfrac{1}{2})\,\omega\big) - \tfrac{191}{120960}f^{\text{v}}\big(a+(i-\tfrac{1}{2})\,\omega\big) + \&c.\big\},$$

which is the required integral between the limits $-\frac{1}{2}$ and i.

161. The methods of integration thus far considered apply to the cases in which but a single integration is required, and when applied to the integration of the differential equations for the variations of the co-ordinates on account of the action of disturbing bodies, they will only give the values of $\frac{d\delta x}{dt}$, $\frac{d\delta y}{dt}$, and $\frac{d\delta z}{dt}$, and another integration becomes necessary in order to obtain the values of δx, δy, and δz. We will therefore proceed to derive formulæ for the determination of the double integral directly.

For the double integral $\iint f(x)\,dx^2$ we have, since $dx^{\cdot\cdot} = \omega^2 dn^2$,

$$\iint f(x)\,dx^2 = \omega^2 \iint f(a + n\omega)\,dn^2.$$

The value of the function designated by $f(a)$ being so taken that when $n = -\frac{1}{2}$,

$$\int f(a + n\omega)\,dn = 0,$$

the equation (23) gives

$$C = \int_{-\frac{1}{2}}^{0} f(a + n\omega)\,dn.$$

Therefore, the general equation is

$$\int f(a + n\omega)\,dn = \int_{-\frac{1}{2}}^{0} f(a + n\omega)\,dn + nf(a) + \tfrac{1}{2}\alpha n^2 + \tfrac{1}{6}\beta n^3 + \tfrac{1}{24}\gamma n^4 + \tfrac{1}{120}\delta n^5 + \&c.$$

the values of α, β, γ, ... being given by the equations (22). Multiplying this by dn, and integrating, we get

$$\iint f(a + n\omega)\,dn^2 = C' + n\int_{-\frac{1}{2}}^{0} f(a + n\omega)\,dn + \tfrac{1}{2}n^2 f(a) + \tfrac{1}{6}\alpha n^3 + \tfrac{1}{24}\beta n^4 + \tfrac{1}{120}\gamma n^5 + \&c.,$$

C' being the new constant of integration. If we take the integral between the limits $-\frac{1}{2}$ and $+\frac{1}{2}$, we find

$$\iint_{-\frac{1}{2}}^{+\frac{1}{2}} f(a + n\omega)\,dn^2 = \int_{-\frac{1}{2}}^{0} f(a + n\omega)\,dn + \tfrac{1}{24}\alpha + \tfrac{1}{1920}\gamma + \tfrac{1}{322560}\varepsilon + \&c.$$

From the equation (32) we get, for $i = 0$,

$$\int_{-\frac{1}{2}}^{0} f(a + n\omega)\,dn = {}'f(a) - \tfrac{1}{12}f'(a) + \tfrac{11}{720}f'''(a) - \tfrac{191}{60480}f^{\text{v}}(a) + \&c. \quad (33)$$

Substituting this value, and also the values of α, γ, ε, &c.,—which are given by the second members of the equations (22),—in the preceding equation, and reducing, we get

$$\iint_{-\frac{1}{2}}^{+\frac{1}{2}} f(a + n\omega)\,dn^2 = {}'f(a) - \tfrac{1}{24}f'(a) + \tfrac{51}{5760}f'''(a) - \tfrac{1835}{967680}f^{\text{v}}(a) + \&c. \quad (34)$$

Hence

$$\iint_{i-\frac{1}{2}}^{i+\frac{1}{2}} f(a+n\omega)\,dn^2 = {}'f(a+i\omega) - \tfrac{1}{24}f'(a+i\omega) + \tfrac{17}{1920}f'''(a+i\omega) - \tfrac{367}{193536}f^{\text{v}}(a+i\omega) + \&\text{c}.$$

and

$$\iint_{-\frac{1}{2}}^{i+\frac{1}{2}} f(a+n\omega)\,dn^2 = \sum_{n=0}^{n=i}{}'f(a+n\omega) - \tfrac{1}{24}\sum_{n=0}^{n=i}f'(a+n\omega) + \tfrac{17}{1920}\sum_{n=0}^{n=i}f'''(a+n\omega) - \tfrac{367}{193536}\sum_{n=0}^{n=i}f^{\text{v}}(a+n\omega) + \&\text{c}. \qquad (35)$$

We may evidently consider $'f(a-\frac{1}{2}\omega)$, $'f(a+\frac{1}{2}\omega)$, &c. as the differences of other functions, the first of which is arbitrary, so that we have

$$\begin{aligned}
'f(a) &= \tfrac{1}{2}'f(a+\tfrac{1}{2}\omega) + \tfrac{1}{2}'f(a-\tfrac{1}{2}\omega) = \tfrac{1}{2}''f(a+\omega) - \tfrac{1}{2}f''(a-\omega),\\
'f(a+\omega) &= \tfrac{1}{2}'f(a+\tfrac{3}{2}\omega) + \tfrac{1}{2}'f(a+\tfrac{1}{2}\omega) = \tfrac{1}{2}''f(a+2\omega) - \tfrac{1}{2}f''(a),\\
&\cdots\\
'f(a+n\omega) &= \tfrac{1}{2}'f(a+(n+\tfrac{1}{2})\omega) + \tfrac{1}{2}'f(a+(n-\tfrac{1}{2})\omega) = \tfrac{1}{2}''f(a+(n+1)\omega) - \tfrac{1}{2}''f(a+(n-1)\omega).
\end{aligned}$$

Therefore

$$\begin{aligned}
\sum_{n=0}^{n=i}{}'f(a+n\omega) &= \tfrac{1}{2}''f(a+(i+1)\omega) + \tfrac{1}{2}''f(a+i\omega) - \tfrac{1}{2}''f(a) - \tfrac{1}{2}''f(a-\omega),\\
\sum_{n=0}^{n=i}f'(a+n\omega) &= \tfrac{1}{2}f(a+(i+1)\omega) + \tfrac{1}{2}f(a+i\omega) - \tfrac{1}{2}f(a) - \tfrac{1}{2}f(a-\omega),\\
\sum_{n=0}^{n=i}f'''(a+n\omega) &= \tfrac{1}{2}f''(a+(i+1)\omega) + \tfrac{1}{2}f''(a+i\omega) - \tfrac{1}{2}f''(a) - \tfrac{1}{2}f''(a-\omega),\\
\sum_{n=0}^{n=i}f^{\text{v}}(a+n\omega) &= \tfrac{1}{2}f^{\text{iv}}(a+(i+1)\omega) + \tfrac{1}{2}f^{\text{iv}}(a+i\omega) - \tfrac{1}{2}f^{\text{iv}}(a) - \tfrac{1}{2}f^{\text{iv}}(a-\omega), \&\text{c}.
\end{aligned}$$

Substituting these values in equation (35), and observing that

$$\begin{aligned}
''f(a) + ''f(a-\omega) &= 2''f(a-\omega) + {}'f(a-\tfrac{1}{2}\omega),\\
f(a) + f(a-\omega) &= 2f(a) - f'(a-\tfrac{1}{2}\omega),\\
f''(a) + f''(a-\omega) &= 2f''(a) - f'''(a-\tfrac{1}{2}\omega), \&\text{c.},
\end{aligned}$$

$$'f(a-\tfrac{1}{2}\omega) = -\tfrac{1}{24}f'(a-\tfrac{1}{2}\omega) + \tfrac{17}{5760}f'''(a-\tfrac{1}{2}\omega) - \tfrac{367}{967680}f^{\text{v}}(a-\tfrac{1}{2}\omega) + \ldots,$$

and that, since $''f(a-\omega)$ is arbitrary, we may put

$$''f(a-\omega) = \tfrac{1}{24}f(a) - \tfrac{17}{5760}(2f''(a) + f''(a-\omega)) + \tfrac{367}{967680}(3f^{\text{iv}}(a) + 2f^{\text{iv}}(a-\omega)) - \&\text{c.}, \qquad (36)$$

the integral becomes

$$\iint\limits_{a-\frac{1}{2}\omega}^{a+(i+\frac{1}{2})\omega} f(x)\,dx^2 = \omega^2 \iint\limits_{-\frac{1}{2}}^{i+\frac{1}{2}} f(a+n\omega)\,dn^2$$

$$\begin{aligned} = \omega^2 \{ \tfrac{1}{2}\,{}''f(a+(i+1)\,\omega) + \tfrac{1}{2}\,{}''f(a+i\omega) - \tfrac{1}{48}f(a+(i+1)\,\omega) \\ - \tfrac{1}{48}f(a+i\omega) + \tfrac{17}{3840}f''(a+(i+1)\,\omega) + \tfrac{17}{3840}f''(a+i\omega) \\ - \tfrac{367}{387072}f^{\mathrm{iv}}(a+(i+1)\,\omega) - \tfrac{367}{387072}f^{\mathrm{iv}}(a+i\omega) + \&c. \}, \end{aligned} \qquad (37)$$

which is the expression for the double integral between the limits $-\frac{1}{2}$ and $i+\frac{1}{2}$.

The value of $''f(a-\omega)$ given by equation (36) is in accordance with the supposition that for $n=-\frac{1}{2}$ the double integral is equal to zero, and this condition is fulfilled in the calculation of the perturbations when the argument $a-\frac{1}{2}\omega$ corresponds to the date for which the osculating elements are given. If, for $n=-\frac{1}{2}$, neither the single nor the double integral is to be taken equal to zero, it is only necessary to add the given value of the single integral for this argument to the value of $'f(a-\frac{1}{2}\omega)$ given by equation (26), and to add the given value of the double integral for the same argument to the value of $''f(a-\omega)$ given by (36).

162. In a similar manner we may find the expressions for the double integral between other limits. Thus, let it be required to find the double integral between the limits $-\frac{1}{2}$ and i.

Between the limits 0 and $\frac{1}{2}$ we have

$$\iint\limits_{0}^{\frac{1}{2}} f(a+n\omega)\,dn^2 = \tfrac{1}{2}\int\limits_{-\frac{1}{2}}^{0} f(a+n\omega)\,dn + \tfrac{1}{8}f(a) + \tfrac{1}{48}\alpha$$
$$+ \tfrac{1}{384}\beta + \tfrac{1}{3840}\gamma + \tfrac{1}{46080}\delta + \&c.$$

which gives

$$\begin{aligned} \iint\limits_{0}^{\frac{1}{2}} f(a+n\omega)\,dn^2 = \tfrac{1}{2}\,{}'f(a) + \tfrac{1}{8}f(a) - \tfrac{1}{48}f'(a) + \tfrac{1}{384}f''(a) + \tfrac{17}{3840}f'''(a) \\ - \tfrac{1}{5120}f^{\mathrm{iv}}(a) - \tfrac{367}{387072}f^{\mathrm{v}}(a) + \tfrac{787}{30965760}f^{\mathrm{vi}}(a) + \&c.; \end{aligned} \qquad (38)$$

and this again, by means of (28), gives

$$\begin{aligned} \iint^{i+\frac{1}{2}} f(a+n\omega)\,dn^2 = \tfrac{1}{2}\,{}'f(a+(i+\tfrac{1}{2})\,\omega) - \tfrac{1}{8}f(a+i\omega) - \tfrac{1}{48}f'(a+(i+\tfrac{1}{2})\,\omega) \\ + \tfrac{5}{384}f''(a+i\omega) + \tfrac{17}{3840}f'''(a+(i+\tfrac{1}{2})\,\omega) - \tfrac{37}{15360}f^{\mathrm{iv}}(a+i\omega) \\ - \tfrac{367}{387072}f^{\mathrm{v}}(a+(i+\tfrac{1}{2})\,\omega) + \tfrac{15467}{30965760}f^{\mathrm{vi}}(a+i\omega) + \&c. \end{aligned}$$

Therefore, since

$$\iint_{-\frac{1}{2}}^{i} f(a+n\omega)\,dn^2 = \iint_{-\frac{1}{2}}^{i+\frac{1}{2}} f(a+n\omega)\,dn^2 - \iint_{i}^{i+\frac{1}{2}} f(a+n\omega)\,dn^2,$$

and

$$\begin{aligned} {}'f(a+(i+\tfrac{1}{2})\omega) &= {}''f(a+(i+1)\omega) - {}''f(a+i\omega), \\ f'(a+(i+\tfrac{1}{2})\omega) &= f(a+(i+1)\omega) - f(a+i\omega), \\ f'''(a+(i+\tfrac{1}{2})\omega) &= f''(a+(i+1)\omega) - f''(a+i\omega), \text{ \&c.} \end{aligned}$$

we shall have

$$\begin{aligned} \iint_{a-\frac{1}{2}\omega}^{a+i\omega} f(x)\,dx^2 &= \omega^2 \iint_{-\frac{1}{2}}^{i} f(a+n\omega)\,dn^2 \\ &= \omega^2 \{ {}''f(a+i\omega) + \tfrac{1}{12} f(a+i\omega) - \tfrac{1}{240} f''(a+i\omega) + \tfrac{31}{60480} f^{\text{iv}}(a+i\omega) - \text{\&c.} \}, \end{aligned} \qquad (39)$$

which gives the required integral between the limits $-\frac{1}{2}$ and i.

163. It will be observed that the coefficients of the several terms of the formulæ of integration converge rapidly, and hence, by a proper selection of the interval at which the values of the function are computed, it will not be necessary to consider the terms which depend on the fourth and higher orders of differences, and rarely those which depend on the second and third differences. The value assigned to the interval ω must be such that we may interpolate with certainty, by means of the values computed directly, all values of the function intermediate to the extreme limits of the integration; and hence, if the fourth and higher orders of differences are sensible, it will be necessary to extend the direct computation of the values of the function beyond the limits which would otherwise be required, in order to obtain correct values of the differences for the beginning and end of the integration. It will be expedient, therefore, to take ω so small that the fourth and higher differences may be neglected, but not smaller than is necessary to satisfy this condition, since otherwise an unnecessary amount of labor would be expended in the direct computation of the values of the function. It is better, however, to have the interval ω smaller than what would appear to be strictly required, in order that there may be no uncertainty with respect to the accuracy of the integration. On account of the rapidity with which the higher orders of differences decrease as we diminish ω, a limit for the magnitude of the adopted interval will speedily be obtained. The magnitude of the interval will therefore be suggested by the rapidity of the change of value of the function. In the com-

putation of the perturbations of the group of small planets between Mars and Jupiter we may adopt uniformly an interval of forty days; but in the determination of the perturbations of comets it will evidently be necessary to adopt different intervals in different parts of the orbit. When the comet is in the neighborhood of its perihelion, and also when it is near a disturbing planet, the interval must necessarily be much smaller than when it is in more remote parts of its orbit or farther from the disturbing body.

It will be observed, further, that since the double integral contains the factor ω^2, if we multiply the computed values of the function by ω^2, this factor will be included in all the differences and sums, and hence it will not appear as a factor in the formulæ of integration. If, however, the values of the function are already multiplied by ω^2, and only the single integral is sought, the result obtained by the formula of integration, neglecting the factor ω^2, will be ω times the actual integral required, and it must be divided by ω in order to obtain the final result.

164. In the computation of the perturbations of one of the asteroid planets for a period of two or three years it will rarely be necessary to take into account the effect of the terms of the second order with respect to the disturbing force. In this case the numerical values of the expressions for the forces will be computed by using the values of the co-ordinates computed from the osculating elements for the beginning of the integration, instead of the actual disturbed values of these co-ordinates as required by the formulæ (8). The values of the second differential coefficients of δx, δy, and δz with respect to the time, will be determined by means of the equations (9). If the interval ω is such that the higher orders of differences may be neglected, the values of the forces must be computed for the successive dates separated by the interval ω, and commencing with the date $t_0 - \frac{1}{2}\omega$ corresponding to the argument $a - \omega$, t_0 being the date to which the osculating elements belong. Then, since the last terms of the formulæ for $\frac{d^2\delta x}{dt^2}$, $\frac{d^2\delta y}{dt^2}$, and $\frac{d^2\delta z}{dt^2}$ involve δx, δy, and δz, which are the quantities sought, the subsequent determination of the differential coefficients must be performed by successive trials. Since the integral must in each case be equal to zero for the date t_0, it will be admissible to assume first, for the dates $t_0 - \frac{1}{2}\omega$ and $t_0 + \frac{1}{2}\omega$ corresponding to the arguments $a - \omega$ and a, that $\delta x = 0$, $\delta y = 0$, and $\delta z = 0$, and hence that the three differential coefficients, for each

date, are respectively equal to X_0, Y_0, and Z_0. We may now by integration derive the actual or the very approximate values of the variations of the co-ordinates for these two dates. Thus, in the case of each co-ordinate, we compute the value of $'f(a - \frac{1}{2}\omega)$ by means of the equation (26), using only the first term, and the value of $''f(a - \omega)$ from (36), using in this case also only the first term. The value of the next function symbolized by $''f$ will be given by

$$''f(a) = ''f(a - \omega) + 'f(a - \tfrac{1}{2}\omega).$$

Then the formula (39), putting first $i = -1$ and then $i = 0$, and neglecting second differences, will give the values of the variations of the co-ordinates for the dates $a - \omega$ and a. These operations will be performed in the case of each of the three co-ordinates; and, by means of the results, the corrected values of the differential coefficients will be obtained from the equations (9), the value of δr being computed by means of (7). With the corrected values thus derived a new table of integration will be commenced; and the values of $'f(a - \frac{1}{2}\omega)$ and $''f(a - \omega)$ will also be recomputed. Then we obtain, also, by adding $'f(a - \frac{1}{2}\omega)$ to $f(a)$, the value of $'f(a + \frac{1}{2}\omega)$, and, by adding this to $''f(a)$, the value of $''f(a + \omega)$.

An approximate value of $f(a + \omega)$ may now be readily estimated, and two terms of the equation (39), putting $i = 1$, will give an approximate value of the integral. This having been obtained for each of the co-ordinates, the corresponding complete values of the differential coefficients may be computed, and these having been introduced into the table of integration, the process may, in a similar manner, be carried one step farther, so as to determine first approximate values of δx, δy, and δz for the date represented by the argument $a + 2\omega$, and then the corresponding values of the differential coefficients. We may thus by successive partial integrations determine the values of the unknown quantities near enough for the calculation of the series of differential coefficients, even when the integrals are involved directly in the values of the differential coefficients. If it be found that the assumed value of the function is, in any case, much in error, a repetition of the calculation may become necessary; but when a few values have been found, the course of the function will indicate at once an approximation sufficiently close, since whatever error remains affects the approximate integral by only one-twelfth part of the amount of this error. Further, it is evident that, in cases of this kind, when the determination of the values of the differential coefficients requires a preliminary approximate integration, it is necessary, in order to avoid the effect of the errors in the values of the higher orders of differences, that the interval ω should be smaller than when the successive values of the function to be integrated are already known. In the case of the small planets an interval of 40 days will afford the required facility in the approximations; but in the case of the comets it may often be necessary to adopt an interval of only a few days. The necessity of a change in the adopted value of ω will be indicated, in the numerical application of the formulæ, by the manner in which the successive assumptions in regard to the value of the function are found to agree with the corrected results.

The values of the differential coefficients, and hence those of the integrals, are conveniently expressed by adopting for unity the unit of the seventh decimal place of their values in terms of the unit of space.

165. Whenever it is considered necessary to commence to take into account the perturbations due to the second and higher powers of the disturbing force, the complete equations (14) must be employed. In this case the forces X, Y, and Z should not be computed at once for the entire period during which the perturbations are to be determined. The values computed by means of the osculating elements will be employed only so long as simply the first power of the disturbing force is considered, and by means of the approximate values of δx, δy, and δz which would be employed in computing, for the next place, the last terms of the equations (9), we must compute also the corrected values of X, Y, and Z. These will be given by the second members of (8), using the values of x, y, and z obtained from

$$x = x_0 + \delta x, \qquad y = y_0 + \delta y, \qquad z = z_0 + \delta z.$$

We compute also q from (12), and then from Table XVII. find the corresponding value of f. The corrected values of $\frac{d^2\delta x}{dt^2}$, $\frac{d^2\delta y}{dt^2}$, and $\frac{d^2\delta z}{dt^2}$ will be given by the equations (14), and these being introduced, in the continuation of the table of integration, we obtain new values of δx, δy, and δz for the date under consideration. If these differ much from those previously assumed, a repetition of the calculation will be necessary in order to secure extreme accuracy. In this repetition, however, it will not be necessary to recompute the coefficients of δx, δy, and δz in the formula for q, their values being given with sufficient accuracy by means of the previous assumption; and generally a repetition of the calculation of X, Y, and Z will not be required.

Next, the values of δx, δy, and δz may be determined approximately, as already explained, for the following date, and by means of these the corresponding values of the forces X, Y, and Z will be found, and also f and the remaining terms of (14), after which the integration will be completed and a new trial made, if it be considered necessary. In the final integration, all the terms of the formulæ of integration which sensibly affect the result may be taken into account. By thus performing the complete calculation of each successive place separately, the determination of the perturbations in the values of the co-ordinates may be effected in reference to all powers of the masses, provided that we regard the masses and co-ordinates of the disturbing bodies as being accurately known; and it is apparent that this complete solution of the problem requires very little more labor than the determination of the perturbations when only the first power of the disturbing force is considered. But although the places of the disturbing bodies as given by the tables of their motion may be regarded as accurately known, there are yet the errors of the adopted osculating elements of the disturbed body to detract from the absolute accuracy of the computed perturbations; and hence the probable errors of these elements should be constantly kept in view, to the end that no useless extension of the calculation may be undertaken. When the osculating elements have been corrected by means of a very extended series of observations, it will be expedient to determine the perturbations with all possible rigor.

When there are several disturbing planets, the forces for all of these may be computed simultaneously and united in a single sum, so that in the equations (14) we shall have ΣX, ΣY, and ΣZ instead of X, Y, and Z respectively; and the integration of the expressions for $\frac{d^2\delta x}{dt^2}$, $\frac{d^2\delta y}{dt^2}$, and $\frac{d^2\delta z}{dt^2}$ will then give the perturbations due to the action of all the disturbing bodies considered. However, when the interval ω for the different disturbing planets may be taken differently, it may be considered expedient to compute the perturbations separately, and especially if the adopted values of the masses of some of the disturbing bodies are regarded as uncertain, and it is desired to separate their action in order to determine the probable corrections to be applied to the values of m, m', &c., or to determine the effect of any subsequent change in these values without repeating the calculation of the perturbations.

166. EXAMPLE.—To illustrate the numerical application of the formulæ for the computation of the perturbations of the rectangular co-ordinates, let it be required to compute the perturbations of *Eurynome* (79) arising from the action of *Jupiter* from 1864 Jan. 1.0 Berlin mean time to 1865 Jan. 15.0 Berlin mean time, assuming the osculating elements to be the following:—

Epoch = 1864 Jan. 1.0 Berlin mean time.

$M_0 =$ 1° 29′ 5″.65
$\pi_0 =$ 44 17 12 .17
$\Omega_0 =$ 206 39 5 .69
$i_0 =$ 4 36 52 .11
(Ecliptic and Mean Equinox 1860.0)
$\varphi_0 =$ 11 15 51 .02
$\log a_0 =$ 0.3881319
$\mu_0 =$ 928″.55745.

From these elements we derive the following values:—

Berlin Mean Time.			x_0	y_0	z_0	$\log r_0$
1863	Dec.	12.0	+ 1.53616	+ 1.23012	— 0.03312	0.294084,
1864	Jan.	21.0	1.15097	1.59918	0.07369	0.294837,
	March	1.0	0.69518	1.87033	0.10978	0.300674,
	April	10.0	+ 0.19817	2.03141	0.13936	0.310864,
	May	20.0	— 0.31012	2.08092	0.16134	0.324298,
	June	29.0	0.80326	2.02602	0.17523	0.339745,
	Aug.	8.0	1.26055	1.87959	0.18122	0.356101,
	Sept.	17.0	1.66729	1.65711	0.17990	0.372469,
	Oct.	27.0	2.01414	1.37473	0.17209	0.388214,
	Dec.	6.0	2.29597	1.04766	0.15870	0.402894,
1865	Jan.	15.0	— 2.51077	+ 0.68978	— 0.14066	0.416240.

The adopted interval is $\omega = 40$ days, and the co-ordinates are referred to the ecliptic and mean equinox of 1860.0. The first date, it will be observed, corresponds to $t_0 - \frac{1}{2}\omega$, and the integration is to commence at 1864 Jan. 1.0.

The places of *Jupiter* derived from the tables give the following values of the co-ordinates of that planet, with which we write also the distances of *Eurynome* from *Jupiter* computed by means of the formula

$$\rho^2 = (x' - x_0)^2 + (y' - y_0)^2 + (z' - z_0)^2.$$

Berlin Mean Time.			x'	y'	z'	$\log r'$	$\log \rho$
1863	Dec.	12.0	—4.09683	—3.55184	+0.10533	0.73425	0.86866,
1864	Jan.	21.0	3.89630	3.76053	0.10152	0.73368	0.86713,
	March	1.0	3.68416	3.95803	0.09744	0.73305	0.86292,
	April	10.0	—3.46098	—4.14366	+0.09304	0.73237	0.85622,

Berlin Mean Time.	x'	y'	z'	$\log r'$	$\log \rho$
1864 May 20.0	−3.22739	−4.31684	+0.08839	0.73164	0.84732,
June 29.0	2.98405	4.47693	0.08346	0.73086	0.83656,
Aug. 8.0	2.73162	4.62343	0.07827	0.73003	0.82428,
Sept. 17.0	2.47085	4.75576	0.07284	0.72915	0.81077,
Oct. 27.0	2.20247	4.87345	0.06720	0.72823	0.79628,
Dec. 6.0	1.92728	4.97606	0.06134	0.72726	0.78098,
1865 Jan. 15.0	−1.64600	−5.06301	+0.05531	0.72625	0.76498.

These co-ordinates are also referred to the ecliptic and mean equinox of 1860.0.

If we neglect the mass of *Eurynome* and adopt for the mass of *Jupiter*

$$m' = \frac{1}{1047.819},$$

we obtain, in units of the seventh decimal place,

$$\omega^2 m' k^2 = 4518.27,$$

and the equations (9) become

$$\begin{aligned}
\omega^2 \frac{d^2\delta x}{dt^2} &= 4518.27\left(\frac{x'-x_0}{\rho^3} - \frac{x'}{r'^3}\right) + \frac{0.47346}{r_0^3}\left(3\frac{x_0}{r_0}\delta r - \delta x\right),\\
\omega^2 \frac{d^2\delta y}{dt^2} &= 4518.27\left(\frac{y'-y_0}{\rho^3} - \frac{y'}{r'^3}\right) + \frac{0.47346}{r_0^3}\left(3\frac{y_0}{r_0}\delta r - \delta y\right),\\
\omega^2 \frac{d^2\delta z}{dt^2} &= 4518.27\left(\frac{z'-z_0}{\rho^3} - \frac{z'}{r'^3}\right) + \frac{0.47346}{r_0^3}\left(3\frac{z_0}{r_0}\delta r - \delta z\right).
\end{aligned} \quad (40)$$

Substituting for the quantities in the first term of the second member of each of these equations the values already found, we obtain

Argument.	Date.	$\omega^2 X_0$	$\omega^2 Y_0$	$\omega^2 Z_0$
$a - \omega$	1863 Dec. 12.0	+ 53.00	+ 47.09	− 1.43,
a	1864 Jan. 21.0	53.71	46.31	0.91,
$a + \omega$	March 1.0	54.23	45.18	− 0.37,
$a + 2\omega$	April 10.0	54.69	43.59	+ 0.22,
$a + 3\omega$	May 20.0	55.23	41.51	0.70,
$a + 4\omega$	June 29.0	56.06	38.96	1.19,
$a + 5\omega$	Aug. 8.0	57.30	35.92	1.66,
$a + 6\omega$	Sept. 17.0	59.09	32.47	2.08,
$a + 7\omega$	Oct. 27.0	61.55	28.60	2.43,
$a + 8\omega$	Dec. 6.0	64.85	24.34	2.69,
$a + 9\omega$	1865 Jan. 15.0	+ 69.09	+ 19.78	+ 2.83,

which are expressed in units of the seventh decimal place.

We now, for a first approximation, regard the perturbations as being equal to zero for the dates Dec. 12.0 and Jan. 21.0, and, in the case of the variation of x, we compute first

$$'f(a-\tfrac{1}{2}\omega) = -\tfrac{1}{24}f'(a-\tfrac{1}{2}\omega) = -\tfrac{1}{24}(53.71-53.00) = -0.03,$$

$$''f(a-\omega) \;\; = \tfrac{1}{24}f(a) = +\frac{53.71}{24} = +2.24,$$

and the approximate table of integration becomes

$$\begin{array}{lll} f(a-\omega) = +53.00 & & ''f(a-\omega) = +2.24, \\ & 'f(a-\tfrac{1}{2}\omega) = -0.03 & \\ f(a) \qquad = +53.71 & & ''f(a) \qquad = +2.21. \end{array}$$

Then the formula (39), putting first $i=-1$, and then $i=0$, gives

$$\text{Dec. 12.0} \qquad \delta x = +2.24 + \frac{53.00}{12} = +6.66,$$

$$\text{Jan. 21.0} \qquad \delta x = +2.21 + \frac{53.71}{12} = +6.69.$$

In a similar manner, we find

Dec. 12.0	$\delta y = +5.85$	$\delta z = -0.16,$
Jan. 21.0	$\delta y = +5.82$	$\delta z = -0.14.$

By means of these results we compute the complete values of the second members of equations (40), δr being found from

$$\delta r = \frac{x_0}{r_0}\delta x + \frac{y_0}{r_0}\delta y + \frac{z_0}{r_0}\delta z,$$

and thus we obtain

Date.	$\omega^2 \frac{d^2\delta x}{dt^2}$	$\omega^2 \frac{d^2\delta y}{dt^2}$	$\omega^2 \frac{d^2\delta z}{dt^2}$	δr
Dec. 12.0	+ 53.86	+ 47.76	− 1.45	+ 8.85,
Jan. 21.0	+ 54.23	+ 47.25	− 0.96	+ 8.63.

We now commence anew the table of integration, namely,

	x			y			z	
f	$'f$	$''f$	f	$'f$	$''f$	f	$'f$	$''f$
		+56.45,			+49.26,			−1.04,
+53.86		+ 2.26,	+47.76		+ 1.97,	−1.45		−0.04,
	− 0.02			+ 0.02			−0.02	
+54.23		+ 2.24,	+47.25		+ 1.99,	−0.96		−0.06,
	+54.21			+47.27			−0.98	

the formation of which is made evident by what precedes.

We may next assume for approximate values of the differential coefficients, for the date March 1.0, + 54.6, + 46.7, and − 0.5, respectively; and these give, for this date,

$$\delta x = +\ 56.45 + \frac{54.6}{12} = +\ 61.00,$$

$$\delta y = +\ 49.26 + \frac{46.7}{12} = +\ 53.15,$$

$$\delta z = -\ \ 1.04 - \frac{0.5}{12} = -\ \ 1.08.$$

By means of these approximate values we obtain the following results:—

1864 March 1.0 $\quad \frac{d^2\delta x}{dt^2} = +\ 55.01, \quad \frac{d^2\delta y}{dt^2} = +\ 53.86, \quad \frac{d^2\delta z}{dt^2} = -1.00,$

$$\delta r = +\ 71.03.$$

Introducing these into the table of integration, we find, for the corresponding values of the integrals,

$$\delta x = +\ 61.03, \qquad \delta y = +\ 53.75, \qquad \delta z = -\ 1.12.$$

These results differ so little from those already derived from the assumed values of the function that a repetition of the calculation is unnecessary. This repetition, however, gives

$$\frac{d^2\delta x}{dt^2} = +\ 55.04, \qquad \frac{d^2\delta y}{dt^2} = +\ 53.91, \qquad \frac{d^2\delta z}{dt^2} = -\ 1.00.$$

Assuming, again, approximate values of the differential coefficients for April 10.0, and computing the corresponding values of δx, δy, and δz, we derive, for this date,

$$\omega^2 \frac{d^2\delta x}{dt^2} = +\ 48.06, \qquad \omega^2 \frac{d^2\delta y}{dt^2} = +\ 63.19, \qquad \omega^2 \frac{d^2\delta z}{dt^2} = -\ 1.54.$$

Introducing these into the table of integration, and thus deriving approximate values of δx, δy, and δz for May 20, we carry the process one step further. In this manner, by successive approximations, we obtain the following results:—

Date.		$\omega^2 \frac{d^2\delta x}{dt^2}$	$\omega^2 \frac{d^2\delta y}{dt^2}$	$\omega^2 \frac{d^2\delta z}{dt^2}$
1863 Dec.	12.0	+ 53.86	+ 47.76	− 1.45,
1864 Jan.	21.0	54.23	47.25	0.96,
March	1.0	55.04	53.91	1.00,
April	10.0	48.06	63.19	1.54,
May	20.0	32.85	65.40	2.07,
June	29.0	16.74	54.48	1.75,
Aug.	8.0	8.62	31.39	− 0.36,
Sept.	17.0	+ 14.20	+ 2.09	+ 1.86,

Date.		$\omega^2 \frac{d^2\delta x}{dt^2}$	$\omega^2 \frac{d^2\delta y}{dt^2}$	$\omega^2 \frac{d^2\delta z}{dt^2}$
1864 Oct.	27.0	+ 34.84	— 26.32	+ 4.44,
Dec.	6.0	68.79	47.87	6.86,
1865 Jan.	15.0	+ 112.64	— 58.39	+ 8.68.

The complete integration may now be effected, and we may use both equation (37) and equation (39), the former giving the integral for the dates Jan. 1.0, Feb. 10.0, March 21.0, &c., and the latter the integrals for the dates in the foregoing table of values of the function. The final results for the perturbations of the rectangular co-ordinates, expressed in units of the seventh decimal place, are thus found to be the following:—

Berlin Mean Time.		δx	δy	δz
1863 Dec.	12.0	+ 6.7	+ 5.9	— 0.2,
1864 Jan.	1.0	0.0	0.0	0.0,
	21.0	+ 6.8	5.9	0.1,
Feb.	10.0	27.1	23.5	0.5,
March	1.0	61.0	53.7	1.1,
	21.0	108.9	97.4	2.0,
April	10.0	169.7	155.7	3.1,
	30.0	242.7	229.9	4.7,
May	20.0	325.7	320.3	6.7,
June	9.0	417.1	427.2	9.3,
	29.0	514.6	549.1	12.3,
July	19.0	616.1	684.9	15.7,
Aug.	8.0	720.8	831.4	19.5,
	28.0	827.4	986.0	23.4,
Sept.	17.0	936.8	1144.6	27.0,
Oct.	7.0	1049.4	1303.8	30.2,
	27.0	1168.2	1460.0	32.6,
Nov.	16.0	1295.4	1609.4	33.9,
Dec.	6.0	1435.6	1749.6	33.8,
	26.0	1592.8	1877.6	32.0,
1865 Jan.	15.0	+ 1772.6	+ 1992.3	— 28.2.

During the interval included by these perturbations, the terms of the second order of the disturbing forces will have no sensible effect; but to illustrate the application of the rigorous formulæ, let us commence at the date 1864 Sept. 17.0 to consider the perturbations of the second order.

In the first place, the components of the disturbing force must be computed by means of the equations

$$\omega^2 X = \omega^2 m' k^2 \left(\frac{x' - x}{\rho^3} - \frac{x'}{r'^3} \right), \qquad \omega^2 Y = \omega^2 m' k^2 \left(\frac{y' - y}{\rho^3} - \frac{y'}{r'^3} \right),$$

$$\omega^2 Z = \omega^2 m' k^2 \left(\frac{z' - z}{\rho^3} - \frac{z'}{r'^3} \right).$$

The approximate values of δx, δy, and δz for Sept. 17.0 given immediately by the table of integration extended to this date, will suffice to furnish the required values of the disturbed co-ordinates by means of

$$x = x_0 + \delta x, \qquad y = y_0 + \delta y, \qquad z = z_0 + \delta z;$$

and to find $\rho = \rho_0 + \delta\rho$, we have

$$\delta\rho = -\frac{x' - x}{\rho}\delta x - \frac{y' - y}{\rho}\delta y - \frac{z' - z}{\rho}\delta z,$$

or

$$\delta \log \rho = -\frac{\lambda_0}{\rho^2}\left((x' - x)\,\delta x + (y' - y)\,\delta y + (z' - z)\,\delta z\right),$$

in which λ_0 is the modulus of the system of logarithms. Thus we obtain, for Sept. 17.0,

$$\delta \log \rho = +\,0.0000084,$$

$$\omega^2 X = +\,59.09, \qquad \omega^2 Y = +\,32.48, \qquad \omega^2 Z = +\,2.08,$$

which require no further correction.

Next, we compute the values of

$$\frac{x_0 + \frac{1}{2}\delta x}{r_0^{\,2}}, \qquad \frac{y_0 + \frac{1}{2}\delta y}{r_0^{\,2}}, \qquad \frac{z_0 + \frac{1}{2}\delta z}{r_0^{\,2}},$$

which also will not require any further correction, and thus we form, according to (12), the equation

$$q = -\,0.29996\delta x + 0.29815\delta y - 0.03237\delta z.$$

The approximate values of δx, δy, and δz being substituted in this equation, we obtain

$$q = +\,0.0000061,$$

corresponding to which Table XVII. gives

$$\log f = 0.477115.$$

Hence we derive

$$\frac{\omega^2 k^2}{r_0^{\,3}}(fqx - \delta x) = -\,44.87, \qquad \frac{\omega^2 k^2}{r_0^{\,3}}(fqy - \delta y) = -\,30.40,$$

$$\frac{\omega^2 k^2}{r_0^{\,3}}(fqz - \delta z) = -\,0.21,$$

and the equations (14) give

$$\omega^2 \frac{d^2\delta x}{dt^2} = +14.22, \qquad \omega^2 \frac{d^2\delta y}{dt^2} = +2.08, \qquad \omega^2 \frac{d^2\delta z}{dt^2} = +1.87.$$

These values being introduced into the table of integration, the resulting values of the integrals are changed so little that a repetition of the calculation is not required.

We now derive approximate values of δx, δy, and δz for Oct. 27.0, and in a similar manner we obtain the corrected values of the differential coefficients for this date; and thus by computing the forces for each place in succession from approximate values of the perturbations, and repeating the calculation whenever it may appear necessary, we may determine the perturbations rigorously for all powers of the masses. The results in the case under consideration are the following:—

Date.	$\omega^2 \frac{d^2\delta x}{dt^2}$	$\omega^2 \frac{d^2\delta y}{dt^2}$	$\omega^2 \frac{d^2\delta z}{dt^2}$
1864 Sept. 17.0	+ 14.22	+ 2.08	+ 1.87,
Oct. 27.0	34.84	— 26.31	4.44,
Dec. 6.0	68.77	47.86	6.86,
1865 Jan. 15.0	+ 112.60	— 58.39	+ 8.68.

Introducing these results into the table of integration, the integrals for Jan. 15.0 are found to be

$$\delta x = +1772.6, \qquad \delta y = +1992.3, \qquad \delta z = -28.2,$$

agreeing exactly with those obtained when terms of the order of the square of the disturbing forces are neglected.

If the perturbations of the rectangular co-ordinates referred to the equator are required, we have, whatever may be the magnitude of the perturbations,

$$\begin{aligned} \delta x_{,} &= \delta x, \\ \delta y_{,} &= \cos\varepsilon\, \delta y - \sin\varepsilon\, \delta z, \\ \delta z_{,} &= \sin\varepsilon\, \delta y + \cos\varepsilon\, \delta z, \end{aligned} \qquad (41)$$

$x_{,,}$ $y_{,,}$ $z_{,}$ being the co-ordinates in reference to the equator as the fundamental plane. Thus we obtain, for 1865 Jan. 15.0,

$$\delta x_{,} = +1772.6, \qquad \delta y_{,} = +1838.9, \qquad \delta z_{,} = +767.2.$$

These values, expressed in seconds of arc of a circle whose radius is the unit of space, are

$$\delta x_{,} = +36''.562, \qquad \delta y_{,} = +37''.930, \qquad \delta z_{,} = +15''.825.$$

The approximate geocentric place of the planet for the same date is

$$\alpha = 183^\circ\ 28', \qquad \delta = -5^\circ\ 39', \qquad \log \Delta = 0.3229,$$

and hence, neglecting terms of the second order, we derive, by means of the equations $(3)_2$, for the perturbations of the geocentric right ascension and declination,

$$\Delta\alpha = -17''.03, \qquad \Delta\delta = +5''.67.$$

167. The values of δx, δy, and δz, computed by means of the co-ordinates referred to the ecliptic and mean equinox of the date t, must be added to the co-ordinates given by the undisturbed elements and referred to the same mean equinox. The co-ordinates referred to the ecliptic and mean equinox of t may be readily transformed into those referred to the ecliptic and mean equinox of another date t'. Thus, let θ denote the longitude of the descending node of the ecliptic of t' on that of t, measured from the mean equinox of t, and let η be the mutual inclination of these planes; then, if we denote by x', y', z' the co-ordinates referred to the ecliptic of t as the fundamental plane, the positive axis of x, however, being directed to the point whose longitude is θ, we shall have

$$\begin{aligned} x' &= x\cos\theta + y\sin\theta, \\ y' &= -x\sin\theta + y\cos\theta, \\ z' &= z. \end{aligned} \tag{42}$$

Let us now denote by x'', y'', z'' the co-ordinates when the ecliptic of t' is the plane of xy, the axis of x remaining the same as in the system of x', y', z'. Then we shall have

$$\begin{aligned} x'' &= x', \\ y'' &= y'\cos\eta - z'\sin\eta, \\ z'' &= y'\sin\eta + z'\cos\eta. \end{aligned} \tag{43}$$

Finally, transforming these so that the axis of z remains unchanged while the positive axis of x is directed to the mean equinox of t', and denoting the new co-ordinates by $x_{\prime}$, $y_{\prime}$, $z_{\prime}$, we get

$$\begin{aligned} x_{\prime} &= x''\cos(\theta + p) - y''\sin(\theta + p), \\ y_{\prime} &= x''\sin(\theta + p) + y''\cos(\theta + p), \\ z_{\prime} &= z'', \end{aligned} \tag{44}$$

in which p denotes the precession during the interval $t' - t$. Eliminating x'', y'', and z'' from these equations by means of (43) and (42), observing that, since η is very small, we may put $\cos\eta = 1$, we get

$$
\begin{aligned}
x_{,} &= x\cos p - y\sin p + \frac{\eta}{s} z\sin(\theta + p),\\
y_{,} &= x\sin p + y\cos p - \frac{\eta}{s} z\cos(\theta + p),\\
z_{,} &= z - \frac{\eta}{s} x\sin\theta + \frac{\eta}{s} y\cos\theta,
\end{aligned}
\tag{45}
$$

in which $s = 206264.8$, η being supposed to be expressed in seconds of arc. If we neglect terms of the order p^3, these equations become

$$
\begin{aligned}
x_{,} &= x - \tfrac{1}{2}\frac{p^2}{s^2} x - \frac{p}{s} y + \frac{\eta}{s}(\sin\theta + p\cos\theta)\, z,\\
y_{,} &= y - \tfrac{1}{2}\frac{p^2}{s^2} y + \frac{p}{s} x - \frac{\eta}{s}(\cos\theta - p\sin\theta)\, z,\\
z_{,} &= z - \frac{\eta}{s} x\sin\theta + \frac{\eta}{s} y\cos\theta.
\end{aligned}
\tag{46}
$$

These formulæ give the co-ordinates referred to the ecliptic and mean equinox of one epoch when those referred to the ecliptic and mean equinox of another date are known. For the values of p, η, and θ, we have

$$
\begin{aligned}
p &= (50''.21129 + 0''.0002442966\tau)\,(t' - t),\\
\eta &= (\ 0''.48892 - 0''.000006143\tau)\,(t' - t),\\
\theta &= 351^\circ\ 36'\ 10'' + 39''.79\,(t - 1750) - 5''.21\,(t' - t),
\end{aligned}
$$

in which $\tau = \frac{1}{2}(t' - t) - 1750$, t and t' being expressed in years from the beginning of the era. If we add the nutation to the value of p, the co-ordinates will be derived for the true equinox of t'.

The equations (45) and (46) serve also to convert the values of δx, δy, and δz belonging to the co-ordinates referred to the ecliptic and mean equinox of t into those to be applied to the co-ordinates referred to the ecliptic and mean equinox of t'. For this purpose it is only necessary to write δx, δy, and δz in place of x, y, and z respectively, and similarly for $x_{,}$, $y_{,}$, $z_{,}$.

In the computation of the perturbations of a heavenly body during a period of several years, it will be convenient to adopt a fixed equinox and ecliptic throughout the calculation; but when the perturbations are to be applied to the co-ordinates, in the calculation of an ephemeris of the body taking into account the perturbations, it will be convenient to compute the co-ordinates directly for the ecliptic and mean equinox of the beginning of the year for which the ephemeris is required, and the values of δx, δy, and δz must be reduced, by means of the equations (45), as already explained, from the ecliptic and mean equinox to which they belong, to the ecliptic and mean equinox adopted in the case of the co-ordinates required.

In a similar manner we may derive formulæ for the transformation of the co-ordinates or of their variations referred to the mean equinox and equator of one date into those referred to the mean equinox and equator of another date; but a transformation of this kind will rarely be required, and, whenever required, it may be effected by first converting the co-ordinates referred to the equator into those referred to the ecliptic, reducing these to the equinox of t' by means of (45) or (46), and finally converting them into the values referred to the equator of t'. Since, in the computation of an ephemeris for the comparison of observations, the co-ordinates are generally required in reference to the equator as the fundamental plane, it would appear preferable to adopt this plane as the plane of xy in the computation of the perturbations, and in some cases this method is most advantageous. But, generally, since the elements of the orbit of the disturbed planet as well as the elements of the orbits of the disturbing bodies are referred to the ecliptic, the calculation of the perturbations will be most conveniently performed by adopting the ecliptic as the fundamental plane. The consideration of the change of the position of the fundamental plane from one epoch to another is thus also rendered more simple. Whenever an ephemeris giving the geocentric right ascension and declination is required, the heliocentric co-ordinates of the body referred to the mean equinox and equator of the beginning of the year will be computed by means of the osculating elements corrected for precession to that epoch, and the perturbations of the co-ordinates referred to the ecliptic and mean equinox of any other date will be first corrected according to the equations (46), and then converted into those to be applied to the co-ordinates referred to the mean equinox and equator. If the perturbations are not of considerable magnitude and the interval $t' - t$ is also not very large, the correction of δx, δy, and δz on account of the change of the position of the ecliptic and of the equinox will be insignificant; and the conversion of the values of these quantities referred to the ecliptic into the corresponding values for the equator, is effected with great facility.

In the determination of the perturbations of comets, ephemerides being required only during the time of describing a small portion of their orbits, it will sometimes be convenient to adopt the plane of the undisturbed orbit as the fundamental plane. In this case the positive axis of x should be directed to the ascending node of this plane on the ecliptic, and the subsequent change to the ecliptic and equinox, whenever it may be required, will be readily effected.

168. The perturbations of a heavenly body may thus be determined rigorously for a long period of time, provided that the osculating elements may be regarded as accurately known. The peculiar object, however, of such calculations is to facilitate the correction of the assumed elements of the orbit by means of additional observations according to the methods which have already been explained; and when the osculating elements have, by successive corrections, been determined with great precision, a repetition of the calculation of the perturbations may become necessary, since changes of the elements which do not sensibly affect the residuals for the given differential equations in the determination of the most probable corrections, may have a much greater influence on the accuracy of the resulting values of the perturbations.

When the calculation of the perturbations is carried forward for a long period, using constantly the same osculating elements,—and those which are supposed to require no correction,—the secular perturbations of the co-ordinates arising from the secular variation of the elements, and the perturbations of long period, will constantly affect the magnitude of the resulting values, so that δx, δy, and δz will not again become simultaneously equal to zero. Hence it appears that even when the adopted elements do not differ much from their mean values, the numerical amount of the perturbations may be very greatly increased by the secular perturbations and by the large perturbations of long period. But when the perturbations are large, the calculation of the complete values of $\frac{d^2\delta x}{dt^2}$, $\frac{d^2\delta y}{dt^2}$, and $\frac{d^2\delta z}{dt^2}$ (which is effected indirectly) cannot be performed with facility, requiring often several repetitions in order to obtain the required accuracy, since any error in the value of the second differential coefficient produces, by the double integration, an error increasing proportionally to the time in the values of the integral. Errors, therefore, in the values of the second differential coefficients which for a moderate period would have no sensible effect, may in the course of a long period produce large errors in the values of the perturbations, and it is evident that, both for convenience in the numerical calculation and for avoiding the accumulation of error, it will be necessary from time to time to apply the perturbations to the elements in order that the integrals may, in the case of each of the co-ordinates, be again equal to zero. The calculation will then be continued until another change of the elements is required.

The transformation from a system of osculating elements for one epoch to that for another epoch is very easily effected by means of the values of the perturbations of the co-ordinates in connection with the corresponding values of the variations of the velocities $\frac{dx}{dt}$, $\frac{dy}{dt}$, and $\frac{dz}{dt}$. The latter will be obtained from the values of the second differential coefficients by means of a single integration according to the equations (27) and (32). Thus, in the case of the example given, we obtain for the date 1865 Jan. 15.0, by means of (32), in units of the seventh decimal place,

$$40\frac{d\delta x}{dt} = +385.9, \qquad 40\frac{d\delta y}{dt} = +214.6, \qquad 40\frac{d\delta z}{dt} = +9.7.$$

The velocities in the case of the disturbed orbit will be given by the formulæ

$$\frac{dx}{dt} = \frac{dx_0}{dt} + \frac{d\delta x}{dt}, \qquad \frac{dy}{dt} = \frac{dy_0}{dt} + \frac{d\delta y}{dt}, \qquad \frac{dz}{dt} = \frac{dz_0}{dt} + \frac{d\delta z}{dt}. \tag{47}$$

To obtain the expressions for the components of the velocity resolved parallel to the co-ordinates, we have, according to the equations $(6)_2$,

$$\begin{aligned}
\frac{dx}{dt} &= \sin a \sin (A + u)\frac{dr}{dt} + r \sin a \cos (A + u)\frac{dv}{dt},\\
\frac{dy}{dt} &= \sin b \sin (B + u)\frac{dr}{dt} + r \sin b \cos (B + u)\frac{dv}{dt},\\
\frac{dz}{dt} &= \sin c \sin (C + u)\frac{dr}{dt} + r \sin c \cos (C + u)\frac{dv}{dt}.
\end{aligned}$$

These equations are applicable in the case of any fundamental plane, if the auxiliaries $\sin a$, $\sin b$, $\sin c$, A, B, and C are determined in reference to that plane. To transform them still further, we have

$$\begin{aligned}
\frac{dr}{dt} &= \frac{k\sqrt{1+m}}{\sqrt{p}}\, e \sin (u - \omega),\\
r\frac{dv}{dt} &= \frac{k\sqrt{p(1+m)}}{r} = \frac{k\sqrt{1+m}}{\sqrt{p}}(1 + e \cos (u - \omega)),
\end{aligned}$$

in which ω denotes the angular distance of the perihelion from the ascending node. Substituting these values, we obtain, by reduction,

$$\frac{dx}{dt}=\frac{k\sqrt{1+m}}{\sqrt{p}}((e\cos\omega+\cos u)\cos A-(e\sin\omega+\sin u)\sin A)\sin a,$$
$$\frac{dy}{dt}=\frac{k\sqrt{1+m}}{\sqrt{p}}((e\cos\omega+\cos u)\cos B-(e\sin\omega+\sin u)\sin B)\sin b,$$
$$\frac{dz}{dt}=\frac{k\sqrt{1+m}}{\sqrt{p}}((e\cos\omega+\cos u)\cos C-(e\sin\omega+\sin u)\sin C)\sin c.$$

Let us now put

$$\begin{aligned}\frac{k\sqrt{1+m}}{\sqrt{p}}(e\sin\omega+\sin u)&=V\sin U,\\ \frac{k\sqrt{1+m}}{\sqrt{p}}(e\cos\omega+\cos u)&=V\cos U,\end{aligned}\tag{48}$$

and we have

$$\begin{aligned}\frac{dx}{dt}&=V\sin a\cos(A+U),\\ \frac{dy}{dt}&=V\sin b\cos(B+U),\\ \frac{dz}{dt}&=V\sin c\cos(C+U).\end{aligned}\tag{49}$$

These equations determine the components of the velocity of a heavenly body resolved in directions parallel to the co-ordinate axes, and for any fundamental plane to which the auxiliaries A, B, &c. belong. When the ecliptic is the fundamental plane, we have

$$\sin c=\sin i,\qquad C=0.$$

The sum of the squares of the equations (48) gives

$$V^2=\frac{k^2(1+m)}{p}(1+e^2+2e\cos(u-\omega))=k^2(1+m)\left(\frac{2}{r}-\frac{1}{a}\right),$$

and hence it appears that V is the linear velocity of the body.

The determination of the osculating elements corresponding to any date for which the perturbations of the co-ordinates and of the velocities have been found, is therefore effected in the following manner:—

First, by means of the osculating elements to which the perturbations belong, we compute accurate values of r_0, x_0, y_0, z_0, and by means of the equations (48) and (49) we compute the values of $\frac{dx_0}{dt}$, $\frac{dy_0}{dt}$, and $\frac{dz_0}{dt}$. Then we apply to these the values of the perturbations, and thus find x, y, z, $\frac{dx}{dt}$, $\frac{dy}{dt}$, and $\frac{dz}{dt}$. These having been found, the equations $(32)_1$ will furnish the values of ☊, i, and p; and the remaining elements may be determined as explained in Art. 112. Thus, from

$$Vr \sin \psi_0 = k\sqrt{p(1+m)},$$
$$Vr \cos \psi_0 = x\frac{dx}{dt} + y\frac{dy}{dt} + z\frac{dz}{dt},$$

we obtain Vr and ψ_0, and from

$$r \sin u = (-x \sin \Omega + y \cos \Omega) \sec i,$$
$$r \cos u = x \cos \Omega + y \sin \Omega,$$

we derive r and u; and hence V from the value of Vr. When i is not very small, we may use, instead of the preceding expression for $r \sin u$,

$$r \sin u = z \operatorname{cosec} i.$$

Next, we compute a from

$$2a - r = \frac{r}{\frac{2}{r} \cdot \frac{k^2(1+m)}{V^2} - 1},$$

and from

$$2ae \sin \omega = -(2a - r) \sin (2\psi_0 + u) - r \sin u,$$
$$2ae \cos \omega = -(2a - r) \cos (2\psi_0 + u) - r \cos u,$$

we find ω and e. The mean daily motion and the mean anomaly or the mean longitude for the epoch will then be determined by means of the usual formulæ.

In the case of a very eccentric orbit, after r and u have been found, $\frac{dr}{dt}$ will be given by equations $(48)_6$, and the values of e and v will be given by the equations $(49)_6$. Then the perihelion distance will be found from

$$q = \frac{p}{1+e},$$

and the time of perihelion passage will be found from v and e by means of Table IX. or Table X.

In the numerical values of the velocities $\frac{dx}{dt}$, $\frac{dy}{dt}$, &c., more decimals must be retained than in the values of the co-ordinates, and enough must be retained to secure the required accuracy of the solution. If it be considered necessary, the different parts of the calculation may be checked by means of various formulæ which have already been given. Thus, the values of ☊ and i must satisfy the equation

$$z\cos i - y\sin i\cos \Omega + x\sin i\sin \Omega = 0.$$

We have, also,

$$V^2 = \left(\frac{dx}{dt}\right)^2 + \left(\frac{dy}{dt}\right)^2 + \left(\frac{dz}{dt}\right)^2,$$
$$r^2 = x^2 + y^2 + z^2,$$
$$z = r\sin u\sin i,$$

which must be satisfied by the resulting values of V, r, and u; and the values of a and e must satisfy the equation

$$p = a(1 - e^2) = a\cos^2\varphi.$$

169. When the plane of the undisturbed orbit is adopted as the fundamental plane, we obtain at once the perturbations

$$\delta(r\cos u), \qquad \delta(r\sin u), \qquad \delta z,$$

and from these the perturbations of the polar co-ordinates are easily derived. There are, however, advantages which may be secured by employing formulæ which give the perturbations of the polar co-ordinates directly, retaining the plane of the orbit for the date t_0 as the fundamental plane.

Let w denote the angle which the projection of the disturbed radius-vector on the plane of xy makes with the axis of x, and β the latitude of the body with respect to the plane of xy; then we shall have

$$\begin{aligned} x &= r\cos\beta\cos w, \\ y &= r\cos\beta\sin w, \\ z &= r\sin\beta. \end{aligned} \tag{50}$$

Let us now denote by X, Y, and Z, respectively, the forces which are expressed by the second members of the equations (1), and the first two of these equations give

$$x\frac{dy}{dt} - y\frac{dx}{dt} = \int (Yx - Xy)\,dt + C,$$

C being the constant of integration. The equations (50) give

$$\frac{dx}{dt} = \cos w\frac{d(r\cos\beta)}{dt} - r\cos\beta\sin w\frac{dw}{dt},$$
$$\frac{dy}{dt} = \sin w\frac{d(r\cos\beta)}{dt} + r\cos\beta\cos w\frac{dw}{dt},$$

and hence

$$x\frac{dy}{dt} - y\frac{dx}{dt} = r^2\cos^2\beta\frac{dw}{dt}.$$

Therefore we have

$$r^2 \cos^2 \beta \frac{dw}{dt} = \int (Yx - Xy)\, dt + C.$$

If we denote by S_0 the component of the disturbing force in a direction perpendicular to the disturbed radius-vector and parallel with the plane of xy, we shall have

$$X = -S_0 \sin w, \qquad Y = S_0 \cos w,$$

and

$$Yx - Xy = S_0\, r \cos \beta.$$

Therefore

$$r^2 \cos^2 \beta \frac{dw}{dt} = \int S_0\, r \cos \beta\, dt + C.$$

In the undisturbed orbit we have $\beta = 0$, and

$$r_0^{\,2} \frac{dw_0}{dt} = k\sqrt{p_0 (1 + m)};$$

and thus the preceding equation becomes

$$r^2 \cos^2 \beta \frac{dw}{dt} = \int S_0\, r \cos \beta\, dt + k\sqrt{p_0 (1 + m)}. \tag{51}$$

The equations (1) also give

$$\frac{1}{r} \cdot \frac{x d^2 x + y d^2 y + z d^2 z}{dt^2} + \frac{k^2 (1 + m)}{r^2} = X\frac{x}{r} + Y\frac{y}{r} + Z\frac{z}{r}. \tag{52}$$

If we denote by R the component of the disturbing force in the direction of the disturbed radius-vector, we have

$$R = X\frac{x}{r} + Y\frac{y}{r} + Z\frac{z}{r}. \tag{53}$$

We have, also,

$$\begin{aligned} x d^2 x + y d^2 y + z d^2 z &= d\,(x dx + y dy + z dz) - (dx^2 + dy^2 + dz^2) \\ &= d\,(r dr) - (dr^2 + r^2 dv^2) = r d^2 r - r^2 dv^2, \end{aligned}$$

v denoting the true anomaly in the disturbed orbit, or, since $dv^2 = \cos^2 \beta\, dw^2 + d\beta^2$,

$$x d^2 x + y d^2 y + z d^2 z = r d^2 r - r^2 \cos^2 \beta\, dw^2 - r^2 d\beta^2.$$

Hence the equation (52) becomes

$$\frac{d^2 r}{dt^2} - r \cos^2 \beta \frac{dw^2}{dt^2} - r\frac{d\beta^2}{dt^2} + \frac{k^2 (1 + m)}{r^2} = R. \tag{54}$$

170. The equations (51) and (54), in connection with the last of equations (1), completely represent the motion of a heavenly body about the sun when acted upon by disturbing forces, and, when completely integrated, they will give the values of w, r, and z for any point of the orbit; but, since they cannot be integrated directly, we must, as in the case of the rectangular co-ordinates, find the equations which give by integration the values of δw, δr, and z. In the case of the undisturbed orbit, we have

$$r_0^2 \frac{dw_0}{dt} = k\sqrt{p_0(1+m)},$$
$$\frac{d^2 r_0}{dt^2} - r_0 \frac{dw_0^2}{dt^2} + \frac{k^2(1+m)}{r_0^2} = 0. \tag{55}$$

If we denote by δw the variation of w arising from the action of the disturbing force, we have $w = w_0 + \delta w$; and hence we easily find, from (51),

$$\frac{d\delta w}{dt} = \frac{1}{r^2 \cos^2 \beta} \int S_0 \, r \cos \beta \, dt - \left(1 - \frac{r_0^2}{r^2 \cos^2 \beta}\right) \frac{k\sqrt{p_0(1+m)}}{r_0^2}. \tag{56}$$

We have, further,

$$r^2 = r_0^2 + 2r_0 \delta r + \delta r^2,$$

which gives

$$\frac{r^2}{r_0^2} = 1 + 2\frac{r_0 + \frac{1}{2}\delta r}{r_0^2} \delta r.$$

Let us now put

$$q' = \left(\frac{r_0 + \frac{1}{2}\delta r}{r_0^2} \cos^2 \beta - \frac{\sin^2 \beta}{2\delta r}\right) \delta r, \qquad f'q' = 1 - \frac{r_0^2}{r^2 \cos^2 \beta}, \tag{57}$$

and we have

$$f' = \frac{2}{1 + 2q'}. \tag{58}$$

The equation (56), therefore, becomes

$$\frac{d\delta w}{dt} = \frac{1}{r^2 \cos^2 \beta} \int S_0 \, r \cos \beta \, dt - g_0 f' q', \tag{59}$$

in which we put

$$g_0 = \frac{dw_0}{dt} = \frac{k\sqrt{p_0(1+m)}}{r_0^2}. \tag{60}$$

If we substitute $r_0 + \delta r$ for r in equation (54), and combine the result with the second of equations (55), we get

$$\frac{d^2 \delta r}{dt^2} = R - g_0^2 r_0 + r \cos^2 \beta \frac{dw^2}{dt^2} + r \frac{d\beta^2}{dt^2} + k^2(1+m)\left(\frac{1}{r_0^2} - \frac{1}{r^2}\right);$$

and if we put

$$q'' = \frac{r_0 + \frac{1}{2}\delta r}{r_0^2}\,\delta r, \qquad f''q'' = 1 - \frac{r_0^2}{r^2}, \tag{61}$$

we have

$$f'' = \frac{2}{1+2q''}, \tag{62}$$

and hence

$$\begin{aligned} \frac{d^2\delta r}{dt^2} &= R + \frac{k^2(1+m)}{r_0^2} f''q'' + g_0^2\delta r + 2g_0 r\frac{d\delta w}{dt} \\ &\quad - r\sin^2\beta\left(g_0 + \frac{d\delta w}{dt}\right)^2 + r\left(\frac{d\delta w}{dt}\right)^2 + r\left(\frac{d\beta}{dt}\right)^2. \end{aligned} \tag{63}$$

Finally, we have, from the last of equations (1),

$$\frac{d^2z}{dt^2} = Z - \frac{k^2(1+m)}{r^3}\,z, \tag{64}$$

by means of which the value of z may be found, since, in the case of the undisturbed motion, we have $z_0 = 0$.

The values of f' corresponding to different values of q' may be tabulated with the argument q', and, since the equation (62) is of the same form as (58), the same table will give the value of f'' when q'' is used as the argument. Table XVII. gives the values of $\log f'$ or $\log f''$ corresponding to values of q' or q'' from -0.03 to $+0.03$. Beyond the limits of this table the required quantities may be computed directly.

171. When we consider only terms of the first order with respect to the disturbing force, we have

$$f'q' = f''q'' = \frac{2\delta r}{r_0},$$

and the equations become

$$\begin{aligned} \frac{d\delta w}{dt} &= \frac{1}{r_0^2}\int S_0 r_0 dt - \frac{2g_0}{r_0}\delta r, \\ \frac{d^2\delta r}{dt^2} &= R + \frac{2g_0}{r_0}\int S_0 r_0 dt + \left(\frac{2k^2(1+m)}{r_0^3} - 3g_0^2\right)\delta r, \\ \frac{d^2z}{dt^2} &= Z - \frac{k^2(1+m)}{r_0^3}\,z. \end{aligned} \tag{65}$$

In determining the perturbations of a heavenly body, we first consider only the terms depending on the first power of the disturbing force, for which these equations will be applied. The value of δr

will be obtained from the second equation by an indirect process, as already illustrated for the case of the variation of the rectangular co-ordinates. Then δw will be obtained directly from the first equation, and, finally, z indirectly from the last equation. Each of the integrals is equal to zero for the date t_0, to which the osculating elements belong.

When the magnitude of the perturbations is such that the terms depending on the squares and products of the masses must be considered, the general equations (59), (63), and (64) will be applied. The values of the perturbations for the dates preceding that for which the complete expressions are to be used, will at once indicate approximate values of δw, δr, and z; and with the values

$$r = r_0 + \delta r, \qquad w = w_0 + \delta w, \qquad \sin\beta = \frac{z}{r},$$

the components of the disturbing force will be computed. We compute also q' from the first of equations (57), and q'' from the first of (61); then, by means of Table XVII., we derive the corresponding values of $\log f'$ and $\log f''$. The coefficients of δr in the expressions for q' and q'' will be given with sufficient accuracy by means of the approximate values of δr and $\sin\beta$, and will not require any further correction. Then we compute $S_0 r\cos\beta$, and find the integral

$$\int S_0 r\cos\beta\, dt;$$

and the complete value of $\frac{d\delta w}{dt}$ will be given by (59). The value of $\frac{d^2\delta r}{dt^2}$ will then be given by equation (63). The term $r\left(\frac{d\beta}{dt}\right)^2$ will always be small, and, unless the inclination of the orbit of the disturbed body is large, it may generally be neglected. Whenever it shall be required, we may put it equal to $\frac{1}{r}\left(\frac{dz}{dt}\right)^2$. The corrected values of the differential coefficients being introduced into the table of integration, the exact or very approximate values of δw, δr, and z will be obtained. Should these results, however, differ much from the corresponding values already assumed, a repetition of the calculation may become necessary. In this manner, by computing each place separately, the terms depending on the squares, products, and higher powers of the disturbing forces may be included in the results. It will, however, be generally possible to estimate the values of δw, δr, and z for two or three intervals in advance to a degree of approximation sufficient for the computation of the forces for these dates.

In order that the quantity ω, representing the interval adopted in the calculation of the perturbations, may not appear in the integration, we should introduce it into the equations as in the case of the variation of the rectangular co-ordinates. Thus, in the determination of δw we compute the values of $\omega \frac{d\delta w}{dt}$, and since the second member of the equation contains the integral $\int S_0 r \cos\beta\, dt$, if we introduce the factor ω^2 under the sign of integration, this integral, omitting the factor ω in the formulæ of integration, will become $\omega \int S_0 r \cos\beta\, dt$, as required. The last term of the equation will be multiplied by ω.

In the case of δr, each term of the equation for $\frac{d^2\delta r}{dt^2}$ must contain the factor ω^2. If the second of equations (65) is employed, the first and third terms of the second member will be multiplied by ω^2; but since the value of S_0 is supposed to be already multiplied by ω^2, the second term will only be multiplied by ω.

The perturbations may be conveniently determined either in units of the seventh decimal place, or expressed in seconds of arc of a circle whose radius is unity. If they are to be expressed in seconds, the factor $s = 206264.8$ must be introduced so as to preserve the homogeneity of the several terms, and finally δr and δz must be converted into their values in terms of the unit of space.

172. It remains yet to derive convenient formulæ for the determination of the forces S_0, R, and Z. For this purpose, it first becomes necessary to determine the position of the orbit of the disturbing planet in reference to the fundamental plane adopted, namely, the plane defined by the osculating elements of the disturbed orbit at the instant t_0. Let i' and Ω' denote the inclination and the longitude of the ascending node of the disturbing body with respect to the ecliptic, and let I denote the inclination of the orbit of the disturbing body with respect to the fundamental plane. Further, let N denote the longitude of its ascending node on the same plane measured from the ascending node of this plane on the ecliptic or from the point whose longitude is Ω_0, and let N' be the angular distance between the ascending node of the orbit of the disturbing body on the ecliptic and the ascending node on the fundamental plane adopted. Then, from the spherical triangle formed by the intersection of the plane of the

ecliptic, the fundamental plane, and the plane of the orbit of the disturbing body with the celestial vault, we have

$$\begin{aligned}\sin\tfrac{1}{2}I\sin\tfrac{1}{2}(N+N') &= \sin\tfrac{1}{2}(\Omega'-\Omega_0)\sin\tfrac{1}{2}(i'+i_0),\\ \sin\tfrac{1}{2}I\cos\tfrac{1}{2}(N+N') &= \cos\tfrac{1}{2}(\Omega'-\Omega_0)\sin\tfrac{1}{2}(i'-i_0),\\ \cos\tfrac{1}{2}I\sin\tfrac{1}{2}(N-N') &= \sin\tfrac{1}{2}(\Omega'-\Omega_0)\cos\tfrac{1}{2}(i'+i_0),\\ \cos\tfrac{1}{2}I\cos\tfrac{1}{2}(N-N') &= \cos\tfrac{1}{2}(\Omega'-\Omega_0)\cos\tfrac{1}{2}(i'-i_0),\end{aligned}\tag{66}$$

from which to find N, N', and I.

Let β' denote the heliocentric latitude of the disturbing planet with respect to the fundamental plane, w' its longitude in this plane measured from the axis of x, as in the case of w, and u_0' the argument of the latitude with respect to this plane. Then, according to the equations $(82)_1$, we have

$$\begin{aligned}\tan(w'-N) &= \tan u_0'\cos I,\\ \tan\beta' &= \tan I\sin(w'-N).\end{aligned}\tag{67}$$

If u' denotes the argument of the latitude of the disturbing planet with respect to the ecliptic, we have

$$u_0' = u' - N'.\tag{68}$$

This formula will give the value of u_0', and then w' and β' will be found from (67). We have, also,

$$\cos u_0' = \cos\beta'\cos(w'-N),$$

which will serve to indicate the quadrant in which $w'-N$ must be taken.

The relations here derived are evidently applicable to the case in which the elements of the orbits of the disturbed and disturbing planets are referred to the equator, the signification of the quantities involved being properly considered.

The co-ordinates of the disturbing planet in reference to the plane of the disturbed orbit at the instant t_0 as the fundamental plane will be given by

$$\begin{aligned}x' &= r'\cos\beta'\cos w',\\ y' &= r'\cos\beta'\sin w',\\ z' &= r'\sin\beta'.\end{aligned}\tag{69}$$

To find the force R, we have

$$R = X\frac{x}{r} + Y\frac{y}{r} + Z\frac{z}{r},$$

and

$$X = m'k^2\left(\frac{x'-x}{\rho^3} - \frac{x'}{r'^3}\right),$$
$$Y = m'k^2\left(\frac{y'-y}{\rho^3} - \frac{y'}{r'^3}\right),$$
$$Z = m'k^2\left(\frac{z'-z}{\rho^3} - \frac{z'}{r'^3}\right).$$

Substituting in these the values of x', y', z' given by (69), and the corresponding values of x, y, z given by (50), and putting

$$h = \frac{1}{\rho^3} - \frac{1}{r'^3}, \tag{70}$$

we get

$$R = m'k^2\left(h\,r' \cos\beta' \cos\beta \cos(w'-w) + h\,r' \sin\beta \sin\beta' - \frac{r}{\rho^3}\right). \tag{71}$$

The equation

$$S_0\, r \cos\beta = Yx - Xy$$

gives

$$S_0 = m'k^2\, h\, r' \cos\beta' \sin(w'-w), \tag{72}$$

from which to find S_0. Finally, we have

$$Z = m'k^2\left(h\,r' \sin\beta' - \frac{z}{\rho^3}\right), \tag{73}$$

from which to find Z.

When we determine the perturbations only with respect to the first power of the disturbing force, the expressions for R, S_0, and Z become

$$\left.\begin{aligned} R &= m'k^2\left(h\,r' \cos\beta' \cos(w'-w_0) - \frac{r_0}{\rho_0^{\,3}}\right),\\ S_0 &= m'k^2\, h\,r' \cos\beta' \sin(w'-w_0),\\ Z &= m'k^2\, h\,r' \sin\beta'. \end{aligned}\right\} \tag{74}$$

To compute the distance ρ, we have

$$\rho^2 = (x'-x)^2 + (y'-y)^2 + (z'-z)^2,$$

which gives

$$\rho^2 = r'^2 + r^2 - 2r\,r' \cos\beta \cos\beta' \cos(w'-w) - 2r\,r' \sin\beta \sin\beta', \tag{75}$$

and, if we neglect terms of the second order, we have

$$\rho_0^{\,2} = r'^2 + r_0^{\,2} - 2r_0\, r' \cos\beta' \cos(w'-w_0). \tag{76}$$

If we put

$$\cos\gamma = \cos\beta \cos\beta' \cos(w'-w) + \sin\beta \sin\beta', \tag{77}$$

we have

$$\begin{aligned} \rho^2 &= r'^2 + r^2 - 2rr' \cos\gamma \\ &= r'^2 \sin^2\gamma + (r - r' \cos\gamma)^2; \end{aligned}$$

and hence we may readily find ρ from

$$\begin{aligned}\rho \sin n &= r' \sin \gamma, \\ \rho \cos n &= r - r' \cos \gamma,\end{aligned} \tag{78}$$

the exact value of the angle n, however, not being required.

Introducing γ into the expression for R, it becomes

$$R = m'k^2 \left(h r' \cos \gamma - \frac{r}{\rho^3} \right), \tag{79}$$

by means of which R may be conveniently determined.

173. When we neglect the terms depending on the squares and higher powers of the masses in the computation of the perturbations, the forces R, S_0, and Z will be computed by means of the equations (74), ρ_0 being found from (76) or from (78), when we put

$$\cos \gamma = \cos \beta' \cos (w' - w_0).$$

But when the terms of the order of the square of the disturbing force are to be taken into account, the complete equations must be used. Thus, we find ρ from (78), S_0 from (72), Z from (73), and R from (71) or (79). The values of δw, δr, and z, computed to the point at which it becomes necessary to consider the terms of the second order, will enable us at once to estimate the values of the perturbations for two or three intervals in advance to a degree of approximation sufficient for the calculation of the forces; and the values of R, S_0, and Z thus found will not require any further correction.

When the places of the disturbing planet are to be derived from an ephemeris giving the heliocentric longitudes and latitudes, the values of Ω' and i' will be obtained from two places separated by a considerable interval, and then the values of u' will be determined by means of the first of equations $(82)_1$ or by means of $(85)_1$. When the inclination i' is very small, it will be sufficient to take

$$u' = l' - \Omega' + s \tan^2 \tfrac{1}{2} i' \sin 2 (l' - \Omega'),$$

in which $s = 206264.8$. But when the tables give directly the longitude in the orbit, $u' + \Omega'$, by subtracting Ω' from each of these longitudes we obtain the required values of u'.

It should be observed, also, that the exact determination of the values of the forces requires that the actual disturbed values of r', w', and β' should be used. The disturbed radius-vector r' will be given immediately by the tables of the motion of the disturbing body, but the determination of the actual values of w' and β' requires that we should use the actual values of N', N, and I in the solution of the equations (68) and (67). Hence the disturbed values of Ω' and i' should be used in the determination of these quantities for each date by means of (66). It will, however, generally be the case that for a moderate period the variation of Ω' and i' may be neglected; and whenever the variation of either of these has a sensible effect, we may compute new values of N, N', and I from time to time, by means of which the true values may be readily interpolated for each date. We may also determine the variations of N, N', and I arising from the variation of Ω' and i', by means of differential formulæ. Thus the relations will be similar to those given by the equations $(71)_2$, so that we have

$$\begin{aligned} \delta N' &= \frac{\sin N'}{\sin(\Omega' - \Omega_0)} \cos N \, \delta\Omega' - \frac{\sin N'}{\sin I} \cos I \, \delta i', \\ \delta N &= \frac{\sin N}{\sin(\Omega' - \Omega_0)} \cos N' \, \delta\Omega' - \frac{\sin N'}{\sin I} \delta i', \\ \delta I &= \sin N' \sin i' \, \delta\Omega' + \cos N' \, \delta i', \end{aligned} \tag{80}$$

from which to find $\delta N'$, δN, and δI.

When the perturbations are computed only in reference to the first power of the mass, the change of Ω' and i' may be entirely neglected; but when the perturbations are to be computed for a long period of time, and the terms depending on the squares and products of the disturbing forces are to be included, it will be advisable to take into account the values of δN, $\delta N'$, and δI, and, using also the value of u' in the actual orbit of the disturbing body, compute the actual values of w' and β'.

In the case of several disturbing bodies, the forces will be determined for each of these, and then, instead of R, S_0, and Z, in the formulæ for the differential coefficients, ΣR, ΣS_0, and ΣZ will be used.

174. By means of the values of δw, δr, and z, the heliocentric or the geocentric place of the disturbed planet may be readily found. Thus, let the positive axis of x be directed to the ascending node of the osculating orbit at the instant t_0 on the plane of the ecliptic; then, in the undisturbed orbit, we shall have

$$w_0 = u_0,$$

u denoting the argument of the latitude. Let $x_{\prime}$, $y_{\prime}$, $z_{\prime}$ be the co-ordinates of the body referred to a system of rectangular co-ordinates in which the ecliptic is the plane of xy, and in which the positive axis of x is directed to the vernal equinox. Then we shall have

$$x_{,} = x\cos\Omega_0 - y\cos i_0\sin\Omega_0 + z\sin i_0\sin\Omega_0,$$
$$y_{,} = x\sin\Omega_0 + y\cos i_0\cos\Omega_0 - z\sin i_0\cos\Omega_0,$$
$$z_{,} = y\sin i_0 + z\cos i_0,$$

or, introducing the values of x and y given by (50),

$$x_{,} = r\cos\beta\cos w\cos\Omega_0 - r\cos\beta\sin w\cos i_0\sin\Omega_0 + z\sin i_0\sin\Omega_0,$$
$$y_{,} = r\cos\beta\cos w\sin\Omega_0 + r\cos\beta\sin w\cos i_0\cos\Omega_0 - z\sin i_0\cos\Omega_0, \quad (81)$$
$$z_{,} = r\cos\beta\sin w\sin i_0 + z\cos i_0.$$

Introducing also the auxiliary constants for the ecliptic according to the equations $(94)_1$ and $(96)_1$, we obtain

$$x_{,} = r\cos\beta\sin a\sin(A + w) + z\cos a,$$
$$y_{,} = r\cos\beta\sin b\sin(B + w) + z\cos b, \quad (82)$$
$$z_{,} = r\cos\beta\sin i_0\sin w \qquad + z\cos i_0,$$

by means of which the heliocentric co-ordinates in reference to the ecliptic may be determined.

If the place of the disturbed body is required in reference to the equator, denoting the heliocentric co-ordinates by $x_{,,}$, $y_{,,}$, $z_{,,}$, and the obliquity of the ecliptic by ε, we have

$$x_{,,} = x_{,}$$
$$y_{,,} = y_{,}\cos\varepsilon - z_{,}\sin\varepsilon,$$
$$z_{,,} = y_{,}\sin\varepsilon + z_{,}\cos\varepsilon.$$

Substituting for $x_{,}$, $y_{,}$, $z_{,}$ their values given by (81), and introducing the auxiliary constants for the equator, according to the equations $(99)_1$ and $(101)_1$, we get

$$x_{,,} = r\cos\beta\sin a\sin(A + w) + z\cos a,$$
$$y_{,,} = r\cos\beta\sin b\sin(B + w) + z\cos b, \quad (83)$$
$$z_{,,} = r\cos\beta\sin c\sin(C + w) + z\cos c.$$

The combination of the values derived from these equations with the corresponding values of the co-ordinates of the sun, will give the required geocentric places of the disturbed body. These equations are applicable to the case of any fundamental plane, provided that the auxiliary constants a, A, b, B, &c. are determined with respect to that plane. In the numerical application of the formulæ, the value of w will be found from

$$w = u_0 + \delta w,$$

u_0 being the argument of the latitude for the fundamental osculating elements, and care must be taken that the proper algebraic sign is assigned to $\cos a$, $\cos b$, and $\cos c$.

If the values of π_0, Ω_0, and i_0 used in the calculation of the perturbations are referred to the ecliptic and mean equinox of the date t_0', and the rectangular co-ordinates of the disturbed body are required in reference to the ecliptic and mean equinox of the date t_0'', the value of w must be found from

$$w = v_0 + \omega_0 + \delta w,$$

the value of ω_0 referred to the ecliptic of t_0' being reduced to that of t_0'', by means of the first of equations $(115)_1$. Then Ω_0 and i_0 should be reduced from the ecliptic and mean equinox of t_0' to the ecliptic and mean equinox of t_0'' by means of the second and third of the equations $(115)_1$, and, using the values thus found in the calculation of the auxiliary constants for the ecliptic, the equations (82) will give the required values of the heliocentric co-ordinates. If the co-ordinates referred to the mean equinox and equator of the date t_0'' are to be determined, the proper corrections having been applied to Ω_0 and i_0, the mean obliquity of the ecliptic for this date will be employed in the determination of the auxiliary constants a, A, &c. with respect to the equator, and the equations (83) will then give the required values of the co-ordinates.

If we differentiate the equations (83), we obtain, by reduction,

$$\begin{aligned}
\frac{dx_{\prime\prime}}{dt} &= r\cos\beta\sin a\cos(A+w)\frac{dw}{dt} + \sec\beta\sin a\sin(A+w)\frac{dr}{dt} \\
&\quad + (\cos a - \tan\beta\sin a\sin(A+w))\frac{dz}{dt}, \\
\frac{dy_{\prime\prime}}{dt} &= r\cos\beta\sin b\cos(B+w)\frac{dw}{dt} + \sec\beta\sin b\sin(B+w)\frac{dr}{dt} \\
&\quad + (\cos b - \tan\beta\sin b\sin(B+w))\frac{dz}{dt}, \\
\frac{dz_{\prime\prime}}{dt} &= r\cos\beta\sin c\cos(C+w)\frac{dw}{dt} + \sec\beta\sin c\sin(C+w)\frac{dr}{dt} \\
&\quad + (\cos c - \tan\beta\sin c\sin(C+w))\frac{dz}{dt},
\end{aligned} \tag{84}$$

by means of which the components of the velocity of the disturbed body in directions parallel to the co-ordinate axes may be determined. The values of $\frac{d\delta r}{dt}$ and $\frac{dz}{dt}$ will be obtained from $\frac{d^2\delta r}{dt^2}$ and $\frac{d^2z}{dt^2}$ by a single integration, and then we have

$$\frac{dw}{dt} = \frac{k\sqrt{p_0(1+m)}}{r_0^2} + \frac{d\delta w}{dt}, \qquad \frac{dr}{dt} = \frac{k\sqrt{1+m}}{\sqrt{p_0}} e_0 \sin v_0 + \frac{d\delta r}{dt}, \quad (85)$$

from which to find $\frac{dw}{dt}$ and $\frac{dr}{dt}$.

175. EXAMPLE.—In order to illustrate the calculation of the perturbations of r, w, and z, let us take the data given in Art. 166, and determine these perturbations instead of those of the rectangular coordinates.

In the first place, we derive from the tables of the motion of *Jupiter* the values

$$\Omega' = 98° \ 58' \ 22''.7, \qquad i' = 1° \ 18' \ 40''.5,$$

which refer to the ecliptic and mean equinox of 1860.0. We find, also, from the data given by the tables the values of u' measured from the ecliptic of 1860.0. Then, by means of the formulæ (66), using the values of Ω_0 and i_0 given in Art. 166, we derive

$$N = 194° \ 0' \ 49''.9, \qquad N' = 301° \ 38' \ 31''.7, \qquad I = 5° \ 9' \ 56''.4.$$

The value of u_0' is given by equation (68), and then w' and β' are found from the equations (67). Thus we have

Berlin Mean Time.	$\log r_0$	$w_0 = u_0$	$\log r'$	w'	β'
1863 Dec. 12.0,	0.294084	192° 4′ 24″.5	0.73425	14° 18′ 54″.6	— 0° 1′ 38″.1
1864 Jan. 21.0,	0.294837	207 40 52 .2	0.73368	17 21 44 .2	0 18 9 .1
March 1.0,	0.300674	223 3 5 .9	0.73305	20 25 5 .2	0 34 39 .9
April 10.0,	0.310864	237 51 38 .3	0.73237	23 28 59 .8	0 51 7 .6
May 20.0,	0.324298	251 52 47 .9	0.73164	26 33 32 .1	1 7 29 .7
June 29.0,	0.339745	264 59 30 .0	0.73086	29 38 44 .8	1 23 43 .5
Aug. 8.0,	0.356101	277 10 24 .6	0.73003	32 44 41 .2	1 39 46 .3
Sept. 17.0,	0.372469	288 28 4 .1	0.72915	35 51 24 .6	1 55 35 .2
Oct. 27.0,	0.388214	298 57 16 .3	0.72823	38 58 57 .5	2 11 7 .5
Dec. 6.0,	0.402894	308 43 48 .7	0.72726	42 7 23 .3	2 26 20 .3
1865 Jan. 15.0,	0.416240	317 53 39 .1	0.72625	45 16 43 .9	— 2 41 10 .6

The values of ρ_0 may be found from (76) or (78) as already given in Art. 166.

The forces R, S_0, and Z may now be determined by means of the equations (74), h being found from (70), and if we introduce the factor ω^2 for convenience in the integration, as already explained, we obtain the following results:

Date.	$\omega^2 R$	$\omega^2 S_0 r_0$	$\omega^2 Z$	$\omega \int S_0 r_0 dt$
1863 Dec. 12.0,	+ 1″.4608	+ 0″.1476	+ 0″.0009	+ 0″.0282
1864 Jan. 21.0,	+ 1 .4223	— 0 .6757	+ 0 .0101	— 0 .2361

Date.	$\omega^2 R$	$\omega^2 S_0 r_0$	$\omega^2 Z$	$\omega\int S_0 r_0 dt$
1864 March 1.0,	+ 1″.2616	− 1″.4512	+ 0″.0190	− 1″.3060
April 10.0,	1 .0018	2 .1226	0 .0273	3 .1035
May 20.0,	0 .6760	2 .6473	0 .0347	5 .5020
June 29.0,	+ 0 .3179	2 .9988	0 .0406	8 .3402
Aug. 8.0,	− 0 .0452	3 .1650	0 .0449	11 .4378
Sept. 17.0,	0 .3944	3 .1437	0 .0470	14 .6076
Oct. 27.0,	0 .7180	2 .9392	0 .0466	17 .6640
Dec. 6.0,	1 .0097	2 .5586	0 .0432	20 .4273
1865 Jan. 15.0,	− 1 .2674	− 2 .0081	+ 0 .0362	− 22 .7245

The integral $\omega\int S_0 r_0 dt$ is obtained from the successive values of $\omega^2 S_0 r_0$ by means of the formula (32).

Next we compute the values of the differential coefficients by means of the formulæ (65). For the dates 1863 Dec. 12.0 and 1864 Jan. 21.0 we may first assume $\delta r = 0$, and, by a preliminary integration, having thus derived very approximate values of δr for these dates, the values of $\frac{d^2\delta r}{dt^2}$ will be recomputed. Then, commencing anew the table of integration, we may at once derive an approximate value of δr for the date March 1.0 with which the last term of the expression for $\frac{d^2\delta r}{dt^2}$ may be computed. Continuing this indirect process, as already illustrated in the case of the perturbations of the rectangular co-ordinates, we obtain the required values of the second differential coefficient. In a similar manner, the values of $\frac{d^2 z}{dt^2}$ will be obtained. The values of $\frac{d\delta w}{dt}$ will then be given directly by means of the first of equations (65); and the final integration will furnish the perturbations required. Thus we derive the following results:—

Date.	$\omega\frac{d\delta w}{dt}$	$\omega^2\frac{d^2\delta r}{dt^2}$	$\omega^2\frac{d^2 z}{dt^2}$	δw	δr	z
1863 Dec. 12.0,	−0″.0423	+1″.4509	+0″.0009	−0″.00	+0″.18	+0″.00
1864 Jan. 21.0,	0 .1086	1 .3405	0 .0101	0 .02	0 .17	0 .00
Mar. 1.0,	0 .7162	+0 .7829	0 .0183	0 .40	1 .47	0 .01
Apr. 10.0,	1 .6114	−0 .0455	0 .0251	1 .55	3 .53	0 .04
May 20.0,	2 .4795	0 .9344	0 .0300	3 .61	5 .54	0 .09
June 29.0,	3 .0807	1 .7333	0 .0326	6 .42	6 .62	0 .18
Aug. 8.0,	3 .2971	2 .3752	0 .0331	9 .64	5 .98	0 .29
Sept. 17.0,	3 .1080	2 .8533	0 .0311	12 .88	+2 .98	0 .44
Oct. 27.0,	−2 .5425	−3 .1872	+0 .0265	−15 .73	−2 .86	+0 .62

Date.	$\omega\frac{d\delta w}{dt}$	$\omega^2\frac{d^2\delta r}{dt^2}$	$\omega^2\frac{d^2z}{dt^2}$	δw	δr	z
1864 Dec. 6.0,	$-1''.6443$	$-3''.4009$	$+0''.0190$	$-17''.85$	$-11''.88$	$+0''.83$
1865 Jan. 15.0,	$-0\ .4511$	$-3\ .5334$	$+0\ .0079$	$-18\ .92$	$-24\ .29$	$+1\ .05$

It has already been found that, during the period included by these results, the perturbations arising from the squares and products of the disturbing forces are insensible, and hence the application of the complete equations for the forces and for the differential coefficients is not required. The equations (83) will give, by means of the results for $w = u_0 + \delta w$, $r = r_0 + \delta r$, and z, the values of the heliocentric co-ordinates of the disturbed body, and the combination of these with the co-ordinates of the sun will give the geocentric place.

When we neglect terms of the second order, we have, according to the equations (84),

$$\begin{aligned} \delta x_{\prime\prime} &= x_0 \cot(A + w)\,\delta w + \frac{x_0}{r_0}\delta r + z\cos a, \\ \delta y_{\prime\prime} &= y_0 \cot(B + w)\,\delta w + \frac{y_0}{r_0}\delta r + z\cos b, \\ \delta z_{\prime\prime} &= z_0 \cot(C + w)\,\delta w + \frac{z_0}{r_0}\delta r + z\cos c, \end{aligned} \tag{86}$$

the heliocentric co-ordinates x_0, y_0, z_0 being referred to the same fundamental plane as the auxiliary constants, a, b, A, &c. Thus, in the case of *Eurynome*, to find the perturbations of the rectangular co-ordinates, referred to the ecliptic and mean equinox of 1860.0, from 1864 Jan. 1.0 to 1865 Jan. 15.0, we have

$$A = 296°\ 34'\ 37''.5, \qquad B = 206°\ 43'\ 34''.4, \qquad C = 0,$$

$$\log\cos a = 8.557354_n, \qquad \log\cos b = 8.856746, \qquad \log\cos c = \log\cos i_0 = 9.998590,$$

$$\log x_0 = 0.399807_n, \qquad \log y_0 = 9.838709, \qquad \log z_0 = 9.148170_n,$$

$$w = w_0 + \delta w = 317°\ 53'\ 20''.2,$$

and hence, by means of (86), we derive

$$\delta x_{\prime} = +\,36''.559, \qquad \delta y_{\prime} = +\,41''.083, \qquad \delta z_{\prime} = -\,0''.588.$$

If we express these in parts of the unit of space, and in units of the seventh decimal place, we obtain

$$\delta x_{\prime} = +\,1772.4, \qquad \delta y_{\prime} = +\,1991.8, \qquad \delta z_{\prime} = -\,28.5,$$

agreeing with the results already obtained by the method of the variation of rectangular co-ordinates, namely,

$$\delta x_{\prime} = +\,1772.6, \qquad \delta y_{\prime} = +\,1992.3, \qquad \delta z_{\prime} = -\,28.2.$$

176. By using the complete formulæ, the perturbations of r, w, and z may be computed with respect to all powers of the disturbing force, and for a long series of years, using constantly the same fundamental osculating elements. But even when these elements are so accurate as not to require correction, on account of the effect of the large perturbations of long period upon the values of δw and δr, the numerical values of the perturbations will at length be such that a change of the osculating elements becomes desirable, so that the integration may again commence with the value zero for the variation of each of the co-ordinates. This change from one system of elements to another system may be readily effected when the values of the perturbations are known. Thus, having found the disturbed values of r, w, and z, we have

$$\frac{dv^2}{dt^2} = \cos^2\beta\frac{dw^2}{dt^2} + \frac{d\beta^2}{dt^2} = \frac{k^2p\,(1+m)}{r^4},$$

p being the semi-parameter of the instantaneous orbit of the disturbed body. In the undisturbed orbit we have

$$g_0 = \frac{dv_0}{dt} = \frac{k\sqrt{p_0(1+m)}}{r_0^{\,2}},$$

and hence we derive

$$p = \frac{p_0 r^4}{g_0^{\,2} r_0^{\,4}}\cdot\frac{dv^2}{dt^2}.$$

Substituting for $\frac{dv}{dt}$ the value above given, there results

$$p = p_0\frac{r^4}{r_0^{\,4}}\left(\cos^2\beta\left(1+\frac{1}{g_0}\cdot\frac{d\delta w}{dt}\right)^2 + \frac{1}{g_0^{\,2}}\cdot\frac{d\beta^2}{dt^2}\right), \tag{87}$$

by means of which p may be determined. To find $\frac{d\beta}{dt}$, we have

$$\frac{d\beta}{dt} = \frac{1}{r\cos\beta}\cdot\frac{dz}{dt} - \frac{\tan\beta}{r}\cdot\frac{dr}{dt}. \tag{88}$$

We have, also,

$$\frac{dr}{dt} = \frac{k\sqrt{1+m}}{\sqrt{p}}\,e\sin v = \frac{k\sqrt{1+m}}{\sqrt{p_0}}\,e_0\sin v_0 + \frac{d\delta r}{dt},$$

and if we put

$$\sqrt{\frac{p}{p_0}} = 1+\alpha, \qquad \gamma = \frac{\sqrt{p}}{k\sqrt{1+m}}\cdot\frac{d\delta r}{dt}, \tag{89}$$

this equation becomes

$$e \sin v = e_0 \sin v_0 + \alpha e_0 \sin v_0 + \gamma. \tag{90}$$

We have, further,

$$e \cos v = \frac{p}{r} - 1,$$

and, putting

$$\frac{p}{p_0} \cdot \frac{r_0}{r} = 1 + \beta, \tag{91}$$

we obtain

$$e \cos v = e_0 \cos v_0 + \beta \frac{p_0}{r_0}.$$

This equation, combined with (90), gives

$$\begin{aligned} e \sin (v - v_0) &= \alpha e_0 \sin v_0 \cos v_0 + \gamma \cos v_0 - \frac{p_0}{r_0} \beta \sin v_0, \\ e \cos (v - v_0) &= e_0 + \alpha e_0 \sin^2 v_0 + \gamma \sin v_0 + \frac{p_0}{r_0} \beta \cos v_0, \end{aligned} \tag{92}$$

by means of which the values of e and v may be found, those of the auxiliaries α, β, γ, being found from (89) and (91). Then we have

$$e = \sin \varphi, \qquad a = p \sec^2 \varphi,$$

$$\mu = \frac{k\sqrt{1+m}}{a^{\frac{3}{2}}}, \qquad \tan \tfrac{1}{2}E = \tan (45° - \tfrac{1}{2}\varphi) \tan \tfrac{1}{2}v,$$

$$M = E - e \sin E,$$

by means of which φ, a, μ, and M may be determined. In the case of orbits of great eccentricity, we find the perihelion distance from

$$q = \frac{p}{1 + e},$$

and the time of perihelion passage will be derived from e and v by means of Table IX. or Table X.

It remains yet to determine the values of Ω, i, and ω or π. Let θ_0 denote the longitude of the ascending node of the instantaneous orbit on the plane of the osculating orbit, defined by Ω_0 and i_0, measured from the origin of w, and let η_0 denote its inclination to this plane. Then we have

$$\begin{aligned} \tan \eta_0 \sin (w - \theta_0) &= \tan \beta, \\ \tan \eta_0 \cos (w - \theta_0) \frac{dw}{dt} &= \sec^2 \beta \frac{d\beta}{dt}, \end{aligned} \tag{93}$$

and hence

$$\tan(w - \theta_0) = \tfrac{1}{2}\sin 2\beta \frac{g_0 + \frac{d\delta w}{dt}}{\frac{d\beta}{dt}}, \tag{94}$$

by means of which θ_0 may be found. The quadrant in which θ_0 is situated is determined by the condition that $\sin(w - \theta_0)$ and $\tan\beta$ must have the same sign. The value of η_0 will be found from the first or the second of equations (93).

If we denote by ζ the argument of the latitude of the disturbed body with respect to the adopted fundamental plane, we have

$$\tan\zeta = \frac{\tan(w - \theta_0)}{\cos\eta_0}, \tag{95}$$

and the angle ζ must be taken in the same quadrant as $w - \theta_0$. Then, from the spherical triangle formed by the intersection of the planes of the ecliptic and instantaneous orbit of the disturbed body, and the fundamental plane, with the celestial vault, we derive

$$\begin{aligned}
\cos\tfrac{1}{2}i\sin\left(\tfrac{1}{2}(u - \zeta) + \tfrac{1}{2}(\Omega - \Omega_0)\right) &= \sin\tfrac{1}{2}\theta_0\cos\tfrac{1}{2}(i_0 - \eta_0),\\
\cos\tfrac{1}{2}i\cos\left(\tfrac{1}{2}(u - \zeta) + \tfrac{1}{2}(\Omega - \Omega_0)\right) &= \cos\tfrac{1}{2}\theta_0\cos\tfrac{1}{2}(i_0 + \eta_0),\\
\sin\tfrac{1}{2}i\sin\left(\tfrac{1}{2}(u - \zeta) - \tfrac{1}{2}(\Omega - \Omega_0)\right) &= \sin\tfrac{1}{2}\theta_0\sin\tfrac{1}{2}(i_0 - \eta_0),\\
\sin\tfrac{1}{2}i\cos\left(\tfrac{1}{2}(u - \zeta) - \tfrac{1}{2}(\Omega - \Omega_0)\right) &= \cos\tfrac{1}{2}\theta_0\sin\tfrac{1}{2}(i_0 + \eta_0).
\end{aligned} \tag{96}$$

These equations will furnish the values of i, $u - \zeta$, and $\Omega - \Omega_0$, and hence, since ζ and Ω_0 are given, those of Ω and u. The value of v having been already found, we have, finally,

$$\begin{aligned}
\omega &= u - v,\\
\pi &= u - v + \Omega,
\end{aligned}$$

and the elements are completely determined. These elements will be referred to the ecliptic and mean equinox to which Ω_0 and i_0 are referred, and they may be reduced to the equinox and ecliptic of any other date by means of the formulæ which have already been given.

The elements of the instantaneous orbit of the disturbed body may also be determined by first computing the values of $x_{,,}$, $y_{,,}$, $z_{,,}$ in reference to the fundamental plane to which Ω and i are to be referred, by means of the equations (83), and also those of $\frac{dx_{,,}}{dt}$, $\frac{dy_{,,}}{dt}$, $\frac{dz_{,,}}{dt}$ by means of (85) and (84), and then determining the elements from the co-ordinates and velocities, as already explained.

It should be observed that when the factor ω^2, or the square of the adopted interval, is introduced into the expressions for the forces and differential coefficients, the first integrals will be

$$\omega\frac{d\delta r}{dt},\qquad \omega\frac{d\delta w}{dt},\qquad \omega\frac{dz}{dt},$$

and that when these quantities are expressed in seconds of arc, they must be converted into their values in parts of the unit of space whenever they are to be combined with quantities which are not expressed in seconds. In other words, the homogeneity of the several terms must be carefully attended to in the actual application of the formulæ.

When the elements which correspond to given values of the perturbations have been determined, if we compute the heliocentric longitude and latitude of the body for the instant to which the elements belong, the results should agree with those obtained by computing the heliocentric place from the fundamental osculating elements and adding the perturbations.

177. The computation of the indirect terms when the perturbations of the co-ordinates r, w, and z are determined, is effected with greater facility than in the case of the rectangular co-ordinates, although the final results are not so convenient for the calculation of an ephemeris for the comparison of observations. This indirect calculation, which, when the perturbations of any system of three co-ordinates are to be computed, cannot in any case be avoided without impairing the accuracy of the results, may be further simplified by determining, in a peculiar form, the perturbations of the mean anomaly, the radius-vector, and the co-ordinate z perpendicular to the fundamental plane adopted.

Let the motion of the disturbed body be, at each instant, referred to the plane of its instantaneous orbit; then we shall have $\beta=0$, and the equations (51) and (54) become

$$\begin{aligned} r^2\frac{dw}{dt} &= \int S\,r\,dt + k\sqrt{p_0(1+m)}, \\ \frac{d^2r}{dt^2} - r\frac{dw^2}{dt^2} &+ \frac{k^2(1+m)}{r^2} = R, \end{aligned} \qquad (97)$$

in which R denotes the component of the disturbing force in the direction of the disturbed radius-vector, and S the component in the plane of the disturbed orbit and perpendicular to the disturbed radius-vector, being positive in the direction of the motion. The effect of the components R and S is to vary the form of the orbit and the angular distance of the perihelion from the node. If we denote by Z the component of the disturbing force perpendicular to the plane of the instantaneous orbit, the effect of this will be to change the position of the plane of the orbit, and hence to vary the elements which depend on the position of this plane.

Let us take a fixed line in the plane of the instantaneous orbit, and suppose it to be directed from the centre of the sun to a point whose angular distance back from the place of the ascending node is σ, and let the value of σ be so taken that, so long as the position of the plane of the orbit is unchanged, we shall have

$$\sigma = \Omega.$$

The line thus taken in the plane of the orbit may be regarded as fixed during all changes in the position of this plane. Let χ denote the angle between this fixed line and the semi-transverse axis; then will

$$\chi = \omega + \sigma, \tag{98}$$

and when the position of the plane of the orbit is unchanged, we have

$$\chi = \pi.$$

But if, on account of the action of the component Z, the position of the plane of the orbit is changed, we have, according to the equations $(72)_2$, the relations

$$\begin{aligned} d\sigma &= \cos i\, d\Omega, \\ d\omega &= d\chi - \cos i\, d\Omega, \\ d\pi &= d\chi + (1 - \cos i)\, d\Omega = d\chi + 2\sin^2 \tfrac{1}{2}i\, d\Omega. \end{aligned} \tag{99}$$

We have, further,

$$u = v + \chi - \sigma, \tag{100}$$

v being the true anomaly in the instantaneous orbit.

The two components of the disturbing force which act in the plane of the disturbed orbit will only vary χ and the elements which determine the dimensions of the conic section. We have, therefore, in the case of the osculating elements, for the instant t_0,

$$\chi_0 = \omega_0 + \Omega_0 = \pi_0.$$

Let us now suppose λ to denote the true longitude in the orbit, so that we have

$$\lambda = v + \pi = v + \omega + \Omega,$$

or

$$\lambda = v + \chi - (\sigma - \Omega);\qquad(101)$$

then, since χ is equal to π when the position of the plane of the orbit is unchanged, it follows that $\sigma - \Omega$ represents the variation of the true longitude in the orbit arising from the action of the component Z of the disturbing force. The elements may refer to the ecliptic or the equator, or to any other fundamental plane which may be adopted.

178. For the instant t we have, in the case of the disturbed motion, the following relations:—

$$\begin{aligned} E - e\sin E &= M + \mu(t - t_0), \\ r\cos v &= a\cos E - ae, \\ r\sin v &= a\sqrt{1 - e^2}\sin E, \\ \lambda &= v + \chi - (\sigma - \Omega). \end{aligned}\qquad(102)$$

Let us first consider only the perturbations arising from the action of the two components of the disturbing force in the plane of the disturbed orbit, and let us put

$$\lambda_{,} = v + \chi.\qquad(103)$$

Further, let $M_0 + \mu_0(t - t_0) + \delta M$ be the mean anomaly which, by means of a system of equations identical in form with the preceding, but in which the values of a_0, e_0, χ_0 are used instead of the instantaneous values a, e, and χ, gives the same longitude $\lambda_{,}$, so that we have

$$\begin{aligned} E_{,} - e_0\sin E_{,} &= M_0 + \mu_0(t - t_0) + \delta M, \\ r_{,}\cos v_{,} &= a_0\cos E_{,} - a_0 e_0, \\ r_{,}\sin v_{,} &= a_0\sqrt{1 - e_0^2}\sin E_{,} \\ \lambda_{,} &= v_{,} + \chi_0 = v_{,} + \pi_0. \end{aligned}\qquad(104)$$

If, therefore, we determine the value of δM so as to satisfy the condition that $\lambda_{,} = v + \chi$, the disturbed value of the true longitude in the orbit, neglecting the effect of the component Z of the disturbing force, will be known. The value of $r_{,}$ will generally differ from that of the disturbed radius-vector r, and hence it becomes necessary to introduce another variable in order to consider completely the effect of the components R and S. Thus, we may put

$$r = r_{,}(1 + \nu),\qquad(105)$$

and ν will always be a very small quantity. When δM and ν have been found, the effect of the disturbing force perpendicular to the plane of the instantaneous orbit may be considered, and thus the complete perturbations will be obtained.

In the equations (97), $\frac{1}{2}r^2\frac{dw}{dt}$ expresses the areal velocity in the instantaneous orbit, and it is evident that, since the true anomaly is not affected by the force Z perpendicular to the plane of the actual orbit, $\frac{1}{2}r^2\frac{dv_{,}}{dt}$ must also represent this areal velocity, and hence the equations become

$$\begin{aligned} r^2\frac{dv_{,}}{dt} &= \int S\,r\,dt + k\sqrt{p_0(1+m)}, \\ \frac{d^2r}{dt^2} - r\left(\frac{dv_{,}}{dt}\right)^2 &+ \frac{k^2(1+m)}{r^2} = R. \end{aligned} \tag{106}$$

179. If we differentiate each of the equations (104), we get

$$\begin{aligned} (1 - e_0\cos E_{,})\frac{dE_{,}}{dt} &= \mu_0 + \frac{d\delta M}{dt}, \\ \cos v_{,}\frac{dr_{,}}{dt} - r_{,}\sin v_{,}\frac{dv_{,}}{dt} &= -a_0\sin E_{,}\frac{dE_{,}}{dt}, \\ \sin v_{,}\frac{dr_{,}}{dt} + r_{,}\cos v_{,}\frac{dv_{,}}{dt} &= a_0\sqrt{1-e_0^2}\cos E_{,}\frac{dE_{,}}{dt}, \\ \frac{d\lambda_{,}}{dt} &= \frac{dv_{,}}{dt}. \end{aligned} \tag{107}$$

From the second and the third of these equations we easily derive

$$r_{,}\frac{dr_{,}}{dt} = (a_0\sqrt{1-e_0^2}\,r_{,}\sin v_{,}\cos E_{,} - a_0 r_{,}\cos v_{,}\sin E_{,})\frac{dE_{,}}{dt}.$$

Substituting in this the values of $r_{,}\sin v_{,}$, $r_{,}\cos v_{,}$, and $\frac{dE_{,}}{dt}$, and reducing, we get

$$r_{,}\frac{dr_{,}}{dt} = a_0^2 e_0\sin E_{,}\left(\mu_0 + \frac{d\delta M}{dt}\right),$$

or

$$\frac{dr_{,}}{dt} = \frac{k\sqrt{1+m}}{\sqrt{p_0}}e_0\sin v_{,}\left(1 + \frac{1}{\mu_0}\cdot\frac{d\delta M}{dt}\right). \tag{108}$$

From the same equations, eliminating $\frac{dr_{,}}{dt}$, we get

$$r_{,}^2\frac{dv_{,}}{dt} = (a_0\sqrt{1-e_0^2}\,r_{,}\cos v_{,}\cos E_{,} + a_0 r_{,}\sin v_{,}\sin E_{,})\frac{dE_{,}}{dt},$$

which reduces to

$$r_{,}^2\frac{dv_{,}}{dt} = k\sqrt{p_0(1+m)}\left(1 + \frac{1}{\mu_0}\cdot\frac{d\delta M}{dt}\right), \tag{109}$$

or

$$r^2\frac{dv_{\prime}}{dt}=k\sqrt{p_0(1+m)}\,(1+\nu)^2\left(1+\frac{1}{\mu_0}\cdot\frac{d\delta M}{dt}\right).$$

Combining this with the first of equations (106), we get

$$\frac{d\delta M}{dt}=\mu_0\left(\frac{1}{(1+\nu)^2}-1\right)+\frac{\mu_0}{(1+\nu)^2}\cdot\frac{1}{k\sqrt{p_0(1+m)}}\int Sr\,dt, \quad (110)$$

from which δM may be found as soon as ν is known.

The equation (105) gives

$$\begin{aligned}\frac{dr}{dt}&=(1+\nu)\frac{dr_{\prime}}{dt}+r_{\prime}\frac{d\nu}{dt},\\ \frac{d^2r}{dt^2}&=(1+\nu)\frac{d^2r_{\prime}}{dt^2}+2\frac{dr_{\prime}}{dt}\cdot\frac{d\nu}{dt}+r_{\prime}\frac{d^2\nu}{dt^2}.\end{aligned} \quad (111)$$

Differentiating equation (108) and substituting for $\frac{dv_{\prime}}{dt}$ its value already found, we obtain

$$\frac{d^2r_{\prime}}{dt^2}=\frac{k^2(1+m)\,e_0\cos v_{\prime}}{r_{\prime}^2}\left(1+\frac{1}{\mu_0}\cdot\frac{d\delta M}{dt}\right)^2+\frac{k\sqrt{1+m}\,e_0\sin v_{\prime}}{\mu_0\sqrt{p_0}}\cdot\frac{d^2\delta M}{dt^2},$$

and the last of the preceding equations becomes

$$\begin{aligned}\frac{d^2r}{dt^2}=r_{\prime}\frac{d^2\nu}{dt^2}&+\frac{k^2(1+m)\,e_0\cos v_{\prime}}{r_{\prime}^2}(1+\nu)\left(1+\frac{1}{\mu_0}\cdot\frac{d\delta M}{dt}\right)^2\\ &+\frac{k\sqrt{1+m}}{\sqrt{p_0}}\,e_0\sin v_{\prime}\left(\frac{1+\nu}{\mu_0}\cdot\frac{d^2\delta M}{dt^2}+2\frac{d\nu}{dt}+\frac{2}{\mu_0}\cdot\frac{d\nu}{dt}\cdot\frac{d\delta M}{dt}\right).\end{aligned}$$

The equation (110) gives

$$\begin{aligned}\frac{1}{\mu_0}\cdot\frac{d^2\delta M}{dt^2}+\frac{2}{(1+\nu)^3}\cdot\frac{d\nu}{dt}+\frac{2}{(1+\nu)^3}\cdot\frac{d\nu}{dt}\cdot\frac{1}{k\sqrt{p_0(1+m)}}\int Sr\,dt&\\ =\frac{1}{(1+\nu)^2}\cdot\frac{Sr}{k\sqrt{p_0(1+m)}},&\end{aligned}$$

which is easily reduced to

$$\frac{1+\nu}{\mu_0}\cdot\frac{d^2\delta M}{dt^2}+2\frac{d\nu}{dt}+\frac{2}{\mu_0}\cdot\frac{d\nu}{dt}\cdot\frac{d\delta M}{dt}=\frac{1}{1+\nu}\cdot\frac{Sr}{k\sqrt{p_0(1+m)}};$$

and hence we derive

$$\frac{d^2r}{dt^2}=r_{\prime}\frac{d^2\nu}{dt^2}+\frac{k^2(1+m)\,e_0\cos v_{\prime}}{r_{\prime}^2}(1+\nu)\left(1+\frac{1}{\mu_0}\cdot\frac{d\delta M}{dt}\right)^2+\frac{e_0\sin v_{\prime}}{p_0(1+\nu)}Sr. \quad (112)$$

The equation (109) gives

$$r_{\prime}\left(\frac{dv_{\prime}}{dt}\right)^2=\frac{k^2p_0(1+m)}{r_{\prime}^3}\left(1+\frac{1}{\mu_0}\cdot\frac{d\delta M}{dt}\right)^2,$$

and, since

$$r_{\prime}=\frac{r}{1+\nu}, \qquad \frac{p_0}{r_{\prime}}=1+e_0\cos v_{\prime},$$

this becomes

$$r\left(\frac{dv_{\prime}}{dt}\right)^2=\frac{k^2(1+m)}{r_{\prime}^2}(1+\nu)\left(1+\frac{1}{\mu_0}\cdot\frac{d\delta M}{dt}\right)^2 + \frac{k^2(1+m)\,e_0\cos v_{\prime}}{r_{\prime}^2}(1+\nu)\left(1+\frac{1}{\mu_0}\cdot\frac{d\delta M}{dt}\right)^2. \qquad (113)$$

Combining equations (112) and (113) with the second of equations (106), we get

$$\frac{d^2\nu}{dt^2}=\frac{1+\nu}{r}R+\frac{k^2(1+m)(1+\nu)^4}{r^3}\left(1+\frac{1}{\mu_0}\cdot\frac{d\delta M}{dt}\right)^2 - \frac{e_0\sin v_{\prime}}{p_0}S-\frac{k^2(1+m)(1+\nu)}{r^3}. \qquad (114)$$

From (110) we derive

$$(1+\nu)^4\left(1+\frac{1}{\mu_0}\cdot\frac{d\delta M}{dt}\right)^2=1+\frac{2}{k\sqrt{p_0(1+m)}}\int Sr\,dt + \left(\frac{1}{k\sqrt{p_0(1+m)}}\int Sr\,dt\right)^2,$$

and the preceding equation becomes

$$\frac{d^2\nu}{dt^2}=\frac{R}{r'}+2\frac{k^2(1+m)}{r^3}\cdot\frac{1}{k\sqrt{p_0(1+m)}}\int Sr\,dt-\frac{e_0\sin v_{\prime}}{p_0}S - \frac{k^2(1+m)}{r^3}\nu+\frac{k^2(1+m)}{r^3}\left(\frac{1}{k\sqrt{p_0(1+m)}}\int Sr\,dt\right)^2, \qquad (115)$$

which is the complete expression for the determination of ν.

180. It remains now to consider the effect of the component of the disturbing force which is perpendicular to the plane of the disturbed orbit. Let $x_{\prime\prime}$, $y_{\prime\prime}$, $z_{\prime}$ denote the co-ordinates of the body referred to the fundamental plane to which the elements belong, and x, y the co-ordinates in the plane of the instantaneous orbit. Further, let α denote the cosine of the angle which the axis of x makes with that of $x_{\prime\prime}$, and β the cosine of the angle which the axis of y makes with that of $y_{\prime\prime}$, and we shall have

$$z_{\prime}=\alpha x+\beta y. \qquad (116)$$

If the position of the plane of the orbit remained unchanged, these cosines α and β would be constant; but on account of the action of the force perpendicular to the plane of the orbit, these quantities are functions of the time. Now, the co-ordinate $z_{\prime}$ is subject to two distinct variations: if the elements remain constant, it varies with the time; and, in the case of the disturbed orbit, it is also subject to a variation arising from the change of the elements themselves. We shall, therefore, have

$$\frac{dz_{\prime}}{dt}=\left(\frac{dz_{\prime}}{dt}\right)+\left[\frac{dz_{\prime}}{dt}\right],$$

in which $\left(\frac{dz_{\prime}}{dt}\right)$ expresses the velocity resulting from the constant elements, and $\left[\frac{dz_{\prime}}{dt}\right]$ that part of the actual velocity which is due to the change of the elements by the action of the disturbing force. But during the element of time dt the elements may be regarded as constant, and hence the velocity $\frac{dz_{\prime}}{dt}$ in a direction parallel to the axis of $z_{\prime}$ may be regarded as constant during the same time, and as receiving an increment only at the end of this instant. Hence we shall have

$$\frac{dz_{\prime}}{dt}=\left(\frac{dz_{\prime}}{dt}\right) \qquad \left[\frac{dz_{\prime}}{dt}\right]=0.$$

Differentiating equation (116), regarding α and β as constant, we get

$$\left(\frac{dz_{\prime}}{dt}\right)=\frac{dz_{\prime}}{dt}=\alpha\frac{dx}{dt}+\beta\frac{dy}{dt}, \tag{117}$$

and differentiating the same equation, regarding x and y as constant, we get

$$\left[\frac{dz_{\prime}}{dt}\right]=x\frac{d\alpha}{dt}+y\frac{d\beta}{dt}=0. \tag{118}$$

Differentiating equation (117), regarding all the quantities involved as variable, the result is

$$\frac{d^2z_{\prime}}{dt^2}=\frac{d\alpha}{dt}\cdot\frac{dx}{dt}+\frac{d\beta}{dt}\cdot\frac{dy}{dt}+\alpha\frac{d^2x}{dt^2}+\beta\frac{d^2y}{dt^2}. \tag{119}$$

Now, we have

$$Z_{\prime}=\alpha X+\beta Y+Z\cos i, \tag{120}$$

in which $Z_{\prime}$ denotes the component of the disturbing force parallel to the axis of $z_{\prime}$, and i the inclination of the instantaneous orbit to the fundamental plane. Substituting for X and Y their values given by the equations (1), and reducing by means of (116), we obtain

$$Z_{\prime} = \alpha \frac{d^2x}{dt^2} + \beta \frac{d^2y}{dt^2} + k^2 (1+m) \frac{z_{\prime}}{r^3} + Z \cos i,$$

or

$$\frac{d^2z_{\prime}}{dt^2} = \alpha \frac{d^2x}{dt^2} + \beta \frac{d^2y}{dt^2} + Z \cos i.$$

Comparing this with (119), there results

$$\frac{d\alpha}{dt} \cdot \frac{dx}{dt} + \frac{d\beta}{dt} \cdot \frac{dy}{dt} = Z \cos i. \qquad (121)$$

181. The equation (120) gives

$$\frac{d^2z_{\prime}}{dt^2} = -\frac{k^2(1+m)}{r^3} z_{\prime} + Z \cos i + \alpha X + \beta Y. \qquad (122)$$

The component of the disturbing force perpendicular to the plane of the disturbed orbit does not affect the radius-vector r; and hence, when we neglect the effect of this component, and consider only the components R and S which act in the plane of the orbit, we have

$$\frac{d^2z_0}{dt^2} = -\frac{k^2(1+m)}{r^3} z_0 + \alpha_0 X + \beta_0 Y, \qquad (123)$$

in which z_0 denotes the value of $z_{\prime}$ obtained when we put $Z = 0$. Let us now denote by $\delta z_{\prime}$ that part of the change in the value of $z_{\prime}$ which arises from the action of the force perpendicular to the plane of the disturbed orbit, so that we shall have

$$z_{\prime} = z_0 + \delta z_{\prime}, \qquad \alpha = \alpha_0 + \delta\alpha, \qquad \beta = \beta_0 + \delta\beta.$$

Substituting these in equation (122) and then subtracting equation (123) from the result, we get

$$\frac{d^2\delta z_{\prime}}{dt^2} = -\frac{k^2(1+m)}{r^3} \delta z_{\prime} + Z \cos i + X\delta\alpha + Y\delta\beta. \qquad (124)$$

The equations (116) and (117) give

$$\delta z_{\prime} = x\delta\alpha + y\delta\beta, \qquad \frac{d\delta z_{\prime}}{dt} = \frac{dx}{dt}\delta\alpha + \frac{dy}{dt}\delta\beta.$$

If we eliminate $\delta\beta$ between these equations, there results

$$\delta\alpha \left(x\frac{dy}{dt} - y\frac{dx}{dt} \right) = \frac{dy}{dt}\delta z_{\prime} - y\frac{d\delta z_{\prime}}{dt},$$

and since the factor of $\delta\alpha$ in this equation is double the areal velocity in the disturbed orbit, we have

$$\delta\alpha = \frac{1}{k\sqrt{p(1+m)}}\left(\frac{dy}{dt}\delta z_{\prime} - y\frac{d\delta z_{\prime}}{dt}\right). \tag{125}$$

Eliminating $\delta\alpha$ from the same equations, we obtain, in a similar manner,

$$\delta\beta = \frac{1}{k\sqrt{p(1+m)}}\left(x\frac{d\delta z_{\prime}}{dt} - \frac{dx}{dt}\delta z_{\prime}\right). \tag{126}$$

Substituting these values in equation (124), it becomes

$$\begin{aligned}\frac{d^2\delta z_{\prime}}{dt^2} = &-\frac{k^2(1+m)}{r^3}\delta z_{\prime} + Z\cos i \\ &+\frac{1}{k\sqrt{p(1+m)}}\left(\left(X\frac{dy}{dt} - Y\frac{dx}{dt}\right)dz_{\prime} + (Yx - Xy)\frac{d\delta z_{\prime}}{dt}\right).\end{aligned} \tag{127}$$

If we introduce the components R and S of the disturbing force, we have

$$X = R\frac{x}{r} - S\frac{y}{r}, \qquad Y = R\frac{y}{r} + S\frac{x}{r},$$

and hence

$$\begin{aligned}X\frac{dy}{dt} - Y\frac{dx}{dt} &= \frac{R}{r}k\sqrt{p(1+m)} - S\frac{dr}{dt}, \\ Yx - Xy &= Sr.\end{aligned}$$

Therefore the equation (127) becomes

$$\begin{aligned}\frac{d^2\delta z_{\prime}}{dt^2} = &-\frac{k^2(1+m)}{r^3}\delta z_{\prime} + Z\cos i \\ &+\left(\frac{R}{r} - \frac{S}{k\sqrt{p(1+m)}}\cdot\frac{dr}{dt}\right)\delta z_{\prime} + \frac{Sr}{k\sqrt{p(1+m)}}\cdot\frac{d\delta z_{\prime}}{dt}.\end{aligned} \tag{128}$$

We have, further,

$$\frac{dr}{dt} = (1+\nu)\frac{dr_{\prime}}{dt} + r_{\prime}\frac{d\nu}{dt},$$

which, by means of the equations (108) and (109), gives

$$\frac{dr}{dt} = \frac{e_0\sin v_{\prime}}{p_0(1+\nu)}r^2\frac{dv_{\prime}}{dt} + r_{\prime}\frac{d\nu}{dt} = \frac{k\sqrt{p(1+m)}}{p_0(1+\nu)}e_0\sin v_{\prime} + r_{\prime}\frac{d\nu}{dt}.$$

Substituting this value in the equation (128), we obtain

$$\begin{aligned}\frac{d^2\delta z_{\prime}}{dt^2} = -\frac{k^2(1+m)}{r^3}\delta z_{\prime} + Z\cos i + \left(\frac{R}{r_{\prime}} - \frac{e_0 \sin v_{\prime}}{p_0}S\right)\frac{\delta z_{\prime}}{1+\nu} \\ + \frac{Sr}{k\sqrt{p(1+m)}}\left(\frac{d\delta z_{\prime}}{dt} - \frac{\delta z_{\prime}}{1+\nu}\cdot\frac{d\nu}{dt}\right),\end{aligned} \tag{129}$$

which is the complete expression for the determination of $\delta z_{\prime}$.

182. The equations (110), (115), and (129) determine the complete perturbations of the disturbed body. The value of ν must first be obtained by an indirect process from the equation (115), and then δM is given directly by means of (110). The value of δz will also be determined by an indirect process by means of (129).

In order to obtain the expressions for the forces R, S, and Z, let w denote the longitude of the disturbed body measured in the plane of the instantaneous orbit from its ascending node on the fundamental plane to which ☊ and i are referred, it being the argument of the latitude in the case of the disturbed motion. Let w' denote the longitude of the disturbing body measured from the same origin and in the plane of the orbit of the disturbed body, and let β' denote its latitude in reference to this plane. Finally, let N, N', I, and u_0' have the same signification in reference to the plane of the instantaneous orbit that they have in reference to the plane of the undisturbed orbit in the case of the equations (66). Then we shall have

$$\begin{aligned}\sin\tfrac{1}{2}I\sin\tfrac{1}{2}(N+N') &= \sin\tfrac{1}{2}(☊'-☊)\sin\tfrac{1}{2}(i'+i),\\ \sin\tfrac{1}{2}I\cos\tfrac{1}{2}(N+N') &= \cos\tfrac{1}{2}(☊'-☊)\sin\tfrac{1}{2}(i'-i),\\ \cos\tfrac{1}{2}I\sin\tfrac{1}{2}(N-N') &= \sin\tfrac{1}{2}(☊'-☊)\cos\tfrac{1}{2}(i'+i),\\ \cos\tfrac{1}{2}I\cos\tfrac{1}{2}(N-N') &= \cos\tfrac{1}{2}(☊'-☊)\cos\tfrac{1}{2}(i'-i),\end{aligned} \tag{130}$$

from which to determine N, N', and I. We have, also,

$$\begin{aligned}u_0' &= u' - N',\\ \tan(w'-N) &= \tan u_0' \cos I,\\ \tan\beta' &= \tan I \sin(w'-N),\end{aligned} \tag{131}$$

from which to find w' and β', u' being the argument of the latitude of the disturbing body in reference to the plane to which ☊ and i are referred.

Since, when the motion of the disturbed body is referred to the plane of its instantaneous orbit, $\beta = 0$, the equations (71), (72), and (73) become

$$\begin{aligned}R &= m'k^2\left(h r' \cos\beta' \cos(w'-w) - \frac{r}{\rho^3}\right),\\ S &= m'k^2 h r' \cos\beta' \sin(w'-w),\\ Z &= m'k^2 h r' \sin\beta',\end{aligned} \tag{132}$$

by means of which the required components of the disturbing force may be found, the value of h being given by

$$h = \frac{1}{\rho^3} - \frac{1}{r'^3}.$$

To find ρ, we have

$$\rho^2 = r'^2 + r^2 - 2rr' \cos\beta' \cos(w' - w), \qquad (133)$$

or, putting

$$\cos\gamma = \cos\beta' \cos(w' - w),$$

the equations

$$\begin{aligned} \rho \sin n &= r' \sin\gamma, \\ \rho \cos n &= r - r' \cos\gamma. \end{aligned} \qquad (134)$$

The values of r' and u' for the actual places of the disturbing body will be given by the tables of its motion, and the actual values of Ω' and i' will also be obtained by means of the tables. The determination of the actual values of r and w requires that the perturbations shall be known. Thus, when δM and ν have been found, we compute, by means of the mean anomaly $M_0 + \mu_0(t - t_0) + \delta M$ and the elements a_0, e_0, the values of $v_{,}$ and $r_{,}$. Then, since $v + \chi = v_{,} + \pi_0$, we have, according to (100),

$$w = v_{,} + \pi_0 - \sigma. \qquad (135)$$

We have, also,

$$r = (1 + \nu)\, r_{,}.$$

In the case of the fundamental osculating elements, we have

$$\sigma_0 = \Omega_0,$$

which may be used as an approximate value of σ; but the complete determination of w requires that $\sigma = \Omega_0 + \delta\sigma$ shall also be determined. The exact determination of the forces also requires that the actual values of Ω and i as well as those of Ω' and i', shall be used in the determination of N, N', and I for each instant. When these have been found, it will be sufficient to compute the actual values of N, N', and I at intervals during the entire period for which the perturbations are required, and to interpolate their values for the intermediate dates. The variations of these quantities arising from the variations of Ω, i, Ω', and i' may also be determined by means of differential formulæ. Thus, from the differential relations of the parts of the spherical triangle from which the equations (130) are derived, we easily find

$$
\begin{aligned}
dN' &= \frac{\sin i}{\sin I} \cos N \, d(\Omega' - \Omega) - \frac{\sin N'}{\sin I} \cos I \, di' + \frac{\sin N}{\sin I} di, \\
dN &= \frac{\sin i'}{\sin I} \cos N' \, d(\Omega' - \Omega) - \frac{\sin N'}{\sin I} di' + \frac{\sin N}{\sin I} \cos I \, di, \\
dI &= \cos N' \, di' - \cos N \, di + \sin i \sin N \, d(\Omega' - \Omega).
\end{aligned} \tag{136}
$$

When i and I are very small, it will be better to use

$$
\frac{\sin i}{\sin I} = \frac{\sin N'}{\sin(\Omega' - \Omega)}, \qquad \frac{\sin i'}{\sin I} = \frac{\sin N}{\sin(\Omega' - \Omega)}, \tag{137}
$$

in finding the numerical values of these coefficients. By means of these formulæ we may derive the values of δN, $\delta N'$, and δI corresponding to given values of $\delta \Omega$, δi, $\delta \Omega'$, and $\delta i'$. The formulæ by means of which $\delta \sigma$, $\delta \Omega$, and δi may be obtained directly, will be presently considered.

The results for δN, $\delta N'$, and δI being applied to the quantities to which they belong, we may compute the actual values of w' and β'. The value of r will be found from the given value of ν, and that of w will be given by means of equation (135). Then, by means of the formulæ (132), the forces R, S, and Z will be obtained. The perturbations will first be computed in reference only to terms depending on the first power of the disturbing force, and, whenever it becomes necessary to consider the terms of the second order, the results already obtained will enable us to estimate the values of the perturbations for two or more intervals in advance with sufficient accuracy for the determination of the three required components of the disturbing force; and when there are two or more disturbing bodies to be considered, the forces for each of these may be computed at once, and the values of each component for the several disturbing bodies may be united into a single sum, thus using ΣR, ΣS, and ΣZ in place of R, S, and Z respectively. The approximate values of the perturbations will also facilitate the indirect calculation in the determination of the complete values of the required differential coefficients.

183. When only the perturbations due to the first power of the disturbing force are required, the osculating elements Ω_0 and i_0 will be used in finding N, N', and I, and r_0, w_0 will be used instead of r and w in the calculation of the values of R, S, and Z. The equations for the determination of the perturbations δM, ν, and $\delta z_{,}$, neglecting terms of the second order, are, according to the equations (110), (115), and (129), the following:—

$$\frac{d\delta M}{dt} = \mu_0 \frac{1}{k\sqrt{p_0(1+m)}} \int S r_0 \, dt - 2\mu_0 \nu,$$
$$\frac{d^2\nu}{dt^2} = \frac{R}{r_0} + \frac{2k^2(1+m)}{r_0^3} \cdot \frac{1}{k\sqrt{p_0(1+m)}} \int S r_0 \, dt - \frac{e_0 \sin v_0}{p_0} S - \frac{k^2(1+m)}{r_0^3} \nu, \tag{138}$$
$$\frac{d^2\delta z_{,}}{dt^2} = Z \cos i_0 - \frac{k^2(1+m)}{r_0^3} \delta z_{,}.$$

The value of ν is first found by integration from the results given by the second of these equations, and then δM is found from the first equation. Finally, $\delta z_{,}$ is found by means of the last equation. The integrals are in each case equal to zero for the dates to which the fundamental osculating elements belong, and the process of integration is analogous, in all respects, to that already illustrated in the case of the variation of the rectangular co-ordinates. It will be observed, however, that the expression for $\frac{d^2\nu}{dt^2}$ involves only one indirect term, the coefficient of which is small, and the same is true in the case of $\frac{d^2\delta z_{,}}{dt^2}$, while $\frac{d\delta M}{dt}$ is given directly. When the perturbations have been found for a few dates, the values for the following date can be estimated so closely that a repetition of the calculation will rarely or never be required; and the actual value of r may be used instead of the approximate value r_0 in these expressions for the differential coefficients. Neglecting terms of the second order, we have

$$\log r = \log r_{,} + \lambda_0 \nu,$$

wherein λ_0 denotes the modulus of the system of logarithms. We may also use $v_{,}$ instead of v_0; but in this case, since $r_{,}$ and $v_{,}$ depend on $\delta M_{,}$ only the quantities required for two or three places may be computed in advance of the integration.

A comparison of the equations (138) with the complete equations (110), (115), and (129) shows that, if the values of β' and w' are known to a sufficient degree of approximation, we may, with very little additional labor, consider the terms depending on the squares and higher powers of the masses. It will, however, appear from what follows, that when we consider the perturbations due to the higher powers of the disturbing forces, the consideration of the effect of the variation of $z_{,}$ in the determination of the heliocentric place of the disturbed body, becomes much more difficult than when the terms of the second order are neglected; and hence it will be found advisable to determine new osculating elements whenever the consideration of these terms becomes troublesome.

The results may be conveniently expressed in seconds of arc, and afterwards ν and $\delta z_,$ may be converted into their values expressed in units of the seventh decimal place, or, giving proper attention to the homogeneity of the several terms of the equations, in the numerical operations, δM may be expressed in seconds of arc, while ν and $\delta z_,$ are obtained directly in units of the seventh decimal place. It will be advisable, also, to introduce the interval ω into the formulæ in such a manner that this quantity may be omitted in the case of the formulæ of integration.

184. In the case of orbits of great eccentricity, the mean anomaly and the mean daily motion cannot be conveniently used in the numerical application of the formulæ. Instead of these we must employ the time of perihelion passage and the elements q and e. Thus, let T_0 be the time of perihelion passage for the osculating elements for the date t_0, and let $T_0 + \delta T$ be the time of perihelion passage to be used in the formulæ in the place of T_0 and in connection with the elements q_0 and e_0 in the determination of the values of $r_,$ and $v_,$, so that we have

$$v + \chi = v_, + \pi_0.$$

In the case of parabolic motion we have, neglecting the mass of the disturbed body,

$$\frac{k(t - (T_0 + \delta T))}{\sqrt{2}\, q_0^{\frac{3}{2}}} = \tan \tfrac{1}{2}v_, + \tfrac{1}{3} \tan^3 \tfrac{1}{2}v_, \qquad (139)$$

the solution of which to find $v_,$ is effected by means of Table VI. as already explained. To find $r_,$, we have

$$r_, = q_0 \sec^2 \tfrac{1}{2}v_,.$$

For the other cases in which the elements M_0 and μ_0 cannot be employed, the solution must be effected by means of Table IX. or Table X. Thus, when Table IX. is used, we compute M from

$$M = (t - (T_0 + \delta T)) \frac{C_0}{q_0^{\frac{3}{2}}} \sqrt{\frac{1 + e_0}{2}},$$

wherein $\log C_0 = 9.9601277$, and with this as the argument we derive from Table VI. the corresponding value of V. Then, having found $i = \dfrac{1 - e_0}{1 + e_0}$, by means of Table IX. we derive the coefficients required in the equation

$$v_, = V + A\,(100i) + B\,(100i)^2 + C(100i)^3, \qquad (140)$$

from which $v_{,}$ will be determined. Finally, $r_{,}$ will be found from

$$r_{,}=\frac{q_0(1+e_0)}{1+e_0\cos v_{,}}. \qquad (141)$$

When Table X. is used, we proceed as explained in Art. 41, using the elements $T=T_0+\delta T$, q_0, and e_0, and thus we obtain the required values of $v_{,}$ and $r_{,}$.

It is evident, therefore, that, for the determination of the perturbations, only the formula for finding the value of δM requires modification in the case of orbits of great eccentricity, and this modification is easily effected. The expression

$$M_0+\mu_0(t-t_0)+\delta M=M,$$

gives

$$\mu_0(t_0-T_0)+\mu_0(t-t_0)+\delta M=\mu_0(t-(T_0+\delta T)),$$

or, simply,

$$\delta M=-\mu_0\delta T,$$

and the equation (110) becomes

$$\frac{d\delta T}{dt}=1-\frac{1}{(1+\nu)^2}-\frac{1}{(1+\nu)^2}\cdot\frac{1}{k\sqrt{p_0}(1+m)}\int Sr\,dt, \qquad (142)$$

by means of which the value δT required in the solution of the equations for $r_{,}$ and $v_{,}$ may be found.

If we denote by $t_{,}$ the time for which the true anomaly and the radius-vector computed by means of the fundamental osculating elements have the values which have been designated by $v_{,}$ and $r_{,}$, respectively, we have

$$\delta M=\mu_0(t_{,}-t), \qquad 1+\frac{1}{\mu_0}\cdot\frac{d\delta M}{dt}=\frac{dt_{,}}{dt},$$

and the equation (110) becomes

$$\frac{dt_{,}}{dt}=\frac{1}{(1+\nu)^2}+\frac{1}{(1+\nu)^2}\cdot\frac{1}{k\sqrt{p_0}(1+m)}\int Sr\,dt, \qquad (143)$$

or, putting $t_{,}=t+\delta t$,

$$\frac{d\delta t}{dt}=\frac{1}{(1+\nu)^2}-1+\frac{1}{(1+\nu)^2}\cdot\frac{1}{k\sqrt{p_0}(1+m)}\int Sr\,dt. \qquad (144)$$

If we determine δt by means of this equation, the values of the radius-vector and true anomaly will be found for the time $t+\delta t$ instead of t, according to the methods for the different conic sections, using the fundamental osculating elements. The results thus obtained are the required values of $r_{,}$ and $v_{,}$ respectively.

185. When the values of the perturbations ν, $\delta z_{,}$, and δM, δT, or δt have been determined, it remains to find the place of the disturbed body. The heliocentric longitude and latitude will be given by

$$\begin{aligned}\cos b\cos(l-\Omega)&=\cos(\lambda-\Omega),\\ \cos b\sin(l-\Omega)&=\sin(\lambda-\Omega)\cos i,\\ \sin b\qquad\quad&=\sin(\lambda-\Omega)\sin i,\end{aligned}$$

or, since $\lambda=\lambda_{,}-\sigma+\Omega$,

$$\begin{aligned}\cos b\cos(l-\Omega)&=\cos(\lambda_{,}-\sigma),\\ \cos b\sin(l-\Omega)&=\sin(\lambda_{,}-\sigma)\cos i,\\ \sin b\qquad\quad&=\sin(\lambda_{,}-\sigma)\sin i,\end{aligned}\tag{145}$$

in which $\lambda_{,}=v_{,}+\pi_0$. If we multiply the first of these equations by $\cos(\Omega-h)$, and the second by $-\sin(\Omega-h)$, in which h may have any value whatever, and add the results; then multiply the first by $\sin(\Omega-h)$, and the second by $\cos(\Omega-h)$, and add, we get

$$\begin{aligned}\cos b\cos(l-h)&=\cos(\lambda_{,}-\sigma)\cos(\Omega-h)-\sin(\lambda_{,}-\sigma)\sin(\Omega-h)\cos i,\\ \cos b\sin(l-h)&=\cos(\lambda_{,}-\sigma)\sin(\Omega-h)+\sin(\lambda_{,}-\sigma)\cos(\Omega-h)\cos i,\\ \sin b\qquad\quad&=\sin(\lambda_{,}-\sigma)\sin i.\end{aligned}$$

But, since $\lambda_{,}-\sigma=(\lambda_{,}-\Omega_0)-(\sigma-\Omega_0)$, these equations may be written

$$\begin{aligned}&\cos b\cos(l-h)\\ &\quad=\cos(\lambda_{,}-\Omega_0)\big(\cos(\sigma-\Omega_0)\cos(\Omega-h)+\sin(\sigma-\Omega_0)\sin(\Omega-h)\cos i\big)\\ &\quad+\sin(\lambda_{,}-\Omega_0)\big(\sin(\sigma-\Omega_0)\cos(\Omega-h)-\cos(\sigma-\Omega_0)\sin(\Omega-h)\cos i\big),\\ &\cos b\sin(l-h)\\ &\quad=\cos(\lambda_{,}-\Omega_0)\big(\cos(\sigma-\Omega_0)\sin(\Omega-h)-\sin(\sigma-\Omega_0)\cos(\Omega-h)\cos i\big)\\ &\quad+\sin(\lambda_{,}-\Omega_0)\big(\sin(\sigma-\Omega_0)\sin(\Omega-h)+\cos(\sigma-\Omega_0)\cos(\Omega-h)\cos i\big),\\ &\sin b=\sin(\lambda_{,}-\Omega_0)\cos(\sigma-\Omega_0)\sin i-\cos(\lambda_{,}-\Omega_0)\sin(\sigma-\Omega_0)\sin i.\end{aligned}\tag{146}$$

Let us now conceive a spherical triangle to be formed, of which two of the sides are $\sigma-\Omega_0$ and $\Omega-h$, respectively, and let the angle included by these sides be i. Since h is entirely arbitrary, we may assign to it a value such that the other angle adjacent to the side $\sigma-\Omega_0$ will be equal to i_0. Let the third side be designated by $h_0-\Omega_0$, and the angle opposite to $\sigma-\Omega_0$ by η'. The auxiliary triangle thus formed gives the following relations:—

$$\begin{aligned}
\cos(h_0-\Omega_0) &= \cos(\sigma-\Omega_0)\cos(\Omega-h)+\sin(\sigma-\Omega_0)\sin(\Omega-h)\cos i,\\
\sin(h_0-\Omega_0)\sin i_0 &= \sin(\Omega-h)\sin i, \qquad (147)\\
\sin(h_0-\Omega_0)\cos i_0 &= \sin(\sigma-\Omega_0)\cos(\Omega-h)-\cos(\sigma-\Omega_0)\sin(\Omega-h)\cos i,\\
\sin(h_0-\Omega_0)\cos\eta' &= \cos(\sigma-\Omega_0)\sin(\Omega-h)-\sin(\sigma-\Omega_0)\cos(\Omega-h)\cos i.
\end{aligned}$$

Combining these with the preceding equations, we easily derive

$$\begin{aligned}
\cos b\cos(l-h) &= \cos(\lambda_{\prime}-\Omega_0)\cos(h_0-\Omega_0)+\sin(\lambda_{\prime}-\Omega_0)\sin(h_0-\Omega_0)\cos i_0,\\
\cos b\sin(l-h) &= \sin(\lambda_{\prime}-\Omega_0)\cos(h_0-\Omega_0)\cos i_0-\cos(\lambda_{\prime}-\Omega_0)\sin(h_0-\Omega_0)\\
&\quad +\cos(\lambda_{\prime}-\Omega_0)\sin(h_0-\Omega_0)(1+\cos\eta') \qquad (148)\\
&\quad +\sin(\lambda_{\prime}-\Omega_0)\big((\cos i-\cos i_0)\cos(h_0-\Omega_0)+\sin(\sigma-\Omega_0)\sin(\Omega-h)\sin^2 i\big),\\
\sin b &= \sin i_0\sin(\lambda_{\prime}-\Omega_0)+\big(\cos(\sigma-\Omega_0)\sin i-\sin i_0\big)\sin(\lambda_{\prime}-\Omega_0)\\
&\quad -\cos(\lambda_{\prime}-\Omega_0)\sin(\sigma-\Omega_0)\sin i.
\end{aligned}$$

Since the action of the component of the disturbing force perpendicular to the plane of the disturbed orbit does not change the radius-vector, we have

$$r\sin b = r\sin i_0\sin(\lambda_{\prime}-\Omega_0)+\delta z_{\prime},$$

and hence the last of these equations gives

$$\begin{aligned}
\frac{\delta z_{\prime}}{r} &= \sin(\lambda_{\prime}-\Omega_0)\big(\cos(\sigma-\Omega_0)\sin i-\sin i_0\big)\\
&\quad -\cos(\lambda_{\prime}-\Omega_0)\sin(\sigma-\Omega_0)\sin i.
\end{aligned} \qquad (149)$$

From the relation of the parts of the auxiliary spherical triangle, we have

$$\begin{aligned}
\sin i\sin(\sigma-\Omega_0) &= \sin\eta'\sin(h_0-\Omega_0),\\
\sin i\cos(\sigma-\Omega_0) &= \sin\eta'\cos(h_0-\Omega_0)\cos i_0+\cos\eta'\sin i_0.
\end{aligned}$$

Therefore,

$$\begin{aligned}
\frac{\delta z_{\prime}}{r} &= \sin(\lambda_{\prime}-\Omega_0)\big(\cos i_0\cos(h_0-\Omega_0)\sin\eta'-\sin i_0(1-\cos\eta')\big),\\
&\quad -\cos(\lambda_{\prime}-\Omega_0)\sin(h_0-\Omega_0)\sin\eta',
\end{aligned} \qquad (150)$$

and

$$\begin{aligned}
\frac{\delta z_{\prime}}{r}\cdot\frac{\sin\eta'}{1-\cos\eta'} &= \sin(\lambda_{\prime}-\Omega_0)\big(\cos i_0\cos(h_0-\Omega_0)(1+\cos\eta')-\sin i_0\sin\eta'\big)\\
&\quad -\cos(\lambda_{\prime}-\Omega_0)\sin(h_0-\Omega_0)(1+\cos\eta').
\end{aligned} \qquad (151)$$

We have, further, from the auxiliary spherical triangle,

$$\cos i = \sin i_0\sin\eta'\cos(h_0-\Omega_0)-\cos i_0\cos\eta',$$

from which we get

$$\cos i-\cos i_0 = \sin i_0\cos(h_0-\Omega_0)\sin\eta'-\cos i_0(1+\cos\eta').$$

We have, also,

$$\begin{aligned}
\sin(\sigma-\Omega_0)\sin i &= \sin\eta'\sin(h_0-\Omega_0),\\
\sin(\Omega-h)\sin i &= \sin i_0\sin(h_0-\Omega_0),
\end{aligned}$$

or

$$\sin(\sigma - \Omega_0)\sin(\Omega - h)\sin^2 i = \sin^2(h_0 - \Omega_0)\sin i_0 \sin\eta'.$$

Hence we derive

$$(\cos i - \cos i_0)\cos(h_0 - \Omega_0) + \sin(\sigma - \Omega_0)\sin(\Omega - h)\sin^2 i = \sin i_0 \sin\eta' \\ -(1+\cos\eta')\cos i_0 \cos(h_0 - \Omega_0).$$

Combining this and the equation (151) with the equations (148), we obtain

$$\begin{aligned}
\cos b\cos(l-h) &= \cos(\lambda_, - \Omega_0)\cos(h_0 - \Omega_0) + \sin(\lambda_, - \Omega_0)\sin(h_0 - \Omega_0)\cos i_0, \\
\cos b\sin(l-h) &= \sin(\lambda_, - \Omega_0)\cos(h_0 - \Omega_0)\cos i_0 - \cos(\lambda_, - \Omega_0)\sin(h_0 - \Omega_0) \\
&\quad - \frac{\sin\eta'}{1-\cos\eta'}\cdot\frac{\delta z_,}{r}, \\
\sin b &= \sin(\lambda_, - \Omega_0)\sin i_0 + \frac{\delta z_,}{r}.
\end{aligned}$$

If we multiply the first of these equations by $\cos(h_0 - \Omega_0)$, and the second by $-\sin(h_0 - \Omega_0)$, and add the results; then multiply the first by $\sin(h_0 - \Omega_0)$, and the second by $\cos(h_0 - \Omega_0)$, and add, we get

$$\begin{aligned}
\cos b\cos\big(l - \Omega_0 - (h - h_0)\big) &= \cos(\lambda_, - \Omega_0) + \sin(h_0 - \Omega_0)\frac{\sin\eta'}{1-\cos\eta'}\cdot\frac{\delta z_,}{r}, \\
\cos b\sin\big(l - \Omega_0 - (h - h_0)\big) &= \sin(\lambda_, - \Omega_0)\cos i_0 - \cos(h_0 - \Omega_0)\frac{\sin\eta'}{1-\cos\eta'}\cdot\frac{\delta z_,}{r}, \\
\sin b &= \sin(\lambda_, - \Omega_0)\sin i_0 + \frac{\delta z_,}{r}.
\end{aligned} \tag{152}$$

Let us now put

$$\begin{aligned}
p' &= \sin(\sigma - \Omega_0)\sin i, \\
q' &= \cos(\sigma - \Omega_0)\sin i - \sin i_0,
\end{aligned} \tag{153}$$

and there results, from (149),

$$\frac{\delta z_,}{r} = q'\sin(\lambda_, - \Omega_0) - p'\cos(\lambda_, - \Omega_0). \tag{154}$$

Comparing this with equation (150), we observe that

$$\begin{aligned}
p' &= \sin\eta'\sin(h_0 - \Omega_0), \\
q' &= \sin\eta'\cos(h_0 - \Omega_0)\cos i_0 - \sin i_0(1-\cos\eta').
\end{aligned}$$

Therefore, we have

$$\begin{aligned}
\frac{\sin\eta'}{1-\cos\eta'}\sin(h_0 - \Omega_0) &= \frac{p'}{1-\cos\eta'}, \\
\frac{\sin\eta'}{1-\cos\eta'}\cos(h_0 - \Omega_0) &= \tan i_0 + \frac{q'}{\cos i_0(1-\cos\eta')},
\end{aligned}$$

and, if we put $\Gamma = h - h_0$, the equations (152) become

$$\cos b \cos(l - \Omega_0 - \Gamma) = \cos(\lambda_, - \Omega_0) + \frac{p'}{1 - \cos\eta'} \cdot \frac{\delta z_,}{r},$$

$$\cos b \sin(l - \Omega_0 - \Gamma) = \sin(\lambda_, - \Omega_0)\cos i_0 - \left(\tan i_0 + \frac{q'}{\cos i_0 (1 - \cos\eta')}\right)\frac{\delta z_,}{r}, \qquad (155)$$

$$\sin b = \sin(\lambda_, - \Omega_0)\sin i_0 + \frac{\delta z_,}{r}.$$

As soon as Γ, p', q', and η' are known, these equations will furnish the exact values of l and b, those of $\lambda_,$ and r being found by means of the perturbations ν and δM.

186. The value of Γ may be expressed in terms of p' and q'. Thus, if we differentiate the first of equations (147) and reduce by means of the remaining equations of the same group, we get

$$d(h_0 - \Omega_0) = \cos\eta' \, d(\Omega - h) + \cos i_0 \, d\sigma + \sin i_0 \sin(\sigma - \Omega_0)\, di,$$

and if we interchange $\Omega - h$ and $h_0 - \Omega_0$ in this equation, we must also interchange i and i_0, which are the angles opposite to these sides, respectively, in the auxiliary spherical triangle, so that we shall have

$$d(\Omega - h) = \cos\eta' \, d(h_0 - \Omega_0) + \cos i \, d\sigma,$$

i_0 being constant. Adding these equations, observing that Ω_0 is also constant, we get

$$(1 - \cos\eta')\, d(\Omega - h + h_0) = \sin i_0 \sin(\sigma - \Omega_0)\, di + (\cos i + \cos i_0)\, d\sigma; \qquad (156)$$

and since $d\sigma = \cos i \, d\Omega$, this becomes

$$(1 - \cos\eta')\, d(h - h_0) = -\sin i_0 \sin(\sigma - \Omega_0)\, di + (\sin^2 i - \cos\eta' - \cos i \cos i_0)\frac{d\sigma}{\cos i},$$

which, since

$$\cos\eta' = \sin i \sin i_0 \cos(\sigma - \Omega_0) - \cos i \cos i_0, \qquad (157)$$

may be written

$$(1 - \cos\eta')\, d\Gamma = -\sin i_0 \sin(\sigma - \Omega_0)\, di + \tan i \left(\sin i - \sin i_0 \cos(\sigma - \Omega_0)\right) d\sigma. \qquad (158)$$

The differentiation of the equations (153) gives

$$dp' = \sin(\sigma - \Omega_0)\cos i \, di + \sin i \cos(\sigma - \Omega_0)\, d\sigma,$$
$$dq' = \cos(\sigma - \Omega_0)\cos i \, di - \sin i \sin(\sigma - \Omega_0)\, d\sigma,$$

from which we derive

$$q'dp' - p'dq' = \sin^2 i\, d\sigma - \sin i_0\, dp'$$
$$= \cos i\left(-\sin i_0 \sin(\sigma - \Omega_0)\, di + \tan i\left(\sin i - \sin i_0 \cos(\sigma - \Omega_0)\right) d\sigma\right).$$

Combining this with equation (158), we get

$$\cos i\,(1 - \cos\eta')\, d\Gamma = q'dp' - p'dq',$$

and hence

$$\Gamma = \int \frac{q'\frac{dp'}{dt} - p'\frac{dq'}{dt}}{\cos i\,(1 - \cos\eta')}\, dt, \tag{159}$$

the integral being equal to zero for the instant to which the fundamental osculating elements belong. It is evident from the equations (153) that p' and q' are of the order of the first power of the disturbing forces, and hence, since η' differs but little from $180° - (i + i_0)$, it follows that, so long as i is not very large, Γ is at least of the second order.

The last of equations (145) gives

$$z_, = r \sin i \sin\lambda_, \cos\sigma - r \sin i \cos\lambda_, \sin\sigma,$$

and since

$$x = r\cos\lambda_{,,}, \qquad y = r \sin\lambda_{,,}$$

this becomes

$$z_, = -x \sin i \sin\sigma + y \sin i \cos\sigma.$$

Comparing this with equation (116), it appears that

$$\alpha = -\sin i \sin\sigma, \qquad \beta = \sin i \cos\sigma, \tag{160}$$

and hence, by means of (153), we derive

$$p' = -\alpha\cos\Omega_0 - \beta \sin\Omega_0,$$
$$q' = -\alpha \sin\Omega_0 + \beta\cos\Omega_0 - \sin i_0,$$

and also

$$\begin{aligned} \frac{dp'}{dt} &= -\cos\Omega_0 \frac{d\alpha}{dt} - \sin\Omega_0 \frac{d\beta}{dt}, \\ \frac{dq'}{dt} &= -\sin\Omega_0 \frac{d\alpha}{dt} + \cos\Omega_0 \frac{d\beta}{dt}. \end{aligned} \tag{161}$$

From the equations (118) and (121), observing that

$$x\frac{dy}{dt} - y\frac{dx}{dt} = k\sqrt{p(1+m)},$$

we derive, by elimination,

$$\frac{d\alpha}{dt} = -\frac{r\sin\lambda_, \cos i}{k\sqrt{p(1+m)}} Z, \qquad \frac{d\beta}{dt} = \frac{r\cos\lambda_, \cos i}{k\sqrt{p(1+m)}} Z.$$

Therefore we shall have

$$\frac{dp'}{dt} = \frac{r\cos i \sin(\lambda_{,} - \Omega_0)}{k\sqrt{p(1+m)}} Z,$$
$$\frac{dq'}{dt} = \frac{r\cos i \cos(\lambda_{,} - \Omega_0)}{k\sqrt{p(1+m)}} Z, \qquad (162)$$

by means of which p' and q' may be found by integration, the integral in each case being zero for the date t_0 at which the determination of the perturbations begins.

When the value of $\delta z_{,}$ has already been found by means of the equation (129), if we compute the value of q', that of p' will be given by means of (154), or

$$p' = q' \tan(\lambda_{,} - \Omega_0) - \frac{\delta z_{,}}{r\cos(\lambda_{,} - \Omega_0)},$$

and if p' is determined, q' will be given by

$$q' = p' \cot(\lambda_{,} - \Omega) + \frac{\delta z_{,}}{r\sin(\lambda_{,} - \Omega_0)}.$$

If both p' and q' are found from the equations (162), $\delta z_{,}$ may be determined directly from (154); but the value thus obtained will be less accurate than that derived by means of equation (129).

Since the formula for $\frac{d^2\delta z_{,}}{dt^2}$ completely determines the perturbations due to the action of the component Z perpendicular to the plane of the instantaneous orbit, instead of determining p' and q' by an independent integration by means of the results given by the equations (162), it will be preferable to derive them directly from $\delta z_{,}$ and $\frac{d\delta z_{,}}{dt}$. The equations (161) give

$$p' = -\cos\Omega_0\,\delta\alpha - \sin\Omega_0\,\delta\beta, \qquad q' = -\sin\Omega_0\,\delta\alpha + \cos\Omega_0\,\delta\beta.$$

Substituting for $\delta\alpha$ and $\delta\beta$ their values given by (125) and (126), and putting

$$x'' = x\cos\Omega_0 + y\sin\Omega_0, \qquad y'' = -x\sin\Omega_0 + y\cos\Omega_0,$$

we obtain

$$p' = \frac{1}{k\sqrt{p(1+m)}}\left(y''\frac{d\delta z_{,}}{dt} - \delta z_{,}\frac{dy''}{dt}\right),$$
$$q' = \frac{1}{k\sqrt{p(1+m)}}\left(x''\frac{d\delta z_{,}}{dt} - \delta z_{,}\frac{dx''}{dt}\right). \qquad (163)$$

Substituting further the values

$$x'' = r\cos(\lambda_{,} - \Omega_0), \qquad y'' = r\sin(\lambda_{,} - \Omega_0),$$

and also

$$\frac{d\lambda_{,}}{dt} = \frac{k\sqrt{p(1+m)}}{r^2},$$

$$\frac{dr}{dt} = \frac{k\sqrt{1+m}}{\sqrt{p}}\, e\sin v = \frac{k\sqrt{p(1+m)}}{r} \cdot \frac{e\sin v}{1 + e\cos v},$$

we easily find, since $\lambda_{,} - v = \chi$,

$$\left.\begin{aligned} p' &= -(\cos(\lambda_{,} - \Omega_0) + e\cos(\chi - \Omega_0))\frac{\delta z_{,}}{p} + \frac{r\sin(\lambda_{,} - \Omega_0)}{k\sqrt{p(1+m)}} \cdot \frac{d\delta z_{,}}{dt}, \\ q' &= +(\sin(\lambda_{,} - \Omega_0) + e\sin(\chi - \Omega_0))\frac{\delta z_{,}}{p} + \frac{r\cos(\lambda_{,} - \Omega_0)}{k\sqrt{p(1+m)}} \cdot \frac{d\delta z_{,}}{dt}, \end{aligned}\right\} \quad (164)$$

which may be used for the determination of $\delta p'$ and $\delta q'$. These equations require, for their exact solution, that the disturbed values e, χ, and p shall be known, but it is evident that the error will be slight, especially when e is small, if we use the undisturbed values e_0, p_0, and $\chi_0 = \pi_0$. The actual values of $\lambda_{,}$ and r are obtained directly from the values of the perturbations.

When p' and q' have been found, it remains only to find $\cos i$, and $1 - \cos\eta'$, in order to be able to obtain Γ by means of the equation (159). From (153) we get

$$p'^2 + q'^2 = \sin^2 i - \sin^2 i_0 - 2q'\sin i_0,$$

and hence

$$\cos i = \sqrt{1 - p'^2 - (q' + \sin i_0)^2}, \qquad (165)$$

from which $\cos i$ may be found. The equation (157) gives

$$1 - \cos\eta' = \cos i_0(\cos i_0 + \cos i) - q'\sin i_0, \qquad (166)$$

by means of which the value of $1 - \cos\eta'$ will be obtained.

If we substitute the values of p', q', $\frac{dp'}{dt}$, and $\frac{dq'}{dt}$ given by the equations (153) and (162) in (159), it is easily reduced to

$$\Gamma = \int \frac{\delta z_{,}}{(1 - \cos\eta')\, k\sqrt{p(1+m)}} Z dt, \qquad (167)$$

which may be used for the determination of Γ. When we neglect terms of the order of the cube of the disturbing force, in finding Γ we may use p_0 in place of p and put $1 - \cos\eta' = 2\cos^2 i_0$, so that the formula becomes

$$\Gamma = \frac{1}{2\cos^2 i_0\, k\sqrt{p_0(1+m)}} \int \delta z_{,} Zdt. \qquad (168)$$

187. By means of the formulæ which have thus been derived, we may find the values of all the quantities required in the solution of the equations (155), in order to obtain the values of l and b for the disturbed motion. From r, l, and b the corresponding geocentric place may be found. The heliocentric longitude and latitude may also be determined directly by means of the equations (145), provided that Ω, σ, and i are known; and the required formulæ for the determination of these elements may be readily derived. Thus, the equations (160) give, by differentiation,

$$\frac{d\alpha}{dt} = -\sin\sigma\cos i\frac{di}{dt} - \sin i\cos\sigma\frac{d\sigma}{dt},$$
$$\frac{d\beta}{dt} = \cos\sigma\cos i\frac{di}{dt} - \sin i\sin\sigma\frac{d\sigma}{dt},$$

whence

$$\sin i\frac{d\sigma}{dt} = -\cos\sigma\frac{d\alpha}{dt} - \sin\sigma\frac{d\beta}{dt},$$
$$\cos i\frac{di}{dt} = -\sin\sigma\frac{d\alpha}{dt} + \cos\sigma\frac{d\beta}{dt}.$$

Introducing the values of $\frac{d\alpha}{dt}$ and $\frac{d\beta}{dt}$ already found into these equations, and putting

$$\sigma = \sigma_0 + \delta\sigma = \Omega_0 + \delta\sigma, \qquad i = i_0 + \delta i, \qquad \Omega = \Omega_0 + \delta\Omega,$$

we obtain

$$\left.\begin{aligned} \frac{d\delta\sigma}{dt} &= \frac{1}{k\sqrt{p(1+m)}}\cot i\sin(\lambda_{,} - \sigma)\, rZ, \\ \frac{d\delta i}{dt} &= \frac{1}{k\sqrt{p(1+m)}}\cos(\lambda_{,} - \sigma)\, rZ, \end{aligned}\right\} \qquad (169)$$

and also, since $d\sigma = \cos i\, d\Omega$,

$$\frac{d\delta\Omega}{dt} = \frac{1}{k\sqrt{p(1+m)}} \cdot \frac{\sin(\lambda_{,} - \sigma)}{\sin i} rZ, \qquad (170)$$

by means of which the variations of σ, i, and Ω due to the action of the disturbing forces, may be determined. The integral is in each case equal to zero at the initial date t_0 to which the fundamental osculating elements belong and at which the integration is to commence.

If we find i, and then $\sigma - \Omega$ from

$$\Omega - \sigma = \int \frac{\tan \frac{1}{2} i}{k \sqrt{p(1+m)}} \sin(\lambda_{,} - \sigma) \, r Z \, dt, \tag{171}$$

the true longitude in the orbit will be obtained from

$$\lambda = \lambda_{,} + \Omega - \sigma.$$

It is evident that since the expressions for $\frac{d\delta i}{dt}$, $\frac{d\delta\sigma}{dt}$, and $\frac{d\delta\Omega}{dt}$ require, for an accurate solution, that the disturbed values i, σ, and p shall be known, and require, besides, that three separate integrations shall be performed, unless the perturbations are computed only in reference to the first power of the disturbing force, in which case we use i_0, p_0, and Ω_0 in place of i, p, and σ, respectively, in the equations (169) and (170), the action of the component Z can be considered in the most advantageous manner by means of the variation of z, arising from this component alone; and even when only the perturbations of the first order are to be determined it will still be preferable to derive $\delta z_{,}$ by the indirect process from the expression for $\frac{d^2 \delta z_{,}}{dt^2}$, and to determine the heliocentric place by means of the equations (155). When we neglect the terms of the second order, these equations become

$$\begin{aligned}
\cos b \cos(l - \Omega_0) &= \cos(\lambda_{,} - \Omega_0), \\
\cos b \sin(l - \Omega_0) &= \sin(\lambda_{,} - \Omega_0) \cos i_0 - \tan i_0 \frac{\delta z_{,}}{r}, \\
\sin b &= \sin(\lambda_{,} - \Omega_0) \sin i_0 + \frac{\delta z_{,}}{r},
\end{aligned} \tag{172}$$

by means of which l and b are determined immediately from the perturbations δM, ν, and $\delta z_{,}$. The peculiar advantage of determining the effect of the action of the component Z by means of the partial variation of z, is apparent when we observe that the expressions for $\frac{d\delta\sigma}{dt}$ and $\frac{d\delta\Omega}{dt}$ involve $\sin i$ as a divisor; and in the case of orbits whose inclination is small, this divisor may be the source of a considerable amount of error.

188. The determination of the perturbations so as to include the higher powers of the masses is readily effected by means of the complete expressions for $\frac{d\delta M}{dt}$, $\frac{d^2\nu}{dt^2}$, and $\frac{d^2\delta z_{,}}{dt^2}$, when the correct values of R, S, Z, i, and p are known. The corrected values of i and p—

which are required only in the case of δz,—may be easily estimated with sufficient accuracy, since we require only $\cos i$, while $\sqrt{p}$ appears as the divisor of a term whose numerical value is generally insignificant. To obtain the actual values of R, S, and Z, the corrections to be applied to N, N', and I must first be determined by means of the formulæ (136). The values of $\delta i'$ and $\delta \Omega'$ will be found by means of the data furnished by the tables of the motion of the disturbing body, and the corresponding corrections for N, N', and I having been found by means of the terms of (136) involving di' and $d\Omega'$, there remain the corrections due to δi and $\delta \Omega$ to be applied. These may be found in terms of the quantities p' and q' already introduced. Thus, the equations

$$dp' = \cos i \sin(\sigma - \Omega_0)\, di + \sin i \cos(\sigma - \Omega_0)\, d\sigma,$$
$$dq' = \cos i \cos(\sigma - \Omega_0)\, di - \sin i \sin(\sigma - \Omega_0)\, d\sigma,$$

give

$$\cos i\, di = \sin(\sigma - \Omega_0)\, dp' + \cos(\sigma - \Omega_0)\, dq',$$
$$\sin i\, d\sigma = \cos(\sigma - \Omega_0)\, dp' - \sin(\sigma - \Omega_0)\, dq'.$$

The equations (136) give, observing that $d\sigma = \cos i\, d\Omega$,

$$dI = -\cos N\, di - \tan i \sin N\, d\sigma,$$
$$dN' = +\frac{\sin N}{\sin I}\, di - \frac{\tan i}{\sin I} \cos N\, d\sigma,$$

and, substituting the preceding values of di and $d\sigma$, these become

$$dI = -\frac{\sin(N + \sigma - \Omega_0)}{\cos i}\, dp' - \frac{\cos(N + \sigma - \Omega_0)}{\cos i}\, dq',$$
$$dN' = -\frac{\cos(N + \sigma - \Omega_0)}{\sin I \cos i}\, dp' + \frac{\sin(N + \sigma - \Omega_0)}{\sin I \cos i}\, dq'.$$

If we neglect the perturbations of the third order, these equations give

$$\delta I = -\sin N \frac{p'}{\cos i_0} - \cos N \frac{q'}{\cos i_0},$$
$$\delta N' = -\operatorname{cosec} I \left(\cos N \frac{p'}{\cos i_0} - \sin N \frac{q'}{\cos i_0} \right), \qquad (173)$$

by means of which δI and δN may be determined, p' and q' being found by means of the equations (164), using e_0, π_0, and p_0 in place of e, χ, and p. The results for δI and $\delta N'$ obtained from (173) being applied to the values of I' and N' as already corrected on account of $\delta i'$ and $\delta \Omega'$, give the required values of these quantities.

When we consider only di and $d\Omega$, since

$$\sin i' \cos N' = \cos i \sin I + \sin i \cos I \cos N,$$

we easily find

$$\delta N = \cos I \,\delta N' - \delta\sigma, \tag{174}$$

and if we add the quantity $\cos I\,\delta N'$ to the value of N already corrected on account of $\delta i'$ and $\delta\Omega'$, and denote the result by $N_{,}$, the required value of N will be $N_{,} - \delta\sigma$. Then, according to (131), we may compute $w' + \delta\sigma$ and β' by means of the formulæ

$$\begin{aligned} u_0' &= u' - N', \\ \tan\big((w' + \delta\sigma) - N_{,}\big) &= \tan u_0' \cos I, \\ \tan \beta' &= \tan I \sin\big((w' + \delta\sigma) - N_{,}\big), \end{aligned} \tag{175}$$

using the values of N' and I as finally corrected. We have, further, according to (135),

$$w + \delta\sigma = v_{,} + \pi_0 - \Omega_0,$$

by means of which we may compute the value of $w + \delta\sigma$; then the value of $w' - w$ required in the equations (132), and also in finding the value of ρ, will be given by

$$w' - w = (w' + \delta\sigma) - (w + \delta\sigma),$$

and the forces R, S, and Z may be accurately determined.

By thus determining the correct values of R, S, and Z from date to date, the perturbations δM, ν, and δz, may be determined in reference to the higher powers of the disturbing forces according to the process already explained. The only difficulty to be encountered is that which arises from the quantities Γ, p', and q', required in the determination of the heliocentric place of the disturbed body by means of the equations (155). If an exact ephemeris for a short period is required, by means of the complete perturbations we may determine new osculating elements, and by means of these the required heliocentric or geocentric places.

189. EXAMPLE.—We will now illustrate the application of the formulæ for the determination of the perturbations δM, ν, and δz, by a numerical example; and for this purpose let it be required to determine the perturbations of *Eurynome* (79) arising from the action of *Jupiter* from 1864 Jan. 1.0 to 1865 Jan. 15.0, Berlin mean

time, the fundamental osculating elements being those given in Art. 166.

In the first place, by means of the formulæ (130), using the values

$$\Omega = 206^\circ\ 39'\ 5''.7, \qquad i = 4^\circ\ 36'\ 52''.1,$$
$$\Omega' = 98\ \ 58\ \ 22\ .7, \qquad i' = 1\ \ 18\ \ 40\ .5,$$

which refer to the ecliptic and mean equinox of 1860.0, we obtain

$$N = 194^\circ\ 0'\ 49''.9, \qquad N' = 301^\circ\ 38'\ 31''.7, \qquad I = 5^\circ\ 9'\ 56''.4.$$

Then, by means of the data furnished by the *Tables of Jupiter*, we find the values of u', the argument of the latitude of *Jupiter* in reference to the ecliptic of 1860.0, and from the equations (131) we derive w' and β'. The values of r' are given by the *Tables of Jupiter*, and the values of r_0 and v_0 are found from the elements given in Art. 166. The results thus obtained are the following:—

Berlin Mean Time.	$\log r_0$	v_0	$\log r'$	w'	β'
1863 Dec. 12.0,	0.294084	354° 26′ 18″.0	0.73425	14° 18′ 54″.6	−0° 1′ 38″.1
1864 Jan. 21.0,	0.294837	10 2 45 .7	0.73368	17 21 44 .2	0 18 9 .1
March 1.0,	0.300674	25 24 59 .4	0.73305	20 25 5 .2	0 34 39 .9
April 10.0,	0.310864	40 13 31 .8	0.73237	23 28 59 .8	0 51 7 .6
May 20.0,	0.324298	54 14 41 .4	0.73164	26 33 32 .1	1 7 29 .7
June 29.0,	0.339745	67 21 23 .5	0.73086	29 38 44 .8	1 23 43 .5
Aug. 8.0,	0.356101	79 32 18 .1	0.73003	32 44 41 .2	1 39 46 .3
Sept. 17.0,	0.372469	90 49 57 .6	0.72915	35 51 24 .6	1 55 35 .2
Oct. 27.0,	0.388214	101 19 9 .8	0.72823	38 58 57 .5	2 11 7 .5
Dec. 6.0,	0.402894	111 5 42 .2	0.72726	42 7 23 .3	2 26 20 .3
1865 Jan. 15.0,	0.416240	120 15 32 .6	0.72625	45 16 43 .9	−2 41 10 .6

The value of w for each date is now found from

$$w = v_0 + \pi_0 - \Omega_0 = v_0 + 197^\circ\ 38'\ 6''.5,$$

and the components of the disturbing force are determined by means of the formulæ (132), ρ being found from (133) or (134), and h from (70). The adopted value of the mass of *Jupiter* is

$$m' = \frac{1}{1047.879},$$

and the results for the components R, S, and Z are expressed in units of the seventh decimal place. The factor ω^2 is introduced for convenience in the integration, ω being the interval in days between the successive dates for which the forces are to be determined. Thus we obtain the following results:—

Date.			$\omega^2 R$	$\omega^2 S r_0$	$\omega^2 Z \cos i_0$	$\omega\int S r_0 dt$
1863	Dec.	12.0,	+ 70.82	+ 7.16	+ 0.04	+ 1.37
1864	Jan.	21.0,	68.95	− 32.76	0.49	− 11.45
	March	1.0,	61.16	70.38	0.92	63.32
	April	10.0,	48.57	102.91	1.32	150.48
	May	20.0,	32.77	128.34	1.68	266.75
	June	29.0,	+ 15.41	145.39	1.96	404.35
	Aug.	8.0,	− 2.19	153.44	2.17	554.54
	Sept.	17.0,	19.12	152.41	2.29	708.21
	Oct.	27.0,	34.81	142.50	2.25	856.39
	Dec.	6.0,	48.95	124.04	2.09	990.36
1865	Jan.	15.0,	− 61.45	− 97.36	+ 1.75	− 1101.73

The single integration to find $\omega\int S r_0 dt$ is effected by means of the formula (32).

The equations for the determination of the required differential coefficients are

$$\omega\frac{d\delta M}{dt} = \mu_0\left(\frac{1}{k\sqrt{p_0}}\,\omega\int S r_0 dt - 2\omega\nu\right),$$

$$\omega^2\frac{d^2\nu}{dt^2} = \frac{\omega^2 R}{r_0} + \frac{2\omega k^2}{r_0^3}\cdot\frac{1}{k\sqrt{p_0}}\,\omega\int S r_0 dt - \frac{e_0 \sin v_0}{p_0}\,\omega^2 S - \frac{\omega^2 k^2}{r_0^3}\,\nu,$$

$$\omega^2\frac{d^2\delta z_{,}}{dt^2} = \omega^2 Z \cos i_0 - \frac{\omega^2 k^2}{r_0^3}\,\delta z_{,}.$$

Substituting in these the results already obtained, and also

$$\log\mu_0 = 2.967809, \qquad \log p_0 = 0.371237, \qquad \log e_0 = 9.290776,$$

we obtain first, by an indirect process, as illustrated in the case of the direct determination of the perturbations of the rectangular co-ordinates, the values of $\omega^2\frac{d^2\nu}{dt^2}$ and $\omega^2\frac{d^2\delta z_{,}}{dt^2}$, and then, having found ν, $\omega\frac{d\delta M}{dt}$ is given directly by the first of these equations. The integration of the results thus derived, by the formulæ for mechanical quadrature, furnishes the required values of ν, δM, and $\delta z_{,}$. The calculation of the indirect terms in the determination of ν and $\delta z_{,}$, there being but one such term in each case, is, on account of the smallness of the coefficient, effected with very great facility.

The final results are the following:—

Date.	$\omega \frac{d\delta M}{dt}$	$\omega^2 \frac{d^2\nu}{dt^2}$	$\omega^2 \frac{d^2\delta z_{,}}{dt^2}$	δM	ν	$\delta z_{,}$
1863 Dec. 12.0,	− 0″.028	+ 36.16	+ 0.04	+ 0″.01	+ 4.41	+ 0.02
1864 Jan. 21.0,	0 .072	33.61	0.49	− 0 .01	4.31	0.04
March 1.0,	0 .499	22.55	0.89	0 .27	37.11	0.54
April 10.0,	1 .213	+ 5.58	1.21	1 .11	91.96	1.93
May 20.0,	2 .070	− 13.52	1.45	2 .75	152.22	4.52
June 29.0,	2 .902	31.59	1.53	5 .24	199.05	8.54
Aug. 8.0,	3 .546	46.65	1.60	8 .49	214.54	14.10
Sept. 17.0,	3 .858	57.88	1.52	12 .22	183.69	21.24
Oct. 27.0,	3 .723	65.19	1.28	16 .05	+ 95.29	29.90
Dec. 6.0,	3 .056	68.83	0.92	19 .49	− 58.00	39.82
1865 Jan. 15.0,	− 1 .800	− 69.19	+ 0.40	− 21 .97	− 279.84	+ 50.64

Since, during the period included by these results, the perturbations of the second order are insensible, we have, for the perturbations of *Eurynome* arising from the action of Jupiter from 1864 Jan. 1.0 to 1865 Jan. 15.0,

$$\delta M = -21''.97, \qquad \nu = -0.00002798, \qquad \delta z_{,} = +0.00000506.$$

It is to be observed that $\delta z_{,}$ is not the complete variation of the co-ordinate z, perpendicular to the ecliptic, but only that part of this variation which is due to the action of the component Z alone; and hence the results for $\delta z_{,}$ differ from the complete values obtained when we compute directly the variations of the rectangular co-ordinates.

Let us now determine the heliocentric longitude and latitude for 1865 Jan. 15.0, Berlin mean time, including the perturbations thus derived. From the equations

$$M_{,} = M_0 + \mu_0 (t - t_0) + \delta M,$$
$$E_{,} - e_0 \sin E_{,} = M_{,},$$
$$r_{,} = a_0 (1 - e_0 \cos E_{,}),$$
$$\sin \tfrac{1}{2} (v_{,} - E_{,}) = \sin \tfrac{1}{2} \varphi_0 \sin E_{,} \sqrt{\frac{a_0}{r_{,}}},$$
$$\lambda_{,} = v_{,} + \pi_0, \qquad r = r_{,} (1 + \nu),$$

we obtain

$$M_{,} = 99° \, 29' \, 35''.51, \qquad E_{,} = 110° \, 0' \, 33''.75,$$
$$\log r_{,} = 0.4162304, \qquad v_{,} = 120 \;\; 15 \;\; 13 .80,$$
$$\log r = 0.4162183, \qquad \lambda_{,} = 164 \;\; 32 \;\; 25 .97.$$

The calculation of the values of $r_{,}$ and $v_{,}$ from the values of $M_{,}$, a_0, and e_0, may be effected by means of the various formulæ for the determination of the radius-vector and true anomaly from given elements. If we substitute these results for $\lambda_{,}$, r, and δz, in the equations (172), we get

$$l = 164^\circ\ 37'\ 59''.05, \qquad b = -3^\circ\ 5'\ 32''.54,$$

which are referred to the ecliptic and mean equinox of 1860.0, and from these we may derive the geocentric place of the disturbed body. If the place of the body is required in reference to the equinox and ecliptic of any other date, it is only necessary to reduce the elements π_0, Ω_0, and i_0 to the equinox and ecliptic of that date; and then, having computed λ, and r, we obtain by means of the equations (172) the required values of l and b. In the determination of the perturbations it will be convenient to adopt a fixed equinox and ecliptic throughout the calculation; and afterwards, when the heliocentric or geocentric places are determined, the proper corrections for precession and nutation may be applied.

In order to compare the results obtained from the perturbations δM, ν, and δz, with those derived by the method of the variation of rectangular co-ordinates, we have, for the date 1865 Jan. 15.0,

$$x_0 = -2.5107584, \qquad y_0 = +0.6897713, \qquad z_0 = -0.1406590;$$

and for the perturbations of these co-ordinates we have found

$$\delta x = +0.0001773, \qquad \delta y = +0.0001992, \qquad \delta z = -0.0000028.$$

Hence we derive

$$x = -2.5105811, \qquad y = +0.6899705, \qquad z = -0.1406618,$$

and from these the corresponding polar co-ordinates, namely,

$$\log r = 0.4162182, \qquad l = 164^\circ\ 37'\ 59''.05, \qquad b = -3^\circ\ 5'\ 32''.54,$$

from which it appears that the agreement of the results obtained by the two methods is complete.

190. When the perturbations become so large that the terms of the second order must be retained, the approximate values which may be obtained for several intervals in advance by extending the columns of differences, will serve to enable us to consider the neglected terms partially or even completely, and thus derive the complete perturbations for a very long period. But on account of the increasing difficulties which present themselves, arising both from the consideration

of the perturbations due to the action of the component Z in computing the place of the body, and from the magnitude of the numerical values of the perturbations, it will be advantageous to determine, from time to time, new osculating elements corresponding to the values of the perturbations for any particular epoch, and thus commencing the integrals again with the value zero, only the terms of the first order will at first be considered, and the indirect part of the calculation will, on account of the smallness of the terms, be effected with great facility. The mode of effecting the calculation when the higher powers of the masses are taken into account has already been explained, and it will present no difficulty beyond that which is inseparably connected with the problem. The determination of Γ, p', and q' may be effected from the results for $\frac{d\Gamma}{dt}$, $\frac{dp'}{dt}$, and $\frac{dq'}{dt}$ by means of the formulæ for integration by mechanical quadrature, as already illustrated, or we may find Γ by a direct integration, and the values of p' and q' by means of the equations (164), $\frac{d\delta z_{\prime}}{dt}$ being found from $\frac{d^2\delta z_{\prime}}{dt^2}$ by a single integration. The other quantities required for the complete solution of the equations for the perturbations will be obtained according to the directions which have been given; and in the numerical application of the formulæ, particular attention should be given to the homogeneity of the several terms, especially since, for convenience, we express some of the quantities in units of the seventh decimal place, and others in seconds of arc.

The magnitude of the perturbations will at length be such that, however completely the terms due to the squares and higher powers of the disturbing forces may be considered, the requirements of the numerical process will render it necessary to determine new osculating elements; and we therefore proceed to develop the formulæ for this purpose.

191. The single integration of the values of $\omega^2\frac{d^2\nu}{dt^2}$ and $\omega^2\frac{d^2\delta z_{\prime}}{dt^2}$ will give the values of $\omega\frac{d\nu}{dt}$ and $\omega\frac{d\delta z_{\prime}}{dt}$, and hence those of $\frac{d\nu}{dt}$ and $\frac{d\delta z_{\prime}}{dt}$, which, in connection with $\frac{d\delta M}{dt}$, are required in the determination of the new system of osculating elements. Since $r^2\frac{dv_{\prime}}{dt}$ represents double the areal velocity in the disturbed orbit, we have

$$\frac{dv_{,}}{dt}=\frac{k\sqrt{p\,(1+m)}}{r^2}.$$

The equation (109) gives

$$\frac{dv_{,}}{dt}=\frac{k\sqrt{p_0\,(1+m)}}{r_{,}^2}\left(1+\frac{1}{\mu_0}\cdot\frac{d\delta M}{dt}\right).$$

Hence, since $r=r_{,}\,(1+\nu)$, we obtain

$$p=p_0\left(1+\frac{1}{\mu_0}\cdot\frac{d\delta M}{dt}\right)^2(1+\nu)^4, \tag{176}$$

by means of which we may derive p. This formula will furnish at once the value of p, which appears in the complete equation for $\frac{d^2\delta z_{,}}{dt^2}$, and also in the equations (164); and the value of $\cos i$ may be determined by means of (165).

In the disturbed orbit we have

$$\frac{dr}{dt}=\frac{k\sqrt{1+m}}{\sqrt{p}}\,e\sin v,$$

and the equations (108) and (111) give

$$\frac{dr}{dt}=\frac{k\sqrt{1+m}}{\sqrt{p_0}}e_0\sin v_{,}\left(1+\frac{1}{\mu_0}\cdot\frac{d\delta M}{dt}\right)(1+\nu)+r_{,}\frac{d\nu}{dt}.$$

Therefore we obtain

$$\sqrt{p_0}\,e\sin v=\sqrt{p}\;e_0\sin v_{,}\left(1+\frac{1}{\mu_0}\cdot\frac{d\delta M}{dt}\right)(1+\nu)+\frac{r_{,}\sqrt{pp_0}}{k\sqrt{1+m}}\cdot\frac{d\nu}{dt},$$

which, by means of (176), becomes

$$e\sin v=e_0\sin v_{,}\left(1+\frac{1}{\mu_0}\cdot\frac{d\delta M}{dt}\right)^2(1+\nu)^3+\frac{r_{,}\sqrt{p}}{k\sqrt{1+m}}\cdot\frac{d\nu}{dt}. \tag{177}$$

The relation between r and $r_{,}$ gives

$$\frac{p}{1+e\cos v}=\frac{p_0}{1+e_0\cos v_{,}}(1+\nu),$$

and, substituting in this the value of p already found, we get

$$e\cos v=(1+e_0\cos v_{,})\left(1+\frac{1}{\mu_0}\cdot\frac{d\delta M}{dt}\right)^2(1+\nu)^3-1. \tag{178}$$

Let us now put

$$\alpha = \left(1 + \frac{1}{\mu_0} \cdot \frac{d\delta M}{dt}\right)^2 (1 + \nu)^3 - 1,$$

$$\beta = \frac{r_{\prime} \sqrt{p}}{k\sqrt{1+m}} \cdot \frac{d\nu}{dt}, \tag{179}$$

α and β being small quantities of the order of the disturbing force, and the equations (177) and (178) become

$$e \sin v = e_0 \sin v_{\prime} + \alpha e_0 \sin v_{\prime} + \beta,$$
$$e \cos v = e_0 \cos v_{\prime} + \alpha e_0 \cos v_{\prime} + \alpha.$$

These equations give, observing that $r_{\prime} (\cos v_{\prime} + e_0) = p_0 \cos E_{\prime}$,

$$e \sin (v_{\prime} - v) = \alpha \sin v_{\prime} - \beta \cos v_{\prime},$$
$$e \cos (v_{\prime} - v) = e_0 + \frac{\alpha p_0}{r_{\prime}} \cos E_{\prime} + \beta \sin v_{\prime}, \tag{180}$$

from which e, $v_{\prime} - v$, and v may be found; and thus, since

$$\chi = \pi_0 + (v_{\prime} - v), \tag{181}$$

we obtain the values of the only remaining unknown quantities in the second members of the equations (164). The determination of p' and q' may now be rigorously effected, and the corresponding value of $\cos i$ being found from (165), $\frac{dp'}{dt}$ and $\frac{dq'}{dt}$ will be given by (162). Then, having found also $1 - \cos \eta'$ by means of (166), Γ may be determined rigorously by the equation (159), and not only the complete values of the perturbations in reference to all powers of the masses, but also the corresponding heliocentric or geocentric places of the body, may be found.

If we put

$$\gamma' = \alpha \sin v_{\prime} - \beta \cos v_{\prime},$$
$$\delta' = \frac{\alpha p_0}{r_{\prime}} \cos E_{\prime} + \beta \sin v_{\prime}, \tag{182}$$

and neglect terms of the third order, the equations (180) give

$$e = e_0 + \delta' + \frac{\gamma'^2}{2e_0},$$
$$v_{\prime} - v = \frac{\gamma'}{e_0} s - \frac{\gamma' \delta'}{e_0^2} s, \tag{183}$$

in which $s = 206264''.8$. These equations are convenient for the determination of e and $v, -v$, and hence χ by means of (181), when the neglected terms are insensible.

The values of p, e, and v having been found, we have

$$\sin\varphi = e, \qquad a = p\sec^2\varphi, \qquad \mu = \frac{k\sqrt{1+m}}{a^{\frac{3}{2}}}, \tag{184}$$
$$\tan\tfrac{1}{2}E = \tan(45^\circ - \tfrac{1}{2}\varphi)\tan\tfrac{1}{2}v, \qquad M = E - e\sin E,$$

from which to find the elements φ, a, μ, and M. The mean anomaly thus found belongs to the date t, and it may be reduced to any other epoch denoted by t_0 by adding to it the quantity $\mu(t_0 - t)$. When we neglect the terms of the third order, we have

$$\varphi - \varphi_0 = \frac{\sin\varphi - \sin\varphi_0}{\cos\varphi_0 - \frac{1}{2}(\varphi - \varphi_0)\sin\varphi_0},$$

and if we substitute for $\sin\varphi - \sin\varphi_0 = e - e_0$ the value given by the first of equations (183), the result is

$$\varphi - \varphi_0 = \frac{2\delta'\sin\varphi_0 + \gamma'^2}{2\sin\varphi_0\cos\varphi_0 - \delta'\sin\varphi_0\tan\varphi_0},$$

from which we get

$$\varphi = \varphi_0 + \frac{\delta'}{\cos\varphi_0}s + \frac{\delta'^2\sin\varphi_0}{2\cos^3\varphi_0}s + \frac{\gamma'^2}{2\sin\varphi_0\cos\varphi_0}s, \tag{185}$$

by means of which φ may be found directly, terms of the third order being neglected.

In the case of the orbits of comets for which e differs but little from unity, instead of δM we compute by means of the formula (142) the value of δT, and since we have

$$\frac{d\delta T}{dt} = -\frac{1}{\mu_0}\cdot\frac{d\delta M}{dt},$$

the equation for p becomes

$$p = p_0\left(1 - \frac{d\delta T}{dt}\right)^2(1+\nu)^4; \tag{186}$$

and for α we have

$$\alpha = \left(1 - \frac{d\delta T}{dt}\right)^2(1+\nu)^3 - 1. \tag{187}$$

Then e, v, and q will be found by means of the equations

$$e \sin (v_{\prime} - v) = \alpha \sin v_{\prime} - \beta \cos v_{\prime\prime},$$
$$e \cos (v_{\prime} - v) = e_0 + \alpha (\cos v_{\prime} + e_0) + \beta \sin v_{\prime\prime}, \qquad (188)$$
$$q = \frac{p}{1+e},$$

and the time of perihelion passage will be derived from e and v by means of Table IX. or Table X.

There remain yet to be found the elements σ, Ω, and i, which determine the position of the plane of the disturbed orbit in space. The values of p' and q' will be found from the equations (164), and Γ, whenever it may be required, will be determined as already explained. Then we shall have

$$\sin i \sin (\sigma - \Omega_0) = p', \qquad (189)$$
$$\sin i \cos (\sigma - \Omega_0) = q' + \sin i_0,$$

from which to find i and σ. When we neglect the terms of the third order, these equations give

$$\sin i - \sin i_0 = q' + \frac{p'q'}{\sin i_0},$$

and hence

$$\sigma = \Omega_0 + \frac{p'}{\sin i_0} s - \frac{p'q'}{\sin^2 i_0} s,$$
$$i = i_0 + \frac{q'}{\cos i_0} s + \frac{q'^2 \sin i_0}{2 \cos^3 i_0} s + \frac{p'^2}{2 \sin i_0 \cos i_0} s, \qquad (190)$$

in which $s = 206264''.8$. The auxiliary spherical triangle which we have employed in the derivation of the equations (155) gives directly

$$\frac{\cos \frac{1}{2} (i + i_0)}{\cos \frac{1}{2} (i - i_0)} = \frac{\tan \frac{1}{2} (\sigma - \Omega_0)}{\tan \frac{1}{2} (\Omega - h + h_0 - \Omega_0)},$$

and since $h - h_0 = \Gamma$, we have

$$\tan \tfrac{1}{2} (\Omega - \Omega_0 - \Gamma) = \frac{\cos \frac{1}{2} (i - i_0)}{\cos \frac{1}{2} (i + i_0)} \tan \tfrac{1}{2} (\sigma - \Omega_0), \qquad (191)$$

by means of which the value of Ω may be found. This equation gives, when we neglect terms of the third order,

$$\Omega = \Omega_0 + \Gamma + \frac{\sigma - \Omega_0}{\cos i_0} + \frac{\sin i_0}{2 \cos^2 i_0} (i - i_0)(\sigma - \Omega_0). \qquad (192)$$

Substituting in this the values of $\sigma - \Omega_0$ and $i - i_0$ given by (190), we get

$$\Omega = \Omega_0 + \frac{p'}{\sin i_0 \cos i_0} s - \frac{1 - \frac{3}{2} \sin^2 i_0}{\sin^2 i_0 \cos^3 i_0} p'q's + \Gamma, \qquad (193)$$

Γ being expressed in seconds of arc. Finally, for the longitude of the perihelion, we have

$$\pi = \chi + \Omega - \sigma, \tag{194}$$

and the elements of the instantaneous orbit are completely determined. When we neglect terms of the third order, this equation, substituting the values given by (190) and (192), becomes

$$\pi = \chi + \frac{\tan \frac{1}{2} i_0}{\cos i_0} p's + \frac{\tan^2 \frac{1}{2} i_0 (1 + 2 \cos i_0)}{2 \cos^3 i_0} p'q's + \Gamma. \tag{195}$$

It should also be observed that the inclination i which appears in these formulæ is supposed to be susceptible of any value from 0° to 180°, and hence when i exceeds 90° and the elements are given in accordance with the distinction of retrograde motion, they are to be changed to the general form by using $180° - i$ instead of i, and $2\Omega - \pi$ instead of π.

The accuracy of the numerical process may be checked by computing the heliocentric place of the body for the date to which the new elements belong by means of these elements, and comparing the results with those obtained directly by means of the equations (155). We may remark, also, that when the inclination does not differ much from 90°, the reduction of the longitudes to the fundamental plane becomes uncertain, and Γ may be very large, and hence, instead of the ecliptic, the equator must be taken as the fundamental plane to which the elements and the longitudes are referred.

192. Although, by means of the formulæ which have been given, the complete perturbations may be determined for a very long period of time, using constantly the same osculating elements, yet, on account of the ease with which new elements may be found from δM, ν, $\delta z_{,}$, $\frac{d\delta M}{dt}$, $\frac{d\nu}{dt}$, and $\frac{d\delta z_{,}}{dt}$, and on account of the facility afforded in the calculation of the indirect terms in the equations for the differential coefficients so long as the values of the perturbations are small, it is evident that the most advantageous process will be to compute δM, ν, and $\delta z_{,}$ only with respect to the first power of the disturbing force, and determine new osculating elements whenever the terms of the second order must be considered. Then the integration will again commence with zero, and will be continued until, on account of the terms of the second order, another change of the elements is required. The frequency of this transformation will necessarily de-

pend on the magnitude of the disturbing force; and if the disturbed body is so near the disturbing body that a very frequent change of the elements becomes necessary, it may be more convenient either to include the terms of the second order directly in the computation of the values of δM, ν, and $\delta z_{,}$, or to adopt one of the other methods which have been given for the determination of the perturbations of a heavenly body. In the case of the asteroid planets, the consideration of the terms of the second order in this manner will only require a change of the osculating elements after an interval of several years, and whenever this transformation shall be required, the equations for φ, i, ☊, and π, in which the terms of the third order are neglected, may be employed. It should be observed, however, that the perturbations of some of the elements are much greater than the perturbations of the co-ordinates, and hence when terms depending on the squares and higher powers of the masses have been neglected in the computation of these perturbations, it may still be necessary to include the values of the terms of the second order in the incomplete equations referred to. No general criterion can be given as to the time at which a change of the osculating elements will be required; but when, on account of the magnitude of the values of δM, ν, and $\delta z_{,}$, it appears probable that the perturbations of the second order ought to be included in the results, by computing a single place, taking into account the neglected terms, we may at once determine whether such is the case and whether new elements are required.

193. We have already found the expressions for the variations of ☊ and i due to the action of the disturbing forces, and we shall now consider those for the variation of the other elements of the orbit directly. Let x, y, z be the co-ordinates of the body at any given time referred to any fixed system of co-ordinates. These will be known functions of the six elements of the orbit and of the time. If the body were not subject to the action of the disturbing forces, these six elements would be rigorously constant, and the co-ordinates would vary only with the time; but on account of the action of these forces the elements must be regarded as continuously varying in order that the relation between the elements and the co-ordinates at any instant shall be expressed by equations of the same form as in the case of the undisturbed motion. The co-ordinates will, therefore, in the disturbed motion, be subject to two distinct variations: that which results from considering the time alone to vary, and that which

results from the variation of the elements themselves. Let these two kinds of partial variations be symbolized respectively by $\left(\frac{dx}{dt}\right)$ and $\left[\frac{dx}{dt}\right]$, and similarly in the case of the other co-ordinates; then will the total variations be given by

$$\frac{dx}{dt}=\left(\frac{dx}{dt}\right)+\left[\frac{dx}{dt}\right], \qquad \frac{dy}{dt}=\left(\frac{dy}{dt}\right)+\left[\frac{dy}{dt}\right],$$
$$\frac{dz}{dt}=\left(\frac{dz}{dt}\right)+\left[\frac{dz}{dt}\right]. \tag{196}$$

But if we differentiate twice in succession the equations which express the values of x, y, and z as functions of the elements and of the time, regarding both the elements and the time as variable, the substitution of the results in the general equations for the motion of the disturbed body will furnish three equations for the determination of the variations of the elements. There are, however, six unknown quantities to be determined; and hence we may assign arbitrarily three other equations of condition. The supposition which affords the required facility in the solution of the problem is that

$$\left[\frac{dx}{dt}\right]=0, \qquad \left[\frac{dy}{dt}\right]=0, \qquad \left[\frac{dz}{dt}\right]=0, \tag{197}$$

and hence that

$$\frac{dx}{dt}=\left(\frac{dx}{dt}\right), \qquad \frac{dy}{dt}=\left(\frac{dy}{dt}\right), \qquad \frac{dz}{dt}=\left(\frac{dz}{dt}\right).$$

It thus appears that in order that the integrals of the equations (1) shall be of the same form as those of the equations (3),—the arbitrary constants of integration which result from the integration of the latter being regarded as variable when the disturbing forces are considered,—the first differential coefficients of the co-ordinates with respect to the time have the same form in the disturbed and undisturbed orbits. But since $\frac{dx}{dt}$, $\frac{dy}{dt}$, and $\frac{dz}{dt}$ are the velocities of the disturbed body in directions parallel to the co-ordinate axes respectively, it follows that during the element of time dt the velocity of the body must be regarded as constant, and as receiving an increment only at the end of this instant. The equations (197) show also that if we differentiate any co-ordinate, rectangular or polar, referred to a fixed plane and measured from a fixed origin, with respect to the elements alone considered as variable, the first differential coefficient must be put equal to zero, and this enables us at once to effect the solution of the problem under consideration. It is to be observed, further, that the functions whose first differential coefficients with respect to the time when only the elements are regarded as variable are thus put equal to zero, must not involve directly the motion of the disturbed body, since the second differential coefficients of the coordinates have not the same form in the case of the disturbed motion as in that of the undisturbed motion.

194. If we suppose the disturbing force to be resolved into three components, namely, R in the direction of the disturbed radius-vector, S in a direction perpendicular to the radius-vector and in the plane of disturbed orbit, positive in the direction of the motion, and Z perpendicular to the plane of the instantaneous orbit, the latter will only vary ☊ and i and the longitude of the perihelion so far as it is affected by the change of the place of the node, while the forces R and S will cause the elements M, π, e, and a to vary without affecting ☊ and i.

Let us now differentiate the equation

$$V^2 = k^2 (1+m)\left(\frac{2}{r} - \frac{1}{a}\right),$$

regarding the elements as variable, and we get

$$-\frac{2}{r^2}\left[\frac{dr}{dt}\right] = -\frac{1}{a^2}\cdot\frac{da}{dt} + \frac{2V}{k^2(1+m)}\cdot\frac{dV}{dt} = 0,$$

or

$$\frac{da}{dt} = \frac{2a^2 V}{k^2(1+m)}\cdot\frac{dV}{dt}.$$

The differential coefficient $\frac{dV}{dt}$ is here the increment of the accelerating force, in the direction of the tangent to the orbit at the given point, due to the action of the disturbing force; and if we designate the angle which the tangent makes with the prolongation of the radius-vector by ψ_0, we shall have

$$\frac{dV}{dt} = R\cos\psi_0 + S\sin\psi_0.$$

Substituting this value in the preceding equation, we obtain

$$\frac{da}{dt}=\frac{2a^2}{k^2(1+m)}(RV\cos\psi_0+SV\sin\psi_0).$$

But we have, according to the equations $(50)_6$,

$$V\cos\psi_0=\left(\frac{dr}{dt}\right)=\frac{k\sqrt{1+m}}{\sqrt{p}}e\sin v,$$

$$V\sin\psi_0=r\left(\frac{dv}{dt}\right)=\frac{k\sqrt{p(1+m)}}{r},$$

in which v denotes the true anomaly in the instantaneous orbit; and hence there results

$$\frac{da}{dt}=\frac{2a^2}{k\sqrt{p(1+m)}}(e\sin vR+\frac{p}{r}S), \tag{198}$$

by means of which the variation of a may be found.

If we introduce the mean daily motion μ, we shall have

$$\frac{d\mu}{dt}=-\frac{\frac{3}{2}\mu}{a}\cdot\frac{da}{dt}, \tag{199}$$

and hence

$$\frac{d\mu}{dt}=-\frac{3a\mu}{k\sqrt{p(1+m)}}(e\sin vR+\frac{p}{r}S), \tag{200}$$

for the determination of $\delta\mu$.

The first of the equations (97) gives

$$\frac{d}{dt}\left(r^2\frac{dv}{dt}\right)=Sr;$$

and hence we obtain

$$\frac{d(\sqrt{p})}{dt}=\frac{Sr}{k\sqrt{1+m}},$$

or

$$\frac{dp}{dt}=\frac{2pr'}{k\sqrt{1+m}}S. \tag{201}$$

The equation $p=a(1-e^2)$ gives

$$\frac{dp}{dt}=\frac{p}{a}\cdot\frac{da}{dt}-2ae\frac{de}{dt}.$$

Equating these values of $\frac{dp}{dt}$, and introducing the value of $\frac{da}{dt}$ already found, we get

$$\frac{de}{dt}=\frac{1}{k\sqrt{p(1+m)}}\left(p\sin vR+\frac{p}{e}\left(\frac{p}{r}-\frac{r}{a}\right)S\right), \tag{202}$$

and since

$$\frac{p}{r} = 1 + e\cos v, \qquad \frac{r}{a} = 1 - e\cos E,$$

E being the eccentric anomaly in the instantaneous orbit, this becomes

$$\frac{de}{dt} = \frac{1}{k\sqrt{p(1+m)}}\left(p\sin vR + p(\cos v + \cos E)S\right), \qquad (203)$$

which will give the variation of e. If we introduce the angle of eccentricity φ, we shall have

$$\frac{de}{dt} = \cos\varphi\frac{d\varphi}{dt}, \qquad p = a\cos^2\varphi,$$

and hence

$$\frac{d\varphi}{dt} = \frac{1}{k\sqrt{p(1+m)}}\left(a\cos\varphi\sin vR + a\cos\varphi(\cos v + \cos E)S\right). \quad (204)$$

195. When we consider only the components R and S of the disturbing force, the longitude in the orbit will be

$$\lambda_{,} = v + \chi.$$

We have, therefore,

$$\frac{p}{r} = 1 + e\cos(\lambda_{,} - \chi),$$

the differentiation of which, regarding the elements as variable, gives

$$\frac{dp}{dt} - \frac{p}{r}\left[\frac{dr}{dt}\right] = r\cos(\lambda_{,} - \chi)\frac{de}{dt} - er\sin(\lambda_{,} - \chi)\left[\frac{d\lambda_{,}}{dt}\right]$$
$$+ er\sin(\lambda_{,} - \chi)\frac{d\chi}{dt},$$

or

$$\frac{dp}{dt} = r\cos v\frac{de}{dt} + er\sin v\frac{d\chi}{dt}.$$

Therefore

$$\frac{d\chi}{dt} = \frac{1}{k\sqrt{p(1+m)}}\cdot\frac{1}{e}\left(-p\cos vR + \frac{p}{\sin v}(2 - \cos^2 v - \cos v\cos E)S\right),$$

and, since $p\cos E = r(\cos v + e)$, we have

$$p(1 - \cos v\cos E) = r\sin^2 v,$$

so that the equation becomes

$$\frac{d\chi}{dt} = \frac{1}{k\sqrt{p(1+m)}} \cdot \frac{1}{e}(-p\cos vR + (p+r)\sin vS), \quad (205)$$

from which the value of $\frac{d\chi}{dt}$ may be derived.

If we introduce the element ω, or the angular distance of the perihelion from the ascending node, it will be necessary to consider also the component Z; and, since $\omega = \chi - \sigma$, we shall have

$$\frac{d\omega}{dt} = \frac{d\chi}{dt} - \frac{d\sigma}{dt} = \frac{d\chi}{dt} - \cos i \frac{d\Omega}{dt},$$

and hence

$$\frac{d\omega}{dt} = \frac{1}{k\sqrt{p(1+m)}} \cdot \frac{1}{e}(-p\cos vR + (p+r)\sin vS) - \cos i \frac{d\Omega}{dt}. \quad (206)$$

In the case of the longitude of the perihelion, we have

$$\frac{d\pi}{dt} = \frac{d\omega}{dt} + \frac{d\Omega}{dt},$$

and therefore

$$\frac{d\pi}{dt} = \frac{1}{k\sqrt{p(1+m)}} \cdot \frac{1}{e}(-p\cos vR + (p+r)\sin vS) + 2\sin^2 \tfrac{1}{2}i \frac{d\Omega}{dt}. \quad (207)$$

The first of the equations $(15)_2$ gives

$$\left[\frac{dr}{dt}\right] = a\tan\varphi\sin v\left(\frac{dM_0}{dt} + (t-t_0)\frac{d\mu}{dt}\right) - \frac{2r}{3\mu}\cdot\frac{d\mu}{dt} - a\cos v\frac{de}{dt} = 0,$$

in which M_0 denotes the mean anomaly at the epoch, which is usually adopted as one of the elements in the case of an elliptic orbit. Substituting for $\frac{d\mu}{dt}$ and $\frac{de}{dt}$ the values already found, we get

$$\frac{dM_0}{dt} = \frac{1}{k\sqrt{p(1+m)}}\{(p\cot\varphi\cos v - 2r\cos\varphi)R - \frac{p}{\sin v}(2-\cos^2 v - \cos v\cos E)\cot\varphi S\} - (t-t_0)\frac{d\mu}{dt},$$

or

$$\frac{dM_0}{dt} = \frac{1}{k\sqrt{p(1+m)}}((p\cot\varphi\cos v - 2r\cos\varphi)R - (p+r)\cot\varphi\sin vS) - (t-t_0)\frac{d\mu}{dt}. \quad (208)$$

The equation (205) gives

$$\frac{1}{k\sqrt{p(1+m)}}(p+r)\cot\varphi\sin v S = \frac{1}{k\sqrt{p(1+m)}}p\cot\varphi\cos v R + \cos\varphi\frac{d\chi}{dt},$$

by means of which (208) reduces to

$$\frac{dM_0}{dt} = -\cos\varphi\frac{d\chi}{dt} - \frac{2r\cos\varphi}{k\sqrt{p(1+m)}}R - (t-t_0)\frac{d\mu}{dt}, \tag{209}$$

which will determine the variation of the mean anomaly at the epoch.

Since the equations for the determination of the place of the body in the case of the disturbed motion are of the same form as those for the undisturbed motion, the mean anomaly at the time t will be given by

$$M = M_0 + \delta M_0 + (t-t_0)(\mu_0 + \delta\mu),$$

in which μ_0 denotes the mean daily motion at the instant t_0. Therefore we shall have

$$M = M_0 + \int\frac{dM_0}{dt}dt + \mu_0(t-t_0) + (t-t_0)\int\frac{d\mu}{dt}dt,$$

the integrals being taken between the limits t_0 and t. The quantity

$$M_0 + \mu_0(t-t_0)$$

expresses the mean anomaly at the time t in the undisturbed orbit; and if we designate by δM the correction to be applied to this in order to obtain the mean anomaly in the disturbed orbit, so that

$$\delta M = \int_{t_0}^{t}\frac{dM}{dt}dt,$$

we shall have

$$M = M_0 + \mu_0(t-t_0) + \int\frac{dM}{dt}dt,$$

and hence

$$\int\frac{dM}{dt}dt = \int\frac{dM_0}{dt}dt + (t-t_0)\int\frac{d\mu}{dt}dt.$$

Differentiating this with respect to t, we get

$$\frac{dM}{dt} = \frac{dM_0}{dt} + (t-t_0)\frac{d\mu}{dt} + \int\frac{d\mu}{dt}dt.$$

Substituting in this the value of $\frac{dM_0}{dt}$ from (209), the result is

$$\frac{dM}{dt} = -\cos\varphi\,\frac{d\chi}{dt} - \frac{2r\cos\varphi}{k\sqrt{p(1+m)}}\,R + \int\frac{d\mu}{dt}\,dt, \qquad (210)$$

which does not involve the factor $t - t_0$ explicitly, and by means of which the mean anomaly in the disturbed orbit, at any instant t, may be found directly from that for the same instant in the undisturbed orbit.

To find the variation of the mean longitude L, we have

$$\frac{dL}{dt} = \frac{dM}{dt} + \frac{d\pi}{dt} = \frac{d\chi}{dt} + \frac{dM}{dt} + (1-\cos i)\,\frac{d\Omega}{dt},$$

and therefore

$$\frac{dL}{dt} = 2\sin^2\tfrac{1}{2}\varphi\frac{d\chi}{dt} + 2\sin^2\tfrac{1}{2}i\frac{d\Omega}{dt} - \frac{2r\cos\varphi}{k\sqrt{p(1+m)}}\,R + \int\frac{d\mu}{dt}\,dt. \qquad (211)$$

To find the variations of Ω and i, since

$$u = \lambda_{\prime} - \sigma,$$

u denoting the argument of the latitude in the disturbed orbit, we have, according to the equations (169) and (170),

$$\frac{d\Omega}{dt} = \frac{1}{k\sqrt{p(1+m)}}\cdot\frac{r\sin u}{\sin i}\,Z,$$
$$\frac{di}{dt} = \frac{1}{k\sqrt{p(1+m)}}\,r\cos u\,Z. \qquad (212)$$

The inclination i may have any value from 0° to 180°; and whenever the elements are given in accordance with the distinction of retrograde motion, they must be converted into those of the general form by taking $180° - i$ in place of the given value of i, and $2\Omega - \pi$ in place of the given value of π, before applying the formulæ which involve these elements.

196. In the case of the orbits of comets in which the eccentricity differs but little from that of the parabola, the perturbations of the perihelion distance q and of the time of perihelion passage T will be determined instead of those of the elements M and a or μ.

The equation

$$p = q(1+e)$$

gives

$$\frac{dq}{dt} = \frac{1}{1+e} \cdot \frac{dp}{dt} - \frac{q}{1+e} \cdot \frac{de}{dt},$$

and substituting in this the value of $\frac{dp}{dt}$ already found, and neglecting the mass of the comet, which is always inconsiderable, we get

$$\frac{dq}{dt} = \frac{2qr}{k\sqrt{p}} S - \frac{q}{1+e} \cdot \frac{de}{dt}, \tag{213}$$

by means of which the variation of q may be found. In the case of elliptic motion the value of $\frac{de}{dt}$ may be found by means of (202) or (203); but in the case of hyperbolic motion the equation (202) will be employed. It should be observed, also, that when the general formulæ for the ellipse are applied to the hyperbola, the semi-transverse axis a must be considered negative.

When the orbit is a parabola, the equation (202) becomes

$$\frac{de}{dt} = \frac{1}{k\sqrt{p}} (p \sin v R + 2p \cos^2 \tfrac{1}{2}v S), \tag{214}$$

and for the value of $\frac{dq}{dt}$ we have

$$\frac{dq}{dt} = \frac{2qr}{k\sqrt{p}} S - \tfrac{1}{2}q \frac{de}{dt}. \tag{215}$$

It remains now to find the formula for the variation of the time of perihelion passage. The relation between T and M_0 is expressed by

$$360° - M_0 = \mu (T - t_0),$$

the differentiation of which gives

$$-\frac{dM_0}{dt} = (T - t_0) \frac{d\mu}{dt} + \mu \frac{dT}{dt};$$

and, substituting for $\frac{dM_0}{dt}$ the value given by equation (209), we get

$$\frac{dT}{dt} = \frac{2ar}{k^2} R + \frac{a\sqrt{p}}{k} \cdot \frac{d\chi}{dt} + (t - T) \frac{1}{\mu} \cdot \frac{d\mu}{dt}.$$

Substituting further the values of $\frac{d\chi}{dt}$ and $\frac{d\mu}{dt}$ given by the equations (205) and (199), the result is

$$\frac{dT}{dt} = \frac{aR}{k^2}\left(2r - \frac{p}{e}\cos v - \frac{3k(t-T)}{\sqrt{p}}\, e\sin v\right)$$
$$+ \frac{aS}{k^2}\left(\frac{p+r}{e}\sin v - \frac{3k(t-T)}{\sqrt{p}}\cdot\frac{p}{r}\right), \tag{216}$$

which may be employed to determine the variation of T whenever the eccentricity is not very nearly equal to unity. It is obvious, however, that when a is very large this equation will not be convenient for numerical calculation, and hence a further transformation of it is desirable. Thus, if we derive the expressions for $\frac{dr}{de}$ and $\frac{dv}{de}$ from the equations $(24)_2$ and $(23)_2$, we easily obtain

$$\frac{2p}{1+e}\cdot\frac{dr}{de} = a\left(2r - \frac{p}{e}\cos v - \frac{3k(t-T)}{\sqrt{p}}\, e\sin v\right) + \frac{p^2}{e(1+e)^2}\cos v,$$

$$\frac{2p}{1+e}\, r\,\frac{dv}{de} = a\left(\frac{p+r}{e}\sin v - \frac{3k(t-T)}{\sqrt{p}}\cdot\frac{p}{r}\right) - \frac{p^2}{e(1+e)^2}\left(1+\frac{r}{p}\right)\sin v.$$

By means of these results the equation (216) is transformed into

$$\frac{dT}{dt} = \frac{qR}{k^2}\left(2\frac{dr}{de} - \frac{q}{e}\cos v\right) + \frac{qS}{k^2}\left(2r\frac{dv}{de} + \frac{q}{e}\left(1+\frac{r}{p}\right)\sin v\right), \tag{217}$$

which may be used for the determination of $\frac{dT}{dt}$, the values of $\frac{dr}{de}$ and $\frac{dv}{de}$ being found by means of the various formulæ developed in Art. 50. When a is very large, its reciprocal denoted by f may often be conveniently introduced as one of the elements, and, for the determination of the variation of f, we derive from equation (198)

$$\frac{df}{dt} = -\frac{2}{k\sqrt{p}}\left(e\sin vR + \frac{p}{r}S\right). \tag{218}$$

In the case of parabolic motion we have $e=1$, and $p=2q$; and if we substitute in (217) for $\frac{dr}{de}$ and $\frac{dv}{de}$ the values given by the equations $(33)_2$ and $(30)_2$, the result is

$$\frac{dT}{dt} = \frac{q^2}{1+\tan^2\frac{1}{2}v}\left(\frac{R}{k^2}\left(-1 + 3\tan^2\tfrac{1}{2}v + \tan^4\tfrac{1}{2}v + \tfrac{1}{5}\tan^6\tfrac{1}{2}v\right)\right.$$
$$\left. + \frac{S}{k^2}\left(4\tan\tfrac{1}{2}v - \tfrac{4}{5}\tan^5\tfrac{1}{2}v\right)\right). \tag{219}$$

197. Instead of the elements usually employed, it may be desirable, in rare and special cases, to introduce other combinations of the elements or constants which determine the circumstances of the undisturbed motion, and the relation between the new elements adopted and those for which the expressions for the differential coefficients have been given, will furnish immediately the necessary formulæ. In the case of the periodic comets, it will often be desired to determine the alteration of the periodic time arising from the action of the disturbing planets. Let us, therefore, suppose that a comet has been identified at two successive returns to the perihelion, and let τ denote the elapsed interval. The observations at each appearance of the comet, however extended they may be, will not indicate with certainty the semi-transverse axis of the orbit, and hence the periodic time. But when τ is known, by eliminating the effect of the disturbing forces, we may determine with accuracy the value of the semi-transverse axis a at each epoch, and, from this and the observed places, the other elements of the orbit according to the process already explained.

Let μ_0 be the mean daily motion at the first epoch, and we shall have

$$\mu_0\tau + \int \frac{dM}{dt}\, dt = 2\pi,$$

in which π denotes the semi-circumference of a circle whose radius is unity. Hence we obtain

$$\mu_0 = \frac{2\pi - \int \frac{dM}{dt}\, dt}{\tau}, \tag{220}$$

by means of which to determine μ_0. Then, to find the mean daily motion μ at the instant of the second return to the perihelion, we have

$$\mu = \mu_0 + \int \frac{d\mu}{dt}\, dt, \tag{221}$$

the integral being taken between the limits 0 and τ. The provisional value of the mean motion as given by the observed interval τ will be sufficiently accurate for the calculation of the variations of M and μ during this interval. The semi-transverse axis will now be derived by means of the formula

$$a = \sqrt[3]{\frac{k^2}{\mu^2}},$$

from the values of μ for the two epochs. Let τ' denote the interval which must elapse before the next succeeding perihelion passage of the comet, and we have

$$2\pi = \mu\tau' + \int \frac{dM}{dt}\,dt,$$

and consequently

$$\tau' = \frac{2\pi - \int \frac{dM}{dt}\,dt}{\mu}, \tag{222}$$

the integral being taken between the limits $t = 0$, corresponding to the beginning of the interval, and $t = \tau'$. We have, therefore,

$$\delta\tau = -\frac{1}{\mu}\int \frac{dM}{dt}\,dt, \tag{223}$$

for the change of the periodic time due to the action of the disturbing forces.

198. The calculation of the values of the components R, S, and Z of the disturbing force will be effected by means of the formulæ given in Art. 182. It will be observed, however, that not only these components of the disturbing force, but also their coefficients in the expressions for the differential coefficients, involve the variable elements, and hence the perturbations which are sought. But if we consider only the perturbations of the first order, the fundamental osculating elements may be employed in place of the actual variable elements, and whenever the perturbations of the second order have a sensible influence, the elements must be corrected for the terms of the first order already obtained. Then, commencing the integration anew at the instant to which the corrected elements belong, the calculation may be continued until another change of the elements becomes necessary. The several quantities required in the computation of the forces may also be corrected from time to time as the elements are changed.

The frequency with which the elements must be changed in order to include in the results all the terms which have a sensible influence in the determination of the place of the disturbed body, will depend entirely on the circumstances of each particular case. In the case of the asteroid planets this change will generally be required only after an interval of about a year; but when the planet approaches very near to Jupiter, the interval may necessarily be much shorter. The magnitude of the resulting values of the perturbations will suggest the necessity of correcting the elements whenever it exists; and if we apply the proper corrections and commence anew the integration for one or more intervals preceding the last date for which the perturbations of the first order have been found, it will appear at once, by a comparison of the results, whether the elements have too long been regarded as constant.

The intervals at which the differential coefficients must be computed directly, will also depend on the relation of the motion of the disturbing body to that of the disturbed body; and although the interval may be greater than in the case of the variations of the coordinates which require an indirect calculation, still it must not be so large that the places of both the disturbing and the disturbed body, as well as the values of the several functions involved, cannot be interpolated with the requisite accuracy for all intermediate dates. In the case of the asteroid planets a uniform interval of about forty days will generally be preferred; but in the case of the comets, which rapidly approach the disturbing body and then again rapidly recede from it, the magnitude of the proper interval for quadrature will be very different at different times, and the necessity of shortening the interval, or the admissibility of extending it, will be indicated, as the numerical calculation progresses, by the manner in which the several functions change value.

If we compute the forces for several disturbing bodies by using ΣR, ΣS, and ΣZ in the formulæ in place of R, S, and Z, respectively, the total perturbations due to the combined action of all of these bodies may be computed at once. But, although the numerical process is thus somewhat abbreviated, yet, if the adopted values of the masses of some of the disturbing bodies are uncertain, and it is desired subsequently to correct the results by means of corrected values of these masses, it will be better to compute the perturbations due to each disturbing body separately, and, since a large part of the numerical process remains unchanged, the additional labor will not be very considerable, especially when, for some of the disturbing bodies, the interval of quadrature may be extended. The successive correction of the elements in order to include in the results the perturbations due to the higher powers of the masses, must, however, involve the perturbations due to all the disturbing bodies considered.

The differential coefficients should be multiplied by the interval ω, so that the formulæ of integration, omitting this factor, will furnish directly the required integrals; and whenever a change of the interval is introduced, the proper caution must be observed in regard to the process of integration. The quantity $s = 206264''.8$ should be introduced into the formulæ in such a manner that the variations of the elements which are expressed in angular measure will be obtained directly in seconds of arc; and the variations of the other elements will be conveniently determined in units of the nth decimal place. It should be observed, also, that if the constants of integration are put equal to zero at the beginning of the integration, the integrals obtained will be the required perturbations of the elements.

199. Example.—We shall now illustrate the calculation of the perturbations of the elements by a numerical example, and for this purpose we shall take that which has already been solved by the other methods which have been given. From 1864 Jan. 1.0 to 1865 Jan. 15.0 the perturbations of the second order are insensible, and hence during the entire period it will be sufficient to use the values of r, v, and E given by the osculating elements for 1864 Jan. 1.0.

The calculation of the forces R, S, and Z is effected precisely as already illustrated in Art. 189, and from the results there given we obtain the following values of the forces, with which we write also the values of E_0:—

Berlin Mean Time.	$40R$	$40S$	$40Z$	E_0
1863 Dec. 12.0,	+ 0″.0365	+ 0″.0019	+ 0″.00002	355° 26′ 8″.2
1864 Jan. 21.0,	0 .0356	− 0 .0086	0 .00025	8 14 57 .8
March 1.0,	0 .0315	0 .0182	0 .00047	20 57 55 .1
April 10.0,	0 .0250	0 .0259	0 .00068	33 26 47 .6
May 20.0,	0 .0169	0 .0314	0 .00087	45 35 25 .3
June 29.0,	+ 0 .0079	0 .0343	0 .00101	57 20 3 .8
Aug. 8.0,	− 0 .0011	0 .0349	0 .00112	68 39 14 .6
Sept. 17.0,	0 .0099	0 .0333	0 .00117	79 33 13 .1
Oct. 27.0,	0 .0179	0 .0301	0 .00116	90 3 23 .2
Dec. 6.0,	0 .0252	0 .0253	0 .00108	100 11 49 .1
1865 Jan. 15.0,	− 0 .0317	− 0 .0193	+ 0 .00090	110 0 54 .3

We compute the values of the required differential coefficients by means of the equations

$$\frac{d\delta\Omega}{dt} = \frac{1}{k\sqrt{p}} \cdot \frac{r \sin u}{\sin i} Z, \qquad \frac{d\delta i}{dt} = \frac{1}{k\sqrt{p}} r \cos u \, Z,$$

$$\frac{d\delta\pi}{dt} = \frac{1}{k\sqrt{p}}\left(- \frac{p \cos v}{\sin \varphi} R + \frac{(p + r) \sin v}{\sin \varphi} S \right) + 2 \sin^2 \tfrac{1}{2} i \frac{d\delta\Omega}{dt},$$

$$\frac{d\delta\varphi}{dt} = \frac{1}{k\sqrt{p}}(a \cos\varphi \sin v R + a \cos\varphi (\cos v + \cos E) S),$$

$$\frac{d\delta\mu}{dt} = -\frac{1}{k\sqrt{p}} \cdot \frac{3a\mu}{s}(\sin\varphi \sin v R + \frac{p}{r} S),$$

$$\frac{d\delta M}{dt} = \frac{1}{k\sqrt{p}}\left(\left(\frac{p \cos v}{\sin\varphi} - 2r\right) R - \frac{(p+r)\sin v}{\sin\varphi} S\right)\cos\varphi + \int\frac{d\delta\mu}{dt}\,dt;$$

and the results are the following:—

Date.	$40\frac{d\delta\Omega}{dt}$	$40\frac{d\delta i}{dt}$	$40\frac{d\delta\pi}{dt}$	$40\frac{d\delta\phi}{dt}$	$1600\frac{d\delta\mu}{dt}$	$40\int\frac{d\delta\mu}{dt}dt$	$40\frac{d\delta M}{dt}$
1863 Dec. 12.0,	−0″.004	−0″.001	−16″.730	+0″.022	−0″.0790	+0″.027	+11″.092
1864 Jan. 21.0,	0 .108	0 .017	17 .255	−0 .992	+0 .4524	0 .162	11 .864
March 1.0,	0 .302	0 .026	19 .578	1 .810	0 .9396	0 .863	15 .381
April 10.0,	0 .555	0 .028	22 .986	2 .294	1 .3321	2 .008	20 .746
May 20.0,	0 .822	0 .022	26 .572	2 .418	1 .6169	3 .492	26 .898
June 29.0,	1 .037	−0 .007	29 .271	2 .228	1 .7750	5 .198	32 .617
Aug. 8.0,	1 .189	+0 .012	30 .698	1 .829	1 .8196	7 .004	37 .293
Sept. 17.0,	1 .233	0 .033	30 .500	1 .406	1 .7591	8 .801	40 .445
Oct. 27.0,	1 .169	0 .052	28 .953	1 .055	1 .6206	10 .498	42 .144
Dec. 6.0,	1 .004	0 .065	26 .498	0 .902	1 .4074	12 .017	42 .741
1865 Jan. 15.0,	−0 .742	+0 .066	−23 .336	−1 .004	+1 .1388	+13 .292	+42 .323

The values thus obtained give, by means of the formulæ for integration by mechanical quadrature, the following perturbations of the elements:—

Berlin Mean Time.	$\delta\Omega$	δi	$\delta\pi$	$\delta\phi$	$\delta\mu$	δM
1863 Dec. 12.0,	+0″.01	−0″.00	+8″.43	+0″.12	+0″.0007	−5″.48
1864 Jan. 21.0,	−0 .04	0 .01	−8 .49	−0 .38	0 .0040	+5 .72
March 1.0,	0 .24	0 .03	26 .78	1 .80	0 .0216	19 .15
April 10.0,	0 .66	0 .06	48 .01	3 .88	0 .0502	37 .11
May 20.0,	1 .35	0 .08	72 .82	6 .27	0 .0875	60 .91
June 29.0,	2 .28	0 .10	100 .83	8 .61	0 .1299	90 .73
Aug. 8.0,	3 .40	0 .09	130 .93	10 .65	0 .1751	125 .79
Sept. 17.0,	4 .63	0 .07	161 .66	12 .26	0 .2206	164 .79
Oct. 27.0,	5 .84	−0 .03	191 .48	13 .48	0 .2624	206 .19
Dec. 6.0,	6 .93	+0 .03	219 .27	14 .44	0 .3004	248 .72
1865 Jan. 15.0,	−7 .81	+0 .10	−244 .24	−15 .37	+0 .3323	+291 .33

Applying the variations of the elements thus obtained to the osculating elements for 1864 Jan. 1.0, as given in Art. 166, the osculating elements for the instant 1865 Jan. 15.0 are found to be the following:—

Epoch = 1865 Jan. 15.0 Berlin mean time.

$$\begin{aligned} M &= 99° \; 34' \; 48''.81 \\ \pi &= 44 \;\; 13 \;\; 7 .93 \\ \Omega &= 206 \;\; 38 \;\; 57 .88 \\ i &= 4 \;\; 36 \;\; 52 .21 \\ \varphi &= 11 \;\; 15 \;\; 35 .65 \\ \log a &= 0.3880283 \\ \mu &= 928''.8897. \end{aligned}$$

(π, Ω, i: Ecliptic and Mean Equinox 1860.0.)

In order to compare the results thus derived with the perturbations computed by the other methods which have been given, let us compute the heliocentric longitude and latitude, in the case of the disturbed orbit, for the date 1865 Jan. 15.0, Berlin mean time. Thus, by means of the new elements, we find

$$\begin{aligned} M &= 99^\circ\ 34'\ 48''.81, & E &= 110^\circ\ \ 5'\ 14''.15, \\ \log r &= 0.4162182, & v &= 120\ \ 19\ \ 18\ .01, \\ l &= 164^\circ\ 37'\ 59''.04, & b &= -3\ \ \ 5\ \ 32\ .54, \end{aligned}$$

agreeing completely with the results already obtained by the other methods. The heliocentric place thus found is referred to the ecliptic and mean equinox of 1860.0, to which the elements π, ☊, and i are referred; and it may be reduced to any other ecliptic and equinox by means of the usual formulæ. Throughout the calculation of the perturbations it will be convenient to adopt a fixed equinox and ecliptic, the results being subsequently reduced by the application of the corrections for precession and nutation.

In the determination of δM, if we denote by $\varDelta M$ the value which is obtained when we neglect the last term of the equation for $\frac{d\delta M}{dt}$, we shall have

$$\delta M = \varDelta M + \iint \frac{d\delta\mu}{dt}\, dt^2,$$

which form is equally convenient in the numerical calculation. Thus, for 1865 Jan. 15.0, we find

$$\varDelta M = +\ 234''.74,$$

and from the several values of $1600\frac{d\delta\mu}{dt}$ we obtain, for the same date, by means of the formula for double integration,

$$\iint \frac{d\delta\mu}{dt}\, dt^2 = +\ 56''.59.$$

Hence we derive

$$\delta M = +\ 234''.74 + 56''.59 = +\ 291''.33,$$

agreeing with the result already obtained.

If we compute the variation of the mean anomaly at the epoch, by means of equation (209), we find, in the case under consideration,

$$\delta M_0 = +\ 165''.29,$$

and since the place of the body in the case of the instantaneous orbit is to be computed precisely as if the planet had been moving constantly in that orbit, we have, for 1865 Jan. 15.0,

$$(t - t_0)\,\delta\mu = +\,126''.27,$$

and hence

$$\delta M = \delta M_0 + (t - t_0)\,\delta\mu = +\,291''.56.$$

The error of this result is $-0''.23$, and arises chiefly from the increase of the accidental and unavoidable errors of the numerical calculation by the factor $t - t_0$, which appears in the last term of the equation (209). Hence it is evident that it will always be preferable to compute the variation of the mean anomaly directly; and if the variation of the mean anomaly at a given epoch be required, it may easily be found from δM by means of the equation

$$\delta M_0 = \delta M - (t - t_0)\,\delta\mu.$$

If the osculating elements of one of the asteroid planets are thus determined for the date of the opposition of the planet, they will suffice, without further change, to compute an ephemeris for the brief period included by the observations in the vicinity of the opposition, unless the disturbed planet shall be very near to Jupiter, in which case the perturbations during the period included by the ephemeris may become sensible. The variation of the geocentric place of the disturbed body arising from the action of the disturbing forces, may be obtained by substituting the corresponding variations of the elements in the differential formulæ as derived from the equation $(1)_2$, whenever the terms of the second order may be neglected. It should be observed, however, that if we substitute the value of δM directly in the equations for the variations of the geocentric co-ordinates, the coefficient of $\delta\mu$ must be that which depends solely on the variation of the semi-transverse axis. But when the coefficient of $\delta\mu$ has been computed so as to involve the effect of this quantity during the interval $t - t_0$, the value of δM_0 must be found from δM and substituted in the equations.

200. It will be observed that, on account of the divisor e in the expressions for $\frac{d\chi}{dt}$, $\frac{d\omega}{dt}$, and $\frac{d\pi}{dt}$, these elements will be subject to large perturbations whenever e is very small, although the absolute effect on the heliocentric place of the disturbed body may be small; and on

account of the divisor $\sin i$ in the expression for $\frac{d\Omega}{dt}$ the variation of Ω will be large whenever i is very small. To avoid the difficulties thus encountered, new elements must be introduced. Thus, in the case of Ω, let us put

$$\alpha'' = \sin i \sin \Omega, \qquad \beta'' = \sin i \cos \Omega; \tag{224}$$

then we shall have

$$\begin{aligned} \frac{d\alpha''}{dt} &= \sin \Omega \cos i \frac{di}{dt} + \sin i \cos \Omega \frac{d\Omega}{dt}, \\ \frac{d\beta''}{dt} &= \cos \Omega \cos i \frac{di}{dt} - \sin i \sin \Omega \frac{d\Omega}{dt}. \end{aligned}$$

Introducing the values of $\frac{di}{dt}$ and $\frac{d\Omega}{dt}$ given by the equations (212), and introducing further the auxiliary constants a, b, A, and B computed by means of the formulæ $(94)_1$ with respect to the fundamental plane to which Ω and i are referred, we obtain

$$\begin{aligned} \frac{d\alpha''}{dt} &= -\frac{1}{k\sqrt{p(1+m)}} rZ \sin a \cos (A + u), \\ \frac{d\beta''}{dt} &= \frac{1}{k\sqrt{p(1+m)}} rZ \sin b \cos (B + u), \end{aligned} \tag{225}$$

by means of which the variations of α'' and β'' may be found. If the integrals are put equal to zero at the beginning of the integration, the values of $\delta\alpha''$ and $\delta\beta''$ will be obtained, so that we shall have

$$\begin{aligned} \sin i \sin \Omega &= \sin i_0 \sin \Omega_0 + \delta\alpha'', \\ \sin i \cos \Omega &= \sin i_0 \cos \Omega_0 + \delta\beta'', \end{aligned}$$

or

$$\begin{aligned} \sin i \sin (\Omega - \Omega_0) &= \cos \Omega_0 \, \delta\alpha'' - \sin \Omega_0 \, \delta\beta'', \\ \sin i \cos (\Omega - \Omega_0) &= \sin i_0 + \sin \Omega_0 \, \delta\alpha'' + \cos \Omega_0 \, \delta\beta'', \end{aligned} \tag{226}$$

by means of which i and $\Omega - \Omega_0$ may be found.

In the case of χ, let us put

$$\eta'' = e \sin \chi, \qquad \zeta'' = e \cos \chi, \tag{227}$$

and we have

$$\begin{aligned} \frac{d\eta''}{dt} &= \sin \chi \frac{de}{dt} + e \cos \chi \frac{d\chi}{dt}, \\ \frac{d\zeta''}{dt} &= \cos \chi \frac{de}{dt} - e \sin \chi \frac{d\chi}{dt}. \end{aligned}$$

Substituting for $\frac{de}{dt}$ and $\frac{d\chi}{dt}$ the values given by the equations (203) and (205), and reducing, we obtain

$$
\begin{aligned}
\frac{d\eta''}{dt} &= \frac{1}{k\sqrt{p(1+m)}}\Big(-p\cos(v+\chi)\,R+\{(p+r)\sin(v+\chi) \\
&\qquad\qquad + er\sin\chi\}\,S\Big), \\
\frac{d\zeta''}{dt} &= \frac{1}{k\sqrt{p(1+m)}}\Big(p\sin(v+\chi)\,R+\{(p+r)\cos(v+\chi) \\
&\qquad\qquad + er\cos\chi\}\,S\Big),
\end{aligned} \tag{228}
$$

by means of which the values of $\delta\eta''$ and $\delta\zeta''$ may be found. Then we shall have

$$
\begin{aligned}
e\sin\chi &= e_0\sin\pi_0+\delta\eta'', \\
e\cos\chi &= e_0\cos\pi_0+\delta\zeta'',
\end{aligned}
$$

or

$$
\begin{aligned}
e\sin(\chi-\pi_0) &= \cos\pi_0\,\delta\eta''-\sin\pi_0\,\delta\zeta'', \\
e\cos(\chi-\pi_0) &= e_0+\sin\pi_0\,\delta\eta''+\cos\pi_0\,\delta\zeta'',
\end{aligned} \tag{229}
$$

from which to find e and χ. If, in order to find the variation of π, we write π instead of χ in these formulæ, the terms $+\,2e\cos\pi\sin^2\tfrac{1}{2}i\frac{d\Omega}{dt}$ and $-\,2e\sin\pi\sin^2\tfrac{1}{2}i\frac{d\Omega}{dt}$ must be added to the second members of (228), respectively.

201. By means of the four methods which we have developed and illustrated, the special perturbations of a heavenly body may be determined with entire accuracy, and the choice of the particular method will depend on the circumstances of the case. By computing the perturbations of the elements, correcting these elements as often as may be required, the terms depending on the higher powers of the masses may be included, and no indirect calculation becomes necessary. The frequent correction of the elements will also render insensible the effect of whatever uncertainty remains in regard to their true values. But, since the perturbations of the elements are in general much greater than those of the co-ordinates, the effect of the terms of the second order will be much greater upon the values of the elements than upon those of the co-ordinates. Hence, the frequency with which a change of the elements will be required will fully compensate the labor of the indirect part of the calculation in the case of the perturbations of the co-ordinates.

The determination of the perturbations of the polar co-ordinates r, w, and z, and that of the perturbations δM, ν, and $\delta z_{\prime}$, are effected with almost equal facility, especially when the effect of the disturbing forces is to be determined for a long interval of time. If the perturbations are required only for a brief period, it will be preferable to determine δM, ν, and δz, rather than δw, δr, and z, since the indirect part of the calculation will thus be effected with less repetition. In both of these cases the values of the perturbations are generally smaller than in the case of the rectangular co-ordinates, and hence they are less affected by terms of the second order; but on account of the simplicity of the formulæ, even when we include the terms depending on the higher powers of the masses, so long as the magnitude of the values of δx, δy, and δz is not so large as to render troublesome the indirect part of the calculation, the method of the variation of rectangular co-ordinates may be advantageously employed when the perturbations are to be determined for a long period.

By whatever method the perturbations are determined, if the fundamental osculating elements are correct, the final elements of the instantaneous orbit will be the same. But, since the effect of the errors of the elements will differ in degree in the different methods of treating the problem, if these elements are affected with small errors, the agreement of the final osculating elements obtained by the different methods, in connection with the corrections derived by the comparison of observations, may not be complete.

When the disturbed body approaches very near to a disturbing planet, the magnitude of the perturbations will be such as to enable us by means of accurate observations to correct the adopted value of the disturbing mass. In this case the perturbations, computed by means of either of the methods applicable, must be converted into the corresponding perturbations of the geocentric spherical co-ordinates. Let the variation of either of the geocentric co-ordinates arising from the action of the disturbing planet be denoted by $\delta\theta$; then, if we suppose the correct value of the disturbing mass to be $1+n$ times the assumed value used in computing $\delta\theta$, the corresponding variation of the geocentric spherical co-ordinate will be

$$(1+n)\,\delta\theta.$$

The value $\delta\theta$ may be included in the determination of the difference between computation and observation in the formation of the equations of condition for finding the corrections to be applied to the elements; and, finally, the term $n\delta\theta$ may be added to each of the equations of condition, so that we thus introduce a new unknown quantity n. The solution of all the equations thus formed, by the method of least squares, will then furnish the most probable values of the corrections to be applied to the adopted elements, and also the value of n, by means of which a corrected value of the mass of the disturbing body will be obtained.

202. If the determination of the perturbations of a heavenly body required that all the disturbing bodies in the system should be constantly considered, the labor would be very great. But, fortunately, it so happens that the masses of many of the planets are so small in comparison with that of the sun, that the sphere of their disturbing influence is very much restricted. Thus, in the determination of the perturbations of the asteroid planets, only the action of Mars, Jupiter, and Saturn need be considered; and of these disturbing planets Jupiter exerts the principal influence. It is true, however, that, on account of the elongated form of the orbits of the periodic comets, they may at different times be sensibly disturbed by each of the planets of the system. But since in the remote parts of their orbits they are very distant from many of the disturbing planets, the determination of their perturbations will then be much facilitated by considering them as revolving around the common centre of gravity of the sun and disturbing planet. When the motion is referred to the centre of the sun, the disturbing force is the difference of the direct action of the disturbing body upon the disturbed body and upon the sun; and in the case of those disturbing planets whose periodic time is short, the term which expresses the action upon the sun will change value so rapidly that it will be necessary to adopt small intervals in the direct numerical calculation. But when we refer the motion to the centre of gravity of the system, which does not receive any motion in virtue of the mutual attractions of the bodies which compose the system, that part of the disturbing force which expresses the action of the disturbing planet upon the sun will disappear, and the magnitude of the disturbing force will be less than that of the force which disturbs the motion of the comet relative to the sun, so that the intervals for quadrature may be greatly extended. It will be observed, further, that, if the distance of the comet from the sun is far greater than the distance of the disturbing body, the direct action of the planet upon the comet becomes so small that its effect upon the motion will be quite insignificant. In this case the motion of the

comet will be sensibly the same as the pure elliptic motion around the common centre of gravity of the sun and disturbing planet.

In order to exhibit these principles more clearly, let us denote by ξ, η, ζ, the co-ordinates of the sun referred to the centre of gravity of the system; by x_0, y_0, z_0, the co-ordinates of the comet; and by x_0', y_0', z_0', the co-ordinates of the disturbing planet referred to the same origin. Let x, y, z be the co-ordinates of the comet, and x', y', z' those of the planet referred to the centre of the sun; then we shall have

$$x_0 = \xi + x, \qquad y_0 = \eta + y, \qquad z_0 = \zeta + z,$$
$$\xi = -m'x_0', \qquad \eta = -m'y_0', \qquad \zeta = -m'z_0',$$

and hence

$$x = x_0 + m'x_0', \qquad y = y_0 + m'y_0', \qquad z = z_0 + m'z_0',$$
$$x' = x_0' + m'x_0', \qquad y' = y_0' + m'y_0', \qquad z' = z_0' + m'z_0',$$
$$r' = r_0' + m'r_0'.$$

From these we derive

$$\xi = -\frac{m'x'}{1+m'}, \qquad \eta = -\frac{m'y'}{1+m'}, \qquad \zeta = -\frac{m'z'}{1+m'}. \qquad (230)$$

The equations $(15)_1$ are now easily transformed into the following:—

$$\begin{aligned}
\frac{d^2x_0}{dt^2} + \frac{k^2(1+m')\,x_0}{r_0^{\,3}} &= m'k^2(x'_0 - x_0)\left(\frac{1}{\rho^3} - \frac{1}{r_0^{\,3}}\right) \\
&\quad + k^2(x_0 + m'x_0')\left(\frac{1}{r_0^{\,3}} - \frac{1}{r^3}\right), \\
\frac{d^2y_0}{dt^2} + \frac{k^2(1+m')\,y_0}{r_0^{\,3}} &= m'k^2(y_0' - y_0)\left(\frac{1}{\rho^3} - \frac{1}{r_0^{\,3}}\right) \qquad (231) \\
&\quad + k^2(y_0 + m'y_0')\left(\frac{1}{r_0^{\,3}} - \frac{1}{r^3}\right), \\
\frac{d^2z_0}{dt^2} + \frac{k^2(1+m')\,z_0}{r_0^{\,3}} &= m'k^2(z_0' - z_0)\left(\frac{1}{\rho^3} - \frac{1}{r_0^{\,3}}\right) \\
&\quad + k^2(z_0 + m'z_0')\left(\frac{1}{r_0^{\,3}} - \frac{1}{r^3}\right),
\end{aligned}$$

which completely determine the motion of the comet about the common centre of gravity of the sun and planet. The second members express the forces which disturb the pure elliptic motion; and it is evident, by an inspection of the terms, that when the comet is remote from both the planet and the sun these forces become extremely small. If, therefore, we compute the perturbations of the motion relative to the sun as far as to the point at which the second members of (231) have not any appreciable influence on the results, it will suffice simply to convert the elements which refer to the centre of the sun into those relative to the common centre of gravity of the sun and disturbing planet, and then to regard the motion as undisturbed until the comet again approaches so near that the direct perturbations must be considered, at which point the motion will again be referred to the centre of the sun.

203. The reduction of the elements from the centre of gravity of the sun to the common centre of gravity of the sun and the disturbing planet, may be easily effected by means of the variations of the rectangular co-ordinates and of the corresponding velocities. To derive the co-ordinates of the comet referred to the centre of gravity of the sun and planet, it is only necessary to add to the heliocentric co-ordinates the co-ordinates of the sun referred to this origin, so that, according to (230), we shall have

$$\delta x = -\frac{m'}{1+m'}x', \qquad \delta y = -\frac{m'}{1+m'}y', \qquad \delta z = -\frac{m'}{1+m'}z', \tag{232}$$

and, also,

$$\delta\frac{dx}{dt} = -\frac{m'}{1+m'}\cdot\frac{dx'}{dt}, \qquad \delta\frac{dy}{dt} = -\frac{m'}{1+m'}\cdot\frac{dy'}{dt}, \qquad \delta\frac{dz}{dt} = -\frac{m'}{1+m'}\cdot\frac{dz'}{dt}. \tag{233}$$

If, therefore, from the elements of the orbit of the disturbing planet we compute the auxiliary constants for the adopted fundamental plane by means of the equations $(94)_1$ or $(99)_1$, and also V' and U' from

$$\frac{k\sqrt{1+m'}}{\sqrt{p'}}(e'\sin\omega' + \sin u') = V'\sin U',$$
$$\frac{k\sqrt{1+m'}}{\sqrt{p'}}(e'\cos\omega' + \cos u') = V'\cos U',$$

the equations $(100)_1$ and (49), in connection with (232) and (233), give

$$\delta x = -\frac{m'}{1+m'}r'\sin a'\sin(A'+u'), \tag{234}$$

$$\delta y = -\frac{m'}{1+m'} r' \sin b' \sin (B' + u'),$$

$$\delta z = -\frac{m'}{1+m'} r' \sin c' \sin (C' + u');$$

$$\delta \frac{dx}{dt} = -\frac{m'}{1+m'} V' \sin a' \cos (A' + U'), \qquad (234)$$

$$\delta \frac{dy}{dt} = -\frac{m'}{1+m'} V' \sin b' \cos (B' + U'),$$

$$\delta \frac{dz}{dt} = -\frac{m'}{1+m'} V' \sin c' \cos (C' + U'),$$

If we add the values of δx, δy, δz, $\delta \frac{dx}{dt}$, $\delta \frac{dy}{dt}$, and $\delta \frac{dz}{dt}$ to the corresponding co-ordinates and velocities of the comet in reference to the centre of gravity of the sun, the results will give the co-ordinates and velocities of the comet in reference to the common centre of gravity of the sun and disturbing planet, and from these the new elements of the orbit may be determined as explained in Art. 168.

The time at which the elements of the orbit of the comet may be referred to the common centre of gravity of the sun and planet, can be readily estimated in the actual application of the formulæ, by means of the magnitude of the disturbing force. In the case of Mercury as the disturbing planet, this transformation may generally be effected when the radius-vector of the comet has attained the value 1.5, and in the case of Venus when it has the value 2.5. It should be remarked, however, that the distance here assigned may be increased or diminished by the relative position of the bodies in their orbits. The motion relative to the common centre of gravity of the sun and planet—disregarding the perturbations produced by the other planets, which should be considered separately—may then be regarded as undisturbed until the comet has again arrived at the point at which the motion must be referred to the centre of the sun, and at which the perturbations of this motion by the planet under consideration must be determined. The reduction to the centre of the sun will be effected by means of the values obtained from (234), when the second member of each of these equations is taken with a contrary sign.

204. In the cases in which the motion of the comet will be referred to the common centre of gravity of the sun and disturbing planet, the resulting variations of the co-ordinates and velocities will be so small that their squares and products may be neglected, and, there-

fore, instead of using the complete formulæ in finding the new elements, it will suffice to employ differential formulæ. The formulæ $(100)_1$ give

$$
\begin{aligned}
\frac{dx}{dt} &= \sin a \sin (A+u) \frac{dr}{dt} + r \sin a \cos (A+u) \frac{dv}{dt}, \\
\frac{dy}{dt} &= \sin b \sin (B+u) \frac{dr}{dt} + r \sin b \cos (B+u) \frac{dv}{dt}, \\
\frac{dz}{dt} &= \sin c \sin (C+u) \frac{dr}{dt} + r \sin c \cos (C+u) \frac{dv}{dt}.
\end{aligned} \tag{235}
$$

If we multiply the first of these equations by δx, the second by δy, and the third by δz; then multiply the first by $\delta \frac{dx}{dt}$, the second by $\delta \frac{dy}{dt}$, and the third by $\delta \frac{dz}{dt}$, and put

$$
\begin{aligned}
P &= \sin a \sin (A+u)\, \delta x + \sin b \sin (B+u)\, \delta y \\
&\quad + \sin c \sin (C+u)\, \delta z, \\
Q &= \sin a \cos (A+u)\, \delta x + \sin b \cos (B+u)\, \delta y \\
&\quad + \sin c \cos (C+u)\, \delta z; \\
P' &= \sin a \sin (A+u)\, \delta \frac{dx}{dt} + \sin b \sin (B+u)\, \delta \frac{dy}{dt} \\
&\quad + \sin c \sin (C+u)\, \delta \frac{dz}{dt}, \\
Q' &= \sin a \cos (A+u)\, \delta \frac{dx}{dt} + \sin b \cos (B+u)\, \delta \frac{dy}{dt} \\
&\quad + \sin c \cos (C+u)\, \delta \frac{dz}{dt},
\end{aligned} \tag{236}
$$

we shall have, observing that $\frac{dr}{dt} = \frac{k}{\sqrt{p}} e \sin v$ and that $\frac{dv}{dt} = \frac{k\sqrt{p}}{r^2}$,

$$
\begin{aligned}
\frac{dx}{dt}\delta x + \frac{dy}{dt}\delta y + \frac{dz}{dt}\delta z &= \frac{k}{\sqrt{p}} e \sin v\, P + \frac{k\sqrt{p}}{r} Q, \\
\frac{dx}{dt}\delta\frac{dx}{dt} + \frac{dy}{dt}\delta\frac{dy}{dt} + \frac{dz}{dt}\delta\frac{dz}{dt} &= \frac{k}{\sqrt{p}} e \sin v\, P' + \frac{k\sqrt{p}}{r} Q'.
\end{aligned} \tag{237}
$$

From the equations

$$
\begin{aligned}
r\frac{dr}{dt} &= x\frac{dx}{dt} + y\frac{dy}{dt} + z\frac{dz}{dt}, \\
V^2 &= \frac{dx^2}{dt^2} + \frac{dy^2}{dt^2} + \frac{dz^2}{dt^2},
\end{aligned}
$$

we get

$$\delta\left(\frac{rdr}{dt}\right)=\frac{dx}{dt}\,\delta x+\frac{dy}{dt}\,\delta y+\frac{dz}{dt}\,\delta z+x\delta\frac{dx}{dt}+y\delta\frac{dy}{dt}+z\delta\frac{dz}{dt},$$

$$V\delta V=\frac{dx}{dt}\,\delta\frac{dx}{dt}+\frac{dy}{dt}\,\delta\frac{dy}{dt}+\frac{dz}{dt}\,\delta\frac{dz}{dt},$$

which by means of (237) become

$$\begin{aligned}\delta\left(\frac{rdr}{dt}\right)&=\frac{k}{\sqrt{p}}\,e\sin v\,P+\frac{k\sqrt{p}}{r}\,Q+P'r,\\ V\delta V&=\frac{k}{\sqrt{p}}\,e\sin v\,P'+\frac{k\sqrt{p}}{r}\,Q'.\end{aligned}\qquad(238)$$

From the equation

$$k^2p=V^2r^2-\frac{r^2dr^2}{dt^2}$$

we get

$$2pk\delta k+k^2\delta p=2r^2V\delta V+2V^2r\delta r-2\frac{rdr}{dt}\,\delta\left(\frac{rdr}{dt}\right).$$

Substituting the values given by (238), observing also that $P=\delta r$, this becomes

$$\frac{\delta k}{k}+\frac{\delta p}{2p}=\frac{V^2r}{k^2p}\,P-\frac{re^2\sin^2 v}{p^2}\,P-\frac{e\sin v}{p}\,Q+\frac{r}{k\sqrt{p}}\,Q';$$

and, since

$$V^2=\frac{k^2}{p}\,(1+2e\cos v+e^2),$$

we obtain

$$\delta\,(\sqrt{p})=\frac{\sqrt{p}}{r}\,P-\frac{e\sin v}{\sqrt{p}}\,Q+\frac{r}{k}\,Q'-\sqrt{p}\,\frac{\delta k}{k},\qquad(239)$$

by means of which the variation of $\sqrt{p}$ may be found.

The equation

$$\frac{k^2}{a}=\frac{2k^2}{r}-V^2$$

gives

$$\delta\frac{1}{a}=-\frac{2}{r^2}\,\delta r-\frac{2}{k^2}\,V\delta V+2\left(\frac{2}{r}-\frac{1}{a}\right)\frac{\delta k}{k},$$

from which we derive

$$\delta\frac{1}{a}=-\frac{2}{r^2}\,P-\frac{2e\sin v}{k\sqrt{p}}\,P'-\frac{2\sqrt{p}}{rk}\,Q'+2\left(\frac{2}{r}-\frac{1}{a}\right)\frac{\delta k}{k},\qquad(240)$$

from which the new value of the semi-transverse axis a may be found. To find $\delta\mu$ we have

$$\delta\mu = \tfrac{3}{2}\mu a \delta \frac{1}{a} + \mu \frac{\delta k}{k}, \tag{241}$$

or

$$\delta\mu = -\frac{3\mu a}{r^2} P - \frac{3\mu a e \sin v}{k\sqrt{p}} P' - \frac{3\mu a \sqrt{p}}{rk} Q' + \left(\frac{6a}{r} - 2\right)\mu \frac{\delta k}{k}. \tag{242}$$

Next, to find δe, we have, from $p = a(1-e^2)$,

$$\delta e = -\frac{p}{2e}\delta\frac{1}{a} - \frac{\sqrt{p}}{ae}\delta(\sqrt{p}), \tag{243}$$

or

$$\delta e = \frac{p \cos E}{r^2} P + \frac{\sin v}{a} Q + \frac{\sin v \sqrt{p}}{k} P' + \frac{\sqrt{p}}{k}(\cos v + \cos E)\, Q' - \frac{2p \cos E}{r} \cdot \frac{\delta k}{k}. \tag{244}$$

The equation $(12)_2$ gives

$$\delta M = \frac{r^2}{a^2 \cos\varphi}\delta v - \frac{r^2 \sin v}{a^2 \cos^3\varphi}(2 + e\cos v)\,\delta e, \tag{245}$$

and from $\frac{p}{r} = 1 + e\cos v$ we get

$$\delta v = \frac{\cos v}{e \sin v}\delta e + \frac{p}{r^2 e \sin v}\delta r - \frac{2\sqrt{p}}{re\sin v}\delta(\sqrt{p}). \tag{246}$$

Substituting this value of δv in (245), and reducing, we find

$$\begin{aligned}\delta M = &-\left(\frac{\cot\phi}{r} + \frac{\tan\phi}{a}\right)\sin v P + \frac{\cos v}{a\tan\phi} Q + \frac{1}{k\sqrt{p}}(p\cot\phi\cos v - 2r\cos\phi)\, P' \\ &- \frac{1}{k\sqrt{p}} \cdot \frac{(p+r)\sin v}{\tan\phi} Q' + \left(\frac{\cot\phi}{r} + \frac{\tan\phi}{a}\right) 2r \sin v \frac{\delta k}{k},\end{aligned} \tag{247}$$

from which to derive the variation of the mean anomaly.

205. Let us now denote by x'', y'', z'' the heliocentric co-ordinates of the comet referred to a system in which the plane of the orbit is the fundamental plane, and in which the positive axis of x is directed to the ascending node on the ecliptic. Let us also denote by x', y', z' the co-ordinates referred to a system in which the plane of the ecliptic is the plane of xy, and in which the positive axis of x is directed to the vernal equinox. Then we shall have

$$x'' = x' \cos \Omega + y' \sin \Omega,$$
$$y'' = -x' \sin \Omega \cos i + y' \cos \Omega \cos i + z' \sin i,$$
$$z'' = x' \sin \Omega \sin i - y' \cos \Omega \sin i + z' \cos i.$$

If we transform the co-ordinates still further, and denote by x, y, z the co-ordinates referred to the equator or to any other plane making the angle ε with the ecliptic, the positive axis of x being directed to the point from which longitudes are measured in this plane; and if we introduce also the auxiliary constants a, A, b, B, &c., we shall have

$$\begin{aligned} \delta x'' &= \sin a \sin A\, \delta x + \sin b \sin B\, \delta y + \sin c \sin C\, \delta z, \\ \delta y'' &= \sin a \cos A\, \delta x + \sin b \cos B\, \delta y + \sin c \cos C\, \delta z, \\ \delta z'' &= \cos a\, \delta x + \cos b\, \delta y + \cos c\, \delta z. \end{aligned} \tag{248}$$

Multiplying the first of these by $-\sin u$, and the second by $\cos u$, adding the results, and introducing Q as given by the second of equations (236), we get

$$\cos u\, \delta y'' - \sin u\, \delta x'' = Q.$$

Substituting for $\delta x''$ and $\delta y''$ the values given by the equations $(73)_2$, the result is

$$r\,(\delta v + \delta \chi) = Q,$$

and, introducing the value of δv given by (246), we obtain

$$\delta \chi = \frac{Q}{r} - \frac{\cos v}{e \sin v}\,\delta e - \frac{p}{r^2 e \sin v}\,\delta r + \frac{2\sqrt{p}}{re \sin v}\,\delta(\sqrt{p}).$$

Substituting further for δe, δr, and $\delta(\sqrt{p})$ the values already obtained, and reducing, we find

$$\delta \chi = \frac{\sin v}{er} P - \frac{\cos E}{er} Q - \frac{\cos v \sqrt{p}}{ek} P' + \frac{(p + r) \sin v}{ek\sqrt{p}} Q' - \frac{2 \sin v}{e} \cdot \frac{\delta k}{k}, \tag{249}$$

by means of which $\delta \chi$ may be found.

If we put

$$\begin{aligned} \cos a\, \delta x + \cos b\, \delta y + \cos c\, \delta z &= R, \\ \cos a\, \delta \frac{dx}{dt} + \cos b\, \delta \frac{dy}{dt} + \cos c\, \delta \frac{dz}{dt} &= R', \end{aligned} \tag{250}$$

the last of the equations (248) gives

$$\delta z'' = R; \tag{251}$$

and if we differentiate the equation

$$\cos a \frac{dx}{dt} + \cos b \frac{dy}{dt} + \cos c \frac{dz}{dt} = 0,$$

which exists in the case of the unchanged elements, we shall have

$$\begin{aligned} 0 = \cos a \, \delta\frac{dx}{dt} + \cos b \, \delta\frac{dy}{dt} + \cos c \, \delta\frac{dz}{dt} \\ - \frac{dx}{dt} \sin a \, \delta a - \frac{dy}{dt} \sin b \, \delta b - \frac{dz}{dt} \sin c \, \delta c. \end{aligned}$$

Substituting for δa, δb, and δc the values given in Art. 60, observing that $\delta \varepsilon = 0$, we have

$$\begin{aligned} 0 = R' + \left(\frac{dx}{dt} \sin a \sin A + \frac{dy}{dt} \sin b \sin B + \frac{dz}{dt} \sin c \sin C \right) \sin i \, \delta \Omega \\ - \left(\frac{dx}{dt} \sin a \cos A + \frac{dy}{dt} \sin b \cos B + \frac{dz}{dt} \sin c \cos C \right) \delta i. \end{aligned} \tag{252}$$

From the equations $(100)_1$, observing that the relations between the auxiliary constants are not changed when the variable u is put equal to zero, or equal to 90°, we get

$$\begin{aligned} \sin^2 a \sin^2 A + \sin^2 b \sin^2 B + \sin^2 c \sin^2 C = 1, \\ \sin^2 a \cos^2 A + \sin^2 b \cos^2 B + \sin^2 c \cos^2 C = 1, \end{aligned} \tag{253}$$

and from (235) we find

$$\sin^2 a \sin A \cos A + \sin^2 b \sin B \cos B + \sin^2 c \sin C \cos C = 0. \tag{254}$$

Substituting in (252) for $\frac{dx}{dt}$, $\frac{dy}{dt}$, and $\frac{dz}{dt}$ the values given by the equations (49), and reducing by means of (253) and (254), we get

$$0 = R' - V \sin U \sin i \, \delta \Omega - V \cos U \, \delta i. \tag{255}$$

Substituting further for $\delta z''$ in (251) the value given by the last of the equations $(73)_2$, there results

$$0 = R + r \cos u \sin i \, \delta \Omega - r \sin u \, \delta i. \tag{256}$$

From these equations we derive, by elimination,

$$\delta\Omega = -\frac{e\cos\omega + \cos u}{p\sin i}R + \frac{1}{k\sqrt{p}}\cdot\frac{r\sin u}{\sin i}R',$$
$$\delta i = \frac{e\sin\omega + \sin u}{p}R + \frac{r\cos u}{k\sqrt{p}}R', \tag{257}$$

by means of which $\delta\Omega$ and δi may be found. To find $\delta\omega$ and $\delta\pi$ we have

$$\delta\omega = \delta\chi - \cos i\delta\Omega, \qquad \delta\pi = \delta\chi + 2\sin^2\tfrac{1}{2}i\delta\Omega, \tag{258}$$

$\delta\chi$ being found from equation (249).

Neglecting the mass of the comet as inappreciable in comparison with that of the sun, the attractive force which acts upon the comet in the case of the undisturbed motion relative to the sun is k^2, but in the case of the motion relative to the common centre of gravity of the sun and planet this force is $k^2(1+m')$. Hence it follows that the increment of this force will be $m'k^2$, and we shall have

$$\frac{\delta k}{k} = \tfrac{1}{2}m', \tag{259}$$

by means of which the value of this factor, which is required in the formulæ for $\delta(\sqrt{p})$, $\delta\frac{1}{a}$, &c., may be found.

206. The formulæ thus derived enable us to effect the required transformation of the elements. In the first place, we compute the values of δx, δy, δz, $\delta\frac{dx}{dt}$, $\delta\frac{dy}{dt}$, and $\delta\frac{dz}{dt}$ by means of the formulæ (234); then, by means of (236) and (250), we compute P, Q, R, P', Q', and R', the auxiliary constants a, A, &c. being determined in reference to the fundamental plane to which the co-ordinates are referred. When the fundamental plane is the plane of the ecliptic, or that to which Ω and i are referred, we have

$$\sin c = \sin i, \qquad C = 0.$$

The algebraic signs of $\cos a$, $\cos b$, and $\cos c$, as indicated by the equations $(101)_1$, must be carefully attended to. The formulæ for the variations of the elements will then give the corrections to be applied to the elements of the orbit relative to the sun in order to obtain those of the orbit relative to the common centre of gravity of the sun and planet. Whenever the elements of the orbit about the sun are again required, the corrections will be determined in the same manner, but will be applied each with a contrary sign.

Since the equations have been derived for the variations of more than the six elements usually employed, the additional formulæ, as well as those which give different relations between the elements employed, may be used to check the numerical calculation; and this proof should not be omitted. It is obvious, also, that these differential formulæ will serve to convert the perturbations of the rectangular co-ordinates into perturbations of the elements, whenever the terms of the second order may be neglected, observing that in this case $\delta k = 0$. If some of the elements considered are expressed in angular measure, and some in parts of other units, the quantity $s = 206264''.8$ should be introduced, in the numerical application, so as to preserve the homogeneity of the formulæ.

When the motion of the comet is regarded as undisturbed about the centre of gravity of the system, the variations of the elements for the instant t in order to reduce them to the centre of gravity of the system, added algebraically to those for the instant t' in order to reduce them again to the centre of the sun, will give the total perturbations of the elements of the orbit relative to the sun during the interval $t' - t$. It should be observed, however, that the value of δM for the instant t should be reduced to that for the instant t', so that the total variation of M during the interval $t' - t$ will be

$$\delta M_t + (t' - t)\,\delta\mu_t + \delta M_{t'}.$$

In this manner, by considering the action of the several disturbing bodies separately, referring the motion of the comet to the common centre of gravity of the sun and planet whenever it may subsequently be regarded as undisturbed about this point, and again referring it to the centre of the sun when such an assumption is no longer admissible, the determination of the perturbations during an entire revolution of the comet is very greatly facilitated.

207. If we consider the position and dimensions of the orbits of the comets, it will at once appear that a very near approach of some of these bodies to a planet may often happen, and that when they approach very near some of the large planets their orbits may be entirely changed. It is, indeed, certainly known that the orbits of comets have been thus modified by a near approach to Jupiter, and there are periodic comets now known which will be eventually thus acted upon. It becomes an interesting problem, therefore, to consider the formulæ applicable to this special case in which the ordinary methods of calculating perturbations cannot be applied.

If we denote by x', y', z', r', the co-ordinates and radius-vector of the planet referred to the centre of the sun, and regard its motion relative to the sun as disturbed by the comet, we shall have

$$\begin{aligned}
\frac{d^2x'}{dt^2} + \frac{k^2(1+m')\,x'}{r'^3} &= mk^2\left(\frac{x-x'}{\rho^3} - \frac{x}{r^3}\right), \\
\frac{d^2y'}{dt^2} + \frac{k^2(1+m')\,y'}{r'^3} &= mk^2\left(\frac{y-y'}{\rho^3} - \frac{y}{r^3}\right), \\
\frac{d^2z'}{dt^2} + \frac{k^2(1+m')\,z'}{r'^3} &= mk^2\left(\frac{z-z'}{\rho^3} - \frac{z}{r^3}\right).
\end{aligned} \tag{260}$$

Let us now denote by ξ, η, ζ the co-ordinates of the comet referred to the centre of gravity of the planet; then will

$$\xi = x - x', \qquad \eta = y - y', \qquad \zeta = z - z'.$$

Substituting the resulting values of x', y', z' in the preceding equations, and subtracting these from the corresponding equations (1) for the disturbed motion of the comet, we derive

$$\begin{aligned}
\frac{d^2\xi}{dt^2} + \frac{k^2(m+m')\,\xi}{\rho^3} &= k^2\left(\frac{x'}{r'^3} - \frac{x'+\xi}{r^3}\right), \\
\frac{d^2\eta}{dt^2} + \frac{k^2(m+m')\,\eta}{\rho^3} &= k^2\left(\frac{y'}{r'^3} - \frac{y'+\eta}{r^3}\right), \\
\frac{d^2\zeta}{dt^2} + \frac{k^2(m+m')\,\zeta}{\rho^3} &= k^2\left(\frac{z'}{r'^3} - \frac{z'+\zeta}{r^3}\right).
\end{aligned} \tag{261}$$

These equations express the motion of the comet relative to the centre of gravity of the disturbing planet; and when the comet approaches very near to the planet, so that the second member of each of these equations becomes very small in comparison with the second term of the first member, we may take, for a first approximation,

$$\begin{aligned}
\frac{d^2\xi}{dt^2} + \frac{k^2(m+m')\,\xi}{\rho^3} &= 0, \\
\frac{d^2\eta}{dt^2} + \frac{k^2(m+m')\,\eta}{\rho^3} &= 0, \\
\frac{d^2\zeta}{dt^2} + \frac{k^2(m+m')\,\zeta}{\rho^3} &= 0;
\end{aligned} \tag{262}$$

and, since $\dfrac{k^2(m+m')}{\rho^2}$ is the sum of the attractive force of the planet on the comet and of the reciprocal action of the comet on the planet, these equations, being of the same form as those for the undisturbed motion of the comet relative to the sun, show that when the action of the disturbing planet on the comet exceeds that of the sun, the result of the first approximation to the motion of the comet is that it describes a conic section around the centre of gravity of the planet. Further, since $-x'$, $-y'$, $-z'$ are the co-ordinates of the sun referred to the centre of gravity of the planet, it appears that the second members of (261) express the disturbing force of the sun on the comet resolved in directions parallel to the co-ordinate axes respectively. Hence when a comet approaches so near a planet that the action of the latter upon it exceeds that of the sun, its motion will be in a conic section relatively to the planet, and will be disturbed by the action of the sun. But the disturbing action of the sun is the difference between its action on the comet and on the planet, and the masses of the larger bodies of the solar system are such that when the comet is equally attracted by the sun and by the planet, the distances of the comet and planet from the sun differ so little that the disturbing force of the sun on the comet, regarded as describing a conic section about the planet, will be extremely small. Thus, in a direction parallel to the co-ordinate ξ the disturbing force exercised by the sun is

$$k^2\left(\frac{x'}{r'^3}-\frac{x'+\xi}{r^3}\right)=k^2\left(\frac{x'}{r'^3}-\frac{x}{r^3}\right),$$

and when the comet approaches very near the planet this force will be extremely small. It is evident, further, that the action of the sun regarded as the disturbing body will be very small even when its direct action upon the comet considerably exceeds that of the planet, and, therefore, that we may consider the orbit of the comet to be a conic section about the planet and disturbed by the sun, when it is actually attracted more by the sun than by the planet.

208. In order to show more clearly that the disturbing force of the sun is very small even when its direct action on the comet exceeds that of the planet, let us suppose the sun, planet, and comet to be situated on the same straight line, in which case the disturbing force of the sun will be a maximum for a given distance of the comet from the planet. Then will the direct action of the sun be $\frac{k^2}{r^2}$, and that of the planet $\frac{m'k^2}{\rho^2}$. The disturbing action of the sun will be

$$\frac{k^2}{r^2} - \frac{k^2}{(r+\rho)^2} = \frac{k^2\rho}{r^2} \cdot \frac{2r+\rho}{(r+\rho)^2},$$

which, since ρ is supposed to be small in comparison with r, may be put equal to

$$\frac{2k^2\rho}{r^3},$$

and hence the ratio of the disturbing action of the sun to the direct action of the planet on the comet cannot exceed

$$R = \frac{2\rho^3}{m'r^3}.$$

If the comet is at a distance, such that the direct action of the sun is equal to the direct action of the planet, we have

$$\rho^2 = m'r^2,$$

and the ratio of the direct action of the sun to its disturbing action cannot in this case exceed $2\sqrt{m'}$. In the case of Jupiter this amounts to only 0.06.

So long as ρ is small, the disturbing action of the planet is very nearly $\frac{m'k^2}{\rho^2}$ in all positions of the comet relative to the planet, and hence the ratio of the disturbing action of the planet to the direct action of the sun cannot exceed

$$R' = \frac{m'r^2}{\rho^2}.$$

At the point for which the value of ρ corresponds to $R = R'$, the comet, sun, and planet being supposed to be situated in the same straight line, it will be immaterial whether we consider the sun or the planet as the disturbing body; but for values of ρ less than this R will be less than R', and the planet must be regarded as the controlling and the sun as the disturbing body. The supposition that R is equal to R' gives

$$\frac{2\rho^3}{m'r^3} = \frac{m'r^2}{\rho^2},$$

and therefore

$$\rho = r\sqrt[5]{\tfrac{1}{2}m'^2}. \qquad (263)$$

Hence we may compute the perturbations of the comet, regarding the planet as the disturbing body, until it approaches so near the planet that ρ has the value given by this equation, after which, so long as ρ does not exceed the value here assigned, the sun must be regarded as the disturbing body.

If ψ represents the angle at the planet between the sun and comet, the disturbing force of the sun, for any position of the comet near the planet, will be very nearly

$$\frac{2k^2\rho}{r^3}\cos\psi,$$

and when this angle is considerable, the disturbing action of the sun will be small even when ρ is greater than $r\sqrt[5]{\tfrac{1}{2}m'^2}$. Hence we may commence to consider the sun as the disturbing body even before the comet reaches the point for which

$$\rho = r\sqrt[5]{\tfrac{1}{2}m'^2},$$

and, since the ratio of the disturbing action of the planet to the direct action of the sun remains nearly the same for all values of ψ, when ρ is within the limits here assigned the sun must in all cases be so considered. Corresponding to the value of ρ given by equation (263), we have

$$R' = \sqrt[5]{4m'},$$

and in the case of a near approach to Jupiter the results are

$$\rho = 0.054r, \qquad R' = 0.33.$$

209. In the actual calculation of the perturbations of any particular comet when very near a large planet, it will be easy to determine the point at which it will be advantageous to commence to regard the sun as the disturbing body; and, having found the elements of the orbit of the comet relative to the planet, the perturbations of these elements or of the co-ordinates will be obtained by means of the formulæ already derived, the necessary distinctions being made in the notation. When the planet again becomes the disturbing body, the elements will be found in reference to the sun; and thus we are enabled to trace the motion of the comet before and subsequent to its being considered as subject principally to the planet. In the case of the first transformation, the co-ordinates and velocities of the comet and planet in reference to the sun being determined for the instant at which the sun is regarded as ceasing to be the controlling body, we shall have

$$\xi = x - x', \qquad \eta = y - y', \qquad \zeta = z - z',$$

$$\frac{d\xi}{dt} = \frac{dx}{dt} - \frac{dx'}{dt}, \qquad \frac{d\eta}{dt} = \frac{dy}{dt} - \frac{dy'}{dt}, \qquad \frac{d\zeta}{dt} = \frac{dz}{dt} - \frac{dz'}{dt};$$

and from ξ, η, ζ, $\frac{d\xi}{dt}$, $\frac{d\eta}{dt}$, and $\frac{d\zeta}{dt}$, the elements of the orbit of the comet about the planet are to be determined precisely as the elements in reference to the sun are found from x, y, z, $\frac{dx}{dt}$, $\frac{dy}{dt}$, and $\frac{dz}{dt}$, and as explained in Art. 168. Having computed the perturbations of the motion relative to the planet to the point at which the planet is again considered as the disturbing body, it only remains to find, for the corresponding time, the co-ordinates and velocities of the comet in reference to the centre of gravity of the planet, and from these the co-ordinates and velocities relative to the centre of the sun, and the elements of the orbit about the sun may be determined. As the interval of time during which the sun will be regarded as the disturbing body will always be small, it will be most convenient to compute the perturbations of the rectangular co-ordinates, in which case the values of ξ, η, ζ, $\frac{d\xi}{dt}$, $\frac{d\eta}{dt}$, and $\frac{d\zeta}{dt}$ will be obtained directly, and then, having found the corresponding co-ordinates x', y', z' and velocities $\frac{dx'}{dt}$, $\frac{dy'}{dt}$, $\frac{dz'}{dt}$ of the planet in reference to the sun, we have

$$x = x' + \xi, \qquad y = y' + \eta, \qquad z = z' + \zeta,$$

$$\frac{dx}{dt} = \frac{dx'}{dt} + \frac{d\xi}{dt}, \qquad \frac{dy}{dt} = \frac{dy'}{dt} + \frac{d\eta}{dt}, \qquad \frac{dz}{dt} = \frac{dz'}{dt} + \frac{d\zeta}{dt},$$

by means of which the elements of the orbit relative to the sun will be found. If it is not considered necessary to compute rigorously the path of the comet before and after it is subject principally to the action of the planet, but simply to find the principal effect of the action of the planet in changing its elements, it will be sufficient, during the time in which the sun is regarded as the disturbing body, to suppose the comet to move in an undisturbed orbit about the planet. For the point at which we cease to regard the sun as the disturbing body, the co-ordinates and velocities of the comet relative to the centre of gravity of the planet will be determined from the elements of the orbit in reference to the planet, precisely as the corresponding quantities are determined in the case of the motion relative to the sun, the necessary distinctions being made in the notation.

210. The results obtained from the observations of the periodic comets at their successive returns to the perihelion, render it probable that there exists in space a resisting medium which opposes the motion of all the heavenly bodies in their orbits; but since the observations of the planets do not exhibit any effect of such a resistance, it is inferred that the density of the ethereal fluid is so slight that it can have an appreciable effect only in the case of rare and attenuated bodies like the comets. If, however, we adopt the hypothesis of a resisting medium in space, in considering the motion of a heavenly body we simply introduce a new disturbing force acting in the direction of the tangent to the instantaneous orbit, and in a sense contrary to that of the motion. The amount of the resistance will depend chiefly on the density of the ethereal fluid and on the velocity of the body. In accordance with what takes place within the limits of our observation, we may assume that the resistance, in a medium of constant density, is proportional to the square of the velocity. The density of the fluid may be assumed to diminish as the distance from the sun increases, and hence it may be expressed as a function of the reciprocal of this distance.

Let ds be the element of the path of the body, and r the radius-vector; then will the resistance be

$$T = -K\varphi\left(\frac{1}{r}\right)\frac{ds^2}{dt^2}, \tag{264}$$

K being a constant quantity depending on the nature of the body, and $\varphi\left(\frac{1}{r}\right)$ the density of the ethereal fluid at the distance r. Since the force acts only in the plane of the orbit, the elements which define the position of this plane will not be changed, and hence we have only to determine the variations of the elements M, e, a, and χ. If we denote by ψ_0 the angle which the tangent makes with the prolongation of the radius-vector, the components R and S will be given by

$$R = T\cos\psi_0, \qquad S = T\sin\psi_0,$$

and, since

$$V\cos\psi_0 = \frac{k}{\sqrt{p}}\,e\sin v, \qquad V\sin\psi_0 = \frac{k\sqrt{p}}{r}, \qquad V = \frac{ds}{dt},$$

we have

$$R = -K\varphi\left(\frac{1}{r}\right)\frac{k}{\sqrt{p}}\,e\sin v\,\frac{ds}{dt}, \qquad S = -K\varphi\left(\frac{1}{r}\right)\frac{k\sqrt{p}}{r}\cdot\frac{ds}{dt}. \tag{265}$$

Substituting these values of R and S in the equation (205), it reduces to

$$e\,d\chi = -\,2K\varphi\left(\frac{1}{r}\right)\sin v\,ds.$$

Now, since

$$V = \frac{k}{\sqrt{p}}\,(1 + 2e\cos v + e^2)^{\frac{1}{2}},$$

we have

$$ds = Vdt = \frac{r^2}{p}\,(1 + 2e\cos v + e^2)^{\frac{1}{2}}dv,$$

and hence

$$e\,d\chi = -\frac{2}{p}\,K\varphi\left(\frac{1}{r}\right)r^2\,(1 + 2e\cos v + e^2)^{\frac{1}{2}}\sin v\,dv. \qquad (266)$$

If we suppose the function

$$K\varphi\left(\frac{1}{r}\right)r^2\,(1 + 2e\cos v + e^2)^{\frac{1}{2}},$$

the value of which is always positive, to be developed in a series arranged in reference to the cosines of v and of its multiples, so that we have

$$K\varphi\left(\frac{1}{r}\right)r^2\,(1 + 2e\cos v + e^2)^{\frac{1}{2}} = A + B\cos v + C\cos 2v + \&c., \qquad (267)$$

in which A, B, &c. are positive and functions of e, the equation (266) becomes

$$e\,d\chi = -\frac{2}{p}\,(A + B\cos v + \ldots.)\sin v\,dv.$$

Hence, by integrating, we derive

$$e\,\delta\chi = \frac{2}{p}\,(A\cos v + \tfrac{1}{4}\,B\cos 2v + \ldots.), \qquad (268)$$

from which it appears that χ is subject only to periodic perturbations on account of the resisting medium.

In a similar manner it may be shown that the second term of the second member of equation (210) produces only periodic terms in the value of δM, so that if we seek only the secular perturbations due to the action of the ethereal fluid, the first and second terms of the second member of (210) will not be considered, and only the secular perturbations arising from the variation of μ will be required.

Let us next consider the elements a and e. Substituting in the equations (198) and (202) the values of R and S given by (265), and reducing, we get

$$da = -\frac{2a^2}{p^2} K\varphi\left(\frac{1}{r}\right) r^2 (1 + 2e\cos v + e^2)^{\frac{3}{2}} dv,$$
$$de = -\frac{2}{p} K\varphi\left(\frac{1}{r}\right) r^2 (1 + 2e\cos v + e^2)^{\frac{1}{2}} (e + \cos v)\, dv. \qquad (269)$$

If we introduce into these the series (267), and integrate, it will be found that, in addition to the periodic terms, the expressions for δa and δe contain each a term multiplied by v, and hence increasing with the time. It is to be observed, further, that since A and B are positive, the secular variation of a, and also that of e, will be negative, and hence the resisting medium acts continuously to diminish both the mean distance and the eccentricity.

211. The magnitude of the disturbing force arising from the action of the resisting medium is so small that the periodic terms have no sensible influence on the place of the comet during the period in which it may be observed; and hence, since the effect of the resistance will be exhibited only by a comparison of observations made at its successive returns to the perihelion, the effect of the planetary perturbations being first completely eliminated, it is only necessary to consider the secular variations. Further, since χ is subject only to periodic changes in virtue of the action of the resistance, and since the mean longitude is subjected to a secular change only through μ, it will suffice to employ the formulæ for $\delta\mu$ and δe or $\delta\varphi$. The variations of these elements may be computed most conveniently by mechanical quadrature from given values of $\frac{d\mu}{dt}$ and $\frac{de}{dt}$ or $\frac{d\varphi}{dt}$, although their values for one complete revolution of the comet may be determined directly, the values of the coefficients A and B which appear in the series (267) being found by means of elliptic functions. The calculation of the effect of the resisting medium will be made in connection with the determination of the planetary perturbations, so that there will be no inconvenience in adding to the results the terms depending on this resistance. Since

$$\frac{d\mu}{dt} = -\frac{3}{2}\frac{\mu}{a}\cdot\frac{da}{dt}, \qquad \frac{d\varphi}{dt} = \sec\varphi\,\frac{de}{dt},$$

the equations (269) give, putting $K = k^2 U$,

$$\frac{d\mu}{dt} = 3a\mu U\varphi\left(\frac{1}{r}\right)V^3,$$
$$\frac{d\varphi}{dt} = -\frac{2k^2 p \cos E}{r \cos\varphi} U\varphi\left(\frac{1}{r}\right)V. \tag{270}$$

It remains now to make an assumption in regard to the law of the density of the resisting medium. In the case of Encke's comet it has been assumed that

$$\varphi\left(\frac{1}{r}\right) = \frac{1}{r^2},$$

and this hypothesis gives results which suffice to represent the observations at its successive returns to the perihelion. Substituting for V its value in terms of r and a, the equations (270) thus become

$$\frac{d\mu}{dt} = 3k^3 U \frac{a\mu}{r^2}\left(\frac{2}{r} - \frac{1}{a}\right)^{\frac{3}{2}},$$
$$\frac{d\varphi}{dt} = -2k^3 U \frac{a \cos\varphi \cos E}{r^3}\left(\frac{2}{r} - \frac{1}{a}\right)^{\frac{1}{2}}, \tag{271}$$

by means of which $\delta\mu$ and $\delta\varphi$ may be found; and from any given value of $\delta\mu$ we may derive the corresponding value of δa. The variation of M, neglecting the periodic terms arising from the first and second terms of the second member of equation (210), will be given by

$$\delta M = \iint \frac{d\mu}{dt}\, dt^2,$$

which will be integrated by mechanical quadrature so as to include the interval of an entire revolution of the comet. The quantity U has been determined, by means of observations of Encke's comet, to be

$$U = \frac{1}{894.892}$$

This value may be corrected by introducing a term in the equations of condition precisely as in the case of the determination of the correction to be applied to the mass of a disturbing planet. Introducing U into the equation (264), and adopting the hypothesis that $\varphi\left(\frac{1}{r}\right) = \frac{1}{r^2}$, the expression for the action of the ethereal fluid becomes

$$T = -\frac{k^2 U}{r^2} V^2.$$

Since the constant U depends on the nature of the comet, the value obtained in the case of Encke's comet may be very different from that in the case of another comet. Thus, in the case of Faye's comet the value has been found to be

$$U = \frac{1}{10.232};$$

and in the application of the formulæ to the motion of any particular body it will be necessary to make an independent determination of this constant.

212. The assumption that the density of the ethereal fluid varies inversely as the square of the distance from the sun, is that which appears to be the most probable, and the results obtained in accordance therewith seem to satisfy the data furnished by observation. It is true, however, that the whole subject is involved in great uncertainty as regards the nature of the resisting medium, so that the results obtained by means of any assumed law of density are not to be regarded as absolutely correct.

From the formulæ which have been given, it appears that, whatever may be the law of the density of the resisting fluid, the mean motion is constantly accelerated and the eccentricity diminished, and we may determine, by means of observations at the successive appearances of the comet, the amount of these secular changes independently of any assumption in regard to the density of the ether. Let x denote the variation of μ during the interval τ, which may be approximately the time of one revolution of the comet, and let y denote the corresponding variation of φ; then, after the lapse of any interval $t - T_0$, we shall have

$$\mu = \mu_0 + \frac{t - T_0}{\tau} x, \qquad \varphi = \varphi_0 + \frac{t - T_0}{\tau} y, \tag{272}$$

and, since the average variation of μ during the interval $t - T_0$ is $\frac{1}{2} \frac{t - T_0}{\tau} x$,

$$M = M_0 + \mu_0 (t - T_0) + \frac{(t - T_0)^2}{2\tau} x. \tag{273}$$

If we introduce x and y as unknown quantities in the equations of condition for the correction of the elements by means of the differences between computation and observation, the secular variations of μ and φ may be determined in connection with the corrections to be applied to the elements. For this purpose the partial differential coefficients of the geocentric spherical co-ordinates with respect to x and y must be determined. Thus, if we substitute the values of μ, φ, and M given by (272) and (273) in the equations $(12)_2$ and $(14)_2$, we obtain

$$\frac{dr}{dx}=a\tan\varphi\sin v\frac{(t-T_0)^2}{2\tau}-\frac{2r}{3\mu}\cdot\frac{t-T_0}{\tau}s,$$
$$\frac{dv}{dx}=\frac{a^2\cos\varphi}{r^2}\cdot\frac{(t-T_0)^2}{2\tau},\qquad\frac{dr}{dy}=-a\cos\varphi\cos v\frac{t-T_0}{\tau},\qquad(274)$$
$$\frac{dv}{dy}=\left(\frac{2}{\cos\varphi}+\tan\varphi\cos v\right)\sin v\frac{t-T_0}{\tau},$$

in which $s=206264''.8$, μ being expressed in seconds of arc. Combining the results thus obtained with the differential coefficients of the geocentric spherical co-ordinates with respect to r and v, as indicated by the equations $(42)_2$, we obtain the required coefficients of x and y to be introduced into the equations of condition. The solution of all the equations of condition by the method of least squares will then furnish the most probable values of y and x, or of the secular variations of the eccentricity and mean motion, without any assumption being made in reference either to the density of the ethereal fluid or to the modifications of the resistance on account of the changes in the form and dimensions of the comet, and the results thus derived may be employed in determining the values of M, μ, and φ for the subsequent returns of the comet to the perihelion.

In all the cases in which the periodic comets have been observed sufficiently, the existence of these secular changes of the elements seems to be well established; and if we grant that they arise from the resistance of an ethereal fluid, the total obliteration of our solar system is to be the final result. The fact that no such inequalities have yet been detected in the case of the motion of any of the planets, shows simply the immensity of the period which must elapse before the final catastrophe, and does not render it any the less certain. Such, indeed, appear to be the present indications of science in regard to this important question; but it is by no means impossible that, as in at least one similar case already, the operation of the simple and unique law of gravitation will alone completely explain these inequalities, and assign a limit which they can never pass, and thus afford a sublime proof of the provident care of the OMNIPOTENT CREATOR.

TABLES.

TABLE I. Angle of the Vertical and Logarithm of the Earth's Radius.

Argument ϕ = Geographical Latitude. Compression $= \frac{1}{299.15}$

ϕ	$\phi - \phi'$	Diff.	$\log \rho$	Diff.	ϕ	$\phi - \phi'$	Diff.	$\log \rho$	Diff.
° ′	′ ″	″			° ′	′ ″	″		
0 0	0 0.00	24.02	0.000 0000	4	**35** 0	10 48.25	1.38	9.999 5248	40
1 0	0 24.02	24.00	9.999 9996	14	10	49.63	1.35	5208	39
2 0	0 48.02	23.93	9982	21	20	50.98	1.33	5169	40
3 0	1 11.95	23.85	9961	31	30	52.31	1.31	5129	40
4 0	1 35.80	23.74	9930	39	40	53.62	1.28	5089	40
5 0	1 59.54	23.58	9891	48	50	54.90	1.26	5049	40
6 0	2 23.12	23.42	9.999 9843	57	**36** 0	10 56.16	1.25	9.999 5009	40
7 0	2 46.54	23.22	9786	65	10	57.41	1.22	4969	40
8 0	3 9.76	22.98	9721	73	20	58.63	1.19	4929	41
9 0	3 32.74	22.73	9648	82	30	10 59.82	1.18	4888	40
10 0	3 55.47	22.45	9566	90	40	11 1.00	1.15	4848	41
11 0	4 17.92	22.14	9476	99	50	2.15	1.13	4807	40
12 0	4 40.06	21.79	9.999 9377	106	**37** 0	11 3.28	1.11	9.999 4767	41
13 0	5 1.85	21.43	9271	114	10	4.39	1.08	4726	40
14 0	5 23.28	21.05	9157	122	20	5.47	1.07	4686	41
15 0	5 44.33	20.62	9035	130	30	6.54	1.04	4645	41
16 0	6 4.95	20.19	8905	137	40	7.58	1.01	4604	41
17 0	6 25.14	19.72	8768	144	50	8.59	1.00	4563	41
18 0	6 44.86	19.23	9.999 8624	152	**38** 0	11 9.59	0.97	9.999 4522	41
19 0	7 4.09	18.71	8472	158	10	10.56	0.95	4481	41
20 0	7 22.80	18.19	8314	165	20	11.51	0.93	4440	41
21 0	7 40.99	17.62	8149	172	30	12.44	0.90	4399	41
22 0	7 58.61	17.05	7977	178	40	13.34	0.88	4358	41
23 0	8 15.66	16.44	7799	185	50	14.22	0.86	4317	41
24 0	8 32.10	15.83	9.999 7614	190	**39** 0	11 15.08	0.84	9.999 4276	42
25 0	8 47.93	15.19	7424	196	10	15.92	0.81	4234	41
26 0	9 3.12	14.53	7228	201	20	16.73	0.79	4193	41
27 0	9 17.65	13.85	7027	207	30	17.52	0.77	4152	42
28 0	9 31.50	13.16	6820	212	40	18.29	0.75	4110	41
29 0	9 44.66	12.46	6608	216	50	19.04	0.72	4069	42
30 0	9 57.12	2.00	9.999 6392	37	**40** 0	11 19.76	0.70	9.999 4027	42
10	9 59.12	1.99	6355	36	10	20.46	0.67	3985	41
20	10 1.11	1.96	6319	37	20	21.13	0.66	3944	42
30	3.07	1.95	6282	37	30	21.79	0.63	3902	42
40	5.02	1.92	6245	37	40	22.42	0.60	3860	41
50	6.94	1.91	6208	37	50	23.02	0.59	3819	42
31 0	10 8.85	1.88	9.999 6171	37	**41** 0	11 23.61	0.56	9.999 3777	42
10	10.73	1.86	6134	38	10	24.17	0.53	3735	42
20	12.59	1.85	6096	37	20	24.70	0.52	3693	42
30	14.44	1.82	6059	38	30	25.22	0.49	3651	42
40	16.26	1.80	6021	37	40	25.71	0.47	3609	42
50	18.06	1.78	5984	38	50	26.18	0.44	3567	42
32 0	10 19.84	1.76	9.999 5946	38	**42** 0	11 26.62	0.42	9.999 3525	42
10	21.60	1.74	5908	38	10	27.04	0.40	3483	42
20	23.34	1.71	5870	38	20	27.44	0.38	3441	42
30	25.05	1.70	5832	38	30	27.82	0.35	3399	42
40	26.75	1.68	5794	39	40	28.17	0.33	3357	42
50	28.43	1.65	5755	38	50	28.50	0.30	3315	42
33 0	10 30.08	1.63	9.999 5717	39	**43** 0	11 28.80	0.28	9.999 3273	43
10	31.71	1.61	5678	38	10	29.08	0.26	3230	42
20	33.32	1.59	5640	39	20	29.34	0.24	3188	42
30	34.91	1.57	5601	39	30	29.58	0.21	3146	42
40	36.48	1.55	5562	39	40	29.79	0.19	3104	42
50	38.03	1.52	5523	39	50	29.98	0.16	3062	43
34 0	10 39.55	1.51	9.999 5484	39	**44** 0	11 30.14	0.15	9.999 3019	42
10	41.06	1.48	5445	39	10	30.29	0.12	2977	42
20	42.54	1.46	5406	39	20	30.41	0.09	2935	43
30	44.00	1.44	5367	40	30	30.50	0.07	2892	42
40	45.44	1.42	5327	39	40	30.57	0.05	2850	42
50	46.86	1.39	5288	40	50	30.62	0.03	2808	42
35 0	10 48.25		9.999 5248		**45** 0	11 30.65		9.999 2766	

TABLE I. Angle of the Vertical and Logarithm of the Earth's Radius.

ϕ' = Geocentric Latitude. ρ = Earth's Radius.

ϕ	$\phi-\phi'$	Diff.	$\log\rho$	Diff.	ϕ	$\phi-\phi'$	Diff.	$\log\rho$	Diff.
° ′	′ ″	″			° ′	′ ″	″		
45 0	11 30.65		9.999 2766		**55** 0	10 49.74		9.999 0275	
10	30.65	0.00	2723	43	10	48.36	1.38	0235	40
20	30.63	0.02	2681	42	20	46.97	1.39	0195	40
30	30.58	0.05	2639	42	30	45.55	1.42	0155	40
40	30.51	0.07	2596	43	40	44.11	1.44	0116	39
50	30.42	0.09	2554	42	50	42.65	1.46	0076	40
46 0	11 30.31	0.11	9.999 2512	42	**56** 0	10 41.16	1.49	9.999 0037	39
10	30.17	0.14	2470	42	10	39.65	1.51	9.998 9998	39
20	30.01	0.16	2427	43	20	38.13	1.52	9958	40
30	29.82	0.19	2385	42	30	36.58	1.55	9919	39
40	29.61	0.21	2343	42	40	35.01	1.57	9880	39
50	29.38	0.23	2300	43	50	33.41	1.60	9841	39
47 0	11 29.12	0.26	9.999 2258	42	**57** 0	10 31.80	1.61	9.998 9802	39
10	28.85	0.27	2216	42	10	30.16	1.64	9764	38
20	28.54	0.31	2174	42	20	28.50	1.66	9725	39
30	28.22	0.32	2132	42	30	26.83	1.67	9686	39
40	27.87	0.35	2089	43	40	25.13	1.70	9648	38
50	27.50	0.37	2047	42	50	23.40	1.73	9610	38
48 0	11 27.10	0.40	9.999 2005	42	**58** 0	10 21.66	1.74	9.998 9571	39
10	26.69	0.41	1963	42	10	19.90	1.76	9533	38
20	26.24	0.45	1921	42	20	18.11	1.79	9495	38
30	25.78	0.46	1879	42	30	16.31	1.80	9457	38
40	25.29	0.49	1837	42	40	14.48	1.83	9419	38
50	24.78	0.51	1795	42	50	12.63	1.85	9382	37
49 0	11 24.24	0.54	9.999 1753	42	**59** 0	10 10.77	1.86	9.998 9344	38
10	23.69	0.55	1711	42	10	8.88	1.89	9307	37
20	23.11	0.58	1669	42	20	6.97	1.91	9269	38
30	22.50	0.61	1627	42	30	5.04	1.93	9232	37
40	21.87	0.63	1586	41	40	3.08	1.96	9195	37
50	21.22	0.65	1544	42	50	10 1.11	1.97	9158	37
50 0	11 20.55	0.67	9.999 1502	42	**60** 0	9 59.12	1.99	9.998 9121	37
10	19.85	0.70	1460	42	**61** 0	9 46.74	12.38	8902	219
20	19.13	0.72	1419	41	**62** 0	9 33.65	13.09	8688	214
30	18.39	0.74	1377	42	**63** 0	9 19.85	13.80	8479	209
40	17.63	0.76	1335	42	**64** 0	9 5.36	14.49	8275	204
50	16.84	0.79	1294	41	**65** 0	8 50.21	15.15	8077	198
51 0	11 16.02	0.82	9.999 1252	42	**66** 0	8 34.40	15.81	9.998 7884	193
10	15.19	0.83	1211	41	**67** 0	8 17.97	16.43	7697	187
20	14.33	0.86	1170	41	**68** 0	8 0.92	17.05	7517	180
30	13.45	0.88	1128	42	**69** 0	7 43.29	17.63	7342	175
40	12.55	0.90	1087	41	**70** 0	7 25.08	18.21	7174	168
50	11.62	0.93	1046	41	**71** 0	7 6.33	18.75	7013	161
52 0	11 10.67	0.95	9.999 1005	41	**72** 0	6 47.06	19.27	9.998 6859	154
10	9.70	0.97	0963	42	**73** 0	6 27.28	19.78	6713	146
20	8.71	0.99	0922	41	**74** 0	6 7.03	20.25	6573	140
30	7.69	1.02	0881	41	**75** 0	5 46.33	20.70	6441	132
40	6.66	1.03	0840	41	**76** 0	5 25.20	21.13	6317	124
50	5.60	1.06	0800	40	**77** 0	5 3.67	21.53	6201	116
53 0	11 4.51	1.09	9.999 0759	41	**78** 0	4 41.77	21.90	9.998 6093	108
10	3.40	1.11	0718	41	**79** 0	4 19.53	22.24	5993	100
20	2.27	1.13	0677	41	**80** 0	3 56.96	22.57	5901	92
30	11 1.12	1.15	0637	40	**81** 0	3 34.10	22.86	5818	83
40	10 59.94	1.18	0596	41	**82** 0	3 10.98	23.12	5743	75
50	58.74	1.20	0556	40	**83** 0	2 47.63	23.35	5676	67
54 0	10 57.52	1.22	9.999 0515	41	**84** 0	2 24.07	23.56	9.998 5619	57
10	56.28	1.24	0475	40	**85** 0	2 0.33	23.74	5570	49
20	55.02	1.26	0435	40	**86** 0	1 36.44	23.89	5530	40
30	53.73	1.29	0395	40	**87** 0	1 12.43	24.01	5498	32
40	52.42	1.31	0355	40	**88** 0	0 48.34	24.09	5476	22
50	51.09	1.33	0315	40	**89** 0	0 24.18	24.16	5463	13
55 0	10 49.74	1.35	9.999 0275	40	**90** 0	0 0.00	24.18	9.998 5458	5

TABLE II.

For converting intervals of Mean Solar Time into equivalent intervals of Sidereal Time.

Hours.		Minutes.		Seconds.		Decimals.	
Mean T.	Sidereal Time.	Mean T.	Sidereal Time.	Mean T.	Sidereal Time.	Mean T.	Sidereal Time.
h	h m s	m	m s	s	s	s	s
1	1 0 9.856	1	1 0.164	1	1.003	0.02	0.020
2	2 0 19.713	2	2 0.329	2	2.005	0.04	0.040
3	3 0 29.569	3	3 0.493	3	3.008	0.06	0.060
4	4 0 39.426	4	4 0.657	4	4.011	0.08	0.080
5	5 0 49.282	5	5 0.821	5	5.014	0.10	0.100
6	6 0 59.139	6	6 0.986	6	6.016	0.12	0.120
7	7 1 8.995	7	7 1.150	7	7.019	0.14	0.140
8	8 1 18.852	8	8 1.314	8	8.022	0.16	0.160
9	9 1 28.708	9	9 1.478	9	9.025	0.18	0.180
10	10 1 38.565	10	10 1.643	10	10.027	0.20	0.201
11	11 1 48.421	11	11 1.807	11	11.030	0.22	0.221
12	12 1 58.278	12	12 1.971	12	12.033	0.24	0.241
13	13 2 8.134	13	13 2.136	13	13.036	0.26	0.261
14	14 2 17.991	14	14 2.300	14	14.038	0.28	0.281
15	15 2 27.847	15	15 2.464	15	15.041	0.30	0.301
16	16 2 37.704	16	16 2.628	16	16.044	0.32	0.321
17	17 2 47.560	17	17 2.793	17	17.047	0.34	0.341
18	18 2 57.416	18	18 2.957	18	18.049	0.36	0.361
19	19 3 7.273	19	19 3.121	19	19.052	0.38	0.381
20	20 3 17.129	20	20 3.285	20	20.055	0.40	0.401
21	21 3 26.986	21	21 3.450	21	21.057	0.42	0.421
22	22 3 36.842	22	22 3.614	22	22.060	0.44	0.441
23	23 3 46.699	23	23 3.778	23	23.063	0.46	0.461
24	24 3 56.555	24	24 3.943	24	24.066	0.48	0.481
		25	25 4.107	25	25.068	0.50	0.501
		26	26 4.271	26	26.071	0.52	0.521
		27	27 4.435	27	27.074	0.54	0.541
		28	28 4.600	28	28.077	0.56	0.562
		29	29 4.764	29	29.079	0.58	0.582
		30	30 4.928	30	30.082	0.60	0.602
		31	31 5.092	31	31.085	0.62	0.622
		32	32 5.257	32	32.088	0.64	0.642
		33	33 5.421	33	33.090	0.66	0.662
		34	34 5.585	34	34.093	0.68	0.682
		35	35 5.750	35	35.096	0.70	0.702
		36	36 5.914	36	36.099	0.72	0.722
		37	37 6.078	37	37.101	0.74	0.742
		38	38 6.242	38	38.104	0.76	0.762
		39	39 6.407	39	39.107	0.78	0.782
		40	40 6.571	40	40.110	0.80	0.802
		41	41 6.735	41	41.112	0.82	0.822
		42	42 6.899	42	42.115	0.84	0.842
		43	43 7.064	43	43.118	0.86	0.862
		44	44 7.228	44	44.120	0.88	0.882
		45	45 7.392	45	45.123	0.90	0.902
		46	46 7.557	46	46.126	0.92	0.923
		47	47 7.721	47	47.129	0.94	0.943
		48	48 7.885	48	48.131	0.96	0.963
		49	49 8.049	49	49.134	0.98	0.983
		50	50 8.214	50	50.137	1.00	1.003
		51	51 8.378	51	51.140		
		52	52 8.542	52	52.142		
		53	53 8.707	53	53.145		
		54	54 8.871	54	54.148		
		55	55 9.035	55	55.151		
		56	56 9.199	56	56.153		
		57	57 9.364	57	57.156		
		58	58 9.528	58	58.159		
		59	59 9.692	59	59.162		
		60	60 9.856	60	60.164		

This table is useful for the conversion of Mean Solar into Sidereal Time.
Sidereal Time required = sidereal time at the preceding mean noon
+ the equivalent to the given mean time.

TABLE III.

For converting intervals of Sidereal Time into equivalent intervals of Mean Solar Time.

Hours.		Minutes.		Seconds.		Decimals.	
Sid. T.	Mean Time.	Sid. T.	Mean Time.	Sid. T.	Mean Time.	Sid. T.	Mean Time.
h	*h m s*	*m*	*m s*	*s*	*s*	*s*	*s*
1	0 59 50.170	1	0 59.836	1	0.997	0.02	0.020
2	1 59 40.341	2	1 59.672	2	1.995	0.04	0.040
3	2 59 30.511	3	2 59.509	3	2.992	0.06	0.060
4	3 59 20.682	4	3 59.345	4	3.989	0.08	0.080
5	4 59 10.852	5	4 59.181	5	4.986	0.10	0.100
6	5 59 1.023	6	5 59.017	6	5.984	0.12	0.120
7	6 58 51.193	7	6 58.853	7	6.981	0.14	0.140
8	7 58 41.363	8	7 58.689	8	7.978	0.16	0.160
9	8 58 31.534	9	8 58.526	9	8.975	0.18	0.180
10	9 58 21.704	10	9 58.362	10	9.973	0.20	0.199
11	10 58 11.875	11	10 58.198	11	10.970	0.22	0.219
12	11 58 2.045	12	11 58.034	12	11.967	0.24	0.239
13	12 57 52.216	13	12 57.870	13	12.964	0.26	0.259
14	13 57 42.386	14	13 57.706	14	13.962	0.28	0.279
15	14 57 32.557	15	14 57.543	15	14.959	0.30	0.299
16	15 57 22.727	16	15 57.379	16	15.956	0.32	0.319
17	16 57 12.897	17	16 57.215	17	16.954	0.34	0.339
18	17 57 3.068	18	17 57.051	18	17.951	0.36	0.359
19	18 56 53.238	19	18 56.887	19	18.948	0.38	0.379
20	19 56 43.409	20	19 56.723	20	19.945	0.40	0.399
21	20 56 33.579	21	20 56.560	21	20.943	0.42	0.419
22	21 56 23.750	22	21 56.396	22	21.940	0.44	0.439
23	22 56 13.920	23	22 56.232	23	22.937	0.46	0.459
24	23 56 4.091	24	23 56.068	24	23.934	0.48	0.479
		25	24 55.904	25	24.932	0.50	0.499
		26	25 55.740	26	25.929	0.52	0.519
		27	26 55.577	27	26.926	0.54	0.539
		28	27 55.413	28	27.924	0.56	0.558
		29	28 55.249	29	28.921	0.58	0.578
		30	29 55.085	30	29.918	0.60	0.598
		31	30 54.921	31	30.915	0.62	0.618
		32	31 54.758	32	31.913	0.64	0.638
		33	32 54.594	33	32.910	0.66	0.658
		34	33 54.430	34	33.907	0.68	0.678
		35	34 54.266	35	34.904	0.70	0.698
		36	35 54.102	36	35.902	0.72	0.718
		37	36 53.938	37	36.899	0.74	0.738
		38	37 53.775	38	37.896	0.76	0.758
		39	38 53.611	39	38.894	0.78	0.778
		40	39 53.447	40	39.891	0.80	0.798
		41	40 53.283	41	40.888	0.82	0.818
		42	41 53.119	42	41.885	0.84	0.838
		43	42 52.955	43	42.883	0.86	0.858
		44	43 52.792	44	43.880	0.88	0.878
		45	44 52.628	45	44.877	0.90	0.898
		46	45 52.464	46	45.874	0.92	0.917
		47	46 52.300	47	46.872	0.94	0.937
		48	47 52.136	48	47.869	0.96	0.957
		49	48 51.972	49	48.866	0.98	0.977
		50	49 51.809	50	49.863	1.00	0.997
		51	50 51.645	51	50.861		
		52	51 51.481	52	51.858		
		53	52 51.317	53	52.855		
		54	53 51.153	54	53.853		
		55	54 50.990	55	54.850		
		56	55 50.826	56	55.847		
		57	56 50.662	57	56.844		
		58	57 50.498	58	57.842		
		59	58 50.334	59	58.839		
		60	59 50.170	60	59.836		

This table is useful for the conversion of Sidereal into Mean Solar Time.
Mean solar time required = mean time at the preceding sidereal noon
+ the equivalent to the given sidereal time.

TABLE IV.

For converting Hours, Minutes, and Seconds into Decimals of a Day.

Hours.	Decimal.	Min.	Decimal.	Min.	Decimal.	Sec.	Decimal.	Sec.	Decimal.
1	0.0416 +	1	.000694 +	31	.021527 +	1	.0000116	31	.0003588
2	.0833 +	2	.001388 +	32	.022222 +	2	.0000231	32	.0003704
3	.1250 +	3	.002083 +	33	.022916 +	3	.0000347	33	.0003819
4	.1666 +	4	.002777 +	34	.023611 +	4	.0000463	34	.0003935
5	.2083 +	5	.003472 +	35	.024305 +	5	.0000579	35	.0004051
6	.2500 +	6	.004166 +	36	.025000 +	6	.0000694	36	.0004167
7	0.2916 +	7	.004861 +	37	.025694 +	7	.0000810	37	.0004282
8	.3333 +	8	.005555 +	38	.026388 +	8	.0000925	38	.0004398
9	.3750 +	9	.006250 +	39	.027083 +	9	.0001042	39	.0004514
10	.4166 +	10	.006944 +	40	.027777 +	10	.0001157	40	.0004630
11	.4583 +	11	.007638 +	41	.028472 +	11	.0001273	41	.0004745
12	.5000 +	12	.008333 +	42	.029166 +	12	.0001389	42	.0004861
13	0.5416 +	13	.009027 +	43	.029861 +	13	.0001505	43	.0004977
14	.5833 +	14	.009722 +	44	.030555 +	14	.0001620	44	.0005093
15	.6250 +	15	.010416 +	45	.031250 +	15	.0001736	45	.0005208
16	.6666 +	16	.011111 +	46	.031944 +	16	.0001852	46	.0005324
17	.7083 +	17	.011805 +	47	.032638 +	17	.0001968	47	.0005440
18	.7500 +	18	.012500 +	48	.033333 +	18	.0002083	48	.0005556
19	0.7916 +	19	.013194 +	49	.034027 +	19	.0002199	49	.0005671
20	.8333 +	20	.013888 +	50	.034722 +	20	.0002315	50	.0005787
21	.8750 +	21	.014583 +	51	.035416 +	21	.0002431	51	.0005903
22	.9166 +	22	.015277 +	52	.036111 +	22	.0002546	52	.0006019
23	0.9583 +	23	.015972 +	53	.036805 +	23	.0002662	53	.0006134
24	1.0000 +	24	.016666 +	54	.037500 +	24	.0002778	54	.0006250
		25	.017361 +	55	.038194 +	25	.0002894	55	.0006366
		26	.018055 +	56	.038888 +	26	.0003009	56	.0006481
		27	.018750 +	57	.039583 +	27	.0003125	57	.0006597
		28	.019444 +	58	.040277 +	28	.0003241	58	.0006713
		29	.020138 +	59	.040972 +	29	.0003356	59	.0006829
		30	.020833 +	60	.041666 +	30	.0003472	60	.0006944

The sign +, appended to numbers in this table, signifies that the last figure repeats to infinity.

TABLE V.

For finding the number of Days from the beginning of the Year.

Date.	Com.	Bis.
January 0.0	0	0
February 0.0	31	31
March 0.0	59	60
April 0.0	90	91
May 0.0	120	121
June 0.0	151	152
July 0.0	181	182
August 0.0	212	213
September 0.0	243	244
October 0.0	273	274
November 0.0	304	305
December 0.0	334	335

TABLE VI.

For finding the True Anomaly or the Time from the Perihelion in a Parabolic Orbit.

v.	0°		1°		2°		3°	
	M.	Diff. 1″.	M.	Diff. 1″.	M.	Diff. 1″.	M.	Diff. 1″.
0′	0.000000	181.81	0.654532	181.83	1.309263	181.92	1.964393	182.05
1	0.010908	181.81	0.665442	181.83	1.320178	181.92	1.975316	182.06
2	0.021817	181.81	0.676352	181.83	1.331093	181.92	1.986240	182.06
3	0.032725	181.81	0.687262	181.84	1.342008	181.92	1.997164	182.06
4	0.043633	181.81	0.698172	181.84	1.352923	181.92	2.008087	182.07
5	0.054542	181.81	0.709082	181.84	1.363839	181.93	2.019011	182.07
6	0.065450	181.81	0.719993	181.84	1.374755	181.93	2.029936	182.07
7	0.076358	181.81	0.730903	181.84	1.385670	181.93	2.040860	182.07
8	0.087267	181.81	0.741813	181.84	1.396586	181.93	2.051785	182.08
9	0.098175	181.81	0.752724	181.84	1.407502	181.93	2.062709	182.08
10	0.109083	181.81	0.763634	181.84	1.418418	181.94	2.073634	182.08
11	0.119992	181.81	0.774545	181.84	1.429334	181.94	2.084559	182.08
12	0.130900	181.81	0.785456	181.84	1.440251	181.94	2.095485	182.09
13	0.141808	181.81	0.796366	181.85	1.451167	181.94	2.106410	182.09
14	0.152717	181.81	0.807277	181.85	1.462083	181.94	2.117335	182.09
15	0.163625	181.81	0.818188	181.85	1.473000	181.95	2.128261	182.10
16	0.174534	181.81	0.829099	181.85	1.483917	181.95	2.139187	182.10
17	0.185442	181.81	0.840010	181.85	1.494834	181.95	2.150114	182.10
18	0.196350	181.81	0.850921	181.85	1.505751	181.95	2.161040	182.11
19	0.207259	181.81	0.861832	181.85	1.516668	181.95	2.171966	182.11
20	0.218167	181.81	0.872743	181.85	1.527585	181.96	2.182894	182.11
21	0.229076	181.81	0.883654	181.86	1.538503	181.96	2.193820	182.12
22	0.239984	181.81	0.894566	181.86	1.549420	181.96	2.204747	182.12
23	0.250893	181.81	0.905478	181.86	1.560338	181.96	2.215674	182.12
24	0.261801	181.81	0.916389	181.86	1.571256	181.96	2.226602	182.13
25	0.272710	181.81	0.927301	181.86	1.582174	181.97	2.237529	182.13
26	0.283619	181.81	0.938212	181.86	1.593092	181.97	2.248457	182.13
27	0.294527	181.81	0.949124	181.86	1.604010	181.97	2.259385	182.14
28	0.305436	181.81	0.960036	181.86	1.614928	181.97	2.270313	182.14
29	0.316345	181.81	0.970948	181.87	1.625847	181.97	2.281242	182.14
30	0.327253	181.81	0.981860	181.87	1.636766	181.98	2.292170	182.14
31	0.338162	181.81	0.992772	181.87	1.647684	181.98	2.303099	182.15
32	0.349071	181.81	1.003684	181.87	1.658603	181.98	2.314028	182.15
33	0.359980	181.81	1.014596	181.87	1.669522	181.98	2.324957	182.15
34	0.370888	181.81	1.025509	181.87	1.680441	181.99	2.335887	182.16
35	0.381797	181.81	1.036421	181.87	1.691361	181.99	2.346816	182.16
36	0.392706	181.81	1.047334	181.87	1.702280	181.99	2.357746	182.16
37	0.403615	181.81	1.058246	181.88	1.713200	181.99	2.368676	182.17
38	0.414524	181.82	1.069159	181.88	1.724120	182.00	2.379606	182.17
39	0.425433	181.82	1.080072	181.88	1.735039	182.00	2.390536	182.17
40	0.436342	181.82	1.090985	181.88	1.745960	182.00	2.401467	182.18
41	0.447251	181.82	1.101898	181.88	1.756880	182.00	2.412398	182.18
42	0.458160	181.82	1.112811	181.89	1.767800	182.01	2.423329	182.18
43	0.469069	181.82	1.123724	181.89	1.778721	182.01	2.434260	182.19
44	0.479979	181.82	1.134637	181.89	1.789641	182.01	2.445191	182.19
45	0.490888	181.82	1.145550	181.89	1.800562	182.01	2.456123	182.19
46	0.501797	181.82	1.156464	181.89	1.811483	182.02	2.467055	182.20
47	0.512706	181.82	1.167377	181.89	1.822404	182.02	2.477987	182.20
48	0.523616	181.82	1.178291	181.89	1.833325	182.02	2.488919	182.20
49	0.534525	181.82	1.189205	181.90	1.844247	182.02	2.499851	182.21
50	0.545435	181.82	1.200119	181.90	1.855168	182.03	2.510784	182.21
51	0.556344	181.82	1.211033	181.90	1.866090	182.03	2.521717	182.22
52	0.567254	181.82	1.221947	181.90	1.877012	182.04	2.532650	182.22
53	0.578163	181.83	1.232861	181.90	1.887934	182.04	2.543583	182.22
54	0.589073	181.83	1.243775	181.91	1.898856	182.04	2.554517	182.23
55	0.599983	181.83	1.254689	181.91	1.909779	182.04	2.565450	182.23
56	0.610892	181.83	1.265604	181.91	1.920701	182.04	2.576384	182.23
57	0.621802	181.83	1.276518	181.91	1.931624	182.05	2.587319	182.24
58	0.632712	181.83	1.287433	181.91	1.942547	182.05	2.598253	182.24
59	0.643622	181.83	1.298348	181.91	1.953470	182.05	2.609187	182.24
60	0.654532	181.83	1.309263	181.92	1.964393	182.05	2.620122	182.25

TABLE VI.

For finding the True Anomaly or the Time from the Perihelion in a Parabolic Orbit.

v.	4°		5°		6°		7°	
	M.	Diff. 1″.	M.	Diff. 1″.	M.	Diff. 1″.	M.	Diff. 1″.
0′	2.620122	182.25	3.276651	182.50	3.934182	182.80	4.592917	183.17
1	2.631057	182.25	3.287602	182.50	3.945151	182.81	4.603907	183.18
2	2.641993	182.26	3.298552	182.51	3.956119	182.82	4.614898	183.18
3	2.652928	182.26	3.309503	182.51	3.967088	182.82	4.625889	183.19
4	2.663864	182.26	3.320454	182.52	3.978058	182.83	4.636880	183.19
5	2.674800	182.27	3.331405	182.52	3.989028	182.83	4.647872	183.20
6	2.685736	182.27	3.342356	182.53	3.999998	182.84	4.658864	183.21
7	2.696672	182.27	3.353308	182.53	4.010968	182.84	4.669857	183.21
8	2.707609	182.28	3.364260	182.54	4.021939	182.85	4.680850	183.22
9	2.718546	182.28	3.375212	182.54	4.032911	182.86	4.691843	183.23
10	2.729483	182.29	3.386165	182.55	4.043882	182.86	4.702837	183.24
11	2.740420	182.29	3.397118	182.55	4.054854	182.87	4.713831	183.24
12	2.751358	182.29	3.408071	182.56	4.065826	182.87	4.724826	183.25
13	2.762295	182.30	3.419024	182.56	4.076799	182.88	4.735821	183.25
14	2.773233	182.30	3.429978	182.57	4.087772	182.88	4.746816	183.26
15	2.784172	182.31	3.440932	182.57	4.098745	182.89	4.757812	183.27
16	2.795110	182.31	3.451887	182.58	4.109718	182.90	4.768809	183.27
17	2.806049	182.31	3.462841	182.58	4.120692	182.90	4.779805	183.28
18	2.816988	182.32	3.473796	182.59	4.131667	182.91	4.790802	183.28
19	2.827927	182.32	3.484752	182.59	4.142641	182.91	4.801800	183.29
20	2.838867	182.33	3.495707	182.60	4.153616	182.92	4.812797	183.30
21	2.849806	182.33	3.506663	182.60	4.164592	182.93	4.823796	183.31
22	2.860746	182.33	3.517619	182.61	4.175568	182.93	4.834795	183.32
23	2.871686	182.34	3.528575	182.61	4.186544	182.94	4.845794	183.32
24	2.882627	182.34	3.539532	182.61	4.197520	182.94	4.856793	183.33
25	2.893567	182.35	3.550489	182.62	4.208497	182.95	4.867793	183.34
26	2.904508	182.35	3.561447	182.62	4.219474	182.95	4.878793	183.34
27	2.915449	182.36	3.572404	182.63	4.230451	182.96	4.889794	183.35
28	2.926391	182.36	3.583362	182.63	4.241429	182.97	4.900795	183.36
29	2.937332	182.36	3.594320	182.64	4.252408	182.97	4.911797	183.36
30	2.948274	182.37	3.605279	182.64	4.263386	182.98	4.922799	183.37
31	2.959217	182.37	3.616238	182.65	4.274365	182.99	4.933801	183.38
32	2.970159	182.37	3.627197	182.65	4.285344	182.99	4.944804	183.38
33	2.981102	182.38	3.638156	182.66	4.296324	183.00	4.955807	183.39
34	2.992045	182.38	3.649116	182.66	4.307304	183.00	4.966811	183.40
35	3.002988	182.39	3.660076	182.67	4.318284	183.01	4.977815	183.41
36	3.013931	182.39	3.671037	182.68	4.329265	183.01	4.988820	183.41
37	3.024875	182.39	3.681997	182.68	4.340246	183.02	4.999825	183.42
38	3.035819	182.40	3.692958	182.69	4.351228	183.03	5.010830	183.43
39	3.046763	182.40	3.703920	182.69	4.362210	183.03	5.021836	183.43
40	3.057707	182.41	3.714881	182.70	4.373192	183.04	5.032842	183.44
41	3.068652	182.41	3.725843	182.70	4.384175	183.05	5.043849	183.45
42	3.079597	182.42	3.736806	182.71	4.395158	183.05	5.054856	183.46
43	3.090542	182.42	3.747768	182.71	4.406141	183.06	5.065864	183.46
44	3.101488	182.43	3.758731	182.72	4.417125	183.06	5.076872	183.47
45	3.112433	182.43	3.769694	182.72	4.428109	183.07	5.087880	183.48
46	3.123379	182.44	3.780658	182.72	4.439093	183.08	5.098889	183.48
47	3.134325	182.44	3.791622	182.73	4.450078	183.08	5.109898	183.49
48	3.145272	182.44	3.802586	182.74	4.461064	183.09	5.120908	183.50
49	3.156219	182.45	3.813551	182.74	4.472049	183.10	5.131918	183.51
50	3.167166	182.45	3.824515	182.75	4.483035	183.10	5.142929	183.51
51	3.178113	182.46	3.835481	182.76	4.494022	183.11	5.153940	183.52
52	3.189061	182.46	3.846446	182.76	4.505008	183.12	5.164951	183.53
53	3.200009	182.47	3.857412	182.77	4.515995	183.12	5.175963	183.54
54	3.210957	182.47	3.868378	182.77	4.526983	183.13	5.186975	183.54
55	3.221905	182.48	3.879345	182.78	4.537971	183.14	5.197988	183.55
56	3.232854	182.48	3.890312	182.78	4.548959	183.14	5.209002	183.56
57	3.243803	182.49	3.901279	182.79	4.559948	183.15	5.220015	183.57
58	3.254752	182.49	3.912246	182.79	4.570937	183.15	5.231029	183.57
59	3.265702	182.49	3.923214	182.80	4.581927	183.16	5.242044	183.58
60	3.276651	182.50	3.934182	182.80	4.592917	183.17	5.253059	183.59

TABLE VI.

For finding the True Anomaly or the Time from the Perihelion in a Parabolic Orbit.

v.	8°		9°		10°		11°	
	M.	Diff. 1″.	M.	Diff. 1″.	M.	Diff. 1″.	M.	Diff. 1″.
0′	5.253059	183.59	5.914815	184.06	6.578391	184.60	7.243997	185.19
1	5.264075	183.59	5.925859	184.07	6.589467	184.61	7.255109	185.20
2	5.275090	183.60	5.936904	184.08	6.600544	184.62	7.266222	185.21
3	5.286107	183.61	5.947949	184.09	6.611622	184.63	7.277335	185.22
4	5.297124	183.62	5.958995	184.10	6.622700	184.64	7.288449	185.23
5	5.308141	183.62	5.970041	184.11	6.633778	184.65	7.299563	185.25
6	5.319159	183.63	5.981087	184.11	6.644857	184.66	7.310678	185.26
7	5.330177	183.64	5.992134	184.12	6.655937	184.67	7.321793	185.27
8	5.341195	183.65	6.003182	184.13	6.667017	184.67	7.332909	185.28
9	5.352214	183.66	6.014230	184.14	6.678098	184.68	7.344026	185.29
10	5.363234	183.66	6.025279	184.15	6.689179	184.69	7.355144	185.30
11	5.374254	183.67	6.036328	184.16	6.700261	184.70	7.366262	185.31
12	5.385275	183.68	6.047378	184.17	6.711343	184.71	7.377381	185.32
13	5.396296	183.69	6.058428	184.18	6.722426	184.72	7.388500	185.33
14	5.407317	183.69	6.069479	184.18	6.733510	184.73	7.399620	185.34
15	5.418339	183.70	6.080530	184.19	6.744594	184.74	7.410741	185.35
16	5.429361	183.71	6.091582	184.20	6.755679	184.75	7.421862	185.36
17	5.440384	183.72	6.102634	184.21	6.766764	184.76	7.432983	185.37
18	5.451407	183.73	6.113687	184.22	6.777850	184.77	7.444106	185.38
19	5.462431	183.73	6.124740	184.23	6.788937	184.78	7.455230	185.39
20	5.473455	183.74	6.135794	184.24	6.800024	184.79	7.466354	185.40
21	5.484480	183.75	6.146849	184.25	6.811112	184.80	7.477478	185.41
22	5.495505	183.75	6.157904	184.25	6.822200	184.81	7.488603	185.42
23	5.506530	183.76	6.168959	184.26	6.833289	184.82	7.499729	185.43
24	5.517556	183.77	6.180015	184.27	6.844378	184.83	7.510855	185.44
25	5.528583	183.78	6.191072	184.28	6.855468	184.84	7.521982	185.46
26	5.539610	183.79	6.202129	184.29	6.866559	184.85	7.533110	185.47
27	5.550637	183.79	6.213187	184.30	6.877650	184.86	7.544239	185.48
28	5.561665	183.80	6.224245	184.31	6.888742	184.87	7.555368	185.49
29	5.572693	183.81	6.235304	184.32	6.899834	184.88	7.566497	185.50
30	5.583722	183.82	6.246363	184.32	6.910927	184.89	7.577628	185.51
31	5.594752	183.83	6.257422	184.33	6.922021	184.90	7.588759	185.52
32	5.605782	183.83	6.268482	184.34	6.933115	184.91	7.599890	185.53
33	5.616812	183.84	6.279543	184.35	6.944210	184.92	7.611022	185.54
34	5.627843	183.85	6.290605	184.36	6.955305	184.93	7.622155	185.55
35	5.638874	183.86	6.301667	184.37	6.966401	184.94	7.633289	185.57
36	5.649906	183.87	6.312729	184.38	6.977498	184.95	7.644423	185.58
37	5.660938	183.87	6.323792	184.39	6.988595	184.96	7.655558	185.59
38	5.671971	183.88	6.334855	184.40	6.999693	184.97	7.666694	185.60
39	5.683004	183.89	6.345919	184.41	7.010791	184.98	7.677830	185.61
40	5.694038	183.90	6.356984	184.41	7.021890	184.99	7.688967	185.62
41	5.705072	183.91	6.368049	184.42	7.032990	185.00	7.700104	185.63
42	5.716106	183.92	6.379115	184.43	7.044090	185.01	7.711242	185.64
43	5.727141	183.92	6.390181	184.44	7.055191	185.02	7.722381	185.65
44	5.738177	183.93	6.401248	184.45	7.066292	185.03	7.733521	185.66
45	5.749213	183.94	6.412315	184.46	7.077394	185.04	7.744661	185.68
46	5.760250	183.95	6.423383	184.47	7.088497	185.05	7.755802	185.69
47	5.771287	183.96	6.434451	184.48	7.099600	185.06	7.766943	185.70
48	5.782325	183.96	6.445520	184.49	7.110704	185.07	7.778085	185.71
49	5.793363	183.97	6.456590	184.50	7.121808	185.08	7.789228	185.72
50	5.804401	183.98	6.467660	184.51	7.132913	185.09	7.800372	185.73
51	5.815440	183.99	6.478731	184.52	7.144019	185.10	7.811516	185.74
52	5.826480	184.00	6.489802	184.52	7.155125	185.11	7.822661	185.75
53	5.837520	184.01	6.500874	184.53	7.166232	185.12	7.833807	185.76
54	5.848561	184.01	6.511946	184.54	7.177340	185.13	7.844953	185.78
55	5.859602	184.02	6.523019	184.55	7.188448	185.14	7.856100	185.79
56	5.870644	184.03	6.534092	184.56	7.199557	185.15	7.867247	185.80
57	5.881686	184.04	6.545166	184.57	7.210666	185.16	7.878396	185.81
58	5.892728	184.05	6.556241	184.58	7.221776	185.17	7.889545	185.82
59	5.903771	184.06	6.567316	184.59	7.232886	185.18	7.900694	185.83
60	5.914815	184.06	6.578391	184.60	7.243997	185.19	7.911845	185.84

TABLE VI.

For finding the True Anomaly or the Time from the Perihelion in a Parabolic Orbit.

v.	12°		13°		14°		15°	
	M.	Diff. 1″.	M.	Diff. 1″.	M.	Diff. 1″.	M.	Diff. 1″.
0′	7.911845	185.84	8.582146	186.56	9.255120	187.33	9.930984	188.16
1	7.922995	185.86	8.593340	186.57	9.266360	187.34	9.942274	188.18
2	7.934147	185.87	8.604535	186.58	9.277601	187.35	9.953565	188.19
3	7.945300	185.88	8.615730	186.59	9.288842	187.37	9.964857	188.21
4	7.956453	185.89	8.626926	186.61	9.300085	187.38	9.976149	188.22
5	7.967606	185.90	8.638123	186.62	9.311328	187.40	9.987443	188.23
6	7.978761	185.91	8.649320	186.63	9.322572	187.41	9.998738	188.25
7	7.989916	185.92	8.660518	186.64	9.333817	187.42	10.010033	188.26
8	8.001072	185.93	8.671717	186.66	9.345063	187.44	10.021329	188.28
9	8.012228	185.95	8.682917	186.67	9.356310	187.45	10.032626	188.29
10	8.023385	185.96	8.694117	186.68	9.367557	187.46	10.043924	188.31
11	8.034543	185.97	8.705318	186.69	9.378805	187.48	10.055223	188.32
12	8.045702	185.98	8.716520	186.71	9.390054	187.49	10.066523	188.34
13	8.056861	185.99	8.727723	186.72	9.401304	187.50	10.077823	188.35
14	8.068021	186.00	8.738927	186.73	9.412555	187.52	10.089125	188.37
15	8.079181	186.02	8.750131	186.74	9.423806	187.53	10.100427	188.38
16	8.090343	186.03	8.761336	186.76	9.435058	187.54	10.111730	188.39
17	8.101505	186.04	8.772542	186.77	9.446311	187.56	10.123035	188.41
18	8.112668	186.05	8.783748	186.78	9.457565	187.57	10.134340	188.42
19	8.123831	186.06	8.794955	186.79	9.468820	187.59	10.145646	188.44
20	8.134995	186.07	8.806163	186.81	9.480076	187.60	10.156952	188.45
21	8.146160	186.09	8.817372	186.82	9.491332	187.61	10.168260	188.47
22	8.157326	186.10	8.828582	186.83	9.502589	187.63	10.179568	188.48
23	8.168492	186.11	8.839792	186.84	9.513847	187.64	10.190878	188.50
24	8.179659	186.12	8.851003	186.86	9.525106	187.65	10.202188	188.51
25	8.190826	186.13	8.862215	186.87	9.536366	187.67	10.213499	188.53
26	8.201995	186.15	8.873427	186.88	9.547626	187.68	10.224812	188.54
27	8.213164	186.16	8.884641	186.90	9.558888	187.70	10.236125	188.56
28	8.224334	186.17	8.895855	186.91	9.570150	187.71	10.247439	188.57
29	8.235504	186.18	8.907070	186.92	9.581413	187.72	10.258753	188.59
30	8.246675	186.19	8.918286	186.93	9.592676	187.74	10.270069	188.60
31	8.257847	186.20	8.929502	186.95	9.603941	187.75	10.281386	188.62
32	8.269020	186.22	8.940719	186.96	9.615207	187.77	10.292703	188.63
33	8.280193	186.23	8.951937	186.97	9.626473	187.78	10.304021	188.65
34	8.291367	186.24	8.963156	186.99	9.637740	187.79	10.315341	188.66
35	8.302542	186.25	8.974376	187.00	9.649008	187.81	10.326661	188.68
36	8.313717	186.26	8.985596	187.01	9.660277	187.82	10.337982	188.69
37	8.324893	186.28	8.996817	187.02	9.671547	187.84	10.349304	188.71
38	8.336070	186.29	9.008039	187.04	9.682817	187.85	10.360627	188.72
39	8.347248	186.30	9.019262	187.05	9.694088	187.86	10.371951	188.74
40	8.358426	186.31	9.030485	187.06	9.705361	187.88	10.383275	188.75
41	8.369605	186.32	9.041709	187.08	9.716634	187.89	10.394601	188.77
42	8.380785	186.34	9.052934	187.09	9.727908	187.91	10.405927	188.78
43	8.391966	186.35	9.064160	187.10	9.739182	187.92	10.417255	188.80
44	8.403147	186.36	9.075387	187.12	9.750458	187.93	10.428583	188.81
45	8.414329	186.37	9.086614	187.13	9.761734	187.95	10.439912	188.83
46	8.425512	186.38	9.097842	187.14	9.773012	187.96	10.451242	188.84
47	8.436695	186.40	9.109071	187.16	9.784290	187.98	10.462573	188.86
48	8.447879	186.41	9.120301	187.17	9.795569	187.99	10.473905	188.87
49	8.459064	186.42	9.131531	187.18	9.806849	188.00	10.485238	188.89
50	8.470250	186.43	9.142763	187.20	9.818129	188.02	10.496572	188.90
51	8.481436	186.45	9.153995	187.21	9.829410	188.03	10.507907	188.92
52	8.492623	186.46	9.165228	187.22	9.840693	188.05	10.519242	188.93
53	8.503811	186.47	9.176462	187.23	9.851977	188.06	10.530579	188.95
54	8.515000	186.48	9.187696	187.25	9.863261	188.08	10.541916	188.97
55	8.526189	186.49	9.198931	187.26	9.874546	188.09	10.553255	188.98
56	8.537379	186.51	9.210167	187.27	9.885832	188.10	10.564594	189.00
57	8.548569	186.52	9.221404	187.29	9.897118	188.12	10.575934	189.01
58	8.559761	186.53	9.232642	187.30	9.908406	188.13	10.587276	189.03
59	8.570953	186.54	9.243880	187.31	9.919694	188.15	10.598618	189.04
60	8.582146	186.56	9.255120	187.33	9.930984	188.16	10.609961	189.06

TABLE VI.

For finding the True Anomaly or the Time from the Perihelion in a Parabolic Orbit.

v.	16°		17°		18°		19°	
	M.	Diff. 1″.	M.	Diff. 1″.	M.	Diff. 1″.	M.	Diff. 1″.
0′	10.609961	189.06	11.292277	190.02	11.978162	191.04	12.667850	192.13
1	10.621305	189.07	11.303679	190.03	11.989625	191.06	12.679379	192.15
2	10.632649	189.09	11.315082	190.05	12.001089	191.08	12.690908	192.17
3	10.643995	189.10	11.326485	190.07	12.012554	191.09	12.702439	192.19
4	10.655342	189.12	11.337889	190.08	12.024021	191.11	12.713970	192.21
5	10.666690	189.14	11.349295	190.10	12.035488	191.13	12.725503	192.22
6	10.678038	189.15	11.360701	190.12	12.046956	191.15	12.737037	192.24
7	10.689388	189.17	11.372109	190.13	12.058425	191.16	12.748573	192.26
8	10.700738	189.18	11.383517	190.15	12.069896	191.18	12.760109	192.28
9	10.712090	189.20	11.394927	190.17	12.081367	191.20	12.771646	192.30
10	10.723442	189.21	11.406337	190.18	12.092840	191.22	12.783185	192.32
11	10.734795	189.23	11.417749	190.20	12.104313	191.24	12.794724	192.34
12	10.746149	189.24	11.429161	190.22	12.115788	191.25	12.806265	192.36
13	10.757505	189.26	11.440575	190.23	12.127264	191.27	12.817807	192.37
14	10.768861	189.28	11.451989	190.25	12.138741	191.29	12.829350	192.39
15	10.780218	189.29	11.463405	190.27	12.150219	191.31	12.840894	192.41
16	10.791576	189.31	11.474821	190.28	12.161698	191.32	12.852440	192.43
17	10.802935	189.32	11.486239	190.30	12.173178	191.34	12.863986	192.45
18	10.814295	189.34	11.497657	190.32	12.184659	191.36	12.875534	192.47
19	10.825655	189.35	11.509077	190.33	12.196141	191.38	12.887082	192.49
20	10.837017	189.37	11.520497	190.35	12.207624	191.40	12.898632	192.51
21	10.848380	189.39	11.531919	190.37	12.219108	191.41	12.910183	192.53
22	10.859744	189.40	11.543342	190.39	12.230594	191.43	12.921736	192.55
23	10.871108	189.42	11.554765	190.40	12.242080	191.45	12.933289	192.56
24	10.882474	189.43	11.566190	190.42	12.253568	191.47	12.944843	192.58
25	10.893840	189.45	11.577616	190.44	12.265057	191.49	12.956399	192.60
26	10.905208	189.47	11.589042	190.45	12.276546	191.50	12.967956	192.62
27	10.916576	189.48	11.600470	190.47	12.288037	191.52	12.979514	192.64
28	10.927946	189.50	11.611899	190.49	12.299529	191.54	12.991073	192.66
29	10.939316	189.51	11.623328	190.50	12.311022	191.56	13.002633	192.68
30	10.950687	189.53	11.634759	190.52	12.322516	191.58	13.014195	192.70
31	10.962059	189.55	11.646191	190.54	12.334011	191.60	13.025757	192.72
32	10.973433	189.56	11.657624	190.56	12.345508	191.61	13.037321	192.74
33	10.984807	189.58	11.669057	190.57	12.357005	191.63	13.048886	192.76
34	10.996182	189.59	11.680492	190.59	12.368503	191.65	13.060452	192.78
35	11.007558	189.61	11.691928	190.61	12.380003	191.67	13.072019	192.80
36	11.018935	189.63	11.703365	190.62	12.391504	191.69	13.083587	192.82
37	11.030313	189.64	11.714803	190.64	12.403006	191.70	13.095157	192.83
38	11.041692	189.66	11.726242	190.66	12.414509	191.72	13.106727	192.85
39	11.053072	189.67	11.737682	190.68	12.426013	191.74	13.118299	192.87
40	11.064453	189.69	11.749123	190.69	12.437517	191.76	13.129872	192.89
41	11.075835	189.71	11.760565	190.71	12.449023	191.78	13.141446	192.91
42	11.087218	189.72	11.772008	190.73	12.460531	191.80	13.153022	192.93
43	11.098602	189.74	11.783452	190.74	12.472039	191.81	13.164598	192.95
44	11.109987	189.76	11.794897	190.76	12.483548	191.83	13.176176	192.97
45	11.121372	189.77	11.806344	190.78	12.495059	191.85	13.187755	192.99
46	11.132759	189.79	11.817791	190.80	12.506571	191.87	13.199335	193.01
47	11.144147	189.80	11.829239	190.81	12.518083	191.89	13.210916	193.03
48	11.155536	189.82	11.840689	190.83	12.529597	191.91	13.222498	193.05
49	11.166925	189.84	11.852139	190.85	12.541112	191.93	13.234082	193.07
50	11.178316	189.85	11.863590	190.87	12.552628	191.94	13.245667	193.09
51	11.189708	189.87	11.875043	190.88	12.564145	191.96	13.257253	193.11
52	11.201100	189.89	11.886496	190.90	12.575664	191.98	13.268840	193.13
53	11.212494	189.90	11.897951	190.92	12.587183	192.00	13.280428	193.15
54	11.223889	189.92	11.909407	190.94	12.598704	192.02	13.292017	193.17
55	11.235284	189.93	11.920863	190.95	12.610225	192.04	13.303608	193.19
56	11.246681	189.95	11.932321	190.97	12.621748	192.06	13.315200	193.21
57	11.258078	189.97	11.943780	190.99	12.633272	192.07	13.326793	193.23
58	11.269477	189.98	11.955239	191.01	12.644797	192.09	13.338387	193.25
59	11.280876	190.00	11.966700	191.02	12.656323	192.11	13.349982	193.27
60	11.292277	190.02	11.978162	191.04	12.667850	192.13	13.361579	193.29

TABLE VI.

For finding the True Anomaly or the Time from the Perihelion in a Parabolic Orbit.

v.	20°		21°		22°		23°	
	M.	Diff. 1″.	M.	Diff. 1″.	M.	Diff. 1″.	M.	Diff. 1″.
0′	13.361579	193.29	14.059591	194.51	14.762133	195.80	15.469459	197.17
1	13.373177	193.31	14.071262	194.53	14.773882	195.83	15.481290	197.19
2	13.384776	193.33	14.082935	194.55	14.785632	195.85	15.493122	197.21
3	13.396376	193.35	14.094608	194.57	14.797384	195.87	15.504956	197.24
4	13.407977	193.37	14.106283	194.59	14.809137	195.89	15.516791	197.26
5	13.419580	193.39	14.117960	194.61	14.820891	195.91	15.528627	197.28
6	13.431183	193.41	14.129637	194.64	14.832647	195.94	15.540465	197.31
7	13.442788	193.43	14.141316	194.66	14.844403	195.96	15.552304	197.33
8	13.454394	193.45	14.152996	194.68	14.856161	195.98	15.564144	197.35
9	13.466002	193.47	14.164677	194.70	14.867921	196.00	15.575986	197.38
10	13.477610	193.49	14.176360	194.72	14.879682	196.03	15.587830	197.40
11	13.489220	193.51	14.188044	194.74	14.891444	196.05	15.599675	197.43
12	13.500831	193.53	14.199729	194.76	14.903208	196.07	15.611521	197.45
13	13.512443	193.55	14.211415	194.78	14.914973	196.09	15.623369	197.47
14	13.524056	193.57	14.223103	194.81	14.926739	196.12	15.635218	197.50
15	13.535671	193.59	14.234792	194.83	14.938506	196.14	15.647068	197.52
16	13.547287	193.61	14.246482	194.85	14.950275	196.16	15.658920	197.54
17	13.558904	193.63	14.258174	194.87	14.962045	196.18	15.670773	197.57
18	13.570522	193.65	14.269867	194.89	14.973817	196.20	15.682628	197.59
19	13.582141	193.67	14.281561	194.91	14.985590	196.23	15.694484	197.61
20	13.593762	193.69	14.293256	194.93	14.997365	196.25	15.706342	197.64
21	13.605383	193.71	14.304953	194.95	15.009140	196.27	15.718201	197.66
22	13.617006	193.73	14.316651	194.98	15.020917	196.30	15.730061	197.69
23	13.628631	193.75	14.328350	195.00	15.032696	196.32	15.741923	197.71
24	13.640256	193.77	14.340050	195.02	15.044475	196.34	15.753786	197.73
25	13.651883	193.79	14.351752	195.04	15.056256	196.36	15.765651	197.76
26	13.663511	193.81	14.363455	195.06	15.068039	196.39	15.777517	197.78
27	13.675140	193.83	14.375159	195.08	15.079823	196.41	15.789385	197.80
28	13.686770	193.85	14.386865	195.10	15.091608	196.43	15.801254	197.83
29	13.698401	193.87	14.398572	195.13	15.103394	196.45	15.813124	197.85
30	13.710034	193.89	14.410280	195.15	15.115182	196.48	15.824996	197.88
31	13.721668	193.91	14.421990	195.17	15.126971	196.50	15.836870	197.90
32	13.733303	193.93	14.433700	195.19	15.138762	196.52	15.848744	197.92
33	13.744940	193.95	14.445412	195.21	15.150554	196.54	15.860620	197.95
34	13.756577	193.97	14.457126	195.23	15.162348	196.57	15.872498	197.97
35	13.768216	193.99	14.468841	195.26	15.174142	196.59	15.884377	198.00
36	13.779856	194.01	14.480557	195.28	15.185938	196.61	15.896258	198.02
37	13.791498	194.03	14.492274	195.30	15.197736	196.64	15.908140	198.04
38	13.803140	194.05	14.503992	195.32	15.209535	196.66	15.920023	198.07
39	13.814784	194.07	14.515712	195.34	15.221335	196.68	15.931908	198.09
40	13.826429	194.09	14.527434	195.36	15.233137	196.70	15.943794	198.12
41	13.838075	194.11	14.539156	195.39	15.244940	196.73	15.955682	198.14
42	13.849723	194.14	14.550880	195.41	15.256744	196.75	15.967571	198.17
43	13.861372	194.16	14.562605	195.43	15.268550	196.77	15.979462	198.19
44	13.873022	194.18	14.574331	195.45	15.280357	196.80	15.991354	198.21
45	13.884673	194.20	14.586059	195.47	15.292165	196.82	16.003248	198.24
46	13.896325	194.22	14.597788	195.50	15.303975	196.84	16.015143	198.26
47	13.907979	194.24	14.609519	195.52	15.315786	196.87	16.027039	198.29
48	13.919634	194.26	14.621250	195.54	15.327599	196.89	16.038937	198.31
49	13.931290	194.28	14.632983	195.56	15.339413	196.91	16.050836	198.34
50	13.942948	194.30	14.644718	195.58	15.351228	196.94	16.062737	198.36
51	13.954606	194.32	14.656453	195.60	15.363045	196.96	16.074639	198.38
52	13.966266	194.34	14.668190	195.63	15.374863	196.98	16.086543	198.41
53	13.977927	194.36	14.679929	195.65	15.386683	197.00	16.098449	198.43
54	13.989590	194.38	14.691668	195.67	15.398504	197.03	16.110355	198.46
55	14.001254	194.41	14.703409	195.69	15.410326	197.05	16.122263	198.48
56	14.012919	194.43	14.715151	195.71	15.422150	197.07	16.134173	198.51
57	14.024585	194.45	14.726895	195.74	15.433975	197.10	16.146084	198.53
58	14.036252	194.47	14.738640	195.76	15.445802	197.12	16.157997	198.56
59	14.047921	194.49	14.750386	195.78	15.457630	197.14	16.169911	198.58
60	14.059591	194.51	14.762133	195.80	15.469459	197.17	16.181826	198.60

TABLE VI.

For finding the True Anomaly or the Time from the Perihelion in a Parabolic Orbit.

v.	24°		25°		26°		27°	
	M.	Diff. 1″.	M.	Diff. 1″.	M.	Diff. 1″.	M.	Diff. 1″.
0′	16.181826	198.60	16.899499	200.12	17.622747	201.70	18.351847	203.37
1	16.193743	198.63	16.911507	200.14	17.634850	201.73	18.364050	203.40
2	16.205662	198.65	16.923516	200.17	17.646954	201.76	18.376255	203.42
3	16.217582	198.68	16.935527	200.19	17.659060	201.78	18.388461	203.45
4	16.229503	198.70	16.947539	200.22	17.671168	201.81	18.400669	203.48
5	16.241426	198.73	16.959553	200.24	17.683278	201.84	18.412879	203.51
6	16.253350	198.75	16.971568	200.27	17.695389	201.87	18.425090	203.54
7	16.265276	198.78	16.983585	200.30	17.707502	201.89	18.437303	203.57
8	16.277204	198.80	16.995604	200.32	17.719616	201.92	18.449518	203.59
9	16.289133	198.83	17.007624	200.35	17.731732	201.95	18.461735	203.62
10	16.301063	198.85	17.019646	200.37	17.743850	201.97	18.473953	203.65
11	16.312995	198.88	17.031669	200.40	17.755969	202.00	18.486173	203.68
12	16.324928	198.90	17.043694	200.43	17.768090	202.03	18.498395	203.71
13	16.336863	198.93	17.055720	200.45	17.780213	202.06	18.510618	203.74
14	16.348799	198.95	17.067748	200.48	17.792337	202.08	18.522843	203.77
15	16.360737	198.97	17.079777	200.50	17.804462	202.11	18.535070	203.80
16	16.372676	199.00	17.091808	200.53	17.816590	202.14	18.547299	203.82
17	16.384617	199.02	17.103841	200.56	17.828719	202.17	18.559529	203.85
18	16.396559	199.05	17.115875	200.58	17.840850	202.19	18.571761	203.88
19	16.408503	199.07	17.127911	200.61	17.852982	202.22	18.583995	203.91
20	16.420448	199.10	17.139948	200.64	17.865116	202.25	18.596230	203.94
21	16.432395	199.12	17.151987	200.66	17.877252	202.28	18.608467	203.97
22	16.444343	199.15	17.164028	200.69	17.889389	202.30	18.620706	204.00
23	16.456292	199.17	17.176070	200.71	17.901528	202.33	18.632947	204.03
24	16.468243	199.20	17.188114	200.74	17.913669	202.36	18.645190	204.05
25	16.480196	199.22	17.200159	200.77	17.925811	202.39	18.657434	204.08
26	16.492151	199.25	17.212206	200.79	17.937955	202.41	18.669679	204.11
27	16.504107	199.27	17.224254	200.82	17.950101	202.44	18.681927	204.14
28	16.516064	199.30	17.236304	200.85	17.962248	202.47	18.694177	204.17
29	16.528022	199.33	17.248356	200.87	17.974397	202.50	18.706428	204.20
30	16.539983	199.35	17.260409	200.90	17.986548	202.52	18.718680	204.23
31	16.551945	199.38	17.272464	200.93	17.998700	202.55	18.730935	204.26
32	16.563908	199.40	17.284520	200.95	18.010854	202.58	18.743191	204.29
33	16.575873	199.43	17.296578	200.98	18.023010	202.61	18.755449	204.32
34	16.587839	199.45	17.308637	201.00	18.035167	202.64	18.767709	204.35
35	16.599807	199.48	17.320698	201.03	18.047326	202.66	18.779971	204.37
36	16.611776	199.50	17.332761	201.06	18.059487	202.69	18.792234	204.40
37	16.623747	199.53	17.344825	201.08	18.071649	202.72	18.804499	204.43
38	16.635719	199.55	17.356891	201.11	18.083813	202.75	18.816767	204.46
39	16.647693	199.58	17.368959	201.14	18.095979	202.78	18.829036	204.49
40	16.659669	199.60	17.381028	201.16	18.108146	202.80	18.841305	204.52
41	16.671646	199.63	17.393098	201.19	18.120315	202.83	18.853577	204.55
42	16.683624	199.65	17.405171	201.22	18.132486	202.86	18.865851	204.58
43	16.695604	199.68	17.417245	201.24	18.144658	202.89	18.878127	204.61
44	16.707586	199.70	17.429320	201.27	18.156832	202.92	18.890404	204.64
45	16.719569	199.73	17.441397	201.30	18.169008	202.94	18.902684	204.67
46	16.731553	199.76	17.453476	201.32	18.181186	202.97	18.914965	204.70
47	16.743539	199.78	17.465556	201.35	18.193365	203.00	18.927247	204.73
48	16.755527	199.81	17.477638	201.38	18.205546	203.03	18.939532	204.76
49	16.767516	199.83	17.489722	201.41	18.217728	203.06	18.951818	204.79
50	16.779507	199.86	17.501807	201.43	18.229912	203.08	18.964106	204.81
51	16.791499	199.88	17.513894	201.46	18.242098	203.11	18.976396	204.84
52	16.803493	199.91	17.525982	201.49	18.254286	203.14	18.988687	204.87
53	16.815488	199.94	17.538072	201.51	18.266475	203.17	19.000981	204.90
54	16.827485	199.96	17.550163	201.54	18.278666	203.20	19.013276	204.93
55	16.839484	199.99	17.562257	201.57	18.290859	203.23	19.025573	204.96
56	16.851484	200.01	17.574352	201.59	18.303053	203.25	19.037871	204.99
57	16.863485	200.04	17.586448	201.62	18.315249	203.28	19.050172	205.02
58	16.875488	200.06	17.598546	201.65	18.327447	203.31	19.062474	205.05
59	16.887493	200.09	17.610646	201.68	18.339646	203.34	19.074778	205.08
60	16.899499	200.12	17.622747	201.70	18.351847	203.37	19.087084	205.11

TABLE VI.

For finding the True Anomaly or the Time from the Perihelion in a Parabolic Orbit.

v.	28° M.	Diff. 1″.	29° M.	Diff. 1″.	30° log M.	Diff. 1″.	31° log M.	Diff. 1″.
0′	19.087084	205.11	19.828747	206.94	1.313 3849	44.08	1.329 0430	42.92
1	19.099391	205.14	19.841164	206.97	.313 6493	44.06	.329 3004	42.91
2	19.111701	205.17	19.853583	207.00	.313 9136	44.04	.329 5578	42.89
3	19.124012	205.20	19.866004	207.03	.314 1778	44.02	.329 8151	42.87
4	19.136325	205.23	19.878427	207.06	.314 4419	44.00	.330 0723	42.85
5	19.148639	205.26	19.890852	207.09	1.314 7058	43.98	1.330 3293	42.83
6	19.160956	205.29	19.903279	207.13	.314 9696	43.96	.330 5862	42.81
7	19.173274	205.32	19.915707	207.16	.315 2333	43.94	.330 8431	42.80
8	19.185594	205.35	19.928137	207.19	.315 4969	43.92	.331 0998	42.78
9	19.197916	205.38	19.940569	207.22	.315 7604	43.90	.331 3564	42.76
10	19.210240	205.41	19.953003	207.25	1.316 0237	43.88	1.331 6129	42.74
11	19.222566	205.44	19.965439	207.28	.316 2869	43.86	.331 8693	42.72
12	19.234893	205.47	19.977877	207.31	.316 5500	43.84	.332 1255	42.70
13	19.247222	205.50	19.990317	207.34	.316 8130	43.82	.332 3817	42.69
14	19.259553	205.53	20.002759	207.38	.317 0759	43.80	.332 6378	42.67
15	19.271885	205.56	20.015202	207.41	1.317 3386	43.78	1.332 8937	42.65
16	19.284220	205.59	20.027647	207.44	.317 6013	43.76	.333 1496	42.63
17	19.296556	205.62	20.040095	207.47	.317 8638	43.74	.333 4053	42.61
18	19.308894	205.65	20.052544	207.50	.318 1262	43.72	.333 6609	42.59
19	19.321234	205.68	20.064995	207.53	.318 3885	43.70	.333 9164	42.58
20	19.333576	205.71	20.077448	207.57	1.318 6506	43.68	1.334 1718	42.56
21	19.345920	205.74	20.089903	207.60	.318 9127	43.67	.334 4271	42.54
22	19.358265	205.77	20.102360	207.63	.319 1746	43.65	.334 6823	42.52
23	19.370612	205.80	20.114818	207.66	.319 4364	43.63	.334 9374	42.50
24	19.382961	205.83	20.127279	207.69	.319 6981	43.61	.335 1924	42.49
25	19.395312	205.86	20.139741	207.72	1.319 9597	43.59	1.335 4472	42.47
26	19.407665	205.89	20.152206	207.76	.320 2212	43.57	.335 7020	42.45
27	19.420019	205.92	20.164672	207.79	.320 4825	43.55	.335 9567	42.43
28	19.432375	205.95	20.177140	207.82	.320 7438	43.53	.336 2112	42.41
29	19.444734	205.98	20.189610	207.85	.321 0049	43.51	.336 4656	42.40
30	19.457094	206.01	20.202082	207.88	1.321 2659	43.49	1.336 7199	42.38
31	19.469455	206.04	20.214556	207.91	.321 5268	43.47	.336 9742	42.36
32	19.481819	206.08	20.227032	207.95	.321 7875	43.45	.337 2283	42.34
33	19.494184	206.11	20.239510	207.98	.322 0482	43.43	.337 4823	42.33
34	19.506551	206.14	20.251989	208.01	.322 3087	43.41	.337 7362	42.31
35	19.518921	206.17	20.264471	208.04	1.322 5692	43.40	1.337 9900	42.29
36	19.531292	206.20	20.276954	208.07	.322 8295	43.38	.338 2437	42.27
37	19.543664	206.23	20.289440	208.11	.323 0897	43.36	.338 4972	42.25
38	19.556039	206.26	20.301927	208.14	.323 3498	43.34	.338 7507	42.24
39	19.568415	206.29	20.314416	208.17	.323 6097	43.32	.339 0041	42.22
40	19.580794	206.32	20.326907	208.20	1.323 8696	43.30	1.339 2573	42.20
41	19.593174	206.35	20.339400	208.24	.324 1294	43.28	.339 5105	42.18
42	19.605556	206.38	20.351895	208.27	.324 3890	43.26	.339 7635	42.17
43	19.617939	206.41	20.364392	208.30	.324 6485	43.24	.340 0165	42.15
44	19.630325	206.44	20.376891	208.33	.324 9079	43.22	.340 2693	42.13
45	19.642713	206.47	20.389392	208.36	1.325 1672	43.21	1.340 5221	42.11
46	19.655102	206.50	20.401895	208.39	.325 4263	43.19	.340 7747	42.10
47	19.667493	206.53	20.414399	208.43	.325 6854	43.17	.341 0272	42.08
48	19.679886	206.57	20.426906	208.46	.325 9443	43.15	.341 2796	42.06
49	19.692281	206.60	20.439415	208.49	.326 2032	43.13	.341 5319	42.04
50	19.704678	206.63	20.451925	208.52	1.326 4619	43.11	1.341 7841	42.03
51	19.717076	206.66	20.464437	208.56	.326 7205	43.09	.342 0362	42.01
52	19.729477	206.69	20.476952	208.59	.326 9790	43.07	.342 2882	41.99
53	19.741879	206.72	20.489468	208.62	.327 2374	43.05	.342 5401	41.97
54	19.754283	206.75	20.501986	208.65	.327 4957	43.04	.342 7919	41.96
55	19.766689	206.78	20.514506	208.69	1.327 7538	43.02	1.343 0436	41.94
56	19.779097	206.81	20.527029	208.72	.328 0119	43.00	.343 2952	41.92
57	19.791507	206.84	20.539553	208.75	.328 2698	42.98	.343 5467	41.90
58	19.803919	206.88	20.552079	208.78	.328 5276	42.96	.343 7980	41.89
59	19.816332	206.91	20.564607	208.82	.328 7853	42.94	.344 0493	41.87
60	19.828747	206.94	20.577137	208.85	1.329 0430	42.92	1.344 3005	41.85

TABLE VI.

For finding the True Anomaly or the Time from the Perihelion in a Parabolic Orbit.

v.	32°		33°		34°		35°	
	log M.	Diff. 1″.	log M.	Diff. 1″.	log M.	Diff. 1″.	log M.	Diff. 1″.
0′	1.344 3005	41.85	1.359 1859	40.86	1.373 7251	39.93	1.387 9418	39.06
1	.344 5515	41.84	.359 4310	40.84	.373 9646	39.91	.388 1761	39.05
2	.344 8025	41.82	.359 6760	40.82	.374 2041	39.90	.388 4104	39.04
3	.345 0534	41.80	.359 9209	40.81	.374 4434	39.88	.388 6446	39.02
4	.345 3041	41.78	.360 1657	40.79	.374 6827	39.87	.388 8787	39.01
5	1.345 5548	41.77	1.360 4104	40.78	1.374 9218	39.85	1.389 1127	38.99
6	.345 8053	41.75	.360 6550	40.76	.375 1609	39.84	.389 3466	38.98
7	.346 0558	41.73	.360 8995	40.74	.375 3999	39.82	.389 5804	38.97
8	.346 3061	41.72	.361 1439	40.73	.375 6388	39.81	.389 8142	38.95
9	.346 5564	41.70	.361 3883	40.71	.375 8776	39.79	.390 0479	38.94
10	1.346 8065	41.68	1.361 6325	40.70	1.376 1164	39.78	1.390 2815	38.93
11	.347 0565	41.66	.361 8766	40.68	.376 3550	39.77	.390 5150	38.91
12	.347 3065	41.65	.362 1207	40.66	.376 5935	39.75	.390 7484	38.90
13	.347 5563	41.63	.362 3646	40.65	.376 8320	39.74	.390 9817	38.88
14	.347 8060	41.61	.362 6084	40.63	.377 0703	39.72	.391 2150	38.87
15	1.348 0557	41.60	1.362 8522	40.62	1.377 3086	39.71	1.391 4482	38.86
16	.348 3052	41.58	.363 0959	40.60	.377 5468	39.69	.391 6813	38.84
17	.348 5546	41.56	.363 3394	40.59	.377 7849	39.68	.391 9143	38.83
18	.348 8040	41.55	.363 5829	40.57	378 0230	39.66	.392 1472	38.82
19	.349 0532	41.53	.363 8263	40.56	.378 2609	39.65	.392 3801	38.80
20	1.349 3023	41.51	1.364 0696	40.54	1.378 4987	39.64	1.392 6128	38.79
21	.349 5513	41.50	.364 3128	40.52	.378 7365	39.62	.392 8455	38.77
22	.349 8003	41.48	.364 5559	40.51	.378 9742	39.61	.393 0781	38.76
23	.350 0491	41.46	.364 7989	40.49	.379 2117	39.59	.393 3107	38.75
24	.350 2978	41.45	.365 0418	40.48	.379 4492	39.58	.393 5431	38.73
25	1.350 5464	41.43	1.365 2846	40.46	1.379 6866	39.56	1.393 7755	38.72
26	.350 7950	41.41	.365 5273	40.45	.379 9240	39.55	.394 0078	38.71
27	.351 0434	41.40	.365 7699	40.43	.380 1612	39.53	.394 2400	38.69
28	.351 2917	41.38	.366 0125	40.41	.380 3983	39.52	.394 4721	38.68
29	.351 5399	41.36	.366 2549	40.40	.380 6354	39.50	.394 7041	38.67
30	1.351 7880	41.35	1.366 4973	40.38	1.380 8724	39.49	1.394 9361	38.65
31	.352 0361	41.33	.366 7395	40.37	.381 1093	39.47	.395 1680	38.64
32	.352 2840	41.31	.366 9817	40.35	.381 3461	39.46	.395 3998	38.63
33	.352 5318	41.30	.367 2238	40.34	.381 5828	39.45	.395 6315	38.61
34	.352 7795	41.28	.367 4657	40.32	.381 8194	39.43	.395 8631	38.60
35	1.353 0272	41.26	1.367 7076	40.31	1.382 0559	39.42	1.396 0947	38.59
36	.353 2747	41.25	.367 9494	40.29	.382 2924	39.40	.396 3262	38.57
37	.353 5221	41.23	.368 1911	40.28	.382 5288	39.39	.396 5576	38.56
38	.353 7694	41.21	.368 4327	40.26	.382 7651	39.37	.396 7889	38.55
39	.354 0167	41.20	.368 6742	40.25	.383 0013	39.36	.397 0201	38.53
40	1.354 2638	41.18	1.368 9157	40.23	1.383 2374	39.35	1.397 2513	38.52
41	.354 5108	41.16	.369 1570	40.21	.383 4734	39.33	.397 4823	38.51
42	.354 7578	41.15	.369 3983	40.20	.383 7093	39.32	.397 7133	38.49
43	.355 0046	41.13	.369 6394	40.18	.383 9452	39.30	.397 9442	38.48
44	.355 2513	41.11	.369 8805	40.17	.384 1809	39.29	.398 1751	38.47
45	1.355 4980	41.10	1.370 1214	40.15	1.384 4166	39.27	1.398 4058	38.45
46	.355 7445	41.08	.370 3623	40.14	.384 6522	39.26	.398 6365	38.44
47	.355 9909	41.07	.370 6031	40.12	.384 8878	39.25	.398 8671	38.43
48	.356 2373	41.05	.370 8438	40.11	.385 1232	39.23	.399 0976	38.41
49	.356 4836	41.03	.371 0844	40.09	.385 3585	39.22	.399 3281	38.40
50	1.356 7297	41.02	1.371 3249	40.08	1.385 5938	39.20	1.399 5584	38.39
51	.356 9758	41.00	.371 5654	40.06	.385 8290	39.19	.399 7887	38.37
52	.357 2217	40.98	.371 8057	40.05	.386 0641	39.18	.400 0189	38.36
53	.357 4676	40.97	.372 0459	40.03	.386 2991	39.16	.400 2491	38.35
54	.357 7134	40.95	.372 2861	40.02	.386 5340	39.15	.400 4791	38.33
55	1.357 9590	40.94	1.372 5261	40.00	1.386 7689	39.13	1.400 7091	38.32
56	.358 2046	40.92	.372 7661	39.99	.387 0036	39.12	.400 9390	38.31
57	.358 4501	40.90	.373 0060	39.97	.387 2383	39.11	.401 1688	38.30
58	.358 6954	40.89	.373 2458	39.96	.387 4729	39.09	.401 3985	38.28
59	.358 9407	40.87	.373 4855	39.94	.387 7074	39.08	.401 6282	38.27
60	1.359 1859	40.86	1.373 7251	39.93	1.387 9418	39.06	1.401 8578	38.26

TABLE VI.

For finding the True Anomaly or the Time from the Perihelion in a Parabolic Orbit.

v.	36°		37°		38°		39°	
	log M.	Diff. 1″.	log M.	Diff. 1″.	log M.	Diff. 1″.	log M.	Diff. 1″.
0′	1.401 8578	38.26	1.415 4930	37.50	1.428 8662	36.80	1.441 9943	36.14
1	.402 0873	38.24	.415 7180	37.49	.429 0869	36.79	.442 2111	36.13
2	.402 3167	38.23	.415 9429	37.47	.429 3076	36.78	.442 4279	36.12
3	.402 5460	38.22	.416 1678	37.46	.429 5283	36.77	.442 6446	36.11
4	.402 7753	38.20	.416 3925	37.45	.429 7488	36.75	.442 8612	36.10
5	1.403 0045	38.19	1.416 6172	37.44	1.429 9693	36.74	1.443 0778	36.09
6	.403 2336	38.18	.416 8419	37.43	.430 1897	36.73	.443 2943	36.08
7	.403 4626	38.17	.417 0664	37.41	.430 4101	36.72	.443 5107	36.07
8	.403 6916	38.15	.417 2909	37.40	.430 6304	36.71	.443 7271	36.06
9	.403 9205	38.14	.417 5153	37.39	.430 8506	36.70	.443 9434	36.05
10	1.404 1493	38.13	1.417 7396	37.38	1.431 0708	36.69	1.444 1597	36.04
11	.404 3780	38.12	.417 9639	37.37	.431 2909	36.68	.444 3758	36.03
12	.404 6067	38.10	.418 1881	37.36	.431 5109	36.66	.444 5920	36.02
13	.404 8352	38.09	.418 4122	37.35	.431 7308	36.65	.444 8080	36.00
14	.405 0637	38.08	.418 6362	37.33	.431 9507	36.64	.445 0240	35.99
15	1.405 2921	38.06	1.418 8602	37.32	1.432 1705	36.63	1.445 2400	35.98
16	.405 5205	38.05	.419 0841	37.31	.432 3903	36.62	.445 4558	35.97
17	.405 7488	38.03	.419 3079	37.30	.432 6100	36.61	.445 6716	35.96
18	.405 9769	38.02	.419 5317	37.29	.432 8296	36.60	.445 8874	35.95
19	.406 2051	38.01	.419 7554	37.27	.433 0491	36.59	.446 1031	35.94
20	1.406 4331	38.00	1.419 9790	37.26	1.433 2686	36.57	1.446 3187	35.93
21	.406 6611	37.99	.420 2026	37.25	.433 4881	36.56	.446 5343	35.92
22	.406 8889	37.97	.420 4260	37.24	.433 7074	36.55	.446 7498	35.91
23	.407 1168	37.96	.420 6494	37.23	.433 9267	36.54	.446 9652	35.90
24	.407 3445	37.95	.420 8728	37.22	.434 1459	36.53	.447 1806	35.89
25	1.407 5721	37.94	1.421 0960	37.20	1.434 3651	36.52	1.447 3959	35.88
26	.407 7997	37.92	.421 3192	37.19	.434 5842	36.51	.447 6112	35.87
27	.408 0272	37.91	.421 5423	37.18	.434 8032	36.50	.447 8263	35.86
28	.408 2547	37.90	.421 7654	37.17	.435 0221	36.49	.448 0415	35.85
29	.408 4820	37.89	.421 9884	37.16	.435 2410	36.48	.448 2565	35.84
30	1.408 7093	37.87	1.422 2113	37.15	1.435 4598	36.47	1.448 4715	35.83
31	.408 9365	37.86	.422 4341	37.13	.435 6786	36.46	.448 6865	35.82
32	.409 1636	37.85	.422 6569	37.12	.435 8973	36.44	.448 9014	35.81
33	.409 3907	37.84	.422 8796	37.11	.436 1159	36.43	.449 1162	35.80
34	.409 6177	37.82	.423 1022	37.10	.436 3345	36.42	.449 3309	35.79
35	1.409 8446	37.81	1.423 3248	37.09	1.436 5530	36.41	1.449 5456	35.78
36	.410 0714	37.80	.423 5473	37.08	.436 7714	36.40	.449 7603	35.77
37	.410 2981	37.78	.423 7697	37.06	.436 9898	36.39	.449 9749	35.76
38	.410 5248	37.77	.423 9920	37.05	.437 2081	36.38	.450 1894	35.75
39	.410 7514	37.76	.424 2143	37.04	.437 4263	36.37	.450 4038	35.74
40	1.410 9780	37.75	1.424 4365	37.03	1.437 6445	36.36	1.450 6182	35.73
41	.411 2044	37.74	.424 6586	37.02	.437 8626	36.35	.450 8325	35.72
42	.411 4308	37.72	.424 8807	37.01	.438 0806	36.34	.451 0468	35.71
43	.411 6571	37.71	.425 1027	36.99	.438 2986	36.32	.451 2610	35.70
44	.411 8833	37.70	.425 3246	36.98	.438 5165	36.31	.451 4752	35.69
45	1.412 1095	37.69	1.425 5465	36.97	1.438 7344	36.30	1.451 6893	35.68
46	.412 3356	37.68	.425 7683	36.96	.438 9522	36.29	.451 9033	35.67
47	.412 5616	37.66	.425 9900	36.95	.439 1699	36.28	.452 1173	35.66
48	.412 7875	37.65	.426 2117	36.94	.439 3875	36.27	.452 3312	35.65
49	.413 0134	37.64	.426 4333	36.92	.439 6051	36.26	.452 5450	35.64
50	1.413 2392	37.63	1.426 6548	36.91	1.439 8226	36.25	1.452 7588	35.63
51	.413 4649	37.61	.426 8762	36.90	.440 0401	36.24	.452 9725	35.62
52	.413 6905	37.60	.427 0976	36.89	.440 2575	36.23	.453 1862	35.61
53	.413 9161	37.59	.427 3189	36.88	.440 4748	36.22	.453 3998	35.60
54	.414 1416	37.58	.427 5402	36.87	.440 6921	36.20	.453 6134	35.59
55	1.414 3670	37.56	1.427 7613	36.86	1.440 9093	36.19	1.453 8269	35.58
56	.414 5924	37.55	.427 9824	36.85	.441 1264	36.18	.454 0403	35.57
57	.414 8176	37.54	.428 2035	36.83	.441 3436	36.17	.454 2537	35.56
58	.415 0429	37.53	.428 4244	36.82	.441 5605	36.16	.454 4670	35.55
59	.415 2680	37.51	.428 6453	36.81	.441 7774	36.15	.454 6802	35.54
60	1.415 4930	37.50	1.428 8662	36.80	1.441 9943	36.14	1.454 8934	35.53

TABLE VI.

For finding the True Anomaly or the Time from the Perihelion in a Parabolic Orbit.

v.	40°		41°		42°		43°	
	log M.	Diff. 1″.	log M.	Diff. 1″.	log M.	Diff. 1″.	log M.	Diff. 1″.
0′	1.454 8934	35.53	1.467 5782	34.95	1.480 0627	34.41	1.492 3597	33.91
1	.455 1065	35.52	.467 7879	34.94	.480 2691	34.40	.492 5631	33.90
2	.455 3196	35.51	.467 9976	34.93	.480 4755	34.40	.492 7665	33.89
3	.455 5326	35.50	.468 2071	34.92	.480 6819	34.39	.492 9698	33.88
4	.455 7456	35.49	.468 4166	34.91	.480 8882	34.38	.493 1731	33.87
5	1.455 9585	35.48	1.468 6261	34.90	1.481 0944	34.37	1.493 3764	33.87
6	.456 1713	35.47	.468 8355	34.90	.481 3006	34.36	.493 5796	33.86
7	.456 3841	35.46	.469 0448	34.89	.481 5068	34.35	.493 7827	33.85
8	.456 5968	35.45	.469 2541	34.88	.481 7129	34.34	.493 9858	33.84
9	.456 8094	35.44	.469 4634	34.87	.481 9189	34.33	.494 1888	33.83
10	1.457 0220	35.43	1.469 6725	34.86	1.482 1249	34.33	1.494 3918	33.83
11	.457 2346	35.42	.469 8817	34.85	.482 3308	34.32	.494 5948	33.82
12	.457 4470	35.41	.470 0907	34.84	.482 5367	34.31	.494 7977	33.81
13	.457 6595	35.40	.470 2998	34.83	.482 7425	34.30	.495 0005	33.80
14	.457 8718	35.39	.470 5087	34.82	.482 9483	34.29	.495 2033	33.79
15	1.458 0841	35.38	1.470 7176	34.81	1.483 1540	34.28	1.495 4061	33.79
16	.458 2964	35.37	.470 9265	34.80	.483 3597	34.28	.495 6088	33.78
17	.458 5086	35.36	.471 1353	34.79	.483 5653	34.27	.495 8114	33.77
18	.458 7207	35.35	.471 3440	34.79	.483 7709	34.26	.496 0140	33.76
19	.458 9328	35.34	.471 5527	34.78	.483 9764	34.25	.496 2166	33.75
20	1.459 1448	35.33	1.471 7613	34.77	1.484 1819	34.24	1.496 4191	33.75
21	.459 3567	35.32	.471 9699	34.76	.484 3873	34.23	.496 6216	33.74
22	.459 5686	35.31	.472 1784	34.75	.484 5927	34.22	.496 8240	33.73
23	.459 7805	35.30	.472 3869	34.74	.484 7980	34.22	.497 0264	33.72
24	.459 9922	35.29	.472 5953	34.73	.485 0033	34.21	.497 2287	33.71
25	1.460 2040	35.28	1.472 8037	34.73	1.485 2085	34.20	1.497 4310	33.71
26	.460 4156	35.27	.473 0120	34.72	.485 4137	34.19	.497 6332	33.70
27	.460 6272	35.26	.473 2203	34.71	.485 6188	34.18	.497 8354	33.69
28	.460 8388	35.25	.473 4285	34.70	.485 8239	34.17	.498 0376	33.68
29	.461 0503	35.24	.473 6366	34.69	.486 0289	34.16	.498 2396	33.68
30	1.461 2617	35.23	1.473 8447	34.68	1.486 2338	34.16	1.498 4417	33.67
31	.461 4731	35.23	.474 0527	34.67	.486 4388	34.15	.498 6437	33.66
32	.461 6844	35.22	.474 2607	34.66	.486 6436	34.14	.498 8456	33.65
33	.461 8957	35.21	.474 4686	34.65	.486 8484	34.13	.499 0475	33.65
34	.462 1069	35.20	.474 6765	34.64	.487 0532	34.12	.499 2494	33.64
35	1.462 3180	35.19	1.474 8843	34.63	1.487 2579	34.12	1.499 4512	33.63
36	.462 5291	35.18	.475 0921	34.62	.487 4626	34.11	.499 6530	33.62
37	.462 7401	35.17	.475 2998	34.61	.487 6672	34.10	.499 8547	33.62
38	.462 9511	35.16	.475 5075	34.61	.487 8718	34.09	.500 0563	33.61
39	.463 1620	35.15	.475 7151	34.60	.488 0763	34.08	.500 2580	33.60
40	1.463 3729	35.14	1.475 9227	34.59	1.488 2807	34.07	1.500 4595	33.59
41	.463 5837	35.13	.476 1302	34.58	.488 4852	34.07	.500 6611	33.58
42	.463 7944	35.12	.476 3376	34.57	.488 6895	34.06	.500 8625	33.58
43	.464 0051	35.11	.476 5450	34.56	.488 8939	34.05	.501 0640	33.57
44	.464 2158	35.10	.476 7524	34.55	.489 0981	34.04	.501 2654	33.56
45	1.464 4263	35.09	1.476 9596	34.54	1.489 3023	34.03	1.501 4667	33.55
46	.464 6369	35.08	.477 1669	34.54	.489 5065	34.02	.501 6680	33.55
47	.464 8473	35.07	.477 3741	34.53	.489 7106	34.02	.501 8693	33.54
48	.465 0577	35.06	.477 5812	34.52	.489 9147	34.01	.502 0705	33.53
49	.465 2681	35.05	.477 7883	34.51	.490 1187	34.00	.502 2716	33.52
50	1.465 4784	35.04	1.477 9953	34.50	1.490 3227	33.99	1.502 4727	33.51
51	.465 6886	35.04	.478 2023	34.49	.490 5266	33.98	.502 6738	33.51
52	.465 8988	35.03	.478 4092	34.48	.490 7305	33.97	.502 8748	33.50
53	.466 1090	35.02	.478 6161	34.47	.490 9343	33.96	.503 0758	33.49
54	.466 3190	35.01	.478 8229	34.46	.491 1381	33.95	.503 2767	33.48
55	1.466 5290	35.00	1.479 0297	34.46	1.491 3418	33.95	1.503 4776	33.48
56	.466 7390	34.99	.479 2364	34.45	.491 5455	33.94	.503 6784	33.47
57	.466 9489	34.98	.479 4430	34.44	.491 7491	33.93	.503 8792	33.46
58	.467 1587	34.97	.479 6496	34.43	.491 9527	33.92	.504 0800	33.45
59	.467 3685	34.96	.479 8562	34.42	.492 1562	33.91	.504 2807	33.44
60	1.467 5782	34.95	1.480 0627	34.41	1.492 3597	33.91	1.504 4813	33.44

TABLE VI.

For finding the True Anomaly or the Time from the Perihelion in a Parabolic Orbit.

v.	44°		45°		46°		47°	
	log M.	Diff. 1″.	log M.	Diff. 1″.	log M.	Diff. 1″.	log M.	Diff. 1″.
0′	1.504 4813	33.44	1.516 4390	33.00	1.528 2435	32.59	1.539 9048	32.20
1	.504 6819	33.43	.516 6370	32.99	.528 4390	32.58	.540 0980	32.20
2	.504 8825	33.42	.516 8349	32.98	.528 6344	32.57	.540 2912	32.19
3	.505 0830	33.42	.517 0328	32.98	.528 8299	32.57	.540 4843	32.18
4	.505 2835	33.41	.517 2306	32.97	.529 0252	32.56	.540 6774	32.18
5	1.505 4839	33.40	1.517 4284	32.96	1.529 2206	32.55	1.540 8705	32.17
6	.505 6843	33.39	.517 6262	32.96	.529 4159	32.55	.541 0635	32.17
7	.505 8846	33.39	.517 8239	32.95	.529 6112	32.54	.541 2564	32.16
8	.506 0849	33.38	.518 0216	32.94	.529 8064	32.53	.541 4494	32.15
9	.506 2852	33.37	.518 2192	32.93	.530 0016	32.53	.541 6423	32.15
10	1.506 4854	33.36	1.518 4168	32.93	1.530 1967	32.52	1.541 8352	32.14
11	.506 6855	33.36	.518 6143	32.92	.530 3918	32.51	.542 0280	32.14
12	.506 8856	33.35	.518 8118	32.91	.530 5869	32.51	.542 2208	32.13
13	.507 0857	33.34	.519 0093	32.91	.530 7819	32.50	.542 4135	32.12
14	.507 2857	33.33	.519 2067	32.90	.530 9769	32.49	.542 6063	32.11
15	1.507 4857	33.33	1.519 4041	32.89	1.531 1719	32.49	1.542 7989	32.11
16	.507 6856	33.32	.519 6014	32.89	.531 3668	32.48	.542 9916	32.10
17	.507 8855	33.31	.519 7987	32.88	.531 5616	32.48	.543 1842	32.10
18	.508 0853	33.30	.519 9960	32.87	.531 7565	32.47	.543 3768	32.09
19	.508 2851	33.29	.520 1932	32.86	.531 9513	32.46	.543 5693	32.09
20	1.508 4849	33.29	1.520 3904	32.86	1.532 1460	32.46	1.543 7618	32.08
21	.508 6846	33.28	.520 5875	32.85	.532 3407	32.45	.543 9543	32.08
22	.508 8843	33.27	.520 7846	32.84	.532 5354	32.44	.544 1467	32.07
23	.509 0839	33.27	.520 9816	32.84	.532 7300	32.44	.544 3391	32.06
24	.509 2835	33.26	.521 1786	32.83	.532 9246	32.43	.544 5315	32.06
25	1.509 4830	33.25	1.521 3756	32.82	1.533 1192	32.43	1.544 7238	32.05
26	.509 6825	33.24	.521 5725	32.82	.533 3137	32.42	.544 9161	32.04
27	.509 8819	33.24	.521 7694	32.81	.533 5082	32.42	.545 1083	32.04
28	.510 0813	33.23	.521 9662	32.80	.533 7027	32.41	.545 3005	32.03
29	.510 2807	33.22	.522 1630	32.80	.533 8971	32.40	.545 4927	32.03
30	1.510 4800	33.21	1.522 3598	32.79	1.534 0914	32.39	1.545 6849	32.02
31	.510 6792	33.21	.522 5565	32.78	.534 2858	32.39	.545 8770	32.02
32	.510 8785	33.20	.522 7531	32.78	.534 4801	32.38	.546 0690	32.01
33	.511 0776	33.19	.522 9498	32.78	.534 6743	32.37	.546 2611	32.00
34	.511 2768	33.18	.523 1464	32.77	.534 8685	32.37	.546 4531	32.00
35	1.511 4759	33.18	1.523 3429	32.76	1.535 0627	32.36	1.546 6450	31.99
36	.511 6749	33.17	.523 5394	32.75	.535 2568	32.35	.546 8370	31.98
37	.511 8739	33.16	.523 7359	32.74	.555 4509	32.35	.547 0289	31.98
38	.512 0729	33.15	.523 9323	32.73	.535 6450	32.34	.547 2207	31.97
39	.512 2718	33.15	.524 1287	32.73	.535 8390	32.33	.547 4125	31.97
40	1.512 4707	33.14	1.524 3251	32.72	1.536 0330	32.33	1.547 6043	31.96
41	.512 6695	33.13	.524 5214	32.71	.536 2270	32.32	.547 7961	31.96
42	.512 8683	33.13	.524 7176	32.71	.536 4209	32.32	.547 9878	31.95
43	.513 0670	33.12	.524 9138	32.70	.536 6148	32.31	.548 1795	31.94
44	.513 2657	33.11	.525 1100	32.70	.536 8086	32.30	.548 3711	31.94
45	1.513 4644	33.11	1.525 3062	32.69	1.537 0024	32.30	1.548 5627	31.93
46	.513 6630	33.10	.525 5023	32.68	.537 1962	32.29	.548 7543	31.93
47	.513 8615	33.09	.525 6983	32.67	.537 3899	32.28	.548 9458	31.92
48	.514 0601	33.08	.525 8944	32.67	.537 5836	32.28	.549 1373	31.91
49	.514 2586	33.07	.526 0903	32.66	.537 7772	32.27	.549 3288	31.91
50	1.514 4570	33.07	1.526 2863	32.65	1.537 9708	32.26	1.549 5202	31.90
51	.514 6554	33.06	.526 4822	32.64	.538 1644	32.26	.549 7116	31.90
52	.514 8537	33.05	.526 6780	32.64	.538 3579	32.25	.549 9030	31.89
53	.515 0520	33.05	.526 8739	32.63	.538 5514	32.25	.550 0943	31.88
54	.515 2503	33.04	.527 0696	32.62	.538 7449	32.24	.550 2856	31.88
55	1.515 4485	33.04	1.527 2654	32.62	1.538 9383	32.23	1.550 4769	31.87
56	.515 6467	33.03	.527 4611	32.61	.539 1317	32.23	.550 6681	31.87
57	.515 8449	33.02	.527 6567	32.61	.539 3250	32.22	.550 8593	31.86
58	.516 0430	33.01	.527 8524	32.60	.539 5183	32.21	.551 0504	31.86
59	.516 2410	33.01	.528 0479	32.60	.539 7116	32,21	.551 2416	31.85
60	1.516 4390	33.00	1.528 2435	32.59	1.539 9048	32.20	1.551 4326	31.85

TABLE VI.

For finding the True Anomaly or the Time from the Perihelion in a Parabolic Orbit.

v.	48°		49°		50°		51°	
	log M.	Diff. 1″.	log M.	Diff. 1″.	log M.	Diff. 1″.	log M.	Diff. 1″.
0′	1.551 4326	31.85	1.562 8360	31.51	1.574 1234	31.20	1.585 3031	30.91
1	.551 6237	31.84	.563 0250	31.51	.574 3106	31.20	.585 4886	30.91
2	.551 8147	31.83	.563 2140	31.50	.574 4977	31.19	.585 6740	30.90
3	.552 0057	31.83	.563 4030	31.50	.574 6849	31.19	.585 8594	30.90
4	.552 1966	31.82	.563 5920	31.49	.574 8720	31.18	.586 0448	30.89
5	1.552 3876	31.82	1.563 7809	31.48	1.575 0590	31.18	1.586 2302	30.89
6	.552 5784	31.81	.563 9698	31.48	.575 2461	31.17	.586 4155	30.89
7	.552 7693	31.80	.564 1586	31.47	.575 4331	31.17	.586 6008	30.88
8	.552 9601	31.80	.564 3475	31.47	.575 6201	31.16	.586 7859	30.87
9	.553 1508	31.79	.564 5363	31.46	.575 8070	31.16	.586 9713	30.87
10	1.553 3416	31.79	1.564 7250	31.46	1.575 9939	31.15	1.587 1565	30.87
11	.553 5323	31.78	.564 9138	31.45	.576 1808	31.15	.587 3417	30.86
12	.553 7230	31.78	.565 1025	31.45	.576 3677	31.14	.587 5268	30.86
13	.553 9136	31.77	.565 2911	31.44	.576 5546	31.14	.587 7120	30.85
14	.554 1042	31.76	.565 4798	31.44	.576 7414	31.13	.587 8971	30.85
15	1.554 2948	31.76	1.565 6684	31.43	1.576 9281	31.13	1.588 0821	30.84
16	.554 4853	31.75	.565 8569	31.43	.577 1149	31.12	.588 2672	30.84
17	.554 6758	31.75	.566 0455	31.42	.577 3016	31.12	.588 4522	30.83
18	.554 8663	31.74	.566 2340	31.41	.577 4883	31.11	.588 6372	30.83
19	.555 0567	31.74	.566 4225	31.41	.577 6749	31.11	.588 8222	30.83
20	1.555 2472	31.73	1.566 6109	31.40	1.577 8615	31.10	1.589 0071	30.82
21	.555 4375	31.73	.566 7993	31.40	.578 0481	31.10	.589 1920	30.82
22	.555 6279	31.72	.566 9877	31.39	.578 2347	31.09	.589 3769	30.81
23	.555 8182	31.71	.567 1761	31.39	.578 4213	31.09	.589 5618	30.81
24	.556 0084	31.71	.567 3644	31.38	.578 6078	31.08	.589 7466	30.80
25	1.556 1987	31.70	1.567 5527	31.38	1.578 7942	31.08	1.589 9314	30.80
26	.556 3888	31.70	.567 7409	31.37	.578 9807	31.07	.590 1162	30.79
27	.556 5790	31.69	.567 9291	31.37	.579 1671	31.07	.590 3009	30.79
28	.556 7691	31.68	.568 1173	31.36	.579 3535	31.06	.590 4857	30.78
29	.556 9592	31.68	.568 3055	31.36	.579 5399	31.06	.590 6704	30.78
30	1.557 1493	31.67	1.568 4936	31.35	1.579 7262	31.06	1.590 8550	30.78
31	.557 3393	31.67	.568 6817	31.35	.579 9125	31.05	.591 0397	30.77
32	.557 5293	31.66	.568 8698	31.34	.580 0988	31.04	.591 2243	30.77
33	.557 7193	31.66	.569 0579	31.34	.580 2851	31.04	.591 4089	30.76
34	.557 9092	31.65	.569 2459	31.33	.580 4713	31.03	.591 5935	30.76
35	1.558 0991	31.65	1.569 4338	31.33	1.580 6575	31.03	1.591 7780	30.75
36	.558 2890	31.64	.569 6218	31.32	.580 8436	31.03	.591 9625	30.75
37	.558 4788	31.64	.569 8097	31.32	.581 0298	31.02	.592 1470	30.75
38	.558 6686	31.63	.569 9976	31.31	.581 2159	31.02	.592 3315	30.74
39	.558 8584	31.62	.570 1854	31.30	.581 4020	31.01	.592 5159	30.74
40	1.559 0482	31.62	1.570 3733	31.30	1.581 5880	31.01	1.592 7003	30.73
41	.559 2379	31.61	.570 5611	31.29	.581 7740	31.00	.592 8847	30.73
42	.559 4275	31.61	.570 7488	31.29	.581 9600	31.00	.593 0690	30.72
43	.559 6172	31.60	.570 9366	31.28	.582 1460	30.99	.593 2534	30.72
44	.559 8068	31.60	.571 1243	31.28	.582 3319	30.99	.593 4377	30.72
45	1.559 9963	31.59	1.571 3119	31.28	1.582 5179	30.98	1.593 6219	30.71
46	.560 1859	31.59	.571 4996	31.27	.582 7037	30.98	.593 8062	30.71
47	.560 3754	31.58	.571 6872	31.27	.582 8896	30.97	.593 9904	30.70
48	.560 5648	31.57	.571 8748	31.26	.583 0754	30.97	.594 1746	30.70
49	.560 7543	31.57	.572 0623	31.26	.583 2612	30.96	.594 3588	30.69
50	1.560 9437	31.56	1.572 2499	31.25	1.583 4470	30.96	1.594 5429	30.69
51	.561 1331	31.56	.572 4373	31.25	.583 6327	30.95	.594 7270	30.68
52	.561 3224	31.55	.572 6248	31.24	.583 8184	30.95	.594 9111	30.68
53	.561 5117	31.55	.572 8123	31.24	.584 0041	30.94	.595 0952	30.68
54	.561 7010	31.54	.572 9997	31.23	.584 1898	30.94	.595 2792	30.67
55	1.561 8902	31.54	1.573 1870	31.23	1.584 3754	30.94	1.595 4633	30.67
56	.562 0794	31.53	.573 3743	31.22	.584 5610	30.93	.595 6473	30.66
57	.562 2686	31.53	.573 5616	31.22	.584 7466	30.93	.595 8312	30.66
58	.562 4578	31.52	.573 7489	31.21	.584 9321	30.92	.596 0151	30.65
59	.562 6469	31.52	.573 9362	31.21	.585 1176	30.92	.596 1990	30.65
60	1.562 8360	31.51	1.574 1234	31.20	1.585 3031	30.91	1.596 3829	30.65

TABLE VI.

For finding the True Anomaly or the Time from the Perihelion in a Parabolic Orbit.

v.	52°		53°		54°		55°	
	log M.	Diff. 1″.	log M.	Diff. 1″.	log M.	Diff. 1″.	log M.	Diff. 1″.
0′	1.596 3829	30.65	1.607 3703	30.40	1.618 2724	30.17	1.629 0959	29.96
1	.596 5668	30.64	.607 5527	30.39	.618 4534	30.17	.629 2757	29.96
2	.596 7506	30.64	.607 7350	30.39	.618 6344	30.16	.629 4554	29.96
3	.596 9344	30.63	.607 9174	30.39	.618 8153	30.16	.629 6351	29.95
4	.597 1182	30.63	.608 0997	30.38	.618 9963	30.16	.629 8148	29.95
5	1.597 3020	30.62	1.608 2820	30.38	1.619 1772	30.15	1.629 9945	29.95
6	.597 4857	30.62	.608 4642	30.38	.619 3581	30.15	.630 1742	29.94
7	.597 6694	30.62	.608 6465	30.37	.619 5390	30.15	.630 3538	29.94
8	.597 8531	30.61	.608 8287	30.37	.619 7199	30.14	.630 5335	29.94
9	.598 0368	30.61	.609 0109	30.36	.619 9007	30.14	.630 7131	29.93
10	1.598 2204	30.60	1.609 1931	30.36	1.620 0816	30.14	1.630 8927	29.93
11	.598 4040	30.60	.609 3752	30.36	.620 2623	30.13	.631 0722	29.93
12	.598 5876	30.59	.609 5573	30.35	.620 4431	30.13	.631 2518	29.92
13	.598 7711	30.59	.609 7394	30.35	.620 6239	30.12	.631 4313	29.92
14	.598 9547	30.59	.609 9215	30.34	.620 8046	30.12	.631 6108	29.92
15	1.599 1382	30.58	1.610 1036	30.34	1.620 9853	30.12	1.631 7903	29.91
16	.599 3217	30.58	.610 2856	30.34	.621 1660	30.11	.631 9698	29.91
17	.599 5051	30.57	.610 4676	30.33	.621 3467	30.11	.632 1492	29.91
18	.599 6885	30.57	.610 6496	30.33	.621 5274	30.11	.632 3286	29.90
19	.599 8719	30.57	.610 8315	30.32	.621 7080	30.10	.632 5081	29.90
20	1.600 0553	30.56	1.611 0135	30.32	1.621 8886	30.10	1.632 6875	29.90
21	.600 2387	30.56	.611 1954	30.32	.622 0692	30.10	.632 8668	29.89
22	.600 4220	30.55	.611 3773	30.31	.622 2497	30.09	.633 0462	29.89
23	.600 6053	30.55	.611 5591	30.31	.622 4303	30.09	.633 2255	29.89
24	.600 7886	30.55	.611 7410	30.31	.622 6108	30.09	.633 4048	29.88
25	1.600 9718	30.54	1.611 9228	30.30	1.622 7913	30.08	1.633 5841	29.88
26	.601 1551	30.54	.612 1046	30.30	.622 9718	30.08	.633 7634	29.88
27	.601 3383	30.53	.612 2864	30.29	.623 1523	30.08	.633 9427	29.87
28	.601 5214	30.53	.612 4681	30.29	.623 3327	30.07	.634 1219	29.87
29	.601 7046	30.52	.612 6499	30.29	.623 5131	30.07	.634 3011	29.87
30	1.601 8877	30.52	1.612 8316	30.28	1.623 6935	30.06	1.634 4803	29.86
31	.602 0708	30.52	.613 0132	30.28	.623 8739	30.06	.634 6595	29.86
32	.602 2539	30.51	.613 1949	30.28	.624 0543	30.06	.634 8387	29.86
33	.602 4370	30.51	.613 3765	30.27	.624 2346	30.05	.635 0178	29.86
34	.602 6200	30.50	.613 5582	30.27	.624 4149	30.05	.635 1969	29.85
35	1.602 8030	30.50	1.613 7398	30.26	1.624 5952	30.05	1.635 3760	29.85
36	.602 9860	30.50	.613 9213	30.26	.624 7755	30.04	.635 5551	29.85
37	.603 1690	30.49	.614 1029	30.26	.624 9557	30.04	.635 7342	29.84
38	.603 3519	30.49	.614 2844	30.25	.625 1360	30.04	.635 9132	29.84
39	.603 5348	30.48	.614 4659	30.25	.625 3162	30.03	.636 0922	29.84
40	1.603 7177	30.48	1.614 6474	30.25	1.625 4964	30.03	1.636 2713	29.83
41	.603 9005	30.47	.614 8288	30.24	.625 6765	30.03	.636 4502	29.83
42	.604 0834	30.47	.615 0103	30.24	.625 8567	30.02	.636 6292	29.83
43	.604 2662	30.47	.615 1917	30.23	.626 0368	30.02	.636 8082	29.82
44	.604 4490	30.46	.615 3731	30.23	.626 2169	30.02	.636 9871	29.82
45	1.604 6317	30.46	1.615 5545	30.23	1.626 3970	30.01	1.637 1660	29.82
46	.604 8145	30.45	.615 7358	30.22	.626 5771	30.01	.637 3449	29.82
47	.604 9972	30.45	.615 9171	30.22	.626 7571	30.01	.637 5238	29.81
48	.605 1799	30.45	.616 0984	30.22	.626 9372	30.00	.637 7027	29.81
49	.605 3626	30.44	.616 2797	30.21	.627 1172	30.00	.637 8815	29.81
50	1.605 5452	30.44	1.616 4610	30.21	1.627 2972	30.00	1.638 0603	29.80
51	.605 7278	30.43	.616 6422	30.20	.627 4771	29.99	.638 2391	29.80
52	.605 9104	30.43	.616 8234	30.20	.627 6571	29.99	.638 4179	29.80
53	.606 0930	30.43	.617 0046	30.20	.627 8370	29.99	.638 5967	29.79
54	.606 2755	30.42	.617 1858	30.19	.628 0169	29.98	.638 7754	29.79
55	1.606 4581	30.42	1.617 3669	30.19	1.628 1968	29.98	1.638 9542	29.79
56	.606 6406	30.42	.617 5481	30.19	.628 3766	29.98	.639 1329	29.78
57	.606 8230	30.41	.617 7292	30.18	.628 5565	29.97	.639 3116	29.78
58	.607 0055	30.41	.617 9102	30.18	.628 7363	29.97	.639 4902	29.78
59	.607 1879	30.40	.618 0913	30.17	.628 9161	29.97	.639 6689	29.77
60	1.607 3703	30.40	1.618 2724	30.17	1.629 0959	29.96	1.639 8475	29.77

TABLE VI.

For finding the True Anomaly or the Time from the Perihelion in a Parabolic Orbit.

v.	56°		57°		58°		59°	
	log M.	Diff. 1″.	log M.	Diff. 1″.	log M.	Diff. 1″.	log M.	Diff. 1″.
0′	1.639 8475	29.77	1.650 5336	29.60	1.661 1601	29.44	1.671 7331	29.30
1	.640 0262	29.77	.650 7112	29.60	.661 3368	29.44	.671 9089	29.30
2	.640 2048	29.77	.650 8887	29.59	.661 5134	29.44	.672 0846	29.30
3	.640 3833	29.76	.651 0663	29.59	.661 6900	29.43	.672 2604	29.29
4	.640 5619	29.76	.651 2438	29.59	.661 8666	29.43	.672 4362	29.29
5	1.640 7405	29.76	1.651 4213	29.58	1.662 0432	29.43	1.672 6119	29.29
6	.640 9190	29.75	.651 5988	29.58	.662 2197	29.43	.672 7876	29.29
7	.641 0975	29.75	.651 7763	29.58	.662 3963	29.42	.672 9634	29.28
8	.641 2760	29.75	.651 9538	29.58	.662 5728	29.42	.673 1391	29.28
9	.641 4545	29.74	.652 1312	29.57	.662 7493	29.42	.673 3147	29.28
10	1.641 6329	29.74	1.652 3086	29.57	1.662 9258	29.42	1.673 4904	29.28
11	.641 8114	29.74	.652 4861	29.57	.663 1023	29.41	.673 6661	29.28
12	.641 9898	29.74	.652 6635	29.57	.663 2788	29.41	.673 8417	29.27
13	.642 1682	29.73	.652 8408	29.56	.663 4553	29.41	.674 0174	29.27
14	.642 3466	29.73	.653 0182	29.56	.663 6317	29.41	.674 1930	29.27
15	1.642 5250	29.73	1.653 1956	29.56	1.663 8082	29.40	1.674 3686	29.27
16	.642 7033	29.72	.653 3729	29.55	.663 9846	29.40	.674 5442	29.27
17	.642 8816	29.72	.653 5502	29.55	.664 1610	29.40	.674 7198	29.26
18	.643 0599	29.72	.653 7275	29.55	.664 3374	29.40	.674 8954	29.26
19	.643 2382	29.71	.653 9048	29.55	.664 5137	29.39	.675 0709	29.26
20	1.643 4165	29.71	1.654 0821	29.54	1.664 6901	29.39	1.675 2465	29.26
21	.643 5948	29.71	.654 2593	29.54	.664 8664	29.39	.675 4220	29.25
22	.643 7730	29.71	.654 4366	29.54	.665 0428	29.39	.675 5975	29.25
23	.643 9513	29.70	.654 6138	29.54	.665 2191	29.39	.675 7730	29.25
24	.644 1295	29.70	.654 7910	29.53	.665 3954	29.38	.675 9485	29.25
25	1.644 3077	29.70	1.654 9682	29.53	1.665 5717	29.38	1.676 1240	29.25
26	.644 4858	29.69	.655 1454	29.53	.665 7480	29.38	.676 2995	29.24
27	.644 6640	29.69	.655 3225	29.53	.665 9242	29.38	.676 4749	29.24
28	.644 8421	29.69	.655 4997	29.52	.666 1005	29.37	.676 6504	29.24
29	.645 0203	29.69	.655 6768	29.52	.666 2767	29.37	.676 8258	29.24
30	1.645 1984	29.68	1.655 8539	29.52	1.666 4529	29.37	1.677 0012	29.24
31	.645 3765	29.68	.656 0310	29.51	.666 6291	29.37	.677 1766	29.23
32	.645 5545	29.68	.656 2081	29.51	.666 8053	29.36	.677 3520	29.23
33	.645 7326	29.67	.656 3852	29.51	.666 9815	29.36	.677 5274	29.23
34	.645 9106	29.67	.656 5622	29.51	.667 1577	29.36	.677 7028	29.23
35	1.646 0886	29.67	1.656 7392	29.50	1.667 3338	29.36	1.677 8781	29.23
36	.646 2666	29.67	.656 9163	29.50	.667 5100	29.35	.678 0535	29.22
37	.646 4446	29.66	.657 0933	29.50	.667 6861	29.35	.678 2288	29.22
38	.646 6226	29.66	.657 2703	29.50	.667 8622	29.35	.678 4041	29.22
39	.646 8005	29.66	.657 4472	29.49	.668 0383	29.35	.678 5794	29.22
40	1.646 9785	29.65	1.657 6242	29.49	1.668 2144	29.35	1.678 7547	29.22
41	.647 1564	29.65	.657 8011	29.49	.668 3904	29.34	.678 9300	29.21
42	.647 3343	29.65	.657 9781	29.49	.668 5665	29.34	.679 1053	29.21
43	.647 5122	29.65	.658 1550	29.48	.668 7425	29.34	.679 2806	29.21
44	.647 6900	29.64	.658 3318	29.48	.668 9185	29.34	.679 4558	29.21
45	1.647 8679	29.64	1.658 5087	29.48	1.669 0945	29.33	1.679 6310	29.20
46	.648 0457	29.64	.658 6855	29.48	.669 2705	29.33	.679 8063	29.20
47	.648 2235	29.63	.658 8624	29.47	.669 4465	29.33	.679 9815	29.20
48	.648 4013	29.63	.659 0393	29.47	.669 6225	29.33	.680 1567	29.20
49	.648 5791	29.63	.659 2161	29.47	.669 7984	29.32	.680 3319	29.20
50	1.648 7569	29.63	1.659 3929	29.47	1.669 9744	29.32	1.680 5070	29.19
51	.648 9346	29.62	.659 5697	29.46	.670 1503	29.32	.680 6822	29.19
52	.649 1123	29.62	.659 7465	29.46	.670 3262	29.32	.680 8574	29.19
53	.649 2901	29.62	.659 9232	29.46	.670 5021	29.32	.681 0325	29.19
54	.649 4677	29.61	.660 1000	29.46	.670 6780	29.31	.681 2076	29.19
55	1.649 6454	29.61	1.660 2767	29.45	1.670 8539	29.31	1.681 3827	29.18
56	.649 8231	29.61	.660 4534	29.45	.671 0298	29.31	.681 5578	29.18
57	.650 0007	29.61	.660 6301	29.45	.671 2056	29.31	.681 7329	29.18
58	.650 1784	29.60	.660 8068	29.45	.671 3814	29.30	.681 9080	29.18
59	.650 3560	29.60	.660 9835	29.44	.671 5573	29.30	.682 0831	29.18
60	1.650 5336	29.60	1.661 1601	29.44	1.671 7331	29.30	1.682 2581	29.17

TABLE VI.

For finding the True Anomaly or the Time from the Perihelion in a Parabolic Orbit.

v.	60°		61°		62°		63°	
	log M.	Diff. 1″.	log M.	Diff. 1″.	log M.	Diff. 1″.	log M.	Diff. 1″.
0′	1.682 2581	29.17	1.692 7408	29.07	1.703 1866	28.97	1.713 6006	28.89
1	.682 4332	29.17	.692 9152	29.06	.703 3604	28.97	.713 7739	28.89
2	.682 6082	29.17	.693 0896	29.06	.703 5342	28.97	.713 9473	28.89
3	.682 7832	29.17	.693 2640	29.06	.703 7080	28.97	.714 1206	28.88
4	.682 9582	29.17	.693 4383	29.06	.703 8818	28.96	.714 2939	28.88
5	1.683 1332	29.16	1.693 6127	29.06	1.704 0556	28.96	1.714 4672	28.88
6	.683 3082	29.16	.693 7870	29.05	.704 2293	28.96	.714 6405	28.88
7	.683 4832	29.16	.693 9613	29.05	.704 4031	28.96	.714 8138	28.88
8	.683 6581	29.16	.694 1356	29.05	.704 5768	28.96	.714 9870	28.88
9	.683 8331	29.16	.694 3099	29.05	.704 7506	28.96	.715 1603	28.88
10	1.684 0080	29.16	1.694 4842	29.05	1.704 9243	28.96	1.715 3336	28.88
11	.684 1830	29.15	.694 6585	29.04	.705 0981	28.95	.715 5068	28.88
12	.684 3579	29.15	.694 8328	29.04	.705 2718	28.95	.715 6801	28.87
13	.684 5328	29.15	.695 0070	29.04	.705 4455	28.95	.715 8533	28.87
14	.684 7077	29.15	.695 1813	29.04	.705 6192	28.95	.716 0266	28.87
15	1.684 8826	29.14	1.695 3555	29.04	1.705 7929	28.95	1.716 1998	28.87
16	.685 0574	29.14	.695 5298	29.04	.705 9666	28.95	.716 3730	28.87
17	.685 2323	29.14	.695 7040	29.04	.706 1402	28.95	.716 5462	28.87
18	.685 4071	29.14	.695 8782	29.03	.706 3139	28.94	.716 7194	28.87
19	.685 5820	29.14	.696 0524	29.03	.706 4875	28.94	.716 8926	28.87
20	1.685 7568	29.14	1.696 2266	29.03	1.706 6612	28.94	1.717 0658	28.86
21	.685 9316	29.13	.696 4008	29.03	.706 8348	28.94	.717 2390	28.86
22	.686 1064	29.13	.696 5750	29.03	.707 0085	28.94	.717 4122	28.86
23	.686 2812	29.13	.696 7491	29.03	.707 1821	28.94	.717 5853	28.86
24	.686 4560	29.13	.696 9233	29.02	.707 3557	28.94	.717 7585	28.86
25	1.686 6308	29.13	1.697 0974	29.02	1.707 5293	28.93	1.717 9317	28.86
26	.686 8055	29.13	.697 2716	29.02	.707 7029	28.93	.718 1048	28.86
27	.686 9803	29.12	.697 4457	29.02	.707 8765	28.93	.718 2780	28.86
28	.687 1550	29.12	.697 6198	29.02	.708 0501	28.93	.718 4511	28.86
29	.687 3297	29.12	.697 7939	29.02	.708 2237	28.93	.718 6242	28.85
30	1.687 5044	29.12	1.697 9680	29.02	1.708 3972	28.93	1.718 7974	28.85
31	.687 6791	29.12	.698 1421	29.01	.708 5708	28.93	.718 9705	28.85
32	.687 8538	29.11	.698 3162	29.01	.708 7444	28.92	.719 1436	28.85
33	.688 0285	29.11	.698 4902	29.01	.708 9179	28.92	.719 3167	28.85
34	.688 2032	29.11	.698 6643	29.01	.709 0914	28.92	.719 4898	28.85
35	1.688 3778	29.11	1.698 8383	29.01	1.709 2650	28.92	1.719 6629	28.85
36	.688 5525	29.11	.699 0124	29.01	.709 4385	28.92	.719 8360	28.85
37	.688 7271	29.10	.699 1864	29.00	.709 6120	28.92	.720 0090	28.85
38	.688 9017	29.10	.699 3604	29.00	.709 7855	28.92	.720 1821	28.84
39	.689 0764	29.10	.699 5345	29.00	.709 9590	28.92	.720 3552	28.84
40	1.689 2510	29.10	1.699 7085	29.00	1.710 1325	28.91	1.720 5282	28.84
41	.689 4256	29.10	.699 8824	29.00	.710 3060	28.91	.720 7013	28.84
42	.689 6001	29.09	.700 0564	29.00	.710 4794	28.91	.720 8743	28.84
43	.689 7747	29.09	.700 2304	29.00	.710 6529	28.91	.721 0474	28.84
44	.689 9493	29.09	.700 4044	28.99	.710 8263	28.91	.721 2204	28.84
45	1.690 1238	29.09	1.700 5783	28.99	1.710 9998	28.91	1.721 3934	28.84
46	.690 2984	29.09	.700 7523	28.99	.711 1732	28.91	.721 5665	28.84
47	.690 4729	29.09	.700 9262	28.99	.711 3467	28.90	.721 7395	28.84
48	.690 6474	29.09	.701 1001	28.99	.711 5201	28.90	.721 9125	28.83
49	.690 8219	29.08	.701 2741	28.99	.711 6935	28.90	.722 0855	28.83
50	1.690 9964	29.08	1.701 4480	28.98	1.711 8669	28.90	1.722 2585	28.83
51	.691 1709	29.08	.701 6219	28.98	.712 0403	28.90	.722 4315	28.83
52	.691 3454	29.08	.701 7958	28.98	.712 2137	28.90	.722 6044	28.83
53	.691 5199	29.08	.701 9697	28.98	.712 3871	28.90	.722 7774	28.83
54	.691 6943	29.08	.702 1435	28.98	.712 5605	28.90	.722 9504	28.83
55	1.691 8688	29.07	1.702 3174	28.98	1.712 7339	28.90	1.723 1233	28.83
56	.692 0432	29.07	.702 4913	28.98	.712 9072	28.89	.723 2963	28.83
57	.692 2176	29.07	.702 6651	28.97	.713 0806	28.89	.723 4693	28.82
58	.692 3920	29.07	.702 8389	28.97	.713 2539	28.89	.723 6422	28.82
59	.692 5664	29.07	.703 0128	28.97	.713 4273	28.89	.723 8151	28.82
60	1.692 7408	29.07	1.703 1866	28.97	1.713 6006	28.89	1.723 9881	28.82

TABLE VI.

For finding the True Anomaly or the Time from the Perihelion in a Parabolic Orbit.

v.	64°		65°		66°		67°	
	log M.	Diff. 1″.	log M.	Diff. 1″.	log M.	Diff. 1″.	log M.	Diff. 1″.
0′	1·723 9881	28.82	1·734 3539	28.77	1·744 7031	28.73	1·755 0405	28.70
1	·724 1610	28.82	·734 5265	28.77	·744 8755	28.73	·755 2127	28.70
2	·724 3339	28.82	·734 6991	28.77	·745 0479	28.73	·755 3849	28.70
3	·724 5068	28.82	·734 8718	28.77	·745 2202	28.73	·755 5571	28.70
4	·724 6798	28.82	·735 0444	28.77	·745 3926	28.73	·755 7293	28.70
5	1·724 8527	28.82	1·735 2169	28.76	1·745 5650	28.73	1·755 9015	28.70
6	·725 0256	28.82	·735 3895	28.76	·745 7373	28.73	·756 0737	28.70
7	·725 1984	28.81	·735 5621	28.76	·745 9097	28.73	·756 2459	28.70
8	·725 3713	28.81	·735 7347	28.76	·746 0820	28.72	·756 4181	28.70
9	·725 5442	28.81	·735 9073	28.76	·746 2544	28.72	·756 5903	28.70
10	1·725 7171	28.81	1·736 0798	28.76	1·746 4267	28.72	1·756 7625	28.70
11	·725 8900	28.81	·736 2524	28.76	·746 5991	28.72	·756 9347	28.70
12	·726 0628	28.81	·736 4250	28.76	·746 7714	28.72	·757 1069	28.70
13	·726 2357	28.81	·736 5975	28.76	·746 9437	28.72	·757 2791	28.70
14	·726 4085	28.81	·736 7701	28.76	·747 1161	28.72	·757 4513	28.70
15	1·726 5814	28.81	1·736 9426	28.76	1·747 2884	28.72	1·757 6235	28.70
16	·726 7542	28.81	·737 1152	28.76	·747 4607	28.72	·757 7957	28.70
17	·726 9270	28.81	·737 2877	28.76	·747 6330	28.72	·757 9679	28.70
18	·727 0999	28.80	·737 4602	28.76	·747 8054	28.72	·758 1401	28.70
19	·727 2727	28.80	·737 6328	28.75	·747 9777	28.72	·758 3123	28.70
20	1·727 4455	28.80	1·737 8053	28.75	1·748 1500	28.72	1·758 4844	28.70
21	·727 6183	28.80	·737 9778	28.75	·748 3223	28.72	·758 6566	28.70
22	·727 7911	28.80	·738 1503	28.75	·748 4946	28.72	·758 8288	28.70
23	·727 9639	28.80	·738 3228	28.75	·748 6669	28.72	·759 0010	28.70
24	·728 1367	28.80	·738 4953	28.75	·748 8392	28.72	·759 1731	28.70
25	1·728 3095	28.80	1·738 6679	28.75	1·749 0115	28.72	1·759 3453	28.70
26	·728 4823	28.80	·738 8404	28.75	·749 1838	28.72	·759 5175	28.70
27	·728 6551	28.80	·739 0129	28.75	·749 3561	28.72	·759 6897	28.70
28	·728 8279	28.80	·739 1853	28.75	·749 5284	28.72	·759 8618	28.69
29	·729 0006	28.79	·739 3578	28.75	·749 7007	28.71	·760 0340	28.69
30	1·729 1734	28.79	1·739 5303	28.75	1·749 8730	28.71	1·760 2062	28.69
31	·729 3461	28.79	·739 7028	28.75	·750 0453	28.71	·760 3783	28.69
32	·729 5189	28.79	·739 8753	28.75	·750 2176	28.71	·760 5505	28.69
33	·729 6916	28.79	·740 0477	28.75	·750 3898	28.71	·760 7227	28.69
34	·729 8644	28.79	·740 2202	28.74	·750 5621	28.71	·760 8948	28.69
35	1·730 0371	28.79	1·740 3927	28.74	1·750 7344	28.71	1·761 0670	28.69
36	·730 2099	28.79	·740 5651	28.74	·750 9067	28.71	·761 2392	28.69
37	·730 3826	28.79	·740 7376	28.74	·751 0789	28.71	·761 4113	28.69
38	·730 5553	28.79	·740 9101	28.74	·751 2512	28.71	·761 5835	28.69
39	·730 7280	28.79	·741 0825	28.74	·751 4234	28.71	·761 7556	28.69
40	1·730 9007	28.78	1·741 2550	28.74	1·751 5957	28.71	1·761 9278	28.69
41	·731 0735	28.78	·741 4274	28.74	·751 7680	28.71	·762 0999	28.69
42	·731 2462	28.78	·741 5998	28.74	·751 9402	28.71	·762 2721	28.69
43	·731 4189	28.78	·741 7723	28.74	·752 1125	28.71	·762 4442	28.69
44	·731 5915	28.78	·741 9447	28.74	·752 2847	28.71	·762 6164	28.69
45	1·731 7642	28.78	1·742 1171	28.74	1·752 4570	28.71	1·762 7885	28.69
46	·731 9369	28.78	·742 2896	28.74	·752 6292	28.71	·762 9607	28.69
47	·732 1096	28.78	·742 4620	28.74	·752 8015	28.71	·763 1328	28.69
48	·732 2823	28.78	·742 6344	28.74	·752 9737	28.71	·763 3050	28.69
49	·732 4549	28.78	·742 8068	28.74	·753 1460	28.71	·763 4771	28.69
50	1·732 6276	28.78	1·742 9792	28.74	1·753 3182	28.71	1·763 6493	28.69
51	·732 8002	28.78	·743 1516	28.73	·753 4904	28.71	·763 8214	28.69
52	·732 9729	28.77	·743 3240	28.73	·753 6627	28.71	·763 9936	28.69
53	·733 1455	28.77	·743 4964	28.73	·753 8349	28.71	·764 1657	28.69
54	·733 3182	28.77	·743 6688	28.73	·754 0071	28.70	·764 3379	28.69
55	1·733 4908	28.77	1·743 8412	28.73	1·754 1794	28.70	1·764 5100	28.69
56	·733 6635	28.77	·744 0136	28.73	·754 3516	28.70	·764 6821	28.69
57	·733 8361	28.77	·744 1860	28.73	·754 5238	28.70	·764 8543	28.69
58	·734 0087	28.77	·744 3584	28.73	·754 6960	28.70	·765 0264	28.69
59	·734 1813	28.77	·744 5308	28.73	·754 8682	28.70	·765 1985	28.69
60	1·734 3539	28.77	1·744 7031	28.73	1·755 0405	28.70	1·765 3707	28.69

TABLE VI.

For finding the True Anomaly or the Time from the Perihelion in a Parabolic Orbit.

v.	68° log M.	68° Diff. 1″.	69° log M.	69° Diff. 1″.	70° log M.	70° Diff. 1″.	71° log M.	71° Diff. 1″.
0′	1.765 3707	28.69	1.775 6985	28.69	1.786 0284	28.70	1.796 3650	28.73
1	.765 5428	28.69	.775 8706	28.69	.786 2006	28.70	.796 5374	28.73
2	.765 7150	28.69	.776 0427	28.69	.786 3728	28.70	.796 7097	28.73
3	.765 8871	28.69	.776 2149	28.69	.786 5450	28.70	.796 8821	28.73
4	.766 0592	28.69	.776 3870	28.69	.786 7172	28.70	.797 0545	28.73
5	1.766 2314	28.69	1.776 5591	28.69	1.786 8894	28.70	1.797 2268	28.73
6	.766 4035	28.69	.776 7313	28.69	.787 0617	28.70	.797 3992	28.73
7	.766 5756	28.69	.776 9034	28.69	.787 2339	28.70	.797 5716	28.73
8	.766 7478	28.69	.777 0755	28.69	.787 4061	28.70	.797 7440	28.73
9	.766 9199	28.69	.777 2477	28.69	.787 5783	28.70	.797 9164	28.73
10	1.767 0920	28.69	1.777 4198	28.69	1.787 7506	28.70	1.798 0888	28.73
11	.767 2642	28.69	.777 5920	28.69	.787 9228	28.71	.798 2611	28.73
12	.767 4363	28.69	.777 7641	28.69	.788 0950	28.71	.798 4335	28.73
13	.767 6084	28.69	.777 9363	28.69	.788 2673	28.71	.798 6060	28.73
14	.767 7805	28.69	.778 1084	28.69	.788 4395	28.71	.798 7784	28.73
15	1.767 9527	28.69	1.778 2806	28.69	1.788 6117	28.71	1.798 9508	28.73
16	.768 1248	28.69	.778 4527	28.69	.788 7840	28.71	.799 1232	28.74
17	.768 2969	28.69	.778 6248	28.69	.788 9562	28.71	.799 2956	28.74
18	.768 4691	28.69	.778 7970	28.69	.789 1284	28.71	.799 4680	28.74
19	.768 6412	28.69	.778 9691	28.69	.789 3007	28.71	.799 6404	28.74
20	1.768 8133	28.69	1.779 1413	28.69	1.789 4730	28.71	1.799 8128	28.74
21	.768 9854	28.69	.779 3140	28.69	.789 6452	28.71	.799 9853	28.74
22	.769 1576	28.69	.779 4862	28.69	.789 8175	28.71	.800 1577	28.74
23	.769 3297	28.69	.779 6578	28.69	.789 9897	28.71	.800 3301	28.74
24	.769 5018	28.69	.779 8299	28.69	.790 1620	28.71	.800 5026	28.74
25	1.769 6740	28.69	1.780 0021	28.69	1.790 3342	28.71	1.800 6750	28.74
26	.769 8461	28.69	.780 1742	28.69	.790 5065	28.71	.800 8475	28.74
27	.770 0182	28.69	.780 3464	28.69	.790 6788	28.71	.801 0199	28.74
28	.770 1903	28.69	.780 5185	28.69	.790 8510	28.71	.801 1924	28.74
29	.770 3625	28.69	.780 6907	28.69	.791 0233	28.71	.801 3648	28.74
30	1.770 5346	28.69	1.780 8629	28.69	1.791 1956	28.71	1.801 5373	28.74
31	.770 7067	28.69	.781 0350	28.69	.791 3678	28.71	.801 7107	28.74
32	.770 8788	28.69	.781 2072	28.69	.791 5401	28.71	.801 8822	28.74
33	.771 0510	28.69	.781 3793	28.69	.791 7124	28.71	.802 0547	28.75
34	.771 2231	28.69	.781 5515	28.69	.791 8847	28.71	.802 2271	28.75
35	1.771 3952	28.69	1.781 7237	28.69	1.792 0570	28.71	1.802 3996	28.75
36	.771 5673	28.69	.781 8959	28.69	.792 2293	28.71	.802 5721	28.75
37	.771 7395	28.69	.782 0680	28.70	.792 4016	28.72	.802 7446	28.75
38	.771 9116	28.69	.782 2402	28.70	.792 5738	28.72	.802 9171	28.75
39	.772 0837	28.69	.782 4124	28.70	.792 7461	28.72	.803 0896	28.75
40	1.772 2559	28.69	1.782 5845	28.70	1.792 9184	28.72	1.803 2621	28.75
41	.772 4280	28.69	.782 7567	28.70	.793 0907	28.72	.803 4346	28.75
42	.772 6001	28.69	.782 9289	28.70	.793 2630	28.72	.803 6071	28.75
43	.772 7722	28.69	.783 1011	28.70	.793 4354	28.72	.803 7796	28.75
44	.772 9444	28.69	.783 2732	28.70	.793 6077	28.72	.803 9521	28.75
45	1.773 1165	28.69	1.783 4454	28.70	1.793 7800	28.72	1.804 1246	28.75
46	.773 2886	28.69	.783 6176	28.70	.793 9523	28.72	.804 2971	28.75
47	.773 4607	28.69	.783 7898	28.70	.794 1246	28.72	.804 4697	28.75
48	.773 6329	28.69	.783 9620	28.70	.794 2969	28.72	.804 6422	28.76
49	.773 8050	28.69	.784 1342	28.70	.794 4693	28.72	.804 8147	28.76
50	1.773 9771	28.69	1.784 3064	28.70	1.794 6416	28.72	1.804 9873	28.76
51	.774 1493	28.69	.784 4786	28.70	.794 8139	28.72	.805 1598	28.76
52	.774 3214	28.69	.784 6508	28.70	.794 9862	28.72	.805 3324	28.76
53	.774 4935	28.69	.784 8230	28.70	.795 1586	28.72	.805 5049	28.76
54	.774 6657	28.69	.784 9952	28.70	.795 3309	28.72	.805 6775	28.76
55	1.774 8378	28.69	1.785 1674	28.70	1.795 5033	28.72	1.805 8500	28.76
56	.775 0099	28.69	.785 3396	28.70	.795 6756	28.72	.806 0226	28.76
57	.775 1821	28.69	.785 5118	28.70	.795 8480	28.72	.806 1952	28.76
58	.775 3542	28.69	.785 6840	28.70	.796 0203	28.73	.806 3677	28.76
59	.775 5263	28.69	.785 8562	28.70	.796 1927	28.73	.806 5403	28.76
60	1.775 6985	28.69	1.786 0284	28.70	1.796 3650	28.73	1.806 7129	28.76

TABLE VI.

For finding the True Anomaly or the Time from the Perihelion in a Parabolic Orbit.

v.	72°		73°		74°		75°	
	log M.	Diff. 1″.	log M.	Diff. 1″.	log M.	Diff. 1″.	log M.	Diff. 1″.
0′	1.806 7129	28.76	1.817 0765	28.81	1.827 4602	28.88	1.837 8686	28.95
1	.806 8855	28.76	.817 2494	28.81	.827 6335	28.88	.838 0423	28.95
2	.807 0581	28.77	.817 4222	28.82	.827 8068	28.88	.838 2160	28.95
3	.807 2307	28.77	.817 5951	28.82	.827 9800	28.88	.838 3898	28.95
4	.807 4033	28.77	.817 7680	28.82	.828 1533	28.88	.838 5635	28.96
5	1.807 5759	28.77	1.817 9410	28.82	1.828 3266	28.88	1.838 7372	28.96
6	.807 7485	28.77	.818 1139	28.82	.828 4999	28.88	.838 9110	28.96
7	.807 9211	28.77	.818 2868	28.82	.828 6732	28.88	.839 0847	28.96
8	.808 0937	28.77	.818 4597	28.82	.828 8465	28.88	.839 2585	28.96
9	.808 2663	28.77	.818 6326	28.82	.829 0198	28.89	.839 4323	28.96
10	1.808 4389	28.77	1.818 8056	28.82	1.829 1931	28.89	1.839 6060	28.96
11	.808 6116	28.77	.818 9785	28.82	.829 3665	28.89	.839 7798	28.97
12	.808 7842	28.77	.819 1515	28.83	.829 5398	28.89	.839 9536	28.97
13	.808 9568	28.77	.819 3244	28.83	.829 7131	28.89	.840 1274	28.97
14	.809 1295	28.77	.819 4974	28.83	.829 8865	28.89	.840 3012	28.97
15	1.809 3021	28.78	1.819 6704	28.83	1.830 0599	28.89	1.840 4751	28.97
16	.809 4748	28.78	.819 8433	28.83	.830 2332	28.89	.840 6489	28.97
17	.809 6474	28.78	.820 0163	28.83	.830 4066	28.90	.840 8227	28.97
18	.809 8201	28.78	.820 1893	28.83	.830 5800	28.90	.840 9966	28.97
19	.809 9928	28.78	.820 3623	28.83	.830 7533	28.90	.841 1704	28.98
20	1.810 1655	28.78	1.820 5353	28.83	1.830 9267	28.90	1.841 3443	28.98
21	.810 3381	28.78	.820 7083	28.83	.831 1001	28.90	.841 5182	28.98
22	.810 5108	28.78	.820 8813	28.84	.831 2735	28.90	.841 6921	28.98
23	.810 6835	28.78	.821 0543	28.84	.831 4470	28.90	.841 8659	28.98
24	.810 8562	28.78	.821 2273	28.84	.831 6204	28.90	.842 0398	28.98
25	1.811 0289	28.78	1.821 4003	28.84	1.831 7938	28.91	1.842 2138	28.98
26	.811 2016	28.78	.821 5734	28.84	.831 9672	28.91	.842 3877	28.99
27	.811 3743	28.78	.821 7464	28.84	.832 1407	28.91	.842 5616	28.99
28	.811 5470	28.79	.821 9194	28.84	.832 3141	28.91	.842 7355	28.99
29	.811 7197	28.79	.822 0925	28.84	.832 4876	28.91	.842 9095	28.99
30	1.811 8924	28.79	1.822 2656	28.84	1.832 6611	28.91	1.843 0834	28.99
31	.812 0652	28.79	.822 4386	28.84	.832 8345	28.91	.843 2574	28.99
32	.812 2379	28.79	.822 6117	28.85	.833 0080	28.92	.843 4313	29.00
33	.812 4106	28.79	.822 7848	28.85	.833 1815	28.92	.843 6053	29.00
34	.812 5834	28.79	.822 9578	28.85	.833 3550	28.92	.843 7793	29.00
35	1.812 7561	28.79	1.823 1309	28.85	1.833 5285	28.92	1.843 9533	29.00
36	.812 9289	28.79	.823 3040	28.85	.833 7020	28.92	.844 1273	29.00
37	.813 1016	28.79	.823 4771	28.85	.833 8755	28.92	.844 3013	29.00
38	.813 2744	28.79	.823 6502	28.85	.834 0491	28.92	.844 4753	29.00
39	.813 4472	28.79	.823 8233	28.85	.834 2226	28.92	.844 6494	29.01
40	1.813 6199	28.80	1.823 9965	28.85	1.834 3961	28.92	1.844 8234	29.01
41	.813 7927	28.80	.824 1696	28.85	.834 5697	28.93	.844 9974	29.01
42	.813 9655	28.80	.824 3427	28.86	.834 7432	28.93	.845 1715	29.01
43	.814 1383	28.80	.824 5159	28.86	.834 9168	28.93	.845 3456	29.01
44	.814 3111	28.80	.824 6890	28.86	.835 0904	28.93	.845 5196	29.01
45	1.814 4839	28.80	1.824 8622	28.86	1.835 2640	28.93	1.845 6937	29.01
46	.814 6567	28.80	.825 0353	28.86	.835 4376	28.93	.845 8678	29.02
47	.814 8295	28.80	.825 2085	28.86	.835 6112	28.93	.846 0419	29.02
48	.815 0023	28.80	.825 3816	28.86	.835 7848	28.93	.846 2160	29.02
49	.815 1751	28.80	.825 5548	28.86	.835 9584	28.94	.846 3901	29.02
50	1.815 3479	28.80	1.825 7280	28.86	1.836 1320	28.94	1.846 5643	29.02
51	.815 5208	28.81	.825 9012	28.87	.836 3056	28.94	.846 7384	29.02
52	.815 6936	28.81	.826 0744	28.87	.836 4792	28.94	.846 9125	29.03
53	.815 8664	28.81	.826 2476	28.87	.836 6529	28.94	.847 0867	29.03
54	.816 0393	28.81	.826 4208	28.87	.836 8265	28.94	.847 2609	29.03
55	1.816 2121	28.81	1.826 5940	28.87	1.837 0002	28.94	1.847 4350	29.03
56	.816 3850	28.81	.826 7673	28.87	.837 1739	28.95	.847 6092	29.03
57	.816 5578	28.81	.826 9405	28.87	.837 3475	28.95	.847 7834	29.03
58	.816 7307	28.81	.827 1137	28.87	.837 5212	28.95	.847 9576	29.03
59	.816 9036	28.81	.827 2870	28.87	.837 6949	28.95	.848 1318	29.04
60	1.817 0765	28.81	1.827 4602	28.88	1.837 8686	28.95	1.848 3060	29.04

TABLE VI.

For finding the True Anomaly or the Time from the Perihelion in a Parabolic Orbit.

v.	76° log M.	76° Diff. 1″.	77° log M.	77° Diff. 1″.	78° log M.	78° Diff. 1″.	79° log M.	79° Diff. 1″.
0′	1.848 3060	29.04	1.858 7769	29.14	1.869 2857	29.25	1.879 8369	29.37
1	.848 4803	29.04	.858 9517	29.14	.869 4612	29.25	.880 0131	29.37
2	.848 6545	29.04	.859 1266	29.14	.869 6367	29.25	.880 1894	29.38
3	.848 8287	29.04	.859 3014	29.14	.869 8122	29.25	.880 3656	29.38
4	.849 0030	29.04	.859 4763	29.15	.869 9878	29.26	.880 5419	29.38
5	1.849 1773	29.04	1.859 6512	29.15	1.870 1633	29.26	1.880 7182	29.38
6	.849 3515	29.05	.859 8260	29.15	.870 3389	29.26	.880 8945	29.38
7	.849 5258	29.05	.860 0009	29.15	.870 5144	29.26	.881 0708	29.39
8	.849 7001	29.05	.860 1758	29.15	.870 6900	29.26	.881 2471	29.39
9	.849 8744	29.05	.860 3507	29.15	.870 8656	29.26	.881 4235	29.39
10	1.850 0487	29.05	1.860 5256	29.15	1.871 0412	29.27	1.881 5998	29.39
11	.850 2231	29.05	.860 7006	29.16	.871 2168	29.27	.881 7762	29.39
12	.850 3974	29.06	.860 8755	29.16	.871 3924	29.27	.881 9526	29.40
13	.850 5717	29.06	.861 0505	29.16	.871 5681	29.27	.882 1290	29.40
14	.850 7461	29.06	.861 2254	29.16	.871 7437	29.28	.882 3054	29.40
15	1.850 9204	29.06	1.861 4004	29.16	1.871 9194	29.28	1.882 4818	29.40
16	.851 0948	29.06	.861 5754	29.16	.872 0950	29.28	.882 6582	29.41
17	.851 2692	29.06	.861 7504	29.17	.872 2707	29.28	.882 8347	29.41
18	.851 4436	29.07	.861 9254	29.17	.872 4464	29.28	.883 0112	29.41
19	.851 6180	29.07	.862 1004	29.17	.872 6221	29.29	.883 1876	29.41
20	1.851 7924	29.07	1.862 2754	29.17	1.872 7979	29.29	1.883 3641	29.42
21	.851 9668	29.07	.862 4505	29.17	.872 9736	29.29	.883 5406	29.42
22	.852 1412	29.07	.862 6255	29.18	.873 1493	29.29	.883 7171	29.42
23	.852 3157	29.07	.862 8006	29.18	.873 3251	29.29	.883 8937	29.42
24	.852 4901	29.07	.862 9756	29.18	.873 5008	29.30	.884 0702	29.42
25	1.852 6646	29.08	1.863 1507	29.18	1.873 6766	29.30	1.884 2468	29.43
26	.852 8391	29.08	.863 3258	29.18	.873 8524	29.30	.884 4233	29.43
27	.853 0135	29.08	.863 5009	29.18	.874 0282	29.30	.884 5999	29.43
28	.853 1880	29.08	.863 6760	29.19	.874 2041	29.30	.884 7765	29.43
29	.853 3625	29.08	.863 8512	29.19	.874 3799	29.31	.884 9531	29.44
30	1.853 5370	29.09	1.864 0263	29.19	1.874 5557	29.31	1.885 1297	29.44
31	.853 7115	29.09	.864 2015	29.19	.874 7316	29.31	.885 3064	29.44
32	.853 8861	29.09	.864 3766	29.19	.874 9074	29.31	.885 4830	29.44
33	.854 0606	29.09	.864 5518	29.20	.875 0833	29.31	.885 6597	29.45
34	.854 2351	29.09	.864 7270	29.20	.875 2592	29.32	.885 8364	29.45
35	1.854 4097	29.09	1.864 9022	29.20	1.875 4351	29.32	1.886 0131	29.45
36	.854 5843	29.10	.865 0774	29.20	.875 6111	29.32	.886 1898	29.45
37	.854 7588	29.10	.865 2526	29.20	.875 7870	29.32	.886 3665	29.45
38	.854 9334	29.10	.865 4278	29.20	.875 9629	29.32	.886 5432	29.46
39	.855 1080	29.10	.865 6030	29.21	.876 1389	29.33	.886 7200	29.46
40	1.855 2826	29.10	1.865 7783	29.21	1.876 3148	29.33	1.886 8967	29.46
41	.855 4572	29.10	.865 9536	29.21	.876 4908	29.33	.887 0735	29.46
42	.855 6319	29.11	.866 1288	29.21	.876 6668	29.33	.887 2503	29.47
43	.855 8065	29.11	.866 3041	29.21	.876 8428	29.33	.887 4271	29.47
44	.855 9811	29.11	.866 4794	29.22	.877 0188	29.34	.887 6039	29.47
45	1.856 1558	29.11	1.866 6547	29.22	1.877 1949	29.34	1.887 7807	29.47
46	.856 3305	29.11	.866 8301	29.22	.877 3709	29.34	.887 9576	29.48
47	.856 5052	29.11	.867 0054	29.22	.877 5470	29.34	.888 1344	29.48
48	.856 6799	29.12	.867 1807	29.22	.877 7230	29.34	.888 3113	29.48
49	.856 8546	29.12	.867 3561	29.23	.877 8991	29.35	.888 4882	29.48
50	1.857 0293	29.12	1.867 5314	29.23	1.878 0752	29.35	1.888 6651	29.48
51	.857 2040	29.12	.867 7068	29.23	.878 2513	29.35	.888 8420	29.49
52	.857 3787	29.12	.867 8822	29.23	.878 4275	29.35	.889 0189	29.49
53	.857 5534	29.12	.868 0576	29.23	.878 6036	29.35	.889 1959	29.49
54	.857 7282	29.13	.868 2330	29.24	.878 7797	29.36	.889 3728	29.49
55	1.857 9030	29.13	1.868 4084	29.24	1.878 9559	29.36	1.889 5498	29.49
56	.858 0777	29.13	.868 5839	29.24	.879 1321	29.36	.889 7268	29.50
57	.858 2525	29.13	.868 7593	29.24	.879 3082	29.36	.889 8038	29.50
58	.858 4273	29.13	.868 9348	29.24	.879 4844	29.36	.890 0808	29.50
59	.858 6021	29.13	.869 1102	29.25	.879 6606	29.37	.890 2578	29.51
60	1.858 7769	29.14	1.869 2857	29.25	1.879 8369	29.37	1.890 4349	29.51

TABLE VI.

For finding the True Anomaly or the Time from the Perihelion in a Parabolic Orbit.

v.	80° log M.	80° Diff. 1″.	81° log M.	81° Diff. 1″.	82° log M.	82° Diff. 1″.	83° log M.	83° Diff. 1″.
0′	1.890 4349	29.51	1.901 0841	29.66	1.911 7893	29.82	1.922 5548	29.99
1	.890 6119	29.51	.901 2621	29.66	.911 9682	29.82	.922 7347	29.99
2	.890 7890	29.51	.901 4400	29.66	.912 1471	29.82	.922 9147	30.00
3	.890 9661	29.51	.901 6180	29.66	.912 3261	29.83	.923 0947	30.00
4	.891 1432	29.52	.901 7960	29.67	.912 5050	29.83	.923 2747	30.00
5	1.891 3203	29.52	1.901 9740	29.67	1.912 6840	29.83	1.923 4548	30.01
6	.891 4974	29.52	.902 1521	29.67	.912 8630	29.84	.923 6348	30.01
7	.891 6745	29.52	.902 3301	29.67	.913 0420	29.84	.923 8149	30.01
8	.891 8517	29.53	.902 5082	29.68	.913 2211	29.84	.923 9950	30.02
9	.892 0289	29.53	.902 6862	29.68	.913 4001	29.84	.924 1751	30.02
10	1.892 2061	29.53	1.902 8643	29.68	1.913 5792	29.85	1.924 3552	30.02
11	.892 3833	29.53	.903 0424	29.69	.913 7583	29.85	.924 5354	30.03
12	.892 5605	29.54	.903 2105	29.69	.913 9374	29.85	.924 7155	30.03
13	.892 7377	29.54	.903 3987	29.69	.914 1165	29.85	.924 8957	30.03
14	.892 9149	29.54	.903 5768	29.69	.914 2956	29.86	.925 0759	30.03
15	1.893 0922	29.54	1.903 7550	29.70	1.914 4748	29.86	1.925 2561	30.04
16	.893 2695	29.55	.903 9332	29.70	.914 6540	29.86	.925 4364	30.04
17	.893 4467	29.55	.904 1114	29.70	.914 8331	29.87	.925 6166	30.04
18	.893 6240	29.55	.904 2896	29.70	.915 0124	29.87	.925 7969	30.05
19	.893 8013	29.55	.904 4678	29.71	.915 1916	29.87	.925 9772	30.05
20	1.893 9787	29.56	1.904 6461	29.71	1.915 3708	29.87	1.926 1575	30.05
21	.894 1560	29.56	.904 8243	29.71	.915 5501	29.88	.926 3378	30.06
22	.894 3334	29.56	.905 0026	29.71	.915 7294	29.88	.926 5182	30.06
23	.894 5108	29.56	.905 1809	29.72	.915 9087	29.88	.926 6986	30.06
24	.894 6882	29.57	.905 3592	29.72	.916 0880	29.89	.926 8789	30.07
25	1.894 8656	29.57	1.905 5376	29.72	1.916 2673	29.89	1.927 0593	30.07
26	.895 0430	29.57	.905 7159	29.73	.916 4466	29.89	.927 2398	30.07
27	.895 2204	29.57	.905 8943	29.73	.916 6260	29.90	.927 4202	30.08
28	.895 3979	29.58	.906 0726	29.73	.916 8054	29.90	.927 6007	30.08
29	.895 5753	29.58	.906 2510	29.73	.916 9848	29.90	.927 7811	30.08
30	1.895 7528	29.58	1.906 4294	29.74	1.917 1642	29.90	1.927 9616	30.08
31	.895 9303	29.58	.906 6079	29.74	.917 3436	29.91	.928 1422	30.09
32	.896 1078	29.59	.906 7863	29.74	.917 5231	29.91	.928 3227	30.09
33	.896 2854	29.59	.906 9648	29.74	.917 7025	29.91	.928 5032	30.09
34	.896 4628	29.59	.907 1432	29.75	.917 8820	29.92	.928 6838	30.10
35	1.896 6404	29.59	1.907 3217	29.75	1.918 0615	29.92	1.928 8644	30.10
36	.896 8180	29.60	.907 5002	29.75	.918 2410	29.92	.929 0450	30.10
37	.896 9955	29.60	.907 6787	29.75	.918 4206	29.92	.929 2256	30.11
38	.897 1732	29.60	.907 8573	29.76	.918 6001	29.93	.929 4063	30.11
39	.897 3508	29.60	.908 0358	29.76	.918 7797	29.93	.929 5869	30.11
40	1.897 5284	29.61	1.908 2144	29.76	1.918 9593	29.93	1.929 7676	30.12
41	.897 7060	29.61	.908 3930	29.77	.919 1389	29.94	.929 9483	30.12
42	.897 8837	29.61	.908 5716	29.77	.919 3185	29.94	.930 1291	30.12
43	.898 0614	29.61	.908 7502	29.77	.919 4982	29.94	.930 3098	30.13
44	.898 2390	29.62	.908 9288	29.77	.919 6778	29.94	.930 4906	30.13
45	1.898 4168	29.62	1.909 1075	29.78	1.919 8575	29.95	1.930 6713	30.13
46	.898 5945	29.62	.909 2862	29.78	.920 0372	29.95	.930 8521	30.13
47	.898 7722	29.62	.909 4648	29.78	.920 2169	29.95	.931 0330	30.14
48	.898 9500	29.63	.909 6436	29.78	.920 3966	29.96	.931 2138	30.14
49	.899 1277	29.63	.909 8223	29.79	.920 5764	29.96	.931 3946	30.14
50	1.899 3055	29.63	1.910 0010	29.79	1.920 7561	29.96	1.931 5755	30.15
51	.899 4833	29.63	.910 1798	29.79	.920 9359	29.97	.931 7564	30.15
52	.899 6611	29.64	.910 3585	29.80	.921 1157	29.97	.931 9373	30.15
53	.899 8389	29.64	.910 5373	29.80	.921 2956	29.97	.932 1183	30.16
54	.900 0168	29.64	.910 7161	29.80	.921 4754	29.98	.932 2992	30.16
55	1.900 1946	29.64	1.910 8949	29.80	1.921 6552	29.98	1.932 4802	30.16
56	.900 3725	29.65	.911 0738	29.81	.921 8351	29.98	.932 6612	30.17
57	.900 5504	29.65	.911 2526	29.81	.922 0150	29.98	.932 8422	30.17
58	.900 7283	29.65	.911 4315	29.81	.922 1949	29.99	.933 0232	30.17
59	.900 9062	29.66	.911 6104	29.82	.922 3748	29.99	.933 2043	30.18
60	1.901 0841	29.66	1.911 7893	29.82	1.922 5548	29.99	1.933 3853	30.18

TABLE VI.

For finding the True Anomaly or the Time from the Perihelion in a Parabolic Orbit.

v.	84° log M.	84° Diff. 1″.	85° log M.	85° Diff. 1″.	86° log M.	86° Diff. 1″.	87° log M.	87° Diff. 1″.
0′	1.933 3853	30.18	1.944 2856	30.38	1.955 2602	30.59	1.966 3140	30.82
1	.933 5664	30.18	.944 4678	30.38	.955 4438	30.60	.966 4990	30.82
2	.933 7475	30.19	.944 6502	30.39	.955 6274	30.60	.966 6839	30.83
3	.933 9287	30.19	.944 8325	30.39	.955 8110	30.60	.966 8689	30.83
4	.934 1098	30.19	.945 0148	30.39	.955 9946	30.61	.967 0539	30.84
5	1.934 2910	30.20	1.945 1972	30.40	1.956 1783	30.61	1.967 2389	30.84
6	.934 4722	30.20	.945 3796	30.40	.956 3619	30.61	.967 4240	30.84
7	.934 6533	30.20	.945 5620	30.40	.956 5456	30.62	.967 6090	30.85
8	.934 8346	30.21	.945 7444	30.41	.956 7294	30.62	.967 7941	30.85
9	.935 0158	30.21	.945 9269	30.41	.956 9131	30.63	.967 9792	30.85
10	1.935 1971	30.21	1.946 1094	30.41	1.957 0969	30.63	1.968 1644	30.86
11	.935 3784	30.22	.946 2919	30.42	.957 2807	30.63	.968 3496	30.86
12	.935 5597	30.22	.946 4744	30.42	.957 4645	30.64	.968 5347	30.87
13	.935 7410	30.22	.946 6569	30.42	.957 6483	30.64	.968 7200	30.87
14	.935 9223	30.22	.946 8395	30.43	.957 8322	30.64	.968 9052	30.87
15	1.936 1037	30.23	1.947 0221	30.43	1.958 0160	30.65	1.969 0905	30.88
16	.936 2851	30.23	.947 2047	30.44	.958 1999	30.65	.969 2757	30.88
17	.936 4665	30.23	.947 3873	30.44	.958 3839	30.66	.969 4610	30.89
18	.936 6479	30.24	.947 5699	30.44	.958 5678	30.66	.969 6464	30.89
19	.936 8293	30.24	.947 7526	30.45	.958 7518	30.66	.969 8317	30.89
20	1.937 0108	30.24	1.947 9353	30.45	1.958 9358	30.67	1.970 0171	30.90
21	.937 1922	30.25	.948 1180	30.45	.959 1198	30.67	.970 2025	30.90
22	.937 3737	30.25	.948 3007	30.46	.959 3038	30.67	.970 3879	30.91
23	.937 5553	30.25	.948 4834	30.46	.959 4879	30.68	.970 5734	30.91
24	.937 7368	30.26	.948 6662	30.46	.959 6720	30.68	.970 7589	30.91
25	1.937 9184	30.26	1.948 8490	30.47	1.959 8561	30.69	1.970 9443	30.92
26	.938 0999	30.26	.949 0318	30.47	.960 0402	30.69	.971 1299	30.92
27	.938 2815	30.27	.949 2146	30.47	.960 2243	30.69	.971 3154	30.93
28	.938 4632	30.27	.949 3975	30.48	.960 4085	30.70	.971 5010	30.93
29	.938 6448	30.27	.949 5804	30.48	.960 5927	30.70	.971 6866	30.93
30	1.938 8264	30.28	1.949 7633	30.48	1.960 7769	30.70	1.971 8722	30.94
31	.939 0081	30.28	.949 9462	30.49	.960 9612	30.71	.972 0578	30.94
32	.939 1898	30.28	.950 1291	30.49	.961 1454	30.71	.972 2435	30.95
33	.939 3715	30.29	.950 3121	30.50	.961 3297	30.71	.972 4292	30.95
34	.939 5533	30.29	.950 4951	30.50	.961 5140	30.72	.972 6149	30.95
35	1.939 7350	30.29	1.950 6781	30.50	1.961 6983	30.72	1.972 8006	30.96
36	.939 9168	30.30	.950 8611	30.51	.961 8827	30.73	.972 9864	30.96
37	.940 0986	30.30	.951 0441	30.51	.962 0671	30.73	.973 1722	30.97
38	.940 2804	30.30	.951 2272	30.51	.962 2515	30.73	.973 3580	30.97
39	.940 4623	30.31	.951 4103	30.52	.962 4359	30.74	.973 5438	30.97
40	1.940 6441	30.31	1.951 5934	30.52	1.962 6203	30.74	1.973 7297	30.98
41	.940 8260	30.31	.951 7766	30.52	.962 8048	30.75	.973 9156	30.98
42	.941 0079	30.32	.951 9597	30.53	.962 9893	30.75	.974 1015	30.99
43	.941 1898	30.32	.952 1429	30.53	.963 1738	30.75	.974 2874	30.99
44	.941 3717	30.32	.952 3261	30.53	.963 3583	30.76	.974 4734	30.99
45	1.941 5537	30.33	1.952 5093	30.54	1.963 5429	30.76	1.974 6593	31.00
46	.941 7357	30.33	.952 6925	30.54	.963 7275	30.77	.974 8454	31.00
47	.941 9177	30.34	.952 8758	30.55	.963 9121	30.77	.975 0314	31.01
48	.942 0997	30.34	.953 0591	30.55	.964 0967	30.77	.975 2174	31.01
49	.942 2817	30.34	.953 2424	30.55	.964 2814	30.78	.975 4035	31.01
50	1.942 4638	30.35	1.953 4257	30.56	1.964 4660	30.78	1.975 5896	31.02
51	.942 6459	30.35	.953 6091	30.56	.964 6507	30.78	.975 7757	31.02
52	.942 8280	30.35	.953 7924	30.56	.964 8354	30.79	.975 9619	31.03
53	.943 0101	30.36	.953 9758	30.57	.965 0202	30.79	.976 1481	31.03
54	.943 1923	30.36	.954 1592	30.57	.965 2050	30.80	.976 3343	31.04
55	1.943 3744	30.36	1.954 3427	30.57	1.965 3897	30.80	1.976 5205	31.04
56	.943 5566	30.37	.954 5262	30.58	.965 5746	30.80	.976 7067	31.04
57	.943 7388	30.37	.954 7096	30.58	.965 7594	30.81	.976 8930	31.05
58	.943 9211	30.37	.954 8931	30.59	.965 9442	30.81	.977 0793	31.05
59	.944 1033	30.38	.955 0766	30.59	.966 1291	30.81	.977 2656	31.06
60	1.944 2856	30.38	1.955 2602	30.59	1.966 3140	30.82	1.977 4520	31.06

TABLE VI.

For finding the True Anomaly or the Time from the Perihelion in a Parabolic Orbit.

v.	88°		89°		90°		91°	
	log M.	Diff. 1″.	log M.	Diff. 1″.	log M.	Diff. 1″.	log M.	Diff. 1″.
0′	1.977 4520	31.06	1.988 6789	31.31	2.000 0000	31.58	2.011 4203	31.87
1	.977 6383	31.06	.988 8668	31.32	.000 1895	31.59	.011 6115	31.87
2	.977 8247	31.07	.989 0548	31.32	.000 3790	31.59	.011 8027	31.88
3	.978 0112	31.07	.989 2427	31.33	.000 5686	31.60	.011 9940	31.88
4	.978 1976	31.08	.989 4307	31.33	.000 7582	31.60	.012 1853	31.89
5	1.978 3841	31.08	1.989 6187	31.34	2.000 9478	31.60	2.012 3766	31.89
6	.978 5706	31.08	.989 8067	31.34	.001 1375	31.61	.012 5680	31.89
7	.978 7571	31.09	.989 9948	31.34	.001 3272	31.61	.012 7594	31.90
8	.978 9436	31.09	.990 1829	31.35	.001 5169	31.62	.012 9508	31.90
9	.979 1302	31.10	.990 3710	31.35	.001 7066	31.62	.013 1422	31.91
10	1.979 3168	31.10	1.990 5591	31.36	2.001 8963	31.63	2.013 3337	31.91
11	.979 5034	31.11	.990 7473	31.36	.002 0861	31.63	.013 5252	31.92
12	.979 6901	31.11	.990 9355	31.37	.002 2759	31.64	.013 7167	31.92
13	.979 8768	31.11	.991 1237	31.37	.002 4658	31.64	.013 9083	31.93
14	.980 0635	31.12	.991 3119	31.38	.002 6557	31.65	.014 0999	31.93
15	1.980 2502	31.12	1.991 5002	31.38	2.002 8456	31.65	2.014 2915	31.94
16	.980 4369	31.13	.991 6885	31.38	.003 0355	31.66	.014 4831	31.94
17	.980 6237	31.13	.991 8768	31.39	.003 2254	31.66	.014 6748	31.95
18	.980 8105	31.13	.992 0651	31.39	.003 4154	31.67	.014 8665	31.95
19	.980 9973	31.14	.992 2535	31.40	.003 6054	31.67	.015 0582	31.96
20	1.981 1842	31.14	1.992 4419	31.40	2.003 7955	31.68	2.015 2500	31.96
21	.981 3710	31.15	.992 6304	31.41	.003 9855	31.68	.015 4418	31.97
22	.981 5579	31.15	.992 8188	31.41	.004 1756	31.68	.015 6336	31.97
23	.981 7449	31.16	.993 0073	31.42	.004 3658	31.69	.015 8255	31.98
24	.981 9318	31.16	.993 1958	31.42	.004 5559	31.69	.016 0174	31.98
25	1.982 1188	31.16	1.993 3843	31.42	2.004 7461	31.70	2.016 2093	31.99
26	.982 3058	31.17	.993 5729	31.43	.004 9363	31.70	.016 4012	31.99
27	.982 4928	31.17	.993 7615	31.43	.005 1265	31.71	.016 5932	32.00
28	.982 6798	31.18	.993 9501	31.44	.005 3168	31.71	.016 7852	32.00
29	.982 8669	31.18	.994 1387	31.44	.005 5071	31.72	.016 9772	32.01
30	1.983 0540	31.18	1.994 3274	31.45	2.005 6974	31.72	2.017 1693	32.01
31	.983 2411	31.19	.994 5161	31.45	.005 8878	31.73	.017 3614	32.02
32	.983 4283	31.19	.994 7048	31.46	.006 0781	31.73	.017 5535	32.02
33	.983 6155	31.20	.994 8936	31.46	.006 2685	31.74	.017 7456	32.03
34	.983 8027	31.20	.995 0823	31.46	.006 4590	31.74	.017 9378	32.03
35	1.983 9899	31.21	1.995 2711	31.47	2.006 6494	31.75	2.018 1300	32.04
36	.984 1772	31.21	.995 4600	31.47	.006 8399	31.75	.018 3223	32.04
37	.984 3644	31.22	.995 6488	31.48	.007 0304	31.76	.018 5145	32.05
38	.984 5517	31.22	.995 8377	31.48	.007 2210	31.76	.018 7068	32.05
39	.984 7391	31.22	.996 0266	31.49	.007 4116	31.77	.018 8992	32.06
40	1.984 9264	31.23	1.996 2155	31.49	2.007 6022	31.77	2.019 0915	32.06
41	.985 1138	31.23	.996 4045	31.50	.007 7928	31.77	.019 2839	32.07
42	.985 3012	31.24	.996 5935	31.50	.007 9835	31.78	.019 4763	32.07
43	.985 4886	31.24	.996 7825	31.51	.008 1742	31.78	.019 6688	32.08
44	.985 6761	31.24	.996 9716	31.51	.008 3649	31.79	.019 8613	32.08
45	1.985 8636	31.25	1.997 1606	31.51	2.008 5556	31.79	2.020 0538	32.09
46	.986 0511	31.25	.997 3497	31.52	.008 7464	31.80	.020 2463	32.09
47	.986 2386	31.26	.997 5389	31.52	.008 9372	31.80	.020 4389	32.10
48	.986 4262	31.26	.997 7280	31.53	.009 1280	31.81	.020 6315	32.10
49	.986 6138	31.27	.997 9172	31.53	.009 3189	31.81	.020 8241	32.11
50	1.986 8014	31.27	1.998 1064	31.54	2.009 5098	31.82	2.021 0168	32.11
51	.986 9890	31.28	.998 2956	31.54	.009 7007	31.82	.021 2095	32.12
52	.987 1767	31.28	.998 4849	31.55	.009 8917	31.83	.021 4022	32.12
53	.987 3644	31.28	.998 6742	31.55	.010 0826	31.83	.021 5949	32.13
54	.987 5521	31.29	.998 8635	31.56	.010 2736	31.84	.021 7877	32.13
55	1.987 7398	31.29	1.999 0529	31.56	2.010 4647	31.84	2.021 9805	32.14
56	.987 9276	31.30	.999 2422	31.56	.010 6557	31.85	.022 1734	32.14
57	.988 1154	31.30	.999 4316	31.57	.010 8468	31.85	.022 3662	32.15
58	.988 3032	31.31	.999 6211	31.57	.011 0380	31.86	.022 5591	32.15
59	.988 4911	31.31	.999 8105	31.58	.011 2291	31.86	.022 7521	32.16
60	1.988 6789	31.31	2.000 0000	31.58	2.011 4203	31.87	2.022 9450	32.16

TABLE VI.

For finding the True Anomaly or the Time from the Perihelion in a Parabolic Orbit.

v.	92°		93°		94°		95°	
	log M.	Diff. 1″.	log M.	Diff. 1″.	log M.	Diff. 1″.	log M.	Diff. 1″.
0′	2.022 9450	32.16	2.034 5797	32.48	2.046 3296	32.80	2.058 2005	33.15
1	.023 1380	32.17	.034 7745	32.48	.046 5264	32.81	.058 3994	33.15
2	.023 3311	32.17	.034 9694	32.49	.046 7233	32.82	.058 5983	33.16
3	.023 5241	32.18	.035 1644	32.49	.046 9202	32.82	.058 7973	33.16
4	.023 7172	32.18	.035 3593	32.50	.047 1172	32.83	.058 9963	33.17
5	2.023 9103	32.19	2.035 5543	32.50	2.047 3141	32.83	2.059 1953	33.18
6	.024 1035	32.19	.035 7494	32.51	.047 5111	32.84	.059 3944	33.18
7	.024 2967	32.20	.035 9444	32.51	.047 7082	32.84	.059 5935	33.19
8	.024 4899	32.20	.036 1395	32.52	.047 9053	32.85	.059 7927	33.19
9	.024 6831	32.21	.036 3347	32.52	.048 1024	32.85	.059 9919	33.20
10	2.024 8764	32.21	2.036 5298	32.53	2.048 2995	32.86	2.060 1911	33.21
11	.025 0697	32.22	.036 7250	32.53	.048 4967	32.87	.060 3904	33.21
12	.025 2630	32.22	.036 9202	32.54	.048 6939	32.87	.060 5897	33.22
13	.025 4564	32.23	.037 1155	32.54	.048 8912	32.88	.060 7890	33.22
14	.025 6498	32.23	.037 3108	32.55	.049 0884	32.88	.060 9884	33.23
15	2.025 8432	32.24	2.037 5061	32.55	2.049 2857	32.89	2.061 1878	33.24
16	.026 0367	32.24	.037 7015	32.56	.049 4831	32.89	.061 3872	33.24
17	.026 2301	32.25	.037 8969	32.57	.049 6805	32.90	.061 5867	33.25
18	.026 4236	32.26	.038 0923	32.57	.049 8879	32.90	.061 7862	33.25
19	.026 6172	32.26	.038 2877	32.58	.050 0753	32.91	.061 9857	33.26
20	2.026 8108	32.27	2.038 4832	32.58	2.050 2728	32.92	2.062 1853	33.27
21	.027 0044	32.27	.038 6787	32.59	.050 4703	32.92	.062 3849	33.27
22	.027 1980	32.28	.038 8743	32.59	.050 6679	32.93	.062 5846	33.28
23	.027 3917	32.28	.039 0699	32.60	.050 8655	32.93	.062 7842	33.28
24	.027 5854	32.29	.039 2655	32.61	.051 0631	32.94	.062 9840	33.29
25	2.027 7791	32.29	2.039 4611	32.61	2.051 2608	32.95	2.063 1837	33.30
26	.027 9729	32.30	.039 6568	32.62	.051 4585	32.95	.063 3835	33.30
27	.028 1667	32.30	.039 8525	32.62	.051 6562	32.96	.063 5833	33.31
28	.028 3605	32.31	.040 0482	32.63	.051 8539	32.96	.063 7832	33.31
29	.028 5544	32.31	.040 2440	32.63	.052 0517	32.97	.063 9831	33.32
30	2.028 7483	32.32	2.040 4399	32.64	2.052 2496	32.97	2.064 1831	33.33
31	.028 9422	32.32	.040 6357	32.64	.052 4474	32.98	.064 3830	33.33
32	.029 1361	32.33	.040 8316	32.65	.052 6453	32.98	.064 5830	33.34
33	.029 3301	32.33	.041 0275	32.65	.052 8432	32.99	.064 7831	33.34
34	.029 5241	32.34	.041 2234	32.66	.053 0412	33.00	.064 9832	33.35
35	2.029 7182	32.34	2.041 4194	32.67	2.053 2392	33.00	2.065 1833	33.36
36	.029 9123	32.35	.041 6154	32.67	.053 4372	33.01	.065 3834	33.36
37	.030 1064	32.35	.041 8114	32.68	.053 6353	33.01	.065 5836	33.37
38	.030 3005	32.36	.042 0075	32.68	.053 8334	33.02	.065 7839	33.37
39	.030 4947	32.36	.042 2036	32.69	.054 0315	33.03	.065 9841	33.38
40	2.030 6889	32.37	2.042 3998	32.69	2.054 2297	33.03	2.066 1844	33.39
41	.030 8831	32.37	.042 5960	32.70	.054 4279	33.04	.066 3847	33.39
42	.031 0774	32.38	.042 7922	32.70	.054 6262	33.04	.066 5851	33.40
43	.031 2717	32.39	.042 9884	32.71	.054 8244	33.05	.066 7855	33.40
44	.031 4660	32.39	.043 1847	32.71	.055 0227	33.05	.066 9860	33.41
45	2.031 6604	32.40	2.043 3810	32.72	2.055 2211	33.06	2.067 1865	33.42
46	.031 8548	32.40	.043 5773	32.73	.055 4195	33.07	.067 3870	33.42
47	.032 0492	32.41	.043 7737	32.73	.055 6179	33.07	.067 5875	33.43
48	.032 2437	32.41	.043 9701	32.74	.055 8163	33.08	.067 7881	33.43
49	.032 4382	32.42	.044 1665	32.74	.056 0148	33.08	.067 9887	33.44
50	2.032 6327	32.42	2.044 3630	32.75	2.056 2133	33.09	2.068 1894	33.45
51	.032 8272	32.43	.044 5595	32.75	.056 4119	33.10	.068 3901	33.45
52	.033 0218	32.43	.044 7561	32.76	.056 6105	33.10	.068 5908	33.46
53	.033 2164	32.44	.044 9526	32.76	.056 8091	33.11	.068 7916	33.47
54	.033 4111	32.44	.045 1492	32.77	.057 0078	33.11	.068 9924	33.47
55	2.033 6058	32.45	2.045 3459	32.78	2.057 2065	33.12	2.069 1933	33.48
56	.033 8005	32.45	.045 5426	32.78	.057 4052	33.12	.069 3942	33.48
57	.033 9952	32.46	.045 7393	32.79	.057 6040	33.13	.069 5951	33.49
58	.034 1900	32.47	.045 9360	32.79	.057 8028	33.14	.069 7960	33.50
59	.034 3848	32.47	.046 1328	32.80	.058 0016	33.14	.069 9970	33.50
60	2.034 5797	32.48	2.046 3296	32.80	2.058 2005	33.15	2.070 1980	33.51

TABLE VI.

For finding the True Anomaly or the Time from the Perihelion in a Parabolic Orbit.

v.	96°		97°		98°		99°	
	log M.	Diff. 1″.	log M.	Diff. 1″.	log M.	Diff. 1″.	log M.	Diff. 1″.
0′	2.070 1980	33.51	2.082 3282	33.88	2.094 5971	34.28	2.107 0109	34.69
1	.070 3991	33.51	.082 5316	33.89	.094 8028	34.29	.107 2190	34.70
2	.070 6002	33.52	.082 7349	33.90	.095 0085	34.29	.107 4272	34.70
3	.070 8014	33.53	.082 9383	33.90	.095 2143	34.30	.107 6355	34.71
4	.071 0025	33.53	.083 1418	33.91	.095 4201	34.31	.107 8437	34.72
5	2.071 2037	33.54	2.083 3453	33.92	2.095 6260	34.31	2.108 0521	34.72
6	.071 4050	33.54	.083 5488	33.92	.095 8318	34.32	.108 2604	34.73
7	.071 6063	33.55	.083 7523	33.93	.096 0378	34.33	.108 4689	34.74
8	.071 8076	33.56	.083 9559	33.94	.096 2438	34.33	.108 6773	34.75
9	.072 0090	33.56	.084 1596	33.94	.096 4498	34.34	.108 8858	34.75
10	2.072 2104	33.57	2.084 3633	33.95	2.096 6558	34.35	2.109 0944	34.76
11	.072 4118	33.58	.084 5670	33.96	.096 8619	34.35	.109 3029	34.77
12	.072 6133	33.58	.084 7707	33.96	.097 0681	34.36	.109 5116	34.77
13	.072 8148	33.59	.084 9745	33.97	.097 2742	34.37	.109 7202	34.78
14	.073 0163	33.59	.085 1783	33.98	.097 4804	34.37	.109 9289	34.79
15	2.073 2179	33.60	2.085 3822	33.98	2.097 6867	34.38	2.110 1377	34.80
16	.073 4195	33.61	.085 5861	33.99	.097 8930	34.39	.110 3465	34.80
17	.073 6212	33.61	.085 7901	33.99	.098 0993	34.39	.110 5553	34.81
18	.073 8229	33.62	.085 9941	34.00	.098 3057	34.40	.110 7642	34.82
19	.074 0246	33.63	.086 1981	34.01	.098 5121	34.41	.110 9731	34.82
20	2.074 2264	33.63	2.086 4021	34.01	2.098 7186	34.41	2.111 1821	34.83
21	.074 4282	33.64	.086 6062	34.02	.098 9251	34.42	.111 3911	34.84
22	.074 6301	33.64	.086 8104	34.03	.099 1316	34.43	.111 6001	34.85
23	.074 8320	33.65	.087 0146	34.03	.099 3382	34.43	.111 8092	34.85
24	.075 0339	33.66	.087 2188	34.04	.099 5449	34.44	.112 0184	34.86
25	2.075 2358	33.66	2.087 4231	34.05	2.099 7515	34.45	2.112 2275	34.87
26	.075 4378	33.67	.087 6274	34.05	.099 9582	34.45	.112 4368	34.87
27	.075 6399	33.67	.087 8317	34.06	.100 1650	34.46	.112 6460	34.88
28	.075 8419	33.68	.088 0361	34.07	.100 3718	34.47	.112 8553	34.89
29	.076 0440	33.69	.088 2405	34.07	.100 5786	34.48	.113 0647	34.90
30	2.076 2462	33.69	2.088 4449	34.08	2.100 7855	34.48	2.113 2741	34.90
31	.076 4484	33.70	.088 6494	34.09	.100 9924	34.49	.113 4835	34.91
32	.076 6507	33.71	.088 8540	34.09	.101 1993	34.50	.113 6930	34.92
33	.076 8529	33.71	.089 0586	34.10	.101 4063	34.50	.113 9025	34.92
34	.077 0552	33.72	.089 2632	34.11	.101 6134	34.51	.114 1121	34.93
35	2.077 2575	33.73	2.089 4678	34.11	2.101 8204	34.52	2.114 3217	34.94
36	.077 4599	33.73	.089 6725	34.12	.102 0276	34.52	.114 5313	34.95
37	.077 6623	33.74	.089 8772	34.12	.102 2347	34.53	.114 7410	34.95
38	.077 8647	33.74	.090 0820	34.13	.102 4419	34.54	.114 9508	34.96
39	.078 0672	33.75	.090 2868	34.14	.102 6492	34.54	.115 1605	34.97
40	2.078 2697	33.76	2.090 4917	34.15	2.102 8564	34.55	2.115 3704	34.97
41	.078 4723	33.76	.090 6966	34.15	.103 0638	34.56	.115 5802	34.98
42	.078 6749	33.77	.090 9015	34.16	.103 2711	34.56	.115 7901	34.99
43	.078 8775	33.78	.091 1065	34.17	.103 4785	34.57	.116 0001	35.00
44	.079 0802	33.78	.091 3115	34.17	.103 6860	34.58	.116 2101	35.00
45	2.079 2829	33.79	2.091 5165	34.18	2.103 8935	34.59	2.116 4201	35.01
46	.079 4857	33.80	.091 7216	34.19	.104 1010	34.59	.116 6301	35.02
47	.079 6885	33.80	.091 9268	34.19	.104 3086	34.60	.116 8403	35.02
48	.079 8913	33.81	.092 1319	34.20	.104 5162	34.61	.117 0505	35.03
49	.080 0942	33.81	.092 3371	34.20	.104 7239	34.61	.117 2607	35.04
50	2.080 2971	33.82	2.092 5424	34.21	2.104 9316	34.62	2.117 4710	35.05
51	.080 5000	33.83	.092 7477	34.22	.105 1393	34.63	.117 6813	35.05
52	.080 7030	33.83	.092 9530	34.22	.105 3471	34.63	.117 8916	35.06
53	.080 9060	33.84	.093 1584	34.23	.105 5549	34.64	.118 1020	35.07
54	.081 1091	33.85	.093 3638	34.24	.105 7628	34.65	.118 3124	35.08
55	2.081 3122	33.85	2.093 5692	34.25	2.105 9707	34.66	2.118 5229	35.08
56	.081 5153	33.86	.093 7747	34.25	.106 1786	34.66	.118 7334	35.09
57	.081 7185	33.87	.093 9803	34.26	.106 3866	34.67	.118 9440	35.10
58	.081 9217	33.87	.094 1858	34.27	.106 5947	34.68	.119 1546	35.10
59	.082 1249	33.88	.094 3914	34.27	.106 8027	34.68	.119 3652	35.11
60	2.082 3282	33.88	2.094 5971	34.28	2.107 0109	34.69	2.119 5759	35.12

TABLE VI.

For finding the True Anomaly or the Time from the Perihelion in a Parabolic Orbit.

v.	100°		101°		102°		103°	
	log M.	Diff. 1″.	log M.	Diff. 1″.	log M.	Diff. 1″.	log M.	Diff. 1″.
0′	2.119 5759	35.12	2.132 2989	35.57	2.145 1866	36.03	2.158 2460	36.52
1	.119 7867	35.13	.132 5123	35.57	.145 4028	36.04	.158 4652	36.53
2	.119 9974	35.13	.132 7258	35.58	.145 6191	36.05	.158 6844	36.54
3	.120 2083	35.14	.132 9393	35.59	.145 8354	36.06	.158 9036	36.55
4	.120 4191	35.15	.133 1529	35.60	.146 0518	36.07	.159 1229	36.55
5	2.120 6301	35.16	2.133 3665	35.61	2.146 2682	36.07	2.159 3423	36.56
6	.120 8410	35.16	.133 5802	35.61	.146 4847	36.08	.159 5617	36.57
7	.121 0520	35.17	.133 7939	35.62	.146 7012	36.09	.159 7811	36.58
8	.121 2630	35.18	.134 0076	35.63	.146 9178	36.10	.160 0006	36.59
9	.121 4741	35.19	.134 2214	35.64	.147 1344	36.11	.160 2202	36.60
10	2.121 6853	35.19	2.134 4352	35.64	2.147 3510	36.11	2.160 4398	36.60
11	.121 8965	35.20	.134 6491	35.65	.147 5677	36.12	.160 6594	36.61
12	.122 1077	35.21	.134 8631	35.66	.147 7845	36.13	.160 8791	36.62
13	.122 3190	35.21	.135 0770	35.67	.148 0013	36.14	.161 0989	36.63
14	.122 5303	35.22	.135 2910	35.67	.148 2182	36.15	.161 3187	36.64
15	2.122 7416	35.23	2.135 5051	35.68	2.148 4351	36.15	2.161 5385	36.65
16	.122 9530	35.24	.135 7192	35.69	.148 6520	36.16	.161 7584	36.65
17	.123 1644	35.24	.135 9334	35.70	.148 8690	36.17	.161 9784	36.66
18	.123 3759	35.25	.136 1476	35.71	.149 0861	36.18	.162 1984	36.67
19	.123 5875	35.26	.136 3619	35.71	.149 3032	36.19	.162 4185	36.68
20	2.123 7990	35.27	2.136 5762	35.72	2.149 5203	36.19	2.162 6386	36.69
21	.124 0107	35.27	.136 7905	35.73	.149 7375	36.20	.162 8587	36.70
22	.124 2223	35.28	.137 0049	35.74	.149 9547	36.21	.163 0789	36.70
23	.124 4340	35.29	.137 2193	35.74	.150 1720	36.22	.163 2992	36.71
24	.124 6458	35.30	.137 4338	35.75	.150 3893	36.23	.163 5195	36.72
25	2.124 8576	35.30	2.137 6484	35.76	2.150 6067	36.23	2.163 7398	36.73
26	.125 0694	35.31	.137 8630	35.77	.150 8242	36.24	.163 9602	36.74
27	.125 2813	35.32	.138 0776	35.77	.151 0417	36.25	.164 1807	36.74
28	.125 4933	35.33	.138 2922	35.78	.151 2592	36.26	.164 4012	36.75
29	.125 7052	35.33	.138 5070	35.79	.151 4768	36.27	.164 6218	36.76
30	2.125 9173	35.34	2.138 7217	35.80	2.151 6944	36.28	2.164 8424	36.77
31	.126 1293	35.35	.138 9365	35.81	.151 9121	36.28	.165 0630	36.78
32	.126 3414	35.35	.139 1514	35.81	.152 1298	36.29	.165 2837	36.79
33	.126 5536	35.36	.139 3663	35.82	.152 3476	36.30	.165 5045	36.80
34	.126 7658	35.37	.139 5813	35.83	.152 5654	36.31	.165 7253	36.81
35	2.126 9780	35.38	2.139 7963	35.84	2.152 7833	36.32	2.165 9462	36.81
36	.127 1903	35.39	.140 0113	35.84	.153 0012	36.32	.166 1671	36.82
37	.127 4027	35.39	.140 2264	35.85	.153 2192	36.33	.166 3881	36.83
38	.127 6151	35.40	.140 4415	35.86	.153 4372	36.34	.166 6091	36.84
39	.127 8275	35.41	.140 6567	35.87	.153 6552	36.35	.166 8301	36.85
40	2.128 0400	35.42	2.140 8720	35.88	2.153 8734	36.35	2.167 0513	36.86
41	.128 2525	35.42	.141 0873	35.88	.154 0915	36.36	.167 2724	36.87
42	.128 4650	35.43	.141 3026	35.89	.154 3097	36.37	.167 4936	36.87
43	.128 6776	35.44	.141 5180	35.90	.154 5280	36.38	.167 7149	36.88
44	.128 8903	35.45	.141 7334	35.91	.154 7463	36.39	.167 9362	36.89
45	2.129 1030	35.45	2.141 9489	35.92	2.154 9647	36.40	2.168 1576	36.90
46	.129 3157	35.46	.142 1644	35.92	.155 1831	36.41	.168 3790	36.91
47	.129 5285	35.47	.142 3799	35.93	.155 4015	36.41	.168 6005	36.92
48	.129 7414	35.48	.142 5955	35.94	.155 6200	36.42	.168 8220	36.93
49	.129 9542	35.48	.142 8112	35.95	.155 8386	36.43	.169 0436	36.93
50	2.130 1672	35.49	2.143 0269	35.96	2.156 0572	36.44	2.169 2652	36.94
51	.130 3801	35.50	.143 2427	35.96	.156 2759	36.45	.169 4869	36.95
52	.130 5931	35.51	.143 4585	35.97	.156 4946	36.46	.169 7087	36.96
53	.130 8062	35.51	.143 6743	35.98	.156 7133	36.46	.169 9304	36.97
54	.131 0193	35.52	.143 8902	35.99	.156 9321	36.47	.170 1523	36.98
55	2.131 2325	35.53	2.144 1062	36.00	2.157 1510	36.48	2.170 3742	36.99
56	.131 4457	35.54	.144 3222	36.00	.157 3699	36.49	.170 5961	36.99
57	.131 6589	35.54	.144 5382	36.01	.157 5889	36.50	.170 8181	37.00
58	.131 8722	35.55	.144 7543	36.02	.157 8079	36.50	.171 0401	37.01
59	.132 0855	35.56	.144 9704	36.03	.158 0269	36.51	.171 2622	37.02
60	2.132 2989	35.57	2.145 1866	36.03	2.158 2460	36.52	2.171 4844	37.03

TABLE VI.

For finding the True Anomaly or the Time from the Perihelion in a Parabolic Orbit.

v.	104°		105°		106°		107°	
	log M.	Diff. 1″.	log M.	Diff. 1″.	log M.	Diff. 1″.	log M.	Diff. 1″.
0′	2.171 4844	37.03	2.184 9092	37.56	2.198 5282	38.11	2.212 3493	38.68
1	.171 7066	37.04	.185 1346	37.57	.198 7568	38.12	.212 5814	38.69
2	.171 9288	37.05	.185 3600	37.57	.198 9856	38.13	.212 8136	38.70
3	.172 1511	37.05	.185 5855	37.58	.199 2144	38.14	.213 0458	38.71
4	.172 3735	37.06	.185 8110	37.59	.199 4432	38.14	.213 2781	38.72
5	2.172 5959	37.07	2.186 0366	37.60	2.199 6721	38.15	2.213 5104	38.73
6	.172 8184	37.08	.186 2622	37.61	.199 9010	38.16	.213 7428	38.74
7	.173 0409	37.09	.186 4879	37.62	.200 1300	38.17	.213 9753	38.75
8	.173 2634	37.10	.186 7137	37.63	.200 3591	38.18	.214 2078	38.76
9	.173 4860	37.11	.186 9395	37.64	.200 5882	38.19	.214 4404	38.77
10	2.173 7087	37.12	2.187 1653	37.65	2.200 8174	38.20	2.214 6730	38.78
11	.173 9314	37.12	.187 3912	37.66	.201 0467	38.21	.214 9057	38.79
12	.174 1542	37.13	.187 6172	37.67	.201 2760	38.22	.215 1385	38.80
13	.174 3770	37.14	.187 8432	37.67	.201 5053	38.23	.215 3713	38.81
14	.174 5999	37.15	.188 0693	37.68	.201 7347	38.24	.215 6042	38.82
15	2.174 8228	37.16	2.188 2954	37.69	2.201 9642	38.25	2.215 8371	38.83
16	.175 0458	37.17	.188 5216	37.70	.202 1937	38.26	.216 0701	38.84
17	.175 2688	37.18	.188 7478	37.71	.202 4233	38.27	.216 3032	38.85
18	.175 4919	37.18	.188 9741	37.72	.202 6529	38.28	.216 5363	38.86
19	.175 7150	37.19	.189 2005	37.73	.202 8826	38.29	.216 7694	38.87
20	2.175 9382	37.20	2.189 4269	37.74	2.203 1123	38.30	2.217 0027	38.88
21	.176 1615	37.21	.189 6533	37.75	.203 3421	38.31	.217 2360	38.89
22	.176 3848	37.22	.189 8798	37.76	.203 5720	38.31	.217 4693	38.90
23	.176 6081	37.23	.190 1064	37.77	.203 8019	38.32	.217 7027	38.91
24	.176 8315	37.24	.190 3330	37.77	.204 0319	38.33	.217 9362	38.92
25	2.177 0550	37.25	2.190 5597	37.78	2.204 2619	38.34	2.218 1697	38.93
26	.177 2785	37.25	.190 7864	37.79	.204 4920	38.35	.218 4033	38.94
27	.177 5020	37.26	.191 0132	37.80	.204 7222	38.36	.218 6369	38.95
28	.177 7256	37.27	.191 2401	37.81	.204 9524	38.37	.218 8706	38.96
29	.177 9493	37.28	.191 4670	37.82	.205 1826	38.38	.219 1044	38.97
30	2.178 1730	37.29	2.191 6939	37.83	2.205 4129	38.39	2.219 3382	38.98
31	.178 3968	37.30	.191 9209	37.84	.205 6433	38.40	.219 5721	38.99
32	.178 6206	37.31	.192 1480	37.85	.205 8737	38.41	.219 8061	39.00
33	.178 8445	37.32	.192 3751	37.86	.206 1042	38.42	.220 0401	39.01
34	.179 0684	37.33	.192 6023	37.87	.206 3348	38.43	.220 2741	39.02
35	2.179 2924	37.33	2.192 8295	37.88	2.206 5654	38.44	2.220 5082	39.03
36	.179 5164	37.34	.193 0568	37.88	.206 7961	38.45	.220 7424	39.04
37	.179 7405	37.35	.193 2841	37.89	.207 0268	38.46	.220 9767	39.05
38	.179 9646	37.36	.193 5115	37.90	.207 2575	38.47	.221 2110	39.06
39	.180 1888	37.37	.193 7389	37.91	.207 4884	38.48	.221 4453	39.07
40	2.180 4131	37.38	2.193 9664	37.92	2.207 7193	38.49	2.221 6797	39.08
41	.180 6374	37.39	.194 1940	37.93	.207 9502	38.50	.221 9142	39.09
42	.180 8617	37.40	.194 4216	37.94	.208 1812	38.51	.222 1488	39.10
43	.181 0861	37.41	.194 6493	37.95	.208 4123	38.52	.222 3834	39.11
44	.181 3106	37.41	.194 8770	37.96	.208 6434	38.53	.222 6180	39.12
45	2.181 5351	37.42	2.195 1048	37.97	2.208 8746	38.54	2.222 8528	39.13
46	.181 7597	37.43	.195 3326	37.98	.209 1058	38.54	.223 0876	39.14
47	.181 9843	37.44	.195 5605	37.99	.209 3371	38.55	.223 3224	39.15
48	.182 1089	37.45	.195 7885	38.00	.209 5685	38.56	.223 5573	39.16
49	.182 4337	37.46	.196 0165	38.00	.209 7999	38.57	.223 7923	39.17
50	2.182 6584	37.47	2.196 2445	38.01	2.210 0314	38.58	2.224 0273	39.18
51	.182 8833	37.48	.196 4726	38.02	.210 2629	38.59	.224 2624	39.19
52	.183 1082	37.49	.196 7008	38.03	.210 4945	38.60	.224 4975	39.20
53	.183 3331	37.49	.196 9290	38.04	.210 7261	38.61	.224 7327	39.21
54	.183 5581	37.50	.197 1573	38.05	.210 9578	38.62	.224 9680	39.22
55	2.183 7831	37.51	2.197 3856	38.06	2.211 1896	38.63	2.225 2033	39.23
56	.184 0082	37.52	.197 6140	38.07	.211 4214	38.64	.225 4387	39.24
57	.184 2334	37.53	.197 8425	38.08	.211 6533	38.65	.225 6741	39.25
58	.184 4586	37.54	.198 0710	38.09	.211 8852	38.66	.225 9096	39.26
59	.184 6839	37.55	.198 2995	38.10	.212 1172	38.67	.226 1452	39.27
60	2.184 9092	37.56	2.198 5282	38.11	2.212 3493	38.68	2.226 3808	39.28

TABLE VI.

For finding the True Anomaly or the Time from the Perihelion in a Parabolic Orbit.

v.	108°		109°		110°		111°	
	log M.	Diff. 1″.	log M.	Diff. 1″.	log M.	Diff. 1″.	log M.	Diff. 1″.
0′	2.226 3808	39.28	2.240 6314	39.90	2.255 1099	40.54	2.269 8255	41.21
1	.226 6165	39.29	.240 8708	39.91	.255 3532	40.55	.270 0728	41.23
2	.226 8523	39.30	.241 1103	39.92	.255 5965	40.56	.270 3202	41.24
3	.227 0881	39.31	.241 3498	39.93	.255 8399	40.58	.270 5676	41.25
4	.227 3240	39.32	.241 5894	39.94	.256 0834	40.59	.270 8152	41.26
5	2.227 5599	39.33	2.241 8291	39.95	2.256 3270	40.60	2.271 0628	41.27
6	.227 7959	39.34	.242 0688	39.96	.256 5706	40.61	.271 3104	41.28
7	.228 0320	39.35	.242 3086	39.97	.256 8143	40.62	.271 5582	41.29
8	.228 2681	39.36	.242 5485	39.98	.257 0580	40.63	.271 8060	41.30
9	.228 5043	39.37	.242 7884	39.99	.257 3019	40.64	.272 0538	41.32
10	2.228 7405	39.38	2.243 0284	40.00	2.257 5458	40.65	2.272 3018	41.33
11	.228 9768	39.39	.243 2685	40.01	.257 7897	40.66	.272 5498	41.34
12	.229 2131	39.40	.243 5086	40.02	.258 0337	40.68	.272 7979	41.35
13	.229 4496	39.41	.243 7488	40.03	.258 2778	40.69	.273 0460	41.36
14	.229 6861	39.42	.243 9890	40.05	.258 5220	40.70	.273 2942	41.38
15	2.229 9226	39.43	2.244 2293	40.06	2.258 7662	40.71	2.273 5425	41.39
16	.230 1592	39.44	.244 4697	40.07	.259 0105	40.72	.273 7909	41.40
17	.230 3959	39.45	.244 7101	40.08	.259 2548	40.73	.274 0393	41.41
18	.230 6326	39.46	.244 9506	40.09	.259 4992	40.74	.274 2878	41.42
19	.230 8694	39.47	[illegible] 1912	40.10	.259 7437	40.75	.274 5364	41.43
20	2.231 1063	39.48	2.245 4318	40.11	2.259 9883	40.76	2.274 7850	41.44
21	.231 3432	39.49	.245 6725	40.12	.260 2329	40.78	.275 0337	41.46
22	.231 5802	39.50	.245 9132	40.13	.260 4776	40.79	.275 2825	41.47
23	.231 8172	39.51	.246 1541	40.14	.260 7223	40.80	.275 5313	41.48
24	.232 0543	39.52	.246 3949	40.15	.260 9671	40.81	.275 7802	41.49
25	2.232 2915	39.53	2.246 6359	40.16	2.261 2120	40.82	2.276 0292	41.50
26	.232 5287	39.54	.246 8769	40.17	.261 4570	40.83	.276 2783	41.51
27	.232 7660	39.55	.247 1180	40.18	.261 7020	40.84	.276 5274	41.53
28	.233 0033	39.56	.247 3591	40.19	.261 9471	40.85	.276 7766	41.54
29	.233 2407	39.57	.247 6003	40.21	.262 1922	40.86	.277 0258	41.55
30	2.233 4782	39.58	2.247 8416	40.22	2.262 4374	40.88	2.277 2752	41.56
31	.233 7157	39.59	.248 0829	40.23	.262 6827	40.89	.277 5246	41.57
32	.233 9533	39.60	.248 3243	40.24	.262 9281	40.90	.277 7740	41.58
33	.234 1910	39.61	.248 5658	40.25	.263 1735	40.91	.278 0236	41.60
34	.234 4287	39.63	.248 8073	40.26	.263 4190	40.92	.278 2732	41.61
35	2.234 6665	39.64	2.249 0489	40.27	2.263 6645	40.93	2.278 5229	41.62
36	.234 9043	39.65	.249 2906	40.28	.263 9102	40.94	.278 7726	41.63
37	.235 1422	39.66	.249 5323	40.29	.264 1559	40.95	.279 0224	41.64
38	.235 3802	39.67	.249 7741	40.30	.264 4016	40.96	.279 2723	41.65
39	.235 6183	39.68	.250 0159	40.31	.264 6474	40.98	.279 5223	41.67
40	2.235 8563	39.69	2.250 2578	40.32	2.264 8933	40.99	2.279 7723	41.68
41	.236 0945	39.70	.250 4998	40.34	.265 1393	41.00	.280 0224	41.69
42	.236 3327	39.71	.250 7419	40.35	.265 3853	41.01	.280 2726	41.70
43	.236 5710	39.72	.250 9840	40.36	.265 6314	41.02	.280 5228	41.71
44	.236 8093	39.73	.251 2262	40.37	.265 8776	41.03	.280 7731	41.72
45	2.237 0478	39.74	2.251 4684	40.38	2.266 1238	41.04	2.281 0235	41.74
46	.237 2862	39.75	.251 7107	40.39	.266 3701	41.06	.281 2740	41.75
47	.237 5247	39.76	.251 9531	40.40	.266 6165	41.07	.281 5245	41.76
48	.237 7633	39.77	.252 1955	40.41	.266 8629	41.08	.281 7751	41.77
49	.238 0020	39.78	.252 4380	40.42	.267 1094	41.09	.282 0258	41.78
50	2.238 2407	39.79	2.252 6806	40.43	2.267 3560	41.10	2.282 2765	41.80
51	.238 4795	39.80	.252 9232	40.44	.267 6026	41.11	.282 5273	41.81
52	.238 7284	39.81	.253 1659	40.46	.267 8493	41.12	.282 7782	41.82
53	.238 9573	39.82	.253 4087	40.47	.268 0961	41.13	.283 0291	41.83
54	.239 1962	39.83	.253 6515	40.48	.268 3430	41.15	.283 2801	41.84
55	2.239 4353	39.84	2.253 8944	40.49	2.268 5899	41.16	2.283 5312	41.85
56	.239 6744	39.86	.254 1374	40.50	.268 8369	41.17	.283 7824	41.87
57	.239 9235	39.87	.254 3804	40.51	.269 0839	41.18	.284 0336	41.88
58	.240 1528	39.88	.254 6235	40.52	.269 3310	41.19	.284 2849	41.89
59	.240 3921	39.89	.254 8666	40.53	.269 5782	41.20	.284 5363	41.90
60	2.240 6314	39.90	2.255 1099	40.54	2.269 8255	41.21	2.284 7878	41.91

TABLE VI.

For finding the True Anomaly or the Time from the Perihelion in a Parabolic Orbit.

v.	112°		113°		114°		115°	
	log M.	Diff. 1″.	log M.	Diff. 1″.	log M.	Diff. 1″.	log M.	Diff. 1″.
0′	2.284 7878	41.91	2.300 0067	42.64	2.315 4927	43.40	2.331 2564	44.18
1	.285 0393	41.93	.300 2626	42.65	.315 7531	43.41	.331 5216	44.20
2	.285 2909	41.94	.300 5186	42.67	.316 0136	43.42	.331 7868	44.21
3	.285 5425	41.95	.300 7746	42.68	.316 2742	43.44	.332 0521	44.22
4	.285 7943	41.96	.301 0307	42.69	.316 5348	43.45	.332 3175	44.24
5	2.286 0461	41.97	2.301 2869	42.70	2.316 7956	43.46	2.332 5830	44.25
6	.286 2979	41.99	.301 5431	42.72	.317 0564	43.47	.332 8485	44.26
7	.286 5499	42.00	.301 7995	42.73	.317 3173	43.49	.333 1141	44.28
8	.286 8019	42.01	.302 0559	42.74	.317 5782	43.50	.333 3799	44.29
9	.287 0540	42.02	.302 3123	42.75	.317 8393	43.51	.333 6456	44.31
10	2.287 3062	42.03	2.302 5689	42.76	2.318 1004	43.53	2.333 9115	44.32
11	.287 5584	42.04	.302 8255	42.78	.318 3616	43.54	.334 1775	44.33
12	.287 8107	42.06	.303 0822	42.79	.318 6229	43.55	.334 4435	44.34
13	.288 0631	42.07	.303 3390	42.80	.318 8842	43.56	.334 7096	44.36
14	.288 3155	42.08	.303 5958	42.81	.319 1456	43.58	.334 9758	44.37
15	2.288 5680	42.09	2.303 8528	42.83	2.319 4072	43.59	2.335 2421	44.39
16	.288 8206	42.10	.304 1098	42.84	.319 6687	43.60	.335 5084	44.40
17	.289 0733	42.12	.304 3668	42.85	.319 9304	43.62	.335 7749	44.41
18	.289 3260	42.13	.304 6240	42.86	.320 1921	43.63	.336 0414	44.43
19	.289 5788	42.14	.304 8812	42.88	.320 454[illegible]	[illegible]3.64	.336 3080	44.44
20	2.289 8317	42.15	2.305 1385	42.89	2.320 7159	43.66	2.336 5747	44.45
21	.290 0847	42.16	.305 3959	42.90	.320 9778	43.67	.336 8414	44.47
22	.290 3377	42.18	.305 6533	42.91	.321 2399	43.68	.337 1083	44.48
23	.290 5908	42.19	.305 9109	42.93	.321 5020	43.69	.337 3752	44.49
24	.290 8440	42.20	.306 1685	42.94	.321 7642	43.70	.337 6422	44.51
25	2.291 0972	42.21	2.306 4261	42.95	2.322 0265	43.72	2.337 9093	44.52
26	.291 3505	42.22	.306 6839	42.96	.322 2889	43.73	.338 1765	44.53
27	.291 6039	42.24	.306 9417	42.98	.322 5513	43.75	.338 4437	44.55
28	.291 8574	42.25	.307 1996	42.99	.322 8139	43.76	.338 7111	44.56
29	.292 1109	42.26	.307 4576	43.00	.323 0765	43.77	.338 9785	44.58
30	2.292 3645	42.27	2.307 7157	43.02	2.323 3391	43.79	2.339 2460	44.59
31	.292 6182	42.29	.307 9738	43.03	.323 6019	43.80	.339 5135	44.60
32	.292 8719	42.30	.308 2320	43.04	.323 8647	43.81	.339 7812	44.62
33	.293 1258	42.31	.308 4903	43.05	.324 1277	43.83	.340 0490	44.63
34	.293 3797	42.32	.308 7486	43.07	.324 3907	43.84	.340 3168	44.64
35	2.293 6336	42.33	2.309 0071	43.08	2.324 6537	43.85	2.340 5847	44.66
36	.293 8877	42.35	.309 2656	43.09	.324 9169	43.87	.340 8527	44.67
37	.294 1418	42.36	.309 5242	43.10	.325 1801	43.88	.341 1207	44.69
38	.294 3960	42.37	.309 7828	43.12	.325 4434	43.89	.341 3889	44.70
39	.294 6503	42.38	.310 0416	43.13	.325 7068	43.91	.341 6571	44.71
40	2.294 9046	42.40	2.310 3004	43.14	2.325 9703	43.92	2.341 9255	44.73
41	.295 1590	42.41	.310 5593	43.15	.326 2339	43.93	.342 1939	44.74
42	.295 4135	42.42	.310 8182	43.17	.326 4975	43.94	.342 4623	44.75
43	.295 6680	42.43	.311 0773	43.18	.326 7612	43.96	.342 7309	44.77
44	.295 9227	42.44	.311 3364	43.19	.327 0250	43.97	.342 9995	44.78
45	2.296 1774	42.46	2.311 5956	43.21	2.327 2889	43.98	2.343 2683	44.80
46	.296 4321	42.47	.311 8549	43.22	.327 5528	44.00	.343 5371	44.81
47	.296 6870	42.48	.312 1142	43.23	.327 8168	44.01	.343 8060	44.82
48	.296 9419	42.49	.312 3736	43.24	.328 0809	44.02	.344 0750	44.84
49	.297 1969	42.51	.312 6331	43.26	.328 3451	44.04	.344 3440	44.85
50	2.297 4520	42.52	2.312 8927	43.27	2.328 6094	44.05	2.344 6132	44.86
51	.297 7071	42.53	.313 1524	43.28	.328 8737	44.06	.344 8824	44.88
52	.297 9623	42.54	.313 4121	43.29	.329 1382	44.08	.345 1517	44.89
53	.298 2176	42.55	.313 6719	43.31	.329 4027	44.09	.345 4211	44.91
54	.298 4730	42.57	.313 9318	43.32	.329 6672	44.10	.345 6906	44.92
55	2.298 7284	42.58	2.314 1917	43.33	2.329 9319	44.12	2.345 9601	44.93
56	.298 9839	42.59	.314 4518	43.35	.330 1967	44.13	.346 2298	44.95
57	.299 2395	42.60	.314 7119	43.36	.330 4615	44.14	.346 4995	44.96
58	.299 4952	42.61	.314 9721	43.37	.330 7264	44.16	.346 7693	44.97
59	.299 7509	42.63	.315 2323	43.38	.330 9914	44.17	.347 0392	44.99
60	2.300 0067	42.64	2.315 4927	43.40	2.331 2564	44.18	2.347 3092	45.00

TABLE VI.

For finding the True Anomaly or the Time from the Perihelion in a Parabolic Orbit.

v.	116°		117°		118°		119°	
	log M.	Diff. 1″.	log M.	Diff. 1″.	log M.	Diff. 1″.	log M.	Diff. 1″.
0′	2.347 3092	45.00	2.363 6626	45.86	2.380 3290	46.74	2.397 3210	47.66
1	·347 5792	45.02	·363 9378	45.87	·380 6095	46.76	·397 6070	47.68
2	·347 8494	45.03	·364 2131	45.88	·380 8901	46.77	·397 8931	47.70
3	·348 1196	45.04	·364 4885	45.90	·381 1708	46.79	·398 1794	47.71
4	·348 3899	45.06	·364 7639	45.91	·381 4515	46.80	·398 4657	47.73
5	2.348 6603	45.07	2.365 0394	45.93	2.381 7324	46.82	2.398 7521	47.74
6	·348 9308	45.09	·365 3150	45.94	·382 0133	46.83	·399 0386	47.76
7	·349 2014	45.10	·365 5907	45.96	·382 2944	46.85	·399 3252	47.77
8	·349 4720	45.11	·365 8665	45.97	·382 5755	46.86	·399 6119	47.79
9	·349 7428	45.13	·366 1423	45.99	·382 8567	46.88	·399 8987	47.81
10	2.350 0136	45.14	2.366 4183	46.00	2.383 1380	46.89	2.400 1856	47.82
11	·350 2845	45.16	·366 6944	46.01	·383 4194	46.91	·400 4725	47.84
12	·350 5554	45.17	·366 9705	46.03	·383 7009	46.92	·400 7596	47.85
13	·350 8265	45.18	·367 2467	46.04	·383 9825	46.94	·401 0468	47.87
14	·351 0977	45.20	·367 5230	46.06	·384 2642	46.95	·401 3340	47.89
15	2.351 3689	45.21	2.367 7994	46.07	2.384 5460	46.97	2.401 6214	47.90
16	·351 6402	45.23	·368 0759	46.09	·384 8278	46.98	·401 9088	47.92
17	·351 9116	45.24	·368 3525	46.10	·385 1098	46.99	·402 1964	47.93
18	·352 1831	45.25	[illegible] 6291	46.12	·385 3918	47.01	·402 4840	47.95
19	·352 4547	45.27	[illegible] 9059	46.13	·385 6739	47.03	·402 7718	47.97
20	2.352 7263	45.28	2.369 1827	46.15	2.385 9562	47.05	2.403 0596	47.98
21	·352 9981	45.30	·369 4596	46.16	·386 2385	47.06	·403 3475	48.00
22	·353 2699	45.31	·369 7367	46.18	·386 5209	47.08	·403 6356	48.01
23	·353 5418	45.33	·370 0138	46.19	·386 8034	47.09	·403 9237	48.03
24	·353 8138	45.34	·370 2909	46.21	·387 0860	47.11	·404 2119	48.04
25	2.354 0859	45.35	2.370 5682	46.22	2.387 3687	47.12	2.404 5002	48.06
26	·354 3581	45.37	·370 8456	46.24	·387 6514	47.14	·404 7886	48.08
27	·354 6303	45.38	·371 1230	46.25	·387 9343	47.15	·405 0771	48.09
28	·354 9027	45.40	·371 4006	46.26	·388 2173	47.17	·405 3657	48.11
29	·355 1751	45.41	·371 6782	46.28	·388 5003	47.18	·405 6544	48.12
30	2.355 4476	45.42	2.371 9559	46.29	2.388 7835	47.20	2.405 9432	48.14
31	·355 7202	45.44	·372 2337	46.31	·389 0667	47.21	·406 2321	48.16
32	·355 9928	45.45	·372 5116	46.32	·389 3500	47.23	·406 5211	48.17
33	·356 2656	45.47	·372 7896	46.34	·389 6335	47.24	·406 8102	48.19
34	·356 5385	45.48	·373 0677	46.35	·389 9170	47.26	·407 0993	48.20
35	2.356 8114	45.50	2.373 3459	46.37	2.390 2006	47.28	2.407 3886	48.22
36	·357 0844	45.51	·373 6241	46.38	·390 4843	47.29	·407 6780	48.24
37	·357 3575	45.52	·373 9024	46.40	·390 7681	47.31	·407 9674	48.25
38	·357 6307	45.54	·374 1809	46.41	·391 0519	47.32	·408 2570	48.27
39	·357 9040	45.55	·374 4594	46.43	·391 3359	47.34	·408 5467	48.28
40	2.358 1773	45.57	2.374 7380	46.44	2.391 6200	47.35	2.408 8364	48.30
41	·358 4508	45.58	·375 0167	46.46	·392 9042	47.37	·409 1263	48.32
42	·358 7243	45.60	·375 2955	46.47	·392 1884	47.38	·409 4162	48.33
43	·358 9979	45.61	·375 5744	46.49	·392 4728	47.40	·409 7063	48.35
44	·359 2716	45.62	·375 8533	46.50	·392 7572	47.41	·409 9964	48.37
45	2.359 5454	45.64	2.376 1324	46.51	2.393 0417	47.43	2.410 2866	48.38
46	·359 8193	45.65	·376 4115	46.53	·393 3264	47.45	·410 5770	48.40
47	·360 0933	45.67	·376 6908	46.55	·393 6111	47.46	·410 8674	48.41
48	·360 3673	45.68	·376 9701	46.56	·393 8959	47.48	·411 1579	48.43
49	·360 6415	45.70	·377 2495	46.58	·394 1808	47.49	·411 4486	48.45
50	2.360 9157	45.71	2.377 5290	46.59	2.394 4658	47.51	2.411 7393	48.46
51	·361 1900	45.72	·377 8086	46.60	·394 7509	47.52	·412 0301	48.48
52	·361 4644	45.74	·378 0883	46.62	·395 0361	47.54	·412 3210	48.49
53	·361 7389	45.75	·378 3681	46.64	·395 3214	47.55	·412 6120	48.51
54	·362 0134	45.77	·378 6479	46.65	·395 6067	47.57	·412 9031	48.53
55	2.362 2881	45.78	2.378 9279	46.67	2.395 8922	47.59	2.413 1944	48.54
56	·362 5628	45.80	·379 2079	46.68	·396 1778	47.60	·413 4857	48.56
57	·362 8376	45.81	·379 4881	46.70	·396 4634	47.62	·413 7771	48.58
58	·363 1126	45.82	·379 7683	46.71	·396 7492	47.63	·414 0686	48.59
59	·363 3876	45.84	·380 0486	46.73	·397 0350	47.65	·414 3602	48.61
60	2.363 6626	45.86	2.380 3290	46.74	2.397 3210	47.66	2.414 6519	48.62

TABLE VI.

For finding the True Anomaly or the Time from the Perihelion in a Parabolic Orbit.

v.	120°		121°		122°		123°	
	log M.	Diff. 1″.	log M.	Diff. 1″.	log M.	Diff. 1″.	log M.	Diff. 1″.
0′	2.414 6519	48.62	2.432 3356	49.62	2.450 3868	50.67	2.468 8205	51.75
1	·414 9437	48.64	·432 6334	49.64	·450 6908	50.68	·469 1311	51.77
2	·415 2356	48.66	·432 9313	49.66	·450 9950	50.70	·469 4418	51.79
3	·415 5276	48.67	·433 2293	49.68	·451 2992	50.72	·469 7526	51.81
4	·415 8197	48.69	·433 5274	49.69	·451 6036	50.74	·470 0634	51.82
5	2.416 1119	48.71	2.433 8257	49.71	2.451 9081	50.75	2.470 3744	51.84
6	·416 4042	48.72	·434 1240	49.73	·452 2127	50.77	·470 6856	51.86
7	·416 6965	48.74	·434 4224	49.74	·452 5174	50.79	·470 9968	51.88
8	·416 9890	48.76	·434 7209	49.76	·452 8222	50.81	·471 3081	51.90
9	·417 2816	48.77	·435 0195	49.78	·453 1271	50.83	·471 6196	51.92
10	2.417 5743	48.79	2.435 3182	49.80	2.453 4321	50.84	2.471 9311	51.94
11	·417 8671	48.81	·435 6171	49.81	·453 7372	50.86	·472 2428	51.95
12	·418 1600	48.82	·435 9160	49.83	·454 0424	50.88	·472 5546	51.97
13	·418 4529	48.84	·436 2150	49.85	·454 3477	50.90	·472 8665	51.99
14	·418 7460	48.85	·436 5141	49.86	·454 6532	50.92	·473 1785	52.01
15	2.419 0392	48.87	2.436 8134	49.88	2.454 9587	50.93	2.473 4906	52.03
16	·419 3325	48.89	·437 1127	49.90	·455 2644	50.95	·473 8028	52.05
17	·419 6258	48.90	·437 4122	49.92	·455 5701	50.97	·474 1152	52.07
18	·419 9193	48.92	·437 7117	49.93	·455 8760	50.99	·474 4276	52.09
19	·420 2129	48.94	·438 0114	49.95	·456 1820	[illegible]1.00	·474 7402	52.10
20	2.420 5066	48.95	2.438 3111	49.97	2.456 4881	51.02	2.475 0529	52.12
21	·420 8003	48.97	·438 6110	49.98	·456 7943	51.04	·475 3657	52.14
22	·421 0942	48.99	·438 9109	50.00	·457 1006	51.06	·475 6786	52.16
23	·421 3882	49.00	·439 2110	50.02	·457 4070	51.08	·475 9916	52.18
24	·421 6822	49.02	·439 5112	50.04	·457 7135	51.09	·476 3047	52.20
25	2.421 9764	49.03	2.439 8114	50.05	2.458 0201	51.11	2.476 6180	52.22
26	·422 2707	49.05	·440 1118	50.07	·458 3268	51.13	·476 9313	52.23
27	·422 5650	49.07	·440 4123	50.09	·458 6337	51.15	·477 2448	52.25
28	·422 8595	49.09	·440 7129	50.11	·458 9406	51.17	·477 5584	52.27
29	·423 1541	49.10	·441 0136	50.12	·459 2477	51.18	·477 8721	52.29
30	2.423 4488	49.12	2.441 3143	50.14	2.459 5548	51.20	2.478 1859	52.31
31	·423 7435	49.14	·441 6152	50.16	·459 8621	51.22	·478 4998	52.33
32	·424 0384	49.15	·441 9162	50.18	·460 1695	51.24	·478 8138	52.35
33	·424 3334	49.17	·442 2173	50.19	·460 4770	51.26	·479 1280	52.37
34	·424 6284	49.19	·442 5185	50.21	·460 7846	51.28	·479 4422	52.39
35	2.424 9236	49.20	2.442 8199	50.23	2.461 0923	51.29	2.479 7566	52.40
36	·425 2189	49.22	·443 1213	50.24	·461 4001	51.31	·480 0711	52.42
37	·425 5142	49.24	·443 4228	50.26	·461 7080	51.33	·480 3857	52.44
38	·425 8097	49.25	·443 7244	50.28	·462 0161	51.35	·480 7004	52.46
39	·426 1053	49.27	·444 0261	50.30	·462 3242	51.37	·481 0152	52.48
40	2.426 4010	49.29	2.444 3280	50.31	2.462 6325	51.38	2.481 3301	52.50
41	·426 6967	49.30	·444 6299	50.33	·462 9408	51.40	·481 6452	52.52
42	·426 9926	49.32	·444 9320	50.35	·463 2493	51.42	·481 9604	52.54
43	·427 2886	49.34	·445 2341	50.37	·463 5579	51.44	·482 2756	52.56
44	·427 5847	49.35	·445 5364	50.38	·463 8666	51.46	·482 5910	52.58
45	2.427 8808	49.37	2.445 8387	50.40	2.464 1754	51.48	2.482 9065	52.59
46	·428 1771	49.39	·446 1412	50.42	·464 4843	51.49	·483 2222	52.61
47	·428 4735	49.40	·446 4437	50.44	·464 7933	51.51	·483 5379	52.63
48	·428 7700	49.42	·446 7464	50.45	·465 1024	51.53	·483 8537	52.65
49	·429 0665	49.44	·447 0492	50.47	·465 4116	51.55	·484 1697	52.67
50	2.429 3632	49.46	2.447 3521	50.49	2.465 7210	51.57	2.484 4858	52.69
51	·429 6600	49.47	·447 6551	50.51	·466 0305	51.59	·484 8020	52.71
52	·429 9569	49.49	·447 9582	50.53	·466 3400	51.60	·485 1183	52.73
53	·430 2539	49.51	·448 2614	50.54	·466 6497	51.62	·485 4347	52.75
54	·430 5510	49.52	·448 5647	50.56	·466 9595	51.64	·485 7513	52.77
55	2.430 8482	49.54	2.448 8681	50.58	2.467 2694	51.66	2.486 0679	52.78
56	·431 1455	49.56	·449 1716	50.60	·467 5794	51.68	·486 3847	52.80
57	·431 4428	49.57	·449 4753	50.61	·467 8895	51.70	·486 7016	52.82
58	·431 7403	49.59	·449 7790	50.63	·468 1997	51.71	·487 0186	52.84
59	·432 0379	49.61	·450 0828	50.65	·468 5101	51.73	·487 3357	52.86
60	2.432 3356	49.62	2.450 3868	50.67	2.468 8205	51.75	2.487 6529	52.88

TABLE VI.

For finding the True Anomaly or the Time from the Perihelion in a Parabolic Orbit.

v.	124°		125°		126°		127°	
	log M.	Diff. 1″.	log M.	Diff. 1″.	log M.	Diff. 1″.	log M.	Diff. 1″.
0′	2.487 6529	52.88	2.506 9006	54.06	2.526 5813	55.29	2.546 7135	56.57
1	.487 9702	52.90	.507 2251	54.08	.526 9131	55.31	.547 0530	56.59
2	.488 2877	52.92	.507 5496	54.10	.527 2450	55.33	.547 3926	56.61
3	.488 6053	52.94	.507 8742	54.12	.527 5771	55.35	547 7323	56.63
4	.488 9230	52.96	.508 1990	54.14	.527 9092	55.37	548 0722	56.65
5	2.489 2408	52.98	2.508 5239	54.16	2.528 2415	55.39	2.548 4122	56.68
6	.489 5587	53.00	.508 8489	54.18	.528 5739	55.41	.548 7523	56.70
7	.489 8767	53.02	.509 1741	54.20	.528 9065	55.43	.549 0926	56.72
8	.490 1949	53.03	.509 4993	54.22	.529 2391	55.45	.549 4330	56.74
9	.490 5132	53.05	.509 8247	54.24	.529 5719	55.48	.549 7735	56.76
10	2.490 8315	53.07	2.510 1502	54.26	2.529 9048	55.50	2.550 1141	56.79
11	.491 1500	53.09	.510 4758	54.28	.530 2379	55.52	.550 4549	56.81
12	.491 4686	53.11	.510 8016	54.30	.530 5710	55.54	.550 7958	56.83
13	.491 7874	53.13	.511 1274	54.32	.530 9043	55.56	.551 1369	56.85
14	.492 1063	53.15	.511 4534	54.34	.531 2378	55.58	.551 4781	56.87
15	2.492 4252	53.17	2.511 7795	54.36	2.531 5713	55.60	2.551 8194	56.90
16	.492 7443	53.19	.512 1057	54.38	.531 9050	55.62	.552 1608	56.92
17	.493 0635	53.21	.512 4321	54.40	.532 2388	55.64	.552 5024	56.94
18	.493 3828	53.23	.512 7586	54.42	.532 5727	55.67	.552 8441	56.96
19	.493 7023	53.25	.513 0852	54.44	.532 9068	55.69	.553 1859	56.98
20	2.494 0218	53.27	2.513 4119	54.46	2.533 2410	55.71	2.553 5279	57.01
21	.494 3415	53.29	.513 7387	54.48	.533 5753	55.73	.553 8700	57.03
22	.494 6613	53.31	.514 0657	54.50	.533 9097	55.75	.554 2122	57.05
23	.494 9812	53.33	.514 3927	54.52	.534 2443	55.77	.554 5546	57.07
24	.495 3012	53.35	.514 7199	54.54	.534 5790	55.79	.554 8971	57.10
25	2.495 6213	53.37	2.515 0473	54.56	2.534 9138	55.81	2.555 2398	57.12
26	.495 9416	53.39	.515 3747	54.58	.535 2487	55.84	.555 5825	57.14
27	.496 2619	53.41	.515 7023	54.60	.535 5838	55.86	.555 9254	57.16
28	.496 5824	53.42	.516 0300	54.63	.535 9190	55.88	.556 2685	57.18
29	.496 9030	53.44	.516 3578	54.65	.536 2543	55.90	.556 6116	57.21
30	2.497 2238	53.46	2.516 6857	54.67	2.536 5898	55.92	2.556 9549	57.23
31	.497 5446	53.48	.517 0138	54.69	.536 9254	55.94	.557 2984	57.25
32	.497 8656	53.50	.517 3420	54.71	.537 2611	55.96	.557 6420	57.27
33	.498 1867	53.52	.517 6703	54.73	.537 5970	55.98	.557 9857	57.29
34	.498 5079	53.54	.517 9987	54.75	.537 9329	56.01	.558 3295	57.32
35	2.498 8292	53.56	2.518 3273	54.77	2.538 2690	56.03	2.558 6735	57.34
36	.499 1506	53.58	.518 6559	54.79	.538 6052	56.05	.559 0176	57.36
37	.499 4721	53.60	.518 9847	54.81	.538 9416	56.07	.559 3618	57.38
38	.499 7938	53.62	.519 3137	54.83	.539 2781	56.09	.559 7062	57.41
39	.500 1156	53.64	.519 6427	54.85	.539 6147	56.11	.560 0507	57.43
40	2.500 4375	53.66	2.519 9719	54.87	2.539 9514	56.13	2.560 3953	57.45
41	.500 7595	53.68	.520 3012	54.89	.540 2883	56.15	.560 7401	57.47
42	.501 0817	53.70	.520 6306	54.91	.540 6253	56.18	.561 0850	57.50
43	.501 4039	53.72	.520 9601	54.93	.540 9625	56.20	.561 4301	57.52
44	.501 7263	53.74	.521 2898	54.95	.541 2997	56.22	.561 7753	57.54
45	2.502 0488	53.76	2.521 6196	54.97	2.541 6371	56.24	2.562 1206	57.56
46	.502 3714	53.78	.521 9495	54.99	.541 9746	56.26	.562 4660	57.59
47	.502 6942	53.80	.522 2795	55.02	.542 3123	56.29	.562 8116	57.61
48	.503 0170	53.82	.522 6097	55.04	.542 6500	56.31	.563 1574	57.63
49	.503 3400	53.84	.522 9400	55.06	.542 9880	56.33	.563 5032	57.65
50	2.503 6631	53.86	2.523 2704	55.08	2.543 3260	56.35	2.563 8492	57.68
51	.503 9863	53.88	.523 6009	55.10	.543 6641	56.37	.564 1953	57.70
52	.504 3096	53.90	.523 9316	55.12	.544 0024	56.39	.564 5416	57.72
53	.504 6331	53.92	.524 2624	55.14	.544 3409	56.42	.564 8880	57.74
54	.504 9567	53.94	.524 5933	55.16	.544 6794	56.44	.565 2345	57.77
55	2.505 2804	53.96	2.524 9243	55.18	2.545 0181	56.46	2.565 5812	57.79
56	.505 6042	53.98	.525 2555	55.20	.545 3569	56.48	.565 9280	57.81
57	.505 9282	54.00	.525 5867	55.22	.545 6959	56.50	.566 2750	57.84
58	.506 2522	54.02	.525 9181	55.24	.546 0350	56.52	.566 6221	57.86
59	.506 5763	54.04	.526 2497	55.26	.546 3742	56.55	.566 9693	57.88
60	2.506 9006	54.06	2.526 5813	55.29	2.546 7135	56.57	2.567 3166	57.90

TABLE VI.

For finding the True Anomaly or the Time from the Perihelion in a Parabolic Orbit.

v.	128°		129°		130°		131°	
	log M.	Diff. 1″.	log M.	Diff. 1″.	log M.	Diff. 1″.	log M.	Diff. 1″.
0′	2.567 3166	57.90	2.588 4112	59.30	2.610 0188	60.75	2.632 1622	62.28
1	.567 6641	57.93	.588 7670	59.32	.610 3834	60.78	.632 5360	62.30
2	.568 0117	57.95	.589 1230	59.35	.610 7481	60.80	.632 9099	62.33
3	.568 3595	57.97	.589 4792	59.37	.611 1130	60.83	.633 2839	62.35
4	.568 7074	57.99	.589 8355	59.39	.611 4781	60.85	.633 6581	62.38
5	2.569 0554	58.02	2.590 1919	59.42	2.611 8433	60.88	2.634 0325	62.41
6	.569 4036	58.04	.590 5485	59.44	.612 2086	60.90	.634 4070	62.43
7	.569 7519	58.06	.590 9052	59.47	.612 5741	60.93	.634 7817	62.46
8	.570 1004	58.09	.591 2620	59.49	.612 9397	60.95	.635 1565	62.48
9	.570 4490	58.11	.591 6190	59.51	.613 3055	60.98	.635 5315	62.51
10	2.570 7977	58.13	2.591 9762	59.54	2.613 6715	61.00	2.635 9066	62.54
11	.571 1465	58.15	.592 3335	59.56	.614 0376	61.03	.636 2819	62.56
12	.571 4955	58.18	.592 6909	59.58	.614 4038	61.05	.636 6573	62.59
13	.571 8447	58.20	.593 0485	59.61	.614 7702	61.08	.637 0329	62.61
14	.572 1939	58.22	.593 4062	59.63	.615 1368	61.10	.637 4087	62.64
15	2.572 5434	58.25	2.593 7641	59.66	2.615 5035	61.13	2.637 7846	62.67
16	.572 8929	58.27	.594 1221	59.68	.615 8703	61.15	.638 1607	62.69
17	.573 2426	58.29	.594 4803	59.70	.616 2373	61.18	.638 5369	62.72
18	.573 5924	58.32	.594 8386	59.73	.616 6045	61.20	.638 9133	62.75
19	.573 9424	58.34	.595 1970	59.75	.616 9718	61.23	.639 2899	62.77
20	2.574 2925	58.36	2.595 5556	59.78	2.617 3392	61.25	2.639 6666	62.80
21	.574 6427	58.38	.595 9143	59.80	.617 7068	61.28	.640 0435	62.82
22	.574 9931	58.41	.596 2732	59.82	.618 0746	61.30	.640 4205	62.85
23	.575 3436	58.43	.596 6322	59.85	.618 4425	61.33	.640 7977	62.88
24	.575 6943	58.45	.596 9914	59.87	.618 8105	61.36	.641 1750	62.90
25	2.576 0451	58.48	2.597 3507	59.90	2.619 1787	61.38	2.641 5525	62.93
26	.576 3960	58.50	.597 7102	59.92	.619 5471	61.41	.641 9302	62.96
27	.576 7471	58.52	.598 0698	59.95	.619 9156	61.44	.642 3080	62.98
28	.577 0983	58.55	.598 4295	59.97	.620 2843	61.46	.642 6860	63.01
29	.577 4496	58.57	.598 7894	59.99	.620 6531	61.48	.643 0641	63.04
30	2.577 8011	58.59	2.599 1494	60.02	2.621 0220	61.51	2.643 4424	63.06
31	.578 1528	58.62	.599 5096	60.04	.621 3911	61.53	.643 8209	63.09
32	.578 5045	58.64	.599 8699	60.07	.621 7604	61.56	.644 1995	63.12
33	.578 8564	58.66	.600 2304	60.09	.622 1298	61.58	.644 5783	63.14
34	.579 2085	58.69	.600 5910	60.12	.622 4994	61.61	.644 9572	63.17
35	2.579 5607	58.71	2.600 9518	60.14	2.622 8691	61.63	2.645 3363	63.19
36	.579 9130	58.73	.601 3127	60.16	.623 2390	61.66	.645 7155	63.22
37	.580 2655	58.76	.601 6738	60.19	.623 6091	61.68	.646 0949	63.25
38	.580 6181	58.78	.602 0350	60.21	.623 9793	61.71	.646 4745	63.27
39	.580 9708	58.80	.602 3963	60.24	.624 3496	61.74	.646 8542	63.30
40	2.581 3237	58.83	2.602 7578	60.26	2.624 7201	61.76	2.647 2341	63.33
41	.581 6768	58.85	.603 1195	60.29	.625 0907	61.79	.647 6142	63.35
42	.582 0299	58.87	.603 4813	60.31	.625 4615	61.81	.647 9944	63.38
43	.582 3832	58.90	.603 8432	60.34	.625 8325	61.84	.648 3748	63.41
44	.582 8267	58.92	.604 2053	60.36	.626 2036	61.86	.648 7553	63.44
45	2.583 0903	58.94	2.604 5675	60.38	2.626 5748	61.89	2.649 1360	63.46
46	.583 4440	58.97	.604 9299	60.41	.626 9462	61.91	.649 5168	63.49
47	.583 7979	58.99	.605 2924	60.43	.627 3178	61.94	.649 8978	63.52
48	.584 1519	59.01	.605 6551	60.46	.627 6895	61.97	.650 2790	63.54
49	.584 5061	59.04	.606 0179	60.48	.628 0614	61.99	.650 6603	63.57
50	2.584 8604	59.06	2.606 3809	60.51	2.628 4334	62.02	2.651 0418	63.60
51	.585 2148	59.09	.606 7440	60.53	.628 8056	62.04	.651 4235	63.62
52	.585 5694	59.11	.607 1073	60.56	.629 1780	62.07	.651 8053	63.65
53	.585 9241	59.13	.607 4707	60.58	.629 5505	62.09	.652 1873	63.68
54	.586 2790	59.16	.607 8343	60.61	.629 9231	62.12	.652 5695	63.70
55	2.586 6340	59.18	2.608 1980	60.63	2.630 2959	62.15	2.652 9518	63.73
56	.586 9891	59.20	.608 5618	60.66	.630 6689	62.17	.653 3342	63.76
57	.587 3444	59.23	.608 9258	60.68	.631 0420	62.20	.653 7168	63.79
58	.587 6999	59.25	.609 2901	60.70	.631 4152	62.22	.654 0996	63.81
59	.588 0555	59.27	.609 6544	60.73	.631 7887	62.25	.654 4826	63.84
60	2.588 4112	59.30	2.610 0188	60.75	2.632 1622	62.28	2.654 8657	63.87

TABLE VI.

For finding the True Anomaly or the Time from the Perihelion in a Parabolic Orbit.

v.	132°		133°		134°		135°	
	log M.	Diff. 1″.	log M.	Diff. 1″.	log M.	Diff. 1″.	log M.	Diff. 1″.
0′	2.654 8657	63.87	2.678 1547	65.53	2.702 0562	67.27	2.726 5990	69.09
1	.655 2490	63.89	.678 5480	65.56	.702 4600	67.30	.727 0137	69.12
2	.655 6324	63.92	.678 9414	65.59	.702 8638	67.33	.727 4285	69.15
3	.656 0160	63.95	.679 3350	65.61	.703 2679	67.36	.727 8435	69.19
4	.656 3998	63.97	.679 7288	65.64	.703 6721	67.39	.728 2587	69.22
5	2.656 7837	64.00	2.680 1227	65.67	2.704 0766	67.42	2.728 6741	69.25
6	.657 1678	64.03	.680 5168	65.70	.704 4812	67.45	.729 0897	69.28
7	.657 5521	64.06	.680 9111	65.73	.704 8860	67.48	.729 5055	69.31
8	.657 9365	64.08	.681 3056	65.76	.705 2909	67.51	.729 9215	69.34
9	.658 3211	64.11	.681 7002	65.79	.705 6961	67.54	.730 3376	69.37
10	2.658 7058	64.14	2.682 0950	65.81	2.706 1014	67.57	2.730 7539	69.40
11	.659 0907	64.17	.682 4900	65.84	.706 5069	67.60	.731 1705	69.44
12	.659 4758	64.19	.682 8851	65.87	.706 9126	67.63	.731 5872	69.47
13	.659 8611	64.22	.683 2804	65.90	.707 3184	67.66	.732 0041	69.50
14	.660 2465	64.25	.683 6759	65.93	.707 7244	67.69	.732 4212	69.53
15	2.660 6320	64.28	2.684 0716	65.96	2.708 1307	67.72	2.732 8385	69.56
16	.661 0178	64.30	.684 4674	65.99	.708 5371	67.75	.733 2559	69.59
17	.661 4037	64.33	.684 8634	66.01	.708 9436	67.78	.733 6736	69.62
18	.661 7897	64.36	.685 2596	66.04	.709 3504	67.81	.734 0914	69.66
19	.662 1760	64.38	.685 6559	66.07	.709 7573	67.84	.734 5094	69.69
20	2.662 5623	64.41	2.686 0524	66.10	2.710 1645	67.87	2.734 9277	69.72
21	.662 9489	64.44	.686 4491	66.13	.710 5718	67.90	.735 3461	69.75
22	.663 3356	64.47	.686 8460	66.16	.710 9792	67.93	.735 7647	69.78
23	.663 7225	64.49	.687 2430	66.19	.711 3869	67.96	.736 1835	69.81
24	.664 1096	64.52	.687 6402	66.22	.711 7947	67.99	.736 6025	69.85
25	2.664 4968	64.55	2.688 0376	66.25	2.712 2028	68.02	2.737 0216	69.88
26	.664 8842	64.57	.688 4352	66.27	.712 6110	68.05	.737 4410	69.91
27	.665 2717	64.60	.688 8329	66.30	.713 0194	68.08	.737 8605	69.94
28	.665 6594	64.63	.689 2308	66.33	.713 4279	68.11	.738 2803	69.97
29	.666 0473	64.66	.689 6289	66.36	.713 8367	68.14	.738 7002	70.00
30	2.666 4354	64.69	2.690 0272	66.39	2.714 2456	68.17	2.739 1203	70.04
31	.666 8236	64.72	.690 4256	66.42	.714 6547	68.20	.739 5406	70.07
32	.667 2120	64.74	.690 8242	66.45	.715 0640	68.23	.739 9612	70.10
33	.667 6005	64.77	.691 2230	66.48	.715 4735	68.26	.740 3819	70.13
34	.667 9892	64.80	.691 6219	66.51	.715 8832	68.29	.740 8027	70.16
35	2.668 3781	64.83	2.692 0210	66.54	2.716 2930	68.32	2.741 2238	70.20
36	.668 7672	64.86	.692 4203	66.56	.716 7031	68.35	.741 6451	70.23
37	.669 1564	64.88	.692 8198	66.59	.717 1133	68.38	.742 0666	70.26
38	.669 5457	64.91	.693 2194	66.62	.717 5237	68.41	.742 4882	70.29
39	.669 9353	64.94	.693 6193	66.65	.717 9342	68.44	.742 9101	70.32
40	2.670 3250	64.97	2.694 0193	66.68	2.718 3450	68.48	2.743 3321	70.36
41	.670 7149	65.00	.694 4194	66.71	.718 7560	68.51	.743 7543	70.39
42	.671 1050	65.02	.694 8198	66.74	.719 1671	68.54	.744 1768	70.42
43	.671 4952	65.05	.695 2203	66.77	.719 5784	68.57	.744 5994	70.45
44	.671 8856	65.08	.695 6210	66.80	.719 9899	68.60	.745 0222	70.48
45	2.672 2761	65.11	2.696 0219	66.83	2.720 4016	68.63	2.745 4452	70.52
46	.672 6668	65.13	.696 4229	66.86	.720 8135	68.66	.745 8684	70.55
47	.673 0577	65.16	.696 8242	66.89	.721 2255	68.69	.746 2918	70.58
48	.673 4488	65.19	.697 2256	66.92	.721 6377	68.72	.746 7154	70.61
49	.673 8400	65.22	.697 6272	66.95	.722 0502	68.75	.747 1391	70.65
50	2.674 2314	65.25	2.698 0289	66.97	2.722 4628	68.78	2.747 5631	70.68
51	.674 6230	65.28	.698 4308	67.00	.722 8756	68.81	.747 9873	70.71
52	.675 0147	65.30	.698 8330	67.03	.723 2885	68.84	.748 4116	70.74
53	.675 4066	65.33	.699 2353	67.06	.723 7017	68.88	.748 8362	70.78
54	.675 7987	65.36	.699 6377	67.09	.724 1150	68.91	.749 2609	70.81
55	2.676 1909	65.39	2.700 0404	67.12	2.724 5286	68.94	2.749 6859	70.84
56	.676 5833	65.42	.700 4432	67.15	.724 9423	68.97	.750 1110	70.87
57	.676 9759	65.44	.700 8462	67.18	.725 3562	69.00	.750 5364	70.90
58	.677 3687	65.47	.701 2494	67.21	.725 7703	69.03	.750 9619	70.94
59	.677 7616	65.50	.701 6527	67.24	.726 1846	69.06	.751 3876	70.97
60	2.678 1547	65.53	2.702 0562	67.27	2.726 5990	69.09	2.751 8135	71.00

TABLE VI.

For finding the True Anomaly or the Time from the Perihelion in a Parabolic Orbit.

v.	136°		137°		138°		139°	
	log M.	Diff. 1″.	log M.	Diff. 1″.	log M.	Diff. 1″.	log M.	Diff. 1″.
0′	2.751 8135	71.00	2.777 7322	73.01	2.804 3895	75.11	2.831 8224	77.32
1	.752 2396	71.03	.778 1703	73.04	.804 8403	75.14	.832 2864	77.35
2	.752 6659	71.07	.778 6087	73.07	.805 2912	75.18	.832 7506	77.39
3	.753 0925	71.10	.779 0472	73.11	.805 7424	75.21	.833 2151	77.43
4	.753 5192	71.13	.779 4859	73.14	.806 1938	75.25	.833 6798	77.47
5	2.753 9461	71.17	2.779 9249	73.18	2.806 6454	75.29	2.834 1447	77.50
6	.754 3732	71.20	.780 3641	73.21	.807 0973	75.32	.834 6098	77.54
7	.754 8004	71.23	.780 8034	73.24	.807 5493	75.36	.835 0752	77.58
8	.755 2279	71.26	.781 2430	73.28	.808 0016	75.40	.835 5408	77.62
9	.755 6556	71.30	.781 6828	73.31	.808 4541	75.43	.836 0066	77.66
10	2.756 0835	71.33	2.782 1228	73.35	2.808 9068	75.47	2.836 4727	77.69
11	.756 5116	71.36	.782 5630	73.38	.809 3597	75.50	.836 9390	77.73
12	.756 9399	71.40	.783 0034	73.42	.809 8128	75.54	.837 4055	77.77
13	.757 3683	71.43	.783 4440	73.45	.810 2662	75.58	.837 8722	77.81
14	.757 7970	71.46	.783 8848	73.49	.810 7197	75.61	.838 3392	77.85
15	2.758 2259	71.49	2.784 3258	73.53	2.811 1735	75.65	2.838 8064	77.89
16	.758 6549	71.53	.784 7671	73.56	.811 6275	75.69	.839 2738	77.92
17	.759 0842	71.56	.785 2085	73.59	.812 0817	75.72	.839 7414	77.96
18	.759 5137	71.59	.785 6502	73.63	.812 5362	75.76	.840 2093	78.00
19	.759 9433	71.63	.786 0920	73.66	.812 9908	75.79	.840 6774	78.04
20	2.760 3732	71.66	2.786 5341	73.70	2.813 4457	75.83	2.841 1458	78.08
21	.760 8032	71.69	.786 9764	73.73	.813 9008	75.87	.841 6144	78.11
22	.761 2335	71.73	.787 4189	73.76	.814 3561	75.90	.842 0832	78.15
23	.761 6639	71.76	.787 8615	73.80	.814 8117	75.94	.842 5522	78.19
24	.762 0946	71.79	.788 3044	73.83	.815 2674	75.98	.843 0215	78.23
25	2.762 5255	71.83	2.788 7476	73.87	2.815 7234	76.01	2.843 4909	78.27
26	.762 9565	71.86	.789 1909	73.90	.816 1796	76.05	.843 9607	78.31
27	.763 3878	71.89	.789 6344	73.94	.816 6360	76.09	.844 4306	78.35
28	.763 8192	71.93	.790 0781	73.97	.817 0927	76.12	.844 9008	78.38
29	.764 2509	71.96	.790 5221	74.01	.817 5495	76.16	.845 3712	78.42
30	2.764 6827	71.99	2.790 9662	74.04	2.818 0066	76.20	2.845 8419	78.46
31	.765 1148	72.03	.791 4106	74.08	.818 4639	76.23	.846 3128	78.50
32	.765 5470	72.06	.791 8552	74.11	.818 9214	76.27	.846 7839	78.54
33	.765 9795	72.09	.792 3000	74.15	.819 3792	76.31	.847 2553	78.58
34	.766 4121	72.13	.792 7450	74.18	.819 8371	76.34	.847 7268	78.62
35	2.766 8450	72.16	2.793 1902	74.22	2.820 2953	76.38	2.848 1986	78.66
36	.767 2781	72.19	.793 6356	74.25	.820 7537	76.42	.848 6707	78.69
37	.767 7113	72.23	.794 0813	74.29	.821 2123	76.46	.849 1430	78.73
38	.768 1448	72.26	.794 5271	74.32	.821 6712	76.49	.849 6155	78.77
39	.768 5784	72.29	.794 9731	74.36	.822 1302	76.53	.850 0882	78.81
40	2.769 0123	72.33	2.795 4194	74.40	2.822 5895	76.57	2.850 5612	78.85
41	.769 4464	72.36	.795 8659	74.43	.823 0491	76.60	.851 0344	78.89
42	.769 8806	72.39	.796 3126	74.47	.823 5088	76.64	.851 5079	78.93
43	.770 3151	72.43	.796 7595	74.50	.823 9688	76.68	.851 9816	78.97
44	.770 7498	72.46	.797 2066	74.54	.824 4289	76.72	.852 4555	79.01
45	2.771 1846	72.50	2.797 6539	74.58	2.824 8894	76.75	2.852 9297	79.05
46	.771 6197	72.53	.798 1015	74.61	.825 3500	76.79	.853 4041	79.08
47	.772 0550	72.56	.798 5492	74.64	.825 8108	76.83	.853 8787	79.12
48	.772 4905	72.60	.798 9972	74.68	.826 2719	76.87	.854 3535	79.16
49	.772 9262	72.63	.799 4454	74.71	.826 7332	76.90	.854 8286	79.20
50	2.773 3621	72.67	2.799 8938	74.75	2.827 1947	76.94	2.855 3040	79.24
51	.773 7982	72.70	.800 3424	74.79	.827 6565	76.98	.855 7795	79.28
52	.774 2344	72.73	.800 7912	74.82	.828 1185	77.01	.856 2553	79.32
53	.774 6709	72.77	.801 2402	74.86	.828 5807	77.05	.856 7314	79.36
54	.775 1077	72.80	.801 6895	74.89	.829 0431	77.09	.857 2077	79.40
55	2.775 5446	72.84	2.802 1390	74.93	2.829 5058	77.13	2.857 6842	79.44
56	.775 9817	72.87	.802 5886	74.96	.829 9686	77.16	.858 1609	79.48
57	.776 4190	72.90	.803 0385	75.00	.830 4317	77.20	.858 6379	79.52
58	.776 8565	72.94	.803 4886	75.04	.830 8951	77.24	.859 1151	79.56
59	.777 2942	72.97	.803 9390	75.08	.831 3586	77.28	.859 5926	79.60
60	2.777 7322	73.01	2.804 3895	75.11	2.831 8224	77.32	2.860 0703	79.64

TABLE VI.

For finding the True Anomaly or the Time from the Perihelion in a Parabolic Orbit.

v.	140°		141°		142°		143°	
	log M.	Diff. 1″.	log M.	Diff. 1″.	log M.	Diff. 1″.	log M.	Diff. 1″.
0′	2.860 0703	79.64	2.889 1754	82.08	2.919 1831	84.65	2.950 1420	87.37
1	.860 5482	79.68	.889 6680	82.12	.919 6911	84.70	.950 6664	87.41
2	.861 0264	79.72	.890 1609	82.16	.920 1994	84.74	.951 1910	87.46
3	.861 5048	79.76	.890 6540	82.20	.920 7080	84.78	.951 7159	87.50
4	.861 9835	79.80	.891 1473	82.25	.921 2169	84.83	.952 2411	87.55
5	2.862 4624	79.84	2.891 6409	82.29	2.921 7260	84.87	2.952 7665	87.60
6	.862 9415	79.88	.892 1348	82.33	.922 2353	84.92	.953 2923	87.65
7	.863 4209	79.92	.892 6289	82.37	.922 7450	84.96	.953 8183	87.69
8	.863 9005	79.96	.893 1233	82.41	.923 2549	85.01	.954 3446	87.74
9	.864 3803	80.00	.893 6179	82.46	.923 7650	85.05	.954 8711	87.79
10	2.864 8604	80.04	2.894 1127	82.50	2.924 2755	85.10	2.955 3980	87.83
11	.865 3408	80.08	.894 6078	82.54	.924 7862	85.14	.955 9251	87.88
12	.865 8213	80.12	.895 1032	82.58	.925 2972	85.18	.956 4525	87.93
13	.866 3021	80.16	.895 5989	82.63	.925 8084	85.23	.956 9802	87.97
14	.866 7832	80.20	.896 0948	82.67	.926 3199	85.27	.957 5082	88.02
15	2.867 2645	80.24	2.896 5909	82.71	2.926 8317	85.32	2.958 0365	88.07
16	.867 7460	80.28	.897 0873	82.75	.927 3437	85.36	.958 5651	88.11
17	.868 2278	80.32	.897 5839	82.79	.927 8560	85.41	.959 0939	88.16
18	.868 7098	80.36	.898 0808	82.84	.928 3686	85.45	.959 6230	88.21
19	.869 1921	80.40	.898 5780	82.88	.928 8814	85.50	.960 1524	88.26
20	2.869 6746	80.44	2.899 0754	82.92	2.929 3945	85.54	2.960 6821	88.30
21	.870 1573	80.48	.899 5730	82.96	.929 9079	85.59	.961 2120	88.35
22	.870 6403	80.52	.900 0709	83.01	.930 4216	85.63	.961 7423	88.40
23	.871 1235	80.56	.900 5691	83.05	.930 9355	85.68	.962 2728	88.45
24	.871 6070	80.60	.901 0675	83.09	.931 4497	85.72	.962 7036	88.49
25	2.872 0907	80.64	2.901 5662	83.13	2.931 9641	85.77	2.963 3347	88.54
26	.872 5747	80.68	.902 0651	83.18	.932 4788	85.81	.963 8661	88.59
27	.873 0589	80.72	.902 5643	83.22	.932 9938	85.86	.964 3978	88.64
28	.873 5433	80.76	.903 0638	83.26	.933 5091	85.91	.964 9297	88.68
29	.874 0280	80.80	.903 5635	83.31	.934 0247	85.95	.965 4620	88.73
30	2.874 5129	80.84	2.904 0635	83.35	2.934 5405	85.99	2.965 9945	88.78
31	.874 9981	80.88	.904 5637	83.39	.935 0565	86.04	.966 5273	88.83
32	.875 4835	80.92	.905 0642	83.43	.935 5729	86.08	.967 0604	88.87
33	.875 9692	80.96	.905 5649	83.48	.936 0895	86.13	.967 5938	88.92
34	.876 4551	81.01	.906 0659	83.52	.936 6064	86.17	.968 1275	88.97
35	2.876 9413	81.05	2.906 5672	83.56	2.937 1236	86.22	2.968 6615	89.02
36	.877 4277	81.09	.907 0687	83.61	.937 6410	86.26	.969 1957	89.07
37	.877 9143	81.13	.907 5704	83.65	.938 1587	86.31	.969 7303	89.12
38	.878 4012	81.17	.908 0725	83.69	.938 6767	86.35	.970 2651	89.17
39	.878 8883	81.21	.908 5748	83.74	.939 1950	86.40	.970 8002	89.21
40	2.879 3757	81.25	2.909 0773	83.78	2.939 7135	86.45	2.971 3356	89.26
41	.879 8633	81.29	.909 5801	83.82	.940 2323	86.49	.971 8713	89.31
42	.880 3512	81.33	.910 0832	83.87	.940 7514	86.54	.972 4073	89.36
43	.880 8393	81.37	.910 5865	83.91	.941 2708	86.58	.972 9436	89.40
44	.881 3277	81.42	.911 0901	83.95	.941 7904	86.63	.973 4801	89.45
45	2.881 8163	81.46	2.911 5940	83.99	2.942 3103	86.67	2.974 0170	89.50
46	.882 3052	81.50	.912 0981	84.04	.942 8305	86.72	.974 5541	89.55
47	.882 7943	81.54	.912 6024	84.08	.943 3510	86.77	.975 0916	89.60
48	.883 2837	81.58	.913 1070	84.13	.943 8717	86.81	.975 6293	89.65
49	.883 7733	81.62	.913 6119	84.17	.944 3927	86.86	.976 1673	89.69
50	2.884 2631	81.66	2.914 1171	84.22	2.944 9140	86.90	2.976 7056	89.74
51	.884 7532	81.70	.914 6225	84.26	.945 4355	86.95	.977 2442	89.79
52	.885 2436	81.75	.915 1282	84.30	.945 9574	87.00	.977 7831	89.84
53	.885 7342	81.79	.915 6341	84.34	.946 4795	87.04	.978 3223	89.89
54	.886 2251	81.83	.916 1403	84.39	.947 0019	87.09	.978 8618	89.94
55	2.886 7162	81.87	2.916 6468	84.43	2.947 5245	87.13	2.979 4015	89.99
56	.887 2075	81.91	.917 1535	84.48	.948 0475	87.18	.979 9416	90.03
57	.887 6991	81.95	.917 6605	84.52	.948 5707	87.23	.980 4820	90.08
58	.888 1910	81.99	.918 1678	84.56	.949 0942	87.27	.981 1226	90.13
59	.888 6831	82.04	.918 6753	84.61	.949 6180	87.32	.981 6636	90.18
60	2.889 1754	82.08	2.919 1831	84.65	2.950 1420	87.37	2.982 1048	90.23

TABLE VI.

For finding the True Anomaly or the Time from the Perihelion in a Parabolic Orbit.

v.	144°		145°		146°		147°	
	log M.	Diff. 1″.	log M.	Diff. 1″.	log M.	Diff. 1″.	log M.	Diff. 1″.
0′	2.982 1048	90.23	3.015 1281	93.26	3.049 2733	96.47	3.084 6070	99.87
1	.982 6463	90.28	.015 6878	93.31	.049 8522	96.52	.085 2064	99.92
2	.983 1882	90.33	.016 2478	93.36	.050 4315	96.58	.085 8061	99.98
3	.983 7303	90.38	.016 8082	93.42	.051 0112	96.63	.086 4062	100.04
4	.984 2727	90.43	.017 3688	93.47	.051 5911	96.69	.087 0066	100.10
5	2.984 8154	90.48	3.017 9298	93.52	3.052 1714	96.74	3.087 6073	100.16
6	.985 3584	90.53	.018 4911	93.57	.052 7520	96.80	.088 2085	100.22
7	.985 9017	90.58	.019 0526	93.62	.053 3329	96.85	.088 8099	100.28
8	.986 4453	90.63	.019 6145	93.68	.053 9142	96.91	.089 4118	100.33
9	.986 9892	90.67	.020 1768	93.73	.054 4959	96.96	.090 0140	100.39
10	2.987 5334	90.72	3.020 7393	93.78	3.055 0778	97.01	3.090 6165	100.45
11	.988 0779	90.77	.021 3021	93.83	.055 6601	97.07	.091 2194	100.51
12	.988 6227	90.82	.021 8653	93.89	.056 2427	97.13	.091 8226	100.57
13	.989 1678	90.87	.022 4288	93.94	.056 8256	97.19	.092 4262	100.63
14	.989 7132	90.92	.022 9926	93.99	.057 4089	97.24	.093 0302	100.69
15	2.990 2589	90.97	3.023 5567	94.04	3.057 9925	97.30	3.093 6345	100.75
16	.990 8049	91.02	.024 1211	94.10	.058 5765	97.35	.094 2392	100.81
17	.991 3512	91.07	.024 6859	94.15	.059 1608	97.41	.094 8442	100.87
18	.991 8977	91.12	.025 2509	94.20	.059 7454	97.47	.095 4496	100.93
19	.992 4446	91.17	.025 8163	94.26	.060 3304	97.52	.096 0553	100.98
20	2.992 9918	91.22	3.026 3820	94.31	3.060 9157	97.58	3.096 6614	101.04
21	.993 5393	91.27	.026 9480	94.36	.061 5013	97.63	.097 2678	101.10
22	.994 0871	91.32	.027 5143	94.41	.062 0873	97.69	.097 8746	101.16
23	.994 6351	91.37	.028 0810	94.47	.062 6736	97.75	.098 4818	101.22
24	.995 1835	91.42	.028 6479	94.52	.063 2602	97.80	.099 0893	101.28
25	2.995 7322	91.47	3.029 2152	94.57	3.063 8472	97.86	3.099 6972	101.34
26	.996 2812	91.52	.029 7828	94.63	.064 4345	97.91	.100 3054	101.40
27	.996 8305	91.57	.030 3507	94.68	.065 0222	97.97	.100 9140	101.46
28	.997 3801	91.62	.030 9190	94.73	.065 6101	98.03	.101 5230	101.52
29	.997 9300	91.67	.031 4875	94.79	.066 1985	98.08	.102 1323	101.58
30	2.998 4802	91.72	3.032 0564	94.84	3.066 7872	98.14	3.102 7420	101.64
31	.999 0307	91.77	.032 6256	94.89	.067 3762	98.20	.103 3520	101.70
32	.999 5815	91.82	.033 1951	94.94	.067 9655	98.25	.103 9624	101.76
33	3.000 1326	91.87	.033 7650	95.00	.068 5552	98.31	.104 5732	101.82
34	.000 6840	91.93	.034 3351	95.05	.069 1453	98.37	.105 1843	101.88
35	3.001 2357	91.98	3.034 9056	95.11	3.069 7357	98.42	3.105 7958	101.94
36	.001 7877	92.03	.035 4764	95.16	.070 3264	98.48	.106 4076	102.00
37	.002 3400	92.08	.036 0475	95.22	.070 9174	98.54	.107 0198	102.07
38	.002 8926	92.13	.036 6190	95.27	.071 5088	98.60	.107 6324	102.13
39	.003 4456	92.18	.037 1908	95.32	.072 1006	98.65	.108 2454	102.19
40	3.003 9988	92.23	3.037 7629	95.38	3.072 6927	98.71	3.108 8587	102.25
41	.004 5523	92.28	.038 3353	95.43	.073 2851	98.77	.109 4723	102.31
42	.005 1062	92.33	.038 9080	95.48	.073 8779	98.82	.110 0864	102.37
43	.005 6603	92.38	.039 4811	95.54	.074 4710	98.88	.110 7008	102.43
44	.006 2148	92.44	.040 0545	95.60	.075 0645	98.94	.111 3155	102.49
45	3.006 7696	92.49	3.040 6282	95.65	3.075 6583	99.00	3.111 9306	102.55
46	.007 3246	92.54	.041 2023	95.70	.076 2524	99.05	.112 5461	102.61
47	.007 8800	92.59	.041 7767	95.76	.076 8469	99.11	.113 1620	102.67
48	.008 4357	92.64	.042 3514	95.81	.077 4418	99.17	.113 7782	102.73
49	.008 9917	92.69	.042 9264	95.86	.078 0370	99.23	.114 3948	102.80
50	3.009 5480	92.74	3.043 5017	95.92	3.078 6325	99.28	3.115 0118	102.86
51	.010 1046	92.79	.044 0774	95.97	.079 2284	99.34	.115 6291	102.92
52	.010 6615	92.85	.044 6534	96.03	.079 8246	99.40	.116 2468	102.98
53	.011 2188	92.90	.045 2297	96.08	.080 4212	99.46	.116 8649	103.04
54	.011 7763	92.95	.045 8064	96.14	.081 0181	99.52	.117 4833	103.10
55	3.012 3342	93.00	3.046 3834	96.19	3.081 6154	99.57	3.118 1022	103.16
56	.012 8923	93.05	.046 9607	96.25	.082 2130	99.63	.118 7213	103.23
57	.013 4508	93.10	.047 5383	96.30	.082 8110	99.69	.119 3409	103.29
58	.014 0096	93.16	.048 1163	96.36	.083 4093	99.75	.119 9608	103.35
59	.014 5687	93.21	.048 6946	96.41	.084 0080	99.81	.120 5811	103.41
60	3.015 1281	93.26	3.049 2733	96.47	3.084 6070	99.87	3.121 2018	103.48

TABLE VI.

For finding the True Anomaly or the Time from the Perihelion in a Parabolic Orbit.

v.	148°		149°		150°		151°	
	log M.	Diff. 1″.	log M.	Diff. 1″.	log M.	Diff. 1″.	log M.	Diff. 1″.
0′	3.121 2018	103.48	3.159 1367	107.31	3.198 4984	111.41	3.239 3820	115.77
1	.121 8228	103.54	.159 7808	107.38	.199 1671	111.48	.240 0768	115.85
2	.122 4442	103.60	.160 4253	107.45	.199 8361	111.55	.240 7722	115.92
3	.123 0660	103.66	.161 0702	107.51	.200 5056	111.62	.241 4680	116.00
4	.123 6882	103.72	.161 7154	107.58	.201 1755	111.69	.242 1642	116.08
5	3.124 3107	103.79	3.162 3611	107.65	3.201 8459	111.76	3.242 8608	116.15
6	.124 9336	103.85	.163 0072	107.71	.202 5166	111.83	.243 5580	116.23
7	.125 5569	103.91	.163 6536	107.78	.203 1878	111.90	.244 2556	116.30
8	.126 1805	103.97	.164 3005	107.85	.203 8594	111.97	.244 9536	116.38
9	.126 8045	104.04	.164 9478	107.91	.204 5315	112.04	.245 6521	116.45
10	3.127 4289	104.10	3.165 5955	107.98	3.205 2040	112.11	3.246 3511	116.53
11	.128 0537	104.16	.166 2435	108.04	.205 8769	112.18	.247 0505	116.61
12	.128 6789	104.22	.166 8920	108.11	.206 5502	112.26	.247 7503	116.68
13	.129 3044	104.29	.167 5409	108.18	.207 2239	112.33	.248 4507	116.76
14	.129 9303	104.35	.168 1901	108.25	.207 8981	112.40	.249 1515	116.84
15	3.130 5566	104.41	3.168 8398	108.31	3.208 5727	112.47	3.249 8527	116.91
16	.131 1833	104.48	.169 4899	108.38	.209 2478	112.54	.250 5544	116.99
17	.131 8103	104.54	.170 1404	108.45	.209 9232	112.61	.251 2566	117.07
18	.132 4377	104.60	.170 7913	108.51	.210 5991	112.69	.251 9592	117.14
19	.133 0655	104.67	.171 4426	108.58	.211 2755	112.76	.252 6623	117.22
20	3.133 6937	104.73	3.172 0942	108.65	3.211 9522	112.83	3.253 3658	117.30
21	.134 3223	104.79	.172 7463	108.72	.212 6294	112.90	.254 0698	117.37
22	.134 9512	104.86	.173 3988	108.78	.213 3070	112.97	.254 7743	117.45
23	.135 5805	104.92	.174 0517	108.85	.213 9851	113.05	.255 4792	117.53
24	.136 2102	104.98	.174 7051	108.92	.214 6636	113.12	.256 1846	117.60
25	3.136 8403	105.05	3.175 3588	108.99	3.215 3425	113.19	3.256 8905	117.68
26	.137 4708	105.11	.176 0129	109.06	.216 0219	113.26	.257 5968	117.76
27	.138 1016	105.17	.176 6674	109.12	.216 7017	113.34	.258 3036	117.84
28	.138 7329	105.24	.177 3224	109.19	.217 3819	113.41	.259 0109	117.91
29	.139 3645	105.30	.177 9777	109.26	.218 0626	113.48	.259 7186	117.99
30	3.139 9965	105.36	3.178 6335	109.33	3.218 7437	113.55	3.260 4268	118.07
31	.140 6289	105.43	.179 2897	109.40	.219 4252	113.63	.261 1354	118.15
32	.141 2616	105.49	.179 9462	109.46	.220 1072	113.70	.261 8446	118.23
33	.141 8948	105.55	.180 6032	109.53	.220 7896	113.77	.262 5542	118.30
34	.142 5283	105.62	.181 2606	109.60	.221 4724	113.84	.263 2642	118.38
35	3.143 1622	105.68	3.181 9184	109.67	3.222 1557	113.92	3.263 9747	118.46
36	.143 7965	105.75	.182 5766	109.74	.222 8395	113.99	.264 6857	118.54
37	.144 4312	105.81	.183 2353	109.81	.223 5236	114.06	.265 3972	118.62
38	.145 0663	105.87	.183 8943	109.87	.224 2082	114.14	.266 1091	118.70
39	.145 7018	105.94	.184 5538	109.94	.224 8933	114.21	.266 8216	118.77
40	3.146 3376	106.00	3.185 2136	110.01	3.225 5788	114.28	3.267 5345	118.85
41	.146 9739	106.07	.185 8739	110.08	.226 2647	114.36	.268 2478	118.93
42	.147 6105	106.14	.186 5346	110.15	.226 9511	114.43	.268 9616	119.01
43	.148 2475	106.20	.187 1957	110.22	.227 6379	114.51	.269 6759	119.09
44	.148 8849	106.27	.187 8572	110.29	.228 3252	114.58	.270 3907	119.17
45	3.149 5227	106.33	3.188 5192	110.36	3.229 0129	114.65	3.271 1060	119.25
46	.150 1609	106.40	.189 1815	110.43	.229 7010	114.73	.271 8217	119.33
47	.150 7995	106.46	.189 8443	110.50	.230 3896	114.80	.272 5379	119.41
48	.151 4385	106.53	.190 5075	110.57	.231 0786	114.88	.273 2546	119.49
49	.152 0778	106.59	.191 1711	110.64	.231 7681	114.95	.273 9717	119.57
50	3.152 7176	106.66	3.191 8351	110.71	3.232 4581	115.03	3.274 6894	119.65
51	.153 3577	106.72	.192 4996	110.77	.233 1484	115.10	.275 4075	119.73
52	.153 9983	106.79	.193 1644	110.84	.233 8392	115.17	.276 1261	119.81
53	.154 6392	106.85	.193 8297	110.91	.234 5305	115.25	.276 8452	119.89
54	.155 2805	106.92	.194 4954	110.98	.235 2222	115.32	.277 5647	119.97
55	3.155 9222	106.99	3.195 1615	111.05	3.235 9144	115.40	3.278 2848	120.05
56	.156 5643	107.05	.195 8281	111.12	.236 6070	115.47	.279 0053	120.13
57	.157 2068	107.12	.196 4950	111.19	.237 3001	115.55	.279 7263	120.21
58	.157 8497	107.18	.197 1624	111.26	.237 9936	115.62	.280 4477	120.29
59	.158 4930	107.25	.197 8302	111.34	.238 6876	115.70	.281 1697	120.37
60	3.159 1367	107.31	3.198 4984	111.41	3.239 3820	115.77	3.281 8921	120.45

TABLE VI.

For finding the True Anomaly or the Time from the Perihelion in a Parabolic Orbit.

v.	152°		153°		154°		155°	
	log M.	Diff. 1″.	log M.	Diff. 1″.	log M.	Diff. 1″.	log M.	Diff. 1″.
0′	3.281 8921	120.45	3.326 1448	125.46	3.372 2684	130.85	3.420 4064	136.66
1	.282 6151	120.53	.326 8978	125.55	.373 0538	130.94	.421 2266	136.76
2	.283 3385	120.61	.327 6513	125.63	.373 8397	131.04	.422 0475	136.86
3	.284 0624	120.69	.328 4054	125.72	.374 6262	131.13	.422 8690	136.96
4	.284 7868	120.77	.329 1600	125.81	.375 4133	131.22	.423 6910	137.06
5	3.285 5116	120.85	3.329 9151	125.89	3.376 2009	131.32	3.424 5137	137.16
6	.286 2370	120.93	.330 6707	125.98	.376 9890	131.41	.425 3370	137.26
7	.286 9628	121.01	.331 4268	126.07	.377 7778	131.50	.426 1609	137.37
8	.287 6891	121.10	.332 1835	126.16	.378 5671	131.60	.426 9854	137.47
9	.288 4160	121.18	.332 9407	126.24	.379 3570	131.69	.427 8105	137.57
10	3.289 1433	121.26	3.333 6984	126.33	3.380 1474	131.79	3.428 6362	137.67
11	.289 8711	121.34	.334 4567	126.42	.380 9384	131.88	.429 4626	137.77
12	.290 5993	121.42	.335 2154	126.51	.381 7300	131.98	.430 2895	137.88
13	.291 3281	121.50	.335 9747	126.59	.382 5221	132.07	.431 1171	137.98
14	.292 0574	121.59	.336 7346	126.68	.383 3148	132.16	.431 9452	138.08
15	3.292 7872	121.67	3.337 4949	126.77	3.384 1081	132.26	3.432 7740	138.18
16	.293 5174	121.75	.338 2558	126.86	.384 9019	132.35	.433 6034	138.29
17	.294 2481	121.83	.339 0172	126.95	.385 6963	132.45	.434 4334	138.39
18	.294 9794	121.91	.339 7792	127.03	.386 4913	132.54	.435 2641	138.49
19	.295 7111	122.00	.340 5417	127.12	.387 2869	132.64	.436 0953	138.59
20	3.296 4433	122.08	3.341 3047	127.21	3.388 0830	132.73	3.436 9272	138.70
21	.297 1761	122.16	.342 0682	127.30	.388 8797	132.83	.437 7597	138.80
22	.297 9093	122.24	.342 8323	127.39	.389 6770	132.93	.438 5928	138.90
23	.298 6430	122.33	.343 5969	127.48	.390 4749	133.02	.439 4266	139.01
24	.299 3772	122.41	.344 3620	127.57	.391 2733	133.12	.440 2609	139.11
25	3.300 1119	122.49	3.345 1277	127.66	3.392 0723	133.22	3.441 0959	139.22
26	.300 8471	122.58	.345 8939	127.75	.392 8719	133.31	.441 9315	139.32
27	.301 5828	122.66	.346 6606	127.84	.393 6720	133.41	.442 7677	139.42
28	.302 3190	122.74	.347 4279	127.93	.394 4728	133.50	.443 6046	139.53
29	.303 0557	122.83	.348 1958	128.02	.395 2741	133.60	.444 4421	139.63
30	3.303 7929	122.91	3.348 9641	128.11	3.396 0760	133.70	3.445 2802	139.74
31	.304 5306	122.99	.349 7330	128.19	.396 8785	133.79	.446 1189	139.84
32	.305 2688	123.08	.350 5024	128.28	.397 6815	133.89	.446 9583	139.95
33	.306 0075	123.16	.351 2724	128.37	.398 4852	133.99	.447 7983	140.05
34	.306 7468	123.24	.352 0429	128.46	.399 2894	134.09	.448 6389	140.16
35	3.307 4865	123.33	3.352 8140	128.55	3.400 0942	134.19	3.449 4802	140.26
36	.308 2267	123.41	.353 5856	128.65	.400 8996	134.28	.450 3221	140.37
37	.308 9674	123.50	.354 3577	128.74	.401 7056	134.38	.451 1646	140.47
38	.309 7086	123.58	.355 1304	128.83	.402 5122	134.48	.452 0077	140.57
39	.310 4504	123.66	.355 9037	128.92	.403 3193	134.57	.452 8515	140.68
40	3.311 1926	123.75	3.356 6774	129.01	3.404 1270	134.67	3.453 6959	140.79
41	.311 9354	123.83	.357 4517	129.10	.404 9354	134.77	.454 5410	140.90
42	.312 6786	123.92	.358 2266	129.19	.405 7443	134.87	.455 3867	141.00
43	.313 4224	124.00	.359 0020	129.28	.406 5538	134.97	.456 2330	141.11
44	.314 1667	124.09	.359 7780	129.37	.407 3639	135.07	.457 0800	141.21
45	3.314 9115	124.17	3.360 5545	129.46	3.408 1746	135.16	3.457 9276	141.32
46	.315 6567	124.26	.361 3316	129.56	.408 9859	135.26	.458 7759	141.43
47	.316 4025	124.34	.362 1092	129.65	.409 7977	135.36	.459 6248	141.54
48	.317 1489	124.43	.362 8873	129.74	.410 6102	135.46	.460 4743	141.64
49	.317 8957	124.51	.363 6660	129.83	.411 4233	135.56	.461 3245	141.75
50	3.318 6430	124.60	3.364 4453	129.92	3.412 2369	135.66	3.462 1753	141.86
51	.319 3909	124.68	.365 2251	130.01	.413 0512	135.76	.463 0268	141.97
52	.320 1392	124.77	.366 0055	130.11	.413 8660	135.86	.463 8789	142.07
53	.320 8881	124.86	.366 7864	130.20	.414 6815	135.96	.464 7317	142.18
54	.321 6375	124.94	.367 5679	130.29	.415 4975	136.06	.465 5851	142.29
55	3.322 3874	125.03	3.368 3499	130.38	3.416 3142	136.16	3.466 4392	142.40
56	.323 1379	125.11	.369 1325	130.48	.417 1314	136.26	.467 2939	142.51
57	.323 8888	125.20	.369 9156	130.57	.417 9492	136.36	.468 1492	142.61
58	.324 6403	125.29	.370 6993	130.66	.418 7677	136.46	.469 0052	142.72
59	.325 3923	125.37	.371 4836	130.76	.419 5867	136.56	.469 8619	142.83
60	3.326 1448	125.46	3.372 2684	130.85	3.420 4064	136.66	3.470 7192	142.94

TABLE VI.

For finding the True Anomaly or the Time from the Perihelion in a Parabolic Orbit.

v.	156°		157°		158°		159°	
	log M.	Diff. 1″.	log M.	Diff. 1″.	log M.	Diff. 1″.	log M.	Diff. 1″.
0′	3.470 7192	142.94	3.523 3875	149.75	3.578 6154	157.17	3.636 6351	165.28
1	.471 5772	143.05	.524 2864	149.87	.579 5588	157.30	.637 6272	165.42
2	.472 4358	143.16	.525 1860	149.99	.580 5030	157.43	.638 6202	165.56
3	.473 2951	143.27	.526 0863	150.11	.581 4480	157.56	.639 6140	165.71
4	.474 1550	143.38	.526 9873	150.23	.582 3937	157.69	.640 6087	165.85
5	3.475 0156	143.49	3.527 8890	150.35	3.583 3403	157.82	3.641 6042	165.99
6	.475 8769	143.60	.528 7915	150.47	.584 2876	157.95	.642 6006	166.13
7	.476 7388	143.71	.529 6947	150.59	.585 2357	158.08	.643 5978	166.28
8	.477 6014	143.82	.530 5985	150.71	.586 1846	158.21	.644 5959	166.42
9	.478 4646	143.93	.531 5031	150.83	.587 1342	158.34	.645 5948	166.56
10	3.479 3285	144.04	3.532 4085	150.95	3.588 0847	158.47	3.646 5946	166.71
11	.480 1931	144.15	.533 3145	151.07	.589 0359	158.61	.647 5953	166.85
12	.481 0583	144.26	.534 2213	151.19	.589 9880	158.74	.648 5968	166.99
13	.481 9242	144.37	.535 1288	151.31	.590 9408	158.87	.649 5992	167.14
14	.482 7907	144.48	.536 0370	151.43	.591 8944	159.00	.650 6025	167.28
15	3.483 6579	144.59	3.536 9459	151.55	3.592 8488	159.13	3.651 6066	167.42
16	.484 5258	144.70	.537 8556	151.67	.593 8040	159.26	.652 6116	167.57
17	.485 3944	144.81	.538 7660	151.79	.594 7600	159.40	.653 6175	167.72
18	.486 2636	144.93	.539 6771	151.91	.595 7167	159.53	.654 6242	167.86
19	.487 1335	145.04	.540 5890	152.04	.596 6743	159.66	.655 6318	168.01
20	3.488 0040	145.15	3.541 5015	152.16	3.597 6327	159.79	3.656 6403	168.15
21	.488 8752	145.26	.542 4148	152.28	.598 5919	159.93	.657 6497	168.30
22	.489 7472	145.37	.543 3289	152.40	.599 5518	160.06	.658 6599	168.45
23	.490 6198	145.49	.544 2436	152.52	.600 5126	160.19	.659 6710	168.59
24	.491 4930	145.60	.545 1591	152.65	.601 4742	160.33	.660 6830	168.74
25	3.492 3670	145.71	3.546 0754	152.77	3.602 4365	160.46	3.661 6959	168.89
26	.493 2416	145.82	.546 9924	152.89	.603 3997	160.60	.662 7096	169.03
27	.494 1168	145.94	.547 9101	153.01	.604 3637	160.73	.663 7243	169.18
28	.494 9928	146.05	.548 8285	153.14	.605 3285	160.87	.664 7398	169.33
29	.495 8695	146.16	.549 7477	153.26	.606 2941	161.00	.665 7562	169.48
30	3.496 7468	146.28	3.550 6677	153.38	3.607 2605	161.14	3.666 7735	169.62
31	.497 6248	146.39	.551 5883	153.51	.608 2277	161.27	.667 7917	169.77
32	.498 5035	146.50	.552 5097	153.63	.609 1957	161.41	.668 8108	169.92
33	.499 3828	146.62	.553 4319	153.75	.610 1646	161.54	.669 8308	170.07
34	.500 2629	146.73	.554 3548	153.88	.611 1342	161.68	.670 8516	170.22
35	3.501 1436	146.85	3.555 2785	154.00	3.612 1047	161.81	3.671 8734	170.37
36	.502 0250	146.96	.556 2029	154.13	.613 0760	161.95	.672 8961	170.52
37	.502 9071	147.08	.557 1280	154.25	.614 0481	162.09	.673 9196	170.67
38	.503 7899	147.19	.558 0539	154.38	.615 0210	162.22	.674 9441	170.82
39	.504 6734	147.31	.558 9806	154.50	.615 9948	162.36	.675 9694	170.97
40	3.505 5576	147.42	3.559 9080	154.63	3.616 9693	162.50	3.676 9957	171.12
41	.506 4425	147.54	.560 8361	154.75	.617 9447	162.63	.678 0228	171.27
42	.507 3280	147.65	.561 7650	154.88	.618 9209	162.77	.679 0509	171.42
43	.508 2143	147.77	.562 6947	155.01	.619 8980	162.91	.680 0799	171.57
44	.509 1012	147.88	.563 6251	155.13	.620 8758	163.05	.681 1098	171.72
45	3.509 9889	148.00	3.564 5562	155.26	3.621 8545	163.18	3.682 1406	171.87
46	.510 8772	148.11	.565 4882	155.38	.622 8340	163.32	.683 1723	172.03
47	.511 7662	148.23	.566 4209	155.51	.623 8144	163.46	.684 2049	172.18
48	.512 6560	148.34	.567 3543	155.64	.624 7956	163.60	.685 2384	172.33
49	.513 5464	148.46	.568 2885	155.76	.625 7776	163.74	.686 2728	172.48
50	3.514 4375	148.58	3.569 2235	155.89	3.626 7604	163.88	3.687 3082	172.64
51	.515 3294	148.70	.570 1592	156.02	.627 7441	164.02	.688 3445	172.79
52	.516 2219	148.81	.571 0957	156.15	.628 7287	164.16	.689 3817	172.94
53	.517 1151	148.93	.572 0330	156.27	.629 7140	164.30	.690 4198	173.10
54	.518 0090	149.05	.572 9710	156.40	.630 7002	164.44	.691 4588	173.25
55	3.518 9037	149.17	3.573 9098	156.53	3.631 6873	164.58	3.692 4988	173.40
56	.519 7990	149.28	.574 8494	156.66	.632 6751	164.72	.693 5397	173.56
57	.520 6951	149.40	.575 7897	156.79	.633 6638	164.86	.694 5815	173.71
58	.521 5918	149.52	.576 7308	156.92	.634 6534	165.00	.695 6243	173.87
59	.522 4893	149.64	.577 6727	157.04	.635 6438	165.14	.696 6680	174.02
60	3.523 3875	149.75	3.578 6154	157.17	3.636 6351	165.28	3.697 7126	174.18

TABLE VI.

For finding the True Anomaly or the Time from the Perihelion in a Parabolic Orbit.

v.	160°		161°		162°		163°	
	log M.	Diff. 1″.	log M.	Diff. 1″.	log M.	Diff. 1″.	log M.	Diff. 1″.
0′	3.697 7126	174.18	3.762 1539	183.99	3.830 3147	194.87	3.902 6107	207.00
1	.698 7581	174.34	.763 2584	184.16	.831 4845	195.06	.903 8534	207.21
2	.699 8046	174.49	.764 3639	184.34	.832 6554	195.25	.905 0973	207.43
3	.700 8520	174.65	.765 4704	184.51	.833 8275	195.44	.906 3425	207.64
4	.701 9003	174.80	.766 5780	184.68	.835 0008	195.64	.907 5890	207.86
5	3.702 9496	174.96	3.767 6867	184.86	3.836 1752	195.83	3.908 8368	208.08
6	.703 9999	175.12	.768 7963	185.03	.837 3508	196.02	.910 0859	208.29
7	.705 0511	175.28	.769 9070	185.20	.838 5275	196.22	.911 3363	208.51
8	.706 1032	175.43	.771 0187	185.38	.839 7054	196.41	.912 5880	208.72
9	.707 1562	175.59	.772 1315	185.55	.840 8844	196.60	.913 8410	208.94
10	3.708 2102	175.75	3.773 2454	185.73	3.842 0646	196.80	3.915 0953	209.16
11	.709 2652	175.91	.774 3603	185.90	.843 2460	196.99	.916 3509	209.38
12	.710 3211	176.07	.775 4762	186.08	.844 4286	197.19	.917 6078	209.60
13	.711 3780	176.22	.776 5932	186.25	.845 6123	197.38	.918 8661	209.81
14	.712 4358	176.38	.777 7112	186.43	.846 7972	197.58	.920 1256	210.03
15	3.713 4946	176.54	3.778 8303	186.60	3.847 9833	197.78	3.921 3865	210.25
16	.714 5543	176.70	.779 9505	186.78	.849 1705	197.97	.922 6487	210.48
17	.715 6150	176.86	.781 0717	186.96	.850 3589	198.17	.923 9122	210.70
18	.716 6766	177.02	.782 1940	187.14	.851 5486	198.37	.925 1770	210.92
19	.717 7392	177.18	.783 3174	187.31	.852 7394	198.57	.926 4432	211.14
20	3.718 8028	177.34	3.784 4418	187.49	3.853 9314	198.76	3.927 7107	211.36
21	.719 8673	177.50	.785 5672	187.67	.855 1245	198.96	.928 9795	211.58
22	.720 9328	177.66	.786 6938	187.85	.856 3189	199.16	.930 2497	211.81
23	.721 9993	177.83	.787 8214	188.03	.857 5145	199.36	.931 5212	212.03
24	.723 0668	178.00	.788 9501	188.21	.858 7112	199.56	.932 7940	212.25
25	3.724 1352	178.15	3.790 0799	188.39	3.859 9092	199.76	3.934 0682	212.48
26	.725 2045	178.31	.791 2108	188.57	.861 1084	199.96	.935 3438	212.70
27	.726 2749	178.47	.792 3427	188.75	.862 3087	200.16	.936 6207	212.93
28	.727 3462	178.63	.793 4757	188.93	.863 5103	200.36	.937 8989	213.15
29	.728 4185	178.80	.794 6098	189.11	.864 7131	200.56	.939 1785	213.38
30	3.729 4918	178.96	3.795 7450	189.29	3.865 9171	200.77	3.940 4595	213.61
31	.730 5661	179.13	.796 8812	189.47	.867 1223	200.97	.941 7418	213.83
32	.731 6413	179.29	.798 0186	189.65	.868 3287	201.17	.943 0254	214.06
33	.732 7176	179.45	.799 1571	189.83	.869 5363	201.37	.944 3105	214.29
34	.733 7948	179.62	.800 2966	190.01	.870 7452	201.58	.945 5969	214.52
35	3.734 8730	179.78	3.801 4372	190.20	3.871 9552	201.78	3.946 8847	214.74
36	.735 9522	179.95	.802 5790	190.38	.873 1665	201.98	.948 1738	214.97
37	.737 0324	180.11	.803 7218	190.56	.874 3791	202.19	.949 4644	215.20
38	.738 1136	180.28	.804 8657	190.65	.875 5928	202.39	.950 7563	215.43
39	.739 1957	180.45	.806 0108	190.93	.876 8078	202.60	.952 0496	215.66
40	3.740 2789	180.61	3.807 1569	191.11	3.878 0240	202.80	3.953 3443	216.90
41	.741 3631	180.78	.808 3041	191.30	.879 2414	203.01	.954 6403	216.13
42	.742 4482	180.94	.809 4525	191.48	.880 4601	203.22	.955 9378	216.36
43	.743 5344	181.11	.810 6020	191.67	.881 6800	203.42	.957 2366	216.59
44	.744 6216	181.28	.811 7525	191.86	.882 9012	203.63	.958 5369	216.82
45	3.745 7097	181.45	3.812 9042	192.04	3.884 1236	203.84	3.959 8385	217.06
46	.746 7989	181.61	.814 0570	192.23	.885 3473	204.05	.961 1416	217.29
47	.747 8891	181.78	.815 2110	192.41	.886 5722	204.26	.962 4460	217.53
48	.748 9803	181.95	.816 3660	192.60	.887 7983	204.46	.963 7519	217.76
49	.750 0725	182.12	.817 5222	192.79	.889 0257	204.67	.965 0592	218.00
50	3.751 1657	182.29	3.818 6795	192.98	3.890 2544	204.88	3.966 3678	218.23
51	.752 2599	182.46	.819 8379	193.16	.891 4843	205.09	.967 6779	218.47
52	.753 3552	182.63	.820 9974	193.35	.892 7155	205.31	.968 9895	218.70
53	.754 4514	182.80	.822 1581	193.54	.893 9480	205.52	.970 3024	218.94
54	.755 5487	182.97	.823 3199	193.73	.895 1817	205.73	.971 6168	219.18
55	3.756 6470	183.14	3.824 4829	193.92	3.896 4167	205.94	3.972 9326	219.42
56	.757 7464	183.31	.825 6470	194.11	.897 6529	206.15	.974 2498	219.66
57	.758 8467	183.48	.826 8122	194.30	.898 8905	206.36	.975 5684	219.90
58	.759 9481	183.65	.827 9785	194.49	.900 1293	206.57	.976 8885	220.13
59	.761 0505	183.82	.829 1460	194.68	.901 3694	206.79	.978 2100	220.37
60	3.762 1539	183.99	3.830 3147	194.87	3.902 6107	207.00	3.979 5330	220.61

TABLE VI.

For finding the True Anomaly or the Time from the Perihelion in a Parabolic Orbit.

v.	164°		165°		166°		167°	
	log M.	Diff. 1″.	log M.	Diff. 1″.	log M.	Diff. 1″.	log M.	Diff. 1″.
0′	3.979 5330	220.62	4.061 6673	236.01	4.149 7198	253.57	4.244 5537	273.78
1	.980 8574	220.86	.063 0842	236.28	.151 2422	253.88	.246 1975	274.14
2	.982 1833	221.10	.064 5027	236.56	.152 7664	254.19	.247 8434	274.51
3	.983 5106	221.34	.065 9229	236.83	.154 2925	254.51	.249 4916	274.87
4	.984 8394	221.58	.067 3447	237.11	.155 8205	254.83	.251 1419	275.24
5	3.986 1696	221.83	4.068 7682	237.39	4.157 3504	255.14	4.252 7944	275.60
6	.987 5013	222.07	.070 1933	237.66	.158 8822	255.46	.254 4491	275.97
7	.988 8345	222.31	.071 6201	237.94	.160 4159	255.78	.256 1061	276.34
8	.990 1691	222.56	.073 0486	238.22	.161 9515	256.10	.257 7652	276.71
9	.991 5051	222.80	.074 4787	238.50	.163 4891	256.42	.259 4266	277.08
10	3.992 8427	223.05	4.075 9106	238.78	4.165 0285	256.74	4.261 0902	277.45
11	.994 1817	223.29	.077 3441	239.06	.166 5699	257.06	.262 7560	277.82
12	.995 5222	223.54	.078 7792	239.34	.168 1132	257.38	.264 4240	278.20
13	.996 8642	223.79	.080 2161	239.62	.169 6585	257.70	.266 0943	278.57
14	.998 2077	224.03	.081 6546	239.90	.171 2056	258.02	.267 7669	278.95
15	3.999 5527	224.28	4.083 0948	240.18	4.172 7547	258.35	4.269 4417	279.32
16	4.000 8991	224.53	.084 5368	240.46	.174 3058	258.67	.271 1187	279.70
17	.002 2471	224.78	.085 9804	240.75	.175 8588	259.00	.272 7981	280.08
18	.003 5965	225.03	.087 4257	241.03	.177 4138	259.33	.274 4797	280.46
19	.004 9474	225.28	.088 8728	241.32	.178 9707	259.65	.276 1635	280.84
20	4.006 2999	225.53	4.090 3215	241.60	4.180 5296	259.98	4.277 8497	281.22
21	.007 6538	225.78	.091 7720	241.89	.182 0905	260.31	.279 5381	281.60
22	.009 0093	226.04	.093 2242	242.08	.183 6534	260.64	.281 2289	281.98
23	.010 3663	226.29	.094 6781	242.56	.185 2182	260.97	.282 9219	282.36
24	.011 7248	226.54	.096 1337	242.75	.186 7850	261.30	.284 6173	282.75
25	4.013 0848	226.79	4.097 5911	243.04	4.188 3538	261.63	4.286 3149	283.14
26	.014 4463	227.05	.099 0502	243.33	.189 9246	261.96	.288 0149	283.52
27	.015 8093	227.30	.100 5110	243.62	.191 4974	262.30	.289 7172	283.91
28	.017 1739	227.55	.101 9736	243.91	.193 0722	262.63	.291 4218	284.30
29	.018 5400	227.81	.103 4379	244.20	.194 6490	262.97	.293 1288	284.69
30	4.019 9077	228.06	4.104 9040	244.49	4.196 2278	263.30	4.294 8381	285.08
31	.021 2769	228.32	.106 3718	244.78	.197 8086	263.64	.296 5498	285.47
32	.022 6476	228.58	.107 8414	245.08	.199 3915	263.98	.298 2638	285.87
33	.024 0199	228.84	.109 3127	245.37	.200 9764	264.32	.299 9802	286.26
34	.025 3937	229.09	.110 7858	245.67	.202 5633	264.66	.301 6990	286.66
35	4.026 7691	229.35	4.112 2607	245.96	4.204 1523	265.00	4.303 4201	287.05
36	.028 1460	229.62	.113 7374	246.26	.205 7433	265.34	.305 1436	287.45
37	.029 5245	229.88	.115 2158	246.55	.207 3363	265.68	.306 8695	287.85
38	.030 9045	230.14	.116 6960	246.85	.208 9314	266.02	.308 5978	288.25
39	.032 2861	230.40	.118 1780	247.15	.210 5286	266.37	.310 3285	288.65
40	4.033 6693	230.66	4.119 6618	247.45	4.212 1278	266.71	4.312 0616	289.05
41	.035 0540	230.92	.121 1474	247.75	.213 7291	267.06	.313 7971	289.45
42	.036 4404	231.18	.122 6348	248.05	.215 3325	267.40	.315 5350	289.86
43	.037 8283	231.45	.124 1239	248.35	.216 9379	267.75	.317 2753	290.26
44	.039 2177	231.71	.125 6149	248.65	.218 5455	268.10	.319 0181	290.67
45	4.040 6088	231.97	4.127 1077	248.95	4.220 1551	268.44	4.320 7633	291.07
46	.042 0015	232.24	.128 6023	249.25	.221 7668	268.79	.322 5110	291.48
47	.043 3957	232.51	.130 0988	249.56	.223 3806	269.14	.324 2611	291.89
48	.044 7915	232.77	.131 5970	249.86	.224 9965	269.50	.326 0137	292.30
49	.046 1890	233.04	.133 0971	250.17	.226 6146	269.85	.327 7688	292.71
50	4.047 5880	233.31	4.134 5990	250.47	4.228 2347	270.20	4.329 5263	293.13
51	.048 9887	233.57	.136 1028	250.78	.229 8570	270.55	.331 2863	293.54
52	.050 3909	233.84	.137 6084	251.08	.231 4814	270.91	.333 0487	293.95
53	.051 7948	234.11	.139 1158	251.39	.233 1079	271.27	.334 8137	294.37
54	.053 2003	234.38	.140 6251	251.70	.234 7366	271.62	.336 5812	294.79
55	4.054 6074	234.65	4.142 1362	252.01	4.236 3674	271.98	4.338 3511	295.20
56	.056 0161	234.92	.143 6492	252.32	.238 0003	272.34	.340 1236	295.62
57	.057 4264	235.19	.145 1641	252.63	.239 6354	272.70	.341 8986	296.04
58	.058 8384	235.46	.146 6808	252.94	.241 2727	273.06	.343 6762	296.47
59	.060 2520	235.73	.148 1994	253.25	.242 9121	273.42	.345 4562	296.89
60	4.061 6673	236.01	4.149 7198	253.57	4.244 5537	273.78	4.347 2388	297.31

TABLE VI.

For finding the True Anomaly or the Time from the Perihelion in a Parabolic Orbit.

v.	168°		169°		170°		171°	
	log M.	Diff. 1″.	log M.	Diff. 1″.	log M.	Diff. 1″.	log M.	Diff. 1″.
0′	4.347 2388	297.31	4.459 1242	325.07	4.581 9445	358.31	4.717 9835	398.87
1	.349 0240	297.74	.461 0761	325.57	.584 0962	358.92	.720 3790	399.62
2	.350 8117	298.16	.463 0311	326.08	.586 2516	359.53	.722 7790	400.38
3	.352 6019	298.59	.464 9891	326.59	.588 4106	360.15	.725 1835	401.14
4	.354 3948	299.02	.466 9501	327.10	.590 5734	360.76	.727 5926	401.90
5	4.356 1902	299.45	4.468 9142	327.61	4.592 7398	361.38	4.730 0063	402.66
6	.357 9882	299.88	.470 8814	328.12	.594 9100	362.00	.732 4245	403.43
7	.359 7888	300.31	.472 8517	328.64	.597 0838	362.62	.734 8474	404.19
8	.361 5919	300.75	.474 8250	329.15	.599 2615	363.25	.737 2749	404.96
9	.363 3977	301.18	.476 8015	329.67	.601 4428	363.88	.739 7070	405.74
10	4.365 2061	301.62	4.478 7811	330.19	4.603 6280	364.50	4.742 1438	406.52
11	.367 0171	302.05	.480 7637	330.71	.605 8169	365.14	.744 5852	407.30
12	.368 8308	302.49	.482 7495	331.23	.608 0096	365.77	.747 0314	408.08
13	.370 6470	302.93	.484 7385	331.75	.610 2061	366.40	.749 4822	408.87
14	.372 4659	303.37	.486 7306	332.28	.612 4064	367.04	.751 9378	409.66
15	4.374 2875	303.81	4.488 7258	332.81	4.614 6106	367.68	4.754 3981	410.45
16	.376 1117	304.26	.490 7242	333.33	.616 8186	368.32	.756 8632	411.24
17	.377 9386	304.70	.492 7258	333.86	.619 0304	368.96	.759 3330	412.04
18	.379 7681	305.15	.494 7306	334.40	.621 2461	369.61	.761 8077	412.84
19	.381 6003	305.59	.496 7386	334.93	.623 4657	370.26	.764 2872	413.65
20	4.383 4352	306.04	4.498 7498	335.46	4.625 6892	370.91	4.766 7715	414.46
21	.385 2728	306.49	.500 7642	336.00	.627 9166	371.56	.769 2606	415.27
22	.387 1131	306.94	.502 7818	336.54	.630 1480	372.21	.771 7547	416.08
23	.388 9561	307.39	.504 8026	337.08	.632 3832	372.87	.774 2536	416.90
24	.390 8019	307.85	.506 8267	337.62	.634 6224	373.53	.776 7574	417.72
25	4.392 6503	308.30	4.508 8541	338.16	4.636 8656	374.19	4.779 2662	418.54
26	.394 5015	308.76	.510 8847	338.71	.639 1127	374.86	.781 7799	419.37
27	.396 3554	309.21	.512 9186	339.26	.641 3639	375.52	.784 2986	420.20
28	.398 2121	309.67	.514 9558	339.80	.643 6190	376.19	.786 8222	421.03
29	.400 0715	310.13	.516 9962	340.35	.645 8781	376.86	.789 3509	421.86
30	4.401 9337	310.59	4.519 0400	340.91	4.648 1413	377.53	4.791 8846	422.70
31	.403 7986	311.06	.521 0871	341.46	.650 4085	378.21	.794 4233	423.54
32	.405 6663	311.52	.523 1376	342.02	.652 6798	378.89	.796 9671	424.39
33	.407 5368	311.99	.525 1913	342.57	.654 9552	379.57	.799 5160	425.24
34	.409 4102	312.45	.527 2484	343.13	.657 2346	380.25	.802 0700	426.09
35	4.411 2863	312.92	4.529 3089	343.69	4.659 5182	380.93	4.804 6291	426.95
36	.413 1652	313.39	.531 3728	344.26	.661 8059	381.62	.807 1934	427.81
37	.415 0469	313.86	.533 4400	344.82	.664 0977	382.31	.809 7628	428.67
38	.416 9315	314.33	.535 5106	345.39	.666 3936	383.00	.812 3374	429.53
39	.418 8189	314.80	.537 5846	345.95	.668 6937	383.70	.814 9172	430.40
40	4.420 7091	315.28	4.539 6620	346.52	4.670 9980	384.39	4.817 5022	431.28
41	.422 6022	315.75	.541 7429	347.09	.673 3064	385.09	.820 0925	432.15
42	.424 4982	316.23	.543 8272	347.67	.675 6191	385.80	.822 6881	433.03
43	.426 3970	316.71	.545 9149	348.24	.677 9360	386.50	.825 2889	433.91
44	.428 2987	317.19	.548 0061	348.82	.680 2571	387.21	.827 8950	434.80
45	4.430 2033	317.67	4.550 1007	349.40	4.682 5825	387.92	4.830 5065	435.69
46	.432 1108	318.16	.552 1989	349.98	.684 9121	388.63	.833 1234	436.59
47	.434 0212	318.64	.554 3005	350.56	.687 2460	389.34	.835 7456	437.48
48	.435 9345	319.13	.556 4056	351.15	.689 5842	390.06	.838 3732	438.38
49	.437 8507	319.61	.558 5143	351.73	.691 9268	390.78	.841 0062	439.29
50	4.439 7698	320.10	4.560 6264	352.32	4.694 2736	391.50	4.843 6446	440.20
51	.441 6919	320.59	.562 7421	352.91	.696 6248	392.23	.846 2886	441.11
52	.443 6169	321.08	.564 8614	353.50	.698 9803	392.96	.848 9380	442.03
53	.445 5449	321.58	.566 9842	354.10	.701 3402	393.68	.851 5929	442.95
54	.447 4758	322.07	.569 1106	354.69	.703 7046	394.42	.854 2533	443.87
55	4.449 4097	322.57	4.571 2405	355.29	4.706 0733	395.15	4.856 9193	444.80
56	.451 3466	323.06	.573 3741	355.89	.708 4464	395.89	.859 5909	445.73
57	.453 2865	323.56	.575 5113	356.49	.710 8240	396.63	.862 2680	446.66
58	.455 2294	324.06	.577 6521	357.10	.713 2060	397.38	.864 9508	447.60
59	.457 1753	324.56	.579 7965	357.70	.715 5925	398.12	.867 6392	448.54
60	4.459 1242	325.07	4.581 9445	358.31	4.717 9835	398.87	4.870 3333	449.49

TABLE VI.

For finding the True Anomaly or the Time from the Perihelion in a Parabolic Orbit.

v.	172°		173°		174°		175°	
	log M.	Diff. 1″.	log M.	Diff. 1″.	log M.	Diff. 1″.	log M.	Diff. 1″.
0′	4.870 3333	449.49	5.043 3285	514.47	5.243 3165	601.00	5.480 1373	722.00
1	.873 0331	450.44	.046 4191	515.71	.246 9276	602.69	.484 4765	724.42
2	.875 7386	451.39	.049 5171	516.96	.250 5488	604.38	.488 8304	726.87
3	.878 4499	452.35	.052 6226	518.21	.254 1802	606.08	.493 1989	729.33
4	.881 1668	453.31	.055 7356	519.47	.257 8218	607.80	.497 5823	731.80
5	4.883 8896	454.28	5.058 8562	520.73	5.261 4738	609.53	5.501 9806	734.30
6	.886 6182	455.25	.061 9843	522.00	.265 1361	611.26	.506 3939	736.81
7	.889 3526	456.23	.065 1202	523.28	.268 8089	613.00	.510 8223	739.33
8	.892 0929	457.20	.068 2637	524.56	.272 4922	614.75	.515 2659	741.87
9	.894 8391	458.19	.071 4149	525.85	.276 1860	616.52	.519 7248	744.44
10	4.897 5912	459.17	5.074 5738	527.14	5.279 8904	618.29	5.524 1992	747.02
11	.900 3492	460.16	.077 7406	528.44	.283 6055	620.08	.528 6890	749.61
12	.903 1132	461.16	.080 9151	529.75	.287 3313	621.87	.533 1946	752.23
13	.905 8831	462.16	.084 0976	531.06	.291 0680	623.67	.537 7158	754.86
14	.908 6591	463.16	.087 2879	532.38	.294 8154	625.49	.542 2529	757.51
15	4.911 4411	464.17	5.090 4862	533.71	5.298 5738	627.31	5.546 8060	760.18
16	.914 2291	465.18	.093 6924	535.04	.302 3432	629.15	.551 3751	762.87
17	.917 0233	466.20	.096 9067	536.38	.306 1237	631.00	.555 9605	765.58
18	.919 8235	467.22	.100 1290	537.73	.309 9152	632.85	.560 5621	768.31
19	.922 6299	468.25	.103 3594	539.08	.313 7179	634.72	.565 1802	771.05
20	4.925 4425	469.28	5.106 5980	540.44	5.317 5319	636.60	5.569 8148	773.82
21	.928 2612	470.31	.109 8447	541.81	.321 3571	638.49	.574 4661	776.61
22	.931 0862	471.35	.113 0997	543.18	.325 1938	640.39	.579 1341	779.41
23	.933 9174	472.39	.116 3629	544.56	.329 0418	642.30	.583 8190	782.24
24	.936 7549	473.44	.119 6344	545.95	.332 9014	644.23	.588 5210	785.08
25	4.939 5987	474.49	5.122 9143	547.34	5.336 7726	646.16	5.593 2401	787.95
26	.942 4489	475.55	.126 2026	548.74	.340 6554	648.11	.597 9764	790.84
27	.945 3053	476.61	.129 4992	550.15	.344 5499	650.07	.602 7302	793.75
28	.948 1682	477.68	.132 8044	551.57	.348 4562	652.04	.607 5014	796.68
29	.951 0375	478.75	.136 1181	552.99	.352 3744	654.02	.612 2903	799.63
30	4.953 9132	479.83	5.139 4403	554.42	5.356 3045	656.01	5.617 0970	802.60
31	.956 7954	480.91	.142 7711	555.86	.360 2466	658.02	.621 9216	805.60
32	.959 6841	481.99	.146 1106	557.30	.364 2007	660.04	.626 7642	808.62
33	.962 5793	483.08	.149 4588	558.75	.368 1671	662.07	.631 6250	811.66
34	.965 4811	484.18	.152 8157	560.21	.372 1456	664.11	.636 5041	814.72
35	4.968 3894	485.28	5.156 1813	561.68	5.376 1364	666.17	5.641 4017	817.81
36	.971 3044	486.38	.159 5558	563.16	.380 1396	668.24	.646 3179	820.92
37	.974 2260	487.49	.162 9392	564.64	.384 1553	670.32	.651 2528	824.05
38	.977 1543	488.61	.166 3315	566.13	.388 1834	672.41	.656 2065	827.21
39	.980 0893	489.73	.169 7328	567.63	.392 2242	674.52	.661 1793	830.39
40	4.983 0311	490.85	5.173 1431	569.13	5.396 2777	676.64	5.666 1713	833.60
41	.985 9795	491.98	.176 5624	570.65	.400 3439	678.77	.671 1825	836.83
42	.988 9348	493.12	.179 9908	572.17	.404 4229	680.92	.676 2132	840.08
43	.991 8970	494.26	.183 4284	573.70	.408 5149	683.08	.681 2635	843.36
44	.994 8659	495.40	.186 8752	575.24	.412 6199	685.25	.686 3336	846.67
45	4.997 8418	496.55	5.190 3312	576.78	5.416 7379	687.44	5.691 4236	850.00
46	5.000 8246	497.71	.193 7966	578.34	.420 8692	689.64	.696 5337	853.36
47	.003 8143	498.87	.197 2713	579.90	.425 0136	691.85	.701 6640	856.75
48	.006 8111	500.04	.200 7554	581.47	.429 1714	694.08	.706 8147	860.16
49	.009 8148	501.21	.204 2489	583.05	.433 3427	696.33	.711 9860	863.60
50	5.012 8256	502.39	5.207 7520	584.64	5.437 5274	698.59	5.717 1779	867.06
51	.015 8435	503.57	.211 2646	586.23	.441 7258	700.86	.722 3908	870.56
52	.018 8685	504.76	.214 7868	587.84	.445 9378	703.15	.727 6247	874.08
53	.021 9006	505.95	.218 3186	589.45	.450 1636	705.45	.732 8798	877.63
54	.024 9399	507.15	.221 8602	591.07	.454 4032	707.77	.738 1563	881.21
55	5.027 9864	508.36	5.225 4116	592.71	5.458 6568	710.10	5.743 4544	884.82
56	.031 0402	509.57	.228 9727	594.35	.462 9244	712.45	.748 7742	888.46
57	.034 1013	510.79	.232 5437	596.00	.467 2062	714.81	.754 1159	892.13
58	.037 1697	512.01	.236 1247	597.66	.471 5022	717.19	.759 4798	895.83
59	.040 2454	513.24	.239 7156	599.32	.475 8125	719.59	.764 8659	899.56
60	5.043 3285	514.47	5.243 3165	601.00	5.480 1373	722.00	5.770 2745	903.31

TABLE VI.

For finding the True Anomaly or the Time from the Perihelion in a Parabolic Orbit.

v.	176°		177°		178°		179°	
	log M.	Diff. 1″.	log M.	Diff. 1″.	log M.	Diff. 1″.	log M.	Diff. 1″.
0′	5.770 2745	903.3	6.144 6289	1205.3	6.672 5724	1808.8	7.575 4640	3619
1	.775 7058	907.1	.151 8807	1212.0	.683 4709	1824.0	.597 3596	3680
2	.781 1599	910.9	.159 1733	1218.8	.694 4613	1839.5	.619 6295	3744
3	.786 6370	914.8	.166 5070	1225.7	.705 5454	1855.3	.642 2868	3809
4	.792 1374	918.7	.173 8823	1232.7	.716 7248	1871.3	.665 3452	3877
5	5.797 6612	922.6	6.181 2997	1239.8	6.728 0010	1887.5	7.688 8192	3948
6	.803 2086	926.6	.188 7597	1246.9	.739 3758	1904.1	.712 7239	4021
7	.808 7798	930.6	.196 2628	1254.1	.750 8509	1921.0	.737 0756	4097
8	.814 3751	934.6	.203 8095	1261.4	.762 4279	1938.2	.761 8913	4176
9	.819 9946	938.6	.211 4002	1268.8	.774 1090	1955.6	.787 1889	4257
10	5.825 6386	942.7	6.219 0354	1276.3	6.785 8958	1973.4	7.812 9876	4343
11	.831 3073	946.8	.226 7158	1283.8	.797 7904	1991.5	.839 3075	4431
12	.837 0008	951.0	.234 4419	1291.5	.809 7946	2010.0	.866 1702	4524
13	.842 7195	955.2	.242 2142	1299.2	.821 9106	2028.8	.893 5986	4620
14	.848 4634	959.5	.250 0333	1307.1	.834 1404	2048.0	.921 6170	4720
15	5.854 2329	963.7	6.257 8997	1315.0	6.846 4863	2067.5	7.950 2513	4825
16	.860 0282	968.0	.265 8139	1323.0	.858 9503	2087.3	7.979 5292	4935
17	.865 8495	972.4	.273 7766	1331.1	.871 5348	2107.6	8.009 4802	5050
18	.871 6970	976.8	.281 7884	1339.4	.884 2422	2128.3	.040 1361	5170
19	.877 5710	981.2	.289 8499	1347.7	.897 0749	2149.4	.071 [illegible]309	5296
20	5.883 4717	985.7	6.297 9617	1356.2	6.910 0353	2170.9	8.103 7011	5428
21	.889 3993	990.2	.306 1244	1364.7	.923 1261	2192.8	.136 6857	5568
22	.895 3542	994.8	.314 3387	1373.3	.936 3498	2215.2	.170 5274	5714
23	.901 3365	999.4	.322 6052	1382.1	.949 7093	2238.0	.205 2717	5869
24	.907 3465	1004.0	.330 9247	1391.0	.963 2073	2261.4	.240 9679	6032
25	5.913 3845	1008.7	6.339 2977	1400.0	6.976 8466	2285.2	8.277 6700	6204
26	.919 4507	1013.4	.347 7249	1409.1	6.990 6304	2309.6	.315 4361	6387
27	.925 5454	1018.1	.356 2072	1418.3	7.004 5616	2334.3	.354 3298	6580
28	.931 6688	1022.9	.364 7451	1427.6	.018 6437	2359.7	.394 4205	6786
29	.937 8213	1027.8	.373 3395	1437.1	.032 8796	2385.7	.435 7842	7004
30	5.944 0030	1032.7	6.381 9910	1446.7	7.047 2729	2412.2	8.478 5044	7238
31	.950 2144	1037.6	.390 7005	1456.4	.061 8271	2439.4	.522 6731	7488
32	.956 4556	1042.6	.399 4687	1466.2	.076 5458	2467.1	.568 3920	7755
33	.962 7269	1047.7	.408 2965	1476.2	.091 4329	2495.4	.615 7739	8042
34	.969 0287	1052.9	.417 1846	1486.4	.106 4921	2524.5	.664 9442	8352
35	5.975 3613	1058.0	6.426 1337	1496.7	7.121 7276	2554.2	8.716 0431	8686
36	.981 7249	1063.2	.435 1449	1507.0	.137 1434	2584.6	.769 2286	9048
37	.988 1198	1068.4	.444 2191	1517.6	.152 7440	2615.8	.824 6779	9441
38	5.994 5464	1073.7	.453 3569	1528.3	.168 5336	2647.6	.882 5925	9870
39	6.001 0050	1079.1	.462 5594	1539.2	.184 5171	2680.4	.943 2018	10340
40	6.007 4958	1084.5	6.471 8275	1550.2	7.200 6993	2713.9	9.006 7690	10857
41	.014 0192	1089.9	.481 1620	1561.3	.217 0850	2748.3	.073 5974	11429
42	.020 5756	1095.4	.490 5641	1572.6	.233 6796	2783.5	.144 0401	12064
43	.027 1652	1101.0	.500 0346	1584.1	.250 4884	2819.7	.218 5102	12773
44	.033 7885	1106.7	.509 5746	1595.8	.267 5170	2856.8	.297 4963	13572
45	6.040 4457	1112.4	6.519 1850	1607.7	7.284 7712	2894.8	9.381 5820	14476
46	.047 1372	1118.1	.528 8669	1619.6	.302 2571	2934.1	.471 4711	15510
47	.053 8634	1123.9	.538 6216	1631.8	.319 9810	2974.2	.568 0247	16704
48	.060 6246	1129.8	.548 4499	1644.2	.337 9494	3015.6	.672 3106	18096
49	.067 4212	1135.7	.558 3530	1656.8	.356 1692	3058.1	.785 6758	19741
50	6.074 2535	1141.7	6.568 3320	1669.6	7.374 6475	3101.7	9.909 8535	21715
51	.081 1219	1147.7	.578 3881	1682.4	.393 3918	3146.8	10.047 1256	24127
52	.088 0269	1153.8	.588 5227	1695.6	.412 4099	3193.0	.200 5829	27144
53	.094 9687	1160.0	.598 7368	1708.9	.431 7097	3240.7	.374 5584	31023
54	.101 9479	1166.3	.609 0317	1722.6	.451 2999	3289.9	.575 3986	36197
55	6.108 9647	1172.6	6.619 4086	1736.4	7.471 1892	3340.3	10.812 9421	43450
56	.116 0196	1179.0	.629 8689	1750.3	.491 3870	3392.6	11.103 6719	
57	.123 1131	1185.4	.640 4141	1764.5	.511 9029	3446.5	11.478 4880	
58	.130 2455	1192.0	.651 0455	1779.0	.532 7472	3502.1	12.006 7617	
59	.137 4173	1198.6	.661 7645	1793.8	.553 9305	3559.6	12.909 8516	
60	6.144 6289	1205.3	6.672 5724	1808.8	7.575 4640	3618.7		

TABLE VII.

For finding the True Anomaly in a Parabolic Orbit when v is nearly 180°.

w	Δ_0	Diff.	w	Δ_0	Diff.	w	Δ_0	Diff.
° ′	′ ″	″	° ′	′ ″	″	° ′	′ ″	″
155 0	3 23.09	3.35	**160** 0	1 6.70	1.37	**165** 0	0 15.85	0.87
5	19.74	3.31	5	5.33	1.36	10	14.98	0.82
10	16.43	3.26	10	3.97	1.33	20	14.16	0.78
15	13.17	3.22	15	2.64	1.31	30	13.38	0.75
20	9.95	3.18	20	1.33	1.29	40	12.63	0.72
25	6.77	3.14	25	0.04	1.26	50	11.91	0.69
155 30	3 3.63	3.09	**160** 30	0 58.78	1.24	**166** 0	0 11.22	0.65
35	0.54	3.05	35	57.54	1.23	10	10.57	0.62
40	2 57.49	3.01	40	56.31	1.20	20	9.95	0.59
45	54.48	2.97	45	55.11	1.18	30	9.36	0.56
50	51.51	2.93	50	53.93	1.16	40	8.80	0.54
55	48.58	2.89	55	52.77	1.14	50	8.26	0.51
156 0	2 45.69	2.85	**161** 0	0 51.63	1.13	**167** 0	0 7.75	0.48
5	42.84	2.81	5	50.50	1.10	10	7.27	0.46
10	40.03	2.77	10	49.40	1.08	20	6.81	0.44
15	37.26	2.73	15	48.32	1.06	30	6.37	0.41
20	34.53	2.70	20	47.26	1.05	40	5.96	0.39
25	31.83	2.66	25	46.21	1.02	50	5.57	0.37
156 30	2 29.17	2.62	**161** 30	0 45.19	1.01	**168** 0	0 5.20	0.36
35	26.55	2.58	35	44.18	0.99	10	4.84	0.33
40	23.97	2.54	40	43.19	0.97	20	4.51	0.31
45	21.43	2.51	45	42.22	0.96	30	4.20	0.30
50	18.92	2.48	50	41.26	0.93	40	3.90	0.28
55	16.44	2.44	55	40.33	0.92	50	3.62	0.26
157 0	2 14.00	2.41	**162** 0	0 39.41	0.90	**169** 0	0 3.36	0.25
5	11.59	2.37	5	38.51	0.89	10	3.11	0.23
10	9.22	2.33	10	37.62	0.87	20	2.88	0.22
15	6.89	2.31	15	36.75	0.85	30	2.66	0.20
20	4.58	2.27	20	35.90	0.84	40	2.46	0.19
25	2.31	2.23	25	35.06	0.82	50	2.27	0.18
157 30	2 0.08	2.19	**162** 30	0 34.24	0.81	**170** 0	0 2.09	0.17
35	1 57.89	2.17	35	33.43	0.79	10	1.92	0.16
40	55.72	2.15	40	32.64	0.78	20	1.76	0.14
45	53.57	2.11	45	31.86	0.76	30	1.62	0.14
50	51.46	2.07	50	31.10	0.75	40	1.48	0.13
55	49.39	2.04	55	30.35	0.73	50	1.35	0.12
158 0	1 47.35	2.01	**163** 0	0 29.62	0.72	**171** 0	0 1.23	0.11
5	45.34	1.99	5	28.90	0.70	10	1.12	0.10
10	43.35	1.96	10	28.20	0.69	20	1.02	0.09
15	41.39	1.92	15	27.51	0.68	30	0.93	0.09
20	39.47	1.90	20	26.83	0.67	40	0.84	0.08
25	37.57	1.87	25	26.16	0.65	50	0.76	0.08
158 30	1 35.70	1.83	**163** 30	0 25.51	0.63	**172** 0	0 0.68	0.07
35	33.87	1.81	35	24.88	0.63	10	0.61	0.06
40	32.06	1.78	40	24.25	0.61	20	0.55	0.06
45	30.28	1.76	45	23.64	0.60	30	0.49	0.05
50	28.52	1.72	50	23.04	0.59	40	0.44	0.05
55	26.80	1.70	55	22.45	0.57	50	0.39	0.04
159 0	1 25.10	1.67	**164** 0	0 21.88	0.57	**173** 0	0 0.35	0.04
5	23.43	1.65	5	21.31	0.55	10	0.31	0.04
10	21.78	1.62	10	20.76	0.54	20	0.27	0.03
15	20.16	1.59	15	20.22	0.53	30	0.24	0.03
20	18.57	1.57	20	19.69	0.51	40	0.21	0.02
25	17.00	1.55	25	19.18	0.51	50	0.19	0.03
159 30	1 15.45	1.51	**164** 30	0 18.67	0.50	**174** 0	0 0.16	0.09
35	13.94	1.50	35	18.17	0.48	**175** 0	0.07	0.05
40	12.44	1.47	40	17.69	0.48	**176** 0	0.02	0.01
45	10.97	1.44	45	17.21	0.46	**177** 0	0.01	0.01
50	9.53	1.43	50	16.75	0.46	**178** 0	0.00	0.00
55	8.10	1.40	55	16.29	0.44	**179** 0	0.00	0.00
160 0	1 6.70		**165** 0	0 15.85		**180** 0	0 0.00	

TABLE VIII.

For finding the Time from the Perihelion in a Parabolic Orbit.

v °	′	log N	Diff.	v °	′	log N	Diff.	v °	′	log N	Diff.
0	0	0.025 5763	14	**30**	0	0.020 7913	1545	**60**	0	0.008 8644	2186
	30	.025 5749	42		30	.020 6368	1566		30	.008 6458	2181
1	0	.025 5707	69	**31**	0	.020 4802	1587	**61**	0	.008 4277	2174
	30	.025 5638	96		30	.020 3215	1608		30	.008 2103	2169
2	0	.025 5542	124	**32**	0	.020 1607	1628	**62**	0	.007 9934	2160
	30	.025 5418	152		30	.019 9979	1649		30	.007 7774	2153
3	0	0.025 5266	179	**33**	0	0.019 8330	1668	**63**	0	0.007 5621	2144
	30	.025 5087	206		30	.019 6662	1688		30	.007 3477	2134
4	0	.025 4881	234	**34**	0	.019 4974	1707	**64**	0	.007 1343	2123
	30	.025 4647	261		30	.019 3267	1727		30	.006 9220	2112
5	0	.025 4386	289	**35**	0	.019 1540	1745	**65**	0	.006 7108	2100
	30	.025 4097	316		30	.018 9795	1765		30	.006 5008	2086
6	0	0.025 3781	344	**36**	0	0.018 8030	1782	**66**	0	0.006 2922	2073
	30	.025 3437	371		30	.018 6248	1800		30	.006 0849	2057
7	0	.025 3066	398	**37**	0	.018 4448	1819	**67**	0	.005 8792	2042
	30	.025 2668	425		30	.018 2629	1835		30	.005 6750	2025
8	0	.025 2243	452	**38**	0	.018 0794	1853	**68**	0	.005 4725	2008
	30	.025 1791	480		30	.017 8941	1869		30	.005 2717	1988
9	0	0.025 1311	506	**39**	0	0.017 7072	1886	**69**	0	0.005 0729	1969
	30	.025 0805	534		30	.017 5186	1903		30	.004 8760	1949
10	0	.025 0271	560	**40**	0	.017 3283	1918	**70**	0	.004 6811	1927
	30	.024 9711	587		30	.017 1365	1933		30	.004 4884	1904
11	0	.024 9124	614	**41**	0	.016 9432	1949	**71**	0	.004 2980	1880
	30	.024 8510	641		30	.016 7483	1963		30	.004 1100	1855
12	0	0.024 7869	668	**42**	0	0.016 5520	1978	**72**	0	0.003 9245	1829
	30	.024 7201	694		30	.016 3542	1992		30	.003 7416	1803
13	0	.024 6507	721	**43**	0	.016 1550	2005	**73**	0	.003 5613	1774
	30	.024 5786	747		30	.015 9545	2019		30	.003 3839	1745
14	0	.024 5039	773	**44**	0	.015 7526	2031	**74**	0	.003 2094	1714
	30	.024 4266	800		30	.015 5495	2045		30	.003 0380	1682
15	0	0.024 3466	825	**45**	0	0.015 3450	2056	**75**	0	0.002 8698	1649
	30	.024 2641	852		30	.015 1394	2068		30	.002 7049	1616
16	0	.024 1789	878	**46**	0	.014 9326	2079	**76**	0	.002 5433	1579
	30	.024 0911	903		30	.014 7247	2090		30	.002 3854	1543
17	0	.024 0008	929	**47**	0	.014 5157	2100	**77**	0	.002 2311	1505
	30	.023 9079	954		30	.014 3057	2110		30	.002 0806	1465
18	0	0.023 8125	980	**48**	0	0.014 0947	2120	**78**	0	0.001 9341	1424
	30	.023 7145	1005		30	.013 8827	2129		30	.001 7917	1382
19	0	.023 6140	1031	**49**	0	.013 6698	2137	**79**	0	.001 6535	1339
	30	.023 5109	1055		30	.013 4561	2145		30	.001 5196	1293
20	0	.023 4054	1081	**50**	0	.013 2416	2153	**80**	0	.001 3903	1247
	30	.023 2973	1105		30	.013 0263	2160		30	.001 2656	1198
21	0	0.023 1868	1130	**51**	0	0.012 8103	2167	**81**	0	0.001 1458	1149
	30	.023 0738	1154		30	.012 5936	2172		30	.001 0309	1098
22	0	.022 9584	1179	**52**	0	.012 3764	2179	**82**	0	.000 9211	1045
	30	.022 8405	1203		30	.012 1585	2183		30	.000 8166	991
23	0	.022 7202	1227	**53**	0	.011 9402	2187	**83**	0	.000 7175	935
	30	.022 5975	1251		30	.011 7215	2191		30	.000 6240	876
24	0	0.022 4724	1275	**54**	0	0.011 5024	2195	**84**	0	0.000 5364	818
	30	.022 3449	1298		30	.011 2829	2197		30	.000 4546	756
25	0	.022 2151	1322	**55**	0	.011 0632	2200	**85**	0	.000 3790	694
	30	.022 0829	1345		30	.010 8432	2201		30	.000 3096	628
26	0	.021 9484	1368	**56**	0	.010 6231	2202	**86**	0	.000 2468	562
	30	.021 8116	1390		30	.010 4029	2202		30	.000 1906	493
27	0	0.021 6726	1414	**57**	0	0.010 1827	2202	**87**	0	0.000 1413	423
	30	.021 5312	1436		30	.009 9625	2201		30	.000 0990	351
28	0	.021 3876	1458	**58**	0	.009 7424	2199	**88**	0	.000 0639	276
	30	.021 2418	1480		30	.009 5225	2197		30	.000 0363	200
29	0	.021 0938	1502	**59**	0	.009 3028	2194	**89**	0	.000 0163	122
	30	.020 9436	1523		30	.009 0834	2190		30	.000 0041	41
30	0	0.020 7913		**60**	0	0.008 8644		**90**	0	0.000 0000	

TABLE VIII.

For finding the Time from the Perihelion in a Parabolic Orbit.

v		log *N′*	Diff.	*v*		log *N′*	Diff.	*v*		log *N′*	Diff.
°	′			°	′			°	′		
90	0	0.000 0000		**120**	0	9.963 1069		**150**	0	9.889 0321	
	30	9.999 9876	124		30	.962 0074	10995		30	.887 8738	11583
91	0	.999 9507	369	**121**	0	.960 8971	11103	**151**	0	.886 7259	11479
	30	.999 8893	614		30	.959 7764	11207		30	.885 5887	11372
92	0	.999 8039	854	**122**	0	.958 6454	11310	**152**	0	.884 4627	11260
	30	.999 6944	1095		30	.957 5046	11408		30	.883 3481	11146
93	0	9.999 5613	1331	**123**	0	9.956 3542	11504	**153**	0	9.882 2455	11026
	30	.999 4046	1567		30	.955 1945	11597		30	.881 1552	10903
94	0	.999 2246	1800	**124**	0	.954 0258	11687	**154**	0	.880 0775	10777
	30	.999 0215	2031		30	.952 8483	11775		30	.879 0129	10646
95	0	.998 7955	2260	**125**	0	.951 6624	11859	**155**	0	.877 9616	10513
	30	.998 5468	2487		30	.950 4684	11940		30	.876 9242	10374
96	0	9.998 2757	2711	**126**	0	9.949 2666	12018	**156**	0	9.875 9010	10232
	30	.997 9824	2933		30	.948 0573	12093		30	.874 8922	10088
97	0	.997 6669	3155	**127**	0	.946 8408	12165	**157**	0	.873 8984	9938
	30	.997 3297	3372		30	.945 6174	12234		30	.872 9198	9786
98	0	.996 9708	3589	**128**	0	.944 3875	12299	**158**	0	.871 9569	9629
	30	.996 5906	3802		30	.943 1513	12362		30	.871 0099	9470
99	0	9.996 1891	4015	**129**	0	9.941 9092	12421	**159**	0	9.870 0792	9307
	30	.995 7666	4225		30	.940 6615	12477		30	.869 1652	9140
100	0	.995 3234	4432	**130**	0	.939 4085	12530	**160**	0	.868 2683	8969
	30	.994 8596	4638		30	.938 1506	12579		30	.867 3886	8797
101	0	.994 3755	4841	**131**	0	.936 8881	12625	**161**	0	.866 5266	8620
	30	.993 8712	5043		30	.935 6213	12668		30	.865 6827	8439
102	0	9.993 3470	5242	**132**	0	9.934 3506	12707	**162**	0	9.864 8570	8257
	30	.992 8031	5439		30	.933 0763	12743		30	.864 0500	8070
103	0	.992 2397	5634	**133**	0	.931 7987	12776	**163**	0	.863 2620	7880
	30	.991 6570	5827		30	.930 5183	12804		30	.862 4932	7688
104	0	.991 0553	6017	**134**	0	.929 2353	12830	**164**	0	.861 7439	7493
	30	.990 4347	6206		30	.927 9501	12852		30	.861 0145	7294
105	0	9.989 7956	6391	**135**	0	9.926 6630	12871	**165**	0	9.860 3053	7092
	30	.989 1380	6576		30	.925 3745	12885		30	.859 6164	6889
106	0	.988 4622	6758	**136**	0	.924 0848	12897	**166**	0	.858 9482	6682
	30	.987 7685	6937		30	.922 7943	12905		30	.858 3010	6472
107	0	.987 0571	7114	**137**	0	.921 5035	12908	**167**	0	.857 6750	6260
	30	.986 3281	7290		30	.920 2126	12909		30	.857 0704	6046
108	0	9.985 5819	7462	**138**	0	9.918 9220	12906	**168**	0	9.856 4875	5829
	30	.984 8186	7633		30	.917 6321	12899		30	.855 9266	5609
109	0	.984 0385	7801	**139**	0	.916 3433	12888	**169**	0	.855 3878	5388
	30	.983 2418	7967		30	.915 0559	12874		30	.854 8714	5164
110	0	.982 4288	8130	**140**	0	.913 7703	12856	**170**	0	.854 3775	4939
	30	.981 5996	8292		30	.912 4870	12833		30	.853 9065	4710
111	0	9.980 7545	8451	**141**	0	9.911 2062	12808	**171**	0	9.853 4584	4481
	30	.979 8938	8607		30	.909 9283	12779		30	.853 0335	4249
112	0	.979 0177	8761	**142**	0	.908 6538	12745	**172**	0	.852 6319	4016
	30	.978 1264	8913		30	.907 3831	12707		30	.852 2538	3781
113	0	.977 2202	9062	**143**	0	.906 1164	12667	**173**	0	.851 8994	3544
	30	.976 2993	9209		30	.904 8542	12622		30	.851 5687	3307
114	0	9.975 3640	9353	**144**	0	9.903 5969	12573	**174**	0	9.851 2620	3067
	30	.974 4145	9495		30	.902 3449	12520		30	.850 9794	2826
115	0	.973 4510	9635	**145**	0	.901 0985	12464	**175**	0	.850 7209	2585
	30	.972 4739	9771		30	.899 8582	12403		30	.850 4868	2341
116	0	.971 4833	9906	**146**	0	.898 6243	12339	**176**	0	.850 2770	2098
	30	.970 4796	10037		30	.897 3972	12271		30	.850 0917	1853
117	0	9.969 4629	10167	**147**	0	9.896 1774	12198	**177**	0	9.849 9309	1608
	30	.968 4337	10292		30	.894 9652	12122		30	.849 7948	1361
118	0	.967 3920	10417	**148**	0	.893 7610	12042	**178**	0	.849 6833	1115
	30	.966 3382	10538		30	.892 5652	11958		30	.849 5966	867
119	0	.965 2726	10656	**149**	0	.891 3782	11870	**179**	0	.849 5346	620
	30	.964 1954	10772		30	.890 2004	11778		30	.849 4974	372
120	0	9.963 1069	10885	**150**	0	9.889 0321	11683	**180**	0	9.849 4850	124

TABLE IX.

For finding the True Anomaly or the Time from the Perihelion in Orbits of great eccentricity.

x	A	Diff.	B	Diff.	C	B'	Diff.	C'
°	″	″	″	″	″	″	″	″
0	0.00	0.00	0.000		0.000	0.000		0.000
1	0.00	0.01	0.000		0.000	0.000		0.000
2	0.01	0.04	0.000		0.000	0.000		0.000
3	0.05	0.07	0.000		0.000	0.000		0.000
4	0.12	0.11	0.000		0.000	0.000		0.000
5	0.23	0.16	0.000		0.000	0.000		0.000
6	0.39	0.23	0.000		0.000	0.000		0.000
7	0.62	0.31	0.000		0.000	0.000		0.000
8	0.93	0.40	0.000		0.000	0.000		0.000
9	1.33	0.49	0.000		0.000	0.000		0.000
10	1.82	0.60	0.000		0.000	0.000		0.000
11	2.42	0.72	0.000		0.000	0.000		0.000
12	3.14	0.85	0.000		0.000	0.000		0.000
13	3.99	1.00	0.000		0.000	0.000		0.000
14	4.99	1.14	0.001		0.000	0.001		0.000
15	6.13	1.30	0.001	.001	0.000	0.001	.000	0.000
16	7.43	1.47	0.002	.000	0.000	0.001	.001	0.000
17	8.90	1.65	0.002	.001	0.000	0.002	.000	0.000
18	10.55	1.85	0.003	.001	0.000	0.002	.001	0.000
19	12.40	2.05	0.004	.001	0.000	0.003	.001	0.000
20	14.45	2.25	0.005	.001	0.000	0.004	.001	0.000
21	16.70	2.48	0.006	.002	0.000	0.005	.001	0.000
22	19.18	2.71	0.008	.002	0.000	0.006	.002	0.000
23	21.89	2.94	0.010	.002	0.000	0.008	.002	0.000
24	24.83	3.20	0.012	.002	0.000	0.010	.002	0.000
25	28.03	3.45	0.014	.003	0.000	0.012	.002	0.000
26	31.48	3.72	0.017	.003	0.000	0.014	.003	0.000
27	35.20	3.99	0.020	.005	0.000	0.017	.003	0.000
28	39.19	4.28	0.025	.005	0.000	0.020	.004	0.000
29	43.47	4.57	0.030	.005	0.000	0.024	004	0.000
30	48.04	4.87	0.035	.006	0.000	0.028	.005	0.000
31	52.91	5.18	0.041	.006	0.000	0.033	.006	0.000
32	58.09	5.50	0.047	.008	0.000	0.039	.006	0.000
33	63.59	5.83	0.055	.009	0.000	0.045	.007	0.000
34	69.42	6.15	0.064	.009	0.000	0.052	.008	0.000
35	75.57	6.50	0.073	.011	0.000	0.060	.008	0.000
36	82.07	6.85	0.084	.012	0.000	0.068	.010	0.000
37	88.92	7.20	0.096	.013	0.000	0.078	.010	0.000
38	96.12	7.56	0.109	.014	0.000	0.088	.012	0.000
39	103.68	7.93	0.123	.016	0.000	0.100	.013	0.000
40	111.61	8.31	0.139	.017	0.000	0.113	.014	0.000
41	119.92	8.70	0.156	.019	0.000	0.127	.015	0.000
42	128.62	9.08	0.175	.021	0.000	0.142	.017	0.000
43	137.70	9.48	0.196	.022	0.000	0.159	.018	0.000
44	147.18	9.87	0.218	.025	0.000	0.177	.020	0.000
45	157.05	10.29	0.243	.026	0.000	0.197	.022	0.000
46	167.34	10.70	0.269	.029	0.000	0.219	.023	0.000
47	178.04	11.12	0.298	.030	0.000	0.242	.025	0.000
48	189.16	11.55	0.328	.033	0.000	0.267	.027	0.000
49	200.71	11.98	0.361	.036	0.000	0.294	.029	0.000
50	212.69	12.41	0.397	.039	0.000	0.323	.031	0.000
51	225.10	12.85	0.436	.041	0.000	0.354	.034	0.000
52	237.95	13.30	0.477	.044	0.001	0.388	.036	0.000
53	251.25	13.76	0.521	.046	0.001	0.424	.038	0.000
54	265.01	14.20	0.567	.050	0.001	0.462	.040	0.000
55	279.21	14.67	0.617	.054	0.001	0.502	.044	0.000
56	293.88	15.14	0.671	.056	0.002	0.546	.046	0.001
57	309.02	15.60	0.727	.060	0.002	0.592	.049	0.001
58	324.62	16.08	0.787	.064	0.002	0.641	.052	0.001
59	340.70	16.56	0.851	.068	0.002	0.693	.056	0.001
60	357.26		0.919		0.003	0.749		0.002

TABLE IX.

For finding the True Anomaly or the Time from the Perihelion in Orbits of great eccentricity.

x	A	Diff.	B	Diff.	C	B′	Diff.	C′
°	″	″	″	″	″	″	″	″
60	357.26	17.04	0.919	.071	0.003	0.749	.058	0.002
61	374.30	17.54	0.990	.076	0.003	0.807	.062	0.002
62	391.84	18.02	1.066	.079	0.003	0.869	.066	0.002
63	409.86	18.52	1.145	.085	0.004	0.935	.069	0.002
64	428.38	19.02	1.230	.088	0.004	1.004	.073	0.002
65	447.40	19.52	1.318	.093	0.004	1.077	.077	0.003
66	466.92	20.04	1.411	.099	0.005	1.154	.081	0.003
67	486.96	20.55	1.510	.103	0.005	1.235	.086	0.003
68	507.51	21.07	1.613	.108	0.006	1.321	.090	0.004
69	528.58	21.59	1.721	.114	0.006	1.411	.094	0.004
70	550.17	22.12	1.835	.119	0.007	1.505	.100	0.004
71	572.29	22.65	1.954	.124	0.007	1.605	.104	0.005
72	594.94	23.18	2.078	.131	0.008	1.709	.110	0.005
73	618.12	23.73	2.209	.136	0.009	1.819	.115	0.006
74	641.85	24.28	2.345	.143	0.009	1.934	.121	0.006
75	666.13	24.83	2.488	.149	0.010	2.055	.126	0.007
76	690.96	25.38	2.637	.156	0.011	2.181	.133	0.007
77	716.34	25.95	2.793	.163	0.012	2.314	.139	0.008
78	742.29	26.52	2.956	.169	0.013	2.453	.146	0.008
79	768.81	27.09	3.125	.177	0.014	2.599	.153	0.009
80	795.90	27.67	3.302	.184	0.015	2.752	.160	0.010
81	823.57	28.27	3.486	.192	0.016	2.912	.167	0.011
82	851.84	28.86	3.678	.200	0.017	3.079	.176	0.012
83	880.70	29.46	3.878	.209	0.018	3.255	.184	0.013
84	910.16	30.07	4.087	.216	0.020	3.439	.192	0.014
85	940.23	30.69	4.303	.226	0.021	3.631	.202	0.015
86	970.92	31.32	4.529	.235	0.023	3.833	.211	0.016
87	1002.24	31.96	4.764	.244	0.024	4.044	.222	0.018
88	1034.20	32.61	5.008	.254	0.026	4.266	.232	0.019
89	1066.81	33.27	5.262	.265	0.028	4.498	.243	0.021
90	1100.08	33.94	5.527	.274	0.030	4.741	.255	0.023
91	1134.02	34.62	5.801	.286	0.032	4.996	.267	0.025
92	1168.64	35.31	6.087	.298	0.034	5.263	.281	0.027
93	1203.95	36.02	6.385	.309	0.036	5.544	.294	0.029
94	1239.97	36.75	6.694	.322	0.038	5.838	.309	0.032
95	1276.72	37.49	7.016	.334	0.041	6.147	.324	0.035
96	1314.21	38.24	7.350	.348	0.044	6.471	.341	0.038
97	1352.45	39.01	7.698	.362	0.047	6.812	.359	0.041
98	1391.46	39.81	8.060	.377	0.050	7.171	.378	0.045
99	1431.27	40.61	8.437	.392	0.053	7.549	.397	0.049
100 0	1471.88	20.62	8.829	.203	0.056	7.946	.206	0.053
30	1492.50	20.83	9.032	.206	0.058	8.152	.212	0.055
101 0	1513.33	21.05	9.238	.211	0.060	8.364	.218	0.058
30	1534.38	21.26	9.449	.215	0.062	8.582	.223	0.060
102 0	1555.64	21.48	9.664	.219	0.064	8.805	.230	0.063
30	1577.12	21.70	9.883	.225	0.066	9.035	.236	0.066
103 0	1598.82	21.93	10.108	.229	0.068	9.271	.242	0.069
30	1620.75	22.16	10.337	.233	0.070	9.513	.248	0.072
104 0	1642.91	22.39	10.570	.239	0.072	9.761	.256	0.075
30	1665.30	22.63	10.809	.244	0.074	10.017	.263	0.078
105 0	1687.93	22.87	11.053	.249	0.077	10.280	.270	0.082
30	1710.80	23.12	11.302	.255	0.079	10.550	.278	0.085
106 0	1733.92	23.36	11.557	.260	0.082	10.828	.286	0.089
30	1757.28	23.62	11.817	.266	0.084	11.114	.294	0.093
107 0	1780.90	23.87	12.083	.271	0.087	11.408	.303	0.098
30	1804.77	24.13	12.354	.278	0.090	11.711	.311	0.102
108 0	1828.90	24.40	12.632	.284	0.093	12.022	.321	0.107
30	1853.30	24.67	12.916	.291	0.096	12.343	.330	0.112
109 0	1877.97		13.207		0.099	12.673		0.117

TABLE IX.

For finding the True Anomaly or the Time from the Perihelion in Orbits of great eccentricity.

x		A	Diff.	B	Diff.	C	Diff.	B'	Diff.	C'	Diff.
°	′	″	″	″	″	″	″	″	″	″	″
109	0	1877.97	24.94	13.207	.297	0.099	.003	12.673	.340	0.117	.005
	30	1902.91	25.22	13.504	.304	0.102	.004	13.013	.350	0.122	.006
110	0	1928.13	25.51	13.808	.311	0.106	.003	13.363	.361	0.128	.006
	30	1953.64	25.80	14.119	.319	0.109	.004	13.724	.371	0.134	.007
111	0	1979.44	26.10	14.438	.326	0.113	.003	14.095	.383	0.141	.007
	30	2005.54	26.40	14.764	.333	0.116	.004	14.478	.396	0.148	.007
112	0	2031.94	26.70	15.097	.342	0.120	.004	14.874	.408	0.155	.007
	30	2058.64	27.02	15.439	.350	0.124	.004	15.282	.420	0.162	.008
113	0	2085.66	27.34	15.789	.359	0.128	.004	15.702	.433	0.170	.008
	30	2113.00	27.66	16.148	.367	0.132	.005	16.135	.448	0.178	.009
114	0	2140.66	28.00	16.515	.377	0.137	.005	16.583	.462	0.187	.009
	30	2168.66	28.34	16.892	.386	0.142	.005	17.045	.477	0.196	.010
115	0	2197.00	28.69	17.278	.396	0.147	.005	17.522	.493	0.206	.010
	30	2225.69	29.04	17.674	.406	0.152	.005	18.015	.509	0.216	.011
116	0	2254.73	29.40	18.080	.416	0.157	.005	18.524	.526	0.227	.012
	30	2284.13	29.78	18.496	.428	0.162	.006	19.050	.544	0.239	.012
117	0	2313.91	30.15	18.924	.439	0.168	.006	19.594	.562	0.251	.013
	30	2344.06	30.54	19.363	.450	0.174	.006	20.156	.582	0.264	.013
118	0	2374.60	30.94	19.813	.463	0.180	.006	20.738	.601	0.277	.014
	30	2405.54	31.34	20.276	.475	0.186	.007	21.339	.623	0.291	.015
119	0	2436.88	31.76	20.751	.489	0.193	.007	21.962	.644	0.306	.016
	30	2468.64	32.19	21.240	.502	0.200	.007	22.606	.667	0.322	.017
120	0	2500.83	32.62	21.742	.516	0.207	.007	23.273	.691	0.339	.018
	30	2533.45	33.06	22.258	.531	0.214	.008	23.964	.716	0.357	.019
121	0	2566.51	33.52	22.789	.547	0.222	.008	24.680	.742	0.376	.020
	30	2600.03	33.99	23.336	.562	0.230	.009	25.422	.769	0.396	.021
122	0	2634.02	34.47	23.898	.579	0.239	.009	26.191	.797	0.417	.022
	30	2668.49	34.97	24.477	.596	0.248	.010	26.988	.827	0.439	.024
123	0	2703.46	35.47	25.073	.614	0.258	.010	27.815	.858	0.463	.025
	30	2738.93	35.98	25.687	.633	0.268	.010	28.673	.891	0.488	.027
124	0	2774.91	36.52	26.320	.653	0.278	.011	29.564	.925	0.515	.029
	30	2811.43	37.07	26.973	.673	0.289	.011	30.489	.961	0.544	.030
125	0	2848.50	37.63	27.646	.695	0.300	.012	31.450	.998	0.574	.032
	30	2886.13	38.20	28.341	.716	0.312	.013	32.448	1.037	0.606	034
126	0	2924.33	38.79	29.057	.740	0.325	.013	33.485	1.078	0.640	.036
	30	2963.12	39.41	29.797	.765	0.338	.014	34.563	1.122	0.676	.039
127	0	3002.53	40.03	30.562	.789	0.352	.015	35.685	1.167	0.715	.042
	30	3042.56	40.67	31.351	.816	0.367	.015	36.852	1.215	0.757	.043
128	0	3083.23	41.34	32.167	.844	0.382	.016	38.067	1.264	0.800	.046
	30	3124.57	42.02	33.011	.874	0.398	.017	39.331	1.318	0.846	.050
129	0	3166.59	42.72	33.885	.904	0.415	.018	40.649	1.373	0.896	.053
	30	3209.31	43.45	34.789	.936	0.433	.019	42.022	1.430	0.949	.056
130	0	3252.76	29.37	35.725	.642	0.452	.013	43.452	0.987	1.005	.040
	20	3282.13	29.72	36.367	.658	0.465	.014	44.439	1.016	1.045	.042
	40	3311.85	30.05	37.025	.674	0.479	.014	45.455	1.045	1.087	.043
131	0	3341.90	30.41	37.699	.690	0.493	.015	46.500	1.075	1.130	.045
	20	3372.31	30.78	38.389	.708	0.508	.015	47.575	1.107	1.175	.048
	40	3403.09	31.14	39.097	.725	0.523	.016	48.682	1.138	1.223	.050
132	0	3434.23	31.51	39.822	.742	0.539	.016	49.820	1.172	1.273	.052
	20	3465.74	31.89	40.564	.762	0.555	.017	50.992	1.207	1.325	.054
	40	3497.63	32.28	41.326	.782	0.572	.018	52.199	1.243	1.379	.057
133	0	3529.91	32.69	42.108	.802	0.590	.019	53.442	1.281	1.436	.059
	20	3562.60	33.09	42.910	.823	0.609	.020	54.723	1.319	1.495	.063
	40	3595.69	33.51	43.733	.843	0.629	.020	56.042	1.359	1.558	.065
134	0	3629.20	33.93	44.576	.866	0.649	.020	57.401	1.401	1.623	.069
	20	3663.13	34.37	45.442	.889	0.669	.022	58.802	1.445	1.692	.072
	40	3697.50	34.81	46.331	.914	0.691	.023	60.247	1.489	1.764	.075
135	0	3732.31	35.27	47.245	.938	0.714	.024	61.736	1.537	1.839	.078
	20	3767.58	35.73	48.183	.964	0.738	.025	63.273	1.584	1.917	.083
	40	3803.31	36.21	49.147	.991	0 763	.025	64.857	1.634	2.000	.087
136	0	3839.52		50.138		0.788		66.491		2.087	

TABLE IX.

For finding the True Anomaly or the Time from the Perihelion in Orbits of great eccentricity

x	A	Diff.	B	Diff.	C	Diff.	B′	Diff.	C′	Diff.
° ′	″	″	″	″	″	″	″	″	″	″
136 0	3839.52	36.69	50.138	1.018	0.788	.027	66.491	1.687	2.087	.091
20	3876.21	37.20	51.156	1.047	0.815	.028	68.178	1.742	2.178	.096
40	3913.41	37.71	52.203	1.077	0.843	.030	69.920	1.798	2.274	.101
137 0	3951.12	38.23	53.280	1.108	0.873	.031	71.718	1.857	2.375	.105
20	3989.35	38.76	54.388	1.140	0.904	.032	73.575	1.918	2.480	.111
40	4028.11	39.31	55.528	1.174	0.936	.033	75.493	1.982	2.591	.117
138 0	4067.42	39.86	56.702	1.208	0.969	.035	77.475	2.048	2.708	.123
20	4107.28	40.44	57.910	1.244	1.004	.037	79.523	2.118	2.831	.129
40	4147.72	41.03	59.154	1.282	1.041	.038	81.641	2.189	2.960	.136
139 0	4188.75	41.63	60.436	1.321	1.079	.040	83.830	2.264	3.096	.143
20	4230.38	42.25	61.757	1.362	1.119	.042	86.094	2.342	3.239	.151
40	4272.63	42.89	63.119	1.404	1.161	.044	88.436	2.424	3.390	.159
140 0	4315.52	43.54	64.523	1.448	1.205	.046	90.860	2.509	3.549	.168
20	4359.06	44.20	65.971	1.494	1.251	.048	93.369	2.598	3.717	.176
40	4403.26	44.89	67.465	1.542	1.299	.051	95.967	2.690	3.893	.187
141 0	4448.15	45.58	69.007	1.592	1.350	.054	98.657	2.786	4.080	.197
20	4493.73	46.30	70.599	1.644	1.404	.056	101.443	2.888	4.277	.207
40	4540.03	47.04	72.243	1.698	1.460	.058	104.331	2.993	4.484	.220
142 0	4587.07	23.81	73.941	0.870	1.518	.031	107.324	1.537	4.704	.115
10	4610.88	24.00	74.811	0.884	1.549	.031	108.861	1.566	4.819	.117
20	4634.88	24.19	75.695	0.900	1.580	.032	110.427	1.595	4.936	.121
30	4659.07	24.39	76.595	0.914	1.612	.033	112.022	1.624	5.057	.124
40	4683.46	24.59	77.509	0.930	1.645	.034	113.646	1.655	5.181	.128
50	4708.05	24.79	78.439	0.946	1.679	.035	115.301	1.685	5.309	.131
143 0	4732.84	25.00	79.385	0.962	1.714	.035	116.986	1.718	5.440	.135
10	4757.84	25.21	80.347	0.978	1.749	.037	118.704	1.748	5.575	.140
20	4783.05	25.41	81.325	0.996	1.786	.037	120.452	1.781	5.715	.143
30	4808.46	25.64	82.321	1.012	1.823	.039	122.233	1.816	5.858	.147
40	4834.10	25.85	83.333	1.030	1.862	.039	124.049	1.850	6.005	.152
50	4859.95	26.07	84.363	1.048	1.901	.041	125.899	1.886	6.157	.156
144 0	4886.02	26.29	85.411	1.067	1.942	.042	127.785	1.922	6.313	.160
10	4912.31	26.52	86.478	1.086	1.984	.042	129.707	1.959	6.473	.166
20	4938.83	26.75	87.564	1.104	2.026	.044	131.666	1.997	6.639	.170
30	4965.58	26.98	88.668	1.125	2.070	.046	133.663	2.035	6.809	.175
40	4992.56	27.22	89.793	1.145	2.116	.046	135.698	2.076	6.984	.181
50	5019.78	27.45	90.938	1.165	2.162		137.774	2.116	7.165	.186
145 0	5047.23	27.70	92.103	1.187	2.210	.049	139.890	2.158	7.351	.192
10	5074.93	27.95	93.290	1.208	2.259	.050	142.048	2.201	7.543	.197
20	5102.88	28.20	94.498	1.231	2.309	.052	144.249	2.245	7.740	.203
30	5131.08	28.45	95.729	1.253	2.361	.053	146.494	2.290	7.943	.210
40	5159.53	28.71	96.982	1.277	2.414	.055	148.784	2.336	8.153	.216
50	5188.24	28.97	98.259	1.300	2.469	.057	151.120	2.383	8.369	.223
146 0	5217.21	29.24	99.559	1.325	2.526	.058	153.503	2.431	8.592	.230
10	5246.45	29.50	100.884	1.350	2.584	.059	155.934	2.481	8.822	.238
20	5275.95	29.78	102.234	1.376	2.643	.061	158.415	2.532	9.060	.244
30	5305.73	30.06	103.610	1.402	2.704	.063	160.947	2.584	9.304	.251
40	5335.79	30.34	105.012	1.429	2.767	.066	163.531	2.637	9.555	.260
50	5366.13	30.63	106.441	1.456	2.833	.067	166.168	2.692	9.815	.268
147 0	5396.76	30.91	107.897	1.485	2.900	.069	168.860	2.748	10.083	.276
10	5427.67	31.21	109.382	1.514	2.969	.071	171.608	2.806	10.359	.286
20	5458.88	31.51	110.896	1.543	3.040	.073	174.414	2.866	10.645	.295
30	5490.39	31.81	112.439	1.574	3.113	.075	177.280	2.926	10.940	.304
40	5522.20	32.13	114.013	1.606	3.188	.078	180.206	2.988	11.244	.314
50	5554.33	32.44	115.619	1.637	3.266	.080	183.194	3.052	11.558	.325
148 0	5586.77	32.75	117.256	1.670	3.346	.082	186.246	3.118	11.883	.335
10	5619.52	33.08	118.926	1.705	3.428	.085	189.364	3.185	12.218	.346
20	5652.60	33.41	120.631	1.739	3.513	.088	192.549	3.255	12.564	.357
30	5686.01	33.74	122.370	1.774	3.601	.090	195.804	3.326	12.921	.370
40	5719.75	34.08	124.144	1.811	3.691	.093	199.130	3.398	13.291	.382
50	5753.83	34.43	125.955	1.849	3.784	.097	202.528	3.474	13.673	.394
149 0	5788.26		127.804		3.881		206.002		14.067	

TABLE X.

For finding the True Anomaly or the Time from the Perihelion in Elliptic and Hyperbolic Orbits.

A	Ellipse.					Hyperbola.				
	log B	Diff.	log C	log I. Diff.	log half II. Diff.	log B	Diff.	log C	log I. Diff.	log half II. Diff.
	0.000					0.000				
0.00	0000	7	0.000 0000	4.23990	1.778	0000	7	0.000 0000	4.23982$_n$	1.771
.01	0007	23	.001 7432	.24286	.783	0007	23	9.998 2688	.23686	.767
.02	0030	37	.003 4985	.24583	.788	0030	37	.996 5493	.23392	.762
.03	0067	53	.005 2659	.24885	.794	0067	51	.994 8414	.23098	.758
.04	0120	68	.007 0457	.25190	.799	0118	66	.993 1450	.22807	.753
0.05	0188	84	0.008 8381	4.25497	1.805	0184	81	9.991 4599	4.22518$_n$	1.748
.06	0272	99	.010 6432	.25806	.811	0265	94	.989 7859	.22230	.743
.07	0371	114	.012 4613	.26116	.816	0359	109	.988 1231	.21943	.739
.08	0485	130	.014 2924	.26427	.821	0468	123	.986 4711	.21659	.734
.09	0615	147	.016 1367	.26741	.827	0591	137	.984 8298	.21376	.730
0.10	0762	162	0.017 9945	4.27057	1.833	0728	152	9.983 1992	4.21094$_n$	1.725
.11	0924	178	.019 8659	.27376	.839	0880	165	.981 5791	.20815	.720
.12	1102	194	.021 7511	.27697	.845	1045	178	.979 9694	.20537	.716
.13	1296	211	.023 6503	.28020	.851	1223	193	.978 3699	.20260	.711
.14	1507	227	.025 5637	.28344	.857	1416	206	.976 7805	.19986	.706
0.15	1734	243	0.027 4916	4.28670	1.863	1622	220	9.975 2011	4.19712$_n$	1.700
.16	1977	261	.029 4340	.28999	.869	1842	233	.973 6316	.19440	.695
.17	2238	277	.031 3913	.29331	.875	2075	246	.972 0719	.19170	.690
.18	2515	294	.033 3636	.29665	.882	2321	260	.970 5218	.18901	.685
.19	2809	311	.035 3511	.30001	.888	2581	273	.968 9813	.18633	.679
0.20	3120	328	0.037 3542	4.30339	1.895	2854	286	9.967 4502	4.18367$_n$	1.672
.21	3448	345	.039 3730	.30679	.901	3140	299	.965 9285	.18102	.666
.22	3793	363	.041 4077	.31022	.908	3439	312	.964 4159	.17840	.661
.23	4156	381	.043 4585	.31368	.915	3751	325	.962 9124	.17579	.655
.24	4537	398	.045 5259	.31716	.922	4076	338	.961 4180	.17319	.649
0.25	4935	416	0.047 6099	4.32066	1.929	4414	351	9.959 9324	4.17061$_n$	1.643
.26	5351	434	.049 7109	.32418	.936	4765	363	.958 4556	.16803	.637
.27	5785	452	.051 8290	.32773	.943	5128	376	.956 9875	.16547	.631
.28	6237	471	.053 9646	.33131	.951	5504	389	.955 5281	.16292	.625
.29	6708	488	.056 1179	.33492	.958	5893	401	.954 0771	.16038	.618
0.30	7196		0.058 2893	4.33856	1.966	6294		9.952 6346	4.15785$_n$	1.613

TABLE X. Part II.

T	Ellipse.		Hyperbola.		T	Ellipse.		Hyperbola.	
	A	Diff.	A	Diff.		A	Diff.	A	Diff.
0.00	0.00000	992	0.00000	1008	0.20	0.17266	742	0.23867	1442
.01	.00992	977	.01008	1025	.21	.18008	732	.25309	1470
.02	.01969	961	.02033	1041	.22	.18740	722	.26779	1501
.03	.02930	947	.03074	1058	.23	.19462	712	.28280	1533
.04	.03877	931	.04132	1077	.24	.20174	704	.29813	1564
0.05	0.04808	918	0.05209	1094	0.25	0.20878	695	0.31377	
.06	.05726	904	.06303	1114	.26	.21573	685		
.07	.06630	891	.07417	1133	.27	.22258	677		
.08	.07521	877	.08550	1152	.28	.22935	669		
.09	.08398	865	.09702	1173	.29	.23604	661		
0.10	0.09263	853	0.10875	1194	0.30	0.24265	652		
.11	.10116	840	.12069	1216	.31	.24917	644		
.12	.10956	827	.13285	1237	.32	.25561	637		
.13	.11783	816	.14522	1260	.33	.26198	628		
.14	.12599	805	.15782	1285	.34	.26826	621		
0.15	0.13404	794	0.17067	1308	0.35	0.27447	614		
.16	.14198	783	.18375	1334	.36	.28061	607		
.17	.14981	772	.19709	1359	.37	.28668	600		
.18	.15753	762	.21068	1386	.38	.29268	592		
.19	.16515	751	.22454	1413	.39	.29860	586		
0.20	0.17266		0.23867		0.40	0.30446			

TABLE XI.

For the Motion in a Parabolic Orbit.

η	$\log \mu$	Diff.	η	$\log \mu$	Diff.	η	$\log \mu$	Diff.
0.000	0.000 0000	0	0.060	0.000 0652	22	0.120	0.000 2617	44
.001	.000 0000	1	.061	.000 0674	23	.121	.000 2661	44
.002	.000 0001	1	.062	.000 0697	22	.122	.000 2705	45
.003	.000 0002	1	.063	.000 0719	23	.123	.000 2750	45
.004	.000 0003	1	.064	.000 0742	24	.124	.000 2795	46
0.005	0.000 0004	2	0.065	0.000 0766	24	0.125	0.000 2841	45
.006	.000 0006	3	.066	.000 0790	24	.126	.000 2886	47
.007	.000 0009	3	.067	.000 0814	24	.127	.000 2933	46
.008	.000 0012	3	.068	.000 0838	25	.128	.000 2979	47
.009	.000 0015	3	.069	.000 0863	25	.129	.000 3026	48
0.010	0.000 0018	4	0.070	0.000 0888	26	0.130	0.000 3074	47
.011	.000 0022	4	.071	.000 0914	26	.131	.000 3121	48
.012	.000 0026	5	.072	.000 0940	26	.132	.000 3169	49
.013	.000 0031	4	.073	.000 0966	27	.133	.000 3218	49
.014	.000 0035	6	.074	.000 0993	27	.134	.000 3267	49
0.015	0.000 0041	5	0.075	0.000 1020	27	0.135	0.000 3316	49
.016	.000 0046	6	.076	.000 1047	28	.136	.000 3365	50
.017	.000 0052	7	.077	.000 1075	28	.137	.000 3415	51
.018	.000 0059	6	.078	.000 1103	29	.138	.000 3466	50
.019	.000 0065	7	.079	.000 1132	29	.139	.000 3516	51
0.020	0.000 0072	8	0.080	0.000 1161	29	0.140	0.000 3567	52
.021	.000 0080	8	.081	.000 1190	29	.141	.000 3619	52
.022	.000 0088	8	.082	.000 1219	30	.142	.000 3671	52
.023	.000 0096	8	.083	.000 1249	31	.143	.000 3723	52
.024	.000 0104	9	.084	.000 1280	31	.144	.000 3775	53
0.025	0.000 0113	9	0.085	0.000 1311	31	0.145	0.000 3828	54
.026	.000 0122	10	.086	.000 1342	31	.146	.000 3882	53
.027	.000 0132	10	.087	.000 1373	32	.147	.000 3935	54
.028	.000 0142	10	.088	.000 1405	32	.148	.000 3989	55
.029	.000 0152	11	.089	.000 1437	33	.149	.000 4044	55
0.030	0.000 0163	11	0.090	0.000 1470	32	0.150	0.000 4099	55
.031	.000 0174	11	.091	.000 1502	34	.151	.000 4154	55
.032	.000 0185	12	.092	.000 1536	33	.152	.000 4209	56
.033	.000 0197	12	.093	.000 1569	34	.153	.000 4265	57
.034	.000 0209	13	.094	.000 1603	35	.154	.000 4322	56
0.035	0.000 0222	13	0.095	0.000 1638	35	0.155	0.000 4378	57
.036	.000 0235	13	.096	.000 1673	35	.156	.000 4435	58
.037	.000 0248	14	.097	.000 1708	35	.157	.000 4493	58
.038	.000 0262	13	.098	.000 1743	36	.158	.000 4551	58
.039	.000 0275	15	.099	.000 1779	36	.159	.000 4609	59
0.040	0.000 0290	14	0.100	0.000 1815	37	0.160	0.000 4668	58
.041	.000 0304	16	.101	.000 1852	37	.161	.000 4726	60
.042	.000 0320	15	.102	.000 1889	37	.162	.000 4786	60
.043	.000 0335	16	.103	.000 1926	38	.163	.000 4846	60
.044	.000 0351	16	.104	.000 1964	38	.164	.000 4906	60
0.045	0.000 0367	16	0.105	0.000 2002	38	0.165	0.000 4966	61
.046	.000 0383	17	.106	.000 2040	39	.166	.000 5027	61
.047	.000 0400	17	.107	.000 2079	39	.167	.000 5088	62
.048	.000 0417	18	.108	.000 2118	40	.168	.000 5150	62
.049	.000 0435	18	.109	.000 2158	40	.169	.000 5212	62
0.050	0.000 0453	18	0.110	0.000 2198	40	0.170	0.000 5274	63
.051	.000 0471	19	.111	.000 2238	41	.171	.000 5337	63
.052	.000 0490	19	.112	.000 2279	41	.172	.000 5400	64
.053	.000 0509	19	.113	.000 2320	41	.173	.000 5464	64
.054	.000 0528	20	.114	.000 2361	42	.174	.000 5528	64
0.055	0.000 0548	20	0.115	0.000 2403	42	0.175	0.000 5592	65
.056	.000 0568	21	.116	.000 2445	42	.176	.000 5657	65
.057	.000 0589	21	.117	.000 2487	43	.177	.000 5722	65
.058	.000 0610	21	.118	.000 2530	43	.178	.000 5787	66
.059	.000 0631	21	.119	.000 2573	44	.179	.000 5853	66
0.060	0.000 0652		0.120	0.000 2617		0.180	0.000 5919	

TABLE XI.

For the Motion in a Parabolic Orbit.

η	$\log \mu$	Diff.	η	$\log \mu$	Diff.	η	$\log \mu$	Diff.
0.180	0.000 5919	67	0.240	0.001 0603	90	0.300	0.001 6733	115
.181	.000 5986	67	.241	.001 0693	91	.301	.001 6848	115
.182	.000 6053	67	.242	.001 0784	91	.302	.001 6963	116
.183	.000 6120	68	.243	.001 0875	91	.303	.001 7079	116
.184	.000 6188	68	.244	.001 0966	92	.304	.001 7195	117
0.185	0.000 6256	69	0.245	0.001 1058	92	0.305	0.001 7312	117
.186	.000 6325	68	.246	.001 1150	92	.306	.001 7429	117
.187	.000 6393	70	.247	.001 1242	93	.307	.001 7546	118
.188	.000 6463	69	.248	.001 1335	94	.308	.001 7664	119
.189	.000 6532	70	.249	.001 1429	93	.309	.001 7783	118
0.190	0.000 6602	71	0.250	0.001 1522	95	0.310	0.001 7901	119
.191	.000 6673	71	.251	.001 1617	94	.311	.001 8020	120
.192	.000 6744	71	.252	.001 1711	95	.312	.001 8140	120
.193	.000 6815	72	.253	.001 1806	95	.313	.001 8260	121
.194	.000 6887	72	.254	.001 1901	96	.314	.001 8381	121
0.195	0.000 6959	72	0.255	0.001 1997	96	0.315	0.001 8502	121
.196	.000 7031	73	.256	.001 2093	97	.316	.001 8623	122
.197	.000 7104	73	.257	.001 2190	97	.317	.001 8745	122
.198	.000 7177	73	.258	.001 2287	97	.318	.001 8867	122
.199	.000 7250	74	.259	.001 2384	98	.319	.001 8989	124
0.200	0.000 7324	75	0.260	0.001 2482	98	0.320	0.001 9113	123
.201	.000 7399	74	.261	.001 2580	99	.321	.001 9236	124
.202	.000 7473	75	.262	.001 2679	99	.322	.001 9360	124
.203	.000 7548	76	.263	.001 2778	99	.323	.001 9484	125
.204	.000 7624	76	.264	.001 2877	100	.324	.001 9609	125
0.205	0.000 7700	76	0.265	0.001 2977	100	0.325	0.001 9734	126
.206	.000 7776	77	.266	.001 3077	101	.326	.001 9860	126
.207	.000 7853	77	.267	.001 3178	101	.327	.001 9986	127
.208	.000 7930	77	.268	.001 3279	102	.328	.002 0113	127
.209	.000 8007	78	.269	.001 3381	101	.329	.002 0240	127
0.210	0.000 8085	78	0.270	0.001 3482	103	0.330	0.002 0367	128
.211	.000 8163	79	.271	.001 3585	103	.331	.002 0495	129
.212	.000 8242	79	.272	.001 3688	103	.332	.002 0624	128
.213	.000 8321	79	.273	.001 3791	103	.333	.002 0752	130
.214	.000 8400	80	.274	.001 3894	104	.334	.002 0882	129
0.215	0.000 8480	80	0.275	0.001 3998	105	0.335	0.002 1011	130
.216	.000 8560	81	.276	.001 4103	104	.336	.002 1141	131
.217	.000 8641	81	.277	.001 4207	106	.337	.002 1272	131
.218	.000 8722	81	.278	.001 4313	105	.338	.002 1403	131
.219	.000 8803	82	.279	.001 4418	106	.339	.002 1534	132
0.220	0.000 8885	82	0.280	0.001 4524	107	0.340	0.002 1666	133
.221	.000 8967	83	.281	.001 4631	107	.341	.002 1799	132
.222	.000 9050	82	.282	.001 4738	107	.342	.002 1931	134
.223	.000 9132	84	.283	.001 4845	108	.343	.002 2065	133
.224	.000 9216	84	.284	.001 4953	108	.344	.002 2198	135
0.225	0.000 9300	84	0.285	0.001 5061	108	0.345	0.002 2333	134
.226	.000 9384	84	.286	.001 5169	109	.346	.002 2467	135
.227	.000 9468	85	.287	.001 5278	110	.347	.002 2602	136
.228	.000 9553	85	.288	.001 5388	109	.348	.002 2738	136
.229	.000 9638	86	.289	.001 5497	111	.349	.002 2874	136
0.230	0.000 9724	86	0.290	0.001 5608	110	0.350	0.002 3010	137
.231	.000 9810	87	.291	.001 5718	111	.351	.002 3147	137
.232	.000 9897	87	.292	.001 5829	112	.352	.002 3284	138
.233	.000 9984	87	.293	.001 5941	112	.353	.002 3422	138
.234	.001 0071	88	.294	.001 6053	112	.354	.002 3560	139
0.235	0.001 0159	88	0.295	0.001 6165	113	0.355	0.002 3699	139
.236	.001 0247	88	.296	.001 6278	113	.356	.002 3838	139
.237	.001 0335	89	.297	.001 6391	114	.357	.002 3977	140
.238	.001 0424	89	.298	.001 6505	114	.358	.002 4117	141
.239	.001 0513	90	.299	.001 6619	114	.359	.002 4258	141
0.240	0.001 0603		0.300	0.001 6733		0.360	0.002 4399	

TABLE XI.

For the Motion in a Parabolic Orbit.

η	log μ	Diff.	η	log μ	Diff.	η	log μ	Diff.
0.360	0.002 4399	141	0.420	0.003 3720	170	0.480	0.004 4858	203
.361	.002 4540	142	.421	.003 3890	171	.481	.004 5061	202
.362	.002 4682	142	.422	.003 4061	171	.482	.004 5263	204
.363	.002 4824	143	.423	.003 4232	172	.483	.004 5467	203
.364	.002 4967	143	.424	.003 4404	172	.484	.004 5670	205
0.365	0.002 5110	144	0.425	0.003 4576	173	0.485	0.004 5875	205
.366	.002 5254	144	.426	.003 4749	174	.486	.004 6080	205
.367	.002 5398	145	.427	.003 4923	173	.487	.004 6285	207
.368	.002 5543	145	.428	.003 5096	175	.488	.004 6492	206
.369	.002 5688	146	.429	.003 5271	174	.489	.004 6698	208
0.370	0.002 5834	146	0.430	0.003 5445	176	0.490	0.004 6906	207
.371	.002 5980	146	.431	.003 5621	176	.491	.004 7113	209
.372	.002 6126	147	.432	.003 5797	176	.492	.004 7322	209
.373	.002 6273	148	.433	.003 5973	177	.493	.004 7531	209
.374	.002 6421	147	.434	.003 6150	177	.494	.004 7740	211
0.375	0.002 6568	149	0.435	0.003 6327	178	0.495	0.004 7951	210
.376	.002 6717	149	.436	.003 6505	178	.496	.004 8161	212
.377	.002 6866	149	.437	.003 6683	179	.497	.004 8373	212
.378	.002 7015	150	.438	.003 6862	180	.498	.004 8585	212
.379	.002 7165	150	.439	.003 7042	180	.499	.004 8797	213
0.380	0.002 7315	151	0.440	0.003 7222	180	0.500	0.004 9010	2163
.381	.002 7466	151	.441	.003 7402	181	.51	.005 1173	2224
.382	.002 7617	152	.442	.003 7583	182	.52	.005 3397	2284
.383	.002 7769	152	.443	.003 7765	182	.53	.005 5681	2348
.384	.002 7921	152	.444	.003 7947	183	.54	.005 8029	2412
0.385	0.002 8073	153	0.445	0.003 8130	183	0.55	0.006 0441	2478
.386	.002 8226	154	.446	.003 8313	183	.56	.006 2919	2545
.387	.002 8380	154	.447	.003 8496	184	.57	.006 5464	2615
.388	.002 8534	155	.448	.003 8680	185	.58	.006 8079	2686
.389	.002 8689	155	.449	.003 8865	185	.59	.007 0765	2760
0.390	0.002 8844	155	0.450	0.003 9050	186	0.60	0.007 3525	2836
.391	.002 8999	156	.451	.003 9236	186	.61	.007 6361	2913
.392	.002 9155	156	.452	.003 9422	187	.62	.007 9274	2994
.393	.002 9311	157	.453	.003 9609	188	.63	.008 2268	3077
.394	.002 9468	158	.454	.003 9797	187	.64	.008 5345	3163
0.395	0.002 9626	158	0.455	0.003 9984	189	0.65	0.008 8508	3251
.396	.002 9784	158	.456	.004 0173	189	.66	.009 1759	3344
.397	.002 9942	159	.457	.004 0362	189	.67	.009 5103	3439
.398	.003 0101	159	.458	.004 0551	190	.68	.009 8542	3539
.399	.003 0260	160	.459	.004 0741	191	.69	.010 2081	3642
0.400	0.003 0420	160	0.460	0.004 0932	191	0.70	0.010 5723	3750
.401	.003 0580	161	.461	.004 1123	192	.71	.010 9473	3863
.402	.003 0741	162	.462	.004 1315	192	.72	.011 3336	3980
.403	.003 0903	161	.463	.004 1507	193	.73	.011 7316	4103
.404	.003 1064	163	.464	.004 1700	193	.74	.012 1419	4233
0.405	0.003 1227	162	0.465	0.004 1893	194	0.75	0.012 5652	4370
.406	.003 1389	164	.466	.004 2087	194	.76	.013 0022	4514
.407	.003 1553	163	.467	.004 2281	195	.77	.013 4536	4666
.408	.003 1716	165	.468	.004 2476	196	.78	.013 9202	4829
.409	.003 1881	164	.469	.004 2672	196	.79	.014 4031	5002
0.410	0.003 2045	166	0.470	0.004 2868	196	0.80	0.014 9033	5186
.411	.003 2211	165	.471	.004 3064	197	.81	.015 4219	5384
.412	.003 2376	167	.472	.004 3261	198	.82	.015 9603	5599
.413	.003 2543	166	.473	.004 3459	198	.83	.016 5202	5831
.414	.003 2709	168	.474	.004 3657	199	.84	.017 1033	6087
0.415	0.003 2877	167	0.475	0.004 3856	199	0.85	0.017 7120	6366
.416	.003 3044	169	.476	.004 4055	200	.86	.018 3486	6679
.417	.003 3213	168	.477	.004 4255	201	.87	.019 0165	7030
.418	.003 3381	169	.478	.004 4456	201	.88	.019 7195	7434
.419	.003 3550	170	.479	.004 4657	201	.89	.020 4629	7900
0.420	0.003 3720		0.480	0.004 4858		0.90	0.021 2529	

TABLE XII.

ζ	log m_1	log m_2	z_1' m_1	z_1' m_2	z_2' m_2	z_2' m_1	z_3' m_1	z_3' m_2	z_4' m_2	z_4' m_1
° ′			° ′	° ′	° ′	° ′	° ′	° ′	° ′	° ′
— 0 0	∞	0.0000	0 0	90 0	90 0	180 0	180 0	180 0	0 0	0 0
1	4.2976	9.9999	2 23	90 20	90 20	178 40	178 40	179 0	359 0	359 5
2	3.3950	9.9996	4 46	90 40	90 40	177 20	177 20	178 0	358 0	358 9
3	2.8675	9.9992	7 8	91 0	91 0	176 0	176 0	177 0	357 0	357 14
4	2.4938	9.9986	9 32	91 20	91 20	174 40	174 40	176 0	356 0	356 18
5	2.2044	9.9978	11 55	91 41	91 41	173 19	173 19	175 0	355 0	355 23
6	1.9686	9.9968	14 19	92 1	92 1	171 59	171 59	174 0	354 0	354 28
7	1.7698	9.9957	16 42	92 22	92 22	170 38	170 38	172 59	353 1	353 32
8	1.5981	9.9943	19 7	92 42	92 42	169 18	169 18	171 59	352 1	352 37
9	1.4473	9.9928	21 32	93 3	93 3	167 57	167 57	170 58	351 2	351 42
10	1.3130	9.9911	23 57	93 25	93 25	166 35	166 35	169 57	350 3	350 47
11	1.1922	9.9892	26 23	93 46	93 46	165 14	165 14	168 55	349 4	349 52
12	1.0824	9.9871	28 50	94 8	94 8	163 52	163 52	167 54	348 6	348 56
13	0.9821	9.9848	31 17	94 31	94 31	162 29	162 29	166 51	347 8	348 1
14	0.8898	9.9823	33 46	94 53	94 53	161 7	161 7	165 48	346 11	347 6
15	0.8045	9.9796	36 15	95 17	95 17	159 43	159 43	164 44	345 14	346 11
16	0.7254	9.9767	38 46	95 40	95 40	158 20	158 20	163 40	344 17	345 16
17	0.6518	9.9736	41 18	96 5	96 5	156 55	156 55	162 34	343 21	344 21
18	0.5830	9.9702	43 51	96 30	96 30	155 30	155 30	161 27	342 27	343 27
19	0.5185	9.9667	46 26	96 56	96 56	154 4	154 4	160 19	341 32	342 32
20	0.4581	9.9629	49 2	97 23	97 23	152 37	152 37	159 9	340 38	341 37
21	0.4013	9.9588	51 41	97 50	97 50	151 10	151 10	157 58	339 45	340 43
22	0.3479	9.9545	54 22	98 19	98 19	149 41	149 41	156 45	338 53	339 49
23	0.2976	9.9499	57 5	98 49	98 49	148 11	148 11	155 29	338 0	338 54
24	0.2501	9.9451	59 51	99 20	99 20	146 40	146 40	154 11	337 9	338 0
25	0.2053	9.9400	62 40	99 53	99 53	145 7	145 7	152 50	336 19	337 6
26	0.1631	9.9345	65 33	100 28	100 28	143 32	143 32	151 25	335 28	336 13
27	0.1232	9.9287	68 30	101 5	101 5	141 55	141 55	149 56	334 38	335 19
28	0.0857	9.9226	71 33	101 45	101 45	140 15	140 15	148 22	333 49	334 25
29	0.0503	9.9161	74 41	102 27	102 27	138 33	138 33	146 42	333 1	333 32
30	0.0170	9.9092	77 58	103 13	103 13	136 46	136 46	144 55	332 12	332 39
31	9.9857	9.9019	81 23	104 4	104 4	134 56	134 56	142 59	331 24	331 46
32	9.9565	9.8940	85 0	105 1	105 1	132 59	132 59	140 51	330 37	330 54
33	9.9292	9.8856	88 54	106 6	106 6	130 54	130 54	138 27	329 49	330 2
34	9.9040	9.8765	93 11	107 22	107 22	128 38	128 38	135 39	329 2	329 10
35	9.8808	9.8665	98 7	108 58	108 58	126 2	126 2	132 13	328 14	328 19
36	9.8600	9.8555	104 20	111 13	111 13	122 47	122 47	127 29	327 27	327 28
—36 52.2	9.8443	9.8443	116 34	116 34	116 34	116 34	116 34	116 34	326 45	326 45

This table exhibits the limits of the roots of the equation

$$\sin(z' - \zeta) = m_0 \sin^4 z',$$

when there are four real roots. The quantities m_1 and m_2 are the limiting values of m_0, and the values of z_1', z_2', z_3', and z_4', corresponding to each of these, give the limits of the four real roots of the equation.

TABLE XII.

ζ	$\log m_1$	$\log m_2$	z_1'		z_2'		z_3'		z_4'	
			m_2	m_1	m_1	m_2	m_2	m_1	m_1	m_2
° ′			° ′	° ′	° ′	° ′	° ′	° ′	° ′	° ′
+ 0 0	∞	0.0000	0 0	0 0	0 0	90 0	90 0	180 0	180 0	180 0
1	4.2976	9.9999	1 0	1 20	1 20	89 40	89 40	177 37	180 55	181 0
2	3.3950	9.9996	2 0	2 40	2 40	89 20	89,20	175 14	181 51	182 0
3	2.8675	9.9992	3 0	4 0	4. 0	89 0	89 0	172 52	182 46	183 0
4	2.4938	9.9986	4 0	5 20	5 20	88 40	88 40	170 28	183 42	184 0
5	2.2044	9.9978	5 0	6 41	6 41	88 19	88 19	168 5	184 37	185 0
6	1.9686	9.9968	6 0	8 1	8 1	87 59	87 59	165 41	185 32	186 0
7	1.7698	9.9957	7 1	9 22	9 22	87 38	87 38	163 18	186 28	186 59
8	1.5981	9.9943	8 1	10 42	10 42	87 18	87 18	160 53	187 23	187 59
9	1.4473	9.9928	9 2	12 3	12 3	86 57	86 57	158 28	188 18	188 58
10	1.3130	9.9911	10 3	13 25	13 25	86 35	86 35	156 3	189 13	189 57
11	1.1922	9.9892	11 5	14 46	14 46	86 14	86 14	153 37	190 8	190 56
12	1.0824	9.9871	12 6	16 8	16 8	85 52	85 52	151 10	191 4	191 54
13	0.9821	9.9848	13 9	17 31	17 31	85 29	85 29	148 43	191 59	192 52
14	0.8898	9.9823	14 12	18 53	18 53	85 7	85 7	146 14	192 54	193 49
15	0.8045	9.9796	15 16	20 17	20 17	84 43	84 43	143 45	193 49	194 46
16	0.7254	9.9767	16 20	21 40	21 40	84 20	84 20	141 14	194 44	195 43
17	0.6518	9.9736	17 26	23 5	23 5	83 55	83 55	138 42	195 39	196 39
18	0.5830	9.9702	18 33	24 30	24 30	83 30	83 30	136 9	196 33	197 33
19	0.5185	9.9667	19 41	25 56	25 56	83 4	83 4	133 34	197 28	198 28
20	0.4581	9.9629	20 51	27 23	27 23	82 37	82 37	130 58	198 23	199 22
21	0.4013	9.9588	22 2	28 50	28 50	82 10	82 10	128 19	199 17	200 15
22	0.3479	9.9545	23 15	30 19	30 19	81 41	81 41	125 38	200 11	201 07
23	0.2976	9.9499	24 31	31 49	31 49	81 11	81 11	122 55	201 6	202 0
24	0.2501	9.9451	25 49	33 20	33 20	80 40	80 40	120 9	202 0	202 51
25	0.2053	9.9400	27 10	34 53	34 53	80 7	80 7	117 20	202 54	203 41
26	0.1631	9.9345	28 35	36 28	36 28	79 32	79 32	114 27	203 47	204 32
27	0.1232	9.9287	30 4	38 5	38 5	78 55	78 55	111 30	204 41	205 22
28	0.0857	9.9226	31 38	39 45	39 45	78 15	78 15	108 27	205 35	206 11
29	0.0503	9.9161	33 18	41 27	41 27	77 33	77 33	105 19	206 28	206 59
30	0.0170	9.9092	35 5	43 13	43 13	76 47	76 47	102 3	207 21	207 48
31	9.9857	9.9019	37 1	45 4	45 4	75 56	75 56	98 37	208 14	208 36
32	9.9565	9.8940	39 9	47 1	47 1	74 59	74 59	95 0	209 06	209 23
33	9.9292	9.8856	41 33	49 6	49 6	73 54	73 54	91 6	209 58	210 11
34	9.9040	9.8765	44 21	51 22	51 22	72 38	72 38	86 49	210 50	210 58
35	9.8808	9.8665	47 47	53 58	53 58	71 2	71 2	81 53	211 41	211 46
36	9.8600	9.8555	52 31	57 13	57 13	68 47	68 47	75 40	212 32	212 33
+36 52.2	9.8443	9.8443	63 26	63 26	63 26	63 26	63 26	63 26	213 15	213 15

This table exhibits the limits of the roots of the equation

$$\sin (z' - \zeta) = m_0 \sin^4 z',$$

when there are four real roots. The quantities m_1 and m_2 are the limiting values of m_0, and the values of z_1', z_2', z_3', and z_4', corresponding to each of these, give the limits of the four real roots of the equation.

TABLE XIII.

For finding the Ratio of the Sector to the Triangle.

η	log s^2	Diff.	η	log s^2	Diff.	η	log s^2	Diff.
0.0000	0.000 0000	965	0.0060	0.005 7298	945	0.0120	0.011 3417	926
.0001	.000 0965	965	.0061	.005 8243	944	.0121	.011 4343	925
.0002	.000 1930	964	.0062	.005 9187	944	.0122	.011 5268	925
.0003	.000 2894	964	.0063	.006 0131	944	.0123	.011 6193	925
.0004	.000 3858	963	.0064	.006 1075	944	.0124	.011 7118	925
0.0005	0.000 4821	963	0.0065	0.006 2019	943	0.0125	0.011 8043	924
.0006	.000 5784	963	.0066	.006 2962	943	.0126	.011 8967	923
.0007	.000 6747	963	.0067	.006 3905	942	.0127	.011 9890	924
.0008	.000 7710	962	.0068	.006 4847	943	.0128	.012 0814	923
.0009	.000 8672	962	.0069	.006 5790	942	.0129	.012 1737	923
0.0010	0.000 9634	961	0.0070	0.006 6732	941	0.0130	0.012 2660	923
.0011	.001 0595	961	.0071	.006 7673	941	.0131	.012 3583	922
.0012	.001 1556	961	.0072	.006 8614	941	.0132	.012 4505	922
.0013	.001 2517	961	.0073	.006 9555	941	.0133	.012 5427	921
.0014	.001 3478	960	.0074	.007 0496	940	.0134	.012 6348	921
0.0015	0.001 4438	960	0.0075	0.007 1436	940	0.0135	0.012 7269	921
.0016	.001 5398	959	.0076	.007 2376	940	.0136	.012 8190	921
.0017	.001 6357	959	.0077	.007 3316	939	.0137	.012 9111	921
.0018	.001 7316	959	.0078	.007 4255	939	.0138	.013 0032	920
.0019	.001 8275	959	.0079	.007 5194	939	.0139	.013 0952	919
0.0020	0.001 9234	958	0.0080	0.007 6133	938	0.0140	0.013 1871	920
.0021	.002 0192	958	.0081	.007 7071	938	.0141	.013 2791	919
.0022	.002 1150	957	.0082	.007 8009	938	.0142	.013 3710	919
.0023	.002 2107	957	.0083	.007 8947	937	.0143	.013 4629	918
.0024	.002 3064	957	.0084	.007 9884	937	.0144	.013 5547	918
0.0025	0.002 4021	956	0.0085	0.008 0821	937	0.0145	0.013 6465	918
.0026	.002 4977	956	.0086	.008 1758	936	.0146	.013 7383	918
.0027	.002 5933	956	.0087	.008 2694	936	.0147	.013 8301	917
.0028	.002 6889	956	.0088	.008 3630	936	.0148	.013 9218	917
.0029	.002 7845	955	.0089	.008 4566	936	.0149	.014 0135	917
0.0030	0.002 8800	955	0.0090	0.008 5502	935	0.0150	0.014 1052	916
.0031	.002 9755	954	.0091	.008 6437	935	.0151	.014 1968	916
.0032	.003 0709	954	.0092	.008 7372	934	.0152	.014 2884	916
.0033	.003 1663	954	.0093	.008 8306	934	.0153	.014 3800	916
.0034	.003 2617	953	.0094	.008 9240	934	.0154	.014 4716	915
0.0035	0.003 3570	953	0.0095	0.009 0174	934	0.0155	0.014 5631	915
.0036	.003 4523	953	.0096	.009 1108	933	.0156	.014 6546	914
.0037	.003 5476	952	.0097	.009 2041	933	.0157	.014 7460	914
.0038	.003 6428	952	.0098	.009 2974	932	.0158	.014 8374	914
.0039	.003 7380	952	.0099	.009 3906	932	.0159	.014 9288	914
0.0040	0.003 8332	952	0.0100	0.009 4838	932	0.0160	0.015 0202	913
.0041	.003 9284	951	.0101	.009 5770	932	.0161	.015 1115	913
.0042	.004 0235	951	.0102	.009 6702	931	.0162	.015 2028	913
.0043	.004 1186	950	.0103	.009 7633	931	.0163	.015 2941	913
.0044	.004 2136	950	.0104	.009 8564	931	.0164	.015 3854	912
0.0045	0.004 3086	950	0.0105	0.009 9495	930	0.0165	0.015 4766	912
.0046	.004 4036	949	.0106	.010 0425	930	.0166	.015 5678	911
.0047	.004 4985	949	.0107	.010 1355	930	.0167	.015 6589	911
.0048	.004 5934	949	.0108	.010 2285	930	.0168	.015 7500	911
.0049	.004 6883	949	.0109	.010 3215	929	.0169	.015 8411	911
0.0050	0.004 7832	948	0.0110	0.010 4144	929	0.0170	0.015 9322	910
.0051	.004 8780	948	.0111	.010 5073	928	.0171	.016 0232	910
.0052	.004 9728	947	.0112	.010 6001	928	.0172	.016 1142	910
.0053	.005 0675	947	.0113	.010 6929	928	.0173	.016 2052	909
.0054	.005 1622	947	.0114	.010 7857	928	.0174	.016 2961	909
0.0055	0.005 2569	946	0.0115	0.010 8785	927	0.0175	0.016 3870	909
.0056	.005 3515	946	.0116	.010 9712	927	.0176	.016 4779	909
.0057	.005 4461	946	.0117	.011 0639	926	.0177	.016 5688	908
.0058	.005 5407	946	.0118	.011 1565	926	.0178	.016 6596	908
.0059	.005 6353	945	.0119	.011 2491	926	.0179	.016 7504	908
0.0060	0.005 7298		0.0120	0.011 3417		0.0180	0.016 8412	

TABLE XIII.

For finding the Ratio of the Sector to the Triangle.

η	log s^2	Diff.	η	log s^2	Diff.	η	log s^2	Diff.
0.0180	0.016 8412	907	0.0240	0.022 2330	890	0.0300	0.027 5218	873
.0181	.016 9319	907	.0241	.022 3220	889	.0301	.027 6091	873
.0182	.017 0226	907	.0242	.022 4109	889	.0302	.027 6964	872
.0183	.017 1133	906	.0243	.022 4998	889	.0303	.027 7836	872
.0184	.017 2039	906	.0244	.022 5887	889	.0304	.027 8708	872
0.0185	0.017 2945	906	0.0245	0.022 6776	888	0.0305	0.027 9580	872
.0186	.017 3851	906	.0246	.022 7664	888	.0306	.028 0452	871
.0187	.017 4757	905	.0247	.022 8552	888	.0307	.028 1323	871
.0188	.017 5662	905	.0248	.022 9440	888	.0308	.028 2194	871
.0189	.017 6567	904	.0249	.023 0328	887	.0309	.028 3065	871
0.0190	0.017 7471	905	0.0250	0.023 1215	887	0.0310	0.028 3936	870
.0191	.017 8376	904	.0251	.023 2102	886	.0311	.028 4806	870
.0192	.017 9280	903	.0252	.023 2988	887	.0312	.028 5676	870
.0193	.018 0183	904	.0253	.023 3875	886	.0313	.028 6546	869
.0194	.018 1087	903	.0254	.023 4761	886	.0314	.028 7415	869
0.0195	0.018 1990	903	0.0255	0.023 5647	885	0.0315	0.028 8284	869
.0196	.018 2893	903	.0256	.023 6532	885	.0316	.028 9153	869
.0197	.018 3796	902	.0257	.023 7417	885	.0317	.029 0022	868
.0198	.018 4698	902	.0258	.023 8302	885	.0318	.029 0890	868
.0199	.018 5600	901	.0259	.023 9187	884	.0319	.029 1758	868
0.0200	0.018 6501	902	0.0260	0.024 0071	885	0.0320	0.029 2626	868
.0201	.018 7403	901	.0261	.024 0956	883	.0321	.029 3494	867
.0202	.018 8304	901	.0262	.024 1839	884	.0322	.029 4361	867
.0203	.018 9205	900	.0263	.024 2723	883	.0323	.029 5228	867
.0204	.019 0105	900	.0264	.024 3606	883	.0324	.029 6095	866
0.0205	0.019 1005	900	0.0265	0.024 4489	883	0.0325	0.029 6961	866
.0206	.019 1905	900	.0266	.024 5372	882	.0326	.029 7827	866
.0207	.019 2805	899	.0267	.024 6254	882	.0327	.029 8693	866
.0208	.019 3704	899	.0268	.024 7136	882	.0328	.029 9559	865
.0209	.019 4603	899	.0269	.024 8018	882	.0329	.030 0424	866
0.0210	0.019 5502	899	0.0270	0.024 8900	881	0.0330	0.030 1290	864
.0211	.019 6401	898	.0271	.024 9781	881	.0331	.030 2154	865
.0212	.019 7299	898	.0272	.025 0662	881	.0332	.030 3019	864
.0213	.019 8197	897	.0273	.025 1543	880	.0333	.030 3883	864
.0214	.019 9094	898	.0274	.025 2423	880	.0334	.030 4747	864
0.0215	0.019 9992	897	0.0275	0.025 3303	880	0.0335	0.030 5611	864
.0216	.020 0889	896	.0276	.025 4183	880	.0336	.030 6475	863
.0217	.020 1785	897	.0277	.025 5063	879	.0337	.030 7338	863
.0218	.020 2682	896	.0278	.025 5942	879	.0338	.030 8201	863
.0219	.020 3578	896	.0279	.025 6821	879	.0339	.030 9064	862
0.0220	0.020 4474	895	0.0280	0.025 7700	879	0.0340	0.030 9926	862
.0221	.020 5369	895	.0281	.025 8579	878	.0341	.031 0788	862
.0222	.020 6264	895	.0282	.025 9457	878	.0342	.031 1650	862
.0223	.020 7159	895	.0283	.026 0335	878	.0343	.031 2512	861
.0224	.020 8054	894	.0284	.026 1213	877	.0344	.031 3373	861
0.0225	0.020 8948	894	0.0285	0.026 2090	877	0.0345	0.031 4234	861
.0226	.020 9842	894	.0286	.026 2967	877	.0346	.031 5095	861
.0227	.021 0736	894	.0287	.026 3844	877	.0347	.031 5956	860
.0228	.021 1630	893	.0288	.026 4721	876	.0348	.031 6816	860
.0229	.021 2523	893	.0289	.026 5597	876	.0349	.031 7676	860
0.0230	0.021 3416	893	0.0290	0.026 6473	876	0.0350	0.031 8536	860
.0231	.021 4309	892	.0291	.026 7349	875	.0351	.031 9396	859
.0232	.021 5201	892	.0292	.026 8224	875	.0352	.032 0255	859
.0233	.021 6093	892	.0293	.026 9099	875	.0353	.032 1114	859
.0234	.021 6985	891	.0294	.026 9974	875	.0354	.032 1973	858
0.0235	0.021 7876	892	0.0295	0.027 0849	874	0.0355	0.032 2831	858
.0236	.021 8768	891	.0296	.027 1723	874	.0356	.032 3689	858
.0237	.021 9659	890	.0297	.027 2597	874	.0357	.032 4547	858
.0238	.022 0549	891	.0298	.027 3471	874	.0358	.032 5405	857
.0239	.022 1440	890	.0299	.027 4345	873	.0359	.032 6262	858
0.0240	0.022 2330		0.0300	0.027 5218		0.0360	0.032 7120	

TABLE XIII.

For finding the Ratio of the Sector to the Triangle.

η	$\log s^2$	Diff.	η	$\log s^2$	Diff.	η	$\log s^2$	Diff.
0.0360	0.032 7120	856	0.060	0.052 5626	7976	0.120	0.096 8849	6843
.0361	.032 7976	857	.061	.053 3602	7954	.121	.097 5692	6828
.0362	.032 8833	856	.062	.054 1556	7932	.122	.098 2520	6811
.0363	.032 9689	857	.063	.054 9488	7909	.123	.098 9331	6796
.0364	.033 0546	855	.064	.055 7397	7888	.124	.099 6127	6780
0.0365	0.033 1401	856	0.065	0.056 5285	7865	0.125	0.100 2907	6765
.0366	.033 2257	855	.066	.057 3150	7844	.126	.100 9672	6749
.0367	.033 3112	855	.067	.058 0994	7823	.127	.101 6421	6733
.0368	.033 3967	855	.068	.058 8817	7801	.128	.102 3154	6719
.0369	.033 4822	855	.069	.059 6618	7780	.129	.102 9873	6703
0.0370	0.033 5677	854	0.070	0.060 4398	7759	0.130	0.103 6576	6688
.0371	.033 6531	854	.071	.061 2157	7738	.131	.104 3264	6672
.0372	.033 7385	854	.072	.061 9895	7717	.132	.104 9936	6658
.0373	.033 8239	853	.073	.062 7612	7696	.133	.105 6594	6643
.0374	.033 9092	854	.074	.063 5308	7676	.134	.106 3237	6628
0.0375	0.033 9946	853	0.075	0.064 2984	7655	0.135	0.106 9865	6613
.0376	.034 0799	852	.076	.065 0639	7635	.136	.107 6478	6598
.0377	.034 1651	853	.077	.065 8274	7614	.137	.108 3076	6584
.0378	.034 2504	852	.078	.066 5888	7594	.138	.108 9660	6569
.0379	.034 3356	852	.079	.067 3482	7575	.139	.109 6229	6554
0.0380	0.034 4208	851	0.080	0.068 1057	7555	0.140	0.110 2783	6540
.0381	.034 5059	852	.081	.068 8612	7534	.141	.110 9323	6526
.0382	.034 5911	851	.082	.069 6146	7515	.142	.111 5849	6511
.0383	.034 6762	851	.083	.070 3661	7496	.143	.112 2360	6497
.0384	.034 7613	851	.084	.071 1157	7476	.144	.112 8857	6483
0.0385	0.034 8464	850	0.085	0.071 8633	7457	0.145	0.113 5340	6469
.0386	.034 9314	850	.086	.072 6090	7437	.146	.114 1809	6455
.0387	.035 0164	850	.087	.073 3527	7418	.147	.114 8264	6440
.0388	.035 1014	850	.088	.074 0945	7400	.148	.115 4704	6427
.0389	.035 1864	849	.089	.074 8345	7380	.149	.116 1131	6413
0.0390	0.035 2713	849	0.090	0.075 5725	7362	0.150	0.116 7544	6399
.0391	.035 3562	849	.091	.076 3087	7343	.151	.117 3943	6386
.0392	.035 4411	848	.092	.077 0430	7324	.152	.118 0329	6372
.0393	.035 5259	849	.093	.077 7754	7306	.153	.118 6701	6358
.0394	.035 6108	848	.094	.078 5060	7288	.154	.119 3059	6345
0.0395	0.035 6956	848	0.095	0.079 2348	7269	0.155	0.119 9404	6331
.0396	.035 7804	847	.096	.079 9617	7251	.156	.120 5735	6318
.0397	.035 8651	848	.097	.080 6868	7233	.157	.121 2053	6304
.0398	.035 9499	847	.098	.081 4101	7215	.158	.121 8357	6292
.0399	.036 0346	846	.099	.082 1316	7197	.159	.122 4649	6278
0.040	0.036 1192	8454	0.100	0.082 8513	7180	0.160	0.123 0927	6265
.041	.036 9646	8429	.101	.083 5693	7161	.161	.123 7192	6252
.042	.037 8075	8403	.102	.084 2854	7145	.162	.124 3444	6238
.043	.038 6478	8378	.103	.084 9999	7126	.163	.124 9682	6226
.044	.039 4856	8353	.104	.085 7125	7110	.164	.125 5908	6213
0.045	0.040 3209	8328	0.105	0.086 4235	7092	0.165	0.126 2121	6200
.046	.041 1537	8304	.106	.087 1327	7074	.166	.126 8321	6187
.047	.041 9841	8280	.107	.087 8401	7058	.167	.127 4508	6175
.048	.042 8121	8255	.108	.088 5459	7041	.168	.128 0683	6162
.049	.043 6376	8231	.109	.089 2500	7023	.169	.128 6845	6149
0.050	0.044 4607	8207	0.110	0.089 9523	7007	0.170	0.129 2994	6137
.051	.045 2814	8183	.111	.090 6530	6990	.171	.129 9131	6124
.052	.046 0997	8160	.112	.091 3520	6974	.172	.130 5255	6112
.053	.046 9157	8137	.113	.092 0494	6957	.173	.131 1367	6099
.054	.047 7294	8113	.114	.092 7451	6940	.174	.131 7466	6087
0.055	0.048 5407	8089	0.115	0.093 4391	6924	0.175	0.132 3553	6075
.056	.049 3496	8067	.116	.094 1315	6908	.176	.132 9628	6062
.057	.050 1563	8044	.117	.094 8223	6891	.177	.133 5690	6050
.058	.050 9607	8021	.118	.095 5114	6876	.178	.134 1740	6038
.059	.051 7628	7998	.119	.096 1990	6859	.179	.134 7778	6026
0.060	0.052 5626		0.120	0.096 8849		0.180	0.135 3804	

TABLE XIII.

For finding the Ratio of the Sector to the Triangle.

η	log s^2	Diff.	η	log s^2	Diff.	η	log s^2	Diff.
0.180	0.135 3804	6014	0.240	0.169 5092	5378	0.300	0.200 2285	4872
.181	.135 9818	6003	.241	.170 0470	5368	.301	.200 7157	4864
.182	.136 5821	5990	.242	.170 5838	5359	.302	.201 2021	4857
.183	.137 1811	5978	.243	.171 1197	5350	.303	.201 6878	4849
.184	.137 7789	5966	.244	.171 6547	5340	.304	.202 1727	4842
0.185	0.138 3755	5955	0.245	0.172 1887	5331	0.305	0.202 6569	4834
.186	.138 9710	5943	.246	.172 7218	5322	.306	.203 1403	4827
.187	.139 5653	5932	.247	.173 2540	5313	.307	.203 6230	4820
.188	.140 1585	5919	.248	.173 7853	5303	.308	.204 1050	4812
.189	.140 7504	5908	.249	.174 3156	5295	.309	.204 5862	4805
0.190	0.141 3412	5897	0.250	0.174 8451	5285	0.310	0.205 0667	4797
.191	.141 9309	5885	.251	.175 3736	5277	.311	.205 5464	4790
.192	.142 5194	5874	.252	.175 9013	5267	.312	.206 0254	4783
.193	.143 1068	5863	.253	.176 4280	5258	.313	.206 5037	4776
.194	.143 6931	5851	.254	.176 9538	5250	.314	.206 9813	4768
0.195	0.144 2782	5840	0.255	0.177 4788	5241	0.315	0.207 4581	4761
.196	.144 8622	5828	.256	.178 0029	5232	.316	.207 9342	4754
.197	.145 4450	5818	.257	.178 5261	5223	.317	.208 4096	4747
.198	.146 0268	5806	.258	.179 0484	5214	.318	.208 8843	4739
.199	.146 6074	5795	.259	.179 5698	5205	.319	.209 3582	4733
0.200	0.147 1869	5784	0.260	0.180 0903	5197	0.320	0.209 8315	4725
.201	.147 7653	5774	.261	.180 6100	5188	.321	.210 3040	4719
.202	.148 3427	5762	.262	.181 1288	5179	.322	.210 7759	4711
.203	.148 9189	5751	.263	.181 6467	5171	.323	.211 2470	4704
.204	.149 4940	5741	.264	.182 1638	5162	.324	.211 7174	4697
0.205	0.150 0681	5730	0.265	0.182 6800	5153	0.325	0.212 1871	4691
.206	.150 6411	5719	.266	.183 1953	5145	.326	.212 6562	4683
.207	.151 2130	5708	.267	.183 7098	5137	.327	.213 1245	4676
.208	.151 7838	5697	.268	.184 2235	5128	.328	.213 5921	4670
.209	.152 3535	5687	.269	.184 7363	5120	.329	.214 0591	4662
0.210	0.152 9222	5677	0.270	0.185 2483	5111	0.330	0.214 5253	4656
.211	.153 4899	5666	.271	.185 7594	5102	.331	.214 9909	4649
.212	.154 0565	5655	.272	.186 2696	5095	.332	.215 4558	4642
.213	.154 6220	5645	.273	.186 7791	5086	.333	.215 9200	4635
.214	.155 1865	5634	.274	.187 2877	5078	.334	.216 3835	4629
0.215	0.155 7499	5624	0.275	0.187 7955	5069	0.335	0.216 8464	4621
.216	.156 3123	5614	.276	.188 3024	5061	.336	.217 3085	4615
.217	.156 8737	5603	.277	.188 8085	5053	.337	.217 7700	4608
.218	.157 4340	5593	.278	.189 3138	5045	.338	.218 2308	4602
.219	.157 9933	5583	.279	.189 8183	5037	.339	.218 6910	4595
0.220	0.158 5516	5573	0.280	0.190 3220	5029	0.340	0.219 1505	4588
.221	.159 1089	5563	.281	.190 8249	5020	.341	.219 6093	4582
.222	.159 6652	5552	.282	.191 3269	5012	.342	.220 0675	4575
.223	.160 2204	5543	.283	.191 8281	5005	.343	.220 5250	4568
.224	.160 7747	5532	.284	.192 3286	4996	.344	.220 9818	4562
0.225	0.161 3279	5523	0.285	0.192 8282	4989	0.345	0.221 4380	4555
.226	.161 8802	5513	.286	.193 3271	4980	.346	.221 8935	4548
.227	.162 4315	5502	.287	.193 8251	4973	.347	.222 3483	4542
.228	.162 9817	5493	.288	.194 3224	4964	.348	.222 8025	4536
.229	.163 5310	5483	.289	.194 8188	4957	.349	.223 2561	4529
0.230	0.164 0793	5474	0.290	0.195 3145	4949	0.350	0.223 7090	4523
.231	.164 6267	5463	.291	.195 8094	4941	.351	.224 1613	4517
.232	.165 1730	5454	.292	.196 3035	4933	.352	.224 6130	4510
.233	.165 7184	5444	.293	.196 7968	4926	.353	.225 0640	4503
.234	.166 2628	5435	.294	.197 2894	4917	.354	.225 5143	4497
0.235	0.166 8063	5425	0.295	0.197 7811	4910	0.355	0.225 9640	4491
.236	.167 3488	5415	.296	.198 2721	4903	.356	.226 4131	4484
.237	.167 8903	5406	.297	.198 7624	4894	.357	.226 8615	4478
.238	.168 4309	5396	.298	.199 2518	4888	.358	.227 3093	4472
.239	.168 9705	5387	.299	.199 7406	4879	.359	.227 7565	4466
0.240	0.169 5092		0.300	0.200 2285		0.360	0.228 2031	

TABLE XIII.

For finding the Ratio of the Sector to the Triangle.

η	log s^2	Diff.	η	log s^2	Diff.	η	log s^2	Diff.
0.360	0.228 2031	4459	0.420	0.253 9153	4116	0.480	0.277 7272	3824
.361	.228 6490	4453	.421	.254 3269	4110	.481	.278 1096	3820
.362	.229 0943	4447	.422	.254 7379	4105	.482	.278 4916	3816
.363	.229 5390	4441	.423	.255 1484	4100	.483	.278 8732	3811
.364	.229 9831	4434	.424	.255 5584	4095	.484	.279 2543	3806
0.365	0.230 4265	4429	0.425	0.255 9679	4090	0.485	0.279 6349	3802
.366	.230 8694	4422	.426	.256 3769	4084	.486	.280 0151	3798
.367	.231 3116	4416	.427	.256 7853	4079	.487	.280 3949	3794
.368	.231 7532	4410	.428	.257 1932	4074	.488	.280 7743	3789
.369	.232 1942	4404	.429	.257 6006	4069	.489	.281 1532	3784
0.370	0.232 6346	4397	0.430	0.258 0075	4064	0.490	0.281 5316	3780
.371	.233 0743	4392	.431	.258 4139	4059	.491	.281 9096	3776
.372	.233 5135	4386	.432	.258 8198	4054	.492	.282 2872	3772
.373	.233 9521	4379	.433	.259 2252	4048	.493	.282 6644	3767
.374	.234 3900	4374	.434	.259 6300	4044	.494	.283 0411	3762
0.375	0.234 8274	4368	0.435	0.260 0344	4038	0.495	0.283 4173	3759
.376	.235 2642	4361	.436	.260 4382	4033	.496	.283 7932	3754
.377	.235 7003	4356	.437	.260 8415	4029	.497	.284 1686	3750
.378	.236 1359	4350	.438	.261 2444	4023	.498	.284 5436	3745
.379	.236 5709	4344	.439	.261 6467	4019	.499	.284 9181	3742
0.380	0.237 0053	4338	0.440	0.262 0486	4013	0.500	0.285 2923	3737
.381	.237 4391	4332	.441	.262 4499	4008	.501	.285 6660	3732
.382	.237 8723	4327	.442	.262 8507	4004	.502	.286 0392	3729
.383	.238 3050	4320	.443	.263 2511	3998	.503	.286 4121	3724
.384	.238 7370	4315	.444	.263 6509	3994	.504	.286 7845	3720
0.385	0.239 1685	4308	0.445	0.264 0503	3989	0.505	0.287 1565	3716
.386	.239 5993	4303	.446	.264 4492	3983	.506	.287 5281	3711
.387	.240 0296	4298	.447	.264 8475	3979	.507	.287 8992	3708
.388	.240 4594	4291	.448	.265 2454	3974	.508	.288 2700	3703
.389	.240 8885	4286	.449	.265 6428	3969	.509	.288 6403	3699
0.390	0.241 3171	4280	0.450	0.266 0397	3965	0.510	0.289 0102	3695
.391	.241 7451	4274	.451	.266 4362	3959	.511	.289 3797	3690
.392	.242 1725	4269	.452	.266 8321	3955	.512	.289 7487	3687
.393	.242 5994	4263	.453	.267 2276	3950	.513	.290 1174	3682
.394	.243 0257	4257	.454	.267 6226	3945	.514	.290 4856	3679
0.395	0.243 4514	4252	0.455	0.268 0171	3940	0.515	0.290 8535	3674
.396	.243 8766	4246	.456	.268 4111	3935	.516	.291 2209	3670
.397	.244 3012	4240	.457	.268 8046	3931	.517	.291 5879	3666
.398	.244 7252	4235	.458	.269 1977	3926	.518	.291 9545	3662
.399	.245 1487	4229	.459	.269 5903	3921	.519	.292 3207	3657
0.400	0.245 5716	4224	0.460	0.269 9824	3917	0.520	0.292 6864	3654
.401	.245 9940	4218	.461	.270 3741	3911	.521	.293 0518	3650
.402	.246 4158	4213	.462	.270 7652	3907	.522	.293 4168	3645
.403	.246 8371	4207	.463	.271 1559	3903	.523	.293 7813	3642
.404	.247 2578	4201	.464	.271 5462	3898	.524	.294 1455	3637
0.405	0.247 6779	4196	0.465	0.271 9360	3893	0.525	0.294 5092	3634
.406	.248 0975	4191	.466	.272 3253	3888	.526	.294 8726	3629
.407	.248 5166	4185	.467	.272 7141	3884	.527	.295 2355	3626
.408	.248 9351	4180	.468	.273 1025	3879	.528	.295 5981	3621
.409	.249 3531	4174	.469	.273 4904	3874	.529	.295 9602	3618
0.410	0.249 7705	4169	0.470	0.273 8778	3870	0.530	0.296 3220	3613
.411	.250 1874	4164	.471	.274 2648	3865	.531	.296 6833	3610
.412	.250 6038	4158	.472	.274 6513	3861	.532	.297 0443	3606
.413	.251 0196	4153	.473	.275 0374	3856	.533	.297 4049	3601
.414	.251 4349	4147	.474	.275 4230	3852	.534	.297 7650	3598
0.415	0.251 8496	4142	0.475	0.275 8082	3847	0.535	0.298 1248	3594
.416	.252 2638	4137	.476	.276 1929	3842	.536	.298 4842	3590
.417	.252 6775	4131	.477	.276 5771	3838	.537	.298 8432	3586
.418	.253 0906	4126	.478	.276 9609	3834	.538	.299 2018	3582
.419	.253 5032	4121	.479	.277 3443	3829	.539	.299 5600	3578
0.420	0.253 9153		0.480	0.277 7272		0.540	0.299 9178	

TABLE XIII.

For finding the Ratio of the Sector to the Triangle.

η	$\log s^2$	Diff.	η	$\log s^2$	Diff.	η	$\log s^2$	Diff.
0.540	0.299 9178	3574	0.560	0.306 9938	3499	0.580	0.313 9215	3426
.541	.300 2752	3571	.561	.307 3437	3494	.581	.314 2641	3423
.542	.300 6323	3567	.562	.307 6931	3491	.582	.314 6064	3419
.543	.300 9890	3562	.563	.308 0422	3488	.583	.314 9483	3415
.544	.301 3452	3559	.564	.308 3910	3484	.584	.315 2898	3412
0.545	0.301 7011	3555	0.565	0.308 7394	3480	0.585	0.315 6310	3409
.546	.302 0566	3551	.566	.309 0874	3476	.586	.315 9719	3405
.547	.302 4117	3547	.567	.309 4350	3473	.587	.316 3124	3401
.548	.302 7664	3544	.568	.309 7823	3469	.588	.316 6525	3398
.549	.303 1208	3540	.569	.310 1292	3466	.589	.316 9923	3395
0.550	0.303 4748	3536	0.570	0.310 4758	3462	0.590	0.317 3318	3391
.551	.303 8284	3532	.571	.310 8220	3458	.591	.317 6709	3387
.552	.304 1816	3528	.572	.311 1678	3455	.592	.318 0096	3384
.553	.304 5344	3525	.573	.311 5133	3451	.593	.318 3480	3381
.554	.304 8869	3521	.574	.311 8584	3447	.594	.318 6861	3377
0.555	0.305 2390	3517	0.575	0.312 2031	3444	0.595	0.319 0238	3374
.556	.305 5907	3513	.576	.312 5475	3440	.596	.319 3612	3371
.557	.305 9420	3510	.577	.312 8915	3437	.597	.319 6983	3367
.558	.306 2930	3506	.578	.313 2352	3433	.598	.320 0350	3364
.559	.306 6436	3502	.579	.313 5785	3430	.599	.320 3714	3360
0.560	0.306 9938		0.580	0.313 9215		0.600	0.320 7074	

TABLE XIV.

For finding the Ratio of the Sector to the Triangle.

x	ξ				x	ξ			
	Ellipse.	Diff.	Hyperbola.	Diff.		Ellipse.	Diff.	Hyperbola.	Diff.
0.000	0.000 0000	1	0.000 0000	1	0.030	0.000 0523	36	0.000 0506	33
.001	.000 0001	1	.000 0001	1	.031	.000 0559	37	.000 0539	36
.002	.000 0002	3	.000 0002	3	.032	.000 0596	38	.000 0575	36
.003	.000 0005	4	.000 0005	4	.033	.000 0634	40	.000 0611	37
.004	.000 0009	5	.000 0009	5	.034	.000 0674	40	.000 0648	38
0.005	0.000 0014	7	0.000 0014	6	0.035	0.000 0714	42	0.000 0686	40
.006	.000 0021	7	.000 0020	8	.036	.000 0756	43	.000 0726	40
.007	.000 0028	9	.000 0028	8	.037	.000 0799	45	.000 0766	41
.008	.000 0037	10	.000 0036	10	.038	.000 0844	45	.000 0807	43
.009	.000 0047	11	.000 0046	11	.039	.000 0889	47	.000 0850	44
0.010	0.000 0058	12	0.000 0057	12	0.040	0.000 0936	48	0.000 0894	44
.011	.000 0070	13	.000 0069	13	.041	.000 0984	49	.000 0938	46
.012	.000 0083	14	.000 0082	14	.042	.000 1033	51	.000 0984	47
.013	.000 0097	16	.000 0096	15	.043	.000 1084	51	.000 1031	48
.014	.000 0113	17	.000 0111	16	.044	.000 1135	53	.000 1079	49
0.015	0.000 0130	18	0.000 0127	18	0.045	0.000 1188	54	0.000 1128	50
.016	.000 0148	19	.000 0145	19	.046	.000 1242	56	.000 1178	51
.017	.000 0167	20	.000 0164	19	.047	.000 1298	56	.000 1229	52
.018	.000 0187	22	.000 0183	21	.048	.000 1354	58	.000 1281	53
.019	.000 0209	22	.000 0204	22	.049	.000 1412	59	.000 1334	55
0.020	0.000 0231	24	0.000 0226	23	0.050	0.000 1471	61	0.000 1389	55
.021	.000 0255	25	.000 0249	24	.051	.000 1532	61	.000 1444	56
.022	.000 0280	26	.000 0273	25	.052	.000 1593	63	.000 1500	58
.023	.000 0306	28	.000 0298	27	.053	.000 1656	64	.000 1558	58
.024	.000 0334	28	.000 0325	27	.054	.000 1720	65	.000 1616	59
0.025	0.000 0362	30	0.000 0352	29	0.055	0.000 1785	67	0.000 1675	61
.026	.000 0392	31	.000 0381	29	.056	.000 1852	68	.000 1736	62
.027	.000 0423	32	.000 0410	31	.057	.000 1920	69	.000 1798	62
.028	.000 0455	34	.000 0441	32	.058	.000 1989	71	.000 1860	64
.029	.000 0489	34	.000 0473	33	.059	.000 2060	71	.000 1924	64
0.030	0.000 0523		0.000 0506		0.060	0.000 2131		0.000 1988	

TABLE XIV.

For finding the Ratio of the Sector to the Triangle.

x	ξ Ellipse.	Diff.	ξ Hyperbola.	Diff.	x	ξ Ellipse.	Diff.	ξ Hyperbola.	Diff.
0.060	0.000 2131	73	0.000 1988	66	0.120	0.000 8845	154	0.000 7698	124
.061	.000 2204	74	.000 2054	67	.121	.000 8999	155	.000 7822	126
.062	.000 2278	76	.000 2121	68	.122	.000 9154	157	.000 7948	126
.063	.000 2354	77	.000 2189	68	.123	.000 9311	158	.000 8074	128
.064	.000 2431	78	.000 2257	70	.124	.000 9469	159	.000 8202	128
0.065	0.000 2509	79	0.000 2327	71	0.125	0.000 9628	161	0.000 8330	129
.066	.000 2588	81	.000 2398	72	.126	.000 9789	162	.000 8459	131
.067	.000 2669	82	.000 2470	73	.127	.000 9951	164	.000 8590	131
.068	.000 2751	83	.000 2543	74	.128	.001 0115	165	.000 8721	132
.069	.000 2834	84	.000 2617	74	.129	.001 0280	167	.000 8853	133
0.070	0.000 2918	86	0.000 2691	76	0.130	0.001 0447	168	0.000 8986	134
.071	.000 3004	87	.000 2767	77	.131	.001 0615	169	.000 9120	135
.072	.000 3091	89	.000 2844	78	.132	.001 0784	171	.000 9255	135
.073	.000 3180	89	.000 2922	79	.133	.001 0955	173	.000 9390	137
.074	.000 3269	91	.000 3001	80	.134	.001 1128	173	.000 9527	138
0.075	0.000 3360	93	0.000 3081	81	0.135	0.001 1301	176	0.000 9665	138
.076	.000 3453	93	.000 3162	82	.136	.001 1477	177	.000 9803	140
.077	.000 3546	95	.000 3244	83	.137	.001 1654	178	.000 9943	140
.078	.000 3641	97	.000 3327	84	.138	.001 1832	180	.001 0083	141
.079	.000 3738	97	.000 3411	85	.139	.001 2012	181	.001 0224	142
0.080	0.000 3835	99	0.000 3496	86	0.140	0.001 2193	183	0.001 0366	143
.081	.000 3934	100	.000 3582	87	.141	.001 2376	184	.001 0509	144
.082	.000 4034	102	.000 3669	88	.142	.001 2560	185	.001 0653	145
.083	.000 4136	103	.000 3757	89	.143	.001 2745	188	.001 0798	146
.084	.000 4239	104	.000 3846	90	.144	.001 2933	188	.001 0944	147
0.085	0.000 4343	105	0.000 3936	91	0.145	0.001 3121	190	0.001 1091	147
.086	.000 4448	107	.000 4027	92	.146	.001 3311	192	.001 1238	149
.087	.000 4555	108	.000 4119	93	.147	.001 3503	193	.001 1387	149
.088	.000 4663	110	.000 4212	94	.148	.001 3696	195	.001 1536	150
.089	.000 4773	111	.000 4306	95	.149	.001 3891	196	.001 1686	152
0.090	0.000 4884	112	0.000 4401	95	0.150	0.001 4087	198	0.001 1838	152
.091	.000 4996	113	.000 4496	97	.151	.001 4285	199	.001 1990	153
.092	.000 5109	115	.000 4593	98	.152	.001 4484	200	.001 2143	153
.093	.000 5224	117	.000 4691	99	.153	.001 4684	202	.001 2296	155
.094	.000 5341	117	.000 4790	100	.154	.001 4886	204	.001 2451	156
0.095	0.000 5458	119	0.000 4890	101	0.155	0.001 5090	205	0.001 2607	156
.096	.000 5577	120	.000 4991	101	.156	.001 5295	207	.001 2763	158
.097	.000 5697	122	.000 5092	103	.157	.001 5502	208	.001 2921	158
.098	.000 5819	123	.000 5195	104	.158	.001 5710	210	.001 3079	159
.099	.000 5942	124	.000 5299	104	.159	.001 5920	211	.001 3238	160
0.100	0.000 6066	126	0.000 5403	106	0.160	0.001 6131	213	0.001 3398	161
.101	.000 6192	127	.000 5509	107	.161	.001 6344	215	.001 3559	162
.102	.000 6319	129	.000 5616	107	.162	.001 6559	216	.001 3721	162
.103	.000 6448	130	.000 5723	109	.163	.001 6775	217	.001 3883	164
.104	.000 6578	131	.000 5832	109	.164	.001 6992	219	.001 4047	164
0.105	0.000 6709	133	0.000 5941	111	0.165	0.001 7211	221	0.001 4211	166
.106	.000 6842	134	.000 6052	111	.166	.001 7432	222	.001 4377	166
.107	.000 6976	135	.000 6163	112	.167	.001 7654	224	.001 4543	167
.108	.000 7111	137	.000 6275	114	.168	.001 7878	225	.001 4710	168
.109	.000 7248	138	.000 6389	114	.169	.001 8103	227	.001 4878	169
0.110	0.000 7386	140	0.000 6503	115	0.170	0.001 8330	228	0.001 5047	169
.111	.000 7526	141	.000 6618	116	.171	.001 8558	230	.001 5216	171
.112	.000 7667	142	.000 6734	117	.172	.001 8788	232	.001 5387	171
.113	.000 7809	144	.000 6851	118	.173	.001 9020	233	.001 5558	172
.114	.000 7953	145	.000 6969	119	.174	.001 9253	234	.001 5730	173
0.115	0.000 8098	147	0.000 7088	120	0.175	0.001 9487	237	0.001 5903	174
.116	.000 8245	148	.000 7208	121	.176	.001 9724	237	.001 6077	175
.117	.000 8393	149	.000 7329	122	.177	.001 9961	240	.001 6252	176
.118	.000 8542	151	.000 7451	123	.178	.002 0201	241	.001 6428	176
.119	.000 8693	152	.000 7574	124	.179	.002 0442	243	.001 6604	178
0.120	0.000 8845		0.000 7698		0.180	0.002 0685		0.001 6782	

TABLE XIV.

For finding the Ratio of the Sector to the Triangle.

x	ξ Ellipse.	Diff.	ξ Hyperbola.	Diff.
0.180	0.002 0685	244	0.001 6782	178
.181	.002 0929	246	.001 6960	179
.182	.002 1175	247	.001 7139	180
.183	.002 1422	249	.001 7319	181
.184	.002 1671	251	.001 7500	181
0.185	0.002 1922	252	0.001 7681	183
.186	.002 2174	254	.001 7864	183
.187	.002 2428	255	.001 8047	184
.188	.002 2683	258	.001 8231	185
.189	.002 2941	258	.001 8416	186
0.190	0.002 3199	261	0.001 8602	187
.191	.002 3460	262	.001 8789	187
.192	.002 3722	263	.001 8976	189
.193	.002 3985	266	.001 9165	189
.194	.002 4251	267	.001 9354	190
0.195	0.002 4518	268	0.001 9544	191
.196	.002 4786	270	.001 9735	191
.197	.002 5056	272	.001 9926	193
.198	.002 5328	274	.002 0119	193
.199	.002 5602	275	.002 0312	195
0.200	0.002 5877	277	0.002 0507	195
.201	.002 6154	279	.002 0702	195
.202	.002 6433	280	.002 0897	197
.203	.002 6713	282	.002 1094	198
.204	.002 6995	283	.002 1292	198
0.205	0.002 7278	286	0.002 1490	199
.206	.002 7564	287	.002 1689	200
.207	.002 7851	288	.002 1889	201
.208	.002 8139	290	.002 2090	201
.209	.002 8429	293	.002 2291	203
0.210	0.002 8722	293	0.002 2494	203
.211	.002 9015	296	.002 2697	204
.212	.002 9311	297	.002 2901	205
.213	.002 9608	299	.002 3106	205
.214	.002 9907	300	.002 3311	207
0.215	0.003 0207	302	0.002 3518	207
.216	.003 0509	305	.002 3725	207
.217	.003 0814	305	.002 3932	210
.218	.003 1119	308	.002 4142	210
.219	.003 1427	309	.002 4352	210
0.220	0.003 1736	311	0.002 4562	212
.221	.003 2047	312	.002 4774	212
.222	.003 2359	315	.002 4986	213
.223	.003 2674	316	.002 5199	213
.224	.003 2990	318	.002 5412	215
0.225	0.003 3308	319	0.002 5627	215
.226	.003 3627	322	.002 5842	216
.227	.003 3949	323	.002 6058	217
.228	.003 4272	325	.002 6275	218
.229	.003 4597	327	.002 6493	218
0.230	0.003 4924	328	0.002 6711	220
.231	.003 5252	330	.002 6931	220
.232	.003 5582	332	.002 7151	220
.233	.003 5914	334	.002 7371	222
.234	.003 6248	336	.002 7593	223
0.235	0.003 6584	337	0.002 7816	223
.236	.003 6921	339	.002 8039	224
.237	.003 7260	341	.002 8263	224
.238	.003 7601	343	.002 8487	226
.239	.003 7944	345	.002 8713	226
0.240	0.003 8289		0.002 8939	

x	ξ Ellipse.	Diff.	ξ Hyperbola.	Diff.
0.240	0.003 8289	346	0.002 8939	227
.241	.003 8635	348	.002 9166	228
.242	.003 8983	350	.002 9394	229
.243	.003 9333	352	.002 9623	229
.244	.003 9685	354	.002 9852	231
0.245	0.004 0039	355	0.003 0083	231
.246	.004 0394	358	.003 0314	231
.247	.004 0752	359	.003 0545	233
.248	.004 1111	361	.003 0778	233
.249	.004 1472	363	.003 1011	234
0.250	0.004 1835	364	0.003 1245	235
.251	.004 2199	367	.003 1480	236
.252	.004 2566	368	.003 1716	236
.253	.004 2934	371	.003 1952	237
.254	.004 3305	372	.003 2189	238
0.255	0.004 3677	374	0.003 2427	239
.256	.004 4051	376	.003 2666	239
.257	.004 4427	377	.003 2905	241
.258	.004 4804	380	.003 3146	241
.259	.004 5184	382	.003 3387	241
0.260	0.004 5566	383	0.003 3628	243
.261	.004 5949	385	.003 3871	243
.262	.004 6334	387	.003 4114	244
.263	.004 6721	390	.003 4358	245
.264	.004 7111	391	.003 4603	245
0.265	0.004 7502	392	0.003 4848	246
.266	.004 7894	395	.003 5094	247
.267	.004 8289	397	.003 5341	248
.268	.004 8686	399	.003 5589	249
.269	.004 9085	400	.003 5838	249
0.270	0.004 9485	403	0.003 6087	250
.271	.004 9888	404	.003 6337	250
.272	.005 0292	407	.003 6587	252
.273	.005 0699	408	.003 6839	252
.274	.005 1107	410	.003 7091	253
0.275	0.005 1517	413	0.003 7344	254
.276	.005 1930	414	.003 7598	254
.277	.005 2344	416	.003 7852	255
.278	.005 2760	418	.003 8107	256
.279	.005 3178	420	.003 8363	257
0.280	0.005 3598	422	0.003 8620	257
.281	.005 4020	424	.003 8877	258
.282	.005 4444	426	.003 9135	259
.283	.005 4870	428	.003 9394	260
.284	.005 5298	430	.003 9654	260
0.285	0.005 5728	432	0.003 9914	261
.286	.005 6160	434	.004 0175	262
.287	.005 6594	436	.004 0437	263
.288	.005 7030	438	.004 0700	263
.289	.005 7468	440	.004 0963	264
0.290	0.005 7908	442	0.004 1227	264
.291	.005 8350	445	.004 1491	266
.292	.005 8795	446	.004 1757	266
.293	.005 9241	448	.004 2023	267
.294	.005 9689	450	.004 2290	267
0.295	0.006 0139	452	0.004 2557	269
.296	.006 0591	454	.004 2826	269
.297	.006 1045	457	.004 3095	269
.298	.006 1502	458	.004 3364	271
.299	.006 1960	461	.004 3635	271
0.300	0.006 2421		0.004 3906	

TABLE XV.

For Elliptic Orbits of great eccentricity.

ϵ or δ	log B_0 or log B_0'	Diff.	log N	Diff.	ϵ or δ	log B_0 or log B_0'	Diff.	log N	Diff.
°					°				
0	0.000 0000	0	0.000 0000	7	**30**	0.000 0066	9	0.000 6400	436
1	.000 0000	0	.000 0007	21	**31**	.000 0075	11	.000 6836	450
2	.000 0000	0	.000 0028	36	**32**	.000 0086	11	.000 7286	464
3	.000 0000	0	.000 0064	49	**33**	.000 0097	12	.000 7750	479
4	.000 0000	0	.000 0113	64	**34**	.000 0109	13	.000 8229	493
5	0.000 0000	0	0.000 0177	78	**35**	0.000 0122	15	0.000 8722	508
6	.000 0000	0	.000 0255	92	**36**	.000 0137	16	.000 9230	523
7	.000 0000	0	.000 0347	107	**37**	.000 0153	18	.000 9753	537
8	.000 0000	1	.000 0454	120	**38**	.000 0171	19	.001 0290	552
9	.000 0001	0	.000 0574	135	**39**	.000 0190	20	.001 0842	567
10	0.000 0001	0	0.000 0709	149	**40**	0.000 0210	22	0.001 1409	581
11	.000 0001	1	.000 0858	163	**41**	.000 0232	23	.001 1990	596
12	.000 0002	0	.000 1021	178	**42**	.000 0255	26	.001 2586	611
13	.000 0002	1	.000 1199	191	**43**	.000 0281	27	.001 3197	626
14	.000 0003	1	.000 1390	206	**44**	.000 0308	29	.001 3823	640
15	0.000 0004	1	0.000 1596	220	**45**	0.000 0337	31	0.001 4463	655
16	.000 0005	2	.000 1816	235	**46**	.000 0368	33	.001 5118	670
17	.000 0007	2	.000 2051	248	**47**	.000 0401	36	.001 5788	685
18	.000 0009	2	.000 2299	263	**48**	.000 0437	38	.001 6473	700
19	.000 0011	2	.000 2562	277	**49**	.000 0475	40	.001 7173	715
20	0.000 0013	3	0.000 2839	292	**50**	0.000 0515	43	0.001 7888	730
21	.000 0016	3	.000 3131	306	**51**	.000 0558	46	.001 8618	744
22	.000 0019	4	.000 3437	320	**52**	.000 0604	48	.001 9362	760
23	.000 0023	4	.000 3757	334	**53**	.000 0652	51	.002 0122	775
24	.000 0027	5	.000 4091	349	**54**	.000 0703	54	.002 0897	790
25	0.000 0032	5	0.000 4440	363	**55**	0.000 0757	58	0.002 1687	806
26	.000 0037	6	.000 4803	378	**56**	.000 0815	60	.002 2493	820
27	.000 0043	7	.000 5181	392	**57**	.000 0875	64	.002 3313	836
28	.000 0050	7	.000 5573	407	**58**	.000 0939	68	.002 4149	851
29	.000 0057	9	.000 5980	420	**59**	.000 1007	71	.002 5000	866
30	0.000 0066		0.000 6400		**60**	0.000 1078		0.002 5866	

TABLE XVI.

For Hyperbolic Orbits.

m or n	log Q or log Q'	log I. Diff.	log half II. Diff.	m or n	log Q or log Q'	log I. Diff.	log half II. Diff.
0.00	0.000 0000	—	2.1149_n	0.10	9.998 7021	3.41256_n	2.1046_n
.01	9.999 9870	2.41597_n	2.1146_n	.11	.998 4308	3.45326_n	2.1025_n
.02	.999 9479	2.71675_n	2.1142_n	.12	.998 1342	3.49028_n	2.1003_n
.03	.999 8828	2.89259_n	2.1137_n	.13	.997 8123	3.52423_n	2.0978_n
.04	.999 7917	3.01741_n	2.1130_n	.14	.997 4654	3.55547_n	2.0952_n
0.05	9.999 6746	3.11411_n	2.1121_n	0.15	9.997 0936	3.58453_n	2.0923_n
.06	.999 5316	3.19290_n	2.1110_n	.16	.996 6971	3.61154_n	2.0892_n
.07	.999 3628	3.25940_n	2.1097_n	.17	.996 2760	3.63679_n	2.0860_n
.08	.999 1682	3.31687_n	2.1082_n	.18	.995 8305	3.66048_n	2.0826_n
.09	.998 9479	3.36745_n	2.1065_n	.19	.995 3608	3.68276_n	2.0790_n
0.10	9.998 7021	3.41256_n	2.1046_n	0.20	9.994 8671	3.70378_n	2.0752_n

TABLE XVII.

For special Perturbations.

q, q', q''	For positive values of the Argument.				For negative values of the Argument.			
	log f	Diff.	log f', log f''	Diff.	log f	Diff.	log f', log f''	Diff.
0.0000	0.477 1213	1086	0.301 0300	869	0.477 1213	1086	0.301 0300	869
.0001	.477 0127	1085	.300 9431	868	.477 2299	1086	.301 1169	868
.0002	.476 9042	1085	.300 8563	868	.477 3385	1086	.301 2037	869
.0003	.476 7957	1085	.300 7695	868	.477 4471	1087	.301 2906	870
.0004	.476 6872	1085	.300 6827	868	.477 5558	1087	.301 3776	869
0.0005	0.476 5787	1085	0.300 5959	867	0.477 6645	1087	0.301 4645	870
.0006	.476 4702	1084	.300 5092	868	.477 7732	1087	.301 5515	869
.0007	.476 3618	1084	.300 4224	867	.477 8819	1087	.301 6384	870
.0008	.476 2534	1084	.300 3357	867	.477 9906	1088	.301 7254	870
.0009	.476 1450	1083	.300 2490	867	.478 0994	1088	.301 8124	871
0.0010	0.476 0367	1083	0.300 1623	867	0.478 2082	1088	0.301 8995	870
.0011	.475 9284	1083	.300 0756	867	.478 3170	1089	.301 9865	871
.0012	.475 8201	1083	.299 9889	866	.478 4259	1089	.302 0736	870
.0013	.475 7118	1083	.299 9023	866	.478 5348	1089	.302 1606	871
.0014	.475 6035	1082	.299 8157	866	.478 6437	1089	.302 2477	871
0.0015	0.475 4953	1082	0.299 7291	866	0.478 7526	1089	0.302 3348	872
.0016	.475 3871	1082	.299 6425	866	.478 8615	1090	.302 4220	871
.0017	.475 2789	1082	.299 5559	866	.478 9705	1090	.302 5091	872
.0018	.475 1707	1081	.299 4693	865	.479 0795	1090	.302 5963	872
.0019	.475 0626	1081	.299 3828	865	.479 1885	1090	.302 6835	872
0.0020	0.474 9545	1081	0.299 2963	865	0.479 2975	1090	0.302 7707	872
.0021	.474 8464	1081	.299 2098	865	.479 4065	1091	.302 8579	872
.0022	.474 7383	1080	.299 1233	865	.479 5156	1091	.302 9451	873
.0023	.474 6303	1080	.299 0368	864	.479 6247	1091	.303 0324	872
.0024	.474 5223	1080	.298 9504	865	.479 7338	1092	.303 1196	873
0.0025	0.474 4143	1080	0.298 8639	864	0.479 8430	1092	0.303 2069	873
.0026	.474 3063	1080	.298 7775	864	.479 9522	1092	.303 2942	873
.0027	.474 1983	1079	.298 6911	864	.480 0614	1092	.303 3815	874
.0028	.474 0904	1079	.298 6047	863	.480 1706	1092	.303 4689	873
.0029	.473 9825	1079	.298 5184	864	.480 2798	1093	.303 5562	874
0.0030	0.473 8746	1079	0.298 4320	863	0.480 3891	1093	0.303 6436	874
.0031	.473 7667	1078	.298 3457	863	.480 4984	1093	.303 7310	874
.0032	.473 6589	1078	.298 2594	863	.480 6077	1093	.303 8184	874
.0033	.473 5511	1078	.298 1731	863	.480 7170	1094	.303 9058	875
.0034	.473 4433	1078	.298 0868	863	.480 8264	1094	.303 9933	874
0.0035	0.473 3355	1077	0.298 0005	862	0.480 9358	1094	0.304 0807	875
.0036	.473 2278	1077	.297 9143	863	.481 0452	1095	.304 1682	875
.0037	.473 1201	1077	.297 8280	862	.481 1547	1094	.304 2557	875
.0038	.473 0124	1077	.297 7418	862	.481 2641	1095	.304 3432	876
.0039	.472 9047	1077	.297 6556	861	.481 3736	1095	.304 4308	875
0.0040	0.472 7970	1076	0.297 5695	862	0.481 4831	1095	0.304 5183	876
.0041	.472 6894	1076	.297 4833	861	.481 5926	1096	.304 6059	876
.0042	.472 5818	1076	.297 3972	862	.481 7022	1096	.304 6935	876
.0043	.472 4742	1076	.297 3110	861	.481 8118	1096	.304 7811	876
.0044	.472 3666	1075	.297 2249	861	.481 9214	1096	.304 8687	876
0.0045	0.472 2591	1075	0.297 1388	860	0.482 0310	1097	0.304 9563	877
.0046	.472 1516	1075	.297 0528	861	.482 1407	1097	.305 0440	877
.0047	.472 0441	1075	.296 9667	860	.482 2504	1097	.305 1317	877
.0048	.471 9366	1074	.296 8807	861	.482 3601	1097	.305 2194	877
.0049	.471 8292	1074	.296 7946	860	.482 4698	1098	.305 3071	877
0.0050	0.471 7218	1074	0.296 7086	860	0.482 5796	1098	0.305 3948	877
.0051	.471 6144	1074	.296 6226	859	.482 6894	1098	.305 4825	878
.0052	.471 5070	1074	.296 5367	860	.482 7992	1098	.305 5703	878
.0053	.471 3996	1073	.296 4507	859	.482 9090	1098	.305 6581	878
.0054	.471 2923	1073	.296 3648	860	.483 0188	1099	.305 7459	878
0.0055	0.471 1850	1073	0.296 2788	859	0.483 1287	1099	0.305 8337	878
.0056	.471 0777	1073	.296 1929	859	.483 2386	1099	.305 9215	879
.0057	.470 9704	1072	.296 1070	858	.483 3485	1099	.306 0094	879
.0058	.470 8632	1072	.296 0212	859	.483 4584	1100	.306 0973	878
.0059	.470 7560	1072	.295 9353	858	.483 5684	1100	.306 1851	879
.0060	.470 6488		.295 8495		.483 6784		.306 2730	

TABLE XVII.

For special Perturbations.

q, q′, q″	For positive values of the Argument. log f	Diff.	log f′, log f″	Diff.	For negative values of the Argument. log f	Diff.	log f′, log f″	Diff.
0.0060	0.470 6488	1072	0.295 8495	858	0.483 6784	1100	0.306 2730	880
.0061	.470 5416	1071	.295 7637	858	.483 7884	1100	.306 3610	879
.0062	.470 4345	1071	.295 6779	858	.483 8984	1101	.306 4489	880
.0063	.470 3274	1071	.295 5921	858	.484 0085	1101	.306 5369	879
.0064	.470 2203	1071	.295 5063	858	.484 1186	1101	.306 6248	880
0.0065	0.470 1132	1070	0.295 4205	857	0.484 2287	1101	0.306 7128	881
.0066	.470 0062	1070	.295 3348	857	.484 3388	1102	.306 8009	880
.0067	.469 8992	1070	.295 3491	857	.484 4490	1102	.306 8889	880
.0068	.469 7922	1070	.295 1634	857	.484 5592	1102	.306 9769	881
.0069	.469 6852	1070	.295 0777	857	.484 6694	1102	.307 0650	881
0.0070	0.469 5782	1069	0.294 9920	856	0.484 7796	1102	0.307 1531	881
.0071	.469 4713	1069	.294 9064	856	.484 8898	1103	.307 2412	881
.0072	.469 3644	1069	.294 8208	857	.485 0001	1103	.307 3293	881
.0073	.469 2575	1069	.294 7351	856	.485 1104	1103	.307 4174	882
.0074	.469 1506	1069	.294 6495	855	.485 2207	1104	.307 5056	882
0.0075	0.469 0437	1068	0.294 5640	856	0.485 3311	1104	0.307 5938	882
.0076	.468 9369	1068	.294 4784	856	.485 4415	1104	.307 6820	882
.0077	.468 8301	1068	.294 3928	855	.485 5519	1104	.307 7702	882
.0078	.468 7233	1068	.294 3073	855	.485 6623	1105	.307 8584	882
.0079	.468 6165	1067	.294 2218	855	.485 7728	1105	.307 9466	883
0.0080	0.468 5098	1067	0.294 1363	855	0.485 8833	1105	0.308 0349	883
.0081	.468 4031	1067	.294 0508	855	.485 9938	1105	.308 1232	883
.0082	.468 2964	1067	.293 9653	854	.486 1043	1106	.308 2115	883
.0083	.468 1897	1066	.293 8799	854	.486 2149	1106	.308 2998	883
.0084	.468 0831	1066	.293 7945	855	.486 3255	1106	.308 3881	884
0.0085	0.467 9765	1066	0.293 7090	854	0.486 4361	1106	0.308 4765	883
.0086	.467 8699	1066	.293 6236	853	.486 5467	1106	.308 5648	884
.0087	.467 7633	1066	.293 5383	854	.486 6573	1107	.308 6532	884
.0088	.467 6567	1065	.293 4529	854	.486 7680	1107	.308 7416	885
.0089	.467 5502	1065	.293 3675	853	.486 8787	1107	.308 8301	884
0.0090	0.467 4437	1065	0.293 2822	853	0.486 9894	1107	0.308 9185	885
.0091	.467 3372	1065	.293 1969	853	.487 1001	1108	.309 0070	884
.0092	.467 2307	1064	.293 1116	853	.487 2109	1108	.309 0954	885
.0093	.467 1243	1064	.293 0263	852	.487 3217	1108	.309 1839	886
.0094	.467 0179	1064	.292 9411	853	.487 4325	1108	.309 2725	885
0.0095	0.466 9115	1064	0.292 8558	852	0.487 5433	1109	0.309 3610	885
.0096	.466 8051	1063	.292 7706	852	.487 6542	1109	.309 4495	886
.0097	.466 6988	1063	.292 6854	852	.487 7651	1109	.309 5381	886
.0098	.466 5925	1063	.292 6002	852	.487 8760	1109	.309 6267	886
.0099	.466 4862	1063	.292 5150	852	.487 9869	1110	.309 7153	886
0.0100	0.466 3799	1063	0.292 4298	851	0.488 0979	1110	0.309 8039	887
.0101	.466 2736	1062	.292 3447	852	.488 2089	1110	.309 8926	886
.0102	.466 1674	1062	.292 2595	851	.488 3199	1110	.309 9812	887
.0103	.466 0612	1062	.292 1744	851	.488 4309	1111	.310 0699	887
.0104	.465 9550	1062	.292 0893	850	.488 5420	1111	.310 1586	887
0.0105	0.465 8488	1061	0.292 0043	851	0.488 6531	1111	0.310 2473	887
.0106	.465 7427	1061	.291 9192	851	.488 7642	1111	.310 3360	888
.0107	.465 6366	1061	.291 8341	850	.488 8753	1112	.310 4248	888
.0108	.465 5305	1061	.291 7491	850	.488 9865	1112	.310 5136	887
.0109	.465 4244	1061	.291 6641	850	.489 0977	1112	.310 6023	888
0.0110	0.465 3183	1060	0.291 5791	850	0.489 2089	1112	0.310 6911	889
.0111	.465 2123	1060	.291 4941	849	.489 3201	1113	.310 7800	888
.0112	.465 1063	1060	.291 4092	850	.489 4314	1113	.310 8688	889
.0113	.465 0003	1060	.291 3242	849	.489 5427	1113	.310 9577	888
.0114	.464 8943	1059	.291 2393	849	.489 6540	1113	.311 0465	889
0.0115	0.464 7884	1059	0.291 1544	849	0.489 7653	1114	0.311 1354	889
.0116	.464 6825	1059	.291 0695	849	.489 8767	1114	.311 2243	890
.0117	.464 5766	1059	.290 9846	849	.489 9881	1114	.311 3133	889
.0118	.464 4707	1059	.290 8997	848	.490 0995	1114	.311 4022	890
.0119	.464 3648	1058	.290 8149	849	.490 2109	1114	.311 4912	890
.0120	.464 2590		.290 7300		.490 3223		.311 5802	

TABLE XVII.

For special Perturbations.

q, q′, q″	For positive values of the Argument.				For negative values of the Argument.			
	log f	Diff.	log f′, log f″	Diff.	log f	Diff.	log f′, log f″	Diff.
0.0120	0.464 2590	1058	0.290 7300	848	0.490 3223	1115	0.311 5802	890
.0121	.464 1532	1058	.290 6452	848	.490 4338	1115	.311 6692	890
.0122	.464 0474	1058	.290 5604	848	.490 5453	1115	.311 7582	890
.0123	.463 9416	1057	.290 4756	847	.490 6568	1116	.311 8472	891
.0124	.463 8359	1057	.290 3909	848	.490 7684	1116	.311 9363	891
0.0125	0.463 7302	1057	0.290 3061	847	0.490 8800	1116	0.312 0254	891
.0126	.463 6245	1057	.290 2214	847	.490 9916	1116	.312 1145	891
.0127	.463 5188	1056	.290 1367	847	.491 1032	1117	.312 2036	891
.0128	.463 4132	1056	.290 0520	847	.491 2149	1117	.312 2927	892
.0129	.463 3076	1056	.289 9673	847	.491 3266	1117	.312 3819	891
0.0130	0.463 2020	1056	0.289 8826	846	0.491 4383	1117	0.312 4710	892
.0131	.463 0964	1056	.289 7980	846	.491 5500	1118	.312 5602	892
.0132	.462 9908	1055	.289 7134	847	.491 6618	1118	.312 6494	893
.0133	.462 8853	1055	.289 6287	846	.491 7736	1118	.312 7387	892
.0134	.462 7798	1055	.289 5441	845	.491 8854	1118	.312 8279	893
0.0135	0.462 6743	1055	0.289 4596	846	0.491 9972	1119	0.313 9172	892
.0136	.462 5688	1055	.289 3750	846	.492 1091	1119	.313 0064	893
.0137	.462 4633	1054	.289 2904	845	.492 2210	1119	.313 0957	893
.0138	.462 3579	1054	.289 2059	845	.492 3329	1119	.313 1850	894
.0139	.462 2525	1054	.289 1214	845	.492 4448	1119	.313 2744	893
0.0140	0.462 1471	1054	0.289 0369	845	0.492 5567	1120	0.313 3637	894
.0141	.462 0417	1053	.288 9524	845	.492 6687	1120	.313 4531	894
.0142	.461 9364	1053	.288 8679	844	.492 7807	1120	.313 5425	894
.0143	.461 8311	1053	.288 7835	845	.492 8927	1120	.313 6319	894
.0144	.461 7258	1053	.288 6990	844	.493 0047	1121	.313 7213	895
0.0145	0.461 6205	1052	0.288 6146	844	0.493 1168	1121	0.313 8108	894
.0146	.461 5153	1052	.288 5302	844	.493 2289	1121	.313 9002	895
.0147	.461 4101	1052	.288 4458	843	.493 3410	1122	.313 9897	895
.0148	.461 3049	1052	.288 3615	844	.493 4532	1122	.314 0792	895
.0149	.461 1997	1052	.288 2771	843	.493 5654	1122	.314 1687	896
0.0150	0.461 0945	1051	0.288 1928	843	0.493 6776	1122	0.314 2583	895
.0151	.460 9894	1051	.288 1085	844	.493 7898	1123	.314 3478	896
.0152	.460 8843	1051	.288 0241	842	.493 9021	1123	.314 4374	896
.0153	.460 7792	1051	.287 9399	843	.494 0144	1123	.314 5270	896
.0154	.460 6741	1051	.287 8556	843	.494 1267	1123	.314 6166	896
0.0155	0.460 5690	1050	0.287 7713	842	0.494 2390	1124	0.314 7062	897
.0156	.460 4640	1050	.287 6871	842	.494 3514	1124	.314 7959	896
.0157	.460 3590	1050	.287 6029	842	.494 4638	1124	.314 8855	897
.0158	.460 2540	1050	.287 5187	842	.494 5762	1124	.314 9752	897
.0159	.460 1490	1049	.287 4345	842	.494 6886	1124	.315 0649	897
0.0160	0.460 0441	1049	0.287 3503	842	0.494 8010	1125	0.315 1546	898
.0161	.459 9392	1049	.287 2661	841	.494 9135	1125	.315 2444	897
.0162	.459 8343	1049	.287 1820	841	.495 0260	1125	.315 3341	898
.0163	.459 7294	1049	.287 0979	841	.495 1385	1125	.315 4239	898
.0164	.459 6245	1048	.287 0138	841	.495 2510	1126	.315 5137	898
0.0165	0.459 5197	1048	0.286 9297	841	0.495 3636	1126	0.315 6035	899
.0166	.459 4149	1048	.286 8456	841	.495 4762	1126	.315 6934	898
.0167	.459 3101	1048	.286 7615	840	.495 5888	1127	.315 7832	899
.0168	.459 2053	1047	.286 6775	840	.495 7015	1127	.315 8731	899
.0169	.459 1006	1047	.286 5935	840	.495 8142	1127	.315 9630	899
0.0170	0.458 9959	1047	0.286 5095	840	0.495 9269	1127	0.316 0529	899
.0171	.458 8912	1047	.286 4255	840	.496 0396	1128	.316 1428	899
.0172	.458 7865	1047	.286 3415	840	.496 1524	1128	.316 2327	900
.0173	.458 6818	1046	.286 2575	839	.496 2652	1128	.316 3227	900
.0174	.458 5772	1046	.286 1736	840	.496 3780	1128	.316 4127	900
0.0175	0.458 4726	1046	0.286 0896	839	0.496 4908	1129	0.316 5027	900
.0176	.458 3680	1046	.286 0057	839	.496 6037	1129	.316 5927	900
.0177	.458 2634	1045	.285 9218	838	.496 7166	1129	.316 6827	901
.0178	.458 1589	1045	.285 8380	839	.496 8295	1129	.316 7728	901
.0179	.458 0544	1045	.285 7541	839	.496 9424	1130	.316 8629	901
.0180	.457 9499		.285 6702		.497 0554		.316 9530	

TABLE XVII.

For special Perturbations.

q, q', q''	For positive values of the Argument.				For negative values of the Argument.			
	log f	Diff.	log f', log f''	Diff.	log f	Diff.	log f', log f''	Diff.
0.0180	0.457 9499	1045	0.285 6702	838	0.497 0554	1130	0.316 9530	901
.0181	.457 8454	1045	.285 5864	838	.497 1684	1130	.317 0431	901
.0182	.457 7409	1044	.285 5026	838	.497 2814	1130	.317 1332	902
.0183	.457 6365	1044	.285 4188	838	.497 3944	1131	.317 2234	901
.0184	.457 5321	1044	.285 3350	838	.497 5075	1131	.317 3135	902
0.0185	0.457 4277	1044	0.285 2512	837	0.497 6206	1131	0.317 4037	902
.0186	.457 3233	1044	.285 1675	837	.497 7337	1131	.317 4939	902
.0187	.457 2189	1043	.285 0838	838	.497 8468	1132	.317 5841	903
.0188	.457 1146	1043	.285 0000	837	.497 9600	1132	.317 6744	902
.0189	.457 0103	1043	.284 9163	837	.498 0732	1132	.317 7646	903
0.0190	0.456 9060	1043	0.284 8326	836	0.498 1864	1132	0.317 8549	903
.0191	.456 8017	1042	.284 7490	837	.498 2996	1133	.317 9452	903
.0192	.456 6975	1042	.284 6653	836	.498 4129	1133	.318 0355	904
.0193	.456 5933	1042	.284 5817	836	.498 5262	1133	.318 1259	903
.0194	.456 4891	1042	.284 4981	836	.498 6395	1133	.318 2162	904
0.0195	0.456 3849	1041	0.284 4145	836	0.498 7528	1134	0.318 3066	904
.0196	.456 2808	1041	.284 3309	836	.498 8662	1134	.318 3970	904
.0197	.456 1767	1041	.284 2473	836	.498 9796	1134	.318 4874	904
.0198	.456 0726	1041	.284 1637	835	.499 0930	1134	.318 5778	905
.0199	.455 9685	1041	.284 0802	835	.499 2064	1135	.318 5683	905
0.0200	0.455 8644	1040	0.283 9967	835	0.499 3199	1135	0.318 7588	904
.0201	.455 7604	1040	.283 9132	835	.499 4334	1135	.318 8492	906
.0202	.455 6564	1040	.283 8297	835	.499 5469	1135	.318 9398	905
.0203	.455 5524	1040	.283 7462	835	.499 6604	1136	.319 0303	905
.0204	.455 4484	1040	.283 6627	834	.499 7740	1136	.319 1208	906
0.0205	0.455 3444	1039	0.283 5793	835	0.499 8876	1136	0.319 2114	906
.0206	.455 2405	1039	.283 4958	834	.500 0012	1137	.319 3020	906
.0207	.455 1366	1039	.283 4124	834	.500 1149	1137	.319 3926	906
.0208	.455 0327	1039	.283 3290	834	.500 2286	1137	.319 4832	906
.0209	.454 9288	1039	.283 2456	833	.500 3423	1137	.319 5738	907
0.0210	0.454 8249	1038	0.283 1623	834	0.500 4560	1137	0.319 6645	907
.0211	.454 7211	1038	.283 0789	833	.500 5697	1138	.319 7552	907
.0212	.454 6173	1038	.282 9956	833	.500 6835	1138	.319 8459	907
.0213	.454 5135	1038	.282 9123	833	.500 7973	1138	.319 9366	907
.0214	.454 4097	1037	.282 8290	833	.500 9111	1139	.320 0273	908
0.0215	0.454 3060	1037	0.282 7457	833	0.501 0250	1139	0.320 1181	907
.0216	.454 2023	1037	.282 6624	832	.501 1389	1139	.320 2088	908
.0217	.454 0986	1037	.282 5792	833	.501 2528	1139	.320 2996	908
.0218	.453 9949	1037	.282 4959	832	.501 3667	1140	.320 3904	909
.0219	.453 8912	1036	.282 4127	832	.501 4807	1140	.320 4813	908
0.0220	0.453 7876	1036	0.282 3295	832	0.501 5947	1140	0.320 5721	909
.0221	.453 6840	1036	.282 2463	832	.501 7087	1140	.320 6630	909
.0222	.453 5804	1036	.282 1631	831	.501 8227	1141	.320 7539	909
.0223	.453 4768	1035	.282 0800	832	.501 9368	1141	.320 8448	909
.0224	.453 3733	1035	.281 9968	831	.502 0509	1141	.320 9357	909
0.0225	0.453 2698	1035	0.281 9137	831	0.502 1650	1141	0.321 0266	910
.0226	.453 1663	1035	.281 8306	831	.502 2791	1142	.321 1176	910
.0227	.453 0628	1035	.281 7475	831	.502 3933	1142	.321 2086	910
.0228	.452 9593	1035	.281 6644	830	.502 5075	1142	.321 2996	910
.0229	.452 8558	1034	.281 5814	831	.502 6217	1143	.321 3906	910
0.0230	0.452 7524	1034	0.281 4983	830	0.502 7360	1143	0.321 4816	911
.0231	.452 6490	1034	.281 4153	830	.502 8503	1143	.321 5727	910
.0232	.452 5456	1034	.281 3323	830	.502 9646	1143	.321 6637	911
.0233	.452 4422	1033	.281 2493	830	.503 0789	1143	.321 7548	912
.0234	.452 3389	1033	.281 1663	830	.503 1932	1144	.321 8460	911
0.0235	0.452 2356	1033	0.281 0833	829	0.503 3076	1144	0.321 9371	911
.0236	.452 1323	1033	.281 0004	830	.503 4220	1144	.322 0282	912
.0237	.452 0290	1032	.280 9174	829	.503 5364	1144	.322 1194	912
.0238	.451 9258	1032	.280 8345	829	.503 6508	1145	.322 2106	912
.0239	.451 8226	1032	.280 7516	829	.503 7653	1145	.322 3018	912
.0240	.451 7194		.280 6687		.503 8798		.322 3930	

TABLE XVII.

For special Perturbations.

q, q', q''	For positive values of the Argument.				For negative values of the Argument.			
	log f	Diff.	log f', log f''	Diff.	log f	Diff.	log f', log f''	Diff.
0.0240	0.451 7194	1032	0.280 6687	829	0.503 8798	1145	0.322 3930	913
.0241	.451 6162	1032	.280 5858	828	.503 9943	1146	.322 4843	913
.0242	.451 5130	1031	.280 5030	829	.504 1089	1146	.322 5756	912
.0243	.451 4099	1031	.280 4201	828	.504 2235	1146	.322 6668	913
.0244	.451 3068	1031	.280 3373	828	.504 3381	1146	.322 7581	914
0.0245	0.451 2037	1031	0.280 2545	828	0.504 4527	1147	0.322 8495	913
.0246	.451 1006	1031	.280 1717	828	.504 5674	1147	.322 9408	914
.0247	.450 9975	1030	.280 0889	827	.504 6821	1147	.323 0322	914
.0248	.450 8945	1030	.280 0062	828	.504 7968	1147	.323 1236	914
.0249	.450 7915	1030	.279 9234	827	.504 9115	1148	.323 2150	914
0.0250	0.450 6885	1030	0.279 8407	827	0.505 0263	1148	0.323 3064	914
.0251	.450 5855	1030	.279 7580	827	.505 1411	1148	.323 3978	915
.0252	.450 4825	1029	.279 6753	827	.505 2559	1148	.323 4893	915
.0253	.450 3796	1029	.279 5926	827	.505 3707	1149	.323 5808	915
.0254	.450 2767	1029	.279 5099	826	.505 4856	1149	.323 6723	915
0.0255	0.450 1738	1029	0.279 4273	827	0.505 6005	1149	0.323 7638	915
.0256	.450 0709	1028	.279 3446	826	.505 7154	1149	.323 8553	916
.0257	.449 9681	1028	.279 2620	826	.505 8303	1150	.323 9469	915
.0258	.449 8653	1028	.279 1794	826	.505 9453	1150	.324 0384	916
.0259	.449 7625	1028	.279 0968	825	.506 0603	1150	.324 1300	917
0.0260	0.449 6597	1028	0.279 0143	826	0.506 1753	1150	0.324 2217	916
.0261	.449 5569	1027	.278 9317	825	.506 2903	1151	.324 3133	916
.0262	.449 4542	1027	.278 8492	826	.506 4054	1151	.324 4049	917
.0263	.449 3515	1027	.278 7666	825	.506 5205	1151	.324 4966	917
.0264	.449 2488	1027	.278 6841	825	.506 6356	1152	.324 5883	917
0.0265	0.449 1461	1026	0.278 6016	825	0.506 7508	1152	0.324 6800	917
.0266	.449 0435	1026	.278 5191	824	.506 8660	1153	.324 7717	918
.0267	.448 9409	1026	.278 4367	825	.506 9813	1152	.324 8635	918
.0268	.448 8383	1026	.278 3542	824	.507 0965	1152	.324 9553	917
.0269	.448 7357	1026	.278 2718	824	.507 2117	1153	.325 0470	919
0.0270	0.448 6331	1026	0.278 1894	824	0.507 3270	1153	0.325 1389	918
.0271	.448 5305	1025	.278 1070	824	.507 4423	1154	.325 2307	918
.0272	.448 4280	1025	.278 0246	824	.507 5577	1154	.325 3225	919
.0273	.448 3255	1025	.277 9422	823	.507 6731	1154	.325 4144	919
.0274	.448 2230	1025	.277 8599	824	.507 7885	1154	.325 5063	919
0.0275	0.448 1205	1024	0.277 7775	823	0.507 9039	1155	0.325 5982	919
.0276	.448 0181	1024	.277 6952	823	.508 0194	1155	.325 6901	920
.0277	.447 9157	1024	.277 6129	823	.508 1349	1155	.325 7821	919
.0278	.447 8133	1024	.277 5306	823	.508 2504	1155	.325 8740	920
.0279	.447 7109	1024	.277 4483	822	.508 3659	1155	.325 9660	920
0.0280	0.447 6085	1023	0.277 3661	823	0.508 4814	1156	0.326 0580	920
.0281	.447 5062	1023	.277 2838	822	.508 5970	1156	.326 1500	921
.0282	.447 4039	1023	.277 2016	822	.508 7126	1156	.326 2421	920
.0283	.447 3016	1023	.277 1194	822	.508 8282	1157	.326 3341	921
.0284	.447 2993	1023	.277 0372	822	.508 9439	1157	.326 4262	921
0.0285	0.447 0970	1022	0.276 9550	822	0.509 0596	1157	0.326 5183	921
.0286	.446 9948	1022	.276 8728	821	.509 1753	1157	.326 6104	922
.0287	.446 8926	1022	.276 7907	821	.509 2910	1158	.326 7026	921
.0288	.446 7904	1022	.276 7086	822	.509 4068	1158	.326 7947	922
.0289	.446 6882	1021	.276 6264	821	.509 5226	1158	.326 8869	922
0.0290	0.446 5861	1021	0.276 5443	821	0.509 6384	1159	0.326 9791	922
.0291	.446 4840	1021	.276 4622	820	.509 7543	1159	.327 0713	922
.0292	.446 3819	1021	.276 3802	821	.509 8702	1159	.327 1635	923
.0293	.446 2798	1021	.276 2981	820	.509 9861	1159	.327 2558	923
.0294	.446 1777	1021	.276 2161	821	.510 1020	1159	.327 3481	923
0.0295	0.446 0756	1020	0.276 1340	820	0.510 2179	1160	0.327 4404	923
.0296	.445 9736	1020	.276 0520	820	.510 3339	1160	.327 5327	923
.0297	.445 8716	1020	.275 9700	820	.510 4499	1160	.327 6250	924
.0298	.445 7696	1020	.275 8880	819	.510 5659	1160	.327 7174	923
.0299	.445 6676	1019	.275 8061	820	.510 6819	1161	.327 8097	924
.0300	.445 5657		.275 7241		.510 7980		.327 9021	

TABLE XVIII.

Elements of the Orbits of Comets which have been observed.

No.	T	π	Ω	i	e	log q	Motion.	Computed by
	h m s	° ′ ″	° ′ ″	° ′ ″				
1	66 Jan. 14, 5 0 0	325 0 0	32 40 0	40 30 0	1.0	9.6480	Retrograde.	Hind.
2	141 March 29, 2 0 0	251 55 0	12 50 0	17 0 0	1.0	9.8573	"	"
3	240 Nov. 10, 0 0 0	271 0 0	189 0 0	44 0 0	1.0	9.5700	Direct.	Burckhardt.
4	539 Oct. 20, 15 0 0	313 30 0	58° or 238°	10 0 0	1.0	9.53307	"	"
5	565 July 9, 0 0 0	88 0 0	158 0 0	62 0 0	1.0	9.85686	Retrograde.	"
6	568 Aug. 28, 6 28 49	316 47 0	294 36 0	4 2 0	1.0	9.9491	Direct.	Hind.
7	574 April 7, 6 43 14	143 39 0	128 17 0	46 31 0	1.0	9.9836	"	"
8	770 June 6, 14 6 1	357 7 0	90 59 0	61 49 0	1.0	9.807664	Retrograde.	Laugier.
9	837 March 1, 0 0 0	289 3 0	206 33 0	11 0 0	1.0	9.763428	"	Pingré.
10	961 Dec. 30, 3 50 25	268 3 0	350 35 0	79 33 0	1.0	9.7418	"	Hind.
11	989 Sept. 12, 0 0 0	264 0 0	84 0 0	17 0 0	1.0	9.7546	"	Burckhardt.
12	1066 April 1, 0 0 0	264 55 0	25 50 0	17 0 0	1.0	9.8573	"	Hind.
13	1092 Feb. 15, 0 0 0	156 20 0	125 40 0	28 55 0	1.0	9.9676	Direct.	"
14	1097 Sept. 21, 21 26 39	332 30 0	207 30 0	73 30 0	1.0	9.86832	"	Burckhardt.
15	1231 Jan. 30, 7 12 40	134 48 0	13 30 0	6 5 0	1.0	9.9767	"	Pingré.
16	1264 July 12, 13 31 0	241 38 0	157 40 0	35 5 0	1.0	9.4938	"	Hoek.
17	1299 March 31, 7 29 0	3 20 0	107 8 0	68 57 0	1.0	9.50233	Retrograde.	Pingré.
18	1337 June 15, 1 46 0	2 20 0	93 1 0	40 28 0	1.0	9.91815	"	Laugier.
19	1366 Oct. 13, 0 0 0	66 0 0	212 0 0	6 0 0	1.0	9.98140	Direct.	Peirce.
20	1378 Nov. 8, 18 19 27	299 31 0	47 17 0	17 56 0	1.0	9.76604	Retrograde.	Laugier.
21	1385 Oct. 16, 6 14 25	101 47 0	268 31 0	52 15 0	1.0	9.88860	"	Hind.
22	1433 Nov. 4, 10 9 51	281 2 0	133 49 0	79 1 0	1.0	9.53079	"	Laugier.
23	1456 June 8, 22 0 40	301 0 0	48 30 0	17 56 0	1.0	9.76754	"	Pingré.
24	1468 Oct. 7, 9 49 40	356 3 0	61 15 0	44 19 0	1.0	9.93109	"	Laugier.
25	1472 Feb. 28, 5 13 13	48 3 0	207 32 0	1 55 0	1.0	9.751718	"	"
26	1490 Dec. 24, 11 16 50	58 40 0	288 45 0	51 37 0	1.0	9.8678	Direct.	Hind.
27	1491 Jan. 4, 21 35 0	113 0 0	268 0 0	75 0 0	1.0	9.8780	Retrograde.	Peirce.
28	1506 Sept. 3, 15 52 34	250 37 0	132 50 0	45 1 0	1.0	9.586565	"	Laugier.
29	1531 Aug. 25, 19 0 40	301 12 0	45 30 0	17 0 0	0.967391	9.763380	"	Halley.
30	1532 Oct. 19, 14 53 0	135 44 0	119 8 0	42 27 0	1.0	9.787141	Direct.	Méchain.
31	1533 June 14, 21 11 25	217 40 0	299 19 0	28 14 0	1.0	9.514362	"	Olbers.
32	1556 April 22, 0 25 0	274 15 0	175 26 0	30 12 0	1.0	9.70323	"	Hind.
33	1558 Aug. 10, 12 24 45	329 49 0	332 36 0	73 29 0	1.0	9.76140	Retrograde.	Olbers.
34	1577 Oct 26, 22 44 36	129 42 0	25 20 24	75 9 42	1.0	9.24920	"	Woldstedt.
35	1580 Nov. 28, 13 6 39	108 29 20	19 7 25	64 33 55	0.998631	9.77982	Direct.	Schjellerup.

TABLE XVIII.

Elements of the Orbits of Comets which have been observed.

No.	T		π	Ω	i	e	log q	Motion.	Computed by
		h m s	° ′ ″	° ′ ″	° ′ ″				
36	1582 May 6,	9 51 22	256 15 18	229 18 1	60 47 3	1.0	9.226156	Retrograde.	D'Arrest.
37	1585 Oct. 8,	0 38 44	8 8 26	37 41 15	6 5 52	1.0	0.0393531	Direct.	Peters and Sawitsch.
38	1590 Feb. 8,	0 39 4	217 57 12	165 36 56	29 29 44	1.0	9.7541386	Retrograde.	Hind.
39	1593 July 18,	13 39 0	176 19 0	164 15 0	87 58 0	1.0	8.949940	Direct.	La Caille.
40	1596 July 25,	5 8 38	270 54 35	330 20 49	51 58 10	1.0	9.7537024	Retrograde.	Hind.
41	1607 Oct. 26,	17 10 58	301 38 10	48 40 28	17 12 17	0.9670888	9.769358	"	Bessel.
42	1618 Aug. 17,	3 2 0	318 20 0	293 25 0	21 18 0	1.0	9.710100	Direct.	Pingré.
43	1618 Nov. 8,	8 25 1	3 5 21	75 44 10	37 11 31	1.0	9.590556	"	Bessel.
44	1652 Nov. 12,	15 41 0	28 18 40	88 10 0	79 28 0	1.0	9.928140	"	Halley.
45	1661 Jan. 26,	21 9 0	115 16 8	81 54 0	33 0 55	1.0	9.646131	"	Méchain.
46	1664 Dec. 4,	11 36 5	130 33 15	81 15 52	21 18 12	1.0	0.010949	Retrograde.	Lindelôf.
47	1665 April 24,	5 16 0	71 54 30	228 2 0	76 5 0	1.0	9.027309	"	Halley.
48	1668 Feb. 24,	18 46 6	40 9 0	193 26 0	27 7 0	1.0	9.39990	Direct.	Henderson.
49	1672 March 1,	8 38 0	46 59 30	297 30 30	83 22 10	1.0	9.843476	"	Halley.
50	1677 May 6,	0 38 0	137 37 5	236 49 10	79 3 15	1.0	9.448072	Retrograde.	"
51	1678 Aug. 18,	7 34 0	322 47 37	163 20 0	2 52 0	0.626970	0.058919	Direct.	Le Verrier.
52	1680 Dec. 17,	23 46 9	262 49 5	272 9 29	60 40 16	0.999985417	7.7939551	"	Encke.
53	1682 Sept. 14,	19 4 53	301 55 37	51 11 18	17 44 45	0.96792019	9.7655898	Retrograde.	Rosenberger.
54	1683 July 13,	17 25 15	86 31 15	173 17 48	83 47 46	0.9832470	9.7430148	"	Clausen.
55	1684 June 8,	10 17 0	238 52 0	268 15 0	65 48 40	1.0	9.982339	Direct.	Halley.
56	1686 Sept. 16,	14 34 0	77 0 30	350 34 40	31 21 40	1.0	9.511883	"	"
57	1689 Nov. 29,	4 48 1	269 41 0	90 25 0	59 5 0	1.0	8.27720	Retrograde.	Vogel.
58	1695 Nov. 9,	17 0 0	60 0 0	216 0 0	22 0 0	1.0	9.9261	Direct.	Burckhardt.
59	1698 Oct. 18,	16 58 0	270 51 15	267 44 15	11 46 0	1.0	9.839660	Retrograde.	Halley.
60	1699 Jan. 13,	8 23 0	212 31 6	321 45 35	69 20 0	1.0	9.871570	"	La Caille.
61	1701 Oct. 17,	9 51 0	133 41 0	298 41 0	41 39 0	1.0	9.77278	"	Burckhardt.
62	1702 March 13,	14 33 22	138 46 34	188 59 10	4 24 44	1.0	9.810790	Direct.	"
63	1706 Jan. 30,	4 57 0	72 36 25	13 11 23	55 14 5	1.0	9.630291	"	Struyck.
64	1707 Dec. 11,	23 30 0	79 54 56	52 46 35	88 36 0	1.0	9.934368	"	La Caille.
65	1718 Jan. 14,	21 44 16	121 39 55	127 55 29	31 8 6	1.0	0.010908	Retrograde.	Argelander.
66	1723 Sept. 27,	15 4 9	42 52 35	14 14 17	50 0 18		9.9994743	"	Spoerer.
67	1729 June 13,	6 19 27	320 31 22	310 38 0	77 5 18	1.0050334	0.6067570	Direct.	Burckhardt.
68	1737 Jan. 30,	8 21 0	325 55 0	226 22 0	18 20 45	1.0	9.347960	"	Bradley.
69	1737 June 8,	7 39 0	262 36 39	123 53 43	39 14 5	1.0	9.93802	"	Daussy.
70	1739 June 17,	10 0 0	102 38 40	207 25 14	55 42 44	1.0	9.828388	Retrograde.	La Caille.

TABLE XVIII.

Elements of the Orbits of Comets which have been observed.

No.	T	π	☊	i	e	log q	Motion.	Computed by
	h m s	° ′ ″	° ′ ″	° ′ ″				
71	1742 Feb. 8, 4 21 14	217 33 44	185 34 45	67 4 11	1.0	9.883976	Retrograde.	Struyck.
72	1743 Jan. 10, 20 20 16	92 57 51	67 31 57	2 16 16	1.0	9.923338	Direct.	Olbers.
73	1743 Sept. 20, 14 11 13	247 15 37	6 15 29	45 38 10	1.0	9.719016	Retrograde.	D'Arrest.
74	1744 March 1, 7 55 39	197 13 58	45 47 54	47 7 41	1.0	9.346842	Direct.	Wolfers.
75	1747 March 3, 9 57 19	277 2 5	147 18 42	79 6 45	1.0	0.342144	Retrograde.	Maraldi.
76	1748 April 28, 19 25 24	215 0 50	232 52 16	85 26 57	1.0	9.924626	〃	〃
77	1748 June 18, 21 18 1	278 47 10	33 8 29	67 3 28	1.0	9.976128	Direct.	Bessel.
78	1757 Oct. 21, 7 54 39	122 58 0	214 12 50	12 50 20	1.0	9.528328	〃	Bradley.
79	1758 June 11, 3 17 39	267 38 0	230 50 0	68 19 0	1.0	9.333148	〃	Pingré.
80	1759 March 12, 13 14 34	303 10 28	53 50 27	17 36 52	0.96768436	9.7667989	Retrograde.	Rosenberger.
81	1759 Nov. 27, 0 33 58	53 38 4	139 40 15	79 3 19	1.0	9.904218	Direct.	Chappe.
82	1759 Dec. 16, 12 48 51	139 3 52	79 20 24	4 42 10	1.0	9.983064	Retrograde.	〃
83	1762 May 28, 8 1 42	104 2 0	348 33 5	85 38 13	1.0	0.003912	Direct.	Burckhardt.
84	1763 Nov. 1, 20 54 58	84 57 27	356 17 38	72 34 10	0.9954268	9.6974946	〃	Lexell.
85	1764 Feb. 12, 13 42 15	15 14 52	120 4 33	52 53 31	1.0	9.744462	Retrograde.	Pingré.
86	1766 Feb. 17, 8 41 0	143 15 25	244 10 50	40 50 20	1.0	9.703570	〃	〃
87	1766 April 26, 23 43 55	251 13 0	74 11 0	8 1 45	0.864000	9.6009521	Direct.	Burckhardt.
88	1769 Oct. 7, 14 53 22	144 11 29	175 3 59	40 45 50	0.99924901	9.089039	〃	Bessel.
89	1770 Aug. 14, 0 38 36	356 16 27	131 59 34	1 34 31	0.786839	9.8288597	〃	Le Verrier.
90	1770 Nov. 22, 5 39 0	208 22 44	108 42 10	31 25 55	1.0	9.722833	Retrograde.	Pingré.
91	1771 April 19, 5 6 19	104 3 16	57 51 55	11 15 19	1.0093698	9.9559104	Direct.	Encke.
92	1772 Feb. 16, 15 43 40	110 8 35	257 15 38	17 3 8	0.724510	9.993890	〃	Hubbard.
93	1773 Sept. 5, 14 1 50	75 17 0	121 8 20	61 15 11	1.0024901	0.052420	〃	Lexell.
94	1774 Aug. 15, 19 55 21	317 27 40	180 44 34	83 20 26	1.0282955	0.1562065	〃	Burckhardt.
95	1779 Jan. 4, 2 4 20	87 14 27	25 4 10	32 30 57	1.0	9.853186	〃	Zach.
96	1780 Sept. 30, 22 13 53	246 35 59	123 41 18	54 23 12	0.9999460	8.9836418	Retrograde.	Clüver.
97	1780 Nov. 28, 20 21 0	246 52 0	142 1 0	72 3 30	1.0	9.712041	〃	Olbers.
98	1781 July 7, 4 31 59	239 11 25	83 0 38	81 43 26	1.0	9.889784	Direct.	Méchain.
99	1781 Nov. 29, 12 33 25	16 3 7	77 22 55	27 12 4	1.0	9.982723	Retrograde.	Legendre.
100	1783 Nov. 19, 11 50 50	50 3 8	55 45 20	44 53 24	0.5395345	0.1626829	Direct.	Burckhardt.
101	1784 Jan. 21, 4 47 26	80 44 24	56 49 21	51 9 12	1.0	9.849946	Retrograde.	Méchain.
102	1785 Jan. 27, 7 48 43	109 51 56	264 12 15	70 14 12	1.0	0.058198	Direct.	〃
103	1785 April 8, 8 58 51	297 29 33	64 33 36	87 31 54	1.0	9.630733	Retrograde.	〃
104	1786 Jan. 30, 20 57 51	156 38 0	334 8 0	13 36 0	0.84836	9.524810	Direct.	Encke.
105	1786 July 8, 13 37 10	158 38 30	195 23 32	50 58 33	1.0	9.595763	〃	Reggio.

TABLE XVIII.

Elements of the Orbits of Comets which have been observed.

No.	T		π	☊	i	e	log q	Motion.	Computed by
		h m s	° ′ ″	° ′ ″	° ′ ″				
106	1787 May 10,	19 48 39	7 44 9	106 51 35	48 15 51	1.0	9.542714	Retrograde.	Saron.
107	1788 Nov. 10,	7 25 26	99 8 7	156 56 43	12 27 40	1.0	0.026538	″	Méchain.
108	1788 Nov. 20,	7 15 39	22 49 54	352 24 26	64 30 24	1.0	9.879276	Direct.	″
109	1790 Jan. 16,	18 58 9	58 24 45	172 50 2	29 44 7	1.0	9.873516	Retrograde.	Saron.
110	1790 Jan. 28,	7 36 9	111 44 37	267 8 37	56 58 13	1.0	0.026650	Direct.	Méchain.
111	1790 May 21,	5 46 54	273 43 27	33 11 2	63 52 27	1.0	9.901981	Retrograde.	″
112	1792 Jan. 13,	12 50 15	36 20 32	190 42 9	39 45 47	1.0	0.111456	″	Zach.
113	1792 Dec. 27,	7 47 9	135 52 35	283 14 44	49 7 14	1.0	9.985350	″	Piazzi.
114	1793 Nov. 4,	20 12 0	228 42 0	108 29 0	60 21 0	1.0	9.605736	″	Saron.
115	1793 Nov. 20,	5 6 21	71 54 3	2 0 12	51 31 10	0.9734211	0.1746744	Direct.	D'Arrest.
116	1795 Dec. 21,	10 35 1	156 41 20	334 39 22	13 42 30	0.8488828	9.5243046	″	Encke.
117	1796 April 2,	19 47 42	192 44 13	17 2 16	64 54 33	1.0	0.198151	Retrograde.	Olbers.
118	1797 July 9,	2 31 10	49 27 8	329 15 37	50 40 34	1.0	9.721489	″	″
119	1798 April 4,	11 58 16	105 6 57	122 12 21	43 44 42	1.0	9.685370	Direct.	″
120	1798 Dec. 31,	13 17 3	34 27 27	249 30 30	42 26 4	1.0	9.891829	Retrograde.	Burckhardt.
121	1799 Sept. 7,	5 50 36	3 38 16	99 23 3	51 2 27	1.0	9.924437	″	Wahl.
122	1799 Dec. 25,	18 3 46	190 22 46	326 30 18	77 5 4	1.0	9.795483	″	″
123	1801 Aug. 8,	13 23 0	183 49 0	44 28 0	21 20 0	1.0	9.417804	″	Burckhardt.
124	1802 Sept. 9,	21 23 5	332 9 4	310 15 39	57 0 47	1.0	0.039061	″	Olbers.
125	1804 Feb. 13,	14 6 55	148 44 51	176 47 58	56 28 40	1.0	0.029858	Direct.	Gauss.
126	1805 Nov. 21,	11 59 50	156 47 24	334 20 10	13 33 30	0.84617529	9.5320168	″	Encke.
127	1806 Jan. 1,	22 1 10	109 28 25	251 16 19	13 36 34	0.7457068	9.9576440	″	Hubbard.
128	1806 Dec. 28,	22 9 2	97 3 24	322 23 16	35 2 33	1.010182	0.034189	Retrograde.	Hensel
129	1807 Sept. 18,	17 43 59	270 54 42	266 47 11	63 10 28	0.99548781	9.8103158	Direct.	Bessel.
130	1808 May 12,	22 52 4	69 12 57	322 58 36	45 43 7	1.0	9.59091	Retrograde.	Encke.
131	1808 July 12,	4 0 58	252 38 50	24 11 15	39 18 59	1.0	9.783870	″	Bessel.
132	1810 Sept. 29,	2 23 31	52 44 42	310 21 2	61 11 15	1.0	9.989355	Direct.	Triesnecker.
133	1811 Sept. 12,	6 10 32	75 0 34	140 24 44	73 2 21	0.99509330	0.0151178	Retrograde.	Argelander.
134	1811 Nov. 10,	23 46 17	47 27 27	93 1 52	31 17 11	0.98271088	0.1992359	Direct.	Nicolai.
135	1812 Sept. 15,	7 31 31	92 18 44	253 1 2	72 57 3	0.9545412	9.8904995	″	Encke.
136	1813 March 4,	12 38 10	69 56 8	60 48 24	21 13 33	1.0	9.8445579	Retrograde.	Nicollet.
137	1813 May 19,	10 1 7	197 43 8	42 40 15	81 2 12	1.0	0.0849212	″	Gerling.
138	1815 April 25,	23 48 42	149 1 56	83 28 34	44 29 55	0.93121968	0.0838109	Direct.	Bessel.
139	1816 March 1,	8 18 0	267 35 33	323 14 56	43 5 26	1.0	8.685769	″	Burckhardt.
140	1818 Feb. 7,	10 55 0	95 7 0	250 4 0	20 2 24	1.0	9.865260	″	Pogson.

TABLE XVIII.

Elements of the Orbits of Comets which have been observed.

No.	T	π	☊	i	e	log q	Motion.	Computed by
	h m s	° ′ ″	° ′ ″	° ′ ″				
141	1818 Feb. 25, 23 0 49	182 45 22	70 26 11	89 43 48	1.0	0.0783711	Direct.	Encke
142	1818 Dec. 4, 2 10 2	103 7 5	90 7 29	62 40 50	1.0	9.928324	Retrograde.	Bessel.
143	1819 Jan. 27, 6 8 53	156 59 12	334 33 19	13 36 54	0.8485841	9.5253771	Direct.	Encke.
144	1819 June 27, 16 52 9	287 5 5	273 43 44	80 45 53	1.0	9.5328194	〃	Brinkley.
145	1819 July 18, 21 36 18	274 40 51	113 10 46	10 42 48	0.75519035	9.8885382	〃	Encke.
146	1819 Nov. 20, 5 53 34	67 18 48	77 13 57	9 1 16	0.6867458	9.9506368	〃	〃
147	1821 March 21, 12 52 39	239 29 25	48 40 56	73 33 7	1.0	8.9629523	Retrograde.	Rosenberger.
148	1822 May 5, 13 34 52	192 47 45	177 25 4	53 35 34	1.0	9.7025976	〃	Gambart.
149	1822 May 23, 23 6 40	157 11 44	334 25 9	13 20 17	0.8444643	9.5390382	Direct.	Encke.
150	1822 July 16, 0 35 2	219 53 48	97 51 23	37 43 4	1.0	9.927430	Retrograde.	v. Heiligenstein.
151	1822 Oct. 23, 18 28 29	271 40 17	92 44 42	52 39 10	0.99630211	0.0588305	〃	Encke.
152	1823 Dec. 9, 10 39 29	274 34 30	303 3 0	76 11 57	1.0	9.3550726	〃	〃
153	1824 July 11, 12 18 40	260 16 32	234 19 9	54 34 9	1.0	9.7717807	〃	Rümker.
154	1824 Sept. 29, 1 23 58	4 31 7	279 15 39	54 36 59	1.0017345	0.0212469	Direct.	Encke.
155	1825 May 30, 13 6 39	273 55 1	20 6 8	56 41 6	1.0	9.9489616	Retrograde.	Clausen.
156	1825 Aug. 18, 17 3 55	10 14 25	192 56 10	89 41 47	1.0	9.9461924	Direct.	〃
157	1825 Sept. 16, 6 33 18	157 14 31	334 27 30	13 21 24	0.8448885	9.5376348	〃	Encke.
158	1825 Dec. 10, 16 7 28	318 46 39	215 43 22	33 32 53	0.9954285	0.0937180	Retrograde.	Hubbard.
159	1826 March 18, 10 43 9	109 48 47	251 27 19	13 33 54	0.7466012	9.9554082	Direct.	〃
160	1826 April 21, 23 27 46	117 11 14	197 30 19	39 57 24	1.0089597	0.3016581	〃	Nicolai.
161	1826 April 29, 0 56 13	35 48 13	40 29 13	5 17 2	1.0	9.2744275	Retrograde.	Clüver.
162	1826 Oct. 8, 22 51 14	57 48 24	44 6 28	25 57 18	1.0	9.930852	Direct.	Argelander.
163	1826 Nov. 18, 9 47 55	315 29 39	235 6 11	89 22 9	1.0	8.4295812	Retrograde.	Gambart.
164	1827 Feb. 4, 22 7 4	33 30 16	184 27 49	77 35 35	1.0	9.704600	〃	v. Heiligenstein.
165	1827 June 7, 20 11 15	297 31 42	318 10 28	43 38 45	1.0	9.907494	〃	〃
166	1827 Sept. 11, 16 37 44	250 57 12	149 39 11	54 4 42	0.99927305	9.1393857	〃	Clüver.
167	1829 Jan. 9, 17 54 7	157 17 53	334 29 32	13 20 34	0.8446245	9.5385038	Direct.	Encke.
168	1830 April 9, 6 43 30	212 11 38	206 21 36	21 16 27	1.0	9.9644642	〃	Carlini.
169	1830 Dec. 27, 15 50 58	310 59 19	337 53 7	44 45 30	1.0	9.0999822	Retrograde.	Wolfers.
170	1832 May 3, 23 24 45	157 21 1	334 32 9	13 22 9	0.8454141	9.5358905	Direct.	Encke.
171	1832 Sept. 25, 12 38 58	227 54 36	72 26 49	43 18 41	1.0	0.0731607	Retrograde.	Peters.
172	1832 Nov. 26, 9 36 44	109 56 24	248 11 49	13 11 48	0.7513780	9.9441275	Direct.	Santini.
173	1833 Sept. 10, 9 29 30	224 21 23	323 28 17	7 18 17	1.0	9.666836	〃	Hartwig.
174	1834 April 2, 15 55 11	276 33 49	226 48 52	5 56 52	1.0	9.7118304	〃	Petersen.
175	1835 March 30, 16 29 51	206 9 24	58 55 57	9 2 42	1.0	0.3120691	Retrograde.	Rümker.

TABLE XVIII.

Elements of the Orbits of Comets which have been observed.

No.	T		π	Ω	i	e	log q	Motion.	Computed by
		h m s	° ′ ″	° ′ ″	° ′ ″				
176	1835 Aug. 26,	8 39 32	157 23 29	334 34 59	13 21 15	0.8450356	9.5371089	Direct.	Encke.
177	1835 Nov. 15,	22 32 1	304 31 32	55 9 59	17 45 5	0.96739091	9.7683194	Retrograde.	Westphalen.
178	1838 Dec. 19,	0 17 38	157 27 4	334 36 41	13 21 18	0.8451775	9.5366085	Direct.	Encke.
179	1840 Jan. 4,	10 13 42	192 11 50	119 57 46	53 5 52	1.0002050	9.7913017	〃	Peters and O. Struve.
180	1840 March 12,	23 46 32	80 18 10	236 49 6	59 13 20	0.9978836	0.0868563	Retrograde.	Plantamour.
181	1840 April 2,	11 53 27	324 12 27	186 2 45	79 51 52	1.0	9.8740948	Direct.	Rümker.
182	1840 Nov. 13,	15 27 55	22 31 40	248 56 22	57 57 23	0.96985265	0.1705070	〃	Goetze.
183	1842 April 12,	0 26 9	157 29 27	334 39 10	13 20 26	0.8447904	9.5378361	〃	Encke.
184	1842 Dec. 15,	22 57 39	327 16 13	207 49 1	73 33 37	1.0	9.7026605	Retrograde.	Laugier.
185	1843 Feb. 27,	9 51 9	278 40 17	1 14 55	35 40 39	0.999915717	7.7433765	〃	Hubbard.
186	1843 May 6,	1 20 33	281 29 43	157 14 54	52 44 46	1.0001798	0.2085316	Direct.	Goetze.
187	1843 Oct. 17,	3 33 46	49 33 52	209 29 36	11 22 33	0.5558997	0.2284632	〃	Möller.
188	1844 Sept. 2,	11 22 36	342 30 50	63 49 0	2 54 50	0.6176539	0.0742308	〃	Brünnow.
189	1844 Oct. 17,	8 15 15	179 35 57	31 39 6	48 36 1	0.9996083	9.9321644	Retrograde.	Plantamour.
190	1844 Dec. 13,	16 11 42	296 2 18	118 19 22	45 38 47	1.00035303	9.4009126	Direct.	Bond.
191	1845 Jan. 8,	3 58 19	91 20 22	336 44 13	46 50 39	1.0	9.9567652	〃	Hind.
192	1845 April 21,	0 44 37	192 33 19	347 6 45	56 23 36	1.0	0.0985330	〃	Faye.
193	1845 June 5,	16 9 44	262 2 56	337 48 56	48 41 59	0.9898742	9.603823	Retrograde.	D'Arrest.
194	1845 Aug. 9,	15 1 50	157 44 21	334 19 33	13 7 34	0.8474362	9.5291008	Direct.	Encke.
195	1846 Jan. 22,	2 15 11	89 6 22	111 8 26	47 26 6	0.9924026	0.1704680	〃	Jelinek.
196	1846 Feb. 10,	22 10 22	109 2 54	245 54 17	12 34 55	0.7566060	9.9327096	〃	Hubbard.
197	1846 Feb. 25,	8 58 39	116 28 15	102 40 58	30 55 53	0.7933880	9.8129825	〃	Brünnow.
198	1846 March 5,	13 5 18	90 27 0	77 33 33	85 5 42	0.96208911	9.8219813	〃	Van Deinse.
199	1846 May 27,	19 44 55	82 39 20	161 18 29	57 36 24	1.0	0.1382020	Retrograde.	Graham.
200	1846 June 1,	5 5 53	240 7 35	260 28 59	30 24 24	0.7213385	0.1842997	Direct.	C. H. F. Peters.
201	1846 June 5,	11 30 5	162 5 40	261 52 51	29 18 47	0.9899389	9.8018857	Retrograde.	Oudemans.
202	1846 Oct. 29,	21 59 57	98 47 15	4 38 18	49 39 3	0.9933127	9.9187601	Direct.	Quirling.
203	1847 March 30,	6 49 29	276 2 22	21 41 52	48 39 50	0.99991293	8.6293024	〃	Hornstein.
204	1847 June 12,	9 1 39	137 41 34	173 25 50	80 16 57	1.0	0.3257617	Retrograde.	D'Arrest.
205	1847 Aug. 9,	8 50 44	246 45 11	338 16 57	83 26 15	0.9985879	0.2470052	〃	Mauvais.
206	1847 Aug. 9,	6 13 10	21 20 41	76 42 10	32 38 24	0.9974348	0.1715154	〃	Schweizer.
207	1847 Sept. 9,	13 1 31	79 12 6	309 48 49	19 8 25	0.972560	9.688297	Direct.	D'Arrest.
208	1847 Nov. 14,	9 36 39	274 12 57	190 49 53	71 50 56	1.0001326	9.5172334	Retrograde.	Rümker.
209	1848 Sept. 8,	1 20 40	310 34 36	211 34 36	84 28 22	1.0	9.5048748	〃	〃
210	1848 Nov. 26,	2 44 10	157 47 8	334 22 12	13 8 36	0.8478280	9.5276718	Direct.	Encke.

TABLE XVIII.

Elements of the Orbits of Comets which have been observed.

No.	T		π	☊	i	e	log q	Motion.	Computed by
		h m s	° ′ ″	° ′ ″	° ′ ″				
211	1849 Jan. 19,	8 31 37	63 14 56	215 12 51	85 2 13	1.0	9.9820756	Direct.	Hensel.
212	1849 May 26,	12 37 26	235 45 15	202 33 27	67 7 50	0.9978863	0.0641120	〃	Weyer.
213	1849 June 8,	4 53 15	267 6 8	30 32 0	66 55 19	0.997830	9.951525	〃	D'Arrest.
214	1850 July 23,	12 40 16	273 25 5	92 53 28	68 11 24	0.9988519	0.0340060	〃	Carrington.
215	1850 Oct. 19,	8 14 20	89 16 3	205 59 31	40 8 53	1.0	9.7522749	〃	Mauvais.
216	1851 April 1,	22 25 17	49 42 10	209 31 16	11 21 38	0.5549601	0.2304281	〃	Möller.
217	1851 July 9,	2 39 15	322 55 55	148 24 51	13 55 8	0.6592674	0.0694270	〃	Schulze.
218	1851 Aug. 26,	5 37 52	310 58 49	223 40 33	38 9 2	0.9968586	9.9931272	〃	Brorsen.
219	1851 Sept. 30,	19 8 58	338 46 26	44 21 30	73 58 37	1.0	9.1521784	〃	Klinkerfues.
220	1852 March 14,	19 6 25	157 51 2	334 23 21	13 7 55	0.8476726	9.5282054	〃	Encke.
221	1852 April 19,	15 15 6	278 42 18	317 29 30	49 11 8	1.0525041	9.9604040	Retrograde.	Hartwig.
222	1852 Sept. 22,	22 38 25	109 8 16	245 51 28	12 33 19	0.7558650	9.9348124	Direct.	Hubbard.
223	1852 Oct. 12,	18 0 57	43 13 42	346 10 0	40 55 0	0.91891698	0.0968963	〃	Westphal.
224	1853 Feb. 23,	23 55 49	153 44 19	69 33 36	20 13 20	0.990412	0.0381820	Retrograde.	Hartwig.
225	1853 May 9,	19 39 59	201 44 37	40 57 37	57 49 3	0.9893194	9.9584172	〃	Rümker.
226	1853 Sept. 1,	16 54 26	310 56 59	140 31 22	61 30 11	0.7294246	9.4871354	Direct.	Stockwell.
227	1853 Oct. 16,	14 31 44	302 14 53	220 5 52	60 59 44	1.0012289	9.2372363	Retrograde.	D'Arrest.
228	1854 Jan. 2,	17 19 36	56 38 52	227 0 44	66 0 44	1.0	0.3108246	〃	Klinkerfues.
229	1854 March 24,	0 20 41	213 49 14	315 27 27	82 32 43	1.0	9.4425551	〃	Mathieu.
230	1854 June 22,	2 1 43	272 58 6	347 48 45	71 8 21	1.0	9.8111244	〃	Bruhns.
231	1854 Oct. 27,	12 13 4	94 24 18	324 28 31	40 54 38	0.9933246	9.902384	Direct.	Lesser.
232	1854 Dec. 15,	17 11 27	165 9 25	238 7 54	14 8 50	0.9864041	0.1327551	〃	Adam.
233	1855 Feb. 5,	1 8 11	226 37 34	189 43 33	51 24 19	0.9651850	0.3411427	Retrograde.	Tiele.
234	1855 May 29,	10 58 4	239 28 46	260 10 48	23 9 54	0.9039970	9.751970	〃	Schulze.
235	1855 July 1,	4 40 0	157 53 12	334 26 24	13 8 9	0.8477869	9.5277600	Direct.	Encke.
236	1855 Nov. 25,	9 8 58	86 2 13	51 34 31	10 11 19	0.997255	0.090728	Retrograde.	Hoek.
237	1857 March 21,	8 43 38	74 43 59	313 9 37	87 56 13	0.9992144	9.8878700	Direct.	Schulze.
238	1857 March 28,	16 4 19	115 46 25	101 45 15	29 48 53	0.8022946	9.7928091	〃	Bruhns.
239	1857 July 17,	23 33 10	249 36 1	23 41 28	58 57 51	0.9989984	9.5652331	Retrograde.	Villarceau.
240	1857 Aug. 23,	23 54 59	21 46 51	200 49 16	32 46 24	0.9803714	9.8732267	Direct.	Möller.
241	1857 Sept. 30,	21 7 5	250 7 38	14 57 48	56 3 21	0.9969135	9.7504285	Retrograde.	Linsser.
242	1857 Nov. 19,	1 42 31	44 13 16	139 18 42	37 48 55	0.9969918	0.003889	〃	Auwers.
243	1857 Nov. 28,	19 36 14	323 3 9	148 27 7	13 56 1	0.6598094	0.0683373	Direct.	Schulze.
244	1858 Feb. 23,	12 34 20	115 51 35	269 3 13	54 24 10	0.820903	0.010940	〃	Bruhns.
245	1858 May 2,	1 24 32	275 39 54	113 30 59	10 47 55	0.7541036	9.8858281	〃	Hänsel.

TABLE XVIII.

Elements of the Orbits of Comets which have been observed.

No.	T	π	☊	i	e	log q	Motion.	Computed by
	h m s	° ′ ″	° ′ ″	° ′ ″				
246	1858 May 2, 7 42 37	195 58 44	170 42 56	22 59 49	1.0	0.0826760	Direct.	Watson.
247	1858 June 5, 7 5 39	226 6 5	324 58 8	80 2 42	1.0	9.7358072	Retrograde.	Auwers.
248	1858 Sept. 29, 23 8 51	36 12 31	165 19 13	63 1 49	0.99629326	9.7622804	"	Hill.
249	1858 Oct. 18, 8 41 33	157 57 30	334 28 34	13 4 15	0.8463915	9.5324034	Direct.	Encke.
250	1858 Sept. 13, 21 26 37	49 51 54	209 40 2	11 22 11	0.5577360	0.2291239	"	Möller.
251	1858 Oct. 12, 19 26 46	4 13 18	159 45 3	21 16 37	1.0	0.1544245	Retrograde.	Weiss.
252	1859 May 29, 5 25 38	75 20 31	357 20 44	83 31 45	1.0	9.303265	"	Hertzsprung.
253	1860 Feb. 16, 16 9 30	173 45 21	324 3 25	79 35 55	1.0	0.078219	Direct.	Liais.
254	1860 March 5, 17 12 25	50 16 5	8 56 9	48 13 4	1.0	0.1167062	"	Seeling.
255	1860 June 16, 0 20 56	161 31 10	84 42 50	79 17 38	0.997240	9.465570	"	Liais.
256	1860 Sept. 28, 6 49 0	111 59 0	104 14 0	28 14 0	1.0	9.9795	Retrograde.	Valz.
257	1861 June 3, 9 21 30	243 22 2	29 55 42	79 45 31	0.983463143	9.9641181	Direct.	Oppolzer.
258	1861 June 11, 12 17 7	249 4 27	278 57 59	85 26 28	0.9853832	9.9150740	"	Sawitsch.
259	1861 Dec. 7, 4 17 18	173 30 36	145 6 58	41 57 23	1.0	9.923813	Retrograde.	Pape.
260	1862 Feb. 6, 4 7 49	158 0 10	334 30 50	13 5 0	0.8467094	9.5313486	Direct.	Encke.
261	1862 June 22, 0 43 59	229 20 27	326 32 53	7 54 ·26	1.0	9.991818	Retrograde.	Seeling.
262	1862 Aug. 22, 21 53 32	344 41 26	137 26 53	66 25 33	0.9612708	9.9834648	"	Oppolzer.
263	1862 Dec. 28, 8 33 28	125 9 43	355 44 58	42 22 53	1.0	9.904475	"	Engelmann.
264	1863 Feb. 3, 11 47 16	191 22 45	116 55 33	85 21 56	0.9999470	9.9002349	Direct.	"
265	1863 April 4, 21 42 13	247 15 25	251 15 35	67 22 13	1.0	0.0286067	Retrograde.	Frischauf.
266	1863 April 20, 20 39 7	305 31 6	249 59 22	85 28 44	1.0	9.798266	Direct.	Karlinski.
267	1863 Nov. 9, 11 35 16	94 43 17	97 29 56	78 5 21	1.0	9.849171	"	Stampfer.
268	1863 Dec. 27, 18 19 44	60 24 28	304 43 26	64 28 46	1.0	9.887344	"	Weiss.
269	1863 Dec. 29, 4 0 45	183 7 18	105 1 24	83 19 17	1.0006499	0.1183045	"	Rosén.
270	1864 July 27, 19 50 29	185 31 54	174 51 6	65 1 19	1.0	9.822162	Retrograde.	Valentiner.
271	1864 Aug. 15, 13 46 54	304 11 52	95 14 27	1 52 10	0.9967771	9.9587003	"	Kowalczyk.
272	1864 Oct. 11, 9 41 54	159 18 2	31 45 26	70 18 2	0.99995324	9.9690407	"	von Asten.
273	1864 Dec. 22, 11 7 31	321 42 31	203 13 12	48 52 20	1.0	9.886982	Direct.	Tietjen.
274	1864 Dec. 27, 17 16 20	162 23 36	160 54 22	17 7 23	1.0	0.0471352	Retrograde.	Valentiner.
275	1865 Jan. 14, 8 10 23	141 15 37	253 3 15	87 32 20	1.0	8.4152071	"	Tebbutt.
276	1866 Jan. 11, 3 12 47	60 28 48	231 26 3	17 18 5	0.9054198	9.9896813	"	Oppolzer.
277	1866 Feb. 14, 0 29 48	49 56 55	209 41 53	11 22 7	0.5575382	0.2258707	Direct.	Möller.
278	1867 Jan. 19, 20 39 15	75 52 15	78 35 45	18 12 35	0.8490551	0.1965869	"	Searle.
279	1867 Feb. 27, 20 17 25	162 40 17	168 35 31	6 7 0	1.0	0.050900	"	C. F. W. Peters.
280								

TABLE XIX.

Elements of the Orbits of the Minor Planets.

No.	Name.	Epoch and Mean Equinox. Berlin Mean Time.	M	π	☊	i	φ	μ	log a	Date of Discovery.	Discoverer.
			° ′ ″	° ′ ″	° ′ ″	° ′ ″	° ′ ″	″			
1	Ceres.	1866 Jan. 21.0	337 10 35.7	148 22 8.4	80 50 7.2	10 36 28.8	4 36 2.8	771.02418	0.4419590	1801 Jan. 1	Piazzi.
2	Pallas.	1866 June 19.0	11 56 49.0	122 1 16.8	172 43 55.6	34 42 38.8	13 53 17.5	769.80966	0.442415	1802 March 28	Olbers.
3	Juno.	1865 Nov. 3.0	329 20 8.9	54 56 31.9	170 49 36.8	13 1 21.3	14 54 25.8	814.0068	0.4262524	1804 Sept. 1	Harding.
4	Vesta.	1810 Jan. 0.0	216 42 25.8	249 19 28.6	103 11 22.1	7 8 5.0	5 5 36.3	977.6338563	0.3732203	1807 March 29	Olbers.
5	Astræa.	1865 Sept. 19.0	234 23 32.5	135 14 48.1	141 26 18.3	5 19 9.0	10 48 30.1	857.60520	0.4111462	1845 Dec. 8	Hencke.
6	Hebe.	1866 June 30.0	283 17 20.5	15 6 12.7	138 39 17.3	14 46 43.9	11 41 34.8	939.08225	0.3848687	1847 July 1	Hencke.
7	Iris.	1850 Jan. 0.0	166 7 9.0	41 23 21.1	259 47 55.8	5 28 3.0	13 20 50.2	962.580602	0.3777130	1847 Aug. 13	Hind.
8	Flora.	1848 Jan. 1.0	35 54 3.6	32 54 28.3	110 17 48.6	5 53 8.0	9 0 56.3	1086.33098	0.3426963	1847 Oct. 18	Hind.
9	Metis.	1858 June 30.0	57 4 34.7	71 3 52.1	68 31 35.2	5 36 0.3	7 5 2.4	962.33898	0.3777857	1848 April 25	Graham.
10	Hygeia.	1864 Feb. 22.0	199 13 22.0	235 10 29.2	286 43 1.8	3 49 0.2	5 44 56.4	634.31180	0.4984692	1849 April 12	Gasparis.
11	Parthenope.	1865 March 27.0	239 14 15.1	317 14 31.4	125 7 27.9	4 37 1.6	5 42 54.1	924.15366	0.3895083	1850 May 11	Gasparis.
12	Victoria.	1851 Jan. 0.0	66 2 39.9	301 39 25.0	235 34 41.7	8 23 17.7	12 38 44.9	994.83472	0.3681389	1850 Sept. 13	Hind.
13	Egeria.	1866 Aug. 29.0	220 54 41.3	120 5 15.0	43 15 56.3	16 30 48.8	4 59 47.1	857.87961	0.411054	1850 Nov. 2	Gasparis.
14	Irene.	1864 Nov. 28.0	134 55 9.2	179 52 6.8	86 42 23.7	9 7 37.5	9 33 23.7	853.20824	0.4126344	1851 May 19	Hind.
15	Eunomia.	1854 Jan. 0.0	122 5 31.5	27 52 0.5	293 52 14.5	11 44 17.4	10 47 32.2	825.4550	0.422209	1851 July 29	Gasparis.
16	Psyche.	1867 Jan. 0.0	115 10 46.6	15 26 27.0	150 33 17.6	3 3 57.2	7 47 0.3	709.7603	0.465930	1852 March 17	Gasparis.
17	Thetis.	1866 July 1.5	177 17 24.1	260 24 17.6	125 23 4.2	5 36 6.2	7 20 12.3	912.06563	0.393320	1852 April 17	Luther.
18	Melpomene.	1854 Jan. 0.0	80 4 37.0	15 5 31.0	150 3 49.7	10 9 16.9	12 34 20.2	1020.1198	0.360903	1852 June 24	Hind.
19	Fortuna.	1863 June 24.0	258 15 3.3	30 57 54.2	211 22 29.1	1 32 44.8	9 7 30.2	930.2787	0.3875957	1852 Aug. 22	Hind.
20	Massalia.	1866 June 15.5	161 43 44.2	98 29 31.8	206 45 6.7	0 41 9.5	8 15 13.7	948.55878	0.381962	1852 Sept. 19	Gasparis.
21	Lutetia.	1853 Jan. 2.0	74 20 5.1	327 3 8.4	80 27 7.2	3 5 9.5	9 19 44.6	933.55438	0.3865780	1852 Nov. 15	Goldschmidt.
22	Calliope.	1866 Aug. 30.5	289 37 46.9	58 15 36.1	66 35 39.8	13 43 47.4	5 39 18.6	714.51387	0.463998	1852 Nov. 16	Hind.
23	Thalia.	1867 Jan. 0.0	68 14 16.3	123 49 41.6	67 40 47.2	10 13 26.6	13 25 8.8	833.1087	0.419537	1852 Dec. 15	Hind.
24	Themis.	1864 Aug. 20.0	40 14 0.7	140 8 26.5	36 12 12.6	0 48 52.1	6 42 52.9	636.76345	0.4973523	1853 April 5	Gasparis.
25	Phocæa.	1865 Nov. 12.0	79 17 21.8	302 49 53.4	214 5 7.3	21 34 36.3	14 43 58.4	953.82327	0.380360	1853 April 6	Chacornac.
26	Proserpina.	1853 June 11.0	351 5 55.6	236 25 15.0	45 54 59.3	3 35 47.7	5 0 37.3	819.68468	0.4242399	1853 May 5	Luther.
27	Euterpe.	1866 May 26.5	149 7 51.3	87 35 3.6	93 48 1.5	1 35 29.8	9 58 29.2	986.99048	0.370463	1853 Nov. 8	Hind.
28	Bellona.	1862 March 24.0	303 8 27.8	122 55 29.6	144 41 9.9	9 21 26.3	8 37 57.5	766.12228	0.4438057	1854 March 1	Luther.
29	Amphitrite.	1866 March 10.0	104 21 32.3	56 56 1.8	356 30 5.2	6 7 49.3	4 14 35.3	869.33444	0.407214	1854 March 1	Marth.
30	Urania.	1865 Aug. 18.0	306 32 25.0	31 28 57.9	308 9 39.2	2 6 6.9	7 16 6.3	975.27438	0.373920	1854 July 22	Hind.
31	Euphrosyne.	1867 Jan. 0.0	11 8 2.0	93 42 6.6	31 31 45.9	26 27 5.0	12 44 10.3	633.8508	0.498680	1854 Sept. 1	Ferguson.
32	Pomona.	1855 Jan. 5.0	222 54 24.0	194 21 32.1	220 48 14.5	5 29 5.0	4 43 43.7	852.5769	0.4128487	1854 Oct. 28	Goldschmidt.
33	Polyhymnia.	1866 Feb. 11.0	144 10 45.7	342 31 6.7	9 5 54.9	1 56 19.9	19 47 58.6	731.6869	0.457121	1854 Oct. 28	Chacornac.
34	Circe.	1865 Aug. 20.0	170 13 2.5	150 3 19.2	184 48 36.5	5 26 28.9	6 9 44.1	805.85537	0.4291663	1855 April 6	Chacornac.
35	Leucothea.	1866 June 22.0	47 39 33.7	201 40 29.0	355 51 35.8	8 10 47.6	12 22 51.7	680.7841	0.477998	1855 April 19	Luther.

TABLE XIX.

Elements of the Orbits of the Minor Planets.

No.	Name.	Epoch and Mean Equinox. Berlin Mean Time.	M	π	Ω	i	φ	μ	log a	Date of Discovery.	Discoverer.
			° ′ ″	° ′ ″	° ′ ″	° ′ ″	° ′ ″	″			
36	Atalanta.	1866 Feb. 21.0	74 52 38.3	42 47 47.7	359 11 14.9	18 42 14.8	17 31 53.2	779.6936	0.438721	1855 Oct. 5	Goldschmidt.
37	Fides.	1853 Oct. 5.0	266 46 29.0	66 20 17.3	8 12 29.4	3 7 12.3	10 10 46.1	826.54485	0.4218268	1855 Oct. 5	Luther.
38	Leda.	1856 Jan. 0.0	12 6 43.3	100 51 44.3	296 27 34.9	6 58 25.3	8 56 30.7	782.2500	0.4377740	1856 Jan. 12	Chacornac.
39	Lætitia.	1866 May 2.0	231 39 4.8	2 30 27.3	157 21 11.5	10 22 5.1	6 35 2.2	770.85681	0.4420219	1856 Feb. 8	Chacornac.
40	Harmonia.	1866 March 3.0	160 34 22.3	1 27 26.1	93 35 58.8	4 15 54.8	2 41 7.6	1039.45323	0.3554678	1856 March 31	Goldschmidt.
41	Daphne.	1866 July 29.5	55 45 17.5	220 12 14.1	179 6 58.7	15 59 12.1	15 25 19.7	769.99685	0.442346	1856 May 22	Goldschmidt.
42	Isis.	1860 Jan. 0.0	289 29 25.4	318 0 48.7	84 30 40.4	8 34 33.0	13 2 20.6	930.9057	0.3874006	1856 May 23	Pogson.
43	Ariadne.	1866 Jan. 1.0	184 54 15.1	277 48 9.6	264 37 43.9	3 27 40.5	9 38 37.8	1084.93658	0.3430683	1857 April 15	Pogson.
44	Nysa.	1866 Oct. 9.0	283 21 50.5	112 5 31.5	131 3 31.2	3 41 57.6	8 40 17.9	941.35966	0.3841674	1857 May 27	Goldschmidt.
45	Eugenia.	1866 June 4.0	19 22 1.6	230 50 34.9	148 6 3.7	6 35 25.0	4 35 2.2	790.4322	0.434762	1857 June 27	Goldschmidt.
46	Hestia.	1865 July 26.0	322 11 46.6	354 10 34.9	181 26 45.3	2 17 32.1	9 26 55.7	883.5638	0.4025124	1857 Aug. 16	Pogson.
47	Aglaia.	1859 June 17.0	162 29 40.5	314 3 45.0	4 12 34.2	5 0 8.5	7 35 15.7	725.4987	0.4595800	1857 Sept. 15	Luther.
48	Doris.	1862 July 25.0	235 11 27.8	74 20 42.4	185 5 29.6	6 29 28.2	4 23 42.9	647.12954	0.4926769	1857 Sept. 19	Goldschmidt.
49	Pales.	1863 Nov. 14.0	20 0 30.8	32 14 49.7	290 32 17.4	3 8 46.4	13 43 18.3	655.62089	0.4889025	1857 Sept. 19	Goldschmidt.
50	Virginia.	1863 Jan. 18.0	83 27 18.9	9 53 21.4	173 31 59.2	2 47 48.4	16 40 22.5	822.94439	0.4230907	1857 Oct. 4	Ferguson.
51	Nemausa.	1865 Jan. 17.0	316 39 29.6	174 52 0.6	175 43 6.3	9 56 52.8	3 47 40.7	975.13844	0.3739602	1858 Jan. 22	Laurent.
52	Europa.	1858 Jan. 0.0	34 25 7.3	101 56 14.8	129 57 16.0	7 24 41.0	5 49 14.3	650.0877	0.4913564	1858 Feb. 6	Goldschmidt.
53	Calypso.	1866 Jan. 4.0	7 11 44.0	92 53 30.3	144 1 9.0	5 6 39.0	11 45 54.8	836.80511	0.4182540	1858 April 4	Luther.
54	Alexandra.	1863 Nov. 14.0	83 37 8.2	295 27 8.7	314 5 8.4	11 46 41.9	11 21 24.0	794.32164	0.4333401	1858 Sept. 10	Goldschmidt.
55	Pandora.	1863 Oct. 25.0	35 42 11.7	11 9 47.8	10 52 9.6	7 13 49.8	8 19 19.2	774.2176	0.4407624	1858 Sept. 10	Searle.
56	Melete.	1865 June 20.0	344 40 12.6	293 29 25.0	194 27 23.7	8 1 40.9	13 44 9.5	848.33049	0.4142944	1857 Sept. 9	Goldschmidt.
57	Mnemosyne.	1860 Jan. 1.0	335 30 22.2	53 7 9.9	200 5 31.5	15 8 8.6	5 58 17.1	632.68967	0.4992106	1859 Sept. 22	Luther.
58	Concordia.	1865 Jan. 7.0	21 50 58.8	188 41 55.0	161 19 35.6	5 1 53.2	2 26 15.2	799.63132	0.4314112	1860 March 24	Luther.
59	Elpis.	1865 Jan. 7.0	334 18 42.6	18 18 54.2	170 20 28.8	8 37 13.5	6 44 1.3	793.974093	0.4334669	1860 Sept. 12	Chacornac.
60	Echo.	1866 Jan. 0.0	65 44 37.1	98 33 32.6	192 2 9.0	3 34 18.5	10 38 45.8	958.47412	0.3879508	1860 Sept. 15	Ferguson.
61	Danaë.	1865 Aug. 19.0	345 54 41.2	341 25 28.5	334 11 50.0	18 15 25.6	9 17 59.3	688.08150	0.4749112	1860 Sept. 19	Goldschmidt.
62	Erato.	1865 May 7.0	279 40 20.8	34 8 29.1	126 11 42.1	2 12 17.5	9 46 4.3	640.85910	0.4954961	1860 Sept. 14	Foerster, Lesser.
63	Ausonia.	1865 April 17.0	307 24 5.0	269 32 49.0	338 6 58.3	5 47 16.3	7 13 45.3	957.32042	0.3792995	1861 Feb. 10	Gasparis.
64	Angelina.	1865 Jan. 7.0	355 46 41.1	123 37 49.1	311 9 7.2	1 19 52.0	7 21 58.9	808.30600	0.4282872	1861 March 4	Tempel.
65	Cybele.	1861 Jan. 0.0	281 57 34.7	258 20 36.9	158 53 34.8	3 28 9.8	6 54 36.4	560.8775	0.534092	1861 March 8	Tempel.
66	Maia.	1865 Jan. 27.0	87 7 3.2	44 25 0.6	8 15 23.7	3 4 15.1	9 5 46.9	821.9211	0.4234510	1861 April 9	Tuttle.
67	Asia.	1865 Jan. 7.0	296 2 14.0	306 8 6.9	202 43 29.0	5 59 35.9	10 39 58.6	941.4909	0.3841270	1861 April 17	Pogson.
68	Leto.	1863 Dec. 20.0	93 53 22.4	345 4 58.2	44 53 11.4	7 57 34.9	10 51 46.8	765.323	0.444108	1861 April 29	Luther.
69	Hesperia.	1861 June 3.0	54 46 56.9	109 6 25.4	187 1 7.5	8 28 19.2	10 0 38.3	692.6300	0.473004	1861 April 29	Schiaparelli.
70	Panopæa.	1861 May 28.0	308 41 11.5	300 3 30.3	48 14 42.6	11 38 30.2	10 33 7.5	839.90600	0.417184	1861 May 5	Goldschmidt.

TABLE XIX. Elements of the Orbits of the Minor Planets.

No.	Name.	Epoch and Mean Equinox. Berlin Mean Time.	M	π	Ω	i	ϕ	μ	log a	Date of Discovery.	Discoverer.
			° ′ ″	° ′ ″	° ′ ″	° ′ ″	° ′ ″	″			
71	Niobe.	1864 Jan. 23.0	283 10 47.6	222 4 26.8	316 19 7.0	23 18 51.2	10 0 15.1	775.73290	0.4401964	1861 Aug. 13	Luther.
72	Feronia.	1866 Jan. 0.0	31 17 25.1	307 54 49.5	207 44 59.6	5 23 54.5	6 52 45.9	1040.14680	0.3552747	1861 May 29	Peters.
73	Clytia.	1864 Oct. 4.0	325 18 55.8	59 59 11.0	7 34 19.1	2 24 39.5	2 27 0.5	814.84338	0.425955	1862 April 7	Tuttle.
74	Galatea.	1866 Jan. 0.0	249 23 12.1	7 22 10.2	197 58 59.3	3 58 54.6	13 46 49.1	766.4390	0.4436860	1862 Aug. 29	Tempel.
75	Eurydice.	1864 Feb. 2.0	133 39 40.8	334 27 46.0	359 56 43.4	5 0 4.2	17 51 2.1	812.9517	0.426628	1862 Sept. 22	Peters.
76	Freia.	1863 July 27.0	355 31 36.1	93 13 58.1	212 58 21.4	2 1 50.8	10 49 12.0	569.0505	0.5299038	1862 Oct. 21	D'Arrest.
77	Frigga.	1866 Jan. 0.0	228 36 16.6	58 11 32.0	2 9 27.6	2 27 56.6	7 48 20.4	812.40096	0.4268241	1862 Nov. 12	Peters.
78	Diana.	1865 Oct. 4.0	256 20 50.5	121 42 47.5	333 55 48.4	8 38 39.9	11 51 34.5	835.35315	0.4187577	1863 March 15	Luther.
79	Eurynome.	1864 Jan. 1.0	1 30 56.7	44 17 58.1	206 42 42.6	4 36 46.5	11 14 53.1	929.1286	0.3879539	1863 Sept. 14	Watson.
80	Sappho.	1865 Oct. 7.0	50 11 5.7	355 5 12.5	218 31 45.0	8 36 51.3	11 33 5.6	1019.6804	0.3610284	1864 May 2	Pogson.
81	Terpsichore.	1864 Oct. 6.0	333 26 18.1	43 33 7.9	2 32 1.6	7 55 40.8	12 13 31.5	735.0244	0.4558032	1864 Sept. 30	Tempel.
82	Alcmene.	1865 Feb. 16.0	332 33 22.9	131 18 19.7	26 56 51.5	2 51 15.0	13 3 43.1	773.711	0.440952	1864 Nov. 27	Luther.
83	Beatrix.	1865 May 4.0	17 1 59.0	188 28 20.9	27 34 9.1	5 2 11.3	4 49 38.8	937.415	0.385383	1865 April 26	Gasparis.
84	Clio.	1865 Nov. 13.0	14 36 45.5	339 12 0.1	327 22 1.5	9 22 16.0	13 39 34.8	977.5422	0.3732474	1865 Aug. 25	Luther.
85	Io.	1866 Jan. 0.0	56 49 20.9	322 32 28.9	203 52 33.3	11 53 12.8	11 0 53.1	820.7120	0.4238772	1865 Sept. 19	Peters.
86	Semele.	1866 Jan. 8.0	8 23 14.6	28 39 3.9	87 55 49.6	4 47 44.6	11 49 36.5	652.9848	0.490069	1866 Jan. 4	Tietjen.
87	Sylvia.	1866 May 16.5	274 4 2.3	337 21 48.6	76 23 59.0	10 51 22.0	4 39 22.6	543.5800	0.5431620	1866 May 16	Pogson.
88	Thisbe.	1866 Aug. 4.5	356 5 1.4	308 55 30.5	277 44 7.8	5 14 58.1	9 29 55.7	769.561	0.442509	1866 June 15	Peters.
89		1866 Sept. 1.0	339 44 19.2	349 30 29.8	311 31 7.5	16 32 38.0	9 37 22.2	872.656	0.406109	1866 Aug. 6	Stephan.
90	Antiope.	1866 Oct. 18.0	52 6 9.2	294 3 7.3	71 0 54.0	2 17 25.2	11 39 2.7	632.35913	0.4993618	1866 Oct. 1	Luther.
91		1866 Dec. 21.0	336 46 5.4	75 16 23.5	11 19 10.4	2 9 25.0	5 4 27.2	867.0876	0.4079624	1866 Nov. 4	Stephan.

TABLE XX. Elements of the Orbits of the Major Planets.

Name.	Epoch and Mean Equinox. Greenwich Mean Time.	L	π	$\Delta\pi$	Ω	$\Delta\Omega$	i	Δi	e	Δe	a
		° ′ ″	° ′ ″	′ ″	° ′ ″	′ ″	° ′ ″	″			
Mercury.	1801 Jan. 1.0	166 0 43.2	74 21 37.2	+ 9 44	45 58 20.2	— 13 2	7 0 4.5	+ 18.1	0.2056003	+ 0.00000387	0.3870984
Venus.	"	11 33 3.0	128 43 53.1	— 4 28	74 54 12.9	— 21 11	3 23 28.5	+ 4.5	0.0068607	— 0.00006275	0.7233316
Earth.	"	100 39 10.2	99 30 5.0	+ 19 41					0.0167836	— 0.00004359	1.0000000
Mars.	"	64 22 55.5	332 23 56.6	+ 26 22	48 0 3.5	— 38 49	1 51 6.2	— 0.3	0.0933070	+ 0.00009019	1.5236923
Jupiter.	"	112 15 23.0	11 8 34.6	+ 11 5	98 26 18.9	— 26 21	1 18 51.3	— 22.6	0.0481621	+ 0.00016036	5.2027760
Saturn.	"	135 20 6.5	89 9 29.8	+ 32 17	111 56 37.4	— 32 22	2 29 35.7	— 15.5	0.0561505	— 0.00031240	9.5387861
Uranus.	"	177 48 23.0	167 31 16.1	+ 4 0	72 59 35.3	— 59 59	0 46 28.0	+ 3.1	0.0466794	— 0.00002521	19.1823900
Neptune.	1850 Jan. 0.0	335 5 38.9	43 17 30.3		130 7 31.8		1 47 1.7		0.0084962		30.0705520

TABLE XXI. Constants, &c.

		log
Base of Naperian logarithms	$e = 2.71828183$	0.43429448
Modulus of the common logarithms	$\lambda_0 = 0.43429448$	9.63778431 — 10
Radius of a Circle in seconds	$r = 206264.806$	5.31442513
〃 〃 〃 〃 minutes	$r = 3437.7468$	3.53627388
〃 〃 〃 〃 degrees	$r = 57.29578$	1.75812263
Circumference of a Circle in seconds	1296000	6.11260500
〃 〃 〃 when $r = 1$	$\pi = 3.14159265$	0.49714987
Sine of 1 second	0.000004848137	4.68557487
Equatorial horizontal parallax of the sun, according to Encke	8″.57116	0.9330396
Length of the sidereal year, according to Hansen and Olufsen	365.2563582 days	2.56259778
Length of the tropical year, according to Hansen and Olufsen	365.2422008 〃	2.56258095

This value of the length of the tropical year is for 1850.0. The annual variation is — 0.^{d}0000000624.

Time occupied by the passage of light over a distance equal to the mean distance of the earth from the sun, according to Struve	497.^{s}827	2.6970785
Attractive force of the sun, according to Gauss .	$k = 0.017202099$	8.23558144 — 10
〃 〃 〃 〃 〃 〃 〃 in seconds of arc	3548.18761	3.55000657

Constant of Aberration, according to Struve	20″.4451
〃 〃 Nutation, 〃 〃 Peters	9″.2231

Mean Obliquity of the ecliptic for $1750 + t$, according to Bessel	23° 28′ 18″.00 — 0″.48368t — 0″.0000027229$5t^2$
Mean Obliquity of the ecliptic for $1800 + t$, according to Struve and Peters . .	23° 27′ 54″.22 — 0″.4738t — 0″.000001$4t^2$

General Precession for the year $1750 + t$, according to Bessel	50″.21129 + 0″.0002442966t
〃 〃 〃 〃 〃 〃 Struve	50″.22980 + 0″.000226t

Masses of the Planets, the Mass of the Sun being the unit.

Mercury	$m = \frac{1}{4865751}$,	Jupiter	$m = \frac{1}{1047.879}$,
Venus	$\frac{1}{390000}$,	Saturn	$\frac{1}{3501.6}$,
Earth	$\frac{1}{354936}$,	Uranus	$\frac{1}{24905}$,
Mars	$\frac{1}{2680637}$,	Neptune	$\frac{1}{18780}$.

EXPLANATION OF THE TABLES.

TABLE I. contains the values of the *angle of the vertical* and of the logarithm of the earth's radius, with the geographical latitude as the argument. The adopted elements are those derived by Bessel. Denoting by ρ the radius of the earth, by φ the geographical latitude, and by φ' the geocentric latitude, we have

$$\varphi' = \varphi - 11' \, 30''.65 \sin 2\varphi + 1''.16 \sin 4\varphi - \&c.,$$
$$\log \rho = 9.9992747 + 0.0007271 \cos 2\varphi - 0.0000018 \cos 4\varphi + \&c.,$$

ρ being expressed in parts of the equatorial radius as the unit. These quantities are required in the determination of the parallax of a heavenly body. The formulæ for the parallax in right ascension and in declination are given in Art. 61.

TABLE II. gives the intervals of sidereal time corresponding to given intervals of mean time. It is required for the conversion of mean solar into sidereal time.

TABLE III. gives the intervals of mean time corresponding to given intervals of sidereal time. It is required for the conversion of sidereal into mean solar time.

TABLE IV. furnishes the numbers required in converting hours, minutes, and seconds into decimals of a day. Thus, to convert 13*h* 19*m* 43.5*s* into the decimal of a day, we find from the Table

$$\begin{aligned} 13h &= 0.5416667 \\ 19m &= 0.0131944 \\ 43s &= 0.0004977 \\ 0.5s &= \underline{0.0000058} \\ \text{Therefore } 13h\ 19m\ 43.5s &= 0.5553646 \end{aligned}$$

The decimal corresponding to 0.5*s* is found from that for 5*s* by changing the place of the decimal point.

TABLE V. serves to find, for any instant, the number of days from the beginning of the year. Thus, for 1863 Sept. 14, 15*h* 53*m* 37.2*s*, we have

$$\begin{aligned} \text{Sept. } 0.0 &= 243.00000 \text{ days from the beginning of the year.} \\ 14d\ 15h\ 53m\ 37.2s &= \underline{\ \ 14.66224\ \ } \\ \text{Required number of days} &= 257.66224 \end{aligned}$$

TABLE VI. contains the values of $M = 75 \tan \frac{1}{2}v + 25 \tan^3 \frac{1}{2}v$ for values of v at intervals of one minute from 0° to 180°. For an explanation of its construction and use, see Articles 22, 27, 29, 41, and 72.

In the case of parabolic motion the formulæ are

$$m = \frac{C_0}{q^{\frac{3}{2}}}, \qquad\qquad M = m\,(t - T),$$

wherein $\log C_0 = 9.9601277$. From these, by means of the Table, v may be found when $t - T$ is given, or $t - T$ when v is known. From $v = 30°$ to $v = 180°$ the Table contains the values of $\log M$.

TABLE VII., the construction of which is explained in Art. 23, serves to determine, in the case of parabolic motion, the true anomaly or the time from the perihelion when v approaches near to 180°. The formulæ are

$$\sin w = \sqrt[3]{\frac{200}{M}}, \qquad v = w + \Delta_0, \qquad t - T = \frac{200}{C_0} \cdot \frac{q^{\frac{3}{2}}}{\sin^3 w},$$

w being taken in the second quadrant. The Table gives the values of Δ_0 with w as the argument. As an example, let it be required to find the true anomaly corresponding to the values $t - T = 22.5$ days and $\log q = 7.902720$. From these we derive

$$\log M = 4.4582302.$$

Table VI. gives for this value of $\log M$, taking into account the second differences,

$$v = 168°\ 59'\ 32''.49;$$

but, using Table VII., we have

$$w = 168°\ 59'\ 29''.11, \qquad \Delta_0 = 3''.37,$$

and hence

$$v = w + \Delta_0 = 168^\circ\ 59'\ 32''.48,$$

the two results agreeing completely.

TABLE VIII. serves to find the time from the perihelion in the case of parabolic motion. For an explanation of its construction and use, see Articles 24, 69, and 72.

TABLE IX. is used in the determination of the true anomaly or the time from the perihelion in the case of orbits of great eccentricity. Its construction is fully explained in Art. 28, and its use in Art. 41.

TABLE X. serves to find the value of v or of $t - T$ in the case of elliptic or hyperbolic orbits. The construction of this Table is explained in Art. 29. The first part gives the values of log B and log C, with A as the argument, for the ellipse and the hyperbola. In the case of log C there are given also log I. Diff. and log half II. Diff., expressed in units of the seventh decimal place, by means of which the interpolation is facilitated. Thus, if we denote by log (C) the value which the Table gives directly for the argument next less than the given value of A, and by ΔA the difference between this argument and the given value of A, expressed in units of the second decimal place, we have, for the required value,

$$\log C = \log (C) + \Delta A \times \text{I. Diff.} + \Delta A^2 \times \text{half II. Diff.}$$

For example, let it be required to find the value of log C corresponding to $A = 0.02497944$, and the process will be:—

			(1)	(2)
Arg. 0.02,	$\log (C) =$	0.0034986	log I. Diff. $= 4.24585$	log half II. Diff. $= 1.778$
	$(1) =$	8770.6	$\log \Delta A = 9.69718$	$2 \log \Delta A = 9.394$
$\Delta A = 0.497944,$	$(2) =$	14.8	3.94303	1.172
	$\log C =$	0.0043771		

The second part of the Table gives the values of A corresponding to given values of τ.

TABLE XI. serves to determine the chord of the orbit when the extreme radii-vectores and the time of describing the parabolic arc are given. For an explanation of the construction and use of this Table, see Articles 68, 72, and 117.

TABLE XII. exhibits the limits of the real roots of the equation

$$\sin(z' - \zeta) = m_0 \sin^4 z'.$$

The construction and use of this table are fully explained in Articles 84 and 93.

TABLES XIII. and XIV. are used in finding the ratio of the sector included by two radii-vectores to the triangle included by the same radii-vectores and the chord joining their extremities. For an explanation of the construction and use of these Tables, see Articles 88, 89, 93, and 101.

TABLE XV. is used in the determination of the chord of the part of the orbit described in a given time in the case of very eccentric elliptic motion, and in the determination of the interval of time whenever the chord is known. For an explanation of its construction and use, see Articles 116, 117, and 119.

TABLE XVI. is used in finding the chord or the interval of time in the case of hyperbolic motion. See Articles 118 and 119 for an explanation of the use of the Table, and also the explanation of Table X. for an illustration of the use of the columns headed log I. Diff. and log half II. Diff.

TABLE XVII. is used in the computation of special perturbations when the terms depending on the squares and higher powers of the masses are taken into account. For an explanation of its construction and use, see Articles 157, 165, 166, 170, and 171.

TABLE XVIII. contains the elements of the orbits of the comets which have been observed. These elements are: T, the time of perihelion passage (mean time at Greenwich); π, the longitude of the perihelion; Ω, the longitude of the ascending node; i, the inclination of the orbit to the plane of the ecliptic; e, the eccentricity of the orbit; and q, the perihelion distance. The longitudes for Nos. 1, 2, 12, 16, 91, 92, 115, 127, 138, 155, 156, 159, 160, 162, 171, 173–175. 180, 181, 185, 191, 192, 195–199, 201, 203, 204, 207, 208, 212–215, 217–219, 221–228, 230, 233, 234, 237–248, 251–258, 261–267, 269–275, 277–279, are in each case measured from the mean equinox of the beginning of the year. In the case of Nos. 134, 146, 172, 182, 189, 190, 205, 231, 232, 236, 259, and 268, the longitudes are measured from the mean equinox of the beginning of the next year. The longitudes for Nos. 19 and 27 are measured from the mean equinox of 1850.0; for No. 186, from the mean equinox of July 3; for No. 187, from the mean equinox of Nov. 9; for No. 200, from the mean equinox of July 1; for No. 202, from the mean equinox of Oct. 1; for No. 206, from the mean equinox of Oct. 7; for No. 211, from the mean equinox of 1848.0; for No. 216, from the mean equinox of Feb. 20; for No. 229, from the mean equinox of April 1; for No. 250, from the mean equinox of Oct. 1; and for No. 276, from the mean equinox of 1865 Oct. 4.0.

Nos. 1, 2, 11, 12, 20, 23, 29, 41, 53, 80, and 177 give the elements for the successive appearances of Halley's comet; Nos. 104, 116, 126, 143, 149, 157, 167, 170, 176, 178, 183, 194, 210, 220, 235, 249, and 260, those for Encke's comet, the longitudes being measured from the mean equinox for the instant of the perihelion passage. Nos. 92, 127, 159, 172, 196, and 222 give the elements for the successive appearances of Biela's comet; Nos. 187, 216, 250, and 276, those for Faye's comet; Nos. 197 and 238, those for Brorsen's comet; Nos. 217 and 243, those for D'Arrest's comet; and Nos. 145 and 245, those for Winnecke's comet. For epochs previous to 1583 the dates are given according to the old style.

This Table is useful for identifying a comet which may appear with one previously observed, by means of a similarity of the elements, its periodic character being otherwise unknown or at least uncertain. The elements given are those which appear to represent the observations most completely. For a collection of elements by various computers, and also for information in regard to the observations made and in regard to the place and manner of their publication, consult Carl's *Repertorium der Cometen-Astronomie* (Munich, 1864), or Galle's *Cometen-Verzeichniss* appended to the latest edition of Olbers's *Methode die Bahn eines Cometen zu berechnen.*

TABLE XIX. contains the elements of the orbits of the minor planets, derived chiefly from the *Berliner Astronomisches Jahrbuch für 1868.* The epoch is given in Berlin mean time; M denotes the mean anomaly, φ the angle of eccentricity, μ the mean daily motion, and a the semi-transverse axis. The elements of Vesta, Iris, Flora, Metis, Victoria, Eunomia, Melpomene, Lutetia, Proserpina, and Pomona are mean elements; the others are osculating for the epoch. The date of the discovery of the planet, and the name of the discoverer, are also added.

TABLE XX. contains the mean elements of the orbits of the major planets, together with the amount of their variations during a period of one hundred years. The epoch is expressed in Greenwich mean time, and L denotes the mean longitude of the planet.

TABLE XXI. gives the values of the masses of the major planets, and also various constants which are used in astronomical calculations.

APPENDIX.

A. Precession.—If we adopt the values for the precession and for the variation of the position of the plane of the ecliptic given in Art. 40, and put

$$M = 171^\circ\ 36'\ 10'' + 39''.79\ (t - 1750),$$

the formulæ for the annual precession in longitude (λ) and latitude (β) become, for the instant t,

$$\begin{aligned}\frac{d\lambda}{dt} &= 50''.2113 + 0''.0002443\ (t - 1750)\\ &\quad + \big(0''.4889 - 0''.00000614\ (t - 1750)\big) \cos(\lambda - M) \tan \beta, \qquad (1)\\ \frac{d\beta}{dt} &= -\big(0''.4889 - 0''.00000614\ (t - 1750)\big) \sin(\lambda - M).\end{aligned}$$

If we denote the planetary precession by a, the luni-solar precession by $l_{\prime}$, and the obliquity of the fixed ecliptic, at the time $1750 + \tau$, by ε_0, we have, according to Bessel,

$$\begin{aligned}\frac{da}{dt} &= 0''.17926 - 0''.0005320786\ \tau,\\ \frac{dl_{\prime}}{dt} &= 50''.37572 - 0''.000243589\ \tau,\\ \varepsilon_0 &= 23^\circ\ 28'\ 18''.0 + 0''.0000098423\ \tau^2,\end{aligned}$$

and if we put

$$\cos \varepsilon_0 \frac{dl_{\prime}}{dt} - \frac{da}{dt} = m, \qquad \sin \varepsilon_0 \frac{dl_{\prime}}{dt} = n,$$

the formulæ for the annual precession in right ascension (α) and declination (δ) become

$$\frac{d\alpha}{dt} = m + n \tan \delta \sin \alpha, \qquad \frac{d\delta}{dt} = n \cos \alpha, \qquad (2)$$

and the numerical values of m and n are, for the instant t,

$$m = 46''.02824 + 0''.0003086450\,(t - 1750),$$
$$n = 20''.06442 - 0''.0000970204\,(t - 1750).$$

To determine the precession during the interval $t' - t$, we compute the annual variation for the instant $\frac{1}{2}(t' + t)$ and this variation multiplied by $t' - t$ furnishes the required result.

B. Nutation.—The expressions for the equation of the equinoxes and for the nutation of the obliquity of the ecliptic are, according to Peters,

$$\begin{aligned} \Delta\lambda = &- 17''.2405 \sin \Omega + 0''.2073 \sin 2\Omega - 0''.2041 \sin 2☾ + 0''.0677 \sin (☾ - \Gamma') \\ &- 1''.2694 \sin 2\odot + 0''.1279 \sin (\odot - \Gamma) \\ &- 0''.0213 \sin (\odot + \Gamma), \\ \Delta\varepsilon = &+ 9''.2231 \cos \Omega - 0''.0897 \cos 2\Omega + 0''.0886 \cos 2☾ \\ &+ 0''.5510 \cos 2\odot + 0''.0093 \cos (\odot + \Gamma), \end{aligned} \quad (3)$$

for the year 1800, and

$$\begin{aligned} \Delta\lambda = &- 17''.2577 \sin \Omega + 0''.2073 \sin 2\Omega - 0''.2041 \sin 2☾ + 0''.0677 \sin (☾ - \Gamma') \\ &- 1''.2695 \sin 2\odot + 0''.1275 \sin (\odot - \Gamma) \\ &- 0''.0213 \sin (\odot + \Gamma), \\ \Delta\varepsilon = &+ 9''.2240 \cos \Omega - 0''.0896 \cos 2\Omega + 0''.0885 \cos 2☾ \\ &+ 0''.5507 \cos 2\odot + 0''.0092 \cos (\odot + \Gamma), \end{aligned}$$

for the year 1900. In these equations ☊ denotes the longitude of the ascending node of the moon's orbit, referred to the mean equinox, ☾ the true longitude of the moon, ☉ the true longitude of the sun, Γ the true longitude of the sun's perigee, and Γ' the true longitude of the moon's perigee. The values of these quantities may be derived from the solar and lunar tables, and thus the required values of $\Delta\lambda$ and $\Delta\varepsilon$ may be found. The equations give the corrections for the reduction from the mean equinox to the true equinox.

To find the nutation in right ascension and in declination, if we consider only the terms of the first order, we have

$$\begin{aligned} \Delta\alpha &= \frac{d\alpha}{d\lambda}\Delta\lambda + \frac{d\alpha}{d\varepsilon}\Delta\varepsilon, \\ \Delta\delta &= \frac{d\delta}{d\lambda}\Delta\lambda + \frac{d\delta}{d\varepsilon}\Delta\varepsilon. \end{aligned} \quad (4)$$

The values of $\Delta\lambda$ and $\Delta\varepsilon$ are found from the preceding equations, and for the differential coefficients we have

$$\frac{d\alpha}{d\lambda} = \cos\varepsilon + \sin\varepsilon\tan\delta\sin\alpha, \qquad \frac{d\delta}{d\lambda} = \cos\alpha\sin\varepsilon,$$
$$\frac{d\alpha}{d\varepsilon} = -\cos\alpha\tan\delta, \qquad \frac{d\delta}{d\varepsilon} = \sin\alpha. \tag{5}$$

The terms of the second order are of sensible magnitude only when the body is very near the pole, and in this case by computing the second differential coefficients the complete values may be found.

In the reduction of the place of a planet or comet from the mean equinox of one date t to the true equinox of another date t', the determination of the correction for precession and of that for nutation may be effected simultaneously. Thus, let τ denote the interval $t'-t$ expressed in parts of a year, and the sum of the corrections for precession and nutation gives

$$\begin{aligned}\Delta\alpha &= m\tau + \Delta\lambda\cos\varepsilon + (n\tau + \Delta\lambda\sin\varepsilon)\sin\alpha\tan\delta - \Delta\varepsilon\cos\alpha\tan\delta,\\ \Delta\delta &= (n\tau + \Delta\lambda\sin\varepsilon)\cos\alpha + \Delta\varepsilon\sin\alpha.\end{aligned} \tag{6}$$

Let us now put

$$\begin{aligned} m\tau + \Delta\lambda\cos\varepsilon &= f,\\ n\tau + \Delta\lambda\sin\varepsilon &= g\sin G,\\ -\Delta\varepsilon &= g\cos G,\end{aligned} \tag{7}$$

and the equations (6) become

$$\begin{aligned}\Delta\alpha &= f + g\sin(G+\alpha)\tan\delta,\\ \Delta\delta &= g\cos(G+\alpha),\end{aligned} \tag{8}$$

as already given in Art. 40.

The astronomical ephemerides give at intervals of a few days the values of the quantities f, g, and G for the reduction of the place of the body from the mean equinox of the beginning of the year to the true equinox of the date; and, in order to obtain uniformity and accuracy, the beginning of the year is taken at the instant when the mean longitude of the sun is 280°. When these tables are not available, the values of f, g, and G may be found directly by means of the equations (7). The reduction from the true equinox of t' to the mean equinox of t will be obtained by changing the signs of the corrections.

C. Aberration.—The aberration in the case of the planets and comets may be considered in three different modes:—

1. If we subtract from the observed time the interval occupied by

the light in passing to the earth, the result will be the time for which the true place is identical with the apparent place for the observed time.

2. If we compute the time occupied by light in traversing the distance between the body and the earth, and, by means of the rate of the variation of the geocentric spherical co-ordinates, compute the motion during this interval, we may derive the true place at the instant of observation.

3. We may consider the observed place corrected for the aberration of the fixed stars as the true place at the instant when the light was emitted, but as seen from the place of the earth at the instant of observation.

The formulæ for the actual aberration of the fixed stars are—

$$\begin{aligned} \Delta\lambda &= -\,20''.4451 \cos(\lambda - \odot) \sec\beta - 0''.3429 \cos(\lambda - \Gamma) \sec\beta, \\ \Delta\beta &= +\,20''.4451 \sin(\lambda - \odot) \sin\beta + 0''.3429 \sin(\lambda - \Gamma) \sin\beta), \end{aligned} \quad (9)$$

in the case of the longitude and latitude, and

$$\begin{aligned} \Delta\alpha = &-\,20''.4451 (\cos\odot \cos\varepsilon \cos\alpha + \sin\odot \sin\alpha) \sec\delta \\ &- 0''.3429 (\cos\Gamma \cos\varepsilon \cos\alpha + \sin\Gamma \sin\alpha) \sec\delta, \\ \Delta\delta = &+\,20''.4451 \cos\odot (\sin\alpha \sin\delta \cos\varepsilon - \cos\delta \sin\varepsilon) \\ &- 20''.4451 \sin\odot \cos\alpha \sin\delta \\ &+ 0''.3429 \cos\Gamma (\sin\alpha \sin\delta \cos\varepsilon - \cos\delta \sin\varepsilon) \\ &- 0''.3429 \sin\Gamma \cos\alpha \sin\delta, \end{aligned} \quad (10)$$

in the case of the right ascension and declination. In these formulæ Γ denotes the longitude of the sun's perigee, and they give the corrections for the reduction from the true place to the apparent place.

D. Intensity of Light.—If we denote by r the distance of a planet or comet from the sun, by Δ its distance from the earth, and by C a constant quantity depending on the magnitude of the body and on its capacity for reflecting the light, the intensity of the light of the body as seen from the earth will be

$$I = \frac{C}{r^2 \Delta^2}. \quad (11)$$

When the constant C is unknown, we may determine the relative brilliancy of the comet at different times by means of the formula

$$B = \frac{r^2 \Delta^2}{r'^2 \Delta'^2}. \quad (12)$$

In the case of the planets we adopt as the unit of the intensity of light the value of I when the planet is in opposition and both it and the earth are at their mean distances from the sun. Thus we obtain

$$C = a^2 (a - 1)^2,$$

and hence

$$I = \frac{a^2 (a - 1)^2}{r^2 \Delta^2}. \tag{13}$$

Let us now denote by R the ratio of the intensities of the light for two consecutive stellar magnitudes; then, if we denote by M the apparent stellar magnitude of the planet when $I = 1$, and by m the magnitude for any value of I, we shall have

$$I = \frac{R^M}{R^m},$$

and hence

$$m = M - \frac{\log I}{\log R}. \tag{14}$$

By means of photometric determinations of the relative brilliancy of the stars, it has been found that

$$R = 2.56,$$

and hence we derive

$$m = M - 2.45 \log I, \tag{15}$$

by means of which the apparent stellar magnitude of a planet may be determined, I being found by means of equation (13). The value of M must be determined for each planet by means of observed values of m.

EXAMPLE.—The value of M for *Eurynome* is 10.4; required the apparent stellar magnitude of the planet when $\log a = 0.38795$, $\log r = 0.2956$, and $\log \Delta = 9.9952$.

The equation (13) gives

$$\log I = 0.5129,$$

and from (15) we derive

$$m = 10.4 - 1.3 = 9.1.$$

For the values $\log r = 0.4338$, $\log \Delta = 0.2357$, we obtain

$$\log I = 9.7555 - 10,$$

and

$$m = 10.4 + 2.45 \times 0.2445 = 11.0.$$

E. Numerical Calculations.—The extended numerical calculations required in many of the problems of Theoretical Astronomy, render it important that a judicious arrangement of the details should be effected. The beginner will not, in general, be able to effect such an arrangement at the outset; and it would only confuse to attempt to give any specific directions. Familiarity with the formulæ to be applied, and practice in the performance of calculations of this character, will speedily suggest those various devices of arrangement by which skillful computers expedite the mechanical part of the solution. There are, however, a few general suggestions which may be of service. Thus, it will always facilitate the calculation, when several values of a variable are to be computed, to arrange it so that the values of each function involved shall appear in the same vertical or horizontal column. The course of the differences will then indicate the existence of errors which might not otherwise be discovered until the greater part if not the entire calculation has been completed; and, besides, by carrying along the several parts simultaneously the use of the logarithmic and other tables will be facilitated. Numbers which are to be frequently used may be written on slips of paper and applied wherever they may be required; and by performing the addition or subtraction of two logarithms or of two numbers from left to right (which will be effected easily and certainly after a little practice), the sum or difference to be used as the argument in the tables may be retained in the memory, and thus the required number or arc may be written down directly. The number of the decimal figures of the logarithms to be used will depend on the character of the data as well as on the accuracy sought to be obtained, and the use of approximate formulæ will be governed by the same considerations. Whenever the formulæ furnish checks or tests of the accuracy of the numerical process, they should be applied; and whenever these are not provided, the use of differences for the same purpose should not be overlooked. By proper attention to these suggestions, much time and labor will be saved. The agreement of the several proofs will beget confidence, relieve the mind from much anxiety, and thus greatly facilitate the progress of the work.

THE END.

www.ingramcontent.com/pod-product-compliance
Lightning Source LLC
LaVergne TN
LVHW021053110826
845150LV00001B/65

* 9 7 8 1 4 2 5 5 6 7 3 8 5 *